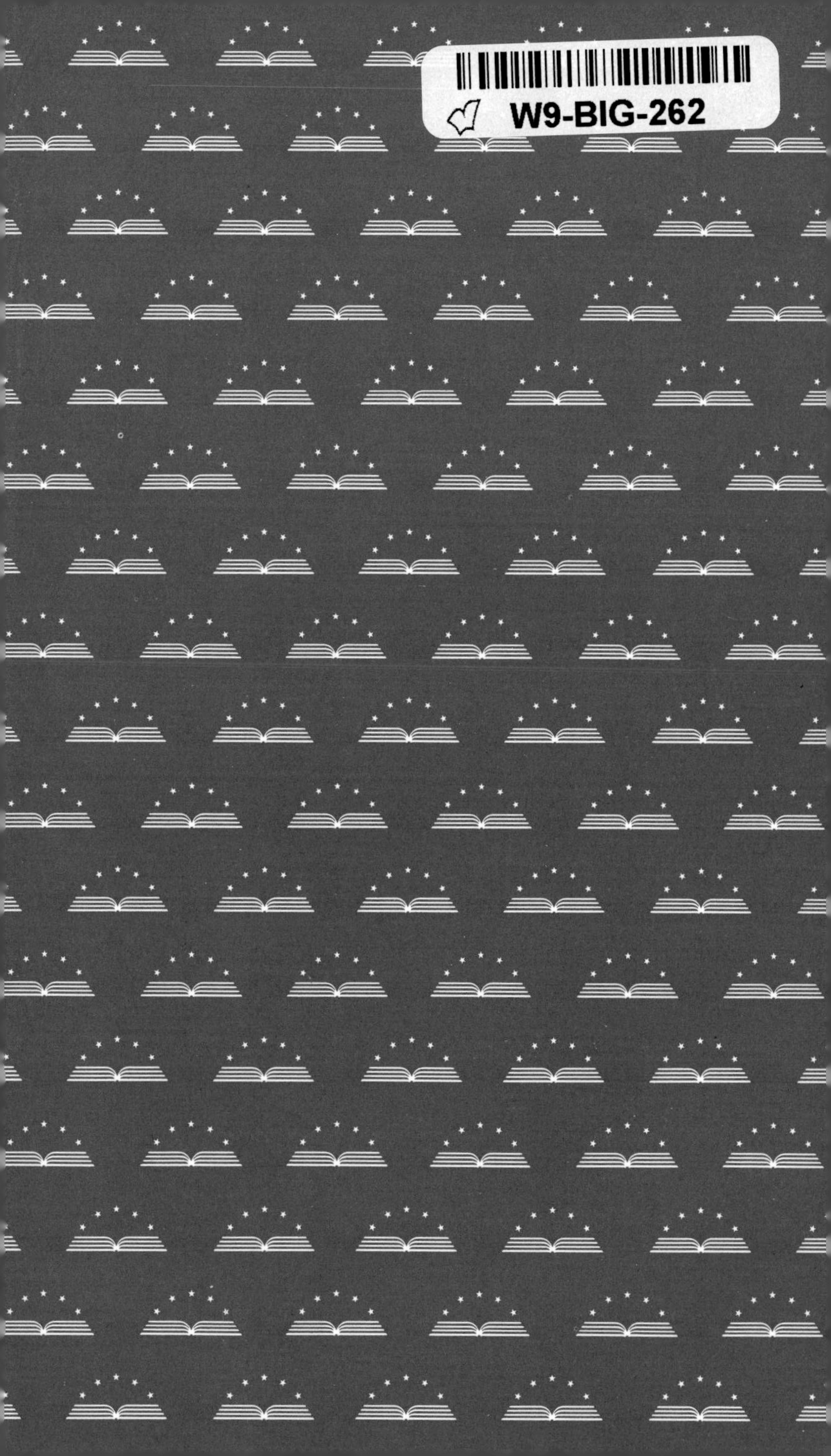
W9-BIG-262

W.E.B. DU BOIS

W.E.B. Du Bois

WRITINGS

The Suppression of the African Slave-Trade

The Souls of Black Folk

Dusk of Dawn

Essays and Articles

THE LIBRARY OF AMERICA

The paper used in this publication meets the
minimum requirements of the American National Standard
for Information Sciences—Permanence of Paper for
Printed Library Materials, ANSI Z39.48–1984.

Distributed to the trade in the United States
and Canada by the Viking Press.

Published outside North America by the Press Syndicate
of the University of Cambridge,
The Pitt Building, Trumpington Street, Cambridge CB2 1RP, England
ISBN 0521 32482 3

Library of Congress Catalog Card Number: 86-10565
For cataloging information, see end of *Notes* section.
ISBN 0–940450–33—X

First Printing

Manufactured in the United States of America

Nathan Huggins
wrote the notes and selected
the texts for this volume

Grateful acknowledgement is made to the National Endowment for the Humanities and the Ford Foundation for their generous financial support of this series.

Contents

THE SUPPRESSION OF THE AFRICAN SLAVE-TRADE TO THE UNITED STATES OF AMERICA 1638–1870

Preface

THIS monograph was begun during my residence as Rogers Memorial Fellow at Harvard University, and is based mainly upon a study of the sources, i. e., national, State, and colonial statutes, Congressional documents, reports of societies, personal narratives, etc. The collection of laws available for this research was, I think, nearly complete; on the other hand, facts and statistics bearing on the economic side of the study have been difficult to find, and my conclusions are consequently liable to modification from this source.

The question of the suppression of the slave-trade is so intimately connected with the questions as to its rise, the system of American slavery, and the whole colonial policy of the eighteenth century, that it is difficult to isolate it, and at the same time to avoid superficiality on the one hand, and unscientific narrowness of view on the other. While I could not hope entirely to overcome such a difficulty, I nevertheless trust that I have succeeded in rendering this monograph a small contribution to the scientific study of slavery and the American Negro.

I desire to express my obligation to Dr. Albert Bushnell Hart, of Harvard University, at whose suggestion I began this work and by whose kind aid and encouragement I have brought it to a close; also I have to thank the trustees of the John F. Slater Fund, whose appointment made it possible to test the conclusions of this study by the general principles laid down in German universities.

W. E. BURGHARDT DU BOIS.

WILBERFORCE UNIVERSITY,
March, 1896.

Contents

CHAPTER I

Introductory

CHAPTER II

The Planting Colonies

CHAPTER III

The Farming Colonies

CHAPTER IV

The Trading Colonies

CHAPTER V

The Period of the Revolution, 1774–1787

CHAPTER VI

The Federal Convention, 1787

CHAPTER VII

Toussaint L'Ouverture and Anti-Slavery Effort, 1787–1807

CHAPTER VIII

The Period of Attempted Suppression, 1807–1825

CHAPTER IX

The International Status of the Slave-Trade, 1783–1862

CHAPTER X

The Rise of the Cotton Kingdom, 1820–1850

CHAPTER XI

The Final Crisis, 1850–1870

CHAPTER XII

The Essentials in the Struggle

APPENDICES

Chapter I

INTRODUCTORY.

1. Plan of the Monograph.
2. The Rise of the English Slave-Trade.

---

1. **Plan of the Monograph.** This monograph proposes to set forth the efforts made in the United States of America, from early colonial times until the present, to limit and suppress the trade in slaves between Africa and these shores.

The study begins with the colonial period, setting forth in brief the attitude of England and, more in detail, the attitude of the planting, farming, and trading groups of colonies toward the slave-trade. It deals next with the first concerted effort against the trade and with the further action of the individual States. The important work of the Constitutional Convention follows, together with the history of the trade in that critical period which preceded the Act of 1807. The attempt to suppress the trade from 1807 to 1830 is next recounted. A chapter then deals with the slave-trade as an international problem. Finally the development of the crises up to the Civil War is studied, together with the steps leading to the final suppression; and a concluding chapter seeks to sum up the results of the investigation. Throughout the monograph the institution of slavery and the interstate slave-trade are considered only incidentally.

2. **The Rise of the English Slave-Trade.** Any attempt to consider the attitude of the English colonies toward the African slave-trade must be prefaced by a word as to the attitude of England herself and the development of the trade in her hands.[1]

Sir John Hawkins's celebrated voyage took place in 1562, but probably not until 1631[2] did a regular chartered company

[1] This account is based largely on the *Report of the Lords of the Committee of Council*, etc. (London, 1789).

[2] African trading-companies had previously been erected (e. g. by Elizabeth in 1585 and 1588, and by James I. in 1618); but slaves are not specifically mentioned in their charters, and they probably did not trade in slaves. Cf. Bandinel, *Account of the Slave Trade* (1842), pp. 38–44.

undertake to carry on the trade.[1] This company was unsuccessful,[2] and was eventually succeeded by the "Company of Royal Adventurers trading to Africa," chartered by Charles II. in 1662, and including the Queen Dowager and the Duke of York.[3] The company contracted to supply the West Indies with three thousand slaves annually; but contraband trade, misconduct, and war so reduced it that in 1672 it surrendered its charter to another company for £34,000.[4] This new corporation, chartered by Charles II. as the "Royal African Company," proved more successful than its predecessors, and carried on a growing trade for a quarter of a century.

In 1698 Parliamentary interference with the trade began. By the Statute 9 and 10 William and Mary, chapter 26, private traders, on payment of a duty of 10% on English goods exported to Africa, were allowed to participate in the trade. This was brought about by the clamor of the merchants, especially the "American Merchants," who "in their Petition suggest, that it would be a great Benefit to the Kingdom to secure the Trade by maintaining Forts and Castles there, with an equal Duty upon all Goods exported."[5] This plan, being a compromise between maintaining the monopoly intact and entirely abolishing it, was adopted, and the statute declared the trade "highly Beneficial and Advantageous to this Kingdom, and to the Plantations and Colonies thereunto belonging."

Having thus gained practically free admittance to the field, English merchants sought to exclude other nations by securing a monopoly of the lucrative Spanish colonial slave-trade.

[1] Chartered by Charles I. Cf. Sainsbury, *Cal. State Papers, Col. Ser., America and W. Indies, 1574–1660*, p. 135.

[2] In 1651, during the Protectorate, the privileges of the African trade were granted anew to this same company for fourteen years. Cf. Sainsbury, *Cal. State Papers, Col. Ser., America and W. Indies, 1574–1660*, pp. 342, 355.

[3] Sainsbury, *Cal. State Papers, Col. Ser., America and W. Indies, 1661–1668*, § 408.

[4] Sainsbury, *Cal. State Papers, Col. Ser., America and W. Indies, 1669–1674*, §§ 934, 1095.

[5] Quoted in the above *Report*, under "Most Material Proceedings in the House of Commons," Vol. I. Part I. An import duty of 10% on all goods, except Negroes, imported from Africa to England and the colonies was also laid. The proceeds of these duties went to the Royal African Company.

Their object was finally accomplished by the signing of the Assiento in 1713.[1]

The Assiento was a treaty between England and Spain by which the latter granted the former a monopoly of the Spanish colonial slave-trade for thirty years, and England engaged to supply the colonies within that time with at least 144,000 slaves, at the rate of 4,800 per year. England was also to advance Spain 200,000 crowns, and to pay a duty of 33½ crowns for each slave imported. The kings of Spain and England were each to receive one-fourth of the profits of the trade, and the Royal African Company were authorized to import as many slaves as they wished above the specified number in the first twenty-five years, and to sell them, except in three ports, at any price they could get.

It is stated that, in the twenty years from 1713 to 1733, fifteen thousand slaves were annually imported into America by the English, of whom from one-third to one-half went to the Spanish colonies.[2] To the company itself the venture proved a financial failure; for during the years 1729–1750 Parliament assisted the Royal Company by annual grants which amounted to £90,000,[3] and by 1739 Spain was a creditor to the extent of £68,000, and threatened to suspend the treaty. The war interrupted the carrying out of the contract, but the Peace of Aix-la-Chapelle extended the limit by four years. Finally, October 5, 1750, this privilege was waived for a money consideration paid to England; the Assiento was ended, and the Royal Company was bankrupt.

By the Statute 23 George II., chapter 31, the old company was dissolved and a new "Company of Merchants trading to Africa" erected in its stead.[4] Any merchant so desiring was allowed to engage in the trade on payment of certain small duties, and such merchants formed a company headed by nine directors. This marked the total abolition of monopoly in the

[1] Cf. Appendix A.

[2] Bandinel, *Account of the Slave Trade*, p. 59. Cf. Bryan Edwards, *History of the British Colonies in the W. Indies* (London, 1798), Book VI.

[3] From 1729 to 1788, including compensation to the old company, Parliament expended £705,255 on African companies. Cf. *Report*, etc., as above.

[4] Various amendatory statutes were passed: e. g., 24 George II. ch. 49, 25 George II. ch. 40, 4 George III. ch. 20, 5 George III. ch. 44, 23 George III. ch. 65.

slave-trade, and was the form under which the trade was carried on until after the American Revolution.

That the slave-trade was the very life of the colonies had, by 1700, become an almost unquestioned axiom in British practical economics. The colonists themselves declared slaves "the strength and sinews of this western world,"[1] and the lack of them "the grand obstruction"[2] here, as the settlements "cannot subsist without supplies of them."[3] Thus, with merchants clamoring at home and planters abroad, it easily became the settled policy of England to encourage the slave-trade. Then, too, she readily argued that what was an economic necessity in Jamaica and the Barbadoes could scarcely be disadvantageous to Carolina, Virginia, or even New York. Consequently, the colonial governors were generally instructed to "give all due encouragement and invitation to merchants and others, . . . and in particular to the royal African company of England."[4] Duties laid on the importer, and all acts in any way restricting the trade, were frowned upon and very often disallowed. "Whereas," ran Governor Dobbs's instructions, "Acts have been passed in some of our Plantations in America for laying duties on the importation and exportation of Negroes to the great discouragement of the Merchants trading thither from the coast of Africa . . . It is our Will and Pleasure that you do not give your assent to or pass any Law imposing duties upon Negroes imported into our Province of North Carolina."[5]

The exact proportions of the slave-trade to America can be but approximately determined. From 1680 to 1688 the African Company sent 249 ships to Africa, shipped there 60,783

[1] Renatus Enys from Surinam, in 1663: Sainsbury, *Cal. State Papers, Col. Ser., America and W. Indies, 1661–68*, § 577.

[2] Thomas Lynch from Jamaica, in 1665: Sainsbury, *Cal. State Papers, Col. Ser., America and W. Indies, 1661–68*, § 934.

[3] Lieutenant-Governor Willoughby of Barbadoes, in 1666: Sainsbury, *Cal. State Papers, Col. Ser., America and W. Indies, 1661–68*, § 1281.

[4] Smith, *History of New Jersey* (1765), p. 254; Sainsbury, *Cal. State Papers, Col. Ser., America and W. Indies, 1669–74*, §§ 367, 398, 812.

[5] *N. C. Col. Rec.*, V. 1118. For similar instructions, cf. *Penn. Archives*, I. 306; *Doc. rel. Col. Hist. New York*, VI. 34; Gordon, *History of the American Revolution*, I. letter 2; *Mass. Hist. Soc. Coll.*, 4th Ser. X. 642.

Negro slaves, and after losing 14,387 on the middle passage, delivered 46,396 in America. The trade increased early in the eighteenth century, 104 ships clearing for Africa in 1701; it then dwindled until the signing of the Assiento, standing at 74 clearances in 1724. The final dissolution of the monopoly in 1750 led—excepting in the years 1754–57, when the closing of Spanish marts sensibly affected the trade—to an extraordinary development, 192 clearances being made in 1771. The Revolutionary War nearly stopped the traffic; but by 1786 the clearances had risen again to 146.

To these figures must be added the unregistered trade of Americans and foreigners. It is probable that about 25,000 slaves were brought to America each year between 1698 and 1707. The importation then dwindled, but rose after the Assiento to perhaps 30,000. The proportion, too, of these slaves carried to the continent now began to increase. Of about 20,000 whom the English annually imported from 1733 to 1766, South Carolina alone received some 3,000. Before the Revolution, the total exportation to America is variously estimated as between 40,000 and 100,000 each year. Bancroft places the total slave population of the continental colonies at 59,000 in 1714, 78,000 in 1727, and 293,000 in 1754. The census of 1790 showed 697,897 slaves in the United States.[1]

In colonies like those in the West Indies and in South Carolina and Georgia, the rapid importation into America of a multitude of savages gave rise to a system of slavery far different from that which the late Civil War abolished. The strikingly harsh and even inhuman slave codes in these colonies show this. Crucifixion, burning, and starvation were legal modes of punishment.[2] The rough and brutal character of the time and place was partly responsible for this, but a more decisive reason lay in the fierce and turbulent character of the imported Negroes. The docility to which long years of bondage and strict discipline gave rise was absent, and in-

[1]These figures are from the above-mentioned *Report*, Vol. II. Part IV. Nos. 1, 5. See also Bancroft, *History of the United States* (1883), II. 274 ff; Bandinel, *Account of the Slave Trade*, p. 63; Benezet, *Caution to Great Britain*, etc., pp. 39–40, and *Historical Account of Guinea*, ch. xiii.

[2]Compare earlier slave codes in South Carolina, Georgia, Jamaica, etc.; also cf. Benezet, *Historical Account of Guinea*, p. 75; *Report*, etc., as above.

surrections and acts of violence were of frequent occurrence.[1] Again and again the danger of planters being "cut off by their own negroes"[2] is mentioned, both in the islands and on the continent. This condition of vague dread and unrest not only increased the severity of laws and strengthened the police system, but was the prime motive back of all the earlier efforts to check the further importation of slaves.

On the other hand, in New England and New York the Negroes were merely house servants or farm hands, and were treated neither better nor worse than servants in general in those days. Between these two extremes, the system of slavery varied from a mild serfdom in Pennsylvania and New Jersey to an aristocratic caste system in Maryland and Virginia.

[1] Sainsbury, *Cal. State Papers, Col. Ser., America and W. Indies, 1574–1660*, pp. 229, 271, 295; *1661–68*, §§ 61, 412, 826, 1270, 1274, 1788; *1669–74*, §§ 508, 1244; Bolzius and Von Reck, *Journals* (in Force, *Tracts*, Vol. IV. No. 5, pp. 9, 18); *Proceedings of Governor and Assembly of Jamaica in regard to the Maroon Negroes* (London, 1796).

[2] Sainsbury, *Cal. State Papers, Col. Ser., America and W. Indies, 1661–68*, § 1679.

Chapter II

THE PLANTING COLONIES.

---

3. **Character of these Colonies.** The planting colonies are those Southern settlements whose climate and character destined them to be the chief theatre of North American slavery. The early attitude of these communities toward the slave-trade is therefore of peculiar interest; for their action was of necessity largely decisive for the future of the trade and for the institution in North America. Theirs was the only soil, climate, and society suited to slavery; in the other colonies, with few exceptions, the institution was by these same factors doomed from the beginning. Hence, only strong moral and political motives could in the planting colonies overthrow or check a traffic so favored by the mother country.

4. **Restrictions in Georgia.** In Georgia we have an example of a community whose philanthropic founders sought to impose upon it a code of morals higher than the colonists wished. The settlers of Georgia were of even worse moral fibre than their slave-trading and whiskey-using neighbors in Carolina and Virginia; yet Oglethorpe and the London proprietors prohibited from the beginning both the rum and the slave traffic, refusing to "suffer slavery (which is against the Gospel as well as the fundamental law of England) to be authorised under our authority."[1] The trustees sought to win the colonists over to their belief by telling them that money could be better expended in transporting white men than Negroes; that slaves would be a source of weakness to the

[1] Hoare, *Memoirs of Granville Sharp* (1820), p. 157. For the act of prohibition, see W. B. Stevens, *History of Georgia* (1847), I. 311.

colony; and that the "Produces designed to be raised in the Colony would not require such Labour as to make Negroes necessary for carrying them on."[1]

This policy greatly displeased the colonists, who from 1735, the date of the first law, to 1749, did not cease to clamor for the repeal of the restrictions.[2] As their English agent said, they insisted that "In Spight of all Endeavours to disguise this Point, it is as clear as Light itself, that Negroes are as essentially necessary to the Cultivation of *Georgia*, as Axes, Hoes, or any other Utensil of Agriculture."[3] Meantime, evasions and infractions of the laws became frequent and notorious. Negroes were brought across from Carolina and "hired" for life.[4] "Finally, purchases were openly made in Savannah from African traders: some seizures were made by those who opposed the principle, but as a majority of the magistrates were favorable to the introduction of slaves into the province, legal decisions were suspended from time to time, and a strong disposition evidenced by the courts to evade the operation of the law."[5] At last, in 1749, the colonists prevailed on the trustees and the government, and the trade was thrown open under careful restrictions, which limited importation, required a registry and quarantine on all slaves brought in, and laid a duty.[6] It is probable, however, that these restrictions were never enforced, and that the trade thus established continued unchecked until the Revolution.

5. **Restrictions in South Carolina.**[7] South Carolina had the largest and most widely developed slave-trade of any of

[1] [B. Martyn], *Account of the Progress of Georgia* (1741), pp. 9–10.

[2] Cf. Stevens, *History of Georgia*, I. 290 ff.

[3] Stephens, *Account of the Causes*, etc., p. 8. Cf. also *Journal of Trustees*, II. 210; cited by Stevens, *History of Georgia*, I. 306.

[4] McCall, *History of Georgia* (1811), I. 206–7.

[5] *Ibid.*

[6] *Pub. Rec. Office, Board of Trade*, Vol. X.; cited by C. C. Jones, *History of Georgia* (1883), I. 422–5.

[7] The following is a summary of the legislation of the colony of South Carolina; details will be found in Appendix A:—

1698,	Act to encourage the immigration of white servants.
1703,	Duty Act: 10*s*. on Africans, 20*s*. on other Negroes.
1714,	" " additional duty.
1714,	" " £2.

the continental colonies. This was owing to the character of her settlers, her nearness to the West Indian slave marts, and the early development of certain staple crops, such as rice, which were adapted to slave labor.[1] Moreover, this colony suffered much less interference from the home government than many other colonies; thus it is possible here to trace the untrammeled development of slave-trade restrictions in a typical planting community.

As early as 1698 the slave-trade to South Carolina had reached such proportions that it was thought that "the great number of negroes which of late have been imported into this Collony may endanger the safety thereof." The immigration of white servants was therefore encouraged by a special law.[2] Increase of immigration reduced this disproportion, but Negroes continued to be imported in such numbers as to afford considerable revenue from a moderate duty on them. About the time when the Assiento was signed, the slave-trade so increased that, scarcely a year after the consummation of that momentous agreement, two heavy duty acts were passed, because "the number of Negroes do extremely increase in this Province, and through the afflicting providence of God, the white persons do not proportionately multiply, by reason whereof, the safety of the said Province is greatly endangered."[3]

1714–15,	Duty Act:	additional duty.
1716,	" "	£3 on Africans, £30 on colonial Negroes.
1717,	" "	£40 in addition to existing duties.
1719,	" "	£10 on Africans, £30 on colonial Negroes. The Act of 1717, etc., was repealed.
1721,	" "	£10 on Africans, £50 on colonial Negroes.
1722,	" "	" " " " "
1740,	" "	£100 on Africans, £150 on colonial Negroes.
1751,	" "	£10 " " £50 " "
1760,	Act prohibiting importation (Disallowed).	
1764,	Duty Act:	additional duty of £100.
1783,	" "	£3 on Africans, £20 on colonial Negroes.
1784,	" "	" " £5 " "
1787,	Act and Ordinance prohibiting importation.	

[1] Cf. Hewatt, *Historical Account of S. Carolina and Georgia* (1779), I. 120 ff.; reprinted in *S. C. Hist. Coll.* (1836), I. 108 ff.

[2] Cooper, *Statutes at Large of S. Carolina*, II. 153.

[3] The text of the first act is not extant: cf. Cooper, *Statutes*, III. 56. For the second, see Cooper, VII. 365, 367.

The trade, however, by reason of the encouragement abroad and of increased business activity in exporting naval stores at home, suffered scarcely any check, although repeated acts, reciting the danger incident to a "great importation of Negroes," were passed, laying high duties.[1] Finally, in 1717, an additional duty of £40,[2] although due in depreciated currency, succeeded so nearly in stopping the trade that, two years later, all existing duties were repealed and one of £10 substituted.[3] This continued during the time of resistance to the proprietary government, but by 1734 the importation had again reached large proportions. "We must therefore beg leave," the colonists write in that year, "to inform your Majesty, that, amidst our other perilous circumstances, we are subject to many intestine dangers from the great number of negroes that are now among us, who amount at least to twenty-two thousand persons, and are three to one of all your Majesty's white subjects in this province. Insurrections against us have been often attempted."[4] In 1740 an insurrection under a slave, Cato, at Stono, caused such widespread alarm that a prohibitory duty of £100 was immediately laid.[5] Importation was again checked; but in 1751 the colony sought to devise a plan whereby the slightly restricted immigration of Negroes should provide a fund to encourage the importation of white servants, "to prevent the mischiefs that may be attended by the great importation of negroes into this Province."[6] Many white servants were thus encouraged to settle in the colony; but so much larger was the influx of black slaves that the colony, in 1760, totally prohibited the slave-trade. This act was promptly disallowed by the Privy Council and

[1] Cf. Grimké, *Public Laws of S. Carolina*, p. xvi, No. 362; Cooper, *Statutes*, II. 649. Cf. also *Governor Johnson to the Board of Trade*, Jan. 12, 1719–20; reprinted in Rivers, *Early History of S. Carolina* (1874), App., xii.

[2] Cooper, *Statutes*, VII. 368.

[3] *Ibid.*, III. 56.

[4] From a memorial signed by the governor, President of the Council, and Speaker of the House, dated April 9, 1734, printed in Hewatt, *Historical Account of S. Carolina and Georgia* (1779), II. 39; reprinted in *S. C. Hist. Coll.* (1836), I. 305–6. Cf. *N. C. Col. Rec.*, II. 421.

[5] Cooper, *Statutes*, III. 556; Grimké, *Public Laws*, p. xxxi, No. 694. Cf. Ramsay, *History of S. Carolina*, I. 110.

[6] Cooper, *Statutes*, III. 739.

the governor reprimanded;[1] but the colony declared that "an importation of negroes, equal in number to what have been imported of late years, may prove of the most dangerous consequence in many respects to this Province, and the best way to obviate such danger will be by imposing such an additional duty upon them as may totally prevent the evils."[2] A prohibitive duty of £100 was accordingly imposed in 1764.[3] This duty probably continued until the Revolution.

The war made a great change in the situation. It has been computed by good judges that, between the years 1775 and 1783, the State of South Carolina lost twenty-five thousand Negroes, by actual hostilities, plunder of the British, runaways, etc. After the war the trade quickly revived, and considerable revenue was raised from duty acts until 1787, when by act and ordinance the slave-trade was totally prohibited.[4] This prohibition, by renewals from time to time, lasted until 1803.

6. **Restrictions in North Carolina.** In early times there were few slaves in North Carolina;[5] this fact, together with the troubled and turbulent state of affairs during the early colonial period, did not necessitate the adoption of any settled policy toward slavery or the slave-trade. Later the slave-trade to the colony increased; but there is no evidence of any effort to restrict or in any way regulate it before 1786, when it was declared that "the importation of slaves into this State is productive of evil consequences and highly impolitic,"[6] and a prohibitive duty was laid on them.

7. **Restrictions in Virginia.**[7] Next to South Carolina, Virginia had probably the largest slave-trade. Her situation,

[1] The text of this law has not been found. Cf. Burge, *Commentaries on Colonial and Foreign Laws*, I. 737, note; Stevens, *History of Georgia*, I. 286. See instructions of the governor of New Hampshire, June 30, 1761, in Gordon, *History of the American Revolution*, I. letter 2.

[2] Cooper, *Statutes*, IV. 187.

[3] This duty avoided the letter of the English instructions by making the duty payable by the first purchasers, and not by the importers. Cf. Cooper, *Statutes*, IV. 187.

[4] Grimké, *Public Laws*, p. lxviii, Nos. 1485, 1486; Cooper, *Statutes*, VII. 430.

[5] Cf. *N. C. Col. Rec.*, IV. 172.

[6] Martin, *Iredell's Acts of Assembly*, I. 413, 492.

[7] The following is a summary of the legislation of the colony of Virginia; details will be found in Appendix A:—

however, differed considerably from that of her Southern neighbor. The climate, the staple tobacco crop, and the society of Virginia were favorable to a system of domestic slavery, but one which tended to develop into a patriarchal serfdom rather than into a slave-consuming industrial hierarchy. The labor required by the tobacco crop was less unhealthy than that connected with the rice crop, and the Virginians were, perhaps, on a somewhat higher moral plane than the Carolinians. There was consequently no such insatiable demand for slaves in the larger colony. On the other hand, the power of the Virginia executive was peculiarly strong, and it was not possible here to thwart the slave-trade policy of the home government as easily as elsewhere.

Considering all these circumstances, it is somewhat difficult to determine just what was the attitude of the early Virginians toward the slave-trade. There is evidence, however, to show that although they desired the slave-trade, the rate at which the Negroes were brought in soon alarmed them. In 1710 a duty of £5 was laid on Negroes, but Governor Spotswood "soon perceived that the laying so high a Duty on Negros was intended to discourage the importation," and vetoed the measure.[1] No further restrictive legislation was attempted for some years, but whether on account of the attitude of the governor or the desire of the inhabitants, is not clear. With

1710,	Duty Act:	proposed duty of £5.
1723,	" "	prohibitive (?).
1727,	" "	"
1732,	" "	5%.
1736,	" "	"
1740,	" "	additional duty of 5%.
1754,	" "	" " 5%.
1755,	" "	" " 10% (Repealed, 1760).
1757,	" "	" " 10% (Repealed, 1761).
1759,	" "	20% on colonial slaves.
1766,	" "	additional duty of 10% (Disallowed?).
1769,	" "	" " " "
1772,	" "	£5 on colonial slaves.
	Petition of Burgesses *vs.* Slave-trade.	
1776,	Arraignment of the king in the adopted Frame of Government.	
1778,	Importation prohibited.	

[1] *Letters of Governor Spotswood*, in *Va. Hist. Soc. Coll.*, New Ser., I. 52.

1723 begins a series of acts extending down to the Revolution, which, so far as their contents can be ascertained, seem to have been designed effectually to check the slave-trade. Some of these acts, like those of 1723 and 1727, were almost immediately disallowed.[1] The Act of 1732 laid a duty of 5%, which was continued until 1769,[2] and all other duties were in addition to this; so that by such cumulative duties the rate on slaves reached 25% in 1755,[3] and 35% at the time of Braddock's expedition.[4] These acts were found "very burthensome," "introductive of many frauds," and "very inconvenient,"[5] and were so far repealed that by 1761 the duty was only 15%. As now the Burgesses became more powerful, two or more bills proposing restrictive duties were passed, but disallowed.[6] By 1772 the anti-slave-trade feeling had become considerably developed, and the Burgesses petitioned the king, declaring that "The importation of slaves into the colonies from the coast of Africa hath long been considered as a trade of great inhumanity, and under its present encouragement, we have too much reason to fear *will endanger the very existence* of your Majesty's American dominions. . . . Deeply impressed with these sentiments, we most humbly beseech your Majesty to remove *all those restraints* on your Majesty's governors of this colony, *which inhibit their assenting to such laws as might check so very pernicious a commerce.*"[7]

Nothing further appears to have been done before the war. When, in 1776, the delegates adopted a Frame of Government, it was charged in this document that the king had perverted his high office into a "detestable and insupportable tyranny, by . . . prompting our negroes to rise in arms among us, those very negroes whom, by an inhuman use of his negative, he hath refused us permission to exclude by law."[8] Two years later, in 1778, an "Act to prevent the further

[1] Hening, *Statutes at Large of Virginia*, IV. 118, 182.

[2] *Ibid.*, IV. 317, 394; V. 28, 160, 318; VI. 217, 353; VII. 281; VIII. 190, 336, 532.

[3] *Ibid.*, V. 92; VI. 417, 419, 461, 466.

[4] *Ibid.*, VII. 69, 81.

[5] *Ibid.*, VII. 363, 383.

[6] *Ibid.*, VIII. 237, 337.

[7] *Miscellaneous Papers, 1672–1865*, in *Va. Hist. Soc. Coll.*, New Ser., VI. 14; Tucker, *Blackstone's Commentaries*, I. Part II. App., 51.

[8] Hening, *Statutes*, IX. 112.

importation of Slaves" stopped definitively the legal slave-trade to Virginia.[1]

8. **Restrictions in Maryland.**[2] Not until the impulse of the Assiento had been felt in America, did Maryland make any attempt to restrain a trade from which she had long enjoyed a comfortable revenue. The Act of 1717, laying a duty of 40*s.*,[3] may have been a mild restrictive measure. The duties were slowly increased to 50*s.* in 1754,[4] and £4 in 1763.[5] In 1771 a prohibitive duty of £9 was laid;[6] and in 1783, after the war, all importation by sea was stopped and illegally imported Negroes were freed.[7]

Compared with the trade to Virginia and the Carolinas, the slave-trade to Maryland was small, and seems at no time to have reached proportions which alarmed the inhabitants. It was regulated to the economic demand by a slowly increasing tariff, and finally, after 1769, had nearly ceased of its own accord before the restrictive legislation of Revolutionary times.[8] Probably the proximity of Maryland to Vir-

[1] Importation by sea or by land was prohibited, with a penalty of £1000 for illegal importation and £500 for buying or selling. The Negro was freed, if illegally brought in. This law was revised somewhat in 1785. Cf. Hening, *Statutes*, IX. 471; XII. 182.

[2] The following is a summary of the legislation of the colony of Maryland; details will be found in Appendix A:—

1695,	Duty Act:		10*s.*						
1704,	"	"	20*s.*						
1715,	"	"	"						
1717,	"	"	additional duty of 40*s.* (?).						
1754,	"	"	"	"	10*s.*,	total	50*s.*		
1756,	"	"	"	"	20*s.*	"	40*s.* (?).		
1763,	"	"	"	"	£2	"	£4.		
1771,	"	"	"	"	£5	"	£9.		
1783,	Importation prohibited.								

[3] *Compleat Coll. Laws of Maryland* (ed. 1727), p. 191; Bacon, *Laws of Maryland at Large*, 1728, ch. 8.

[4] Bacon, *Laws*, 1754, ch. 9, 14.

[5] *Ibid.*, 1763, ch. 28.

[6] *Laws of Maryland since 1763*: 1771, ch. 7. Cf. *Ibid.*: 1777, sess. Feb.–Apr., ch. 18.

[7] *Ibid.*: 1783, sess. Apr.–June, ch. 23.

[8] "The last importation of slaves into Maryland was, as I am credibly informed, in the year 1769": William Eddis, *Letters from America* (London, 1792), p. 65, note.

The number of slaves in Maryland has been estimated as follows:—

ginia made an independent slave-trade less necessary to her.

9. **General Character of these Restrictions.** We find in the planting colonies all degrees of advocacy of the trade, from the passiveness of Maryland to the clamor of Georgia. Opposition to the trade did not appear in Georgia, was based almost solely on political fear of insurrection in Carolina, and sprang largely from the same motive in Virginia, mingled with some moral repugnance. As a whole, it may be said that whatever opposition to the slave-trade there was in the planting colonies was based principally on the political fear of insurrection.

In 1704,	4,475.	*Doc. rel. Col. Hist. New York*, V. 605.
" 1710,	7,935.	*Ibid.*
" 1712,	8,330.	Scharf, *History of Maryland*, I. 377.
" 1719,	25,000.	*Doc. rel. Col. Hist. New York*, V. 605.
" 1748,	36,000.	McMahon, *History of Maryland*, I. 313.
" 1755,	46,356.	*Gentleman's Magazine*, XXXIV. 261.
" 1756,	46,225.	McMahon, *History of Maryland*, I. 313.
" 1761,	49,675.	Dexter, *Colonial Population*, p. 21, note.
" 1782,	83,362.	*Encyclopædia Britannica* (9th ed.), XV. 603.
" 1787,	80,000.	Dexter, *Colonial Population*, p. 21, note.

Chapter III

THE FARMING COLONIES.

---

10. **Character of these Colonies.** The colonies of this group, occupying the central portion of the English possessions, comprise those communities where, on account of climate, physical characteristics, and circumstances of settlement, slavery as an institution found but a narrow field for development. The climate was generally rather cool for the newly imported slaves, the soil was best suited to crops to which slave labor was poorly adapted, and the training and habits of the great body of settlers offered little chance for the growth of a slave system. These conditions varied, of course, in different colonies; but the general statement applies to all. These communities of small farmers and traders derived whatever opposition they had to the slave-trade from three sorts of motives,—economic, political, and moral. First, the importation of slaves did not pay, except to supply a moderate demand for household servants. Secondly, these colonies, as well as those in the South, had a wholesome political fear of a large servile population. Thirdly, the settlers of many of these colonies were of sterner moral fibre than the Southern cavaliers and adventurers, and, in the absence of great counteracting motives, were more easily led to oppose the institution and the trade. Finally, it must be noted that these colonies did not so generally regard themselves as temporary commercial investments as did Virginia and Carolina. Intending to found permanent States, these settlers from the first more carefully studied the ultimate interests of those States.

11. **The Dutch Slave-Trade.** The Dutch seem to have commenced the slave-trade to the American continent, the Middle colonies and some of the Southern receiving supplies from

them. John Rolfe relates that the last of August, 1619, there came to Virginia "a dutch man of warre that sold us twenty Negars."[1] This was probably one of the ships of the numerous private Dutch trading-companies which early entered into and developed the lucrative African slave-trade. Ships sailed from Holland to Africa, got slaves in exchange for their goods, carried the slaves to the West Indies or Brazil, and returned home laden with sugar.[2] Through the enterprise of one of these trading-companies the settlement of New Amsterdam was begun, in 1614. In 1621 the private companies trading in the West were all merged into the Dutch West India Company, and given a monopoly of American trade. This company was very active, sending in four years 15,430 Negroes to Brazil,[3] carrying on war with Spain, supplying even the English plantations,[4] and gradually becoming the great slave carrier of the day.

The commercial supremacy of the Dutch early excited the envy and emulation of the English. The Navigation Ordinance of 1651 was aimed at them, and two wars were necessary to wrest the slave-trade from them and place it in the hands of the English. The final terms of peace among other things surrendered New Netherland to England, and opened the way for England to become henceforth the world's greatest slave-trader. Although the Dutch had thus commenced the continental slave-trade, they had not actually furnished a very large number of slaves to the English colonies outside the West Indies. A small trade had, by 1698, brought a few thousand to New York, and still fewer to New Jersey.[5] It was left to the English, with their strong policy in its favor, to develop this trade.

12. **Restrictions in New York.**[6] The early ordinances of

[1] Smith, *Generall Historie of Virginia* (1626 and 1632), p. 126.

[2] Cf. Southey, *History of Brazil*.

[3] De Laet, in O'Callaghan, *Voyages of the Slavers*, etc., p. viii.

[4] See, e. g., Sainsbury, *Cal. State Papers; Col. Ser., America and W. Indies, 1574–1660*, p. 279.

[5] Cf. below, pp. 27, 32, notes; also *Freedoms*, XXX., in O'Callaghan, *Laws of New Netherland, 1638–74* (ed. 1868), p. 10; Brodhead, *History of New York*, I. 312.

[6] The following is a summary of the legislation of the colony of New York; details will be found in Appendix A:—

the Dutch, laying duties, generally of ten per cent, on slaves, probably proved burdensome to the trade, although this was not intentional.[1] The Biblical prohibition of slavery and the slave-trade, copied from New England codes into the Duke of York's Laws, had no practical application,[2] and the trade continued to be encouraged in the governors' instructions. In 1709 a duty of £3 was laid on Negroes from elsewhere than Africa.[3] This was aimed at West India slaves, and was prohibitive. By 1716 the duty on all slaves was £1 12½*s.*, which was probably a mere revenue figure.[4] In 1728 a duty of 40*s.* was laid, to be continued until 1737.[5] It proved restrictive, however, and on the "humble petition of the Merchants and

---

1709,	Duty Act: £3 on Negroes not direct from Africa (Continued by the Acts of 1710, 1711).
1711,	Bill to lay further duty, lost in Council.
1716,	Duty Act: 5 oz. plate on Africans in colony ships.
	10 " " " " other ships.
1728,	" " 40*s.* on Africans, £4 on colonial Negroes.
1732,	" " " " " " "
1734,	" " (?)
1753,	" " 40*s.* " " " "
	(This act was annually continued.)
[1777,	Vermont Constitution does not recognize slavery.]
1785,	Sale of slaves in State prohibited.
[1786,	" " Vermont prohibited.]
1788,	" " State "

[1] O'Callaghan, *Laws of New Netherland, 1638–74*, pp. 31, 348, etc. The colonists themselves were encouraged to trade, but the terms were not favorable enough: *Doc. rel. Col. Hist. New York*, I. 246; *Laws of New Netherland*, pp. 81–2, note, 127. The colonists declared "that they are inclined to a foreign Trade, and especially to the Coast of *Africa*, . . . in order to fetch thence Slaves": O'Callaghan, *Voyages of the Slavers*, etc., p. 172.

[2] *Charter to William Penn*, etc. (1879), p. 12. First published on Long Island in 1664. Possibly Negro slaves were explicitly excepted. Cf. *Magazine of American History*, XI. 411, and *N. Y. Hist. Soc. Coll.*, I. 322.

[3] *Acts of Assembly, 1691–1718*, pp. 97, 125, 134; *Doc. rel. Col. Hist. New York*, V. 178, 185, 293.

[4] The Assembly attempted to raise the slave duty in 1711, but the Council objected (*Doc. rel. Col. Hist. New York*, V. 292 ff.), although, as it seems, not on account of the slave duty in particular. Another act was passed between 1711 and 1716, but its contents are not known (cf. title of the Act of 1716). For the Act of 1716, see *Acts of Assembly, 1691–1718*, p. 224.

[5] *Doc. rel. Col. Hist. New York*, VI. 37, 38.

Traders of the City of Bristol" was disallowed in 1735, as "greatly prejudicial to the Trade and Navigation of this Kingdom."[1] Governor Cosby was also reminded that no duties on slaves payable by the importer were to be laid. Later, in 1753, the 40*s.* duty was restored, but under the increased trade of those days was not felt.[2] No further restrictions seem to have been attempted until 1785, when the sale of slaves in the State was forbidden.[3]

The chief element of restriction in this colony appears to have been the shrewd business sense of the traders, who never flooded the slave market, but kept a supply sufficient for the slowly growing demand. Between 1701 and 1726 only about 2,375 slaves were imported, and in 1774 the total slave population amounted to 21,149.[4] No restriction was ever put by New York on participation in the trade outside the colony, and in spite of national laws New York merchants continued to be engaged in this traffic even down to the Civil War.[5]

Vermont, who withdrew from New York in 1777, in her

[1] *Doc. rel. Col. Hist. New York*, VI. 32–4.

[2] *Ibid.*, VII. 907. This act was annually renewed. The slave duty remained a chief source of revenue down to 1774. Cf. *Report of Governor Tryon*, in *Doc. rel. Col. Hist. New York*, VIII. 452.

[3] *Laws of New York, 1785–88* (ed. 1886), ch. 68, p. 121. Substantially the same act reappears in the revision of the laws of 1788: *Ibid.*, ch. 40, p. 676.

[4] The slave population of New York has been estimated as follows:—

In 1698,	2,170.	*Doc. rel. Col. Hist. New York*, IV. 420.
" 1703,	2,258.	*N. Y. Col. MSS.*, XLVIII.; cited in Hough, *N. Y. Census, 1855*, Introd.
" 1712,	2,425.	*Ibid.*, LVII., LIX. (a partial census).
" 1723,	6,171.	*Doc. rel. Col. Hist. New York*, V. 702.
" 1731,	7,743.	*Ibid.*, V. 929.
" 1737,	8,941.	*Ibid.*, VI. 133.
" 1746,	9,107.	*Ibid.*, VI. 392.
" 1749,	10,692.	*Ibid.*, VI. 550.
" 1756,	13,548.	*London Doc.*, XLIV. 123; cited in Hough, as above.
" 1771,	19,863.	*Ibid.*, XLIV. 144; cited in Hough, as above.
" 1774,	21,149.	*Ibid.*, " " " " "
" 1786,	18,889.	*Deeds in office Sec. of State*, XXII. 35.

Total number of Africans imported from 1701 to 1726, 2,375, of whom 802 were from Africa: O'Callaghan, *Documentary History of New York*, I. 482.

[5] Cf. below, Chapter XI.

first Constitution[1] declared slavery illegal, and in 1786 stopped by law the sale and transportation of slaves within her boundaries.[2]

13. **Restrictions in Pennsylvania and Delaware.**[3] One of the first American protests against the slave-trade came from certain German Friends, in 1688, at a Weekly Meeting held in Germantown, Pennsylvania. "These are the reasons," wrote "Garret henderich, derick up de graeff, Francis daniell Pastorius, and Abraham up Den graef," "why we are against the traffick of men-body, as followeth: Is there any that would be done or handled at this manner? . . . Now, tho they are black, we cannot conceive there is more liberty to have them slaves, as it is to have other white ones. There is a saying, that we shall doe to all men like as we will be done ourselves; making no difference of what generation, descent or colour they are. And those who steal or robb men, and those who

[1] *Vermont State Papers, 1779–86*, p. 244. The return of sixteen slaves in Vermont, by the first census, was an error: *New England Record*, XXIX. 249.

[2] *Vermont State Papers*, p. 505.

[3] The following is a summary of the legislation of the colony of Pennsylvania and Delaware; details will be found in Appendix A:—

1705,	Duty Act:		(?).
1710,	"	"	40*s*. (Disallowed).
1712,	"	"	£20 "
1712,	"	"	supplementary to the Act of 1710.
1715,	"	"	£5 (Disallowed).
1718,	"	"	
1720,	"	"	(?).
1722,	"	"	(?).
1725–6,	"	"	£10.
1726,	"	"	
1729,	"	"	£2.
1761,	"	"	£10.
1761,	"	"	(?).
1768,	"	"	re-enactment of the Act of 1761.
1773,	"	"	perpetual additional duty of £10; total, £20.
1775,	Bill to prohibit importation vetoed by the governor (Delaware).		
1775,	Bill to prohibit importation vetoed by the governor.		
1778,	Back duties on slaves ordered collected.		
1780,	Act for the gradual abolition of slavery.		
1787,	Act to prevent the exportation of slaves (Delaware).		
1788,	Act to prevent the slave-trade.		

buy or purchase them, are they not all alike?"[1] This little leaven helped slowly to work a revolution in the attitude of this great sect toward slavery and the slave-trade. The Yearly Meeting at first postponed the matter, "It having so General a Relation to many other Parts."[2] Eventually, however, in 1696, the Yearly Meeting advised "That Friends be careful not to encourage the bringing in of any more Negroes."[3] This advice was repeated in stronger terms for a quarter-century,[4] and by that time Sandiford, Benezet, Lay, and Woolman had begun their crusade. In 1754 the Friends took a step farther and made the purchase of slaves a matter of discipline.[5] Four years later the Yearly Meeting expressed itself clearly as "against every branch of this practice," and declared that if "any professing with us should persist to vindicate it, and be concerned in importing, selling or purchasing slaves, the respective Monthly Meetings to which they belong should manifest their disunion with such persons."[6] Further, manumission was recommended, and in 1776 made compulsory.[7] The effect of this attitude of the Friends was early manifested in the legislation of all the colonies where the sect was influential, and particularly in Pennsylvania.

One of the first duty acts (1710) laid a restrictive duty of 40*s.* on slaves, and was eventually disallowed.[8] In 1712 William Southeby petitioned the Assembly totally to abolish slavery. This the Assembly naturally refused to attempt; but the same year, in response to another petition "signed by many hands," they passed an "Act to prevent the Importation of Negroes and Indians,"[9]—the first enactment of its kind in

[1] From fac-simile copy, published at Germantown in 1880. Cf. Whittier's poem, "Pennsylvania Hall" (*Poetical Works*, Riverside ed., III. 62); and Proud, *History of Pennsylvania* (1797), I. 219.

[2] From fac-simile copy, published at Germantown in 1880.

[3] Bettle, *Notices of Negro Slavery*, in *Penn. Hist. Soc. Mem.* (1864), I. 383.

[4] Cf. Bettle, *Notices of Negro Slavery, passim.*

[5] Janney, *History of the Friends*, III. 315–7.

[6] *Ibid.*, III. 317.

[7] Bettle, in *Penn. Hist. Soc. Mem.*, I. 395.

[8] *Penn. Col. Rec.* (1852), II. 530; Bettle, in *Penn. Hist. Soc. Mem.*, I. 415.

[9] *Laws of Pennsylvania, collected*, etc., 1714, p. 165; Bettle, in *Penn. Hist. Soc. Mem.*, I. 387.

America. This act was inspired largely by the general fear of insurrection which succeeded the "Negro-plot" of 1712 in New York. It declared: "Whereas, divers Plots and Insurrections have frequently happened, not only in the Islands but on the Main Land of *America*, by Negroes, which have been carried on so far that several of the inhabitants have been barbarously Murthered, an Instance whereof we have lately had in our Neighboring Colony of *New York*,"[1] etc. It then proceeded to lay a prohibitive duty of £20 on all slaves imported. These acts were quickly disposed of in England. Three duty acts affecting Negroes, including the prohibitory act, were in 1713 disallowed, and it was directed that "the Dep^ty^ Govr Council and Assembly of Pensilvania, be & they are hereby Strictly Enjoyned & required not to permit the said Laws . . . to be from henceforward put in Execution."[2] The Assembly repealed these laws, but in 1715 passed another laying a duty of £5, which was also eventually disallowed.[3] Other acts, the provisions of which are not clear, were passed in 1720 and 1722,[4] and in 1725–1726 the duty on Negroes was raised to the restrictive figure of £10.[5] This duty, for some reason not apparent, was lowered to £2 in 1729,[6] but restored again in 1761.[7] A struggle occurred over this last measure, the Friends petitioning for it, and the Philadelphia merchants against it, declaring that "We, the subscribers, ever desirous

[1] See preamble of the act.

[2] The Pennsylvanians did not allow their laws to reach England until long after they were passed: *Penn. Archives*, I. 161–2; *Col. Rec.*, II. 572–3. These acts were disallowed Feb. 20, 1713. Another duty act was passed in 1712, supplementary to the Act of 1710 (*Col. Rec.*, II. 553). The contents are unknown.

[3] *Acts and Laws of Pennsylvania, 1715*, p. 270; Chalmers, *Opinions*, II. 118. Before the disallowance was known, the act had been continued by the Act of 1718: Carey and Bioren, *Laws of Pennsylvania, 1700–1802*, I. 118; *Penn. Col. Rec.*, III. 38.

[4] Carey and Bioren, *Laws*, I. 165; *Penn. Col. Rec.*, III. 171; Bettle, in *Penn. Hist. Soc. Mem.*, I. 389, note.

[5] Carey and Bioren, *Laws*, I. 214; Bettle, in *Penn. Hist. Soc. Mem.*, I. 388. Possibly there were two acts this year.

[6] *Laws of Pennsylvania* (ed. 1742), p. 354, ch. 287. Possibly some change in the currency made this change appear greater than it was.

[7] Carey and Bioren, *Laws*, I. 371; *Acts of Assembly* (ed. 1782), p. 149; Dallas, *Laws*, I. 406, ch. 379. This act was renewed in 1768: Carey and Bioren, *Laws*, I. 451; *Penn. Col. Rec.*, IX. 472, 637, 641.

to extend the Trade of this Province, have seen, for some time past, the many inconveniencys the Inhabitants have suffer'd for want of Labourers and artificers, . . . have for some time encouraged the importation of Negroes;" they prayed therefore at least for a delay in passing the measure.[1] The law, nevertheless, after much debate and altercation with the governor, finally passed.

These repeated acts nearly stopped the trade, and the manumission or sale of Negroes by the Friends decreased the number of slaves in the province. The rising spirit of independence enabled the colony, in 1773, to restore the prohibitive duty of £20 and make it perpetual.[2] After the Revolution unpaid duties on slaves were collected and the slaves registered,[3] and in 1780 an "Act for the gradual Abolition of Slavery" was passed.[4] As there were probably at no time before the war more than 11,000 slaves in Pennsylvania,[5] the task thus accomplished was not so formidable as in many other States. As it was, participation in the slave-trade outside the colony was not prohibited until 1788.[6]

It seems probable that in the original Swedish settlements along the Delaware slavery was prohibited.[7] This measure had, however, little practical effect; for as soon as the Dutch got control the slave-trade was opened, although, as it appears, to no large extent. After the fall of the Dutch Delaware came into English hands. Not until 1775 do we find any legislation on the slave-trade. In that year the colony attempted

[1] *Penn. Col. Rec.*, VIII. 576.

[2] A large petition called for this bill. Much altercation ensued with the governor: Dallas, *Laws*, I. 671, ch. 692; *Penn. Col. Rec.*, X. 77; Bettle, in *Penn. Hist. Soc. Mem.*, I. 388–9.

[3] Dallas, *Laws*, I. 782, ch. 810.

[4] *Ibid.*, I. 838, ch. 881.

[5] There exist but few estimates of the number of slaves in this colony:—

In 1721, 2,500–5,000. *Doc. rel. Col. Hist. New York*, V. 604.
" 1754, 11,000. Bancroft, *Hist. of United States* (1883), II. 391.
" 1760, "very few." Burnaby, *Travels through N. Amer.* (2d ed.), p. 81.
" 1775, 2,000. *Penn. Archives*, IV. 597.

[6] Dallas, *Laws*, II. 586.

[7] Cf. *Argonautica Gustaviana*, pp. 21–3; *Del. Hist. Soc. Papers*, III. 10; *Hazard's Register*, IV. 221, §§ 23, 24; *Hazard's Annals*, p. 372; Armstrong, *Record of Upland Court*, pp. 29–30, and notes.

to prohibit the importation of slaves, but the governor vetoed the bill.[1] Finally, in 1776 by the Constitution, and in 1787 by law, importation and exportation were both prohibited.[2]

14. **Restrictions in New Jersey.**[3] Although the freeholders of West New Jersey declared, in 1676, that "all and every Person and Persons Inhabiting the said Province, shall, as far as in us lies, be free from Oppression and Slavery,"[4] yet Negro slaves are early found in the colony.[5] The first restrictive measure was passed, after considerable friction between the Council and the House, in 1713; it laid a duty of £10, currency.[6] Governor Hunter explained to the Board of Trade that the bill was "calculated to Encourage the Importation of white Servants for the better Peopeling that Country."[7] How long this act continued does not appear; probably, not long. No further legislation was enacted until 1762 or 1763, when a prohibitive duty was laid on account of "the inconvenience the Province is exposed to in lying open to the free importation of Negros, when the Provinces on each side have laid duties on them."[8] The Board of Trade declared that while they did not object to "the Policy of imposing a reasonable duty," they could not assent to this, and the act was disallowed.[9] The Act of 1769 evaded the technical objection of the Board of Trade, and laid a duty of £15 on the first purchasers of Negroes, because, as the act declared, "Duties on the Im-

[1] Force, *American Archives*, 4th Ser., II. 128–9.

[2] *Ibid.*, 5th Ser., I. 1178; *Laws of Delaware, 1797* (Newcastle ed.), p. 884, ch. 145 b.

[3] The following is a summary of the legislation of the colony of New Jersey; details will be found in Appendix A:—

1713, Duty Act: £10.
1763 (?), Duty Act.
1769, " " £15.
1774, " " £5 on Africans, £10 on colonial Negroes.
1786, Importation prohibited.

[4] Leaming and Spicer, *Grants, Concessions*, etc., p. 398. Probably this did not refer to Negroes at all.

[5] Cf. Vincent, *History of Delaware*, I. 159, 381.

[6] *Laws and Acts of New Jersey, 1703–17* (ed. 1717), p. 43.

[7] *N. J. Archives*, IV. 196. There was much difficulty in passing the bill: *Ibid.*, XIII. 516–41.

[8] *Ibid.*, IX. 345–6. The exact provisions of the act I have not found.

[9] *Ibid.*, IX. 383, 447, 458. Chiefly because the duty was laid on the importer.

portation of Negroes in several of the neighbouring Colonies hath, on Experience, been found beneficial in the Introduction of sober, industrious Foreigners."[1] In 1774 a bill which, according to the report of the Council to Governor Morris, "plainly intended an entire Prohibition of all Slaves being imported from foreign Parts," was thrown out by the Council.[2] Importation was finally prohibited in 1786.[3]

15. **General Character of these Restrictions.** The main difference in motive between the restrictions which the planting and the farming colonies put on the African slave-trade, lay in the fact that the former limited it mainly from fear of insurrection, the latter mainly because it did not pay. Naturally, the latter motive worked itself out with much less legislation than the former; for this reason, and because they held a smaller number of slaves, most of these colonies have fewer actual statutes than the Southern colonies. In Pennsylvania alone did this general economic revolt against the trade acquire a distinct moral tinge. Although even here the institution was naturally doomed, yet the clear moral insight of the Quakers checked the trade much earlier than would otherwise have happened. We may say, then, that the farming colonies checked the slave-trade primarily from economic motives.

[1] Allinson, *Acts of Assembly*, pp. 315–6.

[2] *N. J. Archives*, VI. 222.

[3] *Acts of the 10th General Assembly*, May 2, 1786. There are two estimates of the number of slaves in this colony:—

In 1738,	3,981.	*American Annals*,	II. 127.
" 1754,	4,606.	" "	II. 143.

Chapter IV

THE TRADING COLONIES.

---

16. **Character of these Colonies.** The rigorous climate of New England, the character of her settlers, and their pronounced political views gave slavery an even slighter basis here than in the Middle colonies. The significance of New England in the African slave-trade does not therefore lie in the fact that she early discountenanced the system of slavery and stopped importation; but rather in the fact that her citizens, being the traders of the New World, early took part in the carrying slave-trade and furnished slaves to the other colonies. An inquiry, therefore, into the efforts of the New England colonies to suppress the slave-trade would fall naturally into two parts: first, and chiefly, an investigation of the efforts to stop the participation of citizens in the carrying slave-trade; secondly, an examination of the efforts made to banish the slave-trade from New England soil.

17. **New England and the Slave-Trade.** Vessels from Massachusetts,[1] Rhode Island,[2] Connecticut,[3] and, to a less extent, from New Hampshire,[4] were early and largely engaged in the carrying slave-trade. "We know," said Thomas Pemberton in 1795, "that a large trade to Guinea was carried on for many years by the citizens of Massachusetts Colony, who were the proprietors of the vessels and their cargoes, out and

[1] Cf. Weeden, *Economic and Social History of New England*, II. 449–72; G. H. Moore, *Slavery in Massachusetts*; Charles Deane, *Connection of Massachusetts with Slavery*.

[2] Cf. *American Historical Record*, I. 311, 338.

[3] Cf. W. C. Fowler, *Local Law in Massachusetts and Connecticut*, etc., pp. 122–6.

[4] *Ibid.*, p. 124.

home. Some of the slaves purchased in Guinea, and I suppose the greatest part of them, were sold in the West Indies."[1] Dr. John Eliot asserted that "it made a considerable branch of our commerce. . . . It declined very little till the Revolution."[2] Yet the trade of this colony was said not to equal that of Rhode Island. Newport was the mart for slaves offered for sale in the North, and a point of reshipment for all slaves. It was principally this trade that raised Newport to her commercial importance in the eighteenth century.[3] Connecticut, too, was an important slave-trader, sending large numbers of horses and other commodities to the West Indies in exchange for slaves, and selling the slaves in other colonies.

This trade formed a perfect circle. Owners of slavers carried slaves to South Carolina, and brought home naval stores for their ship-building; or to the West Indies, and brought home molasses; or to other colonies, and brought home hogsheads. The molasses was made into the highly prized New England rum, and shipped in these hogsheads to Africa for more slaves.[4] Thus, the rum-distilling industry indicates to some extent the activity of New England in the slave-trade. In May, 1752, one Captain Freeman found so many slavers fitting out that, in spite of the large importations of molasses, he could get no rum for his vessel.[5] In Newport alone twenty-two stills

[1] Deane, *Letters and Documents relating to Slavery in Massachusetts*, in *Mass. Hist. Soc. Coll.*, 5th Ser., III. 392.

[2] *Ibid.*, III. 382.

[3] Weeden, *Economic and Social History of New England*, II. 454.

[4] A typical voyage is that of the brigantine "Sanderson" of Newport. She was fitted out in March, 1752, and carried, beside the captain, two mates and six men, and a cargo of 8,220 gallons of rum, together with "African" iron, flour, pots, tar, sugar, and provisions, shackles, shirts, and water. Proceeding to Africa, the captain after some difficulty sold his cargo for slaves, and in April, 1753, he is expected in Barbadoes, as the consignees write. They also state that slaves are selling at £33 to £56 per head in lots. After a stormy and dangerous voyage, Captain Lindsay arrived, June 17, 1753, with fifty-six slaves, "all in helth & fatt." He also had 40 oz. of gold dust, and 8 or 9 cwt. of pepper. The net proceeds of the sale of all this was £1,324 3*d*. The captain then took on board 55 hhd. of molasses and 3 hhd. 27 bbl. of sugar, amounting to £911 17*s*. 2½*d*., received bills on Liverpool for the balance, and returned in safety to Rhode Island. He had done so well that he was immediately given a new ship and sent to Africa again. *American Historical Record*, I. 315–9, 338–42.

[5] *Ibid.*, I. 316.

were at one time running continuously;[1] and Massachusetts annually distilled 15,000 hogsheads of molasses into this "chief manufacture."[2]

Turning now to restrictive measures, we must first note the measures of the slave-consuming colonies which tended to limit the trade. These measures, however, came comparatively late, were enforced with varying degrees of efficiency, and did not seriously affect the slave-trade before the Revolution. The moral sentiment of New England put some check upon the trade. Although in earlier times the most respectable people took ventures in slave-trading voyages, yet there gradually arose a moral sentiment which tended to make the business somewhat disreputable.[3] In the line, however, of definite legal enactments to stop New England citizens from carrying slaves from Africa to any place in the world, there were, before the Revolution, none. Indeed, not until the years 1787–1788 was slave-trading in itself an indictable offence in any New England State.

The particular situation in each colony, and the efforts to restrict the small importing slave-trade of New England, can best be studied in a separate view of each community.

18. **Restrictions in New Hampshire.** The statistics of slavery in New Hampshire show how weak an institution it always was in that colony.[4] Consequently, when the usual instructions were sent to Governor Wentworth as to the encouragement he must give to the slave-trade, the House replied: "We have considered his Maj[ties] Instruction relating to an Impost on Negroes & Felons, to which this House answers, that there never was any duties laid on either, by this Goverm[t], and so few bro't in

[1] *American Historical Record*, I. 317.

[2] *Ibid.*, I. 344; cf. Weeden, *Economic and Social History of New England*, II. 459.

[3] Cf. *New England Register*, XXXI. 75–6, letter of John Saffin *et al.* to Welstead. Cf. also Sewall, *Protest*, etc.

[4] The number of slaves in New Hampshire has been estimated as follows:

In	1730,	200.	*N. H. Hist. Soc. Coll.*, I. 229.
"	1767,	633.	*Granite Monthly*, IV. 108.
"	1773,	681.	*Ibid.*
"	1773,	674.	*N. H. Province Papers*, X. 636.
"	1775,	479.	*Granite Monthly*, IV. 108.
"	1790,	158.	*Ibid.*

that it would not be worth the Publick notice, so as to make an act concerning them."[1] This remained true for the whole history of the colony. Importation was never stopped by actual enactment, but was eventually declared contrary to the Constitution of 1784.[2] The participation of citizens in the trade appears never to have been forbidden.

19. **Restrictions in Massachusetts.** The early Biblical codes of Massachusetts confined slavery to "lawfull Captives taken in iust warres, & such strangers as willingly selle themselves or are sold to us."[3] The stern Puritanism of early days endeavored to carry this out literally, and consequently when a certain Captain Smith, about 1640, attacked an African village and brought some of the unoffending natives home, he was promptly arrested. Eventually, the General Court ordered the Negroes sent home at the colony's expense, "conceiving themselues bound by ye first oportunity to bear witnes against ye haynos & crying sinn of manstealing, as also to P'scribe such timely redresse for what is past, & such a law for ye future as may sufficiently deterr all oth^{r}s belonging to us to have to do in such vile & most odious courses, iustly abhored of all good & iust men."[4]

The temptation of trade slowly forced the colony from this high moral ground. New England ships were early found in the West Indian slave-trade, and the more the carrying trade developed, the more did the profits of this branch of it attract Puritan captains. By the beginning of the eighteenth century the slave-trade was openly recognized as legitimate commerce; cargoes came regularly to Boston, and "The merchants of Boston quoted negroes, like any other merchandise demanded by their correspondents."[5] At the same time, the Puritan conscience began to rebel against the growth of actual slavery on New England soil. It was a much less violent wrenching of moral ideas of right and wrong to allow Mas-

[1] *N. H. Province Papers*, IV. 617.

[2] *Granite Monthly*, VI. 377; Poore, *Federal and State Constitutions*, pp. 1280–1.

[3] Cf. *The Body of Liberties*, § 91, in Whitmore, *Bibliographical Sketch of the Laws of the Massachusetts Colony*, published at Boston in 1890.

[4] *Mass. Col. Rec.*, II. 168, 176; III. 46, 49, 84.

[5] Weeden, *Economic and Social History of New England*, II. 456.

sachusetts men to carry slaves to South Carolina than to allow cargoes to come into Boston, and become slaves in Massachusetts. Early in the eighteenth century, therefore, opposition arose to the further importation of Negroes, and in 1705 an act "for the Better Preventing of a Spurious and Mixt Issue," laid a restrictive duty of £4 on all slaves imported.[1] One provision of this act plainly illustrates the attitude of Massachusetts: like the acts of many of the New England colonies, it allowed a rebate of the whole duty on re-exportation. The harbors of New England were thus offered as a free exchange-mart for slavers. All the duty acts of the Southern and Middle colonies allowed a rebate of one-half or three-fourths of the duty on the re-exportation of the slave, thus laying a small tax on even temporary importation.

The Act of 1705 was evaded, but it was not amended until 1728, when the penalty for evasion was raised to £100.[2] The act remained in force, except possibly for one period of four years, until 1749. Meantime the movement against importation grew. A bill "for preventing the Importation of Slaves into this Province" was introduced in the Legislature in 1767, but after strong opposition and disagreement between House and Council it was dropped.[3] In 1771 the struggle was renewed. A similar bill passed, but was vetoed by Governor Hutchinson.[4] The imminent war and the discussions incident to it had now more and more aroused public opinion, and there were repeated attempts to gain executive consent to a prohibitory law. In 1774 such a bill was twice passed, but never received assent.[5]

[1] *Mass. Province Laws, 1705–6*, ch. 10.

[2] *Ibid.*, *1728–9*, ch. 16; *1738–9*, ch. 27.

[3] For petitions of towns, cf. Felt, *Annals of Salem* (1849), II. 416; *Boston Town Records, 1758–69*, p. 183. Cf. also Otis's anti-slavery speech in 1761: John Adams, *Works*, X. 315. For proceedings, see *House Journal*, 1767, pp. 353, 358, 387, 390, 393, 408, 409–10, 411, 420. Cf. Samuel Dexter's answer to Dr. Belknap's inquiry, Feb. 23, 1795, in Deane (*Mass. Hist. Soc. Coll.*, 5th Ser., III. 385). A committee on slave importation was appointed in 1764. Cf. *House Journal*, 1763–64, p. 170.

[4] *House Journal*, 1771, pp. 211, 215, 219, 228, 234, 236, 240, 242–3; Moore, *Slavery in Massachusetts*, pp. 131–2.

[5] Felt, *Annals of Salem* (1849), II. 416–7; Swan, *Dissuasion to Great Britain*, etc. (1773), p. x; Washburn, *Historical Sketches of Leicester, Mass.*, pp. 442–3;

The new Revolutionary government first met the subject in the case of two Negroes captured on the high seas, who were advertised for sale at Salem. A resolution was introduced into the Legislature, directing the release of the Negroes, and declaring "That the selling and enslaving the human species is a direct violation of the natural rights alike vested in all men by their Creator, and utterly inconsistent with the avowed principles on which this, and the other United States, have carried their struggle for liberty even to the last appeal." To this the Council would not consent; and the resolution, as finally passed, merely forbade the sale or ill-treatment of the Negroes.[1] Committees on the slavery question were appointed in 1776 and 1777,[2] and although a letter to Congress on the matter, and a bill for the abolition of slavery were reported, no decisive action was taken.

All such efforts were finally discontinued, as the system was already practically extinct in Massachusetts and the custom of importation had nearly ceased. Slavery was eventually declared by judicial decision to have been abolished.[3] The first step toward stopping the participation of Massachusetts citizens in the slave-trade outside the State was taken in 1785, when a committee of inquiry was appointed by the Legislature.[4] No act was, however, passed until 1788, when participation in the trade was prohibited, on pain of £50 forfeit for every slave and £200 for every ship engaged.[5]

Freeman, *History of Cape Cod*, II. 114; Deane, in *Mass. Hist. Soc. Coll.*, 5th Ser., III. 432; Moore, *Slavery in Massachusetts*, pp. 135–40; Williams, *History of the Negro Race in America*, I. 234–6; *House Journal*, March, 1774, pp. 224, 226, 237, etc.; June, 1774, pp. 27, 41, etc. For a copy of the bill, see Moore.

[1] *Mass. Hist. Soc. Proceedings, 1855–58*, p. 196; Force, *American Archives*, 5th Ser., II. 769; *House Journal*, 1776, pp. 105–9; *General Court Records*, March 13, 1776, etc., pp. 581–9; Moore, *Slavery in Massachusetts*, pp. 149–54. Cf. Moore, pp. 163–76.

[2] Moore, *Slavery in Massachusetts*, pp. 148–9, 181–5.

[3] Washburn, *Extinction of Slavery in Massachusetts*; Haynes, *Struggle for the Constitution in Massachusetts*; La Rochefoucauld, *Travels through the United States*, II. 166.

[4] Moore, *Slavery in Massachusetts*, p. 225.

[5] *Perpetual Laws of Massachusetts, 1780–89*, p. 235. The number of slaves in Massachusetts has been estimated as follows:—

20. **Restrictions in Rhode Island.** In 1652 Rhode Island passed a law designed to prohibit life slavery in the colony. It declared that "Whereas, there is a common course practised amongst English men to buy negers, to that end they may have them for service or slaves forever; for the preventinge of such practices among us, let it be ordered, that no blacke mankind or white being forced by covenant bond, or otherwise, to serve any man or his assighnes longer than ten yeares, or untill they come to bee twentie four yeares of age, if they bee taken in under fourteen, from the time of their cominge within the liberties of this Collonie. And at the end or terme of ten yeares to sett them free, as the manner is with the English servants. And that man that will not let them goe free, or shall sell them away elsewhere, to that end that they may bee enslaved to others for a long time, hee or they shall forfeit to the Collonie forty pounds."[1]

This law was for a time enforced,[2] but by the beginning of the eighteenth century it had either been repealed or become a dead letter; for the Act of 1708 recognized perpetual slavery, and laid an impost of £3 on Negroes imported.[3] This duty was really a tax on the transport trade, and produced a steady

In 1676,	200.	Randolph's *Report*, in *Hutchinson's Coll. of Papers*, p. 485.
" 1680,	120.	Deane, *Connection of Mass. with Slavery*, p. 28 ff.
" 1708,	550.	*Ibid.*; Moore, *Slavery in Mass.*, p. 50.
" 1720,	2,000.	*Ibid.*
" 1735,	2,600.	Deane, *Connection of Mass. with Slavery*, p. 28 ff.
" 1749,	3,000.	*Ibid.*
" 1754,	4,489.	*Ibid.*
" 1763,	5,000.	*Ibid.*
" 1764–5,	5,779.	*Ibid.*
" 1776,	5,249.	*Ibid.*
" 1784,	4,377.	Moore, *Slavery in Mass.*, p. 51.
" 1786,	4,371.	*Ibid.*
" 1790,	6,001.	*Ibid.*

[1] *R. I. Col. Rec.*, I. 243.

[2] Cf. letter written in 1681: *New England Register*, XXXI. 75–6. Cf. also Arnold, *History of Rhode Island*, I. 240.

[3] The text of this act is lost (*Col. Rec.*, IV. 34; Arnold, *History of Rhode Island*, II. 31). The Acts of Rhode Island were not well preserved, the first being published in Boston in 1719. Perhaps other whole acts are lost.

income for twenty years.[1] From the year 1700 on, the citizens of this State engaged more and more in the carrying trade, until Rhode Island became the greatest slave-trader in America. Although she did not import many slaves for her own use, she became the clearing-house for the trade of other colonies. Governor Cranston, as early as 1708, reported that between 1698 and 1708 one hundred and three vessels were built in the State, all of which were trading to the West Indies and the Southern colonies.[2] They took out lumber and brought back molasses, in most cases making a slave voyage in between. From this, the trade grew. Samuel Hopkins, about 1770, was shocked at the state of the trade: more than thirty distilleries were running in the colony, and one hundred and fifty vessels were in the slave-trade.[3] "Rhode Island," said he, "has been more deeply interested in the slave-trade, and has enslaved more Africans than any other colony in New England." Later, in 1787, he wrote: "The inhabitants of Rhode Island, especially those of Newport, have had by far the greater share in this traffic, of all these United States. This trade in human species has been the first wheel of commerce in Newport, on which every other movement in business has chiefly depended. That town has been built up, and flourished in times past, at the expense of the blood, the liberty, and happiness of the poor Africans; and the inhabitants have lived on this, and by it have gotten most of their wealth and riches."[4]

The Act of 1708 was poorly enforced. The "good intentions" of its framers " were wholly frustrated" by the clandestine "hiding and conveying said negroes out of the town [Newport] into the country, where they lie concealed."[5] The act was accordingly strengthened by the Acts of 1712 and 1715, and made to apply to importations by land as well as by sea.[6] The Act of 1715, however, favored the trade by admitting

[1] E. g., it was expended to pave the streets of Newport, to build bridges, etc.: *R. I. Col. Rec.*, IV. 191–3, 225.

[2] *Ibid.*, IV. 55–60.

[3] Patten, *Reminiscences of Samuel Hopkins* (1843), p. 80.

[4] Hopkins, *Works* (1854), II. 615.

[5] Preamble of the Act of 1712.

[6] *R. I. Col. Rec.*, IV. 131–5, 138, 143, 191–3.

African Negroes free of duty. The chaotic state of Rhode Island did not allow England often to review her legislation; but as soon as the Act of 1712 came to notice it was disallowed, and accordingly repealed in 1732.[1] Whether the Act of 1715 remained, or whether any other duty act was passed, is not clear.

While the foreign trade was flourishing, the influence of the Friends and of other causes eventually led to a movement against slavery as a local institution. Abolition societies multiplied, and in 1770 an abolition bill was ordered by the Assembly, but it was never passed.[2] Four years later the city of Providence resolved that "as personal liberty is an essential part of the natural rights of mankind," the importation of slaves and the system of slavery should cease in the colony.[3] This movement finally resulted, in 1774, in an act "prohibiting the importation of Negroes into this Colony,"—a law which curiously illustrated the attitude of Rhode Island toward the slave-trade. The preamble of the act declared: "Whereas, the inhabitants of America are generally engaged in the preservation of their own rights and liberties, among which, that of personal freedom must be considered as the greatest; as those who are desirous of enjoying all the advantages of liberty themselves, should be willing to extend personal liberty to others;—Therefore," etc. The statute then proceeded to enact "that for the future, no negro or mulatto slave shall be brought into this colony; and in case any slave shall hereafter be brought in, he or she shall be, and are hereby, rendered immediately free. . . ." The logical ending of such an act would have been a clause prohibiting the participation of Rhode Island citizens in the slave-trade. Not only was such a clause omitted, but the following was inserted instead: "Provided, also, that nothing in this act shall extend, or be deemed to extend, to any negro or mulatto slave brought from the coast of Africa, into the West Indies,

[1] *R. I. Col. Rec.*, IV. 471.

[2] Arnold, *History of Rhode Island*, II. 304, 321, 337. For a probable copy of the bill, see *Narragansett Historical Register*, II. 299.

[3] A man dying intestate left slaves, who became thus the property of the city; they were freed, and the town made the above resolve, May 17, 1774, in town meeting: Staples, *Annals of Providence* (1843), p. 236.

on board any vessel belonging to this colony, and which negro or mulatto slave could not be disposed of in the West Indies, but shall be brought into this colony. Provided, that the owner of such negro or mulatto slave give bond . . . that such negro or mulatto slave shall be exported out of the colony, within one year from the date of such bond; if such negro or mulatto be alive, and in a condition to be removed."[1]

In 1779 an act to prevent the sale of slaves out of the State was passed,[2] and in 1784, an act gradually to abolish slavery.[3] Not until 1787 did an act pass to forbid participation in the slave-trade. This law laid a penalty of £100 for every slave transported and £1000 for every vessel so engaged.[4]

21. **Restrictions in Connecticut.** Connecticut, in common with the other colonies of this section, had a trade for many years with the West Indian slave markets; and though this trade was much smaller than that of the neighboring colonies, yet many of her citizens were engaged in it. A map of Middletown at the time of the Revolution gives, among one hundred families, three slave captains and "three notables" designated as "slave-dealers."[5]

The actual importation was small,[6] and almost entirely un-

[1] *R. I. Col. Rec.*, VII. 251–2.

[2] *Bartlett's Index*, p. 329; Arnold, *History of Rhode Island*, II. 444; *R. I. Col. Rec.*, VIII. 618.

[3] *R. I. Col. Rec.*, X. 7–8; Arnold, *History of Rhode Island*, II. 506.

[4] *Bartlett's Index*, p. 333; *Narragansett Historical Register*, II. 298–9. The number of slaves in Rhode Island has been estimated as follows:—

In 1708,	426.	*R. I. Col. Rec.*, IV. 59.
" 1730,	1,648.	*R. I. Hist. Tracts*, No. 19, pt. 2, p. 99.
" 1749,	3,077.	Williams, *History of the Negro Race in America*, I. 281.
" 1756,	4,697.	*Ibid.*
" 1774,	3,761.	*R. I. Col. Rec.*, VII. 253.

[5] Fowler, *Local Law*, etc., p. 124.

[6] The number of slaves in Connecticut has been estimated as follows:—

In 1680,	30.	*Conn. Col. Rec.*, III. 298.
" 1730,	700.	Williams, *History of the Negro Race in America*, I. 259.
" 1756,	3,636.	Fowler, *Local Law*, etc., p. 140.
" 1762,	4,590.	Williams, *History of the Negro Race in America*, I. 260.
" 1774,	6,562.	Fowler, *Local Law*, etc., p. 140.

restricted before the Revolution, save by a few light, general duty acts. In 1774 the further importation of slaves was prohibited, because "the increase of slaves in this Colony is injurious to the poor and inconvenient." The law prohibited importation under any pretext by a penalty of £100 per slave.[1] This was re-enacted in 1784, and provisions were made for the abolition of slavery.[2] In 1788 participation in the trade was forbidden, and the penalty placed at £50 for each slave and £500 for each ship engaged.[3]

22. **General Character of these Restrictions.** Enough has already been said to show, in the main, the character of the opposition to the slave-trade in New England. The system of slavery had, on this soil and amid these surroundings, no economic justification, and the small number of Negroes here furnished no political arguments against them. The opposition to the importation was therefore from the first based solely on moral grounds, with some social arguments. As to the carrying trade, however, the case was different. Here, too, a feeble moral opposition was early aroused, but it was swept away by the immense economic advantages of the slave traffic to a thrifty seafaring community of traders. This trade no moral suasion, not even the strong "Liberty" cry of the Revolution, was able wholly to suppress, until the closing of the West Indian and Southern markets cut off the demand for slaves.

In 1782,	6,281.	Fowler, *Local Law*, etc., p. 140.
" 1800,	5,281.	*Ibid.*, p. 141.

[1] *Conn. Col. Rec.*, XIV. 329. Fowler (pp. 125–6) says that the law was passed in 1769, as does Sanford (p. 252). I find no proof of this. There was in Connecticut the same Biblical legislation on the trade as in Massachusetts. Cf. *Laws of Connecticut* (repr. 1865), p. 9; also *Col. Rec.*, I. 77. For general duty acts, see *Col. Rec.*, V. 405; VIII. 22; IX. 283; XIII. 72, 125.

[2] *Acts and Laws of Connecticut* (ed. 1784), pp. 233–4.

[3] *Ibid.*, pp. 368, 369, 388.

Chapter V

THE PERIOD OF THE REVOLUTION. 1774–1787.

---

23. **The Situation in 1774.** In the individual efforts of the various colonies to suppress the African slave-trade there may be traced certain general movements. First, from 1638 to 1664, there was a tendency to take a high moral stand against the traffic. This is illustrated in the laws of New England, in the plans for the settlement of Delaware and, later, that of Georgia, and in the protest of the German Friends. The second period, from about 1664 to 1760, has no general unity, but is marked by statutes laying duties varying in design from encouragement to absolute prohibition, by some cases of moral opposition, and by the slow but steady growth of a spirit unfavorable to the long continuance of the trade. The last colonial period, from about 1760 to 1787, is one of pronounced effort to regulate, limit, or totally prohibit the traffic. Beside these general movements, there are many waves of legislation, easily distinguishable, which rolled over several or all of the colonies at various times, such as the series of high duties following the Assiento, and the acts inspired by various Negro "plots."

Notwithstanding this, the laws of the colonies before 1774 had no national unity, the peculiar circumstances of each colony determining its legislation. With the outbreak of the Revolution came unison in action with regard to the slave-trade, as with regard to other matters, which may justly be called national. It was, of course, a critical period,—a period when, in the rapid upheaval of a few years, the complicated and diverse forces of decades meet, combine, act, and react, until the resultant seems almost the work of chance. In the settlement of the fate of slavery and the slave-trade, however, the real crisis came in the calm that succeeded the storm, in that day when, in the opinion of most men, the question seemed already settled. And indeed it needed an exceptionally clear and discerning mind, in 1787, to deny that slavery and the slave-trade in the United States of America were doomed to early annihilation. It seemed certainly a legitimate deduction from the history of the preceding century to conclude that, as the system had risen, flourished, and fallen in Massachusetts, New York, and Pennsylvania, and as South Carolina, Virginia, and Maryland were apparently following in the same legislative path, the next generation would in all probability witness the last throes of the system on our soil.

To be sure, the problem had its uncertain quantities. The motives of the law-makers in South Carolina and Pennsylvania were dangerously different; the century of industrial expansion was slowly dawning and awakening that vast economic revolution in which American slavery was to play so prominent and fatal a rôle; and, finally, there were already in the South faint signs of a changing moral attitude toward slavery, which would no longer regard the system as a temporary makeshift, but rather as a permanent though perhaps unfortunate necessity. With regard to the slave-trade, however, there appeared to be substantial unity of opinion; and there were, in 1787, few things to indicate that a cargo of five hundred African slaves would openly be landed in Georgia in 1860.

24. **The Condition of the Slave-Trade.** In 1760 England, the chief slave-trading nation, was sending on an average to Africa 163 ships annually, with a tonnage of 18,000 tons, carrying exports to the value of £163,818. Only about twenty of these ships regularly returned to England. Most of them carried slaves to the West Indies, and returned laden with sugar and other products. Thus may be formed some idea of the size and importance of the slave-trade at that time, although for a complete view we must add to this the trade under the French, Portuguese, Dutch, and Americans. The trade fell off somewhat toward 1770, but was flourishing again when the Revolution brought a sharp and serious check upon it,

bringing down the number of English slavers, clearing, from 167 in 1774 to 28 in 1779, and the tonnage from 17,218 to 3,475 tons. After the war the trade gradually recovered, and by 1786 had reached nearly its former extent. In 1783 the British West Indies received 16,208 Negroes from Africa, and by 1787 the importation had increased to 21,023. In this latter year it was estimated that the British were taking annually from Africa 38,000 slaves; the French, 20,000; the Portuguese, 10,000; the Dutch and Danes, 6,000; a total of 74,000. Manchester alone sent £180,000 annually in goods to Africa in exchange for Negroes.[1]

25. **The Slave-Trade and the "Association."** At the outbreak of the Revolution six main reasons, some of which were old and of slow growth, others peculiar to the abnormal situation of that time, led to concerted action against the slave-trade. The first reason was the economic failure of slavery in the Middle and Eastern colonies; this gave rise to the presumption that like failure awaited the institution in the South. Secondly, the new philosophy of "Freedom" and the "Rights of man," which formed the corner-stone of the Revolution, made the dullest realize that, at the very least, the slave-trade and a struggle for "liberty" were not consistent. Thirdly, the old fear of slave insurrections, which had long played so prominent a part in legislation, now gained new power from the imminence of war and from the well-founded fear that the British might incite servile uprisings. Fourthly, nearly all the American slave markets were, in 1774–1775, overstocked with slaves, and consequently many of the strongest partisans of the system were "bulls" on the market, and desired to raise the value of their slaves by at least a temporary stoppage of the trade. Fifthly, since the vested interests of the slave-trading merchants were liable to be swept away by the opening of hostilities, and since the price of slaves was low,[2] there was from this quarter little active opposition to a cessation of the trade for a season. Finally, it was long a favorite belief of the supporters of the Revolution that, as English exploitation of

[1] These figures are from the *Report of the Lords of the Committee of Council*, etc. (London, 1789).

[2] Sheffield, *Observations on American Commerce*, p. 28; P. L. Ford, *The Association of the First Congress*, in *Political Science Quarterly*, VI. 615–7.

colonial resources had caused the quarrel, the best weapon to bring England to terms was the economic expedient of stopping all commercial intercourse with her. Since, then, the slave-trade had ever formed an important part of her colonial traffic, it was one of the first branches of commerce which occurred to the colonists as especially suited to their ends.[1]

Such were the complicated moral, political, and economic motives which underlay the first national action against the slave-trade. This action was taken by the "Association," a union of the colonies entered into to enforce the policy of stopping commercial intercourse with England. The movement was not a great moral protest against an iniquitous traffic; although it had undoubtedly a strong moral backing, it was primarily a temporary war measure.

26. **The Action of the Colonies.** The earlier and largely abortive attempts to form non-intercourse associations generally did not mention slaves specifically, although the Virginia House of Burgesses, May 11, 1769, recommended to merchants and traders, among other things, to agree, "That they will not import any slaves, or purchase any imported after the first day of November next, until the said acts are repealed."[2] Later, in 1774, when a Faneuil Hall meeting started the first successful national attempt at non-intercourse, the slave-trade, being at the time especially flourishing, received more attention. Even then slaves were specifically mentioned in the resolutions of but three States. Rhode Island recommended a stoppage of "all trade with Great Britain, Ireland, Africa and the West Indies."[3] North Carolina, in August, 1774, resolved in convention "That we will not import any slave or slaves, or purchase any slave or slaves, imported or brought into this Province by others, from any part of the world, after the first day of *November* next."[4] Virginia gave the slave-trade especial prominence, and was in reality the

[1] Cf., e. g., Arthur Lee's letter to R. H. Lee, March 18, 1774, in which non-intercourse is declared "the only advisable and sure mode of defence": Force, *American Archives*, 4th Ser., I. 229. Cf. also *Ibid.*, p. 240; Ford, in *Political Science Quarterly*, VI. 614–5.

[2] Goodloe, *Birth of the Republic*, p. 260.

[3] Staples, *Annals of Providence* (1843), p. 235.

[4] Force, *American Archives*, 4th Ser., I. 735. This was probably copied from the Virginia resolve.

leading spirit to force her views on the Continental Congress. The county conventions of that colony first took up the subject. Fairfax County thought "that during our present difficulties and distress, no slaves ought to be imported," and said: "We take this opportunity of declaring our most earnest wishes to see an entire stop forever put to such a wicked, cruel, and unnatural trade."[1] Prince George and Nansemond Counties resolved "That the *African* trade is injurious to this Colony, obstructs the population of it by freemen, prevents manufacturers and other useful emigrants from *Europe* from settling amongst us, and occasions an annual increase of the balance of trade against this Colony."[2] The Virginia colonial convention, August, 1774, also declared: "We will neither ourselves import, nor purchase any slave or slaves imported by any other person, after the first day of *November* next, either from *Africa*, the *West Indies*, or any other place."[3]

In South Carolina, at the convention July 6, 1774, decided opposition to the non-importation scheme was manifested, though how much this was due to the slave-trade interest is not certain. Many of the delegates wished at least to limit the powers of their representatives, and the Charleston Chamber of Commerce flatly opposed the plan of an "Association." Finally, however, delegates with full powers were sent to Congress. The arguments leading to this step were not in all cases on the score of patriotism; a Charleston manifesto argued: "The planters are greatly in arrears to the merchants; a stoppage of importation would give them all an opportunity to extricate themselves from debt. The merchants would have time to settle their accounts, and be ready with the return of liberty to renew trade."[4]

27. **The Action of the Continental Congress.** The first Continental Congress met September 5, 1774, and on September 22 recommended merchants to send no more orders for foreign goods.[5] On September 27 "Mr. Lee made a motion for a non-importation," and it was unanimously resolved to

[1] Force, *American Archives*, 4th Ser., I. 600.

[2] *Ibid.*, I. 494, 530. Cf. pp. 523, 616, 641, etc.

[3] *Ibid.*, I. 687.

[4] *Ibid.*, I. 511, 526. Cf. also p. 316.

[5] *Journals of Cong.*, I. 20. Cf. Ford, in *Political Science Quarterly*, VI. 615–7.

import no goods from Great Britain after December 1, 1774.[1] Afterward, Ireland and the West Indies were also included, and a committee consisting of Low of New York, Mifflin of Pennsylvania, Lee of Virginia, and Johnson of Connecticut were appointed "to bring in a Plan for carrying into Effect the Non-importation, Non-consumption, and Non-exportation resolved on."[2] The next move was to instruct this committee to include in the proscribed articles, among other things, "Molasses, Coffee or Piemento from the *British* Plantations or from *Dominica*,"—a motion which cut deep into the slave-trade circle of commerce, and aroused some opposition. "Will, can, the people bear a total interruption of the West India trade?" asked Low of New York; "Can they live without rum, sugar, and molasses? Will not this impatience and vexation defeat the measure?"[3]

The committee finally reported, October 12, 1774, and after three days' discussion and amendment the proposal passed. This document, after a recital of grievances, declared that, in the opinion of the colonists, a non-importation agreement would best secure redress; goods from Great Britain, Ireland, the East and West Indies, and Dominica were excluded; and it was resolved that "We will neither import, nor purchase any Slave imported after the First Day of *December* next; after which Time, we will wholly discontinue the Slave Trade, and will neither be concerned in it ourselves, nor will we hire our Vessels, nor sell our Commodities or Manufactures to those who are concerned in it."[4]

Strong and straightforward as this resolution was, time unfortunately proved that it meant very little. Two years later, in this same Congress, a decided opposition was manifested to branding the slave-trade as inhuman, and it was thirteen years before South Carolina stopped the slave-trade or Massachusetts prohibited her citizens from engaging in it. The passing of so strong a resolution must be explained by the motives before given, by the character of the drafting com-

[1] John Adams, *Works*, II. 382.

[2] *Journals of Cong.*, I. 21.

[3] *Ibid.*, I. 24; Drayton, *Memoirs of the American Revolution*, I. 147; John Adams, *Works*, II. 394.

[4] *Journals of Cong.*, I. 27, 32–8.

mittee, by the desire of America in this crisis to appear well before the world, and by the natural moral enthusiasm aroused by the imminence of a great national struggle.

28. **Reception of the Slave-Trade Resolution.** The unanimity with which the colonists received this "Association" is not perhaps as remarkable as the almost entire absence of comment on the radical slave-trade clause. A Connecticut town-meeting in December, 1774, noticed "with singular pleasure . . . the second Article of the Association, in which it is agreed to import no more Negro Slaves."[1] This comment appears to have been almost the only one. There were in various places some evidences of disapproval; but only in the State of Georgia was this widespread and determined, and based mainly on the slave-trade clause.[2] This opposition delayed the ratification meeting until January 18, 1775, and then delegates from but five of the twelve parishes appeared, and many of these had strong instructions against the approval of the plan. Before this meeting could act, the governor adjourned it, on the ground that it did not represent the province. Some of the delegates signed an agreement, one article of which promised to stop the importation of slaves March 15, 1775, i. e., four months later than the national "Association" had directed. This was not, of course, binding on the province; and although a town like Darien might declare "our disapprobation and abhorrence of the unnatural practice of Slavery in *America*,"[3] yet the powerful influence of Savannah was "not likely soon to give matters a favourable turn. The importers were mostly against any interruption, and the consumers very much divided."[4] Thus the efforts of this Assembly failed, their resolutions being almost unknown, and, as a gentleman writes, "I hope for the honour of the Province ever will remain so."[5] The delegates to the Continental Congress selected by this rump assembly refused to take their seats.

[1] Danbury, Dec. 12, 1774: Force, *American Archives*, 4th Ser., I. 1038. This case and that of Georgia are the only ones I have found in which the slave-trade clause was specifically mentioned.

[2] Force, *American Archives*, 4th Ser., I. 1033, 1136, 1160, 1163; II. 279–281, 1544; *Journals of Cong.*, May 13, 15, 17, 1775.

[3] Force, *American Archives*, 4th Ser., I. 1136.

[4] *Ibid.*, II. 279–81.

[5] *Ibid.*, I. 1160.

Meantime South Carolina stopped trade with Georgia, because it "hath not acceded to the Continental Association,"[1] and the single Georgia parish of St. Johns appealed to the second Continental Congress to except it from the general boycott of the colony. This county had already resolved not to "purchase any Slave imported at *Savannah* (large Numbers of which we understand are there expected) till the Sense of Congress shall be made known to us."[2]

May 17, 1775, Congress resolved unanimously "That all exportations to *Quebec*, *Nova-Scotia*, the Island of *St. John's*, *Newfoundland*, *Georgia*, except the Parish of *St. John's*, and to *East* and *West Florida*, immediately cease."[3] These measures brought the refractory colony to terms, and the Provincial Congress, July 4, 1775, finally adopted the "Association," and resolved, among other things, "That we will neither import or purchase any Slave imported from Africa, or elsewhere, after this day."[4]

The non-importation agreement was in the beginning, at least, well enforced by the voluntary action of the loosely federated nation. The slave-trade clause seems in most States to have been observed with the others. In South Carolina "a cargo of near three hundred slaves was sent out of the Colony by the consignee, as being interdicted by the second article of the Association."[5] In Virginia the vigilance committee of Norfolk "hold up for your just indignation Mr. *John Brown*, Merchant, of this place," who has several times imported slaves from Jamaica; and he is thus publicly censured "to the end that all such foes to the rights of *British America* may be publickly known . . . as the enemies of *American* Liberty, and that every person may henceforth break off all dealings with him."[6]

29. **Results of the Resolution.** The strain of war at last proved too much for this voluntary blockade, and after some

[1] Force, *American Archives*, 4th Ser., I. 1163.
[2] *Journals of Cong.*, May 13, 15, 1775.
[3] *Ibid.*, May 17, 1775.
[4] Force, *American Archives*, 4th Ser., II. 1545.
[5] Drayton, *Memoirs of the American Revolution*, I. 182. Cf. pp. 181–7; Ramsay, *History of S. Carolina*, I. 231.
[6] Force, *American Archives*, 4th Ser., II. 33–4.

hesitancy Congress, April 3, 1776, resolved to allow the importation of articles not the growth or manufacture of Great Britain, except tea. They also voted "That no slaves be imported into any of the thirteen United Colonies."[1] This marks a noticeable change of attitude from the strong words of two years previous: the former was a definitive promise; this is a temporary resolve, which probably represented public opinion much better than the former. On the whole, the conclusion is inevitably forced on the student of this first national movement against the slave-trade, that its influence on the trade was but temporary and insignificant, and that at the end of the experiment the outlook for the final suppression of the trade was little brighter than before. The whole movement served as a sort of social test of the power and importance of the slave-trade, which proved to be far more powerful than the platitudes of many of the Revolutionists had assumed.

The effect of the movement on the slave-trade in general was to begin, possibly a little earlier than otherwise would have been the case, that temporary breaking up of the trade which the war naturally caused. "There was a time, during the late war," says Clarkson, "when the slave trade may be considered as having been nearly abolished."[2] The prices of slaves rose correspondingly high, so that smugglers made fortunes.[3] It is stated that in the years 1772–1778 slave merchants of Liverpool failed for the sum of £710,000.[4] All this, of course, might have resulted from the war, without the "Association;" but in the long run the "Association" aided in frustrating the very designs which the framers of the first resolve had in mind; for the temporary stoppage in the end created an extraordinary demand for slaves, and led to a slave-trade after the war nearly as large as that before.

30. **The Slave-Trade and Public Opinion after the War.** The Declaration of Independence showed a significant drift of public opinion from the firm stand taken in the "Association" resolutions. The clique of political philosophers to which Jefferson belonged never imagined the continued exis-

[1] *Journals of Cong.*, II. 122.

[2] Clarkson, *Impolicy of the Slave-Trade*, pp. 125–8.

[3] *Ibid.*, pp. 25–6.

[4] *Ibid.*

tence of the country with slavery. It is well known that the first draft of the Declaration contained a severe arraignment of Great Britain as the real promoter of slavery and the slave-trade in America. In it the king was charged with waging "cruel war against human nature itself, violating its most sacred rights of life and liberty in the persons of a distant people who never offended him, captivating and carrying them into slavery in another hemisphere, or to incur miserable death in their transportation thither. This piratical warfare, the opprobrium of *infidel* powers, is the warfare of the *Christian* king of Great Britain. Determined to keep open a market where *men* should be bought and sold, he has prostituted his negative for suppressing every legislative attempt to prohibit or to restrain this execrable commerce. And that this assemblage of horrors might want no fact of distinguished die, he is now exciting those very people to rise in arms among us, and to purchase that liberty of which he has deprived them, by murdering the people on whom he also obtruded them: thus paying off former crimes committed against the *liberties* of one people with crimes which he urges them to commit against the *lives* of another."[1]

To this radical and not strictly truthful statement, even the large influence of the Virginia leaders could not gain the assent of the delegates in Congress. The afflatus of 1774 was rapidly subsiding, and changing economic conditions had already led many to look forward to a day when the slave-trade could successfully be reopened. More important than this, the nation as a whole was even less inclined now than in 1774 to denounce the slave-trade uncompromisingly. Jefferson himself says that this clause "was struck out in complaisance to South Carolina and Georgia, who had never attempted to restrain the importation of slaves, and who, on the contrary, still wished to continue it. Our northern brethren also, I believe," said he, "felt a little tender under those censures; for though their people had very few slaves themselves, yet they had been pretty considerable carriers of them to others."[2]

As the war slowly dragged itself to a close, it became in-

[1] Jefferson, *Works* (Washington, 1853–4), I. 23–4. On the Declaration as an anti-slavery document, cf. Elliot, *Debates* (1861), I. 89.

[2] Jefferson, *Works* (Washington, 1853–4), I. 19.

creasingly evident that a firm moral stand against slavery and the slave-trade was not a probability. The reaction which naturally follows a period of prolonged and exhausting strife for high political principles now set in. The economic forces of the country, which had suffered most, sought to recover and rearrange themselves; and all the selfish motives that impelled a bankrupt nation to seek to gain its daily bread did not long hesitate to demand a reopening of the profitable African slave-trade. This demand was especially urgent from the fact that the slaves, by pillage, flight, and actual fighting, had become so reduced in numbers during the war that an urgent demand for more laborers was felt in the South.

Nevertheless, the revival of the trade was naturally a matter of some difficulty, as the West India circuit had been cut off, leaving no resort except to contraband traffic and the direct African trade. The English slave-trade after the peace "returned to its former state," and was by 1784 sending 20,000 slaves annually to the West Indies.[1] Just how large the trade to the continent was at this time there are few means of ascertaining; it is certain that there was a general reopening of the trade in the Carolinas and Georgia, and that the New England traders participated in it. This traffic undoubtedly reached considerable proportions; and through the direct African trade and the illicit West India trade many thousands of Negroes came into the United States during the years 1783–1787.[2]

Meantime there was slowly arising a significant divergence of opinion on the subject. Probably the whole country still regarded both slavery and the slave-trade as temporary; but the Middle States expected to see the abolition of both within a generation, while the South scarcely thought it probable to prohibit even the slave-trade in that short time. Such a difference might, in all probability, have been satisfactorily adjusted, if both parties had recognized the real gravity of the matter. As it was, both regarded it as a problem of secondary importance, to be solved after many other more pressing ones

[1] Clarkson, *Impolicy of the Slave-Trade*, pp. 25–6; *Report*, etc., as above.

[2] Witness the many high duty acts on slaves, and the revenue derived therefrom. Massachusetts had sixty distilleries running in 1783. Cf. Sheffield, *Observations on American Commerce*, p. 267.

had been disposed of. The anti-slavery men had seen slavery die in their own communities, and expected it to die the same way in others, with as little active effort on their own part. The Southern planters, born and reared in a slave system, thought that some day the system might change, and possibly disappear; but active effort to this end on their part was ever farthest from their thoughts. Here, then, began that fatal policy toward slavery and the slave-trade that characterized the nation for three-quarters of a century, the policy of *laissez-faire, laissez-passer*.

31. **The Action of the Confederation.** The slave-trade was hardly touched upon in the Congress of the Confederation, except in the ordinance respecting the capture of slaves, and on the occasion of the Quaker petition against the trade, although, during the debate on the Articles of Confederation, the counting of slaves as well as of freemen in the apportionment of taxes was urged as a measure that would check further importation of Negroes. "It is our duty," said Wilson of Pennsylvania, "to lay every discouragement on the importation of slaves; but this amendment [i. e., to count two slaves as one freeman] would give the *jus trium liberorum* to him who would import slaves."[1] The matter was finally compromised by apportioning requisitions according to the value of land and buildings.

After the Articles went into operation, an ordinance in regard to the recapture of fugitive slaves provided that, if the capture was made on the sea below high-water mark, and the Negro was not claimed, he should be freed. Matthews of South Carolina demanded the yeas and nays on this proposition, with the result that only the vote of his State was recorded against it.[2]

On Tuesday, October 3, 1783, a deputation from the Yearly Meeting of the Pennsylvania, New Jersey, and Delaware Friends asked leave to present a petition. Leave was granted the following day,[3] but no further minute appears. According to the report of the Friends, the petition was against the

[1] Elliot, *Debates*, I. 72–3. Cf. Art. 8 of the Articles of Confederation.

[2] *Journals of Cong.*, 1781, June 25; July 18; Sept. 21, 27; Nov. 8, 13, 30; Dec. 4.

[3] *Ibid.*, 1782–3, pp. 418–9, 425.

slave-trade; and "though the Christian rectitude of the concern was by the Delegates generally acknowledged, yet not being vested with the powers of legislation, they declined promoting any public remedy against the gross national iniquity of trafficking in the persons of fellow-men."[1]

The only legislative activity in regard to the trade during the Confederation was taken by the individual States.[2] Before 1778 Connecticut, Vermont, Pennsylvania, Delaware, and Virginia had by law stopped the further importation of slaves, and importation had practically ceased in all the New England and Middle States, including Maryland. In consequence of the revival of the slave-trade after the War, there was then a lull in State activity until 1786, when North Carolina laid a prohibitive duty, and South Carolina, a year later, began her series of temporary prohibitions. In 1787–1788 the New England States forbade the participation of their citizens in the traffic. It was this wave of legislation against the traffic which did so much to blind the nation as to the strong hold which slavery still had on the country.

[1] *Annals of Cong.*, 1 Cong. 2 sess. p. 1183.

[2] Cf. above, chapters ii., iii., iv.

Chapter VI

THE FEDERAL CONVENTION. 1787.

---

32. **The First Proposition.** Slavery occupied no prominent place in the Convention called to remedy the glaring defects of the Confederation, for the obvious reason that few of the delegates thought it expedient to touch a delicate subject which, if let alone, bade fair to settle itself in a manner satisfactory to all. Consequently, neither slavery nor the slave-trade is specifically mentioned in the delegates' credentials of any of the States, nor in Randolph's, Pinckney's, or Hamilton's plans, nor in Paterson's propositions. Indeed, the debate from May 14 to June 19, when the Committee of the Whole reported, touched the subject only in the matter of the ratio of representation of slaves. With this same exception, the report of the Committee of the Whole contained no reference to slavery or the slave-trade, and the twenty-three resolutions of the Convention referred to the Committee of Detail, July 23 and 26, maintain the same silence.

The latter committee, consisting of Rutledge, Randolph, Gorham, Ellsworth, and Wilson, reported a draft of the Constitution August 6, 1787. The committee had, in its deliberations, probably made use of a draft of a national Constitution made by Edmund Randolph.[1] One clause of this provided that "no State shall lay a duty on imports;" and, also, "1. No duty on exports. 2. No prohibition on such inhabitants as the United States think proper to admit. 3. No duties by way of such prohibition." It does not appear that any reference to Negroes was here intended. In the extant copy, however,

[1] Conway, *Life and Papers of Edmund Randolph*, ch. ix.

notes in Edward Rutledge's handwriting change the second clause to "No prohibition on such inhabitants or people as the several States think proper to admit."[1] In the report, August 6, these clauses take the following form:—

"Article VII. Section 4. No tax or duty shall be laid by the legislature on articles exported from any state; nor on the migration or importation of such persons as the several states shall think proper to admit; nor shall such migration or importation be prohibited."[2]

33. **The General Debate.** This, of course, referred both to immigrants ("migration") and to slaves ("importation").[3] Debate on this section began Tuesday, August 22, and lasted two days. Luther Martin of Maryland precipitated the discussion by a proposition to alter the section so as to allow a prohibition or tax on the importation of slaves. The debate immediately became general, being carried on principally by Rutledge, the Pinckneys, and Williamson from the Carolinas; Baldwin of Georgia; Mason, Madison, and Randolph of Virginia; Wilson and Gouverneur Morris of Pennsylvania; Dickinson of Delaware; and Ellsworth, Sherman, Gerry, King, and Langdon of New England.[4]

In this debate the moral arguments were prominent. Colonel George Mason of Virginia denounced the traffic in slaves as "infernal;" Luther Martin of Maryland regarded it as "inconsistent with the principles of the revolution, and dishonorable to the American character." "Every principle of honor and safety," declared John Dickinson of Delaware, "demands the exclusion of slaves." Indeed, Mason solemnly averred that the crime of slavery might yet bring the judgment of God on the nation. On the other side, Rutledge of South Carolina bluntly declared that religion and humanity had nothing to do with the question, that it was a matter of "interest" alone. Gerry of Massachusetts wished merely to refrain from giving direct sanction to the trade, while others contented themselves with pointing out the inconsistency of condemning the slave-trade and defending slavery.

[1] Conway, *Life and Papers of Edmund Randolph*, p. 78.

[2] Elliot, *Debates*, I. 227.

[3] Cf. Conway, *Life and Papers of Edmund Randolph*, pp. 78–9.

[4] For the following debate, Madison's notes (Elliot, *Debates*, V. 457 ff.) are mainly followed.

The difficulty of the whole argument, from the moral standpoint, lay in the fact that it was completely checkmated by the obstinate attitude of South Carolina and Georgia. Their delegates—Baldwin, the Pinckneys, Rutledge, and others—asserted flatly, not less than a half-dozen times during the debate, that these States "can never receive the plan if it prohibits the slave-trade;" that "if the Convention thought" that these States would consent to a stoppage of the slave-trade, "the expectation is vain."[1] By this stand all argument from the moral standpoint was virtually silenced, for the Convention evidently agreed with Roger Sherman of Connecticut that "it was better to let the Southern States import slaves than to part with those States."

In such a dilemma the Convention listened not unwillingly to the *non possumus* arguments of the States' Rights advocates. The "morality and wisdom" of slavery, declared Ellsworth of Connecticut, "are considerations belonging to the States themselves;" let every State "import what it pleases;" the Confederation has not "meddled" with the question, why should the Union? It is a dangerous symptom of centralization, cried Baldwin of Georgia; the "central States" wish to be the "vortex for everything," even matters of "a local nature." The national government, said Gerry of Massachusetts, had nothing to do with slavery in the States; it had only to refrain from giving direct sanction to the system. Others opposed this whole argument, declaring, with Langdon of New Hampshire, that Congress ought to have this power, since, as Dickinson tartly remarked, "The true question was, whether the national happiness would be promoted or impeded by the importation; and this question ought to be left to the national government, not to the states particularly interested."

Beside these arguments as to the right of the trade and the proper seat of authority over it, many arguments of general expediency were introduced. From an economic standpoint, for instance, General C. C. Pinckney of South Carolina "contended, that the importation of slaves would be for the interest of the whole Union. The more slaves, the more produce." Rutledge of the same State declared: "If the Northern States

[1] Cf. Elliot, *Debates*, V., *passim.*

consult their interest, they will not oppose the increase of slaves, which will increase the commodities of which they will become the carriers." This sentiment found a more or less conscious echo in the words of Ellsworth of Connecticut, "What enriches a part enriches the whole." It was, moreover, broadly hinted that the zeal of Maryland and Virginia against the trade had an economic rather than a humanitarian motive, since they had slaves enough and to spare, and wished to sell them at a high price to South Carolina and Georgia, who needed more. In such case restrictions would unjustly discriminate against the latter States. The argument from history was barely touched upon. Only once was there an allusion to "the example of all the world" "in all ages" to justify slavery,[1] and once came the counter declaration that "Greece and Rome were made unhappy by their slaves."[2] On the other hand, the military weakness of slavery in the late war led to many arguments on that score. Luther Martin and George Mason dwelt on the danger of a servile class in war and insurrection; while Rutledge hotly replied that he "would readily exempt the other states from the obligation to protect the Southern against them;" and Ellsworth thought that the very danger would "become a motive to kind treatment." The desirability of keeping slavery out of the West was once mentioned as an argument against the trade: to this all seemed tacitly to agree.[3]

Throughout the debate it is manifest that the Convention had no desire really to enter upon a general slavery argument. The broader and more theoretic aspects of the question were but lightly touched upon here and there. Undoubtedly, most of the members would have much preferred not to raise the question at all; but, as it was raised, the differences of opinion were too manifest to be ignored, and the Convention, after its first perplexity, gradually and perhaps too willingly set itself to work to find some "middle ground" on which all parties could stand. The way to this compromise was pointed out by the South. The most radical pro-slavery arguments always ended with the opinion that "if the Southern States were let

[1] By Charles Pinckney.

[2] By John Dickinson.

[3] Mentioned in the speech of George Mason.

alone, they will probably of themselves stop importations."[1] To be sure, General Pinckney admitted that, "candidly, he did not think South Carolina would stop her importations of slaves in any short time;" nevertheless, the Convention "observed," with Roger Sherman, "that the abolition of slavery seemed to be going on in the United States, and that the good sense of the several states would probably by degrees complete it." Economic forces were evoked to eke out moral motives: when the South had its full quota of slaves, like Virginia it too would abolish the trade; free labor was bound finally to drive out slave labor. Thus the chorus of *"laissez-faire"* increased; and compromise seemed at least in sight, when Connecticut cried, "Let the trade alone!" and Georgia denounced it as an "evil." Some few discordant notes were heard, as, for instance, when Wilson of Pennsylvania made the uncomforting remark, "If South Carolina and Georgia were themselves disposed to get rid of the importation of slaves in a short time, as had been suggested, they would never refuse to unite because the importation might be prohibited."

With the spirit of compromise in the air, it was not long before the general terms were clear. The slavery side was strongly intrenched, and had a clear and definite demand. The forces of freedom were, on the contrary, divided by important conflicts of interest, and animated by no very strong and decided anti-slavery spirit with settled aims. Under such circumstances, it was easy for the Convention to miss the opportunity for a really great compromise, and to descend to a scheme that savored unpleasantly of "log-rolling." The student of the situation will always have good cause to believe that a more sturdy and definite anti-slavery stand at this point might have changed history for the better.

34. **The Special Committee and the "Bargain."** Since the debate had, in the first place, arisen from a proposition to tax the importation of slaves, the yielding of this point by the South was the first move toward compromise. To all but the doctrinaires, who shrank from taxing men as property, the argument that the failure to tax slaves was equivalent to a

[1] Charles Pinckney. Baldwin of Georgia said that if the State were left to herself, "she may probably put a stop to the evil": Elliot, *Debates*, V. 459.

bounty, was conclusive. With this point settled, Randolph voiced the general sentiment, when he declared that he "was for committing, in order that some middle ground might, if possible, be found." Finally, Gouverneur Morris discovered the "middle ground," in his suggestion that the whole subject be committed, "including the clauses relating to taxes on exports and to a navigation act. These things," said he, "may form a bargain among the Northern and Southern States." This was quickly assented to; and sections four and five, on slave-trade and capitation tax, were committed by a vote of 7 to 3,[1] and section six, on navigation acts, by a vote of 9 to 2.[2] All three clauses were referred to the following committee: Langdon of New Hampshire, King of Massachusetts, Johnson of Connecticut, Livingston of New Jersey, Clymer of Pennsylvania, Dickinson of Delaware, Martin of Maryland, Madison of Virginia, Williamson of North Carolina, General Pinckney of South Carolina, and Baldwin of Georgia.

The fullest account of the proceedings of this committee is given in Luther Martin's letter to his constituents, and is confirmed in its main particulars by similar reports of other delegates. Martin writes: "A committee of *one* member from each state was chosen by ballot, to take this part of the system under their consideration, and to endeavor to agree upon some report which should reconcile those states [i. e., South Carolina and Georgia]. To this committee also was referred the following proposition, which had been reported by the committee of detail, viz.: 'No navigation act shall be passed without the assent of two thirds of the members present in each house'—a proposition which the staple and commercial states were solicitous to retain, lest their commerce should be placed too much under the power of the Eastern States, but which these last States were as anxious to reject. This committee—of which also I had the honor to be a member—met, and took under their consideration the subjects committed to them. I found the *Eastern* States, notwithstanding their *aversion to slavery*, were very willing to indulge the Southern

[1] *Affirmative:* Connecticut, New Jersey, Maryland, Virginia, North Carolina, South Carolina, Georgia,—7. *Negative:* New Hampshire, Pennsylvania, Delaware,—3. *Absent:* Massachusetts,—1.

[2] *Negative:* Connecticut and New Jersey.

States at least with a temporary liberty to prosecute the slave trade, provided the Southern States would, in their turn, gratify *them*, by laying no restriction on navigation acts; and after a very little time, the committee, by a great majority, agreed on a report, by which the general government was to be prohibited from preventing the importation of slaves for a limited time, and the restrictive clause relative to navigation acts was to be omitted."[1]

That the "bargain" was soon made is proven by the fact that the committee reported the very next day, Friday, August 24, and that on Saturday the report was taken up. It was as follows: "Strike out so much of the fourth section as was referred to the committee, and insert 'The migration or importation of such persons as the several states, now existing, shall think proper to admit, shall not be prohibited by the legislature prior to the year 1800; but a tax or duty may be imposed on such migration or importation, at a rate not exceeding the average of the duties laid on imports.' The fifth section to remain as in the report. The sixth section to be stricken out."[2]

35. **The Appeal to the Convention.** The ensuing debate,[3] which lasted only a part of the day, was evidently a sort of appeal to the House on the decisions of the committee. It throws light on the points of disagreement. General Pinckney first proposed to extend the slave-trading limit to 1808, and Gorham of Massachusetts seconded the motion. This brought a spirited protest from Madison: "Twenty years will produce all the mischief that can be apprehended from the liberty to import slaves. So long a term will be more dishonorable to the American character than to say nothing about it in the Constitution."[4] There was, however, evidently another "bargain" here; for, without farther debate, the South and the East voted the extension, 7 to 4, only New Jersey, Pennsylvania, Delaware, and Virginia objecting. The ambiguous phraseology of the whole slave-trade section as reported did not pass without comment; Gouverneur Morris would have it

[1] Luther Martin's letter, in Elliot, *Debates*, I. 373. Cf. explanations of delegates in the South Carolina, North Carolina, and other conventions.

[2] Elliot, *Debates*, V. 471.

[3] Saturday, Aug. 25, 1787.

[4] Elliot, *Debates*, V. 477.

read: "The importation of slaves into North Carolina, South Carolina, and Georgia, shall not be prohibited," etc.[1] This emendation was, however, too painfully truthful for the doctrinaires, and was, amid a score of objections, withdrawn. The taxation clause also was manifestly too vague for practical use, and Baldwin of Georgia wished to amend it by inserting "common impost on articles not enumerated," in lieu of the "average" duty.[2] This minor point gave rise to considerable argument: Sherman and Madison deprecated any such recognition of property in man as taxing would imply; Mason and Gorham argued that the tax restrained the trade; while King, Langdon, and General Pinckney contented themselves with the remark that this clause was "the price of the first part." Finally, it was unanimously agreed to make the duty "not exceeding ten dollars for each person."[3]

Southern interests now being safe, some Southern members attempted, a few days later, to annul the "bargain" by restoring the requirement of a two-thirds vote in navigation acts. Charles Pinckney made the motion, in an elaborate speech designed to show the conflicting commercial interests of the States; he declared that "The power of regulating commerce was a pure concession on the part of the Southern States."[4] Martin and Williamson of North Carolina, Butler of South Carolina, and Mason of Virginia defended the proposition, insisting that it would be a dangerous concession on the part of the South to leave navigation acts to a mere majority vote. Sherman of Connecticut, Morris of Pennsylvania, and Spaight of North Carolina declared that the very diversity of interest was a security. Finally, by a vote of 7 to 4, Maryland, Virginia, North Carolina, and Georgia being in the minority, the Convention refused to consider the motion, and the recommendation of the committee passed.[5]

When, on September 10, the Convention was discussing the amendment clause of the Constitution, the ever-alert

[1] Elliot, *Debates*, V. 477. Dickinson made a similar motion, which was disagreed to: *Ibid.*

[2] *Ibid.*, V. 478.

[3] *Ibid.*

[4] Aug. 29: *Ibid.*, V. 489.

[5] *Ibid.*, V. 492.

Rutledge, perceiving that the results of the laboriously settled "bargain" might be endangered, declared that he "never could agree to give a power by which the articles relating to slaves might be altered by the states not interested in that property."[1] As a result, the clause finally adopted, September 15, had the proviso: "Provided, that no amendment which may be made prior to the year 1808 shall in any manner affect the 1st and 4th clauses in the 9th section of the 1st article."[2]

36. **Settlement by the Convention.** Thus, the slave-trade article of the Constitution stood finally as follows:—

> "Article I. Section 9. The Migration or Importation of such Persons as any of the States now existing shall think proper to admit, shall not be prohibited by the Congress prior to the Year one thousand eight hundred and eight, but a Tax or duty may be imposed on such Importation, not exceeding ten dollars for each Person."

This settlement of the slavery question brought out distinct differences of moral attitude toward the institution, and yet differences far from hopeless. To be sure, the South apologized for slavery, the Middle States denounced it, and the East could only tolerate it from afar; and yet all three sections united in considering it a temporary institution, the cornerstone of which was the slave-trade. No one of them had ever seen a system of slavery without an active slave-trade; and there were probably few members of the Convention who did not believe that the foundations of slavery had been sapped merely by putting the abolition of the slave-trade in the hands of Congress twenty years hence. Here lay the danger; for when the North called slavery "temporary," she thought of twenty or thirty years, while the "temporary" period of the South was scarcely less than a century. Meantime, for at least a score of years, a policy of strict *laissez-faire*, so far as the general government was concerned, was to intervene. Instead of calling the whole moral energy of the people into action, so as gradually to crush this portentous evil, the Federal Convention lulled the nation to sleep by a "bargain," and left to the vacillating and unripe judgment of the States one of the

[1] Elliot, *Debates*, V. 532.
[2] *Ibid.*, I. 317.

most threatening of the social and political ills which they were so courageously seeking to remedy.

37. **Reception of the Clause by the Nation.** When the proposed Constitution was before the country, the slave-trade article came in for no small amount of condemnation and apology. In the pamphlets of the day it was much discussed. One of the points in Mason's "Letter of Objections" was that "the general legislature is restrained from prohibiting the further importation of slaves for twenty odd years, though such importations render the United States weaker, more vulnerable, and less capable of defence."[1] To this Iredell replied, through the columns of the *State Gazette* of North Carolina: "If all the States had been willing to adopt this regulation [i. e., to prohibit the slave-trade], I should as an individual most heartily have approved of it, because even if the importation of slaves in fact rendered us stronger, less vulnerable and more capable of defence, I should rejoice in the prohibition of it, as putting an end to a trade which has already continued too long for the honor and humanity of those concerned in it. But as it was well known that South Carolina and Georgia thought a further continuance of such importations useful to them, and would not perhaps otherwise have agreed to the new constitution, those States which had been importing till they were satisfied, could not with decency have insisted upon their relinquishing advantages themselves had already enjoyed. Our situation makes it necessary to bear the evil as it is. It will be left to the future legislatures to allow such importations or not. If any, in violation of their clear conviction of the injustice of this trade, persist in pursuing it, this is a matter between God and their own consciences. The interests of humanity will, however, have gained something by the prohibition of this inhuman trade, though at a distance of twenty odd years."[2]

"Centinel," representing the Quaker sentiment of Pennsylvania, attacked the clause in his third letter, published in the *Independent Gazetteer, or The Chronicle of Freedom*, November 8, 1787: "We are told that the objects of this article are slaves, and that it is inserted to secure to the southern states the right of

[1] P. L. Ford, *Pamphlets on the Constitution*, p. 331.

[2] *Ibid.*, p. 367.

introducing negroes for twenty-one years to come, against the declared sense of the other states to put an end to an odious traffic in the human species, which is especially scandalous and inconsistent in a people, who have asserted their own liberty by the sword, and which dangerously enfeebles the districts wherein the laborers are bondsmen. The words, dark and ambiguous, such as no plain man of common sense would have used, are evidently chosen to conceal from Europe, that in this enlightened country, the practice of slavery has its advocates among men in the highest stations. When it is recollected that no poll tax can be imposed on *five* negroes, above what *three* whites shall be charged; when it is considered, that the imposts on the consumption of Carolina field negroes must be trifling, and the excise nothing, it is plain that the proportion of contributions, which can be expected from the southern states under the new constitution, will be unequal, and yet they are to be allowed to enfeeble themselves by the further importation of negroes till the year 1808. Has not the concurrence of the five southern states (in the convention) to the new system, been purchased too dearly by the rest?"[1]

Noah Webster's "Examination" (1787) addressed itself to such Quaker scruples: "But, say the enemies of slavery, negroes may be imported for twenty-one years. This exception is addressed to the quakers, and a very pitiful exception it is. The truth is, Congress cannot prohibit the importation of slaves during that period; but the laws against the importation into particular states, stand unrepealed. An immediate abolition of slavery would bring ruin upon the whites, and misery upon the blacks, in the southern states. The constitution has therefore wisely left each state to pursue its own measures, with respect to this article of legislation, during the period of twenty-one years."[2]

The following year the "Examination" of Tench Coxe said: "The temporary reservation of any particular matter must ever be deemed an admission that it should be done away. This appears to have been well understood. In addition to the arguments drawn from liberty, justice and religion, opinions

[1] McMaster and Stone, *Pennsylvania and the Federal Convention*, pp. 599–600. Cf. also p. 773.

[2] See Ford, *Pamphlets*, etc., p. 54.

against this practice [i. e., of slave-trading], founded in sound policy, have no doubt been urged. Regard was necessarily paid to the peculiar situation of our southern fellow-citizens; but they, on the other hand, have not been insensible of the delicate situation of our national character on this subject."[1]

From quite different motives Southern men defended this section. For instance, Dr. David Ramsay, a South Carolina member of the Convention, wrote in his "Address": "It is farther objected, that they have stipulated for a right to prohibit the importation of negroes after 21 years. On this subject observe, as they are bound to protect us from domestic violence, they think we ought not to increase our exposure to that evil, by an unlimited importation of slaves. Though Congress may forbid the importation of negroes after 21 years, it does not follow that they will. On the other hand, it is probable that they will not. The more rice we make, the more business will be for their shipping; their interest will therefore coincide with ours. Besides, we have other sources of supply—the importation of the ensuing 20 years, added to the natural increase of those we already have, and the influx from our northern neighbours who are desirous of getting rid of their slaves, will afford a sufficient number for cultivating all the lands in this state."[2]

Finally, *The Federalist*, No. 41, written by James Madison, commented as follows: "It were doubtless to be wished, that the power of prohibiting the importation of slaves had not been postponed until the year 1808, or rather, that it had been suffered to have immediate operation. But it is not difficult to account, either for this restriction on the General Government, or for the manner in which the whole clause is expressed. It ought to be considered as a great point gained in favor of humanity, that a period of twenty years may terminate forever, within these States, a traffic which has so long and so loudly upbraided the barbarism of modern policy; that within that period, it will receive a considerable discouragement from the Federal Government, and may be totally abolished, by a concurrence of the few States which continue the

[1] Ford, *Pamphlets*, etc., p. 146.

[2] "Address to the Freemen of South Carolina on the Subject of the Federal Constitution": *Ibid*., p. 378.

unnatural traffic, in the prohibitory example which has been given by so great a majority of the Union. Happy would it be for the unfortunate Africans, if an equal prospect lay before them of being redeemed from the oppressions of their European brethren!

"Attempts have been made to pervert this clause into an objection against the Constitution, by representing it on one side as a criminal toleration of an illicit practice, and on another, as calculated to prevent voluntary and beneficial emigrations from Europe to America. I mention these misconstructions, not with a view to give them an answer, for they deserve none; but as specimens of the manner and spirit, in which some have thought fit to conduct their opposition to the proposed Government."[1]

38. **Attitude of the State Conventions.** The records of the proceedings in the various State conventions are exceedingly meagre. In nearly all of the few States where records exist there is found some opposition to the slave-trade clause. The opposition was seldom very pronounced or bitter; it rather took the form of regret, on the one hand that the Convention went so far, and on the other hand that it did not go farther. Probably, however, the Constitution was never in danger of rejection on account of this clause.

Extracts from a few of the speeches, *pro* and *con*, in various States will best illustrate the character of the arguments. In reply to some objections expressed in the Pennsylvania convention, Wilson said, December 3, 1787: "I consider this as laying the foundation for banishing slavery out of this country; and though the period is more distant than I could wish, yet it will produce the same kind, gradual change, which was pursued in Pennsylvania."[2] Robert Barnwell declared in the South Carolina convention, January 17, 1788, that this clause "particularly pleased" him. "Congress," he said, "has guarantied this right for that space of time, and at its expiration may continue it as long as they please. This question then arises—What will their interest lead them to do? The Eastern States, as the honorable gentleman says, will become the carriers of

[1] Published in the *New York Packet*, Jan. 22, 1788; reprinted in Dawson's *Fœderalist*, I. 290–1.

[2] Elliot, *Debates*, II. 452.

America. It will, therefore, certainly be their interest to encourage exportation to as great an extent as possible; and if the quantum of our products will be diminished by the prohibition of negroes, I appeal to the belief of every man, whether he thinks those very carriers will themselves dam up the sources from whence their profit is derived. To think so is so contradictory to the general conduct of mankind, that I am of opinion, that, without we ourselves put a stop to them, the traffic for negroes will continue forever."[1]

In Massachusetts, January 30, 1788, General Heath said: "The gentlemen who have spoken have carried the matter rather too far on both sides. I apprehend that it is not in our power to do anything for or against those who are in slavery in the southern States. . . . Two questions naturally arise, if we ratify the Constitution: Shall we do anything by our act to hold the blacks in slavery? or shall we become partakers of other men's sins? I think neither of them. Each State is sovereign and independent to a certain degree, and they have a right, and will regulate their own internal affairs, as to themselves appears proper."[2] Iredell said, in the North Carolina convention, July 26, 1788: "When the entire abolition of slavery takes place, it will be an event which must be pleasing to every generous mind, and every friend of human nature. . . . But as it is, this government is nobly distinguished above others by that very provision."[3]

Of the arguments against the clause, two made in the Massachusetts convention are typical. The Rev. Mr. Neal said, January 25, 1788, that "unless his objection [to this clause] was removed, he could not put his hand to the Constitution."[4] General Thompson exclaimed, "Shall it be said, that after we have established our own independence and freedom, we make slaves of others?"[5] Mason, in the Virginia convention, June 15, 1788, said: "As much as I value a union of all the states, I would not admit the Southern States into the Union unless they agree to the discontinuance of this disgraceful

[1] Elliot, *Debates*, IV. 296–7.

[2] Published in *Debates of the Massachusetts Convention*, 1788, p. 217 ff.

[3] Elliot, *Debates*, IV. 100–1.

[4] Published in *Debates of the Massachusetts Convention*, 1788, p. 208.

[5] *Ibid.*

trade. . . . Yet they have not secured us the property of the slaves we have already. So that 'they have done what they ought not to have done, and have left undone what they ought to have done.' "[1] Joshua Atherton, who led the opposition in the New Hampshire convention, said: "The idea that strikes those who are opposed to this clause so disagreeably and so forcibly is,—hereby it is conceived (if we ratify the Constitution) that we become *consenters to* and *partakers in* the sin and guilt of this abominable traffic, at least for a certain period, without any positive stipulation that it shall even then be brought to an end."[2]

In the South Carolina convention Lowndes, January 16, 1788, attacked the slave-trade clause. "Negroes," said he, "were our wealth, our only natural resource; yet behold how our kind friends in the north were determined soon to tie up our hands, and drain us of what we had! The Eastern States drew their means of subsistence, in a great measure, from their shipping; and, on that head, they had been particularly careful not to allow of any burdens. . . . Why, then, call this a reciprocal bargain, which took all from one party, to bestow it on the other!"[3]

In spite of this discussion in the different States, only one State, Rhode Island, went so far as to propose an amendment directing Congress to "promote and establish such laws and regulations as may effectually prevent the importation of slaves of every description, into the United States."[4]

39. **Acceptance of the Policy.** As in the Federal Convention, so in the State conventions, it is noticeable that the compromise was accepted by the various States from widely different motives.[5] Nevertheless, these motives were not fixed

[1] Elliot, *Debates*, III. 452–3.

[2] Walker, *Federal Convention of New Hampshire*, App. 113; Elliot, *Debates*, II. 203.

[3] Elliot, *Debates*, IV. 273.

[4] Updike's *Minutes*, in Staples, *Rhode Island in the Continental Congress*, pp. 657–8, 674–9. Adopted by a majority of one in a convention of seventy.

[5] In five States I have found no mention of the subject (Delaware, New Jersey, Georgia, Connecticut, and Maryland). In the Pennsylvania convention there was considerable debate, partially preserved in Elliot's and Lloyd's *Debates*. In the Massachusetts convention the debate on this clause occupied a part of two or three days, reported in published debates. In South Carolina

and unchangeable, and there was still discernible a certain underlying agreement in the dislike of slavery. One cannot help thinking that if the devastation of the late war had not left an extraordinary demand for slaves in the South,—if, for instance, there had been in 1787 the same plethora in the slave-market as in 1774,—the future history of the country would have been far different. As it was, the twenty-one years of *laissez-faire* were confirmed by the States, and the nation entered upon the constitutional period with the slave-trade legal in three States,[1] and with a feeling of quiescence toward it in the rest of the Union.

---

there were several long speeches, reported in Elliot's *Debates*. Only three speeches made in the New Hampshire convention seem to be extant, and two of these are on the slave-trade: cf. Walker and Elliot. The Virginia convention discussed the clause to considerable extent: see Elliot. The clause does not seem to have been a cause of North Carolina's delay in ratification, although it occasioned some discussion: see Elliot. In Rhode Island "much debate ensued," and in this State alone was an amendment proposed: see Staples, *Rhode Island in the Continental Congress*. In New York the Committee of the Whole "proceeded through sections 8, 9 . . . with little or no debate": Elliot, *Debates*, II. 406.

[1] South Carolina, Georgia, and North Carolina. North Carolina had, however, a prohibitive duty.

Chapter VII

TOUSSAINT L'OUVERTURE AND ANTI-SLAVERY EFFORT, 1787–1806.

---

40. **Influence of the Haytian Revolution.** The rôle which the great Negro Toussaint, called L'Ouverture, played in the history of the United States has seldom been fully appreciated. Representing the age of revolution in America, he rose to leadership through a bloody terror, which contrived a Negro "problem" for the Western Hemisphere, intensified and defined the anti-slavery movement, became one of the causes, and probably the prime one, which led Napoleon to sell Louisiana for a song, and finally, through the interworking of all these effects, rendered more certain the final prohibition of the slave-trade by the United States in 1807.

From the time of the reorganization of the Pennsylvania Abolition Society, in 1787, anti-slavery sentiment became active. New York, New Jersey, Rhode Island, Delaware, Maryland, and Virginia had strong organizations, and a national convention was held in 1794. The terrible upheaval in the West Indies, beginning in 1791, furnished this rising movement with an irresistible argument. A wave of horror and fear swept over the South, which even the powerful slave-traders of Georgia did not dare withstand; the Middle States saw their worst dreams realized, and the mercenary trade interests of the East lost control of the New England conscience.

41. **Legislation of the Southern States.** In a few years the growing sentiment had crystallized into legislation. The Southern States took immediate measures to close their ports, first against West India Negroes, finally against all slaves. Georgia, who had had legal slavery only from 1755, and had since passed no restrictive legislation, felt compelled in 1793[1] to stop the entry of free Negroes, and in 1798[2] to prohibit, under heavy penalties, the importation of all slaves. This provision was placed in the Constitution of the State, and, although miserably enforced, was never repealed.

South Carolina was the first Southern State in which the exigencies of a great staple crop rendered the rapid consumption of slaves more profitable than their proper maintenance. Alternating, therefore, between a plethora and a dearth of Negroes, she prohibited the slave-trade only for short periods. In 1788[3] she had forbidden the trade for five years, and in 1792,[4] being peculiarly exposed to the West Indian insurrection, she quickly found it "inexpedient" to allow Negroes "from Africa, the West India Islands, or other place beyond sea" to enter for two years. This act continued to be extended, although with lessening penalties, until 1803.[5] The home demand in view of the probable stoppage of the trade in 1808, the speculative chances of the new Louisiana Territory trade, and the large already existing illicit traffic combined in that year to cause the passage of an act, December 17, reopening the African slave-trade, although still carefully excluding "West India" Negroes.[6] This action profoundly stirred the

[1] Prince, *Digest of the Laws of Georgia*, p. 786; Marbury and Crawford, *Digest of the Laws of Georgia*, pp. 440, 442. The exact text of this act appears not to be extant. Section I. is stated to have been "re-enacted by the constitution." Possibly this act prohibited slaves also, although this is not certain. Georgia passed several regulative acts between 1755 and 1793. Cf. Renne, *Colonial Acts of Georgia*, pp. 73–4, 164, note.

[2] Marbury and Crawford, *Digest*, p. 30, § 11. The clause was penned by Peter J. Carnes of Jefferson. Cf. W. B. Stevens, *History of Georgia* (1847), II. 501.

[3] Grimké, *Public Laws*, p. 466.

[4] Cooper and McCord, *Statutes*, VII. 431.

[5] *Ibid.*, VII. 433–6, 444, 447.

[6] *Ibid.*, VII. 449.

Union, aroused anti-slavery sentiment, led to a concerted movement for a constitutional amendment, and, failing in this, to an irresistible demand for a national prohibitory act at the earliest constitutional moment.

North Carolina had repealed her prohibitory duty act in 1790,[1] but in 1794 she passed an "Act to prevent further importation and bringing of slaves," etc.[2] Even the body-servants of West India immigrants and, naturally, all free Negroes, were eventually prohibited.[3]

42. **Legislation of the Border States.** The Border States, Virginia and Maryland, strengthened their non-importation laws, Virginia freeing illegally imported Negroes,[4] and Maryland prohibiting even the interstate trade.[5] The Middle States took action chiefly in the final abolition of slavery within their borders, and the prevention of the fitting out of slaving vessels in their ports. Delaware declared, in her Act of 1789, that "it is inconsistent with that spirit of general liberty which pervades the constitution of this state, that vessels should be fitted out, or equipped, in any of the ports thereof, for the purpose of receiving and transporting the natives of Africa to places where they are held in slavery,"[6] and forbade such a practice under penalty of £500 for each person so engaged. The Pennsylvania Act of 1788[7] had similar provisions, with a penalty of £1000; and New Jersey followed with an act in 1798.[8]

43. **Legislation of the Eastern States.** In the Eastern States, where slavery as an institution was already nearly defunct, action was aimed toward stopping the notorious participation of citizens in the slave-trade outside the State. The

[1] Martin, *Iredell's Acts of Assembly*, I. 492.

[2] *Ibid.*, II. 53.

[3] Cf. *Ibid.*, II. 94; *Laws of North Carolina* (revision of 1819), I. 786.

[4] Virginia codified her whole slave legislation in 1792 (*Va. Statutes at Large*, New Ser., I. 122), and amended her laws in 1798 and 1806 (*Ibid.*, III. 251).

[5] Dorsey, *Laws of Maryland, 1796*, I. 334.

[6] *Laws of Delaware, 1797* (Newcastle ed.), p. 942, ch. 194 b.

[7] Dallas, *Laws*, II. 586.

[8] Paterson, *Digest of the Laws of New Jersey* (1800), pp. 307–13. In 1804 New Jersey passed an act gradually to abolish slavery. The legislation of New York at this period was confined to regulating the exportation of slave criminals (1790), and to passing an act gradually abolishing slavery (1799). In 1801 she codified all her acts.

prime movers were the Rhode Island Quakers. Having early secured a law against the traffic in their own State, they turned their attention to others. Through their remonstrances Connecticut, in 1788,[1] prohibited participation in the trade by a fine of £500 on the vessel, £50 on each slave, and loss of insurance; this act was strengthened in 1792,[2] the year after the Haytian revolt. Massachusetts, after many fruitless attempts, finally took advantage of an unusually bold case of kidnapping, and passed a similar act in 1788.[3] "This," says Belknap, "was the utmost which could be done by our legislatures; we still have to regret the impossibility of making a law *here*, which shall restrain our citizens from carrying on this trade *in foreign bottoms*, and from committing the crimes which this act prohibits, *in foreign countries*, as it is said some of them have done since the enacting of these laws."[4]

Thus it is seen how, spurred by the tragedy in the West Indies, the United States succeeded by State action in prohibiting the slave-trade from 1798 to 1803, in furthering the cause of abolition, and in preventing the fitting out of slave-trade expeditions in United States ports. The country had good cause to congratulate itself. The national government hastened to supplement State action as far as possible, and the prophecies of the more sanguine Revolutionary fathers seemed about to be realized, when the ill-considered act of South Carolina showed the weakness of the constitutional compromise.

44. **First Debate in Congress, 1789.** The attention of the national government was early directed to slavery and the trade by the rise, in the first Congress, of the question of taxing slaves imported. During the debate on the duty bill introduced by Clymer's committee, Parker of Virginia moved, May 13, 1789, to lay a tax of ten dollars *per capita* on slaves imported. He plainly stated that the tax was designed to check the trade, and that he was "sorry that the Constitution prevented Congress from prohibiting the importation altogether." The proposal was evidently unwelcome, and

[1] *Acts and Laws of Connecticut* (ed. 1784), pp. 368, 369, 388.

[2] *Ibid.*, p. 412.

[3] *Perpetual Laws of Massachusetts, 1780–89*, pp. 235–6.

[4] *Queries Respecting Slavery*, etc., in *Mass. Hist. Soc. Coll.*, 1st Ser., IV. 205.

caused an extended debate.[1] Smith of South Carolina wanted to postpone a matter so "big with the most serious consequences to the State he represented." Roger Sherman of Connecticut "could not reconcile himself to the insertion of human beings as an article of duty, among goods, wares, and merchandise." Jackson of Georgia argued against any restriction, and thought such States as Virginia "ought to let their neighbors get supplied, before they imposed such a burden upon the importation." Tucker of South Carolina declared it "unfair to bring in such an important subject at a time when debate was almost precluded," and denied the right of Congress to "consider whether the importation of slaves is proper or not."

Mr. Parker was evidently somewhat abashed by this onslaught of friend and foe, but he "had ventured to introduce the subject after full deliberation, and did not like to withdraw it." He desired Congress, "if possible," to "wipe off the stigma under which America labored." This brought Jackson of Georgia again to his feet. He believed, in spite of the "fashion of the day," that the Negroes were better off as slaves than as freedmen, and that, as the tax was partial, "it would be the most odious tax Congress could impose." Such sentiments were a distinct advance in pro-slavery doctrine, and called for a protest from Madison of Virginia. He thought the discussion proper, denied the partiality of the tax, and declared that, according to the spirit of the Constitution and his own desire, it was to be hoped "that, by expressing a national disapprobation of this trade, we may destroy it, and save ourselves from reproaches, and our posterity the imbecility ever attendant on a country filled with slaves." Finally, to Burke of South Carolina, who thought "the gentlemen were contending for nothing," Madison sharply rejoined, "If we contend for nothing, the gentlemen who are opposed to us do not contend for a great deal."

It now became clear that Congress had been whirled into a discussion of too delicate and lengthy a nature to allow its further prolongation. Compromising councils prevailed; and it was agreed that the present proposition should be with-

[1] *Annals of Cong.*, 1 Cong. 1 sess. pp. 336–41.

drawn and a separate bill brought in. This bill was, however, at the next session dexterously postponed "until the next session of Congress."[1]

45. **Second Debate in Congress, 1790.** It is doubtful if Congress of its own initiative would soon have resurrected the matter, had not a new anti-slavery weapon appeared in the shape of urgent petitions from abolition societies. The first petition, presented February 11, 1790,[2] was from the same interstate Yearly Meeting of Friends which had formerly petitioned the Confederation Congress.[3] They urged Congress to inquire "whether, notwithstanding such seeming impediments, it be not in reality within your power to exercise justice and mercy, which, if adhered to, we cannot doubt, must produce the abolition of the slave trade," etc. Another Quaker petition from New York was also presented,[4] and both were about to be referred, when Smith of South Carolina objected, and precipitated a sharp debate.[5] This debate had a distinctly different tone from that of the preceding one, and represents another step in pro-slavery doctrine. The key-note of these utterances was struck by Stone of Maryland, who "feared that if Congress took any measures indicative of an intention to interfere with the kind of property alluded to, it would sink it in value very considerably, and might be injurious to a great number of the citizens, particularly in the Southern States. He thought the subject was of general concern, and that the petitioners had no more right to interfere with it than any other members of the community. It was an unfortunate circumstance, that it was the disposition of religious sects to imagine they understood the rights of human nature better than all the world besides."

In vain did men like Madison disclaim all thought of unconstitutional "interference," and express only a desire to see "If anything is within the Federal authority to restrain such violation of the rights of nations and of mankind, as is supposed to be practised in some parts of the United States." A

[1] *Annals of Cong.*, 1 Cong. 1 sess. p. 903.
[2] *Ibid.*, 1 Cong. 2 sess. pp. 1182–3.
[3] *Journals of Cong., 1782–3*, pp. 418–9. Cf. above, pp. 56–57.
[4] *Annals of Cong.*, 1 Cong. 2 sess. p. 1184.
[5] *Ibid.*, pp. 1182–91.

storm of disapproval from Southern members met such sentiments. "The rights of the Southern States ought not to be threatened," said Burke of South Carolina. "Any extraordinary attention of Congress to this petition," averred Jackson of Georgia, would put slave property "in jeopardy," and "evince to the people a disposition towards a total emancipation." Smith and Tucker of South Carolina declared that the request asked for "unconstitutional" measures. Gerry of Massachusetts, Hartley of Pennsylvania, and Lawrence of New York rather mildly defended the petitioners; but after considerable further debate the matter was laid on the table.

The very next day, however, the laid ghost walked again in the shape of another petition from the "Pennsylvania Society for promoting the Abolition of Slavery," signed by its venerable president, Benjamin Franklin. This petition asked Congress to "step to the very verge of the power vested in you for discouraging every species of traffic in the persons of our fellow-men."[1] Hartley of Pennsylvania called up the memorial of the preceding day, and it was read a second time and a motion for commitment made. Plain words now came from Tucker of South Carolina. "The petition," he said, "contained an unconstitutional request." The commitment would alarm the South. These petitions were "mischievous" attempts to imbue the slaves with false hopes. The South would not submit to a general emancipation without "civil war." The commitment would "blow the trumpet of sedition in the Southern States," echoed his colleague, Burke. The Pennsylvania men spoke just as boldly. Scott declared the petition constitutional, and was sorry that the Constitution did not interdict this "most abominable" traffic. "Perhaps, in our Legislative capacity," he said, "we can go no further than to impose a duty of ten dollars, but I do not know how far I might go if I was one of the Judges of the United States, and those people were to come before me and claim their emancipation; but I am sure I would go as far as I could." Jackson of Georgia rejoined in true Southern spirit, boldly defending slavery in the light of religion and history, and asking if it was "good policy to bring forward a business at this moment likely to

[1] *Annals of Cong.*, 1 Cong. 2 sess. pp. 1197–1205.

light up the flame of civil discord; for the people of the Southern States will resist one tyranny as soon as another. The other parts of the Continent may bear them down by force of arms, but they will never suffer themselves to be divested of their property without a struggle. The gentleman says, if he was a Federal Judge, he does not know to what length he would go in emancipating these people; but I believe his judgment would be of short duration in Georgia, perhaps even the existence of such a Judge might be in danger." Baldwin, his New-England-born colleague, urged moderation by reciting the difficulty with which the constitutional compromise was reached, and declaring, "the moment we go to jostle on that ground, I fear we shall feel it tremble under our feet." Lawrence of New York wanted to commit the memorials, in order to see how far Congress might constitutionally interfere. Smith of South Carolina, in a long speech, said that his constituents entered the Union "from political, not from moral motives," and that "we look upon this measure as an attack upon the palladium of the property of our country." Page of Virginia, although a slave owner, urged commitment, and Madison again maintained the appropriateness of the request, and suggested that "regulations might be made in relation to the introduction of them [i. e., slaves] into the new States to be formed out of the Western Territory." Even conservative Gerry of Massachusetts declared, with regard to the whole trade, that the fact that "we have a right to regulate this business, is as clear as that we have any rights whatever."

Finally, by a vote of 43 to 11, the memorials were committed, the South Carolina and Georgia delegations, Bland and Coles of Virginia, Stone of Maryland, and Sylvester of New York voting in the negative.[1] A committee, consisting of Foster of New Hampshire, Huntington of Connecticut, Gerry of Massachusetts, Lawrence of New York, Sinnickson of New Jersey, Hartley of Pennsylvania, and Parker of Virginia, was charged with the matter, and reported Friday, March 5. The absence of Southern members on this committee compelled it to make this report a sort of official manifesto on the aims of

[1] *House Journal* (repr. 1826), 1 Cong. 2 sess. I. 157–8.

Northern anti-slavery politics. As such, it was sure to meet with vehement opposition in the House, even though conservatively worded. Such proved to be the fact when the committee reported. The onslaught to "negative the whole report" was prolonged and bitter, the debate *pro* and *con* lasting several days.[1]

46. **The Declaration of Powers, 1790.** The result is best seen by comparing the original report with the report of the Committee of the Whole, adopted by a vote of 29 to 25 Monday, March 23, 1790:[2] —

REPORT OF THE SELECT COMMITTEE.	REPORT OF THE COMMITTEE OF THE WHOLE.
That, from the nature of the matters contained in these memorials, they were induced to examine the powers vested in Congress, under the present Constitution, relating to the Abolition of Slavery, and are clearly of opinion,	
First. That the General Government is expressly restrained from prohibiting the importation of such persons 'as any of the States now existing shall think proper to admit, until the year one thousand eight hundred and eight.'	*First*. That the migration or importation of such persons as any of the States now existing shall think proper to admit, cannot be prohibited by Congress, prior to the year one thousand eight hundred and eight.
Secondly. That Congress, by a fair construction of the Constitution, are equally restrained from interfering in the emancipation of slaves, who already are, or who may, within the period mentioned, be imported into, or born within, any of the said States.	*Secondly*. That Congress have no authority to interfere in the emancipation of slaves, or in the treatment of them within any of the States; it remaining with the several States alone to provide any regulation therein, which humanity and true policy may require.
Thirdly. That Congress have no authority to interfere in the internal regulations of particular States, relative to the instructions of slaves in the principles of morality and religion; to their comfortable clothing, accommodations, and subsistence; to the regulation of their marriages, and the prevention of the violation of the rights thereof, or to the separation of children from their parents; to a comfortable provision in cases of sickness, age, or infirmity; or to the seizure,	

[1] *Annals of Cong.*, 1 Cong. 2 sess. pp. 1413–7.

[2] For the reports and debates, cf. *Annals of Cong.*, 1 Cong. 2 sess. pp. 1413–7, 1450–74; *House Journal* (repr. 1826), 1 Cong. 2 sess. I. 168–81.

transportation, or sale of free negroes; but have the fullest confidence in the wisdom and humanity of the Legislatures of the several States, that they will revise their laws from time to time, when necessary, and promote the objects mentioned in the memorials, and every other measure that may tend to the happiness of slaves.

Fourthly. That, nevertheless, Congress have authority, if they shall think it necessary, to lay at any time a tax or duty, not exceeding ten dollars for each person of any description, the importation of whom shall be by any of the States admitted as aforesaid.

Fifthly. That Congress have authority to interdict,[1] or (so far as it is or may be carried on by citizens of the United States, for supplying foreigners) to regulate[1] the African trade, and to make provision for the humane treatment of slaves, in all cases while on their passage to the United States, or to foreign ports, so far as respects the citizens of the United States.

Sixthly. That Congress have also authority to prohibit foreigners from fitting out vessels in any port of the United States, for transporting persons from Africa to any foreign port.

Seventhly. That the memorialists be informed, that in all cases to which the authority of Congress extends, they will exercise it for the humane objects of the memorialists, so far as they can be promoted on the principles of justice, humanity, and good policy.

Thirdly. That Congress have authority to restrain the citizens of the United States from carrying on the African trade, for the purpose of supplying foreigners with slaves, and of providing, by proper regulations, for the humane treatment, during their passage, of slaves imported by the said citizens into the States admitting such importation.

Fourthly. That Congress have authority to prohibit foreigners from fitting out vessels in any port of the United States for transporting persons from Africa to any foreign port.

47. **The Act of 1794.** This declaration of the powers of the central government over the slave-trade bore early fruit in the second Congress, in the shape of a shower of petitions from abolition societies in Massachusetts, Rhode Island, Connecticut, New York, Pennsylvania, Maryland, and Virginia.[2] In some of these slavery was denounced as "an outrageous vio-

[1] A clerical error in the original: "interdict" and "regulate" should be interchanged.

[2] See *Memorials presented to Congress*, etc. (1792), published by the Pennsylvania Abolition Society.

lation of one of the most essential rights of human nature,"[1] and the slave-trade as a traffic "degrading to the rights of man" and "repugnant to reason."[2] Others declared the trade "injurious to the true commercial interest of a nation,"[3] and asked Congress that, having taken up the matter, they do all in their power to limit the trade. Congress was, however, determined to avoid as long as possible so unpleasant a matter, and, save an angry attempt to censure a Quaker petitioner,[4] nothing was heard of the slave-trade until the third Congress.

Meantime, news came from the seas southeast of Carolina and Georgia which influenced Congress more powerfully than humanitarian arguments had done. The wild revolt of despised slaves, the rise of a noble black leader, and the birth of a new nation of Negro freemen frightened the pro-slavery advocates and armed the anti-slavery agitation. As a result, a Quaker petition for a law against the transport traffic in slaves was received without a murmur in 1794,[5] and on March 22 the first national act against the slave-trade became a law.[6] It was designed "to prohibit the carrying on the Slave Trade from the United States to any foreign place or country," or the fitting out of slavers in the United States for that country. The penalties for violation were forfeiture of the ship, a fine of $1000 for each person engaged, and of $200 for each slave transported. If the Quakers thought this a triumph of anti-slavery sentiment, they were quickly undeceived. Congress might willingly restrain the country from feeding West Indian turbulence, and yet be furious at a petition like that of 1797,[7] calling attention to "the oppressed state of our brethren of the African race" in this country, and to the interstate slave-trade. "Considering the present extraordinary state of the West India Islands and of Europe," young John Rutledge in-

[1] From the Virginia petition.

[2] From the petition of Baltimore and other Maryland societies.

[3] From the Providence Abolition Society's petition.

[4] *House Journal* (repr. 1826), 2 Cong. 2 sess. I. 627–9; *Annals of Cong.*, 2 Cong. 2 sess. pp. 728–31.

[5] *Annals of Cong.*, 3 Cong. 1 sess. pp. 64, 70, 72; *House Journal* (repr. 1826), 3 Cong. 1 sess. II. 76, 84–5, 96–100; *Senate Journal* (repr. 1820), 3 Cong. 1 sess. II. 51.

[6] *Statutes at Large*, I. 347–9.

[7] *Annals of Cong.*, 5 Cong. 2 sess. pp. 656–70, 945–1033.

sisted "that 'sufficient for the day is the evil thereof,' and that they ought to shut their door against any thing which had a tendency to produce the like confusion in this country." After excited debate and some investigation by a special committee, the petition was ordered, in both Senate and House, to be withdrawn.

48. **The Act of 1800.** In the next Congress, the sixth, another petition threw the House into paroxysms of slavery debate. Waln of Pennsylvania presented the petition of certain free colored men of Pennsylvania praying for a revision of the slave-trade laws and of the fugitive-slave law, and for prospective emancipation.[1] Waln moved the reference of this memorial to a committee already appointed on the revision of the loosely drawn and poorly enforced Act of 1794.[2] Rutledge of South Carolina immediately arose. He opposed the motion, saying, that these petitions were continually coming in and stirring up discord; that it was a good thing the Negroes were in slavery; and that already "too much of this new-fangled French philosophy of liberty and equality" had found its way among them. Others defended the right of petition, and declared that none wished Congress to exceed its powers. Brown of Rhode Island, a new figure in Congress, a man of distinguished services and from a well-known family, boldly set forth the commercial philosophy of his State. "We want money," said he, " we want a navy; we ought therefore to use the means to obtain it. We ought to go farther than has yet been proposed, and repeal the bills in question altogether, for why should we see Great Britain getting all the slave trade to themselves; why may not our country be enriched by that lucrative traffic? There would not be a slave the more sold, but we should derive the benefits by importing from Africa as well as that nation." Waln, in reply, contended that they should look into "the slave trade, much of which was still carrying on from Rhode Island, Boston and Pennsylvania." Hill of North Carolina called the House back from this general discussion to the petition in question, and, while willing to remedy any existing defect in the Act of 1794, hoped the

[1] *Annals of Cong.*, 6 Cong. 1 sess. p. 229.

[2] Dec. 12, 1799: *House Journal* (repr. 1826), 6 Cong. 1 sess. III. 535. For the debate, see *Annals of Cong.*, 6 Cong. 1 sess. pp. 230–45.

petition would not be received. Dana of Connecticut declared that the paper "contained nothing but a farrago of the French metaphysics of liberty and equality;" and that "it was likely to produce some of the dreadful scenes of St. Domingo." The next day Rutledge again warned the House against even discussing the matter, as "very serious, nay, dreadful effects, must be the inevitable consequence." He held up the most lurid pictures of the fatuity of the French Convention in listening to the overtures of the "three emissaries from St. Domingo," and thus yielding "one of the finest islands in the world" to "scenes which had never been practised since the destruction of Carthage." "But, sir," he continued, "we have lived to see these dreadful scenes. These horrid effects have succeeded what was conceived once to be trifling. Most important consequences may be the result, although gentlemen little apprehend it. But we know the situation of things there, although they do not, and knowing we deprecate it. There have been emissaries amongst us in the Southern States; they have begun their war upon us; an actual organization has commenced; we have had them meeting in their club rooms, and debating on that subject. . . . Sir, I do believe that persons have been sent from France to feel the pulse of this country, to know whether these [i. e., the Negroes] are the proper engines to make use of: these people have been talked to; they have been tampered with, and this is going on."

Finally, after censuring certain parts of this Negro petition, Congress committed the part on the slave-trade to the committee already appointed. Meantime, the Senate sent down a bill to amend the Act of 1794, and the House took this bill under consideration.[1] Prolonged debate ensued. Brown of Rhode Island again made a most elaborate plea for throwing open the foreign slave-trade. Negroes, he said, bettered their condition by being enslaved, and thus it was morally wrong and commercially indefensible to impose "a heavy fine and imprisonment . . . for carrying on a trade so advantageous;"

[1] *Senate Journal* (repr. 1821), 6 Cong. 1 sess. III. 72, 77, 88, 92; see *Ibid.*, Index, Bill No. 62; *House Journal* (repr. 1826), 6 Cong. 1 sess. III., Index, House Bill No. 247. For the debate, see *Annals of Cong.*, 6 Cong. 1 sess. pp. 686–700.

or, if the trade must be stopped, then equalize the matter and abolish slavery too. Nichols of Virginia thought that surely the gentlemen would not advise the importation of more Negroes; for while it "was a fact, to be sure," that they would thus improve their condition, "would it be policy so to do?" Bayard of Delaware said that "a more dishonorable item of revenue" than that derived from the slave-trade "could not be established." Rutledge opposed the new bill as defective and impracticable: the former act, he said, was enough; the States had stopped the trade, and in addition the United States had sought to placate philanthropists by stopping the use of our ships in the trade. "This was going very far indeed." New England first began the trade, and why not let them enjoy its profits now as well as the English? The trade could not be stopped.

The bill was eventually recommitted and reported again.[1] "On the question for its passing, a long and warm debate ensued," and several attempts to postpone it were made; it finally passed, however, only Brown of Rhode Island, Dent of Maryland, Rutledge and Huger of South Carolina, and Dickson of North Carolina voting against it, and 67 voting for it.[2] This Act of May 10, 1800,[3] greatly strengthened the Act of 1794. The earlier act had prohibited citizens from equipping slavers for the foreign trade; but this went so far as to forbid them having any interest, direct or indirect, in such voyages, or serving on board slave-ships in any capacity. Imprisonment for two years was added to the former fine of $2000, and United States commissioned ships were directed to capture such slavers as prizes. The slaves though forfeited by the owner, were not to go to the captor; and the act omitted to say what disposition should be made of them.

49. **The Act of 1803.** The Haytian revolt, having been among the main causes of two laws, soon was the direct instigation to a third. The frightened feeling in the South, when freedmen from the West Indies began to arrive in various ports, may well be imagined. On January 17, 1803, the town

[1] *Annals of Cong.*, 6 Cong. 1 sess. p. 697.
[2] *Ibid.*, p. 699–700.
[3] *Statutes at Large*, II. 70.

of Wilmington, North Carolina, hastily memorialized Congress, stating the arrival of certain freed Negroes from Guadeloupe, and apprehending "much danger to the peace and safety of the people of the Southern States of the Union" from the "admission of persons of that description into the United States."[1] The House committee which considered this petition hastened to agree "That the system of policy stated in the said memorial to exist, and to be now pursued in the French colonial government, of the West Indies, is fraught with danger to the peace and safety of the United States. That the fact stated to have occurred in the prosecution of that system of policy, demands the prompt interference of the Government of the United States, as well Legislative as Executive."[2] The result was a bill providing for the forfeiture of any ship which should bring into States prohibiting the same "any negro, mulatto, or other person of color;" the captain of the ship was also to be punished. After some opposition[3] the bill became a law, February 28, 1803.[4]

50. **State of the Slave-Trade from 1789 to 1803.** Meantime, in spite of the prohibitory State laws, the African slave-trade to the United States continued to flourish. It was notorious that New England traders carried on a large traffic.[5] Members stated on the floor of the House that "it was much to be regretted that the severe and pointed statute against the slave trade had been so little regarded. In defiance of its forbiddance and its penalties, it was well known that citizens and vessels of the United States were still engaged in that traffic. . . . In various parts of the nation, outfits were made for slave-voyages, without secrecy, shame, or apprehension. . . . Countenanced by their fellow-citizens at home, who were as ready to buy as they themselves were to collect and to bring to market, they approached our Southern harbors and inlets, and clandestinely disembarked the sooty offspring of the Eastern, upon the ill fated soil of the Western

[1] *Annals of Cong.*, 7 Cong. 2 sess. pp. 385–6.

[2] *Ibid.*, p. 424.

[3] See House Bills Nos. 89 and 101; *Annals of Cong.*, 7 Cong. 2 sess. pp. 424, 459–67. For the debate, see *Ibid.*, pp. 459–72.

[4] *Statutes at Large*, II. 205.

[5] Cf. Fowler, *Local Law in Massachusetts and Connecticut*, etc., p. 126.

hemisphere. In this way, it had been computed that, during the last twelve months, twenty thousand enslaved negroes had been transported from Guinea, and, by smuggling, added to the plantation stock of Georgia and South Carolina. So little respect seems to have been paid to the existing prohibitory statute, that it may almost be considered as disregarded by common consent."[1]

These voyages were generally made under the flag of a foreign nation, and often the vessel was sold in a foreign port to escape confiscation. South Carolina's own Congressman confessed that although the State had prohibited the trade since 1788, she "was unable to enforce" her laws. "With navigable rivers running into the heart of it," said he, "it was impossible, with our means, to prevent our Eastern brethren, who, in some parts of the Union, in defiance of the authority of the General Government, have been engaged in this trade, from introducing them into the country. The law was completely evaded, and, for the last year or two [1802–3], Africans were introduced into the country in numbers little short, I believe, of what they would have been had the trade been a legal one."[2] The same tale undoubtedly might have been told of Georgia.

51. **The South Carolina Repeal of 1803.** This vast and apparently irrepressible illicit traffic was one of three causes which led South Carolina, December 17, 1803, to throw aside all pretence and legalize her growing slave-trade; the other two causes were the growing certainty of total prohibition of the traffic in 1808, and the recent purchase of Louisiana by the United States, with its vast prospective demand for slave labor. Such a combination of advantages, which meant fortunes to planters and Charleston slave-merchants, could not longer be withheld from them; the prohibition was repealed, and the United States became again, for the first time in at least five years, a legal slave mart. This action shocked the nation, frightening Southern States with visions of an influx of untrained barbarians and servile insurrections, and arousing and

[1] Speech of S. L. Mitchell of New York, Feb. 14, 1804: *Annals of Cong.*, 8 Cong. 1 sess. p. 1000. Cf. also speech of Bedinger: *Ibid.*, pp. 997–8.

[2] Speech of Lowndes in the House, Feb. 14, 1804: *Annals of Cong.*, 8 Cong., 1 sess. p. 992. Cf. Stanton's speech later: *Ibid.*, 9 Cong. 2 sess. p. 240.

intensifying the anti-slavery feeling of the North, which had long since come to think of the trade, so far as legal enactment went, as a thing of the past.

Scarcely a month after this repeal, Bard of Pennsylvania solemnly addressed Congress on the matter. "For many reasons," said he, "this House must have been justly surprised by a recent measure of one of the Southern States. The impressions, however, which that measure gave my mind, were deep and painful. Had I been informed that some formidable foreign Power had invaded our country, I would not, I ought not, be more alarmed than on hearing that South Carolina had repealed her law prohibiting the importation of slaves. . . . Our hands are tied, and we are obliged to stand confounded, while we see the flood-gate opened, and pouring incalculable miseries into our country."[1] He then moved, as the utmost legal measure, a tax of ten dollars per head on slaves imported.

Debate on this proposition did not occur until February 14, when Lowndes explained the circumstances of the repeal, and a long controversy took place.[2] Those in favor of the tax argued that the trade was wrong, and that the tax would serve as some slight check; the tax was not inequitable, for if a State did not wish to bear it she had only to prohibit the trade; the tax would add to the revenue, and be at the same time a moral protest against an unjust and dangerous traffic. Against this it was argued that if the tax furnished a revenue it would defeat its own object, and make prohibition more difficult in 1808; it was inequitable, because it was aimed against one State, and would fall exclusively on agriculture; it would give national sanction to the trade; it would look "like an attempt in the General Government to correct a State for the undisputed exercise of its constitutional powers;" the revenue would be inconsiderable, and the United States had nothing to do with the moral principle; while a prohibitory tax would be defensible, a small tax like this would be useless as a protection and criminal as a revenue measure.

The whole debate hinged on the expediency of the

[1] *Annals of Cong.*, 8 Cong. 1 sess. pp. 820, 876.

[2] *Ibid.*, pp. 992–1036.

measure, few defending South Carolina's action.[1] Finally, a bill was ordered to be brought in, which was done on the 17th.[2] Another long debate took place, covering substantially the same ground. It was several times hinted that if the matter were dropped South Carolina might again prohibit the trade. This, and the vehement opposition, at last resulted in the postponement of the bill, and it was not heard from again during the session.

52. **The Louisiana Slave-Trade, 1803–1805.** About this time the cession of Louisiana brought before Congress the question of the status of slavery and the slave-trade in the Territories. Twice or thrice before had the subject called for attention. The first time was in the Congress of the Confederation, when, by the Ordinance of 1787,[3] both slavery and the slave-trade were excluded from the Northwest Territory. In 1790 Congress had accepted the cession of North Carolina back lands on the express condition that slavery there be undisturbed.[4] Nothing had been said as to slavery in the South Carolina cession (1787),[5] but it was tacitly understood that the provision of the Northwest Ordinance would not be applied. In 1798 the bill introduced for the cession of Mississippi contained a specific declaration that the anti-slavery clause of 1787 should not be included.[6] The bill passed the Senate, but caused long and excited debate in the House.[7] It was argued, on the one hand, that the case in Mississippi was different from that in the Northwest Territory, because slavery was a legal institution in all the surrounding country, and to prohibit the institution was virtually to prohibit the settling of the country. On the other hand, Gallatin declared that if this amendment should

[1] Huger of South Carolina declared that the whole South Carolina Congressional delegation opposed the repeal of the law, although they maintained the State's right to do so if she chose: *Annals of Cong.*, 8 Cong. 1 sess. p. 1005.

[2] *Ibid.*, pp. 1020–36; *House Journal* (repr. 1826), 8 Cong. 1 sess. IV. 523, 578, 580, 581–5.

[3] On slavery in the Territories, cf. Welling, in *Report Amer. Hist. Assoc.*, 1891, pp. 133–60.

[4] *Statutes at Large*, I. 108.

[5] *Journals of Cong.*, XII. 137–8.

[6] *Annals of Cong.*, 5 Cong. 1 sess. pp. 511, 515, 532–3.

[7] *Ibid.*, 5 Cong. 2 sess. pp. 1235, 1249, 1277–84, 1296–1313.

not obtain, "he knew not how slaves could be prevented from being introduced by way of New Orleans, by persons who are not citizens of the United States." It was moved to strike out the excepting clause; but the motion received only twelve votes,—an apparent indication that Congress either did not appreciate the great precedent it was establishing, or was reprehensibly careless. Harper of South Carolina then succeeded in building up the Charleston slave-trade interest by a section forbidding the slave traffic from "without the limits of the United States." Thatcher moved to strike out the last clause of this amendment, and thus to prohibit the interstate trade, but he failed to get a second.[1] Thus the act passed, punishing the introduction of slaves from without the country by a fine of $300 for each slave, and freeing the slave.[2]

In 1804 President Jefferson communicated papers to Congress on the status of slavery and the slave-trade in Louisiana.[3] The Spanish had allowed the traffic by edict in 1793, France had not stopped it, and Governor Claiborne had refrained from interference. A bill erecting a territorial government was already pending.[4] The Northern "District of Louisiana" was placed under the jurisdiction of Indiana Territory, and was made subject to the provisions of the Ordinance of 1787. Various attempts were made to amend the part of the bill referring to the Southern Territory: first, so as completely to prohibit the slave-trade;[5] then to compel the emancipation at a certain age of all those imported;[6] next, to confine all importation to that from the States;[7] and, finally, to limit it further to slaves imported before South Carolina opened her ports.[8] The last two amendments prevailed, and the final act also extended to the Territory the Acts of 1794 and 1803. Only slaves imported before May 1, 1798, could be

[1] *Annals of Cong.*, 5 Cong. 2 sess. p. 1313.

[2] *Statutes at Large*, I. 549.

[3] *Amer. State Papers, Miscellaneous*, I. No. 177.

[4] *Annals of Cong.*, 8 Cong. 1 sess. pp. 106, 211, 223, 231, 233–4, 238.

[5] *Ibid.*, pp. 240, 1186.

[6] *Ibid.*, p. 241.

[7] *Ibid.*, p. 240.

[8] *Ibid.*, p. 242.

introduced, and those must be slaves of actual settlers.[1] All slaves illegally imported were freed.

This stringent act was limited to one year. The next year, in accordance with the urgent petition of the inhabitants, a bill was introduced against these restrictions.[2] By dexterous wording, this bill, which became a law March 2, 1805,[3] swept away all restrictions upon the slave-trade except that relating to foreign ports, and left even this provision so ambiguous that, later, by judicial interpretation of the law,[4] the foreign slave-trade was allowed, at least for a time.

Such a stream of slaves now poured into the new Territory that the following year a committee on the matter was appointed by the House.[5] The committee reported that they "are in possession of the fact, that African slaves, lately imported into Charleston, have been thence conveyed into the territory of Orleans, and, in their opinion, this practice will be continued to a very great extent, while there is no law to prevent it."[6] The House ordered a bill checking this to be prepared; and such a bill was reported, but was soon dropped.[7] Importations into South Carolina during this time reached enormous proportions. Senator Smith of that State declared from official returns that, between 1803 and 1807,

[1] For further proceedings, see *Annals of Cong.*, 8 Cong. 1 sess. pp. 240–55, 1038–79, 1128–9, 1185–9. For the law, see *Statutes at Large*, II. 283–9.

[2] First, a bill was introduced applying the Northwest Ordinance to the Territory (*Annals of Cong.*, 8 Cong. 2 sess. pp. 45–6); but this was replaced by a Senate bill (*Ibid.*, p. 68; *Senate Journal*, repr. 1821, 8 Cong. 2 sess. III. 464). For the petition of the inhabitants, see *Annals of Cong.*, 8 Cong. 2 sess. p. 727–8.

[3] The bill was hurried through, and there are no records of debate. Cf. *Annals of Cong.*, 8 Cong. 2 sess. pp. 28–69, 727, 871, 957, 1016–20, 1213–5. In *Senate Journal* (repr. 1821), III., see Index, Bill No. 8. Importation of slaves was allowed by a clause erecting a Frame of Government "similar" to that of the Mississippi Territory.

[4] *Annals of Cong.*, 9 Cong. 1 sess. p. 443. The whole trade was practically foreign, for the slavers merely entered the Negroes at Charleston and immediately reshipped them to New Orleans. Cf. *Annals of Cong.*, 16 Cong. 1 sess. p. 264.

[5] *House Journal* (repr. 1826), 9 Cong. 1 sess. V. 264; *Annals of Cong.*, 9 Cong. 1 sess. pp. 445, 878.

[6] *House Reports*, 9 Cong. 1 sess. Feb. 17, 1806.

[7] House Bill No. 123.

39,075 Negroes were imported into Charleston, most of whom went to the Territories.[1]

53. **Last Attempts at Taxation, 1805–1806.** So alarming did the trade become that North Carolina passed a resolution in December, 1804,[2] proposing that the States give Congress power to prohibit the trade. Massachusetts,[3] Vermont,[4] New Hampshire,[5] and Maryland[6] responded; and a joint resolution was introduced in the House, proposing as an amendment to the Constitution "That the Congress of the United States shall have power to prevent the further importation of slaves into the United States and the Territories thereof."[7]

[1] *Annals of Cong.*, 16 Cong. 2 sess. pp. 73–7. This report covers the time from Jan. 1, 1804, to Dec. 31, 1807. During that time the following was the number of ships engaged in the traffic:—

From Charleston,	61	From Connecticut,	1
" Rhode Island,	59	" Sweden,	1
" Baltimore,	4	" Great Britain,	70
" Boston,	1	" France,	3
" Norfolk,	2		202

The consignees of these slave ships were natives of

Charleston	13
Rhode Island	88
Great Britain	91
France	10
	202

The following slaves were imported:—

By British vessels	19,949	
" French "	1,078	
		21,027
By American vessels:—		
" Charleston merchants	2,006	
" Rhode Island "	7,958	
" Foreign "	5,717	
" other Northern "	930	
" " Southern "	1,437	18,048
Total number of slaves imported, 1804–7		39,075

It is, of course, highly probable that the Custom House returns were much below the actual figures.

[2] McMaster, *History of the People of the United States*, III. p. 517.

[3] *House Journal* (repr. 1826), 8 Cong. 2 sess. V. 171; *Mass. Resolves*, May, 1802, to March, 1806, Vol. II. A. (State House ed., p. 239).

[4] *House Journal* (repr. 1826), 9 Cong. 1 sess. V. 238.

[5] *Ibid.*, V. 266.

[6] *Senate Journal* (repr. 1821), 9 Cong. 1 sess. IV. 76, 77, 79.

[7] *House Journal* (repr. 1826), 8 Cong. 2 sess. V. 171.

Nothing came of this effort; but meantime the project of taxation was revived. A motion to this effect, made in February, 1805, was referred to a Committee of the Whole, but was not discussed. Early in the first session of the ninth Congress the motion of 1805 was renewed; and although again postponed on the assurance that South Carolina was about to stop the trade,[1] it finally came up for debate January 20, 1806.[2] Then occurred a most stubborn legislative battle, which lasted during the whole session.[3] Several amendments to the motion were first introduced, so as to make it apply to all immigrants, and again to all "persons of color." As in the former debate, it was proposed to substitute a resolution of censure on South Carolina. All these amendments were lost. A long debate on the expediency of the measure followed, on the old grounds. Early of Georgia dwelt especially on the double taxation it would impose on Georgia; others estimated that a revenue of one hundred thousand dollars might be derived from the tax, a sum sufficient to replace the tax on pepper and medicines. Angry charges and counter-charges were made,—e. g., that Georgia, though ashamed openly to avow the trade, participated in it as well as South Carolina. "Some recriminations ensued between several members, on the participation of the traders of some of the New England States in carrying on the slave trade." Finally, January 22, by a vote of 90 to 25, a tax bill was ordered to be brought in.[4] One was reported on the 27th.[5] Every sort of opposition was resorted to. On the one hand, attempts were made to amend it so as to prohibit importation after 1807, and to prevent importation into the Territories; on the other hand, attempts were made to recommit and postpone the measure. It finally got a third reading, but was recommitted to a select committee, and disappeared until February 14.[6] Being then amended so as to provide for the forfeiture of smuggled cargoes, but saying nothing as to the disposition of the slaves, it was again relegated to a

[1] *Annals of Cong.*, 9 Cong. 1 sess. p. 274.

[2] *Ibid.*, pp. 272–4, 323.

[3] *Ibid.*, pp. 346–52, 358–75, etc., to 520.

[4] *Ibid.*, pp. 374–5.

[5] See House Bill No. 94.

[6] *Annals of Cong.*, 9 Cong. 1 sess. p. 466.

committee, after a vote of 69 to 42 against postponement.[1] On March 4 it appeared again, and a motion to reject it was lost. Finally, in the midst of the war scare and the question of non-importation of British goods, the bill was apparently forgotten, and the last attempt to tax imported slaves ended, like the others, in failure.

54. **Key-Note of the Period.** One of the last acts of this period strikes again the key-note which sounded throughout the whole of it. On February 20, 1806, after considerable opposition, a bill to prohibit trade with San Domingo passed the Senate.[2] In the House it was charged by one side that the measure was dictated by France, and by the other, that it originated in the fear of countenancing Negro insurrection. The bill, however, became a law, and by continuations remained on the statute-books until 1809. Even at that distance the nightmare of the Haytian insurrection continued to haunt the South, and a proposal to reopen trade with the island caused wild John Randolph to point out the "dreadful evil" of a "direct trade betwixt the town of Charleston and the ports of the island of St. Domingo."[3]

Of the twenty years from 1787 to 1807 it can only be said that they were, on the whole, a period of disappointment so far as the suppression of the slave-trade was concerned. Fear, interest, and philanthropy united for a time in an effort which bade fair to suppress the trade; then the real weakness of the constitutional compromise appeared, and the interests of the few overcame the fears and the humanity of the many.

[1] *Annals of Cong.*, 9 Cong. 1 sess. pp. 519–20.

[2] *Ibid.*, pp. 21, 52, 75, etc., to 138, 485–515, 1228. See House Bill No. 168. Cf. *Statutes at Large*, II. 421–2.

[3] A few months later, at the expiration of the period, trade was quietly reopened. *Annals of Cong.*, 11 Cong. 1 sess. pp. 443–6.

Chapter VIII

THE PERIOD OF ATTEMPTED SUPPRESSION. 1807–1825.

55. The Act of 1807.
56. The First Question: How shall illegally imported Africans be disposed of?
57. The Second Question: How shall Violations be punished?
58. The Third Question: How shall the Interstate Coastwise Slave-Trade be protected?
59. Legislative History of the Bill.
60. Enforcement of the Act.
61. Evidence of the Continuance of the Trade.
62. Apathy of the Federal Government.
63. Typical Cases.
64. The Supplementary Acts, 1818–1820.
65. Enforcement of the Supplementary Acts, 1818–1825.

---

55. **The Act of 1807.** The first great goal of anti-slavery effort in the United States had been, since the Revolution, the suppression of the slave-trade by national law. It would hardly be too much to say that the Haytian revolution, in addition to its influence in the years from 1791 to 1806, was one of the main causes that rendered the accomplishment of this aim possible at the earliest constitutional moment. To the great influence of the fears of the South was added the failure of the French designs on Louisiana, of which Toussaint L'Ouverture was the most probable cause. The cession of Louisiana in 1803 challenged and aroused the North on the slavery question again; put the Carolina and Georgia slave-traders in the saddle, to the dismay of the Border States; and brought the whole slave-trade question vividly before the public conscience. Another scarcely less potent influence was, naturally, the great anti-slavery movement in England, which after a mighty struggle of eighteen years was about to gain its first victory in the British Act of 1807.

President Jefferson, in his pacificatory message of December 2, 1806, said: "I congratulate you, fellow-citizens, on the approach of the period at which you may interpose your authority constitutionally, to withdraw the citizens of the United States from all further participation in those violations of human rights which have been so long continued on the unoffending inhabitants of Africa, and which the morality, the reputation, and the best interests of our country, have long been eager to proscribe. Although no law you may pass can take prohibitory effect till the first day of the year one thousand eight hundred and eight, yet the intervening period is not too long to prevent, by timely notice, expeditions which cannot be completed before that day."[1]

In pursuance of this recommendation, the very next day Senator Bradley of Vermont introduced into the Senate a bill which, after a complicated legislative history, became the Act of March 2, 1807, prohibiting the African slave-trade.[2]

Three main questions were to be settled by this bill: first, and most prominent, that of the disposal of illegally imported Africans; second, that of the punishment of those concerned in the importation; third, that of the proper limitation of the interstate traffic by water.

The character of the debate on these three questions, as well as the state of public opinion, is illustrated by the fact that forty of the sixty pages of officially reported debates are devoted to the first question, less than twenty to the second, and only two to the third. A sad commentary on the previous enforcement of State and national laws is the readiness with which it was admitted that wholesale violations of the law would take place; indeed, Southern men declared that no strict law against the slave-trade could be executed in the South, and that it was only by playing on the motives of personal interest that the trade could be checked. The question of punishment indicated the slowly changing moral attitude of the South toward the slave system. Early boldly said, "A large majority of people in the Southern States do not consider slavery as even an evil."[3] The South, in fact, insisted on regarding man-stealing as a minor offence, a "misdemeanor" rather than a "crime." Finally, in the short and sharp debate on the interstate coastwise trade, the growing economic side of the slavery question came to the front, the vested interests' argument was squarely put, and the future interstate trade almost consciously provided for.

[1] *House Journal* (repr. 1826), 9 Cong. 2 sess. V. 468.

[2] Cf. below, § 59.

[3] *Annals of Cong.*, 9 Cong. 2 sess. p. 238.

From these considerations, it is doubtful as to how far it was expected that the Act of 1807 would check the slave traffic; at any rate, so far as the South was concerned, there seemed to be an evident desire to limit the trade, but little thought that this statute would definitively suppress it.

56. **The First Question: How shall illegally imported Africans be disposed of?** The dozen or more propositions on the question of the disposal of illegally imported Africans may be divided into two chief heads, representing two radically opposed parties: 1. That illegally imported Africans be free, although they might be indentured for a term of years or removed from the country. 2. That such Africans be sold as slaves.[1] The arguments on these two propositions, which were many and far-reaching, may be roughly divided into three classes, political, constitutional, and moral.

[1]There were at least twelve distinct propositions as to the disposal of the Africans imported:—

1. That they be forfeited and sold by the United States at auction (Early's bill, reported Dec. 15: *Annals of Cong.*, 9 Cong. 2 sess. pp. 167–8).

2. That they be forfeited and left to the disposal of the States (proposed by Bidwell and Early: *Ibid.*, pp. 181, 221, 477. This was the final settlement.)

3. That they be forfeited and sold, and that the proceeds go to charities, education, or internal improvements (Early, Holland, and Masters: *Ibid.*, p. 273).

4. That they be forfeited and indentured for life (Alston and Bidwell: *Ibid.*, pp. 170–1).

5. That they be forfeited and indentured for 7, 8, or 10 years (Pitkin: *Ibid.*, p. 186).

6. That they be forfeited and given into the custody of the President, and by him indentured in free States for a term of years (bill reported from the Senate Jan. 28: *House Journal* (repr. 1826), 9 Cong. 2 sess. V. 575; *Annals of Cong.*, 9 Cong. 2 sess. p. 477. Cf. also *Ibid.*, p. 272).

7. That the Secretary of the Treasury dispose of them, at his discretion, in service (Quincy: *Ibid.*, p. 183).

8. That those imported into slave States be returned to Africa or bound out in free States (Sloan: *Ibid.*, p. 254).

9. That all be sent back to Africa (Smilie: *Ibid.*, p. 176).

10. That those imported into free States be free, those imported into slave States be returned to Africa or indentured (Sloan: *Ibid.*, p. 226).

11. That they be forfeited but not sold (Sloan and others: *Ibid.*, p. 270).

12. That they be free (Sloan: *Ibid.*, p. 168; Bidwell: *House Journal* (repr. 1826), 9 Cong. 2 sess. V. 515).

The political argument, reduced to its lowest terms, ran thus: those wishing to free the Negroes illegally imported declared that to enslave them would be to perpetrate the very evil which the law was designed to stop. "By the same law," they said, "we condemn the man-stealer and become the receivers of his stolen goods. We punish the criminal, and then step into his place, and complete the crime."[1] They said that the objection to free Negroes was no valid excuse; for if the Southern people really feared this class, they would consent to the imposing of such penalties on illicit traffic as would stop the importation of a single slave.[2] Moreover, "forfeiture" and sale of the Negroes implied a property right in them which did not exist.[3] Waiving this technical point, and allowing them to be "forfeited" to the government, then the government should either immediately set them free, or, at the most, indenture them for a term of years; otherwise, the law would be an encouragement to violators. "It certainly will be," said they, "if the importer can find means to evade the penalty of the act; for there he has all the advantage of a market enhanced by our ineffectual attempt to prohibit."[4] They claimed that even the indenturing of the ignorant barbarian for life was better than slavery; and Sloan declared that the Northern States would receive the freed Negroes willingly rather than have them enslaved.[5]

The argument of those who insisted that the Negroes should be sold was tersely put by Macon: "In adopting our measures on this subject, we must pass such a law as can be executed."[6] Early expanded this: "It is a principle in legislation, as correct as any which has ever prevailed, that to give effect to laws you must not make them repugant to the passions and wishes of the people among whom they are to operate. How then, in this instance, stands the fact? Do not gentlemen from every quarter of the Union prove, on the discussion of every question that has ever arisen in the House,

[1] Bidwell, Cook, and others: *Annals of Cong.*, 9 Cong. 2 sess. p. 201.
[2] Bidwell: *Ibid.*, p. 172.
[3] Fisk: *Ibid.*, pp. 224–5; Bidwell: *Ibid.*, p. 221.
[4] Quincy: *Ibid.*, p. 184.
[5] *Annals of Cong.*, 9 Cong. 2 sess. p. 478; Bidwell: *Ibid.*, p. 171.
[6] *Ibid.*, p. 172.

having the most remote bearing on the giving freedom to the Africans in the bosom of our country, that it has excited the deepest sensibility in the breasts of those where slavery exists? And why is this so? It is, because those who, from experience, know the extent of the evil, believe that the most formidable aspect in which it can present itself, is by making these people free among them. Yes, sir, though slavery is an evil, regretted by every man in the country, to have among us in any considerable quantity persons of this description, is an evil far greater than slavery itself. Does any gentleman want proof of this? I answer that all proof is useless; no fact can be more notorious. With this belief on the minds of the people where slavery exists, and where the importation will take place, if at all, we are about to turn loose in a state of freedom all persons brought in after the passage of this law. I ask gentlemen to reflect and say whether such a law, opposed to the ideas, the passions, the views, and the affections of the people of the Southern States, can be executed? I tell them, no; it is impossible—why? Because no man will inform—why? Because to inform will be to lead to an evil which will be deemed greater than the offence of which information is given, because it will be opposed to the principle of self-preservation, and to the love of family. No, no man will be disposed to jeopard his life, and the lives of his countrymen. And if no one dare inform, the whole authority of the Government cannot carry the law into effect. The whole people will rise up against it. Why? Because to enforce it would be to turn loose, in the bosom of the country, firebrands that would consume them."[1]

This was the more tragic form of the argument; it also had a mercenary side, which was presented with equal emphasis. It was repeatedly said that the only way to enforce the law was to play off individual interests against each other. The profit from the sale of illegally imported Negroes was declared to be the only sufficient "inducement to give information of their importation."[2] "Give up the idea of forfeiture, and I challenge the gentleman to invent fines, penalties, or punishments of any sort, sufficient to restrain the slave

[1] *Annals of Cong.*, 9 Cong. 2 sess. pp. 173–4.

[2] Alston: *Ibid.*, p. 170.

trade."[1] If such Negroes be freed, "I tell you that slaves will continue to be imported as heretofore. . . . You cannot get hold of the ships employed in this traffic. Besides, slaves will be brought into Georgia from East Florida. They will be brought into the Mississippi Territory from the bay of Mobile. You cannot inflict any other penalty, or devise any other adequate means of prevention, than a forfeiture of the Africans in whose possession they may be found after importation."[2] Then, too, when foreigners smuggled in Negroes, "who then . . . could be operated on, but the purchasers? There was the rub—it was their interest alone which, by being operated on, would produce a check. Snap their purse-strings, break open their strong box, deprive them of their slaves, and by destroying the temptation to buy, you put an end to the trade, . . . nothing short of a forfeiture of the slave would afford an effectual remedy."[3] Again, it was argued that it was impossible to prevent imported Negroes from becoming slaves, or, what was just as bad, from being sold as vagabonds or indentured for life.[4] Even our own laws, it was said, recognize the title of the African slave factor in the transported Negroes; and if the importer have no title, why do we legislate? Why not let the African immigrant alone to get on as he may, just as we do the Irish immigrant?[5] If he should be returned to Africa, his home could not be found, and he would in all probability be sold into slavery again.[6]

The constitutional argument was not urged as seriously as the foregoing; but it had a considerable place. On the one hand, it was urged that if the Negroes were forfeited, they were forfeited to the United States government, which could dispose of them as it saw fit;[7] on the other hand, it was said that the United States, as owner, was subject to State laws, and could not free the Negroes contrary to such laws.[8] Some alleged that the freeing of such Negroes struck at the

[1] D. R. Williams: *Annals of Cong.*, 9 Cong. 2 sess. p. 183.
[2] Early: *Ibid.*, pp. 184–5.
[3] Lloyd, Early, and others: *Ibid.*, p. 203.
[4] Alston: *Ibid.*, p. 170.
[5] Quincy: *Ibid.*, p. 222; Macon: *Ibid.*, p. 225.
[6] Macon: *Ibid.*, p. 177.
[7] Barker: *Ibid.*, p. 171; Bidwell: *Ibid.*, p. 172.
[8] Clay, Alston, and Early: *Ibid.*, p. 266.

title to all slave property;[1] others thought that, as property in slaves was not recognized in the Constitution, it could not be in a statute.[2] The question also arose as to the source of the power of Congress over the slave-trade. Southern men derived it from the clause on commerce, and declared that it exceeded the power of Congress to declare Negroes imported into a slave State, free, against the laws of that State; that Congress could not determine what should or should not be property in a State.[3] Northern men replied that, according to this principle, forfeiture and sale in Massachusetts would be illegal; that the power of Congress over the trade was derived from the restraining clause, as a non-existent power could not be restrained; and that the United States could act under her general powers as executor of the Law of Nations.[4]

The moral argument as to the disposal of illegally imported Negroes was interlarded with all the others. On the one side, it began with the "Rights of Man," and descended to a stickling for the decent appearance of the statute-book; on the other side, it began with the uplifting of the heathen, and descended to a denial of the applicability of moral principles to the question. Said Holland of North Carolina: "It is admitted that the condition of the slaves in the Southern States is much superior to that of those in Africa. Who, then, will say that the trade is immoral?"[5] But, in fact, "morality has nothing to do with this traffic,"[6] for, as Joseph Clay declared, "it must appear to every man of common sense, that the question could be considered in a commercial point of view only."[7] The other side declared that, "by the laws of God and man," these captured Negroes are "entitled to their freedom as clearly and absolutely as we are;"[8] nevertheless, some were willing to leave them to the tender mercies of the slave States,

[1] Clay, Alston, and Early: *Annals of Cong.*, 9 Cong. 2 sess. p. 266.

[2] Bidwell: *Ibid.*, p. 221.

[3] Sloan and others: *Ibid.*, p. 271; Early and Alston: *Ibid.*, pp. 168, 171.

[4] Ely, Bidwell, and others: *Ibid.*, pp. 179, 181, 271; Smilie and Findley: *Ibid.*, pp. 225, 226.

[5] *Ibid.*, p. 240. Cf. Lloyd: *Ibid.*, p. 236.

[6] Holland: *Ibid.*, p. 241.

[7] *Ibid.*, p. 227; Macon: *Ibid.*, p. 225.

[8] Bidwell, Cook, and others: *Ibid.*, p. 201.

so long as the statute-book was disgraced by no explicit recognition of slavery.[1] Such arguments brought some sharp sarcasm on those who seemed anxious "to legislate for the honor and glory of the statute book;"[2] some desired "to know what honor you will derive from a law that will be broken every day of your lives."[3] They would rather boldly sell the Negroes and turn the proceeds over to charity.

The final settlement of the question was as follows:—

"SECTION 4. . . . And neither the importer, nor any person or persons claiming from or under him, shall hold any right or title whatsoever to any negro, mulatto, or person of color, nor to the service or labor thereof, who may be imported or brought within the United States, or territories thereof, in violation of this law, but the same shall remain subject to any regulations not contravening the provisions of this act, which the Legislatures of the several States or Territories at any time hereafter may make, for disposing of any such negro, mulatto, or person of color."[4]

57. **The Second Question: How shall Violations be punished?** The next point in importance was that of the punishment of offenders. The half-dozen specific propositions reduce themselves to two: 1. A violation should be considered a crime or felony, and be punished by death; 2. A violation should be considered a misdemeanor, and be punished by fine and imprisonment.[5]

Advocates of the severer punishment dwelt on the enormity

[1] Bidwell: *Annals of Cong.*, 9 Cong. 2 sess. p. 221. Cf. *Ibid.*, p. 202.

[2] Early: *Ibid.*, p. 239.

[3] *Ibid.*

[4] *Ibid.*, p. 1267.

[5] There were about six distinct punishments suggested:—

1. Forfeiture, and fine of $5000 to $10,000 (Early's bill: *Ibid.*, p. 167).

2. Forfeiture and imprisonment (amendment to Senate bill: *Ibid.*, pp. 231, 477, 483).

3. Forfeiture, imprisonment from 5 to 10 years, and fine of $1000 to $10,000 (amendment to amendment of Senate bill: *Ibid.*, pp. 228, 483).

4. Forfeiture, imprisonment from 5 to 40 years, and fine of $1000 to $10,000 (Chandler's amendment: *Ibid.*, p. 228).

5. Forfeiture of all property, and imprisonment (Pitkin: *Ibid.*, p. 188).

6. Death (Smilie: *Ibid.*, pp. 189–90; bill reported to House, Dec. 19: *Ibid.*, p. 190; Senate bill as reported to House, Jan. 28).

of the offence. It was "one of the highest crimes man could commit," and "a captain of a ship engaged in this traffic was guilty of murder."[1] The law of God punished the crime with death, and any one would rather be hanged than be enslaved.[2] It was a peculiarly deliberate crime, in which the offender did not act in sudden passion, but had ample time for reflection.[3] Then, too, crimes of much less magnitude are punished with death. Shall we punish the stealer of $50 with death, and the man-stealer with imprisonment only?[4] Piracy, forgery, and fraudulent sinking of vessels are punishable with death, "yet these are crimes only against property; whereas the importation of slaves, a crime committed against the liberty of man, and inferior only to murder or treason, is accounted nothing but a misdemeanor."[5] Here, indeed, lies the remedy for the evil of freeing illegally imported Negroes,—in making the penalty so severe that none will be brought in; if the South is sincere, "they will unite to a man to execute the law."[6] To free such Negroes is dangerous; to enslave them, wrong; to return them, impracticable; to indenture them, difficult,—therefore, by a death penalty, keep them from being imported.[7] Here the East had a chance to throw back the taunts of the South, by urging the South to unite with them in hanging the New England slave-traders, assuring the South that "so far from charging their Southern brethren with cruelty or severity in hanging them, they would acknowledge the favor with gratitude."[8] Finally, if the Southerners would refuse to execute so severe a law because they did not consider the offence great, they would probably refuse to execute any law at all for the same reason.[9]

The opposition answered that the death penalty was more

[1] Smilie: *Annals of Cong.*, 9 Cong. 2 sess. pp. 189–90.
[2] Tallmadge: *Ibid.*, p. 233; Olin: *Ibid.*, p. 237.
[3] Ely: *Ibid.*, p. 237.
[4] Smilie: *Ibid.*, p. 236. Cf. Sloan: *Ibid.*, p. 232.
[5] Hastings: *Ibid.*, p. 228.
[6] Dwight: *Ibid.*, p. 241; Ely: *Ibid.*, p. 232.
[7] Mosely: *Ibid.*, pp. 234–5.
[8] Tallmadge: *Ibid.*, pp. 232, 234. Cf. Dwight: *Ibid.*, p. 241.
[9] Varnum: *Ibid.*, p. 243.

than proportionate to the crime, and therefore "immoral."[1] "I cannot believe," said Stanton of Rhode Island, "that a man ought to be hung for only stealing a negro."[2] It was argued that the trade was after all but a "transfer from one master to another;"[3] that slavery was worse than the slave-trade, and the South did not consider slavery a crime: how could it then punish the trade so severely and not reflect on the institution?[4] Severity, it was said, was also inexpedient: severity often increases crime; if the punishment is too great, people will sympathize with offenders and will not inform against them. Said Mr. Mosely: "When the penalty is excessive or disproportioned to the offence, it will naturally create a repugnance to the law, and render its execution odious."[5] John Randolph argued against even fine and imprisonment, "on the ground that such an excessive penalty could not, in such case, be constitutionally imposed by a Government possessed of the limited powers of the Government of the United States."[6]

The bill as passed punished infractions as follows:—

For equipping a slaver, a fine of $20,000 and forfeiture of the ship.

For transporting Negroes, a fine of $5000 and forfeiture of the ship and Negroes.

For transporting and selling Negroes, a fine of $1000 to $10,000, imprisonment from 5 to 10 years, and forfeiture of the ship and Negroes.

For knowingly buying illegally imported Negroes, a fine of $800 for each Negro, and forfeiture.

58. **The Third Question: How shall the Interstate Coastwise Slave-Trade be protected?** The first proposition was to prohibit the coastwise slave-trade altogether,[7] but an

[1] Elmer: *Annals of Cong.*, 9 Cong. 2 sess. p. 235.

[2] *Ibid.*, p. 240.

[3] Holland: *Ibid.*, p. 240.

[4] Early: *Ibid.*, pp. 238–9; Holland: *Ibid.*, p. 239.

[5] *Ibid.*, p. 233. Cf. Lloyd: *Ibid.*, p. 237; Ely: *Ibid.*, p. 232; Early: *Ibid.*, pp. 238–9.

[6] *Ibid.*, p. 484.

[7] This was the provision of the Senate bill as reported to the House. It was over the House amendment to this that the Houses disagreed. Cf. *Ibid.*, p. 484.

amendment reported to the House allowed it "in any vessel or species of craft whatever." It is probable that the first proposition would have prevailed, had it not been for the vehement opposition of Randolph and Early.[1] They probably foresaw the value which Virginia would derive from this trade in the future, and consequently Randolph violently declared that if the amendment did not prevail, "the Southern people would set the law at defiance. He would begin the example." He maintained that by the first proposition "the proprietor of sacred and chartered rights is prevented the Constitutional use of his property."[2] The Conference Committee finally arranged a compromise, forbidding the coastwise trade for purposes of sale in vessels under forty tons.[3] This did not suit Early, who declared that the law with this provision "would not prevent the introduction of a single slave."[4] Randolph, too, would "rather lose the bill, he had rather lose all the bills of the session, he had rather lose every bill passed since the establishment of the Government, than agree to the provision contained in this slave bill."[5] He predicted the severance of the slave and the free States, if disunion should ever come. Congress was, however, weary with the dragging of the bill, and it passed both Houses with the compromise provision. Randolph was so dissatisfied that he had a committee appointed the next day, and introduced an amendatory bill. Both this bill and another similar one, introduced at the next session, failed of consideration.[6]

59. **Legislative History of the Bill.**[7] On December 12, 1805, Senator Stephen R. Bradley of Vermont gave notice of a bill to prohibit the introduction of slaves after 1808. By a

[1] Cf. *Annals of Cong.*, 9 Cong. 2 sess. pp. 527–8.

[2] *Ibid.*, p. 528.

[3] *Ibid.*, p. 626.

[4] *Ibid.*

[5] *Ibid.*

[6] *Ibid.*, pp. 636–8; *House Journal* (repr. 1826), 9 Cong. 2 sess. V. 616, and House Bill No. 219; *Ibid.*, 10 Cong. 1 sess. VI. 27, 50; *Annals of Cong.*, 10 Cong. 1 sess. pp. 854–5, 961.

[7] On account of the meagre records it is difficult to follow the course of this bill. I have pieced together information from various sources, and trust that this account is approximately correct.

vote of 18 to 9 leave was given, and the bill read a first time on the 17th. On the 18th, however, it was postponed until "the first Monday in December, 1806." The presidential message mentioning the matter, Senator Bradley, December 3, 1806, gave notice of a similar bill, which was brought in on the 8th, and on the 9th referred to a committee consisting of Bradley, Stone, Giles, Gaillard, and Baldwin. This bill passed, after some consideration, January 27. It provided, among other things, that violations of the act should be felony, punishable with death, and forbade the interstate coast-trade.[1]

Meantime, in the House, Mr. Bidwell of Massachusetts had proposed, February 4, 1806, as an amendment to a bill taxing slaves imported, that importation after December 31, 1807, be prohibited, on pain of fine and imprisonment and forfeiture of ship.[2] This was rejected by a vote of 86 to 17. On December 3, 1806, the House, in appointing committees on the message, "*Ordered*, That Mr. Early, Mr. Thomas M. Randolph, Mr. John Campbell, Mr. Kenan, Mr. Cook, Mr. Kelly, and Mr. Van Rensselaer be appointed a committee" on the slave-trade. This committee reported a bill on the 15th, which was considered, but finally, December 18, recommitted. It was reported in an amended form on the 19th, and amended in Committee of the Whole so as to make violation a misdemeanor punishable by fine and imprisonment, instead of a felony punishable by death.[3] A struggle over the disposal of the cargo then ensued. A motion by Bidwell to except the cargo from forfeiture was lost, 77 to 39. Another motion by Bidwell may be considered the crucial vote on the whole bill: it was an amendment to the forfeiture clause, and read, *"Provided, that no person shall be sold as a slave by virtue of this act."*[4]

[1] Cf. *Senate Journal* (repr. 1821), 9 Cong. 2 sess. IV., Senate Bill No. 41.

[2] *Annals of Cong.*, 9 Cong. 1 sess. p. 438. Cf. above, § 53.

[3] This amendment of the Committee of the Whole was adopted by a vote of 63 to 53. The New England States stood 3 to 2 for the death penalty; the Middle States were evenly divided, 3 and 3; and the South stood 5 to 0 against it, with Kentucky evenly divided. Cf. *House Journal* (repr. 1826), 9 Cong. 2 sess. V. 504.

[4] *Ibid.*, V. 514–5.

This resulted in a tie vote, 60 to 60; but the casting vote of the Speaker, Macon of North Carolina, defeated it. New England voted solidly in favor of it, the Middle States stood 4 for and 2 against it, and the six Southern States stood solid against it. On January 8 the bill went again to a select committee of seventeen, by a vote of 76 to 46. The bill was reported back amended January 20, and on the 28th the Senate bill was also presented to the House. On the 9th, 10th, and 11th of February both bills were considered in Committee of the Whole, and the Senate bill finally replaced the House bill, after several amendments had been made.[1] The bill was then passed, by a vote of 113 to 5.[2] The Senate agreed to the amendments, including that substituting fine and imprisonment for the death penalty, but asked for a conference on the provision which left the interstate coast-trade free. The six conferees succeeded in bringing the Houses to agree, by limiting the trade to vessels over forty tons and requiring registry of the slaves.[3]

The following diagram shows in graphic form the legislative history of the act:—[4]

[1] The substitution of the Senate bill was a victory for the anti-slavery party, as all battles had to be fought again. The Southern party, however, succeeded in carrying all its amendments.

[2] Messrs. Betton of New Hampshire, Chittenden of Vermont, Garnett and Trigg of Virginia, and D. R. Williams of South Carolina voted against the bill: *House Journal* (repr. 1826), 9 Cong. 2 sess. V. 585–6.

[3] *Annals of Cong.*, 9 Cong. 2 sess. pp. 626–7.

[4] The unassigned dates refer to debates, etc. The history of the amendments and debates on the measure may be traced in the following references:—

Senate (Bill No. 41).

Annals of Cong., 9 Cong. 1 sess. pp. 20–1; 9 Cong. 2 sess. pp. 16, 19, 23, 33, 36, 45, 47, 68, 69, 70, 71, 79, 87, 93, etc.

Senate Journal (repr. 1826), 9 Cong. 1–2 sess. IV. 11, 112, 123, 124, 132, 133, 150, 158, 164, 165, 167, 168, etc.

House (Bill No. 148).

Annals of Cong., 9 Cong. 1 sess. p. 438; 9 Cong. 2 sess. pp. 114, 151, 167–8, 173–4, 180, 183, 189, 200, 202–4, 220, 228, 231, 240, 254, 264, 266–7, 270, 273, 373, 427, 477, 481, 484–6, 527, 528, etc.

House Journal (repr. 1826), 9 Cong. 1–2 sess. V. 470, 482, 488, 490, 491, 496, 500, 504, 510, 513–6, 517, 540, 557, 575, 579, 581, 583–4, 585, 592, 594, 610, 613–5, 623, 638, 640, etc.

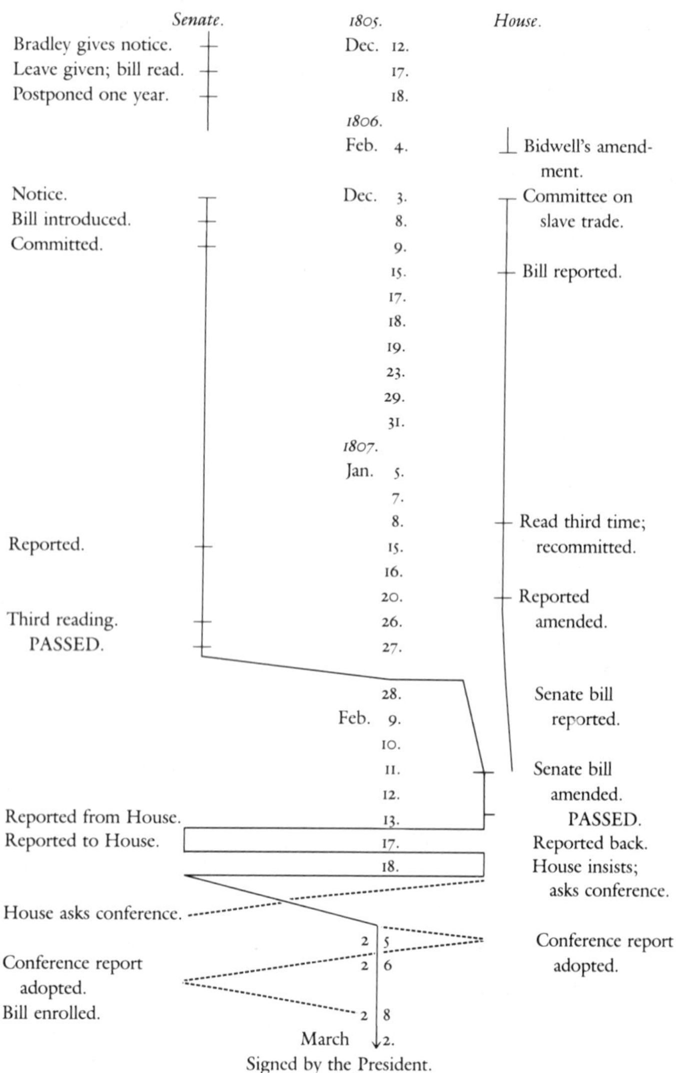

This bill received the approval of President Jefferson, March 2, 1807, and became thus the "Act to prohibit the importation of Slaves into any port or place within the jurisdiction of the United States, from and after the first day of January, in the year of our Lord one thousand eight hundred and eight."[1] The debates in the Senate were not reported. Those in the House were prolonged and bitter, and hinged especially on the disposal of the slaves, the punishment of offenders, and the coast-trade. Men were continually changing their votes, and the bill see-sawed backward and forward, in committee and out, until the House was thoroughly worn out. On the whole, the strong anti-slavery men, like Bidwell and Sloan, were outgeneraled by Southerners, like Early and Williams; and, considering the immense moral backing of the anti-slavery party from the Revolutionary fathers down, the bill of 1807 can hardly be regarded as a great anti-slavery victory.

60. **Enforcement of the Act.** The period so confidently looked forward to by the constitutional fathers had at last arrived; the slave-trade was prohibited, and much oratory and poetry were expended in celebration of the event. In the face of this, let us see how the Act of 1807 was enforced and what it really accomplished. It is noticeable, in the first place, that there was no especial set of machinery provided for the enforcement of this act. The work fell first to the Secretary of the Treasury, as head of the customs collection. Then, through the activity of cruisers, the Secretary of the Navy gradually came to have oversight, and eventually the whole matter was lodged with him, although the Departments of State and War were more or less active on different occasions. Later, at the advent of the Lincoln government, the Department of the Interior was charged with the enforcement of the slave-trade laws. It would indeed be surprising if, amid so much uncertainty and shifting of responsibility, the law were not poorly enforced. Poor enforcement, moreover, in the years 1808 to 1820 meant far

[1] *Statutes at Large*, II. 426. There were some few attempts to obtain laws of relief from this bill: see, e. g., *Annals of Cong.*, 10 Cong. 1 sess. p. 1243; 11 Cong. 1 sess. pp. 34, 36–9, 41, 43, 48, 49, 380, 465, 688, 706, 2209; *House Journal* (repr. 1826), 11 Cong. 1–2 sess. VII. 100, 102, 124, etc., and Index, Senate Bill No. 8. Cf. *Amer. State Papers, Miscellaneous*, II. No. 269. There was also one proposed amendment to make the prohibition perpetual: *Amer. State Papers, Miscellaneous*, I. No. 244.

more than at almost any other period; for these years were, all over the European world, a time of stirring economic change, and the set which forces might then take would in a later period be unchangeable without a cataclysm. Perhaps from 1808 to 1814, in the midst of agitation and war, there was some excuse for carelessness. From 1814 on, however, no such palliation existed, and the law was probably enforced as the people who made it wished it enforced.

Most of the Southern States rather tardily passed the necessary supplementary acts disposing of illegally imported Africans. A few appear not to have passed any. Some of these laws, like the Alabama-Mississippi Territory Act of 1815,[1] directed such Negroes to be "sold by the proper officer of the court, to the highest bidder, at public auction, for ready money." One-half the proceeds went to the informer or to the collector of customs, the other half to the public treasury. Other acts, like that of North Carolina in 1816,[2] directed the Negroes to "be sold and disposed of for the use of the state." One-fifth of the proceeds went to the informer. The Georgia Act of 1817[3] directed that the slaves be either sold or given to the Colonization Society for transportation, providing the society reimburse the State for all expense incurred, and pay for the transportation. In this manner, machinery of somewhat clumsy build and varying pattern was provided for the carrying out of the national act.

61. **Evidence of the Continuance of the Trade.** Undoubtedly, the Act of 1807 came very near being a dead letter. The testimony supporting this view is voluminous. It consists of presidential messages, reports of cabinet officers, letters of collectors of revenue, letters of district attorneys, reports of committees of Congress, reports of naval commanders, statements made on the floor of Congress, the testimony of eye-witnesses, and the complaints of home and foreign anti-slavery societies.

"When I was young," writes Mr. Fowler of Connecticut, "the slave-trade was still carried on, by Connecticut ship-masters and Merchant adventurers, for the supply of south-

[1] Toulmin, *Digest of the Laws of Alabama*, p. 637.
[2] *Laws of North Carolina* (revision of 1819), II. 1350.
[3] Prince, *Digest*, p. 793.

ern ports. This trade was carried on by the consent of the Southern States, under the provisions of the Federal Constitution, until 1808, and, after that time, clandestinely. There was a good deal of conversation on the subject, in private circles." Other States were said to be even more involved than Connecticut.[1] The African Society of London estimated that, down to 1816, fifteen of the sixty thousand slaves annually taken from Africa were shipped by Americans. "Notwithstanding the prohibitory act of America, which was passed in 1807, ships bearing the American flag continued to trade for slaves until 1809, when, in consequence of a decision in the English prize appeal courts, which rendered American slave ships liable to capture and condemnation, that flag suddenly disappeared from the coast. Its place was almost instantaneously supplied by the Spanish flag, which, with one or two exceptions, was now seen for the first time on the African coast, engaged in covering the slave trade. This sudden substitution of the Spanish for the American flag seemed to confirm what was established in a variety of instances by more direct testimony, that the slave trade, which now, for the first time, assumed a Spanish dress, was in reality only the trade of other nations in disguise."[2]

So notorious did the participation of Americans in the traffic become, that President Madison informed Congress in his message, December 5, 1810, that "it appears that American citizens are instrumental in carrying on a traffic in enslaved Africans, equally in violation of the laws of humanity, and in defiance of those of their own country. The same just and benevolent motives which produced the interdiction in force against this criminal conduct, will doubtless be felt by Congress, in devising further means of suppressing the evil."[3] The Secretary of the Navy wrote the same year to Charleston, South Carolina: "I hear, not without great concern, that the law prohibiting the importation of slaves has been violated in frequent instances,

[1] Fowler, *Historical Status of the Negro in Connecticut*, in *Local Law*, etc., pp. 122, 126.

[2] *House Reports*, 17 Cong. 1 sess. II. No. 92, p. 32.

[3] *House Journal* (repr. 1826), 11 Cong. 3 sess. VII. p. 435.

near St. Mary's."[1] Testimony as to violations of the law and suggestions for improving it also came in from district attorneys.[2]

The method of introducing Negroes was simple. A slave smuggler says: "After resting a few days at St. Augustine, . . . I agreed to accompany Diego on a land trip through the United States, where a *kaffle* of negroes was to precede us, for whose disposal the shrewd Portuguese had already made arrangements with my uncle's consignees. I soon learned how readily, and at what profits, the Florida negroes were sold into the neighboring American States. The *kaffle*, under charge of negro drivers, was to strike up the Escambia River, and thence cross the boundary into Georgia, where some of our wild Africans were mixed with various squads of native blacks, and driven inland, till sold off, singly or by couples, on the road. At this period [1812], the United States had declared the African slave trade illegal, and passed stringent laws to prevent the importation of negroes; yet the Spanish possessions were thriving on this inland exchange of negroes and mulattoes; Florida was a sort of nursery for slave-breeders, and many American citizens grew rich by trafficking in Guinea negroes, and smuggling them continually, in small parties, through the southern United States. At the time I mention, the business was a lively one, owing to the war then going on between the States and England, and the unsettled condition of affairs on the border."[3]

The Spanish flag continued to cover American slave-traders. The rapid rise of privateering during the war was not caused solely by patriotic motives; for many armed ships fitted out in the United States obtained a thin Spanish disguise at Havana, and transported thousands of slaves to Brazil and the West Indies. Sometimes all disguise was thrown aside, and the American flag appeared on the slave coast, as in the cases

[1] *House Doc.*, 15 Cong. 2 sess. IV. No. 84, p. 5.

[2] See, e. g., *House Journal* (repr. 1826), 11 Cong. 3 sess. VII. p. 575.

[3] Drake, *Revelations of a Slave Smuggler*, p. 51. Parts of this narrative are highly colored and untrustworthy; this passage, however, has every earmark of truth, and is confirmed by many incidental allusions.

of the "Paz,"[1] the "Rebecca," the "Rosa"[2] (formerly the privateer "Commodore Perry"), the "Dorset" of Baltimore,[3] and the "Saucy Jack."[4] Governor McCarthy of Sierra Leone wrote, in 1817: "The slave trade is carried on most vigorously by the Spaniards, Portuguese, Americans and French. I have had it affirmed from several quarters, and do believe it to be a fact, that there is a greater number of vessels employed in that traffic than at any former period."[5]

62. **Apathy of the Federal Government.** The United States cruisers succeeded now and then in capturing a slaver, like the "Eugene," which was taken when within four miles of the New Orleans bar.[6] President Madison again, in 1816, urged Congress to act on account of the "violations and evasions which, it is suggested, are chargeable on unworthy citizens, who mingle in the slave trade under foreign flags, and with foreign ports; and by collusive importations of slaves into the United States, through adjoining ports and territories."[7] The executive was continually in receipt of ample evidence of this illicit trade and of the helplessness of officers of the law. In 1817 it was reported to the Secretary of the Navy that most of the goods carried to Galveston were brought into the United States; "the more valuable, and the slaves are smuggled in through the numerous inlets to the westward, where the people are but too much disposed to render them every possible assistance. Several hundred slaves are now at Galveston, and persons have gone from New-Orleans to

[1] For accounts of these slavers, see *House Reports*, 17 Cong. 1 sess. II. No. 92, pp. 30–50. The "Paz" was an armed slaver flying the American flag.

[2] Said to be owned by an Englishman, but fitted in America and manned by Americans. It was eventually captured by H. M. S. "Bann," after a hard fight.

[3] Also called Spanish schooner "Triumvirate," with American supercargo, Spanish captain, and American, French, Spanish, and English crew. It was finally captured by a British vessel.

[4] An American slaver of 1814, which was boarded by a British vessel. All the above cases, and many others, were proven before British courts.

[5] *House Reports*, 17 Cong. 1 sess. II. No. 92, p. 51.

[6] *House Doc.*, 15 Cong. 1 sess. II. No. 12, pp. 22, 38. This slaver was after capture sent to New Orleans,—an illustration of the irony of the Act of 1807.

[7] *House Journal*, 14 Cong. 2 sess. p. 15.

purchase them. Every exertion will be made to intercept them, but I have little hopes of success."[1] Similar letters from naval officers and collectors showed that a system of slave piracy had arisen since the war, and that at Galveston there was an establishment of organized brigands, who did not go to the trouble of sailing to Africa for their slaves, but simply captured slavers and sold their cargoes into the United States. This Galveston nest had, in 1817, eleven armed vessels to prosecute the work, and "the most shameful violations of the slave act, as well as our revenue laws, continue to be practised."[2] Cargoes of as many as three hundred slaves were arriving in Texas. All this took place under Aury, the buccaneer governor; and when he removed to Amelia Island in 1817 with the McGregor raid, the illicit traffic in slaves, which had been going on there for years,[3] took an impulse that brought it even to the somewhat deaf ears of Collector Bullock. He reported, May 22, 1817: "I have just received information from a source on which I can implicitly rely, that it has already become the practice to introduce into the state of Georgia, across the St. Mary's River, from Amelia Island, East Florida, Africans, who have been carried into the Port of Fernandina, subsequent to the capture of it by the Patriot army now in possession of it . . . ; were the legislature to pass an act giving compensation in some manner to informers, it would have a tendency in a great degree to prevent the practice; as the thing now is, no citizen will take the trouble of searching for and detecting the slaves. I further understand, that the evil will not be confined altogether to Africans, but will be extended to the worst class of West India slaves."[4]

[1] *House Doc.*, 16 Cong. 1 sess. III. No. 36, p. 5.

[2] *Ibid.*, 15 Cong. 1 sess. II. No. 12, pp. 8–14. See Chew's letter of Oct. 17, 1817: *Ibid.*, pp. 14–16.

[3] By the secret Joint Resolution and Act of 1811 (*Statutes at Large*, III. 471), Congress gave the President power to suppress the Amelia Island establishment, which was then notorious. The capture was not accomplished until 1817.

[4] *House Doc.*, 16 Cong. 1 sess. III. No. 42, pp. 10–11. Cf. Report of the House Committee, Jan. 10, 1818: "It is but too notorious that numerous infractions of the law prohibiting the importation of slaves into the United States have been perpetrated with impunity upon our southern frontier." *Amer. State Papers, Miscellaneous*, II. No. 441.

Undoubtedly, the injury done by these pirates to the regular slave-trading interests was largely instrumental in exterminating them. Late in 1817 United States troops seized Amelia Island, and President Monroe felicitated Congress and the country upon escaping the "annoyance and injury" of this illicit trade.[1] The trade, however, seems to have continued, as is shown by such letters as the following, written three and a half months later:—

PORT OF DARIEN, March 14, 1818.

. . . It is a painful duty, sir, to express to you, that I am in possession of undoubted information, that African and West India negroes are almost daily illicitly introduced into Georgia, for sale or settlement, or passing through it to the territories of the United States for similar purposes; these facts are notorious; and it is not unusual to see such negroes in the streets of St. Mary's, and such too, recently captured by our vessels of war, and ordered to Savannah, were illegally bartered by hundreds in that city, *for* this bartering or bonding (as *it is called*, but in reality *selling*,) actually took place before any decision had [been] passed by the court respecting them. I cannot but again express to you, sir, that these irregularities and mocking of the laws, by men who understand them, and who, it was presumed, would have respected them, are such, that it requires the immediate interposition of Congress to effect a suppression of this traffic; for, as things are, should a faithful officer of the government apprehend such negroes, to avoid the penalties imposed by the laws, the proprietors disclaim them, and some agent of the executive demands a delivery of the same to him, who may employ them as he pleases, or effect a sale by way of a bond, for the restoration of the negroes when legally called on so to do; which bond, it is *understood*, is to be *forfeited*, as the amount of the bond is so much less than the value of the property. . . . There are many negroes . . . recently introduced into this state and the Alabama territory, and which can be apprehended. The undertaking would be great; but to be sensible that we shall possess your approbation, and that we are carrying the views and wishes of the government into execution, is all we wish, and it shall be done, independent of every personal consideration.

I have, etc.[2]

This "approbation" failed to come to the zealous collector,

[1] Special message of Jan. 13, 1818: *House Journal*, 15 Cong. 1 sess. pp. 137–9.

[2] Collector McIntosh, of the District of Brunswick, Ga., to the Secretary of the Treasury. *House Doc.*, 16 Cong. 1 sess. III. No. 42, pp. 8–9.

and on the 5th of July he wrote that, "not being favored with a reply," he has been obliged to deliver over to the governor's agents ninety-one illegally imported Negroes.[1] Reports from other districts corroborate this testimony. The collector at Mobile writes of strange proceedings on the part of the courts.[2] General D. B. Mitchell, ex-governor of Georgia and United States Indian agent, after an investigation in 1821 by Attorney-General Wirt, was found "guilty of having prostituted his power, as agent for Indian affairs at the Creek agency, to the purpose of aiding and assisting in a conscious breach of the act of Congress of 1807, in prohibition of the slave trade—and this from mercenary motives."[3] The indefatigable Collector Chew of New Orleans wrote to Washington that, "to put a stop to that traffic, a naval force suitable to those waters is indispensable," and that "vast numbers of slaves will be introduced to an alarming extent, unless prompt and effectual measures are adopted by the general government."[4] Other collectors continually reported infractions, complaining that they could get no assistance from the citizens,[5] or plaintively asking the services of "one small cutter."[6]

Meantime, what was the response of the government to such representations, and what efforts were made to enforce the act? A few unsystematic and spasmodic attempts are recorded. In 1811 some special instructions were sent out,[7] and the President was authorized to seize Amelia Island.[8] Then came the war; and as late as November 15, 1818, in spite of the complaints of collectors, we find no revenue cutter on the Gulf coast.[9] During the years 1817 and 1818[10] some cruisers

[1] *House Doc.*, 16 Cong. 1 sess. III. No. 42, pp. 6–7.

[2] *Ibid.*, pp. 11–12.

[3] *Amer. State Papers, Miscellaneous*, II. No. 529.

[4] *House Doc.*, 16 Cong. 1 sess. III. No. 42, p. 7.

[5] *Ibid.*, p. 6.

[6] *House Reports*, 21 Cong. 1 sess. III. No. 348, p. 82.

[7] They were not general instructions, but were directed to Commander Campbell. Cf. *House Doc.*, 15 Cong. 2 sess. IV. No. 84, pp. 5–6.

[8] *Statutes at Large*, III. 471 ff.

[9] *House Doc.*, 15 Cong. 2 sess. VI. No. 107, pp. 8–9.

[10] *Ibid.*, IV. No. 84. Cf. Chew's letters in *House Reports*, 21 Cong. 1 sess. III. No. 348.

went there irregularly, but they were too large to be effective; and the partial suppression of the Amelia Island pirates was all that was accomplished. On the whole, the efforts of the government lacked plan, energy, and often sincerity. Some captures of slavers were made;[1] but, as the collector at Mobile wrote, anent certain cases, "this was owing rather to accident, than any well-timed arrangement." He adds: "from the Chandalier Islands to the Perdido river, including the coast, and numerous other islands, we have only a small boat, with four men and an inspector, to oppose to the whole confederacy of smugglers and pirates."[2]

To cap the climax, the government officials were so negligent that Secretary Crawford, in 1820, confessed to Congress that "it appears, from an examination of the records of this office, that no particular instructions have ever been given, by the Secretary of the Treasury, under the original or supplementary acts prohibiting the introduction of slaves into the United States."[3] Beside this inactivity, the government was criminally negligent in not prosecuting and punishing offenders when captured. Urgent appeals for instruction from prosecuting attorneys were too often received in official silence; complaints as to the violation of law by State officers went unheeded;[4] informers were unprotected and sometimes driven from home.[5] Indeed, the most severe comment on the whole period is the report, January 7, 1819, of the Register of the Treasury, who, after the wholesale and open violation of the Act of 1807, reported, in response to a request from the House, "that it doth not appear, from an examination of the records of this office, and particularly of the accounts (to the date of their last settlement) of the

[1] *House Doc.*, 15 Cong. 1 sess. II. No. 12, pp. 22, 38; 15 Cong. 2 sess. VI. No. 100, p. 13; 16 Cong. 1 sess. III. No. 42, p. 9, etc.; *House Reports*, 21 Cong. 1 sess. III. No. 348, p. 85.

[2] *House Doc.*, 15 Cong. 2 sess. VI. No. 107, pp. 8–9.

[3] *House Reports*, 21 Cong. 1 sess. III. No. 348, p. 77.

[4] Cf. *House Doc.*, 16 Cong. 1 sess. III. No. 42, p. 11: "The Grand Jury found true bills against the owners of the vessels, masters, and a supercargo—all of whom are discharged; why or wherefore I cannot say, except that it could not be for want of proof against them."

[5] E. g., in July, 1818, one informer "will have to leave that part of the country to save his life": *Ibid.*, 15 Cong. 2 sess. VI. No. 100, p. 9.

collectors of the customs, and of the several marshals of the United States, that any forfeitures had been incurred under the said act."[1]

63. **Typical Cases.** At this date (January 7, 1819), however, certain cases were stated to be pending, a history of which will fitly conclude this discussion. In 1818 three American schooners sailed from the United States to Havana; on June 2 they started back with cargoes aggregating one hundred and seven slaves. The schooner "Constitution" was captured by one of Andrew Jackson's officers under the guns of Fort Barancas. The "Louisa" and "Marino" were captured by Lieutenant McKeever of the United States Navy. The three vessels were duly proceeded against at Mobile, and the case began slowly to drag along. The slaves, instead of being put under the care of the zealous marshal of the district, were placed in the hands of three bondsmen, friends of the judge. The marshal notified the government of this irregularity, but apparently received no answer. In 1822 the three vessels were condemned as forfeited, but the court "reserved" for future order the distribution of the slaves. Nothing whatever either then or later was done to the slave-traders themselves. The owners of the ships promptly appealed to the Supreme Court of the United States, and that tribunal, in 1824, condemned the three vessels and the slaves on two of them.[2] These slaves, considerably reduced in number "from various causes," were sold at auction for the benefit of the State, in spite of the Act of 1819. Meantime, before the decision of the Supreme Court, the judge of the Supreme Court of West Florida had awarded to certain alleged Spanish claimants of the slaves indemnity for nearly the whole number seized, at the price of $650 per head, and the Secretary of the Treasury had actually paid the claim.[3] In 1826 Lieutenant McKeever urgently petitions Con-

[1] Joseph Nourse, Register of the Treasury, to Hon. W. H. Crawford, Secretary of the Treasury: *Ibid.*, 15 Cong. 2 sess. VI. No. 107, p. 5.

[2] The slaves on the "Constitution" were not condemned, for the technical reason that she was not captured by a commissioned officer of the United States navy.

[3] These proceedings are very obscure, and little was said about them. The Spanish claimants were, it was alleged with much probability, but representatives of Americans. The claim was paid under the provisions of the Treaty of Florida, and included slaves whom the court afterward declared forfeited.

gress for his prize-money of $4,415.15, which he has not yet received.[1] The "Constitution" was for some inexplicable reason released from bond, and the whole case fades in a very thick cloud of official mist. In 1831 Congress sought to inquire into the final disposition of the slaves. The information given was never printed; but as late as 1836 a certain Calvin Mickle petitions Congress for reimbursement for the slaves sold, for their hire, for their natural increase, for expenses incurred, and for damages.[2]

64. **The Supplementary Acts, 1818–1820.** To remedy the obvious defects of the Act of 1807 two courses were possible: one, to minimize the crime of transportation, and, by encouraging informers, to concentrate efforts against the buying of smuggled slaves; the other, to make the crime of transportation so great that no slaves would be imported. The Act of 1818 tried the first method; that of 1819, the second.[3] The latter was obviously the more upright and logical, and the only method deserving thought even in 1807; but the Act of 1818 was the natural descendant of that series of compromises which began in the Constitutional Convention, and which, instead of postponing the settlement of critical questions to more favorable times, rather aggravated and complicated them.

The immediate cause of the Act of 1818 was the Amelia Island scandal.[4] Committees in both Houses reported bills, but

[1] An act to relieve him was finally passed, Feb. 8, 1827, nine years after the capture. See *Statutes at Large*, VI. 357.

[2] It is difficult to get at the exact facts in this complicated case. The above statement is, I think, much milder than the real facts would warrant, if thoroughly known. Cf. *House Reports*, 19 Cong. 1 sess. II. No. 231; 21 Cong. 1 sess. III. No. 348, pp. 62–3, etc.; 24 Cong. 1 sess. I. No. 209; *Amer. State Papers, Naval*, II. No. 308.

[3] The first method, represented by the Act of 1818, was favored by the South, the Senate, and the Democrats; the second method, represented by the Act of 1819, by the North, the House, and by the as yet undeveloped but growing Whig party.

[4] Committees on the slave-trade were appointed by the House in 1810 and 1813; the committee of 1813 recommended a revision of the laws, but nothing was done: *Annals of Cong.*, 11 Cong. 3 sess. p. 387; 12 Cong. 2 sess. pp. 1074, 1090. The presidential message of 1816 led to committees on the trade in both Houses. The committee of the House of Representatives reported a joint resolution on abolishing the traffic and colonizing the Negroes, also looking

that of the Senate finally passed. There does not appear to have been very much debate.[1] The sale of Africans for the benefit of the informer and of the United States was strongly urged "as the only means of executing the laws against the slave trade as experience had fully demonstrated since the origin of the prohibition."[2] This proposition was naturally opposed as "inconsistent with the principles of our Government, and calculated to throw as wide open the door to the importation of slaves as it was before the existing prohibition."[3] The act, which became a law April 20, 1818,[4] was a poorly constructed compromise, which virtually acknowledged the failure of efforts to control the trade, and sought to remedy defects by pitting cupidity against cupidity, informer against thief. One-half of all forfeitures and fines were to go to the informer, and penalties for violation were changed as follows:—

For equipping a slaver, instead of a fine of $20,000, a fine of $1000 to $5000 and imprisonment from 3 to 7 years.

For transporting Negroes, instead of a fine of $5000 and forfeiture of ship and Negroes, a fine of $1000 to $5000 and imprisonment from 3 to 7 years.

For actual importation, instead of a fine of $1000 to $10,000 and

---

toward international action. This never came to a vote: *Senate Journal*, 14 Cong. 2 sess. pp. 46, 179, 180; *House Journal*, 14 Cong. 2 sess. pp. 25, 27, 380; *House Doc.*, 14 Cong. 2 sess. II. No. 77. Finally, the presidential message of 1817 (*House Journal*, 15 Cong. 1 sess. p. 11), announcing the issuance of orders to suppress the Amelia Island establishment, led to two other committees in both Houses. The House committee under Middleton made a report with a bill (*Amer. State Papers, Miscellaneous*, II. No. 441), and the Senate committee also reported a bill.

[1] The Senate debates were entirely unreported, and the report of the House debates is very meagre. For the proceedings, see *Senate Journal*, 15 Cong. 1 sess. pp. 243, 304, 315, 333, 338, 340, 348, 377, 386, 388, 391, 403, 406; *House Journal*, 15 Cong. 1 sess. pp. 19, 20, 29, 51, 92, 131, 362, 410, 450, 452, 456, 468, 479, 484, 492, 505.

[2] Simkins of South Carolina, Edwards of North Carolina, and Pindall: *Annals of Cong.*, 15 Cong. 1 sess. p. 1740.

[3] Hugh Nelson of Virginia: *Annals of Cong.*, 15 Cong. 1 sess. p. 1740.

[4] *Statutes at Large*, III. 450. By this act the first six sections of the Act of 1807 were repealed.

imprisonment from 5 to 10 years, a fine of $1000 to $10,000, and imprisonment from 3 to 7 years.

For knowingly buying illegally imported Negroes, instead of a fine of $800 for each Negro and forfeiture, a fine of $1000 for each Negro.

The burden of proof was laid on the defendant, to the extent that he must prove that the slave in question had been imported at least five years before the prosecution. The slaves were still left to the disposal of the States.

This statute was, of course, a failure from the start,[1] and at the very next session Congress took steps to revise it. A bill was reported in the House, January 13, 1819, but it was not discussed till March.[2] It finally passed, after "much debate."[3] The Senate dropped its own bill, and, after striking out the provision for the death penalty, passed the bill as it came from the House.[4] The House acquiesced, and the bill became a law, March 3, 1819,[5] in the midst of the Missouri trouble. This act directed the President to use armed cruisers on the coasts of the United States and Africa to suppress the slave-trade; one-half the proceeds of the condemned ship were to go to the captors as bounty, provided the Africans were safely lodged with a United States marshal and the crew with the civil authorities. These provisions were seriously marred by a proviso which Butler of Louisiana, had inserted, with a "due regard for the interests of the State which he represented," viz., that a captured

[1] Or, more accurately speaking, every one realized, in view of the increased activity of the trade, that it would be a failure.

[2] Nov. 18, 1818, the part of the presidential message referring to the slave-trade was given to a committee of the House, and this committee also took in hand the House bill of the previous session which the Senate bill had replaced: *House Journal*, 15 Cong. 2 sess. pp. 9–19, 42, 150, 179, 330, 334, 341, 343, 352.

[3] Of which little was reported: *Annals of Cong.*, 15 Cong. 2 sess. pp. 1430–31. Strother opposed, "for various reasons of expediency," the bounties for captors. Nelson of Virginia advocated the death penalty, and, aided by Pindall, had it inserted. The vote on the bill was 57 to 45.

[4] The Senate had also had a committee at work on a bill which was reported Feb. 8, and finally postponed: *Senate Journal*, 15 Cong. 2 sess. pp. 234, 244, 311–2, 347. The House bill was taken up March 2: *Annals of Cong.*, 15 Cong. 2 sess. p. 280.

[5] *Statutes at Large*, III. 532.

slaver must always be returned to the port whence she sailed.[1] This, of course, secured decided advantages to Southern slave-traders. The most radical provision of the act was that which directed the President to "make such regulations and arrangements as he may deem expedient for the safe keeping, support, and removal beyond the limits of the United States, of all such negroes, mulattoes, or persons of colour, as may be so delivered and brought within their jurisdiction;" and to appoint an agent in Africa to receive such Negroes.[2] Finally, an appropriation of $100,000 was made to enforce the act.[3] This act was in some measure due to the new colonization movement; and the return of Africans recaptured was a distinct recognition of its efforts, and the real foundation of Liberia.

To render this straightforward act effective, it was necessary to add but one measure, and that was a penalty commensurate with the crime of slave stealing. This was accomplished by the Act of May 15, 1820,[4] a law which may be regarded as the last of the Missouri Compromise measures. The act originated from the various bills on piracy which were introduced early in the sixteenth Congress. The House bill, in spite of opposition, was amended so as to include slave-trading under

[1] *Annals of Cong.*, 15 Cong. 2 sess. p. 1430. This insured the trial of slave-traders in a sympathetic slave State, and resulted in the "disappearance" of many captured Negroes.

[2] *Statutes at Large*, III. 533.

[3] The first of a long series of appropriations extending to 1869, of which a list is given on the next page. The totals are only approximately correct. Some statutes may have escaped me, and in the reports of moneys the surpluses of previous years are not always clearly distinguishable.

[4] In the first session of the sixteenth Congress, two bills on piracy were introduced into the Senate, one of which passed, April 26. In the House there was a bill on piracy, and a slave-trade committee reported recommending that the slave-trade be piracy. The Senate bill and this bill were considered in Committee of the Whole, May 11, and a bill was finally passed declaring, among other things, the traffic piracy. In the Senate there was "some discussion, rather on the form than the substance of these amendments," and "they were agreed to without a division": *Senate Journal*, 16 Cong. 1 sess. pp. 238, 241, 268, 287, 314, 331, 346, 350, 409, 412, 417, 420, 422, 424, 425; *House Journal*, 16 Cong. 1 sess. pp. 113, 280, 453, 454, 494, 518, 520, 522, 537; *Annals of Cong.*, 16 Cong. 1 sess. pp. 693–4, 2231, 2236–7, etc. The debates were not reported.

piracy, and passed. The Senate agreed without a division. This law provided that direct participation in the slave-trade should be piracy, punishable with death.[1]

Statutes at Large.		Date.	Amount Appropriated.
VOL.	PAGE		
III.	533–4	March 3, 1819	$100,000
"	764	" 3, 1823	50,000
IV.	141	" 14, 1826	32,000
"	208	March 2, 1827	{ 36,710 20,000
"	302	May 24, 1828	30,000
"	354	March 2, 1829	16,000
"	462	" 2, 1831	16,000
"	615	Feb. 20, 1833	5,000
"	671	Jan. 24, 1834	5,000
V.	157–8	March 3, 1837	11,413.57
"	501	Aug. 4, 1842	10,543.42
"	615	March 3, 1843	5,000
IX.	96	Aug. 10, 1846	25,000
XI.	90	" 18, 1856	8,000
"	227	March 3, 1857	8,000
"	404	" 3, 1859	75,000
XII.	21	May 26, 1860	40,000
"	132	Feb. 19, 1861	900,000
"	219	March 2, 1861	900,000
"	639	Feb. 4, 1863	17,000
XIII.	424	Jan. 24, 1865	17,000
XIV.	226	July 25, 1866	17,000
"	415	Feb. 28, 1867	17,000
XV.	58	March 30, 1868	12,500
"	321	March 3, 1869	12,500

Total, 50 years	$2,386,666.99
Minus surpluses re-appropriated (approximate)	48,666.99?
	$2,338,000
Cost of squadron, 1843–58, @ $384,500 per year (*House Exec. Doc.*, 31 Cong. 1 sess. IX. No. 73)	5,767,500
Returning slaves on "Wildfire" (*Statutes at Large*, XII. 41) . .	250,000
Approximate cost of squadron, 1858–66, probably not less than $500,000 per year	4,000,000?
Approximate money cost of suppressing the slave-trade	$12,355,500?

Cf. Kendall's Report: *Senate Doc.*, 21 Cong. 2 sess. I. No. 1, pp. 211–8; *Amer. State Papers, Naval*, III. No. 429 E.; also Reports of the Secretaries of the Navy from 1819 to 1860.

---

[1] *Statutes at Large*, III. 600–1. This act was in reality a continuation of the piracy Act of 1819, and was only temporary. The provision was, however, continued by several acts, and finally made perpetual by the Act of Jan. 30,

65. **Enforcement of the Supplementary Acts, 1818–1825.** A somewhat more sincere and determined effort to enforce the slave-trade laws now followed; and yet it is a significant fact that not until Lincoln's administration did a slave-trader suffer death for violating the laws of the United States. The participation of Americans in the trade continued, declining somewhat between 1825 and 1830, and then reviving, until it reached its highest activity between 1840 and 1860. The development of a vast internal slave-trade, and the consequent rise in the South of vested interests strongly opposed to slave smuggling, led to a falling off in the illicit introduction of Negroes after 1825, until the fifties; nevertheless, smuggling never entirely ceased, and large numbers were thus added to the plantations of the Gulf States.

Monroe had various constitutional scruples as to the execution of the Act of 1819;[1] but, as Congress took no action, he at last put a fair interpretation on his powers, and appointed Samuel Bacon as an agent in Africa to form a settlement for recaptured Africans. Gradually the agency thus formed became merged with that of the Colonization Society on Cape Mesurado; and from this union Liberia was finally evolved.[2]

Meantime, during the years 1818 to 1820, the activity of the slave-traders was prodigious. General James Tallmadge declared in the House, February 15, 1819: "Our laws are already highly penal against their introduction, and yet, it is a well known fact, that about fourteen thousand slaves have been brought into our country this last year."[3] In the same year Middleton of South Carolina and Wright of Virginia esti-

---

1823: *Statutes at Large*, III. 510–4, 721. On March 3, 1823, it was slightly amended so as to give district courts jurisdiction.

[1] Attorney-General Wirt advised him, October, 1819, that no part of the appropriation could be used to purchase land in Africa or tools for the Negroes, or as salary for the agent: *Opinions of Attorneys-General*, I. 314–7. Monroe laid the case before Congress in a special message Dec. 20, 1819 (*House Journal*, 16 Cong. 1 sess. p. 57); but no action was taken there.

[2] Cf. Kendall's Report, August, 1830: *Senate Doc.*, 21 Cong. 2 sess. I. No. 1, pp. 211–8; also see below, Chapter X.

[3] Speech in the House of Representatives, Feb. 15, 1819, p. 18; published in Boston, 1849.

mated illicit introduction at 13,000 and 15,000 respectively.[1] Judge Story, in charging a jury, took occasion to say: "We have but too many proofs from unquestionable sources, that it [the slave-trade] is still carried on with all the implacable rapacity of former times. Avarice has grown more subtle in its evasions, and watches and seizes its prey with an appetite quickened rather than suppressed by its guilty vigils. American citizens are steeped to their very mouths (I can hardly use too bold a figure) in this stream of iniquity."[2] The following year, 1820, brought some significant statements from various members of Congress. Said Smith of South Carolina: "Pharaoh was, for his temerity, drowned in the Red Sea, in pursuing them [the Israelites] contrary to God's express will; but our Northern friends have not been afraid even of that, in their zeal to furnish the Southern States with Africans. They are better seamen than Pharaoh, and calculate by that means to elude the vigilance of Heaven; which they seem to disregard, if they can but elude the violated laws of their country."[3] As late as May he saw little hope of suppressing the traffic.[4] Sergeant of Pennsylvania declared: "It is notorious that, in spite of the utmost vigilance that can be employed, African negroes are clandestinely brought in and sold as slaves."[5] Plumer of New Hampshire stated that "of the unhappy beings, thus in violation of all laws transported to our shores, and thrown by force into the mass of our black population, scarcely one in a hundred is ever detected by the officers of the General Government, in a part of the country, where, if we are to believe the statement of Governor Rabun, 'an officer who would perform his duty, by attempting to enforce the law [against the slave trade] is, by many, considered as an officious meddler, and treated with derision and contempt;' . . . I have been told by a gentleman, who has attended particularly to this subject, that ten thousand slaves were in one year smuggled into the United States; and that,

[1] Jay, *Inquiry into American Colonization* (1838), p. 59, note.

[2] Quoted in Friends' *Facts and Observations on the Slave Trade* (ed. 1841), pp. 7–8.

[3] *Annals of Cong.*, 16 Cong. 1 sess. pp. 270–1.

[4] *Ibid.*, p. 698.

[5] *Ibid.*, p. 1207.

even for the last year, we must count the number not by hundreds, but by thousands."[1] In 1821 a committee of Congress characterized prevailing methods as those "of the grossest fraud that could be practised to deceive the officers of government."[2] Another committee, in 1822, after a careful examination of the subject, declare that they "find it impossible to measure with precision the effect produced upon the American branch of the slave trade by the laws above mentioned, and the seizures under them. They are unable to state, whether those American merchants, the American capital and seamen which heretofore aided in this traffic, have abandoned it altogether, or have sought shelter under the flags of other nations." They then state the suspicious circumstance that, with the disappearance of the American flag from the traffic, "the trade, notwithstanding, increases annually, under the flags of other nations." They complain of the spasmodic efforts of the executive. They say that the first United States cruiser arrived on the African coast in March, 1820, and remained a "few weeks;" that since then four others had in two years made five visits in all; but "since the middle of last November, the commencement of the healthy season on that coast, no vessel has been, nor, as your committee is informed, is, under orders for that service."[3] The United States African agent, Ayres, reported in 1823: "I was informed by an American officer who had been on the coast in 1820, that he had boarded 20 American vessels in one morning, lying in the port of Gallinas, and fitted for the reception of slaves. It is a lamentable fact, that most of the harbours, between the Senegal and the line, were visited by an equal number of American vessels, and for the sole purpose of carrying away slaves. Although for some years the coast had been occasionally

[1] *Annals of Cong.*, 16 Cong. 1 sess. p. 1433.

[2] Referring particularly to the case of the slaver "Plattsburg." Cf. *House Reports*, 17 Cong. 1 sess. II. No. 92, p. 10.

[3] *House Reports*, 17 Cong. 1 sess. II. No. 92, p. 2. The President had in his message spoken in exhilarating tones of the success of the government in suppressing the trade. The House Committee appointed in pursuance of this passage made the above report. Their conclusions are confirmed by British reports: *Parliamentary Papers*, 1822, Vol. XXII., *Slave Trade*, Further Papers, III. p. 44. So, too, in 1823, Ashmun, the African agent, reports that thousands of slaves are being abducted.

visited by our cruizers, their short stay and seldom appearance had made but slight impression on those traders, rendered hardy by repetition of crime, and avaricious by excessive gain. They were enabled by a regular system to gain intelligence of any cruizer being on the coast."[1]

Even such spasmodic efforts bore abundant fruit, and indicated what vigorous measures might have accomplished. Between May, 1818, and November, 1821, nearly six hundred Africans were recaptured and eleven American slavers taken.[2] Such measures gradually changed the character of the trade, and opened the international phase of the question. American slavers cleared for foreign ports, there took a foreign flag and papers, and then sailed boldly past American cruisers, although their real character was often well known. More stringent clearance laws and consular instructions might have greatly reduced this practice; but nothing was ever done, and gradually the laws became in large measure powerless to deal with the bulk of the illicit trade. In 1820, September 16, a British officer, in his official report, declares that, in spite of United States laws, "American vessels, American subjects, and American capital, are unquestionably engaged in the trade, though under other colours and in disguise."[3] The United States ship "Cyane" at one time reported ten captures within a few days, adding: "Although they are evidently owned by Americans, they are so completely covered by Spanish papers that it is impossible to condemn them."[4] The governor of Sierra Leone reported the rivers Nunez and Pongas full of renegade European and American slave-traders;[5] the trade was said to be carried on "to an extent that almost staggers

[1] Ayres to the Secretary of the Navy, Feb. 24, 1823; reprinted in *Friends' View of the African Slave-Trade* (1824), p. 31.

[2] *House Reports*, 17 Cong. 1 sess. II. No. 92, pp. 5–6. The slavers were the "Ramirez," "Endymion," "Esperanza," "Plattsburg," "Science," "Alexander," "Eugene," "Mathilde," "Daphne," "Eliza," and "La Pensée." In these 573 Africans were taken. The naval officers were greatly handicapped by the size of the ships, etc. (cf. *Friends' View*, etc., pp. 33–41). They nevertheless acted with great zeal.

[3] *Parliamentary Papers*, 1821, Vol. XXIII., *Slave Trade*, Further Papers, A, p. 76. The names and description of a dozen or more American slavers are given: *Ibid.*, pp. 18–21.

[4] *House Reports*, 17 Cong. 1 sess. II. No. 92, pp. 15–20.

[5] *House Doc.*, 18 Cong. 1 sess. VI. No. 119, p. 13.

belief."[1] Down to 1824 or 1825, reports from all quarters prove this activity in slave-trading.

The execution of the laws within the country exhibits grave defects and even criminal negligence. Attorney-General Wirt finds it necessary to assure collectors, in 1819, that "it is against public policy to dispense with prosecutions for violation of the law to prohibit the Slave trade."[2] One district attorney writes: "It appears to be almost impossible to enforce the laws of the United States against offenders after the negroes have been landed in the state."[3] Again, it is asserted that "when vessels engaged in the slave trade have been detained by the American cruizers, and sent into the slave-holding states, there appears at once a difficulty in securing the freedom to these captives which the laws of the United States have decreed for them."[4] In some cases, one man would smuggle in the Africans and hide them in the woods; then his partner would "rob" him, and so all trace be lost.[5] Perhaps 350 Africans were officially reported as brought in contrary to law from 1818 to 1820: the absurdity of this figure is apparent.[6] A circular letter to the marshals, in 1821, brought reports of only a few well-known cases, like that of the "General Ramirez;" the marshal of Louisiana had "no information."[7]

There appears to be little positive evidence of a large illicit importation into the country for a decade after 1825. It is hardly possible, however, considering the activity in the trade, that slaves were not largely imported. Indeed, when we note how the laws were continually broken in other respects, absence of evidence of petty smuggling becomes presumptive evidence that collusive or tacit understanding of officers and citizens allowed the trade to some extent.[8] Finally, it must be

[1] *Parliamentary Papers*, 1823, Vol. XVIII., *Slave Trade*, Further Papers, A, pp. 10–11.

[2] *Opinions of Attorneys-General*, V. 717.

[3] R. W. Habersham to the Secretary of the Navy, August, 1821; reprinted in *Friends' View*, etc., p. 47.

[4] *Ibid.*, p. 42.

[5] *Ibid.*, p. 43.

[6] Cf. above, pp. 126–7.

[7] *Friends' View*, etc., p. 42.

[8] A few accounts of captures here and there would make the matter less suspicious; these, however, do not occur. How large this suspected illicit

noted that during all this time scarcely a man suffered for participating in the trade, beyond the loss of the Africans and, more rarely, of his ship. Red-handed slavers, caught in the act and convicted, were too often, like La Coste of South Carolina, the subjects of executive clemency.[1] In certain cases there were those who even had the effrontery to ask Congress to cancel their own laws. For instance, in 1819 a Venezuelan privateer, secretly fitted out and manned by Americans in Balti-

---

traffic was, it is of course impossible to say; there is no reason why it may not have reached many hundreds per year.

[1]Cf. editorial in *Niles's Register*, XXII. 114. Cf. also the following instances of pardons:—

PRESIDENT JEFFERSON: March 1, 1808, Phillip M. Topham, convicted for "carrying on an illegal slave-trade" (pardoned twice). *Pardons and Remissions*, I. 146, 148–9.

PRESIDENT MADISON: July 29, 1809, fifteen vessels arrived at New Orleans from Cuba, with 666 white persons and 683 negroes. Every penalty incurred under the Act of 1807 was remitted. (Note: "Several other pardons of this nature were granted.") *Ibid.*, I. 179.

Nov. 8, 1809, John Hopkins and Lewis Le Roy, convicted for importing a slave. *Ibid.*, I. 184–5.

Feb. 12, 1810, William Sewall, convicted for importing slaves. *Ibid.*, I. 194, 235, 240.

May 5, 1812, William Babbit, convicted for importing slaves. *Ibid.*, I. 248.

PRESIDENT MONROE: June 11, 1822, Thomas Shields, convicted for bringing slaves into New Orleans. *Ibid.*, IV. 15.

Aug. 24, 1822, J. F. Smith, sentenced to five years' imprisonment and $3000 fine; served twenty-five months and was then pardoned. *Ibid.*, IV. 22.

July 23, 1823, certain parties liable to penalties for introducing slaves into Alabama. *Ibid.*, IV. 63.

Aug. 15, 1823, owners of schooner "Mary," convicted of importing slaves. *Ibid.*, IV. 66.

PRESIDENT J. Q. ADAMS: March 4, 1826, Robert Perry; his ship was forfeited for slave-trading. *Ibid.*, IV. 140.

Jan. 17, 1827, Jesse Perry; forfeited ship, and was convicted for introducing slaves. *Ibid.*, IV. 158.

Feb. 13, 1827, Zenas Winston; incurred penalties for slave-trading. *Ibid.*, IV. 161. The four following cases are similar to that of Winston:—

Feb. 24, 1827, John Tucker and William Morbon. *Ibid.*, IV. 162.

March 25, 1828, Joseph Badger. *Ibid.*, IV. 192.

Feb. 19, 1829, L. R. Wallace. *Ibid.*, IV. 215.

PRESIDENT JACKSON: Five cases. *Ibid.*, IV. 225, 270, 301, 393, 440.

The above cases were taken from manuscript copies of the Washington records, made by Mr. W. C. Endicott, Jr., and kindly loaned me.

more, succeeded in capturing several American, Portuguese, and Spanish slavers, and appropriating the slaves; being finally wrecked herself, she transferred her crew and slaves to one of her prizes, the "Antelope," which was eventually captured by a United States cruiser and the 280 Africans sent to Georgia. After much litigation, the United States Supreme Court ordered those captured from Spaniards to be surrendered, and the others to be returned to Africa. By some mysterious process, only 139 Africans now remained, 100 of whom were sent to Africa. The Spanish claimants of the remaining thirty-nine sold them to a certain Mr. Wilde, who gave bond to transport them out of the country. Finally, in December, 1827, there came an innocent petition to Congress to *cancel this bond.*[1] A bill to that effect passed and was approved, May 2, 1828,[2] and in consequence these Africans remained as slaves in Georgia.

On the whole, it is plain that, although in the period from 1807 to 1820 Congress laid down broad lines of legislation sufficient, save in some details, to suppress the African slave trade to America, yet the execution of these laws was criminally lax. Moreover, by the facility with which slavers could disguise their identity, it was possible for them to escape even a vigorous enforcement of our laws. This situation could properly be met only by energetic and sincere international co-operation. The next chapter will review efforts directed toward this end.[3]

[1] See *Senate Journal*, 20 Cong. 1 sess. pp. 60, 66, 340, 341, 343, 348, 352, 355; *House Journal*, 20 Cong. 1 sess. pp. 59, 76, 123, 134, 156, 169, 173, 279, 634, 641, 646, 647, 688, 692.

[2] *Statutes at Large*, VI. 376.

[3] Among interesting minor proceedings in this period were two Senate bills to register slaves so as to prevent illegal importation. They were both dropped in the House; a House proposition to the same effect also came to nothing: *Senate Journal*, 15 Cong. 1 sess. pp. 147, 152, 157, 165, 170, 188, 201, 203, 232, 237; 15 Cong. 2 sess. pp. 63, 74, 77, 202, 207, 285, 291, 297; *House Journal*, 15 Cong. 1 sess. p. 332; 15 Cong. 2 sess. pp. 303, 305, 316; 16 Cong. 1 sess. p. 150. Another proposition was contained in the Meigs resolution presented to the House, Feb. 5, 1820, which proposed to devote the public lands to the suppression of the slave-trade. This was ruled out of order. It was presented again and laid on the table in 1821: *House Journal*, 16 Cong. 1 sess. pp. 196, 200, 227; 16 Cong. 2 sess. p. 238.

Chapter IX

THE INTERNATIONAL STATUS OF THE SLAVE-TRADE. 1783–1862.

---

66. **The Rise of the Movement against the Slave-Trade, 1788–1807.** At the beginning of the nineteenth century England held 800,000 slaves in her colonies; France, 250,000; Denmark, 27,000; Spain and Portugal, 600,000; Holland, 50,000; Sweden, 600; there were also about 2,000,000 slaves in Brazil, and about 900,000 in the United States.[1] This was the powerful basis of the demand for the slave-trade; and against the economic forces which these four and a half millions of enforced laborers represented, the battle for freedom had to be fought.

Denmark first responded to the denunciatory cries of the eighteenth century against slavery and the slave-trade. In 1792, by royal order, this traffic was prohibited in the Danish possessions after 1802. The principles of the French Revolution logically called for the extinction of the slave system by France. This was, however, accomplished more precipitately than the Convention anticipated; and in a whirl of enthusiasm engendered by the appearance of the Dominican deputies, slavery and the slave-trade were abolished in all French colonies February 4, 1794.[2] This abolition was short-lived; for at the command of the First Consul slavery and the slave-

[1] Cf. Augustine Cochin, in Lalor, *Cyclopædia*, III. 723.

[2] By a law of Aug. 11, 1792, the encouragement formerly given to the trade was stopped. Cf. *Choix de rapports, opinions et discours prononcés à la tribune nationale depuis 1789* (Paris, 1821), XIV. 425; quoted in Cochin, *The Results of Emancipation* (Booth's translation, 1863), pp. 33, 35–8.

trade was restored in An X (1799).[1] The trade was finally abolished by Napoleon during the Hundred Days by a decree, March 29, 1815, which briefly declared: "À dater de la publication du présent Décret, la Traite des Noirs est abolie."[2] The Treaty of Paris eventually confirmed this law.[3]

In England, the united efforts of Sharpe, Clarkson, and Wilberforce early began to arouse public opinion by means of agitation and pamphlet literature. May 21, 1788, Sir William Dolben moved a bill regulating the trade, which passed in July and was the last English measure countenancing the traffic.[4] The report of the Privy Council on the subject in 1789[5] precipitated the long struggle. On motion of Pitt, in 1788, the House had resolved to take up at the next session the question of the abolition of the trade.[6] It was, accordingly, called up by Wilberforce, and a remarkable parliamentary battle ensued, which lasted continuously until 1805. The Grenville-Fox ministry now espoused the cause. This ministry first prohibited the trade with such colonies as England had acquired by conquest during the Napoleonic wars; then, in 1806, they prohibited the foreign slave-trade; and finally, March 25, 1807, enacted the total abolition of the traffic.[7]

67. **Concerted Action of the Powers, 1783–1814.** During the peace negotiations between the United States and Great Britain in 1783, it was proposed by Jay, in June, that there be

[1] Cochin, *The Results of Emancipation* (Booth's translation, 1863), pp. 42–7.

[2] *British and Foreign State Papers*, 1815–6, p. 196.

[3] *Ibid.*, pp. 195–9, 292–3; 1816–7, p. 755. It was eventually confirmed by royal ordinance, and the law of April 15, 1818.

[4] *Statute 28 George III.*, ch. 54. Cf. *Statute 29 George III.*, ch. 66.

[5] Various petitions had come in praying for an abolition of the slave-trade; and by an order in Council, Feb. 11, 1788, a committee of the Privy Council was ordered to take evidence on the subject. This committee presented an elaborate report in 1739. See published *Report*, London, 1789.

[6] For the history of the Parliamentary struggle, cf. Clarkson's and Copley's histories. The movement was checked in the House of Commons in 1789, 1790, and 1791. In 1792 the House of Commons resolved to abolish the trade in 1796. The Lords postponed the matter to take evidence. A bill to prohibit the foreign slave-trade was lost in 1793, passed the next session, and was lost in the House of Lords. In 1795, 1796, 1798, and 1799 repeated attempts to abolish the trade were defeated. The matter then rested until 1804, when the battle was renewed with more success.

[7] *Statute 46 George III.*, ch. 52, 119; *47 George III.*, sess. I. ch. 36.

a proviso inserted as follows: "Provided that the subjects of his Britannic Majesty shall not have any right or claim under the convention, to carry or import, into the said States any slaves from any part of the world; it being the intention of the said States entirely to prohibit the importation thereof."[1] Fox promptly replied: "If that be their policy, it never can be competent to us to dispute with them their own regulations."[2] No mention of this was, however, made in the final treaty, probably because it was thought unnecessary.

In the proposed treaty of 1806, signed at London December 31, Article 24 provided that "The high contracting parties engage to communicate to each other, without delay, all such laws as have been or shall be hereafter enacted by their respective Legislatures, as also all measures which shall have been taken for the abolition or limitation of the African slave trade; and they further agree to use their best endeavors to procure the co-operation of other Powers for the final and complete abolition of a trade so repugnant to the principles of justice and humanity."[3]

This marks the beginning of a long series of treaties between England and other powers looking toward the prohibition of the traffic by international agreement. During the years 1810–1814 she signed treaties relating to the subject with Portugal, Denmark, and Sweden.[4] May 30, 1814, an additional article to the Treaty of Paris, between France and Great Britain, engaged these powers to endeavor to induce the approaching Congress at Vienna "to decree the abolition of the Slave Trade, so that the said Trade shall cease universally, as it shall cease definitively, under any circumstances, on the part of the French Government, in the course of 5 years; and that during the said period no Slave Merchant shall import or sell Slaves, except in the Colonies of the State of which he is a Subject."[5] In addition to this, the next day a circular letter was despatched by Castlereagh to Austria, Russia, and

[1] Sparks, *Diplomatic Correspondence*, X. 154.

[2] Fox to Hartley, June 10, 1783; quoted in Bancroft, *History of the Constitution of the United States*, I. 61.

[3] *Amer. State Papers, Foreign*, III. No. 214, p. 151.

[4] *British and Foreign State Papers*, 1815–6, pp. 886, 937 (quotation).

[5] *Ibid.*, pp. 890–1.

Prussia, expressing the hope "that the Powers of Europe, when restoring Peace to Europe, with one common interest, will crown this great work by interposing their benign offices in favour of those Regions of the Globe, which yet continue to be desolated by this unnatural and inhuman traffic."[1] Meantime additional treaties were secured: in 1814 by royal decree Netherlands agreed to abolish the trade;[2] Spain was induced by her necessities to restrain her trade to her own colonies, and to endeavor to prevent the fraudulent use of her flag by foreigners;[3] and in 1815 Portugal agreed to abolish the slave-trade north of the equator.[4]

68. **Action of the Powers from 1814 to 1820.** At the Congress of Vienna, which assembled late in 1814, Castlereagh was indefatigable in his endeavors to secure the abolition of the trade. France and Spain, however, refused to yield farther than they had already done, and the other powers hesitated to go to the lengths he recommended. Nevertheless, he secured the institution of annual conferences on the matter, and a declaration by the Congress strongly condemning the trade and declaring that "the public voice in all civilized countries was raised to demand its suppression as soon as possible," and that, while the definitive period of termination would be left to subsequent negotiation, the sovereigns would not consider their work done until the trade was entirely suppressed.[5]

In the Treaty of Ghent, between Great Britain and the United States, ratified February 17, 1815, Article 10, proposed by Great Britain, declared that, "Whereas the traffic in slaves is irreconcilable with the principles of humanity and justice," the two countries agreed to use their best endeavors in abolishing the trade.[6] The final overthrow of Napoleon was marked by a second declaration of the powers, who, "desiring to give effect to the measures on which they deliberated at

[1] *British and Foreign State Papers*, 1815–6, p. 887. Russia, Austria, and Prussia returned favorable replies: *Ibid.*, pp. 887–8.

[2] *Ibid.*, p. 889.

[3] She desired a loan, which England made on this condition: *Ibid.*, pp. 921–2.

[4] *Ibid.*, pp. 937–9. Certain financial arrangements secured this concession.

[5] *Ibid.*, pp. 939–75.

[6] *Amer. State Papers, Foreign*, III. No. 271, pp. 735–48; *U. S. Treaties and Conventions* (ed. 1889), p. 405.

the Congress of Vienna, relative to the complete and universal abolition of the Slave Trade, and having, each in their respective Dominions, prohibited without restriction their Colonies and Subjects from taking any part whatever in this Traffic, engage to renew conjointly their efforts, with the view of securing final success to those principles which they proclaimed in the Declaration of the 4th February, 1815, and of concerting, without loss of time, through their Ministers at the Courts of London and of Paris, the most effectual measures for the entire and definitive abolition of a Commerce so odious, and so strongly condemned by the laws of religion and of nature."[1]

Treaties further restricting the trade continued to be made by Great Britain: Spain abolished the trade north of the equator in 1817,[2] and promised entire abolition in 1820; Spain, Portugal, and Holland also granted a mutual limited Right of Search to England, and joined in establishing mixed courts.[3] The effort, however, to secure a general declaration of the powers urging, if not compelling, the abolition of the trade in 1820, as well as the attempt to secure a qualified international Right of Visit, failed, although both propositions were strongly urged by England at the Conference of 1818.[4]

69. **The Struggle for an International Right of Search, 1820–1840.** Whatever England's motives were, it is certain that only a limited international Right of Visit on the high seas could suppress or greatly limit the slave-trade. Her diplomacy was therefore henceforth directed to this end. On the

[1]This was inserted in the Treaty of Paris, Nov. 20, 1815: *British and Foreign State Papers*, 1815–6, p. 292.

[2]*Ibid.*, 1816–7, pp. 33–74 (English version, 1823–4, p. 702 ff.).

[3]Cf. *Ibid.*, 1817–8, p. 125 ff.

[4]This was the first meeting of the London ministers of the powers according to agreement; they assembled Dec. 4, 1817, and finally called a meeting of plenipotentiaries on the question of suppression at Aix-la-Chapelle, beginning Oct. 24, 1818. Among those present were Metternich, Richelieu, Wellington, Castlereagh, Hardenberg, Bernstorff, Nesselrode, and Capodistrias. Castlereagh made two propositions: 1. That the five powers join in urging Portugal and Brazil to abolish the trade May 20, 1820; 2. That the powers adopt the principle of a mutual qualified Right of Search. Cf. *British and Foreign State Papers*, 1818–9, pp. 21–88; *Amer. State Papers, Foreign*, V. No. 346, pp. 113–122.

other hand, the maritime supremacy of England, so successfully asserted during the Napoleonic wars, would, in case a Right of Search were granted, virtually make England the policeman of the seas; and if nations like the United States had already, under present conditions, had just cause to complain of violations by England of their rights on the seas, might not any extension of rights by international agreement be dangerous? It was such considerations that for many years brought the powers to a dead-lock in their efforts to suppress the slave-trade.

At first it looked as if England might attempt, by judicial decisions in her own courts, to seize even foreign slavers.[1] After the war, however, her courts disavowed such action,[2] and the right was sought for by treaty stipulation. Castlereagh took early opportunity to approach the United States on the matter, suggesting to Minister Rush, June 20, 1818, a mutual but strictly limited Right of Search.[3] Rush was ordered to give him assurances of the solicitude of the United States to suppress the traffic, but to state that the concessions asked for appeared of a character not adaptable to our institutions. Negotiations were then transferred to Washington; and the new British minister, Mr. Stratford Canning, approached Adams with full instructions in December, 1820.[4]

Meantime, it had become clear to many in the United States that the individual efforts of States could never suppress or even limit the trade without systematic co-operation. In 1817 a committee of the House had urged the opening of negotiations looking toward such international co-operation,[5] and a Senate motion to the same effect had caused long debate.[6] In 1820 and 1821 two House committee reports, one of which recommended the granting of a Right of Search, were

[1] For cases, see *1 Acton*, 240, the "Amedie," and *1 Dodson*, 81, the "Fortuna;" quoted in U. S. Reports, *10 Wheaton*, 66.

[2] Cf. the case of the French ship "Le Louis": *2 Dodson*, 238; and also the case of the "San Juan Nepomuceno": *1 Haggard*, 267.

[3] *British and Foreign State Papers*, 1819–20, pp. 375–9; also pp. 220–2.

[4] *Ibid.*, 1820–21, pp. 395–6.

[5] *House Doc.*, 14 Cong. 2 sess. II. No. 77.

[6] *Annals of Cong.*, 15 Cong. 1 sess. pp. 71, 73–78, 94–109. The motion was opposed largely by Southern members, and passed by a vote of 17 to 16.

adopted by the House, but failed in the Senate.[1] Adams, notwithstanding this, saw constitutional objections to the plan proposed by Canning, and wrote to him, December 30: "A Compact, giving the power to the Naval Officers of one Nation to search the Merchant Vessels of another for Offenders and offences against the Laws of the latter, backed by a further power to seize and carry into a Foreign Port, and there subject to the decision of a Tribunal composed of at least one half Foreigners, irresponsible to the Supreme Corrective tribunal of this Union, and not amendable to the controul of impeachment for official misdemeanors, was an investment of power, over the persons, property and reputation of the Citizens of this Country, not only unwarranted by any delegation of Sovereign Power to the National Government, but so adverse to the elementary principles and indispensable securities of individual rights, . . . that not even the most unqualified approbation of the ends . . . could justify the transgression." He then suggested co-operation of the fleets on the coast of Africa, a proposal which was promptly accepted.[2]

The slave-trade was again a subject of international consideration at the Congress of Verona in 1822. Austria, France, Great Britain, Russia, and Prussia were represented. The English delegates declared that, although only Portugal and Brazil allowed the trade, yet the traffic was at that moment carried on to a greater extent than ever before. They said that in seven months of the year 1821 no less than 21,000 slaves were abducted, and three hundred and fifty-two vessels entered African ports north of the equator. "It is obvious," said they, "that this crime is committed in contravention of the Laws of every Country of Europe, and of America, excepting only of one, and that it requires something more than the ordinary operation of Law to prevent it." England therefore recommended: —

[1]One was reported, May 9, 1820, by Mercer's committee, and passed May 12: *House Journal*, 16 Cong. 1 sess. pp. 497, 518, 520, 526; *Annals of Cong.*, 16 Cong. 1 sess. pp. 697–9. A similar resolution passed the House next session, and a committee reported in favor of the Right of Search: *Ibid.*, 16 Cong. 2 sess. pp. 1064–71. Cf. *Ibid.*, pp. 476, 743, 865, 1469.

[2]*British and Foreign State Papers*, 1820–21, pp. 397–400.

1. That each country denounce the trade as piracy, with a view of founding upon the aggregate of such separate declarations a general law to be incorporated in the Law of Nations.

2. A withdrawing of the flags of the Powers from persons not natives of these States, who engage in the traffic under the flags of these States.

3. A refusal to admit to their domains the produce of the colonies of States allowing the trade, a measure which would apply to Portugal and Brazil alone.

These proposals were not accepted. Austria would agree to the first two only; France refused to denounce the trade as piracy; and Prussia was non-committal. The utmost that could be gained was another denunciation of the trade couched in general terms.[1]

70. **Negotiations of 1823–1825.** England did not, however, lose hope of gaining some concession from the United States. Another House committee had, in 1822, reported that the only method of suppressing the trade was by granting a Right of Search.[2] The House agreed, February 28, 1823, to request the President to enter into negotiations with the maritime powers of Europe to denounce the slave-trade as piracy; an amendment "that we agree to a qualified right of search" was, however, lost.[3] Meantime, the English minister was continually pressing the matter upon Adams, who proposed in turn to denounce the trade as piracy. Canning agreed to this, but only on condition that it be piracy under the Law of Nations and not merely by statute law. Such an agreement, he said, would involve a Right of Search for its enforcement; he proposed strictly to limit and define this right, to allow captured ships to be tried in their own courts, and not to commit the United States in any way to the question of the belligerent Right of Search. Adams finally sent a draft of a proposed treaty to England, and agreed to recognize the slave-traffic "as piracy under the law of nations, namely: that, although seizable by the officers and authorities of every nation, they

[1] *British and Foreign State Papers*, 1822–3, pp. 94–110.

[2] *House Reports*, 17 Cong. 1 sess. II. No. 92.

[3] *House Journal*, 17 Cong. 2 sess. pp. 212, 280; *Annals of Cong.*, 17 Cong. 2 sess. pp. 922, 1147–1155.

should be triable only by the tribunals of the country of the slave trading vessel."[1]

Rush presented this *project* to the government in January, 1824. England agreed to all the points insisted on by the United States; viz., that she herself should denounce the trade as piracy; that slavers should be tried in their own country; that the captor should be laid under the most effective responsibility for his conduct; and that vessels under convoy of a ship of war of their own country should be exempt from search. In addition, England demanded that citizens of either country captured under the flag of a third power should be sent home for trial, and that citizens of either country chartering vessels of a third country should come under these stipulations.[2]

This convention was laid before the Senate April 30, 1824, but was not acted upon until May 21, when it was so amended as to make it terminable at six months' notice. The same day, President Monroe, "apprehending, from the delay in the decision, that some difficulty exists," sent a special message to the Senate, giving at length the reasons for signing the treaty, and saying that "should this Convention be adopted, there is every reason to believe, that it will be the commencement of a system destined to accomplish the entire Abolition of the Slave Trade." It was, however, a time of great political pot-boiling, and consequently an unfortunate occasion to ask senators to settle any great question. A systematic attack, led by Johnson of Louisiana, was made on all the vital provisions of the treaty: the waters of America were excepted from its application, and those of the West Indies barely escaped exception; the provision which, perhaps, aimed the deadliest blow at American slave-trade interests was likewise struck out; namely, the application of the Right of Search to citizens chartering the vessels of a third nation.[3]

The convention thus mutilated was not signed by England, who demanded as the least concession the application of the Right of Search to American waters. Meantime the United

[1] *British and Foreign State Papers*, 1823–4, pp. 409–21; 1824–5, pp. 828–47; *Amer. State Papers, Foreign*, V. No. 371, pp. 333–7.

[2] *Ibid.*

[3] *Ibid.*, No. 374, p. 344 ff., No. 379, pp. 360–2.

States had invited nearly all nations to denounce the trade as piracy; and the President, the Secretary of the Navy, and a House committee had urgently favored the granting of the Right of Search. The bad faith of Congress, however, in the matter of the Colombian treaty broke off for a time further negotiations with England.[1]

71. **The Attitude of the United States and the State of the Slave-Trade.** In 1824 the Right of Search was established between England and Sweden, and in 1826 Brazil promised to abolish the trade in three years.[2] In 1831 the cause was greatly advanced by the signing of a treaty between Great Britain and France, granting mutually a geographically limited Right of Search.[3] This led, in the next few years, to similar treaties with Denmark, Sardinia,[4] the Hanse towns,[5] and Naples.[6] Such measures put the trade more and more in the hands of Americans, and it began greatly to increase. Mercer sought repeatedly in the House to have negotiations reopened with England, but without success.[7] Indeed, the chances of success were now for many years imperilled by the recurrence of de-

[1] *House Reports*, 18 Cong. 2 sess. I. No. 70; *Amer. State Papers, Foreign*, V. No. 379, pp. 364–5, No. 414, p. 783, etc. Among the nations invited by the United States to co-operate in suppressing the trade was the United States of Colombia. Mr. Anderson, our minister, expressed "the certain belief that the Republic of Colombia will not permit herself to be behind any Government in the civilized world in the adoption of energetic measures for the suppression of this disgraceful traffic": *Ibid.*, No. 407, p. 729. The little republic replied courteously; and, as a *projet* for a treaty, Mr. Anderson offered the proposed English treaty of 1824, including the Senate amendments. Nevertheless, the treaty thus agreed to was summarily rejected by the Senate, March 9, 1825: *Ibid.*, p. 735. Another result of this general invitation of the United States was a proposal by Colombia that the slave-trade and the status of Hayti be among the subjects for discussion at the Panama Congress. As a result of this, a Senate committee recommended that the United States take no part in the Congress. This report was finally disagreed to by a vote of 19 to 24: *Ibid.*, No. 423, pp. 837, 860, 876, 882.

[2] *British and Foreign State Papers*, 1823–4, and 1826–7. Brazil abolished the trade in 1830.

[3] This treaty was further defined in 1833: *Ibid.*, 1830–1, p. 641 ff.; 1832–3, p. 286 ff.

[4] *Ibid.*, 1833–4, pp. 218 ff., 1059 ff.

[5] *Ibid.*, 1837–8, p. 268 ff.

[6] *Ibid.*, 1838–9, p. 792 ff.

[7] Viz., Feb. 28, 1825; April 7, 1830; Feb. 16, 1831; March 3, 1831. The last resolution passed the House: *House Journal*, 21 Cong. 2 sess. pp. 426–8.

liberate search of American vessels by the British.[1] In the majority of cases the vessels proved to be slavers, and some of them fraudulently flew the American flag; nevertheless, their molestation by British cruisers created much feeling, and hindered all steps toward an understanding: the United States was loath to have her criminal negligence in enforcing her own laws thus exposed by foreigners. Other international questions connected with the trade also strained the relations of the two countries: three different vessels engaged in the domestic slave-trade, driven by stress of weather, or, in the "Creole" case, captured by Negroes on board, landed slaves in British possessions; England freed them, and refused to pay for such as were landed after emancipation had been proclaimed in the West Indies.[2] The case of the slaver "L'Amistad" also raised difficulties with Spain. This Spanish vessel, after the Negroes on board had mutinied and killed their owners, was seized by a United States vessel and brought into port for adjudication. The court, however, freed the Negroes, on the ground that under Spanish law they were not legally slaves; and although the Senate repeatedly tried to indemnify the owners, the project did not succeed.[3]

Such proceedings well illustrate the new tendency of the pro-slavery party to neglect the enforcement of the slave-trade laws, in a frantic defence of the remotest ramparts of slave property. Consequently, when, after the treaty of 1831, France and England joined in urging the accession of the United States to it, the British minister was at last compelled to inform Palmerston, December, 1833, that "the Executive at

[1] Cf. *House Doc.*, 26 Cong. 2 sess. V. No. 115, pp. 35–6, etc.; *House Reports*, 27 Cong. 3 sess. III. No. 283, pp. 730–55, etc.

[2] These were the celebrated cases of the "Encomium," "Enterprize," and "Comet." Cf. *Senate Doc.*, 24 Cong. 2 sess. II. No. 174; 25 Cong. 3 sess. III. No. 216. Cf. also case of the "Creole": *Ibid.*, 27 Cong. 2 sess. II.–III. Nos. 51, 137.

[3] *Ibid.*, 26 Cong. 2 sess. IV. No. 179; *Senate Exec. Doc.*, 31 Cong. 2 sess. III. No. 29; 32 Cong. 2 sess. III. No. 19; *Senate Reports*, 31 Cong. 2 sess. No. 301; 32 Cong. 1 sess. I. No. 158; 35 Cong. 1 sess. I. No. 36; *House Doc.*, 26 Cong. 1 sess. IV. No. 185; 27 Cong. 3 sess. V. No. 191; 28 Cong. 1 sess. IV. No. 83; *House Exec. Doc.*, 32 Cong. 2 sess. III. No. 20; *House Reports*, 26 Cong. 2 sess. No. 51; 28 Cong. 1 sess. II. No. 426; 29 Cong. 1 sess. IV. No. 753; also Decisions of the U. S. Supreme Court, *15 Peters*, 518. Cf. Drake, *Revelations of a Slave Smuggler*, p. 98.

Washington appears to shrink from bringing forward, in any shape, a question, upon which depends the completion of their former object—the utter and universal Abolition of the Slave Trade—from an apprehension of alarming the Southern States."[1] Great Britain now offered to sign the proposed treaty of 1824 as amended; but even this Forsyth refused, and stated that the United States had determined not to become "a party of any Convention on the subject of the Slave Trade."[2]

Estimates as to the extent of the slave-trade agree that the traffic to North and South America in 1820 was considerable, certainly not much less than 40,000 slaves annually. From that time to about 1825 it declined somewhat, but afterward increased enormously, so that by 1837 the American importation was estimated as high as 200,000 Negroes annually. The total abolition of the African trade by American countries then brought the traffic down to perhaps 30,000 in 1842. A large and rapid increase of illicit traffic followed; so that by 1847 the importation amounted to nearly 100,000 annually. One province of Brazil is said to have received 173,000 in the years 1846–1849. In the decade 1850–1860 this activity in slave-trading continued, and reached very large proportions.

The traffic thus carried on floated under the flags of France, Spain, and Portugal, until about 1830; from 1830 to 1840 it began gradually to assume the United States flag; by 1845, a large part of the trade was under the stars and stripes; by 1850 fully one-half the trade, and in the decade, 1850–1860 nearly all the traffic, found this flag its best protection.[3]

[1] *British and Foreign State Papers*, 1834–5, p. 136.

[2] *Ibid.*, pp. 135–47. Great Britain made treaties meanwhile with Hayti, Uruguay, Venezuela, Bolivia, Argentine Confederation, Mexico, Texas, etc. Portugal prohibited the slave-trade in 1836, except between her African colonies. Cf. *Ibid.*, from 1838 to 1841.

[3] These estimates are from the following sources: *Ibid.*, 1822–3, pp. 94–110; *Parliamentary Papers*, 1823, XVIII., *Slave Trade*, Further Papers, A., pp. 10–11; 1838–9, XLIX., *Slave Trade*, Class A, Further Series, pp. 115, 119, 121; *House Doc.*, 19 Cong. 1 sess. I. No. 1, p. 93; 20 Cong. 1 sess. III. No. 99; 26 Cong. 1 sess. VI. No. 211; *House Exec. Doc.*, 31 Cong. 2 sess. I. No. 1, p. 193; *House Reports*, 21 Cong. 1 sess. III. No. 348; *Senate Doc.*, 28 Cong. 1 sess. IV. No. 217; 31 Cong. 1 sess. XIV. No. 66; 31 Cong. 2 sess. II. No. 6; *Amer. State Papers, Naval*, I. No. 249; Buxton, *The African Slave Trade and its Remedy*, pp. 44–59; Friends' *Facts and Observations on the Slave Trade* (ed. 1841);

72. **The Quintuple Treaty, 1839–1842.** In 1839 Pope Gregory XVI. stigmatized the slave-trade "as utterly unworthy of the Christian name;" and at the same time, although proscribed by the laws of every civilized State, the trade was flourishing with pristine vigor. Great advantage was given the traffic by the fact that the United States, for two decades after the abortive attempt of 1824, refused to co-operate with the rest of the civilized world, and allowed her flag to shelter and protect the slave-trade. If a fully equipped slaver sailed from New York, Havana, Rio Janeiro, or Liverpool, she had only to hoist the stars and stripes in order to proceed unmolested

---

Friends' *Exposition of the Slave Trade, 1840–50*; *Annual Reports of the American and Foreign Anti-Slavery Society*.

The annexed table gives the dates of the abolition of the slave-trade by the various nations:—

Date.	Slave-trade Abolished by	Right of Search Treaty with Great Britain, made by	Arrangements for Joint Cruising with Great Britain, made by
1802	Denmark.		
1807	Great Britain; United States.		
1813	Sweden.		
1814	Netherlands.		
1815	Portugal (north of the equator).		
1817	Spain (north of the equator).	Portugal; Spain.	
1818	France.	Netherlands.	
1820	Spain.		
1824		Sweden.	
1829	Brazil (?).		
1830	Portugal.		
1831–33		France.	
1833–39		Denmark, Hanse Towns, etc.	
1841		Quintuple Treaty (Austria, Russia, Prussia).	
1842			United States.
1844		Texas.	
1845		Belgium.	France.
1862		United States.	

on her piratical voyage; for there was seldom a United States cruiser to be met with, and there were, on the other hand, diplomats at Washington so jealous of the honor of the flag that they would prostitute it to crime rather than allow an English or a French cruiser in any way to interfere. Without doubt, the contention of the United States as to England's pretensions to a Right of Visit was technically correct. Nevertheless, it was clear that if the slave-trade was to be suppressed, each nation must either zealously keep her flag from fraudulent use, or, as a labor-saving device, depute to others this duty for limited places and under special circumstances. A failure of any one nation to do one of these two things meant that the efforts of all other nations were to be fruitless. The United States had invited the world to join her in denouncing the slave-trade as piracy; yet, when such a pirate was waylaid by an English vessel, the United States complained or demanded reparation. The only answer which this country for years returned to the long-continued exposures of American slave-traders and of the fraudulent use of the American flag, was a recital of cases where Great Britain had gone beyond her legal powers in her attempt to suppress the slave-trade.[1] In the face of overwhelming evidence to the contrary, Secretary of State Forsyth declared, in 1840, that the duty of the United States in the matter of the slave-trade "has been faithfully performed, and if the traffic still exists as a disgrace to humanity, it is to be imputed to nations with whom Her Majesty's Government has formed and maintained the most intimate connexions, and to whose Governments Great Britain has paid for the right of active intervention in order to its complete extirpation."[2] So zealous was Stevenson, our minister to England, in denying the Right of Search, that he boldly informed Palmerston, in 1841, "that there is no shadow of pretence for excusing, much less justifying, the exercise of any such right. That it is wholly immaterial, whether the vessels be equipped for, or actually engaged in slave traffic or not, and consequently the right to search or detain even slave vessels, must be confined to the ships or vessels of those

[1] Cf. *British and Foreign State Papers*, from 1836 to 1842.
[2] *Ibid.*, 1839–40, p. 940.

nations with whom it may have treaties on the subject."[1] Palmerston courteously replied that he could not think that the United States seriously intended to make its flag a refuge for slave-traders;[2] and Aberdeen pertinently declared: "Now, it can scarcely be maintained by Mr. Stevenson that Great Britain should be bound to permit her own subjects, with British vessels and British capital, to carry on, before the eyes of British officers, this detestable traffic in human beings, which the law has declared to be piracy, merely because they had the audacity to commit an additional offence by fraudulently usurping the American flag."[3] Thus the dispute, even after the advent of Webster, went on for a time, involving itself in metaphysical subtleties, and apparently leading no nearer to an understanding.[4]

In 1838 a fourth conference of the powers for the consideration of the slave-trade took place at London. It was attended by representatives of England, France, Russia, Prussia, and Austria. England laid the *projet* of a treaty before them, to which all but France assented. This so-called Quintuple Treaty, signed December 20, 1841, denounced the slave-trade as piracy, and declared that "the High Contracting Parties agree by common consent, that those of their ships of war which shall be provided with special warrants and orders . . . may search every merchant-vessel belonging to any one of the High Contracting Parties which shall, on reasonable grounds, be suspected of being engaged in the traffic in slaves." All captured slavers were to be sent to their own countries for trial.[5]

While the ratification of this treaty was pending, the United States minister to France, Lewis Cass, addressed an official note to Guizot at the French foreign office, protesting against the institution of an international Right of Search, and rather grandiloquently warning the powers against the use of force to accomplish their ends.[6] This extraordinary epistle, issued

[1] *House Doc.*, 27 Cong. 1 sess. No. 34, pp. 5–6.
[2] *Senate Doc.*, 29 Cong. 1 sess. VIII. No. 377, p. 56.
[3] *Ibid.*, p. 72.
[4] *Ibid.*, pp. 133–40, etc.
[5] *British and Foreign State Papers*, 1841–2, p. 269 ff.
[6] See below, Appendix B.

on the minister's own responsibility, brought a reply denying that the creation of any "new principle of international law, whereby the vessels even of those powers which have not participated in the arrangement should be subjected to the right of search," was ever intended, and affirming that no such extraordinary interpretation could be deduced from the Convention. Moreover, M. Guizot hoped that the United States, by agreeing to this treaty, would "aid, by its most sincere endeavors, in the definitive abolition of the trade."[1] Cass's theatrical protest was, consciously or unconsciously, the manifesto of that growing class in the United States who wanted no further measures taken for the suppression of the slave-trade; toward that, as toward the institution of slavery, this party favored a policy of strict *laissez-faire*.

73. **Final Concerted Measures, 1842–1862.** The Treaty of Washington, in 1842, made the first effective compromise in the matter and broke the unpleasant dead-lock, by substituting joint cruising by English and American squadrons for the proposed grant of a Right of Search. In submitting this treaty, Tyler said: "The treaty which I now submit to you proposes no alteration, mitigation, or modification of the rules of the law of nations. It provides simply that each of the two Governments shall maintain on the coast of Africa a sufficient squadron to enforce separately and respectively the laws, rights, and obligations of the two countries for the suppression of the slave trade."[2] This provision was a part of the treaty to settle the boundary disputes with England. In the Senate, Benton moved to strike out this article; but the attempt was defeated by a vote of 37 to 12, and the treaty was ratified.[3]

This stipulation of the treaty of 1842 was never properly carried out by the United States for any length of time.[4] Con-

[1] *Senate Doc.*, 29 Cong. 1 sess. VIII. No. 377, p. 201.

[2] *Senate Exec. Journal*, VI. 123.

[3] *U. S. Treaties and Conventions* (ed. 1889), pp. 436–7. For the debates in the Senate, see *Congressional Globe*, 27 Cong. 3 sess. Appendix. Cass resigned on account of the acceptance of this treaty without a distinct denial of the Right of Search, claiming that this compromised his position in France. Cf. *Senate Doc.*, 27 Cong. 3 sess. II., IV. Nos. 52, 223; 29 Cong. 1 sess. VIII. No. 377.

[4] Cf. below, Chapter X.

sequently the same difficulties as to search and visit by English vessels continued to recur. Cases like the following were frequent. The "Illinois," of Gloucester, Massachusetts, while lying at Whydah, Africa, was boarded by a British officer, but having American papers was unmolested. Three days later she hoisted Spanish colors and sailed away with a cargo of slaves. Next morning she fell in with another British vessel and hoisted American colors; the British ship had then no right to molest her; but the captain of the slaver feared that she would, and therefore ran his vessel aground, slaves and all. The senior English officer reported that "had Lieutenant Cumberland brought to and boarded the 'Illinois,' notwithstanding the American colors which she hoisted, . . . the American master of the 'Illinois' . . . would have complained to his Government of the detention of his vessel."[1] Again, a vessel which had been boarded by British officers and found with American flag and papers was, a little later, captured under the Spanish flag with four hundred and thirty slaves. She had in the interim complained to the United States government of the boarding.[2]

Meanwhile, England continued to urge the granting of a Right of Search, claiming that the stand of the United States really amounted to the wholesale protection of pirates under her flag.[3] The United States answered by alleging that even the Treaty of 1842 had been misconstrued by England,[4] whereupon there was much warm debate in Congress, and several attempts were made to abrogate the slave-trade article of the treaty.[5] The pro-slavery party had become more and more suspicious of England's motives, since they had seen her abolition of the slave-trade blossom into abolition of the system itself, and they seized every opportunity to prevent cooperation with her. At the same time, European interest in the question showed some signs of weakening, and no de-

[1] *Senate Exec. Doc.*, 28 Cong. 2 sess. IX. No. 150, p. 72.

[2] *Ibid.*, p. 77.

[3] *House Doc.*, 27 Cong. 3 sess. V. No. 192, p. 4. Cf. *British and Foreign State Papers*, 1842–3, p. 708 ff.

[4] *House Journal*, 27 Cong. 3 sess. pp. 431, 485–8. Cf. *House Doc.*, 27 Cong. 3 sess. V. No. 192.

[5] Cf. below, Chapter X.

cided action was taken. In 1845 France changed her Right of Search stipulations of 1833 to one for joint cruising,[1] while the Germanic Federation,[2] Portugal,[3] and Chili[4] denounced the trade as piracy. In 1844 Texas granted the Right of Search to England,[5] and in 1845 Belgium signed the Quintuple Treaty.[6]

Discussion between England and the United States was revived when Cass held the State portfolio, and, strange to say, the author of "Cass's Protest" went farther than any of his predecessors in acknowledging the justice of England's demands. Said he, in 1859: "If The United States maintained that, by carrying their flag at her masthead, any vessel became thereby entitled to the immunity which belongs to American vessels, they might well be reproached with assuming a position which would go far towards shielding crimes upon the ocean from punishment; but they advance no such pretension, while they concede that, if in the honest examination of a vessel sailing under American colours, but accompanied by strongly-marked suspicious circumstances, a mistake is made, and she is found to be entitled to the flag she bears, but no injury is committed, and the conduct of the boarding party is irreproachable, no Government would be likely to make a case thus exceptional in its character a subject of serious reclamation."[7] While admitting this and expressing a desire to co-operate in the suppression of the slave-trade, Cass nevertheless steadily refused all further overtures toward a mutual Right of Search.

The increase of the slave-traffic was so great in the decade 1850–1860 that Lord John Russell proposed to the governments of the United States, France, Spain, Portugal, and Brazil, that they instruct their ministers to meet at London in May or June, 1860, to consider measures for the final abolition

[1] With a fleet of 26 vessels, reduced to 12 in 1849: *British and Foreign State Papers*, 1844–5, p. 4 ff.; 1849–50, p. 480.

[2] *Ibid.*, 1850–1, p. 953.

[3] Portugal renewed her Right of Search treaty in 1842: *Ibid.*, 1841–2, p. 527 ff.; 1842–3, p. 450.

[4] *Ibid.*, 1843–4, p. 316.

[5] *Ibid.*, 1844–5, p. 592. There already existed some such privileges between England and Texas.

[6] *Ibid.*, 1847–8, p. 397 ff.

[7] *Ibid.*, 1858–9, pp. 1121, 1129.

of the trade. He stated: "It is ascertained, by repeated instances, that the practice is for vessels to sail under the American flag. If the flag is rightly assumed, and the papers correct, no British cruizer can touch them. If no slaves are on board, even though the equipment, the fittings, the water-casks, and other circumstances prove that the ship is on a Slave Trade venture, no American cruizer can touch them."[1] Continued representations of this kind were made to the paralyzed United States government; indeed, the slave-trade of the world seemed now to float securely under her flag. Nevertheless, Cass refused even to participate in the proposed conference, and later refused to accede to a proposal for joint cruising off the coast of Cuba.[2] Great Britain offered to relieve the United States of any embarrassment by receiving all captured Africans into the West Indies; but President Buchanan "could not contemplate any such arrangement," and obstinately refused to increase the suppressing squadron.[3]

On the outbreak of the Civil War, the Lincoln administration, through Secretary Seward, immediately expressed a willingness to do all in its power to suppress the slave-trade.[4] Accordingly, June 7, 1862, a treaty was signed with Great Britain granting a mutual limited Right of Search, and establishing mixed courts for the trial of offenders at the Cape of Good Hope, Sierra Leone, and New York.[5] The efforts of a half-century of diplomacy were finally crowned; Seward wrote to Adams, "Had such a treaty been made in 1808, there would now have been no sedition here."[6]

[1] *British and Foreign State Papers*, 1859–60, pp. 902–3.

[2] *House Exec. Doc.*, 36 Cong. 2 sess. IV. No. 7.

[3] *Ibid.*

[4] *Senate Exec. Doc.*, 37 Cong. 2 sess. V. No. 57.

[5] *Senate Exec. Journal*, XII. 230–1, 240, 254, 256, 391, 400, 403; *Diplomatic Correspondence*, 1862, pp. 141, 158; *U. S. Treaties and Conventions* (ed. 1889), pp. 454–9.

[6] *Diplomatic Correspondence*, 1862, pp. 64–5. This treaty was revised in 1863. The mixed court in the West Indies had, by February, 1864, liberated 95,206 Africans: *Senate Exec. Doc.*, 38 Cong. 1 sess. No. 56, p. 24.

Chapter X

THE RISE OF THE COTTON KINGDOM. 1820–1850.

---

74. **The Economic Revolution.** The history of slavery and the slave-trade after 1820 must be read in the light of the industrial revolution through which the civilized world passed in the first half of the nineteenth century. Between the years 1775 and 1825 occurred economic events and changes of the highest importance and widest influence. Though all branches of industry felt the impulse of this new industrial life, yet, "if we consider single industries, cotton manufacture has, during the nineteenth century, made the most magnificent and gigantic advances."[1] This fact is easily explained by the remarkable series of inventions that revolutionized this industry between 1738 and 1830, including Arkwright's, Watt's, Compton's, and Cartwright's epoch-making contrivances.[2] The effect which these inventions had on the manufacture of cotton goods is

[1] Beer, *Geschichte des Welthandels im 19ten Jahrhundert*, II. 67.

[2] A list of these inventions most graphically illustrates this advance:—

1738, John Jay, fly-shuttle.
John Wyatt, spinning by rollers.
1748, Lewis Paul, carding-machine.
1760, Robert Kay, drop-box.
1769, Richard Arkwright, water-frame and throstle.
James Watt, steam-engine.
1772, James Lees, improvements on carding-machine.
1775, Richard Arkwright, series of combinations.
1779, Samuel Compton, mule.
1785, Edmund Cartwright, power-loom.
1803–4, Radcliffe and Johnson, dressing-machine.
1817, Roberts, fly-frame.
1818, William Eaton, self-acting frame.
1825–30, Roberts, improvements on mule.

Cf. Baines, *History of the Cotton Manufacture*, pp. 116–231; *Encyclopædia Britannica*, 9th ed., article "Cotton."

best illustrated by the fact that in England, the chief cotton market of the world, the consumption of raw cotton rose steadily from 13,000 bales in 1781, to 572,000 in 1820, to 871,000 in 1830, and to 3,366,000 in 1860.[1] Very early, therefore, came the query whence the supply of raw cotton was to come. Tentative experiments on the rich, broad fields of the Southern United States, together with the indispensable invention of Whitney's cotton-gin, soon answered this question: a new economic future was opened up to this land, and immediately the whole South began to extend its cotton culture, and more and more to throw its whole energy into this one staple.

Here it was that the fatal mistake of compromising with slavery in the beginning, and of the policy of *laissez-faire* pursued thereafter, became painfully manifest; for, instead now of a healthy, normal, economic development along proper industrial lines, we have the abnormal and fatal rise of a slave-labor large-farming system, which, before it was realized, had so intertwined itself with and braced itself upon the economic forces of an industrial age, that a vast and terrible civil war was necessary to displace it. The tendencies to a patriarchal serfdom, recognizable in the age of Washington and Jefferson, began slowly but surely to disappear; and in the second quarter of the century Southern slavery was irresistibly changing from a family institution to an industrial system.

The development of Southern slavery has heretofore been viewed so exclusively from the ethical and social standpoint that we are apt to forget its close and indissoluble connection with the world's cotton market. Beginning with 1820, a little after the close of the Napoleonic wars, when the industry of cotton manufacture had begun its modern development and the South had definitely assumed her position as chief producer of raw cotton, we find the average price of cotton per pound, 8½*d*. From this time until 1845 the price steadily fell, until in the latter year it reached 4*d*.; the only exception to this fall was in the years 1832–1839, when, among other things, a strong increase in the English demand, together with an attempt of the young slave power to "corner" the

[1] Baines, *History of the Cotton Manufacture*, p. 215. A bale weighed from 375 lbs. to 400 lbs.

market, sent the price up as high as 11*d*. The demand for cotton goods soon outran a crop which McCullough had pronounced "prodigious," and after 1845 the price started on a steady rise, which, except for the checks suffered during the continental revolutions and the Crimean War, continued until 1860.[1] The steady increase in the production of cotton explains the fall in price down to 1845. In 1822 the crop was a half-million bales; in 1831, a million; in 1838, a million and a half; and in 1840–1843, two million. By this time the world's consumption of cotton goods began to increase so rapidly that, in spite of the increase in Southern crops, the price kept rising. Three million bales were gathered in 1852, three and a half million in 1856, and the remarkable crop of five million bales in 1860.[2]

Here we have data to explain largely the economic development of the South. By 1822 the large-plantation slave system had gained footing; in 1838–1839 it was able to show its power in the cotton "corner;" by the end of the next decade it had not only gained a solid economic foundation, but it had built a closed oligarchy with a political policy. The changes in price during the next few years drove out of competition many survivors of the small-farming free-labor system, and put the slave *régime* in position to dictate the policy of the nation. The zenith of the system and the first inevitable signs of decay came in the years 1850–1860, when the rising price of cotton threw the whole economic energy of the South into its cultivation, leading to a terrible consumption of soil and slaves, to a great increase in the size of plantations, and to increasing power and effrontery on the part of the slave barons. Finally, when a rising moral crusade conjoined with threatened economic disaster, the oligarchy, encouraged by the state of the cotton market, risked all on a political *coup-d'état*, which failed in the war of 1861–1865.[3]

75. **The Attitude of the South.** The attitude of the South toward the slave-trade changed *pari passu* with this development of the cotton trade. From 1808 to 1820 the South half

[1]The prices cited are from Newmarch and Tooke, and refer to the London market. The average price in 1855–60 was about 7*d*.

[2]From United States census reports.

[3]Cf. United States census reports; and Olmsted, *The Cotton Kingdom*.

wished to get rid of a troublesome and abnormal institution, and yet saw no way to do so. The fear of insurrection and of the further spread of the disagreeable system led her to consent to the partial prohibition of the trade by severe national enactments. Nevertheless, she had in the matter no settled policy: she refused to support vigorously the execution of the laws she had helped to make, and at the same time she acknowledged the theoretical necessity of these laws. After 1820, however, there came a gradual change. The South found herself supplied with a body of slave laborers, whose number had been augmented by large illicit importations, with an abundance of rich land, and with all other natural facilities for raising a crop which was in large demand and peculiarly adapted to slave labor. The increasing crop caused a new demand for slaves, and an interstate slave-traffic arose between the Border and the Gulf States, which turned the former into slave-breeding districts, and bound them to the slave States by ties of strong economic interest.

As the cotton crop continued to increase, this source of supply became inadequate, especially as the theory of land and slave consumption broke down former ethical and prudential bounds. It was, for example, found cheaper to work a slave to death in a few years, and buy a new one, than to care for him in sickness and old age; so, too, it was easier to despoil rich, new land in a few years of intensive culture, and move on to the Southwest, than to fertilize and conserve the soil.[1] Consequently, there early came a demand for land and slaves greater than the country could supply. The demand for land showed itself in the annexation of Texas, the conquest of Mexico, and the movement toward the acquisition of Cuba. The demand for slaves was manifested in the illicit traffic that noticeably increased about 1835, and reached large proportions by 1860. It was also seen in a disposition to attack the government for stigmatizing the trade as criminal,[2] then in a disinclination to take any measures which would have rendered our repressive laws effective; and finally in such articulate

[1] Cf. United States census reports; and Olmsted, *The Cotton Kingdom*.

[2] As early as 1836 Calhoun declared that he should ever regret that the term "piracy" had been applied to the slave-trade in our laws: Benton, *Abridgment of Debates*, XII. 718.

declarations by prominent men as this: "Experience having settled the point, that this Trade *cannot be abolished by the use of force*, and that blockading squadrons serve only to make it more profitable and more cruel, I am surprised that the attempt is persisted in, unless as it serves as a cloak to some other purposes. It would be far better than it now is, for the African, if the trade was free from all restrictions, and left to the mitigation and decay which time and competition would surely bring about."[1]

76. **The Attitude of the North and Congress.** With the North as yet unawakened to the great changes taking place in the South, and with the attitude of the South thus in process of development, little or no constructive legislation could be expected on the subject of the slave-trade. As the divergence in sentiment became more and more pronounced, there were various attempts at legislation, all of which proved abortive. The pro-slavery party attempted, as early as 1826, and again in 1828, to abolish the African agency and leave the Africans practically at the mercy of the States;[2] one or two attempts were made to relax the few provisions which restrained the coastwise trade;[3] and, after the treaty of 1842, Benton proposed to stop appropriations for the African squadron until England defined her position on the Right of Search question.[4] The anti-slavery men presented several bills to amend and strengthen previous laws;[5] they sought, for instance, in vain to regulate the Texan trade, through which numbers of slaves indirectly reached the

[1] Governor J. H. Hammond of South Carolina, in *Letters to Clarkson*, No. 1, p. 2.

[2] In 1826 Forsyth of Georgia attempted to have a bill passed abolishing the African agency, and providing that the Africans imported be disposed of in some way that would entail no expense on the public treasury: *House Journal*, 19 Cong. 1 sess. p. 258. In 1828 a bill was reported to the House to abolish the agency and make the Colonization Society the agents, if they would agree to the terms. The bill was so amended as merely to appropriate money for suppressing the slave-trade: *Ibid.*, 20 Cong. 1 sess., House Bill No. 190.

[3] *Ibid.*, pp. 121, 135; 20 Cong. 2 sess. pp. 58–9, 84, 215.

[4] *Congressional Globe*, 27 Cong. 3 sess. pp. 328, 331–6.

[5] Cf. Mercer's bill, *House Journal*, 21 Cong. 1 sess. p. 512; also Strange's two bills, *Senate Journal*, 25 Cong. 3 sess. pp. 200, 313; 26 Cong. 1 sess., Senate Bill No. 123.

United States.[1] Presidents and consuls earnestly recommended legislation to restrict the clearances of vessels bound on slave-trading voyages, and to hinder the facility with which slavers obtained fraudulent papers.[2] Only one such bill succeeded in passing the Senate, and that was dropped in the House.[3]

The only legislation of this period was confined to a few appropriation bills. Only one of these acts, that of 1823, appropriating $50,000,[4] was designed materially to aid in the suppression of the trade, all the others relating to expenses incurred after violations. After 1823 the appropriations dwindled, being made at intervals of one, two, and three years, down to 1834, when the amount was $5,000. No further appropriations were made until 1842, when a few thousands above an unexpended surplus were appropriated. In 1843 $5,000 were given, and finally, in 1846, $25,000 were secured; but this was the last sum obtainable until 1856.[5] Nearly all of these meagre appropriations went toward reimbursing Southern plantation owners for the care and support of illegally imported Africans, and the rest to the maintenance of the African agency. Suspiciously large sums were paid for the first purpose, considering the fact that such Africans were always worked hard by those to whom they were farmed out, and often "disappeared" while in their hands. In the accounts we nevertheless find many items like that of $20,286.98 for the maintenance of Negroes imported on the "Ramirez;"[6] in 1827, $5,442.22 for the "bounty, subsistence, clothing, medicine," etc., of fifteen Africans;[7] in 1835, $3,613 for the support of

[1] *Senate Journal*, 25 Cong. 2 sess. pp. 297–8, 300.

[2] *Senate Doc.*, 28 Cong. 1 sess. IV. No. 217, p. 19; *Senate Exec. Doc.*, 31 Cong. 2 sess. II. No. 6, pp. 3, 10, etc.; 33 Cong. 1 sess. VIII. No. 47, pp. 5–6; 34 Cong. 1 sess. XV. No. 99, p. 80; *House Journal*, 26 Cong. 1 sess. pp. 117–8; cf. *Ibid.*, 20 Cong. 1 sess. p. 650, etc.; 21 Cong. 2 sess. p. 194; 27 Cong. 1 sess. pp. 31, 184; *House Doc.*, 29 Cong. 1 sess. III. No. 43, p. 11; *House Exec. Doc.*, 31 Cong. 1 sess. III. pt. 1, No. 5, pp. 7–8.

[3] *Senate Journal*, 26 Cong. 1 sess., Senate Bill No. 335; *House Journal*, 26 Cong. 1 sess. pp. 1138, 1228, 1257.

[4] *Statutes at Large*, III. 764.

[5] Cf. above, Chapter VIII. p. 125.

[6] Cf. *Report of the Secretary of the Navy*, 1827.

[7] *Ibid.*

thirty-eight slaves for two months (including a bill of $1,038 for medical attendance).[1]

The African agency suffered many vicissitudes. The first agent, Bacon, who set out early in 1820, was authorized by President Monroe "to form an establishment on the island of Sherbro, or elsewhere on the coast of Africa," and to build barracks for three hundred persons. He was, however, warned "not to connect your agency with the views or plans of the Colonization Society, with which, under the law, the Government of the United States has no concern." Bacon soon died, and was followed during the next four years by Winn and Ayres; they succeeded in establishing a government agency on Cape Mesurado, in conjunction with that of the Colonization Society. The agent of that Society, Jehudi Ashmun, became after 1822, the virtual head of the colony; he fortified and enlarged it, and laid the foundations of an independent community. The succeeding government agents came to be merely official representatives of the United States, and the distribution of free rations for liberated Africans ceased in 1827.

Between 1819 and 1830 two hundred and fifty-two recaptured Africans were sent to the agency, and $264,710 were expended. The property of the government at the agency was valued at $18,895. From 1830 to 1840, nearly $20,000 more were expended, chiefly for the agents' salaries. About 1840 the appointment of an agent ceased, and the colony became gradually self-supporting and independent. It was proclaimed as the Republic of Liberia in 1847.[2]

[1] *House Reports*, 24 Cong. 1 sess. I. No. 223.

[2] This account is taken exclusively from government documents: *Amer. State Papers, Naval*, III. Nos. 339, 340, 357, 429 E; IV. Nos. 457 R (1 and 2), 486 H, I, p. 161 and 519 R, 564 P, 585 P; *House Reports*, 19 Cong. 1 sess. I. No. 65; *House Doc.*, 19 Cong. 2 sess. IV. No. 69; 21 Cong. 2 sess. I. No. 2, pp. 42–3, 211–8; 22 Cong. 1 sess. I. No. 2, pp. 45, 272–4; 22 Cong. 2 sess. I. No. 2, pp. 48, 229; 23 Cong. 1 sess. I. No. 1, pp. 238, 269; 23 Cong. 2 sess. I. No. 2, pp. 315, 363; 24 Cong. 1 sess. I. No. 2, pp. 336, 378; 24 Cong. 2 sess. I. No. 2, pp. 450, 506; 25 Cong. 2 sess. I. No. 3, pp. 771, 850; 26 Cong. 1 sess. I. No. 2, pp. 534, 612; 26 Cong. 2 sess. I. No. 2, pp. 405, 450. It is probable that the agent became eventually the United States consul and minister; I cannot however cite evidence for this supposition.

77. **Imperfect Application of the Laws.** In reviewing efforts toward the suppression of the slave-trade from 1820 to 1850, it must be remembered that nearly every cabinet had a strong, if not a predominating, Southern element, and that consequently the efforts of the executive were powerfully influenced by the changing attitude of the South. Naturally, under such circumstances, the government displayed little activity and no enthusiasm in the work. In 1824 a single vessel of the Gulf squadron was occasionally sent to the African coast to return by the route usually followed by the slavers; no wonder that "none of these or any other of our public ships have found vessels engaged in the slave trade under the flag of the United States, . . . although it is known that the trade still exists to a most lamentable extent."[1] Indeed, all that an American slaver need do was to run up a Spanish or a Portuguese flag, to be absolutely secure from all attack or inquiry on the part of United States vessels. Even this desultory method of suppression was not regular: in 1826 "no vessel has been despatched to the coast of Africa for several months,"[2] and from that time until 1839 this country probably had no slave-trade police upon the seas, except in the Gulf of Mexico. In 1839 increasing violations led to the sending of two fast-sailing vessels to the African coast, and these were kept there more or less regularly;[3] but even after the signing of the treaty of 1842 the Secretary of the Navy reports: "On the coast of Africa we have *no* squadron. The small appropriation of the present year was believed to be scarcely sufficient."[4] Between 1843 and 1850 the coast squadron varied from two to six vessels, with from thirty to ninety-eight guns;[5] "but the force habitually and actively engaged in cruizing on the ground frequented by slavers has probably been less by one-fourth, if we consider the size of the ships employed and their withdrawal for purposes of recreation and health, and the movement of the reliefs, whose arrival does not correspond

[1] *Report of the Secretary of the Navy*, 1824.
[2] *Ibid.*, 1826.
[3] *Ibid.*, 1839.
[4] *Ibid.*, 1842.
[5] *British and Foreign State Papers*, 1857–8, p. 1250.

exactly with the departure of the vessels whose term of service has expired."[1] The reports of the navy show that in only four of the eight years mentioned was the fleet, at the time of report, at the stipulated size of eighty guns; and at times it was much below this, even as late as 1848, when only two vessels are reported on duty along the African coast.[2] As the commanders themselves acknowledged, the squadron was too small and the cruising-ground too large to make joint cruising effective.[3]

The same story comes from the Brazil station: "Nothing effectual can be done towards stopping the slave trade, as our squadron is at present organized," wrote the consul at Rio Janeiro in 1847; "when it is considered that the Brazil station extends from north of the equator to Cape Horn on this continent, and includes a great part of Africa south of the equator, on both sides of the Cape of Good Hope, it must be admitted that one frigate and one brig is a very insufficient force to protect American commerce, and repress the participation in the slave trade by our own vessels."[4] In the Gulf of Mexico cruisers were stationed most of the time, although even here there were at times urgent representations that the scarcity or the absence of such vessels gave the illicit trade great license.[5]

Owing to this general negligence of the government, and also to its anxiety on the subject of the theoretic Right of Search, many officials were kept in a state of chronic deception in regard to the trade. The enthusiasm of commanders

[1] Lord Napier to Secretary of State Cass, Dec. 24, 1857: *British and Foreign State Papers*, 1857–8, p. 1249.

[2] *Parliamentary Papers*, 1847–8, Vol. LXIV. No. 133, *Papers Relative to the Suppression of the Slave Trade on the Coast of Africa*, p. 2.

[3] Report of Perry: *Senate Doc.*, 28 Cong. 2 sess. IX. No. 150, p. 118.

[4] Consul Park at Rio Janeiro to Secretary Buchanan, Aug. 20, 1847: *House Exec. Doc.*, 30 Cong. 2 sess. VII. No. 61, p. 7.

[5] Suppose "an American vessel employed to take in negroes at some point on this coast. There is no American man-of-war here to obtain intelligence. What risk does she run of being searched? But suppose that there is a man-of-war in port. What is to secure the master of the merchantman against her [the man-of-war's] commander's knowing all about his [the merchant-man's] intention, or suspecting it in time to be upon him [the merchant-man] before he shall have run a league on his way to Texas?" Consul Trist to Commander Spence: *House Doc.*, 27 Cong. 1 sess. No. 34, p. 41.

was dampened by the lack of latitude allowed and by the repeated insistence in their orders on the non-existence of a Right of Search.[1] When one commander, realizing that he could not cover the trading-track with his fleet, requested English commanders to detain suspicious American vessels until one of his vessels came up, the government annulled the agreement as soon as it reached their ears, rebuked him, and the matter was alluded to in Congress long after with horror.[2] According to the orders of cruisers, only slavers with slaves actually on board could be seized. Consequently, fully equipped slavers would sail past the American fleet, deliberately make all preparations for shipping a cargo, then, when the English were not near, "sell" the ship to a Spaniard, hoist the Spanish flag, and again sail gayly past the American fleet with a cargo of slaves. An English commander reported: "The officers of the United States' navy are extremely active and zealous in the cause, and no fault can be attributed to them, but it is greatly to be lamented that this blemish should in so great a degree nullify our endeavours."[3]

78. **Responsibility of the Government.** Not only did the government thus negatively favor the slave-trade, but also many conscious, positive acts must be attributed to a spirit hostile to the proper enforcement of the slave-trade laws. In cases of doubt, when the law needed executive interpretation, the decision was usually in favor of the looser construction of the law; the trade from New Orleans to Mobile was, for instance, declared not to be coastwise trade, and consequently, to the joy of the Cuban smugglers, was left utterly free and unrestricted.[4] After the conquest of Mexico, even

[1] A typical set of instructions was on the following plan: 1. You are charged with the protection of legitimate commerce. 2. While the United States wishes to suppress the slave-trade, she will not admit a Right of Search by foreign vessels. 3. You are to arrest slavers. 4. You are to allow in no case an exercise of the Right of Search or any great interruption of legitimate commerce.—To Commodore Perry, March 30, 1843: *House Exec. Doc.*, 35 Cong. 2 sess. IX. No. 104.

[2] *House Reports*, 27 Cong. 3 sess. III. No. 283, pp. 765–8. Cf. Benton's speeches on the treaty of 1842.

[3] Report of Hotham to Admiralty, April 7, 1847: *Parliamentary Papers*, 1847–8, Vol. LXIV. No. 133, *Papers Relative to the Suppression of the Slave Trade on the Coast of Africa*, p. 13.

[4] *Opinions of Attorneys-General*, III. 512.

vessels bound to California, by the way of Cape Horn, were allowed to clear coastwise, thus giving our flag to "the slave-pirates of the whole world."[1] Attorney-General Nelson declared that the selling to a slave-trader of an American vessel, to be delivered on the coast of Africa, was not aiding or abetting the slave-trade.[2] So easy was it for slavers to sail that corruption among officials was hinted at. "There is certainly a want of proper vigilance at Havana," wrote Commander Perry in 1844, "and perhaps at the ports of the United States;" and again, in the same year, "I cannot but think that the custom-house authorities in the United States are not sufficiently rigid in looking after vessels of suspicious character."[3]

In the courts it was still next to impossible to secure the punishment of the most notorious slave-trader. In 1847 a consul writes: "The slave power in this city [i. e., Rio Janeiro] is extremely great, and a consul doing his duty needs to be supported kindly and effectually at home. In the case of the 'Fame,' where the vessel was diverted from the business intended by her owners and employed in the slave trade—both of which offences are punishable with death, if I rightly read the laws—I sent home the two mates charged with these offences, for trial, the first mate to Norfolk, the second mate to Philadelphia. What was done with the first mate I know not. In the case of the man sent to Philadelphia, Mr. Commissioner Kane states that a clear prima facie case is made out, and then holds him to bail in the sum of *one thousand dollars*, which would be paid by any slave trader in Rio, on the *presentation of a draft*. In all this there is little encouragement for exertion."[4] Again, the "Perry" in 1850 captured a slaver which was about to ship 1,800 slaves. The captain admitted his guilt, and was condemned in the United States District Court at New York. Nevertheless, he was admitted to bail of $5,000; this being afterward reduced to $3,000, he forfeited it and

[1] *Tenth Annual Report of the Amer. and Foreign Anti-Slav. Soc.*, May 7, 1850, p. 149.

[2] *Opinions of Attorneys-General*, IV. 245.

[3] *Senate Doc.*, 28 Cong. 2 sess. IX. No. 150, pp. 108, 132.

[4] *House Exec. Doc.*, 30 Cong. 2 sess. VII. No. 61, p. 18.

escaped. The mate was sentenced to two years in the penitentiary.[1] Also several slavers sent home to the United States by the British, with clear evidence of guilt, escaped condemnation through technicalities.[2]

79. **Activity of the Slave-Trade, 1820–1850.** The enhanced price of slaves throughout the American slave market, brought about by the new industrial development and the laws against the slave-trade, was the irresistible temptation that drew American capital and enterprise into that traffic. In the United States, in spite of the large interstate traffic, the average price of slaves rose from about $325 in 1840, to $360 in 1850, and to $500 in 1860.[3] Brazil and Cuba offered similar inducements to smugglers, and the American flag was ready to protect such pirates. As a result, the American slave-trade finally came to be carried on principally by United States capital, in United States ships, officered by United States citizens, and under the United States flag.

Executive reports repeatedly acknowledged this fact. In 1839 "a careful revision of these laws" is recommended by the President, in order that "the integrity and honor of our flag may be carefully preserved."[4] In June, 1841, the President declares: "There is reason to believe that the traffic is on the increase," and advocates "vigorous efforts."[5] His message in December of the same year acknowledges: "That the American flag is grossly abused by the abandoned and profligate of other nations is but too probable."[6] The special message of 1845 explains at length that "it would seem" that a regular policy of evading the laws is carried on: American vessels with the knowledge of the owners are chartered by notorious slave dealers in Brazil, aided by English capitalists, with this intent.[7] The message of 1849 "earnestly" invites the attention of Congress "to an amendment of our existing laws relating to

[1] Foote, *Africa and the American Flag*, pp. 286–90.
[2] *British and Foreign State Papers*, 1839–40, pp. 913–4.
[3] Cf. United States census reports; and Olmsted, *Cotton Kingdom*.
[4] *House Journal*, 26 Cong. 1 sess. p. 118.
[5] *Ibid.*, 27 Cong. 1 sess. pp. 31, 184.
[6] *Ibid.*, 27 Cong. 2 sess. pp. 14, 15, 86, 113.
[7] *Senate Journal*, 28 Cong. 2 sess. pp. 191, 227.

the African slave-trade, with a view to the effectual suppression of that barbarous traffic. It is not to be denied," continues the message, "that this trade is still, in part, carried on by means of vessels built in the United States, and owned or navigated by some of our citizens."[1] Governor Buchanan of Liberia reported in 1839: "The chief obstacle to the success of the very active measures pursued by the British government for the suppression of the slave-trade on the coast, is the *American flag*. Never was the proud banner of freedom so extensively used by those pirates upon liberty and humanity, as at this season."[2] One well-known American slaver was boarded fifteen times and twice taken into port, but always escaped by means of her papers.[3] Even American officers report that the English are doing all they can, but that the American flag protects the trade.[4] The evidence which literally poured in from our consuls and ministers at Brazil adds to the story of the guilt of the United States.[5] It was proven that the participation of United States citizens in the trade was large and systematic. One of the most notorious slave merchants of Brazil said: "I am worried by the Americans, who insist upon my hiring their vessels for slave-trade."[6] Minister Proffit stated, in 1844, that the "slave-trade is almost entirely carried on under our flag, in American-built vessels."[7] So, too, in Cuba: the British commissioners affirm that American citizens were openly engaged in the traffic; vessels arrived undisguised at Havana from the United States, and cleared for Africa as slavers after an alleged sale.[8] The American consul, Trist, was proven to have consciously

[1] *House Exec. Doc.*, 31 Cong. 1 sess. III. pt. I. No. 5, p. 7.

[2] Foote, *Africa and the American Flag*, p. 152.

[3] *Ibid.*, pp. 152–3.

[4] *Ibid.*, p. 241.

[5] Cf. e. g. *House Doc.*, 28 Cong. 2 sess. IV. pt. I. No. 148; 29 Cong. 1 sess. III. No. 43; *House Exec. Doc.*, 30 Cong. 2 sess. VII. No. 61; *Senate Exec. Doc.*, 30 Cong. 1 sess. IV. No. 28; 31 Cong. 2 sess. II. No. 6; 33 Cong. 1 sess. VIII. No. 47.

[6] Foote, *Africa and the American Flag*, p. 218.

[7] *Ibid.*, p. 221.

[8] Palmerston to Stevenson: *House Doc.*, 26 Cong. 2 sess. V. No. 115, p. 5. In 1836 five such slavers were known to have cleared; in 1837, eleven; in 1838, nineteen; and in 1839, twenty-three: *Ibid.*, pp. 220–1.

or unconsciously aided this trade by the issuance of blank clearance papers.[1]

The presence of American capital in these enterprises, and the connivance of the authorities, were proven in many cases and known in scores. In 1837 the English government informed the United States that from the papers of a captured slaver it appeared that the notorious slave-trading firm, Blanco and Carballo of Havana, who owned the vessel, had correspondents in the United States: "at Baltimore, Messrs. Peter Harmony and Co., in New York, Robert Barry, Esq."[2] The slaver "Martha" of New York, captured by the "Perry," contained among her papers curious revelations of the guilt of persons in America who were little suspected.[3] The slaver "Prova," which was allowed to lie in the harbor of Charleston, South Carolina, and refit, was afterwards captured with two hundred and twenty-five slaves on board.[4] The real reason that prevented many belligerent Congressmen from pressing certain search claims against England lay in the fact that the unjustifiable detentions had unfortunately revealed so much American guilt that it was deemed wiser to let the matter end in talk. For instance, in 1850 Congress demanded information as to illegal searches, and President Fillmore's report showed the uncomfortable fact that, of the ten American ships wrongly detained by English men-of-war, nine were proven red-handed slavers.[5]

The consul at Havana reported, in 1836, that whole cargoes of slaves fresh from Africa were being daily shipped to Texas in American vessels, that 1,000 had been sent within a few months, that the rate was increasing, and that many of these slaves "can scarcely fail to find their way into the United States." Moreover, the consul acknowledged that ships frequently cleared for the United States in ballast, taking on a

[1] *Parliamentary Papers*, 1839, Vol. XLIX., *Slave Trade*, class A, Further Series, pp. 58–9; class B, Further Series, p. 110; class D, Further Series, p. 25. Trist pleaded ignorance of the law: Trist to Forsyth, *House Doc.*, 26 Cong. 2 sess. V. No. 115.

[2] *House Doc.*, 26 Cong. 2 sess. V. No. 115.

[3] Foote, *Africa and the American Flag*, p. 290.

[4] *House Doc.*, 26 Cong. 2 sess. V. No. 115, pp. 121, 163–6.

[5] *Senate Exec. Doc.*, 31 Cong. 1 sess. XIV. No. 66.

cargo at some secret point.[1] When with these facts we consider the law facilitating "recovery" of slaves from Texas,[2] the repeated refusals to regulate the Texan trade, and the shelving of a proposed congressional investigation into these matters,[3] conjecture becomes a practical certainty. It was estimated in 1838 that 15,000 Africans were annually taken to Texas, and "there are even grounds for suspicion that there are other places . . . where slaves are introduced."[4] Between 1847 and 1853 the slave smuggler Drake had a slave depot in the Gulf, where sometimes as many as 1,600 Negroes were on hand, and the owners were continually importing and shipping. "The joint-stock company," writes this smuggler, "was a very extensive one, and connected with leading American and Spanish mercantile houses. Our island[5] was visited almost weekly, by agents from Cuba, New York, Baltimore, Philadelphia, Boston, and New Orleans. . . . The seasoned and instructed slaves were taken to Texas, or Florida, overland, and to Cuba, in sailing-boats. As no squad contained more than half a dozen, no difficulty was found in posting them to the United States, without discovery, and generally without suspicion. . . . The Bay Island plantation sent ventures weekly to the Florida Keys. Slaves were taken into the great American swamps, and there kept till wanted for the market. Hundreds were sold as captured runaways from the Florida wilderness. We had agents in every slave State; and our coasters were built in Maine, and came out with lumber. I could tell curious stories . . . of this business of smuggling Bozal negroes into the United States. It is growing more profitable every year, and if you should hang all the Yankee merchants

[1] Trist to Forsyth: *House Doc.*, 26 Cong. 2 sess. V. No. 115. "The business of supplying the United States with Africans from this island is one that must necessarily exist," because "slaves are a hundred *per cent*, or more, higher in the United States than in Cuba," and this profit "is a temptation which it is not in human nature as modified by American institutions to withstand": *Ibid.*

[2] *Statutes at Large*, V. 674.

[3] Cf. above, p. 157, note 1.

[4] Buxton, *The African Slave Trade and its Remedy*, pp. 44–5. Cf. *2d Report of the London African Soc.*, p. 22.

[5] I. e., Bay Island in the Gulf of Mexico, near the coast of Honduras.

engaged in it, hundreds would fill their places."[1] Inherent probability and concurrent testimony confirm the substantial truth of such confessions. For instance, one traveller discovers on a Southern plantation Negroes who can speak no English.[2] The careful reports of the Quakers "apprehend that many [slaves] are also introduced into the United States."[3] Governor Mathew of the Bahama Islands reports that "in more than one instance, Bahama vessels with coloured crews have been purposely wrecked on the coast of Florida, and the crews forcibly sold." This was brought to the notice of the United States authorities, but the district attorney of Florida could furnish no information.[4]

Such was the state of the slave-trade in 1850, on the threshold of the critical decade which by a herculean effort was destined finally to suppress it.

[1] *Revelations of a Slave Smuggler*, p. 98.

[2] Mr. H. Moulton in *Slavery as it is*, p. 140; cited in *Facts and Observations on the Slave Trade* (Friends' ed. 1841), p. 8.

[3] In a memorial to Congress, 1840: *House Doc.*, 26 Cong. 1 sess. VI. No. 211.

[4] *British and Foreign State Papers*, 1845–6, pp. 883, 968, 989–90. The governor wrote in reply: "The United States, if properly served by their law officers in the Floridas, will not experience any difficulty in obtaining the requisite knowledge of these illegal transactions, which, I have reason to believe, were the subject of common notoriety in the neighbourhood where they occurred, and of boast on the part of those concerned in them": *British and Foreign State Papers*, 1845–6, p. 990.

Chapter XI

THE FINAL CRISIS. 1850–1870.

---

80. **The Movement against the Slave-Trade Laws.** It was not altogether a mistaken judgment that led the constitutional fathers to consider the slave-trade as the backbone of slavery. An economic system based on slave labor will find, sooner or later, that the demand for the cheapest slave labor cannot long be withstood. Once degrade the laborer so that he cannot assert his own rights, and there is but one limit below which his price cannot be reduced. That limit is not his physical well-being, for it may be, and in the Gulf States it was, cheaper to work him rapidly to death; the limit is simply the cost of procuring him and keeping him alive a profitable length of time. Only the moral sense of a community can keep helpless labor from sinking to this level; and when a community has once been debauched by slavery, its moral sense offers little resistance to economic demand. This was the case in the West Indies and Brazil; and although better moral stamina held the crisis back longer in the United States, yet even here the ethical standard of the South was not able to maintain itself against the demands of the cotton industry. When, after 1850, the price of slaves had risen to a monopoly height, the leaders of the plantation system, brought to the edge of bankruptcy by the crude and reckless farming necessary under a slave *régime*, and baffled, at least temporarily, in their quest of new rich land to exploit, began instinctively to

feel that the only salvation of American slavery lay in the reopening of the African slave-trade.

It took but a spark to put this instinctive feeling into words, and words led to deeds. The movement first took definite form in the ever radical State of South Carolina. In 1854 a grand jury in the Williamsburg district declared, "as our unanimous opinion, that the Federal law abolishing the African Slave Trade is a public grievance. We hold this trade has been and would be, if re-established, a blessing to the American people, and a benefit to the African himself."[1] This attracted only local attention; but when, in 1856, the governor of the State, in his annual message, calmly argued at length for a reopening of the trade, and boldly declared that "if we cannot supply the demand for slave labor, then we must expect to be supplied with a species of labor we do not want,"[2] such words struck even Southern ears like "a thunder clap in a calm day."[3] And yet it needed but a few years to show that South Carolina had merely been the first to put into words the inarticulate thought of a large minority, if not a majority, of the inhabitants of the Gulf States.

81. **Commercial Conventions of 1855–56.** The growth of the movement is best followed in the action of the Southern Commercial Convention, an annual gathering which seems to have been fairly representative of a considerable part of Southern opinion. In the convention that met at New Orleans in 1855, McGimsey of Louisiana introduced a resolution instructing the Southern Congressmen to secure the repeal of the slave-trade laws. This resolution went to the Committee on Resolutions, and was not reported.[4] In 1856, in the convention at Savannah, W. B. Goulden of Georgia moved that the members of Congress be requested to bestir themselves energetically to have repealed all laws which forbade the slave-trade. By a vote of 67 to 18 the convention refused to debate the motion, but appointed a committee to present at the next convention the facts relating to a reopening of the trade.[5] In

[1] *British and Foreign State Papers*, 1854–5, p. 1156.

[2] Cluskey, *Political Text-Book* (14th ed.), p. 585.

[3] *De Bow's Review*, XXII. 223; quoted from Andrew Hunter of Virginia.

[4] *Ibid.*, XVIII. 628.

[5] *Ibid.*, XXII. 91, 102, 217, 221–2.

regard to this action a pamphlet of the day said: "There were introduced into the convention two leading measures, viz.: the laying of a State tariff on northern goods, and the reopening of the slave-trade; the one to advance our commercial interest, the other our agricultural interest, and which, when taken together, as they were doubtless intended to be, and although they have each been attacked by presses of doubtful service to the South, are characterized in the private judgment of politicians as one of the completest southern remedies ever submitted to popular action. . . . The proposition to revive, or more properly to reopen, the slave trade is as yet but imperfectly understood, in its intentions and probable results, by the people of the South, and but little appreciated by them. It has been received in all parts of the country with an undefined sort of repugnance, a sort of squeamishness, which is incident to all such violations of moral prejudices, and invariably wears off on familiarity with the subject. The South will commence by enduring, and end by embracing the project."[1] The matter being now fully before the public through these motions, Governor Adams's message, and newspaper and pamphlet discussion, the radical party pushed the project with all energy.

82. **Commercial Conventions of 1857–58.** The first piece of regular business that came before the Commercial Convention at Knoxville, Tennessee, August 10, 1857, was a proposal to recommend the abrogation of the 8th Article of the Treaty of Washington, on the slave-trade. An amendment offered by Sneed of Tennessee, declaring it inexpedient and against settled policy to reopen the trade, was voted down, Alabama, Arkansas, Florida, Louisiana, Mississippi, South Carolina, and Virginia refusing to agree to it. The original motion then passed; and the radicals, satisfied with their success in the first skirmish, again secured the appointment of a committee to report at the next meeting on the subject of reopening the slave-trade.[2] This next meeting assembled May 10, 1858, in a

[1] From a pamphlet entitled "A New Southern Policy, or the Slave Trade as meaning Union and Conservatism;" quoted in Etheridge's speech, Feb. 21, 1857: *Congressional Globe*, 34 Cong. 3 sess., Appendix, p. 366.

[2] *De Bow's Review*, XXIII. 298–320. A motion to table the motion on the 8th article was supported only by Kentucky, Tennessee, North Carolina, and

Gulf State, Alabama, in the city of Montgomery. Spratt of South Carolina, the slave-trade champion, presented an elaborate majority report from the committee, and recommended the following resolutions:—

1. *Resolved*, That slavery is right, and that being right, there can be no wrong in the natural means to its formation.

2. *Resolved*, That it is expedient and proper that the foreign slave trade should be re-opened, and that this Convention will lend its influence to any legitimate measure to that end.

3. *Resolved*, That a committee, consisting of one from each slave State, be appointed to consider of the means, consistent with the duty and obligations of these States, for re-opening the foreign slave-trade, and that they report their plan to the next meeting of this Convention.

Yancey, from the same committee, presented a minority report, which, though it demanded the repeal of the national prohibitory laws, did not advocate the reopening of the trade by the States.

Much debate ensued. Pryor of Virginia declared the majority report "a proposition to dissolve the Union." Yancey declared that "he was for disunion now. [Applause.]" He defended the principle of the slave-trade, and said: "If it is right to buy slaves in Virginia and carry them to New Orleans, why is it not right to buy them in Cuba, Brazil, or Africa, and carry them there?" The opposing speeches made little attempt to meet this uncomfortable logic; but, nevertheless, opposition enough was developed to lay the report on the table until the next convention, with orders that it be printed, in the mean time, as a radical campaign document. Finally the convention passed a resolution:—

That it is inexpedient for any State, or its citizens, to attempt to re-open the African slave-trade while that State is one of the United States of America.[1]

Maryland. Those voting for Sneed's motion were Georgia, Maryland, North Carolina, and Tennessee. The appointment of a slave-trade committee was at first defeated by a vote of 48 to 44. Finally a similar motion was passed, 52 to 40.

[1] *De Bow's Review*, XXIV. 473–491, 579–605. The Louisiana delegation alone did not vote for the last resolution, the vote of her delegation being evenly divided.

83. **Commercial Convention of 1859.** The Convention of 1859 met at Vicksburg, Mississippi, May 9–19, and the slave-trade party came ready for a fray. On the second day Spratt called up his resolutions, and the next day the Committee on Resolutions recommended that, *"in the opinion of this Convention, all laws, State or Federal, prohibiting the African slave trade, ought to be repealed."* Two minority reports accompanied this resolution: one proposed to postpone action, on account of the futility of the attempt at that time; the other report recommended that, since repeal of the national laws was improbable, nullification by the States impracticable, and action by the Supreme Court unlikely, therefore the States should bring in the Africans as apprentices, a system the legality of which "is incontrovertible." "The only difficult question," it was said, "is the future status of the apprentices after the expiration of their term of servitude."[1] Debate on these propositions began in the afternoon. A brilliant speech on the resumption of the importation of slaves, says Foote of Mississippi, "was listened to with breathless attention and applauded vociferously. Those of us who rose in opposition were looked upon by the excited assemblage present as *traitors* to the best interests of the South, and only worthy of expulsion from the body. The excitement at last grew so high that personal violence was menaced, and some dozen of the more conservative members of the convention withdrew from the hall in which it was holding its sittings."[2] "It was clear," adds De Bow, "that the people of Vicksburg looked upon it [i. e., the convention] with some distrust."[3] When at last a ballot was taken, the first resolution passed by a vote of 40 to 19.[4] Finally, the 8th Article of the Treaty of Washington was again condemned; and it was also suggested, in the newspaper which was the official organ of the meeting, that "the Convention raise a fund to be dispensed in premiums for the

[1] *De Bow's Review*, XXVII. 94–235.

[2] H. S. Foote, in *Bench and Bar of the South and Southwest*, p. 69.

[3] *De Bow's Review*, XXVII. 115.

[4] *Ibid.*, p. 99. The vote was:—

best sermons in favor of reopening the African Slave Trade."[1]

84. **Public Opinion in the South.** This record of the Commercial Conventions probably gives a true reflection of the development of extreme opinion on the question of reopening the slave-trade. First, it is noticeable that on this point there was a distinct divergence of opinion and interest between the Gulf and the Border States, and it was this more than any moral repugnance that checked the radicals. The whole movement represented the economic revolt of the slave-consuming cotton-belt against their base of labor supply. This revolt was only prevented from gaining its ultimate end by the fact that the Gulf States could not get on without the active political co-operation of the Border States. Thus, although such hot-heads as Spratt were not able, even as late as 1859, to carry a substantial majority of the South with them in an attempt to reopen the trade at all hazards, yet the agitation did succeed in sweeping away nearly all theoretical opposition to the trade, and left the majority of Southern people in an attitude which regarded the reopening of the African slave-trade as merely a question of expediency.

This growth of Southern opinion is clearly to be followed in the newspapers and pamphlets of the day, in Congress, and in many significant movements. The Charleston *Standard* in a series of articles strongly advocated the reopening of the trade; the Richmond *Examiner*, though opposing the scheme as a Virginia paper should, was brought to "acknowledge that the laws which condemn the Slave-trade imply an aspersion

Yea.			*Nay.*		
Alabama,	5	votes.	Tennessee,	12	votes.
Arkansas,	4	"	Florida,	3	"
South Carolina,	4	"	South Carolina,	4	"
Louisiana,	6	"	Total	19	
Texas,	4	"			
Georgia,	10	"			
Mississippi,	7	"			
Total	40				

Virginia, Maryland, Kentucky, and North Carolina did not vote; they either withdrew or were not represented.

[1] Quoted in *26th Report of the Amer. Anti-slav. Soc.*, p. 38. The official organ was the *True Southron*.

upon the character of the South.[1] In March, 1859, the *National Era* said: "There can be no doubt that the idea of reviving the African Slave Trade is gaining ground in the South. Some two months ago we could quote strong articles from ultra Southern journals against the traffic; but of late we have been sorry to observe in the same journals an ominous silence upon the subject, while the advocates of 'free trade in negroes' are earnest and active."[2] The Savannah *Republican*, which at first declared the movement to be of no serious intent, conceded, in 1859, that it was gaining favor, and that nine-tenths of the Democratic Congressional Convention favored it, and that even those who did not advocate a revival demanded the abolition of the laws.[3] A correspondent from South Carolina writes, December 18, 1859: "The nefarious project of opening it [i. e., the slave trade] has been started here in that prurient temper of the times which manifests itself in disunion schemes. . . . My State is strangely and terribly infected with all this sort of thing. . . . One feeling that gives a countenance to the opening of the slave trade is, that it will be a sort of spite to the North and defiance of their opinions."[4] The New Orleans *Delta* declared that those who voted for the slave-trade in Congress were men " whose names will be honored hereafter for the unflinching manner in which they stood up for principle, for truth, and consistency, as well as the vital interests of the South."[5]

85. **The Question in Congress.** Early in December, 1856, the subject reached Congress; and although the agitation was then new, fifty-seven Southern Congressmen refused to declare a re-opening of the slave-trade "shocking to the moral sentiment of the enlightened portion of mankind," and eight refused to call the reopening even "unwise" and "inexpe-

[1] Quoted in *24th Report of the Amer. Anti-slav. Soc.*, p. 54.

[2] Quoted in *26th Report*, *Ibid.*, p. 43.

[3] *27th Report*, *Ibid.*, pp. 19–20.

[4] Letter of W. C. Preston, in the *National Intelligencer*, April 3, 1863. Also published in the pamphlet, *The African Slave Trade: The Secret Purpose*, etc., p. 26.

[5] Quoted in Etheridge's speech: *Congressional Globe*, 34 Cong. 3 sess. Appen., p. 366.

dient."[1] Three years later, January 31, 1859, it was impossible, in a House of one hundred and ninety-nine members, to get a two-thirds vote in order even to consider Kilgore's resolutions, which declared "that no legislation can be too thorough in its measures, nor can any penalty known to the catalogue of modern punishment for crime be too severe against a traffic so inhuman and unchristian."[2]

Congressmen and other prominent men hastened with the rising tide.[3] Dowdell of Alabama declared the repressive acts "highly offensive;" J. B. Clay of Kentucky was "opposed to all these laws;"[4] Seward of Georgia declared them "wrong, and a violation of the Constitution;"[5] Barksdale of Mississippi agreed with this sentiment; Crawford of Georgia threatened a reopening of the trade; Miles of South Carolina was for "sweeping away" all restrictions;[6] Keitt of South Carolina wished to withdraw the African squadron, and to cease to brand slave-trading as piracy;[7] Brown of Mississippi "would repeal the law instantly;"[8] Alexander Stephens, in his farewell address to his constituents, said: "Slave states cannot be made without Africans. . . . [My object is] to bring clearly to your mind the great truth that without an increase of African slaves from abroad, you may not expect or look for many more slave States."[9] Jefferson Davis strongly denied "any coincidence of opinion with those who prate of the inhumanity and sinfulness of the trade. The interest of Mississippi," said he, "not of the African, dictates my conclusion." He opposed the immediate reopening of the trade in Mississippi for fear of a paralyzing influx of Negroes, but carefully added: "This con-

[1] *House Journal*, 34 Cong. 3 sess. pp. 105–10; *Congressional Globe*, 34 Cong. 3 sess. pp. 123–6; Cluskey, *Political Text-Book* (14th ed.), p. 589.

[2] *House Journal*, 35 Cong. 2 sess. pp. 298–9. Cf. *26th Report of the Amer. Anti-slav. Soc.*, p. 45.

[3] Cf. *Reports of the Amer. Anti-slav. Soc.*, especially the 26th, pp. 43–4.

[4] *Ibid.*, p. 43. He referred especially to the Treaty of 1842.

[5] *Ibid.*; *Congressional Globe*, 35 Cong. 2 sess., Appen., pp. 248–50.

[6] *26th Report of the Amer. Anti-slav. Soc.*, p. 44.

[7] *Ibid.*; *27th Report*, pp. 13–4.

[8] *26th Report*, *Ibid.*, p. 44.

[9] Quoted in Lalor, *Cyclopædia*, III. 733; Cairnes, *The Slave Power* (New York, 1862), p. 123, note; *27th Report of the Amer. Anti-slav. Soc.*, p. 15.

clusion, in relation to Mississippi, is based upon my view of her *present* condition, *not* upon any *general theory*. It is not supposed to be applicable to Texas, to New Mexico, or to any *future acquisitions* to be made south of the Rio Grande."[1] John Forsyth, who for seven years conducted the slave-trade diplomacy of the nation, declared, about 1860: "But one stronghold of its [i. e., slavery's] enemies remains to be carried, to *complete its triumph* and assure its welfare,—that is the existing prohibition of the African Slave-trade."[2] Pollard, in his *Black Diamonds*, urged the importation of Africans as "laborers." "This I grant you," said he, "would be practically the re-opening of the African slave trade; but . . . you will find that it very often becomes necessary to evade the letter of the law, in some of the greatest measures of social happiness and patriotism."[3]

86. **Southern Policy in 1860.** The matter did not rest with mere words. During the session of the Vicksburg Convention, an "African Labor Supply Association" was formed, under the presidency of J. D. B. De Bow, editor of *De Bow's Review*, and ex-superintendent of the seventh census. The object of the association was "to promote the supply of African labor."[4] In 1857 the committee of the South Carolina legislature to whom the Governor's slave-trade message was referred made an elaborate report, which declared in italics: *"The South at large does need a re-opening of the African slave trade."* Pettigrew, the only member who disagreed to this report, failed of re-election. The report contained an extensive argument to prove the kingship of cotton, the perfidy of English philanthropy, and the lack of slaves in the South, which, it was said, would show a deficit of six hundred thousand slaves by 1878.[5] In Georgia, about this time, an attempt to expunge the slave-trade prohibition in the State Constitution lacked but one vote of passing.[6] From these slower and more

[1] Quoted in Cairnes, *The Slave Power*, p. 123, note; *27th Report of the Amer. Anti-slav. Soc.*, p. 19.

[2] *27th Report*, *Ibid.*, p. 16; quoted from the Mobile *Register*.

[3] Edition of 1859, pp. 63–4.

[4] *De Bow's Review*, XXVII. 121, 231–5.

[5] *Report of the Special Committee*, etc. (1857), pp. 24–5.

[6] *26th Report of the Amer. Anti-slav. Soc.*, p. 40. The vote was 47 to 46.

legal movements came others less justifiable. The long argument on the "apprentice" system finally brought a request to the collector of the port at Charleston, South Carolina, from E. Lafitte & Co., for a clearance to Africa for the purpose of importing African "emigrants." The collector appealed to the Secretary of the Treasury, Howell Cobb of Georgia, who flatly refused to take the bait, and replied that if the "emigrants" were brought in as slaves, it would be contrary to United States law; if as freemen, it would be contrary to their own State law.[1] In Louisiana a still more radical movement was attempted, and a bill passed the House of Representatives authorizing a company to import two thousand five hundred Africans, "indentured" for fifteen years "at least." The bill lacked but two votes of passing the Senate.[2] It was said that the *Georgian*, of Savannah, contained a notice of an agricultural society which "unanimously resolved to offer a premium of $25 for the best specimen of a live African imported into the United States within the last twelve months."[3]

It would not be true to say that there was in the South in 1860 substantial unanimity on the subject of reopening the slave-trade; nevertheless, there certainly was a large and influential minority, including perhaps a majority of citizens of the Gulf States, who favored the project, and, in defiance of law and morals, aided and abetted its actual realization. Various movements, it must be remembered, gained much of their strength from the fact that their success meant a partial nullification of the slave-trade laws. The admission of Texas added probably seventy-five thousand recently imported slaves to the Southern stock; the movement against Cuba, which culminated in the "Ostend Manifesto" of Buchanan, Mason, and Soulé, had its chief impetus in the thousands of slaves whom Americans had poured into the island. Finally, the series of filibustering expeditions against Cuba, Mexico, and Central America were but the wilder and more irresponsible attempts to secure both slave territory and slaves.

[1] *House Exec. Doc.*, 36 Cong. 2 sess. IV. No. 7, pp. 632–6. For the State law, cf. above, Chapter II. This refusal of Cobb's was sharply criticised by many Southern papers. Cf. *26th Report of the Amer. Anti-slav. Soc.*, p. 39.

[2] New York *Independent*, March 11 and April 1, 1858.

[3] *26th Report of the Amer. Anti-slav. Soc.*, p. 41.

87. **Increase of the Slave-Trade from 1850 to 1860.** The long and open agitation for the reopening of the slave-trade, together with the fact that the South had been more or less familiar with violations of the laws since 1808, led to such a remarkable increase of illicit traffic and actual importations in the decade 1850–1860, that the movement may almost be termed a reopening of the slave-trade.

In the foreign slave-trade our own officers continue to report "how shamefully our flag has been used;"[1] and British officers write "that at least one half of the successful part of the slave trade is carried on under the American flag," and this because "the number of American cruisers on the station is so small, in proportion to the immense extent of the slave-dealing coast."[2] The fitting out of slavers became a flourishing business in the United States, and centred at New York City. "Few of our readers," writes a periodical of the day, "are aware of the extent to which this infernal traffic is carried on, by vessels clearing from New York, and in close alliance with our legitimate trade; and that down-town merchants of wealth and respectability are extensively engaged in buying and selling African Negroes, and have been, with comparatively little interruption, for an indefinite number of years."[3] Another periodical says: "The number of persons engaged in the slave-trade, and the amount of capital embarked in it, exceed our powers of calculation. The city of New York has been until of late [1862] the principal port of the world for this infamous commerce; although the cities of Portland and Boston are only second to her in that distinction. Slave dealers added largely to the wealth of our commercial metropolis; they contributed liberally to the treasuries of political organizations, and their bank accounts were largely depleted to carry elections in New Jersey, Pennsylvania, and Connecticut."[4] During eighteen months of the years 1859–1860 eighty-

[1] Gregory to the Secretary of the Navy, June 8, 1850: *Senate Exec. Doc.*, 31 Cong. 1 sess. XIV. No. 66, p. 2. Cf. *Ibid.*, 31 Cong. 2 sess. II. No. 6.

[2] Cumming to Commodore Fanshawe, Feb. 22, 1850: *Senate Exec. Doc.*, 31 Cong. 1 sess. XIV. No. 66, p. 8.

[3] New York *Journal of Commerce*, 1857; quoted in *24th Report of the Amer. Anti-slav. Soc.*, p. 56.

[4] "The Slave-Trade in New York," in the *Continental Monthly*, January, 1862, p. 87.

five slavers are reported to have been fitted out in New York harbor,[1] and these alone transported from 30,000 to 60,000 slaves annually.[2] The United States deputy marshal of that district declared in 1856 that the business of fitting out slavers "was never prosecuted with greater energy than at present. The occasional interposition of the legal authorities exercises no apparent influence for its suppression. It is seldom that one or more vessels cannot be designated at the wharves, respecting which there is evidence that she is either in or has been concerned in the Traffic."[3] On the coast of Africa "it is a well-known fact that most of the Slave ships which visit the river are sent from New York and New Orleans."[4]

The absence of United States war-ships at the Brazilian station enabled American smugglers to run in cargoes, in spite of the prohibitory law. One cargo of five hundred slaves was landed in 1852, and the *Correio Mercantil* regrets "that it was the flag of the United States which covered this act of piracy, sustained by citizens of that great nation."[5] When the Brazil trade declined, the illicit Cuban trade greatly increased, and the British consul reported: "Almost all the slave expeditions for some time past have been fitted out in the United States, chiefly at New York."[6]

88. **Notorious Infractions of the Laws.** This decade is especially noteworthy for the great increase of illegal importations into the South. These became bold, frequent, and notorious. Systematic introduction on a considerable scale probably commenced in the forties, although with great secrecy. "To have boldly ventured into New Orleans, with negroes freshly imported from Africa, would not only have

[1] New York *Evening Post*; quoted in Lalor, *Cyclopædia*, III. 733.

[2] Lalor, *Cyclopædia*, III. 733; quoted from a New York paper.

[3] *Friends' Appeal on behalf of the Coloured Races* (1858), Appendix, p. 41; quoted from the *Journal of Commerce*.

[4] *26th Report of the Amer. Anti-slav. Soc.*, pp. 53–4; quoted from the African correspondent of the Boston *Journal*. From April, 1857, to May, 1858, twenty-one of twenty-two slavers which were seized by British cruisers proved to be American, from New York, Boston, and New Orleans. Cf. *25th Report*, *Ibid.*, p. 122. De Bow estimated in 1856 that forty slavers cleared annually from Eastern harbors, clearing yearly $17,000,000: *De Bow's Review*, XXII. 430–1.

[5] *Senate Exec. Doc.*, 33 Cong. 1 sess. VIII. No. 47, p. 13.

[6] *House Exec. Doc.*, 34 Cong. 1 sess. XII. No. 105, p. 38.

brought down upon the head of the importer the vengeance of our very philanthropic Uncle Sam, but also the anathemas of the whole sect of philanthropists and negrophilists everywhere. To import them for years, however, into quiet places, evading with impunity the penalty of the law, and the ranting of the thin-skinned sympathizers with Africa, was gradually to popularize the traffic by creating a demand for laborers, and thus to pave the way for the *gradual revival of the slave trade*. To this end, a few men, bold and energetic, determined, ten or twelve years ago [1848 or 1850], to commence the business of importing negroes, slowly at first, but surely; and for this purpose they selected a few secluded places on the coast of Florida, Georgia and Texas, for the purpose of concealing their stock until it could be sold out. Without specifying other places, let me draw your attention to a deep and abrupt pocket or indentation in the coast of Texas, about thirty miles from Brazos Santiago. Into this pocket a slaver could run at any hour of the night, because there was no hindrance at the entrance, and here she could discharge her cargo of movables upon the projecting bluff, and again proceed to sea inside of three hours. The live stock thus landed could be marched a short distance across the main island, over a porous soil which refuses to retain the recent foot-prints, until they were again placed in boats, and were concealed upon some of the innumerable little islands which thicken on the waters of the Laguna in the rear. These islands, being covered with a thick growth of bushes and grass, offer an inscrutable hiding place for the 'black diamonds.' "[1] These methods became, however, toward 1860, too slow for the radicals, and the trade grew more defiant and open. The yacht "Wanderer," arrested on suspicion in New York and released, landed in Georgia six months later four hundred and twenty slaves, who were never recovered.[2] The Augusta *Despatch* says: "Citizens of our city are probably interested in the enterprise. It is hinted that this is the third cargo landed by the same company, during the

[1] New York *Herald*, Aug. 5, 1860; quoted in Drake, *Revelations of a Slave Smuggler*, Introd., pp. vii.–viii.

[2] *House Exec. Doc.*, 35 Cong. 2 sess. IX. No. 89. Cf. *26th Report of the Amer. Anti-slav. Soc.*, pp. 45–9.

last six months."[1] Two parties of Africans were brought into Mobile with impunity. One bark, strongly suspected of having landed a cargo of slaves, was seized on the Florida coast; another vessel was reported to be landing slaves near Mobile; a letter from Jacksonville, Florida, stated that a bark had left there for Africa to ship a cargo for Florida and Georgia.[2] Stephen A. Douglas said "that there was not the shadow of doubt that the Slave-trade had been carried on quite extensively for a long time back, and that there had been more Slaves imported into the southern States, during the last year, than had ever been imported before in any one year, even when the Slave-trade was legal. It was his confident belief, that over fifteen thousand Slaves had been brought into this country during the past year [1859.] He had seen, with his own eyes, three hundred of those recently-imported, miserable beings, in a Slave-pen in Vicksburg, Miss., and also large numbers at Memphis, Tenn."[3] It was currently reported that depots for these slaves existed in over twenty large cities and towns in the South, and an interested person boasted to a senator, about 1860, that "twelve vessels would discharge their living freight upon our shores within ninety days from the 1st of June last," and that between sixty and seventy cargoes had been successfully introduced in the last eighteen months.[4] The New York *Tribune* doubted the statement; but John C. Underwood, formerly of Virginia, wrote to the paper saying that he was satisfied that the correspondent was correct. "I have," he said, "had ample evidences of the fact, that reopening the African Slave-trade is a thing already accomplished, and the traffic is brisk, and rapidly increasing. In fact, the most vital question of the day is not the opening of this trade, but its suppression. The arrival of cargoes of negroes, fresh from Africa, in our southern ports, is an event of frequent occurrence."[5]

[1] Quoted in *26th Report of the Amer. Anti-slav. Soc.*, p. 46.

[2] For all the above cases, cf. *Ibid.*, p. 49.

[3] Quoted in *27th Report, Ibid.*, p. 20. Cf. *Report of the Secretary of the Navy*, 1859: *Senate Exec. Doc.*, 36 Cong. 1 sess. III. No. 2.

[4] *27th Report of the Amer. Anti-slav. Soc.*, p. 21.

[5] Quoted in *Ibid.*

Negroes, newly landed, were openly advertised for sale in the public press, and bids for additional importations made. In reply to one of these, the Mobile *Mercury* facetiously remarks: "Some negroes who never learned to talk English, went up the railroad the other day."[1] Congressmen declared on the floor of the House: "The slave trade may therefore be regarded as practically re-established;"[2] and petitions like that from the American Missionary Society recited the fact that "this piratical and illegal trade—this inhuman invasion of the rights of men,—this outrage on civilization and Christianity—this violation of the laws of God and man—is openly countenanced and encouraged by a portion of the citizens of some of the States of this Union."[3]

From such evidence it seems clear that the slave-trade laws, in spite of the efforts of the government, in spite even of much opposition to these extra-legal methods in the South itself, were grossly violated, if not nearly nullified, in the latter part of the decade 1850–1860.

89. **Apathy of the Federal Government.** During the decade there was some attempt at reactionary legislation, chiefly directed at the Treaty of Washington. June 13, 1854, Slidell, from the Committee on Foreign Relations, made an elaborate report to the Senate, advocating the abrogation of the 8th Article of that treaty, on the ground that it was costly, fatal

[1] Issue of July 22, 1860; quoted in Drake, *Revelations of a Slave Smuggler*, Introd., p. vi. The advertisement referred to was addressed to the "Ship-owners and Masters of our Mercantile Marine," and appeared in the Enterprise (Miss.) *Weekly News*, April 14, 1859. William S. Price and seventeen others state that they will "pay three hundred dollars per head for one thousand native Africans, between the ages of fourteen and twenty years, (of sexes equal,) likely, sound, and healthy, to be delivered within twelve months from this date, at some point accessible by land, between Pensacola, Fla., and Galveston, Texas; the contractors giving thirty days' notice as to time and place of delivery": Quoted in *26th Report of the Amer. Anti-slav. Soc.*, pp. 41–2.

[2] *Congressional Globe*, 35 Cong. 1 sess. p. 1362. Cf. the speech of a delegate from Georgia to the Democratic Convention at Charleston, 1860: "If any of you northern democrats will go home with me to my plantation, I will show you some darkies that I bought in Virginia, some in Delaware, some in Florida, and I will also show you the pure African, the noblest Roman of them all. I represent the African slave trade interest of my section:" Lalor, *Cyclopædia*, III. 733.

[3] *Senate Misc. Doc.*, 36 Cong. 1 sess. No. 8.

to the health of the sailors, and useless, as the trade had actually increased under its operation.[1] Both this and a similar attempt in the House failed,[2] as did also an attempt to substitute life imprisonment for the death penalty.[3] Most of the actual legislation naturally took the form of appropriations. In 1853 there was an attempt to appropriate $20,000.[4] This failed, and the appropriation of $8,000 in 1856 was the first for ten years.[5] The following year brought a similar appropriation,[6] and in 1859[7] and 1860[8] $75,000 and $40,000 respectively were appropriated. Of attempted legislation to strengthen the laws there was plenty: e. g., propositions to regulate the issue of sea-letters and the use of our flag;[9] to prevent the "coolie" trade, or the bringing in of "apprentices" or "African laborers;"[10] to stop the coastwise trade;[11] to assent to a Right of Search;[12] and to amend the Constitution by forever prohibiting the slave-trade.[13]

The efforts of the executive during this period were crim-

[1] *Senate Journal*, 34 Cong. 1–2 sess. pp. 396, 695–8; *Senate Reports*, 34 Cong. 1 sess. I. No. 195.

[2] *House Journal*, 31 Cong. 2 sess. p. 64. There was still another attempt by Sandidge. Cf. *26th Report of the Amer. Anti-Slav. Soc.*, p. 44.

[3] *Senate Journal*, 36 Cong. 1 sess. p. 274; *Congressional Globe*, 36 Cong. 1 sess. p. 1245.

[4] *Congressional Globe*, 32 Cong. 2 sess. p. 1072.

[5] I. e., since 1846: *Statutes at Large*, XI. 90.

[6] *Ibid.*, XI. 227.

[7] *Ibid.*, XI. 404.

[8] *Ibid.*, XII. 21.

[9] E. g., Clay's resolutions: *Congressional Globe*, 31 Cong. 2 sess. pp. 304–9. Clayton's resolutions: *Senate Journal*, 33 Cong. 1 sess. p. 404; *House Journal*, 33 Cong. 1 sess. pp. 1093, 1332–3; *Congressional Globe*, 33 Cong. 1 sess. pp. 1591–3, 2139. Seward's bill: *Senate Journal*, 33 Cong. 1 sess. pp. 448, 451.

[10] Mr. Blair of Missouri asked unanimous consent in Congress, Dec. 23, 1858, to a resolution instructing the Judiciary Committee to bring in such a bill; Houston of Alabama objected: *Congressional Globe*, 35 Cong. 2 sess. p. 198; *26th Report of the Amer. Anti-slav. Soc.*, p. 44.

[11] This was the object of attack in 1851 and 1853 by Giddings: *House Journal*, 32 Cong. 1 sess. p. 42; 33 Cong. 1 sess. p. 147. Cf. *House Journal*, 38 Cong. 1 sess. p. 46.

[12] By Mr. Wilson, March 20, 1860: *Senate Journal*, 36 Cong. 1 sess. p. 274.

[13] Four or five such attempts were made: Dec. 12, 1860, *House Journal*, 36 Cong. 2 sess. pp. 61–2; Jan. 7, 1861, *Congressional Globe*, 36 Cong. 2 sess. p. 279; Jan. 23, 1861, *Ibid.*, p. 527; Feb. 1, 1861, *Ibid.*, p. 690; Feb. 27, 1861, *Ibid.*, pp. 1243, 1259.

inally lax and negligent. "The General Government did not exert itself in good faith to carry out either its treaty stipulations or the legislation of Congress in regard to the matter. If a vessel was captured, her owners were permitted to bond her, and thus continue her in the trade; and if any man was convicted of this form of piracy, the executive always interposed between him and the penalty of his crime. The laws providing for the seizure of vessels engaged in the traffic were so constructed as to render the duty unremunerative; and marshals now find their fees for such services to be actually less than their necessary expenses. No one who bears this fact in mind will be surprised at the great indifference of these officers to the continuing of the slave-trade; in fact, he will be ready to learn that the laws of Congress upon the subject had become a dead letter, and that the suspicion was well grounded that certain officers of the Federal Government had actually connived at their violation."[1] From 1845 to 1854, in spite of the well-known activity of the trade, but five cases obtained cognizance in the New York district. Of these, Captains Mansfield and Driscoll forfeited their bonds of $5,000 each, and escaped; in the case of the notorious Canot, nothing had been done as late as 1856, although he was arrested in 1847; Captain Jefferson turned State's evidence, and, in the case of Captain Mathew, a *nolle prosequi* was entered.[2] Between 1854 and 1856 thirty-two persons were indicted in New York, of whom only thirteen had at the latter date been tried, and only one of these convicted.[3] These dismissals were seldom on account of insufficient evidence. In the notorious case of the "Wanderer," she was arrested on suspicion, released, and soon after she landed a cargo of slaves in Georgia; some who attempted to seize the Negroes were arrested for larceny, and in spite of the efforts of Congress the captain was never punished. The yacht was afterwards started on another voyage, and being brought back to Boston was sold to her former owner for about one third

[1] "The Slave-Trade in New York," in the *Continental Monthly*, January, 1862, p. 87.

[2] New York *Herald*, July 14, 1856.

[3] *Ibid.* Cf. *Senate Exec. Doc.*, 37 Cong. 2 sess. V. No. 53.

her value.[1] The bark "Emily" was seized on suspicion and released, and finally caught red-handed on the coast of Africa; she was sent to New York for trial, but "disappeared" under a certain slave captain, Townsend, who had, previous to this, in the face of the most convincing evidence, been acquitted at Key West.[2]

The squadron commanders of this time were by no means as efficient as their predecessors, and spent much of their time, apparently, in discussing the Right of Search. Instead of a number of small light vessels, which by the reports of experts were repeatedly shown to be the only efficient craft, the government, until 1859, persisted in sending out three or four great frigates. Even these did not attend faithfully to their duties. A letter from on board one of them shows that, out of a fifteen months' alleged service, only twenty-two days were spent on the usual cruising-ground for slavers, and thirteen of these at anchor; eleven months were spent at Madeira and Cape Verde Islands, 300 miles from the coast and 3,000 miles from the slave market.[3] British commanders report the apathy of American officers and the extreme caution of their instructions, which allowed many slavers to escape.[4]

The officials at Washington often remained in blissful, and perhaps willing, ignorance of the state of the trade. While Americans were smuggling slaves by the thousands into Brazil, and by the hundreds into the United States, Secretary Graham was recommending the abrogation of the 8th Article of the Treaty of Washington;[5] so, too, when the Cuban slave-trade was reaching unprecedented activity, and while slavers were being fitted out in every port on the Atlantic seaboard, Secretary Kennedy naïvely reports. "The time has come, perhaps, when it may be properly commended to the notice of Congress to inquire into the necessity of further continuing the regular employment of a squadron on this [i. e., the

[1] *27th Report of the Amer. Anti-slav. Soc.*, pp. 25–6. Cf. *26th Report*, *Ibid.*, pp. 45–9.

[2] *27th Report*, *Ibid.*, pp. 26–7.

[3] *26th Report*, *Ibid.*, p. 54.

[4] *British and Foreign State Papers*, 1859–60, pp. 899, 973.

[5] Nov. 29, 1851: *House Exec. Doc.*, 32 Cong. 1 sess. II. pt. 2, No. 2, p. 4.

African] coast."[1] Again, in 1855, the government has "advices that the slave trade south of the equator is entirely broken up;"[2] in 1856, the reports are "favorable;"[3] in 1857 a British commander writes: "No vessel has been seen here for one year, certainly; I think for nearly three years there have been no American cruizers on these waters, where a valuable and extensive American commerce is carried on. I cannot, therefore, but think that this continued absence of foreign cruizers looks as if they were intentionally withdrawn, and as if the Government did not care to take measures to prevent the American flag being used to cover Slave Trade transactions;"[4] nevertheless, in this same year, according to Secretary Toucey, "the force on the coast of Africa has fully accomplished its main object."[5] Finally, in the same month in which the "Wanderer" and her mates were openly landing cargoes in the South, President Buchanan, who seems to have been utterly devoid of a sense of humor, was urging the annexation of Cuba to the United States as the only method of suppressing the slave-trade![6]

About 1859 the frequent and notorious violations of our laws aroused even the Buchanan government; a larger appropriation was obtained, swift light steamers were employed, and, though we may well doubt whether after such a carnival illegal importations "entirely" ceased, as the President informed Congress,[7] yet some sincere efforts at suppression were certainly begun. From 1850 to 1859 we have few notices of captured slavers, but in 1860 the increased appropriation of the thirty-fifth Congress resulted in the capture of twelve ves-

[1] Dec. 4, 1852: *House Exec. Doc.*, 32 Cong. 2 sess. I. pt. 2, No. 1, p. 293.

[2] *Ibid.*, 34 Cong. 1 sess. I. pt. 3, No. 1, p. 5.

[3] *Ibid.*, 34 Cong. 3 sess. I. pt. 2, No. 1, p. 407.

[4] Commander Burgess to Commodore Wise, Whydah, Aug. 12, 1857: *Parliamentary Papers*, 1857–8, vol. LXI. *Slave Trade*, Class A, p. 136.

[5] *House Exec. Doc.*, 35 Cong. 1 sess. II. pt. 3, No. 2, p. 576.

[6] *Ibid.*, 35 Cong. 2 sess. II. pt. 1, No. 2, pp. 14–15, 31–33.

[7] *Senate Exec. Doc.*, 36 Cong. 2 sess. I. No. 1, p. 24. The Report of the Secretary of the Navy, 1859, contains this ambiguous passage: "What the effect of breaking up the trade will be upon the United States or Cuba it is not necessary to inquire; certainly, under the laws of Congress and our treaty obligations, it is the duty of the executive government to see that our citizens shall not be engaged in it": *Ibid.*, 36 Cong. 1 sess. III. No. 2, pp. 1138–9.

sels with 3,119 Africans.[1] The Act of June 16, 1860, enabled the President to contract with the Colonization Society for the return of recaptured Africans; and by a long-needed arrangement cruisers were to proceed direct to Africa with such cargoes, instead of first landing them in this country.[2]

90. **Attitude of the Southern Confederacy.** The attempt, initiated by the constitutional fathers, to separate the problem of slavery from that of the slave-trade had, after a trial of half a century, signally failed, and for well-defined economic reasons. The nation had at last come to the parting of the ways, one of which led to a free-labor system, the other to a slave system fed by the slave-trade. Both sections of the country naturally hesitated at the cross-roads: the North clung to the delusion that a territorially limited system of slavery, without a slave-trade, was still possible in the South; the South hesitated to fight for her logical object—slavery and free trade in Negroes—and, in her moral and economic dilemma, sought to make autonomy and the Constitution her object. The real line of contention was, however, fixed by years of development, and was unalterable by the present whims or wishes of the contestants, no matter how important or interesting these might be: the triumph of the North meant free labor; the triumph of the South meant slavery and the slave-trade.

It is doubtful if many of the Southern leaders ever deceived themselves by thinking that Southern slavery, as it then was, could long be maintained without a general or a partial reopening of the slave-trade. Many had openly declared this a few years before, and there was no reason for a change of opinion. Nevertheless, at the outbreak of actual war and secession, there were powerful and decisive reasons for relegating the question temporarily to the rear. In the first place, only by this means could the adherence of important Border States be secured, without the aid of which secession was folly. Secondly, while it did no harm to laud the independence of the South and the kingship of cotton in "stump" speeches and conventions, yet, when it came to actual hostilities, the South sorely needed the aid of Europe; and this a nation fighting for slavery and the slave-trade stood poor

[1] *Senate Exec. Doc.*, 36 Cong. 2 sess. III. pt. 1, No. 1, pp. 8–9.

[2] *Statutes at Large*, XII. 40.

chance of getting. Consequently, after attacking the slave-trade laws for a decade, and their execution for a quarter-century, we find the Southern leaders inserting, in both the provisional and the permanent Constitutions of the Confederate States, the following article:—

> The importation of negroes of the African race, from any foreign country other than the slaveholding States or Territories of the United States of America, is hereby forbidden; and Congress is required to pass such laws as shall effectually prevent the same.
>
> Congress shall also have power to prohibit the introduction of slaves from any State not a member of, or Territory not belonging to, this Confederacy.[1]

The attitude of the Confederate government toward this article is best illustrated by its circular of instructions to its foreign ministers:—

> It has been suggested to this Government, from a source of unquestioned authenticity, that, after the recognition of our independence by the European Powers, an expectation is generally entertained by them that in our treaties of amity and commerce a clause will be introduced making stipulations against the African slave trade. It is even thought that neutral Powers may be inclined to insist upon the insertion of such a clause as a *sine qua non*.
>
> You are well aware how firmly fixed in our Constitution is the policy of this Confederacy against the opening of that trade, but we are informed that false and insidious suggestions have been made by the agents of the United States at European Courts of our intention to change our constitution as soon as peace is restored, and of authorizing the importation of slaves from Africa. If, therefore, you should find, in your intercourse with the Cabinet to which you are accredited, that any such impressions are entertained, you will use every proper effort to remove them, and if an attempt is made to introduce into any treaty which you may be charged with negotiating stipulations on the subject just mentioned, you will assume, in behalf of your Government, the position which, under the direction of the President, I now proceed to develop.
>
> The Constitution of the Confederate States is an agreement made between independent States. By its terms all the powers of Government are separated into classes as follows, viz.:—

[1] *Confederate States of America Statutes at Large*, 1861, p. 15, Constitution, Art. 1, sect. 9, §§ 1, 2.

1st. Such powers as the States delegate to the General Government.

2d. Such powers as the States agree to refrain from exercising, although they do not delegate them to the General Government.

3d. Such powers as the States, without delegating them to the General Government, thought proper to exercise by direct agreement between themselves contained in the Constitution.

4th. All remaining powers of sovereignty, which not being delegated to the Confederate States by the Constitution nor prohibited by it to the States, are reserved to the States respectively, or to the people thereof. . . . Especially in relation to the importation of African negroes was it deemed important by the States that no power to permit it should exist in the Confederate Government. . . . It will thus be seen that no power is delegated to the Confederate Government over this subject, but that it is included in the third class above referred to, of powers exercised directly by the States. . . . This Government unequivocally and absolutely denies its possession of any power whatever over the subject, and cannot entertain any proposition in relation to it. . . . The policy of the Confederacy is as fixed and immutable on this subject as the imperfection of human nature permits human resolve to be. No additional agreements, treaties, or stipulations can commit these States to the prohibition of the African slave trade with more binding efficacy than those they have themselves devised. A just and generous confidence in their good faith on this subject exhibited by friendly Powers will be far more efficacious than persistent efforts to induce this Government to assume the exercise of powers which it does not possess. . . . We trust, therefore, that no unnecessary discussions on this matter will be introduced into your negotiations. If, unfortunately, this reliance should prove ill-founded, you will decline continuing negotiations on your side, and transfer them to us at home. . . .[1]

This attitude of the conservative leaders of the South, if it meant anything, meant that individual State action could, when it pleased, reopen the slave-trade. The radicals were, of course, not satisfied with any veiling of the ulterior purpose of the new slave republic, and attacked the constitutional pro-

[1] From an intercepted circular despatch from J. P. Benjamin, "Secretary of State," addressed in this particular instance to Hon. L. Q. C. Lamar, "Commissioner, etc., St. Petersburg, Russia," and dated Richmond, Jan. 15, 1863; published in the *National Intelligencer*, March 31, 1863; cf. also the issues of Feb. 19, 1861, April 2, 3, 25, 1863; also published in the pamphlet, *The African Slave-Trade: The Secret Purpose*, etc. The editors vouch for its authenticity, and state it to be in Benjamin's own handwriting.

vision violently. "If," said one, "the clause be carried into the permanent government, our whole movement is defeated. It will abolitionize the Border Slave States—it will brand our institution. Slavery cannot share a government with Democracy,—it cannot bear a brand upon it; thence another revolution . . . having achieved one revolution to escape democracy at the North, it must still achieve another to escape it at the South. That it will ultimately triumph none can doubt."[1]

91. **Attitude of the United States.** In the North, with all the hesitation in many matters, there existed unanimity in regard to the slave-trade; and the new Lincoln government ushered in the new policy of uncompromising suppression by hanging the first American slave-trader who ever suffered the extreme penalty of the law.[2] One of the earliest acts of President Lincoln was a step which had been necessary since 1808, but had never been taken, viz., the unification of the whole work of suppression into the hands of one responsible department. By an order, dated May 2, 1861, Caleb B. Smith, Secretary of the Interior, was charged with the execution of the slave-trade laws,[3] and he immediately began energetic work. Early in 1861, as soon as the withdrawal of the Southern members untied the hands of Congress, two appropriations of $900,000 each were made to suppress the slave trade, the first appropriations commensurate with the vastness of the task. These were followed by four appropriations of $17,000 each in the years 1863 to 1867, and two of $12,500 each in 1868 and 1869.[4] The first work of the new secretary was to obtain a corps of efficient assistants. To this end, he assembled all the marshals of the loyal seaboard States at New York, and gave

[1] L. W. Spratt of South Carolina, in the *Southern Literary Messenger*, June, 1861, XXXII. 414, 420. Cf. also the Charleston *Mercury*, Feb. 13, 1861, and the *National Intelligencer*, Feb. 19, 1861.

[2] Captain Gordon of the slaver "Erie;" condemned in the U. S. District Court for Southern New York in 1862. Cf. *Senate Exec. Doc.*, 37 Cong. 2 sess. I. No. 1, p. 13.

[3] *Ibid.*, pp. 453–4.

[4] *Statutes at Large*, XII. 132, 219, 639; XIII. 424; XIV. 226, 415; XV. 58, 321. The sum of $250,000 was also appropriated to return the slaves on the "Wildfire": *Ibid.*, XII. 40–41.

them instruction and opportunity to inspect actual slavers. Congress also, for the first time, offered them proper compensation.[1] The next six months showed the effect of this policy in the fact that five vessels were seized and condemned, and four slave-traders were convicted and suffered the penalty of their crimes. "This is probably the largest number [of convictions] ever obtained, and certainly the only ones for many years."[2]

Meantime the government opened negotiations with Great Britain, and the treaty of 1862 was signed June 7, and carried out by Act of Congress, July 11.[3] Specially commissioned war vessels of either government were by this agreement authorized to search merchant vessels on the high seas and specified coasts, and if they were found to be slavers, or, on account of their construction or equipment, were suspected to be such, they were to be sent for condemnation to one of the mixed courts established at New York, Sierra Leone, and the Cape of Good Hope. These courts, consisting of one judge and one arbitrator on the part of each government, were to judge the facts without appeal, and upon condemnation by them, the culprits were to be punished according to the laws of their respective countries. The area in which this Right of Search could be exercised was somewhat enlarged by an additional article to the treaty, signed in 1863. In 1870 the mixed courts were abolished, but the main part of the treaty was left in force. The Act of July 17, 1862, enabled the President to contract with foreign governments for the apprenticing of recaptured Africans in the West Indies,[4] and in 1864 the coastwise slave-trade was forever prohibited.[5] By these measures the trade was soon checked, and before the end of the war entirely suppressed.[6] The vigilance of the government, however, was not checked, and as late as 1866 a squadron of ten ships,

[1] *Statutes at Large*, XII. 368–9.

[2] *Senate Exec. Doc.*, 37 Cong. 2 sess. I. No. 1, pp. 453–4.

[3] *Statutes at Large*, XII. 531.

[4] For a time not exceeding five years: *Ibid.*, pp. 592–3.

[5] By section 9 of an appropriation act for civil expenses, July 2, 1864: *Ibid.*, XIII. 353.

[6] British officers attested this: *Diplomatic Correspondence*, 1862, p. 285.

with one hundred and thirteen guns, patrolled the slave coast.[1] Finally, the Thirteenth Amendment legally confirmed what the war had already accomplished, and slavery and the slave-trade fell at one blow.[2]

[1] *Report of the Secretary of the Navy*, 1866; *House Exec. Doc.*, 39 Cong. 2 sess. IV. p. 12.

[2] There were some later attempts to legislate. Sumner tried to repeal the Act of 1803: *Congressional Globe*, 41 Cong. 2 sess. pp. 2894, 2932, 4953, 5594. Banks introduced a bill to prohibit Americans owning or dealing in slaves abroad: *House Journal*, 42 Cong. 2 sess. p. 48. For the legislation of the Confederate States, cf. Mason, *Veto Power*, 2d ed., Appendix C, No. 1.

Chapter XII

THE ESSENTIALS IN THE STRUGGLE.

92. **How the Question Arose.** We have followed a chapter of history which is of peculiar interest to the sociologist. Here was a rich new land, the wealth of which was to be had in return for ordinary manual labor. Had the country been conceived of as existing primarily for the benefit of its actual inhabitants, it might have waited for natural increase or immigration to supply the needed hands; but both Europe and the earlier colonists themselves regarded this land as existing chiefly for the benefit of Europe, and as designed to be exploited, as rapidly and ruthlessly as possible, of the boundless wealth of its resources. This was the primary excuse for the rise of the African slave-trade to America.

Every experiment of such a kind, however, where the moral standard of a people is lowered for the sake of a material advantage, is dangerous in just such proportion as that advantage is great. In this case it was great. For at least a century, in the West Indies and the southern United States, agriculture flourished, trade increased, and English manufactures were nourished, in just such proportion as Americans stole Negroes and worked them to death. This advantage, to be sure, became much smaller in later times, and at one critical period was, at least in the Southern States, almost *nil*; but energetic efforts were wanting, and, before the nation was aware, slavery had seized a new and well-nigh immovable footing in the Cotton Kingdom.

The colonists averred with perfect truth that they did not commence this fatal traffic, but that it was imposed upon them from without. Nevertheless, all too soon did they lay aside scruples against it and hasten to share its material benefits. Even those who braved the rough Atlantic for the highest moral motives fell early victims to the allurements of this system. Thus, throughout colonial history, in spite of many honest attempts to stop the further pursuit of the slave-trade, we notice back of nearly all such attempts a certain moral apathy, an indisposition to attack the evil with the sharp weapons which its nature demanded. Consequently, there developed steadily, irresistibly, a vast social problem, which required two centuries and a half for a nation of trained European stock and boasted moral fibre to solve.

93. **The Moral Movement.** For the solution of this problem there were, roughly speaking, three classes of efforts made during this time,—moral, political, and economic: that is to say, efforts which sought directly to raise the moral standard of the nation; efforts which sought to stop the trade by legal enactment; efforts which sought to neutralize the economic advantages of the slave-trade. There is always a certain glamour about the idea of a nation rising up to crush an evil simply because it is wrong. Unfortunately, this can seldom be realized in real life; for the very existence of the evil usually argues a moral weakness in the very place where extraordinary moral strength is called for. This was the case in the early history of the colonies; and experience proved that an appeal to moral rectitude was unheard in Carolina when rice had become a great crop, and in Massachusetts when the rum-slave-traffic was paying a profit of 100%. That the various abolition societies and anti-slavery movements did heroic work in rousing the national conscience is certainly true; unfortunately, however, these movements were weakest at the most critical times. When, in 1774 and 1804, the material advantages of the slave-trade and the institution of slavery were least, it seemed possible that moral suasion might accomplish the abolition of both. A fatal spirit of temporizing, however, seized the nation at these points; and although the slave-trade was, largely for political reasons, forbidden, slavery was left untouched. Beyond this point, as years rolled by, it was found well-nigh impossible to rouse the moral sense of the nation. Even in the matter of enforcing its own laws and co-operating with the civilized world, a lethargy seized the country, and it did not awake until slavery was about to destroy it. Even then, after a long and earnest crusade, the national sense of

right did not rise to the entire abolition of slavery. It was only a peculiar and almost fortuitous commingling of moral, political, and economic motives that eventually crushed African slavery and its handmaid, the slave-trade in America.

94. **The Political Movement.** The political efforts to limit the slave-trade were the outcome partly of moral reprobation of the trade, partly of motives of expediency. This legislation was never such as wise and powerful rulers may make for a nation, with the ulterior purpose of calling in the respect which the nation has for law to aid in raising its standard of right. The colonial and national laws on the slave-trade merely registered, from time to time, the average public opinion concerning this traffic, and are therefore to be regarded as negative signs rather than as positive efforts. These signs were, from one point of view, evidences of moral awakening; they indicated slow, steady development of the idea that to steal even Negroes was wrong. From another point of view, these laws showed the fear of servile insurrection and the desire to ward off danger from the State; again, they often indicated a desire to appear well before the civilized world, and to rid the "land of the free" of the paradox of slavery. Representing such motives, the laws varied all the way from mere regulating acts to absolute prohibitions. On the whole, these acts were poorly conceived, loosely drawn, and wretchedly enforced. The systematic violation of the provisions of many of them led to a widespread belief that enforcement was, in the nature of the case, impossible; and thus, instead of marking ground already won, they were too often sources of distinct moral deterioration. Certainly the carnival of lawlessness that succeeded the Act of 1807, and that which preceded final suppression in 1861, were glaring examples of the failure of the efforts to suppress the slave-trade by mere law.

95. **The Economic Movement.** Economic measures against the trade were those which from the beginning had the best chance of success, but which were least tried. They included tariff measures; efforts to encourage the immigration of free laborers and the emigration of the slaves; measures for changing the character of Southern industry; and, finally, plans to restore the economic balance which slavery destroyed, by raising the condition of the slave to that of complete freedom

and responsibility. Like the political efforts, these rested in part on a moral basis; and, as legal enactments, they were also themselves often political measures. They differed, however, from purely moral and political efforts, in having as a main motive the economic gain which a substitution of free for slave labor promised.

The simplest form of such efforts was the revenue duty on slaves that existed in all the colonies. This developed into the prohibitive tariff, and into measures encouraging immigration or industrial improvements. The colonization movement was another form of these efforts; it was inadequately conceived, and not altogether sincere, but it had a sound, although in this case impracticable, economic basis. The one great measure which finally stopped the slave-trade forever was, naturally, the abolition of slavery, i. e., the giving to the Negro the right to sell his labor at a price consistent with his own welfare. The abolition of slavery itself, while due in part to direct moral appeal and political sagacity, was largely the result of the economic collapse of the large-farming slave system.

96. **The Lesson for Americans.** It may be doubted if ever before such political mistakes as the slavery compromises of the Constitutional Convention had such serious results, and yet, by a succession of unexpected accidents, still left a nation in position to work out its destiny. No American can study the connection of slavery with United States history, and not devoutly pray that his country may never have a similar social problem to solve, until it shows more capacity for such work than it has shown in the past. It is neither profitable nor in accordance with scientific truth to consider that whatever the constitutional fathers did was right, or that slavery was a plague sent from God and fated to be eliminated in due time. We must face the fact that this problem arose principally from the cupidity and carelessness of our ancestors. It was the plain duty of the colonies to crush the trade and the system in its infancy: they preferred to enrich themselves on its profits. It was the plain duty of a Revolution based upon "Liberty" to take steps toward the abolition of slavery: it preferred promises to straightforward action. It was the plain duty of the Constitutional Convention, in founding a new nation, to

compromise with a threatening social evil only in case its settlement would thereby be postponed to a more favorable time: this was not the case in the slavery and the slave-trade compromises; there never was a time in the history of America when the system had a slighter economic, political, and moral justification than in 1787; and yet with this real, existent, growing evil before their eyes, a bargain largely of dollars and cents was allowed to open the highway that led straight to the Civil War. Moreover, it was due to no wisdom and foresight on the part of the fathers that fortuitous circumstances made the result of that war what it was, nor was it due to exceptional philanthropy on the part of their descendants that that result included the abolition of slavery.

With the faith of the nation broken at the very outset, the system of slavery untouched, and twenty years' respite given to the slave-trade to feed and foster it, there began, with 1787, that system of bargaining, truckling, and compromising with a moral, political, and economic monstrosity, which makes the history of our dealing with slavery in the first half of the nineteenth century so discreditable to a great people. Each generation sought to shift its load upon the next, and the burden rolled on, until a generation came which was both too weak and too strong to bear it longer. One cannot, to be sure, demand of whole nations exceptional moral foresight and heroism; but a certain hard common-sense in facing the complicated phenomena of political life must be expected in every progressive people. In some respects we as a nation seem to lack this; we have the somewhat inchoate idea that we are not destined to be harassed with great social questions, and that even if we are, and fail to answer them, the fault is with the question and not with us. Consequently we often congratulate ourselves more on getting rid of a problem than on solving it. Such an attitude is dangerous; we have and shall have, as other peoples have had, critical, momentous, and pressing questions to answer. The riddle of the Sphinx may be postponed, it may be evasively answered now; sometime it must be fully answered.

It behooves the United States, therefore, in the interest both of scientific truth and of future social reform, carefully to study such chapters of her history as that of the suppression of the slave-trade. The most obvious question which this study suggests is: How far in a State can a recognized moral wrong safely be compromised? And although this chapter of history can give us no definite answer suited to the ever-varying aspects of political life, yet it would seem to warn any nation from allowing, through carelessness and moral cowardice, any social evil to grow. No persons would have seen the Civil War with more surprise and horror than the Revolutionists of 1776; yet from the small and apparently dying institution of their day arose the walled and castled Slave-Power. From this we may conclude that it behooves nations as well as men to do things at the very moment when they ought to be done.

APPENDIX A.

A CHRONOLOGICAL CONSPECTUS OF COLONIAL AND STATE LEGISLATION RESTRICTING THE AFRICAN SLAVE-TRADE.

1641–1787.

1641. Massachusetts: Limitations on Slavery.

"Liberties of Forreiners & Strangers": 91. "There shall never be any bond slaverie villinage or Captivitie amongst vs, unles it be lawfull Captives taken in iust warres, & such strangers as willingly selle themselves or are sold to us. And those shall have all the liberties & Christian usages w[ch] y[e] law of god established in Jsraell concerning such p/[sons] doeth morally require. This exempts none from servitude who shall be Judged there to by Authoritie."

"Capitall Laws": 10. "If any man stealeth aman or mankinde, he shall surely be put to death" (marginal reference, Exodus xxi. 16). Re-enacted in the codes of 1649, 1660, and 1672. Whitmore, *Reprint of Colonial Laws of 1660*, etc. (1889), pp. 52, 54, 71–117.

1642, April 3. New Netherland: Ten per cent Duty.

"Ordinance of the Director and Council of New Netherland, imposing certain Import and Export Duties." O'Callaghan, *Laws of New Netherland* (1868), p. 31.

1642, Dec. 1. Connecticut: Man-Stealing made a Capital Offence.

"Capitall Lawes," No. 10. Re-enacted in Ludlow's code, 1650. *Colonial Records*, I. 77.

1646, Nov. 4. Massachusetts: Declaration against Man-Stealing.

Testimony of the General Court. For text, see above, page 37. *Colonial Records*, II. 168; III. 84.

1652, April 4. New Netherland: Duty of 15 Guilders.

"Conditions and Regulations" of Trade to Africa. O'Callaghan, *Laws of New Netherland*, pp. 81, 127.

1652, May 18–20. Rhode Island: Perpetual Slavery Prohibited.

For text, see above, page 40. *Colonial Records*, I. 243.

1655, Aug. 6. New Netherland: Ten per cent Export Duty.

"Ordinance of the Director General and Council of New Netherland, imposing a Duty on exported Negroes." O'Callaghan, *Laws of New Netherland*, p. 191.

1664, March 12. Duke of York's Patent: Slavery Regulated.

"Lawes establisht by the Authority of his Majesties Letters patents, granted to his Royall Highnes James Duke of Yorke and Albany; Bearing Date the 12th Day of March in the Sixteenth year of the Raigne of our Soveraigne Lord Kinge Charles the Second." First published at Long Island in 1664.

"Bond slavery": "No Christian shall be kept in Bond-slavery villenage or Captivity, Except Such who shall be Judged thereunto by Authority, or such as willingly have sould, or shall sell themselves," etc. Apprenticeship allowed. *Charter to William Penn, and Laws of the Province of Pennsylvania* (1879), pp. 3, 12.

1672, October. Connecticut: Law against Man-Stealing.

"The General Laws and Liberties of Conecticut Colonie."

"Capital Laws": 10. "If any Man stealeth a Man or Man kinde, and selleth him, or if he be found in his hand, he shall be put to death. Exod. 21. 16." *Laws of Connecticut*, 1672 (repr. 1865), p. 9.

1676, March 3. West New Jersey: Slavery Prohibited (?).

"The Concessions and Agreements of the Proprietors, Freeholders and Inhabitants of the Province of West New-Jersey, in America."

Chap. XXIII. "That in all publick Courts of Justice for Tryals of Causes, Civil or Criminal, any Person or Persons, Inhabitants of the said Province, may freely come into, and attend the said Courts, . . . that all and every Person and Persons Inhabiting the said Province, shall, as far as in us lies, be free from Oppression and Slavery." Leaming and Spicer, *Grants, Concessions*, etc., pp. 382, 398.

1688, Feb. 18. Pennsylvania: First Protest of Friends against Slave-Trade.

"At Monthly Meeting of Germantown Friends." For text, see above, pages 28–29. *Fac-simile Copy* (1880).

1695, May. Maryland: 10s. Duty Act.

"An Act for the laying an Imposition upon Negroes, Slaves, and White Persons imported into this Province." Re-enacted in 1696, and included in Acts of 1699 and 1704. Bacon, *Laws*, 1695, ch. ix.; 1696, ch. vii.; 1699, ch. xxiii.; 1704, ch. ix.

1696. Pennsylvania: Protest of Friends.

"That Friends be careful not to encourage the bringing in of any more negroes." Bettle, *Notices of Negro Slavery*, in *Penn. Hist. Soc. Mem.* (1864), I. 383.

1698, Oct. 8. South Carolina: White Servants Encouraged.

"An Act for the Encouragement of the Importation of White Servants."

"Whereas, the great number of negroes which of late have been imported into this Collony may endanger the safety thereof if speedy care be not taken and encouragement given for the importation of white servants."

§ 1. £13 are to be given to any ship master for every male white servant (Irish excepted), between sixteen and forty years, whom he shall bring into Ashley river; and £12 for boys between twelve and sixteen years. Every servant must have at least four years to serve, and every boy seven years.

§ 3. Planters are to take servants in proportion of one to every six male Negroes above sixteen years.

§ 5. Servants are to be distributed by lot.

§ 8. This act to continue three years. Cooper, *Statutes*, II. 153.

1699, April. Virginia: 20s. Duty Act.

"An act for laying an imposition upon servants and slaves imported into this country, towards building the Capitoll." For three years; continued in

August, 1701, and April, 1704. Hening, *Statutes*, III. 193, 212, 225.

1703, May 6. South Carolina: Duty Act.

"An Act for the laying an Imposition on Furrs, Skinns, Liquors and other Goods and Merchandize, Imported into and Exported out of this part of this Province, for the raising of a Fund of Money towards defraying the publick charges and expenses of this Province, and paying the debts due for the Expedition against St. Augustine." 10*s.* on Africans and 20*s.* on others. Cooper, *Statutes*, II. 201.

1704, October. Maryland: 20s. Duty Act.

"An Act imposing Three Pence per Gallon on Rum and Wine, Brandy and Spirits; and Twenty Shillings per Poll for Negroes; for raising a Supply to defray the Public Charge of this Province; and Twenty Shillings per Poll on Irish Servants, to prevent the importing too great a Number of Irish Papists into this Province." Revived in 1708 and 1712. Bacon, *Laws*, 1704, ch. xxxiii.; 1708, ch. xvi.; 1712, ch. xxii.

1705, Jan. 12. Pennsylvania: 10s. Duty Act.

"An Act for Raising a Supply of Two pence half penny per Pound & ten shillings per Head. Also for Granting an Impost & laying on Sundry Liquors & negroes Imported into this Province for the Support of Governmt., & defraying the necessary Publick Charges in the Administration thereof." *Colonial Records* (1852), II. 232, No. 50.

1705, October. Virginia: 6d. Tax on Imported Slaves.

"An act for raising a publick revenue for the better support of the Government," etc. Similar tax by Act of October, 1710. Hening, *Statutes*, III. 344, 490.

1705, October. Virginia: 20s. Duty Act.

"An act for laying an Imposition upon Liquors and Slaves." For two years; re-enacted in October, 1710, for three years, and in October, 1712. *Ibid.*, III. 229, 482; IV. 30.

1705, Dec. 5. Massachusetts: £4 Duty Act.

"An act for the Better Preventing of a Spurious and Mixt Issue," etc.

§ 6. On and after May 1, 1706, every master importing Negroes shall enter his number, name, and sex in the impost office, and insert them in the bill of lading; he shall pay to the commissioner and receiver of the impost £4 per head for every such Negro. Both master and ship are to be security for the payment of the same.

§ 7. If the master neglect to enter the slaves, he shall forfeit £8 for each Negro, one-half to go to the informer and one-half to the government.

§ 8. If any Negro imported shall, within twelve months, be exported and sold in any other plantation, and a receipt from the collector there be shown, a drawback of the whole duty will be allowed. Like drawback will be allowed a purchaser, if any Negro sold die within six weeks after importation. *Mass. Province Laws, 1705–6*, ch. 10.

1708, February. Rhode Island: £3 Duty Act.

No title or text found. Slightly amended by Act of April, 1708; strengthened by Acts of February, 1712, and July 5, 1715; proceeds disposed of by Acts of July, 1715, October, 1717, and June, 1729. *Colonial Records*, IV. 34, 131–5, 138, 143, 191–3, 225, 423–4.

1709, Sept. 24. New York: £3 Duty Act.

"An Act for Laying a Duty on the Tonnage of Vessels and Slaves." A duty of £3 was laid on slaves not imported directly from their native country. Continued by Act of Oct. 30, 1710. *Acts of Assembly, 1691–1718*, pp. 97, 125, 134; Laws of New York, 1691–1773, p. 83.

1710, Dec. 28. Pennsylvania: 40s. Duty Act.

"An impost Act, laying a duty on Negroes, wine, rum and other spirits, cyder and vessels." Repealed by order in Council Feb. 20, 1713. Carey and Bioren, *Laws*, I. 82; Bettle, *Notices of Negro Slavery*, in *Penn. Hist. Soc. Mem.* (1864), I. 415.

1710. Virginia: £5 Duty Act.

"Intended to discourage the importation" of slaves. Title and text not found. Disallowed (?). *Governor Spotswood to the Lords of Trade*, in *Va. Hist. Soc. Coll.*, New Series, I. 52.

1711, July–Aug. New York: Act of 1709 Strengthened.

"An Act for the more effectual putting in Execution an Act of General Assembly, Intituled, An Act for Laying a Duty on the Tonnage of Vessels and Slaves." *Acts of Assembly, 1691–1718*, p. 134.

1711, December. New York: Bill to Increase Duty.

Bill for laying a further duty on slaves. Passed Assembly; lost in Council. *Doc. rel. Col. Hist. New York*, V. 293.

1711. Pennsylvania: Testimony of Quakers.

". . . the Yearly Meeting of Philadelphia, on a representation from the Quarterly Meeting of Chester, that the buying and encouraging the importation of negroes was still practised by some of the members of the society, again repeated and enforced the observance of the advice issued in 1696, and further directed all merchants and factors to write to their correspondents and discourage their sending any more negroes." Bettle, *Notices of Negro Slavery*, in *Penn. Hist. Soc. Mem.* (1864), I. 386.

1712, June 7. Pennsylvania: Prohibitive (?) Duty Act.

"A supplementary Act to an act, entituled, An impost act, laying a duty on Negroes, rum," etc. Disallowed by Great Britain, 1713. Carey and Bioren, *Laws*, I. 87, 88. Cf. *Colonial Records* (1852), II. 553.

1712, June 7. Pennsylvania: Prohibitive Duty Act.

"An act to prevent the Importation of Negroes and Indians into this Province."

"Whereas Divers Plots and Insurrections have frequently happened, not only in the Islands, but on the Main Land of *America*, by Negroes, which have been carried on so far that several of the Inhabitants have been thereby barbarously Murthered, an instance whereof we have lately had in our neighboring Colony of *New York*. And whereas the Importation of Indian Slaves hath given our Neighboring *Indians* in this Province some umbrage of Suspicion and Dis-satisfaction. For Prevention of all which for the future,

"*Be it Enacted* . . . , That from and after the Publication of this Act, upon the Importation of any Negro or Indian, by Land or Water, into this Province, there shall be paid by the Importer, Owner or Possessor thereof, the sum of *Twenty Pounds per head*, for every Negro or Indian so imported or brought in (except Negroes directly brought in from the *West India Islands* before the first Day of the Month called *August* next) unto the proper Officer herein after named, or that shall be appointed according to the Directions of this Act to receive the same," etc. Disallowed by Great Britain, 1713. *Laws of Pennsylvania, collected*, etc. (ed. 1714), p. 165; *Colonial Records* (1852), II. 553; Burge, *Commentaries*, I. 737, note; *Penn. Archives*, I. 162.

1713, March 11. New Jersey: £10 Duty Act.

"An Act for laying a Duty on Negro, Indian and Mulatto Slaves, imported and brought into this Province."

"*Be it Enacted* . . . , That every Person or Persons that shall hereafter Import or bring in, or cause to be imported or brought into this Province, any Negro Indian or Mulatto Slave or Slaves, every such Person or Persons so importing or bringing in, or causing to be imported or brought in, such Slave or Slaves, shall enter with one of the Collectors of her Majestie's Customs of this Province, every such Slave or Slaves, within Twenty Four Hours after such Slave or Slaves is so Imported, and pay the Sum of *Ten Pounds* Money as appointed by her Majesty's Proclamation, for each Slave so imported, or give sufficient Security that the said Sum of *Ten Pounds*, Money aforesaid, shall be well and truly paid within three Months after such Slave or Slaves are so imported, to the

Collector or his Deputy of the District into which such Slave or Slaves shall be imported, for the use of her Majesty, her Heirs and Successors, toward the Support of the Government of this Province." For seven years; violations incur forfeiture and sale of slaves at auction; slaves brought from elsewhere than Africa to pay £10, etc. *Laws and Acts of New Jersey, 1703–1717* (ed. 1717), p. 43; *N. J. Archives*, 1st Series, XIII. 516, 517, 520, 522, 523, 527, 532, 541.

1713, March 26. Great Britain and Spain: The Assiento.

"The Assiento, or Contract for allowing to the Subjects of Great Britain the Liberty of importing Negroes into the Spanish America. Signed by the Catholick King at Madrid, the 26th Day of March, 1713."

Art. I. "First then to procure, by this means, a mutual and reciprocal advantage to the sovereigns and subjects of both crowns, her British majesty does offer and undertake for the persons, whom she shall name and appoint, That they shall oblige and charge themselves with the bringing into the West-Indies of America, belonging to his catholick majesty, in the space of the said 30 years, to commence on the 1st day of May, 1713, and determine on the like day, which will be in the year 1743, *viz.* 144000 negroes, *Piezas de India*, of both sexes, and of all ages, at the rate of 4800 negroes, *Piezas de India*, in each of the said 30 years, with this condition, That the persons who shall go to the West-Indies to take care of the concerns of the assiento, shall avoid giving any offence, for in such case they shall be prosecuted and punished in the same manner, as they would have been in Spain, if the like misdemeanors had been committed there."

Art. II. Assientists to pay a duty of 33 pieces of eight (*Escudos*) for each Negro, which should include all duties.

Art. III. Assientists to advance to his Catholic Majesty

200,000 pieces of eight, which should be returned at the end of the first twenty years, etc. John Almon, *Treaties of Peace, Alliance, and Commerce, between Great-Britain and other Powers* (London, 1772), I. 83–107.

1713, July 13. Great Britain and Spain: Treaty of Utrecht.

"Treaty of Peace and Friendship between the most serene and most potent princess Anne, by the grace of God, Queen of Great Britain, France, and Ireland, Defender of the Faith, &c. and the most serene and most potent Prince Philip V. the Catholick King of Spain, concluded at Utrecht, the 2/13 Day of July, 1713."

Art. XII. "The Catholick King doth furthermore hereby give and grant to her Britannick majesty, and to the company of her subjects appointed for that purpose, as well the subjects of Spain, as all others, being excluded, the contract for introducing negroes into several parts of the dominions of his Catholick Majesty in America, commonly called *el Pacto de el Assiento de Negros*, for the space of thirty years successively, beginning from the first day of the month of May, in the year 1713, with the same conditions on which the French enjoyed it, or at any time might or ought to enjoy the same, together with a tract or tracts of Land to be allotted by the said Catholick King, and to be granted to the company aforesaid, commonly called *la Compania de el Assiento*, in some convenient place on the river of Plata, (no duties or revenues being payable by the said company on that account, during the time of the abovementioned contract, and no longer) and this settlement of the said society, or those tracts of land, shall be proper and sufficient for planting, and sowing, and for feeding cattle for the subsistence of those who are in the service of the said company, and of their negroes; and that the said negroes may be there kept in safety till they are sold; and moreover, that the ships belonging to the said company may come close to land, and be secure from any danger. But it shall always be lawful for the Catholick King, to appoint an officer in the said place or settlement, who may take care that nothing be done or practised contrary to his royal interests. And all who manage the affairs of the said company there, or belong to it, shall be subject to the inspection of the aforesaid officer, as to all matters relating to the tracts of land abovementioned. But if any doubts, difficulties, or controversies, should arise between the said officer and the managers for the said company, they shall be referred to the determination of the governor of Buenos Ayres. The Catholick King has been likewise pleased to grant to the said company, several other extraordinary advantages, which are more fully and amply explained in the contract of the Assiento, which was made and concluded at Madrid, the 26th day of the month of March, of this present year 1713. Which contract, or *Assiento de Negros*, and all the clauses, conditions, privileges and immunities contained therein, and which are not contrary to this article, are and shall be deemed, and taken to be, part of this treaty, in the same manner as if they had been here inserted word for word." John Almon, *Treaties of Peace, Alliance, and Commerce, between Great-Britain and other Powers*, I. 168–80.

1714, Feb. 18. South Carolina: Duty on American Slaves.

"An Act for laying an additional duty on all Negro Slaves imported into this Province from any part of America." Title quoted in Act of 1719, § 30, *q. v.*

1714, Dec. 18. South Carolina: Prohibitive Duty.

"An additional Act to an Act entitled 'An Act for the better Ordering and Governing Negroes and all other Slaves.' "

§ 9. "And *whereas*, the number of negroes do extremely increase in this Province, and through the afflicting providence of God, the white persons do not proportionably multiply, by reason whereof, the safety of the said Province is greatly endangered; for the prevention of which for the future,

"*Be it further enacted* by the authority aforesaid, That all negro slaves from twelve years old and upwards, imported into this part of this Province from any part of Africa, shall pay such additional duties as is hereafter named, that is to say:—that every merchant or other person whatsoever, who shall, six months after the ratification of this Act, import any negro slaves as aforesaid, shall, for every such slave, pay unto the public receiver for the time being, (within thirty days after such importation,) the sum of two pounds current money of this Province." Cooper, *Statutes*, VII. 365.

1715, Feb. 18. South Carolina: Duty on American Negroes.

"*An additional Act* to an act entitled *an act for raising the sum of £2000, of and from the estates real and personal of the inhabitants of this Province, ratified in open Assembly the 18th day of December, 1714*; and for laying an additional duty on all Negroe slaves imported into this Province from any part of America." Title only given. Grimké, *Public Laws*, p. xvi, No. 362.

1715, May 28. Pennsylvania: £5 Duty Act.

"An Act for laying a Duty on *Negroes* imported into this province." Disallowed by Great Britain, 1719. *Acts and Laws of Pennsylvania, 1715*, p. 270; *Colonial Records* (1852), III. 75–6; Chalmers, *Opinions*, II. 118.

1715, June 3. Maryland: 20s. Duty Act.

"An Act laying an Imposition on Negroes . . . ; and also on Irish Servants, to prevent the importing too great a Number of Irish Papists into this Province." Supplemented April 23, 1735, and July 25, 1754. *Compleat Collection of the Laws of Maryland* (ed. 1727), p. 157; Bacon, *Laws*, 1715, ch. xxxvi. § 8; 1735, ch. vi. §§ 1–3; *Acts of Assembly, 1754*, p. 10.

1716, June 30. South Carolina: £3 Duty Act.

"An Act for laying an Imposition on Liquors, Goods

and Merchandizes, Imported into and Exported out of this Province, for the raising of a Fund of Money towards the defraying the publick charges and expences of the Government." A duty of £3 was laid on African slaves, and £30 on American slaves. Cooper, *Statutes*, II. 649.

1716. New York: 5 oz. and 10 oz. plate Duty Act.

"An Act to Oblige all Vessels Trading into this Colony (except such as are therein excepted) to pay a certain Duty; and for the further Explanation and rendring more Effectual certain Clauses in an Act of General Assembly of this Colony, Intituled, An Act by which a Duty is laid on Negroes, and other Slaves, imported into this Colony." The act referred to is not to be found. *Acts of Assembly, 1691–1718*, p. 224.

1717, June 8. Maryland: Additional 20s. Duty Act.

"An Act for laying an Additional Duty of Twenty Shillings Current Money per Poll on all Irish Servants, . . . also, the Additional Duty of Twenty Shillings Current Money per Poll on all Negroes, for raising a Fund for the Use of Publick Schools," etc. Continued by Act of 1728. *Compleat Collection of the Laws of Maryland* (ed. 1727), p. 191; Bacon, *Laws*, 1728, ch. viii.

1717, Dec. 11. South Carolina: Prohibitive Duty.

"A further additional Act to an Act entitled An Act for the better ordering and governing of Negroes and all other Slaves; and to an additional Act to an Act entitled An Act for the better ordering and governing of Negroes and all other Slaves."

§ 3. "And *whereas*, the great importation of negroes to this Province, in proportion to the white inhabitants of the same, whereby the future safety of this Province will be greatly endangered; for the prevention whereof,

"*Be it enacted* by the authority aforesaid, That all negro slaves of any age or condition whatsoever, imported or otherwise brought into this Province, from any part of the world, shall pay such additional duties as is hereafter named, that is to say:—that every merchant or other person whatsoever, who shall, eighteen months after the ratification of this Act, import any negro slave as aforesaid, shall, for every such slave, pay unto the public receiver for the time being, at the time of each importation, over and above all the duties already charged on negroes, by any law in force in this Province, the additional sum of forty pounds current money of this Province," etc.

§ 4. This section on duties to be in force for four years after ratification, and thence to the end of the next session of the General Assembly. Cooper, *Statutes*, VII. 368.

1718, Feb. 22. Pennsylvania: Duty Act.

"An Act for continuing a duty on Negroes brought into this province." Carey and Bioren, *Laws*, I. 118.

1719, March 20. South Carolina: £10 Duty Act.

"An Act for laying an Imposition on Negroes, Liquors, and other Goods and Merchandizes, imported, and exported out of this Province, for the raising of a Fund of Money towards the defraying the Publick Charges and Expences of this Government; as also to Repeal several Duty Acts, and Clauses and Paragraphs of Acts, as is herein mentioned." This repeals former duty acts (e. g. that of 1714), and lays a duty of £10 on African slaves, and £30 on American slaves. Cooper, *Statutes*, III. 56.

1721, Sept. 21. South Carolina: £10 Duty Act.

"An Act for granting to His Majesty a Duty and Imposition on Negroes, Liquors, and other Goods and Merchandize, imported into and exported out of this Province." This was a continuation of the Act of 1719. *Ibid.*, III. 159.

1722, Feb. 23. South Carolina: £10 Duty Act.

"An Act for Granting to His Majesty a Duty and Imposition on Negroes, Liquors, and other Goods and Merchandizes, for the use of the Publick of this Province."

§ 1. " . . . on all negro slaves imported from Africa directly, or any other place whatsoever, Spanish negroes excepted, if above ten years of age, ten pounds; on all negroes under ten years of age, (sucking children excepted) five pounds," etc.

§ 3. "And whereas, it has proved to the detriment of some of the inhabitants of this Province, who have purchased negroes imported here from the Colonies of America, that they were either transported thence by the Courts of justice, or sent off by private persons for their ill behaviour and misdemeanours, to prevent which for the future,

"*Be it enacted* by the authority aforesaid, That all negroes imported in this Province from any part of America, after the ratification of this Act, above ten years of age, shall pay unto the Publick Receiver as a duty, the sum of fifty pounds, and all such negroes under the age of ten years, (sucking children excepted) the sum of five pounds of like current money, unless the owner or agent shall produce a testimonial under the hand and seal of any Notary Publick of the Colonies or plantations from whence such negroes came last, before whom it was proved upon oath, that the same are new negroes, and have not been six months on shoar in any part of America," etc.

§ 4. "And whereas, the importation of Spanish Indians, mustees, negroes, and mulattoes, may be of dangerous consequence by inticing the slaves belonging to the inhabitants of this Province to desert with them to the Spanish settlements near us,

"*Be it therefore enacted* That all such Spanish negroes, Indians, mustees, or mulattoes, so imported into this Province, shall pay unto the Publick Receiver, for the use of this Province, a duty of one hundred and fifty pounds, current money of this Province."

§ 19. Rebate of three-fourths of the duty allowed in case of re-exportation in six months.

§ 31. Act of 1721 repealed.

§ 36. This act to continue in force for three years, and thence to the end of the next session of the General Assembly, and no longer. Cooper, *Statutes*, III. 193.

1722, May 12. Pennsylvania: Duty Act.

"An Act for laying a duty on Negroes imported into this province." Carey and Bioren, *Laws*, I. 165.

1723, May. Virginia: Duty Act.

"An Act for laying a Duty on Liquors and Slaves." Title only; repealed by proclamation Oct. 27, 1724. Hening, *Statutes*, IV. 118.

1723, June 18. Rhode Island: Back Duties Collected.

Resolve appointing the attorney-general to collect back duties on Negroes. *Colonial Records*, IV. 330.

1726, March 5. Pennsylvania: £10 Duty Act.

"An Act for the better regulating of Negroes in this province." Carey and Bioren, *Laws*, I. 214; Bettle, *Notices of Negro Slavery*, in *Penn. Hist. Soc. Mem.* (1864), I. 388.

1726, March 5. Pennsylvania: Duty Act.

"An Act for laying a duty on Negroes imported into this province." Carey and Bioren, *Laws*, I. 213.

1727, February. Virginia: Prohibitive Duty Act (?).

"An Act for laying a Duty on Slaves imported; and for appointing a Treasurer." Title only found; the duty was probably prohibitive; it was enacted with a suspending clause, and was not assented to by the king. Hening, *Statutes*, IV. 182.

1728, Aug. 31. New York: £2 and £4 Duty Act.

"An Act to repeal some Parts and to continue and enforce other Parts of the Act therein mentioned, and for granting several Duties to His Majesty, for supporting His Government in the Colony of New York" from Sept. 1, 1728, to Sept. 1, 1733. Same duty continued by Act of 1732. *Laws of New York, 1691–1773*, pp. 148, 171; *Doc. rel. Col. Hist. New York*, VI. 32, 33, 34, 37, 38.

1728, Sept. 14. Massachusetts: Act of 1705 Strengthened.

"An Act more effectually to secure the Duty on the Importation of Negroes." For seven years; substantially the same law re-enacted Jan. 26, 1738, for ten years. *Mass. Province Laws, 1728–9*, ch. 16; *1738–9*, ch. 27.

1729, May 10. Pennsylvania: 40s. Duty Act.

"An Act for laying a Duty on Negroes imported into this Province." *Laws of Pennsylvania* (ed. 1742), p. 354, ch. 287.

1732, May. Rhode Island: Repeal of Act of 1712.

"Whereas, there was an act made and passed by the General Assembly, at their session, held at Newport, the 27th day of February, 1711 [O. S., N. S. = 1712], entitled 'An Act for laying a duty on negro slaves that shall be imported into this colony,' and this Assembly being directed by His Majesty's instructions to repeal the same;—

"Therefore, be it enacted by the General Assembly . . . that the said act . . . be, and it is hereby repealed, made null and void, and of none effect for the future." If this is the act mentioned under Act of 1708, the title is wrongly cited; if not, the act is lost. *Colonial Records*, IV. 471.

1732, May. Virginia: Five per cent Duty Act.

"An Act for laying a Duty upon Slaves, to be paid by the Buyers." For four years; continued and slightly amended by Acts of 1734, 1736, 1738, 1742, and 1745; revived February, 1752, and continued by Acts of November, 1753, February, 1759, November, 1766, and 1769; revived (or continued?) by Act of February, 1772, until 1778. Hening, *Statutes*, IV. 317, 394, 469; V. 28, 160, 318; VI. 217, 353; VII. 281; VIII. 190, 336, 530.

1734, November. New York: Duty Act.

"An act to lay a duty on Negroes & a tax on the Slaves therein mentioned during the time and for the uses within mentioned." The tax was 1*s.* yearly per slave. *Doc. rel. Col. Hist. New York*, VI. 38.

1734, Nov. 28. New York: £2 and £4 (?) Duty Act.

"An Act to lay a Duty on the Goods, and a Tax on the Slaves therein mentioned, during the Time, and for the Uses mentioned in the same." Possibly there were two acts this year. *Laws of New York, 1691–1773*, p. 186; *Doc. rel. Col. Hist. New York*, VI. 27.

1735. Georgia: Prohibitive Act.

An "act for rendering the colony of Georgia more defensible by prohibiting the importation and use of black slaves or negroes into the same." W. B. Stevens, *History of Georgia*, I. 311; [B. Martyn], *Account of the Progress of Georgia* (1741), pp. 9–10; Prince Hoare, *Memoirs of Granville Sharp* (London, 1820), p. 157.

1740, April 5. South Carolina: £100 Prohibitive Duty Act.

"An Act for the better strengthening of this Province, by granting to His Majesty certain taxes and impositions on the purchasers of Negroes imported," etc. The duty on slaves from America was £150. Continued to 1744. Cooper, *Statutes*, III. 556. Cf. *Abstract Evidence on Slave-Trade before Committee of House of Commons, 1790–91* (London, 1791), p. 150.

1740, May. Virginia: Additional Five per cent Duty Act.

"An Act, for laying an additional Duty upon Slaves, to be paid by the Buyer, for encouraging persons to enlist in his Majesty's service: And for preventing desertion." To continue until July 1, 1744. Hening, *Statutes*, V. 92.

1751, June 14. South Carolina: White Servants Encouraged.

"An Act for the better strengthening of this Province, by granting to His Majesty certain Taxes and Impositions on the purchasers of Negroes and other slaves imported, and for appropriating the same to the uses therein mentioned, and for granting to His Majesty a duty on Liquors and other Goods and Merchandize, for the uses therein mentioned, and for exempting the purchasers of Negroes and other slaves imported from payment of the Tax, and the Liquors and other Goods and Merchandize from the duties imposed by any former Act or Acts of the General Assembly of this Province."

"Whereas, the best way to prevent the mischiefs that may be attended by the great importation of negroes into this Province, will be to establish a method by which such importation should be made a necessary means of introducing a proportionable number of white inhabitants into the same; therefore for the effectual raising and appropriating a fund sufficient for the better settling of this Province with white inhabitants, we, his Majesty's most dutiful and loyal subjects, the House of Assembly now met in General Assembly, do cheerfully give and grant unto the King's most excellent Majesty, his heirs and successors, the several taxes and impositions hereinafter mentioned, for the uses and to be raised, appropriated, paid and applied as is hereinafter directed and appointed, and not otherwise, and do humbly pray his most sacred Majesty that it may be enacted,

§ 1. "*And be it enacted*, by his Excellency James Glen, Esquire, Governor in chief and Captain General in and over the Province of South Carolina, by and with the advice and consent of his Majesty's honorable Council, and the House of Assembly of the said Province, and by the authority of the same, That from and immediately after the passing of this Act, there shall be imposed on and paid by all and every the inhabitants of this Province, and other person and persons whosoever, first purchasing any negro or other slave, hereafter to be imported, a certain tax or sum of ten pounds current money for every such negro and other slave of the height of four feet two inches and upwards; and for every one under that height, and above three feet two inches, the sum of five pounds like money; and for all under three feet two inches, (sucking children excepted) two pounds and ten shillings like money, which every such inhabitant of this Province, and other person and persons whosoever shall so purchase or buy as aforesaid, which said sums of ten pounds and five pounds and two pounds and ten shillings respectively, shall be paid by such purchaser for every such slave, at the time of his, her or their purchasing of the same, to the public treasurer of this Province for the time being, for the uses hereinafter mentioned, set down and appointed, under pain of forfeiting all and every such negroes and slaves, for which the said taxes or impositions shall not be paid, pursuant to the directions of this Act, to be sued for, recovered and applied in the manner hereinafter directed."

§ 6. "*And be it further enacted* by the authority aforesaid, That the said tax hereby imposed on negroes and other slaves, paid or to be paid by or on the behalf of the purchasers as aforesaid, by virtue of this Act, shall be applied and appropriated as followeth, and to no other use, or in any other manner whatever, (that is to say) that three-fifth parts (the whole into five equal parts to be divided) of the net sum arising by the said tax, for and during the term of five years from the time of passing this Act, be applied and the same is hereby applied for payment of the sum of six pounds proclamation money to every poor foreign protestant whatever from Europe, or other poor protestant (his Majesty's subject) who shall produce a certificate under the seal of any corporation, or a certificate under the hands of the minister and church-wardens of any parish, or the minister and elders of any church, meeting or congregation in Great Britain or Ireland, of the good character of such poor protestant, above the age of twelve and under the age of fifty years, and for payment of the sum of three pounds like money, to every such poor protestant under the age of twelve and above the age of two years; who shall come into this Province within the first three years of the said term of five years, and settle on any part of the southern frontier lying between Pon Pon and Savannah rivers, or in the central parts of this Province," etc. For the last two years the bounty is £4 and £2.

§ 7. After the expiration of this term of five years, the sum is appropriated to the protestants settling anywhere in the State, and the bounty is £2 13*s.* 4*d.*, and £1 6*s.* 8*d.*

§ 8. One other fifth of the tax is appropriated to survey lands, and the remaining fifth as a bounty for ship-building, and for encouraging the settlement of ship-builders.

§ 14. Rebate of three-fourths of the tax allowed in case of re-exportation of the slaves in six months.

§ 16. "*And be it further enacted* by the authority aforesaid, That every person or persons who after the passing this Act shall purchase any slave or slaves which shall be brought or imported into this Province, either by land or water, from any of his Majesty's plantations or colonies in America, that have been in any such colony or plantation for the space of six months; and if such slave or slaves have not been so long in such colony or plantation, the importer shall be obliged to make oath or produce a proper certificate thereof, or otherwise every such importer shall pay a further tax or imposition of fifty pounds, over and besides the tax hereby imposed for every such slave which he or they shall purchase as aforesaid." Actual settlers bringing slaves are excepted.

§ 41. This act to continue in force ten years from its passage, and thence to the end of the next session of the General Assembly, and no longer. Cooper, *Statutes*, III. 739.

1753, Dec. 12. New York: 5 oz. and 10 oz. plate Duty Act.

"An Act for granting to His Majesty the several Duties and Impositions, on Goods, Wares and Merchandizes imported into this Colony, therein mentioned." Annually continued until 1767, or perhaps until 1774. *Laws of New York, 1752–62*, p. 21, ch. xxvii.; *Doc. rel. Col. Hist. New York*, VII. 907; VIII. 452.

1754, February. Virginia: Additional Five per cent Duty Act.

"An Act for the encouragement and protection of the settlers upon the waters of the Mississippi." For three years; continued in 1755 and 1763; revived in 1772, and continued until 1778. Hening, *Statutes*, VI. 417, 468; VII. 639; VIII. 530.

1754, July 25. Maryland: Additional 10s. Duty Act.

"An Act for his Majesty's Service." Bacon, *Laws*, 1754, ch. ix.

1755, May. Virginia: Additional Ten per cent Duty Act.

"An act to explain an act, intituled, An act for raising the sum of twenty thousand pounds, for the protection of his majesty's subjects, against the insults and encroachments of the French; and for other purposes therein mentioned."

§ 10. " . . . from and after the passing of this act, there shall be levied and paid to our sovereign lord the king, his heirs and successors, for all slaves imported, or brought into this colony and dominion for sale, either by land or water, from any part [port] or place whatsoever, by the buyer, or purchaser, after the rate of ten per centum, on the amount of each respective purchase, over and above the several duties already laid on slaves, imported as aforesaid, by an act or acts of Assembly, now subsisting, and also over and above the duty laid by" the Act of 1754. Repealed by Act of May, 1760, § 11, " . . . inasmuch as the same prevents the importation of slaves, and thereby lessens the fund arising from the duties upon slaves." Hening, *Statutes*, VI. 461; VII. 363. Cf. *Dinwiddie Papers*, II. 86.

1756, March 22. Maryland: Additional 20s. Duty Act.

"An Act for granting a Supply of Forty Thousand

Pounds, for his Majesty's Service," etc. For five years. Bacon, *Laws*, 1756, ch. v.

1757, April. Virginia: Additional Ten per cent Duty Act.

"An Act for granting an aid to his majesty for the better protection of this colony, and for other purposes therein mentioned."

§ 22. " . . . from and after the ninth day of July, one thousand seven hundred and fifty-eight, during the term of seven years, there shall be paid for all slaves imported into this colony, for sale, either by land or water, from any port or place whatsoever, by the buyer or purchaser thereof, after the rate of ten per centum on the amount of each respective purchase, over and above the several duties already laid upon slaves imported, as aforesaid, by any act or acts of Assembly now subsisting in this colony," etc. Repealed by Act of March, 1761, § 6, as being "found very inconvenient." Hening, *Statutes*, VII. 69, 383.

1759, November. Virginia: Twenty per cent Duty Act.

"An Act to oblige the persons bringing slaves into this colony from Maryland, Carolina, and the West-Indies, for their own use, to pay a duty."

§ 1. " . . . from and after the passing of this act, there shall be paid . . . for all slaves imported or brought into this colony and dominion from Maryland, North-Carolina, or any other place in America, by the owner or importer thereof, after the rate of twenty per centum on the amount of each respective purchase," etc. This act to continue until April 20, 1767; continued in 1766 and 1769, until 1773; altered by Act of 1772, *q. v. Ibid.*, VII. 338; VIII. 191, 336.

1760. South Carolina: Total Prohibition.

Text not found; act disallowed by Great Britain. Cf. Burge, *Commentaries*, I. 737, note; W. B. Stevens, *History of Georgia*, I. 286.

1761, March 14. Pennsylvania: £10 Duty Act.

"An Act for laying a duty on Negroes and Mulattoe slaves, imported into this province." Continued in

1768; repealed (or disallowed) in 1780. Carey and Bioren, *Laws*, I. 371, 451; *Acts of Assembly* (ed. 1782), p. 149; *Colonial Records* (1852),.VIII. 576.

1761, April 22. Pennsylvania: Prohibitive Duty Act.

"A Supplement to an act, entituled An Act for laying a duty on Negroes and Mulattoe slaves, imported into this province." Continued in 1768. Carey and Bioren, *Laws*, I. 371, 451; Bettle, *Notices of Negro Slavery*, in *Penn. Hist. Soc. Mem.* (1864), I. 388–9.

1763, Nov. 26. Maryland: Additional £2 Duty Act.

"An Act for imposing an additional Duty of Two Pounds per Poll on all Negroes Imported into this Province."

§ 1. All persons importing Negroes by land or water into this province, shall at the time of entry pay to the naval officer the sum of two pounds, current money, over and above the duties now payable by law, for every Negro so imported or brought in, on forfeiture of £10 current money for every Negro so brought in and not paid for. One half of the penalty is to go to the informer, the other half to the use of the county schools. The duty shall be collected, accounted for, and paid by the naval officers, in the same manner as former duties on Negroes.

§ 2. But persons removing from any other of his Majesty's dominions in order to settle and reside within this province, may import their slaves for carrying on their proper occupations at the time of removal, duty free.

§ 3. Importers of Negroes, exporting the same within two months of the time of their importation, on application to the naval officer shall be paid the aforesaid duty. Bacon, *Laws*, 1763, ch. xxviii.

1763 (circa). New Jersey: Prohibitive Duty Act.

"An Act for laying a duty on Negroes and Mulatto Slaves Imported into this Province." Disallowed (?) by Great Britain. *N. J. Archives*, IX. 345–6, 383, 447, 458.

1764, Aug. 25. South Carolina: Additional £100 Duty Act.

"An Act for laying an additional duty upon all Negroes hereafter to be imported into this Province, for the time therein mentioned, to be paid by the first purchasers of such Negroes." Cooper, *Statutes*, IV. 187.

1766, November. Virginia: Proposed Duty Act.

"An act for laying an additional duty upon slaves imported into this colony."

§ 1. " . . . from and after the passing of this act there shall be levied and paid . . . for all slaves imported or brought into this colony for sale, either by land or water from any port or place whatsoever, by the buyer or purchaser, after the rate of ten per centum on the amount of each respective purchase over and above the several duties already laid upon slaves imported or brought into this colony as aforesaid," etc. To be suspended until the king's consent is given, and then to continue seven years. The same act was passed again in 1769. Hening, *Statutes*, VIII. 237, 337.

1766. Rhode Island: Restrictive Measure (?).

Title and text not found. Cf. *Digest* of 1798, under "Slave Trade;" *Public Laws of Rhode Island* (revision of 1822), p. 441.

1768, Feb. 20. Pennsylvania: Re-enactment of Acts of 1761.

Titles only found. Dallas, *Laws*, I. 490; *Colonial Records* (1852), IX. 472, 637, 641.

1769, Nov. 16. New Jersey: £15 Duty Act.

"An Act for laying a Duty on the Purchasers of Slaves imported into this Colony."

"Whereas Duties on the Importation of Negroes in several of the neighbouring Colonies hath, on Experience, been found beneficial in the Introduction of sober, industrious Foreigners, to settle under His Majesty's Allegiance, and the promoting a Spirit of Industry among the Inhabitants in general: *In order therefore* to promote the same good Designs in this Government, and that such as choose to purchase Slaves may contribute some equitable Proportion of the publick Burdens," etc. A duty of "*Fifteen Pounds*, Proclamation Money, is laid." *Acts of Assembly* (Allinson, 1776), p. 315.

1769 (circa). Connecticut: Importation Prohibited (?).

Title and text not found. "Whereas, the increase of slaves is injurious to the poor, and inconvenient, therefore," etc. Fowler, *Historical Status of the Negro in Connecticut*, in *Local Law*, etc., p. 125.

1770. Rhode Island: Bill to Prohibit Importation.

Bill to prohibit importation of slaves fails. Arnold, *History of Rhode Island* (1859), II. 304, 321, 337.

1771, April 12. Massachusetts: Bill to Prevent Importation.

Bill passes both houses and fails of Governor Hutchinson's assent. *House Journal*, pp. 211, 215, 219, 228, 234, 236, 240, 242–3.

1771. Maryland: Additional £5 Duty Act.

"An Act for imposing a further additional duty of five pounds current money per poll on all negroes imported into this province." For seven years. *Laws of Maryland since 1763*: 1771, ch. vii.; cf. 1773, sess. Nov.–Dec., ch. xiv.

1772, April 1. Virginia: Address to the King.

" . . . The importation of slaves into the colonies from the coast of Africa hath long been considered as a trade of great inhumanity, and under its *present encouragement*, we have too much reason to fear *will endanger the very existence* of your majesty's American dominions. . . .

"Deeply impressed with these sentiments, we most humbly beseech your majesty to *remove all those restraints* on your majesty's governors of this colony, *which inhibit their assenting to such laws as might check so very pernicious a commerce*." *Journals of the House of Burgesses*, p. 131; quoted in Tucker, *Dissertation on Slavery* (repr. 1861), p. 43.

1773, Feb. 26. Pennsylvania: Additional £10 Duty Act.

"An Act for making perpetual the act . . . [of 1761] . . . and laying an additional duty on the said slaves." Dallas, *Laws*, I. 671; *Acts of Assembly* (ed. 1782), p. 149.

1774, March, June. Massachusetts: Bills to Prohibit Importation.

Two bills designed to prohibit the importation of slaves fail of the governor's assent. First bill: *General Court Records*, XXX. 248, 264; *Mass. Archives, Domestic Relations, 1643–1774*, IX. 457. Second bill: *General Court Records*, XXX. 308, 322.

1774, June. Rhode Island: Importation Restricted.

"An Act prohibiting the importation of Negroes into this Colony."

"Whereas, the inhabitants of America are generally engaged in the preservation of their own rights and liberties, among which, that of personal freedom must be considered as the greatest; as those who are desirous of enjoying all the advantages of liberty themselves, should be willing to extend personal liberty to others;—

"Therefore, be it enacted . . . that for the future, no negro or mulatto slave shall be brought into this colony; and in case any slave shall hereafter be brought in, he or she shall be, and are hereby, rendered immediately free, so far as respects personal freedom, and the enjoyment of private property, in the same manner as the native Indians."

"Provided that the slaves of settlers and travellers be excepted.

"Provided, also, that nothing in this act shall extend, or be deemed to extend, to any negro or mulatto slave brought from the coast of Africa, into the West Indies, on board any vessel belonging to this colony, and which negro or mulatto slave could not be disposed of in the West Indies, but shall be brought into this colony.

"Provided, that the owner of such negro or mulatto slave give bond to the general treasurer of the said colony, within ten days after such arrival in the sum of £100, lawful money, for each and every such negro or mulatto slave so brought in, that such negro or mulatto slave shall be exported out of the colony, within one year from the date of such bond; if such negro or mulatto be alive, and in a condition to be removed."

"Provided, also, that nothing in this act shall extend, or be deemed to extend, to any negro or mulatto slave that may be on board any vessel belonging to this colony, now at sea, in her present voyage." Heavy penalties are laid for bringing in Negroes in order to free them. *Colonial Records*, VII. 251–3.

[1784, February: "It is voted and resolved, that the whole of the clause contained in an act of this Assembly, passed at June session, A. D. 1774, permitting slaves brought from the coast of Africa into the West Indies, on board any vessel belonging to this (then colony, now) state, and who could not be disposed of in the West Indies, &c., be, and the same is, hereby repealed." *Colonial Records*, X. 8.]

1774, October. Connecticut: Importation Prohibited.

"An Act for prohibiting the Importation of Indian, Negro or Molatto Slaves."

" . . . no indian, negro or molatto Slave shall at any time hereafter be brought or imported into this Colony, by sea or land, from any place or places whatsoever, to be disposed of, left or sold within this Colony." This was re-enacted in the revision of 1784, and slaves born after 1784 were ordered to be emancipated at the age of twenty-five. *Colonial Records*, XIV. 329; *Acts and Laws of Connecticut* (ed. 1784), pp. 233–4.

1774. New Jersey: Proposed Prohibitive Duty.

"A Bill for laying a Duty on Indian, Negroe and Molatto Slaves, imported into this Colony." Passed the Assembly, and was rejected by the Council as "plainly" intending "an intire Prohibition," etc. *N. J. Archives*, 1st Series, VI. 222.

1775, March 27. Delaware: Bill to Prohibit Importation.

Passed the Assembly and was vetoed by the governor. Force, *American Archives*, 4th Series, II. 128–9.

1775, Nov. 23. Virginia: On Lord Dunmore's Proclamation.

Williamsburg Convention to the public: "Our Assemblies have repeatedly passed acts, laying heavy duties upon imported Negroes, by which they meant altogether to prevent the horrid traffick; but their humane intentions have been as often frustrated by the cruelty and covetousness of a set of *English* merchants." . . . The Americans would, if possible, "not only prevent any more Negroes from losing their freedom, but restore it to such as have already unhappily lost it." This is evidently addressed in part to Negroes, to keep them from joining the British. *Ibid.*, III. 1387.

1776, June 29. Virginia: Preamble to Frame of Government.

Blame for the slave-trade thrown on the king. See above, page 21. Hening, *Statutes*, IX. 112–3.

1776, Aug.–Sept. Delaware: Constitution.

"The Constitution or system of Government agreed to and resolved upon by the Representatives in full Convention of the Delaware State," etc.

§ 26. "No person hereafter imported into this State from *Africa* ought to be held in slavery on any pretence whatever; and no Negro, Indian, or Mulatto slave ought to be brought into this State, for sale, from any part of the world." Force, *American Archives*, 5th Series, I. 1174–9.

1777, July 2. Vermont: Slavery Condemned.

The first Constitution declares slavery a violation of "natural, inherent and unalienable rights." *Vermont State Papers, 1779–86*, p. 244.

1777. Maryland: Negro Duty Maintained.

"An Act concerning duties."

" . . . no duties imposed by act of assembly on any article or thing imported into or exported out of this state (except duties imposed on the importation of negroes), shall be taken or received within two years from the end of the present session of the general assembly." *Laws of Maryland since 1763*: 1777, sess. Feb.–Apr., ch. xviii.

1778, Sept. 7. Pennsylvania: Act to Collect Back Duties.

"An Act for the recovery of the duties on Negroes and Mulattoe slaves, which on the fourth day of July, one thousand seven hundred and seventy-six, were due to this state," etc. Dallas, *Laws*, I. 782.

1778, October. Virginia: Importation Prohibited.

"An act for preventing the farther importation of Slaves.

§ 1. "For preventing the farther importation of slaves into this commonwealth, *Be it enacted by the General Assembly*, That from and after the passing of this act no slave or slaves shall hereafter be imported into this commonwealth by sea or land, nor shall any slaves so imported be sold or bought by any person whatsoever.

§ 2. "Every person hereafter importing slaves into this commonwealth contrary to this act shall forfeit and pay the sum of one thousand pounds for every slave so imported, and every person selling or buying any such slaves shall in like manner forfeit and pay the sum of five hundred pounds for every slave so sold or bought," etc.

§ 3. "*And be it farther enacted*, That every slave imported into this commonwealth, contrary to the true intent and meaning of this act, shall, upon such importation become free."

§ 4. Exceptions are *bona fide* settlers with slaves not imported later than Nov. 1, 1778, nor intended to be sold; and transient travellers. Re-enacted in substance in the revision of October, 1785. For a temporary exception to this act, as concerns citizens of Georgia and South Carolina during the war, see Act of May, 1780. Hening, *Statutes*, IX. 471; X. 307; XII. 182.

1779, October. Rhode Island: Slave-Trade Restricted.

"An Act prohibiting slaves being sold out of the state, against their consent." Title only found. *Colonial Records*, VIII. 618; Arnold, *History of Rhode Island*, II. 449.

1779. Vermont: Importation Prohibited.

"An Act for securing the general privileges of the people," etc. The act abolished slavery. *Vermont State Papers, 1779–86*, p. 287.

1780. Massachusetts: Slavery Abolished.

Passage in the Constitution which was held by the courts to abolish slavery: "Art. I. All men are born free and equal, and have certain, natural, essential, and unalienable rights; among which may be reckoned the right of enjoying and defending their lives and liberties," etc. *Constitution of Massachusetts*, Part I., Art. 1; prefixed to *Perpetual Laws* (1789).

1780, March 1. Pennsylvania: Slavery Abolished.

"An Act for the gradual abolition of slavery."

§ 5. All slaves to be registered before Nov. 1.

§ 10. None but slaves "registered as aforesaid, shall, at any time hereafter, be deemed, adjudged, or holden, within the territories of this commonwealth, as slaves or servants for life, but as free men and free women; except the domestic slaves attending upon Delegates in Congress from the other American States," and those of travellers not remaining over six months, foreign ministers, etc., "provided such domestic slaves be not aliened or sold to any inhabitant," etc.

§ 11. Fugitive slaves from other states may be taken back.

§ 14. Former duty acts, etc., repealed. Dallas, *Laws*, I. 838. Cf. *Penn. Archives*, VII. 79; VIII. 720.

1783, April. Confederation: Slave-Trade in Treaty of 1783.

"To the earnest wish of Jay that British ships should have no right under the convention to carry into the states any slaves from any part of the world, it being the intention of the United States entirely to prohibit their importation, Fox answered promptly: 'If that be their policy, it never can be competent to us to dispute with them their own regulations.'" Fox to Hartley, June 10, 1783, in Bancroft, *History of the Constitution*, I. 61. Cf.

Sparks, *Diplomatic Correspondence*, X. 154, June, 1783.

1783. Maryland: Importation Prohibited.

"An Act to prohibit the bringing slaves into this state."

". . . it shall not be lawful, after the passing this act, to import or bring into this state, by land or water, any negro, mulatto, or other slave, for sale, or to reside within this state; and any person brought into this state as a slave contrary to this act, if a slave before, shall thereupon immediately cease to be a slave, and shall be free; provided that this act shall not prohibit any person, being a citizen of some one of the United States, coming into this state, with a *bona fide* intention of settling therein, and who shall actually reside within this state for one year at least, . . . to import or bring in any slave or slaves which before belonged to such person, and which slave or slaves had been an inhabitant of some one of the United States, for the space of three whole years next preceding such importation," etc. *Laws of Maryland since 1763*: 1783, sess. April–June, ch. xxiii.

1783, Aug. 13. South Carolina: £3 and £20 Duty Act.

"An Act for levying and collecting certain duties and imposts therein mentioned, in aid of the public revenue." Cooper, *Statutes*, IV. 576.

1784, February. Rhode Island: Manumission.

"An Act authorizing the manumission of negroes, mulattoes, and others, and for the gradual abolition of slavery." Persons born after March, 1784, to be free. Bill framed pursuant to a petition of Quakers. *Colonial Records*, X. 7–8; Arnold, *History of Rhode Island*, II. 503.

1784, March 26. South Carolina: £3 and £5 Duty Act.

"An Act for levying and collecting certain Duties," etc. Cooper, *Statutes*, IV. 607.

1785, April 12. New York: Partial Prohibition.

"An Act granting a bounty on hemp to be raised

within this State, and imposing an additional duty on sundry articles of merchandise, and for other purposes therein mentioned."

" . . . *And be it further enacted by the authority aforesaid*, That if any negro or other person to be imported or brought into this State from any of the United States or from any other place or country after the first day of June next, shall be sold as a slave or slaves within this State, the seller or his or her factor or agent, shall be deemed guilty of a public offence, and shall for every such offence forfeit the sum of one hundred pounds lawful money of New York, to be recovered by any person," etc.

"*And be it further enacted* . . . That every such person imported or brought into this State and sold contrary to the true intent and meaning of this act shall be freed." *Laws of New York, 1785–88* (ed. 1886), pp. 120–21.

1785. Rhode Island: Restrictive Measure (?).

Title and text not found. Cf. *Public Laws of Rhode Island* (revision of 1822), p. 441.

1786, March 2. New Jersey: Importation Prohibited.

"An Act to prevent the importation of Slaves into the State of New Jersey, and to authorize the Manumission of them under certain restrictions, and to prevent the Abuse of Slaves."

"Whereas the Principles of Justice and Humanity require that the barbarous Custom of bringing the unoffending African from his native Country and Connections into a State of Slavery ought to be discountenanced, and as soon as possible prevented; and sound Policy also requires, in order to afford ample Support to such of the Community as depend upon their Labour for their daily Subsistence, that the Importation of Slaves into this State from any other State or Country whatsoever, ought to be prohibited under certain Restrictions; and that such as are under Servitude in the State ought to be protected by Law from those Exercises of Wanton Cruelty too often practiced upon them; and that every unnecessary Obstruction in the Way of freeing Slaves should be removed; therefore,

§ 1. "*Be it Enacted by the Council and General Assembly of this State, and it is hereby Enacted by the Authority of the same*, That from and after the Publication of this Act, it shall not be lawful for any Person or Persons whatsoever to bring into this State, either for Sale or for Servitude, any Negro Slave brought from Africa since the Year Seventeen Hundred and Seventy-six; and every Person offending by bringing into this State any such Negro Slave shall, for each Slave, forfeit and Pay the Sum of Fifty Pounds, to be sued for and recovered with Costs by the Collector of the Township into which such Slave shall be brought, to be applied when recovered to the Use of the State.

§ 2. "*And be it further Enacted by the Authority aforesaid*, That if any Person shall either bring or procure to be brought into this State, any Negro or Mulatto Slave, who shall not have been born in or brought from Africa since the Year above mentioned, and either sell or buy, or cause such Negro or Mulatto Slave to be sold or remain in this State, for the Space of six Months, every such Person so bringing or procuring to be brought or selling or purchasing such Slave, not born in or brought from Africa since the Year aforesaid, shall for every such Slave, forfeit and pay the Sum of Twenty Pounds, to be sued for and recovered with Costs by the Collector of the Township into which such Slave shall be brought or remain after the Time limited for that Purpose, the Forfeiture to be applied to the Use of the State as aforesaid.

§ 3. "*Provided always, and be it further Enacted by the Authority aforesaid*, That Nothing in this Act contained shall be construed to prevent any Person who shall remove into the State, to take a settled Residence here, from bringing all his or her Slaves without incurring the Penalties aforesaid, excepting such Slaves as shall have been brought from Africa since the Year first above mentioned, or to prevent any Foreigners or others having only a temporary Residence in this State, for the Purpose of transacting any particular Business, or on their Travels, from bringing and employing such Slaves as Servants, during the Time of his or her Stay here, provided such Slaves shall not be sold or disposed of in this State." *Acts of the Tenth General Assembly* (Tower Collection of Laws).

1786, Oct. 30. Vermont: External Trade Prohibited.

"An act to prevent the sale and transportation of Negroes and Molattoes out of this State." £100 penalty. *Statutes of Vermont* (ed. 1787), p. 105.

1786. North Carolina: Prohibitive Duty.

"An act to impose a duty on all slaves brought into this state by land or water."

"Whereas the importation of slaves into this state is productive of evil consequences, and highly impolitic," etc. A prohibitive duty is imposed. The exact text was not found.

§ 6. Slaves introduced from States which have passed emancipation acts are to be returned in three months; if not, a bond of £50 is to be forfeited, and a fine of £100 imposed.

§ 8. Act to take effect next Feb. 1; repealed by Act of 1790, ch. 18. Martin, *Iredell's Acts of Assembly*, I. 413, 492.

1787, Feb. 3. Delaware: Exportation Prohibited.

"An Act to prevent the exportation of slaves, and for other purposes." *Laws of Delaware* (ed. 1797), p. 884, ch. 145 b.

1787, March 28. South Carolina: Total Prohibition.

"An Act to regulate the recovery and payment of debts and for prohibiting the importation of negroes for the time therein mentioned." Title only given. Grimké, *Public Laws*, p. lxviii, No. 1485.

1787, March 28. South Carolina: Importation Prohibited.

"An Ordinance to impose a Penalty on any person

who shall import into this State any Negroes, contrary to the Instalment Act."

1. "*Be it ordained*, by the honorable the Senate and House of Representatives, met in General Assembly, and by the authority of the same, That any person importing or bringing into this State a negro slave, contrary to the Act to regulate the recovery of debts and prohibiting the importation of negroes, shall, besides the forfeiture of such negro or slave, be liable to a penalty of one hundred pounds, to the use of the State, for every such negro or slave so imported and brought in, in addition to the forfeiture in and by the said Act prescribed." Cooper, *Statutes*, VII. 430.

1787, October. Rhode Island: Importation Prohibited.

"An act to prevent the slave trade and to encourage the abolition of slavery." This act prohibited and censured trade under penalty of £100 for each person and £1,000 for each vessel. Bartlett, *Index to the Printed Acts and Resolves*, p. 333; *Narragansett Historical Register*, II. 298–9.

APPENDIX B.

A CHRONOLOGICAL CONSPECTUS OF STATE, NATIONAL, AND INTERNATIONAL LEGISLATION.

1788–1871.

As the State statutes and Congressional reports and bills are difficult to find, the significant parts of such documents are printed in full. In the case of national statutes and treaties, the texts may easily be found through the references.

1788, Feb. 22. New York: Slave-Trade Prohibited.

"An Act concerning slaves."

"Whereas in consequence of the act directing a revision of the laws of this State, it is expedient that the several existing laws relative to slaves, should be revised, and comprized in one. Therefore, *Be it enacted*," etc.

"And to prevent the further importation of slaves into this State, *Be it further enacted by the authority aforesaid*, That if any person shall sell as a slave within this State any negro, or other person, who has been imported or brought into this State, after" June 1, 1785, "such seller, or his or her factor or agent, making such sale, shall be deemed guilty of a public offence, and shall for every such offence, forfeit the sum of one hundred pounds. . . . *And further*, That every person so imported . . . shall be free." The purchase of slaves for removal to another State is prohibited under penalty of £100. *Laws of New York, 1785–88* (ed. 1886), pp. 675–6.

1788, March 25. Massachusetts: Slave-Trade Prohibited.

"An Act to prevent the Slave-Trade, and for granting Relief to the Families of such unhappy Persons as may be kidnapped or decoyed away from this Commonwealth."

"Whereas by the African trade for slaves, the lives and liberties of many innocent persons have been from time to time sacrificed to the lust of gain: And whereas some persons residing in this Commonwealth may be so regardless of the rights of human kind, as to be concerned in that unrighteous commerce:

§ 1. "Be it therefore enacted by the Senate and House of Representatives, in General Court assembled, and by the authority of the same, That no citizen of this Commonwealth, or other person residing within the same, shall for himself, or any other person whatsoever, either as master, factor, supercargo, owner or hirer, in whole or in part, of any vessel, directly or indirectly, import or transport, or buy or sell, or receive on board, his or their vessel, with intent to cause to be imported or transported, any of the inhabitants of any State or Kingdom, in that part of the world called *Africa*, as slaves, or as servants for term of years." Any person convicted of doing this shall forfeit and pay the sum of £50 for every person received on board, and the sum of £200 for every vessel fitted out for the trade, "to be recovered by action of debt, in any Court within this Commonwealth, proper to try the same; the one moiety thereof to the use of this Commonwealth, and the other moiety to the person who shall prosecute for and recover the same."

§ 2. All insurance on said vessels and cargo shall be null and void; "and this act may be given in evidence under the general issue, in any suit or action commenced for the recovery of insurance so made," etc.

§ 4. "*Provided* . . . That this act do not extend to vessels which have already sailed, their owners, factors, or commanders, for and during their present voyage, or to any insurance that shall have been made, previous to the passing of the same." *Perpetual Laws of Massachusetts, 1780–89* (ed. 1789), p. 235.

1788, March 29. Pennsylvania: Slave-Trade Prohibited.

"An Act to explain and amend an act, entituled, 'An Act for the gradual abolition of slavery.' "

§ 2. Slaves brought in by persons intending to settle shall be free.

§ 3. " . . . no negro or mulatto slave, or servant for term of years," except servants of congressmen, consuls, etc., "shall be removed out of this state, with the design and intention that the place of abode or residence of such slave or servant shall be thereby altered or changed, or with the design and intention that such slave or servant, if a female, and pregnant, shall be detained and kept out of this state till her delivery of the child of which she is or shall be pregnant, or with the design and intention that such slave or servant shall be brought again into this state, after the expiration of six months from the time of such slave or servant having been first brought into this state, without his or her consent, if of full age, testified upon a private examination, before two Justices of the peace of the city or county in which he or she shall reside, or, being under the age of twenty-one years, without his or her consent, testified in manner aforesaid, and also without the consent of his or her parents," etc. Penalty for every such offence, £75.

§ 5. " . . . if any person or persons shall build, fit, equip, man, or otherwise prepare any ship or vessel, within any port of this state, or shall cause any ship or other vessel to sail from any port of this state, for the purpose of carrying on a trade or traffic in slaves, to, from, or between Europe, Asia, Africa or America, or any places or countries whatever, or of transporting slaves to or from one port or place to another, in any part or parts of the world, such ship or vessel, her tackle, furniture, apparel, and other appurtenances, shall be forfeited to the commonwealth. . . . And, moreover, all and every person and persons so building, fitting out," etc., shall forfeit £1000. Dallas, *Laws*, II. 586.

1788, October. Connecticut: Slave-Trade Prohibited.

"An Act to prevent the Slave-Trade."

"*Be it enacted by the Governor, Council and Representatives in General Court assembled, and by the Authority of the same*, That no Citizen or Inhabitant of this State, shall for himself, or any other Person, either as Master, Factor, Supercargo, Owner or Hirer, in Whole, or in Part, of any Vessel, directly or indirectly, import or transport, or buy or sell, or receive on board his or her Vessel, with Intent to cause to be imported or transported, any of the Inhabitants of any Country in Africa, as Slaves or Servants, for Term of Years; upon Penalty of *Fifty Pounds*, for every Person so received on board, as aforesaid; and of *Five Hundred Pounds* for every such Vessel employed in the Importation or Transportation aforesaid; to be recovered by Action, Bill, Plaint or Information; the one Half to the Plaintiff, and the other Half to the Use of this State." And all insurance on vessels and slaves shall be void. This act to be given as evidence under general issue, in any suit commenced for recovery of such insurance.

". . . if any Person shall kidnap . . . any free Negro," etc., inhabitant of this State, he shall forfeit £100. Every vessel clearing for the coast of Africa or any other part of the world, and suspected to be in the slave-trade, must give bond in £1000. Slightly amended in 1789. *Acts and Laws of Connecticut* (ed. 1784), pp. 368–9, 388.

1788, Nov. 4. South Carolina: Temporary Prohibition.

"An Act to regulate the Payment and Recovery of Debts, and to prohibit the Importation of Negroes, for the Time therein limited."

§ 16. "No negro or other slave shall be imported or brought into this State either by land or water on or before the first of January, 1793, under the penalty of forfeiting every such slave or slaves to any person who will sue or inform for the same; and under further penalty of paying £100 to the use of the State for every such negro or slave so imported or brought in: *Provided*, That nothing in this prohibition contained shall extend to such slaves as are now the property of citizens of the United States, and at the time of passing this act shall be within the limits of the said United States.

§ 17. "All former instalment laws, and an ordinance imposing a penalty on persons importing negroes into this State, passed the 28th day of March 1787, are hereby repealed." Grimké, *Public Laws*, p. 466.

1789, Feb. 3. Delaware: Slave-Trade Prohibited.

"*An additional Supplementary* ACT *to an act, intituled*, An act to prevent the exportation of slaves, and for other purposes."

"Whereas it is inconsistent with that spirit of general liberty which pervades the constitution of this state, that vessels should be fitted out, or equipped, in any of the ports thereof, for the purpose of receiving and transporting the natives of Africa to places where they are held in slavery; or that any acts should be deemed lawful, which tend to encourage or promote such iniquitous traffic among us:

§ 1. "*Be it therefore enacted by the General Assembly of Delaware*, That if any owner or owners, master, agent, or factor, shall fit out, equip, man, or otherwise prepare, any ship or vessel within any port or place in this state, or shall cause any ship, or other vessel, to sail from any port or place in this state, for the purpose of carrying on a trade or traffic in slaves, to, from, or between, Europe, Asia, Africa, or America, or any places or countries whatever, or of transporting slaves to, or from, one port or place to another, in any part or parts of the world; such ship or vessel, her tackle, furniture, apparel, and other appurtenances, shall be forfeited to this state. . . . And moreover, all and every person and persons so fitting out . . . any ship or vessel . . . shall severally forfeit and pay the sum of Five Hundred Pounds;" one-half to the state, and one-half to the informer.

§ 2. "*And whereas* it has been found by experience, that the act, intituled, *An act to prevent the exportation of slaves, and for other purposes*, has not produced all the good effects expected therefrom," any one exporting a slave to Maryland, Virginia, North Carolina, South Carolina, Georgia, or the West Indies, without license, shall forfeit £100 for each slave exported and £20 for each attempt.

§ 3. Slaves to be tried by jury for capital offences. *Laws of Delaware* (ed. 1797), p. 942, ch. 194 b.

1789, May 13. Congress (House): Proposed Duty on Slaves Imported.

A tax of $10 per head on slaves imported, moved by Parker of Virginia. After debate, withdrawn. *Annals of Cong.*, 1 Cong. 1 sess. pp. 336–42.

1789, Sept. 19. Congress (House): Bill to Tax Slaves Imported.

A committee under Parker of Virginia reports, "a bill concerning the importation of certain persons prior to the year 1808." Read once and postponed until next session. *House Journal* (repr. 1826), 1 Cong. 1 sess. I. 37, 114; *Annals of Cong.*, 1 Cong. 1 sess., pp. 366, 903.

1790, March 22. Congress (House): Declaration of Powers.

See above, pages 82–83.

1790, March 22. New York: Amendment of Act of 1788.

"An Act to amend the act entitled 'An act concerning slaves.' "

"Whereas many inconveniences have arisen from the prohibiting the exporting of slaves from this State. Therefore

"*Be it enacted* . . . , That where any slave shall hereafter be convicted of a crime under the degree of a capital offence, in the supreme court, or the court of oyer and terminer, and general gaol delivery, or a court of general sessions of the peace within this State, it shall and may be lawful to and for the master or mistress to cause such slave to be transported out of this State," etc. *Laws of New York, 1789–96* (ed. 1886), p. 151.

1792, May. Connecticut: Act of 1788 Strengthened.

"An Act in addition to an Act, entitled 'An Act to prevent the Slave Trade.' "

This provided that persons directly or indirectly aiding or assisting in slave-trading should be fined £100. All notes, bonds, mortgages, etc., of any kind, made or executed in payment for any slave imported contrary to this act, are declared null and void. Persons removing from the State might carry away their slaves. *Acts and Laws of Connecticut* (ed. 1784), pp. 412–3.

1792, Dec. 17. Virginia: Revision of Acts.

"An Act to reduce into one, the several acts concerning slaves, free negroes, and mulattoes."

§ 1. "*Be it enacted* . . . , That no persons shall henceforth be slaves within this commonwealth, except such as were so on the seventeenth day of October," 1785, "and the descendants of the females of them.

§ 2. "Slaves which shall hereafter be brought into this commonwealth, and kept therein one whole year together, or so long at different times as shall amount to one year, shall be free."

§ 4. "*Provided*, That nothing in this act contained, shall be construed to extend to those who may incline to remove from any of the United States and become citizens of this, if within sixty days after such removal, he or she shall take the following oath before some justice of the peace of this commonwealth: '*I, A. B., do swear, that my removal into the state of Virginia, was with no intent of evading the laws for preventing the further importation of slaves, nor have I brought with me any slaves, with an intention of selling them, nor have any of the slaves which I have brought with me, been imported from Africa, or any of the West India islands, since the first day of November,*' " 1778, etc.

§ 53. This act to be in force immediately. *Statutes at Large of Virginia, New Series*, I. 122.

1792, Dec. 21. South Carolina: Importation Prohibited until 1795.

"An Act to prohibit the importation of Slaves from Africa, or other places beyond sea, into this State, for two years; and also to prohibit the importation or bringing in Slaves, or Negroes, Mulattoes, Indians, Moors or Mestizoes, bound for a term of years, from any of the United States, by land or by water."

"Whereas, it is deemed inexpedient to increase the number of slaves within this State, in our present circumstances and situation;

§ 1. "*Be it therefore enacted* . . . , That no slave shall be imported into this State from Africa, the West India Islands, or other place beyond sea, for and during the term of two years, commencing from the first day of January next, which will be in the year of our Lord one thousand seven hundred and ninety-three."

§ 2. No slaves, Negroes, Indians, etc., bound for a term of years, to be brought in from any of the United States or bordering countries. Settlers may bring their slaves. Cooper, *Statutes*, VII. 431.

1793, Dec. 19. Georgia: Importation Prohibited.

"An act to prevent the importation of negroes into this state from the places herein mentioned." Title only. Re-enacted (?) by the Constitution of 1798. Marbury and Crawford, *Digest*, p. 442; Prince, *Digest*, p. 786.

1794, North Carolina: Importation Prohibited.

"An act to prevent the further importation and bringing of slaves and indented servants of colour into this state."

§ 1. "*Be it enacted* . . . , That from and after the first day of May next, no slave or indented servant of colour shall be imported or brought into this state by land or water; nor shall any slave or indented servant of colour, who may be imported or brought contrary to the intent and meaning of this act, be bought, sold or hired by any person whatever."

§ 2. Penalty for importing, £100 per slave; for buying or selling, the same.

§ 4. Persons removing, travelling, etc., are excepted. The act was amended slightly in 1796. Martin, *Iredell's Acts of Assembly*, II. 53, 94.

1794, March 22. United States Statute: Export Slave-Trade Forbidden.

"An Act to prohibit the carrying on the Slave Trade from the United States to any foreign place or country." *Statutes at Large*, I. 347. For proceedings in Congress, see *Senate Journal* (repr. 1820), 3 Cong. 1 sess. II. 51; *House Journal* (repr. 1826), 3 Cong. 1 sess. II. 76, 84, 85, 96, 98, 99, 100; *Annals of Cong.*, 3 Cong. 1 sess. pp. 64, 70, 72.

1794, Dec. 20. South Carolina: Act of 1792 Extended.

"An Act to revive and extend an Act entitled 'An Act to prohibit the importation of Slaves from Africa, or other places beyond Sea, into this State, for two years; and also, to prohibit the importation or bringing in of Negro Slaves, Mulattoes, Indians, Moors or Mestizoes, bound for a term of years, from any of the United States, by Land or Water.' "

§ 1. Act of 1792 extended until Jan. 1, 1797.

§ 2. It shall not be lawful hereafter to import slaves, free Negroes, etc., from the West Indies, any part of America outside the United States, "or from other parts beyond sea." Such slaves are to be forfeited and sold; the importer to be fined £50; free Negroes to be re-transported. Cooper, *Statutes*, VII. 433.

1795. North Carolina: Act against West Indian Slaves.

"An act to prevent any person who may emigrate from any of the West India or Bahama islands, or the French, Dutch or Spanish settlements on the southern coast of America, from bringing slaves into this state, and also for imposing certain restrictions on free persons of colour who may hereafter come into this state." Penalty, £100 for each slave over 15 years of age. *Laws of North Carolina* (revision of 1819), I. 786.

1796. Maryland: Importation Prohibited.

"An Act relating to Negroes, and to repeal the acts of assembly therein mentioned."

"*Be it enacted* . . . , That it shall not be lawful, from and after the passing of this act, to import or bring into this state, by land or water, any negro, mulatto or other slave, for sale, or to reside within this state; and any person brought into this state as a slave contrary to this act, if a slave before, shall thereupon immediately cease to be the property of the person or persons so importing or bringing such slave within this state, and shall be free."

§ 2. Any citizen of the United States, coming into the State to take up *bona fide* residence, may bring with him, or within one year import, any slave which was his property at the time of removal, "which slaves, or the mother of which slaves, shall have been a resident of the United States, or some one of them, three whole years next preceding such removal."

§ 3. Such slaves cannot be sold within three years, except by will, etc. In 1797, "A Supplementary Act," etc., slightly amended the preceding, allowing guardians, executors, etc., to import the slaves of the estate. Dorsey, *Laws*, I. 334, 344.

1796, Dec. 19. South Carolina: Importation Prohibited until 1799.

"An Act to prohibit the importation of Negroes, until the first day of January, one thousand seven hundred and ninety-nine."

"Whereas, it appears to be highly impolitic to import negroes from Africa, or other places beyond seas," etc. Extended by acts of Dec. 21, 1798, and Dec. 20, 1800, until Jan. 1, 1803. Cooper, *Statutes*, VII. 434, 436.

1797, Jan. 18. Delaware: Codification of Acts.

"An Act concerning Negro and Mulatto slaves."

§ 5. " . . . any Negro or Mulatto slave, who hath been or shall be brought into this state contrary to the intent and meaning of [the act of 1787]; and any Negro or Mulatto slave who hath been or shall be exported, or sold with an intention for exportation, or carried out for sale from this state, contrary to the intent and meaning of [the act of 1793], shall be, and are hereby declared free; any thing in this act to the contrary notwithstanding." *Laws of Delaware* (ed. 1797), p. 1321, ch. 124 c.

1798, Jan. 31. Georgia: Importation Prohibited.

"An act to prohibit the further importation of slaves into this state."

§ 1. " . . . six months after the passing of this act, it shall be unlawful for any person or persons to import into this state, from Africa or elsewhere, any negro or negroes of any age or sex." Every person so offending shall forfeit for the first offence the sum of $1,000 for every negro so imported, and for every subsequent offence the sum of $ 1,000, one half for the use of the informer, and one half for the use of the State.

§ 2. Slaves not to be brought from other States for sale after three months.

§ 3. Persons convicted of bringing slaves into this State with a view to sell them, are subject to the same penalties as if they had sold them. Marbury and Crawford, *Digest*, p. 440.

1798, March 14. New Jersey: Slave-Trade Prohibited.

"An Act respecting slaves."

§ 12. "*And be it enacted*, That from and after the passing of this act, it shall not be lawful for any person or persons whatsoever, to bring into this state, either for sale or for servitude, any negro or other slave whatsoever." Penalty, $140 for each slave; travellers and temporary residents excepted.

§ 17. Any persons fitting out vessels for the slave-trade shall forfeit them. Paterson, *Digest*, p. 307.

1798, April 7. United States Statute: Importation into Mississippi Territory Prohibited.

"An Act for an amicable settlement of limits with the state of Georgia, and authorizing the establishment of a government in the Mississippi territory." *Statutes at Large*, I. 549. For proceedings in Congress, see *Annals of Cong.*, 5 Cong. 2 sess. pp. 511, 512, 513, 514, 515, 532, 533, 1235, 1249, 1277–84, 1296, 1298–1312, 1313, 1318.

1798, May 30. Georgia: Constitutional Prohibition.

Constitution of Georgia:—

Art. IV. § 11. "There shall be no future importation of slaves into this state from Africa, or any foreign place, after the first day of October next. The legislature shall have no power to pass laws for the emancipation of slaves, without the consent of each of their respective owners previous to such emancipation. They shall have no power to prevent emigrants, from either of the United States to this state, from bringing with them such persons as may be deemed slaves, by the laws of any one of the United States." Marbury and Crawford, *Digest*, p. 30.

1800, May 10. United States Statute: Americans Forbidden to Trade from one Foreign Country to Another.

"An Act in addition to the act intituled 'An act to prohibit the carrying on the Slave Trade from the United States to any foreign place or country.'" *Statutes at Large*, II. 70. For proceedings in Congress, see *Senate Journal* (repr. 1821), 6 Cong. 1 sess. III. 72, 77, 88, 92.

1800, Dec. 20. South Carolina: Slaves and Free Negroes Prohibited.

"An Act to prevent Negro Slaves and other persons of Colour, from being brought into or entering this State." Supplemented Dec. 19, 1801, and amended Dec. 18, 1802. Cooper, *Statutes*, VII. 436, 444, 447.

1801, April 8. New York: Slave-Trade Prohibited.

"An Act concerning slaves and servants."

" . . . *And be it further enacted*, That no slave shall hereafter be imported or brought into this State, unless the person importing or bringing such slave shall be coming into this State with intent to reside permanently therein and shall have resided without this State, and also have owned such slave at least during one year next preceding the importing or bringing in of such slave," etc. A certificate, sworn to, must be obtained; any violation of this act or neglect to take out such certificate will result in freedom to the slave. Any sale or limited transfer of any person hereafter imported to be a public offence, under penalty of $250, and freedom to the slave transferred. The export of slaves or of any person freed by this act is forbidden, under penalty of $250 and freedom to the slave. Transportation for crime is permitted. Re-enacted with amendments March 31, 1817. *Laws of New York, 1801* (ed. 1887), pp. 547–52; *Laws of New York, 1817* (ed. 1817), p. 136.

1803, Feb. 28. United States Statute: Importation into States Prohibiting Forbidden.

"An Act to prevent the importation of certain persons into certain states, where, by the laws thereof, their admission is prohibited." *Statutes at Large*, II. 205. For copy of the proposed bill which this replaced, see *Annals of Cong.*, 7 Cong. 2 sess. p. 467. For proceedings in Congress, see *House Journal* (repr. 1826), 7 Cong. 2 sess. IV. 304, 324, 347; *Senate Journal* (repr. 1821), 7 Cong. 2 sess. III. 267, 268, 269–70, 273, 275, 276, 279.

1803, Dec. 17. South Carolina: African Slaves Admitted.

"An Act to alter and amend the several Acts respecting the importation or bringing into this State, from beyond seas, or elsewhere, Negroes and other persons of colour; and for other purposes therein mentioned."

§ 1. Acts of 1792, 1794, 1796, 1798, 1800, 1802, hereby repealed.

§ 2. Importation of Negroes from the West Indies prohibited.

§ 3. No Negro over fifteen years of age to be imported from the United States except under certificate of good character.

§ 5. Negroes illegally imported to be forfeited and sold, etc. Cooper, *Statutes*, VII. 449.

1804. [Denmark.

Act of 1792 abolishing the slave-trade goes into effect.]

1804, Feb. 14. Congress (House): Proposed Censure of South Carolina.

Representative Moore of South Carolina offered the following resolution, as a substitute to Mr. Bard's taxing proposition of Jan. 6:—

"*Resolved*, That this House receive with painful sensibility information that one of the Southern States, by a repeal of certain prohibitory laws, have permitted a traffic unjust in its nature, and highly impolitic in free Governments." Ruled out of order by the chairman of the Committee of the Whole. *Annals of Cong.*, 8 Cong. 1 sess. p. 1004.

1804, Feb. 15. Congress (House): Proposed Duty.

"*Resolved*, That a tax of ten dollars be imposed on every slave imported into any part of the United States."

"*Ordered*, That a bill, or bills, be brought in, pursuant to the said resolution," etc. Feb. 16 "a bill laying a duty on slaves imported into the United States" was read, but was never considered. *House Journal* (repr. 1826), 8 Cong. 1 sess. IV. 523, 578, 580, 581–2, 585; *Annals of Cong.*, 8 Cong. 1 sess. pp. 820, 876, 991, 1012, 1020, 1024–36.

1804, March 26. United States Statute: Slave-Trade Limited.

"An Act erecting Louisiana into two territories," etc. Acts of 1794 and 1803 extended to Louisiana. *Statutes at Large*, II. 283. For proceedings in Congress, see *Annals of Cong.*, 8 Cong. 1 sess. pp. 106, 211, 223, 231, 233–4, 238, 255, 1038, 1054–68, 1069–79, 1128–30, 1185–9.

1805, Feb. 15. Massachusetts: Proposed Amendment.

"Resolve requesting the Governor to transmit to the Senators and Representatives in Congress, and the Executives of the several States this Resolution, as an amendment to the Constitution of the United States, respecting Slaves." June 8, Governor's message; Connecticut answers that it is inexpedient; Maryland opposes the proposition. *Massachusetts Resolves*, February, 1805, p. 55; June, 1805, p. 18. See below, March 3, 1805.

1805, March 2. United States Statute: Slave-Trade to Orleans Territory Permitted.

"An Act further providing for the government of the territory of Orleans."

§ 1. A territorial government erected similar to Mississippi, with same rights and privileges.

§ 5. 6th Article of Ordinance of 1787, on slaves, not to extend to this territory.

Statutes at Large, II. 322. For proceedings in Congress, see *Annals of Cong.*, 8 Cong. 2 sess. pp. 28, 30, 45–6, 47, 48, 54, 59–61, 69, 727–8, 871–2, 957, 1016–9, 1020–1, 1201, 1209–10, 1211. Cf. *Statutes at Large*, II. 331; *Annals of Cong.*, 8 Cong. 2 sess., pp. 50, 51, 52, 57, 68, 69, 1213, 1215. In *Journals*, see Index, Senate Bills Nos. 8, 11.

1805, March 3. Congress (House): Massachusetts Proposition to Amend Constitution.

Mr. Varnum of Massachusetts presented the resolution of the Legislature of Massachusetts, "instructing the Senators, and requesting the Representatives in Congress, from the said State, to take all legal and necessary steps, to use their utmost exertions, as soon as the same is practicable, to obtain an amendment to the Federal Constitution, so as to authorize and empower the Congress of the United States to pass a law, whenever they may deem it expedient, to prevent the further importation of slaves from any of the West India Islands, from the coast of Africa, or elsewhere, into the United States, or any part thereof." A motion was made that Congress have power to prevent further importation; it was read and ordered to lie on the table. *House Journal* (repr. 1826), 8 Cong. 2 sess. V. 171; *Annals of Cong.*, 8 Cong. 2 sess. pp. 1221–2. For the original resolution, see *Massachusetts Resolves*, May, 1802, to March, 1806, Vol. II. A. (State House ed., p. 239.)

1805, Dec. 17. Congress (Senate): Proposition to Prohibit Importation.

A "bill to prohibit the importation of certain persons therein described into any port or place within the jurisdiction of the United States, from and after" Jan. 1, 1808, was read twice and postponed. *Senate Journal* (repr. 1821), 9 Cong. 1 sess. IV. 10–11; *Annals of Cong.*, 9 Cong. 1 sess. pp. 20–1.

1806, Jan. 20. Congress (House): Vermont Proposed Amendment.

"Mr. Olin, one of the Representatives from the State of Vermont, presented to the House certain resolutions of the General Assembly of the said State, proposing an article of amendment to the Constitution of the United States, to prevent the further importation of slaves, or people of color, from any of the West India Islands, from the coast of Africa, or elsewhere, into the United States, or any part thereof; which were read, and ordered to lie on the table." No further mention found. *House Journal* (repr. 1826), 9 Cong. 1 sess. V. 238; *Annals of Cong.*, 9 Cong. 1 sess. pp. 343–4.

1806, Jan. 25. Virginia: Imported Slaves to be Sold.

"An Act to amend the several laws concerning slaves."

§ 5. If the jury before whom the importer is brought "shall find that the said slave or slaves were brought into this commonwealth, and have remained therein, contrary to the provisions of this act, the court shall make an order, directing him, her or them to be delivered to the overseers of the poor, to be by them sold for cash and applied as herein directed."

§ 8. Penalty for bringing slaves, $400 per slave; the

same for buying or hiring, knowingly, such a slave.

§ 16. This act to take effect May 1, 1806. *Statutes at Large of Virginia*, New Series, III. 251.

1806, Jan. 27. Congress (House): Bill to Tax Slaves Imported.

"A Bill laying a duty on slaves imported into any of the United States." Finally dropped. *House Journal* (repr. 1826), 8 Cong. 2 sess. V. 129; *Ibid.*, 9 Cong. 1 sess. V. 195, 223, 240, 242, 243–4, 248, 260, 262, 264, 276–7, 287, 294, 305, 309, 338; *Annals of Cong.*, 9 Cong. 1 sess. pp. 273, 274, 346, 358, 372, 434, 442–4, 533.

1806, Feb. 4. Congress (House): Proposition to Prohibit Slave-Trade after 1807.

Mr. Bidwell moved that the following section be added to the bill for taxing slaves imported,—that any ship so engaged be forfeited. The proposition was rejected, yeas, 17, nays, 86 (?). *Annals of Cong.*, 9 Cong. 1 sess. p. 438.

1806, Feb. 10. Congress (House): New Hampshire Proposed Amendment.

"Mr. Tenney . . . presented to the House certain resolutions of the Legislature of the State of New Hampshire, 'proposing an amendment to the Constitution of the United States, so as to authorize and empower Congress to pass a law, whenever they may deem it expedient, to prevent the further importation of slaves,' or people of color, into the United States, or any part thereof." Read and laid on the table. *House Journal* (repr. 1826), 9 Cong. 1 sess. V. 266; *Annals of Cong.*, 9 Cong. 1 sess. p. 448.

1806, Feb. 17. Congress (House): Proposition on Slave-Trade.

The committee on the slave-trade reported a resolution:—

"*Resolved*, That it shall not be lawful for any person or persons, to import or bring into any of the Territories of the United States, any slave or slaves that may hereafter be imported into the United States." *House Journal*, 9 Cong. 1 sess. V. 264, 278, 308, 345–6; *House Reports*, 9 Cong. 1 sess. II. Feb. 17, 1806; *Annals of Cong.*, 9 Cong. 1 sess. pp. 472–3.

1806, April 7. Congress (Senate): Maryland Proposed Amendment.

"Mr. Wright communicated a resolution of the legislature of the state of Maryland instructing their Senators and Representatives in Congress to use their utmost exertions to obtain an amendment to the constitution of the United States to prevent the further importation of slaves; whereupon, Mr. Wright submitted the following resolutions for the consideration of the Senate. . . .

"*Resolved*, That the migration or importation of slaves into the United States, or any territory thereof, be prohibited after the first day of January, 1808." Considered April 10, and further consideration postponed until the first Monday in December next. *Senate Journal* (repr. 1821), 9 Cong. 1 sess. IV. 76–7, 79; *Annals of Cong.*, 9 Cong. 1 sess. pp. 229, 232.

1806, Dec. 2. President Jefferson's Message.

See above, pages 97–98. *House Journal* (repr. 1826), 9 Cong. 2 sess. V. 468.

1806, Dec. 15. Congress (House): Proposition on Slave-Trade.

"A bill to prohibit the importation or bringing of slaves into the United States, etc.," after Dec. 31, 1807. Finally merged into Senate bill. *Ibid.*, House Bill No. 148.

1806, Dec. 17. Congress (House): Sloan's Proposition.

Proposition to amend the House bill by inserting after the article declaring the forfeiture of an illegally imported slave, "And such person or slave shall be entitled to his freedom." Lost. *Annals of Cong.*, 9 Cong. 2 sess. pp. 167–77, 180–89.

1806, Dec. 29. Congress (House): Sloan's Second Proposition.

Illegally imported Africans to be either freed, apprenticed, or returned to Africa. Lost; Jan. 5, 1807, a somewhat similar proposition was also lost. *Ibid.*, pp. 226–8, 254.

1806, Dec. 31. Great Britain: Rejected Treaty.

"Treaty of amity, commerce, and navigation, between His Britannic Majesty and the United States of America."

"Art. XXIV. The high contracting parties engage to communicate to each other, without delay, all such laws as have been or shall be hereafter enacted by their respective Legislatures, as also all measures which shall have been taken for the abolition or limitation of the African slave trade; and they further agree to use their best endeavors to procure the co-operation of other Powers for the final and complete abolition of a trade so repugnant to the principles of justice and humanity." *Amer. State Papers, Foreign*, III. 147, 151.

1807, March 25. [**England: Slave-Trade Abolished.**

"An Act for the Abolition of the Slave Trade." *Statute 47 George III.*, 1 sess. ch. 36.]

1807, Jan. 7. Congress (House): Bidwell's Proposition.

"Provided, that no person shall be sold as a slave by virtue of this act." Offered as an amendment to § 3 of House bill; defeated 60 to 61, Speaker voting. A similar proposition was made Dec. 23, 1806. *House Journal* (repr. 1826), 9 Cong. 2 sess. V. 513–6. Cf. *Annals of Cong.*, 9 Cong. 2 sess. pp. 199–203, 265–7.

1807, Feb. 9. Congress (House): Section Seven of House Bill.

§ 7 of the bill reported to the House by the committee provided that all Negroes imported should be conveyed whither the President might direct and there be indentured as apprentices, or employed in whatever way the President might deem best for them and the country; provided that no such Negroes should be indentured or employed except in some State in which provision is now made for the gradual abolition of slavery. Blank spaces were left for limiting the term of indenture. The report was never acted on. *Annals of Cong.*, 9 Cong. 2 sess. pp. 477–8.

1807, March 2. United States Statute: Importation Prohibited.

"An Act to prohibit the importation of Slaves into any port or place within the jurisdiction of the United States, from and after the first day of January, in the year of our Lord one thousand eight hundred and eight." Bills to amend § 8, so as to make less ambiguous the permit given to the internal traffic, were introduced Feb. 27 and Nov. 27. *Statutes at Large*, II. 426. For proceedings in Senate, see *Senate Journal* (repr. 1821), 9 Cong. 1–2 sess. IV. 11, 112, 123, 124, 132, 133, 150, 158, 164, 165, 167, 168; *Annals of Cong.*, 9 Cong. 2 sess. pp. 16, 19, 23, 33, 36, 45, 47, 68, 69, 70, 71, 79, 87, 93. For proceedings in House, see *House Journal* (repr. 1826), 9 Cong. 2 sess. V. 470, 482, 488, 490, 491, 496, 500, 504, 510, 513–6, 517, 540, 557, 575, 579, 581, 583–4, 585, 592, 594, 610, 613–4, 616, 623, 638, 640; 10 Cong. 1 sess. VI. 27, 50; *Annals of Cong.*, 9 Cong. 2 sess. pp. 167, 180, 200, 220, 231, 254, 264, 270.

1808, Feb. 23. Congress (Senate): Proposition to Amend Constitution.

"Agreeably to instructions from the legislature of the state of Pennsylvania to their Senators in Congress, Mr. Maclay submitted the following resolution, which was read for consideration:—

"*Resolved* . . . , That the Constitution of the United States be so altered and amended, as to prevent the Congress of the United States, and the legislatures of any state in the Union, from authorizing the importation of slaves." No further mention. *Senate Journal* (repr. 1821), 10 Cong. 1 sess. IV. 235; *Annals of Cong.*, 10 Cong. 1 sess. p. 134. For the full text of the instructions, see *Amer. State Papers, Miscellaneous*, I. 716.

1810, Dec. 5. President Madison's Message.

"Among the commercial abuses still committed under

the American flag, . . . it appears that American citizens are instrumental in carrying on a traffic in enslaved Africans, equally in violation of the laws of humanity, and in defiance of those of their own country. The same just and benevolent motives which produced the interdiction in force against this criminal conduct, will doubtless be felt by Congress, in devising further means of suppressing the evil." *House Journal* (repr. 1826), 11 Cong. 3 sess. VII. 435.

1811, Jan. 15. United States Statute: Secret Act and Joint Resolution against Amelia Island Smugglers.

Statutes at Large, III. 471 ff.

1815, March 29. [**France: Abolition of Slave-Trade.**

Napoleon on his return from Elba decrees the abolition of the slave-trade. Decree re-enacted in 1818 by the Bourbon dynasty. *British and Foreign State Papers*, 1815–16, p. 196, note; 1817–18, p. 1025.]

1815, Feb. 18. Great Britain: Treaty of Ghent.

"Treaty of peace and amity. Concluded December 24, 1814; Ratifications exchanged at Washington February 17, 1815; Proclaimed February 18, 1815."

Art. X. "Whereas the traffic in slaves is irreconcilable with the principles of humanity and justice, and whereas both His Majesty and the United States are desirous of continuing their efforts to promote its entire abolition, it is hereby agreed that both the contracting parties shall use their best endeavors to accomplish so desirable an object." *U. S. Treaties and Conventions* (ed. 1889), p. 405.

1815, Dec. 8. Alabama and Mississippi Territory: Act to Dispose of Illegally Imported Slaves.

"An Act concerning Slaves brought into this Territory, contrary to the Laws of the United States." Slaves to be sold at auction, and the proceeds to be divided between the territorial treasury and the collector or informer. Toulmin, *Digest of the Laws of Alabama*, p. 637; *Statutes of Mississippi digested*, etc. (ed. 1816), p. 389.

1816, Nov. 18. North Carolina: Act to Dispose of Illegally Imported Slaves.

"An act to direct the disposal of negroes, mulattoes and persons of colour, imported into this state, contrary to the provisions of an act of the Congress of the United States, entitled 'an act to prohibit the importation of slaves into any port or place, within the jurisdiction of the United States, from and after the first day of January, in the year of our Lord one thousand eight hundred and eight.' "

§ 1. Every slave illegally imported after 1808 shall be sold for the use of the State.

§ 2. The sheriff shall seize and sell such slave, and pay the proceeds to the treasurer of the State.

§ 3. If the slave abscond, the sheriff may offer a reward not exceeding one-fifth of the value of the slave. *Laws of North Carolina, 1816*, ch. xii. p. 9; *Laws of North Carolina* (revision of 1819), II. 1350.

1816, Dec. 3. President Madison's Message.

"The United States having been the first to abolish, within the extent of their authority, the transportation of the natives of Africa into slavery, by prohibiting the introduction of slaves, and by punishing their citizens participating in the traffick, cannot but be gratified at the progress, made by concurrent efforts of other nations, towards a general suppression of so great an evil. They must feel, at the same time, the greater solicitude to give the fullest efficacy to their own regulations. With that view, the interposition of Congress appears to be required by the violations and evasions which, it is suggested, are chargeable on unworthy citizens, who mingle in the slave trade under foreign flags, and with foreign ports; and by collusive importations of slaves into the United States, through adjoining ports and territories. I present the subject to Congress, with a full assurance of their disposition to apply all the remedy which can be afforded by an amendment of the law. The regulations which were intended to guard against abuses of a kindred character, in the trade between the several States, ought also to be rendered more effectual for their humane object." *House Journal*, 14 Cong. 2 sess. pp. 15–6.

1817, Feb. 11. Congress (House): Proposed Joint Resolution.

"Joint Resolution for abolishing the traffick in Slaves, and the Colinization [*sic*] of the Free People of Colour of the United States."

"*Resolved*, . . . That the President be, and he is hereby authorized to consult and negotiate with all the governments where ministers of the United States are, or shall be accredited, on the means of effecting an entire and immediate abolition of the traffick in slaves. And, also, to enter into a convention with the government of Great Britain, for receiving into the colony of Sierra Leone, such of the free people of colour of the United States as, with their own consent, shall be carried thither. . . .

"*Resolved*, That adequate provision shall hereafter be made to defray any necessary expenses which may be incurred in carrying the preceding resolution into effect." Reported on petition of the Colonization Society by the committee on the President's Message. No further record. *House Journal*, 14 Cong. 2 sess. pp. 25–7, 380; *House Doc.*, 14 Cong. 2 sess. No. 77.

1817, July 28. [Great Britain and Portugal: First Concession of Right of Search.

"By this treaty, ships of war of each of the nations might visit merchant vessels of both, if suspected of having slaves on board, acquired by illicit traffic." This "related only to the trade north of the equator; for the slave-trade of Portugal within the regions of western Africa, to the south of the equator, continued long after this to be carried on with great vigor." Woolsey, *International Law*

(1874), § 197, pp. 331–2; *British and Foreign State Papers*, 1816–17, pp. 85–118.]

1817, Sept. 23. [Great Britain and Spain: Abolition of Trade North of Equator.

"By the treaty of Madrid, . . . Great Britain obtained from Spain, for the sum of four hundred thousand pounds, the immediate abolition of the trade north of the equator, its entire abolition after 1820, and the concession of the same mutual right of search, which the treaty with Portugal had just established." Woolsey, *International Law* (1874), § 197, p. 332; *British and Foreign State Papers*, 1816–17, pp. 33–74.]

1817, Dec. 2. President Monroe's Message on Amelia Island, etc.

"A just regard for the rights and interests of the United States required that they [i. e., the Amelia Island and Galveston pirates] should be suppressed, and orders have been accordingly issued to that effect. The imperious considerations which produced this measure will be explained to the parties whom it may, in any degree, concern." *House Journal*, 15 Cong. 1 sess. p. 11.

1817, Dec. 19. Georgia: Act to Dispose of Illegally Imported Slaves.

"An Act for disposing of any such negro, mulatto, or person of color, who has been or may hereafter be imported or brought into this State in violation of an act of the United States, entitled an act to prohibit the importation of slaves," etc.

§ 1. The governor by agent shall receive such Negroes, and,

§ 2. sell them, or,

§ 3. give them to the Colonization Society to be transported, on condition that the Society reimburse the State for all expense, and transport them at their own cost. Prince, *Digest*, p. 793.

1818, Jan. 10. Congress (House): Bill to Supplement Act of 1807.

Mr. Middleton, from the committee on so much of the

President's Message as related to the illicit introduction of slaves into the United States from Amelia Island, reported a bill in addition to former acts prohibiting the introduction of slaves into the United States. This was read twice and committed; April 1 it was considered in Committee of the Whole; Mr. Middleton offered a substitute, which was ordered to be laid on table and to be printed; it became the Act of 1819. See below, March 3, 1819. *House Journal*, 15 Cong. 1 sess. pp. 131, 410.

1818, Jan. 13. President Monroe's Special Message.

"I have the satisfaction to inform Congress, that the establishment at Amelia Island has been suppressed, and without the effusion of blood. The papers which explain this transaction, I now lay before Congress," etc. *Ibid.*, pp. 137–9.

1818, Feb. 9. Congress (Senate): Bill to Register (?) Slaves.

"A bill respecting the transportation of persons of color, for sale, or to be held to labor." Passed Senate, dropped in House; similar bill Dec. 9, 1818, also dropped in House. *Senate Journal*, 15 Cong. 1 sess. pp. 147, 152, 157, 165, 170, 188, 201, 203, 232, 237; 15 Cong. 2 sess. pp. 63, 74, 77, 202, 207, 285, 291, 297; *House Journal*, 15 Cong. 1 sess. p. 332; 15 Cong. 2 sess. pp. 303, 305, 316.

1818, April 4. Congress (House): Proposition to Amend Constitution.

Mr. Livermore's resolution:—

"No person shall be held to service or labour as a slave, nor shall slavery be tolerated in any state hereafter admitted into the Union, or made one of the United States of America." Read, and on the question, "Will the House consider the same?" it was determined in the negative. *House Journal*, 15 Cong. 1 sess. pp. 420–1; *Annals of Cong.*, 15 Cong. 1 sess. pp. 1675–6.

1818, April 20. United States Statute: Act in Addition to Act of 1807.

"An Act in addition to 'An act to prohibit the introduction [importation] of slaves into any port or place within the jurisdiction of the United States, from and after the first day of January, in the year of our Lord one thousand eight hundred and eight,' and to repeal certain parts of the same." *Statutes at Large*, III. 450. For proceedings in Congress, see *Senate Journal*, 15 Cong. 1 sess. pp. 243, 304, 315, 333, 338, 340, 348, 377, 386, 388, 391, 403, 406; *House Journal*, 15 Cong. 1 sess. pp. 450, 452, 456, 468, 479, 484, 492, 505.

1818, May 4. [Great Britain and Netherlands: Treaty.

Right of Search granted for the suppression of the slave-trade. *British and Foreign State Papers*, 1817–18, pp. 125–43.]

1818, Dec. 19. Georgia: Act of 1817 Reinforced.

No title found. "*Whereas* numbers of African slaves have been illegally introduced into the State, in direct violation of the laws of the United States and of this State, *Be it therefore enacted*," etc. Informers are to receive one-tenth of the net proceeds from the sale of illegally imported Africans, "*Provided*, nothing herein contained shall be so construed as to extend farther back than the year 1817." Prince, *Digest*, p. 798.

1819, Feb. 8. Congress (Senate): Bill in Addition to Former Acts.

"A bill supplementary to an act, passed the 2d day of March, 1807, entitled," etc. Postponed. *Senate Journal*, 15 Cong. 2 sess. pp. 234, 244, 311–2, 347.

1819, March 3. United States Statute: Cruisers Authorized, etc.

"An Act in addition to the Acts prohibiting the slave trade." *Statutes at Large*, III. 532. For proceedings in Congress, see *Senate Journal*, 15 Cong. 2 sess. pp. 338, 339, 343, 345, 350, 362; *House Journal*, 15 Cong. 2 sess. pp. 9–19, 42–3, 150, 179, 330, 334, 341, 343, 352.

1819, Dec. 7. President Monroe's Message.

"Due attention has likewise been paid to the suppression of the slave trade, in compliance with a law of the last session. Orders have been given to the commanders of all our public ships to seize all vessels navigated under our flag, engaged in that trade, and to bring them in, to be proceeded against, in the manner prescribed by that law. It is hoped that these vigorous measures, supported by like acts by other nations, will soon terminate a commerce so disgraceful to the civilized world." *House Journal*, 16 Cong. 1 sess. p. 18.

1820, Jan. 19. Congress (House): Proposed Registry of Slaves.

"On motion of Mr. Cuthbert,

"Resolved, That the Committee on the Slave Trade be instructed to enquire into the expediency of establishing a registry of slaves, more effectually to prevent the importation of slaves into the United States, or the territories thereof." No further mention. *Ibid.*, p. 150.

1820, Feb. 5. Congress (House): Proposition on Slave-Trade.

"Mr. Meigs submitted the following preamble and resolution:

"Whereas, slavery in the United States is an evil of great and increasing magnitude; one which merits the greatest efforts of this nation to remedy: Therefore,

"Resolved, That a committee be appointed to enquire into the expediency of devoting the public lands as a fund for the purpose of,

"1st, Employing a naval force competent to the annihilation of the slave trade;

"2dly, The emancipation of slaves in the United States; and,

"3dly, Colonizing them in such way as shall be conducive to their comfort and happiness, in Africa, their mother country." Read, and, on motion of Walker of North Carolina, ordered to lie on the table. Feb. 7, Mr. Meigs moved that the House now consider the above-mentioned resolution, but it was decided in the negative. Feb. 18, he made a similar motion and proceeded to discussion, but was ruled out of order by the Speaker. He appealed, but the Speaker was sustained, and the House refused to take up the resolution. No further record appears. *Ibid.*, pp. 196, 200, 227.

1820, Feb. 23. Massachusetts: Slavery in Western Territory.

"Resolve respecting Slavery":—

"The Committee of both Houses, who were appointed to consider 'what measures it may be proper for the Legislature of this Commonwealth to adopt, in the expression of their sentiments and views, relative to the interesting subject, now before Congress, of interdicting slavery in the New States, which may be admitted into the Union, beyond the River Mississippi,' respectfully submit the following report: . . .

"Nor has this question less importance as to its influence on the slave trade. Should slavery be further permitted, an immense new market for slaves would be opened. It is well known that notwithstanding the strictness of our laws, and the vigilance of the government, thousands are now annually imported from Africa," etc. *Massachusetts Resolves*, May, 1819, to February, 1824, pp. 147–51.

1820, May 12. Congress (House): Resolution for Negotiation.

"Resolved by the Senate and House of Representatives of the United States of America in Congress assembled, That the President of the United States be requested to negociate with all the governments where ministers of the United States are or shall be accredited, on the means of effecting an entire and immediate abolition of the slave trade." Passed House, May 12, 1820; lost in Senate, May 15, 1820. *House Journal*, 16 Cong. 1 sess. pp. 497, 518, 520–21, 526; *Annals of Cong.*, 16 Cong. 1 sess. pp. 697–700.

1820, May 15. United States Statute: Slave-Trade made Piracy.

"An act to continue in force 'An act to protect the

commerce of the United States, and punish the crime of piracy,' and also to make further provisions for punishing the crime of piracy." Continued by several statutes until passage of the Act of 1823, *q. v. Statutes at Large*, III. 600. For proceedings in Congress, see *Senate Journal*, 16 Cong. 1 sess. pp. 238, 241, 268, 286–7, 314, 331, 346, 350, 409, 412, 417, 422, 424, 425; *House Journal*, 16 Cong. 1 sess. pp. 453, 454, 494, 518, 520, 522, 537, 539, 540, 542. There was also a House bill, which was dropped: cf. *House Journal*, 16 Cong. 1 sess. pp. 21, 113, 280, 453, 494.

1820, Nov. 14. President Monroe's Message.

"In execution of the law of the last session, for the suppression of the slave trade, some of our public ships have also been employed on the coast of Africa, where several captures have already been made of vessels engaged in that disgraceful traffic." *Senate Journal*, 16 Cong. 2 sess. pp. 16–7.

1821, Feb. 15. Congress (House): Meigs's Resolution.

Mr. Meigs offered in modified form the resolutions submitted at the last session:—

"Whereas slavery, in the United States, is an evil, acknowledged to be of great and increasing magnitude, . . . therefore,

"Resolved, That a committee be appointed to inquire into the expediency of devoting five hundred million acres of the public lands, next west of the Mississippi, as a fund for the purpose of, in the

"*First place*; Employing a naval force, competent to the annihilation of the slave trade," etc. Question to consider decided in the affirmative, 63 to 50; laid on the table, 66 to 55. *House Journal*, 16 Cong. 2 sess. p. 238; *Annals of Cong.*, 16 Cong. 2 sess. pp. 1168–70.

1821, Dec. 3. President Monroe's Message.

"Like success has attended our efforts to suppress the slave trade. Under the flag of the United States, and the sanction of their papers, the trade may be considered as entirely suppressed; and, if any of our citizens are engaged in it, under the flag and papers of other powers, it is only from a respect to the rights of those powers, that these offenders are not seized and brought home, to receive the punishment which the laws inflict. If every other power should adopt the same policy, and pursue the same vigorous means for carrying it into effect, the trade could no longer exist." *House Journal*, 17 Cong. 1 sess. p. 22.

1822, April 12. Congress (House): Proposed Resolution.

"*Resolved*, That the President of the United States be requested to enter into such arrangements as he may deem suitable and proper, with one or more of the maritime powers of Europe, for the effectual abolition of the slave trade." *House Reports*, 17 Cong. 1 sess. II. No. 92, p. 4; *Annals of Cong.*, 17 Cong. 1 sess. p. 1538.

1822, June 18. Mississippi: Act on Importation, etc.

"An act, to reduce into one, the several acts, concerning slaves, free negroes, and mulattoes."

§ 2. Slaves born and resident in the United States, and not criminals, may be imported.

§ 3. No slave born or resident outside the United States shall be brought in, under penalty of $1,000 per slave. Travellers are excepted. *Revised Code of the Laws of Mississippi* (Natchez, 1824), p. 369.

1822, Dec. 3. President Monroe's Message.

"A cruise has also been maintained on the coast of Africa, when the season would permit, for the suppression of the slave-trade; and orders have been given to the commanders of all our public ships to seize our own vessels, should they find any engaged in that trade, and to bring them in for adjudication." *House Journal*, 17 Cong. 2 sess. pp. 12, 21.

1823, Jan. 1. Alabama: Act to Dispose of Illegally Imported Slaves.

"An Act to carry into effect the laws of the United States prohibiting the slave trade."

§ 1. "*Be it enacted*, . . . That the Governor of this state be . . . authorized and required to appoint some suitable person, as the agent of the state, to receive all and every slave or slaves or persons of colour, who may have been brought into this state in violation of the laws of the United States, prohibiting the slave trade: *Provided*, that the authority of the said agent is not to extend to slaves who have been condemned and sold."

§ 2. The agent must give bonds.

§ 3. "*And be it further enacted*, That the said slaves, when so placed in the possession of the state, as aforesaid, shall be employed on such public work or works, as shall be deemed by the Governor of most value and utility to the public interest."

§ 4. A part may be hired out to support those employed in public work.

§ 5. "*And be it further enacted*, That in all cases in which a decree of any court having competent authority, shall be in favor of any or claimant or claimants, the said slaves shall be truly and faithfully, by said agent, delivered to such claimant or claimants: but in case of their condemnation, they shall be sold by such agent for cash to the highest bidder, by giving sixty days notice," etc. *Acts of the Assembly of Alabama, 1822* (Cahawba, 1823), p. 62.

1823, Jan. 30. United States Statute: Piracy Act made Perpetual.

"An Act in addition to 'An act to continue in force "An act to protect the commerce of the United States, and punish the crime of piracy,"'" etc. *Statutes at Large*, III. 510–14, 721, 789. For proceedings in Congress, see *Senate Journal*, 17 Cong. 2 sess. pp. 61, 64, 70, 83, 98, 101, 106, 110, 111, 122, 137; *House Journal*, 17 Cong. 2 sess. pp. 73, 76, 156, 183, 189.

1823, Feb. 10. Congress (House): Resolution on Slave-Trade.

Mr. Mercer offered the following resolution:—

"*Resolved*, That the President of the United States be requested to enter upon, and to prosecute, from time to time, such negotiations with the several maritime powers of Europe and America, as he may deem expedient, for the effectual abolition of the African slave trade, and its ultimate denunciation as piracy, under the law of nations, by the consent of the civilized world." Agreed to Feb. 28; passed Senate. *House Journal*, 17 Cong. 2 sess. pp. 212, 280–82; *Annals of Cong.*, 17 Cong. 2 sess. pp. 928, 1147–55.

1823, March 3. United States Statute: Appropriation.

"An Act making appropriations for the support of the navy," etc.

"To enable the President of the United States to carry into effect the act" of 1819, $50,000. *Statutes at Large*, III. 763, 764.

1823. President: Proposed Treaties.

Letters to various governments in accordance with the resolution of 1823: April 28, to Spain; May 17, to Buenos Ayres; May 27, to United States of Colombia; Aug. 14, to Portugal. See above, Feb. 10, 1823. *House Doc.*, 18 Cong. 1 sess. VI. No. 119.

1823, June 24. Great Britain: Proposed Treaty.

Adams, March 31, proposes that the trade be made piracy. Canning, April 8, reminds Adams of the treaty of Ghent and asks for the granting of a mutual Right of Search to suppress the slave-trade. The matter is further discussed until June 24. Minister Rush is empowered to propose a treaty involving the Right of Search, etc. This treaty was substantially the one signed (see below, March 13, 1824), differing principally in the first article.

"Article I. The two high contracting Powers, having each separately, by its own laws, subjected their subjects and citizens, who may be convicted of carrying on the illicit traffic in slaves on the coast of Africa, to the penalties of piracy, do hereby agree to use their influence, respectively, with the other maritime and civilized nations of the world, to the end that the said African slave trade may be recognized, and declared to be, piracy, under the law of nations." *House Doc.*, 18 Cong. 1 sess. VI. No. 119.

1824, Feb. 6. Congress (House): Proposition to Amend Constitution.

Mr. Abbot's resolution on persons of color:—

"That no part of the constitution of the United States ought to be construed, or shall be construed to authorize the importation or ingress of any person of color into any one of the United States, contrary to the laws of such state." Read first and second time and committed to the Committee of the Whole. *House Journal*, 18 Cong. 1 sess. p. 208; *Annals of Cong.*, 18 Cong. 1 sess. p. 1399.

1824, March 13. Great Britain: Proposed Treaty of 1824.

"The Convention:"—

Art. I. "The commanders and commissioned officers of each of the two high contracting parties, duly authorized, under the regulations and instructions of their respective Governments, to cruize on the coasts of Africa, of America, and of the West Indies, for the suppression of the slave trade," shall have the power to seize and bring into port any vessel owned by subjects of the two contracting parties, found engaging in the slave-trade. The vessel shall be taken for trial to the country where she belongs.

Art. II. Provides that even if the vessel seized does not belong to a citizen or citizens of either of the two contracting parties, but is chartered by them, she may be seized in the same way as if she belonged to them.

Art. III. Requires that in all cases where any vessel of either party shall be boarded by any naval officer of the other party, on suspicion of being concerned in the slave-trade, the officer shall deliver to the captain of the vessel so boarded a certificate in writing, signed by the naval officer, specifying his rank, etc., and the object of his visit. Provision is made for the delivery of ships and papers to the tribunal before which they are brought.

Art. IV. Limits the Right of Search, recognized by the Convention, to such investigation as shall be necessary to ascertain the fact whether the said vessel is or is not engaged in the slave-trade. No person shall be taken out of the vessel so visited unless for reasons of health.

Art. V. Makes it the duty of the commander of either nation, having captured a vessel of the other under the treaty, to receive unto his custody the vessel captured, and send or carry it into some port of the vessel's own country for adjudication, in which case triplicate declarations are to be signed, etc.

Art. VI. Provides that in cases of capture by the officer of either party, on a station where no national vessel is cruising, the captor shall either send or carry his prize to some convenient port of its own country for adjudication, etc.

Art. VII. Provides that the commander and crew of the captured vessel shall be proceeded against as pirates, in the ports to which they are brought, etc.

Art. VIII. Confines the Right of Search, under this treaty, to such officers of both parties as are especially authorized to execute the laws of their countries in regard to the slave-trade. For every abusive exercise of this right, officers are to be personally liable in costs and damages, etc.

Art. IX. Provides that the government of either nation shall inquire into abuses of this Convention and of the laws of the two countries, and inflict on guilty officers the proper punishment.

Art. X. Declares that the right, reciprocally conceded by this treaty, is wholly and exclusively founded on the consideration that the two nations have by their laws made the slave-trade piracy, and is not to be taken to affect in any other way the rights of the parties, etc.; it further engages that each power shall use its influence with all other civilized powers, to procure from them the acknowledgment that the slave-trade is piracy under the law of nations.

Art. XI. Provides that the ratifications of the treaty shall be exchanged at London within twelve months, or as much sooner as possible. Signed by Mr. Rush, Minister to the Court of St. James, March 13, 1824.

The above is a synopsis of the treaty as it was laid before the Senate. It was ratified by the Senate with certain conditions, one of which was that the duration of this treaty should be limited to the pleasure of the two parties on six months' notice; another was that the Right of Search should be limited to the African and West Indian seas: i. e., the word "America" was struck out. This treaty as amended and passed by the Senate (cf. above, p. 141) was rejected by Great Britain. A counter project was suggested by her, but not accepted (cf. above, p. 144). The striking out of the word "America" was declared to be the insuperable objection. *Senate Doc.*, 18 Cong. 2 sess. I. No. 1, pp. 15–20; *Niles's Register*, 3rd Series, XXVI. 230–2. For proceedings in Senate, see *Amer. State Papers, Foreign*, V. 360–2.

1824, March 31. [**Great Britain: Slave-Trade made Piracy.**

"An Act for the more effectual Suppression of the *African* Slave Trade."

Any person engaging in the slave-trade "shall be deemed and adjudged guilty of Piracy, Felony and Robbery, and being convicted thereof shall suffer Death without Benefit of Clergy, and Loss of Lands, Goods and Chattels, as Pirates, Felons and Robbers upon the Seas ought to suffer," etc. *Statute 5 George IV.*, ch. 17; *Amer. State Papers, Foreign*, V. 342.]

1824, April 16. Congress (House): Bill to Suppress Slave-Trade.

"Mr. Govan, from the committee to which was

referred so much of the President's Message as relates to the suppression of the Slave Trade, reported a bill respecting the slave trade; which was read twice, and committed to a Committee of the Whole."

§ 1. Provided a fine not exceeding $5,000, imprisonment not exceeding 7 years, and forfeiture of ship, for equipping a slaver even for the foreign trade; and a fine not exceeding $3,000, and imprisonment not exceeding 5 years, for serving on board any slaver. *Annals of Cong.*, 18 Cong. 1 sess. pp. 2397–8; *House Journal*, 18 Cong. 1 sess. pp. 26, 180, 181, 323, 329, 356, 423.

1824, May 21. President Monroe's Message on Treaty of 1824.

Amer. State Papers, Foreign, V. 344–6.

1824, Nov. 6. [Great Britain and Sweden: Treaty.

Right of Search granted for the suppression of the slave-trade. *British and Foreign State Papers*, 1824–5, pp. 3–28.]

1824, Nov. 6. Great Britain: Counter Project of 1825.

Great Britain proposes to conclude the treaty as amended by the Senate, if the word "America" is reinstated in Art. I. (Cf. above, March 13, 1824.) February 16, 1825, the House Committee favors this project; March 2, Addington reminds Adams of this counter proposal; April 6, Clay refuses to reopen negotiations on account of the failure of the Colombian treaty. *Amer. State Papers, Foreign*, V. 367; *House Reports*, 18 Cong. 2 sess. I. No. 70; *House Doc.*, 19 Cong. 1 sess. I. No. 16.

1824, Dec. 7. President Monroe's Message.

"It is a cause of serious regret, that no arrangement has yet been finally concluded between the two Governments, to secure, by joint co-operation, the suppression of the slave trade. It was the object of the British Government, in the early stages of the negotiation, to adopt a plan for the suppression, which should include the concession of the mutual right of search by the ships of war of each party, of the vessels of the other, for suspected offenders. This was objected to by this Government, on the principle that, as the right of search was a right of war of a belligerant towards a neutral power, it might have an ill effect to extend it, by treaty, to an offence which had been made comparatively mild, to a time of peace. Anxious, however, for the suppression of this trade, it was thought adviseable, in compliance with a resolution of the House of Representatives, founded on an act of Congress, to propose to the British Government an expedient, which should be free from that objection, and more effectual for the object, by making it piratical. . . . A convention to this effect was concluded and signed, in London," on the 13th of March, 1824, "by plenipotentiaries duly authorized by both Governments, to the ratification of which certain obstacles have arisen, which are not yet entirely removed." [For the removal of which, the documents relating to the negotiation are submitted for the action of Congress]. . . .

"In execution of the laws for the suppression of the slave trade, a vessel has been occasionally sent from that squadron to the coast of Africa, with orders to return thence by the usual track of the slave ships, and to seize any of our vessels which might be engaged in that trade. None have been found, and, it is believed, that none are thus employed. It is well known, however, that the trade still exists under other flags." *House Journal*, 18 Cong. 2 sess. pp. 11, 12, 19, 27, 241; *House Reports*, 18 Cong. 2 sess. I. No. 70; Gales and Seaton, *Register of Debates*, I. 625–8, and Appendix, p. 2 ff.

1825, Feb. 21. United States of Colombia: Proposed Treaty.

The President sends to the Senate a treaty with the United States of Colombia drawn, as United States Minister Anderson said, similar to that signed at London, with the alterations made by the Senate. March 9, 1825, the Senate rejects this treaty. *Amer. State Papers, Foreign*, V. 729–35.

1825, Feb. 28. Congress (House): Proposed Resolution on Slave-Trade.

Mr. Mercer laid on the table the following resolution:—

"*Resolved*, That the President of the United States be requested to enter upon, and prosecute from time to time, such negotiations with the several maritime powers of Europe and America, as he may deem expedient for the effectual abolition of the slave trade, and its ultimate denunciation, as piracy, under the law of nations, by the consent of the civilized world." The House refused to consider the resolution. *House Journal*, 18 Cong. 2 sess. p. 280; Gales and Seaton, *Register of Debates*, I. 697, 736.

1825, March 3. Congress (House): Proposed Resolution against Right of Search.

"Mr. Forsyth submitted the following resolution:

"*Resolved*, That while this House anxiously desires that the Slave Trade should be, universally, denounced as Piracy, and, as such, should be detected and punished under the law of nations, it considers that it would be highly inexpedient to enter into engagements with any foreign power, by which *all* the merchant vessels of the United States would be exposed to the inconveniences of any regulation of search, from which any merchant vessels of that foreign power would be exempted." Resolution laid on the table. *House Journal*, 18 Cong. 2 sess. pp. 308–9; Gales and Seaton, *Register of Debates*, I. 739.

1825, Dec. 6. President Adams's Message.

"The objects of the West India Squadron have been, to carry into execution the laws for the suppression of the African Slave Trade: for the protection of our commerce against vessels of piratical character. . . . These objects, during the present year, have been accomplished more effectually than at any former period. The African Slave Trade has long been excluded from the use of our flag; and if some few citizens of our country have continued to set the laws of the Union, as well as those of nature and humanity, at defiance, by persevering in that abominable traffic, it has been only by sheltering themselves under the banners of other nations, less earnest for the total extinction of the trade than ours." *House Journal*, 19 Cong. 1 sess. pp. 20, 96, 296–7, 305, 323, 329, 394–5, 399, 410, 414, 421, 451, 640.

1826, Feb. 14. Congress (House): Proposition to Repeal Parts of Act of 1819.

"Mr. Forsyth submitted the following resolutions, viz.:

1. "*Resolved*, That it is expedient to repeal so much of the act of the 3d March, 1819, entitled, 'An act in addition to the acts prohibiting the slave trade,' as provides for the appointment of agents on the coast of Africa.
2. "*Resolved*, That it is expedient so to modify the said act of the 3d of March, 1819, as to release the United States from all obligation to support the negroes already removed to the coast of Africa, and to provide for such a disposition of those taken in slave ships who now are in, or who may be, hereafter, brought into the United States, as shall secure to them a fair opportunity of obtaining a comfortable subsistence, without any aid from the public treasury." Read and laid on the table. *Ibid.*, p. 258.

1826, March 14. United States Statute: Appropriation.

"An Act making appropriations for the support of the navy," etc.

"For the agency on the coast of Africa, for receiving the negroes," etc., $32,000. *Statutes at Large*, IV. 140, 141.

1827, March 2. United States Statute: Appropriation.

"An Act making appropriations for the support of the Navy," etc.

"For the agency on the coast of Africa," etc., $56,710. *Ibid.*, IV. 206, 208.

1827, March 11. Texas: Introduction of Slaves Prohibited.

Constitution of the State of Coahuila and Texas. Preliminary Provisions: —

Art. 13. "From and after the promulgation of the constitution in the capital of each district, no one shall be born a slave in the state, and after six months the introduction of slaves under any pretext shall not be permitted." *Laws and Decrees of Coahuila and Texas* (Houston, 1839), p. 314.

1827, Sept. 15. Texas: Decree against Slave-Trade.

"The Congress of the State of Coahuila and Texas decrees as follows:"

Art. 1. All slaves to be registered.

Art. 2, 3. Births and deaths to be recorded.

Art. 4. "Those who introduce slaves, after the expiration of the term specified in article 13 of the Constitution, shall be subject to the penalties established by the general law of the 13th of July, 1824." *Ibid.*, pp. 78–9.

1828, Feb. 25. Congress (House): Proposed Bill to Abolish African Agency, etc.

"Mr. McDuffie, from the Committee of Ways and Means, . . . reported the following bill:

"A bill to abolish the Agency of the United States on the Coast of Africa, to provide other means of carrying into effect the laws prohibiting the slave trade, and for other purposes." This bill was amended so as to become the act of May 24, 1828 (see below). *House Reports*, 21 Cong. 1 sess. III. No. 348, p. 278.

1828, May 24. United States Statute: Appropriation.

"An Act making an appropriation for the suppression of the slave trade." *Statutes at Large*, IV. 302; *House Journal*, 20 Cong. 1 sess., House Bill No. 190.

1829, Jan. 28. Congress (House): Bill to Amend Act of 1807.

The Committee on Commerce reported "a bill (No.

399) to amend an act, entitled 'An act to prohibit the importation of slaves,'" etc. Referred to Committee of the Whole. *House Journal*, 20 Cong. 2 sess. pp. 58, 84, 215. Cf. *Ibid.*, 20 Cong. 1 sess. pp. 121, 135.

1829, March 2. United States Statute: Appropriation.

"An Act making additional appropriations for the support of the navy," etc.

"For the reimbursement of the marshal of Florida for expenses incurred in the case of certain Africans who were wrecked on the coast of the United States, and for the expense of exporting them to Africa," $16,000. *Statutes at Large*, IV. 353, 354.

1830, April 7. Congress (House): Resolution against Slave-Trade.

Mr. Mercer reported the following resolution:—

"*Resolved*, That the President of the United States be requested to consult and negotiate with all the Governments where Ministers of the United States are, or shall be accredited, on the means of effecting an entire and immediate abolition of the African slave trade; and especially, on the expediency, with that view, of causing it to be universally denounced as piratical." Referred to Committee of the Whole; no further action recorded. *House Journal*, 21 Cong. 1 sess. p. 512.

1830, April 7. Congress (House): Proposition to Amend Act of March 3, 1819.

Mr. Mercer, from the committee to which was referred the memorial of the American Colonization Society, and also memorials, from the inhabitants of Kentucky and Ohio, reported with a bill (No. 412) to amend "An act in addition to the acts prohibiting the slave trade," passed March 3, 1819. Read twice and referred to Committee of the Whole. *Ibid.*

1830, May 31. Congress (Statute): Appropriation.

"An Act making a re-appropriation of a sum heretofore appropriated for the suppression of the slave trade." *Statutes at Large*, IV. 425; *Senate Journal*,

21 Cong. 1 sess. pp. 359, 360, 383; *House Journal*, 21 Cong. 1 sess. pp. 624, 808–11.

1830. [Brazil: Prohibition of Slave-Trade.

Slave-trade prohibited under severe penalties.]

1831, 1833. [Great Britain and France: Treaty Granting Right of Search.

Convention between Great Britain and France granting a mutual limited Right of Search on the East and West coasts of Africa, and on the coasts of the West Indies and Brazil. *British and Foreign State Papers*, 1830–1, p. 641 ff; 1832–3, p. 286 ff.]

1831, Feb. 16. Congress (House): Proposed Resolution on Slave-Trade.

"Mr. Mercer moved to suspend the rule of the House in regard to motions, for the purpose of enabling himself to submit a resolution requesting the Executive to enter into negotiations with the maritime Powers of Europe, to induce them to enact laws declaring the African slave trade piracy, and punishing it as such." The motion was lost. Gales and Seaton, *Register of Debates*, VII. 726.

1831, March 2. United States Statute: Appropriation.

"An Act making appropriations for the naval service," etc.

"For carrying into effect the acts for the suppression of the slave trade," etc., $16,000. *Statutes at Large*, IV. 460, 462.

1831, March 3. Congress (House): Resolution as to Treaties.

"Mr. Mercer moved to suspend the rule to enable him to submit the following resolution:

"*Resolved*, That the President of the United States be requested to renew, and to prosecute from time to time, such negotiations with the several maritime powers of Europe and America as he may deem expedient for the effectual abolition of the African slave trade, and its ultimate denunciation as piracy, under the laws of nations, by the consent of the civilized world." The rule was suspended by a vote of 108 to 36, and the resolution passed, 118 to 32. *House Journal*, 21 Cong. 2 sess. pp. 426–8.

1833, Feb. 20. United States Statute: Appropriation.

"An Act making appropriations for the naval service," etc.

" . . . for carrying into effect the acts for the suppression of the slave trade," etc., $5,000. *Statutes at Large*, IV. 614, 615.

1833, August. Great Britain and France: Proposed Treaty with the United States.

British and French ministers simultaneously invited the United States to accede to the Convention just concluded between them for the suppression of the slave-trade. The Secretary of State, Mr. M'Lane, deferred answer until the meeting of Congress, and then postponed negotiations on account of the irritable state of the country on the slave question. Great Britain had proposed that "A reciprocal right of search . . . be conceded by the United States, limited as to place, and subject to specified restrictions. It is to be employed only in repressing the Slave Trade, and to be exercised under a written and specific authority, conferred on the Commander of the visiting ship." In the act of accession, "it will be necessary that the right of search should be extended to the coasts of the United States," and Great Britain will in turn extend it to the British West Indies. This proposal was finally refused, March 24, 1834, chiefly, as stated, because of the extension of the Right of Search to the coasts of the United States. This part was waived by Great Britain, July 7, 1834. On Sept. 12 the French Minister joined in urging accession. On Oct. 4, 1834, Forsyth states that the determination has "been definitely formed, not to make the United States a party to any Convention on the subject of the Slave Trade." *Parliamentary Papers*, 1835, Vol. LI., *Slave Trade*, Class B., pp. 84–92.

1833, Dec. 23. Georgia: Slave-Trade Acts Amended.

"An Act to reform, amend, and consolidate the penal laws of the State of Georgia."

13th Division. "Offences relative to Slaves": —

§ 1. "If any person or persons shall bring, import, or introduce into this State, or aid or assist, or knowingly become concerned or interested, in bringing, importing, or introducing into this State, either by land or by water, or in any manner whatever, any slave or slaves, each and every such person or persons so offending, shall be deemed principals in law, and guilty of a high misdemeanor, and . . . on conviction, shall be punished by a fine not exceeding five hundred dollars each, for each and every slave, . . . and imprisonment and labor in the penitentiary for any time not less than one year, nor longer than four years." Residents, however, may bring slaves for their own use, but must register and swear they are not for sale, hire, mortgage, etc.

§ 6. Penalty for knowingly receiving such slaves, $500. Slightly amended Dec. 23, 1836, e. g., emigrants were allowed to hire slaves out, etc.; amended Dec. 19, 1849, so as to allow importation of slaves from "any other slave holding State of this Union." Prince, *Digest*, pp. 619, 653, 812; Cobb, *Digest*, II. 1018.

1834, Jan. 24. United States Statute: Appropriation.

"An Act making appropriations for the naval service," etc.

"For carrying into effect the acts for the suppression of the slave trade," etc., $5,000. *Statutes at Large*, IV. 670, 671.

1836, March 17. Texas: African Slave-Trade Prohibited.

Constitution of the Republic of Texas: General Provisions: —

§ 9. All persons of color who were slaves for life before coming to Texas shall remain so. "Congress shall pass no laws to prohibit emigrants from bringing their slaves into the republic with them, and holding them by the same tenure by which such slaves were held in the United States; . . . the importation or admission of Africans or negroes into this republic, excepting from the United States of America, is forever prohibited, and declared to be piracy." *Laws of the Republic of Texas* (Houston, 1838), I. 19.

1836, Dec. 21. Texas: Slave-Trade made Piracy.

"An Act supplementary to an act, for the punishment of Crimes and Misdemeanors."

§ 1. "*Be it enacted* . . . , That if any person or persons shall introduce any African negro or negroes, contrary to the true intent and meaning of the ninth section of the general provisions of the constitution, . . . except such as are from the United States of America, and had been held as slaves therein, be considered guilty of piracy; and upon conviction thereof, before any court having cognizance of the same, shall suffer death, without the benefit of clergy."

§ 2. The introduction of Negroes from the United States of America, except of those legally held as slaves there, shall be piracy. *Ibid.*, I. 197. Cf. *House Doc.*, 27 Cong. 1 sess. No. 34, p. 42.

1837, March 3. United States Statute: Appropriation.

"An Act making appropriations for the naval service," etc.

"For carrying into effect the acts for the suppression of the slave trade," etc., $11,413.57. *Statutes at Large*, V. 155, 157.

1838, March 19. Congress (Senate): Slave-Trade with Texas, etc.

"Mr. Morris submitted the following motion for consideration:

"*Resolved*, That the Committee on the Judiciary be instructed to inquire whether the present laws of the United States, on the subject of the slave trade, will prohibit that trade being carried on between citizens of the United States and citizens of the Republic of Texas, either by land or by sea; and whether it would be lawful in vessels owned by citizens of that Republic, and not lawful in vessels owned by citizens of this, or lawful in both, and by citizens of both countries; and also whether a slave carried from the United States into a foreign country, and brought back, on returning into the United States, is considered a free person, or is liable to be sent back, if demanded, as a slave, into that country from which he or she last came; and also whether any additional legislation by Congress is necessary on any of these subjects." March 20, the motion of Mr. Walker that this resolution "lie on the table," was determined in the affirmative, 32 to 9. *Senate Journal*, 25 Cong. 2 sess. pp. 297–8, 300.

1839, Feb. 5. Congress (Senate): Bill to Amend Slave-Trade Acts.

"Mr. Strange, on leave, and in pursuance of notice given, introduced a bill to amend an act entitled an act to prohibit the importation of slaves into any port in the jurisdiction of the United States; which was read twice, and referred to the Committee on Commerce." March 1, the Committee was discharged from further consideration of the bill. *Congressional Globe*, 25 Cong. 3 sess. p. 172; *Senate Journal*, 25 Cong. 3 sess. pp. 200, 313.

1839, Dec. 24. President Van Buren's Message.

"It will be seen by the report of the Secretary of the navy respecting the disposition of our ships of war, that it has been deemed necessary to station a competent force on the coast of Africa, to prevent a fraudulent use of our flag by foreigners.

"Recent experience has shown that the provisions in our existing laws which relate to the sale and transfer of American vessels while abroad, are extremely defective. Advantage has been taken of these defects to give to vessels wholly belonging to foreigners, and navigating the ocean, an apparent American ownership. This character has been so well simulated as to afford them comparative security in prosecuting the slave trade, a traffic emphatically denounced in our statutes, regarded with abhorrence by our citizens, and of which the effectual suppression is nowhere more sincerely desired than in the United States. These circumstances make it proper to recommend to your early attention a careful revision of these laws, so that . . . the integrity and honor of our flag may be carefully preserved." *House Journal*, 26 Cong. 1 sess. pp. 117–8.

1840, Jan. 3. Congress (Senate): Bill to Amend Act of 1807.

"Agreeably to notice, Mr. Strange asked and obtained leave to bring in a bill (Senate, No. 123) to amend an act entitled 'An act to prohibit the importation of slaves into any port or place within the jurisdiction of the United States from and after the 1st day of January, in the year 1808,' approved the 2d day of March, 1807; which was read the first and second times, by unanimous consent, and referred to the Committee on the Judiciary." Jan. 8, it was reported without amendment; May 11, it was considered, and, on motion by Mr. King, "*Ordered*, That it lie on the table." *Senate Journal*, 26 Cong. 1 sess. pp. 73, 87, 363.

1840, May 4. Congress (Senate): Bill on Slave-Trade.

"Mr. Davis, from the Committee on Commerce, reported a bill (Senate, No. 335) making further provision to prevent the abuse of the flag of the United States, and the use of unauthorized papers in the foreign slavetrade, and for other purposes." This passed the Senate, but was dropped in the House. *Ibid.*, pp. 356, 359, 440, 442; *House Journal*, 26 Cong. 1 sess. pp. 1138, 1228, 1257.

1841, June 1. Congress (House): President Tyler's Message.

"I shall also, at the proper season, invite your attention to the statutory enactments for the suppression of the slave trade, which may require to be rendered more efficient in their provisions. There is reason to believe that the traffic is on the increase. Whether such increase is to be ascribed to the abolition of slave labor in the British possessions in our vicinity, and an attendant diminution in the supply of those articles which enter into the general consumption of the world, thereby augmenting the demand from other quarters, . . . it were needless to inquire. The highest considerations of public honor, as well as the strongest promptings of humanity, require a resort to the most vigorous efforts to suppress the trade." *House Journal*, 27 Cong. 1 sess. pp. 31, 184.

1841, Dec. 7. President Tyler's Message.

Though the United States is desirous to suppress the slave-trade, she will not submit to interpolations into the maritime code at will by other nations. This government has expressed its repugnance to the trade by several laws. It is a matter for deliberation whether we will enter upon treaties containing mutual stipulations upon the subject with other governments. The United States will demand indemnity for all depredations by Great Britain.

"I invite your attention to existing laws for the suppression of the African slave trade, and recommend all such alterations as may give to them greater force and efficacy. That the American flag is grossly abused by the abandoned and profligate of other nations is but too probable. Congress has, not long since, had this subject under its consideration, and its importance well justifies renewed and anxious attention." *House Journal*, 27 Cong. 2 sess. pp. 14–5, 86, 113.

1841, Dec. 20. [Great Britain, Austria, Russia, Prussia, and France: Quintuple Treaty.] *British and Foreign State Papers*, 1841–2, p. 269 ff.

1842, Feb. 15. Right of Search: Cass's Protest.

Cass writes to Webster, that, considering the fact that the signing of the Quintuple Treaty would oblige the participants to exercise the Right of Search denied by the United States, or to make a change in the hitherto recognized law of nations, he, on his own responsibility, addressed the following protest to the French Minister of Foreign Affairs, M. Guizot:—

"LEGATION OF THE UNITED STATES,
"PARIS, FEBRUARY 13, 1842.

"SIR: The recent signature of a treaty, having for its object the suppression of the African slave trade, by five of the powers of Europe, and to which France is a party, is a fact of such general notoriety that it may be assumed as the basis of any diplomatic representations which the subject may fairly require."

The United States is no party to this treaty. She denies the Right of Visitation which England asserts. [Quotes from the presidential message of Dec. 7, 1841.] This principle is asserted by the treaty.

" . . . The moral effect which such a union of five great powers, two of which are eminently maritime, but three of which have perhaps never had a vessel engaged in that traffic, is calculated to produce upon the United States, and upon other nations who, like them, may be indisposed to these combined movements, though it may be regretted, yet furnishes no just cause of complaint. But the subject assumes another aspect when they are told by one of the parties that their vessels are to be forcibly entered and examined, in order to carry into effect these stipulations. Certainly the American Government does not believe that the high powers, contracting parties to this treaty, have any wish to compel the United States, by force, to adopt their measures to its provisions, or to adopt its stipulations . . . ; and they will see with pleasure the prompt disavowal made by yourself, sir, in the name of your country, . . . of any intentions of this nature. But were it otherwise, . . . They would prepare themselves with apprehension, indeed, but without dismay—with regret, but with firmness—for one of those desperate struggles which have sometimes occurred in the history of the world."

If, as England says, these treaties cannot be executed without visiting United States ships, then France must pursue the same course. It is hoped, therefore, that his Majesty will, before signing this treaty, carefully examine the pretensions of England and their compatibility with the law of nations and the honor of the United States. *Senate Doc.*, 27 Cong. 3 sess. II. No. 52, and IV. No. 223; 29 Cong. 1 sess. VIII. No. 377, pp. 192–5.

1842, Feb. 26. Mississippi: Resolutions on Creole Case.

The following resolutions were referred to the Committee on Foreign Affairs in the United States Congress, House of Representatives, May 10, 1842:

"Whereas, the right of search has never been yielded to Great Britain," and the brig Creole has not been surrendered by the British authorities, etc., therefore,

§ 1. "*Be it resolved by the Legislature of the State of Mississippi*, That . . . the right of search cannot be conceded to Great Britain without a manifest servile submission, unworthy a free nation. . . .

§ 2. "*Resolved*, That any attempt to detain and search our vessels, by British cruisers, should be held and esteemed an unjustifiable outrage on the part of the Queen's Government; and that any such outrage, which may have occurred since Lord Aberdeen's note to our envoy at the Court of St. James, of date October thirteen, eighteen hundred and forty-one, (if any,) may well be deemed, by our Government, just cause of war."

§ 3. "*Resolved*, That the Legislature of the State, in view of the late murderous insurrection of the slaves on board the Creole, their reception in a British port, the absolute connivance at their crimes, manifest in the protection extended to them by the British authorities, most solemnly declare their firm conviction that, if the conduct of those authorities be submitted to, compounded for by the payment of money, or in any other manner, or atoned for in any mode except by the surrender of the actual criminals to the Federal Government, and the delivery of the other identical slaves to their rightful owner or owners, or his or their agents, the slaveholding States would have most just cause to apprehend that the American flag is powerless to protect American property; that the Federal Government is not sufficiently energetic in the maintenance and preservation of their peculiar rights; and that these rights, therefore, are in imminent danger."

§ 4. *Resolved*, That restitution should be demanded "at all hazards." *House Doc.*, 27 Cong. 2 sess. IV. No. 215.

1842, March 21. Congress (House): Giddings's Resolutions.

Mr. Giddings moved the following resolutions:—

§ 5. "*Resolved*, That when a ship belonging to the citizens of any State of this Union leaves the waters and territory of such State, and enters upon the high seas, the persons on board cease to be subject to the slave laws of such State, and therefore are governed in their relations to each other by, and are amenable to, the laws of the United States."

§ 6. *Resolved*, That the slaves in the brig Creole are amenable only to the laws of the United States.

§ 7. *Resolved*, That those slaves by resuming their natural liberty violated no laws of the United States.

§ 8. *Resolved*, That all attempts to re-enslave them are unconstitutional, etc.

Moved that these resolutions lie on the table; defeated, 53 to 125. Mr. Giddings withdrew the resolutions. Moved to censure Mr. Giddings, and he was finally censured. *House Journal*, 27 Cong. 2 sess. pp. 567–80.

1842, May 10. Congress (House): Remonstrance of Mississippi against Right of Search.

"Mr. Gwin presented resolutions of the Legislature of the State of Mississippi, against granting the right of search to Great Britain for the purpose of suppressing the African slave trade; urging the Government to demand of the British Government redress and restitution in relation to the case of the brig Creole and the slaves on board." Referred to the Committee on Foreign Affairs. *House Journal*, 27 Cong. 2 sess. p. 800.

1842, Aug. 4. United States Statute: Appropriation.

"An Act making appropriations for the naval service," etc.

"For carrying into effect the acts for the suppression of the slave trade," etc. $10,543.42. *Statutes at Large*, V. 500, 501.

1842, Nov. 10. Joint-Cruising Treaty with Great Britain.

"Treaty to settle and define boundaries; for the final suppression of the African slave-trade; and for the giving up of criminals fugitive from justice. Concluded August 9, 1842; ratifications exchanged at London October 13, 1842; proclaimed November 10, 1842." Articles VIII., and IX. Ratified by the Senate by a vote of 39 to 9, after several unsuccessful attempts to amend it. *U. S. Treaties and Conventions* (1889), pp. 436–7; *Senate Exec. Journal*, VI. 118–32.

1842, Dec. 7. President Tyler's Message.

The treaty of Ghent binds the United States and Great Britain to the suppression of the slave-trade. The Right of Search was refused by the United States, and our Minister in France for that reason protested against the Quintuple Treaty; his conduct had the approval of the administration. On this account the eighth article was inserted, causing each government to keep a flotilla in African waters to enforce the laws. If this should be done by all the powers, the trade would be swept from the ocean. *House Journal*, 27 Cong. 3 sess. pp. 16–7.

1843, Feb. 22. Congress (Senate): Appropriation Opposed.

Motion by Mr. Benton, during debate on naval appropriations, to strike out appropriation "for the support of Africans recaptured on the coast of Africa or elsewhere, and returned to Africa by the armed vessels of the United States, $5,000." Lost; similar proposition by Bagby, lost. Proposition to strike out appropriation for squadron, lost. March 3, bill becomes a law, with appropriation for Africans, but without that for squadron. *Congressional Globe*, 27 Cong. 3 sess. pp. 328, 331–6; *Statutes at Large*, V. 615.

1845, Feb. 20. President Tyler's Special Message to Congress.

Message on violations of Brazilian slave-trade laws by Americans. *House Journal*, 28 Cong. 2 sess. pp. 425, 463; *House Doc.*, 28 Cong. 2 sess. IV. No. 148. Cf. *Ibid.*, 29 Cong. 1 sess. III. No. 43.

1846, Aug. 10. United States Statute: Appropriation.

"For carrying into effect the acts for the suppression of the slave trade, including the support of recaptured Africans, and their removal to their country, twenty-five thousand dollars." *Statutes at Large*, IX. 96.

1849, Dec. 4. President Taylor's Message.

"Your attention is earnestly invited to an amendment of our existing laws relating to the African slave-trade, with a view to the effectual suppression of that barbarous traffic. It is not to be denied that this trade is still, in part, carried on by means of vessels built in the United States, and owned or navigated by some of our citizens." *House Exec. Doc.*, 31 Cong. 1 sess. III. No. 5, pp. 7–8.

1850, Aug. 1. Congress (House): Bill for War Steamers.

"A bill (House, No. 367) to establish a line of war steamers to the coast of Africa for the suppression of the slave trade and the promotion of commerce and colonization." Read twice, and referred to Committee of the Whole. *House Journal*, 31 Cong. 1 sess. pp. 1022, 1158, 1217.

1850, Dec. 16. Congress (House): Treaty of Washington.

"Mr. Burt, by unanimous consent, introduced a joint resolution (No. 28) 'to terminate the eighth article of the treaty between the United States and Great Britain concluded at Washington the ninth day of August, 1842.'" Read twice, and referred to the Committee on Naval Affairs. *Ibid.*, 31 Cong. 2 sess. p. 64.

1851, Jan. 22. Congress (Senate): Resolution on Sea Letters.

"The following resolution, submitted by Mr. Clay the 20th instant, came up for consideration:—

"*Resolved*, That the Committee on Commerce be instructed to inquire into the expediency of making more effectual provision by law to prevent the employment of American vessels and American seamen in the African slave trade, and especially as to the expediency of granting sea letters or other evidence of national character to American vessels clearing out of the ports of the empire of Brazil for the western coast of Africa." Agreed to. *Congressional Globe*, 31 Cong. 2 sess. pp. 304–9; *Senate Journal*, 31 Cong. 2 sess. pp. 95, 102–3.

1851, Feb. 19. Congress (Senate): Bill on Slave-Trade.

"A bill (Senate, No. 472) concerning the intercourse and trade of vessels of the United States with certain places on the eastern and western coasts of Africa, and for other purposes." Read once. *Senate Journal*, 31 Cong. 2 sess. pp. 42, 45, 84, 94, 159, 193–4; *Congressional Globe*, 31 Cong. 2 sess. pp. 246–7.

1851, Dec. 3. Congress (House): Bill to Amend Act of 1807.

Mr. Giddings gave notice of a bill to repeal §§ 9 and 10 of the act to prohibit the importation of slaves, etc. from and after Jan. 1, 1808. *House Journal*, 32 Cong. 1 sess. p. 42. Cf. *Ibid.*, 33 Cong. 1 sess. p. 147.

1852, Feb. 5. Alabama: Illegal Importations.

By code approved on this date:—

§§ 2058–2062. If slaves have been imported contrary to law, they are to be sold, and one fourth paid to the agent or informer and the residue to the treasury. An agent is to be appointed to take charge of such slaves, who is to give bond. Pending controversy, he may hire the slaves out. Ormond, *Code of Alabama*, pp. 392–3.

1853, March 3. Congress (Senate): Appropriation Proposed.

A bill making appropriations for the naval service for the year ending June 30, 1854. Mr. Underwood offered the following amendment:—

"For executing the provisions of the act approved 3d of March, 1819, entitled 'An act in addition to the acts prohibiting the slave trade,' $20,000." Amendment agreed to, and bill passed. It appears, however, to have been subsequently amended in the House, and the appropriation does not stand in the final act. *Congressional Globe*, 32 Cong. 2 sess. p. 1072; *Statutes at Large*, X. 214.

1854, May 22. Congress (Senate): West India Slave-Trade.

Mr. Clayton presented the following resolution, which was unanimously agreed to:—

"*Resolved*, That the Committee on Foreign Relations be instructed to inquire into the expediency of providing by law for such restrictions on the power of American consuls residing in the Spanish West India islands to issue sea letters on the transfer of American vessels in those islands, as will prevent the abuse of the American flag in protecting persons engaged in the African slave trade." June 26, 1854, this committee reported "a bill (Senate, No. 416) for the more effectual suppression of the slave-trade in American built vessels." Passed Senate, postponed in House. *Senate Journal*, 33 Cong. 1 sess. pp. 404, 457–8, 472–3, 476; *House Journal*, 33 Cong. 1 sess. pp. 1093, 1332–3; *Congressional Globe*, 33 Cong. 1 sess. pp. 1257–61, 1511–3, 1591–3, 2139.

1854, May 29. Congress (Senate): Treaty of Washington.

Resolved, "that, in the opinion of the Senate, it is expedient, and in conformity with the interests and sound policy of the United States, that the eighth article of the treaty between this government and

Great Britain, of the 9th of August, 1842, should be abrogated." Introduced by Slidell, and favorably reported from Committee on Foreign Relations in Executive Session, June 13, 1854. *Senate Journal*, 34 Cong. 1–2 sess. pp. 396, 695–8; *Senate Reports*, 34 Cong. 1 sess. I. No. 195.

1854, June 21. Congress (Senate): Bill Regulating Navigation.

"Mr. Seward asked and obtained leave to bring in a bill (Senate, No. 407) to regulate navigation to the coast of Africa in vessels owned by citizens of the United States, in certain cases; which was read and passed to a second reading." June 22, ordered to be printed. *Senate Journal*, 33 Cong. 1 sess. pp. 448, 451; *Congressional Globe*, 33 Cong. 1 sess. pp. 1456, 1461, 1472.

1854, June 26. Congress (Senate): Bill to Suppress Slave-Trade.

"A bill for the more effectual suppression of the slave trade in American built vessels." See references to May 22, 1854, above.

1856, June 23. Congress (House): Proposition to Amend Act of 1818.

Notice given of a bill to amend the Act of April 20, 1818. *House Journal*, 34 Cong. 1 sess. II. 1101.

1856, Aug. 18. United States Statute: Appropriation.

To carry out the Act of March 3, 1819, and subsequent acts, $8,000. *Statutes at Large*, XI. 90.

1856, Nov. 24. South Carolina: Governor's Message.

Governor Adams, in his annual message to the legislature, said:—

"It is apprehended that the opening of this trade [*i. e.*, the slave-trade] will lessen the value of slaves, and ultimately destroy the institution. It is a sufficient answer to point to the fact, that unrestricted immigration has not diminished the value of labor in the Northwestern section of the confederacy. The cry there is, want of labor, notwithstanding capital has the pauperism of the old world to press into its grinding service. If we cannot supply the demand for slave labor, then we must expect to be supplied with a species of labor we do not want, and which is, from the very nature of things, antagonistic to our institutions. It is much better that our drays should be driven by slaves—that our factories should be worked by slaves—that our hotels should be served by slaves—that our locomotives should be manned by slaves, than that we should be exposed to the introduction, from any quarter, of a population alien to us by birth, training, and education, and which, in the process of time, must lead to that conflict between capital and labor, 'which makes it so difficult to maintain free institutions in all wealthy and highly civilized nations where such institutions as ours do not exist.' In all slaveholding States, true policy dictates that the superior race should direct, and the inferior perform all menial service. Competition between the white and black man for this service, may not disturb Northern sensibility, but it does not exactly suit our latitude." *South Carolina House Journal*, 1856, p. 36; Cluskey, *Political Text-Book*, 14 edition, p. 585.

1856, Dec. 15. Congress (House): Reopening of Slave-Trade.

"*Resolved*, That this House of Representatives regards all suggestions and propositions of every kind, by whomsoever made, for a revival of the African slave trade, as shocking to the moral sentiment of the enlightened portion of mankind; and that any action on the part of Congress conniving at or legalizing that horrid and inhuman traffic would justly subject the government and citizens of the United States to the reproach and execration of all civilized and Christian people throughout the world." Offered by Mr. Etheridge; agreed to, 152 to 57. *House Journal*, 34 Cong. 3 sess. pp. 105–11; *Congressional Globe*, 34 Cong. 3 sess. pp. 123–5, and Appendix, pp. 364–70.

1856, Dec. 15. Congress (House): Reopening of Slave-Trade.

"*Resolved*, That it is inexpedient to repeal the laws prohibiting the African slave trade." Offered by Mr. Orr; not voted upon. *Congressional Globe*, 34 Cong. 3 sess. p. 123.

1856, Dec. 15. Congress (House): Reopening of Slave-Trade.

"*Resolved*, That it is inexpedient, unwise, and contrary to the settled policy of the United States, to repeal the laws prohibiting the African slave trade." Offered by Mr. Orr; agreed to, 183 to 8. *House Journal*, 34 Cong. 3 sess. pp. 111–3; *Congressional Globe*, 34 Cong. 3 sess. pp. 125–6.

1856, Dec. 15. Congress (House): Reopening of Slave-Trade.

"*Resolved*, That the House of Representatives, expressing, as they believe, public opinion both North and South, are utterly opposed to the reopening of the slave trade." Offered by Mr. Boyce; not voted upon. *Congressional Globe*, 34 Cong. 3 sess. p. 125.

1857. South Carolina: Report of Legislative Committee.

Special committee of seven on the slave-trade clause in the Governor's message report: majority report of six members, favoring the reopening of the African slave-trade; minority report of Pettigrew, opposing it. *Report of the Special Committee*, etc., published in 1857.

1857, March 3. United States Statute: Appropriation.

To carry out the Act of March 3, 1819, and subsequent acts, $8,000. *Statutes at Large*, XI. 227; *House Journal*, 34 Cong. 3 sess. p. 397. Cf. *House Exec. Doc.*, 34 Cong. 3 sess. IX. No. 70.

1858, March (?). Louisiana: Bill to Import Africans.

Passed House; lost in Senate by two votes. Cf. *Congressional Globe*, 35 Cong. 1 sess. p. 1362.

1858, Dec. 6. President Buchanan's Message.

"The truth is, that Cuba in its existing colonial condition, is a constant source of injury and annoyance to the American people. It is the only spot in the civilized world where the African slave trade is tolerated; and we are bound by treaty with Great Britain to maintain a naval force on the coast of Africa, at much expense both of life and treasure, solely for the purpose of arresting slavers bound to that island. The late serious difficulties between the United States and Great Britain respecting the right of search, now so happily terminated, could never have arisen if Cuba had not afforded a market for slaves. As long as this market shall remain open, there can be no hope for the civilization of benighted Africa. . . .

"It has been made known to the world by my predecessors that the United States have, on several occasions, endeavored to acquire Cuba from Spain by honorable negotiation. If this were accomplished, the last relic of the African slave trade would instantly disappear. We would not, if we could, acquire Cuba in any other manner. This is due to our national character. . . . This course we shall ever pursue, unless circumstances should occur, which we do not now anticipate, rendering a departure from it clearly justifiable, under the imperative and overruling law of self-preservation." *House Exec. Doc.*, 35 Cong. 2 sess. II. No. 2, pp. 14–5. See also *Ibid.*, pp. 31–3.

1858, Dec. 23. Congress (House): Resolution on Slave-Trade.

On motion of Mr. Farnsworth,

"*Resolved*, That the Committee on Naval Affairs be requested to inquire and report to this House if any, and what, further legislation is necessary on the part of the United States to fully carry out and perform the stipulations contained in the eighth article of the treaty with Great Britain (known as the 'Ashburton treaty') for the suppression of the slave trade." *House Journal*, 35 Cong. 2 sess. pp. 115–6.

1859, Jan. 5. Congress (Senate): Resolution on Slave-Trade.

On motion of Mr. Seward, Dec. 21, 1858,

"*Resolved*, That the Committee on the Judiciary inquire whether any amendments to existing laws ought to be made for the suppression of the African slave trade." *Senate Journal*, 35 Cong. 2 sess. pp. 80, 108, 115.

1859, Jan. 13. Congress (Senate): Bill on Slave-Trade.

Mr. Seward introduced "a bill (Senate, No. 510) in addition to the acts which prohibit the slave trade." Referred to committee, reported, and dropped. *Ibid.*, pp. 134, 321.

1859, Jan. 31. Congress (House): Reopening of Slave-Trade.

"Mr. Kilgore moved that the rules be suspended, so as to enable him to submit the following preamble and resolutions, viz:

"Whereas the laws prohibiting the African slave trade have become a topic of discussion with newspaper writers and political agitators, many of them boldly denouncing these laws as unwise in policy and disgraceful in their provisions, and insisting on the justice and propriety of their repeal, and the revival of the odious traffic in African slaves; and whereas recent demonstrations afford strong reasons to apprehend that said laws are to be set at defiance, and their violation openly countenanced and encouraged by a portion of the citizens of some of the States of this Union; and whereas it is proper in view of said facts that the sentiments of the people's representatives in Congress should be made public in relation thereto: Therefore—

"*Resolved*, That while we recognize no right on the part of the federal government, or any other law-making power, save that of the States wherein it exists, to interfere with or disturb the institution of domestic slavery where it is established or protected by State legislation, we do hold that Congress has power to prohibit the foreign traffic, and that no legislation can be too thorough in its measures, nor can any penalty known to the catalogue of modern punishment for crime be too severe against a traffic so inhuman and unchristian.

"*Resolved*, That the laws in force against said traffic are founded upon the broadest principles of philanthropy, religion, and humanity; that they should remain unchanged, except so far as legislation may be needed to render them more efficient; that they should be faithfully and promptly executed by our government, and respected by all good citizens.

"*Resolved*, That the Executive should be sustained and commended for any proper efforts whenever and wherever made to enforce said laws, and to bring to speedy punishment the wicked violators thereof, and all their aiders and abettors."

Failed of the two-thirds vote necessary to suspend the rules—the vote being 115 to 84—and was dropped. *House Journal*, 35 Cong. 2 sess. pp. 298–9.

1859, March 3. United States Statute: Appropriation.

To carry out the Act of March 3, 1819, and subsequent acts, and to pay expenses already incurred, $75,000. *Statutes at Large*, XI. 404.

1859, Dec. 19. President Buchanan's Message.

"All lawful means at my command have been employed, and shall continue to be employed, to execute the laws against the African slave trade. After a most careful and rigorous examination of our coasts, and a thorough investigation of the subject, we have not been able to discover that any slaves have been imported into the United States except the cargo by the Wanderer, numbering between three and four hundred. Those engaged in this unlawful enterprise have been rigorously prosecuted, but not with as much success as their crimes have deserved. A number of them are still under prosecution. [Here follows a history of our slave-trade legislation.]

"These acts of Congress, it is believed, have, with very rare and insignificant exceptions, accomplished their purpose. For a period of more than half a century there has been no perceptible addition to the number of our domestic slaves. . . . Reopen the trade, and it would be difficult to determine whether the effect would be more deleterious on the interests of the master, or on those of the native born slave, . . ." *Senate Exec. Doc.*, 36 Cong. 1 sess. I. No. 2, pp. 5–8.

1860, March 20. Congress (Senate): Proposed Resolution.

"Mr. Wilson submitted the following resolution; which was considered, by unanimous consent, and agreed to:—

"*Resolved*, That the Committee on the Judiciary be instructed to inquire into the expediency of so amending the laws of the United States in relation to the suppression of the African slave trade as to provide a penalty of imprisonment for life for a participation in such trade, instead of the penalty of forfeiture of life, as now provided; and also an amendment of such laws as will include in the punishment for said offense all persons who fit out or are in any way connected with or interested in fitting out expeditions or vessels for the purpose of engaging in such slave trade." *Senate Journal*, 36 Cong. 1 sess. p. 274.

1860, March 20. Congress (Senate): Right of Search.

"Mr. Wilson asked, and by unanimous consent obtained, leave to bring in a joint resolution (Senate, No. 20) to secure the right of search on the coast of Africa, for the more effectual suppression of the African slave trade." Read twice, and referred to Committee on Foreign Relations. *Ibid.*

1860, March 20. Congress (Senate): Steam Vessels for Slave-Trade.

"Mr. Wilson asked, and by unanimous consent obtained, leave to bring in a bill (Senate, No. 296) for the construction of five steam screw sloops-of-war, for service on the African coast." Read twice, and referred to Committee on Naval Affairs; May 23, reported with an amendment. *Ibid.*, pp. 274, 494–5.

1860, March 26. Congress (House): Proposed Resolutions.

"Mr. Morse submitted . . . the following resolutions; which were read and committed to the Committee of the Whole House on the state of the Union, viz:

"*Resolved*, That for the more effectual suppression of the African slave trade the treaty of 1842 . . . , requiring each country to keep *eighty* guns on the coast of Africa for that purpose, should be so changed as to require a specified and sufficient number of small steamers and fast sailing brigs or schooners to be kept on said coast. . . .

"*Resolved*, That as the African slave trade appears to be rapidly increasing, some effective mode of identifying the nationality of a vessel on the coast of Africa suspected of being in the slave trade or of wearing false colors should be immediately adopted and carried into effect by the leading maritime nations of the earth; and that the government of the United States has thus far, by refusing to aid in establishing such a system, shown a strange neglect of one of the best means of suppressing said trade.

"*Resolved*, That the African slave trade is against the moral sentiment of mankind and a crime against human nature; and that as the most highly civilized nations have made it a criminal offence or piracy under their own municipal laws, it ought at once and without hesitation to be declared a crime by the code of international law; and that . . . the President be requested to open negotiations on this subject with the leading powers of Europe." . . . *House Journal*, 36 Cong. 1 sess. I. 588–9.

1860, April 16. Congress (Senate): Bill on Slave-Trade.

"Mr. Wilson asked, and by unanimous consent

obtained, leave to bring in a bill (Senate, No. 408) for the more effectual suppression of the slave trade." Bill read twice, and ordered to lie on the table; May 21, referred to Committee on the Judiciary, and printed. *Senate Journal*, 36 Cong. 1 sess. pp. 394, 485; *Congressional Globe*, 36 Cong. 1 sess. pp. 1721, 2207–11.

1860, May 21. Congress (House): Buyers of Imported Negroes.

"Mr. Wells submitted the following resolution, and debate arising thereon, it lies over under the rule, viz:

"*Resolved*, That the Committee on the Judiciary be instructed to report forthwith a bill providing that any person purchasing any negro or other person imported into this country in violation of the laws for suppressing the slave trade, shall not by reason of said purchase acquire any title to said negro or person; and where such purchase is made with a knowledge that such negro or other person has been so imported, shall forfeit not less than one thousand dollars, and be punished by imprisonment for a term not less than six months." *House Journal*, 36 Cong. 1 sess. II. 880.

1860, May 26. United States Statute: Appropriation.

To carry out the Act of March 3, 1819, and subsequent acts, $40,000. *Statutes at Large*, XII. 21.

1860, June 16. United States Statute: Additional Act to Act of 1819.

"An Act to amend an Act entitled 'An Act in addition to the Acts Prohibiting the Slave Trade.' " *Ibid.*, XII. 40–1; *Senate Journal*, 36 Cong. 1 sess., Senate Bill No. 464.

1860, July 11. Great Britain: Proposed Co-operation.

Lord John Russell suggested for the suppression of the trade:—

"1st. A systematic plan of cruising on the coast of Cuba by the vessels of Great Britain, Spain, and the United States.

"2d. Laws of registration and inspection in the Island

of Cuba, by which the employment of slaves, imported contrary to law, might be detected by the Spanish authorities.

"3d. A plan of emigration from China, regulated by the agents of European nations, in conjunction with the Chinese authorities." President Buchanan refused to co-operate on this plan. *House Exec. Doc.*, 36 Cong. 2 sess. IV. No. 7, pp. 441–3, 446–8.

1860, Dec. 3. President Buchanan's Message.

"It is with great satisfaction I communicate the fact that since the date of my last annual message not a single slave has been imported into the United States in violation of the laws prohibiting the African slave trade. This statement is founded upon a thorough examination and investigation of the subject. Indeed, the spirit which prevailed some time since among a portion of our fellow-citizens in favor of this trade seems to have entirely subsided." *Senate Exec. Doc.*, 36 Cong. 2 sess. I. No. 1, p. 24.

1860, Dec. 12. Congress (House): Proposition to Amend Constitution.

Mr. John Cochrane's resolution:—

"The migration or importation of slaves into the United States or any of the Territories thereof, from any foreign country, is hereby prohibited." *House Journal*, 36 Cong. 2 sess. pp. 61–2; *Congressional Globe*, 36 Cong. 2 sess. p. 77.

1860, Dec. 24. Congress (Senate): Bill on Slave-Trade.

"Mr. Wilson asked, and by unanimous consent obtained, leave to bring in a bill (Senate, No. 529) for the more effectual suppression of the slave trade." Read twice, and referred to Committee on the Judiciary; not mentioned again. *Senate Journal*, 36 Cong. 2 sess. p. 62; *Congressional Globe*, 36 Cong. 2 sess. p. 182.

1861, Jan. 7. Congress (House): Proposition to Amend Constitution.

Mr. Etheridge's resolution:—

§ 5. "The migration or importation of persons held to service or labor for life, or a term of years, into any of the States, or the Territories belonging to the United States, is perpetually prohibited; and Congress shall pass all laws necessary to make said prohibition effective." *Congressional Globe*, 36 Cong. 2 sess. p. 279.

1861, Jan. 23. Congress (House): Proposition to Amend Constitution.

Resolution of Mr. Morris of Pennsylvania:—

"Neither Congress nor a Territorial Legislature shall make any law respecting slavery or involuntary servitude, except as a punishment for crime; but Congress may pass laws for the suppression of the African slave trade, and the rendition of fugitives from service or labor in the States." Mr. Morris asked to have it printed, that he might at the proper time move it as an amendment to the report of the select committee of thirty-three. It was ordered to be printed. *Ibid.*, p. 527.

1861, Feb. 1. Congress (House): Proposition to Amend Constitution.

Resolution of Mr. Kellogg of Illinois:—

§ 16. "The migration or importation of persons held to service or involuntary servitude into any State, Territory, or place within the United States, from any place or country beyond the limits of the United States or Territories thereof, is forever prohibited." Considered Feb. 27, 1861, and lost. *Ibid.*, pp. 690, 1243, 1259–60.

1861, Feb. 8. Confederate States of America: Importation Prohibited.

Constitution for the Provisional Government of the Confederate States of America, Article I. Section 7:—

"1. The importation of African negroes from any foreign country other than the slave-holding States of the United States, is hereby forbidden; and Congress are required to pass such laws as shall effectually prevent the same.

"2. The Congress shall also have power to prohibit the introduction of slaves from any State not a member of this Confederacy." March 11, 1861, this article was placed in the permanent Constitution. The first line was changed so as to read "negroes of the African race." *C. S. A. Statutes at Large, 1861–2*, pp. 3, 15.

1861, Feb. 9. Confederate States of America: Statutory Prohibition.

"*Be it enacted by the Confederate States of America in Congress assembled*, That all the laws of the United States of America in force and in use in the Confederate States of America on the first day of November last, and not inconsistent with the Constitution of the Confederate States, be and the same are hereby continued in force until altered or repealed by the Congress." *Ibid.*, p. 27.

1861, Feb. 19. United States Statute: Appropriation.

To supply deficiencies in the fund hitherto appropriated to carry out the Act of March 3, 1819, and subsequent acts, $900,000. *Statutes at Large*, XII. 132.

1861, March 2. United States Statute: Appropriation.

To carry out the Act of March 3, 1819, and subsequent acts, and to provide compensation for district attorneys and marshals, $900,000. *Ibid.*, XII. 218–9.

1861, Dec. 3. President Lincoln's Message.

"The execution of the laws for the suppression of the African slave trade has been confided to the Department of the Interior. It is a subject of gratulation that the efforts which have been made for the suppression of this inhuman traffic have been recently attended with unusual success. Five vessels being fitted out for the slave trade have been seized and condemned. Two mates of vessels engaged in the trade, and one person in equipping a vessel as a slaver, have been convicted and subjected to the penalty of fine and imprisonment, and one captain, taken with a cargo of Africans on board his vessel, has been convicted of the highest grade of offence under our laws, the punishment of which is death." *Senate Exec. Doc.*, 37 Cong. 2 sess. I. No. 1, p. 13.

1862, Jan. 27. Congress (Senate): Bill on Slave-Trade.

"Agreeably to notice Mr. Wilson, of Massachusetts, asked and obtained leave to bring in a bill (Senate, No. 173), for the more effectual suppression of the slave trade." Read twice, and referred to Committee on the Judiciary; Feb. 11, 1863, reported adversely, and postponed indefinitely. *Senate Journal*, 37 Cong. 2 sess. p. 143; 37 Cong. 3 sess. pp. 231–2.

1862, March 14. United States Statute: Appropriation.

For compensation to United States marshals, district attorneys, etc., for services in the suppression of the slave-trade, so much of the appropriation of March 2, 1861, as may be expedient and proper, not exceeding in all $10,000. *Statutes at Large*, XII. 368–9.

1862, March 25. United States Statute: Prize Law.

"An Act to facilitate Judicial Proceedings in Adjudications upon Captured Property, and for the better Administration of the Law of Prize." Applied to captures under the slave-trade law. *Ibid.*, XII. 374–5; *Congressional Globe*, 37 Cong. 2 sess., Appendix, pp. 346–7.

1862, June 7. Great Britain: Treaty of 1862.

"Treaty for the suppression of the African slave trade. Concluded at Washington April 7, 1862; ratifications exchanged at London May 20, 1862; proclaimed June 7, 1862." Ratified unanimously by the Senate. *U. S. Treaties and Conventions* (1889), pp. 454–66. See also *Senate Exec. Journal*, XII. pp. 230, 231, 240, 254, 391, 400, 403.

1862, July 11. United States Statute: Treaty of 1862 Carried into Effect.

"An Act to carry into Effect the Treaty between the United States and her Britannic Majesty for the Suppression of the African Slave-Trade." *Statutes at Large*, XII. 531; *Senate Journal* and *House Journal*, 37 Cong. 2 sess., Senate Bill No. 352.

1862, July 17. United States Statute: Former Acts Amended.

"An Act to amend an Act entitled 'An Act to amend an Act entitled "An Act in Addition to the Acts prohibiting the Slave Trade."' " *Statutes at Large*, XII. 592–3; *Senate Journal* and *House Journal*, 37 Cong. 2 sess., Senate Bill No. 385.

1863, Feb. 4. United States Statute: Appropriation.

To carry out the treaty with Great Britain, proclaimed July 11, 1862, $17,000. *Statutes at Large*, XII. 639.

1863, March 3. Congress: Joint Resolution.

"Joint Resolution respecting the Compensation of the Judges and so forth, under the Treaty with Great Britain and other Persons employed in the Suppression of the Slave Trade." *Statutes at Large*, XII. 829.

1863, April 22. Great Britain: Treaty of 1862 Amended.

"Additional article to the treaty for the suppression of the African slave trade of April 7, 1862." Concluded February 17, 1863; ratifications exchanged at London April 1, 1863; proclaimed April 22, 1863.

Right of Search extended. *U. S. Treaties and Conventions* (1889), pp. 466–7.

1863, Dec. 17. Congress (House): Resolution on Coastwise Slave-Trade.

Mr. Julian introduced a bill to repeal portions of the Act of March 2, 1807, relative to the coastwise slave-trade. Read twice, and referred to Committee on the Judiciary. *Congressional Globe*, 38 Cong. 1 sess. p. 46.

1864, July 2. United States Statute: Coastwise Slave-Trade Prohibited Forever.

§ 9 of Appropriation Act repeals §§ 8 and 9 of Act of 1807. *Statutes at Large*, XIII. 353.

1864, Dec. 7. Great Britain: International Proposition.

"The crime of trading in human beings has been for many years branded by the reprobation of all civilized nations. Still the atrocious traffic subsists, and many persons flourish on the gains they have derived from that polluted source.

"Her Majesty's government, contemplating, on the one hand, with satisfaction the unanimous abhorrence which the crime inspires, and, on the other hand, with pain and disgust the slave-trading speculations which still subist [*sic*], have come to the conclusion that no measure would be so effectual to put a stop to these wicked acts as the punishment of all persons who can be proved to be guilty of carrying slaves across the sea. Her Majesty's government, therefore, invite the government of the United States to consider whether it would not be practicable, honorable, and humane——

"1st. To make a general declaration, that the governments who are parties to it denounce the slave trade as piracy.

"2d. That the aforesaid governments should propose to their legislatures to affix the penalties of piracy already existing in their laws—provided, only, that the penalty in this case be that of death—to all persons, being subjects or citizens of one of the contracting powers, who shall be convicted in a court which takes cognizance of piracy, of being concerned in carrying human beings across the sea for the purpose of sale, or for the purpose of serving as slaves, in any country or colony in the world." Signed,

"RUSSELL."

Similar letters were addressed to France, Spain, Portugal, Austria, Prussia, Italy, Netherlands, and Russia. *Diplomatic Correspondence*, 1865, pt. ii. pp. 4, 58–9, etc.

1865, Jan. 24. United States Statute: Appropriation.

To carry out the treaty with Great Britain, proclaimed July 11, 1862, $17,000. *Statutes at Large*, XIII. 424.

1866, April 7. United States Statute: Compensation to Marshals, etc.

For additional compensation to United States marshals, district attorneys, etc., for services in the suppression of the slave-trade, so much of the appropriation of March 2, 1861, as may be expedient and proper, not exceeding in all $10,000; and also so much as may be necessary to pay the salaries of judges and the expenses of mixed courts. *Ibid.*, XIV. 23.

1866, July 25. United States Statute: Appropriation.

To carry out the treaty with Great Britain, proclaimed July 11, 1862, $17,000. *Ibid.*, XIV. 226.

1867, Feb. 28. United States Statute: Appropriation.

To carry out the treaty with Great Britain, proclaimed July 11, 1862, $17,000. *Ibid.*, XIV. 414–5.

1868, March 30. United States Statute: Appropriation.

To carry out the treaty with Great Britain, proclaimed July 11, 1862, $12,500. *Ibid.*, XV. 58.

1869, Jan. 6. Congress (House): Abrogation of Treaty of 1862.

Mr. Kelsey asked unanimous consent to introduce the following resolution:—

"Whereas the slave trade has been practically suppressed; and whereas by our treaty with Great Britain for the suppression of the slave trade large appropriations are annually required to carry out the provisions thereof: Therefore,

"*Resolved*, That the Committee on Foreign Affairs are hereby instructed to inquire into the expediency of taking proper steps to secure the abrogation or modification of the treaty with Great Britain for the suppression of the slave trade." Mr. Arnell objected. *Congressional Globe*, 40 Cong. 3 sess. p. 224.

1869, March 3. United States Statute: Appropriation.

To carry out the treaty with Great Britain, proclaimed July 11, 1862, $12,500; provided that the salaries of judges be paid only on condition that they reside where the courts are held, and that Great Britain be asked to consent to abolish mixed courts. *Statutes at Large*, XV. 321.

1870, April 22. Congress (Senate): Bill to Repeal Act of 1803.

Senate Bill No. 251, to repeal an act entitled "An act to prevent the importation of certain persons into certain States where by the laws thereof their admission is prohibited." Mr. Sumner said that the bill had passed the Senate once, and that he hoped it would now pass. Passed; title amended by adding "approved February 28, 1803;" June 29, bill passed over in House; July 14, consideration again postponed on Mr. Woodward's objection. *Congressional Globe*, 41 Cong. 2 sess. pp. 2894, 2932, 4953, 5594.

1870, Sept. 16. Great Britain: Additional Treaty.

"Additional convention to the treaty of April 7, 1862, respecting the African slave trade." Concluded June 3, 1870; ratifications exchanged at London August 10, 1870; proclaimed September 16, 1870. *U. S. Treaties and Conventions* (1889), pp. 472–6.

1871, Dec. 11. Congress (House): Bill on Slave-Trade.

On the call of States, Mr. Banks introduced "a bill (House, No. 490) to carry into effect article thirteen of the Constitution of the United States, and to prohibit the owning or dealing in slaves by American citizens in foreign countries." *House Journal*, 42 Cong. 2 sess. p. 48.

APPENDIX C.

TYPICAL CASES OF VESSELS ENGAGED IN THE AMERICAN SLAVE-TRADE.

1619–1864.

THIS chronological list of certain typical American slavers is not intended to catalogue all known cases, but is designed merely to illustrate, by a few selected examples, the character of the licit and the illicit traffic to the United States.

1619. ———. Dutch man-of-war, imports twenty Negroes into Virginia, the first slaves brought to the continent. Smith, *Generall Historie of Virginia* (1626 and 1632), p. 126.

1645. Rainbowe, under Captain Smith, captures and imports African slaves into Massachusetts. The slaves were forfeited and returned. *Massachusetts Colonial Records*, II. 115, 129, 136, 168, 176; III. 13, 46, 49, 58, 84.

1655. Witte paert, first vessel to import slaves into New York. O'Callaghan, *Laws of New Netherland* (ed. 1868), p. 191, note.

1736, Oct. ———. Rhode Island slaver, under Capt. John Griffen. *American Historical Record*, I. 312.

1746. ———. Spanish vessel, with certain free Negroes, captured by Captains John Dennis and Robert Morris, and Negroes sold by them in Rhode Island, Massachusetts, and New York; these Negroes afterward returned to Spanish colonies by the authorities of Rhode Island. *Rhode Island Colonial Records*, V. 170, 176–7; Dawson's *Historical Magazine*, XVIII. 98.

1752. Sanderson, of Newport, trading to Africa and West Indies. *American Historical Record*, I. 315–9, 338–42. Cf. above, p. 35, note 4.

1788 (*circa*). ———. "One or two" vessels fitted out in Connecticut. W. C. Fowler, *Historical Status of the Negro in Connecticut*, in *Local Law*, etc., p. 125.

1801. Sally, of Norfolk, Virginia, equipped slaver; libelled and acquitted; owners claimed damages. *American State Papers, Commerce and Navigation*, I. No. 128.

1803 (?). ———. Two slavers seized with slaves, and

brought to Philadelphia; both condemned, and slaves apprenticed. Robert Sutcliff, *Travels in North America*, p. 219.

1804. ———. Slaver, allowed by Governor Claiborne to land fifty Negroes in Louisiana. *American State Papers, Miscellaneous*, I. No. 177.

1814. Saucy Jack carries off slaves from Africa and attacks British cruiser. *House Reports*, 17 Cong. 1 sess. II. No. 92, p. 46; 21 Cong. 1 sess. III. No. 348, p. 147.

1816 (*circa*). **Paz, Rosa, Dolores, Nueva Paz,** and **Dorset,** American slavers in Spanish-African trade. Many of these were formerly privateers. *Ibid.*, 17 Cong. 1 sess. II. No. 92, pp. 45–6; 21 Cong. 1 sess. III. No. 348, pp. 144–7.

1817, Jan. 17. Eugene, armed Mexican schooner, captured while attempting to smuggle slaves into the United States. *House Doc.*, 15 Cong. 1 sess. II. No. 12, p. 22.

1817, Nov. 19. Tentativa, captured with 128 slaves and brought into Savannah. *Ibid.*, p. 38; *House Reports*, 21 Cong. 1 sess. III. No. 348, p. 81. See *Friends' View of the African Slave Trade* (1824), pp. 44–7.

1818. ———. Three schooners unload slaves in Louisiana. Collector Chew to the Secretary of the Treasury, *House Reports*, 21 Cong. 1 sess. III. No. 348, p. 70.

1818, Jan. 23. English brig **Neptune,** detained by U. S. S. John Adams, for smuggling slaves into the United States. *House Doc.*, 16 Cong. 1 sess. III. No. 36 (3).

1818, June. Constitution, captured with 84 slaves on the Florida coast, by a United States army officer. See references under 1818, June, below.

1818, June. Louisa and **Merino,** captured slavers, smuggling from Cuba to the United States; condemned after five years' litigation. *House Doc.*, 15 Cong. 2 sess. VI. No. 107; 19 Cong. 1 sess. VI.–IX. Nos. 121, 126, 152, 163; *House Reports*, 19 Cong. 1 sess. II. No. 231; *American State Papers, Naval Affairs*, II. No. 308; Decisions of the United States Supreme Court in *9 Wheaton*, 391.

1819. Antelope, or **General Ramirez.** The Colombia (or Arraganta), a Venezuelan privateer, fitted in the United States and manned by Americans, captures slaves from a Spanish slaver, the Antelope, and from other slavers; is wrecked, and transfers crew and slaves to Antelope; the latter, under the name of the General Ramirez, is captured with 280 slaves by a United States ship. The slaves were distributed, some to Spanish claimants, some sent to Africa, and some allowed to remain; many died. *House Reports*, 17 Cong. 1 sess. II. No. 92, pp. 5, 15; 21 Cong. 1 sess. III. No. 348, p. 186; *House Journal*, 20 Cong. 1 sess. pp. 59, 76, 123 to 692, *passim*. Gales and Seaton, *Register of Debates*, IV. pt. 1, pp. 915–6, 955–68, 998, 1005; *Ibid*., pt. 2, pp. 2501–3; *American State Papers, Naval Affairs*, II. No. 319, pp. 750–60; Decisions of the United States Supreme Court in *10 Wheaton*, 66, and *12 Ibid*., 546.

1820. Endymion, Plattsburg, Science, Esperanza, and **Alexander,** captured on the African coast by United States ships, and sent to New York and Boston. *House Reports*, 17 Cong. 1 sess. II. No. 92, pp. 6, 15; 21 Cong. 1 sess. III. No. 348, pp. 122, 144, 187.

1820. General Artigas imports twelve slaves into the United States. *Friends' View of the African Slave Trade* (1824), p. 42.

1821 (?). **Dolphin,** captured by United States officers and sent to Charleston, South Carolina. *Ibid*., pp. 31–2.

1821. La Jeune Eugène, La Daphnée, La Mathilde, and **L'Elize,** captured by U. S. S. Alligator; **La Jeune Eugène** sent to Boston; the rest escape, and are recaptured under the French flag; the French protest. *House Reports*, 21 Cong. 1 sess. III. No. 348, p. 187; *Friends' View of the African Slave Trade* (1824), pp. 35–41.

1821. La Pensée, captured with 220 slaves by the U. S. S. Hornet; taken to Louisiana. *House Reports*, 17 Cong. 1 sess. II. No. 92, p. 5; 21 Cong. 1 sess. III. No. 348, p. 186.

1821. Esencia lands 113 Negroes at Matanzas. *Parliamentary Papers*, 1822, Vol. XXII., *Slave Trade, Further Papers*, III. p. 78.

1826. Fell's Point attempts to land Negroes in the United States. The Negroes were seized. *American State Papers, Naval Affairs*, II. No. 319, p. 751.

1827, Dec. 20. Guerrero, Spanish slaver, chased by British cruiser and grounded on Key West, with 561 slaves; a part (121) were landed at Key West, where they were seized by the collector; 250 were seized by the Spanish and taken to Cuba, etc. *House Journal*, 20 Cong. 1 sess. p. 650; *House*

Reports, 24 Cong. 1 sess. I. No. 268; 25 Cong. 2 sess. I. No. 4; *American State Papers, Naval Affairs*, III. No. 370, p. 210; *Niles's Register*, XXXIII. 373.

1828, March 11. General Geddes brought into St. Augustine for safe keeping 117 slaves, said to have been those taken from the wrecked **Guerrero** and landed at Key West (see above, 1827). *House Doc.*, 20 Cong. 1 sess. VI. No. 262.

1828. Blue-eyed Mary, of Baltimore, sold to Spaniards and captured with 405 slaves by a British cruiser. *Niles's Register*, XXXIV. 346.

1830, June 4. Fenix, with 82 Africans, captured by U. S. S. Grampus, and brought to Pensacola; American built, with Spanish colors. *House Doc.*, 21 Cong. 2 sess. III. No. 54; *House Reports*, 24 Cong. 1 sess. I. No. 223; *Niles's Register*, XXXVIII. 357.

1831, Jan. 3. Comet, carrying slaves from the District of Columbia to New Orleans, was wrecked on Bahama banks and 164 slaves taken to Nassau, in New Providence, where they were freed. Great Britain finally paid indemnity for these slaves. *Senate Doc.*, 24 Cong. 2 sess. II. No. 174; 25 Cong. 3 sess. III. No. 216.

1834, Feb. 4. Encomium, bound from Charleston, South Carolina, to New Orleans, with 45 slaves, was wrecked near Fish Key, Abaco, and slaves were carried to Nassau and freed. Great Britain eventually paid indemnity for these slaves. *Ibid.*

1835, March. Enterprise, carrying 78 slaves from the District of Columbia to Charleston, was compelled by rough weather to put into the port of Hamilton, West Indies, where the slaves were freed. Great Britain refused to pay for these, because, before they landed, slavery in the West Indies had been abolished. *Ibid.*

1836, Aug.–Sept. Emanuel, Dolores, Anaconda, and **Viper,** built in the United States, clear from Havana for Africa. *House Doc.*, 26 Cong. 2 sess. V. No. 115, pp. 4–6, 221.

1837. ———. Eleven American slavers clear from Havana for Africa. *Ibid.*, p. 221.

1837. Washington, allowed to proceed to Africa by the American consul at Havana. *Ibid.*, pp. 488–90, 715 ff.; 27 Cong. 1 sess. No. 34, pp. 18–21.

1838. Prova spends three months refitting in the harbor of Charleston, South Carolina; afterwards captured by the British, with 225 slaves. *Ibid.*, pp. 121, 163–6.

1838. ———. Nineteen American slavers clear from Havana for Africa. *House Doc.*, 26 Cong. 2 sess. V. No. 115, p. 221.

1838–9. Venus, American built, manned partly by Americans, owned by Spaniards. *Ibid.*, pp. 20–2, 106, 124–5, 132, 144–5, 330–2, 475–9.

1839. Morris Cooper, of Philadelphia, lands 485 Negroes in Cuba. *Niles's Register*, LVII. 192.

1839. Edwin and **George Crooks,** slavers, boarded by British cruisers. *House Doc.*, 26 Cong. 2 sess. V. No. 115, pp. 12–4, 61–4.

1839. Eagle, Clara, and **Wyoming,** with American and Spanish flags and papers and an American crew, captured by British cruisers, and brought to New York. The United States government declined to interfere in case of the **Eagle** and the **Clara,** and they were taken to Jamaica. The **Wyoming** was forfeited to the United States. *Ibid.*, pp. 92–104, 109, 112, 118–9, 180–4; *Niles's Register*, LVI. 256; LVII. 128, 208.

1839. Florida, protected from British cruisers by American papers. *House Doc.*, 26 Cong. 2 sess. V. No. 115, pp. 113–5.

1839. ———. Five American slavers arrive at Havana from Africa, under American flags. *Ibid.*, p. 192.

1839. ———. Twenty-three American slavers clear from Havana. *Ibid.*, pp. 190–1, 221.

1839. Rebecca, part Spanish, condemned at Sierra Leone. *House Reports*, 27 Cong. 3 sess. III. No. 283, pp. 649–54, 675–84.

1839. Douglas and **Iago,** American slavers, visited by British cruisers, for which the United States demanded indemnity. *Ibid.*, pp. 542–65, 731–55; *Senate Doc.*, 29 Cong. 1 sess. VIII. No. 377, pp. 39–45, 107–12, 116–24, 160–1, 181–2.

1839, April 9. Susan, suspected slaver, boarded by the British. *House Doc.*, 26 Cong. 2 sess. V. No. 115, pp. 34–41.

1839, July–Sept. Dolphin (or **Constitução), Hound, Mary Cushing** (or **Sete de Avril**), with American and Spanish flags and papers. *Ibid.*, pp. 28, 51–5, 109–10, 136, 234–8; *House Reports*, 27 Cong. 3 sess. III. No. 283, pp. 709–15.

1839, Aug. L'Amistad, slaver, with fifty-three Negroes on board, who mutinied; the vessel was then captured by a United States vessel and brought into Connecticut; the Negroes were declared free. *House Doc.*, 26 Cong. 1 sess. IV. No. 185; 27 Cong. 3 sess. V. No. 191; 28 Cong. 1 sess. IV. No. 83; *House Exec. Doc.*, 32 Cong. 2 sess. III. No. 20; *House Reports*, 26 Cong. 2 sess. No. 51; 28 Cong. 1 sess. II. No. 426; 29 Cong. 1 sess. IV. No. 753; *Senate Doc.*, 26 Cong. 2 sess. IV. No. 179; *Senate Exec. Doc.*, 31 Cong. 2 sess. III. No. 29; 32 Cong. 2 sess. III. No. 19; *Senate Reports*, 31 Cong. 2 sess. No. 301; 32 Cong. 1 sess. I. No. 158; 35 Cong. 1 sess. I. No. 36; Decisions of the United States Supreme Court in *15 Peters*, 518; *Opinions of the Attorneys-General*, III. 484–92.

1839, Sept. My Boy, of New Orleans, seized by a British cruiser, and condemned at Sierra Leone. *Niles's Register*, LVII. 353.

1839, Sept. 23. Butterfly, of New Orleans, fitted as a slaver, and captured by a British cruiser on the coast of Africa. *House Doc.*, 26 Cong. 2 sess. No. 115, pp. 191, 244–7; *Niles's Register*, LVII. 223.

1839, Oct. Catharine, of Baltimore, captured on the African coast by a British cruiser, and brought by her to New York. *House Doc.*, 26 Cong. 2 sess. V. No. 115, pp. 191, 215, 239–44; *Niles's Register*, LVII. 119, 159.

1839. Asp, Laura, and **Mary Ann Cassard,** foreign slavers sailing under the American flag. *House Doc.*, 26 Cong. 2 sess. V. No. 115, pp. 126–7, 209–18; *House Reports*, 27 Cong. 3 sess. III. No. 283, p. 688 ff.

1839. Two Friends, of New Orleans, equipped slaver, with Spanish, Portuguese, and American flags. *House Doc.*, 26 Cong. 2 sess. V. No. 115, pp. 120, 160–2, 305.

1839. Euphrates, of Baltimore, with American papers, seized by British cruisers as Spanish property. Before this she had been boarded fifteen times. *Ibid.*, pp. 41–4; A. H. Foote, *Africa and the American Flag*, pp. 152–6.

1839. Ontario, American slaver, "sold" to the Spanish on shipping a cargo of slaves. *House Doc.*, 26 Cong. 2 sess. V. No. 115, pp. 45–50.

1839. **Mary,** of Philadelphia; case of a slaver whose nationality was disputed. *House Reports*, 27 Cong. 3 sess. III. No. 283, pp. 736–8; *Senate Doc.*, 29 Cong. 1 sess. VIII. No. 377, pp. 19, 24–5.

1840, March. **Sarah Ann,** of New Orleans, captured with fraudulent papers. *House Doc.*, 26 Cong. 2 sess. V. No. 115, pp. 184–7.

1840, June. **Caballero, Hudson,** and **Crawford;** the arrival of these American slavers was publicly billed in Cuba. *Ibid.*, pp. 65–6.

1840. **Tigris,** captured by British cruisers and sent to Boston for kidnapping. *House Reports*, 27 Cong. 3 sess. III. No. 283, pp. 724–9; *Senate Doc.*, 29 Cong. 1 sess. VIII. No. 377, p. 94.

1840. **Jones,** seized by the British. *Senate Doc.*, 29 Cong. 1 sess. VIII. No. 377, pp. 131–2, 143–7, 148–60.

1841, Nov. 7. **Creole,** of Richmond, Virginia, transporting slaves to New Orleans; the crew mutiny and take her to Nassau, British West Indies. The slaves were freed and Great Britain refused indemnity. *Senate Doc.*, 27 Cong. 2 sess. II. No. 51 and III. No. 137.

1841. **Sophia,** of New York, ships 750 slaves for Brazil. *House Doc.*, 29 Cong. 1 sess. III. No. 43, pp. 3–8.

1841. **Pilgrim,** of Portsmouth, N. H., **Solon,** of Baltimore, **William Jones** and **Himmaleh,** of New York, clear from Rio Janeiro for Africa. *Ibid.*, pp. 8–12.

1842, May. **Illinois,** of Gloucester, saved from search by the American flag; escaped under the Spanish flag, loaded with slaves. *Senate Doc.*, 28 Cong. 2 sess. IX. No. 150, p. 72 ff.

1842, June. **Shakespeare,** of Baltimore, with 430 slaves, captured by British cruisers. *Ibid.*

1843. **Kentucky,** of New York, trading to Brazil. *Ibid.*, 30 Cong. 1 sess. IV. No. 28, pp. 71–8; *House Exec. Doc.*, 30 Cong. 2 sess. VII. No. 61, p. 72 ff.

1844. **Enterprise,** of Boston, transferred in Brazil for slave-trade. *Senate Exec. Doc.*, 30 Cong. 1 sess. IV. No. 28, pp. 79–90.

1844. **Uncas,** of New Orleans, protected by United States papers; allowed to clear, in spite of her evident character. *Ibid.*, 28 Cong. 2 sess. IX. No. 150, pp. 106–14.

1844. Sooy, of Newport, without papers, captured by the British sloop Racer, after landing 600 slaves on the coast of Brazil. *House Doc.*, 28 Cong. 2 sess. IV. No. 148, pp. 4, 36–62.

1844. Cyrus, of New Orleans, suspected slaver, captured by the British cruiser Alert. *Ibid.*, pp. 3–41.

1844–5. ———. Nineteen slavers from Beverly, Boston, Baltimore, Philadelphia, New York, Providence, and Portland, make twenty-two trips. *Ibid.*, 30 Cong. 2 sess. VII. No. 61, pp. 219–20.

1844–9. ———. Ninety-three slavers in Brazilian trade. *Senate Exec. Doc.*, 31 Cong. 2 sess. II. No. 6, pp. 37–8.

1845. Porpoise, trading to Brazil. *House Exec. Doc.*, 30 Cong. 2 sess. VII. No. 61, pp. 111–56, 212–4.

1845, May 14. Spitfire, of New Orleans, captured on the coast of Africa, and the captain indicted in Boston. A. H. Foote, *Africa and the American Flag*, pp. 240–1; *Niles's Register*, LXVIII. 192, 224, 248–9.

1845–6. Patuxent, Pons, Robert Wilson, Merchant, and **Panther,** captured by Commodore Skinner. *House Exec. Doc.*, 31 Cong. 1 sess. IX. No. 73.

1847. Fame, of New London, Connecticut, lands 700 slaves in Brazil. *House Exec. Doc.*, 30 Cong. 2 sess. VII. No. 61, pp. 5–6, 15–21.

1847. Senator, of Boston, brings 944 slaves to Brazil. *Ibid.*, pp. 5–14.

1849. Casco, slaver, with no papers; searched, and captured with 420 slaves, by a British cruiser. *Senate Exec. Doc.*, 31 Cong. 1 sess. XIV. No. 66, p. 13.

1850. Martha, of New York, captured when about to embark 1800 slaves. The captain was admitted to bail, and escaped. A. H. Foote, *Africa and the American Flag*, pp. 285–92.

1850. Lucy Ann, of Boston, captured with 547 slaves by the British. *Senate Exec. Doc.*, 31 Cong. 1 sess. XIV. No. 66, pp. 1–10 ff.

1850. Navarre, American slaver, trading to Brazil, searched and finally seized by a British cruiser. *Ibid.*

1850 (*circa*). **Louisa Beaton, Pilot, Chatsworth, Meteor, R. de Zaldo, Chester,** etc., American slavers, searched by British vessels. *Ibid.*, *passim*.

1851, Sept. 18. Illinois brings seven kidnapped West India

Negro boys into Norfolk, Virginia. *House Exec. Doc.*, 34 Cong. 1 sess. XII. No. 105, pp. 12–14.

1852–62. ———. Twenty-six ships arrested and bonded for slave-trading in the Southern District of New York. *Senate Exec. Doc.*, 37 Cong. 2 sess. V. No. 53.

1852. Advance and **Rachel P. Brown,** of New York; the capture of these was hindered by the United States consul in the Cape Verd Islands. *Ibid.*, 34 Cong. 1 sess. XV. No. 99, pp. 41–5; *House Exec. Doc.*, 34 Cong. 1 sess. XII. No. 105, pp. 15–19.

1853. Silenus, of New York, and **General de Kalb,** of Baltimore, carry 900 slaves from Africa. *Senate Exec. Doc.*, 34 Cong. 1 sess. XV. No. 99, pp. 46–52; *House Exec. Doc.*, 34 Cong. 1 sess. XII. No. 105, pp. 20–26.

1853. Jasper carries slaves to Cuba. *Senate Exec. Doc.*, 34 Cong. 1 sess. XV. No. 99, pp. 52–7.

1853. Camargo, of Portland, Maine, lands 500 slaves in Brazil. *Ibid.*, 33 Cong. 1 sess. VIII. No. 47.

1854. Glamorgan, of New York, captured when about to embark nearly 700 slaves. *Ibid.*, 34 Cong. 1 sess. XV. No. 99, pp. 59–60.

1854. Grey Eagle, of Philadelphia, captured off Cuba by British cruiser. *Ibid.*, pp. 61–3.

1854. Peerless, of New York, lands 350 Negroes in Cuba. *Ibid.*, p. 66.

1854. Oregon, of New Orleans, trading to Cuba. *Senate Exec. Doc.*, 34 Cong. 1 sess. XV. No. 99, pp. 69–70.

1856. Mary E. Smith, sailed from Boston in spite of efforts to detain her, and was captured with 387 slaves, by the Brazilian brig Olinda, at port of St. Matthews. *Ibid.*, pp. 71–3.

1857. ———. Twenty or more slavers from New York, New Orleans, etc. *Ibid.*, 35 Cong. 1 sess. XII. No. 49, pp. 14–21, 70–1, etc.

1857. William Clark and **Jupiter,** of New Orleans, **Eliza Jane,** of New York, **Jos. H. Record,** of Newport, and **Onward,** of Boston, captured by British cruisers. *Ibid.*, pp. 13, 25–6, 69, etc.

1857. James Buchanan, slaver, escapes under American colors, with 300 slaves. *Ibid.*, p. 38.

1857. James Titers, of New Orleans, with 1200 slaves, captured by British cruiser. *Ibid.*, pp. 31–4, 40–1.

1857. ———. Four New Orleans slavers on the African coast. *Senate Exec. Doc.*, 35 Cong. 1 sess., XII. No. 49, p. 30.

1857. Cortes, of New York, captured. *Ibid.*, pp. 27–8.

1857. Charles, of Boston, captured by British cruisers, with about 400 slaves. *Ibid.*, pp. 9, 13, 36, 69, etc.

1857. Adams Gray and **W. D. Miller,** of New Orleans, fully equipped slavers. *Ibid.*, pp. 3–5, 13.

1857–8. Charlotte, of New York, **Charles,** of Maryland, etc., reported American slavers. *Ibid.*, *passim.*

1858, Aug. 21. Echo, captured with 306 slaves, and brought to Charleston, South Carolina. *House Exec. Doc.*, 35 Cong. 2 sess. II. pt. 4, No. 2. pt. 4, pp. 5, 14.

1858, Sept. 8. Brothers, captured and sent to Charleston, South Carolina. *Ibid.*, p. 14.

1858. Mobile, Cortez, Tropic Bird; cases of American slavers searched by British vessels. *Ibid.*, 36 Cong. 2 sess. IV. No. 7, p. 97 ff.

1858. Wanderer, lands 500 slaves in Georgia. *Senate Exec. Doc.*, 35 Cong. 2 sess. VII. No. 8; *House Exec. Doc.*, 35 Cong. 2 sess. IX. No. 89.

1859, Dec. 20. Delicia, supposed to be Spanish, but without papers; captured by a United States ship. The United States courts declared her beyond their jurisdiction. *House Exec. Doc.*, 36 Cong. 2 sess. IV. No. 7, p. 434.

1860. Erie, with 897 Africans, captured by a United States ship. *Senate Exec. Doc.*, 36 Cong. 2 sess. I. No. 1, pp. 41–4.

1860. William, with 550 slaves, **Wildfire,** with 507, captured on the coast of Cuba. *Senate Journal*, 36 Cong. 1 sess. pp. 478–80, 492, 543, etc.; *Senate Exec. Doc.*, 36 Cong. 1 sess. XI. No. 44; *House Exec. Doc.*, 36 Cong. 1 sess. XII. No. 83; 36 Cong. 2 sess. V. No. 11; *House Reports*, 36 Cong. 1 sess. IV. No. 602.

1861. Augusta, slaver, which, in spite of the efforts of the officials, started on her voyage. *Senate Exec. Doc.*, 37 Cong. 2 sess. V. No. 40; *New York Tribune*, Nov. 26, 1861.

1861. Storm King, of Baltimore, lands 650 slaves in Cuba. *Senate Exec. Doc.*, 38 Cong. 1 sess. No. 56, p. 3.

1862. Ocilla, of Mystic, Connecticut, lands slaves in Cuba. *Ibid.*, pp. 8–13.

1864. Huntress, of New York, under the American flag, lands slaves in Cuba. *Ibid.*, pp. 19–21.

APPENDIX D.

BIBLIOGRAPHY.

COLONIAL LAWS.

[The Library of Harvard College, the Boston Public Library, and the Charlemagne Tower Collection at Philadelphia are especially rich in Colonial Laws.]

Alabama and Mississippi Territory. Acts of the Assembly of Alabama, 1822, etc.; J. J. Ormond, Code of Alabama, Montgomery, 1852; H. Toulmin, Digest of the Laws of Alabama, Cahawba, 1823; A. Hutchinson, Code of Mississippi, Jackson, 1848; Statutes of Mississippi etc., digested, Natchez, 1816 and 1823.

Connecticut. Acts and Laws of Connecticut, New London, 1784 [–1794], and Hartford, 1796; Connecticut Colonial Records; The General Laws and Liberties of Connecticut Colonie, Cambridge, 1673, reprinted at Hartford in 1865; Statute Laws of Connecticut, Hartford, 1821.

Delaware. Laws of Delaware, 1700–1797, 2 vols., New Castle, 1797.

Georgia. George W. J. De Renne, editor, Colonial Acts of Georgia, Wormsloe, 1881; Constitution of Georgia; T. R. R. Cobb, Digest of the Laws, Athens, Ga., 1851; Horatio Marbury and W. H. Crawford, Digest of the Laws, Savannah, 1802; Oliver H. Prince, Digest of the Laws, 2d edition, Athens, Ga., 1837.

Maryland. James Bisset, Abridgment of the Acts of Assembly, Philadelphia, 1759; Acts of Maryland, 1753–1768, Annapolis, 1754 [–1768]; Compleat Collection of the Laws of Maryland, Annapolis, 1727; Thomas Bacon, Laws of Maryland at Large, Annapolis, 1765; Laws of Maryland since 1763, Annapolis, 1787, year 1771; Clement Dorsey, General Public Statutory Law, etc., 1692–1837, 3 vols., Baltimore, 1840.

Massachusetts. Acts and Laws of His Majesty's Province of the Massachusetts-Bay in New-England, Boston, 1726; Acts and Resolves . . . of the Province of the Massachusetts Bay, 1692–1780 [Massachusetts Province

Laws]; Colonial Laws of Massachusetts, reprinted from the editions of 1660 and 1672, Boston, 1887, 1890; General Court Records; Massachusetts Archives; Massachusetts Historical Society Collections; Perpetual Laws of Massachusetts, 1780–1789, Boston, 1789; Plymouth Colony Records; Records of the Governor and Company of the Massachusetts Bay.

New Jersey. Samuel Allinson, Acts of Assembly, Burlington, 1776; William Paterson, Digest of the Laws, Newark, 1800; William A. Whitehead, editor, Documents relating to the Colonial History of New Jersey, Newark, 1880–93; Joseph Bloomfield, Laws of New Jersey, Trenton, 1811; New Jersey Archives.

New York. Acts of Assembly, 1691–1718, London, 1719; E. B. O'Callaghan, Documentary History of New York, 4 vols., Albany, 1849–51; E. B. O'Callaghan, editor, Documents relating to the Colonial History of New York, 12 vols., Albany, 1856–77; Laws of New York, 1752–1762, New York, 1762; Laws of New York, 1777–1801, 5 vols., republished at Albany, 1886–7.

North Carolina. F. X. Martin, Iredell's Public Acts of Assembly, Newbern, 1804; Laws, revision of 1819, 2 vols., Raleigh, 1821; North Carolina Colonial Records, edited by William L. Saunders, Raleigh, 1886–90.

Pennsylvania. Acts of Assembly, Philadelphia, 1782; Charter and Laws of the Province of Pennsylvania, Harrisburg, 1879; M. Carey and J. Bioren, Laws of Pennsylvania, 1700–1802, 6 vols., Philadelphia, 1803; A. J. Dallas, Laws of Pennsylvania, 1700–1781, Philadelphia, 1797; *Ibid.*, 1781–1790, Philadelphia, 1793; Collection of all the Laws now in force, 1742; Pennsylvania Archives; Pennsylvania Colonial Records.

Rhode Island. John Russell Bartlett, Index to the Printed Acts and Resolves, of . . . the General Assembly, 1756–1850, Providence, 1856; Elisha R. Potter, Reports and Documents upon Public Schools, etc., Providence, 1855; Rhode Island Colonial Records.

South Carolina. J. F. Grimké, Public Laws, Philadelphia, 1790; Thomas Cooper and D. J. McCord, Statutes at Large, 10 vols., Columbia, 1836–41.

Vermont. Statutes of Vermont, Windsor, 1787; Vermont State Papers, Middlebury, 1823.

Virginia. John Mercer, Abridgement of the Acts of Assembly, Glasgow, 1759; Acts of Assembly, Williamsburg, 1769; Collection of Public Acts . . . passed since 1768, Richmond, 1785; Collections of the Virginia Historical Society; W. W. Hening, Statutes at Large, 13 vols., Richmond, etc., 1819–23; Samuel Shepherd, Statutes at Large, New Series (continuation of Hening), 3 vols. Richmond, 1835–6.

UNITED STATES DOCUMENTS.

1789–1836. American State Papers—Class I., *Foreign Relations*, Vols. III. and IV. (Reprint of Foreign Relations, 1789–1828.) Class VI., *Naval Affairs*. (Well indexed.)

1794, Feb. 11. Report of Committee on the Slave Trade. *Amer. State Papers, Miscellaneous*, I. No. 44.

1806, Feb. 17. Report of the Committee appointed on the seventh instant, to inquire whether any, and if any, what Additional Provisions are necessary to Prevent the Importation of Slaves into the Territories of the United States. *House Reports*, 9 Cong. 1 sess. II.

1817, Feb. 11. Joint Resolution for abolishing the traffick in Slaves, and the Colinization [*sic*] of the Free People of Colour of the United States. *House Doc.*, 14 Cong. 2 sess. II. No. 77.

1817, Dec. 15. Message from the President . . . communicating Information of the Proceeding of certain Persons who took Possession of Amelia Island and of Galvezton, [*sic*] during the Summer of the Present Year, and made Establishments there. *House Doc.*, 15 Cong. 1 sess. II. No. 12. (Contains much evidence of illicit traffic.)

1818, Jan. 10. Report of the Committee to whom was referred so much of the President's Message as relates to the introduction of Slaves from Amelia Island. *House Doc.*, 15 Cong. 1 sess. III. No. 46 (cf. *House Reports*, 21 Cong. 1 sess. III. No. 348).

1818, Jan. 13. Message from the President . . . communicating information of the Troops of the United States having taken possession of Amelia Island, in East Florida. *House Doc.*, 15 Cong. 1 sess. III. No. 47. (Contains correspondence.)

1819, Jan. 12. Letter from the Secretary of the Navy, transmitting copies of the instructions which have been issued to Naval Commanders, upon the subject of the Importation of Slaves, etc. *House Doc.*, 15 Cong. 2 sess. IV. No. 84.

1819, Jan. 19. Extracts from Documents in the Departments of State, of the Treasury, and of the Navy, in relation to the Illicit Introduction of Slaves into the United States. *House Doc.*, 15 Cong. 2 sess. VI. No. 100.

1819, Jan. 21. Letter from the Secretary of the Treasury . . . in relation to Ships engaged in the Slave Trade, which have been Seized and Condemned, and the Disposition which has been made of the Negroes, by the several State Governments, under whose Jurisdiction they have fallen. *House Doc.*, 15 Cong. 2 sess. VI. No. 107.

1820, Jan. 7. Letter from the Secretary of the Navy, transmitting information in relation to the Introduction of Slaves into the United States. *House Doc.*, 16 Cong. 1 sess. III. No. 36.

1820, Jan. 13. Letter from the Secretary of the Treasury, transmitting . . . Information in relation to the Illicit Introduction of Slaves into the United States, etc., *Ibid.*, No. 42.

1820, May 8. Report of the Committee to whom was referred . . . so much of the President's Message as relates to the Slave Trade, etc. *House Reports*, 16 Cong. 1 sess. No. 97.

1821, Jan. 5. Message from the President . . . transmitting . . . Information on the Subject of the African Slave Trade. *House Doc.*, 16 Cong. 2 sess. IV. No. 48.

1821, Feb. 7. Report of the Secretary of the Navy. *House Reports*, 17 Cong. 1 sess. No. 92, pp. 15–21.

1821, Feb. 9. Report of the Committee to which was referred so much of the President's message as relates to the Slave Trade. *House Reports*, 16 Cong. 2 sess. No. 59.

1822, April 12. Report of the Committee on the Suppression of the Slave Trade. Also Report of 1821, Feb. 9, reprinted. (Contains discussion of the Right of Search, and papers on European Conference for the Suppression of the Slave Trade.) *House Reports*, 17 Cong. 1 sess. II. No. 92.

1823, Dec. 1. Report of the Secretary of the Navy. *House Doc.*, 18 Cong. 1 sess. I. No. 2, p. 111, ff.; *Amer. State Papers, Naval Affairs*, I. No. 258. (Contains reports on the establishment at Cape Mesurado.)[1]

1824, March 20. Message from the President . . . in relation to the Suppression of the African Slave Trade. *House Doc.*, 18 Cong. 1 sess. VI. No. 119. (Contains correspondence on the proposed treaty of 1824.)

1824, Dec. 1. Report of the Secretary of the Navy. *Amer. State Papers, Naval Affairs*, I. No. 249.

1824, Dec. 7. Documents accompanying the Message of the President . . . to both Houses of Congress, at the commencement of the Second Session of the Eighteenth Congress: Documents from the Department of State. *House Doc.*, 18 Cong. 2 sess. I. No. 1. pp. 1–56. Reprinted in *Senate Doc.*, 18 Cong. 2 sess. I. No. 1. (Matter on the treaty of 1824.)

1825, Feb. 16. Report of the Committee to whom was referred so much of the President's Message, of the 7th of December last, as relates to the Suppression of the Slave Trade. *House Reports*, 18 Cong. 2 sess. I. No. 70. (Report favoring the treaty of 1824.)

1825, Dec. 2. Report of the Secretary of the Navy. *House Doc.*, 19 Cong. 1 sess. I. No. 1. p. 98.

1825, Dec. 27. Slave Trade: Message from the President . . . communicating Correspondence with Great Britain in relation to the Convention for Suppressing the Slave Trade. *House Doc.*, 19 Cong. 1 sess. I. No. 16.

1826, Feb. 6. Appropriation—Slave Trade: Report of the Committee of Ways and Means on the subject of the estimate of appropriations for the service of the year 1826. *House Reports*, 19 Cong. 1 sess. I. No. 65. (Contains report of the Secretary of the Navy and account of expenditures for the African station.)

[1]The Reports of the Secretary of the Navy are found among the documents accompanying the annual messages of the President.

1826, March 8. Slave Ships in Alabama: Message from the President . . . in relation to the Cargoes of certain Slave Ships, etc. *House Doc.*, 19 Cong. 1 sess. VI. No. 121; cf. *Ibid.*, VIII. No. 126, and IX. Nos. 152, 163; also *House Reports*, 19 Cong. 1 sess. II. No. 231. (Cases of the Constitution, Louisa, and Merino.)

1826, Dec. 2. Report of the Secretary of the Navy. (Part IV. of Documents accompanying the President's Message.) *House Doc.*, 19 Cong. 2 sess. I. No. 2, pp. 9, 10, 74–103.

1827, etc. Colonization Society: Reports, etc. *House Doc.*, 19 Cong. 2 sess. IV. Nos. 64, 69; 20 Cong. 1 sess. III. Nos. 99, 126, and V. No. 193; 20 Cong. 2 sess. I. No. 2, pp. 114, 127–8; 21 Cong. 2 sess. I. No. 2, p. 211–18; *House Reports*, 19 Cong. 2 sess. II. No. 101; 21 Cong. 1 sess. II. No. 277, and III. No. 348; 22 Cong. 1 sess. II. No. 277.

1827, Jan. 30. Prohibition of the Slave Trade: Statement showing the Expenditure of the Appropriation for the Prohibition of the Slave Trade, during the year 1826, and an Estimate for 1827. *House Doc.*, 19 Cong. 2 sess. IV. No. 69.

1827, Dec. 1 and Dec. 4. Reports of the Secretary of the Navy. *Amer. State Papers, Naval Affairs*, III. Nos. 339, 340.

1827, Dec. 6. Message from the President . . . transmitting . . . a Report from the Secretary of the Navy, showing the expense annually incurred in carrying into effect the Act of March 2, 1819, for Prohibiting the Slave Trade. *Senate Doc.*, 20 Cong. 1 sess. I. No. 3.

1828, March 12. Recaptured Africans: Letter from the Secretary of the Navy . . . in relation to . . . Recaptured Africans. *House Doc.*, 20 Cong. 1 sess. V. No. 193; cf. *Ibid.*, 20 Cong. 2 sess. I. No. 2, pp. 114, 127–8; also *Amer. State Papers, Naval Affairs*, III. No. 357.

1828, April 30. Africans at Key West: Message from the President . . . relative to the Disposition of the Africans Landed at Key West. *House Doc.*, 20 Cong. 1 sess. VI. No. 262.

1828, Nov. 27. Report of the Secretary of the Navy. *Amer. State Papers, Naval Affairs*, III. No. 370.

1829, Dec. 1. Report of the Secretary of the Navy. *House Doc.*, 21 Cong. 1 sess. I. No. 2, p. 40.

1830, April 7. Slave Trade . . . Report: "The committee to whom were referred the memorial of the American Society for colonizing the free people of color of the United States; also, sundry memorials from the inhabitants of the State of Kentucky, and a memorial from certain free people of color of the State of Ohio, report," etc., 3 pp. Appendix. Collected and arranged by Samuel Burch. 290 pp. *House Reports*, 21 Cong. 1 sess. III. No. 348. (Contains a reprint of legislation and documents from 14 Cong. 2 sess. to 21 Cong. 1 sess. Very valuable.)

1830, Dec. 6. Report of the Secretary of the Navy. *House Doc.*, 21 Cong. 2 sess. I. No. 2, pp. 42–3; *Amer. State Papers, Naval Affairs*, III. No. 429 E.

1830, Dec. 6. Documents communicated to Congress by the President at the opening of the Second Session of the Twenty-first Congress, accompanying the Report of the Secretary of the Navy: Paper E. Statement of expenditures, etc., for the removal of Africans to Liberia. *House Doc.*, 21 Cong. 2 sess. I. No. 2, pp. 211–8.

1831, Jan. 18. Spanish Slave Ship Fenix: Message from the President . . . transmitting Documents in relation to certain captives on board the Spanish slave vessel, called the Fenix. *House Doc.*, 21 Cong. 2 sess. III. No. 54; *Amer. State Papers, Naval Affairs*, III. No. 435.

1831–1835. Reports of the Secretary of the Navy. *House Doc.*, 22 Cong. 1 sess. I. No. 2, pp. 45, 272–4; 22 Cong. 2 sess. I. No. 2, pp. 48, 229; 23 Cong. 1 sess. I. No. 1, pp. 238, 269; 23 Cong. 2 sess. I. No. 2, pp. 315, 363; 24 Cong. 1 sess. I. No. 2, pp. 336, 378. Also *Amer. State Papers, Naval Affairs*, IV. No. 457, R. Nos. 1, 2; No. 486, H. I.; No. 519, R.; No. 564, P.; No. 585, P.

1836, Jan. 26. Calvin Mickle, Ex'r of Nagle & De Frias. *House Reports*, 24 Cong. 1 sess. I. No. 209. (Reports on claims connected with the captured slaver Constitution.)

1836, Jan. 27, etc. [Reports from the Committee of Claims on cases of captured Africans.] *House Reports*, 24 Cong. 1 sess. I. Nos. 223, 268, and III. No. 574. No. 268 is reprinted in *House Reports*, 25 Cong. 2 sess. I. No. 4.

1836, Dec. 3. Report of the Secretary of the Navy. *House Doc.*, 24 Cong. 2 sess. I. No. 2, pp. 450, 506.

1837, Feb. 14. Message from the President . . . with copies of Correspondence in relation to the Seizure of Slaves on board the brigs "Encomium" and "Enterprise." *Senate Doc.*, 24 Cong. 2 sess. II. No. 174; cf. *Ibid.*, 25 Cong. 3 sess. III. No. 216.

1837–1839. Reports of the Secretary of the Navy. *House Doc.*, 25 Cong. 2 sess. I. No. 3, pp. 762, 771, 850; 25 Cong. 3 sess. I. No. 2, p. 613; 26 Cong. 1 sess. I. No. 2, pp. 534, 612.

1839. [L'Amistad Case.] *House Doc.*, 26 Cong. 1 sess. IV. No. 185 (correspondence); 27 Cong. 3 sess. V. No. 191 (correspondence); 28 Cong. 1 sess. IV. No. 83; *House Exec. Doc.*, 32 Cong. 2 sess. III. No. 20; *House Reports*, 26 Cong. 2 sess. No. 51 (case of altered Ms.); 28 Cong. 1 sess. II. No. 426 (Report of Committee); 29 Cong. 1 sess. IV. No. 753 (Report of Committee); *Senate Doc.*, 26 Cong. 2 sess. IV. No. 179 (correspondence); *Senate Exec. Doc.*, 31 Cong. 2 sess. III. No. 29 (correspondence); 32 Cong. 2 sess. III. No. 19; *Senate Reports*, 31 Cong. 2 sess. No. 301 (Report of Committee); 32 Cong. 1 sess. I. No. 158 (Report of Committee); 35 Cong. 1 sess. I. No. 36 (Report of Committee).

1840, May 18. Memorial of the Society of Friends, upon the subject of the foreign slave trade. *House Doc.*, 26 Cong. 1 sess. VI. No. 211. (Results of certain investigations.)

1840, Dec. 5. Report of the Secretary of the Navy. *House Doc.*, 26 Cong. 2 sess. I. No. 2, pp. 405, 450.

1841, Jan. 20. Message from the President . . . communicating . . . copies of correspondence, imputing malpractices to the American consul at Havana, in regard to granting papers to vessels engaged in the slave-trade. *Senate Doc.*, 26 Cong. 2 sess. III. No. 125. (Contains much information.)

1841, March 3. Search or Seizure of American Vessels, etc.: Message from the President . . . transmitting a report from the Secretary of State, in relation to seizures or search of American vessels on the coast of Africa, etc. *House Doc.*, 26 Cong. 2 sess. V. No. 115 (elaborate correspondence). See also *Ibid.*, 27 Cong. 1 sess. No. 34; *House Reports*, 27 Cong. 3 sess. III. No. 283, pp. 478–755 (correspondence).

1841, Dec. 4. Report of the Secretary of the Navy. *House Doc.*, 27 Cong. 2 sess. I. No. 2, pp. 349, 351.

1842, Jan. 20. Message from the President . . . communicating . . . copies of correspondence in relation to the mutiny on board the brig Creole, and the liberation of the slaves who were passengers in the said vessel. *Senate Doc.*, 27 Cong. 2 sess. II. No. 51. See also *Ibid.*, III. No. 137; *House Doc.*, 27 Cong. 3 sess. I. No. 2, p. 114.

1842, May 10. Resolutions of the Legislature of the State of Mississippi in reference to the right of search, and the case of the American brig Creole. *House Doc.*, 27 Cong. 2 sess. IV. No. 215. (Suggestive.)

1842, etc. [Quintuple Treaty and Cass's Protest: Messages of the President, etc.] *House Doc.*, 27 Cong. 2 sess. V. No. 249; *Senate Doc.*, 27 Cong. 3 sess. II. No. 52, and IV. No. 223; 29 Cong. 1 sess. VIII. No. 377.

1842, June 10. Indemnities for slaves on board the Comet and Encomium: Report of the Secretary of State. *House Doc.*, 27 Cong. 2 sess. V. No. 242.

1842, Aug. Suppression of the African Slave Trade—Extradition: Case of the Creole, etc. *House Doc.*, 27 Cong. 3 sess. I. No. 2, pp. 105–136. (Correspondence accompanying Message of President.)

1842, Dec. Report of the Secretary of the Navy. *House Doc.*, 27 Cong. 3 sess. I. No. 2, p. 532.

1842, Dec. 30. Message from the President . . . in relation to the strength and expense of the squadron to be employed on the coast of Africa. *Senate Doc.*, 27 Cong. 3 sess. II. No. 20.

1843, Feb. 28. Construction of the Treaty of Washington, etc.: Message from the President . . . transmitting a report from the Secretary of State, in answer to the resolution of the House of the 22d February, 1843. *House Doc.*, 27 Cong. 3 sess. V. No. 192.

1843, Feb. 28. African Colonization. . . . Report: "The Committee on Commerce, to whom was referred the memorial of the friends of African colonization, assembled in convention in the city of Washington in May last, beg leave to submit the following report," etc. (16 pp.). Appendix. (1071 pp.). *House Reports*, 27 Cong. 3 sess. III. No. 283 [Contents of Appendix: pp. 17–408, identical nearly with the Appendix to *House Reports*, 21 Cong. 1 sess. III. No. 348; pp. 408–478. Congressional history of the slave-trade, case of the Fenix, etc. (cf. *House Doc.*, 21 Cong. 2 sess. III. No. 54); pp. 478–729, search and seizure of American vessels (same as *House Doc.*, 26 Cong. 2 sess. V. No. 115, pp. 1–252); pp. 730–755, correspondence on British search of American vessels, etc.; pp. 756–61, Quintuple Treaty; pp. 762–3, President's Message on Treaty of 1842; pp. 764–96, correspondence on African squadron, etc.; pp. 796–1088, newspaper extracts on the slave-trade and on colonization, report of Colonization Society, etc.]

1843, Nov. 25. Report of the Secretary of the Navy. *House Doc.*, 28 Cong. 1 sess. I. No. 2, pp. 484–5.

1844, March 14. Message from the President . . . communicating . . . information in relation to the abuse of the flag of the United States in . . . the African slave trade, etc. *Senate Doc.*, 28 Cong. 1 sess. IV. No. 217.

1844, March 15. Report: "The Committee on the Judiciary, to whom was referred the petition of . . . John Hanes, . . . praying an adjustment of his accounts for the maintenance of certain captured African slaves, ask leave to report," etc. *Senate Doc.*, 28 Cong. 1 sess. IV. No. 194.

1844, May 4. African Slave Trade: Report: "The Committee on Foreign Affairs, to whom was referred the petition of the American Colonization Society and others, respectfully report," etc. *House Reports*, 28 Cong. 1 sess. II. No. 469.

1844, May 22. Suppression of the Slave-Trade on the coast of

Africa: Message from the President, etc. *House Doc.*, 28 Cong. 1 sess. VI. No. 263.

1844, Nov. 25. Report of the Secretary of the Navy. *House Doc.*, 28 Cong. 2 sess. I. No. 2, p. 514.

1845, Feb. 20. Slave-Trade, etc.: Message from the President . . . transmitting copies of despatches from the American minister at the court of Brazil, relative to the slave-trade, etc. *House Doc.*, 28 Cong. 2 sess. IV. No. 148. (Important evidence, statistics, etc.)

1845, Feb. 26. Message from the President . . . communicating . . . information relative to the operations of the United States squadron, etc. *Senate Doc.*, 28 Cong. 2 sess. IX. No. 150. (Contains reports of Commodore Perry, and statistics of Liberia.)

1845, Dec. 1. Report of the Secretary of the Navy. *House Doc.*, 29 Cong. 1 sess. I. No. 2, p. 645.

1845, Dec. 22. African Slave-Trade: Message from the President . . . transmitting a report from the Secretary of State, together with the correspondence of George W. Slacum, relative to the African slave trade. *House Doc.*, 29 Cong. 1 sess. III. No. 43. (Contains much information.)

1846, June 6. Message from the President . . . communicating . . . copies of the correspondence between the government of the United States and that of Great Britain, on the subject of the right of search; with copies of the protest of the American minister at Paris against the quintuple treaty, etc. *Senate Doc.*, 29 Cong. 1 sess. VIII. No. 377. Cf. *Ibid.*, 27 Cong. 3 sess. II. No. 52, and IV. No. 223; *House Doc.*, 27 Cong. 2 sess. V. No. 249.

1846–1847, Dec. Reports of the Secretary of the Navy. *House Doc.*, 29 Cong. 2 sess. I. No. 4, p. 377; 30 Cong. 1 sess. II. No. 8, p. 946.

1848, March 3. Message from the President . . . communicating a report from the Secretary of State, with the correspondence of Mr. Wise, late United States minister to Brazil, in relation to the slave trade. *Senate Exec. Doc.*, 30 Cong. 1 sess. IV. No. 28. (Full of facts.)

1848, May 12. Report of the Secretary of State, in relation to

. . . the seizure of the brig Douglass by a British cruiser. *Senate Exec. Doc.*, 30 Cong. 1 sess. VI. No. 44.

1848, Dec. 4. Report of the Secretary of the Navy. *House Exec. Doc.*, 30 Cong. 2 sess. I. No. 1, pp. 605, 607.

1849, March 2. Correspondence between the Consuls of the United States at Rio de Janeiro, etc., with the Secretary of State, on the subject of the African Slave Trade: Message of the President, etc. *House Exec. Doc.*, 30 Cong. 2 sess. VII. No. 61. (Contains much evidence.)

1849, Dec. 1. Report of the Secretary of the Navy. *House Exec. Doc.*, 31 Cong. 1 sess. III. pt. 1, No. 5, pt. 1, pp. 427–8.

1850, March 18. Report of the Secretary of the Navy, showing the annual number of deaths in the United States squadron on the coast of Africa, and the annual cost of that squadron. *Senate Exec. Doc.*, 31 Cong. 1 sess. X. No. 40.

1850, July 22. African Squadron: Message from the President . . . transmitting Information in reference to the African squadron. *House Exec. Doc.*, 31 Cong. 1 sess. IX. No. 73. (Gives total expenses of the squadron, slavers captured, etc.)

1850, Aug. 2. Message from the President . . . relative to the searching of American vessels by British ships of war. *Senate Exec. Doc.*, 31 Cong. 1 sess. XIV. No. 66.

1850, Dec. 17. Message of the President . . . communicating . . . a report of the Secretary of State, with documents relating to the African slave trade. *Senate Exec. Doc.*, 31 Cong. 2 sess. II. No. 6.

1851–1853. Reports of the Secretary of the Navy. *House Exec. Doc.*, 32 Cong. 1 sess. II. pt. 2, No. 2, pt. 2, pp. 4–5; 32 Cong. 2 sess. I. pt. 2, No. 1, pt. 2, p. 293; 33 Cong. 1 sess. I. pt. 3, No. 1, pt. 3, pp. 298–9.

1854, March 13. Message from the President . . . communicating . . . the correspondence between Mr. Schenck, United States Minister to Brazil, and the Secretary of State, in relation to the African slave trade. *Senate Exec. Doc.*, 33 Cong. 1 sess. VIII. No. 47.

1854, June 13. Report submitted by Mr. Slidell, from the Committee on Foreign Relations, on a resolution relative to the abrogation of the eighth article of the treaty with Great Britain of the 9th of August, 1842, etc. *Senate Reports*, 34 Cong. 1 sess. I. No. 195. (Injunction of secrecy removed June 26, 1856.)

1854–1855, Dec. Reports of the Secretary of the Navy. *House Exec. Doc.*, 33 Cong. 2 sess. I. pt. 2, No. 1, pt. 2, pp. 386–7; 34 Cong. 1 sess. I. pt. 3, No. 1, pt. 3, p. 5.

1856, May 19. Slave and Coolie Trade: Message from the President . . . communicating information in regard to the Slave and Coolie trade. *House Exec. Doc.*, 34 Cong. 1 sess. XII. No. 105. (Partly reprinted in *Senate Exec. Doc.*, 34 Cong. 1 sess. XV. No. 99.)

1856, Aug. 5. Report of the Secretary of State, in compliance with a resolution of the Senate of April 24, calling for information relative to the coolie trade. *Senate Exec. Doc.*, 34 Cong. 1 sess. XV. No. 99. (Partly reprinted in *House Exec. Doc.*, 34 Cong. 1 sess. XII. No. 105.)

1856, Dec. 1. Report of the Secretary of the Navy. *House Exec. Doc.*, 34 Cong. 3 sess. I. pt. 2, No. 1, pt. 2, p. 407.

1857, Feb. 11. Slave Trade: Letter from the Secretary of State, asking an appropriation for the suppression of the slave trade, etc. *House Exec. Doc.*, 34 Cong. 3 sess. IX. No. 70.

1857, Dec. 3. Report of the Secretary of the Navy. *House Exec. Doc.*, 35 Cong. 1 sess. II. pt. 3, No. 2, pt. 3, p. 576.

1858, April 23. Message of the President . . . communicating . . . reports of the Secretary of State and the Secretary of the Navy, with accompanying papers, in relation to the African slave trade. *Senate Exec. Doc.*, 35 Cong. 1 sess. XII. No. 49. (Valuable.)

1858, Dec. 6. Report of the Secretary of the Navy. *House Exec. Doc.*, 35 Cong. 2 sess. II. pt. 4, No. 2, pt. 4, pp. 5, 13–4.

1859, Jan. 12. Message of the President . . . relative to the landing of the barque Wanderer on the coast of Georgia, etc. *Senate Exec. Doc.*, 35 Cong. 2 sess. VII. No. 8. See also *House Exec. Doc.*, 35 Cong. 2 sess. IX. No. 89.

1859, March 1. Instructions to African squadron: Message from the President, etc. *House Exec. Doc.*, 35 Cong. 2 sess. IX. No. 104.

1859, Dec. 2. Report of the Secretary of the Navy. *Senate Exec. Doc.*, 36 Cong. 1 sess. III. No. 2, pt. 3, pp. 1138–9, 1149–50.

1860, Jan. 25. Memorial of the American Missionary Association, praying the rigorous enforcement of the laws for the suppression of the African slave-trade, etc. *Senate Misc. Doc.*, 36 Cong. 1 sess. No. 8.

1860, April 24. Message from the President . . . in answer to a resolution of the House calling for the number of persons . . . belonging to the African squadron, who have died, etc. *House Exec. Doc.*, 36 Cong. 1 sess. XII. No. 73.

1860, May 19. Message of the President . . . relative to the capture of the slaver Wildfire, etc. *Senate Exec. Doc.*, 36 Cong. 1 sess. XI. No. 44.

1860, May 22. Capture of the slaver "William": Message from the President . . . transmitting correspondence relative to the capture of the slaver "William," etc. *House Exec. Doc.*, 36 Cong. 1 sess. XII. No. 83.

1860, May 31. The Slave Trade . . . Report: "The Committee on the Judiciary, to whom was referred Senate Bill No. 464, . . . together with the messages of the President . . . relative to the capture of the slavers 'Wildfire' and 'William,' . . . respectfully report," etc. *House Reports*, 36 Cong. 1 sess. IV. No. 602.

1860, June 16. Recaptured Africans: Letter from the Secretary of the Interior, on the subject of the return to Africa of recaptured Africans, etc. *House Misc. Doc.*, 36 Cong. 1 sess. VII. No. 96. Cf. *Ibid.*, No. 97, p. 2.

1860, Dec. 1. Report of the Secretary of the Navy. *Senate Exec. Doc.*, 36 Cong. 2 sess. III. pt. 1, No. 1, pt. 3, pp. 8–9.

1860, Dec. 6. African Slave Trade: Message from the President . . . transmitting . . . a report from the Secretary of State in reference to the African slave trade. *House Exec. Doc.*, 36 Cong. 2 sess. IV. No. 7. (Voluminous document, containing chiefly correspondence, orders, etc., 1855–1860.)

1860, Dec. 17. Deficiencies of Appropriation, etc.: Letter from the Secretary of the Interior, communicating estimates for deficiencies in the appropriation for the suppression of the slave trade, etc. *House Exec. Doc.*, 36 Cong. 2 sess. V. No. 11. (Contains names of captured slavers.)

1861, July 4. Report of the Secretary of the Navy. *Senate Exec. Doc.*, 37 Cong. 1 sess. No. 1, pp. 92, 97.

1861, Dec. 2. Report of the Secretary of the Navy. *Senate Exec. Doc.*, 37 Cong. 2 sess. Vol. III. pt. 1, No. 1, pt. 3, pp. 11, 21.

1861, Dec. 18. In Relation to Captured Africans: Letter from the Secretary of the Interior . . . as to contracts for returning and subsistence of captured Africans. *House Exec. Doc.*, 37 Cong. 2 sess. I. No. 12.

1862, April 1. Letter of the Secretary of the Interior . . . in relation to the slave vessel the "Bark Augusta." *Senate Exec. Doc.*, 37 Cong. 2 sess. V. No. 40.

1862, May 30. Letter of the Secretary of the Interior . . . in relation to persons who have been arrested in the southern district of New York, from the 1st day of May, 1852, to the 1st day of May, 1862, charged with being engaged in the slave trade, etc. *Senate Exec. Doc.*, 37 Cong. 2 sess. V. No. 53.

1862, June 10. Message of the President . . . transmitting a copy of the treaty between the United States and her Britannic Majesty for the suppression of the African slave trade. *Senate Exec. Doc.*, 37 Cong. 2 sess. V. No. 57. (Also contains correspondence.)

1862, Dec. 1. Report of the Secretary of the Navy. *House Exec. Doc.*, 37 Cong. 3 sess. III. No. 1, pt. 3, p. 23.

1863, Jan. 7. Liberated Africans: Letter from the Acting Secretary of the Interior . . . transmitting reports from Agent Seys in relation to care of liberated Africans. *House Exec. Doc.*, 37 Cong. 3 sess. V. No. 28.

1864, July 2. Message of the President . . . communicating . . . information in regard to the African slave trade. *Senate Exec. Doc.*, 38 Cong. 1 sess. No. 56.

1866–69. Reports of the Secretary of the Navy. *House Exec. Doc.*, 39 Cong. 2 sess. IV. No. 1, pt. 6, pp. 12, 18–9; 40 Cong. 2 sess. IV. No. 1, p. 11; 40 Cong. 3 sess. IV. No. 1, p. ix; 41 Cong. 2 sess. I. No. 1, pp. 4, 5, 9, 10.

1870, March 2. [Resolution on the slave-trade submitted to the Senate by Mr. Wilson]. *Senate Misc. Doc.*, 41 Cong. 2 sess. No. 66.

GENERAL BIBLIOGRAPHY.

John Quincy Adams. Argument before the Supreme Court of the United States, in the case of the United States, Appellants, *vs.* Cinque, and Others, Africans, captured in the schooner Amistad, by Lieut. Gedney, delivered on the 24th of Feb. and 1st of March, 1841. With a Review of the case of the Antelope. New York, 1841.

An African Merchant (anon.). A Treatise upon the Trade from Great-Britain to Africa; Humbly recommended to the Attention of Government. London, 1772.

The African Slave Trade: Its Nature, Consequences, and Extent. From the Leeds Mercury. [Birmingham, 183–.]

The African Slave Trade: The Secret Purpose of the Insurgents to Revive it. No Treaty Stipulations against the Slave Trade to be entered into with the European Powers, etc. Philadelphia, 1863.

George William Alexander. Letters on the Slave-Trade, Slavery, and Emancipation, etc. London, 1842. (Contains Bibliography.)

American and Foreign Anti-Slavery Society; Reports.

American Anti-Slavery Society. Memorial for the Abolition of Slavery and the Slave Trade. London, 1841.

—— ——. Reports and Proceedings.

American Colonization Society. Annual Reports, 1818–1860. (Cf. above, United States Documents.)

J. A. Andrew and A. G. Browne, proctors. Circuit Court of the United States, Massachusetts District, ss. In Admiralty. The United States, by Information, *vs.* the Schooner Wanderer and Cargo, G. Lamar, Claimant. Boston, 1860.

Edward Armstrong, editor. The Record of the Court at Upland, in Pennsylvania. 1676–1681. Philadelphia, 1860. (In *Memoirs* of the Pennsylvania Historical Society, VII. 11.)

Samuel Greene Arnold. History of the State of Rhode Island and Providence Plantations. 2 vols. New York, 1859–60. (See Index to Vol. II., "Slave Trade.")

Assiento, or, Contract for allowing to the Subjects of Great Britain the Liberty of Importing Negroes into the Spanish America. Sign'd by the Catholick King at Madrid, the Twenty sixth Day of March, 1713. By Her Majesties special Command. London, 1713.

R. S. Baldwin. Argument before the Supreme Court of the United States, in the case of the United States, Appellants, *vs.* Cinque, and Others, Africans of the Amistad. New York, 1841.

James Bandinel. Some Account of the Trade in Slaves from Africa as connected with Europe and America; From the Introduction of the Trade into Modern Europe, down to the present Time; especially with reference to the efforts made by the British Government for its extinction. London, 1842.

Anthony Benezet. Inquiry into the Rise and Progress of the Slave Trade, 1442–1771. (In his Historical Account of Guinea, etc., Philadelphia, 1771.)

—— ——. Notes on the Slave Trade, etc. [1780?].

Thomas Hart Benton. Abridgment of the Debates of Congress, from 1789 to 1856. 16 vols. Washington, 1857–61.

Edward Bettle. Notices of Negro Slavery, as connected with Pennsylvania. (Read before the Historical Society of Pennsylvania, Aug. 7, 1826. Printed in *Memoirs* of the Historical Society of Pennsylvania, Vol. I. Philadelphia, 1864.)

W. O. Blake. History of Slavery and the Slave Trade, Ancient and Modern. Columbus, 1859.

Jeffrey R. Brackett. The Status of the Slave, 1775–1789. (Essay V. in Jameson's *Essays in the Constitutional History of the United States, 1775–89*. Boston, 1889.)

Thomas Branagan. Serious Remonstrances, addressed to the Citizens of the Northern States and their Representatives, on the recent Revival of the Slave Trade in this Republic. Philadelphia, 1805.

British and Foreign Anti-Slavery Society. Annual and Special Reports.

—— ——. Proceedings of the general Anti-Slavery Convention, called by the committee of the British and Foreign Anti-Slavery Society, and held in London, . . . June, 1840. London, 1841.

[A British Merchant.] The African Trade, the Great Pillar

and Support of the British Plantation Trade in America: shewing, etc. London, 1745.

[British Parliament, House of Lords.] Report of the Lords of the Committee of the Council appointed for the Confederation of all Matters relating to Trade and Foreign Plantations, etc. 2 vols. [London,] 1789.

William Brodie. Modern Slavery and the Slave Trade: a Lecture, etc. London, 1860.

Thomas Fowell Buxton. The African Slave Trade and its Remedy. London, 1840.

John Elliot Cairnes. The Slave Power: its Character, Career, and Probable Designs. London, 1862.

Henry C. Carey. The Slave Trade, Domestic and Foreign: why it Exists and how it may be Extinguished. Philadelphia, 1853.

[Lewis Cass]. An Examination of the Question, now in Discussion, . . . concerning the Right of Search. By an American. [Philadelphia, 1842.]

William Ellery Channing. The Duty of the Free States, or Remarks suggested by the case of the Creole. Boston, 1842.

David Christy. Ethiopia, her Gloom and Glory, as illustrated in the History of the Slave Trade, etc. (1442–1857.) Cincinnati, 1857.

Rufus W. Clark. The African Slave Trade. Boston, [1860.]

Thomas Clarkson. An Essay on the Comparative Efficiency of Regulation or Abolition, as applied to the Slave Trade. Shewing that the latter only can remove the evils to be found in that commerce. London, 1789.

—— ——. An Essay on the Impolicy of the African Slave Trade. In two parts. Second edition. London, 1788.

—— ——. An Essay on the Slavery and Commerce of the Human Species, particularly the African. London and Dublin, 1786.

—— ——. The History of the Rise, Progress, and Accomplishment of the Abolition of the African Slave-Trade, by the British Parliament. 2 vols. Philadelphia, 1808.

Michael W. Cluskey. The Political Text-Book, or Encyclopedia . . . for the Reference of Politicians and Statesmen. Fourteenth edition. Philadelphia, 1860.

T. R. R. Cobb. An Historical Sketch of Slavery, from the Earliest Periods. Philadelphia and Savannah. 1858.

T. R. R. Cobb. Inquiry into the Law of Negro Slavery in the United States of America. Vol. I. Philadelphia and Savannah, 1858.

Company of Royal Adventurers. The Several Declarations of the Company of Royal Adventurers of England trading into Africa, inviting all His Majesties Native Subjects in general to Subscribe, and become Sharers in their Joynt-stock, etc. [London,] 1667.

Confederate States of America. By Authority of Congress: The Statutes at Large of the Provisional Government of the Confederate States of America, from the Institution of the Government, Feb. 8, 1861, to its Termination, Feb. 18, 1862, Inclusive, etc. (Contains provisional and permanent constitutions.) Edited by James M. Matthews. Richmond, 1864.

Constitution of a Society for Abolishing the Slave-Trade. With Several Acts of the Legislatures of the States of Massachusetts, Connecticut and Rhode-Island, for that Purpose. Printed by John Carter. Providence, 1789.

Continental Congress. Journals and Secret Journals.

Moncure D. Conway. Omitted Chapters of History disclosed in the Life and Papers of Edmund Randolph, etc. New York and London, 1888.

Thomas Cooper. Letters on the Slave Trade. Manchester, Eng., 1787.

Correspondence with British Ministers and Agents in Foreign Countries, and with Foreign Ministers in England, relative to the Slave Trade, 1859–60. London, 1860.

The Creole Case, and Mr. Webster's Despatch; with the comments of the New York "American." New York, 1842.

B. R. Curtis. Reports of Decisions in the Supreme Court of the United States. With Notes, and a Digest. Fifth edition. 22 vols. Boston, 1870.

James Dana. The African Slave Trade. A Discourse delivered . . . September, 9, 1790, before the Connecticut Society for the Promotion of Freedom. New Haven, 1791.

Henry B. Dawson, editor. The Fœderalist: A Collection of Essays, written in favor of the New Constitution, as agreed upon by the Fœderal Convention, September 17, 1787. Reprinted from the Original Text. With an Historical Introduction and Notes. Vol. I. New York, 1863.

Paul Dean. A Discourse delivered before the African Society . . . in Boston, Mass., on the Abolition of the Slave Trade . . . July 14, 1819. Boston, 1819.

Charles Deane. The Connection of Massachusetts with Slavery and the Slave-Trade, etc. Worcester, 1886. (Also in *Proceedings* of the American Antiquarian Society, October, 1886.)

—— ——. Charles Deane. Letters and Documents relating to Slavery in Massachusetts. (In *Collections* of the Massachusetts Historical Society, 5th Series, III. 373.)

Debate on a Motion for the Abolition of the Slave-Trade, in the House of Commons, on Monday and Tuesday, April 18 and 19, 1791. Reported in detail. London, 1791.

J. D. B. De Bow. The Commercial Review of the South and West. (Also De Bow's Review of the Southern and Western States.) 38 vols. New Orleans, 1846–69.

Franklin B. Dexter. Estimates of Population in the American Colonies. Worcester, 1887.

Captain Richard Drake. Revelations of a Slave Smuggler: being the Autobiography of Capt. Richard Drake, an African Trader for fifty years—from 1807 to 1857, etc. New York, [1860.]

Daniel Drayton. Personal Memoir, etc. Including a Narrative of the Voyage and Capture of the Schooner Pearl. Published by the American and Foreign Anti-Slavery Society, Boston and New York, 1855.

John Drayton. Memoirs of the American Revolution. 2 vols. Charleston, 1821.

Paul Dudley. An Essay on the Merchandize of Slaves and Souls of Men. Boston, 1731.

Edward E. Dunbar. The Mexican Papers, containing the History of the Rise and Decline of Commercial Slavery in America, with reference to the Future of Mexico. First Series, No. 5. New York, 1861.

Jonathan Edwards. The Injustice and Impolicy of the Slave Trade, and of the Slavery of the Africans, etc. [New Haven,] 1791.

Jonathan Elliot. The Debates . . . on the adoption of the Federal Constitution, etc. 4 vols. Washington, 1827–30.

Emerson Etheridge. Speech . . . on the Revival of the African Slave Trade, etc. Washington, 1857.

Alexander Falconbridge. An Account of the Slave Trade on the Coast of Africa. London, 1788.

Andrew H. Foote. Africa and the American Flag. New York, 1854.

—— ——. The African Squadron: Ashburton Treaty: Consular Sea Letters. Philadelphia, 1855.

Peter Force. American Archives, etc. In Six Series. Prepared and Published under Authority of an act of Congress. Fourth and Fifth Series. 9 vols. Washington, 1837–53.

Paul Leicester Ford. The Association of the First Congress. (In Political Science Quarterly, VI. 613.)

—— ——. Pamphlets on the Constitution of the United States, published during its Discussion by the People, 1787–8. (With Bibliography, etc.) Brooklyn, 1888.

William Chauncey Fowler. Local Law in Massachusetts and Connecticut, Historically considered; and The Historical Status of the Negro, in Connecticut, etc. Albany, 1872, and New Haven, 1875.

[Benjamin Franklin.] An Essay on the African Slave Trade. Philadelphia, 1790.

[Friends.] Address to the Citizens of the United States of America on the subject of Slavery, etc. (At New York Yearly Meeting.) New York, 1837.

—— ——. An Appeal on the Iniquity of Slavery and the Slave Trade. (At London Yearly Meeting.) London and Cincinnati, 1844.

—— ——. The Appeal of the Religious Society of Friends in Pennsylvania, New Jersey, Delaware, etc., [Yearly Meeting] to their Fellow-Citizens of the United States on behalf of the Coloured Races. Philadelphia, 1858.

—— ——. A Brief Statement of the Rise and Progress of the Testimony of the Religious Society of Friends against Slavery and the Slave Trade. 1671–1787. (At Yearly Meeting in Philadelphia.) Philadelphia, 1843.

—— ——. The Case of our Fellow-Creatures, the Oppressed Africans, respectfully recommended to the Serious Consideration of the Legislature of Great-Britain, by the People called Quakers. (At London Meeting.) London, 1783 and 1784. (This volume contains many tracts on the African slave-trade, especially in the West Indies; also descriptions of trade, proposed legislation, etc.)

[Friends.] An Exposition of the African Slave Trade, from the year 1840, to 1850, inclusive. Prepared from official documents. Philadelphia, 1857.

—— ——. Extracts and Observations on the Foreign Slave Trade. Philadelphia, 1839.

—— ——. Facts and Observations relative to the Participation of American Citizens in the African Slave Trade. Philadelphia, 1841.

—— ——. Faits relatifs à la Traite des Noirs, et Détails sur Sierra Leone; par la Société des Ames. Paris, 1824.

—— ——. Germantown Friends' Protest against Slavery, 1688. Fac-simile Copy. Philadelphia, 1880.

—— ——. Observations on the Inslaving, importing and purchasing of Negroes; with some Advice thereon, extracted from the Epistle of the Yearly-Meeting of the People called Quakers, held at London in the Year 1748. Second edition. Germantown, 1760.

—— ——. Proceedings in relation to the Presentation of the Address of the [Great Britain and Ireland] Yearly Meeting on the Slave-Trade and Slavery, to Sovereigns and those in Authority in the nations of Europe, and in other parts of the world, where the Christian religion is professed. Cincinnati, 1855.

—— ——. Slavery and the Domestic Slave Trade in the United States. By the committee appointed by the late Yearly Meeting of Friends held in Philadelphia, in 1839. Philadelphia, 1841.

—— ——. A View of the Present State of the African Slave Trade. Philadelphia, 1824.

Carl Gareis. Das Heutige Völkerrecht und der Menschenhandel. Eine völkerrechtliche Abhandlung, zugleich Ausgabe des deutschen Textes der Verträge von 20. Dezember 1841 und 29. März 1879. Berlin, 1879.

—— ——. Der Sklavenhandel, das Völkerrecht, und das deutsche Recht. (In Deutsche Zeit- und Streit-Fragen, No. 13.) Berlin, 1885.

Agénor Étienne de Gasparin. Esclavage et Traite. Paris, 1838.

Joshua R. Giddings. Speech . . . on his motion to reconsider the vote taken upon the final passage of the "Bill for the relief of the owners of slaves lost from on Board the Comet and Encomium." [Washington, 1843.]

Benjamin Godwin. The Substance of a Course of Lectures on British Colonial Slavery, delivered at Bradford, York, and Scarborough. London, 1830.

—— ——. Lectures on Slavery. From the London edition, with additions. Edited by W. S. Andrews. Boston, 1836.

William Goodell. The American Slave Code in Theory and Practice: its Distinctive Features shown by its Statutes, Judicial Decisions, and Illustrative Facts. New York, 1853.

—— ——. Slavery and Anti-Slavery; A History of the great Struggle in both Hemispheres; with a view of the Slavery Question in the United States. New York, 1852.

Daniel R. Goodloe. The Birth of the Republic. Chicago, [1889.]

[Great Britain.] British and Foreign State Papers.

—— ——. Sessional Papers. (For notices of slave-trade in British Sessional Papers, see Bates Hall Catalogue, Boston Public Library, pp. 347 *et seq.*)

[Great Britain: Parliament.] Chronological Table and Index of the Statutes, Eleventh Edition, to the end of the Session 52 and 53 Victoria, (1889.) By Authority. London, 1890.

[Great Britain: Record Commission.] The Statutes of the Realm. Printed by command of His Majesty King George the Third . . . From Original Records and Authentic Manuscripts. 9 vols. London, 1810–22.

George Gregory. Essays, Historical and Moral. Second edition. London, 1788. (Essays 7 and 8: Of Slavery and the Slave Trade; A Short Review, etc.)

Pope Gregory XVI. To Catholic Citizens! The Pope's Bull [for the Abolition of the Slave Trade], and the words of Daniel O'Connell [on American Slavery.] New York, [1856.]

H. Hall. Slavery in New Hampshire. (In *New England Register*, XXIX. 247.)

Isaac W. Hammond. Slavery in New Hampshire in the Olden Time. (In *Granite Monthly*, IV. 108.)

James H. Hammond. Letters on Southern Slavery: addressed to Thomas Clarkson. [Charleston, (?)].

Robert G. Harper. Argument against the Policy of Re-opening the African Slave Trade. Atlanta, Ga., 1858.

Samuel Hazard, editor. The Register of Pennsylvania. 16 vols. Philadelphia, 1828–36.

Hinton R. Helper. The Impending Crisis of the South: How to Meet it. Enlarged edition. New York, 1860.

Lewis and Sir Edward Hertslet, compilers. A Complete Collection of the Treaties and Conventions, and Reciprocal Regulations, at present subsisting between Great Britain and Foreign Powers, and of the Laws, Decrees, and Orders in Council, concerning the same; so far as they relate to Commerce and Navigation, . . . the Slave Trade, etc. 17 vols., (Vol. XVI., Index.) London, 1840–90.

William B. Hodgson. The Foulahs of Central Africa, and the African Slave Trade. [New York, (?)] 1843.

John Codman Hurd. The Law of Freedom and Bondage in the United States. 2 vols. Boston and New York, 1858, 1862.

—— ——. The International Law of the Slave Trade, and the Maritime Right of Search. (In the American Jurist, XXVI. 330.)

—— ——. The Jamaica Movement, for promoting the Enforcement of the Slave-Trade Treaties, and the Suppression of the Slave-Trade; with statements of Fact, Convention, and Law: prepared at the request of the Kingston Committee. London, 1850.

William Jay. Miscellaneous Writings on Slavery. Boston, 1853.

—— ——. A View of the Action of the Federal Government, in Behalf of Slavery. New York, 1839.

T. and J. W. Johnson. Inquiry into the Law of Negro Slavery in the United States.

Alexandre Moreau de Jonnès. Recherches Statistiques sur l'Esclavage Colonial et sur les Moyens de le supprimer. Paris, 1842.

M. A. Juge. The American Planter: or The Bound Labor Interest in the United States. New York, 1854.

Friedrich Kapp. Die Sklavenfrage in den Vereinigten Staaten. Göttingen and New York, 1854.

—— ——. Geschichte der Sklaverei in den Vereinigten Staaten von Amerika. Hamburg, 1861.

Frederic Kidder. The Slave Trade in Massachusetts. (In *New-England Historical and Genealogical Register*, XXXI. 75.)

George Lawrence. An Oration on the Abolition of the Slave Trade . . . Jan. 1, 1813. New York, 1813.

William B. Lawrence. Visitation and Search; or, An Historical Sketch of the British Claim to exercise a Maritime Police over the Vessels of all Nations, in Peace as well as in War. Boston, 1858.

Letter from . . . in London, to his Friend in America, on the . . . Slave Trade, etc. New York, 1784.

Thomas Lloyd. Debates of the Convention of the State of Pennsylvania on the Constitution, proposed for the Government of the United States. In two volumes. Vol. I. Philadelphia, 1788.

London Anti-Slavery Society. The Foreign Slave Trade, A Brief Account of its State, of the Treaties which have been entered into, and of the Laws enacted for its Suppression, from the date of the English Abolition Act to the present time. London, 1837.

—— ——. The Foreign Slave Trade, etc., No. 2. London, 1838.

London Society for the Extinction of the Slave Trade, and for the Civilization of Africa. Proceedings at the first Public Meeting, held at Exeter Hall, on Monday, 1st June, 1840. London, 1840.

Theodore Lyman, Jr. The Diplomacy of the United States, etc. Second edition. 2 vols. Boston, 1828.

Hugh M'Call. The History of Georgia, containing Brief Sketches of the most Remarkable Events, up to the Present Day. 2 vols. Savannah, 1811–16.

Marion J. McDougall. Fugitive Slaves. Boston, 1891.

John Fraser Macqueen. Chief Points in the Laws of War and Neutrality, Search and Blockade, etc. London and Edinburgh, 1862.

R. R. Madden. A Letter to W. E. Channing, D. D., on the subject of the Abuse of the Flag of the United States in the Island of Cuba, and the Advantage taken of its Protection in promoting the Slave Trade. Boston, 1839.

James Madison. Letters and Other Writings of James Madison, Fourth President of the United States. In four volumes. Published by order of Congress. Philadelphia, 1865.

James Madison. The Papers of James Madison, purchased by order of Congress; being his Correspondence and Reports of Debates during the Congress of the Confederation and his Reports of Debates in the Federal Convention. 3 vols. Washington, 1840.

Marana (pseudonym). The Future of America. Considered . . . in View of . . . Re-opening the Slave Trade. Boston, 1858.

E. Marining. Six Months on a Slaver. New York, 1879.

George C. Mason. The African Slave Trade in Colonial Times. (In American Historical Record, I. 311, 338.)

Frederic G. Mather. Slavery in the Colony and State of New York. (In *Magazine of American History*, XI. 408.)

Samuel May, Jr. Catalogue of Anti-Slavery Publications in America, 1750–1863. (Contains bibliography of periodical literature.)

Memorials presented to the Congress of the United States of America, by the Different Societies instituted for promoting the Abolition of Slavery, etc., etc., in the States of Rhode-Island, Connecticut, New-York, Pennsylvania, Maryland, and Virginia. Philadelphia, 1792.

Charles F. Mercer. Mémoires relatifs à l'Abolition de la Traite Africaine, etc. Paris, 1855.

C. W. Miller. Address on Re-opening the Slave Trade . . . August 29, 1857. Columbia, S. C., 1857.

George H. Moore. Notes on the History of Slavery in Massachusetts. New York, 1866.

—— ——. Slavery in Massachusetts. (In *Historical Magazine*, XV. 329.)

Jedidiah Morse. A Discourse . . . July 14, 1808, in Grateful Celebration of the Abolition of the African Slave-Trade by the Governments of the United States, Great Britain and Denmark. Boston, 1808.

John Pennington, Lord Muncaster. Historical Sketches of the Slave Trade and its effect on Africa, addressed to the People of Great Britain. London, 1792.

Edward Needles. An Historical Memoir of the Pennsylvania Society, for Promoting the Abolition of Slavery. Philadelphia, 1848.

New England Anti-Slavery Convention. Proceedings at Boston, May 27, 1834. Boston, 1834.

Hezekiah Niles (*et al.*), editors. The Weekly Register, etc. 71 vols. Baltimore, 1811–1847. (For Slave-Trade, see I. 224; III. 189; V. 30, 46; VI. 152; VII. 54, 96, 286, 350; VIII. 136, 190, 262, 302, Supplement, p. 155; IX. 60, 78, 133, 172, 335; X. 296, 400, 412, 427; XI. 15, 108, 156, 222, 336, 399; XII. 58, 60, 103, 122, 159, 219, 237, 299, 347, 397, 411.)

Robert Norris. A Short Account of the African Slave-Trade. A new edition corrected. London, 1789.

E. B. O'Callaghan, translator. Voyages of the Slavers St. John and Arms of Amsterdam, 1659, 1663; with additional papers illustrative of the Slave Trade under the Dutch. Albany, 1867. (New York Colonial Tracts, No. 3.)

Frederick Law Olmsted. A Journey in the Back Country. New York, 1860.

—— ——. A Journey in the Seaboard Slave States, etc. New York, 1856.

—— ——. A Journey through Texas, etc. New York, 1857.

—— ——. The Cotton Kingdom, etc. 2 vols. New York, 1861.

Sir W. G. Ouseley. Notes on the Slave Trade; with Remarks on the Measures adopted for its Suppression. London, 1850.

Pennsylvania Historical Society. The Charlemagne Tower Collection of American Colonial Laws. (Bibliography.) Philadelphia, 1890.

Edward A. Pollard. Black Diamonds gathered in the Darkey Homes of the South. New York, 1859.

William F. Poole. Anti-Slavery Opinions before the Year 1800. To which is appended a fac-simile reprint of Dr. George Buchanan's Oration on the Moral and Political Evil of Slavery, etc. Cincinnati, 1873.

Robert Proud. History of Pennsylvania. 2 vols. Philadelphia. 1797–8.

[James Ramsay.] An Inquiry into the Effects of putting a Stop to the African Slave Trade, and of granting Liberty to the Slaves in the British Sugar Colonies. London, 1784.

[James Ramsey.] Objections to the Abolition of the Slave Trade, with Answers, etc. Second edition. London, 1788.

[John Ranby.] Observations on the Evidence given before the Committees of the Privy Council and House of Commons in Support of the Bill for Abolishing the Slave Trade. London, 1791.

Remarks on the Colonization of the Western Coast of Africa, by the Free Negroes of the United States, etc. New York, 1850.

Right of Search. Reply to an "American's Examination" of the "Right of Search, etc." By an Englishman. London, 1842.

William Noel Sainsbury, editor. Calendar of State Papers, Colonial Series, America and the West Indies, 1574–1676. 4 vols. London, 1860–93.

George Sauer. La Traite et l'Esclavage des Noirs. London, 1863.

George S. Sawyer. Southern Institutes; or, An Inquiry into the Origin and Early Prevalence of Slavery and the Slave-Trade. Philadelphia, 1858.

Selections from the Revised Statutes: Containing all the Laws relating to Slaves, etc. New York, 1830.

Johann J. Sell. Versuch einer Geschichte des Negersclavenhandels. Halle, 1791.

[Granville Sharp.] Extract of a Letter to a Gentleman in Maryland; Wherein is demonstrated the extreme wickedness of tolerating the Slave Trade. Fourth edition. London, 1806.

A Short Account of that part of Africa Inhabited by the Negroes, . . . and the Manner by which the Slave Trade is carried on. Third edition. London, 1768.

A Short Sketch of the Evidence for the Abolition of the Slave-Trade. Philadelphia, 1792.

Joseph Sidney. An Oration commemorative of the Abolition of the Slave Trade in the United States. . . . Jan. 2. 1809. New York, 1809.

[A Slave Holder.] Remarks upon Slavery and the Slave-Trade, addressed to the Hon. Henry Clay. 1839.

The Slave Trade in New York. (In the *Continental Monthly*, January, 1862, p. 86.)

Joseph Smith. A Descriptive Catalogue of Friends' Books. (Bibliography.) 2 vols. London, 1867.

Capt. William Snelgrave. A New Account of some Parts of Guinea, and the Slave-Trade. London, 1734.

South Carolina. General Assembly (House), 1857. Report of the Special Committee of the House of Representatives . . . on so much of the Message of His Excellency Gov. Jas. H. Adams, as relates to Slavery and the Slave Trade. Columbia, S. C., 1857.

L. W. Spratt. A Protest from South Carolina against a Decision of the Southern Congress: Slave Trade in the Southern Congress. (In Littell's *Living Age*, Third Series, LXVIII. 801.)

—— ——. Speech upon the Foreign Slave Trade, before the Legislature of South Carolina. Columbia, S. C., 1858.

—— ——. The Foreign Slave Trade the Source of Political Power, etc. Charleston, 1858.

William Stith. The History of the First Discovery and Settlement of Virginia. Virginia and London, 1753.

George M. Stroud. A Sketch of the Laws relating to Slavery in the Several States of the United States of America. Philadelphia, 1827.

James Swan. A Dissuasion to Great-Britain and the Colonies: from the Slave-Trade to Africa. Shewing the Injustice thereof, etc. Revised and Abridged. Boston, 1773.

F. T. Texugo. A Letter on the Slave Trade still carried on along the Eastern Coast of Africa, etc. London, 1839.

R. Thorpe. A View of the Present Increase of the Slave Trade, the Cause of that Increase, and a mode for effecting its total Annihilation. London, 1818.

Jesse Torrey. A Portraiture of Domestic Slavery . . . and a Project of Colonial Asylum for Free Persons of Colour. Philadelphia, 1817.

Drs. Tucker and Belknap. Queries respecting the Slavery and Emancipation of Negroes in Massachusetts, proposed by the Hon. Judge Tucker of Virginia, and answered by the Rev. Dr. Belknap. (In Collections of the Massachusetts Historical Society, First Series, IV. 191.)

David Turnbull. Travels in the West. Cuba; with Notices of Porto Rico, and the Slave Trade. London, 1840.

United States Congress. Annals of Congress, 1789–1824; Congressional Debates, 1824–37; Congressional Globe, 1833–73; Congressional Record, 1873–; Documents (House and

Senate); Executive Documents (House and Senate); Journals (House and Senate); Miscellaneous Documents (House and Senate); Reports (House and Senate); Statutes at Large.

United States Supreme Court. Reports of Decisions.

Charles W. Upham. Speech in the House of Representatives, Massachusetts, on the Compromises of the Constitution, with an Appendix containing the Ordinance of 1787. Salem, 1849.

Virginia State Convention. Proceedings and Debates, 1829–30. Richmond, 1830.

G. Wadleigh. Slavery in New Hampshire. (In *Granite Monthly*, VI. 377.)

Emory Washburn. Extinction of Slavery in Massachusetts. (In Proceedings of the Massachusetts Historical Society, May, 1857. Boston, 1859.)

William B. Weeden. Economic and Social History of New England, 1620–1789. 2 vols. Boston, 1890.

Henry Wheaton. Enquiry into the Validity of the British Claim to a Right of Visitation and Search of American Vessels suspected to be engaged in the African Slave-Trade. Philadelphia, 1842.

William H. Whitmore. The Colonial Laws of Massachusetts. Reprinted from the Edition of 1660, with the Supplements to 1772. Containing also the Body of Liberties of 1641. Boston, 1889.

George W. Williams. History of the Negro Race in America from 1619 to 1880. 2 vols. New York, 1883.

Henry Wilson. History of the Antislavery Measures of the Thirty-seventh and Thirty-eighth United-States Congresses, 1861–64. Boston, 1864.

—— ——. History of the Rise and Fall of the Slave Power in America. 3 vols. Boston, 1872–7.

Index

THE SOULS
OF BLACK FOLK

TO

Burghardt and Yolande

THE LOST AND THE FOUND

The Forethought

HEREIN lie buried many things which if read with patience may show the strange meaning of being black here in the dawning of the Twentieth Century. This meaning is not without interest to you, Gentle Reader; for the problem of the Twentieth Century is the problem of the color-line.

I pray you, then, receive my little book in all charity, studying my words with me, forgiving mistake and foible for sake of the faith and passion that is in me, and seeking the grain of truth hidden there.

I have sought here to sketch, in vague, uncertain outline, the spiritual world in which ten thousand thousand Americans live and strive. First, in two chapters I have tried to show what Emancipation meant to them, and what was its aftermath. In a third chapter I have pointed out the slow rise of personal leadership, and criticised candidly the leader who bears the chief burden of his race to-day. Then, in two other chapters I have sketched in swift outline the two worlds within and without the Veil, and thus have come to the central problem of training men for life. Venturing now into deeper detail, I have in two chapters studied the struggles of the massed millions of the black peasantry, and in another have sought to make clear the present relations of the sons of master and man.

Leaving, then, the world of the white man, I have stepped within the Veil, raising it that you may view faintly its deeper recesses,—the meaning of its religion, the passion of its human sorrow, and the struggle of its greater souls. All this I have ended with a tale twice told but seldom written.

Some of these thoughts of mine have seen the light before in other guise. For kindly consenting to their republication here, in altered and extended form, I must thank the publishers of *The Atlantic Monthly*, *The World's Work*, *The Dial*, *The New World*, and the *Annals of the American Academy of Political and Social Science*.

Before each chapter, as now printed, stands a bar of the Sorrow Songs,—some echo of haunting melody from the only American music which welled up from black souls in the dark past. And, finally, need I add that I who speak here am bone of the bone and flesh of the flesh of them that live within the Veil?

W. E. B. Du B.

Atlanta, Ga., Feb. 1, 1903.

Herein is Written

I

Of Our Spiritual Strivings

O water, voice of my heart, crying in the sand,
  All night long crying with a mournful cry,
As I lie and listen, and cannot understand
    The voice of my heart in my side or the voice of the sea,
  O water, crying for rest, is it I, is it I?
    All night long the water is crying to me.

Unresting water, there shall never be rest
  Till the last moon droop and the last tide fail,
And the fire of the end begin to burn in the west;
    And the heart shall be weary and wonder and cry like the sea,
  All life long crying without avail,
    As the water all night long is crying to me.

ARTHUR SYMONS.

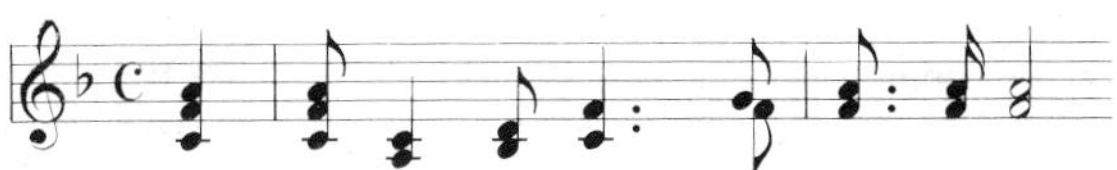

BETWEEN me and the other world there is ever an unasked question: unasked by some through feelings of delicacy; by others through the difficulty of rightly framing it. All, nevertheless, flutter round it. They approach me in a half-hesitant sort of way, eye me curiously or compassionately, and then, instead of saying directly, How does it feel to be a problem? they say, I know an excellent colored man in my town; or, I fought at Mechanicsville; or, Do not these Southern outrages make your blood boil? At these I smile, or am interested, or reduce the boiling to a simmer, as the occasion may require. To the real question, How does it feel to be a problem? I answer seldom a word.

And yet, being a problem is a strange experience,—peculiar even for one who has never been anything else, save perhaps in babyhood and in Europe. It is in the early days of rollicking boyhood that the revelation first bursts upon one, all in a day, as it were. I remember well when the shadow swept across me. I was a little thing, away up in the hills of New England, where the dark Housatonic winds between Hoosac and Taghkanic to the sea. In a wee wooden schoolhouse, something put it into the boys' and girls' heads to buy gorgeous visiting-cards—ten cents a package—and exchange. The exchange was merry, till one girl, a tall newcomer, refused my card,—refused it peremptorily, with a glance. Then it dawned upon me with a certain suddenness that I was different from the others; or like, mayhap, in heart and life and longing, but shut out from their world by a vast veil. I had thereafter no desire to tear down that veil, to creep through; I held all beyond it in common contempt, and lived above it in a region of blue sky and great wandering shadows. That sky was bluest when I could beat my mates at examination-time, or beat them at a foot-race, or even beat their stringy heads. Alas, with the years all this fine contempt began to fade; for the worlds I longed for, and all their dazzling opportunities, were theirs, not mine. But they should not keep these prizes, I said; some, all, I would wrest from them. Just how I would do it I could never decide: by reading law, by healing the sick, by telling the wonderful tales that swam in my head,—some way. With other black boys the strife was not so fiercely sunny: their youth shrunk into tasteless sycophancy, or into silent hatred of the pale world about them and mocking distrust of everything white; or wasted itself in a bitter cry, Why did God make me an outcast and a stranger in mine own house? The shades of the prison-house closed round about us all: walls strait and stubborn to the whitest, but relentlessly narrow, tall, and unscalable to sons of night who must plod darkly on in resignation, or beat unavailing palms against the stone, or steadily, half hopelessly, watch the streak of blue above.

After the Egyptian and Indian, the Greek and Roman, the Teuton and Mongolian, the Negro is a sort of seventh son, born with a veil, and gifted with second-sight in this American world,—a world which yields him no true self-consciousness, but only lets him see himself through the revelation of the other world. It is a peculiar sensation, this double-consciousness, this sense of always looking at one's self through the eyes of others, of measuring one's soul by the tape of a world that looks on in amused contempt and pity. One ever feels his two-ness,—an American, a Negro; two souls, two thoughts, two unreconciled strivings; two warring ideals in one dark body, whose dogged strength alone keeps it from being torn asunder.

The history of the American Negro is the history of this strife,—this longing to attain self-conscious manhood, to merge his double self into a better and truer self. In this merging he wishes neither of the older selves to be lost. He would not Africanize America, for America has too much to teach the world and Africa. He would not bleach his Negro soul in a flood of white Americanism, for he knows that Negro blood has a message for the world. He simply wishes to make it possible for a man to be both a Negro and an American, without being cursed and spit upon by his fellows, without having the doors of Opportunity closed roughly in his face.

This, then, is the end of his striving: to be a co-worker in the kingdom of culture, to escape both death and isolation, to husband and use his best powers and his latent genius. These powers of body and mind have in the past been strangely wasted, dispersed, or forgotten. The shadow of a mighty Negro past flits through the tale of Ethiopia the Shadowy and of Egypt the Sphinx. Throughout history, the powers of single black men flash here and there like falling stars, and die sometimes before the world has rightly gauged their brightness. Here in America, in the few days since Emancipation, the black man's turning hither and thither in hesitant and doubtful striving has often made his very strength to lose effectiveness, to seem like absence of power, like weakness. And yet it is not weakness,—it is the contradiction of double aims. The double-aimed struggle of the black artisan—on the one hand to escape white contempt for a nation of mere hewers of wood and drawers of water, and on the other hand to plough and nail and dig for a poverty-stricken horde—could only result in making him a poor craftsman, for he had but half a heart in either cause. By the poverty and ignorance of his people, the Negro minister or doctor was tempted toward quackery and demagogy; and by the criticism of the other world, toward ideals that made him ashamed of his lowly tasks. The would-be black *savant* was confronted by the paradox that the knowledge his people needed was a twice-told tale to his white neighbors, while the knowledge which would teach the white world was Greek to his own flesh and blood. The innate love of harmony and beauty that set the ruder souls of his people a-dancing and a-singing raised but confusion and doubt in the soul of the black artist; for the beauty revealed to him was the soul-beauty of a race which his larger audience despised, and he could not articulate the message of another people. This waste of double aims, this seeking to satisfy two unreconciled ideals, has wrought sad havoc with the courage and faith and deeds of ten thousand thousand people,—has sent them often wooing false gods and invoking false means of salvation, and at times has even seemed about to make them ashamed of themselves.

Away back in the days of bondage they thought to see in one divine event the end of all doubt and disappointment; few men ever worshipped Freedom with half such unquestioning faith as did the American Negro for two centuries. To him, so far as he thought and dreamed, slavery was indeed the sum of all villainies, the cause of all sorrow, the root of all prejudice; Emancipation was the key to a promised land of sweeter beauty than ever stretched before the eyes of wearied Israelites. In song and exhortation swelled one refrain—Liberty; in his tears and curses the God he implored had Freedom in his right hand. At last it came,—suddenly, fearfully, like a dream. With one wild carnival of blood and passion came the message in his own plaintive cadences:—

> "Shout, O children!
> Shout, you 're free!
> For God has bought your liberty!"

Years have passed away since then,—ten, twenty, forty; forty years of national life, forty years of renewal and development, and yet the swarthy spectre sits in its accustomed seat at the Nation's feast. In vain do we cry to this our vastest social problem:—

> "Take any shape but that, and my firm nerves
> Shall never tremble!"

The Nation has not yet found peace from its sins; the freedman has not yet found in freedom his promised land.

Whatever of good may have come in these years of change, the shadow of a deep disappointment rests upon the Negro people,—a disappointment all the more bitter because the unattained ideal was unbounded save by the simple ignorance of a lowly people.

The first decade was merely a prolongation of the vain search for freedom, the boon that seemed ever barely to elude their grasp,—like a tantalizing will-o'-the-wisp, maddening and misleading the headless host. The holocaust of war, the terrors of the Ku-Klux Klan, the lies of carpet-baggers, the disorganization of industry, and the contradictory advice of friends and foes, left the bewildered serf with no new watchword beyond the old cry for freedom. As the time flew, however, he began to grasp a new idea. The ideal of liberty demanded for its attainment powerful means, and these the Fifteenth Amendment gave him. The ballot, which before he had looked upon as a visible sign of freedom, he now regarded as the chief means of gaining and perfecting the liberty with which war had partially endowed him. And why not? Had not votes made war and emancipated millions? Had not votes enfranchised the freedmen? Was anything impossible to a power that had done all this? A million black men started with renewed zeal to vote themselves into the kingdom. So the decade flew away, the revolution of 1876 came, and left the half-free serf weary, wondering, but still inspired. Slowly but steadily, in the following years, a new vision began gradually to replace the dream of political power,—a powerful movement, the rise of another ideal to guide the unguided, another pillar of fire by night after a clouded day. It was the ideal of "book-learning"; the curiosity, born of compulsory ignorance, to know and test the power of the cabalistic letters of the white man, the longing to know. Here at last seemed to have been discovered the mountain path to Canaan; longer than the highway of Emancipation and law, steep and rugged, but straight, leading to heights high enough to overlook life.

Up the new path the advance guard toiled, slowly, heavily, doggedly; only those who have watched and guided the faltering feet, the misty minds, the dull understandings, of the dark pupils of these schools know how faithfully, how piteously, this people strove to learn. It was weary work. The cold statistician wrote down the inches of progress here and there, noted also where here and there a foot had slipped or some one had fallen. To the tired climbers, the horizon was ever dark, the mists were often cold, the Canaan was always dim and far away. If, however, the vistas disclosed as yet no goal, no resting-place, little but flattery and criticism, the journey at least gave leisure for reflection and self-examination; it changed the child of Emancipation to the youth with dawning self-consciousness, self-realization, self-respect. In those sombre forests of his striving his own soul rose before him, and he saw himself,—darkly as through a veil; and yet he saw in himself some faint revelation of his power, of his mission. He began to have a dim feeling that, to attain his place in the world, he must be himself, and not another. For the first time he sought to analyze the burden he bore upon his back, that dead-weight of social degradation partially masked behind a half-named Negro problem. He felt his poverty; without a cent, without a home, without land, tools, or savings, he had entered into competition with rich, landed, skilled neighbors. To be a poor man is hard, but to be a poor race in a land of dollars is the very bottom of hardships. He felt the weight of his ignorance,—not simply of letters, but of life, of business, of the humanities; the accumulated sloth and shirking and awkwardness of decades and centuries shackled his hands and feet. Nor was his burden all poverty and ignorance. The red stain of bastardy, which two centuries of systematic legal defilement of Negro women had stamped upon his race, meant not only the loss of ancient African chastity, but also the hereditary weight of a mass of corruption from white adulterers, threatening almost the obliteration of the Negro home.

A people thus handicapped ought not to be asked to race with the world, but rather allowed to give all its time and thought to its own social problems. But alas! while sociologists gleefully count his bastards and his prostitutes, the very soul of the toiling, sweating black man is darkened by the shadow of a vast despair. Men call the shadow prejudice, and learnedly explain it as the natural defence of culture against barbarism, learning against ignorance, purity against crime, the "higher" against the "lower" races. To which the Negro cries Amen! and swears that to so much of this strange prejudice as is founded on just homage to civilization, culture, righteousness, and progress, he humbly bows and meekly does obeisance. But before that nameless prejudice that leaps beyond all this he stands helpless, dismayed, and well-nigh speechless; before that personal disrespect and mockery, the ridicule and systematic humiliation, the distortion of fact and wanton license of fancy, the cynical ignoring of the better and the boisterous welcoming of the worse, the all-pervading desire to inculcate disdain for everything black, from Toussaint to the devil,—before this there rises a sickening despair that would disarm and discourage any nation save that black host to whom "discouragement" is an unwritten word.

But the facing of so vast a prejudice could not but bring the inevitable self-questioning, self-disparagement, and lowering of ideals which ever accompany repression and breed in an atmosphere of contempt and hate. Whisperings and portents came borne upon the four winds: Lo! we are diseased and dying, cried the dark hosts; we cannot write, our voting is vain; what need of education, since we must always cook and serve? And the Nation echoed and enforced this self-criticism, saying: Be content to be servants, and nothing more; what need of higher culture for half-men? Away with the black man's ballot, by force or fraud,—and behold the suicide of a race! Nevertheless, out of the evil came something of good,—the more careful adjustment of education to real life, the clearer perception of the Negroes' social responsibilities, and the sobering realization of the meaning of progress.

So dawned the time of *Sturm und Drang*: storm and stress to-day rocks our little boat on the mad waters of the world-sea; there is within and without the sound of conflict, the burning of body and rending of soul; inspiration strives with doubt, and faith with vain questionings. The bright ideals of the past,—physical freedom, political power, the training of brains and the training of hands,—all these in turn have waxed and waned, until even the last grows dim and overcast. Are they all wrong,—all false? No, not that, but each alone was over-simple and incomplete,—the dreams of a credulous race-childhood, or the fond imaginings of the other world which does not know and does not want to know our power. To be really true, all these ideals must be melted and welded into one. The training of the schools we need to-day more than ever,—the training of deft hands, quick eyes and ears, and above all the broader, deeper, higher culture of gifted minds and pure hearts. The power of the ballot we need in sheer self-defence,—else what shall save us from a second slavery? Freedom, too, the long-sought, we still seek,—the freedom of life and limb, the freedom to work and think, the freedom to love and aspire. Work, culture, liberty,—all these we need, not singly but together, not successively but together, each growing and aiding each, and all striving toward that vaster ideal that swims before the Negro people, the ideal of human brotherhood, gained through the unifying ideal of Race; the ideal of fostering and developing the traits and talents of the Negro, not in opposition to or contempt for other races, but rather in large conformity to the greater ideals of the American Republic, in order that some day on American soil two world-races may give each to each those characteristics both so sadly lack. We the darker ones come even now not altogether empty-handed: there are to-day no truer exponents of the pure human spirit of the Declaration of Independence than the American Negroes; there is no true American music but the wild sweet melodies of the Negro slave; the American fairy tales and folk-lore are Indian and African; and, all in all, we black men seem the sole oasis of simple faith and reverence in a dusty desert of dollars and smartness. Will America be poorer if she replace her brutal dyspeptic blundering with light-hearted but determined Negro humility? or her coarse and cruel wit with loving jovial good-humor? or her vulgar music with the soul of the Sorrow Songs?

Merely a concrete test of the underlying principles of the great republic is the Negro Problem, and the spiritual striving of the freedmen's sons is the travail of souls whose burden is almost beyond the measure of their strength, but who bear it in the name of an historic race, in the name of this the land of their fathers' fathers, and in the name of human opportunity.

* * *

And now what I have briefly sketched in large outline let me on coming pages tell again in many ways, with loving emphasis and deeper detail, that men may listen to the striving in the souls of black folk.

II

Of the Dawn of Freedom

Careless seems the great Avenger;
  History's lessons but record
One death-grapple in the darkness
  'Twixt old systems and the Word;
Truth forever on the scaffold,
  Wrong forever on the throne;
Yet that scaffold sways the future,
  And behind the dim unknown
Standeth God within the shadow
  Keeping watch above His own.

LOWELL.

THE PROBLEM of the twentieth century is the problem of the color-line,—the relation of the darker to the lighter races of men in Asia and Africa, in America and the islands of the sea. It was a phase of this problem that caused the Civil War; and however much they who marched South and North in 1861 may have fixed on the technical points of union and local autonomy as a shibboleth, all nevertheless knew, as we know, that the question of Negro slavery was the real cause of the conflict. Curious it was, too, how this deeper question ever forced itself to the surface despite effort and disclaimer. No sooner had Northern armies touched Southern soil than this old question, newly guised, sprang from the earth,—What shall be done with Negroes? Peremptory military commands, this way and that, could not answer the query; the Emancipation Proclamation seemed but to broaden and intensify the difficulties; and the War Amendments made the Negro problems of to-day.

It is the aim of this essay to study the period of history from 1861 to 1872 so far as it relates to the American Negro.

In effect, this tale of the dawn of Freedom is an account of that government of men called the Freedmen's Bureau,—one of the most singular and interesting of the attempts made by a great nation to grapple with vast problems of race and social condition.

The war has naught to do with slaves, cried Congress, the President, and the Nation; and yet no sooner had the armies, East and West, penetrated Virginia and Tennessee than fugitive slaves appeared within their lines. They came at night, when the flickering camp-fires shone like vast unsteady stars along the black horizon: old men and thin, with gray and tufted hair; women, with frightened eyes, dragging whimpering hungry children; men and girls, stalwart and gaunt,—a horde of starving vagabonds, homeless, helpless, and pitiable, in their dark distress. Two methods of treating these newcomers seemed equally logical to opposite sorts of minds. Ben Butler, in Virginia, quickly declared slave property contraband of war, and put the fugitives to work; while Fremont, in Missouri, declared the slaves free under martial law. Butler's action was approved, but Fremont's was hastily countermanded, and his successor, Halleck, saw things differently. "Hereafter," he commanded, "no slaves should be allowed to come into your lines at all; if any come without your knowledge, when owners call for them deliver them." Such a policy was difficult to enforce; some of the black refugees declared themselves freemen, others showed that their masters had deserted them, and still others were captured with forts and plantations. Evidently, too, slaves were a source of strength to the Confederacy, and were being used as laborers and producers. "They constitute a military resource," wrote Secretary Cameron, late in 1861; "and being such, that they should not be turned over to the enemy is too plain to discuss." So gradually the tone of the army chiefs changed; Congress forbade the rendition of fugitives, and Butler's "contrabands" were welcomed as military laborers. This complicated rather than solved the problem, for now the scattering fugitives became a steady stream, which flowed faster as the armies marched.

Then the long-headed man with care-chiselled face who sat in the White House saw the inevitable, and emancipated the slaves of rebels on New Year's, 1863. A month later Congress called earnestly for the Negro soldiers whom the act of July, 1862, had half grudgingly allowed to enlist. Thus the barriers were levelled and the deed was done. The stream of fugitives swelled to a flood, and anxious army officers kept inquiring: "What must be done with slaves, arriving almost daily? Are we to find food and shelter for women and children?"

It was a Pierce of Boston who pointed out the way, and thus became in a sense the founder of the Freedmen's Bureau. He was a firm friend of Secretary Chase; and when, in 1861, the care of slaves and abandoned lands devolved upon the Treasury officials, Pierce was specially detailed from the ranks to study the conditions. First, he cared for the refugees at Fortress Monroe; and then, after Sherman had captured Hilton Head, Pierce was sent there to found his Port Royal experiment of making free workingmen out of slaves. Before his experiment was barely started, however, the problem of the fugitives had assumed such proportions that it was taken from the hands of the over-burdened Treasury Department and given to the army officials. Already centres of massed freedmen were forming at Fortress Monroe, Washington, New Orleans, Vicksburg and Corinth, Columbus, Ky., and Cairo, Ill., as well as at Port Royal. Army chaplains found here new and fruitful fields; "superintendents of contrabands" multiplied, and some attempt at systematic work was made by enlisting the able-bodied men and giving work to the others.

Then came the Freedmen's Aid societies, born of the touching appeals from Pierce and from these other centres of distress. There was the American Missionary Association, sprung from the *Amistad*, and now full-grown for work; the various church organizations, the National Freedmen's Relief Association, the American Freedmen's Union, the Western Freedmen's Aid Commission,—in all fifty or more active organizations, which sent clothes, money, school-books, and teachers southward. All they did was needed, for the destitution of the freedmen was often reported as "too appalling for belief," and the situation was daily growing worse rather than better.

And daily, too, it seemed more plain that this was no ordinary matter of temporary relief, but a national crisis; for here loomed a labor problem of vast dimensions. Masses of

Negroes stood idle, or, if they worked spasmodically, were never sure of pay; and if perchance they received pay, squandered the new thing thoughtlessly. In these and other ways were camp-life and the new liberty demoralizing the freedmen. The broader economic organization thus clearly demanded sprang up here and there as accident and local conditions determined. Here it was that Pierce's Port Royal plan of leased plantations and guided workmen pointed out the rough way. In Washington the military governor, at the urgent appeal of the superintendent, opened confiscated estates to the cultivation of the fugitives, and there in the shadow of the dome gathered black farm villages. General Dix gave over estates to the freedmen of Fortress Monroe, and so on, South and West. The government and benevolent societies furnished the means of cultivation, and the Negro turned again slowly to work. The systems of control, thus started, rapidly grew, here and there, into strange little governments, like that of General Banks in Louisiana, with its ninety thousand black subjects, its fifty thousand guided laborers, and its annual budget of one hundred thousand dollars and more. It made out four thousand pay-rolls a year, registered all freedmen, inquired into grievances and redressed them, laid and collected taxes, and established a system of public schools. So, too, Colonel Eaton, the superintendent of Tennessee and Arkansas, ruled over one hundred thousand freedmen, leased and cultivated seven thousand acres of cotton land, and fed ten thousand paupers a year. In South Carolina was General Saxton, with his deep interest in black folk. He succeeded Pierce and the Treasury officials, and sold forfeited estates, leased abandoned plantations, encouraged schools, and received from Sherman, after that terribly picturesque march to the sea, thousands of the wretched camp followers.

Three characteristic things one might have seen in Sherman's raid through Georgia, which threw the new situation in shadowy relief: the Conqueror, the Conquered, and the Negro. Some see all significance in the grim front of the destroyer, and some in the bitter sufferers of the Lost Cause. But to me neither soldier nor fugitive speaks with so deep a meaning as that dark human cloud that clung like remorse on the rear of those swift columns, swelling at times to half their size, almost engulfing and choking them. In vain were they ordered back, in vain were bridges hewn from beneath their feet; on they trudged and writhed and surged, until they rolled into Savannah, a starved and naked horde of tens of thousands. There too came the characteristic military remedy: "The islands from Charleston south, the abandoned rice-fields along the rivers for thirty miles back from the sea, and the country bordering the St. John's River, Florida, are reserved and set apart for the settlement of Negroes now made free by act of war." So read the celebrated "Field-order Number Fifteen."

All these experiments, orders, and systems were bound to attract and perplex the government and the nation. Directly after the Emancipation Proclamation, Representative Eliot had introduced a bill creating a Bureau of Emancipation; but it was never reported. The following June a committee of inquiry, appointed by the Secretary of War, reported in favor of a temporary bureau for the "improvement, protection, and employment of refugee freedmen," on much the same lines as were afterwards followed. Petitions came in to President Lincoln from distinguished citizens and organizations, strongly urging a comprehensive and unified plan of dealing with the freedmen, under a bureau which should be "charged with the study of plans and execution of measures for easily guiding, and in every way judiciously and humanely aiding, the passage of our emancipated and yet to be emancipated blacks from the old condition of forced labor to their new state of voluntary industry."

Some half-hearted steps were taken to accomplish this, in part, by putting the whole matter again in charge of the special Treasury agents. Laws of 1863 and 1864 directed them to take charge of and lease abandoned lands for periods not exceeding twelve months, and to "provide in such leases, or otherwise, for the employment and general welfare" of the freedmen. Most of the army officers greeted this as a welcome relief from perplexing "Negro affairs," and Secretary Fessenden, July 29, 1864, issued an excellent system of regulations, which were afterward closely followed by General Howard. Under Treasury agents, large quantities of land were leased in the Mississippi Valley, and many Negroes were employed; but in August, 1864, the new regulations were suspended for reasons of "public policy," and the army was again in control.

Meanwhile Congress had turned its attention to the subject; and in March the House passed a bill by a majority of two establishing a Bureau for Freedmen in the War Department. Charles Sumner, who had charge of the bill in the Senate, argued that freedmen and abandoned lands ought to be under the same department, and reported a substitute for the House bill attaching the Bureau to the Treasury Department. This bill passed, but too late for action by the House. The debates wandered over the whole policy of the administration and the general question of slavery, without touching very closely the specific merits of the measure in hand. Then the national election took place; and the administration, with a vote of renewed confidence from the country, addressed itself to the matter more seriously. A conference between the two branches of Congress agreed upon a carefully drawn measure which contained the chief provisions of Sumner's bill, but made the proposed organization a department independent of both the War and the Treasury officials. The bill was conservative, giving the new department "general superintendence of all freedmen." Its purpose was to "establish regulations" for them, protect them, lease them lands, adjust their wages, and appear in civil and military courts as their "next friend." There were many limitations attached to the powers thus granted, and the organization was made permanent. Nevertheless, the Senate defeated the bill, and a new conference committee was appointed. This committee reported a new bill, February 28, which was whirled through just as the session closed, and became the act of 1865 establishing in the War Department a "Bureau of Refugees, Freedmen, and Abandoned Lands."

This last compromise was a hasty bit of legislation, vague and uncertain in outline. A Bureau was created, "to continue during the present War of Rebellion, and for one year thereafter," to which was given "the supervision and management of all abandoned lands and the control of all subjects relating to refugees and freedmen," under "such rules and regulations as may be presented by the head of the Bureau and approved by the President." A Commissioner, appointed by the President and Senate, was to control the Bureau, with an office force not exceeding ten clerks. The President might also appoint assistant commissioners in the seceded States, and to all these offices military officials might be detailed at regular pay. The Secretary of War could issue rations, clothing, and fuel to the destitute, and all abandoned property was placed in the hands of the Bureau for eventual lease and sale to ex-slaves in forty-acre parcels.

Thus did the United States government definitely assume charge of the emancipated Negro as the ward of the nation. It was a tremendous undertaking. Here at a stroke of the pen was erected a government of millions of men,—and not ordinary men either, but black men emasculated by a peculiarly complete system of slavery, centuries old; and now, suddenly, violently, they come into a new birthright, at a time of war and passion, in the midst of the stricken and embittered population of their former masters. Any man might well have hesitated to assume charge of such a work, with vast responsibilities, indefinite powers, and limited resources. Probably no one but a soldier would have answered such a call promptly; and, indeed, no one but a soldier could be called, for Congress had appropriated no money for salaries and expenses.

Less than a month after the weary Emancipator passed to his rest, his successor assigned Major-Gen. Oliver O. Howard to duty as Commissioner of the new Bureau. He was a Maine man, then only thirty-five years of age. He had marched with Sherman to the sea, had fought well at Gettysburg, and but the year before had been assigned to the command of the Department of Tennessee. An honest man, with too much faith in human nature, little aptitude for business and intricate detail, he had had large opportunity of becoming acquainted at first hand with much of the work before him. And of that work it has been truly said that "no approximately correct history of civilization can ever be written which does not throw out in bold relief, as one of the great landmarks of political and social progress, the organization and administration of the Freedmen's Bureau."

On May 12, 1865, Howard was appointed; and he assumed

the duties of his office promptly on the 15th, and began examining the field of work. A curious mess he looked upon: little despotisms, communistic experiments, slavery, peonage, business speculations, organized charity, unorganized almsgiving,—all reeling on under the guise of helping the freedmen, and all enshrined in the smoke and blood of war and the cursing and silence of angry men. On May 19 the new government—for a government it really was—issued its constitution; commissioners were to be appointed in each of the seceded States, who were to take charge of "all subjects relating to refugees and freedmen," and all relief and rations were to be given by their consent alone. The Bureau invited continued coöperation with benevolent societies, and declared: "It will be the object of all commissioners to introduce practicable systems of compensated labor," and to establish schools. Forthwith nine assistant commissioners were appointed. They were to hasten to their fields of work; seek gradually to close relief establishments, and make the destitute self-supporting; act as courts of law where there were no courts, or where Negroes were not recognized in them as free; establish the institution of marriage among ex-slaves, and keep records; see that freedmen were free to choose their employers, and help in making fair contracts for them; and finally, the circular said: "Simple good faith, for which we hope on all hands for those concerned in the passing away of slavery, will especially relieve the assistant commissioners in the discharge of their duties toward the freedmen, as well as promote the general welfare."

No sooner was the work thus started, and the general system and local organization in some measure begun, than two grave difficulties appeared which changed largely the theory and outcome of Bureau work. First, there were the abandoned lands of the South. It had long been the more or less definitely expressed theory of the North that all the chief problems of Emancipation might be settled by establishing the slaves on the forfeited lands of their masters,—a sort of poetic justice, said some. But this poetry done into solemn prose meant either wholesale confiscation of private property in the South, or vast appropriations. Now Congress had not appropriated a cent, and no sooner did the proclamations of general amnesty appear than the eight hundred thousand acres of abandoned lands in the hands of the Freedmen's Bureau melted quickly away. The second difficulty lay in perfecting the local organization of the Bureau throughout the wide field of work. Making a new machine and sending out officials of duly ascertained fitness for a great work of social reform is no child's task; but this task was even harder, for a new central organization had to be fitted on a heterogeneous and confused but already existing system of relief and control of ex-slaves; and the agents available for this work must be sought for in an army still busy with war operations,—men in the very nature of the case ill fitted for delicate social work,—or among the questionable camp followers of an invading host. Thus, after a year's work, vigorously as it was pushed, the problem looked even more difficult to grasp and solve than at the beginning. Nevertheless, three things that year's work did, well worth the doing: it relieved a vast amount of physical suffering; it transported seven thousand fugitives from congested centres back to the farm; and, best of all, it inaugurated the crusade of the New England schoolma'am.

The annals of this Ninth Crusade are yet to be written,—the tale of a mission that seemed to our age far more quixotic than the quest of St. Louis seemed to his. Behind the mists of ruin and rapine waved the calico dresses of women who dared, and after the hoarse mouthings of the field guns rang the rhythm of the alphabet. Rich and poor they were, serious and curious. Bereaved now of a father, now of a brother, now of more than these, they came seeking a life work in planting New England schoolhouses among the white and black of the South. They did their work well. In that first year they taught one hundred thousand souls, and more.

Evidently, Congress must soon legislate again on the hastily organized Bureau, which had so quickly grown into wide significance and vast possibilities. An institution such as that was well-nigh as difficult to end as to begin. Early in 1866 Congress took up the matter, when Senator Trumbull, of Illinois, introduced a bill to extend the Bureau and enlarge its powers. This measure received, at the hands of Congress, far more thorough discussion and attention than its predecessor.

The war cloud had thinned enough to allow a clearer conception of the work of Emancipation. The champions of the bill argued that the strengthening of the Freedmen's Bureau was still a military necessity; that it was needed for the proper carrying out of the Thirteenth Amendment, and was a work of sheer justice to the ex-slave, at a trifling cost to the government. The opponents of the measure declared that the war was over, and the necessity for war measures past; that the Bureau, by reason of its extraordinary powers, was clearly unconstitutional in time of peace, and was destined to irritate the South and pauperize the freedmen, at a final cost of possibly hundreds of millions. These two arguments were unanswered, and indeed unanswerable: the one that the extraordinary powers of the Bureau threatened the civil rights of all citizens; and the other that the government must have power to do what manifestly must be done, and that present abandonment of the freedmen meant their practical re-enslavement. The bill which finally passed enlarged and made permanent the Freedmen's Bureau. It was promptly vetoed by President Johnson as "unconstitutional," "unnecessary," and "extrajudicial," and failed of passage over the veto. Meantime, however, the breach between Congress and the President began to broaden, and a modified form of the lost bill was finally passed over the President's second veto, July 16.

The act of 1866 gave the Freedmen's Bureau its final form,—the form by which it will be known to posterity and judged of men. It extended the existence of the Bureau to July, 1868; it authorized additional assistant commissioners, the retention of army officers mustered out of regular service, the sale of certain forfeited lands to freedmen on nominal terms, the sale of Confederate public property for Negro schools, and a wider field of judicial interpretation and cognizance. The government of the unreconstructed South was thus put very largely in the hands of the Freedmen's Bureau, especially as in many cases the departmental military commander was now made also assistant commissioner. It was thus that the Freedmen's Bureau became a full-fledged government of men. It made laws, executed them and interpreted them; it laid and collected taxes, defined and punished crime, maintained and used military force, and dictated such measures as it thought necessary and proper for the accomplishment of its varied ends. Naturally, all these powers were not exercised continuously nor to their fullest extent; and yet, as General Howard has said, "scarcely any subject that has to be legislated upon in civil society failed, at one time or another, to demand the action of this singular Bureau."

To understand and criticise intelligently so vast a work, one must not forget an instant the drift of things in the later sixties. Lee had surrendered, Lincoln was dead, and Johnson and Congress were at loggerheads; the Thirteenth Amendment was adopted, the Fourteenth pending, and the Fifteenth declared in force in 1870. Guerrilla raiding, the ever-present flickering after-flame of war, was spending its force against the Negroes, and all the Southern land was awakening as from some wild dream to poverty and social revolution. In a time of perfect calm, amid willing neighbors and streaming wealth, the social uplifting of four million slaves to an assured and self-sustaining place in the body politic and economic would have been a herculean task; but when to the inherent difficulties of so delicate and nice a social operation were added the spite and hate of conflict, the hell of war; when suspicion and cruelty were rife, and gaunt Hunger wept beside Bereavement,—in such a case, the work of any instrument of social regeneration was in large part foredoomed to failure. The very name of the Bureau stood for a thing in the South which for two centuries and better men had refused even to argue,—that life amid free Negroes was simply unthinkable, the maddest of experiments.

The agents that the Bureau could command varied all the way from unselfish philanthropists to narrow-minded busybodies and thieves; and even though it be true that the average was far better than the worst, it was the occasional fly that helped spoil the ointment.

Then amid all crouched the freed slave, bewildered between friend and foe. He had emerged from slavery,—not the worst slavery in the world, not a slavery that made all life unbearable, rather a slavery that had here and there something of kindliness, fidelity, and happiness,—but withal slavery, which, so far as human aspiration and desert were concerned, classed the black man and the ox together. And the Negro knew full well that, whatever their deeper convictions may have been, Southern men had fought with desperate energy to perpetuate this slavery under which the black masses, with half-articulate thought, had writhed and shivered. They welcomed freedom with a cry. They shrank from the master who still strove for their chains; they fled to the friends that had freed them, even though those friends stood ready to use them as a club for driving the recalcitrant South back into loyalty. So the cleft between the white and black South grew. Idle to say it never should have been; it was as inevitable as its results were pitiable. Curiously incongruous elements were left arrayed against each other,—the North, the government, the carpet-bagger, and the slave, here; and there, all the South that was white, whether gentleman or vagabond, honest man or rascal, lawless murderer or martyr to duty.

Thus it is doubly difficult to write of this period calmly, so intense was the feeling, so mighty the human passions that swayed and blinded men. Amid it all, two figures ever stand to typify that day to coming ages,—the one, a gray-haired gentleman, whose fathers had quit themselves like men, whose sons lay in nameless graves; who bowed to the evil of slavery because its abolition threatened untold ill to all; who stood at last, in the evening of life, a blighted, ruined form, with hate in his eyes;—and the other, a form hovering dark and mother-like, her awful face black with the mists of centuries, had aforetime quailed at that white master's command, had bent in love over the cradles of his sons and daughters, and closed in death the sunken eyes of his wife,—aye, too, at his behest had laid herself low to his lust, and borne a tawny man-child to the world, only to see her dark boy's limbs scattered to the winds by midnight marauders riding after "cursed Niggers." These were the saddest sights of that woful day; and no man clasped the hands of these two passing figures of the present-past; but, hating, they went to their long home, and, hating, their children's children live to-day.

Here, then, was the field of work for the Freedmen's Bureau; and since, with some hesitation, it was continued by the act of 1868 until 1869, let us look upon four years of its work as a whole. There were, in 1868, nine hundred Bureau officials scattered from Washington to Texas, ruling, directly and indirectly, many millions of men. The deeds of these rulers fall mainly under seven heads: the relief of physical suffering, the overseeing of the beginnings of free labor, the buying and selling of land, the establishment of schools, the paying of bounties, the administration of justice, and the financiering of all these activities.

Up to June, 1869, over half a million patients had been treated by Bureau physicians and surgeons, and sixty hospitals and asylums had been in operation. In fifty months twenty-one million free rations were distributed at a cost of over four million dollars. Next came the difficult question of labor. First, thirty thousand black men were transported from the refuges and relief stations back to the farms, back to the critical trial of a new way of working. Plain instructions went out from Washington: the laborers must be free to choose their employers, no fixed rate of wages was prescribed, and there was to be no peonage or forced labor. So far, so good; but where local agents differed *toto cœlo* in capacity and character, where the *personnel* was continually changing, the outcome was necessarily varied. The largest element of success lay in the fact that the majority of the freedmen were willing, even eager, to work. So labor contracts were written,—fifty thousand in a single State,—laborers advised, wages guaranteed, and employers supplied. In truth, the organization became a vast labor bureau,—not perfect, indeed, notably defective here and there, but on the whole successful beyond the dreams of thoughtful men. The two great obstacles which confronted the officials were the tyrant and the idler,—the slaveholder who was determined to perpetuate slavery under another name; and the freedman who regarded freedom as perpetual rest,—the Devil and the Deep Sea.

In the work of establishing the Negroes as peasant proprietors, the Bureau was from the first handicapped and at last absolutely checked. Something was done, and larger things were planned; abandoned lands were leased so long as they remained in the hands of the Bureau, and a total revenue of nearly half a million dollars derived from black tenants. Some other lands to which the nation had gained title were sold on easy terms, and public lands were opened for settlement to the very few freedmen who had tools and capital. But the vision of "forty acres and a mule"—the righteous and reasonable ambition to become a landholder, which the nation had all but categorically promised the freedmen—was destined in most cases to bitter disappointment. And those men of marvellous hindsight who are to-day seeking to preach the Negro back to the present peonage of the soil know well, or ought to know, that the opportunity of binding the Negro peasant willingly to the soil was lost on that day when the Commissioner of the Freedmen's Bureau had to go to South Carolina and tell the weeping freedmen, after their years of toil, that their land was not theirs, that there was a mistake—somewhere. If by 1874 the Georgia Negro alone owned three hundred and fifty thousand acres of land, it was by grace of his thrift rather than by bounty of the government.

The greatest success of the Freedmen's Bureau lay in the planting of the free school among Negroes, and the idea of free elementary education among all classes in the South. It not only called the schoolmistresses through the benevolent agencies and built them schoolhouses, but it helped discover and support such apostles of human culture as Edmund Ware, Samuel Armstrong, and Erastus Cravath. The opposition to Negro education in the South was at first bitter, and showed itself in ashes, insult, and blood; for the South believed an educated Negro to be a dangerous Negro. And the South was not wholly wrong; for education among all kinds of men always has had, and always will have, an element of danger and revolution, of dissatisfaction and discontent. Nevertheless, men strive to know. Perhaps some inkling of this paradox, even in the unquiet days of the Bureau, helped the bayonets allay an opposition to human training which still to-day lies smouldering in the South, but not flaming. Fisk, Atlanta, Howard, and Hampton were founded in these days, and six million dollars were expended for educational work, seven hundred and fifty thousand dollars of which the freedmen themselves gave of their poverty.

Such contributions, together with the buying of land and various other enterprises, showed that the ex-slave was handling some free capital already. The chief initial source of this was labor in the army, and his pay and bounty as a soldier. Payments to Negro soldiers were at first complicated by the ignorance of the recipients, and the fact that the quotas of colored regiments from Northern States were largely filled by recruits from the South, unknown to their fellow soldiers. Consequently, payments were accompanied by such frauds that Congress, by joint resolution in 1867, put the whole matter in the hands of the Freedmen's Bureau. In two years six million dollars was thus distributed to five thousand claimants, and in the end the sum exceeded eight million dollars. Even in this system fraud was frequent; but still the work put needed capital in the hands of practical paupers, and some, at least, was well spent.

The most perplexing and least successful part of the Bureau's work lay in the exercise of its judicial functions. The regular Bureau court consisted of one representative of the employer, one of the Negro, and one of the Bureau. If the Bureau could have maintained a perfectly judicial attitude, this arrangement would have been ideal, and must in time have gained confidence; but the nature of its other activities and the character of its *personnel* prejudiced the Bureau in favor of the black litigants, and led without doubt to much injustice and annoyance. On the other hand, to leave the Negro in the hands of Southern courts was impossible. In a distracted land where slavery had hardly fallen, to keep the strong from wanton abuse of the weak, and the weak from gloating insolently over the half-shorn strength of the strong, was a thankless, hopeless task. The former masters of the land were peremptorily ordered about, seized, and imprisoned, and punished over and again, with scant courtesy from army officers. The former slaves were intimidated, beaten, raped, and butchered by angry and revengeful men. Bureau courts tended to become centres simply for punishing whites, while the regular civil courts tended to become solely institutions for perpetuating the slavery of blacks. Almost every law and method ingenuity could devise was employed by the legislatures to reduce the Negroes to serfdom,—to make them the slaves of the State, if not of individual owners; while the Bureau officials too often were found striving to put the "bottom rail on top," and give the freedmen a power and independence which they could not yet use. It is all well enough for us of another generation to wax wise with advice to those who bore the burden in the heat of the day. It is full easy now to see that the man who lost home, fortune, and family at a stroke, and saw his land ruled by "mules and niggers," was really benefited by the passing of slavery. It is not difficult now to say to the young freedman, cheated and cuffed about, who has seen his father's head beaten to a jelly and his own mother namelessly assaulted, that the meek shall inherit the earth. Above all, nothing is more convenient than to heap on the Freedmen's Bureau all the evils of that evil day, and damn it utterly for every mistake and blunder that was made.

All this is easy, but it is neither sensible nor just. Some one had blundered, but that was long before Oliver Howard was born; there was criminal aggression and heedless neglect, but without some system of control there would have been far more than there was. Had that control been from within, the Negro would have been re-enslaved, to all intents and purposes. Coming as the control did from without, perfect men and methods would have bettered all things; and even with imperfect agents and questionable methods, the work accomplished was not undeserving of commendation.

Such was the dawn of Freedom; such was the work of the Freedmen's Bureau, which, summed up in brief, may be epitomized thus: For some fifteen million dollars, beside the sums spent before 1865, and the dole of benevolent societies, this Bureau set going a system of free labor, established a beginning of peasant proprietorship, secured the recognition of black freedmen before courts of law, and founded the free common school in the South. On the other hand, it failed to begin the establishment of good-will between ex-masters and freedmen, to guard its work wholly from paternalistic methods which discouraged self-reliance, and to carry out to any considerable extent its implied promises to furnish the freedmen with land. Its successes were the result of hard work, supplemented by the aid of philanthropists and the eager striving of black men. Its failures were the result of bad local agents, the inherent difficulties of the work, and national neglect.

Such an institution, from its wide powers, great responsibilities, large control of moneys, and generally conspicuous position, was naturally open to repeated and bitter attack. It sustained a searching Congressional investigation at the instance of Fernando Wood in 1870. Its archives and few remaining functions were with blunt discourtesy transferred from Howard's control, in his absence, to the supervision of Secretary of War Belknap in 1872, on the Secretary's recommendation. Finally, in consequence of grave intimations of wrong-doing made by the Secretary and his subordinates, General Howard was court-martialed in 1874. In both of these trials the Commissioner of the Freedmen's Bureau was officially exonerated from any wilful misdoing, and his work commended. Nevertheless, many unpleasant things were brought to light,—the methods of transacting the business of the Bureau were faulty; several cases of defalcation were proved, and other frauds strongly suspected; there were some business transactions which savored of dangerous speculation, if not dishonesty; and around it all lay the smirch of the Freedmen's Bank.

Morally and practically, the Freedmen's Bank was part of the Freedmen's Bureau, although it had no legal connection with it. With the prestige of the government back of it, and a directing board of unusual respectability and national reputation, this banking institution had made a remarkable start in the development of that thrift among black folk which slavery had kept them from knowing. Then in one sad day came the crash,—all the hard-earned dollars of the freedmen disappeared; but that was the least of the loss,—all the faith in saving went too, and much of the faith in men; and that was a loss that a Nation which to-day sneers at Negro shiftlessness has never yet made good. Not even ten additional years of slavery could have done so much to throttle the thrift of the freedmen as the mismanagement and bankruptcy of the series of savings banks chartered by the Nation for their especial aid. Where all the blame should rest, it is hard to say; whether the Bureau and the Bank died chiefly by reason of the blows of its selfish friends or the dark machinations of its foes, perhaps even time will never reveal, for here lies unwritten history.

Of the foes without the Bureau, the bitterest were those who attacked not so much its conduct or policy under the law as the necessity for any such institution at all. Such attacks came primarily from the Border States and the South; and they were summed up by Senator Davis, of Kentucky, when he moved to entitle the act of 1866 a bill "to promote strife and conflict between the white and black races . . . by a grant of unconstitutional power." The argument gathered tremendous strength South and North; but its very strength was its weakness. For, argued the plain common-sense of the nation, if it is unconstitutional, unpractical, and futile for the nation to stand guardian over its helpless wards, then there is left but one alternative,—to make those wards their own guardians by arming them with the ballot. Moreover, the path of the practical politician pointed the same way; for, argued this opportunist, if we cannot peacefully reconstruct the South with white votes, we certainly can with black votes. So justice and force joined hands.

The alternative thus offered the nation was not between full and restricted Negro suffrage; else every sensible man, black and white, would easily have chosen the latter. It was rather a choice between suffrage and slavery, after endless blood and gold had flowed to sweep human bondage away. Not a single Southern legislature stood ready to admit a Negro, under any conditions, to the polls; not a single Southern legislature believed free Negro labor was possible without a system of restrictions that took all its freedom away; there was scarcely a white man in the South who did not honestly regard Emancipation as a crime, and its practical nullification as a duty. In such a situation, the granting of the ballot to the black man was a necessity, the very least a guilty nation could grant a wronged race, and the only method of compelling the South to accept the results of the war. Thus Negro suffrage ended a civil war by beginning a race feud. And some felt gratitude toward the race thus sacrificed in its swaddling clothes on the altar of national integrity; and some felt and feel only indifference and contempt.

Had political exigencies been less pressing, the opposition to government guardianship of Negroes less bitter, and the attachment to the slave system less strong, the social seer can well imagine a far better policy,—a permanent Freedmen's Bureau, with a national system of Negro schools; a carefully supervised employment and labor office; a system of impartial protection before the regular courts; and such institutions for social betterment as savings-banks, land and building associations, and social settlements. All this vast expenditure of money and brains might have formed a great school of prospective citizenship, and solved in a way we have not yet solved the most perplexing and persistent of the Negro problems.

That such an institution was unthinkable in 1870 was due in part to certain acts of the Freedmen's Bureau itself. It came to regard its work as merely temporary, and Negro suffrage as a final answer to all present perplexities. The political ambition of many of its agents and *protégés* led it far afield into questionable activities, until the South, nursing its own deep prejudices, came easily to ignore all the good deeds of the Bureau and hate its very name with perfect hatred. So the Freedmen's Bureau died, and its child was the Fifteenth Amendment.

The passing of a great human institution before its work is done, like the untimely passing of a single soul, but leaves a legacy of striving for other men. The legacy of the Freedmen's Bureau is the heavy heritage of this generation. To-day, when new and vaster problems are destined to strain every fibre of the national mind and soul, would it not be well to count this legacy honestly and carefully? For this much all men know: despite compromise, war, and struggle, the Negro is not free. In the backwoods of the Gulf States, for miles and miles, he may not leave the plantation of his birth; in well-nigh the whole rural South the black farmers are peons, bound by law and custom to an economic slavery, from which the only escape is death or the penitentiary. In the most cultured sections and cities of the South the Negroes are a segregated servile caste, with restricted rights and privileges. Before the courts, both in law and custom, they stand on a different and peculiar basis. Taxation without representation is the rule of their political life. And the result of all this is, and in nature must have been, lawlessness and crime. That is the large legacy of the Freedmen's Bureau, the work it did not do because it could not.

* * *

I have seen a land right merry with the sun, where children sing, and rolling hills lie like passioned women wanton with harvest. And there in the King's Highway sat and sits a figure veiled and bowed, by which the traveller's footsteps hasten as they go. On the tainted air broods fear. Three centuries' thought has been the raising and unveiling of that bowed human heart, and now behold a century new for the duty and the deed. The problem of the Twentieth Century is the problem of the color-line.

III

Of Mr. Booker T. Washington and Others

From birth till death enslaved; in word, in deed, unmanned!

. . . .

Hereditary bondsmen! Know ye not
Who would be free themselves must strike the blow?

BYRON.

EASILY the most striking thing in the history of the American Negro since 1876 is the ascendancy of Mr. Booker T. Washington. It began at the time when war memories and ideals were rapidly passing; a day of astonishing commercial development was dawning; a sense of doubt and hesitation overtook the freedmen's sons,—then it was that his leading began. Mr. Washington came, with a simple definite programme, at the psychological moment when the nation was a little ashamed of having bestowed so much sentiment on Negroes, and was concentrating its energies on Dollars. His programme of industrial education, conciliation of the South, and submission and silence as to civil and political rights, was not wholly original; the Free Negroes from 1830 up to wartime had striven to build industrial schools, and the American Missionary Association had from the first taught various trades; and Price and others had sought a way of honorable alliance with the best of the Southerners. But Mr. Washington first indissolubly linked these things; he put enthusiasm, unlimited energy, and perfect faith into this programme, and changed it from a by-path into a veritable Way of Life. And the tale of the methods by which he did this is a fascinating study of human life.

It startled the nation to hear a Negro advocating such a programme after many decades of bitter complaint; it startled and won the applause of the South, it interested and won the admiration of the North; and after a confused murmur of protest, it silenced if it did not convert the Negroes themselves.

To gain the sympathy and coöperation of the various elements comprising the white South was Mr. Washington's first task; and this, at the time Tuskegee was founded, seemed, for a black man, well-nigh impossible. And yet ten years later it was done in the word spoken at Atlanta: "In all things purely social we can be as separate as the five fingers, and yet one as the hand in all things essential to mutual progress." This "Atlanta Compromise" is by all odds the most notable thing in Mr. Washington's career. The South interpreted it in different ways: the radicals received it as a complete surrender of the demand for civil and political equality; the conservatives, as a generously conceived working basis for mutual understanding. So both approved it, and to-day its author is certainly the most distinguished Southerner since Jefferson Davis, and the one with the largest personal following.

Next to this achievement comes Mr. Washington's work in gaining place and consideration in the North. Others less shrewd and tactful had formerly essayed to sit on these two stools and had fallen between them; but as Mr. Washington knew the heart of the South from birth and training, so by singular insight he intuitively grasped the spirit of the age which was dominating the North. And so thoroughly did he learn the speech and thought of triumphant commercialism, and the ideals of material prosperity, that the picture of a lone black boy poring over a French grammar amid the weeds and dirt of a neglected home soon seemed to him the acme of absurdities. One wonders what Socrates and St. Francis of Assisi would say to this.

And yet this very singleness of vision and thorough oneness with his age is a mark of the successful man. It is as though Nature must needs make men narrow in order to give them force. So Mr. Washington's cult has gained unquestioning followers, his work has wonderfully prospered, his friends are legion, and his enemies are confounded. To-day he stands as the one recognized spokesman of his ten million fellows, and one of the most notable figures in a nation of seventy millions. One hesitates, therefore, to criticise a life which, beginning with so little, has done so much. And yet the time is come when one may speak in all sincerity and utter courtesy of the mistakes and shortcomings of Mr. Washington's career, as well as of his triumphs, without being thought captious or envious, and without forgetting that it is easier to do ill than well in the world.

The criticism that has hitherto met Mr. Washington has not always been of this broad character. In the South especially has he had to walk warily to avoid the harshest judgments,—and naturally so, for he is dealing with the one subject of deepest sensitiveness to that section. Twice—once when at the Chicago celebration of the Spanish-American War he alluded to the color-prejudice that is "eating away the vitals of the South," and once when he dined with President Roosevelt—has the resulting Southern criticism been violent enough to threaten seriously his popularity. In the North the feeling has several times forced itself into words, that Mr. Washington's counsels of submission overlooked certain elements of true manhood, and that his educational programme was unnecessarily narrow. Usually, however, such criticism has not found open expression, although, too, the spiritual sons of the Abolitionists have not been prepared to acknowledge that the schools founded before Tuskegee, by men of broad ideals and self-sacrificing spirit, were wholly failures or worthy of ridicule. While, then, criticism has not failed to follow Mr. Washington, yet the prevailing public opinion of the land has been but too willing to deliver the solution of a wearisome problem into his hands, and say, "If that is all you and your race ask, take it."

Among his own people, however, Mr. Washington has encountered the strongest and most lasting opposition, amounting at times to bitterness, and even to-day continuing strong and insistent even though largely silenced in outward expression by the public opinion of the nation. Some of this opposition is, of course, mere envy; the disappointment of displaced demagogues and the spite of narrow minds. But aside from this, there is among educated and thoughtful colored men in all parts of the land a feeling of deep regret, sorrow, and apprehension at the wide currency and ascendancy which some of Mr. Washington's theories have gained. These same men admire his sincerity of purpose, and are willing to forgive much to honest endeavor which is doing something worth the doing. They coöperate with Mr. Washington as far as they conscientiously can; and, indeed, it is no ordinary tribute to this man's tact and power that, steering as he must between so many diverse interests and opinions, he so largely retains the respect of all.

But the hushing of the criticism of honest opponents is a dangerous thing. It leads some of the best of the critics to unfortunate silence and paralysis of effort, and others to burst into speech so passionately and intemperately as to lose listeners. Honest and earnest criticism from those whose interests are most nearly touched,—criticism of writers by readers, of government by those governed, of leaders by those led,—this is the soul of democracy and the safeguard of modern society. If the best of the American Negroes receive by outer pressure a leader whom they had not recognized before, manifestly there is here a certain palpable gain. Yet there is also irreparable loss,—a loss of that peculiarly valuable education which a group receives when by search and criticism it finds and commissions its own leaders. The way in which this is done is at once the most elementary and the nicest problem of social growth. History is but the record of such group-leadership; and yet how infinitely changeful is its type and character! And of all types and kinds, what can be more instructive than the leadership of a group within a group?—that curious double movement where real progress may be negative and actual advance be relative retrogression. All this is the social student's inspiration and despair.

Now in the past the American Negro has had instructive experience in the choosing of group leaders, founding thus a peculiar dynasty which in the light of present conditions is worth while studying. When sticks and stones and beasts form the sole environment of a people, their attitude is largely one of determined opposition to and conquest of natural forces. But when to earth and brute is added an environment of men and ideas, then the attitude of the imprisoned group may take three main forms,—a feeling of revolt and revenge; an attempt to adjust all thought and action to the will of the greater group; or, finally, a determined effort at self-realization and self-development despite environing opinion. The influence of all of these attitudes at various times can be traced in the history of the American Negro, and in the evolution of his successive leaders.

Before 1750, while the fire of African freedom still burned in the veins of the slaves, there was in all leadership or attempted leadership but the one motive of revolt and revenge,—typified in the terrible Maroons, the Danish blacks, and Cato of Stono, and veiling all the Americas in fear of insurrection. The liberalizing tendencies of the latter half of the eighteenth century brought, along with kindlier relations between black and white, thoughts of ultimate adjustment and assimilation. Such aspiration was especially voiced in the earnest songs of Phyllis, in the martyrdom of Attucks, the fighting of Salem and Poor, the intellectual accomplishments of Banneker and Derham, and the political demands of the Cuffes.

Stern financial and social stress after the war cooled much of the previous humanitarian ardor. The disappointment and impatience of the Negroes at the persistence of slavery and serfdom voiced itself in two movements. The slaves in the South, aroused undoubtedly by vague rumors of the Haytian revolt, made three fierce attempts at insurrection,—in 1800 under Gabriel in Virginia, in 1822 under Vesey in Carolina, and in 1831 again in Virginia under the terrible Nat Turner. In the Free States, on the other hand, a new and curious attempt at self-development was made. In Philadelphia and New York color-prescription led to a withdrawal of Negro communicants from white churches and the formation of a peculiar socio-religious institution among the Negroes known as the African Church,—an organization still living and controlling in its various branches over a million of men.

Walker's wild appeal against the trend of the times showed how the world was changing after the coming of the cotton-gin. By 1830 slavery seemed hopelessly fastened on the South, and the slaves thoroughly cowed into submission. The free Negroes of the North, inspired by the mulatto immigrants from the West Indies, began to change the basis of their demands; they recognized the slavery of slaves, but insisted that they themselves were freemen, and sought assimilation and amalgamation with the nation on the same terms with other men. Thus, Forten and Purvis of Philadelphia, Shad of Wilmington, Du Bois of New Haven, Barbadoes of Boston, and others, strove singly and together as men, they said, not as slaves; as "people of color," not as "Negroes." The trend of the times, however, refused them recognition save in individual and exceptional cases, considered them as one with all the despised blacks, and they soon found themselves striving to keep even the rights they formerly had of voting and working and moving as freemen. Schemes of migration and colonization arose among them; but these they refused to entertain, and they eventually turned to the Abolition movement as a final refuge.

Here, led by Remond, Nell, Wells-Brown, and Douglass, a new period of self-assertion and self-development dawned. To be sure, ultimate freedom and assimilation was the ideal before the leaders, but the assertion of the manhood rights of the Negro by himself was the main reliance, and John Brown's raid was the extreme of its logic. After the war and emancipation, the great form of Frederick Douglass, the greatest of American Negro leaders, still led the host. Self-assertion, especially in political lines, was the main programme, and behind Douglass came Elliot, Bruce, and Langston, and the Reconstruction politicians, and, less conspicuous but of greater social significance Alexander Crummell and Bishop Daniel Payne.

Then came the Revolution of 1876, the suppression of the Negro votes, the changing and shifting of ideals, and the seeking of new lights in the great night. Douglass, in his old age, still bravely stood for the ideals of his early manhood,—ultimate assimilation *through* self-assertion, and on no other terms. For a time Price arose as a new leader, destined, it seemed, not to give up, but to re-state the old ideals in a form less repugnant to the white South. But he passed away in his prime. Then came the new leader. Nearly all the former ones had become leaders by the silent suffrage of their fellows, had sought to lead their own people alone, and were usually, save Douglass, little known outside their race. But Booker T. Washington arose as essentially the leader not of one race but of two,—a compromiser between the South, the North, and the Negro. Naturally the Negroes resented, at first bitterly, signs of compromise which surrendered their civil and political rights, even though this was to be exchanged for larger chances of economic development. The rich and dominating North, however, was not only weary of the race problem, but was investing largely in Southern enterprises, and welcomed any method of peaceful coöperation. Thus, by national opinion, the Negroes began to recognize Mr. Washington's leadership; and the voice of criticism was hushed.

Mr. Washington represents in Negro thought the old attitude of adjustment and submission; but adjustment at such a peculiar time as to make his programme unique. This is an age of unusual economic development, and Mr. Washington's programme naturally takes an economic cast, becoming a gospel of Work and Money to such an extent as apparently almost completely to overshadow the higher aims of life. Moreover, this is an age when the more advanced races are coming in closer contact with the less developed races, and the race-feeling is therefore intensified; and Mr. Washington's programme practically accepts the alleged inferiority of the Negro races. Again, in our own land, the reaction from the sentiment of war time has given impetus to race-prejudice against Negroes, and Mr. Washington withdraws many of the high demands of Negroes as men and American citizens. In other periods of intensified prejudice all the Negro's tendency to self-assertion has been called forth; at this period a policy of submission is advocated. In the history of nearly all other races and peoples the doctrine preached at such crises has been that manly self-respect is worth more than lands and houses, and that a people who voluntarily surrender such respect, or cease striving for it, are not worth civilizing.

In answer to this, it has been claimed that the Negro can survive only through submission. Mr. Washington distinctly asks that black people give up, at least for the present, three things,—

First, political power,

Second, insistence on civil rights,

Third, higher education of Negro youth,—

and concentrate all their energies on industrial education, the accumulation of wealth, and the conciliation of the South. This policy has been courageously and insistently advocated for over fifteen years, and has been triumphant for perhaps ten years. As a result of this tender of the palm-branch, what has been the return? In these years there have occurred:

1. The disfranchisement of the Negro.
2. The legal creation of a distinct status of civil inferiority for the Negro.
3. The steady withdrawal of aid from institutions for the higher training of the Negro.

These movements are not, to be sure, direct results of Mr. Washington's teachings; but his propaganda has, without a shadow of doubt, helped their speedier accomplishment. The question then comes: Is it possible, and probable, that nine millions of men can make effective progress in economic lines if they are deprived of political rights, made a servile caste, and allowed only the most meagre chance for developing their exceptional men? If history and reason give any distinct answer to these questions, it is an emphatic *No*. And Mr. Washington thus faces the triple paradox of his career:

1. He is striving nobly to make Negro artisans business men and property-owners; but it is utterly impossible, under modern competitive methods, for workingmen and property-owners to defend their rights and exist without the right of suffrage.
2. He insists on thrift and self-respect, but at the same time counsels a silent submission to civic inferiority such as is bound to sap the manhood of any race in the long run.
3. He advocates common-school and industrial training, and depreciates institutions of higher learning; but neither the Negro common-schools, nor Tuskegee itself, could remain open a day were it not for teachers trained in Negro colleges, or trained by their graduates.

This triple paradox in Mr. Washington's position is the object of criticism by two classes of colored Americans. One class is spiritually descended from Toussaint the Savior, through Gabriel, Vesey, and Turner, and they represent the attitude of revolt and revenge; they hate the white South blindly and distrust the white race generally, and so far as they agree on definite action, think that the Negro's only hope lies in emigration beyond the borders of the United States. And yet, by the irony of fate, nothing has more effectually made this programme seem hopeless than the recent course of the United States toward weaker and darker peoples in the West Indies, Hawaii, and the Philippines,—for where in the world may we go and be safe from lying and brute force?

The other class of Negroes who cannot agree with Mr. Washington has hitherto said little aloud. They deprecate the sight of scattered counsels, of internal disagreement; and especially they dislike making their just criticism of a useful and earnest man an excuse for a general discharge of venom from small-minded opponents. Nevertheless, the questions involved are so fundamental and serious that it is difficult to see how men like the Grimkes, Kelly Miller, J. W. E. Bowen, and other representatives of this group, can much longer be silent. Such men feel in conscience bound to ask of this nation three things:

1. The right to vote.
2. Civic equality.
3. The education of youth according to ability.

They acknowledge Mr. Washington's invaluable service in counselling patience and courtesy in such demands; they do not ask that ignorant black men vote when ignorant whites are debarred, or that any reasonable restrictions in the suffrage should not be applied; they know that the low social level of the mass of the race is responsible for much discrimination against it, but they also know, and the nation knows, that relentless color-prejudice is more often a cause than a result of the Negro's degradation; they seek the abatement of this relic of barbarism, and not its systematic encouragement and pampering by all agencies of social power from the Associated Press to the Church of Christ. They advocate, with Mr. Washington, a broad system of Negro common schools supplemented by thorough industrial training; but they are surprised that a man of Mr. Washington's insight cannot see that no such educational system ever has rested or can rest on any other basis than that of the well-equipped college and university, and they insist that there is a demand for a few such institutions throughout the South to train the best of the Negro youth as teachers, professional men, and leaders.

This group of men honor Mr. Washington for his attitude of conciliation toward the white South; they accept the "Atlanta Compromise" in its broadest interpretation; they recognize, with him, many signs of promise, many men of high purpose and fair judgment, in this section; they know that no easy task has been laid upon a region already tottering under heavy burdens. But, nevertheless, they insist that the way to truth and right lies in straightforward honesty, not in indiscriminate flattery; in praising those of the South who do well and criticising uncompromisingly those who do ill; in taking advantage of the opportunities at hand and urging their fellows to do the same, but at the same time in remembering that only a firm adherence to their higher ideals and aspirations will ever keep those ideals within the realm of possibility. They do not expect that the free right to vote, to enjoy civic rights, and to be educated, will come in a moment; they do not expect to see the bias and prejudices of years disappear at the blast of a trumpet; but they are absolutely certain that the way for a people to gain their reasonable rights is not by voluntarily throwing them away and insisting that they do not want them; that the way for a people to gain respect is not by continually belittling and ridiculing themselves; that, on the contrary, Negroes must insist continually, in season and out of season, that voting is necessary to modern manhood, that color discrimination is barbarism, and that black boys need education as well as white boys.

In failing thus to state plainly and unequivocally the legitimate demands of their people, even at the cost of opposing an honored leader, the thinking classes of American Negroes would shirk a heavy responsibility,—a responsibility to themselves, a responsibility to the struggling masses, a responsibility to the darker races of men whose future depends so largely on this American experiment, but especially a responsibility to this nation,—this common Fatherland. It is wrong to encourage a man or a people in evil-doing; it is wrong to aid and abet a national crime simply because it is unpopular not to do so. The growing spirit of kindliness and reconciliation between the North and South after the frightful differences of a generation ago ought to be a source of deep congratulation to all, and especially to those whose mistreatment caused the war; but if that reconciliation is to be marked by the industrial slavery and civic death of those same black men, with permanent legislation into a position of inferiority, then those black men, if they are really men, are called upon by every consideration of patriotism and loyalty to oppose such a course by all civilized methods, even though such opposition involves disagreement with Mr. Booker T. Washington. We have no right to sit silently by while the inevitable seeds are sown for a harvest of disaster to our children, black and white.

First, it is the duty of black men to judge the South discriminatingly. The present generation of Southerners are not responsible for the past, and they should not be blindly hated or blamed for it. Furthermore, to no class is the indiscriminate endorsement of the recent course of the South toward Negroes more nauseating than to the best thought of the South. The South is not "solid"; it is a land in the ferment of social change, wherein forces of all kinds are fighting for supremacy; and to praise the ill the South is to-day perpetrating is just as wrong as to condemn the good. Discriminating and broad-minded criticism is what the South needs,—needs it for the sake of her own white sons and daughters, and for the insurance of robust, healthy mental and moral development.

To-day even the attitude of the Southern whites toward the blacks is not, as so many assume, in all cases the same; the ignorant Southerner hates the Negro, the workingmen fear his competition, the money-makers wish to use him as a laborer, some of the educated see a menace in his upward development, while others—usually the sons of the masters—wish to help him to rise. National opinion has enabled this last class to maintain the Negro common schools, and to protect the Negro partially in property, life, and limb. Through the pressure of the money-makers, the Negro is in danger of being reduced to semi-slavery, especially in the country districts; the workingmen, and those of the educated who fear the Negro, have united to disfranchise him, and some have urged his deportation; while the passions of the ignorant are easily aroused to lynch and abuse any black man. To praise this intricate whirl of thought and prejudice is nonsense; to inveigh indiscriminately against "the South" is unjust; but to use the same breath in praising Governor Aycock, exposing Senator Morgan, arguing with Mr. Thomas Nelson Page, and denouncing Senator Ben Tillman, is not only sane, but the imperative duty of thinking black men.

It would be unjust to Mr. Washington not to acknowledge that in several instances he has opposed movements in the South which were unjust to the Negro; he sent memorials to the Louisiana and Alabama constitutional conventions, he has spoken against lynching, and in other ways has openly or silently set his influence against sinister schemes and unfortunate happenings. Notwithstanding this, it is equally true to assert that on the whole the distinct impression left by Mr. Washington's propaganda is, first, that the South is justified in its present attitude toward the Negro because of the Negro's degradation; secondly, that the prime cause of the Negro's failure to rise more quickly is his wrong education in the past; and, thirdly, that his future rise depends primarily on his own efforts. Each of these propositions is a dangerous half-truth. The supplementary truths must never be lost sight of: first, slavery and race-prejudice are potent if not sufficient causes of the Negro's position; second, industrial and common-school training were necessarily slow in planting because they had to await the black teachers trained by higher institutions,—it being extremely doubtful if any essentially different development was possible, and certainly a Tuskegee was unthinkable before 1880; and, third, while it is a great truth to say that the Negro must strive and strive mightily to help himself, it is equally true that unless his striving be not simply seconded, but rather aroused and encouraged, by the initiative of the richer and wiser environing group, he cannot hope for great success.

In his failure to realize and impress this last point, Mr. Washington is especially to be criticised. His doctrine has tended to make the whites, North and South, shift the burden of the Negro problem to the Negro's shoulders and stand aside as critical and rather pessimistic spectators; when in fact the burden belongs to the nation, and the hands of none of us are clean if we bend not our energies to righting these great wrongs.

The South ought to be led, by candid and honest criticism,

to assert her better self and do her full duty to the race she has cruelly wronged and is still wronging. The North—her co-partner in guilt—cannot salve her conscience by plastering it with gold. We cannot settle this problem by diplomacy and suaveness, by "policy" alone. If worse come to worst, can the moral fibre of this country survive the slow throttling and murder of nine millions of men?

The black men of America have a duty to perform, a duty stern and delicate,—a forward movement to oppose a part of the work of their greatest leader. So far as Mr. Washington preaches Thrift, Patience, and Industrial Training for the masses, we must hold up his hands and strive with him, rejoicing in his honors and glorying in the strength of this Joshua called of God and of man to lead the headless host. But so far as Mr. Washington apologizes for injustice, North or South, does not rightly value the privilege and duty of voting, belittles the emasculating effects of caste distinctions, and opposes the higher training and ambition of our brighter minds,—so far as he, the South, or the Nation, does this,—we must unceasingly and firmly oppose them. By every civilized and peaceful method we must strive for the rights which the world accords to men, clinging unwaveringly to those great words which the sons of the Fathers would fain forget: "We hold these truths to be self-evident: That all men are created equal; that they are endowed by their Creator with certain unalienable rights; that among these are life, liberty, and the pursuit of happiness."

IV

Of the Meaning of Progress

Willst Du Deine Macht verkünden,
Wähle sie die frei von Sünden,
Steh'n in Deinem ew'gen Haus!
Deine Geister sende aus!
Die Unsterblichen, die Reinen,
Die nicht fühlen, die nicht weinen!
Nicht die zarte Jungfrau wähle,
Nicht der Hirtin weiche Seele!

SCHILLER.

ONCE upon a time I taught school in the hills of Tennessee, where the broad dark vale of the Mississippi begins to roll and crumple to greet the Alleghanies. I was a Fisk student then, and all Fisk men thought that Tennessee—beyond the Veil—was theirs alone, and in vacation time they sallied forth in lusty bands to meet the county school-commissioners. Young and happy, I too went, and I shall not soon forget that summer, seventeen years ago.

First, there was a Teachers' Institute at the county-seat; and there distinguished guests of the superintendent taught the teachers fractions and spelling and other mysteries,—white teachers in the morning, Negroes at night. A picnic now and then, and a supper, and the rough world was softened by laughter and song. I remember how— But I wander.

There came a day when all the teachers left the Institute and began the hunt for schools. I learn from hearsay (for my mother was mortally afraid of fire-arms) that the hunting of ducks and bears and men is wonderfully interesting, but I am sure that the man who has never hunted a country school has something to learn of the pleasures of the chase. I see now the white, hot roads lazily rise and fall and wind before me under the burning July sun; I feel the deep weariness of heart and limb as ten, eight, six miles stretch relentlessly ahead; I feel my heart sink heavily as I hear again and again, "Got a teacher? Yes." So I walked on and on—horses were too expensive—until I had wandered beyond railways, beyond stage lines, to a land of "varmints" and rattlesnakes, where the coming of a stranger was an event, and men lived and died in the shadow of one blue hill.

Sprinkled over hill and dale lay cabins and farmhouses, shut out from the world by the forests and the rolling hills toward the east. There I found at last a little school. Josie told me of it; she was a thin, homely girl of twenty, with a dark-brown face and thick, hard hair. I had crossed the stream at Watertown, and rested under the great willows; then I had gone to the little cabin in the lot where Josie was resting on her way to town. The gaunt farmer made me welcome, and Josie, hearing my errand, told me anxiously that they wanted a school over the hill; that but once since the war had a teacher been there; that she herself longed to learn,—and thus she ran on, talking fast and loud, with much earnestness and energy.

Next morning I crossed the tall round hill, lingered to look at the blue and yellow mountains stretching toward the Carolinas, then plunged into the wood, and came out at Josie's home. It was a dull frame cottage with four rooms, perched just below the brow of the hill, amid peach-trees. The father was a quiet, simple soul, calmly ignorant, with no touch of vulgarity. The mother was different,—strong, bustling, and energetic, with a quick, restless tongue, and an ambition to live "like folks." There was a crowd of children. Two boys had gone away. There remained two growing girls; a shy midget of eight; John, tall, awkward, and eighteen; Jim, younger, quicker, and better looking; and two babies of indefinite age. Then there was Josie herself. She seemed to be the centre of the family: always busy at service, or at home, or berry-picking; a little nervous and inclined to scold, like her mother, yet faithful, too, like her father. She had about her a certain fineness, the shadow of an unconscious moral heroism that would willingly give all of life to make life broader, deeper, and fuller for her and hers. I saw much of this family afterwards, and grew to love them for their honest efforts to be decent and comfortable, and for their knowledge of their own ignorance. There was with them no affectation. The mother would scold the father for being so "easy"; Josie would roundly berate the boys for carelessness; and all knew that it was a hard thing to dig a living out of a rocky side-hill.

I secured the school. I remember the day I rode horseback out to the commissioner's house with a pleasant young white fellow who wanted the white school. The road ran down the bed of a stream; the sun laughed and the water jingled, and we rode on. "Come in," said the commissioner,—"come in. Have a seat. Yes, that certificate will do. Stay to dinner. What do you want a month?" "Oh," thought I, "this is lucky"; but even then fell the awful shadow of the Veil, for they ate first, then I—alone.

The schoolhouse was a log hut, where Colonel Wheeler used to shelter his corn. It sat in a lot behind a rail fence and thorn bushes, near the sweetest of springs. There was an entrance where a door once was, and within, a massive rickety fireplace; great chinks between the logs served as windows. Furniture was scarce. A pale blackboard crouched in the corner. My desk was made of three boards, reinforced at critical points, and my chair, borrowed from the landlady, had to be returned every night. Seats for the children—these puzzled me much. I was haunted by a New England vision of neat little desks and chairs, but, alas! the reality was rough plank benches without backs, and at times without legs. They had the one virtue of making naps dangerous,—possibly fatal, for the floor was not to be trusted.

It was a hot morning late in July when the school opened. I trembled when I heard the patter of little feet down the dusty road, and saw the growing row of dark solemn faces and bright eager eyes facing me. First came Josie and her brothers and sisters. The longing to know, to be a student in the great school at Nashville, hovered like a star above this child-woman amid her work and worry, and she studied doggedly. There were the Dowells from their farm over toward Alexandria,—Fanny, with her smooth black face and wondering eyes; Martha, brown and dull; the pretty girl-wife of a brother, and the younger brood.

There were the Burkes,—two brown and yellow lads, and a tiny haughty-eyed girl. Fat Reuben's little chubby girl came, with golden face and old-gold hair, faithful and solemn. 'Thenie was on hand early,—a jolly, ugly, good-hearted girl, who slyly dipped snuff and looked after her little bow-legged brother. When her mother could spare her, 'Tildy came,—a midnight beauty, with starry eyes and tapering limbs; and her brother, correspondingly homely. And then the big boys,—the hulking Lawrences; the lazy Neills, unfathered sons of mother and daughter; Hickman, with a stoop in his shoulders; and the rest.

There they sat, nearly thirty of them, on the rough benches, their faces shading from a pale cream to a deep brown, the little feet bare and swinging, the eyes full of expectation, with here and there a twinkle of mischief, and the hands grasping Webster's blue-back spelling-book. I loved my school, and the fine faith the children had in the wisdom of their teacher was truly marvellous. We read and spelled together, wrote a little, picked flowers, sang, and listened to stories of the world beyond the hill. At times the school would dwindle away, and I would start out. I would visit Mun Eddings, who lived in two very dirty rooms, and ask why little Lugene, whose flaming face seemed ever ablaze with the dark-red hair uncombed, was absent all last week, or why I missed so often the inimitable rags of Mack and Ed. Then the father, who worked Colonel Wheeler's farm on shares, would tell me how the crops needed the boys; and the thin, slovenly mother, whose face was pretty when washed, assured me that Lugene must mind the baby. "But we 'll start them again next week." When the Lawrences stopped, I knew that the doubts of the old folks about book-learning had conquered again, and so, toiling up the hill, and getting as far into the cabin as possible, I put Cicero "pro Archia Poeta" into the simplest English with local applications, and usually convinced them—for a week or so.

On Friday nights I often went home with some of the children,—sometimes to Doc Burke's farm. He was a great, loud, thin Black, ever working, and trying to buy the seventy-five acres of hill and dale where he lived; but people said that he would surely fail, and the "white folks would get it all." His wife was a magnificent Amazon, with saffron face and shining hair, uncorseted and barefooted, and the children were strong and beautiful. They lived in a one-and-a-half-room cabin in the hollow of the farm, near the spring. The front room was full of great fat white beds, scrupulously neat; and there were bad chromos on the walls, and a tired centre-table. In the tiny back kitchen I was often invited to "take out and help" myself to fried chicken and wheat biscuit, "meat" and corn pone, string-beans and berries. At first I used to be a little alarmed at the approach of bedtime in the one lone bedroom, but embarrassment was very deftly avoided. First, all the children nodded and slept, and were stowed away in one great pile of goose feathers; next, the mother and the father discreetly slipped away to the kitchen while I went to bed; then, blowing out the dim light, they retired in the dark. In the morning all were up and away before I thought of awaking. Across the road, where fat Reuben lived, they all went outdoors while the teacher retired, because they did not boast the luxury of a kitchen.

I liked to stay with the Dowells, for they had four rooms and plenty of good country fare. Uncle Bird had a small, rough farm, all woods and hills, miles from the big road; but he was full of tales,—he preached now and then,—and with his children, berries, horses, and wheat he was happy and prosperous. Often, to keep the peace, I must go where life was less lovely; for instance, 'Tildy's mother was incorrigibly dirty, Reuben's larder was limited seriously, and herds of untamed insects wandered over the Eddingses' beds. Best of all I loved to go to Josie's, and sit on the porch, eating peaches, while the mother bustled and talked: how Josie had bought the sewing-machine; how Josie worked at service in winter, but that four dollars a month was "mighty little" wages; how Josie longed to go away to school, but that it "looked like" they never could get far enough ahead to let her; how the crops failed and the well was yet unfinished; and, finally, how "mean" some of the white folks were.

For two summers I lived in this little world; it was dull and humdrum. The girls looked at the hill in wistful longing, and the boys fretted and haunted Alexandria. Alexandria was "town,"—a straggling, lazy village of houses, churches, and shops, and an aristocracy of Toms, Dicks, and Captains.

Cuddled on the hill to the north was the village of the colored folks, who lived in three- or four-room unpainted cottages, some neat and homelike, and some dirty. The dwellings were scattered rather aimlessly, but they centred about the twin temples of the hamlet, the Methodist, and the Hard-Shell Baptist churches. These, in turn, leaned gingerly on a sad-colored schoolhouse. Hither my little world wended its crooked way on Sunday to meet other worlds, and gossip, and wonder, and make the weekly sacrifice with frenzied priest at the altar of the "old-time religion." Then the soft melody and mighty cadences of Negro song fluttered and thundered.

I have called my tiny community a world, and so its isolation made it; and yet there was among us but a half-awakened common consciousness, sprung from common joy and grief, at burial, birth, or wedding; from a common hardship in poverty, poor land, and low wages; and, above all, from the sight of the Veil that hung between us and Opportunity. All this caused us to think some thoughts together; but these, when ripe for speech, were spoken in various languages. Those whose eyes twenty-five and more years before had seen "the glory of the coming of the Lord," saw in every present hindrance or help a dark fatalism bound to bring all things right in His own good time. The mass of those to whom slavery was a dim recollection of childhood found the world a puzzling thing: it asked little of them, and they answered with little, and yet it ridiculed their offering. Such a paradox they could not understand, and therefore sank into listless indifference, or shiftlessness, or reckless bravado. There were, however, some—such as Josie, Jim, and Ben—to whom War, Hell, and Slavery were but childhood tales, whose young appetites had been whetted to an edge by school and story and half-awakened thought. Ill could they be content, born without and beyond the World. And their weak wings beat against their barriers,—barriers of caste, of youth, of life; at last, in dangerous moments, against everything that opposed even a whim.

The ten years that follow youth, the years when first the realization comes that life is leading somewhere,—these were the years that passed after I left my little school. When they were past, I came by chance once more to the walls of Fisk University, to the halls of the chapel of melody. As I lingered there in the joy and pain of meeting old school-friends, there swept over me a sudden longing to pass again beyond the blue hill, and to see the homes and the school of other days, and to learn how life had gone with my school-children; and I went.

Josie was dead, and the gray-haired mother said simply, "We 've had a heap of trouble since you 've been away." I had feared for Jim. With a cultured parentage and a social caste to uphold him, he might have made a venturesome merchant or a West Point cadet. But here he was, angry with life and reckless; and when Farmer Durham charged him with stealing wheat, the old man had to ride fast to escape the stones which the furious fool hurled after him. They told Jim to run away; but he would not run, and the constable came that afternoon. It grieved Josie, and great awkward John walked nine miles every day to see his little brother through the bars of Lebanon jail. At last the two came back together in the dark night. The mother cooked supper, and Josie emptied her purse, and the boys stole away. Josie grew thin and silent, yet worked the more. The hill became steep for the quiet old father, and with the boys away there was little to do in the valley. Josie helped them to sell the old farm, and they moved nearer town. Brother Dennis, the carpenter, built a new house with six rooms; Josie toiled a year in Nashville, and brought back ninety dollars to furnish the house and change it to a home.

When the spring came, and the birds twittered, and the stream ran proud and full, little sister Lizzie, bold and thoughtless, flushed with the passion of youth, bestowed herself on the tempter, and brought home a nameless child. Josie shivered and worked on, with the vision of schooldays all fled, with a face wan and tired,—worked until, on a summer's day, some one married another; then Josie crept to her mother like a hurt child, and slept—and sleeps.

I paused to scent the breeze as I entered the valley. The Lawrences have gone,—father and son forever,—and the other son lazily digs in the earth to live. A new young widow rents out their cabin to fat Reuben. Reuben is a Baptist preacher now, but I fear as lazy as ever, though his cabin has three rooms; and little Ella has grown into a bouncing woman, and is ploughing corn on the hot hillside. There are babies a-plenty, and one half-witted girl. Across the valley is a house I did not know before, and there I found, rocking one baby and expecting another, one of my schoolgirls, a daughter of Uncle Bird Dowell. She looked somewhat worried with her new duties, but soon bristled into pride over her neat cabin and the tale of her thrifty husband, the horse and cow, and the farm they were planning to buy.

My log schoolhouse was gone. In its place stood Progress; and Progress, I understand, is necessarily ugly. The crazy foundation stones still marked the former site of my poor little cabin, and not far away, on six weary boulders, perched a jaunty board house, perhaps twenty by thirty feet, with three windows and a door that locked. Some of the window-glass was broken, and part of an old iron stove lay mournfully under the house. I peeped through the window half reverently, and found things that were more familiar. The blackboard had grown by about two feet, and the seats were still without backs. The county owns the lot now, I hear, and every year there is a session of school. As I sat by the spring and looked on the Old and the New I felt glad, very glad, and yet—

After two long drinks I started on. There was the great double log-house on the corner. I remembered the broken, blighted family that used to live there. The strong, hard face of the mother, with its wilderness of hair, rose before me. She had driven her husband away, and while I taught school a strange man lived there, big and jovial, and people talked. I felt sure that Ben and 'Tildy would come to naught from such a home. But this is an odd world; for Ben is a busy farmer in Smith County, "doing well, too," they say, and he had cared for little 'Tildy until last spring, when a lover married her. A hard life the lad had led, toiling for meat, and laughed at because he was homely and crooked. There was Sam Carlon, an impudent old skinflint, who had definite notions about "niggers," and hired Ben a summer and would not pay him. Then the hungry boy gathered his sacks together, and in broad daylight went into Carlon's corn; and when the hard-fisted farmer set upon him, the angry boy flew at him like a beast. Doc Burke saved a murder and a lynching that day.

The story reminded me again of the Burkes, and an impatience seized me to know who won in the battle, Doc or the seventy-five acres. For it is a hard thing to make a farm out of nothing, even in fifteen years. So I hurried on, thinking of the Burkes. They used to have a certain magnificent barbarism about them that I liked. They were never vulgar, never immoral, but rather rough and primitive, with an unconventionality that spent itself in loud guffaws, slaps on the back, and naps in the corner. I hurried by the cottage of the misborn Neill boys. It was empty, and they were grown into fat, lazy farm-hands. I saw the home of the Hickmans, but Albert, with his stooping shoulders, had passed from the world. Then I came to the Burkes' gate and peered through; the inclosure looked rough and untrimmed, and yet there were the same fences around the old farm save to the left, where lay twenty-five other acres. And lo! the cabin in the hollow had climbed the hill and swollen to a half-finished six-room cottage.

The Burkes held a hundred acres, but they were still in debt. Indeed, the gaunt father who toiled night and day would scarcely be happy out of debt, being so used to it. Some day he must stop, for his massive frame is showing decline. The mother wore shoes, but the lion-like physique of other days was broken. The children had grown up. Rob, the image of his father, was loud and rough with laughter. Birdie, my school baby of six, had grown to a picture of maiden beauty, tall and tawny. "Edgar is gone," said the mother, with head half bowed,—"gone to work in Nashville; he and his father couldn't agree."

Little Doc, the boy born since the time of my school, took me horseback down the creek next morning toward Farmer Dowell's. The road and the stream were battling for mastery, and the stream had the better of it. We splashed and waded, and the merry boy, perched behind me, chattered and laughed. He showed me where Simon Thompson had bought a bit of ground and a home; but his daughter Lana, a plump, brown, slow girl, was not there. She had married a man and a farm twenty miles away. We wound on down the stream till we came to a gate that I did not recognize, but the boy insisted that it was "Uncle Bird's." The farm was fat with the growing crop. In that little valley was a strange stillness as I rode up; for death and marriage had stolen youth and left age and childhood there. We sat and talked that night after the chores were done. Uncle Bird was grayer, and his eyes did not see so well, but he was still jovial. We talked of the acres bought,—one hundred and twenty-five,—of the new guest-chamber added, of Martha's marrying. Then we talked of death: Fanny and Fred were gone; a shadow hung over the other daughter, and when it lifted she was to go to Nashville to school. At last we spoke of the neighbors, and as night fell, Uncle Bird told me how, on a night like that, 'Thenie came wandering back to her home over yonder, to escape the blows of her husband. And next morning she died in the home that her little bow-legged brother, working and saving, had bought for their widowed mother.

My journey was done, and behind me lay hill and dale, and Life and Death. How shall man measure Progress there where the dark-faced Josie lies? How many heartfuls of sorrow shall balance a bushel of wheat? How hard a thing is life to the lowly, and yet how human and real! And all this life and love and strife and failure,—is it the twilight of nightfall or the flush of some faint-dawning day?

Thus sadly musing, I rode to Nashville in the Jim Crow car.

V

Of the Wings of Atalanta

O black boy of Atlanta!
  But half was spoken;
The slave's chains and the master's
  Alike are broken;
The one curse of the races
  Held both in tether;
They are rising—all are rising—
  The black and white together.

WHITTIER.

SOUTH of the North, yet north of the South, lies the City of a Hundred Hills, peering out from the shadows of the past into the promise of the future. I have seen her in the morning, when the first flush of day had half-roused her; she lay gray and still on the crimson soil of Georgia; then the blue smoke began to curl from her chimneys, the tinkle of bell and scream of whistle broke the silence, the rattle and roar of busy life slowly gathered and swelled, until the seething whirl of the city seemed a strange thing in a sleepy land.

Once, they say, even Atlanta slept dull and drowsy at the foot-hills of the Alleghanies, until the iron baptism of war awakened her with its sullen waters, aroused and maddened her, and left her listening to the sea. And the sea cried to the hills and the hills answered the sea, till the city rose like a widow and cast away her weeds, and toiled for her daily bread; toiled steadily, toiled cunningly,—perhaps with some bitterness, with a touch of *réclame*,—and yet with real earnestness, and real sweat.

It is a hard thing to live haunted by the ghost of an untrue dream; to see the wide vision of empire fade into real ashes and dirt; to feel the pang of the conquered, and yet know that with all the Bad that fell on one black day, something was vanquished that deserved to live, something killed that in justice had not dared to die; to know that with the Right that triumphed, triumphed something of Wrong, something sordid and mean, something less than the broadest and best. All this is bitter hard; and many a man and city and people have found in it excuse for sulking, and brooding, and listless waiting.

Such are not men of the sturdier make; they of Atlanta turned resolutely toward the future; and that future held aloft vistas of purple and gold:—Atlanta, Queen of the cotton kingdom; Atlanta, Gateway to the Land of the Sun; Atlanta, the new Lachesis, spinner of web and woof for the world. So the city crowned her hundred hills with factories, and stored her shops with cunning handiwork, and stretched long iron ways to greet the busy Mercury in his coming. And the Nation talked of her striving.

Perhaps Atlanta was not christened for the winged maiden of dull Bœotia; you know the tale,—how swarthy Atalanta, tall and wild, would marry only him who out-raced her; and how the wily Hippomenes laid three apples of gold in the way. She fled like a shadow, paused, startled over the first apple, but even as he stretched his hand, fled again; hovered over the second, then, slipping from his hot grasp, flew over river, vale, and hill; but as she lingered over the third, his arms fell round her, and looking on each other, the blazing passion of their love profaned the sanctuary of Love, and they were cursed. If Atlanta be not named for Atalanta, she ought to have been.

Atalanta is not the first or the last maiden whom greed of gold has led to defile the temple of Love; and not maids alone, but men in the race of life, sink from the high and generous ideals of youth to the gambler's code of the Bourse; and in all our Nation's striving is not the Gospel of Work befouled by the Gospel of Pay? So common is this that one-half think it normal; so unquestioned, that we almost fear to question if the end of racing is not gold, if the aim of man is not rightly to be rich. And if this is the fault of America, how dire a danger lies before a new land and a new city, lest Atlanta, stooping for mere gold, shall find that gold accursed!

It was no maiden's idle whim that started this hard racing; a fearful wilderness lay about the feet of that city after the

War,—feudalism, poverty, the rise of the Third Estate, serfdom, the re-birth of Law and Order, and above and between all, the Veil of Race. How heavy a journey for weary feet! what wings must Atalanta have to flit over all this hollow and hill, through sour wood and sullen water, and by the red waste of sun-baked clay! How fleet must Atalanta be if she will not be tempted by gold to profane the Sanctuary!

The Sanctuary of our fathers has, to be sure, few Gods,—some sneer, "all too few." There is the thrifty Mercury of New England, Pluto of the North, and Ceres of the West; and there, too, is the half-forgotten Apollo of the South, under whose ægis the maiden ran,—and as she ran she forgot him, even as there in Bœotia Venus was forgot. She forgot the old ideal of the Southern gentleman,—that new-world heir of the grace and courtliness of patrician, knight, and noble; forgot his honor with his foibles, his kindliness with his carelessness, and stooped to apples of gold,—to men busier and sharper, thriftier and more unscrupulous. Golden apples are beautiful—I remember the lawless days of boyhood, when orchards in crimson and gold tempted me over fence and field—and, too, the merchant who has dethroned the planter is no despicable *parvenu*. Work and wealth are the mighty levers to lift this old new land; thrift and toil and saving are the highways to new hopes and new possibilities; and yet the warning is needed lest the wily Hippomenes tempt Atalanta to thinking that golden apples are the goal of racing, and not mere incidents by the way.

Atlanta must not lead the South to dream of material prosperity as the touchstone of all success; already the fatal might of this idea is beginning to spread; it is replacing the finer type of Southerner with vulgar money-getters; it is burying the sweeter beauties of Southern life beneath pretence and ostentation. For every social ill the panacea of Wealth has been urged,—wealth to overthrow the remains of the slave feudalism; wealth to raise the "cracker" Third Estate; wealth to employ the black serfs, and the prospect of wealth to keep them working; wealth as the end and aim of politics, and as the legal tender for law and order; and, finally, instead of Truth, Beauty, and Goodness, wealth as the ideal of the Public School.

Not only is this true in the world which Atlanta typifies, but it is threatening to be true of a world beneath and beyond that world,—the Black World beyond the Veil. To-day it makes little difference to Atlanta, to the South, what the Negro thinks or dreams or wills. In the soul-life of the land he is to-day, and naturally will long remain, unthought of, half forgotten; and yet when he does come to think and will and do for himself,—and let no man dream that day will never come,—then the part he plays will not be one of sudden learning, but words and thoughts he has been taught to lisp in his race-childhood. To-day the ferment of his striving toward self-realization is to the strife of the white world like a wheel within a wheel: beyond the Veil are smaller but like problems of ideals, of leaders and the led, of serfdom, of poverty, of order and subordination, and, through all, the Veil of Race. Few know of these problems, few who know notice them; and yet there they are, awaiting student, artist, and seer,—a field for somebody sometime to discover. Hither has the temptation of Hippomenes penetrated; already in this smaller world, which now indirectly and anon directly must influence the larger for good or ill, the habit is forming of interpreting the world in dollars. The old leaders of Negro opinion, in the little groups where there is a Negro social consciousness, are being replaced by new; neither the black preacher nor the black teacher leads as he did two decades ago. Into their places are pushing the farmers and gardeners, the well-paid porters and artisans, the businessmen,—all those with property and money. And with all this change, so curiously parallel to that of the Other-world, goes too the same inevitable change in ideals. The South laments to-day the slow, steady disappearance of a certain type of Negro,—the faithful, courteous slave of other days, with his incorruptible honesty and dignified humility. He is passing away just as surely as the old type of Southern gentleman is passing, and from not dissimilar causes,—the sudden transformation of a fair far-off ideal of Freedom into the hard reality of bread-winning and the consequent deification of Bread.

In the Black World, the Preacher and Teacher embodied once the ideals of this people,—the strife for another and a juster world, the vague dream of righteousness, the mystery of knowing; but to-day the danger is that these ideals, with their simple beauty and weird inspiration, will suddenly sink to a question of cash and a lust for gold. Here stands this black young Atalanta, girding herself for the race that must be run; and if her eyes be still toward the hills and sky as in the days of old, then we may look for noble running; but what if some ruthless or wily or even thoughtless Hippomenes lay golden apples before her? What if the Negro people be wooed from a strife for righteousness, from a love of knowing, to regard dollars as the be-all and end-all of life? What if to the Mammonism of America be added the rising Mammonism of the re-born South, and the Mammonism of this South be reinforced by the budding Mammonism of its half-awakened black millions? Whither, then, is the new-world quest of Goodness and Beauty and Truth gone glimmering? Must this, and that fair flower of Freedom which, despite the jeers of latter-day striplings, sprung from our fathers' blood, must that too degenerate into a dusty quest of gold,—into lawless lust with Hippomenes?

The hundred hills of Atlanta are not all crowned with factories. On one, toward the west, the setting sun throws three buildings in bold relief against the sky. The beauty of the group lies in its simple unity:—a broad lawn of green rising from the red street with mingled roses and peaches; north and south, two plain and stately halls; and in the midst, half hidden in ivy, a larger building, boldly graceful, sparingly decorated, and with one low spire. It is a restful group,—one never looks for more; it is all here, all intelligible. There I live, and there I hear from day to day the low hum of restful life. In winter's twilight, when the red sun glows, I can see the dark figures pass between the halls to the music of the night-bell. In the morning, when the sun is golden, the clang of the day-bell brings the hurry and laughter of three hundred young hearts from hall and street, and from the busy city below,—children all dark and heavy-haired,—to join their clear young voices in the music of the morning sacrifice. In a half-dozen class-rooms they gather then,—here to follow the love-song of Dido, here to listen to the tale of Troy divine; there to wander among the stars, there to wander among men and nations,—and elsewhere other well-worn ways of knowing this queer world. Nothing new, no time-saving devices,—simply old time-glorified methods of delving for Truth, and searching out the hidden beauties of life, and learning the good of living. The riddle of existence is the college curriculum that was laid before the Pharaohs, that was taught in the groves by Plato, that formed the *trivium* and *quadrivium*, and is to-day laid before the freedmen's sons by Atlanta University. And this course of study will not change; its methods will grow more deft and effectual, its content richer by toil of scholar and sight of seer; but the true college will ever have one goal,—not to earn meat, but to know the end and aim of that life which meat nourishes.

The vision of life that rises before these dark eyes has in it nothing mean or selfish. Not at Oxford or at Leipsic, not at Yale or Columbia, is there an air of higher resolve or more unfettered striving; the determination to realize for men, both black and white, the broadest possibilities of life, to seek the better and the best, to spread with their own hands the Gospel of Sacrifice,—all this is the burden of their talk and dream. Here, amid a wide desert of caste and proscription, amid the heart-hurting slights and jars and vagaries of a deep race-dislike, lies this green oasis, where hot anger cools, and the bitterness of disappointment is sweetened by the springs and breezes of Parnassus; and here men may lie and listen, and learn of a future fuller than the past, and hear the voice of Time:

"Entbehren sollst du, sollst entbehren."

They made their mistakes, those who planted Fisk and Howard and Atlanta before the smoke of battle had lifted; they made their mistakes, but those mistakes were not the things at which we lately laughed somewhat uproariously. They were right when they sought to found a new educational system upon the University: where, forsooth, shall we ground knowledge save on the broadest and deepest knowledge? The roots of the tree, rather than the leaves, are the sources of its life; and from the dawn of history, from Academus to Cambridge, the culture of the University has been the broad foundation-stone on which is built the kindergarten's A B C.

But these builders did make a mistake in minimizing the gravity of the problem before them; in thinking it a matter of years and decades; in therefore building quickly and laying their foundation carelessly, and lowering the standard of knowing, until they had scattered haphazard through the South some dozen poorly equipped high schools and miscalled them universities. They forgot, too, just as their successors are forgetting, the rule of inequality:—that of the million black youth, some were fitted to know and some to dig; that some had the talent and capacity of university men, and some the talent and capacity of blacksmiths; and that true training meant neither that all should be college men nor all artisans, but that the one should be made a missionary of culture to an untaught people, and the other a free workman among serfs. And to seek to make the blacksmith a scholar is almost as silly as the more modern scheme of making the scholar a blacksmith; almost, but not quite.

The function of the university is not simply to teach bread-winning, or to furnish teachers for the public schools, or to be a centre of polite society; it is, above all, to be the organ of that fine adjustment between real life and the growing knowledge of life, an adjustment which forms the secret of civilization. Such an institution the South of to-day sorely needs. She has religion, earnest, bigoted:—religion that on both sides the Veil often omits the sixth, seventh, and eighth commandments, but substitutes a dozen supplementary ones. She has, as Atlanta shows, growing thrift and love of toil; but she lacks that broad knowledge of what the world knows and knew of human living and doing, which she may apply to the thousand problems of real life to-day confronting her. The need of the South is knowledge and culture,—not in dainty limited quantity, as before the war, but in broad busy abundance in the world of work; and until she has this, not all the Apples of Hesperides, be they golden and bejewelled, can save her from the curse of the Bœotian lovers.

The Wings of Atalanta are the coming universities of the South. They alone can bear the maiden past the temptation of golden fruit. They will not guide her flying feet away from the cotton and gold; for—ah, thoughtful Hippomenes!—do not the apples lie in the very Way of Life? But they will guide her over and beyond them, and leave her kneeling in the Sanctuary of Truth and Freedom and broad Humanity, virgin and undefiled. Sadly did the Old South err in human education, despising the education of the masses, and niggardly in the support of colleges. Her ancient university foundations dwindled and withered under the foul breath of slavery; and even since the war they have fought a failing fight for life in the tainted air of social unrest and commercial selfishness, stunted by the death of criticism, and starving for lack of broadly cultured men. And if this is the white South's need and danger, how much heavier the danger and need of the freedmen's sons! how pressing here the need of broad ideals and true culture, the conservation of soul from sordid aims and petty passions! Let us build the Southern university—William and Mary, Trinity, Georgia, Texas, Tulane, Vanderbilt, and the others—fit to live; let us build, too, the Negro universities:—Fisk, whose foundation was ever broad; Howard, at the heart of the Nation; Atlanta at Atlanta, whose ideal of scholarship has been held above the temptation of numbers. Why not here, and perhaps elsewhere, plant deeply and for all time centres of learning and living, colleges that yearly would send into the life of the South a few white men and a few black men of broad culture, catholic tolerance, and trained ability, joining their hands to other hands, and giving to this squabble of the Races a decent and dignified peace?

Patience, Humility, Manners, and Taste, common schools and kindergartens, industrial and technical schools, literature and tolerance,—all these spring from knowledge and culture, the children of the university. So must men and nations build, not otherwise, not upside down.

Teach workers to work,—a wise saying; wise when applied to German boys and American girls; wiser when said of Negro boys, for they have less knowledge of working and none to teach them. Teach thinkers to think,—a needed knowledge in a day of loose and careless logic; and they whose lot is gravest must have the carefulest training to think aright. If these things are so, how foolish to ask what is the best education for one or seven or sixty million souls! shall we teach them trades, or train them in liberal arts? Neither and both: teach the workers to work and the thinkers to think; make carpenters of carpenters, and philosophers of philosophers, and fops of fools. Nor can we pause here. We are training not isolated men but a living group of men,—nay, a group within a group. And the final product of our training must be neither a psychologist nor a brickmason, but a man. And to make men, we must have ideals, broad, pure, and inspiring ends of living,—not sordid money-getting, not apples of gold. The worker must work for the glory of his handiwork, not simply for pay; the thinker must think for truth, not for fame. And all this is gained only by human strife and longing; by ceaseless training and education; by founding Right on righteousness and Truth on the unhampered search for Truth; by founding the common school on the university, and the industrial school on the common school; and weaving thus a system, not a distortion, and bringing a birth, not an abortion.

When night falls on the City of a Hundred Hills, a wind gathers itself from the seas and comes murmuring westward. And at its bidding, the smoke of the drowsy factories sweeps down upon the mighty city and covers it like a pall, while yonder at the University the stars twinkle above Stone Hall. And they say that yon gray mist is the tunic of Atalanta pausing over her golden apples. Fly, my maiden, fly, for yonder comes Hippomenes!

VI

Of the Training of Black Men

Why, if the Soul can fling the Dust aside,
And naked on the Air of Heaven ride,
  Were 't not a Shame—were 't not a Shame for him
In this clay carcase crippled to abide?

OMAR KHAYYÁM (FITZGERALD).

FROM the shimmering swirl of waters where many, many thoughts ago the slave-ship first saw the square tower of Jamestown, have flowed down to our day three streams of thinking: one swollen from the larger world here and overseas, saying, the multiplying of human wants in culture-lands calls for the world-wide coöperation of men in satisfying them. Hence arises a new human unity, pulling the ends of earth nearer, and all men, black, yellow, and white. The larger humanity strives to feel in this contact of living Nations and sleeping hordes a thrill of new life in the world, crying, "If the contact of Life and Sleep be Death, shame on such Life." To be sure, behind this thought lurks the afterthought of force and dominion,—the making of brown men to delve when the temptation of beads and red calico cloys.

The second thought streaming from the death-ship and the curving river is the thought of the older South,—the sincere and passionate belief that somewhere between men and cattle, God created a *tertium quid*, and called it a Negro,—a clownish, simple creature, at times even lovable within its limitations, but straitly foreordained to walk within the Veil. To be sure, behind the thought lurks the afterthought,—some of them with favoring chance might become men, but in sheer self-defence we dare not let them, and we build about them walls so high, and hang between them and the light a veil so thick, that they shall not even think of breaking through.

And last of all there trickles down that third and darker thought,—the thought of the things themselves, the confused, half-conscious mutter of men who are black and whitened, crying "Liberty, Freedom, Opportunity—vouchsafe to us, O boastful World, the chance of living men!" To be sure, behind the thought lurks the afterthought,—suppose, after all, the World is right and we are less than men? Suppose this mad impulse within is all wrong, some mock mirage from the untrue?

So here we stand among thoughts of human unity, even through conquest and slavery; the inferiority of black men, even if forced by fraud; a shriek in the night for the freedom of men who themselves are not yet sure of their right to demand it. This is the tangle of thought and afterthought wherein we are called to solve the problem of training men for life.

Behind all its curiousness, so attractive alike to sage and *dilettante*, lie its dim dangers, throwing across us shadows at once grotesque and awful. Plain it is to us that what the world seeks through desert and wild we have within our threshold,—a stalwart laboring force, suited to the semi-tropics; if, deaf to the voice of the Zeitgeist, we refuse to use and develop these men, we risk poverty and loss. If, on the other hand, seized by the brutal afterthought, we debauch the race thus caught in our talons, selfishly sucking their blood and brains in the future as in the past, what shall save us from national decadence? Only that saner selfishness, which Education teaches men, can find the rights of all in the whirl of work.

Again, we may decry the color-prejudice of the South, yet it remains a heavy fact. Such curious kinks of the human mind exist and must be reckoned with soberly. They cannot be laughed away, nor always successfully stormed at, nor easily abolished by act of legislature. And yet they must not be encouraged by being let alone. They must be recognized as facts, but unpleasant facts; things that stand in the way of civilization and religion and common decency. They can be met in but one way,—by the breadth and broadening of human reason, by catholicity of taste and culture. And so, too, the native ambition and aspiration of men, even though they be black, backward, and ungraceful, must not lightly be dealt with. To stimulate wildly weak and untrained minds is to play with mighty fires; to flout their striving idly is to welcome a harvest of brutish crime and shameless lethargy in our very laps. The guiding of thought and the deft coördination of deed is at once the path of honor and humanity.

And so, in this great question of reconciling three vast and partially contradictory streams of thought, the one panacea of Education leaps to the lips of all:—such human training as will best use the labor of all men without enslaving or brutalizing; such training as will give us poise to encourage the prejudices that bulwark society, and to stamp out those that in sheer barbarity deafen us to the wail of prisoned souls within the Veil, and the mounting fury of shackled men.

But when we have vaguely said that Education will set this tangle straight, what have we uttered but a truism? Training for life teaches living; but what training for the profitable living together of black men and white? A hundred and fifty years ago our task would have seemed easier. Then Dr. Johnson blandly assured us that education was needful solely for the embellishments of life, and was useless for ordinary vermin. To-day we have climbed to heights where we would open at least the outer courts of knowledge to all, display its treasures to many, and select the few to whom its mystery of Truth is revealed, not wholly by birth or the accidents of the stock market, but at least in part according to deftness and aim, talent and character. This programme, however, we are sorely puzzled in carrying out through that part of the land where the blight of slavery fell hardest, and where we are dealing with two backward peoples. To make here in human education that ever necessary combination of the permanent and the contingent—of the ideal and the practical in workable equilibrium—has been there, as it ever must be in every age and place, a matter of infinite experiment and frequent mistakes.

In rough approximation we may point out four varying decades of work in Southern education since the Civil War. From the close of the war until 1876, was the period of uncertain groping and temporary relief. There were army schools, mission schools, and schools of the Freedman's Bureau in chaotic disarrangement seeking system and coöperation. Then followed ten years of constructive definite effort toward the building of complete school systems in the South. Normal schools and colleges were founded for the freedmen, and teachers trained there to man the public schools. There was the inevitable tendency of war to underestimate the prejudices of the master and the ignorance of the slave, and all seemed clear sailing out of the wreckage of the storm. Meantime, starting in this decade yet especially developing from 1885 to 1895, began the industrial revolution of the South. The land saw glimpses of a new destiny and the stirring of new ideals. The educational system striving to complete itself saw new obstacles and a field of work ever broader and deeper. The Negro colleges, hurriedly founded, were inadequately equipped, illogically distributed, and of varying efficiency and grade; the normal and high schools were doing little more than common-school work, and the common schools were training but a third of the children who ought to be in them, and training these too often poorly. At the same time the white South, by reason of its sudden conversion from the slavery ideal, by so much the more became set and strengthened in its racial prejudice, and crystallized it into harsh law and harsher custom; while the marvellous pushing forward of the poor white daily threatened to take even bread and butter from the mouths of the heavily handicapped sons of the freedmen. In the midst, then, of the larger problem of Negro education sprang up the more practical question of work, the inevitable economic quandary that faces a people in the transition from slavery to freedom, and especially those who make that change amid hate and prejudice, lawlessness and ruthless competition.

The industrial school springing to notice in this decade, but coming to full recognition in the decade beginning with 1895, was the proffered answer to this combined educational and economic crisis, and an answer of singular wisdom and timeliness. From the very first in nearly all the schools some attention had been given to training in handiwork, but now was this training first raised to a dignity that brought it in direct touch with the South's magnificent industrial development, and given an emphasis which reminded black folk that before the Temple of Knowledge swing the Gates of Toil.

Yet after all they are but gates, and when turning our eyes from the temporary and the contingent in the Negro problem to the broader question of the permanent uplifting and civilization of black men in America, we have a right to inquire, as this enthusiasm for material advancement mounts to its height, if after all the industrial school is the final and sufficient answer in the training of the Negro race; and to ask gently, but in all sincerity, the ever-recurring query of the ages, Is not life more than meat, and the body more than raiment? And men ask this to-day all the more eagerly because of sinister signs in recent educational movements. The tendency is here, born of slavery and quickened to renewed life by the crazy imperialism of the day, to regard human beings as among the material resources of a land to be trained with an eye single to future dividends. Race-prejudices, which keep brown and black men in their "places," we are coming to regard as useful allies with such a theory, no matter how much they may dull the ambition and sicken the hearts of struggling human beings. And above all, we daily hear that an education that encourages aspiration, that sets the loftiest of ideals and seeks as an end culture and character rather than breadwinning, is the privilege of white men and the danger and delusion of black.

Especially has criticism been directed against the former educational efforts to aid the Negro. In the four periods I have mentioned, we find first, boundless, planless enthusiasm and sacrifice; then the preparation of teachers for a vast public-school system; then the launching and expansion of that school system amid increasing difficulties; and finally the training of workmen for the new and growing industries. This development has been sharply ridiculed as a logical anomaly and flat reversal of nature. Soothly we have been told that first industrial and manual training should have taught the Negro to work, then simple schools should have taught him to read and write, and finally, after years, high and normal schools could have completed the system, as intelligence and wealth demanded.

That a system logically so complete was historically impossible, it needs but a little thought to prove. Progress in human affairs is more often a pull than a push, surging forward of the exceptional man, and the lifting of his duller brethren slowly and painfully to his vantage-ground. Thus it was no accident that gave birth to universities centuries before the common schools, that made fair Harvard the first flower of our wilderness. So in the South: the mass of the freedmen at the end of the war lacked the intelligence so necessary to modern workingmen. They must first have the common school to teach them to read, write, and cipher; and they must have higher schools to teach teachers for the common schools. The white teachers who flocked South went to establish such a common-school system. Few held the idea of founding colleges; most of them at first would have laughed at the idea. But they faced, as all men since them have faced, that central paradox of the South,—the social separation of the races. At that time it was the sudden volcanic rupture of nearly all relations between black and white, in work and government and family life. Since then a new adjustment of relations in economic and political affairs has grown up,—an adjustment subtle and difficult to grasp, yet singularly ingenious, which leaves still that frightful chasm at the color-line across which men pass at their peril. Thus, then and now, there stand in the South two separate worlds; and separate not simply in the higher realms of social intercourse, but also in church and school, on railway and street-car, in hotels and theatres, in streets and city sections, in books and newspapers, in asylums and jails, in hospitals and graveyards. There is still enough of contact for large economic and group coöperation, but the separation is so thorough and deep that it absolutely precludes for the present between the races anything like that sympathetic and effective group-training and leadership of the one by the other, such as the American Negro and all backward peoples must have for effectual progress.

This the missionaries of '68 soon saw; and if effective industrial and trade schools were impracticable before the establishment of a common-school system, just as certainly no adequate common schools could be founded until there were teachers to teach them. Southern whites would not teach them; Northern whites in sufficient numbers could not be had. If the Negro was to learn, he must teach himself, and the most effective help that could be given him was the establishment of schools to train Negro teachers. This conclusion was slowly but surely reached by every student of the situation until simultaneously, in widely separated regions, without consultation or systematic plan, there arose a series of institutions designed to furnish teachers for the untaught. Above the sneers of critics at the obvious defects of this procedure must ever stand its one crushing rejoinder: in a single generation they put thirty thousand black teachers in the South; they wiped out the illiteracy of the majority of the black people of the land, and they made Tuskegee possible.

Such higher training-schools tended naturally to deepen broader development: at first they were common and grammar schools, then some became high schools. And finally, by 1900, some thirty-four had one year or more of studies of college grade. This development was reached with different degrees of speed in different institutions: Hampton is still a high school, while Fisk University started her college in 1871, and Spelman Seminary about 1896. In all cases the aim was identical,—to maintain the standards of the lower training by giving teachers and leaders the best practicable training; and above all, to furnish the black world with adequate standards of human culture and lofty ideals of life. It was not enough that the teachers of teachers should be trained in technical normal methods; they must also, so far as possible, be broad-minded, cultured men and women, to scatter civilization among a people whose ignorance was not simply of letters, but of life itself.

It can thus be seen that the work of education in the South began with higher institutions of training, which threw off as their foliage common schools, and later industrial schools, and at the same time strove to shoot their roots ever deeper toward college and university training. That this was an inevitable and necessary development, sooner or later, goes without saying; but there has been, and still is, a question in many minds if the natural growth was not forced, and if the higher training was not either overdone or done with cheap and unsound methods. Among white Southerners this feeling is widespread and positive. A prominent Southern journal voiced this in a recent editorial.

"The experiment that has been made to give the colored students classical training has not been satisfactory. Even though many were able to pursue the course, most of them did so in a parrot-like way, learning what was taught, but not seeming to appropriate the truth and import of their instruction, and graduating without sensible aim or valuable occupation for their future. The whole scheme has proved a waste of time, efforts, and the money of the state."

While most fair-minded men would recognize this as extreme and overdrawn, still without doubt many are asking, Are there a sufficient number of Negroes ready for college training to warrant the undertaking? Are not too many students prematurely forced into this work? Does it not have the effect of dissatisfying the young Negro with his environment? And do these graduates succeed in real life? Such natural questions cannot be evaded, nor on the other hand must a Nation naturally skeptical as to Negro ability assume an unfavorable answer without careful inquiry and patient openness to conviction. We must not forget that most Americans answer all queries regarding the Negro *a priori*, and that the least that human courtesy can do is to listen to evidence.

The advocates of the higher education of the Negro would be the last to deny the incompleteness and glaring defects of the present system: too many institutions have attempted to do college work, the work in some cases has not been thoroughly done, and quantity rather than quality has sometimes been sought. But all this can be said of higher education throughout the land; it is the almost inevitable incident of educational growth, and leaves the deeper question of the legitimate demand for the higher training of Negroes untouched. And this latter question can be settled in but one way,—by a first-hand study of the facts. If we leave out of view all institutions which have not actually graduated students from a course higher than that of a New England high school, even though they be called colleges; if then we take the thirty-four remaining institutions, we may clear up many misapprehensions by asking searchingly, What kind of institutions are they? what do they teach? and what sort of men do they graduate?

And first we may say that this type of college, including Atlanta, Fisk, and Howard, Wilberforce and Lincoln, Biddle, Shaw, and the rest, is peculiar, almost unique. Through the shining trees that whisper before me as I write, I catch glimpses of a boulder of New England granite, covering a grave, which graduates of Atlanta University have placed there, with this inscription:

"IN GRATEFUL MEMORY OF THEIR
FORMER TEACHER AND FRIEND
AND OF THE UNSELFISH LIFE HE
LIVED, AND THE NOBLE WORK HE
WROUGHT; THAT THEY, THEIR
CHILDREN, AND THEIR CHIL-
DREN'S CHILDREN MIGHT BE
BLESSED."

This was the gift of New England to the freed Negro: not alms, but a friend; not cash, but character. It was not and is not money these seething millions want, but love and sympathy, the pulse of hearts beating with red blood;—a gift which to-day only their own kindred and race can bring to the masses, but which once saintly souls brought to their favored children in the crusade of the sixties, that finest thing in American history, and one of the few things untainted by sordid greed and cheap vainglory. The teachers in these institutions came not to keep the Negroes in their place, but to raise them out of the defilement of the places where slavery had wallowed them. The colleges they founded were social settlements; homes where the best of the sons of the freedmen came in close and sympathetic touch with the best traditions of New England. They lived and ate together, studied and worked, hoped and harkened in the dawning light. In actual formal content their curriculum was doubtless old-fashioned, but in educational power it was supreme, for it was the contact of living souls.

From such schools about two thousand Negroes have gone forth with the bachelor's degree. The number in itself is enough to put at rest the argument that too large a proportion of Negroes are receiving higher training. If the ratio to population of all Negro students throughout the land, in both college and secondary training, be counted, Commissioner Harris assures us "it must be increased to five times its present average" to equal the average of the land.

Fifty years ago the ability of Negro students in any appreciable numbers to master a modern college course would have been difficult to prove. To-day it is proved by the fact that four hundred Negroes, many of whom have been reported as brilliant students, have received the bachelor's degree from Harvard, Yale, Oberlin, and seventy other leading colleges. Here we have, then, nearly twenty-five hundred Negro graduates, of whom the crucial query must be made, How far did their training fit them for life? It is of course extremely difficult to collect satisfactory data on such a point,—difficult to reach the men, to get trustworthy testimony, and to gauge that testimony by any generally acceptable criterion of success. In 1900, the Conference at Atlanta University undertook to study these graduates, and published the results. First they sought to know what these graduates were doing, and succeeded in getting answers from nearly two-thirds of the living. The direct testimony was in almost all cases corroborated by the reports of the colleges where they graduated, so that in the main the reports were worthy of credence. Fifty-three per cent of these graduates were teachers,—presidents of institutions, heads of normal schools, principals of city school-systems, and the like. Seventeen per cent were clergymen; another seventeen per cent were in the professions, chiefly as physicians. Over six per cent were merchants, farmers, and artisans, and four per cent were in the government civil-service. Granting even that a considerable proportion of the third unheard from are unsuccessful, this is a record of usefulness. Personally I know many hundreds of these graduates, and have corresponded with more than a thousand; through others I have followed carefully the life-work of scores; I have taught some of them and some of the pupils whom they have taught, lived in homes which they have builded, and looked at life through their eyes. Comparing them as a class with my fellow students in New England and in Europe, I cannot hesitate in saying that nowhere have I met men and women with a broader spirit of helpfulness, with deeper devotion to their life-work, or with more consecrated determination to succeed in the face of bitter difficulties than among Negro college-bred men. They have, to be sure, their proportion of ne'er-do-weels, their pedants and lettered fools, but they have a surprisingly small proportion of them; they have not that culture of manner which we instinctively associate with university men, forgetting that in reality it is the heritage from cultured homes, and that no people a generation removed from slavery can escape a certain unpleasant rawness and *gaucherie*, despite the best of training.

With all their larger vision and deeper sensibility, these men have usually been conservative, careful leaders. They have seldom been agitators, have withstood the temptation to head the mob, and have worked steadily and faithfully in a thousand communities in the South. As teachers, they have given the South a commendable system of city schools and large numbers of private normal-schools and academies. Colored college-bred men have worked side by side with white college graduates at Hampton; almost from the beginning the backbone of Tuskegee's teaching force has been formed of graduates from Fisk and Atlanta. And to-day the institute is filled with college graduates, from the energetic wife of the principal down to the teacher of agriculture, including nearly half of the executive council and a majority of the heads of departments. In the professions, college men are slowly but surely leavening the Negro church, are healing and preventing the devastations of disease, and beginning to furnish legal protection for the liberty and property of the toiling masses. All this is needful work. Who would do it if Negroes did not? How could Negroes do it if they were not trained carefully for it? If white people need colleges to furnish teachers, ministers, lawyers, and doctors, do black people need nothing of the sort?

If it is true that there are an appreciable number of Negro youth in the land capable by character and talent to receive that higher training, the end of which is culture, and if the two and a half thousand who have had something of this training in the past have in the main proved themselves useful to their race and generation, the question then comes, What place in the future development of the South ought the Negro college and college-bred man to occupy? That the present social separation and acute race-sensitiveness must eventually yield to the influences of culture, as the South grows civilized, is clear. But such transformation calls for singular wisdom and patience. If, while the healing of this vast sore is progressing, the races are to live for many years side by side, united in economic effort, obeying a common government, sensitive to mutual thought and feeling, yet subtly and silently separate in many matters of deeper human intimacy,—if this unusual and dangerous development is to progress amid peace and order, mutual respect and growing intelligence, it will call for social surgery at once the delicatest and nicest in modern history. It will demand broad-minded, upright men, both white and black, and in its final accomplishment American civilization will triumph. So far as white men are concerned, this fact is to-day being recognized in the South, and a happy renaissance of university education seems imminent. But the very voices that cry hail to this good work are, strange to relate, largely silent or antagonistic to the higher education of the Negro.

Strange to relate! for this is certain, no secure civilization can be built in the South with the Negro as an ignorant, turbulent proletariat. Suppose we seek to remedy this by making them laborers and nothing more: they are not fools, they have tasted of the Tree of Life, and they will not cease to think, will not cease attempting to read the riddle of the world. By taking away their best equipped teachers and leaders, by slamming the door of opportunity in the faces of their bolder and brighter minds, will you make them satisfied with their lot? or will you not rather transfer their leading from the hands of men taught to think to the hands of untrained demagogues? We ought not to forget that despite the pressure of poverty, and despite the active discouragement and even ridicule of friends, the demand for higher training steadily increases among Negro youth: there were, in the years from 1875 to 1880, 22 Negro graduates from Northern colleges; from 1885 to 1890 there were 43, and from 1895 to 1900, nearly 100 graduates. From Southern Negro colleges there were, in the same three periods, 143, 413, and over 500 graduates. Here, then, is the plain thirst for training; by refusing to give this Talented Tenth the key to knowledge, can any sane man imagine that they will lightly lay aside their yearning and contentedly become hewers of wood and drawers of water?

No. The dangerously clear logic of the Negro's position will more and more loudly assert itself in that day when increasing wealth and more intricate social organization preclude the South from being, as it so largely is, simply an armed camp for intimidating black folk. Such waste of energy cannot be spared if the South is to catch up with civilization. And as the black third of the land grows in thrift and skill, unless skilfully guided in its larger philosophy, it must more and more brood over the red past and the creeping, crooked present, until it grasps a gospel of revolt and revenge and throws its new-found energies athwart the current of advance. Even to-day the masses of the Negroes see all too clearly the anomalies of their position and the moral crookedness of yours. You may marshal strong indictments against them, but their counter-cries, lacking though they be in formal logic, have burning truths within them which you may not wholly ignore, O Southern Gentlemen! If you deplore their presence here, they ask, Who brought us? When you cry, Deliver us from the vision of intermarriage, they answer that legal marriage is infinitely better than systematic concubinage and prostitution. And if in just fury you accuse their vagabonds of violating women, they also in fury quite as just may reply: The wrong which your gentlemen have done against helpless black women in defiance of your own laws is written on the foreheads of two millions of mulattoes, and written in ineffaceable blood. And finally, when you fasten crime upon this race as its peculiar trait, they answer that slavery was the arch-crime, and lynching and lawlessness its twin abortion; that color and race are not crimes, and yet they it is which in this land receives most unceasing condemnation, North, East, South, and West.

I will not say such arguments are wholly justified,—I will not insist that there is no other side to the shield; but I do say that of the nine millions of Negroes in this nation, there is scarcely one out of the cradle to whom these arguments do not daily present themselves in the guise of terrible truth. I insist that the question of the future is how best to keep these millions from brooding over the wrongs of the past and the difficulties of the present, so that all their energies may be bent toward a cheerful striving and co-operation with their white neighbors toward a larger, juster, and fuller future. That one wise method of doing this lies in the closer knitting of the Negro to the great industrial possibilities of the South is a great truth. And this the common schools and the manual training and trade schools are working to accomplish. But these alone are not enough. The foundations of knowledge in this race, as in others, must be sunk deep in the college and university if we would build a solid, permanent structure. Internal problems of social advance must inevitably come,—problems of work and wages, of families and homes, of morals and the true valuing of the things of life; and all these and other inevitable problems of civilization the Negro must meet and solve largely for himself, by reason of his isolation; and can there be any possible solution other than by study and thought and an appeal to the rich experience of the past? Is there not, with such a group and in such a crisis, infinitely more danger to be apprehended from half-trained minds and shallow thinking than from over-education and over-refinement? Surely we have wit enough to found a Negro college so manned and equipped as to steer successfully between the *dilettante* and the fool. We shall hardly induce black men to believe that if their stomachs be full, it matters little about their brains. They already dimly perceive that the paths of peace winding between honest toil and dignified manhood call for the guidance of skilled thinkers, the loving, reverent comradeship between the black lowly and the black men emancipated by training and culture.

The function of the Negro college, then, is clear: it must maintain the standards of popular education, it must seek the social regeneration of the Negro, and it must help in the solution of problems of race contact and co-operation. And finally, beyond all this, it must develop men. Above our modern socialism, and out of the worship of the mass, must persist and evolve that higher individualism which the centres of culture protect; there must come a loftier respect for the sovereign human soul that seeks to know itself and the world about it; that seeks a freedom for expansion and self-development; that will love and hate and labor in its own way, untrammeled alike by old and new. Such souls aforetime have inspired and guided worlds, and if we be not wholly bewitched by our Rhine-gold, they shall again. Herein the longing of black men must have respect: the rich and bitter depth of their experience, the unknown treasures of their inner life, the strange rendings of nature they have seen, may give the world new points of view and make their loving, living, and doing precious to all human hearts. And to themselves in these the days that try their souls, the chance to soar in the dim blue air above the smoke is to their finer spirits boon and guerdon for what they lose on earth by being black.

I sit with Shakespeare and he winces not. Across the color line I move arm in arm with Balzac and Dumas, where smiling men and welcoming women glide in gilded halls. From out the caves of evening that swing between the strong-limbed earth and the tracery of the stars, I summon Aristotle and Aurelius and what soul I will, and they come all graciously with no scorn nor condescension. So, wed with Truth, I dwell above the Veil. Is this the life you grudge us, O knightly America? Is this the life you long to change into the dull red hideousness of Georgia? Are you so afraid lest peering from this high Pisgah, between Philistine and Amalekite, we sight the Promised Land?

VII
Of the Black Belt

I am black but comely, O ye daughters of Jerusalem,
As the tents of Kedar, as the curtains of Solomon.
Look not upon me, because I am black,
Because the sun hath looked upon me:
My mother's children were angry with me;
They made me the keeper of the vineyards;
But mine own vineyard have I not kept.

THE SONG OF SOLOMON.

OUT of the North the train thundered, and we woke to see the crimson soil of Georgia stretching away bare and monotonous right and left. Here and there lay straggling, unlovely villages, and lean men loafed leisurely at the depots; then again came the stretch of pines and clay. Yet we did not nod, nor weary of the scene; for this is historic ground. Right across our track, three hundred and sixty years ago, wandered the cavalcade of Hernando de Soto, looking for gold and the Great Sea; and he and his foot-sore captives disappeared yonder in the grim forests to the west. Here sits Atlanta, the city of a hundred hills, with something Western, something Southern, and something quite its own, in its busy life. And a little past Atlanta, to the southwest, is the land of the Cherokees, and there, not far from where Sam Hose was crucified, you may stand on a spot which is to-day the centre of the Negro problem,—the centre of those nine million men who are America's dark heritage from slavery and the slave-trade.

Not only is Georgia thus the geographical focus of our Negro population, but in many other respects, both now and yesterday, the Negro problems have seemed to be centered in this State. No other State in the Union can count a million Negroes among its citizens,—a population as large as the slave population of the whole Union in 1800; no other State fought so long and strenuously to gather this host of Africans. Oglethorpe thought slavery against law and gospel; but the circumstances which gave Georgia its first inhabitants were not calculated to furnish citizens over-nice in their ideas about rum and slaves. Despite the prohibitions of the trustees, these Georgians, like some of their descendants, proceeded to take the law into their own hands; and so pliant were the judges, and so flagrant the smuggling, and so earnest were the prayers of Whitefield, that by the middle of the eighteenth century all restrictions were swept away, and the slave-trade went merrily on for fifty years and more.

Down in Darien, where the Delegal riots took place some summers ago, there used to come a strong protest against slavery from the Scotch Highlanders; and the Moravians of Ebenezea did not like the system. But not till the Haytian Terror of Toussaint was the trade in men even checked; while the national statute of 1808 did not suffice to stop it. How the Africans poured in!—fifty thousand between 1790 and 1810, and then, from Virginia and from smugglers, two thousand a year for many years more. So the thirty thousand Negroes of Georgia in 1790 were doubled in a decade,—were over a hundred thousand in 1810, had reached two hundred thousand in 1820, and half a million at the time of the war. Thus like a snake the black population writhed upward.

But we must hasten on our journey. This that we pass as we leave Atlanta is the ancient land of the Cherokees,—that brave Indian nation which strove so long for its fatherland, until Fate and the United States Government drove them beyond the Mississippi. If you wish to ride with me you must come into the "Jim Crow Car." There will be no objection,—already four other white men, and a little white girl with her nurse, are in there. Usually the races are mixed in there; but the white coach is all white. Of course this car is not so good as the other, but it is fairly clean and comfortable. The discomfort lies chiefly in the hearts of those four black men yonder—and in mine.

We rumble south in quite a business-like way. The bare red clay and pines of Northern Georgia begin to disappear, and in their place appears a rich rolling land, luxuriant, and here and there well tilled. This is the land of the Creek Indians; and a hard time the Georgians had to seize it. The towns grow more frequent and more interesting, and brand-new cotton mills rise on every side. Below Macon the world grows darker; for now we approach the Black Belt,—that strange land of shadows, at which even slaves paled in the past, and whence come now only faint and half-intelligible murmurs to the world beyond. The "Jim Crow Car" grows larger and a shade better; three rough field-hands and two or three white loafers accompany us, and the newsboy still spreads his wares at one end. The sun is setting, but we can see the great cotton country as we enter it,—the soil now dark and fertile, now thin and gray, with fruit-trees and dilapidated buildings,—all the way to Albany.

At Albany, in the heart of the Black Belt, we stop. Two hundred miles south of Atlanta, two hundred miles west of the Atlantic, and one hundred miles north of the Great Gulf lies Dougherty County, with ten thousand Negroes and two thousand whites. The Flint River winds down from Andersonville, and, turning suddenly at Albany, the county-seat, hurries on to join the Chattahoochee and the sea. Andrew Jackson knew the Flint well, and marched across it once to avenge the Indian Massacre at Fort Mims. That was in 1814, not long before the battle of New Orleans; and by the Creek treaty that followed this campaign, all Dougherty County, and much other rich land, was ceded to Georgia. Still, settlers fought shy of this land, for the Indians were all about, and they were unpleasant neighbors in those days. The panic of 1837, which Jackson bequeathed to Van Buren, turned the planters from the impoverished lands of Virginia, the Carolinas, and east Georgia, toward the West. The Indians were removed to Indian Territory, and settlers poured into these coveted lands to retrieve their broken fortunes. For a radius of a hundred miles about Albany, stretched a great fertile land, luxuriant with forests of pine, oak, ash, hickory, and poplar; hot with the sun and damp with the rich black swamp-land; and here the corner-stone of the Cotton Kingdom was laid.

Albany is to-day a wide-streeted, placid, Southern town, with a broad sweep of stores and saloons, and flanking rows of homes,—whites usually to the north, and blacks to the south. Six days in the week the town looks decidedly too small for itself, and takes frequent and prolonged naps. But on Saturday suddenly the whole county disgorges itself upon the place, and a perfect flood of black peasantry pours through the streets, fills the stores, blocks the sidewalks, chokes the thoroughfares, and takes full possession of the town. They are black, sturdy, uncouth country folk, good-natured and simple, talkative to a degree, and yet far more silent and brooding than the crowds of the Rhine-pfalz, or Naples, or Cracow. They drink considerable quantities of whiskey, but do not get very drunk; they talk and laugh loudly at times, but seldom quarrel or fight. They walk up and down the streets, meet and gossip with friends, stare at the shop windows, buy coffee, cheap candy, and clothes, and at dusk drive home—happy? well no, not exactly happy, but much happier than as though they had not come.

Thus Albany is a real capital,—a typical Southern county town, the centre of the life of ten thousand souls; their point of contact with the outer world, their centre of news and gossip, their market for buying and selling, borrowing and lending, their fountain of justice and law. Once upon a time we knew country life so well and city life so little, that we illustrated city life as that of a closely crowded country district. Now the world has well-nigh forgotten what the country is, and we must imagine a little city of black people scattered far and wide over three hundred lonesome square miles of land, without train or trolley, in the midst of cotton and corn, and wide patches of sand and gloomy soil.

It gets pretty hot in Southern Georgia in July,—a sort of dull, determined heat that seems quite independent of the sun; so it took us some days to muster courage enough to leave the porch and venture out on the long country roads, that we might see this unknown world. Finally we started. It was about ten in the morning, bright with a faint breeze, and we jogged leisurely southward in the valley of the Flint. We passed the scattered box-like cabins of the brick-yard hands, and the long tenement-row facetiously called "The Ark," and were soon in the open country, and on the confines of the great plantations of other days. There is the "Joe Fields place"; a rough old fellow was he, and had killed many a "nigger" in his day. Twelve miles his plantation used to run,—a regular barony. It is nearly all gone now; only straggling bits belong to the family, and the rest has passed to Jews and Negroes. Even the bits which are left are heavily mortgaged, and, like the rest of the land, tilled by tenants. Here is one of them now,—a tall brown man, a hard worker and a hard drinker, illiterate, but versed in farm-lore, as his nodding crops declare. This distressingly new board house is his, and he has just moved out of yonder moss-grown cabin with its one square room.

From the curtains in Benton's house, down the road, a dark comely face is staring at the strangers; for passing carriages are not every-day occurrences here. Benton is an intelligent yellow man with a good-sized family, and manages a plantation blasted by the war and now the broken staff of the widow. He might be well-to-do, they say; but he carouses too much in Albany. And the half-desolate spirit of neglect born of the very soil seems to have settled on these acres. In times past there were cotton-gins and machinery here; but they have rotted away.

The whole land seems forlorn and forsaken. Here are the remnants of the vast plantations of the Sheldons, the Pellots, and the Rensons; but the souls of them are passed. The houses lie in half ruin, or have wholly disappeared; the fences have flown, and the families are wandering in the world. Strange vicissitudes have met these whilom masters. Yonder stretch the wide acres of Bildad Reasor; he died in war-time, but the upstart overseer hastened to wed the widow. Then he went, and his neighbors too, and now only the black tenant remains; but the shadow-hand of the master's grand-nephew or cousin or creditor stretches out of the gray distance to collect the rack-rent remorselessly, and so the land is uncared-for and poor. Only black tenants can stand such a system, and they only because they must. Ten miles we have ridden to-day and have seen no white face.

A resistless feeling of depression falls slowly upon us, despite the gaudy sunshine and the green cotton-fields. This, then, is the Cotton Kingdom,—the shadow of a marvellous dream. And where is the King? Perhaps this is he,—the sweating ploughman, tilling his eighty acres with two lean mules, and fighting a hard battle with debt. So we sit musing, until, as we turn a corner on the sandy road, there comes a fairer scene suddenly in view,—a neat cottage snugly ensconced by the road, and near it a little store. A tall bronzed man rises from the porch as we hail him, and comes out to our carriage. He is six feet in height, with a sober face that smiles gravely. He walks too straight to be a tenant,—yes, he owns two hundred and forty acres. "The land is run down since the boom-days of eighteen hundred and fifty," he explains, and cotton is low. Three black tenants live on his place, and in his little store he keeps a small stock of tobacco, snuff, soap, and soda, for the neighborhood. Here is his gin-house with new machinery just installed. Three hundred bales of cotton went through it last year. Two children he has sent away to school. Yes, he says sadly, he is getting on, but cotton is down to four cents; I know how Debt sits staring at him.

Wherever the King may be, the parks and palaces of the Cotton Kingdom have not wholly disappeared. We plunge even now into great groves of oak and towering pine, with an undergrowth of myrtle and shrubbery. This was the "home-house" of the Thompsons,—slave-barons who drove their coach and four in the merry past. All is silence now, and ashes, and tangled weeds. The owner put his whole fortune into the rising cotton industry of the fifties, and with the falling prices of the eighties he packed up and stole away. Yonder is another grove, with unkempt lawn, great magnolias, and grass-grown paths. The Big House stands in half-ruin, its great front door staring blankly at the street, and the back part grotesquely restored for its black tenant. A shabby, well-built Negro he is, unlucky and irresolute. He digs hard to pay rent to the white girl who owns the remnant of the place. She married a policeman, and lives in Savannah.

Now and again we come to churches. Here is one now,—Shepherd's, they call it,—a great whitewashed barn of a thing, perched on stilts of stone, and looking for all the world as though it were just resting here a moment and might be expected to waddle off down the road at almost any time. And yet it is the centre of a hundred cabin homes; and sometimes, of a Sunday, five hundred persons from far and near gather here and talk and eat and sing. There is a school-house near,—a very airy, empty shed; but even this is an improvement, for usually the school is held in the church. The churches vary from log-huts to those like Shepherd's, and the schools from nothing to this little house that sits demurely on the county line. It is a tiny plank-house, perhaps ten by twenty, and has within a double row of rough unplaned benches, resting mostly on legs, sometimes on boxes. Opposite the door is a square home-made desk. In one corner are the ruins of a stove, and in the other a dim blackboard. It is the cheerfulest schoolhouse I have seen in Dougherty, save in town. Back of the schoolhouse is a lodge-house two stories high and not quite finished. Societies meet there,—societies "to care for the sick and bury the dead"; and these societies grow and flourish.

We had come to the boundaries of Dougherty, and were about to turn west along the county-line, when all these sights were pointed out to us by a kindly old man, black, white-haired, and seventy. Forty-five years he had lived here, and now supports himself and his old wife by the help of the steer tethered yonder and the charity of his black neighbors. He shows us the farm of the Hills just across the county line in Baker,—a widow and two strapping sons, who raised ten bales (one need not add "cotton" down here) last year. There are fences and pigs and cows, and the soft-voiced, velvet-skinned young Memnon, who sauntered half-bashfully over to greet the strangers, is proud of his home. We turn now to the west along the county line. Great dismantled trunks of pines tower above the green cotton-fields, cracking their naked gnarled fingers toward the border of living forest beyond. There is little beauty in this region, only a sort of crude abandon that suggests power,—a naked grandeur, as it were. The houses are bare and straight; there are no hammocks or easy-chairs, and few flowers. So when, as here at Rawdon's, one sees a vine clinging to a little porch, and home-like windows peeping over the fences, one takes a long breath. I think I never before quite realized the place of the Fence in civilization. This is the Land of the Unfenced, where crouch on either hand scores of ugly one-room cabins, cheerless and dirty. Here lies the Negro problem in its naked dirt and penury. And here are no fences. But now and then the criss-cross rails or straight palings break into view, and then we know a touch of culture is near. Of course Harrison Gohagen,—a quiet yellow man, young, smooth-faced, and diligent,—of course he is lord of some hundred acres, and we expect to see a vision of well-kept rooms and fat beds and laughing children. For has he not fine fences? And those over yonder, why should they build fences on the rack-rented land? It will only increase their rent.

On we wind, through sand and pines and glimpses of old plantations, till there creeps into sight a cluster of buildings,—wood and brick, mills and houses, and scattered cabins. It seemed quite a village. As it came nearer and nearer, however, the aspect changed: the buildings were rotten, the bricks were falling out, the mills were silent, and the store was closed. Only in the cabins appeared now and then a bit of lazy life. I could imagine the place under some weird spell, and was half-minded to search out the princess. An old ragged black man, honest, simple, and improvident, told us the tale. The Wizard of the North—the Capitalist—had rushed down in the seventies to woo this coy dark soil. He bought a square mile or more, and for a time the field-hands sang, the gins groaned, and the mills buzzed. Then came a change. The agent's son embezzled the funds and ran off with them. Then the agent himself disappeared. Finally the new agent stole even the books, and the company in wrath closed its business and its houses, refused to sell, and let houses and furniture and machinery rust and rot. So the Waters-Loring plantation was stilled by the spell of dishonesty, and stands like some gaunt rebuke to a scarred land.

Somehow that plantation ended our day's journey; for I could not shake off the influence of that silent scene. Back toward town we glided, past the straight and thread-like pines, past a dark tree-dotted pond where the air was heavy with a dead sweet perfume. White slender-legged curlews flitted by us, and the garnet blooms of the cotton looked gay against the green and purple stalks. A peasant girl was hoeing in the field, white-turbaned and black-limbed. All this we saw, but the spell still lay upon us.

How curious a land is this,—how full of untold story, of tragedy and laughter, and the rich legacy of human life; shadowed with a tragic past, and big with future promise! This is the Black Belt of Georgia. Dougherty County is the west end of the Black Belt, and men once called it the Egypt of the Confederacy. It is full of historic interest. First there is the Swamp, to the west, where the Chickasawhatchee flows sullenly southward. The shadow of an old plantation lies at its edge, forlorn and dark. Then comes the pool; pendent gray moss and brackish waters appear, and forests filled with wildfowl. In one place the wood is on fire, smouldering in dull red anger; but nobody minds. Then the swamp grows beautiful; a raised road, built by chained Negro convicts, dips down into it, and forms a way walled and almost covered in living green. Spreading trees spring from a prodigal luxuriance of undergrowth; great dark green shadows fade into the black background, until all is one mass of tangled semi-tropical foliage, marvellous in its weird savage splendor. Once we crossed a black silent stream, where the sad trees and writhing creepers, all glinting fiery yellow and green, seemed like some vast cathedral,—some green Milan builded of wildwood. And as I crossed, I seemed to see again that fierce tragedy of seventy years ago. Osceola, the Indian-Negro chieftain, had risen in the swamps of Florida, vowing vengeance. His war-cry reached the red Creeks of Dougherty, and their war-cry rang from the Chattahoochee to the sea. Men and women and children fled and fell before them as they swept into Dougherty. In yonder shadows a dark and hideously painted warrior glided stealthily on,—another and another, until three hundred had crept into the treacherous swamp. Then the false slime closing about them called the white men from the east. Waist-deep, they fought beneath the tall trees, until the war-cry was hushed and the Indians glided back into the west. Small wonder the wood is red.

Then came the black slaves. Day after day the clank of chained feet marching from Virginia and Carolina to Georgia was heard in these rich swamp lands. Day after day the songs of the callous, the wail of the motherless, and the muttered curses of the wretched echoed from the Flint to the Chickasawhatchee, until by 1860 there had risen in West Dougherty perhaps the richest slave kingdom the modern world ever knew. A hundred and fifty barons commanded the labor of nearly six thousand Negroes, held sway over farms with ninety thousand acres of tilled land, valued even in times of cheap soil at three millions of dollars. Twenty thousand bales of ginned cotton went yearly to England, New and Old; and men that came there bankrupt made money and grew rich. In a single decade the cotton output increased four-fold and the value of lands was tripled. It was the heyday of the *nouveau riche*, and a life of careless extravagance reigned among the masters. Four and six bob-tailed thoroughbreds rolled their coaches to town; open hospitality and gay entertainment were the rule. Parks and groves were laid out, rich with flower and vine, and in the midst stood the low wide-halled "big house," with its porch and columns and great fire-places.

And yet with all this there was something sordid, something forced,—a certain feverish unrest and recklessness; for was not all this show and tinsel built upon a groan? "This land was a little Hell," said a ragged, brown, and grave-faced man to me. We were seated near a roadside blacksmith-shop, and behind was the bare ruin of some master's home. "I 've seen niggers drop dead in the furrow, but they were kicked aside, and the plough never stopped. And down in the guard-house, there's where the blood ran."

With such foundations a kingdom must in time sway and fall. The masters moved to Macon and Augusta, and left only the irresponsible overseers on the land. And the result is such ruin as this, the Lloyd "home-place":—great waving oaks, a spread of lawn, myrtles and chestnuts, all ragged and wild; a solitary gate-post standing where once was a castle entrance; an old rusty anvil lying amid rotting bellows and wood in the ruins of a blacksmith shop; a wide rambling old mansion, brown and dingy, filled now with the grandchildren of the slaves who once waited on its tables; while the family of the master has dwindled to two lone women, who live in Macon and feed hungrily off the remnants of an earldom. So we ride on, past phantom gates and falling homes,—past the once flourishing farms of the Smiths, the Gandys, and the Lagores,—and find all dilapidated and half ruined, even there where a solitary white woman, a relic of other days, sits alone in state among miles of Negroes and rides to town in her ancient coach each day.

This was indeed the Egypt of the Confederacy,—the rich granary whence potatoes and corn and cotton poured out to the famished and ragged Confederate troops as they battled for a cause lost long before 1861. Sheltered and secure, it became the place of refuge for families, wealth, and slaves. Yet even then the hard ruthless rape of the land began to tell. The red-clay sub-soil already had begun to peer above the loam. The harder the slaves were driven the more careless and fatal was their farming. Then came the revolution of war and Emancipation, the bewilderment of Reconstruction,—and now, what is the Egypt of the Confederacy, and what meaning has it for the nation's weal or woe?

It is a land of rapid contrasts and of curiously mingled hope and pain. Here sits a pretty blue-eyed quadroon hiding her bare feet; she was married only last week, and yonder in the field is her dark young husband, hoeing to support her, at thirty cents a day without board. Across the way is Gatesby, brown and tall, lord of two thousand acres shrewdly won and held. There is a store conducted by his black son, a blacksmith shop, and a ginnery. Five miles below here is a town owned and controlled by one white New Englander. He owns almost a Rhode Island county, with thousands of acres and hundreds of black laborers. Their cabins look better than most, and the farm, with machinery and fertilizers, is much more business-like than any in the county, although the manager drives hard bargains in wages. When now we turn and look five miles above, there on the edge of town are five houses of prostitutes,—two of blacks and three of whites; and in one of the houses of the whites a worthless black boy was harbored too openly two years ago; so he was hanged for rape. And here, too, is the high whitewashed fence of the "stockade," as the county prison is called; the white folks say it is ever full of black criminals,—the black folks say that only colored boys are sent to jail, and they not because they are guilty, but because the State needs criminals to eke out its income by their forced labor.

The Jew is the heir of the slave-baron in Dougherty; and as we ride westward, by wide stretching cornfields and stubby orchards of peach and pear, we see on all sides within the circle of dark forest a Land of Canaan. Here and there are tales of projects for money-getting, born in the swift days of Reconstruction,—"improvement" companies, wine companies, mills and factories; nearly all failed, and the Jew fell heir. It is a beautiful land, this Dougherty, west of the Flint. The forests are wonderful, the solemn pines have disappeared, and this is the "Oakey Woods," with its wealth of hickories, beeches, oaks, and palmettos. But a pall of debt hangs over the beautiful land; the merchants are in debt to the wholesalers, the planters are in debt to the merchants, the tenants owe the planters, and laborers bow and bend beneath the burden of it all. Here and there a man has raised his head above these murky waters. We passed one fenced stock-farm, with grass and grazing cattle, that looked very homelike after endless corn and cotton. Here and there are black freeholders: there is the gaunt dull-black Jackson, with his hundred acres. "I says, 'Look up! If you don't look up you can't get up,' " remarks Jackson, philosophically. And he's gotten up. Dark Carter's neat barns would do credit to New England. His master helped him to get a start, but when the black man died last fall the master's sons immediately laid claim to the estate. "And them white folks will get it, too," said my yellow gossip.

I turn from these well-tended acres with a comfortable feeling that the Negro is rising. Even then, however, the fields, as we proceed, begin to redden and the trees disappear. Rows of old cabins appear filled with renters and laborers,—cheerless, bare, and dirty, for the most part, although here and there the very age and decay makes the scene picturesque. A young black fellow greets us. He is twenty-two, and just married. Until last year he had good luck renting; then cotton fell, and the sheriff seized and sold all he had. So he moved here, where the rent is higher, the land poorer, and the owner inflexible; he rents a forty-dollar mule for twenty dollars a year. Poor lad!—a slave at twenty-two. This plantation, owned now by a Russian Jew, was a part of the famous Bolton estate. After the war it was for many years worked by gangs of Negro convicts,—and black convicts then were even more plentiful than now; it was a way of making Negroes work, and the question of guilt was a minor one. Hard tales of cruelty and mistreatment of the chained freemen are told, but the county authorities were deaf until the free-labor market was nearly ruined by wholesale migration. Then they took the convicts from the plantations, but not until one of the fairest regions of the "Oakey Woods" had been ruined and ravished into a red waste, out of which only a Yankee or a Jew could squeeze more blood from debt-cursed tenants.

No wonder that Luke Black, slow, dull, and discouraged, shuffles to our carriage and talks hopelessly. Why should he strive? Every year finds him deeper in debt. How strange that Georgia, the world-heralded refuge of poor debtors, should bind her own to sloth and misfortune as ruthlessly as ever England did! The poor land groans with its birth-pains, and brings forth scarcely a hundred pounds of cotton to the acre, where fifty years ago it yielded eight times as much. Of this meagre yield the tenant pays from a quarter to a third in rent, and most of the rest in interest on food and supplies bought on credit. Twenty years yonder sunken-cheeked, old black man has labored under that system, and now, turned day-laborer, is supporting his wife and boarding himself on his wages of a dollar and a half a week, received only part of the year.

The Bolton convict farm formerly included the neighboring plantation. Here it was that the convicts were lodged in the great log prison still standing. A dismal place it still remains, with rows of ugly huts filled with surly ignorant tenants. "What rent do you pay here?" I inquired. "I don't know,—what is it, Sam?" "All we make," answered Sam. It is a depressing place,—bare, unshaded, with no charm of past association, only a memory of forced human toil,—now, then, and before the war. They are not happy, these black men whom we meet throughout this region. There is little of the joyous abandon and playfulness which we are wont to associate with the plantation Negro. At best, the natural good-nature is edged with complaint or has changed into sullenness and gloom. And now and then it blazes forth in veiled but hot anger. I remember one big red-eyed black whom we met by the roadside. Forty-five years he had labored on this farm, beginning with nothing, and still having nothing. To be sure, he had given four children a common-school training, and perhaps if the new fence-law had not allowed unfenced crops in West Dougherty he might have raised a little stock and kept ahead. As it is, he is hopelessly in debt, disappointed, and embittered. He stopped us to inquire after the black boy in Albany, whom it was said a policeman had shot and killed for loud talking on the sidewalk. And then he said slowly: "Let a white man touch me, and he dies; I don't boast this,—I don't say it around loud, or before the children,—but I mean it. I 've seen them whip my father and my old mother in them cotton-rows till the blood ran; by—" and we passed on.

Now Sears, whom we met next lolling under the chubby oak-trees, was of quite different fibre. Happy?—Well, yes; he laughed and flipped pebbles, and thought the world was as it was. He had worked here twelve years and has nothing but a mortgaged mule. Children? Yes, seven; but they hadn't been to school this year,—could n't afford books and clothes, and could n't spare their work. There go part of them to the fields now,—three big boys astride mules, and a strapping girl with bare brown legs. Careless ignorance and laziness here, fierce hate and vindictiveness there;—these are the extremes of the Negro problem which we met that day, and we scarce knew which we preferred.

Here and there we meet distinct characters quite out of the ordinary. One came out of a piece of newly cleared ground, making a wide detour to avoid the snakes. He was an old, hollow-cheeked man, with a drawn and characterful brown face. He had a sort of self-contained quaintness and rough humor impossible to describe; a certain cynical earnestness that puzzled one. "The niggers were jealous of me over on the other place," he said, "and so me and the old woman begged this piece of woods, and I cleared it up myself. Made nothing for two years, but I reckon I 've got a crop now." The cotton looked tall and rich, and we praised it. He curtsied low, and then bowed almost to the ground, with an imperturbable gravity that seemed almost suspicious. Then he continued, "My mule died last week,"—a calamity in this land equal to a devastating fire in town,—"but a white man loaned me another." Then he added, eyeing us, "Oh, I gets along with white folks." We turned the conversation. "Bears? deer?" he answered, " well, I should say there were," and he let fly a string of brave oaths, as he told hunting-tales of the swamp. We left him standing still in the middle of the road looking after us, and yet apparently not noticing us.

The Whistle place, which includes his bit of land, was bought soon after the war by an English syndicate, the "Dixie Cotton and Corn Company." A marvellous deal of style their factor put on, with his servants and coach-and-six; so much so that the concern soon landed in inextricable bankruptcy. Nobody lives in the old house now, but a man comes each winter out of the North and collects his high rents. I know not which are the more touching,—such old empty houses, or the homes of the masters' sons. Sad and bitter tales lie hidden back of those white doors,—tales of poverty, of struggle, of disappointment. A revolution such as that of '63 is a terrible thing; they that rose rich in the morning often slept in paupers' beds. Beggars and vulgar speculators rose to rule over them, and their children went astray. See yonder sad-colored house, with its cabins and fences and glad crops? It is not glad within; last month the prodigal son of the struggling father wrote home from the city for money. Money! Where was it to come from? And so the son rose in the night and killed his baby, and killed his wife, and shot himself dead. And the world passed on.

I remember wheeling around a bend in the road beside a graceful bit of forest and a singing brook. A long low house faced us, with porch and flying pillars, great oaken door, and a broad lawn shining in the evening sun. But the window-panes were gone, the pillars were worm-eaten, and the moss-grown roof was falling in. Half curiously I peered through the unhinged door, and saw where, on the wall across the hall, was written in once gay letters a faded "Welcome."

Quite a contrast to the southwestern part of Dougherty County is the northwest. Soberly timbered in oak and pine, it has none of that half-tropical luxuriance of the southwest. Then, too, there are fewer signs of a romantic past, and more of systematic modern land-grabbing and money-getting. White people are more in evidence here, and farmer and hired labor replace to some extent the absentee landlord and rack-rented tenant. The crops have neither the luxuriance of the richer land nor the signs of neglect so often seen, and there were fences and meadows here and there. Most of this land was poor, and beneath the notice of the slave-baron, before the war. Since then his nephews and the poor whites and the Jews have seized it. The returns of the farmer are too small to allow much for wages, and yet he will not sell off small farms. There is the Negro Sanford; he has worked fourteen years as overseer on the Ladson place, and "paid out enough for fertilizers to have bought a farm," but the owner will not sell off a few acres.

Two children—a boy and a girl—are hoeing sturdily in the fields on the farm where Corliss works. He is smooth-faced and brown, and is fencing up his pigs. He used to run a successful cotton-gin, but the Cotton Seed Oil Trust has forced the price of ginning so low that he says it hardly pays him. He points out a stately old house over the way as the home of "Pa Willis." We eagerly ride over, for "Pa Willis" was the tall and powerful black Moses who led the Negroes for a generation, and led them well. He was a Baptist preacher, and when he died two thousand black people followed him to the grave; and now they preach his funeral sermon each year. His widow lives here,—a weazened, sharp-featured little woman, who curtsied quaintly as we greeted her. Further on lives Jack Delson, the most prosperous Negro farmer in the county. It is a joy to meet him,—a great broad-shouldered, handsome black man, intelligent and jovial. Six hundred and fifty acres he owns, and has eleven black tenants. A neat and tidy home nestled in a flower-garden, and a little store stands beside it.

We pass the Munson place, where a plucky white widow is renting and struggling; and the eleven hundred acres of the Sennet plantation, with its Negro overseer. Then the character of the farms begins to change. Nearly all the lands belong to Russian Jews; the overseers are white, and the cabins are bare board-houses scattered here and there. The rents are high, and day-laborers and "contract" hands abound. It is a keen, hard struggle for living here, and few have time to talk. Tired with the long ride, we gladly drive into Gillonsville. It is a silent cluster of farm-houses standing on the cross-roads, with one of its stores closed and the other kept by a Negro preacher. They tell great tales of busy times at Gillonsville before all the railroads came to Albany; now it is chiefly a memory. Riding down the street, we stop at the preacher's and seat ourselves before the door. It was one of those scenes one cannot soon forget:—a wide, low, little house, whose motherly roof reached over and sheltered a snug little porch. There we sat, after the long hot drive, drinking cool water,—the talkative little storekeeper who is my daily companion; the silent old black woman patching pantaloons and saying never a word; the ragged picture of helpless misfortune who called in just to see the preacher; and finally the neat matronly preacher's wife, plump, yellow, and intelligent. "Own land?" said the wife; "well, only this house." Then she added quietly, "We did buy seven hundred acres up yonder, and paid for it; but they cheated us out of it. Sells was the owner." "Sells!" echoed the ragged misfortune, who was leaning against the balustrade and listening, "he 's a regular cheat. I worked for him thirty-seven days this spring, and he paid me in cardboard checks which were to be cashed at the end of the month. But he never cashed them,—kept putting me off. Then the sheriff came and took my mule and corn and furniture—" "Furniture?" I asked; "but furniture is exempt from seizure by law." "Well, he took it just the same," said the hard-faced man.

VIII

Of the Quest of the Golden Fleece

But the Brute said in his breast, "Till the mills I grind have ceased,
The riches shall be dust of dust, dry ashes be the feast!

"On the strong and cunning few
Cynic favors I will strew;
I will stuff their maw with overplus until their spirit dies;
From the patient and the low
I will take the joys they know;
They shall hunger after vanities and still an-hungered go.
Madness shall be on the people, ghastly jealousies arise;
Brother's blood shall cry on brother up the dead and empty skies."

WILLIAM VAUGHN MOODY.

HAVE you ever seen a cotton-field white with the harvest,—its golden fleece hovering above the black earth like a silvery cloud edged with dark green, its bold white signals waving like the foam of billows from Carolina to Texas across that Black and human Sea? I have sometimes half suspected that here the winged ram Chrysomallus left that Fleece after which Jason and his Argonauts went vaguely wandering into the shadowy East three thousand years ago; and certainly one might frame a pretty and not far-fetched analogy of witchery and dragon's teeth, and blood and armed men, between the ancient and the modern Quest of the Golden Fleece in the Black Sea.

And now the golden fleece is found; not only found, but, in its birthplace, woven. For the hum of the cotton-mills is the newest and most significant thing in the New South today. All through the Carolinas and Georgia, away down to Mexico, rise these gaunt red buildings, bare and homely, and yet so busy and noisy withal that they scarce seem to belong to the slow and sleepy land. Perhaps they sprang from dragons' teeth. So the Cotton Kingdom still lives; the world still bows beneath her sceptre. Even the markets that once defied the *parvenu* have crept one by one across the seas, and then slowly and reluctantly, but surely, have started toward the Black Belt.

To be sure, there are those who wag their heads knowingly and tell us that the capital of the Cotton Kingdom has moved from the Black to the White Belt,—that the Negro of to-day raises not more than half of the cotton crop. Such men forget that the cotton crop has doubled, and more than doubled, since the era of slavery, and that, even granting their contention, the Negro is still supreme in a Cotton Kingdom larger than that on which the Confederacy builded its hopes. So the Negro forms to-day one of the chief figures in a great world-industry; and this, for its own sake, and in the light of historic interest, makes the field-hands of the cotton country worth studying.

We seldom study the condition of the Negro to-day honestly and carefully. It is so much easier to assume that we know it all. Or perhaps, having already reached conclusions in our own minds, we are loth to have them disturbed by facts. And yet how little we really know of these millions,—of their daily lives and longings, of their homely joys and sorrows, of their real shortcomings and the meaning of their crimes! All this we can only learn by intimate contact with the masses, and not by wholesale arguments covering millions separate in time and space, and differing widely in training and culture. To-day, then, my reader, let us turn our faces to the Black Belt of Georgia and seek simply to know the condition of the black farm-laborers of one county there.

Here in 1890 lived ten thousand Negroes and two thousand whites. The country is rich, yet the people are poor. The keynote of the Black Belt is debt; not commercial credit, but debt in the sense of continued inability on the part of the mass of the population to make income cover expense. This is the direct heritage of the South from the wasteful economies of the slave *régime*; but it was emphasized and brought to a crisis by the Emancipation of the slaves. In 1860, Dougherty County had six thousand slaves, worth at least two and a half millions of dollars; its farms were estimated at three millions,—making five and a half millions of property, the value of which depended largely on the slave system, and on the speculative demand for land once marvellously rich but already partially devitalized by careless and exhaustive culture. The war then meant a financial crash; in place of the five and a half millions of 1860, there remained in 1870 only farms valued at less than two millions. With this came increased competition in cotton culture from the rich lands of Texas; a steady fall in the normal price of cotton followed, from about fourteen cents a pound in 1860 until it reached four cents in 1898. Such a financial revolution was it that involved the owners of the cotton-belt in debt. And if things went ill with the master, how fared it with the man?

The plantations of Dougherty County in slavery days were not as imposing and aristocratic as those of Virginia. The Big House was smaller and usually one-storied, and sat very near the slave cabins. Sometimes these cabins stretched off on either side like wings; sometimes only on one side, forming a double row, or edging the road that turned into the plantation from the main thoroughfare. The form and disposition of the laborers' cabins throughout the Black Belt is to-day the same as in slavery days. Some live in the self-same cabins, others in cabins rebuilt on the sites of the old. All are sprinkled in little groups over the face of the land, centering about some dilapidated Big House where the head-tenant or agent lives. The general character and arrangement of these dwellings remains on the whole unaltered. There were in the county, outside the corporate town of Albany, about fifteen hundred Negro families in 1898. Out of all these, only a single family occupied a house with seven rooms; only fourteen have five rooms or more. The mass live in one- and two-room homes.

The size and arrangements of a people's homes are no unfair index of their condition. If, then, we inquire more carefully into these Negro homes, we find much that is unsatisfactory. All over the face of the land is the one-room cabin,—now standing in the shadow of the Big House, now staring at the dusty road, now rising dark and sombre amid the green of the cotton-fields. It is nearly always old and bare, built of rough boards, and neither plastered nor ceiled. Light and ventilation are supplied by the single door and by the square hole in the wall with its wooden shutter. There is no glass, porch, or ornamentation without. Within is a fireplace, black and smoky, and usually unsteady with age. A bed or two, a table, a wooden chest, and a few chairs compose the furniture; while a stray show-bill or a newspaper makes up the decorations for the walls. Now and then one may find such a cabin kept scrupulously neat, with merry steaming fire-place and hospitable door; but the majority are dirty and dilapidated, smelling of eating and sleeping, poorly ventilated, and anything but homes.

Above all, the cabins are crowded. We have come to associate crowding with homes in cities almost exclusively. This is primarily because we have so little accurate knowledge of country life. Here in Dougherty County one may find families of eight and ten occupying one or two rooms, and for every ten rooms of house accommodation for the Negroes there are twenty-five persons. The worst tenement abominations of New York do not have above twenty-two persons for every ten rooms. Of course, one small, close room in a city, without a yard, is in many respects worse than the larger single country room. In other respects it is better; it has glass windows, a decent chimney, and a trustworthy floor. The single great advantage of the Negro peasant is that he may spend most of his life outside his hovel, in the open fields.

There are four chief causes of these wretched homes: First, long custom born of slavery has assigned such homes to Negroes; white laborers would be offered better accommodations, and might, for that and similar reasons, give better work. Secondly, the Negroes, used to such accommodations, do not as a rule demand better; they do not know what better houses mean. Thirdly, the landlords as a class have not yet come to realize that it is a good business investment to raise the standard of living among labor by slow and judicious methods; that a Negro laborer who demands three rooms and fifty cents a day would give more efficient work and leave a larger profit than a discouraged toiler herding his family in one room and working for thirty cents. Lastly, among such conditions of life there are few incentives to make the laborer become a better farmer. If he is ambitious, he moves to town or tries other labor; as a tenant-farmer his outlook is almost hopeless, and following it as a makeshift, he takes the house that is given him without protest.

In such homes, then, these Negro peasants live. The families are both small and large; there are many single tenants,—widows and bachelors, and remnants of broken groups. The system of labor and the size of the houses both tend to the breaking up of family groups: the grown children go away as contract hands or migrate to town, the sister goes into service; and so one finds many families with hosts of babies, and many newly married couples, but comparatively few families with half-grown and grown sons and daughters. The average size of Negro families has undoubtedly decreased since the war, primarily from economic stress. In Russia over a third of the bridegrooms and over half the brides are under twenty; the same was true of the ante-bellum Negroes. To-day, however, very few of the boys and less than a fifth of the Negro girls under twenty are married. The young men marry between the ages of twenty-five and thirty-five; the young women between twenty and thirty. Such postponement is due to the difficulty of earning sufficient to rear and support a family; and it undoubtedly leads, in the country districts, to sexual immorality. The form of this immorality, however, is very seldom that of prostitution, and less frequently that of illegitimacy than one would imagine. Rather, it takes the form of separation and desertion after a family group has been formed. The number of separated persons is thirty-five to the thousand,—a very large number. It would of course be unfair to compare this number with divorce statistics, for many of these separated women are in reality widowed, were the truth known, and in other cases the separation is not permanent. Nevertheless, here lies the seat of greatest moral danger. There is little or no prostitution among these Negroes, and over three-fourths of the families, as found by house-to-house investigation, deserve to be classed as decent people with considerable regard for female chastity. To be sure, the ideas of the mass would not suit New England, and there are many loose habits and notions. Yet the rate of illegitimacy is undoubtedly lower than in Austria or Italy, and the women as a class are modest. The plague-spot in sexual relations is easy marriage and easy separation. This is no sudden development, nor the fruit of Emancipation. It is the plain heritage from slavery. In those days Sam, with his master's consent, "took up" with Mary. No ceremony was necessary, and in the busy life of the great plantations of the Black Belt it was usually dispensed with. If now the master needed Sam's work in another plantation or in another part of the same plantation, or if he took a notion to sell the slave, Sam's married life with Mary was usually unceremoniously broken, and then it was clearly to the master's interest to have both of them take new mates. This widespread custom of two centuries has not been eradicated in thirty years. To-day Sam's grandson "takes up" with a woman without license or ceremony; they live together decently and honestly, and are, to all intents and purposes, man and wife. Sometimes these unions are never broken until death; but in too many cases family quarrels, a roving spirit, a rival suitor, or perhaps more frequently the hopeless battle to support a family, lead to separation, and a broken household is the result. The Negro church has done much to stop this practice, and now most marriage ceremonies are performed by the pastors. Nevertheless, the evil is still deep seated, and only a general raising of the standard of living will finally cure it.

Looking now at the county black population as a whole, it is fair to characterize it as poor and ignorant. Perhaps ten per cent compose the well-to-do and the best of the laborers, while at least nine per cent are thoroughly lewd and vicious. The rest, over eighty per cent, are poor and ignorant, fairly honest and well meaning, plodding, and to a degree shiftless, with some but not great sexual looseness. Such class lines are by no means fixed; they vary, one might almost say, with the price of cotton. The degree of ignorance cannot easily be expressed. We may say, for instance, that nearly two-thirds of them cannot read or write. This but partially expresses the fact. They are ignorant of the world about them, of modern economic organization, of the function of government, of individual worth and possibilities,—of nearly all those things which slavery in self-defence had to keep them from learning. Much that the white boy imbibes from his earliest social atmosphere forms the puzzling problems of the black boy's mature years. America is not another word for Opportunity to *all* her sons.

It is easy for us to lose ourselves in details in endeavoring to grasp and comprehend the real condition of a mass of human beings. We often forget that each unit in the mass is a throbbing human soul. Ignorant it may be, and poverty stricken, black and curious in limb and ways and thought; and yet it loves and hates, it toils and tires, it laughs and weeps its bitter tears, and looks in vague and awful longing at the grim horizon of its life,—all this, even as you and I. These black thousands are not in reality lazy; they are improvident and careless; they insist on breaking the monotony of toil with a glimpse at the great town-world on Saturday; they have their loafers and their rascals; but the great mass of them work continuously and faithfully for a return, and under circumstances that would call forth equal voluntary effort from few if any other modern laboring class. Over eighty-eight per cent of them—men, women, and children—are farmers. Indeed, this is almost the only industry. Most of the children get their schooling after the "crops are laid by," and very few there are that stay in school after the spring work has begun. Child-labor is to be found here in some of its worst phases, as fostering ignorance and stunting physical development. With the grown men of the county there is little variety in work: thirteen hundred are farmers, and two hundred are laborers, teamsters, etc., including twenty-four artisans, ten merchants, twenty-one preachers, and four teachers. This narrowness of life reaches its maximum among the women: thirteen hundred and fifty of these are farm laborers, one hundred are servants and washerwomen, leaving sixty-five housewives, eight teachers, and six seamstresses.

Among this people there is no leisure class. We often forget that in the United States over half the youth and adults are not in the world earning incomes, but are making homes, learning of the world, or resting after the heat of the strife. But here ninety-six per cent are toiling; no one with leisure to turn the bare and cheerless cabin into a home, no old folks to sit beside the fire and hand down traditions of the past; little of careless happy childhood and dreaming youth. The dull monotony of daily toil is broken only by the gayety of the thoughtless and the Saturday trip to town. The toil, like all farm toil, is monotonous, and here there are little machinery and few tools to relieve its burdensome drudgery. But with all this, it is work in the pure open air, and this is something in a day when fresh air is scarce.

The land on the whole is still fertile, despite long abuse. For nine or ten months in succession the crops will come if asked: garden vegetables in April, grain in May, melons in June and July, hay in August, sweet potatoes in September, and cotton from then to Christmas. And yet on two-thirds of the land there is but one crop, and that leaves the toilers in debt. Why is this?

Away down the Baysan road, where the broad flat fields are flanked by great oak forests, is a plantation; many thousands of acres it used to run, here and there, and beyond the great wood. Thirteen hundred human beings here obeyed the call of one,—were his in body, and largely in soul. One of them lives there yet,—a short, stocky man, his dull-brown face seamed and drawn, and his tightly curled hair gray-white. The crops? Just tolerable, he said; just tolerable. Getting on? No—he was n't getting on at all. Smith of Albany "furnishes" him, and his rent is eight hundred pounds of cotton. Can't make anything at that. Why did n't he buy land? *Humph!* Takes money to buy land. And he turns away. Free! The most piteous thing amid all the black ruin of war-time, amid the broken fortunes of the masters, the blighted hopes of mothers and maidens, and the fall of an empire,—the most piteous thing amid all this was the black freedman who threw down his hoe because the world called him free. What did such a mockery of freedom mean? Not a cent of money, not an inch of land, not a mouthful of victuals,—not even ownership of the rags on his back. Free! On Saturday, once or twice a month, the old master, before the war, used to dole out bacon and meal to his Negroes. And after the first flush of freedom wore off, and his true helplessness dawned on the freedman, he came back and picked up his hoe, and old master still doled out his bacon and meal. The legal form of service was theoretically far different; in practice, task-work or "cropping" was substituted for daily toil in gangs; and the slave gradually became a metayer, or tenant on shares, in name, but a laborer with indeterminate wages in fact.

Still the price of cotton fell, and gradually the landlords deserted their plantations, and the reign of the merchant began. The merchant of the Black Belt is a curious institution,—part banker, part landlord, part contractor, and part despot. His store, which used most frequently to stand at the cross-roads and become the centre of a weekly village, has now moved to town; and thither the Negro tenant follows him. The merchant keeps everything,—clothes and shoes, coffee and sugar, pork and meal, canned and dried goods, wagons and ploughs, seed and fertilizer,—and what he has not in stock he can give you an order for at the store across the way. Here, then, comes the tenant, Sam Scott, after he has contracted with some absent landlord's agent for hiring forty acres of land; he fingers his hat nervously until the merchant finishes his morning chat with Colonel Sanders, and calls out, "Well, Sam, what do you want?" Sam wants him to "furnish" him,—*i. e.*, to advance him food and clothing for the year, and perhaps seed and tools, until his crop is raised and sold. If Sam seems a favorable subject, he and the merchant go to a lawyer, and Sam executes a chattel mortgage on his mule and wagon in return for seed and a week's rations. As soon as the green cotton-leaves appear above the ground, another mortgage is given on the "crop." Every Saturday, or at longer intervals, Sam calls upon the merchant for his "rations"; a family of five usually gets about thirty pounds of fat side-pork and a couple of bushels of corn-meal a month. Besides this, clothing and shoes must be furnished; if Sam or his family is sick, there are orders on the druggist and doctor; if the mule wants shoeing, an order on the blacksmith, etc. If Sam is a hard worker and crops promise well, he is often encouraged to buy more,—sugar, extra clothes, perhaps a buggy. But he is seldom encouraged to save. When cotton rose to ten cents last fall, the shrewd merchants of Dougherty County sold a thousand buggies in one season, mostly to black men.

The security offered for such transactions—a crop and chattel mortgage—may at first seem slight. And, indeed, the merchants tell many a true tale of shiftlessness and cheating;

of cotton picked at night, mules disappearing, and tenants absconding. But on the whole the merchant of the Black Belt is the most prosperous man in the section. So skilfully and so closely has he drawn the bonds of the law about the tenant, that the black man has often simply to choose between pauperism and crime; he "waives" all homestead exemptions in his contract; he cannot touch his own mortgaged crop, which the laws put almost in the full control of the land-owner and of the merchant. When the crop is growing the merchant watches it like a hawk; as soon as it is ready for market he takes possession of it, sells it, pays the land-owner his rent, subtracts his bill for supplies, and if, as sometimes happens, there is anything left, he hands it over to the black serf for his Christmas celebration.

The direct result of this system is an all-cotton scheme of agriculture and the continued bankruptcy of the tenant. The currency of the Black Belt is cotton. It is a crop always salable for ready money, not usually subject to great yearly fluctuations in price, and one which the Negroes know how to raise. The landlord therefore demands his rent in cotton, and the merchant will accept mortgages on no other crop. There is no use asking the black tenant, then, to diversify his crops,—he cannot under this system. Moreover, the system is bound to bankrupt the tenant. I remember once meeting a little one-mule wagon on the River road. A young black fellow sat in it driving listlessly, his elbows on his knees. His dark-faced wife sat beside him, stolid, silent.

"Hello!" cried my driver,—he has a most impudent way of addressing these people, though they seem used to it,—"what have you got there?"

"Meat and meal," answered the man, stopping. The meat lay uncovered in the bottom of the wagon,—a great thin side of fat pork covered with salt; the meal was in a white bushel bag.

"What did you pay for that meat?"

"Ten cents a pound." It could have been bought for six or seven cents cash.

"And the meal?"

"Two dollars." One dollar and ten cents is the cash price in town. Here was a man paying five dollars for goods which he could have bought for three dollars cash, and raised for one dollar or one dollar and a half.

Yet it is not wholly his fault. The Negro farmer started behind,—started in debt. This was not his choosing, but the crime of this happy-go-lucky nation which goes blundering along with its Reconstruction tragedies, its Spanish war interludes and Philippine matinees, just as though God really were dead. Once in debt, it is no easy matter for a whole race to emerge.

In the year of low-priced cotton, 1898, out of three hundred tenant families one hundred and seventy-five ended their year's work in debt to the extent of fourteen thousand dollars; fifty cleared nothing, and the remaining seventy-five made a total profit of sixteen hundred dollars. The net indebtedness of the black tenant families of the whole county must have been at least sixty thousand dollars. In a more prosperous year the situation is far better; but on the average the majority of tenants end the year even, or in debt, which means that they work for board and clothes. Such an economic organization is radically wrong. Whose is the blame?

The underlying causes of this situation are complicated but discernible. And one of the chief, outside the carelessness of the nation in letting the slave start with nothing, is the widespread opinion among the merchants and employers of the Black Belt that only by the slavery of debt can the Negro be kept at work. Without doubt, some pressure was necessary at the beginning of the free-labor system to keep the listless and lazy at work; and even to-day the mass of the Negro laborers need stricter guardianship than most Northern laborers. Behind this honest and widespread opinion dishonesty and cheating of the ignorant laborers have a good chance to take refuge. And to all this must be added the obvious fact that a slave ancestry and a system of unrequited toil has not improved the efficiency or temper of the mass of black laborers. Nor is this peculiar to Sambo; it has in history been just as true of John and Hans, of Jacques and Pat, of all grounddown peasantries. Such is the situation of the mass of the Negroes in the Black Belt to-day; and they are thinking about it. Crime, and a cheap and dangerous socialism, are the inevitable results of this pondering. I see now that ragged black man sitting on a log, aimlessly whittling a stick. He muttered to me with the murmur of many ages, when he said: "White man sit down whole year; Nigger work day and night and make crop; Nigger hardly gits bread and meat; white man sittin' down gits all. *It's wrong*." And what do the better classes of Negroes do to improve their situation? One of two things: if any way possible, they buy land; if not, they migrate to town. Just as centuries ago it was no easy thing for the serf to escape into the freedom of town-life, even so to-day there are hindrances laid in the way of county laborers. In considerable parts of all the Gulf States, and especially in Mississippi, Louisiana, and Arkansas, the Negroes on the plantations in the back-country districts are still held at forced labor practically without wages. Especially is this true in districts where the farmers are composed of the more ignorant class of poor whites, and the Negroes are beyond the reach of schools and intercourse with their advancing fellows. If such a peon should run away, the sheriff, elected by white suffrage, can usually be depended on to catch the fugitive, return him, and ask no questions. If he escape to another county, a charge of petty thieving, easily true, can be depended upon to secure his return. Even if some unduly officious person insist upon a trial, neighborly comity will probably make his conviction sure, and then the labor due the county can easily be bought by the master. Such a system is impossible in the more civilized parts of the South, or near the large towns and cities; but in those vast stretches of land beyond the telegraph and the newspaper the spirit of the Thirteenth Amendment is sadly broken. This represents the lowest economic depths of the black American peasant; and in a study of the rise and condition of the Negro freeholder we must trace his economic progress from this modern serfdom.

Even in the better-ordered country districts of the South the free movement of agricultural laborers is hindered by the migration-agent laws. The "Associated Press" recently informed the world of the arrest of a young white man in Southern Georgia who represented the "Atlantic Naval Supplies Company," and who "was caught in the act of enticing hands from the turpentine farm of Mr. John Greer." The crime for which this young man was arrested is taxed five hundred dollars for each county in which the employment agent proposes to gather laborers for work outside the State. Thus the Negroes' ignorance of the labor-market outside his own vicinity is increased rather than diminished by the laws of nearly every Southern State.

Similar to such measures is the unwritten law of the back districts and small towns of the South, that the character of all Negroes unknown to the mass of the community must be vouched for by some white man. This is really a revival of the old Roman idea of the patron under whose protection the new-made freedman was put. In many instances this system has been of great good to the Negro, and very often under the protection and guidance of the former master's family, or other white friends, the freedman progressed in wealth and morality. But the same system has in other cases resulted in the refusal of whole communities to recognize the right of a Negro to change his habitation and to be master of his own fortunes. A black stranger in Baker County, Georgia, for instance, is liable to be stopped anywhere on the public highway and made to state his business to the satisfaction of any white interrogator. If he fails to give a suitable answer, or seems too independent or "sassy," he may be arrested or summarily driven away.

Thus it is that in the country districts of the South, by written or unwritten law, peonage, hindrances to the migration of labor, and a system of white patronage exists over large areas. Besides this, the chance for lawless oppression and illegal exactions is vastly greater in the country than in the city, and nearly all the more serious race disturbances of the last decade have arisen from disputes in the county between master and man,—as, for instance, the Sam Hose affair. As a result of such a situation, there arose, first, the Black Belt; and, second, the Migration to Town. The Black Belt was not, as many assumed, a movement toward fields of labor under more genial climatic conditions; it was primarily a huddling for self-protection,—a massing of the black population for mutual defence in order to secure the peace and tranquillity necessary to economic advance. This movement took place between Emancipation and 1880, and only partially accomplished the desired results. The rush to town since 1880 is the counter-movement of men disappointed in the economic opportunities of the Black Belt.

In Dougherty County, Georgia, one can see easily the results of this experiment in huddling for protection. Only ten per cent of the adult population was born in the county, and yet the blacks outnumber the whites four or five to one. There is undoubtedly a security to the blacks in their very numbers,—a personal freedom from arbitrary treatment, which makes hundreds of laborers cling to Dougherty in spite of low wages and economic distress. But a change is coming, and slowly but surely even here the agricultural laborers are drifting to town and leaving the broad acres behind. Why is this? Why do not the Negroes become land-owners, and build up the black landed peasantry, which has for a generation and more been the dream of philanthropist and statesman?

To the car-window sociologist, to the man who seeks to understand and know the South by devoting the few leisure hours of a holiday trip to unravelling the snarl of centuries,—to such men very often the whole trouble with the black field-hand may be summed up by Aunt Ophelia's word, "Shiftless!" They have noted repeatedly scenes like one I saw last summer. We were riding along the highroad to town at the close of a long hot day. A couple of young black fellows passed us in a mule-team, with several bushels of loose corn in the ear. One was driving, listlessly bent forward, his elbows on his knees,—a happy-go-lucky, careless picture of irresponsibility. The other was fast asleep in the bottom of the wagon. As we passed we noticed an ear of corn fall from the wagon. They never saw it,—not they. A rod farther on we noted another ear on the ground; and between that creeping mule and town we counted twenty-six ears of corn. Shiftless? Yes, the personification of shiftlessness. And yet follow those boys: they are not lazy; to-morrow morning they 'll be up with the sun; they work hard when they do work, and they work willingly. They have no sordid, selfish, money-getting ways, but rather a fine disdain for mere cash. They 'll loaf before your face and work behind your back with good-natured honesty. They 'll steal a watermelon, and hand you back your lost purse intact. Their great defect as laborers lies in their lack of incentive to work beyond the mere pleasure of physical exertion. They are careless because they have not found that it pays to be careful; they are improvident because the improvident ones of their acquaintance get on about as well as the provident. Above all, they cannot see why they should take unusual pains to make the white man's land better, or to fatten his mule, or save his corn. On the other hand, the white land-owner argues that any attempt to improve these laborers by increased responsibility, or higher wages, or better homes, or land of their own, would be sure to result in failure. He shows his Northern visitor the scarred and wretched land; the ruined mansions, the worn-out soil and mortgaged acres, and says, This is Negro freedom!

Now it happens that both master and man have just enough argument on their respective sides to make it difficult for them to understand each other. The Negro dimly personifies in the white man all his ills and misfortunes; if he is poor, it is because the white man seizes the fruit of his toil; if he is ignorant, it is because the white man gives him neither time nor facilities to learn; and, indeed, if any misfortune happens to him, it is because of some hidden machinations of "white folks." On the other hand, the masters and the masters' sons have never been able to see why the Negro, instead of settling down to be day-laborers for bread and clothes, are infected with a silly desire to rise in the world, and why they are sulky, dissatisfied, and careless, where their fathers were happy and dumb and faithful. "Why, you niggers have an easier time than I do," said a puzzled Albany merchant to his black customer. "Yes," he replied, "and so does yo' hogs."

Taking, then, the dissatisfied and shiftless field-hand as a starting-point, let us inquire how the black thousands of Dougherty have struggled from him up toward their ideal, and what that ideal is. All social struggle is evidenced by the rise, first of economic, then of social classes, among a homogeneous population. To-day the following economic classes are plainly differentiated among these Negroes.

A "submerged tenth" of croppers, with a few paupers; forty per cent who are metayers and thirty-nine per cent of semi-metayers and wage-laborers. There are left five per cent of money-renters and six per cent of freeholders,—the "Upper Ten" of the land. The croppers are entirely without capital, even in the limited sense of food or money to keep them from seed-time to harvest. All they furnish is their labor; the land-owner furnishes land, stock, tools, seed, and house; and at the end of the year the laborer gets from a third to a half of the crop. Out of his share, however, comes pay and interest for food and clothing advanced him during the year. Thus we have a laborer without capital and without wages, and an employer whose capital is largely his employees' wages. It is an unsatisfactory arrangement, both for hirer and hired, and is usually in vogue on poor land with hard-pressed owners.

Above the croppers come the great mass of the black population who work the land on their own responsibility, paying rent in cotton and supported by the crop-mortgage system. After the war this system was attractive to the freedmen on account of its larger freedom and its possibilities for making a surplus. But with the carrying out of the crop-lien system, the deterioration of the land, and the slavery of debt, the position of the metayers has sunk to a dead level of practically unrewarded toil. Formerly all tenants had some capital, and often considerable; but absentee landlordism, rising rack-rent, and falling cotton have stripped them well-nigh of all, and probably not over half of them to-day own their mules. The change from cropper to tenant was accomplished by fixing the rent. If, now, the rent fixed was reasonable, this was an incentive to the tenant to strive. On the other hand, if the rent was too high, or if the land deteriorated, the result was to discourage and check the efforts of the black peasantry. There is no doubt that the latter case is true; that in Dougherty County every economic advantage of the price of cotton in market and of the strivings of the tenant has been taken advantage of by the landlords and merchants, and swallowed up in rent and interest. If cotton rose in price, the rent rose even higher; if cotton fell, the rent remained or followed reluctantly. If a tenant worked hard and raised a large crop, his rent was raised the next year; if that year the crop failed, his corn was confiscated and his mule sold for debt. There were, of course, exceptions to this,—cases of personal kindness and forbearance; but in the vast majority of cases the rule was to extract the uttermost farthing from the mass of the black farm laborers.

The average metayer pays from twenty to thirty per cent of his crop in rent. The result of such rack-rent can only be evil,—abuse and neglect of the soil, deterioration in the character of the laborers, and a widespread sense of injustice. "Wherever the country is poor," cried Arthur Young, "it is in the hands of metayers," and "their condition is more wretched than that of day-laborers." He was talking of Italy a century ago; but he might have been talking of Dougherty County to-day. And especially is that true to-day which he declares was true in France before the Revolution: "The metayers are considered as little better than menial servants, removable at pleasure, and obliged to conform in all things to the will of the landlords." On this low plane half the black population of Dougherty County—perhaps more than half the black millions of this land—are to-day struggling.

A degree above these we may place those laborers who receive money wages for their work. Some receive a house with perhaps a garden-spot; then supplies of food and clothing are advanced, and certain fixed wages are given at the end of the year, varying from thirty to sixty dollars, out of which the supplies must be paid for, with interest. About eighteen per cent of the population belong to this class of semi-metayers, while twenty-two per cent are laborers paid by the month or year, and are either "furnished" by their own savings or perhaps more usually by some merchant who takes his chances of payment. Such laborers receive from thirty-five to fifty cents a day during the working season. They are usually young unmarried persons, some being women; and when they marry they sink to the class of metayers, or, more seldom, become renters.

The renters for fixed money rentals are the first of the emerging classes, and form five per cent of the families. The sole advantage of this small class is their freedom to choose their crops, and the increased responsibility which comes through having money transactions. While some of the renters differ little in condition from the metayers, yet on the whole they are more intelligent and responsible persons, and are the ones who eventually become land-owners. Their better character and greater shrewdness enable them to gain, perhaps to demand, better terms in rents; rented farms, varying from forty to a hundred acres, bear an average rental of about fifty-four dollars a year. The men who conduct such farms do not long remain renters; either they sink to metayers, or with a successful series of harvests rise to be land-owners.

In 1870 the tax-books of Dougherty report no Negroes as landholders. If there were any such at that time,—and there may have been a few,—their land was probably held in the name of some white patron,—a method not uncommon during slavery. In 1875 ownership of land had begun with seven hundred and fifty acres; ten years later this had increased to over sixty-five hundred acres, to nine thousand acres in 1890 and ten thousand in 1900. The total assessed property has in this same period risen from eighty thousand dollars in 1875 to two hundred and forty thousand dollars in 1900.

Two circumstances complicate this development and make it in some respects difficult to be sure of the real tendencies; they are the panic of 1893, and the low price of cotton in 1898. Besides this, the system of assessing property in the country districts of Georgia is somewhat antiquated and of uncertain statistical value; there are no assessors, and each man makes a sworn return to a tax-receiver. Thus public opinion plays a large part, and the returns vary strangely from year to year. Certainly these figures show the small amount of accumulated capital among the Negroes, and the consequent large dependence of their property on temporary prosperity. They have little to tide over a few years of economic depression, and are at the mercy of the cotton-market far more than the whites. And thus the land-owners, despite their marvellous efforts, are really a transient class, continually being depleted by those who fall back into the class of renters or metayers, and augmented by newcomers from the masses. Of the one hundred land-owners in 1898, half had bought their land since 1893, a fourth between 1890 and 1893, a fifth between 1884 and 1890, and the rest between 1870 and 1884. In all, one hundred and eighty-five Negroes have owned land in this county since 1875.

If all the black land-owners who had ever held land here had kept it or left it in the hands of black men, the Negroes would have owned nearer thirty thousand acres than the fifteen thousand they now hold. And yet these fifteen thousand acres are a creditable showing,—a proof of no little weight of the worth and ability of the Negro people. If they had been given an economic start at Emancipation, if they had been in an enlightened and rich community which really desired their best good, then we might perhaps call such a result small or even insignificant. But for a few thousand poor ignorant field-hands, in the face of poverty, a falling market, and social stress, to save and capitalize two hundred thousand dollars in a generation has meant a tremendous effort. The rise of a nation, the pressing forward of a social class, means a bitter struggle, a hard and soul-sickening battle with the world such as few of the more favored classes know or appreciate.

Out of the hard economic conditions of this portion of the Black Belt, only six per cent of the population have succeeded in emerging into peasant proprietorship; and these are not all firmly fixed, but grow and shrink in number with the wavering of the cotton-market. Fully ninety-four per cent have struggled for land and failed, and half of them sit in hopeless serfdom. For these there is one other avenue of escape toward which they have turned in increasing numbers, namely, migration to town. A glance at the distribution of land among the black owners curiously reveals this fact. In 1898 the holdings were as follows: Under forty acres, forty-nine families; forty to two hundred and fifty acres, seventeen families; two hundred and fifty to one thousand acres, thirteen families; one thousand or more acres, two families. Now in 1890 there were forty-four holdings, but only nine of these were under forty acres. The great increase of holdings, then, has come in the buying of small homesteads near town, where their owners really share in the town life; this is a part of the rush to town. And for every land-owner who has thus hurried away from the narrow and hard conditions of country life, how many field-hands, how many tenants, how many ruined renters, have joined that long procession? Is it not strange compensation? The sin of the country districts is visited on the town, and the social sores of city life to-day may, here in Dougherty County, and perhaps in many places near and far, look for their final healing without the city walls.

IX

Of the Sons of Master and Man

Life treads on life, and heart on heart;
We press too close in church and mart
To keep a dream or grave apart.

MRS. BROWNING.

THE world-old phenomenon of the contact of diverse races of men is to have new exemplification during the new century. Indeed, the characteristic of our age is the contact of European civilization with the world's undeveloped peoples. Whatever we may say of the results of such contact in the past, it certainly forms a chapter in human action not pleasant to look back upon. War, murder, slavery, extermination, and debauchery,—this has again and again been the result of carrying civilization and the blessed gospel to the isles of the sea and the heathen without the law. Nor does it altogether satisfy the conscience of the modern world to be told complacently that all this has been right and proper, the fated triumph of strength over weakness, of righteousness over evil, of superiors over inferiors. It would certainly be soothing if one could readily believe all this; and yet there are too many ugly facts for everything to be thus easily explained away. We feel and know that there are many delicate differences in race psychology, numberless changes that our crude social measurements are not yet able to follow minutely, which explain much of history and social development. At the same time, too, we know that these considerations have never adequately explained or excused the triumph of brute force and cunning over weakness and innocence.

It is, then, the strife of all honorable men of the twentieth century to see that in the future competition of races the survival of the fittest shall mean the triumph of the good, the beautiful, and the true; that we may be able to preserve for future civilization all that is really fine and noble and strong, and not continue to put a premium on greed and impudence and cruelty. To bring this hope to fruition, we are compelled daily to turn more and more to a conscientious study of the phenomena of race-contact,—to a study frank and fair, and not falsified and colored by our wishes or our fears. And we have in the South as fine a field for such a study as the world affords,—a field, to be sure, which the average American scientist deems somewhat beneath his dignity, and which the average man who is not a scientist knows all about, but nevertheless a line of study which by reason of the enormous race complications with which God seems about to punish this nation must increasingly claim our sober attention, study, and thought, we must ask, what are the actual relations of whites and blacks in the South? and we must be answered, not by apology or fault-finding, but by a plain, unvarnished tale.

In the civilized life of to-day the contact of men and their relations to each other fall in a few main lines of action and communication: there is, first, the physical proximity of homes and dwelling-places, the way in which neighborhoods group themselves, and the contiguity of neighborhoods. Secondly, and in our age chiefest, there are the economic relations,—the methods by which individuals coöperate for earning a living, for the mutual satisfaction of wants, for the production of wealth. Next, there are the political relations, the coöperation in social control, in group government, in laying and paying the burden of taxation. In the fourth place there are the less tangible but highly important forms of intellectual contact and commerce, the interchange of ideas through conversation and conference, through periodicals and libraries; and, above all, the gradual formation for each community of that curious *tertium quid* which we call public opinion. Closely allied with this come the various forms of social contact in everyday life, in travel, in theatres, in house gatherings, in marrying and giving in marriage. Finally, there are the varying forms of religious enterprise, of moral teaching and benevolent endeavor. These are the principal ways in which men living in the same communities are brought into contact with each other. It is my present task, therefore, to indicate, from my point of view, how the black race in the South meet and mingle with the whites in these matters of everyday life.

First, as to physical dwelling. It is usually possible to draw in nearly every Southern community a physical color-line on the map, on the one side of which whites dwell and on the other Negroes. The winding and intricacy of the geographical color line varies, of course, in different communities. I know some towns where a straight line drawn through the middle of the main street separates nine-tenths of the whites from nine-tenths of the blacks. In other towns the older settlement of whites has been encircled by a broad band of blacks; in still other cases little settlements or nuclei of blacks have sprung up amid surrounding whites. Usually in cities each street has its distinctive color, and only now and then do the colors meet in close proximity. Even in the country something of this segregation is manifest in the smaller areas, and of course in the larger phenomena of the Black Belt.

All this segregation by color is largely independent of that natural clustering by social grades common to all communities. A Negro slum may be in dangerous proximity to a white residence quarter, while it is quite common to find a white slum planted in the heart of a respectable Negro district. One thing, however, seldom occurs: the best of the whites and the best of the Negroes almost never live in anything like close proximity. It thus happens that in nearly every Southern town and city, both whites and blacks see commonly the worst of each other. This is a vast change from the situation in the past, when, through the close contact of master and house-servant in the patriarchal big house, one found the best of both races in close contact and sympathy, while at the same time the squalor and dull round of toil among the field-hands was removed from the sight and hearing of the family. One can easily see how a person who saw slavery thus from his father's parlors, and sees freedom on the streets of a great city, fails to grasp or comprehend the whole of the new picture. On the other hand, the settled belief of the mass of the Negroes that the Southern white people do not have the black man's best interests at heart has been intensified in later years by this continual daily contact of the better class of blacks with the worst representatives of the white race.

Coming now to the economic relations of the races, we are on ground made familiar by study, much discussion, and no little philanthropic effort. And yet with all this there are many essential elements in the coöperation of Negroes and whites for work and wealth that are too readily overlooked or not thoroughly understood. The average American can easily conceive of a rich land awaiting development and filled with black laborers. To him the Southern problem is simply that of making efficient workingmen out of this material, by giving them the requisite technical skill and the help of invested capital. The problem, however, is by no means as simple as this, from the obvious fact that these workingmen have been trained for centuries as slaves. They exhibit, therefore, all the advantages and defects of such training; they are willing and good-natured, but not self-reliant, provident, or careful. If now the economic development of the South is to be pushed to the verge of exploitation, as seems probable, then we have a mass of workingmen thrown into relentless competition with the workingmen of the world, but handicapped by a training the very opposite to that of the modern self-reliant democratic laborer. What the black laborer needs is careful personal guidance, group leadership of men with hearts in their bosoms, to train them to foresight, carefulness, and honesty. Nor does it require any fine-spun theories of racial differences to prove the necessity of such group training after the brains of the race have been knocked out by two hundred and fifty years of assiduous education in submission, carelessness, and stealing. After Emancipation, it was the plain duty of some one to assume this group leadership and training of the Negro laborer. I will not stop here to inquire whose duty it was,—whether that of the white ex-master who had profited by unpaid toil, or the Northern philanthropist whose persistence brought on the crisis, or the National Government whose edict freed the bondmen; I will not stop to ask whose duty it was, but I insist it was the duty of some one to see that these workingmen were not left alone and unguided, without capital, without land, without skill, without economic organization, without even the bald protection of law, order, and decency,—left in a great land, not to settle down to slow and careful internal development, but destined to be thrown almost immediately into relentless and sharp competition with the best of modern workingmen under an economic system where every participant is fighting for himself, and too often utterly regardless of the rights or welfare of his neighbor.

For we must never forget that the economic system of the South to-day which has succeeded the old *régime* is not the same system as that of the old industrial North, of England, or of France, with their trades-unions, their restrictive laws, their written and unwritten commercial customs, and their long experience. It is, rather, a copy of that England of the early nineteenth century, before the factory acts,—the England that wrung pity from thinkers and fired the wrath of Carlyle. The rod of empire that passed from the hands of Southern gentlemen in 1865, partly by force, partly by their own petulance, has never returned to them. Rather it has passed to those men who have come to take charge of the industrial exploitation of the New South,—the sons of poor whites fired with a new thirst for wealth and power, thrifty and avaricious Yankees, shrewd and unscrupulous Jews. Into the hands of these men the Southern laborers, white and black, have fallen; and this to their sorrow. For the laborers as such there is in these new captains of industry neither love nor hate, neither sympathy nor romance; it is a cold question of dollars and dividends. Under such a system all labor is bound to suffer. Even the white laborers are not yet intelligent, thrifty, and well trained enough to maintain themselves against the powerful inroads of organized capital. The results among them, even, are long hours of toil, low wages, child labor, and lack of protection against usury and cheating. But among the black laborers all this is aggravated, first, by a race prejudice which varies from a doubt and distrust among the best element of whites to a frenzied hatred among the worst; and, secondly, it is aggravated, as I have said before, by the wretched economic heritage of the freedmen from slavery. With this training it is difficult for the freedman to learn to grasp the opportunities already opened to him, and the new opportunities are seldom given him, but go by favor to the whites.

Left by the best elements of the South with little protection or oversight, he has been made in law and custom the victim of the worst and most unscrupulous men in each community. The crop-lien system which is depopulating the fields of the South is not simply the result of shiftlessness on the part of Negroes, but is also the result of cunningly devised laws as to mortgages, liens, and misdemeanors, which can be made by conscienceless men to entrap and snare the unwary until escape is impossible, further toil a farce, and protest a crime. I have seen, in the Black Belt of Georgia, an ignorant, honest Negro buy and pay for a farm in installments three separate times, and then in the face of law and decency the enterprising Russian Jew who sold it to him pocketed money and deed and left the black man landless, to labor on his own land at thirty cents a day. I have seen a black farmer fall in debt to a white storekeeper, and that storekeeper go to his farm and strip it of every single marketable article,—mules, ploughs, stored crops, tools, furniture, bedding, clocks, looking-glass,—and all this without a warrant, without process of law, without a sheriff or officer, in the face of the law for homestead exemptions, and without rendering to a single responsible person any account or reckoning. And such proceedings can happen, and will happen, in any community where a class of ignorant toilers are placed by custom and race-prejudice beyond the pale of sympathy and race-brotherhood. So long as the best elements of a community do not feel in duty bound to protect and train and care for the weaker members of their group, they leave them to be preyed upon by these swindlers and rascals.

This unfortunate economic situation does not mean the hindrance of all advance in the black South, or the absence of a class of black landlords and mechanics who, in spite of disadvantages, are accumulating property and making good citizens. But it does mean that this class is not nearly so large as a fairer economic system might easily make it, that those who survive in the competition are handicapped so as to accomplish much less than they deserve to, and that, above all, the *personnel* of the successful class is left to chance and accident, and not to any intelligent culling or reasonable methods of selection. As a remedy for this, there is but one possible procedure. We must accept some of the race prejudice in the South as a fact,—deplorable in its intensity, unfortunate in results, and dangerous for the future, but nevertheless a hard fact which only time can efface. We cannot hope, then, in this generation, or for several generations, that the mass of the whites can be brought to assume that close sympathetic and self-sacrificing leadership of the blacks which their present situation so eloquently demands. Such leadership, such social teaching and example, must come from the blacks themselves. For some time men doubted as to whether the Negro could develop such leaders; but to-day no one seriously disputes the capability of individual Negroes to assimilate the culture and common sense of modern civilization, and to pass it on, to some extent at least, to their fellows. If this is true, then here is the path out of the economic situation, and here is the imperative demand for trained Negro leaders of character and intelligence,—men of skill, men of light and leading, college-bred men, black captains of industry, and missionaries of culture; men who thoroughly comprehend and know modern civilization, and can take hold of Negro communities and raise and train them by force of precept and example, deep sympathy, and the inspiration of common blood and ideals. But if such men are to be effective they must have some power,—they must be backed by the best public opinion of these communities, and able to wield for their objects and aims such weapons as the experience of the world has taught are indispensable to human progress.

Of such weapons the greatest, perhaps, in the modern world is the power of the ballot; and this brings me to a consideration of the third form of contact between whites and blacks in the South,—political activity.

In the attitude of the American mind toward Negro suffrage can be traced with unusual accuracy the prevalent conceptions of government. In the fifties we were near enough the echoes of the French Revolution to believe pretty thoroughly in universal suffrage. We argued, as we thought then rather logically, that no social class was so good, so true, and so disinterested as to be trusted wholly with the political destiny of its neighbors; that in every state the best arbiters of their own welfare are the persons directly affected; consequently that it is only by arming every hand with a ballot,—with the right to have a voice in the policy of the state,—that the greatest good to the greatest number could be attained. To be sure, there were objections to these arguments, but we thought we had answered them tersely and convincingly; if some one complained of the ignorance of voters, we answered, "Educate them." If another complained of their venality, we replied, "Disfranchise them or put them in jail." And, finally, to the men who feared demagogues and the natural perversity of some human beings we insisted that time and bitter experience would teach the most hardheaded. It was at this time that the question of Negro suffrage in the South was raised. Here was a defenceless people suddenly made free. How were they to be protected from those who did not believe in their freedom and were determined to thwart it? Not by force, said the North; not by government guardianship, said the South; then by the ballot, the sole and legitimate defence of a free people, said the Common Sense of the Nation. No one thought, at the time, that the ex-slaves could use the ballot intelligently or very effectively; but they did think that the possession of so great power by a great class in the nation would compel their fellows to educate this class to its intelligent use.

Meantime, new thoughts came to the nation: the inevitable period of moral retrogression and political trickery that ever follows in the wake of war overtook us. So flagrant became the political scandals that reputable men began to leave politics alone, and politics consequently became disreputable. Men began to pride themselves on having nothing to do with their own government, and to agree tacitly with those who regarded public office as a private perquisite. In this state of mind it became easy to wink at the suppression of the Negro vote in the South, and to advise self-respecting Negroes to leave politics entirely alone. The decent and reputable citizens of the North who neglected their own civic duties grew hilarious over the exaggerated importance with which the Negro regarded the franchise. Thus it easily happened that more and more the better class of Negroes followed the advice from abroad and the pressure from home, and took no further interest in politics, leaving to the careless and the venal of their race the exercise of their rights as voters. The black vote that still remained was not trained and educated, but further debauched by open and unblushing bribery, or force and fraud; until the Negro voter was thoroughly inoculated with the idea that politics was a method of private gain by disreputable means.

And finally, now, to-day, when we are awakening to the fact that the perpetuity of republican institutions on this continent depends on the purification of the ballot, the civic training of voters, and the raising of voting to the plane of a solemn duty which a patriotic citizen neglects to his peril and to the peril of his children's children,—in this day, when we are striving for a renaissance of civic virtue, what are we going to say to the black voter of the South? Are we going to tell him still that politics is a disreputable and useless form of human activity? Are we going to induce the best class of Negroes to take less and less interest in government, and to give up their right to take such an interest, without a protest? I am not saying a word against all legitimate efforts to purge the ballot of ignorance, pauperism, and crime. But few have pretended that the present movement for disfranchisement in the South is for such a purpose; it has been plainly and frankly declared in nearly every case that the object of the disfranchising laws is the elimination of the black man from politics.

Now, is this a minor matter which has no influence on the main question of the industrial and intellectual development of the Negro? Can we establish a mass of black laborers and artisans and landholders in the South who, by law and public opinion, have absolutely no voice in shaping the laws under which they live and work? Can the modern organization of industry, assuming as it does free democratic government and the power and ability of the laboring classes to compel respect for their welfare,—can this system be carried out in the South when half its laboring force is voiceless in the public councils and powerless in its own defence? To-day the black man of the South has almost nothing to say as to how much he shall be taxed, or how those taxes shall be expended; as to who shall execute the laws, and how they shall do it; as to who shall make the laws, and how they shall be made. It is pitiable that frantic efforts must be made at critical times to get law-makers in some States even to listen to the respectful presentation of the black man's side of a current controversy. Daily the Negro is coming more and more to look upon law and justice, not as protecting safeguards, but as sources of humiliation and oppression. The laws are made by men who have little interest in him; they are executed by men who have absolutely no motive for treating the black people with courtesy or consideration; and, finally, the accused law-breaker is tried, not by his peers, but too often by men who would rather punish ten innocent Negroes than let one guilty one escape.

I should be the last one to deny the patent weaknesses and shortcomings of the Negro people; I should be the last to withhold sympathy from the white South in its efforts to solve its intricate social problems. I freely acknowledge that it is possible, and sometimes best, that a partially undeveloped people should be ruled by the best of their stronger and better neighbors for their own good, until such time as they can start and fight the world's battles alone. I have already pointed out how sorely in need of such economic and spiritual guidance the emancipated Negro was, and I am quite willing to admit that if the representatives of the best white Southern public opinion were the ruling and guiding powers in the South to-day the conditions indicated would be fairly well fulfilled. But the point I have insisted upon, and now emphasize again, is that the best opinion of the South to-day is not the ruling opinion. That to leave the Negro helpless and without a ballot to-day is to leave him, not to the guidance of the best, but rather to the exploitation and debauchment of the worst; that this is no truer of the South than of the North,—of the North than of Europe: in any land, in any country under modern free competition, to lay any class of weak and despised people, be they white, black, or blue, at the political mercy of their stronger, richer, and more resourceful fellows, is a temptation which human nature seldom has withstood and seldom will withstand.

Moreover, the political status of the Negro in the South is closely connected with the question of Negro crime. There can be no doubt that crime among Negroes has sensibly increased in the last thirty years, and that there has appeared in the slums of great cities a distinct criminal class among the blacks. In explaining this unfortunate development, we must note two things: (1) that the inevitable result of Emancipation was to increase crime and criminals, and (2) that the police system of the South was primarily designed to control slaves. As to the first point, we must not forget that under a strict slave system there can scarcely be such a thing as crime. But when these variously constituted human particles are suddenly thrown broadcast on the sea of life, some swim, some sink, and some hang suspended, to be forced up or down by the chance currents of a busy hurrying world. So great an economic and social revolution as swept the South in '63 meant a weeding out among the Negroes of the incompetents and vicious, the beginning of a differentiation of social grades. Now a rising group of people are not lifted bodily from the ground like an inert solid mass, but rather stretch upward like a living plant with its roots still clinging in the mould. The appearance, therefore, of the Negro criminal was a phenomenon to be awaited; and while it causes anxiety, it should not occasion surprise.

Here again the hope for the future depended peculiarly on careful and delicate dealing with these criminals. Their offences at first were those of laziness, carelessness, and impulse, rather than of malignity or ungoverned viciousness. Such misdemeanors needed discriminating treatment, firm but reformatory, with no hint of injustice, and full proof of guilt. For such dealing with criminals, white or black, the South had no machinery, no adequate jails or reformatories; its police system was arranged to deal with blacks alone, and tacitly assumed that every white man was *ipso facto* a member of that police. Thus grew up a double system of justice, which erred on the white side by undue leniency and the practical immunity of red-handed criminals, and erred on the black side by undue severity, injustice, and lack of discrimination. For, as I have said, the police system of the South was originally designed to keep track of all Negroes, not simply of criminals; and when the Negroes were freed and the whole South was convinced of the impossibility of free Negro labor, the first and almost universal device was to use the courts as a means of reënslaving the blacks. It was not then a question of crime, but rather one of color, that settled a man's conviction on almost any charge. Thus Negroes came to look upon courts as instruments of injustice and oppression, and upon those convicted in them as martyrs and victims.

When, now, the real Negro criminal appeared, and instead of petty stealing and vagrancy we began to have highway robbery, burglary, murder, and rape, there was a curious effect on both sides the color-line: the Negroes refused to believe the evidence of white witnesses or the fairness of white juries, so that the greatest deterrent to crime, the public opinion of one's own social caste, was lost, and the criminal was looked upon as crucified rather than hanged. On the other hand, the whites, used to being careless as to the guilt or innocence of accused Negroes, were swept in moments of passion beyond law, reason, and decency. Such a situation is bound to increase crime, and has increased it. To natural viciousness and vagrancy are being daily added motives of revolt and revenge which stir up all the latent savagery of both races and make peaceful attention to economic development often impossible.

But the chief problem in any community cursed with crime is not the punishment of the criminals, but the preventing of the young from being trained to crime. And here again the peculiar conditions of the South have prevented proper precautions. I have seen twelve-year-old boys working in chains on the public streets of Atlanta, directly in front of the schools, in company with old and hardened criminals; and this indiscriminate mingling of men and women and children makes the chain-gangs perfect schools of crime and debauchery. The struggle for reformatories, which has gone on in Virginia, Georgia, and other States, is the one encouraging sign of the awakening of some communities to the suicidal results of this policy.

It is the public schools, however, which can be made, outside the homes, the greatest means of training decent self-respecting citizens. We have been so hotly engaged recently in discussing trade-schools and the higher education that the pitiable plight of the public-school system in the South has almost dropped from view. Of every five dollars spent for public education in the State of Georgia, the white schools get four dollars and the Negro one dollar; and even then the white public-school system, save in the cities, is bad and cries for reform. If this is true of the whites, what of the blacks? I am becoming more and more convinced, as I look upon the system of common-school training in the South, that the national government must soon step in and aid popular education in some way. To-day it has been only by the most strenuous efforts on the part of the thinking men of the South that the Negro's share of the school fund has not been cut down to a pittance in some half-dozen States; and that movement not only is not dead, but in many communities is gaining strength. What in the name of reason does this nation expect of a people, poorly trained and hard pressed in severe economic competition, without political rights, and with ludicrously inadequate common-school facilities? What can it expect but crime and listlessness, offset here and there by the dogged struggles of the fortunate and more determined who are themselves buoyed by the hope that in due time the country will come to its senses?

I have thus far sought to make clear the physical, economic, and political relations of the Negroes and whites in the South, as I have conceived them, including, for the reasons set forth, crime and education. But after all that has been said on these more tangible matters of human contact, there still remains a part essential to a proper description of the South which it is difficult to describe or fix in terms easily understood by strangers. It is, in fine, the atmosphere of the land, the thought and feeling, the thousand and one little actions which go to make up life. In any community or nation it is these little things which are most elusive to the grasp and yet most essential to any clear conception of the group life taken as a whole. What is thus true of all communities is peculiarly true of the South, where, outside of written history and outside of printed law, there has been going on for a generation as deep a storm and stress of human souls, as intense a ferment of feeling, as intricate a writhing of spirit, as ever a people experienced. Within and without the sombre veil of color vast social forces have been at work,—efforts for human betterment, movements toward disintegration and despair, tragedies and comedies in social and economic life, and a swaying and lifting and sinking of human hearts which have made this land a land of mingled sorrow and joy, of change and excitement and unrest.

The centre of this spiritual turmoil has ever been the millions of black freedmen and their sons, whose destiny is so fatefully bound up with that of the nation. And yet the casual observer visiting the South sees at first little of this. He notes the growing frequency of dark faces as he rides along,—but otherwise the days slip lazily on, the sun shines, and this little world seems as happy and contented as other worlds he has visited. Indeed, on the question of questions—the Negro problem—he hears so little that there almost seems to be a conspiracy of silence; the morning papers seldom mention it, and then usually in a far-fetched academic way, and indeed almost every one seems to forget and ignore the darker half of the land, until the astonished visitor is inclined to ask if after all there *is* any problem here. But if he lingers long enough there comes the awakening: perhaps in a sudden whirl of passion which leaves him gasping at its bitter intensity; more likely in a gradually dawning sense of things he had not at first noticed. Slowly but surely his eyes begin to catch the shadows of the color-line: here he meets crowds of Negroes and whites; then he is suddenly aware that he cannot discover a single dark face; or again at the close of a day's wandering he may find himself in some strange assembly, where all faces are tinged brown or black, and where he has the vague, uncomfortable feeling of the stranger. He realizes at last that silently, resistlessly, the world about flows by him in two great streams: they ripple on in the same sunshine, they approach and mingle their waters in seeming carelessness,—then they divide and flow wide apart. It is done quietly; no mistakes are made, or if one occurs, the swift arm of the law and of public opinion swings down for a moment, as when the other day a black man and a white woman were arrested for talking together on Whitehall Street in Atlanta.

Now if one notices carefully one will see that between these two worlds, despite much physical contact and daily intermingling, there is almost no community of intellectual life or point of transference where the thoughts and feelings of one race can come into direct contact and sympathy with the thoughts and feelings of the other. Before and directly after the war, when all the best of the Negroes were domestic servants in the best of the white families, there were bonds of intimacy, affection, and sometimes blood relationship, between the races. They lived in the same home, shared in the family life, often attended the same church, and talked and conversed with each other. But the increasing civilization of the Negro since then has naturally meant the development of higher classes: there are increasing numbers of ministers, teachers, physicians, merchants, mechanics, and independent farmers, who by nature and training are the aristocracy and leaders of the blacks. Between them, however, and the best element of the whites, there is little or no intellectual commerce. They go to separate churches, they live in separate sections, they are strictly separated in all public gatherings, they travel separately, and they are beginning to read different papers and books. To most libraries, lectures, concerts, and museums, Negroes are either not admitted at all, or on terms peculiarly galling to the pride of the very classes who might otherwise be attracted. The daily paper chronicles the doings of the black world from afar with no great regard for accuracy; and so on, throughout the category of means for intellectual communication,—schools, conferences, efforts for social betterment, and the like,—it is usually true that the very representatives of the two races, who for mutual benefit and the welfare of the land ought to be in complete understanding and sympathy, are so far strangers that one side thinks all whites are narrow and prejudiced, and the other thinks educated Negroes dangerous and insolent. Moreover, in a land where the tyranny of public opinion and the intolerance of criticism is for obvious historical reasons so strong as in the South, such a situation is extremely difficult to correct. The white man, as well as the Negro, is bound and barred by the color-line, and many a scheme of friendliness and philanthropy, of broad-minded sympathy and generous fellowship between the two has dropped still-born because some busybody has forced the color-question to the front and brought the tremendous force of unwritten law against the innovators.

It is hardly necessary for me to add very much in regard to the social contact between the races. Nothing has come to replace that finer sympathy and love between some masters and house servants which the radical and more uncompromising drawing of the color-line in recent years has caused almost completely to disappear. In a world where it means so much to take a man by the hand and sit beside him, to look frankly into his eyes and feel his heart beating with red blood; in a world where a social cigar or a cup of tea together means more than legislative halls and magazine articles and speeches,—one can imagine the consequences of the almost utter absence of such social amenities between estranged races, whose separation extends even to parks and street-cars.

Here there can be none of that social going down to the people,—the opening of heart and hand of the best to the worst, in generous acknowledgment of a common humanity and a common destiny. On the other hand, in matters of simple almsgiving, where there can be no question of social contact, and in the succor of the aged and sick, the South, as if stirred by a feeling of its unfortunate limitations, is generous to a fault. The black beggar is never turned away without a good deal more than a crust, and a call for help for the unfortunate meets quick response. I remember, one cold winter, in Atlanta, when I refrained from contributing to a public relief fund lest Negroes should be discriminated against, I afterward inquired of a friend: "Were any black people receiving aid?" "Why," said he, "they were *all* black."

And yet this does not touch the kernel of the problem. Human advancement is not a mere question of almsgiving, but rather of sympathy and coöperation among classes who would scorn charity. And here is a land where, in the higher walks of life, in all the higher striving for the good and noble and true, the color-line comes to separate natural friends and co-workers; while at the bottom of the social group, in the saloon, the gambling-hell, and the brothel, that same line wavers and disappears.

I have sought to paint an average picture of real relations between the sons of master and man in the South. I have not glossed over matters for policy's sake, for I fear we have already gone too far in that sort of thing. On the other hand, I have sincerely sought to let no unfair exaggerations creep in. I do not doubt that in some Southern communities conditions are better than those I have indicated; while I am no less certain that in other communities they are far worse.

Nor does the paradox and danger of this situation fail to interest and perplex the best conscience of the South. Deeply religious and intensely democratic as are the mass of the whites, they feel acutely the false position in which the Negro problems place them. Such an essentially honest-hearted and generous people cannot cite the caste-levelling precepts of Christianity, or believe in equality of opportunity for all men, without coming to feel more and more with each generation that the present drawing of the color-line is a flat contradiction to their beliefs and professions. But just as often as they come to this point, the present social condition of the Negro stands as a menace and a portent before even the most open-minded: if there were nothing to charge against the Negro but his blackness or other physical peculiarities, they argue, the problem would be comparatively simple; but what can we say to his ignorance, shiftlessness, poverty, and crime? can a self-respecting group hold anything but the least possible fellowship with such persons and survive? and shall we let a mawkish sentiment sweep away the culture of our fathers or the hope of our children? The argument so put is of great strength, but it is not a whit stronger than the argument of thinking Negroes: granted, they reply, that the condition of our masses is bad; there is certainly on the one hand adequate historical cause for this, and unmistakable evidence that no small number have, in spite of tremendous disadvantages, risen to the level of American civilization. And when, by proscription and prejudice, these same Negroes are classed with and treated like the lowest of their people, simply *because* they are Negroes, such a policy not only discourages thrift and intelligence among black men, but puts a direct premium on the very things you complain of,—inefficiency and crime. Draw lines of crime, of incompetency, of vice, as tightly and uncompromisingly as you will, for these things must be proscribed; but a color-line not only does not accomplish this purpose, but thwarts it.

In the face of two such arguments, the future of the South depends on the ability of the representatives of these opposing views to see and appreciate and sympathize with each other's position,—for the Negro to realize more deeply than he does at present the need of uplifting the masses of his people, for the white people to realize more vividly than they have yet done the deadening and disastrous effect of a color-prejudice that classes Phillis Wheatley and Sam Hose in the same despised class.

It is not enough for the Negroes to declare that color-prejudice is the sole cause of their social condition, nor for the white South to reply that their social condition is the main cause of prejudice. They both act as reciprocal cause and effect, and a change in neither alone will bring the desired effect. Both must change, or neither can improve to any great extent. The Negro cannot stand the present reactionary tendencies and unreasoning drawing of the color-line indefinitely without discouragement and retrogression. And the condition of the Negro is ever the excuse for further discrimination. Only by a union of intelligence and sympathy across the color-line in this critical period of the Republic shall justice and right triumph,—

> "That mind and soul according well,
> May make one music as before,
> But vaster."

X

Of the Faith of the Fathers

Dim face of Beauty haunting all the world,
  Fair face of Beauty all too fair to see,
Where the lost stars adown the heavens are hurled,—
    There, there alone for thee
    May white peace be.

. . . .

Beauty, sad face of Beauty, Mystery, Wonder,
  What are these dreams to foolish babbling men
Who cry with little noises 'neath the thunder
    Of Ages ground to sand,
    To a little sand.

FIONA MACLEOD.

IT WAS out in the country, far from home, far from my foster home, on a dark Sunday night. The road wandered from our rambling log-house up the stony bed of a creek, past wheat and corn, until we could hear dimly across the fields a rhythmic cadence of song,—soft, thrilling, powerful, that swelled and died sorrowfully in our ears. I was a country school-teacher then, fresh from the East, and had never seen a Southern Negro revival. To be sure, we in Berkshire were not perhaps as stiff and formal as they in Suffolk of olden time; yet we were very quiet and subdued, and I know not what would have happened those clear Sabbath mornings had some one punctuated the sermon with a wild scream, or interrupted the long prayer with a loud Amen! And so most striking to me, as I approached the village and the little plain church perched aloft, was the air of intense excitement that possessed that mass of black folk. A sort of suppressed terror hung in the air and seemed to seize us,—a pythian madness, a demoniac possession, that lent terrible reality to song and word. The black and massive form of the preacher swayed and quivered as the words crowded to his lips and flew at us in singular eloquence. The people moaned and fluttered, and then the gaunt-cheeked brown woman beside me suddenly leaped straight into the air and shrieked like a lost soul, while round about came wail and groan and outcry, and a scene of human passion such as I had never conceived before.

Those who have not thus witnessed the frenzy of a Negro revival in the untouched backwoods of the South can but dimly realize the religious feeling of the slave; as described, such scenes appear grotesque and funny, but as seen they are awful. Three things characterized this religion of the slave,—the Preacher, the Music, and the Frenzy. The Preacher is the most unique personality developed by the Negro on American soil. A leader, a politician, an orator, a "boss," an intriguer, an idealist,—all these he is, and ever, too, the centre of a group of men, now twenty, now a thousand in number. The combination of a certain adroitness with deep-seated earnestness, of tact with consummate ability, gave him his preëminence, and helps him maintain it. The type, of course, varies according to time and place, from the West Indies in the sixteenth century to New England in the nineteenth, and from the Mississippi bottoms to cities like New Orleans or New York.

The Music of Negro religion is that plaintive rhythmic melody, with its touching minor cadences, which, despite caricature and defilement, still remains the most original and beautiful expression of human life and longing yet born on American soil. Sprung from the African forests, where its counterpart can still be heard, it was adapted, changed, and intensified by the tragic soul-life of the slave, until, under the stress of law and whip, it became the one true expression of a people's sorrow, despair, and hope.

Finally the Frenzy or "Shouting," when the Spirit of the Lord passed by, and, seizing the devotee, made him mad with supernatural joy, was the last essential of Negro religion and the one more devoutly believed in than all the rest. It varied in expression from the silent rapt countenance or the low murmur and moan to the mad abandon of physical fervor,—the stamping, shrieking, and shouting, the rushing to and fro and wild waving of arms, the weeping and laughing, the vision and the trance. All this is nothing new in the world, but old as religion, as Delphi and Endor. And so firm a hold did it have on the Negro, that many generations firmly believed that without this visible manifestation of the God there could be no true communion with the Invisible.

These were the characteristics of Negro religious life as developed up to the time of Emancipation. Since under the peculiar circumstances of the black man's environment they were the one expression of his higher life, they are of deep interest to the student of his development, both socially and psychologically. Numerous are the attractive lines of inquiry that here group themselves. What did slavery mean to the African savage? What was his attitude toward the World and Life? What seemed to him good and evil,—God and Devil? Whither went his longings and strivings, and wherefore were his heart-burnings and disappointments? Answers to such questions can come only from a study of Negro religion as a development, through its gradual changes from the heathenism of the Gold Coast to the institutional Negro church of Chicago.

Moreover, the religious growth of millions of men, even though they be slaves, cannot be without potent influence upon their contemporaries. The Methodists and Baptists of America owe much of their condition to the silent but potent influence of their millions of Negro converts. Especially is this noticeable in the South, where theology and religious philosophy are on this account a long way behind the North, and where the religion of the poor whites is a plain copy of Negro thought and methods. The mass of "gospel" hymns which has swept through American churches and well-nigh ruined our sense of song consists largely of debased imitations of Negro melodies made by ears that caught the jingle but not the music, the body but not the soul, of the Jubilee songs. It is thus clear that the study of Negro religion is not only a vital part of the history of the Negro in America, but no uninteresting part of American history.

The Negro church of to-day is the social centre of Negro life in the United States, and the most characteristic expression of African character. Take a typical church in a small Virginian town: it is the "First Baptist"—a roomy brick edifice seating five hundred or more persons, tastefully finished in Georgia pine, with a carpet, a small organ, and stained-glass windows. Underneath is a large assembly room with benches. This building is the central club-house of a community of a thousand or more Negroes. Various organizations meet here,—the church proper, the Sunday-school, two or three insurance societies, women's societies, secret societies, and mass meetings of various kinds. Entertainments, suppers, and lectures are held beside the five or six regular weekly religious services. Considerable sums of money are collected and expended here, employment is found for the idle, strangers are introduced, news is disseminated and charity distributed. At the same time this social, intellectual, and economic centre is a religious centre of great power. Depravity, Sin, Redemption, Heaven, Hell, and Damnation are preached twice a Sunday with much fervor, and revivals take place every year after the crops are laid by; and few indeed of the community have the hardihood to withstand conversion. Back of this more formal religion, the Church often stands as a real conserver of morals, a strengthener of family life, and the final authority on what is Good and Right.

Thus one can see in the Negro church to-day, reproduced in microcosm, all that great world from which the Negro is cut off by color-prejudice and social condition. In the great city churches the same tendency is noticeable and in many respects emphasized. A great church like the Bethel of Philadelphia has over eleven hundred members, an edifice seating fifteen hundred persons and valued at one hundred thousand dollars, an annual budget of five thousand dollars, and a government consisting of a pastor with several assisting local preachers, an executive and legislative board, financial boards and tax collectors; general church meetings for making laws; subdivided groups led by class leaders, a company of militia, and twenty-four auxiliary societies. The activity of a church like this is immense and far-reaching, and the bishops who preside over these organizations throughout the land are among the most powerful Negro rulers in the world.

Such churches are really governments of men, and consequently a little investigation reveals the curious fact that, in the South, at least, practically every American Negro is a church member. Some, to be sure, are not regularly enrolled, and a few do not habitually attend services; but, practically, a proscribed people must have a social centre, and that centre for this people is the Negro church. The census of 1890 showed nearly twenty-four thousand Negro churches in the country, with a total enrolled membership of over two and a half millions, or ten actual church members to every twenty-eight persons, and in some Southern States one in every two persons. Besides these there is the large number who, while not enrolled as members, attend and take part in many of the activities of the church. There is an organized Negro church for every sixty black families in the nation, and in some States for every forty families, owning, on an average, a thousand dollars' worth of property each, or nearly twenty-six million dollars in all.

Such, then, is the large development of the Negro church since Emancipation. The question now is, What have been the successive steps of this social history and what are the present tendencies? First, we must realize that no such institution as the Negro church could rear itself without definite historical foundations. These foundations we can find if we remember that the social history of the Negro did not start in America. He was brought from a definite social environment,—the polygamous clan life under the headship of the chief and the potent influence of the priest. His religion was nature-worship, with profound belief in invisible surrounding influences, good and bad, and his worship was through incantation and sacrifice. The first rude change in this life was the slave ship and the West Indian sugar-fields. The plantation organization replaced the clan and tribe, and the white master replaced the chief with far greater and more despotic powers. Forced and long-continued toil became the rule of life, the old ties of blood relationship and kinship disappeared, and instead of the family appeared a new polygamy and polyandry, which, in some cases, almost reached promiscuity. It was a terrific social revolution, and yet some traces were retained of the former group life, and the chief remaining institution was the Priest or Medicine-man. He early appeared on the plantation and found his function as the healer of the sick, the interpreter of the Unknown, the comforter of the sorrowing, the supernatural avenger of wrong, and the one who rudely but picturesquely expressed the longing, disappointment, and resentment of a stolen and oppressed people. Thus, as bard, physician, judge, and priest, within the narrow limits allowed by the slave system, rose the Negro preacher, and under him the first Afro-American institution, the Negro church. This church was not at first by any means Christian nor definitely organized; rather it was an adaptation and mingling of heathen rites among the members of each plantation, and roughly designated as Voodooism. Association with the masters, missionary effort and motives of expediency gave these rites an early veneer of Christianity, and after the lapse of many generations the Negro church became Christian.

Two characteristic things must be noticed in regard to this church. First, it became almost entirely Baptist and Methodist in faith; secondly, as a social institution it antedated by many decades the monogamic Negro home. From the very circumstances of its beginning, the church was confined to the plantation, and consisted primarily of a series of disconnected units; although, later on, some freedom of movement was allowed, still this geographical limitation was always important and was one cause of the spread of the decentralized and democratic Baptist faith among the slaves. At the same time, the visible rite of baptism appealed strongly to their mystic temperament. To-day the Baptist Church is still largest in membership among Negroes, and has a million and a half communicants. Next in popularity came the churches organized in connection with the white neighboring churches, chiefly Baptist and Methodist, with a few Episcopalian and others. The Methodists still form the second greatest denomination, with nearly a million members. The faith of these two leading denominations was more suited to the slave church from the prominence they gave to religious feeling and fervor. The Negro membership in other denominations has always been small and relatively unimportant, although the Episcopalians and Presbyterians are gaining among the more intelligent classes to-day, and the Catholic Church is making headway in certain sections. After Emancipation, and still earlier in the North, the Negro churches largely severed such affiliations as they had had with the white churches, either by choice or by compulsion. The Baptist churches became independent, but the Methodists were compelled early to unite for purposes of episcopal government. This gave rise to the great African Methodist Church, the greatest Negro organization in the world, to the Zion Church and the Colored Methodist, and to the black conferences and churches in this and other denominations.

The second fact noted, namely, that the Negro church antedates the Negro home, leads to an explanation of much that is paradoxical in this communistic institution and in the morals of its members. But especially it leads us to regard this institution as peculiarly the expression of the inner ethical life of a people in a sense seldom true elsewhere. Let us turn, then, from the outer physical development of the church to the more important inner ethical life of the people who compose it. The Negro has already been pointed out many times as a religious animal,—a being of that deep emotional nature which turns instinctively toward the supernatural. Endowed with a rich tropical imagination and a keen, delicate appreciation of Nature, the transplanted African lived in a world animate with gods and devils, elves and witches; full of strange influences,—of Good to be implored, of Evil to be propitiated. Slavery, then, was to him the dark triumph of Evil over him. All the hateful powers of the Under-world were striving against him, and a spirit of revolt and revenge filled his heart. He called up all the resources of heathenism to aid,—exorcism and witchcraft, the mysterious Obi worship with its barbarous rites, spells, and blood-sacrifice even, now and then, of human victims. Weird midnight orgies and mystic conjurations were invoked, the witch-woman and the voodoo-priest became the centre of Negro group life, and that vein of vague superstition which characterizes the unlettered Negro even to-day was deepened and strengthened.

In spite, however, of such success as that of the fierce Maroons, the Danish blacks, and others, the spirit of revolt gradually died away under the untiring energy and superior strength of the slave masters. By the middle of the eighteenth century the black slave had sunk, with hushed murmurs, to his place at the bottom of a new economic system, and was unconsciously ripe for a new philosophy of life. Nothing suited his condition then better than the doctrines of passive submission embodied in the newly learned Christianity. Slave masters early realized this, and cheerfully aided religious propaganda within certain bounds. The long system of repression and degradation of the Negro tended to emphasize the elements in his character which made him a valuable chattel: courtesy became humility, moral strength degenerated into submission, and the exquisite native appreciation of the beautiful became an infinite capacity for dumb suffering. The Negro, losing the joy of this world, eagerly seized upon the offered conceptions of the next; the avenging Spirit of the Lord enjoining patience in this world, under sorrow and tribulation until the Great Day when He should lead His dark children home,—this became his comforting dream. His preacher repeated the prophecy, and his bards sang,—

"Children, we all shall be free
When the Lord shall appear!"

This deep religious fatalism, painted so beautifully in "Uncle Tom," came soon to breed, as all fatalistic faiths will, the sensualist side by side with the martyr. Under the lax moral life of the plantation, where marriage was a farce, laziness a virtue, and property a theft, a religion of resignation and submission degenerated easily, in less strenuous minds, into a philosophy of indulgence and crime. Many of the worst characteristics of the Negro masses of to-day had their seed in this period of the slave's ethical growth. Here it was that the Home was ruined under the very shadow of the Church, white and black; here habits of shiftlessness took root, and sullen hopelessness replaced hopeful strife.

With the beginning of the abolition movement and the gradual growth of a class of free Negroes came a change. We often neglect the influence of the freedman before the war, because of the paucity of his numbers and the small weight he had in the history of the nation. But we must not forget that his chief influence was internal,—was exerted on the black world; and that there he was the ethical and social leader. Huddled as he was in a few centres like Philadelphia, New York, and New Orleans, the masses of the freedmen sank into poverty and listlessness; but not all of them. The free Negro leader early arose and his chief characteristic was intense earnestness and deep feeling on the slavery question.

Freedom became to him a real thing and not a dream. His religion became darker and more intense, and into his ethics crept a note of revenge, into his songs a day of reckoning close at hand. The "Coming of the Lord" swept this side of Death, and came to be a thing to be hoped for in this day. Through fugitive slaves and irrepressible discussion this desire for freedom seized the black millions still in bondage, and became their one ideal of life. The black bards caught new notes, and sometimes even dared to sing,—

> "O Freedom, O Freedom, O Freedom over me!
> Before I 'll be a slave
> I 'll be buried in my grave,
> And go home to my Lord
> And be free."

For fifty years Negro religion thus transformed itself and identified itself with the dream of Abolition, until that which was a radical fad in the white North and an anarchistic plot in the white South had become a religion to the black world. Thus, when Emancipation finally came, it seemed to the freedman a literal Coming of the Lord. His fervid imagination was stirred as never before, by the tramp of armies, the blood and dust of battle, and the wail and whirl of social upheaval. He stood dumb and motionless before the whirlwind: what had he to do with it? Was it not the Lord's doing, and marvellous in his eyes? Joyed and bewildered with what came, he stood awaiting new wonders till the inevitable Age of Reaction swept over the nation and brought the crisis of to-day.

It is difficult to explain clearly the present critical stage of Negro religion. First, we must remember that living as the blacks do in close contact with a great modern nation, and sharing, although imperfectly, the soul-life of that nation, they must necessarily be affected more or less directly by all the religious and ethical forces that are to-day moving the United States. These questions and movements are, however, overshadowed and dwarfed by the (to them) all-important question of their civil, political, and economic status. They must perpetually discuss the "Negro Problem,"—must live, move, and have their being in it, and interpret all else in its light or darkness. With this come, too, peculiar problems of their inner life,—of the status of women, the maintenance of Home, the training of children, the accumulation of wealth, and the prevention of crime. All this must mean a time of intense ethical ferment, of religious heart-searching and intellectual unrest. From the double life every American Negro must live, as a Negro and as an American, as swept on by the current of the nineteenth while yet struggling in the eddies of the fifteenth century,—from this must arise a painful self-consciousness, an almost morbid sense of personality and a moral hesitancy which is fatal to self-confidence. The worlds within and without the Veil of Color are changing, and changing rapidly, but not at the same rate, not in the same way; and this must produce a peculiar wrenching of the soul, a peculiar sense of doubt and bewilderment. Such a double life, with double thoughts, double duties, and double social classes, must give rise to double words and double ideals, and tempt the mind to pretence or to revolt, to hypocrisy or to radicalism.

In some such doubtful words and phrases can one perhaps most clearly picture the peculiar ethical paradox that faces the Negro of to-day and is tingeing and changing his religious life. Feeling that his rights and his dearest ideals are being trampled upon, that the public conscience is ever more deaf to his righteous appeal, and that all the reactionary forces of prejudice, greed, and revenge are daily gaining new strength and fresh allies, the Negro faces no enviable dilemma. Conscious of his impotence, and pessimistic, he often becomes bitter and vindictive; and his religion, instead of a worship, is a complaint and a curse, a wail rather than a hope, a sneer rather than a faith. On the other hand, another type of mind, shrewder and keener and more tortuous too, sees in the very strength of the anti-Negro movement its patent weaknesses, and with Jesuitic casuistry is deterred by no ethical considerations in the endeavor to turn this weakness to the black man's strength. Thus we have two great and hardly reconcilable streams of thought and ethical strivings; the danger of the one lies in anarchy, that of the other in hypocrisy. The one type of Negro stands almost ready to curse God and die, and the other is too often found a traitor to right and a coward before force; the one is wedded to ideals remote, whimsical, perhaps impossible of realization; the other forgets that life is more than meat and the body more than raiment. But, after all, is not this simply the writhing of the age translated into black,—the triumph of the Lie which to-day, with its false culture, faces the hideousness of the anarchist assassin?

To-day the two groups of Negroes, the one in the North, the other in the South, represent these divergent ethical tendencies, the first tending toward radicalism, the other toward hypocritical compromise. It is no idle regret with which the white South mourns the loss of the old-time Negro,—the frank, honest, simple old servant who stood for the earlier religious age of submission and humility. With all his laziness and lack of many elements of true manhood, he was at least open-hearted, faithful, and sincere. To-day he is gone, but who is to blame for his going? Is it not those very persons who mourn for him? Is it not the tendency, born of Reconstruction and Reaction, to found a society on lawlessness and deception, to tamper with the moral fibre of a naturally honest and straightforward people until the whites threaten to become ungovernable tyrants and the blacks criminals and hypocrites? Deception is the natural defence of the weak against the strong, and the South used it for many years against its conquerors; to-day it must be prepared to see its black proletariat turn that same two-edged weapon against itself. And how natural this is! The death of Denmark Vesey and Nat Turner proved long since to the Negro the present hopelessness of physical defence. Political defence is becoming less and less available, and economic defence is still only partially effective. But there is a patent defence at hand,—the defence of deception and flattery, of cajoling and lying. It is the same defence which the Jews of the Middle Age used and which left its stamp on their character for centuries. To-day the young Negro of the South who would succeed cannot be frank and outspoken, honest and self-assertive, but rather he is daily tempted to be silent and wary, politic and sly; he must flatter and be pleasant, endure petty insults with a smile, shut his eyes to wrong; in too many cases he sees positive personal advantage in deception and lying. His real thoughts, his real aspirations, must be guarded in whispers; he must not criticise, he must not complain. Patience, humility, and adroitness must, in these growing black youth, replace impulse, manliness, and courage. With this sacrifice there is an economic opening, and perhaps peace and some prosperity. Without this there is riot, migration, or crime. Nor is this situation peculiar to the Southern United States,—is it not rather the only method by which undeveloped races have gained the right to share modern culture? The price of culture is a Lie.

On the other hand, in the North the tendency is to emphasize the radicalism of the Negro. Driven from his birthright in the South by a situation at which every fibre of his more outspoken and assertive nature revolts, he finds himself in a land where he can scarcely earn a decent living amid the harsh competition and the color discrimination. At the same time, through schools and periodicals, discussions and lectures, he is intellectually quickened and awakened. The soul, long pent up and dwarfed, suddenly expands in new-found freedom. What wonder that every tendency is to excess,—radical complaint, radical remedies, bitter denunciation or angry silence. Some sink, some rise. The criminal and the sensualist leave the church for the gambling-hell and the brothel, and fill the slums of Chicago and Baltimore; the better classes segregate themselves from the group-life of both white and black, and form an aristocracy, cultured but pessimistic, whose bitter criticism stings while it points out no way of escape. They despise the submission and subserviency of the Southern Negroes, but offer no other means by which a poor and oppressed minority can exist side by side with its masters. Feeling deeply and keenly the tendencies and opportunities of the age in which they live, their souls are bitter at the fate which drops the Veil between; and the very fact that this bitterness is natural and justifiable only serves to intensify it and make it more maddening.

Between the two extreme types of ethical attitude which I have thus sought to make clear wavers the mass of the millions of Negroes, North and South; and their religious life and activity partake of this social conflict within their ranks. Their churches are differentiating,—now into groups of cold, fashionable devotees, in no way distinguishable from similar white groups save in color of skin; now into large social and business institutions catering to the desire for information and amusement of their members, warily avoiding unpleasant questions both within and without the black world, and preaching in effect if not in word: *Dum vivimus, vivamus.*

But back of this still broods silently the deep religious feeling of the real Negro heart, the stirring, unguided might of powerful human souls who have lost the guiding star of the past and are seeking in the great night a new religious ideal. Some day the Awakening will come, when the pent-up vigor of ten million souls shall sweep irresistibly toward the Goal, out of the Valley of the Shadow of Death, where all that makes life worth living—Liberty, Justice, and Right—is marked "For White People Only."

XI

Of the Passing of the First-Born

O sister, sister, thy first-begotten,
The hands that cling and the feet that follow,
The voice of the child's blood crying yet,
Who hath remembered me? who hath forgotten?
Thou hast forgotten, O summer swallow,
But the world shall end when I forget.

SWINBURNE.

UNTO you a child is born," sang the bit of yellow paper that fluttered into my room one brown October morning. Then the fear of fatherhood mingled wildly with the joy of creation; I wondered how it looked and how it felt,—what were its eyes, and how its hair curled and crumpled itself. And I thought in awe of her,—she who had slept with Death to tear a man-child from underneath her heart, while I was unconsciously wandering. I fled to my wife and child, repeating the while to myself half wonderingly, "Wife and child? Wife and child?"—fled fast and faster than boat and steam-car, and yet must ever impatiently await them; away from the hard-voiced city, away from the flickering sea into my own Berkshire Hills that sit all sadly guarding the gates of Massachusetts.

Up the stairs I ran to the wan mother and whimpering babe, to the sanctuary on whose altar a life at my bidding had offered itself to win a life, and won. What is this tiny formless thing, this new-born wail from an unknown world,—all head and voice? I handle it curiously, and watch perplexed its winking, breathing, and sneezing. I did not love it then; it seemed a ludicrous thing to love; but her I loved, my girl-mother, she whom now I saw unfolding like the glory of the morning—the transfigured woman.

Through her I came to love the wee thing, as it grew and waxed strong; as its little soul unfolded itself in twitter and cry and half-formed word, and as its eyes caught the gleam and flash of life. How beautiful he was, with his olive-tinted flesh and dark gold ringlets, his eyes of mingled blue and brown, his perfect little limbs, and the soft voluptuous roll which the blood of Africa had moulded into his features! I held him in my arms, after we had sped far away to our Southern home,—held him, and glanced at the hot red soil of Georgia and the breathless city of a hundred hills, and felt a vague unrest. Why was his hair tinted with gold? An evil omen was golden hair in my life. Why had not the brown of his eyes crushed out and killed the blue?—for brown were his father's eyes, and his father's father's. And thus in the Land of the Color-line I saw, as it fell across my baby, the shadow of the Veil.

Within the Veil was he born, said I; and there within shall he live,—a Negro and a Negro's son. Holding in that little head—ah, bitterly!—the unbowed pride of a hunted race, clinging with that tiny dimpled hand—ah, wearily!—to a hope not hopeless but unhopeful, and seeing with those bright wondering eyes that peer into my soul a land whose freedom is to us a mockery and whose liberty a lie. I saw the shadow of the Veil as it passed over my baby, I saw the cold city towering above the blood-red land. I held my face beside his little cheek, showed him the star-children and the twinkling lights as they began to flash, and stilled with an evensong the unvoiced terror of my life.

So sturdy and masterful he grew, so filled with bubbling life, so tremulous with the unspoken wisdom of a life but eighteen months distant from the All-life,—we were not far from worshipping this revelation of the divine, my wife and I. Her own life builded and moulded itself upon the child; he tinged her every dream and idealized her every effort. No hands but hers must touch and garnish those little limbs; no dress or frill must touch them that had not wearied her fingers; no voice but hers could coax him off to Dreamland, and she and he together spoke some soft and unknown tongue and in it held communion. I too mused above his little white bed; saw the strength of my own arm stretched onward through the ages through the newer strength of his; saw the dream of my black fathers stagger a step onward in the wild phantasm of the world; heard in his baby voice the voice of the Prophet that was to rise within the Veil.

And so we dreamed and loved and planned by fall and winter, and the full flush of the long Southern spring, till the hot winds rolled from the fetid Gulf, till the roses shivered and the still stern sun quivered its awful light over the hills of Atlanta. And then one night the little feet pattered wearily to the wee white bed, and the tiny hands trembled; and a warm flushed face tossed on the pillow, and we knew baby was sick. Ten days he lay there,—a swift week and three endless days, wasting, wasting away. Cheerily the mother nursed him the first days, and laughed into the little eyes that smiled again. Tenderly then she hovered round him, till the smile fled away and Fear crouched beside the little bed.

Then the day ended not, and night was a dreamless terror, and joy and sleep slipped away. I hear now that Voice at midnight calling me from dull and dreamless trance,—crying, "The Shadow of Death! The Shadow of Death!" Out into the starlight I crept, to rouse the gray physician,—the Shadow of Death, the Shadow of Death. The hours trembled on; the night listened; the ghastly dawn glided like a tired thing across the lamplight. Then we two alone looked upon the child as he turned toward us with great eyes, and stretched his string-like hands,—the Shadow of Death! And we spoke no word, and turned away.

He died at eventide, when the sun lay like a brooding sorrow above the western hills, veiling its face; when the winds spoke not, and the trees, the great green trees he loved, stood motionless. I saw his breath beat quicker and quicker, pause, and then his little soul leapt like a star that travels in the night and left a world of darkness in its train. The day changed not; the same tall trees peeped in at the windows, the same green grass glinted in the setting sun. Only in the chamber of death writhed the world's most piteous thing—a childless mother.

I shirk not. I long for work. I pant for a life full of striving. I am no coward, to shrink before the rugged rush of the storm, nor even quail before the awful shadow of the Veil.

But hearken, O Death! Is not this my life hard enough,—is not that dull land that stretches its sneering web about me cold enough,—is not all the world beyond these four little walls pitiless enough, but that thou must needs enter here,—thou, O Death? About my head the thundering storm beat like a heartless voice, and the crazy forest pulsed with the curses of the weak; but what cared I, within my home beside my wife and baby boy? Wast thou so jealous of one little coign of happiness that thou must needs enter there,—thou, O Death?

A perfect life was his, all joy and love, with tears to make it brighter,—sweet as a summer's day beside the Housatonic. The world loved him; the women kissed his curls, the men looked gravely into his wonderful eyes, and the children hovered and fluttered about him. I can see him now, changing like the sky from sparkling laughter to darkening frowns, and then to wondering thoughtfulness as he watched the world. He knew no color-line, poor dear,—and the Veil, though it shadowed him, had not yet darkened half his sun. He loved the white matron, he loved his black nurse; and in his little world walked souls alone, uncolored and unclothed. I—yea, all men—are larger and purer by the infinite breadth of that one little life. She who in simple clearness of vision sees beyond the stars said when he had flown, "He will be happy There; he ever loved beautiful things." And I, far more ignorant, and blind by the web of mine own weaving, sit alone winding words and muttering, "If still he be, and he be There, and there be a There, let him be happy, O Fate!"

Blithe was the morning of his burial, with bird and song and sweet-smelling flowers. The trees whispered to the grass, but the children sat with hushed faces. And yet it seemed a ghostly unreal day,—the wraith of Life. We seemed to rumble down an unknown street behind a little white bundle of posies, with the shadow of a song in our ears. The busy city dinned about us; they did not say much, those pale-faced hurrying men and women; they did not say much,—they only glanced and said, "Niggers!"

We could not lay him in the ground there in Georgia, for the earth there is strangely red; so we bore him away to the northward, with his flowers and his little folded hands. In vain, in vain!—for where, O God! beneath thy broad blue sky shall my dark baby rest in peace,—where Reverence dwells, and Goodness, and a Freedom that is free?

All that day and all that night there sat an awful gladness in my heart,—nay, blame me not if I see the world thus darkly through the Veil,—and my soul whispers ever to me, saying, "Not dead, not dead, but escaped; not bond, but free." No bitter meanness now shall sicken his baby heart till it die a living death, no taunt shall madden his happy boyhood. Fool that I was to think or wish that this little soul should grow choked and deformed within the Veil! I might have known that yonder deep unworldly look that ever and anon floated past his eyes was peering far beyond this narrow Now. In the poise of his little curl-crowned head did there not sit all that wild pride of being which his father had hardly crushed in his own heart? For what, forsooth, shall a Negro want with pride amid the studied humiliations of fifty million fellows? Well sped, my boy, before the world had dubbed your ambition insolence, had held your ideals unattainable, and taught you to cringe and bow. Better far this nameless void that stops my life than a sea of sorrow for you.

Idle words; he might have borne his burden more bravely than we,—aye, and found it lighter too, some day; for surely, surely this is not the end. Surely there shall yet dawn some mighty morning to lift the Veil and set the prisoned free. Not for me,—I shall die in my bonds,—but for fresh young souls who have not known the night and waken to the morning; a morning when men ask of the workman, not "Is he white?" but "Can he work?" When men ask artists, not "Are they black?" but "Do they know?" Some morning this may be, long, long years to come. But now there wails, on that dark shore within the Veil, the same deep voice, *Thou shalt forego!* And all have I foregone at that command, and with small complaint,—all save that fair young form that lies so coldly wed with death in the nest I had builded.

If one must have gone, why not I? Why may I not rest me from this restlessness and sleep from this wide waking? Was not the world's alembic, Time, in his young hands, and is not my time waning? Are there so many workers in the vineyard that the fair promise of this little body could lightly be tossed away? The wretched of my race that line the alleys of the nation sit fatherless and unmothered; but Love sat beside his cradle, and in his ear Wisdom waited to speak. Perhaps now he knows the All-love, and needs not to be wise. Sleep, then, child,—sleep till I sleep and waken to a baby voice and the ceaseless patter of little feet—above the Veil.

XII

Of Alexander Crummell

Then from the Dawn it seemed there came, but faint
As from beyond the limit of the world,
Like the last echo born of a great cry,
Sounds, as if some fair city were one voice
Around a king returning from his wars.

TENNYSON.

THIS is the history of a human heart,—the tale of a black boy who many long years ago began to struggle with life that he might know the world and know himself. Three temptations he met on those dark dunes that lay gray and dismal before the wonder-eyes of the child: the temptation of Hate, that stood out against the red dawn; the temptation of Despair, that darkened noonday; and the temptation of Doubt, that ever steals along with twilight. Above all, you must hear of the vales he crossed,—the Valley of Humiliation and the Valley of the Shadow of Death.

I saw Alexander Crummell first at a Wilberforce commencement season, amid its bustle and crush. Tall, frail, and black he stood, with simple dignity and an unmistakable air of good breeding. I talked with him apart, where the storming of the lusty young orators could not harm us. I spoke to him politely, then curiously, then eagerly, as I began to feel the fineness of his character,—his calm courtesy, the sweetness of his strength, and his fair blending of the hope and truth of life. Instinctively I bowed before this man, as one bows before the prophets of the world. Some seer he seemed, that came not from the crimson Past or the gray To-come, but from the pulsing Now,—that mocking world which seemed to me at once so light and dark, so splendid and sordid. Four-score years had he wandered in this same world of mine, within the Veil.

He was born with the Missouri Compromise and lay a-dying amid the echoes of Manila and El Caney: stirring times for living, times dark to look back upon, darker to look forward to. The black-faced lad that paused over his mud and marbles seventy years ago saw puzzling vistas as he looked down the world. The slave-ship still groaned across the Atlantic, faint cries burdened the Southern breeze, and the great black father whispered mad tales of cruelty into those young ears. From the low doorway the mother silently watched her boy at play, and at nightfall sought him eagerly lest the shadows bear him away to the land of slaves.

So his young mind worked and winced and shaped curiously a vision of Life; and in the midst of that vision ever stood one dark figure alone,—ever with the hard, thick countenance of that bitter father, and a form that fell in vast and shapeless folds. Thus the temptation of Hate grew and shadowed the growing child,—gliding stealthily into his laughter, fading into his play, and seizing his dreams by day and night with rough, rude turbulence. So the black boy asked of sky and sun and flower the never-answered Why? and loved, as he grew, neither the world nor the world's rough ways.

Strange temptation for a child, you may think; and yet in this wide land to-day a thousand thousand dark children brood before this same temptation, and feel its cold and shuddering arms. For them, perhaps, some one will some day lift the Veil,—will come tenderly and cheerily into those sad little lives and brush the brooding hate away, just as Beriah Green strode in upon the life of Alexander Crummell. And before the bluff, kind-hearted man the shadow seemed less dark. Beriah Green had a school in Oneida County, New York, with a score of mischievous boys. "I'm going to bring a black boy here to educate," said Beriah Green, as only a crank and an abolitionist would have dared to say. "Oho!" laughed the boys. "Ye-es," said his wife; and Alexander came. Once before, the black boy had sought a school, had travelled, cold and hungry, four hundred miles up into free New Hampshire, to Canaan. But the godly farmers hitched ninety yoke of oxen to the abolition schoolhouse and dragged it into the middle of the swamp. The black boy trudged away.

The nineteenth was the first century of human sympathy,—the age when half wonderingly we began to descry in others that transfigured spark of divinity which we call Myself; when clodhoppers and peasants, and tramps and thieves, and millionaires and—sometimes—Negroes, became throbbing souls whose warm pulsing life touched us so nearly that we half gasped with surprise, crying, "Thou too! Hast Thou seen Sorrow and the dull waters of Hopelessness? Hast Thou known Life?" And then all helplessly we peered into those Other-worlds, and wailed, "O World of Worlds, how shall man make you one?"

So in that little Oneida school there came to those schoolboys a revelation of thought and longing beneath one black skin, of which they had not dreamed before. And to the lonely boy came a new dawn of sympathy and inspiration. The shadowy, formless thing—the temptation of Hate, that hovered between him and the world—grew fainter and less sinister. It did not wholly fade away, but diffused itself and lingered thick at the edges. Through it the child now first saw the blue and gold of life,—the sun-swept road that ran 'twixt heaven and earth until in one far-off wan wavering line they met and kissed. A vision of life came to the growing boy,—mystic, wonderful. He raised his head, stretched himself, breathed deep of the fresh new air. Yonder, behind the forests, he heard strange sounds; then glinting through the trees he saw, far, far away, the bronzed hosts of a nation calling,—calling faintly, calling loudly. He heard the hateful clank of their chains, he felt them cringe and grovel, and there rose within him a protest and a prophecy. And he girded himself to walk down the world.

A voice and vision called him to be a priest,—a seer to lead the uncalled out of the house of bondage. He saw the headless host turn toward him like the whirling of mad waters,—he stretched forth his hands eagerly, and then, even as he stretched them, suddenly there swept across the vision the temptation of Despair.

They were not wicked men,—the problem of life is not the problem of the wicked,—they were calm, good men, Bishops of the Apostolic Church of God, and strove toward righteousness. They said slowly, "It is all very natural—it is even commendable; but the General Theological Seminary of the Episcopal Church cannot admit a Negro." And when that thin, half-grotesque figure still haunted their doors, they put their hands kindly, half sorrowfully, on his shoulders, and said, "Now,—of course, we—we know how *you* feel about it; but you see it is impossible,—that is—well—it is premature. Sometime, we trust—sincerely trust—all such distinctions will fade away; but now the world is as it is."

This was the temptation of Despair; and the young man fought it doggedly. Like some grave shadow he flitted by those halls, pleading, arguing, half angrily demanding admittance, until there came the final *No*; until men hustled the disturber away, marked him as foolish, unreasonable, and injudicious, a vain rebel against God's law. And then from that Vision Splendid all the glory faded slowly away, and left an earth gray and stern rolling on beneath a dark despair. Even the kind hands that stretched themselves toward him from out the depths of that dull morning seemed but parts of the purple shadows. He saw them coldly, and asked, "Why should I strive by special grace when the way of the world is closed to me?" All gently yet, the hands urged him on,—the hands of young John Jay, that daring father's daring son; the hands of the good folk of Boston, that free city. And yet, with a way to the priesthood of the Church open at last before him, the cloud lingered there; and even when in old St. Paul's the venerable Bishop raised his white arms above the Negro deacon—even then the burden had not lifted from that heart, for there had passed a glory from the earth.

And yet the fire through which Alexander Crummell went did not burn in vain. Slowly and more soberly he took up again his plan of life. More critically he studied the situation. Deep down below the slavery and servitude of the Negro people he saw their fatal weaknesses, which long years of mistreatment had emphasized. The dearth of strong moral character, of unbending righteousness, he felt, was their great shortcoming, and here he would begin. He would gather the best of his people into some little Episcopal chapel and there lead, teach, and inspire them, till the leaven spread, till the children grew, till the world hearkened, till—till—and then across his dream gleamed some faint after-glow of that first fair vision of youth—only an after-glow, for there had passed a glory from the earth.

One day—it was in 1842, and the springtide was struggling merrily with the May winds of New England—he stood at last in his own chapel in Providence, a priest of the Church. The days sped by, and the dark young clergyman labored; he wrote his sermons carefully; he intoned his prayers with a soft, earnest voice; he haunted the streets and accosted the wayfarers; he visited the sick, and knelt beside the dying. He worked and toiled, week by week, day by day, month by month. And yet month by month the congregation dwindled, week by week the hollow walls echoed more sharply, day by day the calls came fewer and fewer, and day by day the third temptation sat clearer and still more clearly within the Veil; a temptation, as it were, bland and smiling, with just a shade of mockery in its smooth tones. First it came casually, in the cadence of a voice: "Oh, colored folks? Yes." Or perhaps more definitely: "What do you *expect*?" In voice and gesture lay the doubt—the temptation of Doubt. How he hated it, and stormed at it furiously! "Of course they are capable," he cried; "of course they can learn and strive and achieve—" and "Of course," added the temptation softly, "they do nothing of the sort." Of all the three temptations, this one struck the deepest. Hate? He had outgrown so childish a thing. Despair? He had steeled his right arm against it, and fought it with the vigor of determination. But to doubt the worth of his life-work,—to doubt the destiny and capability of the race his soul loved because it was his; to find listless squalor instead of eager endeavor; to hear his own lips whispering, "They do not care; they cannot know; they are dumb driven cattle,—why cast your pearls before swine?"—this, this seemed more than man could bear; and he closed the door, and sank upon the steps of the chancel, and cast his robe upon the floor and writhed.

The evening sunbeams had set the dust to dancing in the gloomy chapel when he arose. He folded his vestments, put away the hymn-books, and closed the great Bible. He stepped out into the twilight, looked back upon the narrow little pulpit with a weary smile, and locked the door. Then he walked briskly to the Bishop, and told the Bishop what the Bishop already knew. "I have failed," he said simply. And gaining courage by the confession, he added: "What I need is a larger constituency. There are comparatively few Negroes here, and perhaps they are not of the best. I must go where the field is wider, and try again." So the Bishop sent him to Philadelphia, with a letter to Bishop Onderdonk.

Bishop Onderdonk lived at the head of six white steps,—corpulent, red-faced, and the author of several thrilling tracts on Apostolic Succession. It was after dinner, and the Bishop had settled himself for a pleasant season of contemplation, when the bell must needs ring, and there must burst in upon the Bishop a letter and a thin, ungainly Negro. Bishop Onderdonk read the letter hastily and frowned. Fortunately, his mind was already clear on this point; and he cleared his brow and looked at Crummell. Then he said, slowly and impressively: "I will receive you into this diocese on one condition: no Negro priest can sit in my church convention, and no Negro church must ask for representation there."

I sometimes fancy I can see that tableau: the frail black figure, nervously twitching his hat before the massive abdomen of Bishop Onderdonk; his threadbare coat thrown against the dark woodwork of the book-cases, where Fox's "Lives of the Martyrs" nestled happily beside "The Whole Duty of Man." I seem to see the wide eyes of the Negro wander past the Bishop's broadcloth to where the swinging glass doors of the cabinet glow in the sunlight. A little blue fly is trying to cross the yawning keyhole. He marches briskly up to it, peers into the chasm in a surprised sort of way, and rubs his feelers reflectively; then he essays its depths, and, finding it bottomless, draws back again. The dark-faced priest finds himself wondering if the fly too has faced its Valley of Humiliation, and if it will plunge into it,—when lo! it spreads its tiny wings and buzzes merrily across, leaving the watcher wingless and alone.

Then the full weight of his burden fell upon him. The rich walls wheeled away, and before him lay the cold rough moor winding on through life, cut in twain by one thick granite ridge,—here, the Valley of Humiliation; yonder, the Valley of the Shadow of Death. And I know not which be darker,—no, not I. But this I know: in yonder Vale of the Humble stand to-day a million swarthy men, who willingly would

"... bear the whips and scorns of time,
The oppressor's wrong, the proud man's contumely,
The pangs of despised love, the law's delay,
The insolence of office, and the spurns
That patient merit of the unworthy takes,"

all this and more would they bear did they but know that this were sacrifice and not a meaner thing. So surged the thought within that lone black breast. The Bishop cleared his throat suggestively; then, recollecting that there was really nothing to say, considerately said nothing, only sat tapping his foot impatiently. But Alexander Crummell said, slowly and heavily: "I will never enter your diocese on such terms." And saying this, he turned and passed into the Valley of the Shadow of Death. You might have noted only the physical dying, the shattered frame and hacking cough; but in that soul lay deeper death than that. He found a chapel in New York,—the church of his father; he labored for it in poverty and starvation, scorned by his fellow priests. Half in despair, he wandered across the sea, a beggar with outstretched hands. Englishmen clasped them,—Wilberforce and Stanley, Thirwell and Ingles, and even Froude and Macaulay; Sir Benjamin Brodie bade him rest awhile at Queen's College in Cambridge, and there he lingered, struggling for health of body and mind, until he took his degree in '53. Restless still and unsatisfied, he turned toward Africa, and for long years, amid the spawn of the slave-smugglers, sought a new heaven and a new earth.

So the man groped for light; all this was not Life,—it was the world-wandering of a soul in search of itself, the striving of one who vainly sought his place in the world, ever haunted by the shadow of a death that is more than death,—the passing of a soul that has missed its duty. Twenty years he wandered,—twenty years and more; and yet the hard rasping question kept gnawing within him, "What, in God's name, am I on earth for?" In the narrow New York parish his soul seemed cramped and smothered. In the fine old air of the

English University he heard the millions wailing over the sea. In the wild fever-cursed swamps of West Africa he stood helpless and alone.

You will not wonder at his weird pilgrimage,—you who in the swift whirl of living, amid its cold paradox and marvellous vision, have fronted life and asked its riddle face to face. And if you find that riddle hard to read, remember that yonder black boy finds it just a little harder; if it is difficult for you to find and face your duty, it is a shade more difficult for him; if your heart sickens in the blood and dust of battle, remember that to him the dust is thicker and the battle fiercer. No wonder the wanderers fall! No wonder we point to thief and murderer, and haunting prostitute, and the never-ending throng of unhearsed dead! The Valley of the Shadow of Death gives few of its pilgrims back to the world.

But Alexander Crummell it gave back. Out of the temptation of Hate, and burned by the fire of Despair, triumphant over Doubt, and steeled by Sacrifice against Humiliation, he turned at last home across the waters, humble and strong, gentle and determined. He bent to all the gibes and prejudices, to all hatred and discrimination, with that rare courtesy which is the armor of pure souls. He fought among his own, the low, the grasping, and the wicked, with that unbending righteousness which is the sword of the just. He never faltered, he seldom complained; he simply worked, inspiring the young, rebuking the old, helping the weak, guiding the strong.

So he grew, and brought within his wide influence all that was best of those who walk within the Veil. They who live without knew not nor dreamed of that full power within, that mighty inspiration which the dull gauze of caste decreed that most men should not know. And now that he is gone, I sweep the Veil away and cry, Lo! the soul to whose dear memory I bring this little tribute. I can see his face still, dark and heavy-lined beneath his snowy hair; lighting and shading, now with inspiration for the future, now in innocent pain at some human wickedness, now with sorrow at some hard memory from the past. The more I met Alexander Crummell, the more I felt how much that world was losing which knew so little of him. In another age he might have sat among the elders of the land in purple-bordered toga; in another country mothers might have sung him to the cradles.

He did his work,—he did it nobly and well; and yet I sorrow that here he worked alone, with so little human sympathy. His name to-day, in this broad land, means little, and comes to fifty million ears laden with no incense of memory or emulation. And herein lies the tragedy of the age: not that men are poor,—all men know something of poverty; not that men are wicked,—who is good? not that men are ignorant,—what is Truth? Nay, but that men know so little of men.

He sat one morning gazing toward the sea. He smiled and said, "The gate is rusty on the hinges." That night at star-rise a wind came moaning out of the west to blow the gate ajar, and then the soul I loved fled like a flame across the Seas, and in its seat sat Death.

I wonder where he is to-day? I wonder if in that dim world beyond, as he came gliding in, there rose on some wan throne a King,—a dark and pierced Jew, who knows the writhings of the earthly damned, saying, as he laid those heart-wrung talents down, "Well done!" while round about the morning stars sat singing.

XIII

Of the Coming of John

What bring they 'neath the midnight,
   Beside the River-sea?
They bring the human heart wherein
   No nightly calm can be;
That droppeth never with the wind,
   Nor drieth with the dew;
O calm it, God; thy calm is broad
   To cover spirits too.
      The river floweth on.

MRS. BROWNING.

CARLISLE STREET runs westward from the centre of Johnstown, across a great black bridge, down a hill and up again, by little shops and meat-markets, past single-storied homes, until suddenly it stops against a wide green lawn. It is a broad, restful place, with two large buildings outlined against the west. When at evening the winds come swelling from the east, and the great pall of the city's smoke hangs wearily above the valley, then the red west glows like a dreamland down Carlisle Street, and, at the tolling of the supper-bell, throws the passing forms of students in dark silhouette against the sky. Tall and black, they move slowly by, and seem in the sinister light to flit before the city like dim warning ghosts. Perhaps they are; for this is Wells Institute, and these black students have few dealings with the white city below.

And if you will notice, night after night, there is one dark form that ever hurries last and late toward the twinkling lights of Swain Hall,—for Jones is never on time. A long, straggling fellow he is, brown and hard-haired, who seems to be growing straight out of his clothes, and walks with a half-apologetic roll. He used perpetually to set the quiet dining-room into waves of merriment, as he stole to his place after the bell had tapped for prayers; he seemed so perfectly awkward. And yet one glance at his face made one forgive him much,—that broad, good-natured smile in which lay no bit of art or artifice, but seemed just bubbling good-nature and genuine satisfaction with the world.

He came to us from Altamaha, away down there beneath the gnarled oaks of Southeastern Georgia, where the sea croons to the sands and the sands listen till they sink half drowned beneath the waters, rising only here and there in long, low islands. The white folk of Altamaha voted John a good boy,—fine plough-hand, good in the rice-fields, handy everywhere, and always good-natured and respectful. But they shook their heads when his mother wanted to send him off to school. "It'll spoil him,—ruin him," they said; and they talked as though they knew. But full half the black folk followed him proudly to the station, and carried his queer little trunk and many bundles. And there they shook and shook hands, and the girls kissed him shyly and the boys clapped him on the back. So the train came, and he pinched his little sister lovingly, and put his great arms about his mother's neck, and then was away with a puff and a roar into the great yellow world that flamed and flared about the doubtful pilgrim. Up the coast they hurried, past the squares and palmettos of Savannah, through the cotton-fields and through the weary night, to Millville, and came with the morning to the noise and bustle of Johnstown.

And they that stood behind, that morning in Altamaha, and watched the train as it noisily bore playmate and brother and son away to the world, had thereafter one ever-recurring word,—"When John comes." Then what parties were to be, and what speakings in the churches; what new furniture in the front room,—perhaps even a new front room; and there would be a new schoolhouse, with John as teacher; and then perhaps a big wedding; all this and more—when John comes. But the white people shook their heads.

At first he was coming at Christmas-time,—but the vacation proved too short; and then, the next summer,—but times were hard and schooling costly, and so, instead, he worked in Johnstown. And so it drifted to the next summer, and the next,—till playmates scattered, and mother grew gray, and sister went up to the Judge's kitchen to work. And still the legend lingered,—"When John comes."

Up at the Judge's they rather liked this refrain; for they too had a John—a fair-haired, smooth-faced boy, who had played many a long summer's day to its close with his darker namesake. "Yes, sir! John is at Princeton, sir," said the broad-shouldered gray-haired Judge every morning as he marched down to the post-office. "Showing the Yankees what a Southern gentleman can do," he added; and strode home again with his letters and papers. Up at the great pillared house they lingered long over the Princeton letter,—the Judge and his frail wife, his sister and growing daughters. "It 'll make a man of him," said the Judge, "college is the place." And then he asked the shy little waitress, "Well, Jennie, how 's your John?" and added reflectively, "Too bad, too bad your mother sent him off,—it will spoil him." And the waitress wondered.

Thus in the far-away Southern village the world lay waiting, half consciously, the coming of two young men, and dreamed in an inarticulate way of new things that would be done and new thoughts that all would think. And yet it was singular that few thought of two Johns,—for the black folk thought of one John, and he was black; and the white folk thought of another John, and he was white. And neither world thought the other world's thought, save with a vague unrest.

Up in Johnstown, at the Institute, we were long puzzled at the case of John Jones. For a long time the clay seemed unfit for any sort of moulding. He was loud and boisterous, always laughing and singing, and never able to work consecutively at anything. He did not know how to study; he had no idea of thoroughness; and with his tardiness, carelessness, and appalling good-humor, we were sore perplexed. One night we sat in faculty-meeting, worried and serious; for Jones was in trouble again. This last escapade was too much, and so we solemnly voted "that Jones, on account of repeated disorder and inattention to work, be suspended for the rest of the term."

It seemed to us that the first time life ever struck Jones as a really serious thing was when the Dean told him he must leave school. He stared at the gray-haired man blankly, with great eyes. "Why,—why," he faltered, "but—I have n't graduated!" Then the Dean slowly and clearly explained, reminding him of the tardiness and the carelessness, of the poor lessons and neglected work, of the noise and disorder, until the fellow hung his head in confusion. Then he said quickly, "But you won't tell mammy and sister,—you won't write mammy, now will you? For if you won't I 'll go out into the city and work, and come back next term and show you something." So the Dean promised faithfully, and John shouldered his little trunk, giving neither word nor look to the giggling boys, and walked down Carlisle Street to the great city, with sober eyes and a set and serious face.

Perhaps we imagined it, but someway it seemed to us that the serious look that crept over his boyish face that afternoon never left it again. When he came back to us he went to work with all his rugged strength. It was a hard struggle, for things did not come easily to him,—few crowding memories of early life and teaching came to help him on his new way; but all the world toward which he strove was of his own building, and he builded slow and hard. As the light dawned lingeringly on his new creations, he sat rapt and silent before the vision, or wandered alone over the green campus peering through and beyond the world of men into a world of thought. And the thoughts at times puzzled him sorely; he could not see just why the circle was not square, and carried it out fifty-six decimal places one midnight,—would have gone further, indeed, had not the matron rapped for lights out. He caught terrible colds lying on his back in the meadows of nights, trying to think out the solar system; he had grave doubts as to the ethics of the Fall of Rome, and strongly suspected the Germans of being thieves and rascals, despite his text-books; he pondered long over every new Greek word, and wondered why this meant that and why it could n't mean something else, and how it must have felt to think all things in Greek. So he thought and puzzled along for himself,—pausing perplexed where others skipped merrily, and walking steadily through the difficulties where the rest stopped and surrendered.

Thus he grew in body and soul, and with him his clothes seemed to grow and arrange themselves; coat sleeves got longer, cuffs appeared, and collars got less soiled. Now and then his boots shone, and a new dignity crept into his walk. And we who saw daily a new thoughtfulness growing in his eyes began to expect something of this plodding boy. Thus he passed out of the preparatory school into college, and we who watched him felt four more years of change, which almost transformed the tall, grave man who bowed to us commencement morning. He had left his queer thought-world and come back to a world of motion and of men. He looked now for the first time sharply about him, and wondered he had seen so little before. He grew slowly to feel almost for the first time the Veil that lay between him and the white world; he first noticed now the oppression that had not seemed oppression before, differences that erstwhile seemed natural, restraints and slights that in his boyhood days had gone unnoticed or been greeted with a laugh. He felt angry now when men did not call him "Mister," he clenched his hands at the "Jim Crow" cars, and chafed at the color-line that hemmed in him and his. A tinge of sarcasm crept into his speech, and a vague bitterness into his life; and he sat long hours wondering and planning a way around these crooked things. Daily he found himself shrinking from the choked and narrow life of his native town. And yet he always planned to go back to Altamaha,—always planned to work there. Still, more and more as the day approached he hesitated with a nameless dread; and even the day after graduation he seized with eagerness the offer of the Dean to send him North with the quartette during the summer vacation, to sing for the Institute. A breath of air before the plunge, he said to himself in half apology.

It was a bright September afternoon, and the streets of New York were brilliant with moving men. They reminded John of the sea, as he sat in the square and watched them, so changelessly changing, so bright and dark, so grave and gay. He scanned their rich and faultless clothes, the way they carried their hands, the shape of their hats; he peered into the hurrying carriages. Then, leaning back with a sigh, he said, "This is the World." The notion suddenly seized him to see where the world was going; since many of the richer and brighter seemed hurrying all one way. So when a tall, light-haired young man and a little talkative lady came by, he rose half hesitatingly and followed them. Up the street they went, past stores and gay shops, across a broad square, until with a hundred others they entered the high portal of a great building.

He was pushed toward the ticket-office with the others, and felt in his pocket for the new five-dollar bill he had hoarded. There seemed really no time for hesitation, so he drew it bravely out, passed it to the busy clerk, and received simply a ticket but no change. When at last he realized that he had paid five dollars to enter he knew not what, he stood stock-still amazed. "Be careful," said a low voice behind him; "you must not lynch the colored gentleman simply because he 's in your way," and a girl looked up roguishly into the eyes of her fair-haired escort. A shade of annoyance passed over the escort's face. "You *will* not understand us at the South," he said half impatiently, as if continuing an argument. "With all your professions, one never sees in the North so cordial and intimate relations between white and black as are every-day occurrences with us. Why, I remember my closest play-fellow in boyhood was a little Negro named after me, and surely no two,—*well!*" The man stopped short and flushed to the roots of his hair, for there directly beside his reserved orchestra chairs sat the Negro he had stumbled over in the hallway. He hesitated and grew pale with anger, called the usher and gave him his card, with a few peremptory words, and slowly sat down. The lady deftly changed the subject.

All this John did not see, for he sat in a half-maze minding the scene about him; the delicate beauty of the hall, the faint perfume, the moving myriad of men, the rich clothing and low hum of talking seemed all a part of a world so different from his, so strangely more beautiful than anything he had known, that he sat in dreamland, and started when, after a hush, rose high and clear the music of Lohengrin's swan. The infinite beauty of the wail lingered and swept through every muscle of his frame, and put it all a-tune. He closed his eyes and grasped the elbows of the chair, touching unwittingly the lady's arm. And the lady drew away. A deep longing swelled in all his heart to rise with that clear music out of the dirt and dust of that low life that held him prisoned and befouled. If he could only live up in the free air where birds sang and setting suns had no touch of blood! Who had called him to be the slave and butt of all? And if he had called, what right had he to call when a world like this lay open before men?

Then the movement changed, and fuller, mightier harmony swelled away. He looked thoughtfully across the hall, and wondered why the beautiful gray-haired woman looked so listless, and what the little man could be whispering about. He would not like to be listless and idle, he thought, for he felt with the music the movement of power within him. If he but had some master-work, some life-service, hard,—aye, bitter hard, but without the cringing and sickening servility, without the cruel hurt that hardened his heart and soul. When at last a soft sorrow crept across the violins, there came to him the vision of a far-off home,—the great eyes of his sister, and the dark drawn face of his mother. And his heart sank below the waters, even as the sea-sand sinks by the shores of Altamaha, only to be lifted aloft again with that last ethereal wail of the swan that quivered and faded away into the sky.

It left John sitting so silent and rapt that he did not for some time notice the usher tapping him lightly on the shoulder and saying politely, "Will you step this way, please, sir?" A little surprised, he arose quickly at the last tap, and, turning to leave his seat, looked full into the face of the fair-haired young man. For the first time the young man recognized his dark boyhood playmate, and John knew that it was the Judge's son. The white John started, lifted his hand, and then froze into his chair; the black John smiled lightly, then grimly, and followed the usher down the aisle. The manager was sorry, very, very sorry,—but he explained that some mistake had been made in selling the gentleman a seat already disposed of; he would refund the money, of course,—and indeed felt the matter keenly, and so forth, and—before he had finished John was gone, walking hurriedly across the square and down the broad streets, and as he passed the park he buttoned his coat and said, "John Jones, you 're a natural-born fool." Then he went to his lodgings and wrote a letter, and tore it up; he wrote another, and threw it in the fire. Then he seized a scrap of paper and wrote: "Dear Mother and Sister—I am coming—John."

"Perhaps," said John, as he settled himself on the train, "perhaps I am to blame myself in struggling against my manifest destiny simply because it looks hard and unpleasant. Here is my duty to Altamaha plain before me; perhaps they 'll let me help settle the Negro problems there,—perhaps they won't. 'I will go in to the King, which is not according to the law; and if I perish, I perish.' " And then he mused and dreamed, and planned a life-work; and the train flew south.

Down in Altamaha, after seven long years, all the world knew John was coming. The homes were scrubbed and scoured,—above all, one; the gardens and yards had an unwonted trimness, and Jennie bought a new gingham. With some finesse and negotiation, all the dark Methodists and Presbyterians were induced to join in a monster welcome at the Baptist Church; and as the day drew near, warm discussions arose on every corner as to the exact extent and nature of John's accomplishments. It was noontide on a gray and cloudy day when he came. The black town flocked to the depot, with a little of the white at the edges,—a happy throng, with "Good-mawnings" and "Howdys" and laughing and joking and jostling. Mother sat yonder in the window watching; but sister Jennie stood on the platform, nervously fingering her dress,—tall and lithe, with soft brown skin and loving eyes peering from out a tangled wilderness of hair. John rose gloomily as the train stopped, for he was thinking of the "Jim Crow" car; he stepped to the platform, and paused: a little dingy station, a black crowd gaudy and dirty, a half-mile of dilapidated shanties along a straggling ditch of mud. An overwhelming sense of the sordidness and narrowness of it all seized him; he looked in vain for his mother, kissed coldly the tall, strange girl who called him brother, spoke a short, dry word here and there; then, lingering neither for hand-shaking nor gossip, started silently up the street, raising his hat merely to the last eager old aunty, to her open-mouthed astonishment. The people were distinctly bewildered. This silent, cold man,—was this John? Where was his smile and hearty handgrasp? " 'Peared kind o' down in the mouf," said the Methodist preacher thoughtfully. "Seemed monstus stuck up," complained a Baptist sister. But the white postmaster from the edge of the crowd expressed the opinion of his folks plainly. "That damn Nigger," said he, as he shouldered the mail and arranged his tobacco, "has gone North and got plum full o' fool notions; but they won't work in Altamaha." And the crowd melted away.

The meeting of welcome at the Baptist Church was a failure. Rain spoiled the barbecue, and thunder turned the milk in the ice-cream. When the speaking came at night, the house was crowded to overflowing. The three preachers had especially prepared themselves, but somehow John's manner seemed to throw a blanket over everything,—he seemed so cold and preoccupied, and had so strange an air of restraint that the Methodist brother could not warm up to his theme and elicited not a single "Amen"; the Presbyterian prayer was but feebly responded to, and even the Baptist preacher, though he wakened faint enthusiasm, got so mixed up in his favorite sentence that he had to close it by stopping fully fifteen minutes sooner than he meant. The people moved uneasily in their seats as John rose to reply. He spoke slowly and methodically. The age, he said, demanded new ideas; we were far different from those men of the seventeenth and eighteenth centuries,—with broader ideas of human brotherhood and destiny. Then he spoke of the rise of charity and popular education, and particularly of the spread of wealth and work. The question was, then, he added reflectively, looking at the low discolored ceiling, what part the Negroes of this land would take in the striving of the new century. He sketched in vague outline the new Industrial School that might rise among these pines, he spoke in detail of the charitable and philanthropic work that might be organized, of money that might be saved for banks and business. Finally he urged unity, and deprecated especially religious and denominational bickering. "To-day," he said, with a smile, "the world cares little whether a man be Baptist or Methodist, or indeed a churchman at all, so long as he is good and true. What difference does it make whether a man be baptized in river or wash-bowl, or not at all? Let 's leave all that littleness, and look higher." Then, thinking of nothing else, he slowly sat down. A painful hush seized that crowded mass. Little had they understood of what he said, for he spoke an unknown tongue, save the last word about baptism; that they knew, and they sat very still while the clock ticked. Then at last a low suppressed snarl came from the Amen corner, and an old bent man arose, walked over the seats, and climbed straight up into the pulpit. He was wrinkled and black, with scant gray and tufted hair; his voice and hands shook as with palsy; but on his face lay the intense rapt look of the religious fanatic. He seized the Bible with his rough, huge hands; twice he raised it inarticulate, and then fairly burst into the words, with rude and awful eloquence. He quivered, swayed, and bent; then rose aloft in perfect majesty, till the people moaned and wept, wailed and shouted, and a wild shrieking arose from the corners where all the pent-up feeling of the hour gathered itself and rushed into the air. John never knew clearly what the old man said; he only felt himself held up to scorn and scathing denunciation for trampling on the true Religion, and he realized with amazement that all unknowingly he had put rough, rude hands on something this little world held sacred. He arose silently, and passed out into the night. Down toward the sea he went, in the fitful starlight, half conscious of the girl who followed timidly after him. When at last he stood upon the bluff, he turned to his little sister and looked upon her sorrowfully, remembering with sudden pain how little thought he had given her. He put his arm about her and let her passion of tears spend itself on his shoulder.

Long they stood together, peering over the gray unresting water.

"John," she said, "does it make every one—unhappy when they study and learn lots of things?"

He paused and smiled. "I am afraid it does," he said.

"And, John, are you glad you studied?"

"Yes," came the answer, slowly but positively.

She watched the flickering lights upon the sea, and said

thoughtfully, "I wish I was unhappy,—and—and," putting both arms about his neck, "I think I am, a little, John."

It was several days later that John walked up to the Judge's house to ask for the privilege of teaching the Negro school. The Judge himself met him at the front door, stared a little hard at him, and said brusquely, "Go 'round to the kitchen door, John, and wait." Sitting on the kitchen steps, John stared at the corn, thoroughly perplexed. What on earth had come over him? Every step he made offended some one. He had come to save his people, and before he left the depot he had hurt them. He sought to teach them at the church, and had outraged their deepest feelings. He had schooled himself to be respectful to the Judge, and then blundered into his front door. And all the time he had meant right,—and yet, and yet, somehow he found it so hard and strange to fit his old surroundings again, to find his place in the world about him. He could not remember that he used to have any difficulty in the past, when life was glad and gay. The world seemed smooth and easy then. Perhaps,—but his sister came to the kitchen door just then and said the Judge awaited him.

The Judge sat in the dining-room amid his morning's mail, and he did not ask John to sit down. He plunged squarely into the business. "You 've come for the school, I suppose. Well, John, I want to speak to you plainly. You know I 'm a friend to your people. I 've helped you and your family, and would have done more if you had n't got the notion of going off. Now I like the colored people, and sympathize with all their reasonable aspirations; but you and I both know, John, that in this country the Negro must remain subordinate, and can never expect to be the equal of white men. In their place, your people can be honest and respectful; and God knows, I 'll do what I can to help them. But when they want to reverse nature, and rule white men, and marry white women, and sit in my parlor, then, by God! we 'll hold them under if we have to lynch every Nigger in the land. Now, John, the question is, are you, with your education and Northern notions, going to accept the situation and teach the darkies to be faithful servants and laborers as your fathers were,—I knew your father, John, he belonged to my brother, and he was a good

Nigger. Well—well, are you going to be like him, or are you going to try to put fool ideas of rising and equality into these folks' heads, and make them discontented and unhappy?"

"I am going to accept the situation, Judge Henderson," answered John, with a brevity that did not escape the keen old man. He hesitated a moment, and then said shortly, "Very well,—we 'll try you awhile. Good-morning."

It was a full month after the opening of the Negro school that the other John came home, tall, gay, and headstrong. The mother wept, the sisters sang. The whole white town was glad. A proud man was the Judge, and it was a goodly sight to see the two swinging down Main Street together. And yet all did not go smoothly between them, for the younger man could not and did not veil his contempt for the little town, and plainly had his heart set on New York. Now the one cherished ambition of the Judge was to see his son mayor of Altamaha, representative to the legislature, and—who could say?—governor of Georgia. So the argument often waxed hot between them. "Good heavens, father," the younger man would say after dinner, as he lighted a cigar and stood by the fireplace, "you surely don't expect a young fellow like me to settle down permanently in this—this God-forgotten town with nothing but mud and Negroes?" "*I* did," the Judge would answer laconically; and on this particular day it seemed from the gathering scowl that he was about to add something more emphatic, but neighbors had already begun to drop in to admire his son, and the conversation drifted.

"Heah that John is livenin' things up at the darky school," volunteered the postmaster, after a pause.

"What now?" asked the Judge, sharply.

"Oh, nothin' in particulah,—just his almighty air and uppish ways. B'lieve I did heah somethin' about his givin' talks on the French Revolution, equality, and such like. He 's what I call a dangerous Nigger."

"Have you heard him say anything out of the way?"

"Why, no,—but Sally, our girl, told my wife a lot of rot. Then, too, I don't need to heah: a Nigger what won't say 'sir' to a white man, or—"

"Who is this John?" interrupted the son.

"Why, it 's little black John, Peggy's son,—your old playfellow."

The young man's face flushed angrily, and then he laughed.

"Oh," said he, "it 's the darky that tried to force himself into a seat beside the lady I was escorting—"

But Judge Henderson waited to hear no more. He had been nettled all day, and now at this he rose with a half-smothered oath, took his hat and cane, and walked straight to the schoolhouse.

For John, it had been a long, hard pull to get things started in the rickety old shanty that sheltered his school. The Negroes were rent into factions for and against him, the parents were careless, the children irregular and dirty, and books, pencils, and slates largely missing. Nevertheless, he struggled hopefully on, and seemed to see at last some glimmering of dawn. The attendance was larger and the children were a shade cleaner this week. Even the booby class in reading showed a little comforting progress. So John settled himself with renewed patience this afternoon.

"Now, Mandy," he said cheerfully, "that 's better; but you must n't chop your words up so: 'If—the—man—goes.' Why, your little brother even would n't tell a story that way, now would he?"

"Naw, suh, he cain't talk."

"All right; now let 's try again: 'If the man—' "

"John!"

The whole school started in surprise, and the teacher half arose, as the red, angry face of the Judge appeared in the open doorway.

"John, this school is closed. You children can go home and get to work. The white people of Altamaha are not spending their money on black folks to have their heads crammed with impudence and lies. Clear out! I 'll lock the door myself."

Up at the great pillared house the tall young son wandered aimlessly about after his father's abrupt departure. In the house there was little to interest him; the books were old and stale, the local newspaper flat, and the women had retired with headaches and sewing. He tried a nap, but it was too warm. So he sauntered out into the fields, complaining disconsolately, "Good Lord! how long will this imprisonment last!" He was not a bad fellow,—just a little spoiled and self-indulgent, and as headstrong as his proud father. He seemed a young man pleasant to look upon, as he sat on the great black stump at the edge of the pines idly swinging his legs and smoking. "Why, there is n't even a girl worth getting up a respectable flirtation with," he growled. Just then his eye caught a tall, willowy figure hurrying toward him on the narrow path. He looked with interest at first, and then burst into a laugh as he said, "Well, I declare, if it is n't Jennie, the little brown kitchen-maid! Why, I never noticed before what a trim little body she is. Hello, Jennie! Why, you have n't kissed me since I came home," he said gaily. The young girl stared at him in surprise and confusion,—faltered something inarticulate, and attempted to pass. But a wilful mood had seized the young idler, and he caught at her arm. Frightened, she slipped by; and half mischievously he turned and ran after her through the tall pines.

Yonder, toward the sea, at the end of the path, came John slowly, with his head down. He had turned wearily homeward from the schoolhouse; then, thinking to shield his mother from the blow, started to meet his sister as she came from work and break the news of his dismissal to her. "I 'll go away," he said slowly; "I 'll go away and find work, and send for them. I cannot live here longer." And then the fierce, buried anger surged up into his throat. He waved his arms and hurried wildly up the path.

The great brown sea lay silent. The air scarce breathed. The dying day bathed the twisted oaks and mighty pines in black and gold. There came from the wind no warning, not a whisper from the cloudless sky. There was only a black man hurrying on with an ache in his heart, seeing neither sun nor sea, but starting as from a dream at the frightened cry that woke the pines, to see his dark sister struggling in the arms of a tall and fair-haired man.

He said not a word, but, seizing a fallen limb, struck him with all the pent-up hatred of his great black arm; and the body lay white and still beneath the pines, all bathed in sunshine and in blood. John looked at it dreamily, then walked back to the house briskly, and said in a soft voice, "Mammy, I 'm going away,—I 'm going to be free."

She gazed at him dimly and faltered, "No'th, honey, is yo' gwine No'th agin?"

He looked out where the North Star glistened pale above the waters, and said, "Yes, mammy, I 'm going—North."

Then, without another word, he went out into the narrow lane, up by the straight pines, to the same winding path, and seated himself on the great black stump, looking at the blood where the body had lain. Yonder in the gray past he had played with that dead boy, romping together under the solemn trees. The night deepened; he thought of the boys at Johnstown. He wondered how Brown had turned out, and Carey? And Jones,—Jones? Why, *he* was Jones, and he wondered what they would all say when they knew, when they knew, in that great long dining-room with its hundreds of merry eyes. Then as the sheen of the starlight stole over him, he thought of the gilded ceiling of that vast concert hall, and heard stealing toward him the faint sweet music of the swan. Hark! was it music, or the hurry and shouting of men? Yes, surely! Clear and high the faint sweet melody rose and fluttered like a living thing, so that the very earth trembled as with the tramp of horses and murmur of angry men.

He leaned back and smiled toward the sea, whence rose the strange melody, away from the dark shadows where lay the noise of horses galloping, galloping on. With an effort he roused himself, bent forward, and looked steadily down the pathway, softly humming the "Song of the Bride,"—

"Freudig geführt, ziehet dahin."

Amid the trees in the dim morning twilight he watched their shadows dancing and heard their horses thundering toward him, until at last they came sweeping like a storm, and he saw in front that haggard white-haired man, whose eyes flashed red with fury. Oh, how he pitied him,—pitied him,—and wondered if he had the coiling twisted rope. Then, as the storm burst round him, he rose slowly to his feet and turned his closed eyes toward the Sea.

And the world whistled in his ears.

XIV

The Sorrow Songs

I walk through the churchyard
    To lay this body down;
I know moon-rise, I know star-rise;
I walk in the moonlight, I walk in the starlight;
I 'll lie in the grave and stretch out my arms,
I 'll go to judgment in the evening of the day,
And my soul and thy soul shall meet that day,
    When I lay this body down.

NEGRO SONG.

THEY that walked in darkness sang songs in the olden days—Sorrow Songs—for they were weary at heart. And so before each thought that I have written in this book I have set a phrase, a haunting echo of these weird old songs in which the soul of the black slave spoke to men. Ever since I was a child these songs have stirred me strangely. They came out of the South unknown to me, one by one, and yet at once I knew them as of me and of mine. Then in after years when I came to Nashville I saw the great temple builded of these songs towering over the pale city. To me Jubilee Hall seemed ever made of the songs themselves, and its bricks were red with the blood and dust of toil. Out of them rose for me morning, noon, and night, bursts of wonderful melody, full of the voices of my brothers and sisters, full of the voices of the past.

Little of beauty has America given the world save the rude grandeur God himself stamped on her bosom; the human spirit in this new world has expressed itself in vigor and ingenuity rather than in beauty. And so by fateful chance the Negro folk-song—the rhythmic cry of the slave—stands today not simply as the sole American music, but as the most beautiful expression of human experience born this side the seas. It has been neglected, it has been, and is, half despised, and above all it has been persistently mistaken and misunderstood; but notwithstanding, it still remains as the singular spiritual heritage of the nation and the greatest gift of the Negro people.

Away back in the thirties the melody of these slave songs stirred the nation, but the songs were soon half forgotten. Some, like "Near the lake where drooped the willow," passed into current airs and their source was forgotten; others were caricatured on the "minstrel" stage and their memory died away. Then in war-time came the singular Port Royal experiment after the capture of Hilton Head, and perhaps for the first time the North met the Southern slave face to face and heart to heart with no third witness. The Sea Islands of the Carolinas, where they met, were filled with a black folk of primitive type, touched and moulded less by the world about them than any others outside the Black Belt. Their appearance was uncouth, their language funny, but their hearts were human and their singing stirred men with a mighty power. Thomas Wentworth Higginson hastened to tell of these songs, and Miss McKim and others urged upon the world their rare beauty. But the world listened only half credulously until the Fisk Jubilee Singers sang the slave songs so deeply into the world's heart that it can never wholly forget them again.

There was once a blacksmith's son born at Cadiz, New York, who in the changes of time taught school in Ohio and helped defend Cincinnati from Kirby Smith. Then he fought at Chancellorsville and Gettysburg and finally served in the Freedman's Bureau at Nashville. Here he formed a Sunday-school class of black children in 1866, and sang with them and taught them to sing. And then they taught him to sing, and when once the glory of the Jubilee songs passed into the soul of George L. White, he knew his life-work was to let those Negroes sing to the world as they had sung to him. So in 1871 the pilgrimage of the Fisk Jubilee Singers began. North to Cincinnati they rode,—four half-clothed black boys and five girl-women,—led by a man with a cause and a purpose. They stopped at Wilberforce, the oldest of Negro schools, where a black bishop blessed them. Then they went, fighting cold and starvation, shut out of hotels, and cheerfully sneered at, ever northward; and ever the magic of their song kept thrilling hearts, until a burst of applause in the Congregational Council at Oberlin revealed them to the world. They came to New York and Henry Ward Beecher dared to welcome them, even though the metropolitan dailies sneered at his "Nigger Minstrels." So their songs conquered till they sang across the land and across the sea, before Queen and Kaiser, in Scotland and Ireland, Holland and Switzerland. Seven years they sang, and brought back a hundred and fifty thousand dollars to found Fisk University.

Since their day they have been imitated—sometimes well, by the singers of Hampton and Atlanta, sometimes ill, by straggling quartettes. Caricature has sought again to spoil the quaint beauty of the music, and has filled the air with many debased melodies which vulgar ears scarce know from the real. But the true Negro folk-song still lives in the hearts of those who have heard them truly sung and in the hearts of the Negro people.

What are these songs, and what do they mean? I know little of music and can say nothing in technical phrase, but I know something of men, and knowing them, I know that these songs are the articulate message of the slave to the world. They tell us in these eager days that life was joyous to the black slave, careless and happy. I can easily believe this of some, of many. But not all the past South, though it rose from the dead, can gainsay the heart-touching witness of these songs. They are the music of an unhappy people, of the children of disappointment; they tell of death and suffering and unvoiced longing toward a truer world, of misty wanderings and hidden ways.

The songs are indeed the siftings of centuries; the music is far more ancient than the words, and in it we can trace here and there signs of development. My grandfather's grandmother was seized by an evil Dutch trader two centuries ago; and coming to the valleys of the Hudson and Housatonic, black, little, and lithe, she shivered and shrank in the harsh north winds, looked longingly at the hills, and often crooned a heathen melody to the child between her knees, thus:

Do ba - na co - ba, ge - ne me, ge - ne me!
Do ba - na co - ba, ge - ne me, ge - ne me!
Ben d' nu - li, nu - li, nu - li, nu - li, ben d' le.

The child sang it to his children and they to their children's children, and so two hundred years it has travelled down to us and we sing it to our children, knowing as little as our fathers what its words may mean, but knowing well the meaning of its music.

This was primitive African music; it may be seen in larger form in the strange chant which heralds "The Coming of John":

"You may bury me in the East,
You may bury me in the West,
But I 'll hear the trumpet sound in that morning,"

—the voice of exile.

Ten master songs, more or less, one may pluck from this forest of melody—songs of undoubted Negro origin and wide popular currency, and songs peculiarly characteristic of the slave. One of these I have just mentioned. Another whose strains begin this book is "Nobody knows the trouble I 've seen." When, struck with a sudden poverty, the United States refused to fulfil its promises of land to the freedmen, a brigadier-general went down to the Sea Islands to carry the news. An old woman on the outskirts of the throng began singing this song; all the mass joined with her, swaying. And the soldier wept.

The third song is the cradle-song of death which all men know,—"Swing low, sweet chariot,"—whose bars begin the life story of "Alexander Crummell." Then there is the song of many waters, "Roll, Jordan, roll," a mighty chorus with minor cadences. There were many songs of the fugitive like that which opens "The Wings of Atalanta," and the more familiar "Been a-listening." The seventh is the song of the End and the Beginning—"My Lord, what a mourning! when the stars begin to fall"; a strain of this is placed before "The Dawn of Freedom." The song of groping—"My way 's cloudy"—begins "The Meaning of Progress"; the ninth is the song of this chapter—"Wrestlin' Jacob, the day is a-breaking,"—a pæan of hopeful strife. The last master song is the song of songs—"Steal away,"—sprung from "The Faith of the Fathers."

There are many others of the Negro folk-songs as striking and characteristic as these, as, for instance, the three strains in the third, eighth, and ninth chapters; and others I am sure could easily make a selection on more scientific principles. There are, too, songs that seem to me a step removed from the more primitive types: there is the maze-like medley, "Bright sparkles," one phrase of which heads "The Black Belt"; the Easter carol, "Dust, dust and ashes"; the dirge, "My mother 's took her flight and gone home"; and that burst of melody hovering over "The Passing of the First-Born"—"I hope my mother will be there in that beautiful world on high."

These represent a third step in the development of the slave song, of which "You may bury me in the East" is the first, and songs like "March on" (chapter six) and "Steal away" are the second. The first is African music, the second Afro-American, while the third is a blending of Negro music with the music heard in the foster land. The result is still distinctively Negro and the method of blending original, but the elements are both Negro and Caucasian. One might go further and find a fourth step in this development, where the songs of white America have been distinctively influenced by the slave songs or have incorporated whole phrases of Negro melody, as "Swanee River" and "Old Black Joe." Side by side, too, with the growth has gone the debasements and imitations—the Negro "minstrel" songs, many of the "gospel" hymns, and some of the contemporary "coon" songs,—a mass of music in which the novice may easily lose himself and never find the real Negro melodies.

In these songs, I have said, the slave spoke to the world. Such a message is naturally veiled and half articulate. Words and music have lost each other and new and cant phrases of a dimly understood theology have displaced the older sentiment. Once in a while we catch a strange word of an unknown tongue, as the "Mighty Myo," which figures as a river of death; more often slight words or mere doggerel are joined to music of singular sweetness. Purely secular songs are few in number, partly because many of them were turned into hymns by a change of words, partly because the frolics were seldom heard by the stranger, and the music less often caught. Of nearly all the songs, however, the music is distinctly sorrowful. The ten master songs I have mentioned tell in word and music of trouble and exile, of strife and hiding; they grope toward some unseen power and sigh for rest in the End.

The words that are left to us are not without interest, and, cleared of evident dross, they conceal much of real poetry and meaning beneath conventional theology and unmeaning rhapsody. Like all primitive folk, the slave stood near to Nature's heart. Life was a "rough and rolling sea" like the brown Atlantic of the Sea Islands; the "Wilderness" was the home of God, and the "lonesome valley" led to the way of life. "Winter 'll soon be over," was the picture of life and death to a tropical imagination. The sudden wild thunderstorms of the South awed and impressed the Negroes,—at times the rumbling seemed to them "mournful," at times imperious:

> "My Lord calls me,
> He calls me by the thunder,
> The trumpet sounds it in my soul."

The monotonous toil and exposure is painted in many words. One sees the ploughmen in the hot, moist furrow, singing:

> "Dere 's no rain to wet you,
> Dere 's no sun to burn you,
> Oh, push along, believer,
> I want to go home."

The bowed and bent old man cries, with thrice-repeated wail:

"O Lord, keep me from sinking down,"

and he rebukes the devil of doubt who can whisper:

"Jesus is dead and God 's gone away."

Yet the soul-hunger is there, the restlessness of the savage, the wail of the wanderer, and the plaint is put in one little phrase:

My soul wants some thing that's new, that's new

Over the inner thoughts of the slaves and their relations one with another the shadow of fear ever hung, so that we get but glimpses here and there, and also with them, eloquent omissions and silences. Mother and child are sung, but seldom father; fugitive and weary wanderer call for pity and affection, but there is little of wooing and wedding; the rocks and the mountains are well known, but home is unknown. Strange blending of love and helplessness sings through the refrain:

"Yonder 's my ole mudder,
Been waggin' at de hill so long;
'Bout time she cross over,
Git home bime-by."

Elsewhere comes the cry of the "motherless" and the "Farewell, farewell, my only child."

Love-songs are scarce and fall into two categories—the frivolous and light, and the sad. Of deep successful love there is ominous silence, and in one of the oldest of these songs there is a depth of history and meaning:

Poor Ro - sy, poor gal; Poor Ro - sy,

poor gal; Ro - sy break my poor heart.
Heav'n shall - a - be my home.

A black woman said of the song, "It can't be sung without a full heart and a troubled sperrit." The same voice sings here that sings in the German folk-song:

"Jetz Geh i' an's brunele, trink' aber net."

Of death the Negro showed little fear, but talked of it familiarly and even fondly as simply a crossing of the waters, perhaps—who knows?—back to his ancient forests again. Later days transfigured his fatalism, and amid the dust and dirt the toiler sang:

"Dust, dust and ashes, fly over my grave,
But the Lord shall bear my spirit home."

The things evidently borrowed from the surrounding world undergo characteristic change when they enter the mouth of the slave. Especially is this true of Bible phrases. "Weep, O captive daughter of Zion," is quaintly turned into "Zion, weep-a-low," and the wheels of Ezekiel are turned every way in the mystic dreaming of the slave, till he says:

"There 's a little wheel a-turnin' in-a-my heart."

As in olden time, the words of these hymns were improvised by some leading minstrel of the religious band. The circumstances of the gathering, however, the rhythm of the songs, and the limitations of allowable thought, confined the poetry for the most part to single or double lines, and they seldom were expanded to quatrains or longer tales, although there are some few examples of sustained efforts, chiefly paraphrases of the Bible. Three short series of verses have always attracted me,—the one that heads this chapter, of one line of which Thomas Wentworth Higginson has fittingly said, "Never, it seems to me, since man first lived and suffered was his infinite longing for peace uttered more plaintively." The second and third are descriptions of the Last Judgment, —the one a late improvisation, with some traces of outside influence:

"Oh, the stars in the elements are falling,
And the moon drips away into blood,
And the ransomed of the Lord are returning unto God,
Blessed be the name of the Lord."

And the other earlier and homelier picture from the low coast lands:

"Michael, haul the boat ashore,
Then you 'll hear the horn they blow,
Then you 'll hear the trumpet sound,
Trumpet sound the world around,
Trumpet sound for rich and poor,
Trumpet sound the Jubilee,
Trumpet sound for you and me."

Through all the sorrow of the Sorrow Songs there breathes a hope—a faith in the ultimate justice of things. The minor cadences of despair change often to triumph and calm confidence. Sometimes it is faith in life, sometimes a faith in death, sometimes assurance of boundless justice in some fair world beyond. But whichever it is, the meaning is always clear: that sometime, somewhere, men will judge men by their souls and not by their skins. Is such a hope justified? Do the Sorrow Songs sing true?

The silently growing assumption of this age is that the probation of races is past, and that the backward races of to-day are of proven inefficiency and not worth the saving. Such an assumption is the arrogance of peoples irreverent toward Time and ignorant of the deeds of men. A thousand years ago such an assumption, easily possible, would have made it difficult for the Teuton to prove his right to life. Two thousand years ago such dogmatism, readily welcome, would have scouted the idea of blond races ever leading civilization. So wofully unorganized is sociological knowledge that the meaning of progress, the meaning of "swift" and "slow" in human doing, and the limits of human perfectability, are veiled, unanswered sphinxes on the shores of science. Why should Æschylus have sung two thousand years before Shakespeare was born? Why has civilization flourished in Europe, and flickered, flamed, and died in Africa? So long as the world stands meekly dumb before such questions, shall this nation proclaim its ignorance and unhallowed prejudices by denying freedom of opportunity to those who brought the Sorrow Songs to the Seats of the Mighty?

Your country? How came it yours? Before the Pilgrims landed we were here. Here we have brought our three gifts and mingled them with yours: a gift of story and song—soft, stirring melody in an ill-harmonized and unmelodious land; the gift of sweat and brawn to beat back the wilderness, conquer the soil, and lay the foundations of this vast economic empire two hundred years earlier than your weak hands could have done it; the third, a gift of the Spirit. Around us the history of the land has centred for thrice a hundred years; out of the nation's heart we have called all that was best to throttle and subdue all that was worst; fire and blood, prayer and sacrifice, have billowed over this people, and they have found peace only in the altars of the God of Right. Nor has our gift of the Spirit been merely passive. Actively we have woven ourselves with the very warp and woof of this nation,—we fought their battles, shared their sorrow, mingled our blood with theirs, and generation after generation have pleaded with a headstrong, careless people to despise not Justice, Mercy, and Truth, lest the nation be smitten with a curse. Our song, our toil, our cheer, and warning have been given to this nation in blood-brotherhood. Are not these gifts worth the giving? Is not this work and striving? Would America have been America without her Negro people?

Even so is the hope that sang in the songs of my fathers well sung. If somewhere in this whirl and chaos of things there dwells Eternal Good, pitiful yet masterful, then anon in His good time America shall rend the Veil and the prisoned shall go free. Free, free as the sunshine trickling down the morning into these high windows of mine, free as yonder fresh young voices welling up to me from the caverns of brick and mortar below—swelling with song, instinct with life, tremulous treble and darkening bass. My children, my little children, are singing to the sunshine, and thus they sing:

And the traveller girds himself, and sets his face toward the Morning, and goes his way.

THE AFTER-THOUGHT

Hear my cry, O God the Reader; vouchsafe that this my book fall not still-born into the world-wilderness. Let there spring, Gentle One, from out its leaves vigor of thought and thoughtful deed to reap the harvest wonderful. (Let the ears of a guilty people tingle with truth, and seventy millions sigh for the righteousness which exalteth nations, in this drear day when human brotherhood is mockery and a snare.) Thus in Thy good time may infinite reason turn the tangle straight, and these crooked marks on a fragile leaf be not indeed

THE END

DUSK OF DAWN

An Essay Toward an Autobiography of a Race Concept

TO

KEEP THE MEMORY

OF

Joel Spingarn

SCHOLAR AND KNIGHT

Apology

I have essayed in a half century three sets of thought centering around the hurts and hesitancies that hem the black man in America. The first of these, "The Souls of Black Folk," written thirty-seven years ago was a cry at midnight thick within the veil, when none rightly knew the coming day. The second, "Darkwater," now twenty years old, was an exposition and militant challenge, defiant with dogged hope. This the third book started to record dimly but consciously that subtle sense of coming day which one feels of early mornings even when mist and murk hang low. But midway in its writing, it changed its object and pattern, because of the revelation of a seventieth birthday and the unawaited remarks and comments thereon. It threatened thereupon to become mere autobiography. But in my own experience, autobiographies have had little lure; repeatedly they assume too much or too little: too much in dreaming that one's own life has greatly influenced the world; too little in the reticences, repressions and distortions which come because men do not dare to be absolutely frank. My life had its significance and its only deep significance because it was part of a Problem; but that problem was, as I continue to think, the central problem of the greatest of the world's democracies and so the Problem of the future world. The problem of the future world is the charting, by means of intelligent reason, of a path not simply through the resistances of physical force, but through the vaster and far more intricate jungle of ideas conditioned on unconscious and subconscious reflexes of living things; on blind unreason and often irresistible urges of sensitive matter; of which the concept of race is today one of the most unyielding and threatening. I seem to see a way of elucidating the inner meaning and significance of that race problem by explaining it in terms of the one human life that I know best.

I have written then what is meant to be not so much my autobiography as the autobiography of a concept of race, elucidated, magnified and doubtless distorted in the thoughts and deeds which were mine. If the first two books were written in tears and blood, this is set down no less determinedly but yet with wider hope in some more benign fluid. Wherefore I have not hesitated in calling it "Dusk of Dawn."

Contents

Chapter 1

THE PLOT

FROM 1868 to 1940 stretch seventy-two mighty years, which are incidentally the years of my own life but more especially years of cosmic significance, when one remembers that they rush from the American Civil War to the reign of the second Roosevelt; from Victoria to the Sixth George; from the Franco-Prussian to the two World Wars. They contain the rise and fall of the Hohenzollerns, the shadowy emergence, magnificence and miracle of Russia; the turmoil of Asia in China, India and Japan, and the world-wide domination of white Europe.

In the folds of this European civilization I was born and shall die, imprisoned, conditioned, depressed, exalted and inspired. Integrally a part of it and yet, much more significant, one of its rejected parts; one who expressed in life and action and made vocal to many, a single whirlpool of social entanglement and inner psychological paradox, which always seem to me more significant for the meaning of the world today than other similar and related problems.

Little indeed did I do, or could I conceivably have done, to make this problem or to loose it. Crucified on the vast wheel of time, I flew round and round with the Zeitgeist, waving my pen and lifting faint voices to explain, expound and exhort; to see, foresee and prophesy, to the few who could or would listen. Thus very evidently to me and to others I did little to create my day or greatly change it; but I did exemplify it and thus for all time my life is significant for all lives of men.

What now was this particular social problem which, through the chances of birth and existence, became so peculiarly mine? At bottom and in essence it was as old as human life. Yet in its revelation, through the nineteenth century, it was significantly and fatally new: the differences between men; differences in their appearance, in their physique, in their thoughts and customs; differences so great and so impelling that always from the beginning of time, they thrust themselves forward upon the consciousness of all living things. Culture among human beings came to be and had to be built upon knowledge and recognition of these differences.

But after the scientific method had been conceived in the seventeenth century it came toward the end of the eighteenth century to be applied to man and to man as he appeared then, with no wide or intensive inquiry into what he had been or how he had lived in the past. In the nineteenth century however came the revolution of conceiving the world not as permanent structure but as changing growth and then the study of man as changing and developing physical and social entity had to begin.

But the mind clung desperately to the idea that basic racial differences between human beings had suffered no change; and it clung to this idea not simply from inertia and unconscious action but from the fact that because of the modern African slave trade a tremendous economic structure and eventually an industrial revolution had been based upon racial differences between men; and this racial difference had now been rationalized into a difference mainly of skin color. Thus in the latter part of the nineteenth century when I was born and grew to manhood, color had become an abiding unchangeable fact chiefly because a mass of self-conscious instincts and unconscious prejudices had arranged themselves rank on rank in its defense. Government, work, religion and education became based upon and determined by the color line. The future of mankind was implicit in the race and color of men.

Already in my boyhood this matter of color loomed significantly. My skin was darker than that of my schoolmates. My family confined itself not entirely but largely to people of this same darker hue. Even when in fact the color was lighter, this was an unimportant variation from the norm. As I grew older, and saw the peoples of the land and of the world, the problem changed from a simple thing of color, to a broader, deeper matter of social condition: to millions of folk born of dark slaves, with the slave heritage in mind and home; millions of people spawned in compulsory ignorance; to a whole problem of the uplift of the lowly who formed the darker races.

This social condition pictured itself gradually in my mind as a matter of education, as a matter of knowledge; as a matter of scientific procedure in a world which had become scientific in concept. Later, however, all this frame of concept became blurred and distorted. There was evidently evil and hindrance blocking the way of life. Not science alone could settle this matter, but force must come to its aid. The black world must fight for freedom. It must fight with the weapons of Truth, with the sword of the intrepid, uncompromising Spirit, with organization in boycott, propaganda and mob frenzy. Upon this state of mind after a few years of conspicuous progress fell the horror of World War—of ultimate agitation, propaganda and murder.

The lesson of fighting was unforgettable; it was eternal loss and cost in victory or defeat. And again my problem of human difference, of the color line, of social degradation, of the fight for freedom became transformed. First and natural to the emergence of colder and more mature manhood from hot youth, I saw that the color bar could not be broken by a series of brilliant immediate assaults. Secondly, I saw defending this bar not simply ignorance and ill will; these to be sure; but also certain more powerful motives less open to reason or appeal. There were economic motives, urges to build wealth on the backs of black slaves and colored serfs; there followed those unconscious acts and irrational reactions, unpierced by reason, whose current form depended on the long history of relation and contact between thought and idea. In this case not sudden assault but long siege was indicated; careful planning and subtle campaign with the education of growing generations and propaganda.

For all this, time was needed to move the resistance in vast areas of unreason and especially in the minds of men where conscious present motive had been built on false rationalization. Meantime the immediate problem of the Negro was the question of securing existence, of labor and income, of food and home, of spiritual independence and democratic control of the industrial process. It would not do to concenter all effort on economic well-being and forget freedom and manhood and equality. Rather Negroes must live and eat and strive, and still hold unfaltering commerce with the stars.

Finally, I could see that the scientific task of the twentieth century would be to explore and measure the scope of chance and unreason in human action, which does not yield to argument but changes slowly and with difficulty after long study and careful development.

My intent in this book is to set forth the interaction of this stream and change of my thought, on my work and in relation to what has been going on in the world since my birth. Not so much its causal relation, for that in sheer limitation of opportunity was small; but rather of its intellectual relations, of its psychological interactions, and of the consequent results of these for me and many millions, who with me have had their lives shaped and directed by this course of events.

Chapter 2

A NEW ENGLAND BOY AND RECONSTRUCTION

As I HAVE written elsewhere, "I was born by a golden river and in the shadow of two great hills." My birthplace was Great Barrington, a little town in western Massachusetts in the valley of the Housatonic, flanked by the Berkshire hills. Physically and socially our community belonged to the Dutch valley of the Hudson rather than to Puritan New England, and travel went south to New York more often and more easily than east to Boston. But my birthplace was less important than my birth-time. The Civil War had closed but three years earlier and 1868 was the year in which the freedmen of the South were enfranchised and for the first time as a mass took part in government. Conventions with black delegates voted new constitutions all over the South; and two groups of laborers—freed slaves and poor whites—dominated the former slave states. It was an extraordinary experiment in democracy. Thaddeus Stevens, the clearest-headed leader of this attempt at industrial democracy, made his last speech impeaching Andrew Johnson on February sixteenth and on February twenty-third I was born.

Less than a month after my birth Andrew Johnson passed from the scene and Ulysses Grant became President of the United States. The Fifteenth Amendment enfranchising the Negro as a race became law and the work of abolishing slavery and making Negroes men was accomplished, so far as law could do it. Meanwhile elsewhere in the world there were stirring and change which were to mean much in my life: in Japan the Meiji Emperors rose to power the year I was born; in China the intrepid Empress Dowager was fighting strangulation by England and France; Prussia had fought with Austria and France, and the German Empire arose in 1871. In England, Victoria opened her eighth parliament; the duel of Disraeli and Gladstone began; while in Africa came the Abyssinian expedition and opening of the Suez Canal, so fateful for all my people.

My town was shut in by its mountains and provincialism;

but it was a beautiful place, a little New England town nestled shyly in its valley with something of Dutch cleanliness and English reticence. The Housatonic yellowed by the paper mills, rolled slowly through its center; while Green River, clear and beautiful, joined in to the south. Main Street was lined with ancient elms; the hills held white pines and orchards and then faded up to magnificent rocks and caves which shut out the neighboring world. The people were mainly of English descent with much Dutch blood and with a large migration of Irish and German workers to the mills as laborers.

The social classes of the town were built partly on landholding farmers and more especially on manufacturers and merchants, whose prosperity was due in no little degree to the new and high tariff. The rich people of the town were not very rich nor many in number. The middle class were farmers, merchants and artisans; and beneath these was a small proletariat of Irish and German mill workers. They lived in slums near the woolen mills and across the river clustering about the Catholic Church. The number of colored people in the town and county was small. They were all, save directly after the war, old families, well-known to the old settlers among the whites. The color line was manifest and yet not absolutely drawn. I remember a cousin of mine who brought home a white wife. The chief objection was that he was not able to support her and nobody knew about her family; and knowledge of family history was counted as highly important. Most of the colored people had some white blood from unions several generations past. That they congregated together in their own social life was natural because that was the rule in the town: there were little social knots of people, but not much that today would be called social life, save that which centered about the churches; and there the colored folk often took part. My grandmother was Episcopalian and my mother, Congregational. I grew up in the Congregational Sunday school.

In Great Barrington there were perhaps twenty-five, certainly not more than fifty, colored folk in a population of five thousand. My family was among the oldest inhabitants of the valley. The family had spread slowly through the county intermarrying among cousins and other black folk with some but limited infiltration of white blood. Other dark families had come in and there was some intermingling with local Indians. In one or two cases there were groups of apparently later black immigrants, near Sheffield for instance. There survives there even to this day an isolated group of black folk whose origin is obscure. We knew little of them but felt above them because of our education and economic status.

The economic status was not high. The early members of the family supported themselves on little farms of a few acres; then drifted to town as laborers and servants, but did not go into the mills. Most of them rented homes, but some owned little homes and pieces of land; a few had very pleasant and well-furnished homes, but none had anything like wealth.

My immediate family, which I remember as a young child, consisted of a very dark grandfather, Othello Burghardt, sitting beside the fireplace in a high chair, because of an injured hip. He was good-natured but not energetic. The energy was in my grandmother, Sally, a thin, tall, yellow and hawk-faced woman, certainly beautiful in her youth, and efficient and managing in her age. My mother, Mary Sylvina, was born at Great Barrington, January 14, 1831, and died there in 1885 at the age of fifty-four years. She had at the age of thirty a son, Idelbert, born of her and her cousin, John Burghardt. The circumstances of this romance I never knew. No one talked of it in the family. Perhaps there was an actual marriage. If so, it was not recorded in the family Bible. Perhaps the mating was broken up on account of the consanguinity of the cousins by a family tradition which had a New England strictness in its sex morals. So far as I ever knew there was only one illegitimate child throughout the family in my grandfather's and the two succeeding generations. My mother was brown and rather small with smooth skin and lovely eyes, and hair that curled and crinkled down each side her forehead from the part in the middle. She was rather silent but very determined and very patient. My father, a light mulatto, died in my infancy so that I do not remember him. I shall later speak more intimately of him.

I was born in a rather nice little cottage which belonged to a black South Carolinian, whose own house stood next, at the lower end of one of the pleasant streets of the town. Then for a time I lived in the country at the house of my grandfather, Othello, one of three farming brothers. It was sturdy, small and old-fashioned. Later we moved back to town and lived in quarters over the woodshed of one of the town's better mansions. After that we lived awhile over a store by the railway and during my high school years in a little four room tenement house on the same street where I was born, but farther up, down a lane and in the rear of a home owned by the widow of a New York physician. None of these homes had modern conveniences but they were weatherproof, fairly warm in winter and furnished with some comfort.

For several generations my people had attended schools for longer or shorter periods so most of them could read and write. I was brought up from earliest years with the idea of regular attendance at school. This was partly because the schools of Great Barrington were near at hand, simple but good, well-taught, and truant laws were enforced. I started on one school ground, which I remember vividly, at the age of five or six years, and continued there in school until I was graduated from high school at sixteen. I was seldom absent or tardy, and the school ran regularly ten months in the year with a few vacations. The curriculum was simple: reading, writing, spelling and arithmetic; grammar, geography and history. We learned the alphabet; we were drilled rigorously on the multiplication tables and we drew accurate maps. We could spell correctly and read clearly.

By the time I neared the high school, economic problems and questions of the future began to loom. These were partly settled by my own activities. My mother was then a widow with limited resources of income through boarding the barber, my uncle; supplemented infrequently by day's work, and by some kindly but unobtrusive charity. But I was keen and eager to eke out this income by various jobs: splitting kindling, mowing lawns, doing chores. My first regular wage began as I entered the high school: I went early of mornings and filled with coal one or two of the new so-called "base-burning" stoves in the millinery shop of Madame L'Hommedieu. From then on, all through my high school course, I worked after school and on Saturdays; I sold papers, distributed tea from the new A & P stores in New York; and for a few months, through the good will of Johnny Morgan, actually rose to be local correspondent of the *Springfield Republican.*

Meantime the town and its surroundings were a boy's paradise: there were mountains to climb and rivers to wade and swim; lakes to freeze and hills for coasting. There were orchards and caves and wide green fields; and all of it was apparently property of the children of the town. My earlier contacts with playmates and other human beings were normal and pleasant. Sometimes there was a dearth of available playmates but that was peculiar to the conventions of the town where families were small and children must go to bed early and not loaf on the streets or congregate in miscellaneous crowds. Later, in the high school, there came some rather puzzling distinctions which I can see now were social and racial; but the racial angle was more clearly defined against the Irish than against me. It was a matter of income and ancestry more than color. I have written elsewhere of the case of exchanging visiting cards where one girl, a stranger, did not seem to want mine to my vast surprise.

I presume I was saved evidences of a good deal of actual discrimination by my own keen sensitiveness. My companions did not have a chance to refuse me invitations; they must seek me out and urge me to come as indeed they often did. When my presence was not wanted they had only to refrain from asking. But in the ordinary social affairs of the village—the Sunday school with its picnics and festivals; the temporary skating rink in the town hall; the coasting in crowds on all the hills—in all these, I took part with no thought of discrimination on the part of my fellows, for that I would have been the first to notice.

Later, I was protected in part by the fact that there was little social activity in the high school; there were no fraternities; there were no school dances; there were no honor societies. Whatever of racial feeling gradually crept into my life, its effect upon me in these earlier days was rather one of exaltation and high disdain. They were the losers who did not ardently court me and not I, which seemed to be proven by the fact that I had no difficulty in outdoing them in nearly all competition, especially intellectual. In athletics I was not outstanding. I was only moderately good at baseball and football; but at running, exploring, story-telling and planning of intricate games, I was often if not always the leader. This made discrimination all the more difficult.

When, however, during my high school course the matter of my future career began to loom, there were difficulties. The colored population of the town had been increased a little by "contrabands," who on the whole were well received by the colored group; although the older group held some of its social distinctions and the newcomers astonished us by forming a little Negro Methodist Zion Church, which we sometimes attended. The work open to colored folk was limited. There was day labor; there was farming; there was house-service, particularly work in summer hotels; but for a young, educated and ambitious colored man, what were the possibilities? And the practical answer to this inquiry was: Why encourage a young colored man toward such higher training? I imagine this matter was discussed considerably among my friends, white and black, and in a way it was settled partially before I realized it.

My high school principal was Frank Hosmer, afterward president of Oahu College, Hawaii. He suggested, quite as a matter of fact, that I ought to take the college preparatory course which involved algebra, geometry, Latin and Greek. If Hosmer had been another sort of man, with definite ideas as to a Negro's "place," and had recommended agricultural "science" or domestic economy, I would doubtless have followed his advice, had such "courses" been available. I did not then realize that Hosmer was quietly opening college doors to me, for in those days they were barred with ancient tongues. This meant a considerable expenditure for books which were not free in those days—more than my folk could afford; but the wife of one of the mill-owners, or rather I ought to describe her as the mother of one of my playmates, after some hesitation offered to furnish all the necessary school books. I became therefore a high school student preparing for college and thus occupying an unusual position in the town even among whites, although there had been one or two other colored boys in the past who had gotten at least part of a high school education. In this way I was thrown with the upper rather than the lower social classes and protected in many ways. I came in touch with rich folk, summer boarders, who made yearly incursions from New York. Their beautiful clothes impressed me tremendously but otherwise I found them quite ordinary. The children did not have much sense or training; they were not very strong and rather too well dressed to have a good time playing.

I had little contact with crime and degradation. The slums in the town were not bad and repelled me, partly because they were inhabited by the foreign-born. There was one house among colored folk, where I now realize there must have been a good deal of gambling, drinking and other looseness. The inmates were pleasant to me but I was never asked to enter and of course had no desire. In the whole town, colored and white, there was not much crime. The one excess was drunkenness and there my mother quietly took a firm stand. I was never to enter a liquor saloon. I never did. I donned a Murphy "blue ribbon." And yet perhaps, as I now see, the one solace that this pleasant but spiritually rather drab little town had against the monotony of life was liquor; and rich and poor got drunk more or less regularly. I have seen one of the mill owners staggering home, and my very respectable uncle used to come home now and then walking exceedingly straight.

I was born in a community which conceived itself as having helped put down a wicked rebellion for the purpose of freeing four million slaves. All respectable people belonged to the Republican Party, but Democrats were tolerated, although regarded with some surprise and hint of motive. Most of the older men had been soldiers, including members of my own family. The town approached in politics a pure democracy with annual town meeting and elections of well-known and fairly qualified officials. We were placidly religious. The bulk of the well-to-do people belonged to the Episcopal and Congregational churches, a small number of farmers and artisans to the Methodist Church and the Irish workers to the Catholic Church across the river. The marriage laws and family relations were fairly firm. The chief delinquency was drunkenness and the major social problem of the better classes was the status of women who had little or no opportunity to marry.

My ideas of property and work during my boyhood were vague. They did not present themselves to me as problems. As a family we owned little property and our income was always small. Spending money for me came first as small gifts of pennies or a nickel from relatives; once I received a silver dollar, a huge fortune. Later I earned all my spending funds. I can see now that my mother must have struggled pretty desperately on very narrow resources and that the problem of shoes and clothes for me must have been at times staggering. But these matters seldom bothered me because they were not brought to my attention. My general attitude toward property and income was that all who were willing to work could easily earn a living; that those who had property had earned it and deserved it and could use it as they wished; that poverty was the shadow of crime and connoted lack of thrift and shiftlessness. These were the current patterns of economic thought of the town in my boyhood.

In Great Barrington the first glimpse of the outer and wider world I got, was through Johnny Morgan's news shop which occupied the front end of the post office. There newspapers and books were on display and I remember very early seeing pictures of "U. S." Grant, and of "Bill" Tweed who was beginning his extraordinary career in New York City; and later I saw pictures of Hayes and of the smooth and rather cruel face of Tilden. Of the great things happening in the United States at that time, we were actually touched only by the Panic of 1873. When my uncle came home from a little town east of us where he was the leading barber, he brought me, I remember, a silver dollar which was an extraordinary thing: up to that time I had seen nothing but paper money. I was six when Charles Sumner died and the Freedmen's Bank closed; and when I was eight there came the revolution of 1876 in the South, and Victoria of England became Empress of India; but I did not know the meaning of these events until long after.

In general thought and conduct I became quite thoroughly New England. It was not good form in Great Barrington to express one's thought volubly, or to give way to excessive emotion. We were even sparing in our daily greetings. I am quite sure that in a less restrained and conventional atmosphere I should have easily learned to express my emotions with far greater and more unrestrained intensity; but as it was I had the social heritage not only of a New England clan but Dutch taciturnity. This was later reinforced and strengthened by inner withdrawals in the face of real and imagined discriminations. The result was that I was early thrown in upon myself. I found it difficult and even unnecessary to approach other people and by that same token my own inner life perhaps grew the richer; but the habit of repression often returned to plague me in after years, for so early a habit could not easily be unlearned. The Negroes in the South, when I came to know them, could never understand why I did not naturally greet everyone I passed on the street or slap my friends on the back.

During my high school career I had a chance for the first time to step beyond the shadow of the hills which hemmed in my little valley. My father's father was living in New Bedford and his third wife who had greatly loved my own father wanted my grandfather to know and recognize me. The grandfather, a short thick-set man, "colored" but quite white in appearance, with austere face, was hard and set in his ways, proud and bitter. My father and grandfather had not been able to get along together. Of them, I shall speak more intimately later. I went to New Bedford in 1883 at the age of fifteen. On the way I saw Hartford and Providence. I called on my uncle in Amherst and received a new navy-blue suit. Grandfather was a gentleman in manner, precise and formal. He looked at me coolly, but in the end he was not unpleasant. I went down across the water to Martha's Vineyard and saw what was then "Cottage City" and came home by way of Springfield and Albany where I was a guest of my older half-brother and saw my first electric street light blink and sputter.

I was graduated from high school in 1884 and was of course the only colored student. Once during my course another young dark man had attended the school for a short time but I was very much ashamed of him because he did not excel the whites as I was quite used to doing. All thirteen of us had orations and mine was on "Wendell Phillips." The great anti-slavery agitator had just died in February and I presume that some of my teachers must have suggested the subject, although it is quite possible that I chose it myself. But I was fascinated by his life and his work and took a long step toward a wider conception of what I was going to do. I spoke in June and then came face to face with the problem of my future life.

My mother lived proudly to see me graduate but died in the fall and I went to live with an aunt. I was strongly advised that I was too young to enter college. Williams had been suggested, because most of our few high school graduates who went to college had attended there; but my heart was set on Harvard. It was the greatest and oldest college and I therefore quite naturally thought it was the one I must attend. Of course I did not realize the difficulties: some difficulties in entrance examinations because our high school was not quite up to the Harvard standard; but a major difficulty of money. There must have been in my family and among my friends a good deal of anxious discussion as to my future but finally it was temporarily postponed when I was offered a job and promised that the next fall I should begin my college work.

The job brought me in unexpected touch with the world. There had been a great-uncle of mine, Tom Burghardt, whose tombstone I had seen often in the town graveyard. My family used to say in undertones that the money of Tom Burghardt helped to build the Pacific Railroad and that this came about in this wise: nearly all his life Tom Burghardt had been a servant in the Kellogg family, only the family usually forgot to pay him; but finally they did give him a handsome burial. Then Mark Hopkins, a son or relative of the great Mark, appeared on the scene and married a daughter of the Kelloggs. He became one of the Huntington-Stanford-Crocker Pacific Associates who built, manipulated and cornered the Pacific railroads and with the help of the Kellogg nest-egg, Hopkins made nineteen million dollars in the West by methods not to be inquired into. His widow came back to Great Barrington in the eighties and planned a mansion out of the beautiful blue granite which formed our hills. A host of workmen, masons, stone-cutters and carpenters were assembled, and in the summer of 1884 I was made time-keeper for the contractors who carried on this job. I received the fabulous wage of a dollar a day. It was a most interesting experience and had new and intriguing bits of reality and romance. As time-keeper and the obviously young and inexperienced agent of superiors, I was the one who handed the discharged workers their last wage envelopes. I talked with contractors and saw the problems of employers. I pored over the plans and specifications and even came in contact with the elegant English architect Searles who finally came to direct the work.

The widow had a steward, a fine, young educated colored fellow who had come to be her right-hand man; but the architect supplanted him. He had the glamour of an English gentleman. The steward was gradually pushed aside and down into his place. The architect eventually married the widow and her wealth and the steward killed himself. So the Hopkins millions passed strangely into foreign hands and gave me my first problem of inheritance. But in the meantime the fabrication and growth of this marvelous palace, beautiful beyond anything that Great Barrington had seen, went slowly and majestically on, and always I could sit and watch it grow.

Finally in the fall of 1885, the difficulty of my future education was solved. The whole subtlety of the plan was clear neither to me nor my relatives at the time. Merely I was offered through the Reverend C. C. Painter, once excellent Federal Indian Agent, a scholarship to attend Fisk University in Nashville, Tennessee; the funds were to be furnished by four Connecticut churches which Mr. Painter had formerly pastored. Disappointed though I was at not being able to go to Harvard, I merely regarded this as a temporary change of plan; I would of course go to Harvard in the end. But here and immediately was adventure. I was going into the South; the South of slavery, rebellion and black folk; and above all I was going to meet colored people of my own age and education, of my own ambitions. Once or twice already I had had swift glimpses of the colored world: at Rocky Point on Narragansett Bay, I had attended an annual picnic beside the sea, and had seen in open-mouthed astonishment the whole gorgeous color gamut of the American Negro world; the swaggering men, the beautiful girls, the laughter and gaiety, the unhampered self-expression. I was astonished and inspired. I became aware, once a chance to go to a group of such young people was opened up for me, of the spiritual isolation in which I was living. I heard too in these days for the first time the Negro folk songs. A Hampton Quartet had sung them in the Congregational Church. I was thrilled and moved to tears and seemed to recognize something inherently and deeply my own. I was glad to go to Fisk.

On the other hand my people had undoubtedly a more discriminating and unromantic view of the situation. They said frankly that it was a shame to send me South. I was Northern born and bred and instead of preparing me for work and giving me an opportunity right there in my own town and state, they were bundling me off to the South. This was undoubtedly true. The educated young white folk of Great Barrington became clerks in stores, bookkeepers and teachers, while a few went into professions. Great Barrington was not able to conceive of me in such local position. It was not so much that they were opposed to it, but it did not occur to them as a possibility.

On the other hand there was the call of the black South; teachers were needed. The crusade of the New England schoolmarm was in full swing. The freed slaves, if properly led, had a great future. Temporarily deprived of their full voting privileges, this was but a passing set-back. Black folk were bound in time to dominate the South. They needed trained leadership. I was sent to help furnish it.

I started out and went into Tennessee at the age of seventeen to be a sophomore at Fisk University. It was to me an extraordinary experience. I was thrilled to be for the first time among so many people of my own color or rather of such various and such extraordinary colors, which I had only glimpsed before, but who it seemed were bound to me by new and exciting and eternal ties. Never before had I seen young men so self-assured and who gave themselves such airs, and colored men at that; and above all for the first time I saw beautiful girls. At my home among my white school mates there were a few pretty girls; but either they were not entrancing or because I had known them all my life I did not notice them; but at Fisk at the first dinner I saw opposite me a girl of whom I have often said, no human being could possibly have been as beautiful as she seemed to my young eyes that far-off September night of 1885.

Chapter 3

EDUCATION IN THE LAST DECADES OF THE NINETEENTH CENTURY

TODAY BOTH youth and age look upon a world whose foundations seem to be tottering. They are not sure what the morrow will bring; perhaps the complete overthrow of European civilization, of that great enveloping mass of culture into which they were born. Everything in their environment is a meet subject for criticism. They can dispassionately evaluate the past and speculate upon the future. It is a day of fundamental change. On the other hand when I was a young man, so far as I conceived, the foundations of present culture were laid, the way was charted, the progress toward certain great goals was undoubted and inevitable. There was room for argument concerning details and methods and possible detours in the onsweep of civilization; but the fundamental facts were clear, unquestioned and unquestionable.

Between the years 1885 and 1894 I received my education at Fisk University, Harvard College and the University of Berlin. It was difficult for me at the time to form any critical estimate of any meaning of the world which differed from the conventional unanimity about me. Apparently one consideration alone saved me from complete conformity with the thoughts and confusions of then current social trends; and that was the problems of racial and cultural contacts. Otherwise I might easily have been simply the current product of my day. Even as it was, the struggle for which I was preparing and the situations which I was trying to conceive and study, related themselves primarily to the plight of the comparatively small group of American Negroes with which I was identified, and theoretically to the larger Negro race. I did not face the general plight and conditions of all humankind. That I took for granted, and in the unanimity of thought and development of that day, this was scarcely to be wondered at.

It was a day of Progress with a capital P. Population in all the culture lands was increasing, doubling and more; cities everywhere were growing and expanding and making themselves the centers and almost the only centers of civilization; transportation by land and sea was drawing the nations near and making the lands of the earth increasingly accessible. Invention and technique were a perpetual marvel and their accomplishment infinite in possibility; commerce was madly seeking markets all around the earth; colonies were being seized and countries integrated in Asia, Africa, South America and the islands.

Above all science was becoming religion; psychology was reducing metaphysics to experiment and a sociology of human action was planned. Fighting the vast concept of evolution, religion went into its heresy trials, its struggle with "higher criticism," its discomfort at the "revised version" of the New Testament which was published the year I entered college. Wealth was God. Everywhere men sought wealth and especially in America there was extravagant living; everywhere the poor planned to be rich and the rich planned to be richer; everywhere wider, bigger, higher, better things were set down as inevitable.

All this, of course, dominated education; especially the economic order determined what the next generation should learn and know. On the whole, looking at the marvelous industrial expansion of America, seeing the rise of the western farmer and the wages of the eastern mechanic, all was well; or if not, if there were ominous protests and upheavals, these were but the friction necessary to all advance. "God's in His heaven; All's right with the world," Browning was singing—that colored Robert Browning, who died just after I received my first bachelor's degree.

Had it not been for the race problem early thrust upon me and enveloping me, I should have probably been an unquestioning worshiper at the shrine of the social order and economic development into which I was born. But just that part of that order which seemed to most of my fellows nearest perfection, seemed to me most inequitable and wrong; and starting from that critique, I gradually, as the years went by, found other things to question in my environment. At first, however, my criticism was confined to the relation of my people to the world movement. I was not questioning the world movement in itself. What the white world was doing, its goals and ideals, I had not doubted were quite right. What was wrong was that I and people like me and thousands of others who might have my ability and aspiration, were refused permission to be a part of this world. It was as though moving on a rushing express, my main thought was as to the relations I had to other passengers on the express, and not to its rate of speed and its destination. In the day of my formal education, my interest was concentered upon the race struggle. The fight on the moving car had to do with my relations to the car and its folk; but on the whole, nothing to do with the car's own movement. My attention from the first was focused on democracy and democratic development and upon the problem of the admission of my people into the freedom of democracy. This my school training touched but obliquely. We studied history and politics almost exclusively from the point of view of ancient German freedom, English and New England democracy, and the development of the United States.

Here, however, I could bring criticism from what I knew and saw touching the Negro. I was brought up in the primary democracy of a New England village. I attended the town meeting every spring and in the upper room in that little red brick town hall, fronted by a Roman "Victory" commemorating the Civil War, I listened to the citizens discuss things about which I knew and had opinions: streets and bridges and schools, and particularly the high school. Baretown Beebee, a dirty, ragged old hermit, used regularly to come down from his rocks and woods and denounce high school education and expense. Regularly the responsible citizens of the town sat and listened and then quietly voted the usual appropriation. That one recurring incident was a splendid part of my education.

The rest of my early political knowledge came largely from newspapers which I read outside my curriculum. I read of the contests of the Democratic and Republican parties, from the first seating of Hayes, through the administrations of Garfield and Arthur, Cleveland, Harrison, Cleveland again, and McKinley in 1895. All this complied with the conventional theory of party government, and while the issues were not as clear cut and the motives as unmixed as they ought to have been, nevertheless the increasing triumph of democratic government was in my mind unquestioned. The Populists as a third party movement beginning during this time, did not impress me.

The year before I entered college, England killed the arbitrary power of the Justice of the Peace and the County Squire, doubled the number of its voters and was forced into a struggle to yield Ireland home rule; eventually Japan attempted a constitution with elective representatives; Brazil became a republic while I was at Harvard, and during that time France fought successfully to curtail the political power of the Catholic Church.

My problem then was how, into the inevitable and logical democracy which was spreading over the world, could black folk in America and particularly in the South be openly and effectively admitted; and the colored people of the world allowed their own self-government? I therefore watched, outside my textbooks and without reference to my teachers, the race developments throughout the world. The difficulty here, however, was securing any real and exhaustive knowledge of facts. I could not get any clear picture of the current change in Africa and Asia.

Lynching was a continuing and recurrent horror during my college days: from 1885 through 1894, seventeen hundred Negroes were lynched in America. Each death was a scar upon my soul, and led me on to conceive the plight of other minority groups; for in my college days Italians were lynched in New Orleans, forcing the Federal government to pay $25,000 in indemnity, and the anti-Chinese riots in the West culminated in the Chinese Exclusion Act of 1892. Some echoes of Jewish segregation and pogroms in Russia came through the magazines; I followed the Dreyfus case; and I began to see something of the struggle between East and West in the Sino-Japanese War.

The three years at Fisk were years of growth and development. I learned new things about the world. My knowledge of the race problem became more definite. I saw discrimination in ways of which I had never dreamed; the separation of passengers on the railways of the South was just beginning; the race separation in living quarters throughout the cities and towns was manifest; the public disdain and even insult in race contact on the street continually took my breath; I came in contact for the first time with a sort of violence that I had never realized in New England; I remember going down and looking wide-eyed at the door of a public building, filled with buck-shot, where the editor of the leading daily paper had been publicly murdered the day before. I was astonished to find many of my fellow students carrying fire-arms and to hear their stories of adventure. On the other hand my personal contact with my teachers was inspiring and beneficial as indeed I suppose all personal contacts between human beings must be. Adam Spence of Fisk first taught me to know what the Greek language meant. In a funny little basement room crowded with apparatus, Frederick Chase gave me insight into natural science and talked with me about future study. I knew the President, Erastus Cravath, to be honest and sincere.

I determined to know something of the Negro in the country districts; to go out and teach during the summer vacation. I was not compelled to do this, for my scholarship was sufficient to support me, but that was not the point. I had heard about the country in the South as the real seat of slavery. I wanted to know it. I walked out into east Tennessee ten or more miles a day until at last in a little valley near Alexandria I found a place where there had been a Negro public school only once since the Civil War; and there for two successive terms during the summer I taught at $28 and $30 a month. It was an enthralling experience. I met new and intricate and unconscious discrimination. I was pleasantly surprised when the white school superintendent, on whom I had made a business call, invited me to stay for dinner; and he would have been astonished if he had dreamed that I expected to eat at the table with him and not after he was through. All the appointments of my school were primitive: a windowless log cabin; hastily manufactured benches; no blackboard; almost no books; long, long distances to walk. And on the other hand, I heard the sorrow songs sung with primitive beauty and grandeur. I saw the hard, ugly drudgery of country life and the writhing of landless, ignorant peasants. I saw the race problem at nearly its lowest terms.

At Fisk I began my writing and public speaking. I edited the *Fisk Herald.* I became an impassioned orator and developed a belligerent attitude toward the color bar. I was determined to make a scientific conquest of my environment, which would render the emancipation of the Negro race easier and quicker. The persistence which I had learned in New England stood me now in good stead. Because my first college choice had been Harvard, to Harvard I was still resolved to go. When I heard that Harvard, seeking to shed something of its New England provincialism, was offering scholarships in various parts of the country, I immediately wrote, and to the astonishment of teachers and fellow students, not to mention myself, received Price Greenleaf Aid of $300.

I was graduated from Fisk in 1888 and took as my subject "Bismarck." This choice in itself showed the abyss between my education and the truth in the world. Bismarck was my hero. He had made a nation out of a mass of bickering peoples. He had dominated the whole development with his strength until he crowned an emperor at Versailles. This foreshadowed in my mind the kind of thing that American Negroes must do, marching forth with strength and determination under trained leadership. On the other hand, I did not understand at all, nor had my history courses led me to understand, anything of current European intrigue, of the expansion of European power into Africa, of the Industrial Revolution built on slave trade and now turning into Colonial Imperialism; of the fierce rivalry among white nations for controlling the profits from colonial raw material and labor—of all this I had no clear conception. I was blithely European and imperialist in outlook; democratic as democracy was conceived in America.

So far my formal education had touched politics and religion, but on the whole had avoided economics. At Fisk a very definite attempt was made to see that we did not lose or question our Christian orthodoxy. At first the effort seemed to me entirely superfluous, since I had never questioned my religious upbringing. Its theory had presented no particular difficulties: God ruled the world, Christ loved it, and men did right, or tried to; otherwise they were rightly punished. But the book on "Christian Evidences" which we were compelled to read, affronted my logic. It was to my mind, then and since, a cheap piece of special pleading. Our course in general philosophy under the serious and entirely lovable president was different. It opened vistas. It made me determine to go further in this probing for truth. Eventually it landed me squarely in the arms of William James of Harvard, for which God be praised.

I became critical of religion and resentful of its practice for two reasons: first the heresy trials, particularly the one which expelled Briggs from the Presbyterian Church; and especially the insistence of the local church at Fisk University that dancing was a "sin." I was astonished to find that anybody could possibly think this; as a boy I had attended with my mother little parlor dances; as a youth at Fisk I danced gaily and happily. I was reminded by a smug old hypocrite of the horrible effects my example might have even if my own conscience was clear. I searched my soul with the Pauline text: "If meat maketh my brother to offend," etc. I have never had much respect for Paul since.

After graduation, the members of the Fisk Glee Club went to Lake Minnetonka, a resort in Minnesota, for the summer of 1888, with the idea of working in the dining room and giving concerts. I was to act as their business manager. During college I had developed rather as the executive and planner, the natural secretary of affairs rather than ornamental president and chairman. The only difficulty about the Minnesota excursion was that I had never worked in a hotel in my life; I could not wait on table and therefore became one of the bus boys. It was so unusual a pageant to watch the dining room that I made no tips and for a long time had difficulty in getting enough to eat, not realizing that in that day servants in great hotels were not systematically fed but foraged for food in devious ways. I saw the Americans, rich and near-rich, at play; it was not inspiring. The servility necessary for the successful waiter I could not or would not learn. After the season, I went on ahead and succeeded in making engagements for a respectable number of concerts for the students who followed me down all the way to Chicago; while I went on to Harvard to enter the junior class.

I was happy at Harvard, but for unusual reasons. One of these unusual circumstances was my acceptance of racial segregation. Had I gone from Great Barrington high school directly to Harvard I would have sought companionship with my white fellows and been disappointed and embittered by a discovery of social limitations to which I had not been used. But I came by way of Fisk and the South and there I had accepted and embraced eagerly the companionship of those of my own color. It was, of course, no final end. Eventually with them and in mass assault, led by culture, we were going to break down the boundaries of race; but at present we were banded together in a great crusade and happily so. Indeed, I suspect that the joy of full human intercourse without reservations and annoying distinctions, made me all too willing to consort with mine own and to disdain and forget as far as was possible that outer, whiter world.

Naturally it could not be entirely forgotten, so that now and then I plunged into it, joined its currents and rose or fell with it. The joining was sometimes a matter of social contact. I escorted colored girls, and as pretty ones as I could find, to the vesper exercises and the class day and commencement social functions. Naturally we attracted attention and sometimes the shadow of insult as when in one case a lady seemed determined to mistake me for a waiter. A few times I attempted to enter student organizations, but was not greatly disappointed when the expected refusals came. My voice, for instance, was better than the average. The glee club listened to it but I was not chosen a member. It posed the later recurring problem of a "nigger" on the team.

In general, I asked nothing of Harvard but the tutelage of teachers and the freedom of the library. I was quite voluntarily and willingly outside its social life. I knew nothing of and cared nothing for fraternities and clubs. Most of those which dominated the Harvard life of my day were unknown to me even by name. I asked no fellowship of my fellow students. I found friends and most interesting and inspiring friends among the colored folk of Boston and surrounding places. With them I carried on lively social intercourse, but one which involved little expenditure of money. I called at their homes and ate at their tables. We danced at private parties. We went on excursions down the Bay. Once, with a group of colored students gathered from surrounding institutions, we gave Aristophanes' "The Birds" in a colored church.

So that of the general social intercourse on the campus I consciously missed nothing. Some white students made themselves known to me and a few, a very few, became life-long friends. Most of them, even of my own more than three hundred classmates, I knew neither by sight nor name. Among my Harvard classmates many made their mark in life: Norman Hapgood, Robert Herrick, Herbert Croly, George A. Dorsey, Homer Folks, Augustus Hand, James Brown Scott, and others. I knew practically none of these. For the most part I do not doubt that I was voted a somewhat selfish and self-centered "grind" with a chip on my shoulder and a sharp tongue.

Something of a certain inferiority complex was possibly present: I was desperately afraid of not being wanted; of intruding without invitation; of appearing to desire the company of those who had no desire for me. I should have been pleased if most of my fellow students had desired to associate with me; if I had been popular and envied. But the absence of this made me neither unhappy nor morose. I had my "island within" and it was a fair country.

Only once or twice did I come to the surface of college life. First, by careful calculation, I found that I needed the cash of one of the Boylston prizes to piece out my year's expenses. I got it through winning a second oratorical prize. The occasion was noteworthy by the fact that the first prize went to a black classmate of mine, Clement Morgan. He and I became fast friends and spent a summer giving readings along the North Shore to help our college costs. Later Morgan became the center of a revolt within the college. By unwritten rule, all of the honorary offices of the class went to Bostonians of Back Bay. No Westerner, Southerner, Jew, nor Irishman, much less a Negro, had thought of aspiring to the honor of being class day official. But in 1890, after the oratorical contest, the students of the class staged an unexpected revolt and elected Morgan as class orator. There was national surprise and discussion and later several smaller Northern colleges elected colored class orators.

This cutting of myself off from my fellows did not mean unhappiness nor resentment. I was in my early young manhood, unusually full of high spirits and humor. I thoroughly enjoyed life. I was conscious of understanding and power, and conceited enough still to think, as in high school, that they who did not know me were the losers, not I. On the other hand, I do not think that my classmates found in me anything personally objectionable. I was clean, not well-dressed but decently clothed. Manners I regarded as more or less superfluous and deliberately cultivated a certain brusquerie. Personal adornment I regarded as pleasing but not important. I was in Harvard but not of it and realized all the irony of "Fair Harvard." I sang it because I liked the music.

The Harvard of 1888 was an extraordinary aggregation of great men. Not often since that day have so many distinguished teachers been together in one place and at one time in America. There were William James, the psychologist; Palmer in ethics; Royce and Santayana in philosophy; Shaler in geology and Hart in history. There were Francis Child, Charles Eliot Norton, Justin Winsor, and John Trowbridge; Goodwin, Taussig and Kittridge. The president was the cold, precise but exceedingly just and efficient Charles William Eliot, while Oliver Wendell Holmes and James Russell Lowell were still alive and emeriti.

By good fortune, I was thrown into direct contact with many of these men. I was repeatedly a guest in the house of William James; he was my friend and guide to clear thinking; I was a member of the Philosophical Club and talked with Royce and Palmer; I sat in an upper room and read Kant's Critique with Santayana; Shaler invited a Southerner, who objected to sitting by me, out of his class; I became one of Hart's favorite pupils and was afterwards guided by him through my graduate course and started on my work in Germany.

It was a great opportunity for a young man and a young American Negro, and I realized it. I formed habits of work rather different from those of most of the other students. I burned no midnight oil. I did my studying in the daytime and had my day parceled out almost to the minute. I spent a great deal of time in the library and did my assignments with thoroughness and with prevision of the kind of work I wanted to do later. I have before me a theme which I wrote

October 3, 1890, for Barrett Wendell, then the great pundit of Harvard English. I said: "Spurred by my circumstances, I have always been given to systematically planning my future, not indeed without many mistakes and frequent alterations, but always with what I now conceive to have been a strangely early and deep appreciation of the fact that to live is a serious thing. I determined while in the high school to go to college—partly because other men went, partly because I foresaw that such discipline would best fit me for life. . . . I believe foolishly perhaps, but sincerely, that I have something to say to the world, and I have taken English 12 in order to say it well." Barrett Wendell rather liked that last sentence. He read it out to the class.

It was at Harvard that my education, turning from philosophy, centered in history and then gradually in economics and social problems. Today my course of study would have been called sociology; but in that day Harvard did not recognize any such science. I had taken in high school and at Fisk the old classical course with Latin and Greek, philosophy and some history. At Harvard I started in with philosophy and then turned toward United States history and social problems. The turning was due to William James. He said to me, "If you must study philosophy you will; but if you can turn aside into something else, do so. It is hard to earn a living with philosophy."

So I turned toward history and social science. But there the way was difficult. Harvard had in the social sciences no such leadership of thought and breadth of learning as in philosophy, literature, and physical science. She was then groping and is still groping toward a scientific treatment of human action. She was facing at the end of the century a tremendous economic era. In the United States, finance was succeeding in monopolizing transportation, and raw materials like sugar, coal and oil. The power of the trust and combine was so great that the Sherman Act was passed in 1890. On the other hand, the tariff at the demand of manufacturers continued to rise in height from the McKinley to the indefensible Wilson tariff of 1894. A financial crisis shook the land in 1893 and popular discontent showed itself in the Populist movement and Coxey's Army. The whole question of the burden of taxation began to be discussed and England barred an income tax in 1894.

These things we discussed with some clearness and factual understanding at Harvard. The tendency was toward English free trade and against the American tariff policy. We reverenced Ricardo and wasted long hours on the "Wages-fund." The trusts and monopolies were viewed frankly as dangerous enemies of democracies, but at the same time as inevitable methods of industry. We were strong for the gold standard and fearful of silver. On the other hand, the attitude of Harvard toward labor was on the whole contemptuous and condemnatory. Strikes like that of the anarchists in Chicago, the railway strikes of 1886; the terrible Homestead strike of 1892 and Coxey's Army of 1894 were pictured as ignorant lawlessness, lurching against conditions largely inevitable. Karl Marx was hardly mentioned and Henry George given but tolerant notice. The anarchists of Spain, the Nihilists of Russia, the British miners—all these were viewed not as part of the political development and the tremendous economic organization but as sporadic evil. This was natural. Harvard was the child of its era. The intellectual freedom and flowering of the late eighteenth and early nineteenth centuries were yielding to the deadening economic pressure which made Harvard rich but reactionary. This defender of wealth and capital, already half ashamed of Sumner and Phillips, was willing finally to replace an Eliot with a Lowell. The social community that mobbed Garrison, easily hanged Sacco and Vanzetti.

It was not until I was long out of college and had finished the first phase of my teaching career that I began to see clearly the connection of economics and politics; the fundamental influence of man's efforts to earn a living upon all his other efforts. The politics which we studied in college were conventional, especially when it came to describing and elucidating the current scene in Europe. The Queen's Jubilee in June, 1887, while I was still at Fisk, set the pattern of our thinking. The little old woman of Windsor became a magnificent symbol of Empire. Here was England with her flag draped around the world, ruling more black folk than white and leading the colored peoples of the earth to Christian baptism, civilization and eventual self-rule. Only two years before, in 1885,

Stanley, the traveling reporter, became a hero and symbol of white world leadership in Africa. The wild, fierce fight of the Mahdi and the driving of the English out of the Sudan for sixteen years did not reveal its inner truth to me. I heard only of the martyrdom of the drunken Bible-reader and freebooter, Gordon.

The Congo Free State was established and the Berlin Conference of 1885 was reported to be an act of civilization against the slave trade and liquor. French, English and Germans pushed on in Africa, but I did not question the interpretation which pictured this as the advance of civilization and the benevolent tutelage of barbarians. I read of the confirmation of the Triple Alliance in 1891. Later I saw the celebration of the renewed Triple Alliance on the Tempelhofer Feld, with the new young Emperor Wilhelm II, who, fresh from his dismissal of Bismarck, led the splendid pageantry; and finally the year I left Germany, Nicholas II became Czar of all the Russias. In all this I had not yet linked the political development of Europe with the race problem in America.

In 1890, I took my bachelor's degree from Harvard and was one of the six commencement speakers, taking as my subject "Jefferson Davis." This was a better subject than Bismarck for Davis was no hero of mine; yet the New York *Nation* said, July 3, 1890, that I handled my subject "with absolute good taste, great moderation, and almost contemptuous fairness." I was graduated just at the beginning of the term of President Harrison, when the trusts were dominating industry and the McKinley tariff making that domination easier. The understanding between the Industrial North and the New South was being perfected and in 1890 the series of disfranchising laws began to be enacted by the Southern states destined in the next sixteen years to make voting by Southern Negroes practically impossible.

Already I had received more education than most young white men, having been almost continuously in school from the age of six to the age of twenty-two. But I did not yet feel prepared. I felt that to cope with the new and extraordinary situations then developing in the United States and the world, I needed to go further and that as a matter of fact I had just well begun my training in knowledge of social conditions. On the other hand, I had no resources in wealth nor friends. I applied for a fellowship in the graduate school of Harvard and was appointed Henry Bromsfield Rogers fellow for a year and later the appointment was renewed; so that from 1890 to 1892 I was a fellow in Harvard University, studying in history and political science and what would have been sociology if Harvard had yet recognized such a field. I worked on my thesis, "The Suppression of the Slave Trade," taking my master's degree in 1891 and hoping to get my doctor's degree in another two years.

Then came one of these tricks of fortune which always seem partly due to chance: in 1882, the Slater Fund for the education of Negroes had been established and the board in 1890 was headed by ex-President R. B. Hayes. President Hayes went down to Johns Hopkins University and talked frankly about the plans of the fund. The *Boston Herald* of November 2, 1890, quoted him as saying: "If there is any young colored man in the South whom we find to have a talent for art or literature or any special aptitude for study, we are willing to give him money from the education funds to send him to Europe or give him an advanced education." He added that so far they had been able to find only "orators." This seemed to me a nasty fling at my black classmate, Morgan, who had been Harvard class orator a few months earlier, and indirectly at me.

The Hayes statement was brought to my attention at a card party one evening; it not only made me good and angry but inspired me to write President Hayes and ask for a scholarship. I received a pleasant reply saying that the newspaper quotation was incorrect; that his board had had some such program in the past but had no present plans for such scholarships. I proceeded to collect letters from every person I knew in the Harvard Yard and places outside, and literally deluged the unfortunate chairman of the Slater Fund, intimating that his change of plan did not seem to me fair or honest. He wrote again in apologetic mood and said that he was sorry the plan had been given up; that he recognized that I was a candidate who might otherwise have been given attention.

I sat down and wrote Mr. Hayes a letter that could be

described as nothing less than impudent and flatly accused him of bad faith. He was undoubtedly stirred. He apologized again, re-asserted his good faith, and further promised to take up the matter the next year with the board. Thereupon, the next year I proceeded to write the board: "At the close of the last academic year at Harvard, I received the degree of Master of Arts, and was re-appointed to my fellowship for the year 1891–92. I have spent most of the year in the preparation of my doctor's thesis on the suppression of the slave trade in America. I prepared a preliminary paper on this subject and read it before the American Historical Association at its annual meeting at Washington during the Christmas holidays. . . . Properly to finish my education, careful training in an European university for at least a year is, in my mind and the minds of my professors, absolutely indispensable." I thereupon asked respectfully "aid to study at least a year abroad under the direction of the graduate department of Harvard or other reputable auspices" and if this was not practicable, "that the board loan me a sufficient sum for this purpose." I did not of course believe that this would get me an appointment, but I did think that possibly through the influence of people who thus came to know about my work, I might somehow borrow or beg enough to get to Europe. To my surprise, I was given a fellowship of seven hundred and fifty dollars, half grant and half repayable loan, to study abroad; with the promise that it might possibly be renewed for a second year. I remember rushing down to New York and talking with President Hayes in the old Astor House, and then going out walking on air. I saw an especially delectable shirt in a shop window. I went in and asked about it. It cost three dollars, which was about four times as much as I had ever paid for a shirt in my life; but I bought it.

I sailed in the summer of 1892 on a Dutch boat, the old "Amsterdam," landing in Holland. I wrote gaily, "Holland is an extremely neat and well-ordered mud-puddle, situated at the confluence of the English, French, and German languages." My first memory of it is inextricably interwoven with the smell of clover and the sight of black and white cows.

Europe modified profoundly my outlook on life and my

thought and feeling toward it, even though I was there but two short years with my contacts limited and my friends few. But something of the possible beauty and elegance of life permeated my soul; I gained a respect for manners. I had been before, above all, in a hurry. I wanted a world, hard, smooth and swift, and had no time for rounded corners and ornament, for unhurried thought and slow contemplation. Now at times I sat still. I came to know Beethoven's symphonies and Wagner's Ring. I looked long at the colors of Rembrandt and Titian. I saw in arch and stone and steeple the history and striving of men and also their taste and expression. Form, color, and words took new combinations and meanings.

My introduction to Europe had some characteristic incidents. In my journey up the Rhine I found myself with a Dutch family: a lady, two daughters about my own age or a little younger, and a girl of ten or twelve. They were white and I therefore avoided them; when they strolled to one end of the deck I strolled to the other; but at last they approached and introduced themselves. They spoke both English and German, and I ended by having a delightful trip and by feeling more at home with cultured white folk than I had before in my life. This experience was continued when I spent a summer with Oberpfarrer Dr. Marbach in Eisenach. There were other boarders, German, French, and English, boys and girls; we had a delightful time. There was only one false note, when an American husband and wife from the West came, and were so alarmed about my social relations with German girls that they solemnly warned the Marbach family against racial intermarriage. The warning was quite unnecessary. I had already told the daughter, Dora, with whom I was most frequently coupled, that it would not be fair to marry her and bring her to America. She said she would come "gleich!" but I assured her that she would not be happy; and besides, I had work to do.

In the fall I went up to Berlin and registered in the university. In groups of one hundred we went into a large room with a high ceiling ornamented with busts of Berlin's famous professors. The year's Rector Magnificus was the widely famous Rudolf Virchow. He was a meek and calm little man, white-haired and white-bearded, with kindly face and pleasant voice. I had again at Berlin as at Harvard unusual opportunity. Although a foreigner, I was admitted my first semester to two seminars under Schmoller and Wagner, both of them at the time the most distinguished men in their line; I received eventually from both of them pleasant testimony on my work. That work was in economics, history, and sociology. I sat under the voice of the fire-eating Pan-German, von Treitschke; I heard Sering and Weber; I wrote on American agriculture for Schmoller and discussed social conditions in Europe with teachers and students. Under these teachers and in this social setting, I began to see the race problem in America, the problem of the peoples of Africa and Asia, and the political development of Europe as one. I began to unite my economics and politics; but I still assumed that in these groups of activities and forces, the political realm was dominant.

But more especially, I traveled; living cheaply, I saved good sums for the numerous vacations. I went to the Hansa cities; I made the celebrated Harzreise up to the Brocken in the spring. One Christmas vacation I spent in making a trip through south Germany along with a German-American and an Englishman. We visited Weimar, Frankfort, Heidelberg and Mannheim. Over Christmas Day and New Year's we stopped in a little German "Dorf" in the Rheinpfalz, where I had an excellent opportunity to study the peasant life closely and compare it with country life in the South. We visited perhaps twenty different families, talked, ate and drank with them; listened to their gossip, attended their assemblies, etc. We then went to Strassburg, Stuttgart, Ulm, München, Nürnberg, Prague and Dresden. In those places we stayed from one to five days following our Baedekers closely and paying much attention to the München and Dresden art galleries. The whole trip cost about eighty dollars. Later I went down to Italy; to Genoa, Rome and Naples, and over to Venice and Vienna and Budapest; up to Krakau, where the father of a fellow-student was the head of a Polish library. From this friend, Stanislaus von Estreicher, I learned of the race problems of the Poles. Then by Breslau I came back to Berlin. In 1940, von Estreicher died in a German concentration camp, after he had refused to be one of Germany's puppet rulers of Poland.

I received a renewal of my fellowship and spent a second year in Germany. By that time I knew my Germany well and spoke its tongue. I had associated with some of the lower nobility, many of the "Gelehrten," artists, business men, and members of the Social Democracy.

I returned to the United States by way of Paris where I stayed as long as possible and then, having reduced myself almost to the last cent, took passage to the United States in steerage. It was by no means a pleasant trip, but perhaps it was good introduction to the new life; because now at last at twenty-six years of age and after twenty years of study I was coming home to look for a job and begin work.

I need not dwell on the difficulties of finding that job. It was a disturbed world in which I landed; 1892 saw the high tide of lynching in the United States; Cleveland had entered his second term in 1893 and the Chicago Exposition had taken place. The Dreyfus case had opened in France with his conviction and imprisonment, and he was destined for twelve years to suffer martyrdom. The war between China and Japan broke out the year of my return. I had rejoiced in the million dollar gift of Daniel Hand for education in my graduation year but recognized clearly the blow that democracy received when Congress repealed the so-called Force bills in 1894, refusing longer even to try to protect the legal citizenship rights of Negroes. But on the other hand, I did not at all understand the implications of the Matabele War in 1893. I did not see how the gold and diamonds of South Africa and later the copper, ivory, cocoa, tin and vegetable oils of other parts of Africa and especially black labor force were determining and conditioning the political action of Europe.

I received eventually three offers of work. On August 17, the chair of "classics" at Wilberforce University, Ohio, with a salary of $800 was offered, which I immediately accepted with gratitude. A little later there came an offer of a position at Lincoln Institute in Missouri at $1050; but I stuck to my previous promise; and finally, August 25, I received this telegram: "Can give mathematics if terms suit. Will you accept. Booker T. Washington." It would be interesting to speculate just what would have happened, if I had accepted the last offer of Tuskegee instead of that of Wilberforce.

Chapter 4

SCIENCE AND EMPIRE

FROM THE FALL of 1894 to the spring of 1910, for sixteen years, I was a teacher. For two years I remained at Wilberforce; for something over a year, at the University of Pennsylvania; and for thirteen years at Atlanta University in Georgia. I sought in these years to teach youth the meaning and way of the world. What did I know about the world and how could I teach my knowledge?

The main result of my schooling had been to emphasize science and the scientific attitude. I got some insight into the laws of the physical world at Fisk and in the chemical laboratory and class in geology at Harvard. I was interested in evolution, geology, and the new psychology. I began to conceive of the world as a continuing growth rather than a finished product. In Germany I turned still further from religious dogma and began to grasp the idea of a world of human beings whose actions, like those of the physical world, were subject to law. The triumphs of the scientific world thrilled me: the X-ray and radium came during my teaching term, the airplane and the wireless. The machine increased in technical efficiency and the North and South Poles were invaded.

On the other hand the difficulties of applying scientific law and discovering cause and effect in the social world were still great. Social thinkers were engaged in vague statements and were seeking to lay down the methods by which, in some not too distant future, social law analogous to physical law would be discovered. Herbert Spencer finished his ten volumes of Synthetic Philosophy in 1896. The biological analogy, the vast generalizations, were striking, but actual scientific accomplishment lagged. For me an opportunity seemed to present itself. I could not lull my mind to hypnosis by regarding a phrase like "consciousness of kind" as a scientific law. But turning my gaze from fruitless word-twisting and facing the facts of my own social situation and racial world, I determined to put science into sociology through a study of the condition and problems of my own group.

I was going to study the facts, any and all facts, concerning the American Negro and his plight, and by measurement and comparison and research, work up to any valid generalization which I could. I entered this primarily with the utilitarian object of reform and uplift; but nevertheless, I wanted to do the work with scientific accuracy. Thus, in my own sociology, because of firm belief in a changing racial group, I easily grasped the idea of a changing developing society rather than a fixed social structure.

The decade and a half in which I taught, was riotous with happenings in the world of social development; with economic expansion, with political control, with racial difficulties. Above all, it was the era of empire and while I had some equipment to deal with a scientific approach to social studies, I did not have any clear conception or grasp of the meaning of that industrial imperialism which was beginning to grip the world. My only approach to meanings and helpful study there again was through my interest in race contact.

That interest began to clear my vision and interpret the whirl of events which swept the world on. Japan was rising to national status and through the Chinese War and the Russian War, despite rivalry with Germany, Russia and Great Britain, she achieved a new and nearly equal status in the world, which only the United States refused to recognize. But all this, I began to realize, was but a result of the expansion of Europe into Africa where a fierce fight was precipitated for the labor, gold, and diamonds of South Africa; for domination of the Nile Valley; for the gold, cocoa, raw materials, and labor of West Africa; and for the exploitation of the Belgian Congo. Europe was determined to dominate China and all but succeeded in dividing it between the chief white nations, when Japan stopped the process. After sixteen years, stirred by the triumph of the Abyssinians at Adowa, and pushing forward of the French in North Africa, England returned to the Egyptian Sudan.

The Queen's Jubilee then, I knew, was not merely a sentimental outburst; it was a triumph of English economic aggression around the world and it aroused the cupidity and fear of Germany who proceeded to double her navy, expand into Asia, and consolidate her European position. Germany challenged France and England at Algeciras, prelude to the World War. Imperialism, despite Cleveland's opposition, spread to America, and the Hawaiian sugar fields were annexed. The Spanish war brought Cuban sugar under control and annexed Puerto Rico and the Philippines. The Panama Canal brought the Pacific nearer the Atlantic and we protected capital investment in San Domingo and South America.

All this might have been interpreted as history and politics. Mainly I did so interpret it; but continually I was forced to consider the economic aspects of world movements as they were developing at the time. Chiefly this was because the group in which I was interested were workers, earners of wages, owners of small bits of land, servants. The labor strikes interested and puzzled me. They were for the most part strikes of workers led by organizations to which Negroes were not admitted. There was the great steel strike; the railway strikes, actual and threatened; the teamsters' strike in Chicago; the long strike in Leadville, Colorado. Only in the coal strike were Negroes involved. But there was a difference. During my school days, strikes were regarded as futile and ill-advised struggles against economic laws; and when the government intervened, it was to cow the strikers as law-breakers. But during my teaching period, the plight of the worker began to sift through into the consciousness of the average citizen. Public opinion not only allowed but forced Theodore Roosevelt to intervention in the coal strike, and the steel strikers had widespread sympathy.

Then there were the tariff agitations, the continual raising and shifting and manipulation of tariff rates, always in the end for the purpose of subsidizing the manufacturer and making the consumer pay. The political power of the great organizations of capital in coal, oil and sugar, the extraordinary immunities of the corporations, made the President openly attack the trusts as a kind of super-government and we began to see more and more clearly the outlines of economic battle. The Supreme Court stood staunchly behind capital. It outlawed the labor boycott, it denied the right of the states to make railway rates. It declared the income tax unconstitutional.

With all that, and the memory of the Panic of 1873 not forgotten, came the Panic of 1893 and the financial upheaval of 1907. Into this economic turmoil, politics had to intrude. The older role of free, individual enterprise, with little or no government interference, had to be surrendered and the whole political agitation during these days took on a distinct economic tinge and object. The impassioned plea of Bryan in 1896 that labor be not "crucified upon a cross of gold" could not be wholly ridiculed to silence. The Populist Movement which swept over the West and South, I began now to believe, was a third party movement of deep significance and it was kept from political power on the one hand by the established election frauds of the South, of which I knew, and by the fabulous election fund which made McKinley President of the United States. With this went the diversion of the Spanish war with its sordid scandals of rotten beef, cheating and stealing, fever and death from neglect. Politics and economics thus in those days of my teaching became but two aspects of a united body of action and effort.

I tried to isolate myself in the ivory tower of race. I wanted to explain the difficulties of race and the ways in which these difficulties caused political and economic troubles. It was this concentration of thought and action and effort that really, in the end, saved my scientific accuracy and search for truth. But first came a period of three years when I was casting about to find a way of applying science to the race problem. In these years I was torn with excitement of quick-moving events. Lynching, for instance, was still a continuing horror in the United States at the time of my entrance upon a teaching career. It reached a climax in 1892, when 235 persons were publicly murdered, and in the sixteen years of my teaching nearly two thousand persons were publicly killed by mobs, and not a single one of the murderers punished. The partition, domination and exploitation of Africa gradually centered my thought as part of my problem of race. I saw in Asia and the West Indies the results of race discrimination while right here in America came the wild foray of the exasperated

Negro soldiers at Brownsville and the political-economic riot at Atlanta.

One happening in America linked in my mind the race problem with the general economic development and that was the speech of Booker T. Washington in Atlanta in 1895. When many colored papers condemned the proposition of compromise with the white South, which Washington proposed, I wrote to the *New York Age* suggesting that here might be the basis of a real settlement between whites and blacks in the South, if the South opened to the Negroes the doors of economic opportunity and the Negroes co-operated with the white South in political sympathy. But this offer was frustrated by the fact that between 1895 and 1909 the whole South disfranchised its Negro voters by unfair and illegal restrictions and passed a series of "Jim Crow" laws which made the Negro citizen a subordinate caste.

As a possible offset to this came the endowment of the General Education Board and the Sage Foundation; but they did not to my mind plan clearly to attack the Negro problem; the Sage Foundation ignored us, and the General Education Board in its first years gave its main attention to the education of whites and to black industrial schools. Finally the riot and lynching at Springfield, the birthplace of Abraham Lincoln, one hundred years after his birth, sounded a knell which in the end stopped my teaching career. This, then, was the general setting when I returned to America for work.

Wilberforce was a small colored denominational college, married to a state normal school. The church was too poor to run the college; the State tolerated the normal school so as to keep Negroes out of other state schools. Consequently, there were enormous difficulties in both church and state politics. Into this situation I landed with the cane and gloves of my German student days; with my rather inflated ideas of what a "university" ought to be and with a terrible plainness of speech that was continually getting me into difficulty; when, for instance, the student leader of a prayer meeting into which I had wandered casually to look local religion over, suddenly and without warning announced that "Professor Du Bois would lead us in prayer," I simply answered, "No, he won't," and as a result nearly lost my job. It took a great deal of explaining to the board of bishops why a professor in Wilberforce should not be able at all times and sundry to address God in extemporaneous prayer. I was saved only by the fact that my coming to Wilberforce had been widely advertised and I was so willing to do endless work when the work seemed to me worth doing.

My program for the day at Wilberforce looked almost as long as a week's program now. I taught Latin, Greek, German, and English, and wanted to add sociology. I had charge of some of the most unpleasant duties of discipline and had outside work in investigation. But I met and made many friends: Charles Young, not long graduated from West Point, was one; Charles Burroughs, a gifted reader, was a student in my classes; Paul Laurence Dunbar came over from Dayton and read to us. I had known his work but was astonished to find that he was a Negro. And not least, I met the slender, quiet, and dark-eyed girl who became Mrs. Du Bois in 1896. Her father was chef in the leading hotel of Cedar Rapids, Iowa, and her dead mother a native of Alsace.

We younger teachers had a hard team fight, and after a two years' struggle I knew I was whipped and that it was impossible to stay at Wilberforce. It had a fine tradition, a strategic position, and a large constituency; but its religion was narrow dogma; its finances cramped; its policies too intertwined with intrigue and worse; and its future in grave doubt. When, therefore, a temporary appointment came from the University of Pennsylvania for one year as "assistant instructor" at $600, I accepted forthwith in the fall of 1896; that year Abyssinia overthrew Italy and England, suddenly seeing two black nations threatening her Cape to Cairo plans, threw her army back into the Sudan and re-captured Khartoum. The next year, the free silver controversy of Bryan and McKinley flamed.

The two years at Wilberforce was my uneasy apprenticeship, and with my advent into the University of Pennsylvania, I began a more clearly planned career which had an unusual measure of success, but was in the end pushed aside by forces which, if not entirely beyond my control, were yet of great weight.

The opportunity opened at the University of Pennsylvania

seemed just what I wanted. I had offered to teach social science at Wilberforce outside of my overloaded program, but I was not allowed. My vision was becoming clearer. The Negro problem was in my mind a matter of systematic investigation and intelligent understanding. The world was thinking wrong about race, because it did not know. The ultimate evil was stupidity. The cure for it was knowledge based on scientific investigation. At the University of Pennsylvania I ignored the pitiful stipend. It made no difference to me that I was put down as an "assistant instructor" and even at that, that my name never actually got into the catalogue; it goes without saying that I did no instructing save once to pilot a pack of idiots through the Negro slums.

The fact was that the city of Philadelphia at that time had a theory; and that theory was that this great, rich, and famous municipality was going to the dogs because of the crime and venality of its Negro citizens, who lived largely centered in the slum at the lower end of the seventh ward. Philadelphia wanted to prove this by figures and I was the man to do it. Of this theory back of the plan, I neither knew nor cared. I saw only here a chance to study an historical group of black folk and to show exactly what their place was in the community.

I did it despite extraordinary difficulties both within and without the group. Whites said, Why study the obvious? Blacks said, Are we animals to be dissected and by an unknown Negro at that? Yet, I made a study of the Philadelphia Negro so thorough that it has withstood the criticism of forty years. It was as complete a scientific study and answer as could have then been given, with defective facts and statistics, one lone worker and little money. It revealed the Negro group as a symptom, not a cause; as a striving, palpitating group, and not an inert, sick body of crime; as a long historic development and not a transient occurrence.

Of the methods of my research, I wrote:

"The best available methods of sociological research are at present so liable to inaccuracies that the careful student discloses the results of individual research with diffidence; he knows that they are liable to error from the seemingly ineradicable faults of the statistical method; to even greater error from the methods of general observation; and, above all, he must ever tremble lest some personal bias, some moral conviction or some unconscious trend of thought due to previous training, has to a degree distorted the picture in his view. Convictions on all great matters of human interest one must have to a greater or less degree, and they will enter to some extent into the most cold-blooded scientific research as a disturbing factor.

"Nevertheless, here are some social problems before us demanding careful study, questions awaiting satisfactory answers. We must study, we must investigate, we must attempt to solve; and the utmost that the world can demand is, not lack of human interest and moral conviction, but rather the heart-quality of fairness, and an earnest desire for the truth despite its possible unpleasantness."

At the end of that study, I announced with a certain pride my plan of studying the complete Negro problem in the United States. I spoke at the forty-second meeting of the American Academy of Political and Social Sciences in Philadelphia, November 19, 1897, and my subject was "The Study of the Negro Problems." I began by asserting that in the development of sociological study there was at least one positive answer which years of research and speculation had been able to return, and that was: "The phenomena of society are worth the most careful and systematic study, and whether or not this study may eventually lead to a systematic body of knowledge deserving the name of science, it cannot in any case fail to give the world a mass of truth worth the knowing." I then defined and tried to follow the development of the Negro problem not as one problem, but "rather a plexus of social problems, some new, some old, some simple, some complex; and these problems have their one bond of unity in the fact that they group themselves about those Africans whom two centuries of slave-trading brought into the land."

I insisted on the necessity of carefully studying these problems and said: "The American Negro deserves study for the great end of advancing the cause of science in general. No such opportunity to watch and measure the history and development of a great race of men ever presented itself to the scholars of a modern nation. If they miss this opportunity—

if they do the work in a slip-shod, unsystematic manner—if they dally with the truth to humor the whims of the day, they do far more than hurt the good name of the American people; they hurt the cause of scientific truth the world over, they voluntarily decrease human knowledge of a universe of which we are ignorant enough, and they degrade the high end of truth-seeking in a day when they need more and more to dwell upon its sanctity."

Finally I tried to lay down a plan for the study, postulating only: that the Negro "is a member of the human race, and as one who, in the light of history and experience, is capable to a degree of improvement and culture, is entitled to have his interests considered according to his numbers in all conclusions as to the common weal."

Dividing the prospective scientific study of the Negro into two parts: the social group and his peculiar social environment, I proposed to study the social group by historical investigation, statistical measurement, anthropological measurement and sociological interpretation. Particularly with regard to anthropology I said:

"That there are differences between the white and black races is certain, but just what those differences are is known to none with an approach to accuracy. Yet here in America is the most remarkable opportunity ever offered of studying these differences, of noting influences of climate and physical environment, and particularly of studying the effect of amalgamating two of the most diverse races in the world—another subject which rests under a cloud of ignorance."

In concluding, I said:

"It is to the credit of the University of Pennsylvania that she has been the first to recognize her duty in this respect and in so far as restricted means and opportunity allowed, has attempted to study the Negro problems in a single definite locality. This work needs to be extended to other groups, and carried out with larger system; and here it would seem is the opportunity of the Southern Negro college. We hear much of higher Negro education, and yet all candid people know there does not exist today in the center of Negro population a single first-class fully equipped institution, devoted to the higher education of Negroes; not more than three Negro institutions in the South deserve the name of 'college' at all; and yet what is a Negro college but a vast college settlement for the study of a particular set of peculiarly baffling problems? What more effective or suitable agency could be found in which to focus the scientific efforts of the great universities of the North and East, than an institution situated in the very heart of these social problems, and made the center of careful historical and statistical research? Without doubt the first effective step toward the solving of the Negro question will be the endowment of a Negro college which is not merely a teaching body, but a center of sociological research, in close connection and co-operation with Harvard, Columbia, Johns Hopkins, and the University of Pennsylvania.

"Finally the necessity must again be emphasized of keeping clearly before students the object of all science, amid the turmoil and intense feeling that clouds the discussion of a burning social question. We live in a day when in spite of the brilliant accomplishments of a remarkable century, there is current much flippant criticism of scientific work; when the truth-seeker is too often pictured as devoid of human sympathy, and careless of human ideals. We are still prone in spite of all our culture to sneer at the heroism of the laboratory while we cheer the swagger of the street broil. At such times true lovers of humanity can only hold higher the pure ideals of science, and continue to insist that if we would solve a problem we must study it, and there is but one coward on earth, and that is the coward that dare not know."

I had, at this time, already been approached by President Horace Bumstead of Atlanta University and asked to come there and take charge of the work in sociology, and of the new conferences which they were inaugurating on the Negro problem. With this program in mind, I eagerly accepted the invitation, although at the last moment there came a curious reminiscence of Wilberforce in a little hitch based on that old matter of extemporaneous public prayer. Dr. Bumstead and I compromised on my promise to use the Episcopal prayer book; later I used to add certain prayers of my own composing. I am not sure that they were orthodox or reached heaven, but they certainly reached my audience.

Without thought or consultation I rather peremptorily

changed the plans of the first two Atlanta Conferences. They had been conceived as conferences limited to city problems, contrasting with the increasingly popular conferences on rural problems held at Tuskegee. But I was not thinking of mere conferences. I was thinking of a comprehensive plan for studying a human group and if I could have carried it out as completely as I conceived it, the American Negro would have contributed to the development of social science in this country an unforgettable body of work.

Annually our reports carried this statement of aims: "This study is a further carrying out of a plan of social study by means of recurring decennial inquiries into the same general set of human problems. The object of these studies is primarily scientific—a careful search for truth conducted as thoroughly, broadly, and honestly as the material resources and mental equipment at command will allow; but this is not our sole object; we wish not only to make the Truth clear but to present it in such shape as will encourage and help social reform. Our financial resources are unfortunately meager: Atlanta University is primarily a school and most of its funds and energy go to teaching. It is, however, also a seat of learning and as such it has endeavored to advance knowledge, particularly in matters of racial contact and development which seemed obviously its nearest field. In this work it has received unusual encouragement from the scientific world, and the published results of these studies are used in America, Europe, Asia, and Africa."

Social scientists were then still thinking in terms of theory and vast and eternal laws, but I had a concrete group of living beings artificially set off by themselves and capable of almost laboratory experiment. I laid down an ambitious program for a hundred years of study. I proposed to take up annually in each decade the main aspects of the group life of Negroes with as thorough study and measurement as possible, and repeat the same program in the succeeding decade with additions, changes and better methods. In this way, I proposed gradually to broaden and intensify the study, sharpen the tools of investigation and perfect our methods of work, so that we would have an increasing body of scientifically ascertained fact, instead of the vague mass of the so-called Negro problems. And through this laboratory experiment I hoped to make the laws of social living clearer, surer, and more definite.

Some of this was accomplished, but of course only an approximation of the idea. For thirteen years we poured forth a series of studies; limited, incomplete, only partially conclusive, and yet so much better done than any other attempt of the sort in the nation that they gained attention throughout the world. We studied during the first decade Negro mortality, urbanization, the effort of Negroes for their own social betterment, Negroes in business, college-bred Negroes, the Negro common school, the Negro artisan, the Negro church, and Negro crime. We ended the decade by a general review of the methods and results of this ten year study and a bibliography of the Negro. Taking new breath in 1906 I planned a more logical division of subjects but was not able to carry it out quite as I wished, because of lack of funds. We took up health and physique of American Negroes, economic co-operation and the Negro American family. We made a second study of the efforts for social betterment, the college-bred Negro, the Negro common school, the Negro artisan, and added a study of morals and manners among Negroes instead of further study of the church. In all we published a total of 2,172 pages which formed a current encyclopaedia on the American Negro problems.

These studies with all their imperfections were widely distributed in the libraries of the world and used by scholars. It may be said without undue boasting that between 1896 and 1920 there was no study of the race problem in America made which did not depend in some degree upon the investigations made at Atlanta University; often they were widely quoted and commended.

It must be remembered that the significance of these studies lay not so much in what they were actually able to accomplish, as in the fact that at the time of their publication Atlanta University was the only institution in the world carrying on a systematic study of the Negro and his development, and putting the result in a form available for the scholars of the world.

In addition to the publications, we did something toward

bringing together annually at Atlanta University persons and authorities interested in the problems of the South. Among these were Booker T. Washington, Frank Sanborn, Franz Boas, Jane Addams and Walter Wilcox. We were asked from time to time to co-operate in current studies. I wrote a number of studies for the Bureau of Labor in Washington. I co-operated in the taking of the Twelfth Census and wrote one of the monographs. I not only published the Atlanta Conference reports, but wrote magazine articles in the *World's Work* and in the *Atlantic Monthly* where I joined in a symposium and one of my fellow contributors was Woodrow Wilson. At the same time I joined with the Negro leaders of Georgia in efforts to better local conditions; to stop discrimination in the distribution of school funds; to keep the legislature from making further discriminations in railway travel. I prepared an exhibit showing the condition of the Negro for the Paris Exposition which gained a Grand Prize. I became a member of the American Association for the Advancement of Science in 1900 and was made a fellow in 1904.

I testified before Congressional Commissions in Washington and appeared on the lecture platform with Walter Page, afterwards war ambassador to England; I did a considerable amount of lecturing throughout the United States. I had wide correspondence with men of prominence in America and Europe: Lyman Abbott of the *Outlook*; E. D. Morel, the English expert on Africa; Max Weber of Heidelberg; Professor Wilcox of Cornell; Bliss Perry of the *Atlantic Monthly*; Horace Traubel, the great protagonist for Walt Whitman; Charles Eliot Norton and Talcott Williams. I began to be regarded by many groups and audiences as having definite information on the Negro to which they might listen with profit.

At the very time when my studies were most successful, there cut across this plan which I had as a scientist, a red ray which could not be ignored. I remember when it first, as it were, startled me to my feet: a poor Negro in central Georgia, Sam Hose, had killed his landlord's wife. I wrote out a careful and reasoned statement concerning the evident facts and started down to the Atlanta *Constitution* office, carrying in my pocket a letter of introduction to Joel Chandler Harris. I did not get there. On the way news met me: Sam Hose had been lynched, and they said that his knuckles were on exhibition at a grocery store farther down on Mitchell Street, along which I was walking. I turned back to the University. I began to turn aside from my work. I did not meet Joel Chandler Harris nor the editor of the *Constitution.*

Two considerations thereafter broke in upon my work and eventually disrupted it: first, one could not be a calm, cool, and detached scientist while Negroes were lynched, murdered and starved; and secondly, there was no such definite demand for scientific work of the sort that I was doing, as I had confidently assumed would be easily forthcoming. I regarded it as axiomatic that the world wanted to learn the truth and if the truth was sought with even approximate accuracy and painstaking devotion, the world would gladly support the effort. This was, of course, but a young man's idealism, not by any means false, but also never universally true. The work of the conference for thirteen years including my own salary and small office force did not average five thousand dollars a year. Probably with some effort and sacrifice Atlanta University might have continued to raise this amount if it had not been for the controversy with Booker T. Washington that arose in 1903 and increased in virulence until 1908.

There were, of course, other considerations which made Atlanta University vulnerable to attack at this time. The university from the beginning had taken a strong and unbending attitude toward Negro prejudice and discrimination; white teachers and black students ate together in the same dining room and lived in the same dormitories. The charter of the institution opened the doors of Atlanta University to any student who applied, of any race or color; and when the state in 1887 objected to the presence of a few white students, all children of teachers and professors, the institution gave up the small appropriation from the State rather than repudiate its principles. In fact, this appropriation represented not State funds, but the Negroes' share of the sum received from the Federal government for education. When later there came an attempt on the part of the Southern Education Board and afterwards of the General Education Board to form a working program between educated Negroes and forward-looking whites in the South, it gradually became an understood principle of action that colored teachers should be encouraged in colored schools; that the races in the schools should be separated socially; that colored schools should be chiefly industrial; and that every effort should be made to conciliate Southern white public opinion. Schools which were successfully carrying out this program could look for further help from organized philanthropy. Other schools, and this included Atlanta University, could not.

Even this would not necessarily have excluded Atlanta University from consideration at the hands of the philanthropists. The university had done and was doing excellent and thorough work. Even industrial training in the South was often in the hands of Atlanta graduates. Tuskegee had always been largely manned by graduates of Atlanta and some of the best school systems of the South were directed by persons trained at Atlanta University. The college department was recognized as perhaps the largest and best in the South at the time. But unfortunately, at this time, there came a controversy between myself and Booker Washington, which became more personal and bitter than I had ever dreamed and which necessarily dragged in the University.

It was no controversy of my seeking; quite the contrary. I was in my imagination a scientist, and neither a leader nor an agitator; I had nothing but the greatest admiration for Mr. Washington and Tuskegee, and I had applied at both Tuskegee and Hampton for work. If Mr. Washington's telegram had reached me before the Wilberforce bid, I should have doubtless gone to Tuskegee. Certainly I knew no less about mathematics than I did about Latin and Greek.

Since the controversy between myself and Mr. Washington has become historic, it deserves more careful statement than it has had hitherto, both as to the matters and the motives involved. There was first of all the ideological controversy. I believed in the higher education of a Talented Tenth who through their knowledge of modern culture could guide the American Negro into a higher civilization. I knew that without this the Negro would have to accept white leadership, and that such leadership could not always be trusted to guide this group into self-realization and to its highest cultural possibilities. Mr. Washington, on the other hand, believed that the Negro as an efficient worker could gain wealth and that eventually through his ownership of capital he would be able to achieve a recognized place in American culture and could then educate his children as he might wish and develop his possibilities. For this reason he proposed to put the emphasis at present upon training in the skilled trades and encouragement in industry and common labor.

These two theories of Negro progress were not absolutely contradictory. I recognized the importance of the Negro gaining a foothold in trades and his encouragement in industry and common labor. Mr. Washington was not absolutely opposed to college training, and sent his own children to college. But he did minimize its importance, and discouraged the philanthropic support of higher education; while I openly and repeatedly criticized what seemed to me the poor work and small accomplishment of the Negro industrial school. Moreover, it was characteristic of the Washington statesmanship that whatever he or anybody believed or wanted must be subordinated to dominant public opinion and that opinion deferred to and cajoled until it allowed a deviation toward better ways. This is no new thing in the world, but it is always dangerous.

But beyond this difference of ideal lay another and more bitter and insistent controversy. This started with the rise at Tuskegee Institute, and centering around Booker T. Washington, of what I may call the Tuskegee Machine. Of its existence and work, little has ever been said and almost nothing written. The years from 1899 to 1905 marked the culmination of the career of Booker T. Washington. In 1899 Mr. Washington, Paul Laurence Dunbar, and myself spoke on the same platform at the Hollis Street Theatre, Boston, before a distinguished audience. Mr. Washington was not at his best and friends immediately raised a fund which sent him to Europe for a three months' rest. He was received with extraordinary honors: he had tea with the aged Queen Victoria, but two years before her death; he was entertained by two dukes and other members of the aristocracy; he met James Bryce and Henry M. Stanley; he was received at the Peace Conference at The Hague and was greeted by many distinguished Americans, like ex-President Harrison, Archbishop Ireland and two justices of the Supreme Court. Only a few years before he had received an honorary degree from Harvard; in 1901, he received a LL.D. from Dartmouth and that same year he dined with President Roosevelt to the consternation of the white South.

Returning to America he became during the administrations of Theodore Roosevelt and William Taft, from 1901 to 1912, the political referee in all Federal appointments or action taken with reference to the Negro and in many regarding the white South. In 1903 Andrew Carnegie made the future of Tuskegee certain by a gift of $600,000. There was no question of Booker T. Washington's undisputed leadership of the ten million Negroes in America, a leadership recognized gladly by the whites and conceded by most of the Negroes.

But there were discrepancies and paradoxes in this leadership. It did not seem fair, for instance, that on the one hand Mr. Washington should decry political activities among Negroes, and on the other hand dictate Negro political objectives from Tuskegee. At a time when Negro civil rights called for organized and aggressive defense, he broke down that defense by advising acquiescence or at least no open agitation. During the period when laws disfranchising the Negro were being passed in all the Southern states, between 1890 and 1909, and when these were being supplemented by "Jim Crow" travel laws and other enactments making color caste legal, his public speeches, while they did not entirely ignore this development, tended continually to excuse it, to emphasize the shortcomings of the Negro, and were interpreted widely as putting the chief onus for his condition upon the Negro himself.

All this naturally aroused increasing opposition among Negroes and especially among the younger classes of educated Negroes, who were beginning to emerge here and there, especially from Northern institutions. This opposition began to become vocal in 1901 when two men, Monroe Trotter, Harvard 1895, and George Forbes, Amherst 1895, began the publication of the Boston *Guardian*. The *Guardian* was bitter, satirical, and personal; but it was well-edited, it was earnest, and it published facts. It attracted wide attention among colored people; it circulated among them all over the country; it was quoted and discussed. I did not wholly agree with the *Guardian*, and indeed only a few Negroes did, but nearly all read it and were influenced by it.

This beginning of organized opposition, together with other events, led to the growth at Tuskegee of what I have called the Tuskegee Machine. It arose first quite naturally. Not only did presidents of the United States consult Booker Washington, but governors and congressmen; philanthropists conferred with him, scholars wrote to him. Tuskegee became a vast information bureau and center of advice. It was not merely passive in these matters but, guided by a young unobtrusive minor official who was also intelligent, suave and far-seeing, active efforts were made to concentrate influence at Tuskegee. After a time almost no Negro institution could collect funds without the recommendation or acquiescence of Mr. Washington. Few political appointments were made anywhere in the United States without his consent. Even the careers of rising young colored men were very often determined by his advice and certainly his opposition was fatal. How much Mr. Washington knew of this work of the Tuskegee Machine and was directly responsible, one cannot say, but of its general activity and scope he must have been aware.

Moreover, it must not be forgotten that this Tuskegee Machine was not solely the idea and activity of black folk at Tuskegee. It was largely encouraged and given financial aid through certain white groups and individuals in the North. This Northern group had clear objectives. They were capitalists and employers and yet in most cases sons, relatives, or friends of the abolitionists who had sent teachers into the new Negro South after the war. These younger men believed that the Negro problem could not remain a matter of philanthropy. It must be a matter of business. These Negroes were not to be encouraged as voters in the new democracy, nor were they to be left at the mercy of the reactionary South. They were good laborers and they might be better. They could become a strong labor force and properly guided they would restrain the unbridled demands of white labor, born of the Northern labor unions and now spreading to the South.

One danger must be avoided and that was to allow the silly idealism of Negroes, half-trained in Southern missionary "colleges," to mislead the mass of laborers and keep them stirred-up by ambitions incapable of realization. To this school of thought, the philosophy of Booker Washington came as a godsend and it proposed by building up his prestige and power to control the Negro group. The control was to be drastic. The Negro intelligentsia was to be suppressed and hammered into conformity. The process involved some cruelty and disappointment, but that was inevitable. This was the real force back of the Tuskegee Machine. It had money and it had opportunity, and it found in Tuskegee tools to do its bidding.

There were some rather pitiful results in thwarted ambition and curtailed opportunity. I remember one case which always stands in my memory as typical. There was a young colored man, one of the most beautiful human beings I have ever seen, with smooth brown skin, velvet eyes of intelligence, and raven hair. He was educated and well-to-do. He proposed to use his father's Alabama farm and fortune to build a Negro town and independent economic unit in the South. He furnished a part of the capital but soon needed more and he came North to get it. He struggled for more than a decade; philanthropists and capitalists were fascinated by his personality and story; and when, according to current custom, they appealed to Tuskegee for confirmation, there was silence. Mr. Washington would not say a word in favor of the project. He simply kept still. Will Benson struggled on with ups and downs, but always balked by a whispering galley of suspicion, because his plan was never endorsed by Tuskegee. In the midst of what seemed to us who looked on the beginnings of certain success, Benson died of overwork, worry, and a broken heart.

From facts like this, one may gauge the bitterness of the fight of young Negroes against Mr. Washington and Tuskegee. Contrary to most opinion, the controversy as it developed was not entirely against Mr. Washington's ideas, but became the insistence upon the right of other Negroes to have and express their ideas. Things came to such a pass that when any Negro complained or advocated a course of action, he was silenced with the remark that Mr. Washington did not agree with this. Naturally the bumptious, irritated, young black intelligentsia of the day declared, "I don't care a damn what Booker Washington thinks! This is what I think, and *I have a right to think.*"

It was this point, and not merely disagreement with Mr. Washington's plans, that brought eventually violent outbreak. It was more than opposition to a program of education. It was opposition to a system and that system was part of the economic development of the United States at the time. The fight cut deep: it went into social relations; it divided friends; it made bitter enemies. I can remember that years later, when I went to live in New York and was once invited to a social gathering among Brooklyn colored people, one of the most prominent Negroes of the city refused to be present because of my former attitude toward Mr. Washington.

When the *Guardian* began to increase in influence, determined effort was made to build up a Negro press for Tuskegee. Already Tuskegee filled the horizon so far as national magazines and the great newspapers were concerned. In 1901 the *Outlook*, then the leading weekly, chose two distinguished Americans for autobiographies. Mr. Washington's "Up from Slavery" was so popular that it was soon published and circulated all over the earth. Thereafter, every magazine editor sought articles with his signature and publishing houses continued to ask for books. A number of talented "ghost writers," black and white, took service under Tuskegee, and books and articles poured out of the institution. An annual letter "To My People" went out from Tuskegee to the press. Tuskegee became the capital of the Negro nation. Negro newspapers were influenced and finally the oldest and largest was bought by white friends of Tuskegee. Most of the other papers found it to their advantage certainly not to oppose Mr. Washington, even if they did not wholly agree with him. Negroes who sought high positions groveled for his favor.

I was greatly disturbed at this time, not because I was in absolute opposition to the things that Mr. Washington was advocating, but because I was strongly in favor of more open agitation against wrongs and above all I resented the practical buying up of the Negro press and choking off of even mild and reasonable opposition to Mr. Washington in both the Negro press and the white.

Then, too, during these years there came a series of influences that were brought to bear upon me personally, which increased my discomfort and resentment. I had tried to keep in touch with Hampton and Tuskegee, for I regarded them as great institutions. I attended the conferences which for a long time were held at Hampton, and at one of them I was approached by a committee. It consisted of Walter Hines Page, editor of the *Atlantic Monthly*; William McVickar, Episcopal Bishop of Rhode Island; and Dr. Frissel, principal of Hampton. They asked me about the possibilities of my editing a periodical to be published at Hampton. I told them of my dreams and plans, and afterwards wrote them in detail. But one query came by mail: that was concerning the editorial direction. I replied firmly that editorial decisions were to be in my hands, if I edited the magazine. This was undiplomatic and too sweeping; and yet, it brought to head the one real matter in controversy: would such a magazine be dominated by and subservient to the Tuskegee philosophy, or would it have freedom of thought and discussion? Perhaps if I had been more experienced, the question could have been discussed and some reasonable outcome obtained; but I doubt it. I think any such magazine launched at the time would have been seriously curtailed in its freedom of speech. At any rate, the project was dropped.

Beginning in 1902 considerable pressure was put upon me to give up my work at Atlanta University and go to Tuskegee. There again I was not at first adverse in principle to Tuskegee, except that I wanted to continue what I had begun and if my work was worth support, it was worth support at Atlanta University. Moreover, I was unable to be assured that my studies would be continued at Tuskegee, and that I would not sink to the level of a "ghost writer." I remember a letter came from Wallace Buttrick late in 1902, asking that I attend a private conference in New York with Felix Adler, William H. Baldwin, Jr., George Foster Peabody, and Robert Ogden. The object of the conference was ostensibly the condition of the Negro in New York City. I went to the conference and I did not like it. Most of the more distinguished persons named were not present. The conference itself amounted to little, but I was whisked over to William H. Baldwin's beautiful Long

Island home and there what seemed to me to be the real object of my coming was disclosed. Mr. Baldwin was at that time president of the Long Island Railroad and slated to be president of the Pennsylvania. He was the rising industrial leader of America; also he was a prime mover of the Tuskegee board of trustees. Both he and his wife insisted that my place was at Tuskegee; that Tuskegee was not yet a good school, and needed the kind of development that I had been trained to promote.

This was followed by two interviews with Mr. Washington himself. I was elated at the opportunity and we met twice in New York City. The results to me were disappointing. Booker T. Washington was not an easy person to know. He was wary and silent. He never expressed himself frankly or clearly until he knew exactly to whom he was talking and just what their wishes and desires were. He did not know me, and I think he was suspicious. On the other hand, I was quick, fast-speaking and voluble. I found at the end of the first interview that I had done practically all the talking and that no clear and definite offer or explanation of my proposed work at Tuskegee had been made. In fact, Mr. Washington had said about as near nothing as was possible.

The next interview did not go so well because I myself said little. Finally, we resorted to correspondence. Even then I could get no clear understanding of just what I was going to do at Tuskegee if I went. I was given to understand that the salary and accommodations would be satisfactory. In fact, I was invited to name my price. Later in the year I went to Bar Harbor for a series of speeches in behalf of Atlanta University, and while there met Jacob Schiff, the Schieffelins and Merriam of Webster's dictionary. I had dinner with the Schieffelins and again was urged to go to Tuskegee.

Early in the next year I received an invitation to join Mr. Washington and certain prominent white and colored friends in a conference to be held in New York. The conference was designed to talk over a common program for the American Negro and evidently it was hoped that the growing division of opinion and opposition to Mr. Washington within the ranks of Negroes would thus be overcome. I was enthusiastic over the idea. It seemed to me just what was needed to clear the air.

There was difficulty, however, in deciding what persons ought to be invited to the conference, how far it should include Mr. Washington's extreme opponents, or how far it should be composed principally of his friends. There ensued a long delay and during this time it seemed to me that I ought to make my own position clearer than I had hitherto. I was increasingly uncomfortable under the statements of Mr. Washington's position: his depreciation of the value of the vote; his evident dislike of Negro colleges; and his general attitude which seemed to place the onus of blame for the status of Negroes upon the Negroes themselves rather than upon the whites. And above all, I resented the Tuskegee Machine.

I had been asked sometime before by A. C. McClurg and Company of Chicago if I did not have some material for a book; I planned a social study which should be perhaps a summing up of the work of the Atlanta Conferences, or at any rate, a scientific investigation. They asked, however, if I did not have some essays that they might put together and issue immediately, mentioning my articles in the *Atlantic Monthly* and other places. I demurred because books of essays almost always fall so flat. Nevertheless, I got together a number of my fugitive pieces. I then added a chapter, "Of Mr. Booker T. Washington and Others," in which I sought to make a frank evaluation of Booker T. Washington. I left out the more controversial matter: the bitter resentment which young Negroes felt at the continued and increasing activity of the Tuskegee Machine. I concentrated my thought and argument on Mr. Washington's general philosophy. As I read that statement now, a generation later, I am satisfied with it. I see no word that I would change. The "Souls of Black Folk" was published in 1903 and is still selling today.

My book settled pretty definitely any further question of my going to Tuskegee as an employee. But it also drew pretty hard and fast lines about my future career. Meantime, the matter of the conference in New York dragged on until finally in October, 1903, a circular letter was sent out setting January, 1904, as the date of meeting. The conference took place accordingly in Carnegie Hall, New York. About fifty persons were present, most of them colored and including many well-known persons. There was considerable plain speaking but the whole purpose of the conference seemed revealed by the invited guests and the tone of their message. Several white persons of high distinction came to speak to us, including Andrew Carnegie and Lyman Abbott. Their words were lyric, almost fulsome in praise of Mr. Washington and his work, and in support of his ideas. Even if all they said had been true, it was a wrong note to strike in a conference of conciliation. The conferences ended with two speeches by Mr. Washington and myself, and the appointment of a Committee of Twelve in which we were also included.

The Committee of Twelve which was thus instituted was unable to do any effective work as a steering committee for the Negro race in America. First of all, it was financed, through Mr. Washington, probably by Mr. Carnegie. This put effective control of the committee in Mr. Washington's hands. It was organized during my absence and laid down a plan of work which seemed to me of some value but of no lasting importance and having little to do with the larger questions and issues. I, therefore, soon resigned so as not to be responsible for work and pronouncements over which I would have little influence. My friends and others accused me of refusing to play the game after I had assented to a program of co-operation. I still think, however, that my action was wise.

Meantime, the task of raising money for Atlanta University and my work became increasingly difficult. In the fall of 1904 the printing of our conference report was postponed by the trustees until special funds could be secured. I did not at the time see the handwriting on the wall. I did not realize how strong the forces were back of Tuskegee and how they might interfere with my scientific study of the Negro. My continuing thought was that we must have a vehicle for both opinion and fact which would help me carry on my scientific work and at the same time be a forum less radical than the *Guardian*, and yet more rational than the rank and file of Negro papers now so largely arrayed with Tuskegee. With this in mind, as early as 1904, I helped one of the Atlanta University graduates, who was a good printer, to set up a job office in Memphis.

In 1905 I wrote to Jacob Schiff, reminding him of having met him in Bar Harbor in 1903: "I want to lay before you a plan which I have and ask you if it is of sufficient interest to you for you to be willing to hear more of it and possibly to assist in its realization. The Negro race in America is today in a critical condition. Only united concerted effort will save us from being crushed. This union must come as a matter of education and long continued effort. To this end there is needed a high class of journal to circulate among the intelligent Negroes, tell them of the deeds of themselves and their neighbors, interpret the news of the world to them, and inspire them toward definite ideals. Now we have many small weekly papers and one or two monthlies, and none of them fill the great need I have outlined. I want to establish, therefore, for the nine million American Negroes and eventually for the whole Negro world, a monthly journal. To this end I have already in Memphis a printing establishment which has been running successfully at job work a year under a competent printer—self-sacrificing educated young man. Together we shall have about $2,000 invested in this plant by April 15."

Mr. Schiff wrote back courteously, saying: "Your plans to establish a high class journal to circulate among the intelligent Negroes is in itself interesting, and on its face has my sympathy. But before I could decide whether I can become of advantage in carrying your plans into effect, I would wish to advise with men whose opinion in such a matter I consider of much value." Nothing ever came of this, because, as I might have known, most of Mr. Schiff's friends were strong and sincere advocates of Tuskegee.

It was with difficulty that I came fully to realize the situation that was thus developing: first of all, I could not persuade myself that my program of solving the Negro problem by scientific investigation was wrong, or that it could possibly fail of eventual support when once it was undertaken; that it was understood in widening circles of readers and thinkers, I was convinced, because of the reception accorded the Atlanta University Studies. When, however, in spite of that, the revenue of the University continued to fall off, and no special support came for my particular part of its work, I tried several times by personal effort to see if funds could not be raised.

In 1906 I made two appeals: first and boldly, I outlined the work of the Atlanta Conference to Andrew Carnegie, reminding him that I had been presented to him and Carl Schurz some years before. I hoped that despite his deep friendship for Mr. Washington and the Tuskegee idea, he would see the use and value of my efforts at Atlanta. The response was indirect. At the time a white Mississippi planter, Alfred W. Stone, was popular in the North. He had grave doubts about the future of the Negro race, widely criticized black labor, and once tried to substitute Italians on his own plantations, until they became too handy with the knife. To his direction, Mr. Carnegie and others entrusted a fund for certain studies among Negroes. Why they selected him and neglected an established center like Atlanta University, I cannot imagine; but at any rate, Stone turned to me and offered to give the University a thousand dollars to help finance a special study of the history of economic co-operation among Negroes. I had planned that year, 1907, to study the Negro in politics, but here was needed support and I turned aside and made the study asked for.

About the same time, I approached the United States Commissioner of Labor. For several years I had been able to do now and then certain small studies for the Bureau of Labor, which had been accepted and paid for. It began with a proposal to Carroll D. Wright for a study of the Negro in a Virginia town in 1898, which Mr. Wright authorized me to make on my own responsibility, promising only to print it if he liked it. He did like it. This was followed by a study of the Negro in the Black Belt in 1899 and among Negroes in Georgia in 1901, and I now approached the Bureau with a new proposal.

I asked United States Commissioner of Labor Neill, in 1906, to authorize a study of a Black Belt community. I wanted to take Lownes County, Alabama, in a former slave state with a large majority of Negroes, and make a social and economic study from the earliest times where documents were available, down to the present; supplemented by studies of official records and a house to house canvas. I plied Commissioner Neill with plans and specifications until at last he authorized the study. Helped by Monroe Work, now at

Tuskegee Institute, and R. R. Wright, now a bishop of the A. M. E. Church, and a dozen or more local employees, I settled at the Calhoun School and began the study.

It was carried on with all sorts of difficulties, including financing which was finally arranged by loans from the University, and with the greeting of some of my agents with shotguns in certain parts of the county; but it was eventually finished. The difficult schedules were tabulated and I made chronological maps of the division of the land; I considered the distribution of labor; the relation of landlord and tenant; the political organization and the family life and distribution of the population. The report went to Washington and I spent some weeks there in person, revising and perfecting it. It was accepted by the government, and $2,000 paid for it, most of which went back to the University in repayment of funds which they had kindly furnished me to carry on the work. But the study was not published. I knew the symptoms of this sort of treatment: in 1898, S. S. McClure had sent me to south Georgia to make a study of social situations there. He paid for the report but never published the manuscript and afterward did the same thing in the case of Sir Harry Johnston.

I finally approached the bureau and tried to find out when it would be published and was told that the bureau had decided not to publish the manuscript, since it "touched on political matters." I was astonished and disappointed, but after a year went back to them again and asked if they would allow me to have the manuscript published since they were not going to use it. They told me it had been destroyed. And while I was down in Lownes County finishing this study, there came the news of the Atlanta riot. I took the next train for Atlanta and my family. On the way, I wrote the "Litany of Atlanta."

By this time I was pretty thoroughly disillusioned. It did not seem possible for me to occupy middle ground and try to appease the *Guardian* on the one hand and the Hampton-Tuskegee idea on the other. I began to feel the strength and implacability of the Tuskegee Machine; the Negro newspapers were definitely showing their reaction and publishing jibes and innuendoes at my expense. Filled with increasing indignation, I published in the *Guardian* a statement concerning the venality of certain Negro papers which I charged had sold out to Mr. Washington. It was a charge difficult of factual proof without an expenditure of time and funds not at my disposal. I was really at last openly tilting against the Tuskegee Machine and its methods. These methods have become common enough in our day for all sorts of purposes: the distribution of advertising and favors, the sending out of special correspondence, veiled and open attacks upon recalcitrants, the narrowing of opportunities for employment and promotion. All this is a common method of procedure today, but in 1904 it seemed to me monstrous and dishonest, and I resented it. On the other hand, the public expression of this resentment greatly exercised and annoyed Mr. Washington's friends. Some knew little about these activities at Tuskegee; others knew and approved. The New York *Evening Post* challenged me to present proof of my extraordinary statements and refused to regard my answer as sufficient, which was of course true.

Then came a new and surprising turn to the whole situation which in the end quite changed my life. In the early summer of 1905, Mr. Washington went to Boston and arranged to speak in a colored church to colored people—a thing which he did not often do in the North. Trotter and Forbes, editors of the *Guardian*, determined to heckle him and make him answer publicly certain questions with regard to his attitude toward voting and education. William H. Lewis, a colored lawyer whom I myself had introduced to Mr. Washington, had charge of the meeting, and the result was a disturbance magnified by the newspapers into a riot, which resulted in the arrest of Mr. Trotter. Eventually he served a term in jail.

With this incident I had no direct connection whatsoever. I did not know beforehand of the meeting in Boston, nor of the projected plan to heckle Mr. Washington. But when Trotter went to jail, my indignation overflowed. I did not always agree with Trotter then or later. But he was an honest, brilliant, unselfish man, and to treat as a crime that which was at worst mistaken judgment was an outrage. I sent out from Atlanta in June, 1905, a call to a few selected persons "for organized determination and aggressive action on the part of men who believe in Negro freedom and growth." I proposed a conference during the summer "to oppose firmly present methods of strangling honest criticism; to organize intelligent and honest Negroes; and to support organs of news and public opinion."

Fifty-nine colored men from seventeen different states signed a call for a meeting near Buffalo, New York, during the week of July 9, 1905. I went to Buffalo and hired a little hotel on the Canada side of the river at Fort Erie, and waited for the men to attend the meeting. If sufficient men had not come to pay for the hotel, I should certainly have been in bankruptcy and perhaps in jail; but as a matter of fact, twenty-nine men, representing fourteen states, came. The "Niagara Movement" was organized January 31, 1906, and was incorporated in the District of Columbia.

Its particular business and objects are to advocate and promote the following principles:

1. Freedom of speech and criticism.
2. Unfettered and unsubsidized press.
3. Manhood suffrage.
4. The abolition of all caste distinctions based simply on race and color.
5. The recognition of the principles of human brotherhood as a practical present creed.
6. The recognition of the highest and best human training as the monopoly of no class or race.
7. A belief in the dignity of labor.
8. United effort to realize these ideals under wise and courageous leadership.

The Niagara Movement raised a furor of the most disconcerting criticism. I was accused of acting from motives of envy of a great leader and being ashamed of the fact that I was a member of the Negro race. The leading weekly of the land, the New York *Outlook*, pilloried me with scathing articles. But the movement went on. The next year, 1906, instead of meeting in secret, we met openly at Harper's Ferry, the scene of John Brown's raid, and had in significance if not numbers one of the greatest meetings that American Negroes have ever held. We made pilgrimage at dawn bare-footed to the scene of Brown's martyrdom and we talked some of the plainest English that has been given voice to by black men in America. The resolutions which I wrote expressed with tumult of emotion my creed of 1905:

"The men of the Niagara Movement, coming from the toil of the year's hard work, and pausing a moment from the earning of their daily bread, turn toward the nation and again ask in the name of ten million the privilege of a hearing. In the past year the work of the Negro hater has flourished in the land. Step by step the defenders of the rights of American citizens have retreated. The work of stealing the black man's ballot has progressed and the fifty and more representatives of stolen votes still sit in the nation's capital. Discrimination in travel and public accommodation has so spread that some of our weaker brethren are actually afraid to thunder against color discrimination as such and are simply whispering for ordinary decencies.

"Against this the Niagara Movement eternally protests. We will not be satisfied to take one jot or tittle less than our full manhood rights. We claim for ourselves every single right that belongs to a freeborn American, political, civil, and social; and until we get these rights we will never cease to protest and assail the ears of America. The battle we wage is not for ourselves alone, but for all true Americans. It is a fight for ideals, lest this, our common fatherland, false to its founding, become in truth the land of the Thief and the home of the Slave—a by-word and a hissing among the nations for its sounding pretensions and pitiful accomplishment.

"Never before in the modern age has a great and civilized folk threatened to adopt so cowardly a creed in the treatment of its fellow-citizens, born and bred on its soil. Stripped of verbiage and subterfuge and in its naked nastiness, the new American creed says: fear to let black men even try to rise lest they become the equals of the white. And this is the land that professes to follow Jesus Christ. The blasphemy of such a course is only matched by its cowardice.

"In detail our demands are clear and unequivocal. First, we would vote; with the right to vote goes everything: freedom, manhood, the honor of your wives, the chastity of your daughters, the right to work, and the chance to rise, and let no man listen to those who deny this.

"We want full manhood suffrage, and we want it now, henceforth and forever.

"Second. We want discrimination in public accommodation to cease. Separation in railway and street cars, based simply on race and color, is un-American, undemocratic, and silly. We protest against all such discrimination.

"Third. We claim the right of freemen to walk, talk, and be with them that wish to be with us. No man has a right to choose another man's friends, and to attempt to do so is an impudent interference with the most fundamental human privilege.

"Fourth. We want the laws enforced against rich as well as poor; against Capitalist as well as Laborer; against white as well as black. We are not more lawless than the white race, we are more often arrested, convicted and mobbed. We want justice even for criminals and outlaws. We want the Constitution of the country enforced. We want Congress to take charge of the Congressional elections. We want the Fourteenth Amendment carried out to the letter and every State disfranchised in Congress which attempts to disfranchise its rightful voters. We want the Fifteenth Amendment enforced and no State allowed to base its franchise simply on color.

"The failure of the Republican Party in Congress at the session just closed to redeem its pledge of 1904 with reference to suffrage conditions at the South seems a plain, deliberate, and premeditated breach of promise, and stamps that party as guilty of obtaining votes under false pretense.

"Fifth. We want our children educated. The school system in the country districts of the South is a disgrace and in few towns and cities are the Negro schools what they ought to be. We want the national government to step in and wipe out illiteracy in the South. Either the United States will destroy ignorance, or ignorance will destroy the United States.

"And when we call for education, we mean real education. We believe in work. We ourselves are workers, but work is not necessarily education. Education is the development of power and ideal. We want our children trained as intelligent human beings should be, and we will fight for all time against any proposal to educate black boys and girls simply as servants and underlings, or simply for the use of other people. They have a right to know, to think, to aspire.

"These are some of the chief things which we want. How shall we get them? By voting where we may vote; by persistent, unceasing agitation; by hammering at the truth; by sacrifice and work.

"We do not believe in violence, neither in the despised violence of the raid nor the lauded violence of the soldier, nor the barbarous violence of the mob; but we do believe in John Brown, in that incarnate spirit of justice, that hatred of a lie, that willingness to sacrifice money, reputation, and life itself on the altar of right. And here on the scene of John Brown's martyrdom, we reconsecrate ourselves, our honor, our property to the final emancipation of the race which John Brown died to make free."

Meantime, I refused to give up the idea that a critical periodical for the American Negro might be founded. I had started in Memphis with the help of two graduates of Atlanta University the little printing shop that I have already mentioned, and from this was published weekly a paper called *The Moon* beginning in 1906. *The Moon* was in some sort precursor of *The Crisis*. It was published for a year in Memphis and then the printing office given up and in 1907 in conjunction with two friends in Washington there was issued a miniature monthly called the *Horizon*. The *Horizon* was published from 1907 to 1910, and in the fall of 1910 *The Crisis* was born.

Gradually I began to realize that the difficulty about support for my work in Atlanta University was personal; that on account of my attitude toward Mr. Washington I had become *persona non grata* to powerful interests, and that Atlanta University would not be able to get support for its general work or for its study of the Negro problem so long as I remained at the institution. No one ever said this to me openly, but I sensed it in the worries which encompassed the new young President Ware who had succeeded Dr. Bumstead. I began to realize that I would better look out for work elsewhere.

About this time an offer came from the city of Washington. The merging of the white and colored school systems into one, had thrown colored folk into uproar lest their control of their own schools be eliminated. The new and rather eccentric W. C. Chancellor, superintendent of schools, wanted an assistant superintendent to put in charge of the Negro schools. To my great surprise he offered the position to me, while I was on a chance visit to the city. I asked for time to consider it. My reaction was to refuse even though the salary was twice what I was getting; for I doubted my fitness for such a job; but when I thought the matter over further and my position of Atlanta University, I began to wonder if I should not accept.

I was not called upon to decide, for forces started moving in Washington. The Tuskegee Machine was definitely against me and local interests in the Negro group were opposed. A prominent colored official took the matter straight to President Theodore Roosevelt and emphasized the "danger" of my appointment. He never forgot the "danger" of my personality as later events proved. The offer was never actually withdrawn, but it was not pressed, and I finally realized that it probably would not have gone through even if I had indicated my acceptance.

Still my eventual withdrawal from Atlanta University seemed wise. Young President Ware had received almost categorical promise that under certain circumstances increased contributions from the General Education Board and other sources might be expected, which would make the University secure, and perhaps even permit the continuance of my studies. I was sure that I was at least one of these "circumstances," and so my work in Atlanta and my dream of the settlement of the Negro problem by science faded. I began to be acutely conscious of the difficulty which my attitudes and beliefs were making for Atlanta University.

My career as a scientist was to be swallowed up in my role as master of propaganda. This was not wholly to my liking. I was no natural leader of men. I could not slap people on the back and make friends of strangers. I could not easily break down an inherited reserve; or at all times curb a biting, critical tongue. Nevertheless, having put my hand to the plow, I had to go on. The Niagara Movement with less momentum met in Boston in 1907 and in Oberlin in 1908. It began to suffer internal strain from the dynamic personality of Trotter and my inexperience with organizations. Finally it practically became merged with a new and enveloping organization.

This started with a lynching 100 years after the birth of Abraham Lincoln, in his birthplace. William English Walling dramatized the gruesome happening and a group of liberals formed a committee in New York, which I was invited to join. A conference was held in 1909. After the conference, a new organization, the National Association for the Advancement of Colored People, was formed, which without formal merger absorbed practically the whole membership of the Niagara Movement, save Trotter, who distrusted our white allies and their objects. With some hesitation I was asked to come as Director of Publications and Research, with the idea that my research work was to go on and with the further idea that my activities would be so held in check that the Association would not develop as an organ of attack upon Tuskegee—a difficult order; because how, in 1910, could one discuss the Negro problem and not touch upon Booker T. Washington and Tuskegee? But after all, as I interpreted the matter, it was a question of temperament and manner rather than of subject.

Here was an opportunity to enter the lists in a desperate fight aimed straight at the real difficulty: the question as to how far educated Negro opinion in the United States was going to have the right and opportunity to guide the Negro group. I did not hesitate because I could not. It was the voice without reply, and I went to New York.

One may consider these personal equations and this clash of ideologies as biographical or sociological; as a matter of the actions and thoughts of certain men, or as a development of larger social forces beyond personal control. I suppose the latter aspect is the truer. My thoughts, the thoughts of Washington, Trotter and others, were the expression of social forces more than of our own minds. These forces or ideologies embraced more than our reasoned acts. They included physical, biological and psychological forces; habits, conventions and enactments. Opposed to these came natural reaction: the physical recoil of the victims, the unconscious and irrational urges, as well as reasoned complaints and acts. The total result was the history of our day. That history may be epitomized in one word—Empire; the domination of white

Europe over black Africa and yellow Asia, through political power built on the economic control of labor, income and ideas. The echo of this industrial imperialism in America was the expulsion of black men from American democracy, their subjection to caste control and wage slavery. This ideology was triumphant in 1910.

Chapter 5

THE CONCEPT OF RACE

I WANT now to turn aside from the personal annals of this biography to consider the conception which is after all my main subject. The concept of race lacks something in personal interest, but personal interest in my case has always depended primarily upon this race concept and I wish to examine this now. The history of the development of the race concept in the world and particularly in America, was naturally reflected in the education offered me. In the elementary school it came only in the matter of geography when the races of the world were pictured: Indians, Negroes and Chinese, by their most uncivilized and bizarre representatives; the whites by some kindly and distinguished-looking philanthropist. In the elementary and high school, the matter was touched only incidentally, due I doubt not to the thoughtfulness of the teachers; and again my racial inferiority could not be dwelt upon because the single representative of the Negro race in the school did not happen to be in any way inferior to his fellows. In fact it was not difficult for me to excel them in many ways and to regard this as quite natural.

At Fisk, the problem of race was faced openly and essential racial equality asserted and natural inferiority strenuously denied. In some cases the teachers expressed this theory; in most cases the student opinion naturally forced it. At Harvard, on the other hand, I began to face scientific race dogma: first of all, evolution and the "Survival of the Fittest." It was continually stressed in the community and in classes that there was a vast difference in the development of the whites and the "lower" races; that this could be seen in the physical development of the Negro. I remember once in a museum, coming face to face with a demonstration: a series of skeletons arranged from a little monkey to a tall well-developed white man, with a Negro barely outranking a chimpanzee. Eventually in my classes stress was quietly transferred to brain weight and brain capacity, and at last to the "cephalic index."

In the graduate school at Harvard and again in Germany,

the emphasis again was altered, and race became a matter of culture and cultural history. The history of the world was paraded before the observation of students. Which was the superior race? Manifestly that which had a history, the white race; there was some mention of Asiatic culture, but no course in Chinese or Indian history or culture was offered at Harvard, and quite unanimously in America and Germany, Africa was left without culture and without history. Even when the matter of mixed races was touched upon their evident and conscious inferiority was mentioned. I can never forget that morning in the class of the great Heinrich von Treitschke in Berlin. He was a big aggressive man, with an impediment in his speech which forced him to talk rapidly lest he stutter. His classes were the only ones always on time, and an angry scraping of feet greeted a late comer. Clothed in black, big, bushy-haired, peering sharply at the class, his words rushed out in a flood: "Mulattoes," he thundered, "are inferior." I almost felt his eyes boring into me, although probably he had not noticed me. "Sie fühlen sich niedriger!" "Their actions show it," he asserted. What contradiction could there be to that authoritative dictum?

The first thing which brought me to my senses in all this racial discussion was the continuous change in the proofs and arguments advanced. I could accept evolution and the survival of the fittest, provided the interval between advanced and backward races was not made too impossible. I balked at the usual "thousand years." But no sooner had I settled into scientific security here, than the basis of race distinction was changed without explanation, without apology. I was skeptical about brain weight; surely much depended upon what brains were weighed. I was not sure about physical measurements and social inquiries. For instance, an insurance actuary published in 1890 incontrovertible statistics showing how quickly and certainly the Negro race was dying out in the United States through sheer physical inferiority. I lived to see every assumption of Hoffman's "Race Traits and Tendencies" contradicted; but even before that, I doubted the statistical method which he had used. When the matter of race became a question of comparative culture, I was in revolt. I began to see that the cultural equipment attributed to any people depended largely on who estimated it; and conviction came later in a rush as I realized what in my education had been suppressed concerning Asiatic and African culture.

It was not until I was long out of school and indeed after the World War that there came the hurried use of the new technique of psychological tests, which were quickly adjusted so as to put black folk absolutely beyond the possibility of civilization. By this time I was unimpressed. I had too often seen science made the slave of caste and race hate. And it was interesting to see Odum, McDougall and Brigham eventually turn somersaults from absolute scientific proof of Negro inferiority to repudiation of the limited and questionable application of any test which pretended to measure innate human intelligence.

So far I have spoken of "race" and race problems quite as a matter of course without explanation or definition. That was our method in the nineteenth century. Just as I was born a member of a colored family, so too I was born a member of the colored race. That was obvious and no definition was needed. Later I adopted the designation "Negro" for the race to which I belong. It seemed more definite and logical. At the same time I was of course aware that all members of the Negro race were not black and that the pictures of my race which were current were not authentic nor fair portraits. But all that was incidental. The world was divided into great primary groups of folk who belonged naturally together through heredity of physical traits and cultural affinity.

I do not know how I came first to form my theories of race. The process was probably largely unconscious. The differences of personal appearance between me and my fellows, I must have been conscious of when quite young. Whatever distinctions came because of that did not irritate me; they rather exalted me because, on the whole, while I was still a youth, they gave me exceptional position and a chance to excel rather than handicapping me.

Then of course, when I went South to Fisk, I became a member of a closed racial group with rites and loyalties, with a history and a corporate future, with an art and philosophy. I received these eagerly and expanded them so that when I came to Harvard the theory of race separation was quite in my blood. I did not seek contact with my white fellow students. On the whole I rather avoided them. I took it for granted that we were training ourselves for different careers in worlds largely different. There was not the slightest idea of the permanent subordination and inequality of my world. Nor again was there any idea of racial amalgamation. I resented the assumption that we desired it. I frankly refused the possibility while in Germany and even in America gave up courtship with one "colored" girl because she looked quite white, and I should resent the inference on the street that I had married outside my race.

All this theory, however, was disturbed by certain facts in America, and by my European experience. Despite everything, race lines were not fixed and fast. Within the Negro group especially there were people of all colors. Then too, there were plenty of my colored friends who resented my ultra "race" loyalty and ridiculed it. They pointed out that I was not a "Negro," but a mulatto; that I was not a Southerner but a Northerner, and my object was to be an American and not a Negro; that race distinctions must go. I agreed with this in part and as an ideal, but I saw it leading to inner racial distinction in the colored group. I resented the defensive mechanism of avoiding too dark companions in order to escape notice and discrimination in public. As a sheer matter of taste I wanted the color of my group to be visible. I hotly championed the inclusion of two black school mates whose names were not usually on the invitation list to our social affairs. In Europe my friendships and close contact with white folk made my own ideas waver. The eternal walls between races did not seem so stern and exclusive. I began to emphasize the cultural aspects of race.

It is probably quite natural for persons of low degree, who have reached any status, to search feverishly for distinguished ancestry, as a sort of proof of their inherent desert. This is particularly true in America and has given rise to a number of organizations whose membership depends upon ancestors who have made their mark in the world. Of course, it is clear that there must be here much fable, invention and wishful thinking, facilitated by poor vital statistics and absence of written records. For the mass of Americans, and many Americans who have had the most distinguished careers, have been descended from people who were quite ordinary and even less; America indeed has meant the breaking down of class bars which imprisoned personalities and capabilities and allowing new men and new families to emerge. This is not, as some people assume, a denial of the importance of heredity and family. It is rather its confirmation. It shows us that the few in the past who have emerged are not necessarily the best; and quite certainly are not the only ones worthy of development and distinction; that, on the contrary, only a comparatively few have, under our present economic and social organization, had a chance to show their capabilities.

I early began to take a direct interest in my own family as a group and became curious as to that physical descent which so long I had taken for granted quite unquestioningly. But I did not at first think of any but my Negro ancestors. I knew little and cared less of the white forebears of my father. But this chauvinism gradually changed. There is, of course, nothing more fascinating than the question of the various types of mankind and their intermixture. The whole question of heredity and human gift depends upon such knowledge; but ever since the African slave trade and before the rise of modern biology and sociology, we have been afraid in America that scientific study in this direction might lead to conclusions with which we were loath to agree; and this fear was in reality because the economic foundation of the modern world was based on the recognition and preservation of so-called racial distinctions. In accordance with this, not only Negro slavery could be justified, but the Asiatic coolie profitably used and the labor classes in white countries kept in their places by low wage.

It is not singular then that here in America and in the West Indies, where we have had the most astonishing modern mixture of human types, scientific study of the results and circumstances of this mixture has not only lagged but been almost non-existent. We have not only not studied race and race mixture in America, but we have tried almost by legal process to stop such study. It is for this reason that it has occurred to me just here to illustrate the way in which Africa and Europe have been united in my family. There is nothing unusual about this interracial history. It has been duplicated thousands of times; but on the one hand, the white folk have bitterly resented even a hint of the facts of this intermingling; while black folk have recoiled in natural hesitation and affected disdain in admitting what they know.

I am, therefore, relating the history of my family and centering it around my maternal great-great-grandfather, Tom Burghardt, and my paternal grandfather, Alexander Du Bois.

Absolute legal proof of facts like those here set down is naturally unobtainable. Records of birth are often non-existent, proof of paternity is exceedingly difficult and actual written record rare. In the case of my family I have relied on oral tradition in my mother's family and direct word and written statement from my paternal grandfather; and upon certain general records which I have been able to obtain. I have no doubt of the substantial accuracy of the story that I am to tell.

Of my own immediate ancestors I knew personally only four: my mother and her parents and my paternal grandfather. One other I knew at second hand—my father. I had his picture. I knew what my mother told me about him and what others who had known him, said. So that in all, five of my immediate forebears were known to me. Three others, my paternal great-grandfather and my maternal great-grandfather and great-great-grandfather, I knew about through persons who knew them and through records; and also I knew many of my collateral relatives and numbers of their descendants. My known ancestral family, therefore, consisted of eight or more persons. None of these had reached any particular distinction or were known very far beyond their own families and localities. They were divided into whites, blacks and mulattoes, most of them being mulattoes.

My paternal great-grandfather, Dr. James Du Bois, was white and descended from Chrétien Du Bois who was a French Huguenot farmer and perhaps artisan and resided at Wicres near Lille in French Flanders. It is doubtful if he had any ancestors among the nobility, although his white American descendants love to think so. He had two, possibly three, sons of whom Louis and Jacques came to America to escape religious persecution. Jacques went from France first to

Leiden in the Netherlands, where he was married and had several children, including a second Jacques or James. In 1674 that family came to America and settled at Kingston, New York. James Du Bois appears in the Du Bois family genealogy as a descendant of Jacques in the fifth generation, although the exact line of descent is not clear; but my grandfather's written testimony establishes that James was a physician and a landholder along the Hudson and in the West Indies. He was born in 1750, or later. He may have been a loyalist refugee. One such refugee, Isaac Du Bois, was given a grant of five hundred acres in Eleuthera after the Revolutionary War.

The career of Dr. James Du Bois was chiefly as a plantation proprietor and slave owner in the Bahama Islands with his headquarters at Long Cay. Cousins of his named Gilbert also had plantations near. He never married, but had one of his slaves as his common-law wife, a small brown-skinned woman born on the island. Of this couple two sons were born, Alexander and John. Alexander, my grandfather, was born in 1803, and about 1810, possibly because of the death of the mother, the father brought both these boys to America and planned to give them the education of gentlemen. They were white enough in appearance to give no inkling of their African descent. They were entered in the private Episcopal school at Cheshire, Connecticut, which still exists there and has trained many famous men. Dr. James Du Bois used often to visit his sons there, but about 1812, on his return from a visit, he had a stroke of apoplexy and died. He left no will and his estate descended to a cousin.

The boys were removed from school and bound out as apprentices, my grandfather to a shoemaker. Their connection with the white Du Bois family ceased suddenly, and was never renewed. Alexander Du Bois thus started with a good common school and perhaps some high school training and with the instincts of a gentleman of his day. Naturally he passed through much inner turmoil. He became a rebel, bitter at his lot in life, resentful at being classed as a Negro and yet implacable in his attitude toward whites. Of his brother, John, I have only a picture. He may have been the John Du Bois who helped Bishop Payne to purchase Wilberforce University.

If Alexander Du Bois, following the footsteps of Alexander Hamilton, had come from the West Indies to the United States, stayed with the white group and married and begotten children among them, anyone in after years who had suggested his Negro descent would have been unable to prove it and quite possibly would have been laughed to scorn, or sued for libel. Indeed the legal advisers of the publishers of my last book could write: "We may assume as a general proposition that it is libelous to state erroneously that a white man or woman has colored blood." Lately in Congress the true story, in a WPA history, of miscegenation affecting a high historic personage raised a howl of protest.

Alexander Du Bois did differently from Hamilton. He married into the colored group and his oldest son allied himself with a Negro clan but four generations removed from Africa. He himself first married Sarah Marsh Lewis in 1823 and then apparently set out to make his way in Haiti. There my father was born in 1825, and his elder sister, Augusta, a year earlier, either there or just as the family was leaving the United States. Evidently the situation in Haiti did not please my grandfather or perhaps the death of his young wife when she was scarcely thirty turned him back to America. Within a year he married Emily Basset who seems to have been the widow of a man named Jacklyn and lived in New Milford. Leonard Bacon, a well-known Congregational clergyman, performed his second marriage.

The following year, Alexander began his career in the United States. He lived in New Haven, Springfield, Providence, and finally in New Bedford. For some time, he was steward on the New York–New Haven boat and insisted on better treatment for his colored help. Later about 1848 he ran a grocery store at 23 Washington Street, New Haven, and owned property at different times in the various cities where he lived. By his first wife, my grandmother, he had two children, and by his second wife, one daughter, Henrietta. Three or four children died in infancy. Alexander was a communicant of Trinity Parish, New Haven, and was enrolled there as late as 1845; then something happened, because in 1847 he was among that group of Negroes who formed the new colored Episcopal Parish of St. Luke, where he was for years their senior warden. Probably this indicates one of his bitter fights and rebellions, for nothing but intolerable insult would have led him into a segregated church movement. Alexander Crummell was his first rector here.

As I knew my grandfather, he was a short, stern, upstanding man, sparing but precise in his speech and stiff in manner, evidently long used to repressing his feelings. I remember as a boy of twelve, watching his ceremonious reception of a black visitor, John Freedom; his stately bow, the way in which the red wine was served and the careful almost stilted conversation. I had seen no such social ceremony in my simple western Massachusetts home. The darkened parlor with its horsehair furniture became a very special and important place. I was deeply impressed. My grandfather evidently looked upon me with a certain misgiving if not actual distaste. I was brown, the son of his oldest son, Alfred, and Alfred and his father had never gotten on together.

The boy Alfred was a throwback to his white grandfather. He was small, olive-skinned and handsome and just visibly colored, with curly hair; and he was naturally a play-boy. My only picture of him shows him clothed in the uniform of the Union Army; but he never actually went to the front. In fact, Alfred never actually did much of anything. He was gay and carefree, refusing to settle long at any one place or job. He had a good elementary school training but nothing higher. I think that my father ran away from home several times. Whether he got into any very serious scrapes or not, I do not know, nor do I know whether he was married early in life; I imagine not. I think he was probably a free lance, gallant and lover, yielding only to marital bonds when he found himself in the rather strict clannishness of my mother's family. He was barber, merchant and preacher, but always irresponsible and charming. He had wandered out from eastern New England where his father lived and come to the Berkshire valley in 1867 where he met and married my brown mother.

The second wife of Alexander Du Bois died in 1865. His oldest daughter, Augusta, married a light mulatto and has descendants today who do not know of their Negro blood. Much later Alexander Du Bois married his third wife, Annie

Green, who was the grandmother that I knew, and who knew and liked my father Alfred, and who brought me and my grandfather together. Alexander Du Bois died December 9, 1887, at the age of eighty-four, in New Bedford, and lies buried today in Oak Grove Cemetery near the Yale campus in New Haven, in a lot which he owned and which is next to that of Jehudi Ashmun of Liberian fame.

My father, by some queer chance, came into western Massachusetts and into the Housatonic Valley at the age of forty-two and there met and quickly married my brown mother who was then thirty-six and belonged to the Burghardt clan. This brings us to the history of the black Burghardts.

In 1694, Rev. Benjamin Wadsworth, afterwards president of Harvard College, made a journey through western Massachusetts, and says in regard to the present site of the town of Great Barrington, "Ye greatest part of our road this day was a hideous, howling wilderness." Here it was that a committee of the Massachusetts General Court confirmed a number of land titles in 1733–34, which had previously been in dispute between the English, Dutch, and Indians. In the "fifth division" of this land appears the name of a Dutchman, who signed himself as "Coenraet Borghghardt." This Borghghardt, Bogoert or Burghardt family has been prominent in Dutch colonial history and its descendants have been particularly identified with the annals of the little town of about five thousand inhabitants which today still lies among the hills of middle Berkshire.

Coenrod Burghardt seems to have been a shrewd pushing Dutchman and is early heard of in Kinderhook, together with his son John. This family came into possession of an African Negro named Tom, who had formerly belonged to the family of Etsons (Ettens?) and had come to the Burghardts by purchase or possibly by marriage. This African has had between one hundred and fifty and two hundred descendants, a number of whom are now living and reach to the eighth generation.

Tom was probably born about 1730. His granddaughter writes me that her father told her that Tom was born in Africa and was brought to this country when he was a boy. For many years my youthful imagination painted him as certainly the son of a tribal chief, but there is no warrant for this even in family tradition. Tom was probably just a stolen black boy from the West African Coast, nameless and lost, either a war captive or a tribal pawn. He was probably sent overseas on a Dutch ship at the time when their slave trade was beginning to decline and the vast English expansion to begin. He was in the service of the Burghardts and was a soldier in the Revolutionary War, going to the front probably several times; of only one of these is there official record when he appeared with the rank of private on the muster and payroll of Colonel John Ashley's Berkshire County regiment and Captain John Spoor's company in 1780. The company marched northward by order of Brigadier-General Fellows on an alarm when Fort Anne and Fort George were taken by the enemy. It is recorded that Tom was "reported a Negro." (Record Index of the Military Archives of Massachusetts, Vol. 23, p. 2.)

Tom appears to have been held as a servant and possibly a legal slave first by the family of Etsons or Ettens and then to have come into the possession of the Burghardts who settled at Great Barrington. Eventually, probably after the Revolutionary War, he was regarded as a freeman. There is record of only one son, Jacob Burghardt, who continued in the employ of the Burghardt family, and was born apparently about 1760. He is listed in the census of 1790 as "free" with two in his family. He married a wife named Violet who was apparently newly arrived from Africa and brought with her an African song which became traditional in the family. After her death, Jacob married Mom Bett, a rather celebrated figure in western Massachusetts history. She had been freed under the Bill of Rights of 1780 and the son of the judge who freed her wrote, "Even in her humble station, she had, when occasion required it, an air of command which conferred a degree of dignity and gave her an ascendancy over those of her rank, or color. Her determined and resolute character, which enabled her to limit the ravages of Shays's mob, was manifested in her conduct and deportment during her whole life. She claimed no distinction, but it was yielded to her from her superior experience, energy, skill and sagacity. Having known this woman as familiarly as I knew either of my parents, I cannot believe in the moral or physical inferiority of the race to which she belonged. The degradation of the African must have been otherwise caused than by natural inferiority."

Family tradition has it that her husband, Jacob, took part in suppressing this Shays's Rebellion. Jacob Burghardt had nine children, five sons of whom one was my grandfather, and four daughters. My grandfather's brothers and sisters had many children: Harlow had ten and Ira also ten; Maria had two. Descendants of Harlow and Ira still survive. Three of these sons, Othello, Ira, Harlow, and one daughter Lucinda settled on South Egremont plain near Great Barrington, where they owned small adjoining farms. A small part of one of these farms I continue to own.

Othello was my grandfather. He was born November 18, 1791, and married Sarah Lampman in 1811. Sarah was born in Hillsdale, New York, in 1793, of a mother named Lampman. There is no record of her father. She was probably the child of a Dutchman perhaps with Indian blood. This couple had ten children, three sons and seven daughters. Othello died in 1872 at the age of eighty-one and Sarah or Sally in 1877 at the age of eighty-six. Their sons and daughters married and drifted to town as laborers and servants. I thus had innumerable cousins up and down the valley. I was brought up with the Burghardt clan and this fact determined largely my life and "race." The white relationship and connections were quite lost and indeed unknown until long years after. The black Burghardts were ordinary farmers, laborers and servants. The children usually learned to read and write. I never heard or knew of any of them of my mother's generation or later who were illiterate. I was, however, the first one of the family who finished in the local high school. Afterward, one or two others did. Most of the members of the family left Great Barrington. Parts of the family are living and are fairly prosperous in the Middle West and on the Pacific Coast. I have heard of one or two high school graduates in the Middle West branch of the family.

This, then, was my racial history and as such it was curiously complicated. With Africa I had only one direct cultural connection and that was the African melody which my great-grandmother Violet used to sing. Where she learned it, I do not know. Perhaps she herself was born in Africa or had it of

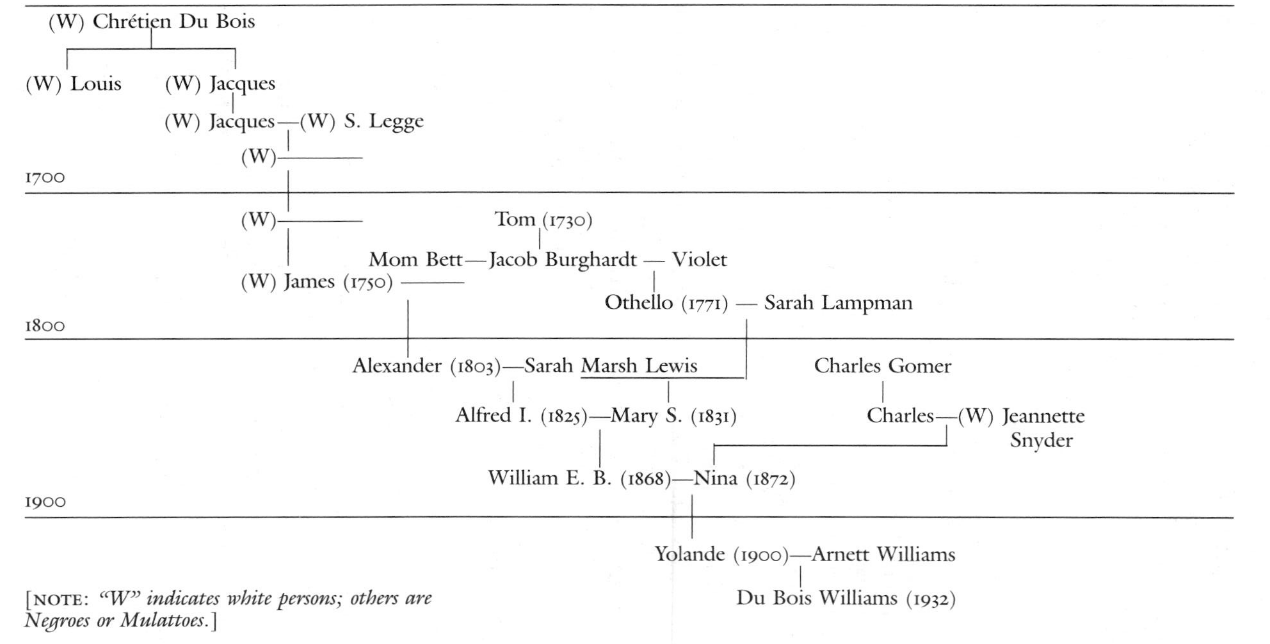

[NOTE: *"W" indicates white persons; others are Negroes or Mulattoes.*]

a mother or father stolen and transported. But at any rate, as I wrote years ago in the "Souls of Black Folk," "coming to the valleys of the Hudson and Housatonic, black, little, and lithe, she shivered and shrank in the harsh north winds, looked longingly at the hills, and often crooned a heathen melody to the child between her knees, thus:

> Do bana coba, gene me, gene me!
> Do bana coba, gene me, gene me!
> Ben d' nuli, nuli, nuli, nuli, ben d' le.

The child sang it to his children and they to their children's children, and so two hundred years it has traveled down to us and we sing it to our children, knowing as little as our fathers what its words may mean, but knowing well the meaning of its music."

Living with my mother's people I absorbed their culture patterns and these were not African so much as Dutch and New England. The speech was an idiomatic New England tongue with no African dialect; the family customs were New England, and the sex mores. My African racial feeling was then purely a matter of my own later learning and reaction; my recoil from the assumptions of the whites; my experience in the South at Fisk. But it was none the less real and a large determinant of my life and character. I felt myself African by "race" and by that token was African and an integral member of the group of dark Americans who were called Negroes.

At the same time I was firm in asserting that these Negroes were Americans. For that reason and on the basis of my great-great-grandfather's Revolutionary record I was accepted as a member of the Massachusetts Society of the Sons of the American Revolution, in 1908. When, however, the notice of this election reached the headquarters in Washington and was emphasized by my requesting a national certificate, the secretary, A. Howard Clark of the Smithsonian Institution, wrote to Massachusetts and demanded "proof of marriage of the ancestor of Tom Burghardt and record of birth of the son." He knew, of course, that the birth record of a stolen African slave could not possibly be produced. My membership was, therefore, suspended.

Countee Cullen sings:

> What is Africa to me:
> Copper sun or scarlet sea,
> Jungle star or jungle track,
> Strong bronzed men, or regal black
> Women from whose loins I sprang
> When the birds of Eden sang?
> *One three centuries removed*
> *From the scenes his fathers loved,*
> *Spicy grove, cinnamon tree,*
> *What is Africa to me?*

What is Africa to me? Once I should have answered the question simply: I should have said "fatherland" or perhaps better "motherland" because I was born in the century when the walls of race were clear and straight; when the world consisted of mutually exclusive races; and even though the edges might be blurred, there was no question of exact definition and understanding of the meaning of the word. One of the first pamphlets that I wrote in 1897 was on "The Conservation of Races" wherein I set down as the first article of a proposed racial creed: "We believe that the Negro people as a race have a contribution to make to civilization and humanity which no other race can make."

Since then the concept of race has so changed and presented so much of contradiction that as I face Africa I ask myself: what is it between us that constitutes a tie which I can feel better than I can explain? Africa is, of course, my fatherland. Yet neither my father nor my father's father ever saw Africa or knew its meaning or cared overmuch for it. My mother's folk were closer and yet their direct connection, in culture and race, became tenuous; still, my tie to Africa is strong. On this vast continent were born and lived a large portion of my direct ancestors going back a thousand years or more. The mark of their heritage is upon me in color and hair. These are obvious things, but of little meaning in themselves; only important as they stand for real and more subtle differences from other men. Whether they do or not, I do not know nor does science know today.

But one thing is sure and that is the fact that since the fifteenth century these ancestors of mine and their other descendants have had a common history; have suffered a common disaster and have one long memory. The actual ties of heritage between the individuals of this group, vary with the ancestors that they have in common and many others: Europeans and Semites, perhaps Mongolians, certainly American Indians. But the physical bond is least and the badge of color relatively unimportant save as a badge; the real essence of this kinship is its social heritage of slavery; the discrimination and insult; and this heritage binds together not simply the children of Africa, but extends through yellow Asia and into the South Seas. It is this unity that draws me to Africa.

When shall I forget the night I first set foot on African soil? I am the sixth generation in descent from forefathers who left this land. The moon was at the full and the waters of the Atlantic lay like a lake. All the long slow afternoon as the sun robed herself in her western scarlet with veils of misty cloud, I had seen Africa afar. Cape Mount—that mighty headland with its twin curves, northern sentinel of the realm of Liberia—gathered itself out of the cloud at half past three and then darkened and grew clear. On beyond flowed the dark low undulating land quaint with palm and breaking sea. The world grew black. Africa faded away, the stars stood forth curiously twisted—Orion in the zenith—the Little Bear asleep and the Southern Cross rising behind the horizon. Then afar, ahead, a lone light shone, straight at the ship's fore. Twinkling lights appeared below, around, and rising shadows. "Monrovia," said the Captain.

Suddenly we swerved to our left. The long arms of the bay enveloped us and then to the right rose the twinkling hill of Monrovia, with its crowning star. Lights flashed on the shore—here, there. Then we sensed a darker shading in the shadows: it lay very still. "It's a boat," one said. "It's two boats!" Then the shadow drifted in pieces and as the anchor roared into the deep, five boats outlined themselves on the waters—great ten-oared barges with men swung into line and glided toward us.

It was nine at night—above, the shadows, there the town, here the sweeping boats. One forged ahead with the flag—

stripes and a lone star flaming behind, the ensign of the customs floating wide; and bending to the long oars, the white caps of ten black sailors. Up the stairway clambered a soldier in khaki, aide-de-camp of the President of the Republic, a customhouse official, the clerk of the American legation—and after them sixty-five lithe, lean black stevedores with whom the steamer would work down to Portuguese Angola and back. A few moments of formalities, greetings and good-bys and I was in the great long boat with the President's aide—a brown major in brown khaki. On the other side, the young clerk and at the back, the black barelegged pilot. Before us on the high thwarts were the rowers: men, boys, black, thin, trained in muscle and sinew, little larger than the oars in thickness, they bent their strength to them and swung upon them.

One in the center gave curious little cackling cries to keep up the rhythm, and for the spurts and the stroke, a call a bit thicker and sturdier; he gave a low guttural command now and then; the boat, alive, quivering, danced beneath the moon, swept a great curve to the bar to breast its narrow teeth of foam—"t'chick-a-tickity, t'chick-a-tickity," sang the boys, and we glided and raced, now between boats, now near the landing—now cast aloft at the dock. And lo! I was in Africa.

Christmas Eve, and Africa is singing in Monrovia. They are Krus and Fanti—men, women and children, and all the night they march and sing. The music was once the music of mission revival hymns. But it is that music now transformed and the silly words hidden in an unknown tongue—liquid and sonorous. It is tricked out and expounded with cadence and turn. And this is that same rhythm I heard first in Tennessee forty years ago: the air is raised and carried by men's strong voices, while floating above in obbligato, come the high mellow voices of women—it is the ancient African art of part singing, so curiously and insistently different.

So they come, gay appareled, lit by transparency. They enter the gate and flow over the high steps and sing and sing and sing. They saunter round the house, pick flowers, drink water and sing and sing and sing. The warm dark heat of the night steams up to meet the moon. And the night is song.

On Christmas Day, 1923, we walk down to the narrow, crooked wharves of Monrovia, by houses old and gray and step-like streets of stone. Before is the wide St. Paul River, double-mouthed, and beyond, the sea, white, curling on the sand. Before us is the isle—the tiny isle, hut-covered and guarded by a cotton tree, where the pioneers lived in 1821. We board the boat, then circle round—then up the river. Great bowing trees, festoons of flowers, golden blossoms, star-faced palms and thatched huts; tall spreading trees lifting themselves like vast umbrellas, low shrubbery with gray and laced and knotted roots—the broad, black, murmuring river. Here a tree holds wide fingers out and stretches them over the water in vast incantation; bananas throw their wide green fingers to the sun. Iron villages, scarred clearings with gray, sheet-iron homes staring, grim and bare, at the ancient tropical flood of green.

The river sweeps wide and the shrubs bow low. Behind, Monrovia rises in clear, calm beauty. Gone are the wharves, the low and clustered houses of the port, the tight-throated business village, and up sweep the villas and the low wall, brown and cream and white, with great mango and cotton trees, with lighthouse and spire, with porch and pillar and the color of shrubbery and blossom.

We climbed the upright shore to a senator's home and received his wide and kindly hospitality—curious blend of feudal lord and modern farmer—sandwiches, cake, and champagne. Again we glided up the drowsy river—five, ten, twenty miles and came to our hostess, a mansion of five generations with a compound of endless native servants and cows under the palm thatches. The daughters of the family wore, on the beautiful black skin of their necks, the exquisite pale gold chains of the Liberian artisan and the slim, black little granddaughter of the house had a wide pink ribbon on the thick curls of her dark hair, that lay like sudden sunlight on the shadows. Double porches, one above the other, welcomed us to ease. A native man, gay with Christmas and a dash of gin, sang and danced in the road. Children ran and played in the blazing sun. We sat at a long broad table and ate duck, chicken, beef, rice, plantain, collards, cake, tea, water and Madeira wine. Then we went and looked at the heavens, the uptwisted sky—Orion and Cassiopeia at zenith; the Little Bear beneath the horizon, now unfamiliar sights in the Milky

Way—all awry, a-living—sun for snow at Christmas, and happiness and cheer.

The shores were lined with old sugar plantations, the buildings rotting and falling. I looked upon the desolation with a certain pain. What had happened, I asked? The owners and planters had deserted these homes and come down to Monrovia, but why? After all, Monrovia had not much to offer in the way of income and occupation. Was this African laziness and inefficiency? No, it was a specimen of the way in which the waves of modern industry broke over the shores of far-off Africa. Here during our Civil War, men hastened to raise sugar and supply New York. They built their own boats and filled the river and sailed the sea. But afterwards, Louisiana came back into the Union, colored Rillieux invented the vacuum pan; the sugar plantations began to spread in Cuba and the Sugar Trust monopoly of refining machinery, together with the new beet sugar industry, drove Liberia quickly from the market. What all this did not do, the freight rates finished. So sugar did not pay in Liberia and other crops rose and fell in the same way.

As I look back and recall the days, which I have called great—the occasions in which I have taken part and which have had for me and others the widest significance, I can remember none like the first of January, 1924. Once I took my bachelor's degree before a governor, a great college president, and a bishop of New England. But that was rather personal in its memory than in any way epochal. Once before the assembled races of the world I was called to speak in London in place of the suddenly sick Sir Harry Johnston. It was a great hour. But it was not greater than the day when I was presented to the President of the Negro Republic of Liberia.

Liberia had been resting under the shock of world war into which the Allies forced her. She had asked and been promised a loan by the United States to bolster and replace her stricken trade. She had conformed to every preliminary requirement and waited when waiting was almost fatal. It was not simply money, it was world prestige and protection at a time when the little republic was sorely beset by creditors and greedy imperial powers. At the last moment, an insurgent Senate peremptorily and finally refused the request and strong recommendation of President Wilson and his advisers, and the loan was refused. The Department of State made no statement to the world, and Liberia stood naked, not only well-nigh bankrupt, but peculiarly defenseless amid scowling and unbelieving powers.

It was then that the United States made a gesture of courtesy; a little thing, and merely a gesture, but one so unusual that it was epochal. President Coolidge, at the suggestion of William H. Lewis, a leading colored lawyer of Boston, named me, an American Negro traveler, Envoy Extraordinary and Minister Plenipotentiary to Liberia—the highest rank ever given by any country to a diplomatic agent in black Africa. And it named this Envoy the special representative of the President of the United States to the President of Liberia, on the occasion of his inauguration; charging the Envoy with a personal word of encouragement and moral support. It was a significant action. It had in it nothing personal. Another appointee would have been equally significant. But Liberia recognized the meaning. She showered upon the Envoy every mark of appreciation and thanks. The Commander of the Liberian Frontier Force was made his special aide, and a sergeant, his orderly. At ten a.m. New Year's morning, 1924, a company of the Frontier Force, in red fez and khaki, presented arms before the American Legation and escorted Solomon Porter Hood, the American Minister Resident, and myself as Envoy Extraordinary and my aide to the Presidential Mansion—a beautiful white, verandaed house, waving with palms and fronting a grassy street.

Ceremonials are old and to some antiquated and yet this was done with such simplicity, grace and seriousness that none could escape its spell. The Secretary of State met us at the door, as the band played the impressive Liberian National hymn, and soldiers saluted:

All hail! Liberia, hail!
In union strong, success is sure.
We cannot fail.
With God above,
Our rights to prove,
We will the world assail.

We mounted a broad stairway and into a great room that stretched across the house. Here in semi-circle were ranged the foreign consuls and the cabinet—the former in white, gilt with orders and swords; the latter in solemn black. Present were England, France, Germany, Spain, Belgium, Holland, and Panama, to be presented to me in order of seniority by the small brown Secretary of State with his perfect poise and ease. The President entered—frock-coated with the star and ribbon of a Spanish order on his breast. The American Minister introduced me, and I said:

"The President of the United States has done me the great honor of designating me as his personal representative on the occasion of your inauguration. In so doing, he has had, I am sure, two things in mind. First, he wished publicly and unmistakably to express before the world the interest and solicitude which the hundred million inhabitants of the United States of America have for Liberia. Liberia is a child of the United States, and a sister Republic. Its progress and success is the progress and success of democracy everywhere and for all men; and the United States would view with sorrow and alarm any misfortune which might happen to this Republic and any obstacle that was placed in her path.

"But special and peculiar bonds draw these two lands together. In America live eleven million persons of African descent; they are citizens, legally invested with every right that inheres in American citizenship. And I am sure that in this special mark of the President's favor, he has had in mind the wishes and hopes of Negro Americans. He knows how proud they are of the hundred years of independence which you have maintained by force of arms and by brawn and brain upon the edge of this mighty continent; he knows that in the great battle against color caste in America, the ability of Negroes to rule in Africa has been and ever will be a great and encouraging reenforcement. He knows that the unswerving loyalty of Negro Americans to their country is fitly accompanied by a pride in their race and lineage, a belief in the potency and promise of Negro blood which makes them eager listeners to every whisper of success from Liberia, and eager helpers in every movement for your aid and comfort. In a special sense, the moral burden of Liberia and the advancement and integrity of Liberia is the sincere prayer of America."

And now a word about the African himself—about this primitive black man: I began to notice a truth as I entered southern France. I formulated it in Portugal. I knew it as a great truth one Sunday in Liberia. And the Great Truth was this: efficiency and happiness do not go together in modern culture. Going south from London, as the world darkens it gets happier. Portugal is deliciously dark. Many leading citizens would have difficulty keeping off a Georgia "Jim Crow" car. But, oh, how lovely a land and how happy a people! And so leisurely. Little use of trying to shop seriously in Lisbon before eleven. It isn't done. Nor at noon; the world is lunching or lolling in the sun. Even after four p.m. one takes chances, for the world is in the Rocio. And the banks are so careless and the hotels so leisurely. How delightfully angry Englishmen get at the "damned, lazy" Portuguese!

But if this of Portugal, what of Africa? Here darkness descends and rests on lovely skins until brown seems luscious and natural. There is sunlight in great gold globules and soft, heavy-scented heat that wraps you like a garment. And laziness; divine, eternal, languor is right and good and true. I remember the morning; it was Sunday, and the night before we heard the leopards crying down there. Today beneath the streaming sun we went down into the gold-green forest. It was silence—silence the more mysterious because life abundant and palpitating pulsed all about us and held us drowsy captives to the day. Ahead the gaunt missionary strode, alert, afire, with his gun. He apologized for the gun, but he did not need to, for I saw the print of a leopard's hind foot. A monkey sentinel screamed, and I heard the whir of the horde as they ran.

Then we came to the village; how can I describe it? Neither London, nor Paris, nor New York has anything of its delicate, precious beauty. It was a town of the Veys and done in cream and pale purple—still, clean, restrained, tiny, complete. It was no selfish place, but the central abode of fire and hospitality, clean-swept for wayfarers, and best seats were bare. They quite expected visitors, morning, noon, and night; and they gave our hands a quick, soft grasp and talked easily.

Their manners were better than those of Park Lane or Park Avenue. Oh, much better and more natural. They showed breeding. The chief's son—tall and slight and speaking good English—had served under the late Colonel Young. He made a little speech of welcome. Long is the history of the Veys and comes down from the Eastern Roman Empire, the great struggle of Islam and the black empires of the Sudan.

We went on to other villages—dun-colored, not so beautiful, but neat and hospitable. In one sat a visiting chief of perhaps fifty years in a derby hat and a robe, and beside him stood a shy young wife done in ebony and soft brown, whose liquid eyes would not meet ours. The chief was taciturn until we spoke of schools. Then he woke suddenly—he had children to "give" to a school. I see the last village fading away; they are plastering the wall of a home, leisurely and carefully. They smiled a good-by—not effusively, with no eagerness, with a simple friendship, as we glided under the cocoa trees and into the silent forest, the gold and silent forest.

And there and elsewhere in two long months I began to learn: primitive men are not following us afar, frantically waving and seeking our goals; primitive men are not behind us in some swift foot-race. Primitive men have already arrived. They are abreast, and in places ahead of us; in others behind. But all their curving advance line is contemporary, not prehistoric. They have used other paths and these paths have led them by scenes sometimes fairer, sometimes uglier than ours, but always toward the Pools of Happiness. Or, to put it otherwise, these folk have the leisure of true aristocracy—leisure for thought and courtesy, leisure for sleep and laughter. They have time for their children—such well-trained, beautiful children with perfect, unhidden bodies. Have you ever met a crowd of children in the east of London or New York, or even on the Avenue at Forty-second or One Hundred and Forty-second Street, and fled to avoid their impudence and utter ignorance of courtesy? Come to Africa, and see well-bred and courteous children, playing happily and never sniffling and whining.

I have read everywhere that Africa means sexual license. Perhaps it does. Most folk who talk sex frantically have all too seldom revealed their source material. I was in West Africa only two months, but with both eyes wide. I saw children quite naked and women usually naked to the waist—with bare bosom and limbs. And in those sixty days I saw less of sex dalliance and appeal than I see daily on Fifth Avenue. This does not mean much, but it is an interesting fact.

The primitive black man is courteous and dignified. If the platforms of Western cities had swarmed with humanity as I have seen the platforms swarm in Senegal, the police would have a busy time. I did not see one respectable quarrel. Wherefore shall we all take to the Big Bush? No. I prefer New York. But my point is that New York and London and Paris must learn of West Africa and may learn.

The one great lack in Africa is communication—communication as represented by human contact, movement of goods, dissemination of knowledge. All these things we have—we have in such crushing abundance that they have mastered us and defeated their real good. We meet human beings in such throngs that we cannot know or even understand them—they become to us inhuman, mechanical, hateful. We are choked and suffocated, tempted and killed by goods accumulated from the ends of the earth; our newspapers and magazines so overwhelm us with knowledge—knowledge of all sorts and kinds from particulars as to our neighbors' underwear to Einstein's mathematics—that one of the great and glorious joys of the African bush is to escape from "news."

On the other hand, African life with its isolation has deeper knowledge of human souls. The village life, the forest ways, the teeming markets, bring in intimate human knowledge that the West misses, sinking the individual in the social. Africans know fewer folk, but know them infinitely better. Their intertwined communal souls, therefore, brook no poverty nor prostitution—these things are to them un-understandable. On the other hand, they are vastly ignorant of what the world is doing and thinking, and of what is known of its physical forces. They suffer terribly from preventable disease, from unnecessary hunger, from the freaks of the weather.

Here, then, is something for Africa and Europe both to learn; and Africa is eager, breathless, to learn—while Europe? Europe laughs with loud guffaws. Learn of Africa? Nonsense.

Poverty cannot be abolished. Democracy and firm government are incompatible. Prostitution is world old and inevitable. And Europe proceeds to use Africa as a means and not as an end; as a hired tool and welter of raw materials and not as a land of human beings.

I think it was in Africa that I came more clearly to see the close connection between race and wealth. The fact that even in the minds of the most dogmatic supporters of race theories and believers in the inferiority of colored folk to white, there was a conscious or unconscious determination to increase their incomes by taking full advantage of this belief. And then gradually this thought was metamorphosed into a realization that the income-bearing value of race prejudice was the cause and not the result of theories of race inferiority; that particularly in the United States the income of the Cotton Kingdom based on black slavery caused the passionate belief in Negro inferiority and the determination to enforce it even by arms.

I have wandered afield from miscegenation in the West Indies to race blending and segregation in America and to a glimpse of present Africa. Now to return to the American concept of race. It was in my boyhood, as I have intimated, an adventure. In my youth, it became the vision of a glorious crusade where I and my fellows were to match our mettle against white folk and show them what black folk could do. But as I grew older the matter became more serious and less capable of jaunty settlement. I not only met plenty of persons equal in ability to myself but often with greater ability and nearly always with greater opportunity. Racial identity presented itself as a matter of trammels and impediments as "tightening bonds about my feet." As I looked out into my racial world the whole thing verged on tragedy. My "way was cloudy" and the approach to its high goals by no means straight and clear. I saw the race problem was not as I conceived, a matter of clear, fair competition, for which I was ready and eager. It was rather a matter of segregation, of hindrance and inhibitions, and my struggles against this and resentment at it began to have serious repercussions upon my inner life.

It is difficult to let others see the full psychological meaning of caste segregation. It is as though one, looking out from a dark cave in a side of an impending mountain, sees the world passing and speaks to it; speaks courteously and persuasively, showing them how these entombed souls are hindered in their natural movement, expression, and development; and how their loosening from prison would be a matter not simply of courtesy, sympathy, and help to them, but aid to all the world. One talks on evenly and logically in this way, but notices that the passing throng does not even turn its head, or if it does, glances curiously and walks on. It gradually penetrates the minds of the prisoners that the people passing do not hear; that some thick sheet of invisible but horribly tangible plate glass is between them and the world. They get excited; they talk louder; they gesticulate. Some of the passing world stop in curiosity; these gesticulations seem so pointless; they laugh and pass on. They still either do not hear at all, or hear but dimly, and even what they hear, they do not understand. Then the people within may become hysterical. They may scream and hurl themselves against the barriers, hardly realizing in their bewilderment that they are screaming in a vacuum unheard and that their antics may actually seem funny to those outside looking in. They may even, here and there, break through in blood and disfigurement, and find themselves faced by a horrified, implacable, and quite overwhelming mob of people frightened for their own very existence.

It is hard under such circumstances to be philosophical and calm, and to think through a method of approach and accommodation between castes. The entombed find themselves not simply trying to make the outer world understand their essential and common humanity but even more, as they become inured to their experience, they have to keep reminding themselves that the great and oppressing world outside is also real and human and in its essence honest. All my life I have had continually to haul my soul back and say, "All white folk are not scoundrels nor murderers. They are, even as I am, painfully human."

One development continually recurs: any person outside of this wall of glass can speak to his own fellows, can assume a facile championship of the entombed, and gain the enthusiastic and even gushing thanks of the victims. But this method is subject to two difficulties: first of all, not being possibly among the entombed or capable of sharing their inner thought and experience, this outside leadership will continually misinterpret and compromise and complicate matters, even with the best of will. And secondly, of course, no matter how successful the outside advocacy is, it remains impotent and unsuccessful until it actually succeeds in freeing and making articulate the submerged caste.

Practically, this group imprisonment within a group has various effects upon the prisoner. He becomes provincial and centered upon the problems of his particular group. He tends to neglect the wider aspects of national life and human existence. On the one hand he is unselfish so far as his inner group is concerned. He thinks of himself not as an individual but as a group man, a "race" man. His loyalty to this group idea tends to be almost unending and balks at almost no sacrifice. On the other hand, his attitude toward the environing race congeals into a matter of unreasoning resentment and even hatred, deep disbelief in them and refusal to conceive honesty and rational thought on their part. This attitude adds to the difficulties of conversation, intercourse, understanding between groups.

This was the race concept which has dominated my life, and the history of which I have attempted to make the leading theme of this book. It had as I have tried to show all sorts of illogical trends and irreconcilable tendencies. Perhaps it is wrong to speak of it at all as "a concept" rather than as a group of contradictory forces, facts and tendencies. At any rate I hope I have made its meaning to me clear. It was for me as I have written first a matter of dawning realization, then of study and science; then a matter of inquiry into the diverse strands of my own family; and finally consideration of my connection, physical and spiritual, with Africa and the Negro race in its homeland. All this led to an attempt to rationalize the racial concept and its place in the modern world.

Chapter 6

THE WHITE WORLD

THE MAJORITY of men resent and always have resented the idea of equality with most of their fellow men. This has had physical, economic, and cultural reasons: the physical fear of attack; the economic strife to avert starvation and secure protection and shelter; but more especially I presume the cultural and spiritual desire to be one's self without interference from others; to enjoy that anarchy of the spirit which is inevitably the goal of all consciousness. It is only in highly civilized times and places that the conception arises of an individual freedom and development, and even that was conceived of as the right of a privileged minority, and was based on the degradation, the exclusion, the slavery of most others. The history of tribes and clans, of social classes and all nations, and of race antipathies in our own world, is an exemplification of this fight against equality and inability even to picture its possibility.

The result is that men are conditioned and their actions forced not simply by their physical environment, powerful as mountains and rain, heat and cold, forest and desert always have been and will be. When we modify the effects of this environment by what we call the social environment, we have conceived a great and important truth. But even this needs further revision. A man lives today not only in his physical environment and in the social environment of ideas and customs, laws and ideals; but that total environment is subjected to a new socio-physical environment of other groups, whose social environment he shares but in part.

A man in the European sixteenth century was born not simply in the valley of the Thames or Seine, but in a certain social class and the environment of that class made and limited his world. He was then, consciously or not, not fully a man; he was an artisan and until he complied with the limitations of that class he was continually knocking his hands, head and heart against an environment, composed of other classes, which limited what he could and could not do and what he must do; and this greater group environment was not a matter of mere ideas and thought; it was embodied in muscles and armed men, in scowling faces, in the majesty of judge and police and in human law which became divine.

Much as I knew of this class structure of the world, I should never have realized it vividly and fully if I had not been born into its modern counterpart, racial segregation; first into a world composed of people with colored skins who remembered slavery and endured discrimination; and who had to a degree their own habits, customs, and ideals; but in addition to this I lived in an environment which I came to call the white world. I was not an American; I was not a man; I was by long education and continual compulsion and daily reminder, a colored man in a white world; and that white world often existed primarily, so far as I was concerned, to see with sleepless vigilance that I was kept within bounds. All this made me limited in physical movement and provincial in thought and dream. I could not stir, I could not act, I could not live, without taking into careful daily account the reaction of my white environing world. How I traveled and where, what work I did, what income I received, where I ate, where I slept, with whom I talked, where I sought recreation, where I studied, what I wrote and what I could get published—all this depended and depended primarily upon an overwhelming mass of my fellow citizens in the United States, from whose society I was largely excluded.

Of course, there was no real wall between us. I knew from the days of my childhood and in the elementary school, on through my walks in the Harvard yard and my lectures in Germany, that in all things in general, white people were just the same as I: their physical possibilities, their mental processes were no different from mine; even the difference in skin color was vastly overemphasized and intrinsically trivial. And yet this fact of racial distinction based on color was the greatest thing in my life and absolutely determined it, because this surrounding group, in alliance and agreement with the white European world, was settled and determined upon the fact that I was and must be a thing apart.

It was impossible to gainsay this. It was impossible for any time and to any distance to withdraw myself and look down upon these absurd assumptions with philosophical calm and humorous self-control. If, as happened to a friend of mine, a lady in a pullman car ordered me to bring her a glass of water, mistaking me for a porter, the incident in its essence was a joke to be chuckled over; but in its hard, cruel significance and its unending inescapable sign of slavery, it was something to drive a man mad.

For long years it seemed to me that this imprisonment of a human group with chains in hands of an environing group, was a singularly unusual characteristic of the Negro in the United States in the nineteenth century. But since then it has been easy for me to realize that the majority of mankind has struggled through this inner spiritual slavery and that while a dream which we have easily and jauntily called democracy envisages a day when the environing group looses the chains and compulsion, and is willing and even eager to grant families, nations, sub-races, and races equality of opportunity among larger groups, that even this grand equality has not come; and until it does, individual equality and the free soul is impossible. All our present frustration in trying to realize individual equality through communism, fascism, and democracy arises from our continual unwillingness to break the intellectual bonds of group and racial exclusiveness.

Thus it is easy to see that scientific definition of race is impossible; it is easy to prove that physical characteristics are not so inherited as to make it possible to divide the world into races; that ability is the monopoly of no known aristocracy; that the possibilities of human development cannot be circumscribed by color, nationality, or any conceivable definition of race; all this has nothing to do with the plain fact that throughout the world today organized groups of men by monopoly of economic and physical power, legal enactment and intellectual training are limiting with determination and unflagging zeal the development of other groups; and that the concentration particularly of economic power today puts the majority of mankind into a slavery to the rest.

There has been an understandable determination in the United States among both Negro and white thinkers to minimize and deny the realities of racial difference. The race problem has been rationalized in every way. It has been called the natural result of slavery; the effect of poverty and ignorance; the situation consequent upon lack of effort and thought on the part of Americans and of other races. But all this reasoning has its logical pitfalls: granted that poverty causes color prejudice, color prejudice certainly is a cause of poverty. Ignorance leads to exploitation and mistreatment, but the black child is more often forced into ignorance and kept there than the white child. Thus it is impossible for the clear-headed student of human action in the United States and in the world, to avoid facing the fact of a white world which is today dominating human culture and working for the continued subordination of the colored races.

It may be objected here that so general a statement is not fair; that there are many white folk who feel the unfairness and crime of color and race prejudice and have toiled and sacrificed to counteract it. This brings up the whole question of social guilt. When, for instance, one says that the action of England toward the darker races has been a course of hypocrisy, force and greed covering four hundred years it does not mean to include in that guilt many persons of the type of William Wilberforce and Granville Sharpe. On the other hand because British history has not involved the guilt of all Britons we cannot jump to the opposite and equally fallacious conclusion that there has been no guilt; that the development of the British Empire is a sort of cosmic process with no individual human being at fault. In the history of England, France, America, Germany and Italy, we have villains who have selfishly and criminally desired and accomplished what made for the suffering and degradation of mankind. We have had others who desired the uplift and worked for the uplift of all men. And we have had a middle class of people who sometimes ignorantly and sometimes consciously shifted the balance now here, and now there; and when, in the end, this balance of public opinion, this effective social action, has made for the degradation of mankind or in so far as it has done this, that part of England which has allowed this or made it possible is blood-guilty of the result. So in America, not the philosophy of Jefferson nor the crusade of Garrison nor the reason of Sumner was able to counterbalance the race superiority doctrines of Calhoun, the imperialism of Jefferson

Davis, nor the race hate of Ben Tillman. As a result white America has crucified, enslaved, and oppressed the Negro group and holds them still, especially in the South, in a legalized position of inferior caste.

With the best will the factual outline of a life misses the essence of its spirit. Thus in my life the chief fact has been race—not so much scientific race, as that deep conviction of myriads of men that congenital differences among the main masses of human beings absolutely condition the individual destiny of every member of a group. Into the spiritual provincialism of this belief I have been born and this fact has guided, embittered, illuminated and enshrouded my life. Yet, how shall I explain and clarify its meaning for a soul? Description fails—I have tried that. Yet, lest I omit the most important thing in the life of an American Negro today and the only thing that adequately explains his success, failures and foibles, let me attempt its exposition by personifying my white and colored environment.

When, for example, the obsession of his race consciousness leaves him, my white friend, Roger Van Dieman (who, I hasten to add, is an abstraction and integration and never existed), is quite companionable; otherwise he is impossible. He has a way of putting an excessive amount of pity in his look and of stating as a general and incontrovertible fact that it is "horrible" to be an Exception. By this he means me. He is more than certain that I prove the rule. He is not a bright person, but of that famous average, standardized and astonished at anything that even seems original. His thesis is simple: the world is composed of Race superimposed on Race; classes superimposed on classes; beneath the whole thing is "Our Family" in capitals, and under that is God. God seems to be a cousin, or at least a blood relative, of the Van Diemans.

"Of course," he says, "you know Negroes are inferior."

I admit nothing of the sort, I maintain. In fact, having known with some considerable intimacy both male and female, the people of the British Isles, of Scandinavia, of Russia, of Germany, north and south, of the three ends of France and the two ends of Italy; specimens from the Balkans and black and white Spain; the three great races of Asia and the melange of Africa, without mentioning America, I sit here and maintain that black folk are much superior to white.

"You are either joking or mad," he says.

Both and neither. This race talk is, of course, a joke, and frequently it has driven me insane and probably will permanently in the future; and yet, seriously and soberly, we black folk are the salvation of mankind.

He regards me with puzzled astonishment and says confidentially:

"Do you know that sometimes I am half afraid that you really believe this? At other times I see clearly the inferiority complex."

The former after lunch, I reply, and the latter before.

"Very well," he says, "let's lunch."

Where? I ask quizzically, we being at the time in the Roaring Forties.

"Why—oh, well—their refusal to serve you lunch at least does not prove your superiority."

Nor yet theirs, I answer; but never mind, come with me to Second Avenue, where Labor lives and food is bad.

We start again with the salad.

"Now, superiority consists of what?" he argues.

Life is, I remark, (1) Beauty and health of body. (2) Mental clearness and creative genius. (3) Spiritual goodness and receptivity. (4) Social adaptability and constructiveness.

"Not bad," he answers. "Not bad at all. Now I contend that the white race conspicuously excels in beauty, genius, and construction, and is well abreast even in goodness."

And I maintain that the black race excels in beauty, goodness, and adaptability, and is well abreast in genius.

"Sheer nonsense and pure balderdash. Compare the Venus of Milo and the Apollo Belvedere with a Harlem or Beale Street couple."

I retort: in short, compare humanity at its worst with the Ideal, and humanity suffers. But black folk in most attributes of physical beauty, in line and height and curve, have the same norms as whites and differ only in small details of color, hair and curve of countenance. Now can there be any question but that as colors, bronze, mahogany, coffee and gold are far lovelier than pink, gray, and marble? Hair is a matter of taste. Some will have it drab and stringy and others in a gray, woven, unmoving mass. Most of us like it somewhere between, in tiny tendrils, smoking curls and sweeping curves. I have loved all these varieties in my day. I prefer the crinkly kind, almost wavy, in black, brown, and glistening gold. In faces, I hate straight features; needles and razors may be sharp—but beautiful, never.

"All that is personal opinion. I prefer the colors of heaven and day: sunlight hair and sky-blue eyes; straight noses and thin lips, and that incomparable air of haughty aloofness and aristocracy."

And I, on the contrary, am the child of twilight and night, and choose intricately curly hair, black eyes, full and luscious features; and that air of humility and wonder which streams from moonlight. Add to this voices that caress instead of rasp, glances that appeal rather than repel, and a sinuous litheness of movement to replace Anglo-Saxon stalking—there you have my ideal. Of course, you can bury any human body in dirt and misery and make it horrible. I have seen the East End of London.

"Beauty seems to be simply opinion, if you put it that way."

To be sure. But whose opinion?

"Bother beauty. Here we shall never agree. But, after all, I doubt if it makes much difference. The real point is Brains: clear thinking, pure reason, mathematical precision and creative genius. Now, without blague, stand and acknowledge that here the white race is supreme."

Quite the contrary. I know no attribute in which the white race has more conspicuously failed. This is white and European civilization; and as a system of culture it is idiotic, addlebrained, unreasoning, topsy-turvy, without precision; and its genius chiefly runs to marvelous contrivances for enslaving the many, and enriching the few, and murdering both. I see absolutely no proof that the average ability of the white man's brain to think clearly is any greater than that of the yellow man or of the black man. If we take even that doubtful but widely heralded test, the frequency of individual creative genius (when a real racial test should be the frequency of ordinary common sense)—if we take the Genius as the savior of mankind, it is only possible for the white race to prove its own incontestable superiority by appointing both judge and jury and summoning its own witnesses.

I freely admit that, according to white writers, white teachers, white historians, and white molders of public opinion, nothing ever happened in the world of any importance that could not or should not be labeled "white." How silly. I place black iron-welding and village democracy, and yellow printing and state building, side by side with white representative government and the steam engine, and unhesitatingly give the palm to the first. I hand the first vast conception of the solar system to the Africanized Egyptians, the creation of Art to the Chinese, the highest conception of Religion to the Asiatic Semites, and then let Europe rave over the Factory system.

"But is not well-being more widely diffused among white folk than among yellow and black, and general intelligence more common?"

True, and why? Ask the geography of Europe, the African Slave Trade and the industrial technique of the nineteenth-century white man. Turn the thing around, and let a single tradition of culture suddenly have thrust into its hands the power to bleed the world of its brawn and wealth, and the willingness to do this, and you will have exactly what we have today, under another name and color.

"Precisely. Then, at least, the white race is more advanced and no more blameworthy than others because, as I insist, its native intelligence is greater. It is germ plasm, seed, that I am talking about. Do you believe in heredity?"

Not blindly; but I should be mildly surprised to see a dog born of a cat.

"Exactly; or a genius born of a fool."

No, no; on the contrary. I rather expect fools of geniuses and geniuses of fools. And while I stoutly maintain that cattiness and dogginess are as far apart as the East from the West, on the other hand, I just as strongly believe that the human ass and the superman have much in common and can often, if not always, spawn each other.

"Is it possible that you have never heard of the Jukes, or of the plain results of hereditary degeneration and the possibilities of careful breeding?"

It is not possible; they have been served up to me ad infinitum. But they are nothing. I know greater wonders: Lincoln from Nancy Hanks, Dumas from a black beast of burden, Kant from a saddler, and Jesus Christ from a manger.

"All of which, instead of disproving, is exact and definite proof of the persistence of good blood."

Precisely, and of the catholicity of its tastes; the method of proof is this: when anything good occurs, it is proof of good blood; when anything bad occurs, it is proof of bad blood. Very well. Now good and bad, native endowment and native deficiency, do not follow racial lines. There is good stock in all races and the outcropping of bad individuals, too; and there has been absolutely no proof that the white race has any larger share of the gifted strains of human heritage than the black race or the yellow race. To be sure, good seed proves itself in the flower and the fruit, but the failure of seed to sprout is no proof that it is not good. It may be proof simply of the absence of manure—or its excessive presence.

Granted, that when time began, there was hidden in a Seed that tiny speck that spelled the world's salvation, do you think today it would manifest itself crudely and baldly in a dash of skin color and a crinkle of hair? Is the subtle mystery of life and consciousness and of ability portrayed in any such slapdash and obvious marks of difference?

"Go out upon the street; choose ten white men and ten colored men. Which can carry on and preserve American civilization?"

The whites.

"Well, then."

You evidently consider that a compliment. Let it pass. Go out upon the street and choose ten men and ten women. Which could best run a Ford car? The men, of course; but hold. Fly out into the sky and look down upon ten children of Podunk and ten children of Chicago. Which would know most about elevated railroads, baseball, zoology, and movies?

"The point is visible, but beyond that, outside of mere experience and education, and harking back to native gift and intelligence, on your honor, which has most, white folk or black folk?"

There you have me deep in the shadows, beyond the

benign guidance of words. Just what is gift and intelligence, especially of the native sort? And when we compare the gift of one human soul with that of another, are we not seeking to measure incommensurable things; trying to lump things like sunlight and music and love? And if a certain shadowy Over-soul can really compare the incomparable with some transcendental yardstick, may we not here emerge into a super-equality of man? At least this I can quite believe.

"But it is a pious belief, not more."

Not more; but a pious belief outweighs an impious unbelief.

Admitting that the problem of native human endowment is obscure, there is no corresponding obscurity in spiritual values. Goodness and unselfishness; simplicity and honor; tolerance, susceptibility to beauty in form, color, and music; courage to look truth in the face; courage to live and suffer in patience and humility, in forgiveness and in hope; eagerness to turn, not simply the other cheek, but the face and the bowed back; capacity to love. In all these mighty things, the greatest things in the world, where do black folk and white folk stand?

Why, man of mine, you would not have the courage to live one hour as a black man in America, or as a Negro in the whole wide world. Ah, yes, I know what you whisper to such accusation. You say dryly that if we had good sense, we would not live either; and that the fact that we do submit to life as it is and yet laugh and dance and dream, is but another proof that we are idiots.

This is the truly marvelous way in which you prove your superiority by admitting that our love of life can only be intelligently explained on the hypothesis of inferiority. What finer tribute is possible to our courage?

What great works of Art have we made? Very few. The Pyramids, Luxor, the Bronzes of Benin, the Spears of the Bongo, "When Malinda Sings" and the Sorrow Song she is always singing. Oh, yes, and the love of her dancing.

But art is not simply works of art; it is the spirit that knows Beauty, that has music in its soul and the color of sunsets in its headkerchiefs; that can dance on a flaming world and make the world dance, too. Such is the soul of the Negro.

Why, do you know the two finest things in the industry of the West, finer than factory, shop or ship? One is the black laborer's Saturday off. Neither the whip of the driver, nor the starvation wage, nor the disgust of the Yankee, nor the call of the cotton crop, has yet convinced the common black variety of plantation laborer that one day in the week is enough for rest and play. He wants two days. And, from California to Texas, from Florida to Trinidad, he takes two days while the planter screams and curses. They have beaten the English slavey, the French and German peasants, and the North Italian contadini into twelve-hour, six-day slaves. They crushed the Chinese and Indian coolie into a twenty-four-hour beast of burden; they have even made the American, free, white and twenty-one, believe that daily toil is one of the Ten Commandments. But not the Negro. From Monday to Friday the field hand is a slave; then for forty-eight golden hours he is free, and through these same forty-eight hours he may yet free the dumb, driven cattle of the world.

Then the second thing, laughter. This race has the greatest of the gifts of God, laughter. It dances and sings; it is humble; it longs to learn; it loves men; it loves women. It is frankly, baldly, deliciously human in an artificial and hypocritical land. If you will hear men laugh, go to Guinea, "Black Bottom," "Niggertown," Harlem. If you want to feel humor too exquisite and subtle for translation, sit invisibly among a gang of Negro workers. The white world has its gibes and cruel caricatures; it has its loud guffaws; but to the black world alone belongs the delicious chuckle.

"But the State; the modern industrial State. Wealth of work, wealth of commerce, factory and mine, skyscrapers; New York, Chicago, Johannesburg, London and Buenos Aires!"

This is the best expression of the civilization in which the white race finds itself today. This is what the white world means by culture.

"Does it not excel the black and yellow race here?"

It does. But the excellence here raises no envy; only regrets. If this vast Frankenstein monster really served its makers; if it were their minister and not their master, god and king; if their machines gave us rest and leisure, instead of the drab uniformity of uninteresting drudgery; if their factories gave us gracious community of thought and feeling; beauty enshrined, free and joyous; if their work veiled them with tender sympathy at human distress and wide tolerance and understanding—then, all hail, White Imperial Industry! But it does not. It is a Beast! Its creators even do not understand it, cannot curb or guide it. They themselves are but hideous, groping higher Hands, doing their bit to oil the raging devastating machinery which kills men to make cloth, prostitutes women to rear buildings and eats little children.

Is this superiority? It is madness. We are the supermen who sit idly by and laugh and look at civilization. We, who frankly want the bodies of our mates and conjure no blush to our bronze cheeks when we own it. We, who exalt the Lynched above the Lyncher, and the Worker above the Owner, and the Crucified above Imperial Rome.

"But why have you black and yellow men done nothing better or even as good in the history of the world?"

We have, often.

"I never heard of it."

Lions have no historians.

"It is idiotic even to discuss it. Look around and see the pageantry of the world. It belongs to white men; it is the expression of white power; it is the product of white brains. Who can have the effrontery to stand for a moment and compare with this white triumph, yellow and brown anarchy and black savagery?"

You are obsessed by the swiftness of the gliding of the sled at the bottom of the hill. You say: what tremendous power must have caused its speed, and how wonderful is Speed. You think of the rider as the originator and inventor of that vast power. You admire his poise and *sang-froid*, his utter self-absorption. You say: surely here is the son of God and he shall reign forever and forever.

You are wrong, quite wrong. Away back on the level stretches of the mountain tops in the forests, amid drifts and driftwood, this sled was slowly and painfully pushed on its little hesitating start. It took power, but the power of sweating, courageous men, not of demigods. As the sled slowly started and gained momentum, it was the Law of Being that gave it speed, and the grace of God that steered its lone, scared passengers. Those passengers, white, black, red and yellow, deserve credit for their balance and pluck. But many times it was sheer luck that made the road not land the white man in the gutter, as it had others so many times before, and as it may him yet. He has gone farther than others because of others whose very falling made hard ways iced and smooth for him to traverse. His triumph is a triumph not of himself alone, but of humankind, from the pusher in the primeval forests to the last flier through the winds of the twentieth century.

And so to leave our parable and come to reality. Great as has been the human advance in the last one thousand years, it is, so far as native human ability, so far as intellectual gift and moral courage are concerned, nothing as compared with any one of ten and more millenniums before, far back in the forests of tropical Africa and in hot India, where brown and black humanity first fought climate and disease and bugs and beasts; where man dared simply to live and propagate himself. There was the hardest and greatest struggle in all the human world. If in sheer exhaustion or in desperate self-defense during this last moment of civilization he has rested, half inert and blinded with the sweat of his efforts, it is only the silly onlooker who sees but the passing moment of time, who can think of him as subhuman and inferior.

All this is Truth, but unknown, unapprehended Truth. Indeed, the greatest and most immediate danger of white culture, perhaps least sensed, is its fear of the Truth, its childish belief in the efficacy of lies as a method of human uplift. The lie is defensible; it has been used widely and often profitably among humankind. But it may be doubted if ever before in the world so many intelligent people believed in it so deeply. We deliberately and continuously deceive not simply others, but ourselves as to the truth about them, us, and the world. We have raised Propaganda to a capital "P" and elaborated an art, almost a science, of how one may make the world believe what is not true, provided the untruth is a widely wished-for thing like the probable extermination of Negroes, the failure of Japanese Imperialism, the incapacity of India for self-rule, the collapse of Russian Revolution. When in other days the world lied, it was a world that expected lies and consciously defended them; when the world lies today it is to a world that pretends to love truth.

"In other words, according to you, white folk are about the meanest and lowest on earth."

They are human, even as you and I.

"Why don't you leave them, then? Get out, go to Africa or to the North Pole; shake the dust of their hospitality from off your feet?"

There are abundant reasons. First, they have annexed the earth and hold it by transient but real power. Thus, by running away, I shall not only not escape them, but succeed in hiding myself in out of the way places where they can work their deviltry on me without photograph, telegraph, or mail service. But even more important than this: I am as bad as they are. In fact, I am related to them and they have much that belongs to me—this land, for instance, for which my fathers starved and fought; I share their sins; in fine, I am related to them.

"By blood?"

By Blood.

"Then you are railing at yourself. You are not black; you are no Negro."

And you? Yellow blood and black has deluged Europe in days past even more than America yesterday. You are not white, as the measurements of your head will show.

"What then becomes of all your argument, if there are no races and we are all so horribly mixed as you maliciously charge?"

Oh, my friend, can you not see that I am laughing at you? Do you suppose this world of men is simply a great layer cake with superimposed slices of inferior and superior races, interlaid with mud?

No, no. Human beings are infinite in variety, and when they are agglutinated in groups, great and small, the groups differ as though they, too, had integrating souls. But they have not. The soul is still individual if it is free. Race is a cultural, sometimes an historical fact. And all that I really have been trying to say is that a certain group that I know and to which I belong, as contrasted with the group you know and to which you belong, and in which you fanatically and glorifyingly believe, bears in its bosom just now the spiritual hope of this land because of the persons who compose it and not by divine command.

"But what is this group; and how do you differentiate it; and how can you call it 'black' when you admit it is not black?"

I recognize it quite easily and with full legal sanction; the black man is a person who must ride "Jim Crow" in Georgia.

My mythical friend Van Dieman is not my only white companion. I have others—many others; one and one especially I want to bring to your attention not because of his attitude toward me but rather because of his attitude toward himself. He represents the way in which my environing white group distorts and frustrates itself even as it strives toward Justice and all because of me. In other words, because of the Negro problem. The average reasonable, conscientious, and fairly intelligent white American faces continuing paradox.

This other friend of mine is free, white, and twenty-one. Which is to say—he is as free as the law and his income, his family and friends, and his formal and informal education allow. He is " white" so far as the records show and as tradition tells; he is not simply twenty-one—he is fifty-one. He is respectable, that is, he belongs to the Episcopal Church, the Union League and Harvard Clubs, and the Republican Party. He is educated, in the sense that he can read if he will, he can write in case his stenographer is absent and he has the privilege of listening to Metropolitan Opera on Tuesdays. He is a Son of the American Revolution, a reserve officer and a member of the American Legion. He reads the *Times* and the *Evening Post* (Saturday); he subscribes for the *Atlantic* and last year he read two books. He also began "Man the Unknown." He owns a home in Westchester assessed at fifty thousand; he drives a Buick. He associates quite often with a wife and a child of fifteen and more often with his fellow employees of the wholesale house which pays him ten thousand a year.

Frankly, my friend faces a dilemma. It is this: his pastor, the Reverend J. Simpson Stodges, D.D., preaches to him Sundays (except July, August and September) a doctrine that sounds like this (I say "sounds" because Dr. Stodges has explanations which mitigate the extremities of his ex cathedra statements): The Doctor asserts in sermons that Peace on Earth is the message of Christ, the Divine leader of men; that this means Good Will to all human beings; that it means Freedom, Toleration of the mistakes, sins and shortcomings of not only your friends but of your enemies. That the Golden Rule of Christianity is to treat others as you want to be treated and that finally you should be willing to sacrifice your comfort, your convenience, your wealth and even your life for mankind; in other words, that Poverty is better than riches and that the meek shall inherit the earth.

Stated thus plainly, this is to my friend's mind pretty stiff doctrine for an ordinary human being in A.D. 1940; and while he believes it in a sense (having been reared in a Godly and Presbyterian household and by a father who spared no rods and spoiled no children), yet, as he puts it to Dr. Stodges in his own parlor, Could a man live up to all that today?

Now, Dr. Stodges out of the pulpit is a most companionable fellow; excellent family, good manners, Oxford accent and Brooks Brothers to-order clothes. He plays keen golf, smokes a rare weed and knows a Bronx cocktail from a Manhattan. Well, the Doctor explained things rather satisfactorily. This Christian business of Peace, Good Will, the Golden Rule, Liberty and Poverty, was, of course, the Ideal. But, bless your soul, man, we can't all always attain the heights, much less live in their rarefied atmosphere. Aim at 'em—that's the point, and in fact, at least live a Gentleman with the "G" capitalized.

Now my friend is exceedingly anxious to be a gentleman. His father, to be sure, sneered at gentlemen and his grandfather for certain obscure reasons both hated them and denied their existence. His great-great-great-grandfather, whose existence the Media Research Bureau had discovered, was, however, high-bred enough to shoulder a pitchfork against England. But at college, at his club, and with his daily companions it appeared altogether desirable to be genteel—to have manners, an "air," and a tailor. As there was no one to preach gentility in plain words, my friend has gathered this rather vague definition: a Gentleman relies on the Police and

Law for protection and self-assertion; he is sustained by a fine sense of Justice for himself and his Family, past and present; he is always courteous in public with "ladies first" and precedence to "gray hairs"; and even in private, he minds his manners and dignity and resists his neighbor's wife; he is charitable, giving to the needy and deserving, to the poor and proud, to inexplicable artists and to the Church. He certainly does not believe in the WPA or other alphabetical ways of encouraging laziness and waste and increasing his taxes. And finally, without ostentation, he is exclusive; picking his associates with care and fine discrimination and appearing socially only where the Best People appear. All this calls for money and a good deal of it. He does not want to be vulgarly and ostentatiously rich. As millionaires go, he is relatively poor, which is poverty as he understands it.

Now my friend knows that this conception lets one in for a certain snobbishness and tendency toward "climbing." And yet it does furnish atmosphere, comfort and a reasonable rule of life for a modern man of position. It is not, of course, the Christianity of the Gospels, nor the career of the Knight Errant; but it is a good, honest, middle path suited to good, honest, middle-aged men.

If the matter halted here, my friend might be vaguely disappointed, but fairly well satisfied. After all, in the workaday life we can't expect moral heroes in quantity. But the trouble is, my friend saw the edges of the Great War (from a swivel chair in America) and he belongs to the American Legion. Also he reads the papers and converses in club lobbies. From this he has assimilated a new and alarming code of action. As Americans we've got to be "prepared" for "defense." Well enough to think of a world of peace, but we haven't got it. Not only that, but the world is not preparing for peace. Everywhere and all over it is not only preparing for war—it is fighting. What is the sense of man, even though he be big, strong, well, sitting down empty-handed while around him are grouped a dozen men armed to the teeth with every device that brains and money can furnish? No, no, this will never do. We've got to have an army and a big army for a big country. We need a militia and a universal draft; we need several big seventy-five million dollar battle-ships with cruisers, airplane carriers and submersibles. We must play expensively at war with elaborate maneuvers. Defense, Preparedness—that's the word.

America must be prepared for all eventualities. England wants her trade, France wants her gold, Germany wants her markets, Russia wants her laborers remade into Bolsheviks. Italy wants her raw material; and above all—Japan! Japan is about to conquer the world for the yellow race and then she'll be ready to swallow America. We must, therefore, be prepared to defend ourselves.

In order to defend America and make an efficient, desirable country, we must have authority and discipline. This may not sound like the Good Will of the Christian but at bottom, it is. There is no use pretending any longer that all men are equal. We know perfectly well that Negroes, Chinamen, Mexicans and a lot of others who are presuming to exercise authority in this country are not our equals. Human beings should be considered as facts and not as possibilities and most of them have no possibilities. Unless, therefore, we have Efficiency—Ability at the top and submission and thrift at the bottom—we are going to come a cropper. Critics may sneer at this and call it caste or fascism, but a country and a world governed by gentlemen for gentlemen is after all the only one worth living in.

There may come some argument as to who should belong to this ruling caste of the Efficient. My friend does not want to be snobbish nor assume too much. Ability will rise. On the whole it would seem that well-bred persons of English descent and New England nurture are the kernel and hope of the land. There will, of course, be modifications in the membership of this group. Without doubt remnants of the Southern slave-holding aristocracy and some of the Mid-Western agrarian stock belong. But we have got to have the best at the top and we know pretty well who the best are.

This hierarchy we should defend vigorously. For this, deliberate propaganda is necessary and permissible; propaganda assists the truth and hurries it on; it may at times exaggerate and distort but all this is for a defensible end and newspapers, radio channels, and news distribution agencies should be owned and used for this end. Here comes the necessity of smoking out radicals. Radicals are insidious intellectuals, themselves usually unsuccessful misfits, envious of success and misled by cranks. They not only advocate impossible panaceas but they undermine the safety of the state. If honest and able, they are even more dangerous. They should be sternly dealt with.

Having thus established a country worth saving, patriotism comes next; and patriotism means standing by your country, thick and thin. It means not simply being an American but feeling proud of America and publicly asserting the fact from time to time. Also, it means seeing to it that other people are patriotic; looking about carefully when the "Star-Spangled Banner" is played to see who is sitting down and why; keeping a watchful eye on the flag. Americans traveling abroad, or at any rate white Americans, should, like the English, have such a panoply thrown about them that street urchins will be afraid to make faces and throw stones.

Finally, my friend learned that a nation must not only be powerful; that power must expand; more territory; more commerce; widened influence and that sort of thing. America must no longer be provincial. It must sit among the great powers of the earth, consulted for all world movements. In fact, it is not too much to think of this marvelous country as a sort of super-power, umpire of humanity, tremendous, irresistible.

Now all these things intrigue my friend. On his trip to Europe last summer he was made to feel more strongly his Americanism, partly in protest against the outrageous misunderstanding and apparent jealousy of America which he met, and partly from the complacency which swelled his breast when he noted what a great country America was in the eyes of Europe and how everybody was hanging on her lightest whisper. Would she please call a peace conference? Would she please restore the gold standard? Would she kindly sell her raw materials cheap? Would she please lend a helping hand in China and Africa? Would she forbear from completely swallowing South America? And so forth and so on.

But there was one difficulty about this code of Americanism which my friend learned; and that was that it led directly and inevitably to another code to which, theoretically, he was definitely opposed, but which, logically, he could not see his way to resist. It was not stated as clearly as any of the other codes; it certainly did not echo in Sunday sermons, although he sometimes suspected it lurked there. It did not enter into his definition of "gentleman" and seemed in fact opposed to it. And yet, somehow, all the gentlemen that he knew were strongly for it. It did seem bound up with his Americanism and yet there again, he resented the logical imputation.

The statement of this fourth code of action was found in unfinished assumption rather than plain words; in unfinished sentences, in novels, in editorials written for country papers by city scriveners; in organizations like the Ku Klux Klan which he thought was extremely silly; or the Security League, which was very respectable. This code rested upon the fact that he was a White Man. Now until my friend had reached the age of thirty he had not known that he was a white man, or at least he had not realized it. Certainly, so far as his skin was concerned, he knew that he was not black, brown, or very yellow. But it never occurred to him that there was any divine significance in that rather negative fact. But lately he had come to realize that his whiteness was fraught with tremendous responsibilities, age-old and infinite in future possibilities. It would seem that colored folks were a threat to the world. They were going to overthrow white folk by sheer weight of numbers, destroy their homes and marry their daughters.

It was this last point that particularly got upon his nerves. He had, as I've said, a girl of fifteen, rather pretty and fragile; and he and his wife were planning already certain advantageous family and economic alliances for the young miss. Much of their social life was already being guided to this end. Now, imagine a world where she would have to repel the advances of Japanese or Negroes!

He had noticed with some disturbed feeling that Negroes in particular were not nearly as agreeable and happy as they used to be. He had not for years been able to get a cheap, good colored cook and the last black yard man asked quite exorbitant wages. He now had white help. They were expensive but in fashion. He had had only last year to join in a neighborhood association to keep a Negro from buying a lot right in the next block!

Now all this led him to understand, if not to sympathize with, a code which began with War. Not only preparedness nor simply defense, but war against the darker races, carried out now and without too nice discrimination as to who were dark: war against the Riff, the Turk, Chinese, Japanese, Indians, Negroes, Mulattoes, Italians and South Americans. Recently this fact, which he knew perfectly well himself, has been confirmed by that great authority, Charles Lindbergh, who flew into wealth and omniscience through one trip to Paris. War and all that goes to implement war: We must hate our enemies. That sounds heathenish; but there can be no effective war, no determination to fight evil to the death, without full-bellied Hate! We need to lay emphasis upon "white": acting like a "White" man, doing things "white"; "white" angels, etc.; efforts to boost novels which paint white heroes, black devils and brown scoundrels with yellow souls; efforts to use the theater and the movies for the same reason; emphasis upon the race element in crime.

In this matter, too, there cannot unfortunately be too nice an honesty. Self-preservation is a First Law; the crimes and shortcomings of white people, while unfortunate, are incidental; news of them must be ignored or suppressed; crimes of colored people are characteristic and must be advertised as stern warnings. He had noted with surprise and satisfaction that the only place in the movies where Negroes were in special evidence was in jails. That was the only way to make that true which ought to be true and which was true but hidden. War, righteous Hate and then Suspicion. It was very easy to be deceived by other races; to think of the Negro as good-natured; of the Chinaman as simply "queer"; of the Japanese as "imitative." No. Look for low subtle methods and death-dealing ideals. Meet them by full-blooded contempt for other races. Teach this to children so that it will become instinctive. Then they won't get into trouble by playing artlessly with colored children or even with colored dolls unless, of course, they are attired as servants.

Next, Exploitation. No use wincing at the word. No sense in letting Roosevelt and the "New Deal" mislead you. The poor must be poor so that the Rich may be Rich. That's clear and true. It merely means using the world for the good of the world and those who own it; bringing out its wealth and abundance; making the lazy and shiftless and ignorant work for their soul's good and for the profit of their betters, who alone are capable of using Wealth to promote Culture.

And finally, Empire: the white race as ruler of all the world and the world working for it, and the world's wealth piled up for the white man's use. This may seem harsh and selfish and yet, of course, it was perfectly natural. Naturally white men would and must rule and any question of their ruling should be met and settled promptly. My friend had not thought that there was any question of this, and there was not before the first World War. There we made the wretched mistake of letting the colored folk dip in, and it turned their weak heads. They almost thought they won the war. He remembered his own disgust at seeing American Negroes actually tricked up as officers—shoulder-straps, Sam Browne belts, and all. He could not conceive of a world where white people did not rule colored people, and certainly if the matter actually came to a trial of force, would he not naturally have to stand for War, Hate, Suspicion and Exploitation in order to put over the Empire of the Whites?

The trouble was, however, that when my friend tabulated all of the codes which he at once and apparently simultaneously was to put in action, he found a most astonishing result, and here it is:

Christian	*Gentleman*	*American*	*White Man*
Peace	Justice	Defense	War
Good Will	Manners	Caste	Hate
Golden Rule	Exclusiveness	Propaganda	Suspicion
Liberty	Police	Patriotism	Exploitation
Poverty	Wealth	Power	Empire

Looking them over, he doesn't know what on earth to do. It is not only dilemma, it is almost quadri-lemma. Perhaps he might put a line between "Christian Gentleman" on the one hand and the "American White Man" on the other, and so arrange a very tremendous and puzzling dilemma.

My friend comes and sits down with me and asks me frankly what to do about it. And I? Why, I appeal to you, Gentle Reader. What should he do about it?

My friend's fault is that he is logical. His reasoning is a clean, simple process like two plus two equal four. This is the cause of his present unrest. Other folk are deliciously impervious to reason. They are pacifists with the help of the police and backed by careful preparation for war. They are filled with Good Will for all men, provided these men are in their places and certain of them kept there by severe discountenance. In that case courtesy smooths human relations. They certainly aim to treat others as they want to be treated themselves, so far as this is consistent with their own necessarily exclusive position. This position must be maintained by propaganda inculcating a perfectly defensible contempt for inferiors and suspicion of strangers and radicals. They believe in liberty under a firm police system backed by patriotism and an organization of work which will yield profit to capital. And, of course, they believe in poverty so long as they have sufficient wealth. This they are certain is the way to make America the greatest country on earth for white supremacy.

This makes my friend tear his pale hair. "How can they do it?" he yells. "It ain't reasonable." I explained patiently: possibly they are playing acrostics. See how they might arrange their meanings?

Peace			
	Manners		
		Propaganda	
			Exploitation
Good Will			
	Exclusiveness		
		Patriotism	
			Empire

			Hate
		Propaganda	
	Police		
Poverty			
			War
		Caste	
	Exclusiveness		
Liberty			

"Fact is," I add, "I've heard them singing in St. Thomas's:

> The Prince of *Peace* goes forth to *War*
> A *Kingly Crown* to ga-a-ain!
> His *blood-red banner* floats afar.
> Who follows *in his Name*!"

"Your quotation is not exact," responds my literal friend.

"Perhaps not, but it comes to the same thing: they combine Peace, War, Empire, Bolshevism and Jesus Christ in one happy family."

My friend waves all this aside. "Outside of spoofing and horse-play," he insists, "it's all both reasonable and impossible. Take each column alone and it is to me absolutely convincing. I believe in it. Think of a world with Peace, Good Will, Freedom, the Golden Rule and Poverty! My God, what a Paradise, despite death and accident, cold and heat—what? That fellow Gandhi is the only human leader today with the right idea. It's magnificent. It's tremendous."

"Plain living and high thinking," I suggest.

"Of course," he responds, "only—well, one wants some Beauty—travel, gowns, palaces, diamonds, and Grand Opera—"

I intervene, "But don't forget the preceding lines: 'never to blend our pleasure or our pride, with sorrow of the meanest thing that feels.' "

"But—well, that brings me down out of the clouds," he complains. "This can't be a world of saints. We have got to have wealth and servants. Servants must be cheap and willing and the mean ought not to be so sensitive. Perhaps they are not. But why not have a world of gentlemen—well-policed, everybody in his place; all the rich, courteous and generous and all the poor appreciative; propaganda for the right, love of country and prosperous business; White World leading the Colored as far as the darkies can go. Certainly despite all your democracy, blood will tell. Now that seems to be *practical.* They've got something like that in England. Or at least, they think they have.

"But if I put this thing to the club, as man to man, no sooner have I mentioned England than they're in arms. England, dammit, has a bigger navy and merchant marine than we, with which she monopolizes the world-carrying trade; she patronizes and despises us, and then pats us on the back when her chestnuts are red-hot; she rules a bigger empire. And France won't pay us and has a big black army; and Russia is stirring up Revolution with a big Red army; and Germany! Good Lord! Hitler is anti-Christ. I tell you what, we got to watch out. America is the greatest nation on earth and the world is jealous of her. We got to be prepared if it takes a billion a year for powder and guns. We've got to be disciplined; a stern, severe code for the lazy and criminal; training for boy scouts and militia. We must put patriotism before everything—make 'em salute the flag, stop radical treason, keep out the dirty foreigners, disfranchise niggers and make America a Power!

"Well, I like America. Darn it! I *love* it. My father died for it, although not in war—and I am reasonably willing to. There's no doubt about it, lambs have got no business prowling about lions and—oh, Hell! Honest to God, what do you think Asia and Africa would do to us, if they got a chance?"

"Skin us alive," I answer cheerfully, loving the "us."

"Well, then! Skin them and skin 'em first and keep 'em skinned. I'm a He-White-Man, get me?

"Then, look at these other columns. Suppose they are not logical, correct, compelling. We cannot run this world without the police and courts of Justice. We must not be discourteous even to the pushing, careless, impudent American fellow-citizen, but something is due our own self-respect. Can we get on without being exclusive? I don't mean downright snobbishness, but be careful, nice, 'aristocratic' in the best meaning of the term. Finally, we of the upper class must have money. We must have it, no matter how we get it, or civilization is lost.

"Well, now, if we cannot do without these things, then, they must become our rule of life. But no sooner have you settled it this way than there comes that business of being an American. Can we give that up? Can we go in for Humanity and the Internation? Lord knows I'd like to but somehow, I can't see it. Suppose America disarmed like Denmark, gave up poison gas, big battleships and dinky little officers in khaki? Suppose we continue to neglect discipline for the mob and stop teaching thick and thin patriotism? I admit it isn't exactly honest business; America isn't so wonderful as nations go, but must we not make Americans believe it wonderful? Can we emphasize the fact that Lincoln told smutty stories and Washington held slaves and Jefferson begat bastards, and Webster drank more than was good for him? Suppose we did not become powerful as well as big? What is going to happen to us? Well, there you are. We've got to be Americans even if we give up being Christians and Gentlemen."

Or again, and here my friend gets a bit embarrassed and red in the face: "You see," he says to me confidentially, "I've got a little daughter, young yet, but a nice little thing. Probably she is going to be pretty, certainly is going to have some money from her aunt as well as a bit from me. She is being educated, and I may say rather expensively educated, in a private school. She may go in for art or some high class profession, or she may not; but certainly, I hope she will marry and marry well. There will be children and grandchildren and great-grandchildren and so on ad infinitum. Now, I tell you frankly, I want them all white. Even if she were a son, while the case wouldn't be so bad, still I don't want to think of colored folk sharing my blood. Can you for a moment conceive a world where brown men and dagoes were giving orders to white men and women? It would spell the end of civilization. Of course, there may be a few exceptions, but the mass of the colored world can't think, they can't rule, they can't direct, and we mustn't let them try. And to keep them from trying we've got to pound them back into their places every time they show their heads above the ramparts!"

Then my friend stopped. He turned red and grew apologetic. "Of course," he stammered, "I don't exactly mean you—you are an Exception, at least in some respects—"

"In some respects?" I rejoin helplessly. But my friend stiffened. Suddenly he ceased speaking and stared at the headlines in the evening paper. The world had gone to war again to defend Democracy!

The democracy which the white world seeks to defend does not exist. It has been splendidly conceived and discussed, but not realized. If it ever is to grow strong enough for self-defense and for embracing the world and developing human culture to its highest, it must include not simply the lower classes among the whites now excluded from voice in the control of industry; but in addition to that it must include the colored peoples of Asia and Africa, now hopelessly imprisoned by poverty and ignorance. Unless these latter are included and in so far as they are not, democracy is a mockery and contains within itself the seeds of its own destruction.

Hitler is the late crude but logical exponent of white world race philosophy since the Conference of Berlin in 1884. Europe had followed the high, ethical dream of a young Jew but twisted that ethic beyond recognition to any end that Europe wanted. If that end was murder, the "Son of God went forth to war!" If that end was slavery, God thundered, "Cursed be Canaan," and Paul echoed "Servants obey your masters!" If poverty was widespread and seemingly inevitable, Christ was poor and alms praiseworthy.

There persisted the mud-sill theory of society that civilization not only permitted but must have the poor, the diseased, the wretched, the criminal upon which to build its temples of light. Western Europe did not and does not want democracy, never believed in it, never practiced it and never without fundamental and basic revolution will accept it. Not the keen, the bold, the brave and the enlightened are the ones which modern individual struggle throws to the fore but rather the lucky and the strong.

How now, not so much in the judgment of the common man, but in the light of science, can the racial attitude of the white world be explained and rationalized and removed from the harsh judgment put upon it by the darker races today? Negroes in Africa, Indians in Asia, mulattoes and mestizoes in the West Indies, Central and South America, all explain the attitude of the white world as sheer malevolence; while the white people of the leading European countries honestly regard themselves as among the great benefactors of mankind and especially of colored mankind.

In this dilemma sociologists of earlier years took refuge in inventing a new entity, the group, which had action, guilt, praise and blame quite apart from the persons composing the group. It was of course a metaphysical hypothesis which had its uses in reasoning, but could not be regarded as corresponding to exact truth. No such group over-soul has been proven to exist.

The facts of the situation however as science today conceives it, are clear. The individual may act consciously and rationally and be responsible for what he does; but on the other hand many of his actions, and indeed, as we are coming to believe, most of his actions, are not rational and many of them arise from subconscious urges. It is our duty to assess praise and blame for the rational and conscious acts of men, but to regard the vast area of the subconscious and the irrational and especially of habit and convention which also produce significant action, as an area where we must apply other remedies and judgments if we would get justice and right to prevail in the world. Above all we must survey these vague and uncharted lands and measure their limits.

Looking at this whole matter of the white race as it confronts the world today, what can be done to make its attitudes rational and consistent and calculated to advance the best interests of the whole world of men? The first point of attack is undoubtedly the economic. The progress of the white world must cease to rest upon the poverty and the ignorance of its own proletariat and of the colored world. Thus industrial imperialism must lose its reason for being and in that way alone can the great racial groups of the world come into normal and helpful relation to each other. The present attitude and action of the white world is not based solely upon rational, deliberate intent. It is a matter of conditioned reflexes; of long followed habits, customs and folkways; of subconscious trains of reasoning and unconscious nervous reflexes. To attack and better all this calls for more than appeal and argument. It needs carefully planned and scientific propaganda; the vision of a world of intelligent men with sufficient income to live decently and with the will to build a beautiful world. It will not be easy to accomplish all this, but the quickest way to bring the reason of the world face to face with this major problem of human progress is to listen to the complaint of those human beings today who are suffering most from white attitudes, from white habits, from the conscious and unconscious wrongs which white folk are today inflicting on their victims. The colored world therefore must be seen as existing not simply for itself but as a group whose insistent cry may yet become the warning which awakens the world to its truer self and its wider destiny.

Chapter 7

THE COLORED WORLD WITHIN

NOT ONLY do white men but also colored men forget the facts of the Negro's double environment. The Negro American has for his environment not only the white surrounding world, but also, and touching him usually much more nearly and compellingly, is the environment furnished by his own colored group. There are exceptions, of course, but this is the rule. The American Negro, therefore, is surrounded and conditioned by the concept which he has of white people and he is treated in accordance with the concept they have of him. On the other hand, so far as his own people are concerned, he is in direct contact with individuals and facts. He fits into this environment more or less willingly. It gives him a social world and mental peace. On the other hand and especially if in education and ambition and income he is above the average culture of his group, he is often resentful of its environing power; partly because he does not recognize its power and partly because he is determined to consider himself part of the white group from which, in fact, he is excluded. This weaving of words does not make the situation entirely clear and yet it does point toward its complications.

It is true, as I have argued, that Negroes are not inherently ugly nor congenitally stupid. They are not naturally criminal and their poverty and ignorance today have clear and well-known and remediable causes. All this is true; and yet what every colored man living today knows is that by practical present measurement Negroes today are inferior to whites. The white folk of the world are richer and more intelligent; they live better; have better government; have better legal systems; have built more impressive cities, larger systems of communication and they control a larger part of the earth than all the colored peoples together.

Against this colored folk may certainly bring many countervailing considerations. But putting these aside, there remains the other fact that the mass of the colored peoples in

Asia and Africa, in North America and the West Indies and in South America and in the South Sea Islands are in the mass ignorant, diseased, and inefficient; that the governments which they have evolved, even allowing for the interested interference of the white world, have seldom reached the degree of efficiency of modern European governments; and that particularly in the use, increase, and distribution of wealth, in the regulation of human services, they have at best fallen behind the accomplishment of modern England, France and the United States.

It may be said, and with very strong probability back of such assertion, there is no reason to doubt, that whatever white folk have accomplished, black, brown and yellow folk might have done possibly in differing ways with different results. Certainly modern civilization is too new and has steered too crooked a course and been too much a matter of chance and fate to make any final judgment as to the abilities of humankind.

All this I strongly believe and yet today we are faced by these uncomforting facts: the ignorance, poverty and inefficiency of the darker peoples; the wealth, power and technical triumph of the whites. It is not enough when the colored people face this situation, that they decry resulting attitudes of the white world. There is a strong suspicion among themselves and a probability often asserted among whites, that were conditions reversed, blacks would have done everything to white people that white people have done to blacks; or going less far afield than this: if yellow folk in the future gain the domination of the world, their program might not be more philanthropic than that of the whites. But here again, this is not the question. Granting its possible truth, it is no answer to the present plight.

The present question is: What is the colored world going to do about the current situations? Present Negro attitudes can be illuminated by turning our attention for a space to colored America, to an average group of Negroes, say, in Harlem, not in their role of agitation and reform, but in their daily human intercourse and play. Imagine a conversation like this, of which I have heard dozens:

* * *

"Just like niggers!"

"This is what colored people always do."

"What can you expect of the 'brother'?"

"I wish to God I had been born white!"

This interchange takes place at midnight. There are no white persons present. Four persons have spent an evening playing bridge, and now are waiting until a fifth, the hostess, brings in the supper. The apartment is small but comfortable; perhaps a little too full of conventional furniture, which does not altogether agree in pattern; but evidently the home of fairly well-to-do people who like each other and are enjoying themselves. But, of course, they have begun to discuss "the problem" which no group of American colored people can long keep from discussing. It is and must be the central interest of their lives.

There is a young colored teacher from the public schools of New York—well-paid and well-dressed, with a comely form and an arresting personality. She is from the South. Her mother had been servant and housekeeper in a wealthy Southern white family. Her grandmother had been a slave of their own grandfather. This teacher is complaining bitterly of her walk through Harlem that night; of the loud and vulgar talking; of the way in which the sidewalks were blocked; of the familiarity and even insults of dark loafers; of the insistent bad manners and resentful attitude of so many of these Harlem black folk.

The lawyer lights a cigar. "It certainly is a question where to live," he says. He had been educated at Fisk University and brought in contact for eight years with Northern white teachers. Then he had gone West and eventually studied law at the University of Michigan. He is big, dark, good-natured and well-dressed. He complains of the crowded conditions of living in Harlem; of the noise and dirt in any Negro community; of the fact that if you went out to a better class white neighborhood you could not rent, you had to buy; if you did buy, first you could place no mortgage; then the whites made your life a hell; if you survived this, the whites became panicky, sold to anyone for anything: pretty soon, in two, three, five years, people of all sorts and kinds came crowding in. Homes were transformed into lodging houses; undesirable elements became your neighbors. "I moved to a nice apartment on Sugar Hill last year. It had just been turned over to colored people. The landlord promised everything. I started out of the apartment last night; there was a pool of blood in front of my door, where there had been a drunken brawl and cutting the night before."

A young, slim, cream-colored physician, native of New York and a graduate of its schools, but compelled to go to Howard in order to finish the clinical work of his medical education, looked uncomfortable. "I don't mind going with colored people; I prefer it, if they are my kind; but if I go out to lunch here in Harlem, I get pork chops and yams which I do not like, served on a table cloth which is not clean, set down negligently by indifferent waiters. In the movies uptown here I find miscellaneous and often ill-smelling neighbors. On my vacation, where shall I—where can I go? The part of Atlantic City open to me, I continue to frequent, because I see so many charming friends of mine from all over the land; but always I get sick at heart not only at the discrimination on the boardwalk, in the restaurants, on the beach, in the amusements—that is bad enough; but I gag at the kind of colored people always in evidence, against whom I want to discriminate myself. We tried to support a colored section of the beach; see who crowded in; we failed."

"Yes, but that is all pleasure or convenience," says the fourth man. He was an insurance agent, playing a difficult game of chance with people who made weekly payments to him and then tried to beat him by malingering; or with others who paid promptly and had their claims disallowed by the higher-ups. "What I am bothered about," he says, "is this poverty, sickness and crime; the cheating of Negroes not only by whites, but by Negroes themselves; the hold-ups and murders of colored people by colored people. I am afraid to go to some places to make my collections. I don't know what is going to become of Negroes at this rate."

Just then, the fifth member of the party, the wife of the insurance agent, emerges from the kitchen where she has been arranging the lunch. She is pretty and olive, a little inclined to be fat. She was the daughter of dark laborers who had gone to Boston after emancipation. There she had been educated in the public schools and was a social worker there before she married. She knew how to cook and liked to, and is accompanied through the swinging door by a delicious aroma of coffee, hot biscuits and fried chicken. She has been listening to the conversation from outside and she came in saying, "What's got me worried to death, is where I am going to send Junior to school. Junior is bright and has got nice manners, if I do say it; but I just can't send him to these Harlem schools. I was visiting them yesterday; dirt, noise, bad manners, filthy tales, no discipline, over-crowded. The teachers aren't half trying. They purposely send green teachers to Harlem for experience. I just can't send Junior there; but where can I send him?"

This is a fairly characteristic colored group of the better class and they are voicing that bitter inner criticism of Negroes directed in upon themselves, which is widespread. It tends often to fierce, angry, contemptuous judgment of nearly all that Negroes do, say, and believe. Of course these words are seldom voiced in the presence of white folk. Every one of these persons, in the presence of whites, would eagerly and fiercely defend their "race."

Such complaints are the natural reaction of people toward the low average of culture among American Negroes. There is some exaggeration here, which the critics themselves, if challenged, would readily admit; and yet, there is sound basis for much of this criticism. Similar phenomena may be noticed always among undeveloped or suppressed peoples or groups undergoing extraordinary experience. None have more pitilessly castigated Jews than the Jewish prophets, ancient and modern. It is the Irish themselves who rail at "dirty Irish tricks." Nothing could exceed the self-abasement of the Germans during the *Sturm und Drang*.

Negro self-criticism recognizes a perfectly obvious fact and that fact is that most Negroes in the United States today occupy a low cultural status; both low in itself and low as compared with the national average in the land. There are cultured individuals and groups among them. All Negroes do not fall culturally below all whites. But if one selects any one of the obviously low culture groups in the United States, the proportion of Negroes who belong to it will be larger than the Negro proportion in the total population. Nor is there anything singular about it; the real miracle would be if this were not so. Former slavery, present poverty and ignorance, with the inevitable resulting sickness and crime, are adequate social explanation.

This low social condition of the majority of Negroes is not solely a problem of the whites; a question of historic guilt in slavery and labor exploitation and of present discrimination; it is not merely a matter of the social uplifting of an alien group within their midst; a problem of social contact and political power. Howsoever it may be thus rationalized and explained, it must be, at any current moment, primarily an inner problem of the Negro group itself, a condition from which they themselves are prime sufferers, and a problem with which this group is forced itself to grapple. No matter what the true reasons are, or where the blame lies, the fact remains that among twelve million American Negroes, there are today poverty, ignorance, bad manners, disease, and crime.

A determined fight has been made upon Negro ignorance, both within and without the group, and the results have been notable. Nevertheless, this is still an ignorant people. One in every six Negroes ten years of age and over admitted in 1930 that he could not read and write. It is probable that one in every three would have been justified in confessing to practical illiteracy, to inexperience and lack of knowledge of the meaning of the modern world. In the South not one-half the colored children from five to sixteen are regularly in school and the majority of these schools are not good schools. Any poor, ignorant people herded by themselves, filled with more or less articulate resentment, are bound to be bad-mannered, for manners are a matter of social environment; and the mass of American Negroes have retrograded in this respect.

There has been striking improvement in the Negro death rate. It was better than that of most South American countries, of Italy, Japan and Spain even before the war. Nevertheless it is still bad and costly, and the toll in tuberculosis, pneumonia, heart disease, syphilis, and homicide is far too high. It is hard to know just what the criminal tendencies of the American Negroes are, for our crime statistics are woefully inadequate. We do know that in proportion to population three times as many Negroes are arrested as whites, but to what extent this measures prejudice and to what extent anti-social ills, who shall say? Many of these ought never to have been arrested; most of them are innocent of grave crimes; but the transgression of the poor and sick is always manifest among Negroes: disorder of all sorts, theft and burglary, fighting, breaking the gambling and liquor laws and especially fighting with and killing each other.

Above all the Negro is poor: poor by heritage from two hundred forty-four years of chattel slavery, by emancipation without land or capital and by seventy-five years of additional wage exploitation and crime peonage. Sudden industrial changes like the Civil War, the World War and the spree in speculation during the twenties have upset him. The Negro worker has been especially hard hit by the current depression. Of the nearly three million Negro families in the United States today, probably the breadwinners of a million are unemployed and another million on the lower margin of decent subsistence. Assuming a gradual restoration of fairly normal conditions it is probable that not more than two per cent of the Negro families in the United States would have an income of $2,500 a year and over; while fifty-eight per cent would have incomes between $500 and $2,500.

This social degradation is intensified and emphasized by discrimination; inability to get work, discrimination in pay, improbability of promotion, and more fundamentally, spiritual segregation from contact with manners, customs, incentives to effort despite handicaps. By outer pressure in most cases, Negroes must live among themselves; neighbors to their own people in segregated parts of the city, in segregated country districts. The segregation is not complete and most of it is customary rather than legal. Nevertheless, most Negroes live with Negroes, in what are on the whole the least pleasant dwelling places, although not necessarily always bad places in themselves.

This means that Negroes live in districts of low cultural level; that their contacts with their fellow men involve contacts with people largely untrained and ignorant, frequently diseased, dirty, and noisy, and sometimes anti-social. These districts are not usually protected by the police—rather victimized and tyrannized over by them. No one who does not know can realize what tyranny a low-grade white policeman can exercise in a colored neighborhood. In court his unsupported word cannot be disputed and the only defense against him is often mayhem and assassination by black criminals, with resultant hue and cry. City services of water, sewerage, garbage-removal, street-cleaning, lighting, noise and traffic regulation, schools and hospitalization are usually neglected or withheld. Saloons, brothels, and gambling seek these areas with open or tacit consent. No matter in what degree or in what way the action of the white population may increase or decrease these social problems, they remain the present problems which must be faced by colored people themselves and by colored people of widely different status.

It goes without saying that while Negroes are thus manifestly of low average culture, in no place nor at any time do they form a homogeneous group. Even in the country districts of the lower South, Allison Davis likens the group to a steeple with wide base tapering to a high pinnacle. This means that while the poor, ignorant, sick and anti-social form a vast foundation, that upward from that base stretch classes whose highest members, although few in number, reach above the average not only of the Negroes but of the whites, and may justly be compared to the better-class white culture. The class structure of the whites, on the other hand, resembles a tower bulging near the center with the lowest classes small in number as compared with the middle and lower middle classes; and the highest classes far more numerous in proportion than those among blacks. This, of course, is what one would naturally expect, but it is easily forgotten. The Negro group is spoken of continually as one undifferentiated low-class mass. The culture of the higher whites is often considered as typical of all the whites.

American Negroes again are of differing descent, from parents with varied education, born in many parts of the land and under all sorts of conditions. In differing degrees these folk have come through periods of great and vital social change; emancipation from slavery, migration from South to North, from country to city; changes in income and intelligence. Above this they have experienced widely different contacts with their own group and with the whites. For instance, during slavery the dark house servant came into close and intimate contact with the master class. This class itself differed in all degrees from cultured aristocrats to brutal tyrants. Many of the Negroes thus received ideals of gracious manners, of swaggering self-assertion, of conspicuous consumption. Later cultural contact came to the best of the Negroes through the mission schools in the South succeeding the war: the more simple and austere intellectual life of New England with its plain living and high thinking; its cleanliness and conscience; this was brought into direct contact with educated Negro life. Its influence is still felt among the descendants of those trained at Fisk and Atlanta, Hampton and Talladega and a score of other schools.

These contacts between the white and colored groups in the United States have gradually changed. On the whole the better cultural contacts have lessened in breadth and time, and greater cultural segregation by race has ensued. The old bonds between servants and masters in the South disappeared. The white New England teachers gradually withdrew from the Southern schools partly by white Southern caste pressure, partly to make place for Negroes whom the Northern teachers had trained. The bonds that replaced these older contacts were less direct, more temporary and casual; and yet, these still involve considerable numbers of persons. In Northern public schools and colleges, numbers of white and colored youth come into direct contact, knowledge and sympathy. Various organizations, movements, and meetings bring white and colored people together; in various occupations they work side by side and in large numbers of cases they meet as employers and employed. Deliberate interracial movements have brought some social contacts in the South.

Thus considerable intercourse between white and black folk in America is current today; and yet on the whole, the more or less clearly defined upper layers of educated and ambitious Negroes find themselves for the most part largely segregated and alone. They are unable, or at least unwilling on the terms offered, to share the social institutions of the cultured whites of the nation, and are faced with inner problems of contact with their own lower classes with which they have few or no social institutions capable of dealing.

The Negro of education and income is jammed beside the careless, ignorant and criminal. He recoils from appeal to the white city even for physical protection against his anti-social elements, for this, he feels, is a form of self-accusation, of attack on the Negro race. It invites the smug rejoinder: "Well, if you can't live with niggers, how do you expect us to?" For escape of the Negro cultured to areas of white culture, with the consequent acceleration of acculturation, there is small opportunity. There is little or no chance for a Negro family to remove to a quiet neighborhood, to a protected suburb or a college town. I tried once to buy a home in the Sage Foundation development at Forest Hills, Long Island. The project was designed for the class of white-collar workers to which I belonged. Robert De Forest and his directors hesitated, but finally and definitely refused, simply and solely because of my dark skin.

What now is the practical path for the solution of the problem? Usually it has been assumed in such cases that the culture recruits rising from a submerged group will be received more or less willingly by corresponding classes of neighboring or enveloping groups. Of course it is clear in the case of immigrant groups and other disadvantaged clusters of folk that this process is by no means easy or natural. Much bitter frustration and social upheaval continually arise from the refusal of the upper social layers to receive recruits from below. Nevertheless, in the United States it has been impossible long or entirely to exclude the better classes of the Irish, the Italians, the Southern poor whites. In the case of the Negro, the unwillingness is greater and public opinion supports it to such a degree, that admission of black folk to cultured circles is slow and difficult. It still remains possible in the United States for a white American to be a gentleman and a scholar, a Christian and a man of integrity, and yet flatly and openly refuse to treat as a fellow human being any person who has Negro ancestry.

The inner contradiction and frustration which this involves is curious. The younger educated Negroes show here vastly different interpretations. One avoids every appearance of segregation. He will not sit in a street car beside a Negro; he will not frequent a Negro church; he will join few, if any, Negro organizations. On the other hand, he will take every opportunity to join in the political and cultural life of the whites. But he pays for this and pays dearly. He so often meets actual insult or more or less veiled rebuffs from the whites that he becomes nervous and truculent through expectation of dislike, even when its manifestation does not always appear. And on the other hand, Negroes more or less withdraw from associating with him. They suspect that he is "ashamed of his race."

Another sort of young educated Negro forms and joins Negro organizations; prides himself on living with "his people"; withdraws from contact with whites, unless there is no obvious alternative. He too pays. His cultural contacts sink of necessity to a lower level. He becomes provincial in his outlook. He attributes to whites a dislike and hatred and racial prejudice of which many of them are quite unconscious and guiltless.

Between these two extremes range all sorts of interracial patterns, and all of them theoretically follow the idea that Negroes must only submit to segregation "when forced." In practically all cases the net result is a more or less clear and definite crystallization of the culture elements among colored people into their own groups for social and cultural contact.

The resultant path which commends itself to many whites is deliberate and planned cultural segregation of the upper classes of Negroes not only from the whites of all classes, but from their own masses. It has been said time and time again: if certain classes of Negroes do not like the squalor, filth and crime of Negro slums, instead of trying to escape to better class white neighborhoods, why do they not establish their own exclusive neighborhoods? In other words, why does not the Negro race build up a class structure of its own, parallel to that of the whites, but separate; and including its own social, economic and religious institutions?

The arresting thing about this advice and program is that even when not planned, this is exactly what Negroes are doing and must do even in the case of those who theoretically resent it. The group with whose conversation this chapter started is a case in point. They form a self-segregated culture group. They have come to know each other partly by chance, partly by design, but form a small integrated clique because of similar likes and ideas, because of corresponding culture. This is happening all over the land among these twelve million Negroes. It is not a matter yet of a few broad superimposed social classes, but rather of smaller cliques and groups gradually integrating and extending out of their neighborhoods into neighboring districts and cities. In this way a distinct social grouping has long been growing among American Negroes and recent studies have emphasized what we all knew, and that is that the education and acculturation of the Negro child is more largely the result of the training through contact with these cultural groups than it is of the caste-conditioned contacts with whites.

The question now comes as to how far this method of acculturation should and could go, and by what conscious planning the uplift of the Negro race can be accomplished through this means. Is cultural separation in the same territory feasible? To force a group of various levels of culture to segregate itself, will certainly retard its advance, since it must put energy not simply into social advance, but in the vast and intricate effort to duplicate, evolve, and contrive new social institutions to maintain their advance and guard against retrogression.

There can be two theories here: one that the rise of a talented tenth within the Negro race, whether or not it succeeds in escaping to the higher cultural classes of the white race, is a threat to the development of the whole Negro group and hurts their chances for salvation. Or it may be said that the rise of classes within the Negro group is precisely a method by which the level of culture in the whole group is going to be raised. But this depends upon the relations that develop between these masses and the cultural aims of the higher classes.

Many assume that an upper social class maintains its status mainly by reason of its superior culture. It may, however, maintain its status because of its wealth and political power and in that case its ranks can be successfully invaded only by the wealthy. In white America, it is in this direction that we have undoubtedly changed the older pattern of social hierarchy. Birth and culture still count, but the main avenue to social power and class domination is wealth: income and oligarchic economic power, the consequent political power and the prestige of those who own and control capital and distribute credit. This makes a less logical social hierarchy and one that can only be penetrated by the will and permission of the ruling oligarchy or the chances of gambling. Education, thrift, hard work and character undoubtedly are influential, but they are implemented with power only as they gain wealth; and as land, natural resources, credit and capital are increasingly monopolized, they gain wealth by permission of the dominating wealthy class.

If now American Negroes plan a vertical parallel of such a structure and such processes, they will find it practically impossible. First of all, they have not the wealth; secondly, they have not the political power which wealth manipulates, and in the realm of their democratic power they are not only already partly disfranchised by law and custom, but they suffer the same general limitation of democratic power in income and industry, in which the white masses are imprisoned.

There would be greater possibility of the Negro imitating the class structure of the white race if those whites who advise and encourage it were ready to help in its accomplishment, ready to furnish the Negro the broadest opportunity for cultural development and in addition to this to open the way for them to accumulate such wealth and receive such income as would make the corresponding structure secure. But, of course, those who most vehemently tell the Negro to develop his own classes and social institutions, have no plan or desire for such help. First of all, and often deliberately, they curtail the education and cultural advantage of black folk and they do this because they are not convinced of the cultural ability or gift of Negroes and have no hope nor wish that the mass of Negroes can be raised even as far as the mass of whites have been. It is this insincere attitude which especially arouses the ire and resentment of the culture groups among American Negroes.

When the Negro despairs of duplicating white development, his despair is not always because the paths to this development are shut in his face, but back of this lurks too often a lack of faith in essential Negro possibilities, parallel to similar attitudes on the part of the whites. Instead of this proving anything concerning the truth, it is simply a natural phenomenon. Negroes, particularly the better class Negroes, are brought up like other Americans despite the various separations and segregations. They share, therefore, average American culture and current American prejudices. It is almost impossible for a Negro boy trained in a white Northern high school and a white college to come out with any high idea of his own people or any abiding faith in what they can do; or for a Negro trained in the segregated schools of the South wholly to escape the deadening environment of insult and caste, even if he happens to have the good teachers and teaching facilities, which poverty almost invariably denies him. He may rationalize his own individual status as exceptional. He can well believe that there are many other exceptions, but he cannot ordinarily believe that the mass of Negro people have possibilities equal to the whites.

It is this sort of thing that leads to the sort of self-criticism that introduces this chapter. My grandfather, Alexander Du Bois, was pushed into the Negro group. He resented it. He wasn't a "Negro," he was a man. He would not attend Negro picnics or join a Negro church, and yet he had to. Now, his situation in 1810 was much different from mine in 1940, because the Negro group today is much more differentiated and has distinct cultural elements. He could go to a Negro picnic today and associate with interesting people of his own level. So much so, indeed, that some Negro thinkers are beginning to be afraid that we will become so enamored of our own internal social contacts, that we will cease to hammer at the doors of the larger group, with all the consequent loss of breadth through lack of the widest cultural contact; and all the danger of ultimate extinction through exacerbated racial repulsions and violence. For any building of a segregated Negro culture in America in those areas where it is by law or custom the rule and where neglect to take positive action would mean a slowing down or stoppage or even retrogression of Negro advance, unusual and difficult and to some extent unprecedented action is called for.

To recapitulate: we cannot follow the class structure of America; we do not have the economic or political power, the ownership of machines and materials, the power to direct the processes of industry, the monopoly of capital and credit. On the other hand, even if we cannot follow this method of structure, nevertheless we must do something. We cannot stand still; we cannot permit ourselves simply to be the victims of exploitation and social exclusion. It is from this paradox that arises the present frustration among American Negroes.

Historically, beginning with their thought in the eighteenth century and coming down to the twentieth, Negroes have tended to choose between these difficulties and emphasize two lines of action: the *first* is exemplified in Walker's Appeal, that tremendous indictment of slavery by a colored man published in 1829, and resulting very possibly in the murder of the author; and coming down through the work of the Niagara Movement and the National Association for the Advancement of Colored People in our day. This program of organized opposition to the action and attitude of the dominant white group, includes ceaseless agitation and insistent demand for equality: the equal right to work, civic and political equality, and social equality. It involves the use of force of every sort: moral suasion, propaganda and where possible even physical resistance.

There are, however, manifest difficulties about such a program. First of all it is not a program that envisages any direct action of Negroes themselves for the uplift of their socially depressed masses; in the very conception of the program, such work is to be attended to by the nation and Negroes are to be the subjects of uplift forces and agencies to the extent of their numbers and need. Another difficulty is that the effective organization of this plan of protest and agitation involves a large degree of inner union and agreement among Negroes. Now for obvious reasons of ignorance and poverty, and the natural envy and bickering of any disadvantaged group, this unity is difficult to achieve. In fact the efforts to achieve it through the Negro conventions of 1833 and thereafter during the fifties; during Reconstruction, and in the formation of the early Equal Rights League and Afro-American Council, were only partly successful.

The largest measure of united effort in the demand for Negro rights was attempted by the NAACP in the decade between 1914 and 1924. The difficulty even in that case was the matter of available funds. The colored people are not today able to furnish enough funds for the kind of campaign against Negro prejudice which is demanded; or at least the necessity of large enough contributions is not clear to a sufficient number of Negroes. Moreover, even if there were the necessary unity and resources available, there are two assumptions usually made in such a campaign, which are not quite true; and that is the assumption on one hand that most race prejudice is a matter of ignorance to be cured by information; and on the other hand that much discrimination is a matter of deliberate deviltry and unwillingness to be just. Admitting widespread ignorance concerning the guilt of American whites for the plight of the Negroes; and the undoubted existence of sheer malevolence, the present attitude of the whites is much more the result of inherited customs and of those irrational and partly subconscious actions of men which control so large a proportion of their deeds. Attitudes and habits thus built up cannot be changed by sudden assault. They call for a long, patient, well-planned and persistent campaign of propaganda.

Moreover, until such a campaign has had a chance to do its work, the minority which is seeking emancipation must remember that they are facing a powerful majority. There is no way in which the American Negro can force this nation to treat him as equal until the unconscious cerebration and folkways of the nation, as well as its rational deliberate thought among the majority of whites, are willing to grant equality.

In the meantime of course the agitating group may resort to a campaign of countermoves. They may organize and collect resources and by every available means teach the white majority and appeal to their sense of justice; but at the very best this means a campaign of waiting and the colored group must be financially able to afford to wait and patient to endure without spiritual retrogression while they wait.

The *second* group effort to which Negroes have turned is more extreme and decisive. One can see it late in the eighteenth century when the Negro union of Newport, Rhode

Island, in 1788 proposed to the Free African Society of Philadelphia a general exodus to Africa on the part at least of free Negroes. This "back to Africa" movement has recurred time and time again in the philosophy of American Negroes and has commended itself not simply to the inexperienced and to demagogues, but to the prouder and more independent type of Negro; to the black man who is tired of begging for justice and recognition from folk who seem to him to have no intention of being just and do not propose to recognize Negroes as men. This thought was strong during the active existence of the Colonization Society and succeeded in convincing leading Negroes like John Russworm, the first Negro college graduate, and Lott Carey, the powerful Virginia preacher. Then it fell into severe disrepute when the objects of the Colonization Society were shown by the Abolitionists to be the perpetuation rather than the amelioration of American slavery.

Later, just before the Civil War, the scheme of migration to Africa or elsewhere was revived and agents sent out to South America, Haiti and Africa. After the Civil War and the disappointments of Reconstruction came Bishop Turner's proposal and recently the crazy scheme of Marcus Garvey. The hard facts which killed all these proposals were first lack of training, education and habits on the part of ex-slaves which unfitted them to be pioneers; and mainly that tremendous industrial expansion of Europe which made colonies in Africa or elsewhere about the last place where colored folk could successfully seek freedom and equality.

These extreme plans tended always to fade to more moderate counsel. First came the planned inner migration of the Negro group: to Canada, to the North, to the West, to cities everywhere. This has been a vast and continuing movement, affecting millions and changing and modifying the Negro problems. One result has been a new system of racial integrations. Groups of Negroes in their own clubs and organizations, in their own neighborhoods and schools, were formed, and were not so much the result of deliberate planning as the rationalization of the segregation into which they were forced by racial prejudice. These groups became physical and spiritual cities of refuge, where sometimes the participants were inspired to efforts for social uplift, learning and ambition; and sometimes reduced to sullen wordless resentment. It is toward this sort of group effort that the thoughts and plans of Booker T. Washington led. He did not advocate a deliberate and planned segregation, but advised submission to segregation in settlement and in work, in order that this bending to the will of a powerful majority might bring from that majority gradually such sympathy and sense of justice that in the long run the best interests of the Negro group would be served; particularly as those interests were, he thought, inseparable from the best interests of the dominant group. The difficulty here was that unless the dominant group saw its best interests bound up with those of the black minority, the situation was hopeless; and in any case the danger was that if the minority ceased to agitate and resist oppression it would grow to accept it as normal and inevitable.

A *third* path of the advance which lately I have been formulating and advocating can easily be mistaken for a program of complete racial segregation and even nationalism among Negroes. Indeed it has been criticized as such. This is a misapprehension. First, ignoring other racial separations, I have stressed the economic discrimination as fundamental and advised concentration of planning here. We need sufficient income for health and home; to supplement our education and recreation; to fight our own crime problem; and above all to finance a continued, planned and intelligent agitation for political, civil and social equality. How can we Negroes in the United States gain such average income as to be able to attend to these pressing matters? The cost of this program must fall first and primarily on us, ourselves. It is silly to expect any large number of whites to finance a program which the overwhelming majority of whites today fear and reject. Setting up as a bogey-man an assumed proposal for an absolute separate Negro economy in America, it has been easy for colored philosophers and white experts to dismiss the matter with a shrug and a laugh. But this is not so easily dismissed. In the first place we have already got a partially segregated Negro economy in the United States. There can be no question about this. We not only build and finance Negro churches, but we furnish a considerable part of the funds for our segregated schools. We furnish most of our own professional services in medicine, pharmacy, dentistry and law. We furnish some part of our food and clothes, our home building and repairing and many retail services. We furnish books and newspapers; we furnish endless personal services like those of barbers, beauty shop keepers, hotels, restaurants. It may be said that this inner economy of the Negro serves but a small proportion of its total needs; but it is growing and expanding in various ways; and what I propose is to so plan and guide it as to take advantage of certain obvious facts.

It is of course impossible that a segregated economy for Negroes in the United States should be complete. It is quite possible that it could never cover more than the smaller part of the economic activities of Negroes. Nevertheless, it is also possible that this smaller part could be so important and wield so much power that its influence upon the total economy of Negroes and the total industrial organization of the United States would be decisive for the great ends toward which the Negro moves.

We are of course obsessed with the vastness of the industrial machine in America, and with the way in which organized wealth dominates our whole government, our education, our intellectual life and our art. But despite this, the American economic class structure—that system of domination of industry and the state through income and monopoly—is breaking down; not simply in America but in the world. We have reached the end of an economic era, which seemed but a few years ago omnipotent and eternal. We have lived to see the collapse of capitalism. It makes no difference what we may say, and how we may boast in the United States of the failures and changed objectives of the New Deal, and the prospective rehabilitation of the rule of finance capital; that is but wishful thinking. In Europe and in the United States as well as in Russia the whole organization and direction of industry is changing. We are not called upon to be dogmatic as to just what the end of this change will be and what form the new organization will take. What we are sure of is the present fundamental change.

There faces the American Negro therefore an intricate and

subtle problem of combining into one object two difficult sets of facts: his present racial segregation which despite anything he can do will persist for many decades; and his attempt by carefully planned and intelligent action to fit himself into the new economic organization which the world faces.

This plan of action would have for its ultimate object, full Negro rights and Negro equality in America; and it would most certainly approve, as one method of attaining this, continued agitation, protest and propaganda to that end. On the other hand my plan would not decline frankly to face the possibility of eventual emigration from America of some considerable part of the Negro population, in case they could find a chance for free and favorable development unmolested and unthreatened, and in case the race prejudice in America persisted to such an extent that it would not permit the full development of the capacities and aspirations of the Negro race. With its eyes open to the necessity of agitation and to possible migration, this plan would start with the racial grouping that today is inevitable and proceed to use it as a method of progress along which we have worked and are now working. Instead of letting this segregation remain largely a matter of chance and unplanned development, and allowing its objects and results to rest in the hands of the white majority or in the accidents of the situation, it would make the segregation a matter of careful thought and intelligent planning on the part of Negroes.

The object of that plan would be two-fold: first to make it possible for the Negro group to await its ultimate emancipation with reasoned patience, with equitable temper and with every possible effort to raise the social status and increase the efficiency of the group. And secondly and just as important, the ultimate object of the plan is to obtain admission of the colored group to co-operation and incorporation into the white group on the best possible terms.

This planned and deliberate recognition of self-segregation on the part of colored people involves many difficulties which have got to be faced. First of all, in what lines and objects of effort should segregation come? This choice is not wide, because so much segregation is compulsory: most colored children, most colored youth, are educated in Negro schools and by Negro teachers. There is more education by race today than there was in the latter part of the nineteenth century; partly because of increased racial consciousness, and partly because more Negroes are applying for education and this would call for larger social contact than ever before, if whites and Negroes went to the same schools.

On the other hand this educational segregation involves, as Negroes know all too well, poorer equipment in the schools and poorer teaching than colored children would have if they were admitted to white schools and treated with absolute fairness. It means that their contact with the better-trained part of the nation, a contact which spells quicker acculturation, is lessened and shortened; and that above all, less money is spent upon their schools. They must submit to double taxation in order to have a minimum of decent equipment. The Rosenwald school houses involved such double taxation on the Negro. The Booker T. Washington High School in Atlanta raises thousands of dollars each year by taxation upon colored students and parents, while city funds furnish only salaries, buildings, books and a minimum of equipment. This is the pattern throughout the South. On the other hand with the present attitude of teachers and the public, even if colored students were admitted to white schools, they would not in most cases receive decent treatment nor real education.

It is not then the theory but a fact that faces the Negro in education. He has group education in large proportion and he must organize and plan these segregated schools so that they become efficient, well-housed, well-equipped, with the best of teachers and with the best results on the children; so that the illiteracy and bad manners and criminal tendencies of young Negroes can be quickly and effectively reduced. Most Negroes would prefer a good school with properly paid colored teachers for educating their children, to forcing their children into white schools which met them with injustice and humiliation and discouraged their efforts to progress.

So too in the church, the activities for ethical teaching, character-building, and organized charity and neighborliness, which are largely concentrated in religious organizations, are segregated racially more completely than any other human activity; a curious and eloquent commentary upon modern

Christianity. These are the facts and the colored church must face them. It is facing them only in part today because a large proportion of the intelligent colored folk do not co-operate with the church and leave the ignorant to make the church a seat of senseless dogma and meaningless ceremonies together with a multitude of activities which have no social significance and lead to no social betterment. On the other hand the Negro church does do immense amounts of needed works of charity and mercy among the poor; but here again it lacks funds.

There has been a larger movement on the part of the Negro intelligentsia toward racial grouping for the advancement of art and literature. There has been a distinct plan for reviving ancient African art through an American Negro art movement; and more especially a thought to use the extremely rich and colorful life of the Negro in America and elsewhere as a basis for painting, sculpture and literature. This has been partly nullified by the fact that if these new artists expect support for their art from the Negro group itself, that group must be deliberately trained and schooled in art appreciation and in willingness to accept new canons of art and in refusal to follow the herd instinct of the nation. Instead of this artistic group following such lines, it has largely tried to get support for the Negro art movement from the white public often with disastrous results. Most whites want Negroes to amuse them; they demand caricature; they demand jazz; and torn between these allegiances: between the extraordinary reward for entertainers of the white world, and meager encouragement to honest self-expression, the artistic movement among American Negroes has accomplished something, but it has never flourished and never will until it is deliberately planned. Perhaps its greatest single accomplishment is Carter Woodson's "Negro History Week."

In the same way there is a demand for a distinct Negro health movement. We have few Negro doctors in proportion to our population and the best training of Negro doctors has become increasingly difficult because of their exclusion from the best medical schools of America. Hospitalization among Negroes is far below their reasonable health needs and the individual medical practitioner depending upon fees is the almost universal pattern in this group. What is needed is a carefully planned and widely distributed system of Negro hospitals and socialized medicine with an adequate number of doctors on salary, with the object of social health and not individual income. "Negro Health Week," originating in Tuskegee, is a step in this direction. The whole planned political program of intelligent Negroes is deliberate segregation of their vote for Negro welfare. William L. Dawson, former alderman of Chicago, recently said, "I am not playing Party politics but race politics"; he urged, irrespective of party, adherence to political groups interested in advancing the political and economic rights of the Negro.

The same need is evident in the attitude of Negroes toward Negro crime; obsessed by the undoubted fact that crime is increased and magnified by race prejudice, we ignore the other fact that we have crime and a great deal of it and that we ourselves have got to do something about it; what we ought to do is to cover the Negro group with the services of legal defense organizations in order to counteract the injustice of the police and of the magistrate courts; and then we need positive organized effort to reclaim young and incipient malefactors. There is little organized effort of that sort among Negroes today, save a few Negro reformatories with meager voluntary support and grudging state aid.

From all the foregoing, it is evident that economic planning to insure adequate income is the crying need of Negroes today. This does not involve plans that envisage a return to the old patterns of economic organization in America and the world. This is the American Negro's present danger. Most of the well-to-do with fair education do not realize the imminence of profound economic change in the modern world. They are thinking in terms of work, thrift, investment and profit. They hope with the late Booker T. Washington to secure better economic conditions for Negroes by wider chances of employment and higher wages. They believe in savings and investment in Negro and in general business, and in the gradual evolution of a Negro capitalist class which will exploit both Negro and white labor.

The younger and more intelligent Negroes, realizing in different degrees and according to their training and acquaintance with the modern world the profound economic change through which the world is passing and is destined to pass, have taken three different attitudes: first, they have been confronted with the Communist solution of present social difficulties. The Communist philosophy was a program for a majority, not for a relatively small minority; it presupposed a class structure based on exploitation of the overwhelming majority by an exploiting minority; it advised the seizure of power by this majority and the future domination of the state by and for this majority through the dictation of a trusted group, who would hold power until the people were intelligent and experienced enough to rule themselves by democratic methods.

This philosophy did not envisage a situation where instead of a horizontal division of classes, there was a vertical fissure, a complete separation of classes by race, cutting square across the economic layers. Even if on one side this color line, the dark masses were overwhelmingly workers, with but an embryonic capitalist class, nevertheless the split between white and black workers was greater than that between white workers and capitalists; and this split depended not simply on economic exploitation but on a racial folk-lore grounded on centuries of instinct, habit and thought and implemented by the conditioned reflex of visible color. This flat and incontrovertible fact, imported Russian Communism ignored, would not discuss. American Negroes were asked to accept a complete dogma without question or alteration. It was first of all emphasized that all racial thought and racial segregation must go and that Negroes must put themselves blindly under the dictatorship of the Communist Party.

American Communists did thoroughly and completely obliterate the color bar within their own party ranks, but by so doing, absolutely blocked any chance they might have had to attract any considerable number of white workers to their ranks. The movement consequently did not get far. First, because of the natural fear of radical action in a group made timid through the heredity of slavery; but also and mainly because the attempt to abolish American race prejudice by a phrase was impossible even for the Communist Party. One result of Communistic agitation among Negroes was, however, far-reaching; and that was to impress the younger intellectuals with the fact that American Negroes were overwhelmingly workers, and that their first duty was to associate themselves with the white labor movement, and thus seek to bridge the gap of color, and eradicate the deep-seated racial instincts.

This formed a second line of action, more in consonance with conservative Negro thought. In accordance with this thought and advice and the pressure of other economic motives, Negro membership in labor unions has increased and is still increasing. This is an excellent development, but it has difficulties and pitfalls. The American labor movement varies from closed skilled labor groups, who are either nascent capitalists or stooges, to masses of beaten, ignorant labor outcasts, quite as helpless as the Negroes. Moreover among the working white masses the same racial repulsion persists as in the case of other cultural contacts. This is only natural. The white laborer has been trained to dislike and fear black labor; to regard the Negro as an unfair competitor, able and willing to degrade the price of labor; and even if the Negro prove a good union man, his treatment as an equal would involve equal status, which the white laborer through his long cultural training bitterly resents as a degradation of his own status. Under these circumstances the American Negro faces in the current labor movement, especially in the A F of L and also even in the CIO, the current racial patterns of America.

To counteract this, a recent study of Negro unionism suggests that like the Jews with their United Hebrew Trades, so the Negroes with a United Negro Trades should fight for equality and opportunity within the labor ranks. This illustrates exactly my plan to use the segregation technique for industrial emancipation. The Negro has but one clear path: to enter the white labor movement wherever and whenever he can; but to enter fighting still within labor ranks for recognition and equal treatment. Certainly unless the Negro by his organization and discipline is in position to bring to the movement something beside ignorance, poverty and ill-health, unionization in itself is no panacea.

There has come a third solution which is really a sophisticated attempt to dodge the whole problem of color in economic change; this proposal says that Negroes should join the labor movement, and also so far as possible should join themselves to capital and become capitalists and employers; and in this way, gradually the color line will dissolve into a class line between employers and employees.

Of course this solution ignores the impending change in capitalist society and hopes whatever that change may be, Negroes will benefit along with their economic class. The difficulty here is threefold: not only would there be the same difficulties of the color line in unions, but additional difficulties and exclusion when Negroes as small capitalists seek larger power through the use of capital and credit. The color bar there is beyond present hope of scaling. But in addition to that, this plan will have inserted into the ranks of the Negro race a new cause of division, a new attempt to subject the masses of the race to an exploiting capitalist class of their own people. Negro labor will be estranged from its own intelligentsia, which represents black labor's own best blood; upper class Negroes and Negro labor will find themselves cutting each other's throats on opposite sides of a desperate economic battle, which will be but replica of the old battle which the white world is seeking to outgrow. Instead of forging ahead to a new relation of capital and labor, we would relapse into the old discredited pattern.

It seems to me that all three of these solutions are less hopeful than a fourth solution and that is a racial attempt to use the power of the Negro as a consumer not only for his economic uplift but in addition to that, for his economic education. What I propose is that into the interstices of this collapse of the industrial machine, the Negro shall search intelligently and carefully and farsightedly plan for his entrance into the new economic world, not as a continuing slave but as an intelligent free man with power in his hands.

I see this chance for planning in the role which the Negro plays as a consumer. In the future reorganization of industry the consumer as against the producer is going to become the key man. Industry is going to be guided according to his wants and needs and not exclusively with regard to the profit of the producers and transporters. Now as a consumer the

Negro approaches economic equality much more nearly than he ever has as producer. Organizing then and conserving and using intelligently the power which twelve million people have through what they buy, it is possible for the American Negro to help in the rebuilding of the economic state.

The American Negro is primarily a consumer in the sense that his place and power in the industrial process is low and small. Nevertheless, he still has a remnant of his political power and that is growing not only in the North but even in the South. He has in addition to that his economic power as a consumer, as one who can buy goods with some discretion as to what goods he buys. It may truly be said that his discretion is not large but it does exist and it may be made the basis of a new instrument of democratic control over industry.

The cultural differentiation among American Negroes has considerably outstripped the economic differences, which sets this group aside as unusual and at the same time opens possibilities for institutional development and changes of great importance. Fundamental in such change would be the building up of new economic institutions suited to minority groups without wide economic differences, and with distinct cultural possibilities.

The fact that the number of Negro college graduates has increased from 215 between 1876 and 1880 to 10,000 between 1931 and 1935 shows that the ability is there if it can act. In addition to mental ability there is demanded an extraordinary moral strength, the strength to endure discrimination and not become discouraged; to face almost universal disparagement and keep one's soul; and to sacrifice for an ideal which the present generation will hardly see fulfilled. This is an unusual demand and no one can say off-hand whether or not the present generation of American Negroes is equal to it. But there is reason to believe that if the high emotional content of the Negro soul could once be guided into channels that promise success, the end might be accomplished.

Despite a low general level of income, Negroes probably spend at least one hundred and fifty million a month under ordinary circumstances, and they live in an era when gradually economic revolution is substituting the consumer as the decisive voice in industry rather than the all-powerful producer of the past. Already in the Negro group the consumer interest is dominant. Outside of agriculture the Negro is a producer only so far as he is an employee and usually a subordinate employee of large interests dominated almost entirely by whites. His social institutions, therefore, are almost entirely the institutions of consumers and it is precisely along the development of these institutions that he can move in general accordance with the economic development of his time and of the larger white group, and also in this way evolve unified organization for his own economic salvation.

The fact is, as the Census of 1930 shows, there is almost no need that a modern group has which Negro workers already trained and at work are not able to satisfy. Already Negroes can raise their own food, build their own homes, fashion their own clothes, mend their own shoes, do much of their repair work, and raise some raw materials like tobacco and cotton. A simple transfer of Negro workers, with only such additional skills as can easily be learned in a few months, would enable them to weave their own cloth, make their own shoes, slaughter their own meat, prepare furniture for their homes, install electrical appliances, make their own cigars and cigarettes.

Appropriate direction and easily obtainable technique and capital would enable Negroes further to take over the whole of their retail distribution, to raise, cut, mine and manufacture a considerable proportion of the basic raw material, to man their own manufacturing plants, to process foods, to import necessary raw materials, to invent and build machines. Processes and monopolized natural resources they must continue to buy, but they could buy them on just as advantageous terms as their competitors if they bought in large quantities and paid cash, instead of enslaving themselves with white usury.

Large numbers of other Negroes working as miners, laborers in industry and transportation, could without difficulty be transferred to productive industries designed to cater to Negro consumers. The matter of skill in such industries is not as important as in the past, with industrial operations massed and standardized.

Without doubt, there are difficulties in the way of this program. The Negro population is scattered. The mouths which the Negro farmers might feed might be hundreds or thousands of miles away, and carpenters and mechanics would have to be concentrated and guaranteed a sufficiency of steady employment. All this would call for careful planning and particularly for such an organization of consumers as would eliminate unemployment, risk and profit. Demand organized and certain must precede the production and transportation of goods. The waste of advertising must be eliminated. The difference between actual cost and selling price must disappear, doing away with exploitation of labor which is the source of profit.

All this would be a realization of democracy in industry led by consumers' organizations and extending to planned production. Is there any reason to believe that such democracy among American Negroes could evolve the necessary leadership in technique and the necessary social institutions which would so guide and organize the masses that a new economic foundation could be laid for a group which is today threatened with poverty and social subordination?

In this process it will be possible to use consumers' organizations already established among the whites. There are such wholesale and manufacturing plants and they welcome patronage; but the Negro co-operative movement cannot rest here. If it does, it will find that quite unconsciously and without planning, Negroes will not be given places of authority or perhaps even of ordinary co-operation in these wider institutions; and the reason will be that white co-operators will not conceive it probable that Negroes could share and guide this work. This the Negro must prove in his own wholesale and manufacturing establishments. Once he has done this and done it thoroughly, there will gradually disappear much of the discrimination in the wider co-operative movement. But that will take a long time.

Meantime, this integration of the single consumers' co-operative into wholesales and factories will intensify the demand for selected leaders and intelligent democratic control over them—for the discovery of ability to manage, of character, of absolute honesty, of inspirational push not toward power but toward efficiency, of expert knowledge in the technique of production and distribution and of scholarship in the past and present of economic development. Nor is this enough. The eternal tendency of such leadership is, once it is established, to assume its own technocratic right to rule, to begin to despise the mass of people who do not know, who have no idea of difficulties of machinery and processes, who succumb to the blandishments of the glib talker, and are willing to select people not because they are honest and sincere but because they wield the glad hand.

Now these people must not be despised, they must be taught. They must be taught in long and lingering conference, in careful marshaling of facts, in the willingness to come to decision slowly and the determination not to tyrannize over minorities. There will be minorities that do not understand. They must patiently be taught to understand. There will be minorities who are stubborn, selfish, self-opinionated. Their real character must be so brought out and exhibited until the overwhelming mass of people who own the co-operative movement and whose votes guide and control it will be able to see just exactly the principles and persons for which they are voting.

The group can socialize most of its professional activities. Certain general and professional services they could change from a private profit to a mutual basis. They could mutualize in reality and not in name, banking and insurance, law and medicine. Health can be put upon the same compulsory basis that we have tried in the case of education, with universal service under physicians paid if possible by the state, or helped by the state, or paid entirely by the group. Hospitals can be as common as churches and used to far better advantage. The legal profession can be socialized and instead of being, as it is now, a defense of property and of the anti-social aggressions of wealth, it can become as it should be, the defense of the young, poor, ignorant and careless.

Banking should be so arranged as to furnish credit to the honest in emergencies or to put unneeded savings to useful and socially necessary work. Banking should not be simply and mainly a method of gambling, theft, tyranny, exploitation and profit-making. Our insurance business should cease to be, as it so largely is, a matter of deliberate gambling and become a co-operative service to equalize the incidence of misfortune equitably among members of the whole group without profit to anybody.

Negroes could not only furnish pupils for their own schools and colleges, but could control their teaching force and policies, their textbooks and ideals. By concentrating their demand, by group buying and by their own plants they could get Negro literature issued by the best publishers without censorship upon expression and they could evolve Negro art for its own sake and for its own beauty and not simply for the entertainment of white folk.

The American Negro must remember that he is primarily a consumer; that as he becomes a producer, it must be at the demand and under the control of organized consumers and according to their wants; that in this way he can gradually build up the absolutely needed co-operation in occupations. Today we work for others at wages pressed down to the limit of subsistence. Tomorrow we may work for ourselves, exchanging services, producing an increasing proportion of the goods which we consume and being rewarded by a living wage and by work under civilized conditions. This will call for self-control. It will eliminate the millionaire and even the rich Negro; it will put the Negro leader upon a salary which will be modest as American salaries go and yet sufficient for a life under modern standards of decency and enjoyment. It will eliminate also the pauper and the industrial derelict.

To a degree, but not completely, this is a program of segregation. The consumer group is in important aspects a self-segregated group. We are now segregated largely without reason. Let us put reason and power beneath this segregation. Here comes tremendous opportunity in the Negro housing projects of New York, Chicago, Atlanta and a dozen other centers; in re-settlement projects like the eight all-Negro farmers' colonies in six Southern states and twenty-three rural projects in twelve states. Rail if you will against the race segregation here involved and condoned, but take advantage of it by planting secure centers of Negro co-operative effort and particularly of economic power to make us spiritually free for initiative and creation in other and wider fields, and for eventually breaking down all segregation based on color or curl of hair.

There are unpleasant eventualities which we must face even if we succeed. For instance, if the Negro in America is successful in welding a mass or large proportion of his people into groups working for their own betterment and uplift, they will certainly, like the Jews, be suspected of sinister designs and inner plotting; and their very success in cultural advance be held against them and used for further and perhaps fatal segregation. There is, of course, always the possibility that the plan of a minority group may be opposed to the best interests of a neighboring or enveloping or larger group; or even if it is not, the larger and more powerful group may think certain policies of a minority are inimical to the national interests. The possibility of this happening must be taken into account.

The Negro group in the United States can establish, for a large proportion of its members, a co-operative commonwealth, finding its authority in the consensus of the group and its intelligent choice of inner leadership. It can see to it that not only no action of this inner group is opposed to the real interests of the nation, but that it works for and in conjunction with the best interests of the nation. It need draw no line of exclusion so long as the outsiders join in the consensus. Within its own group it can, in the last analysis, expel the anti-social and hand him over to the police force of the nation. On the other hand it can avoid all appearance of conspiracy, of seeking goals incompatible with the general welfare of the nation, it can court publicity, it can exhibit results, it can plead for co-operation. Its great advantage will be that it is no longer as now attempting to march face forward into walls of prejudice. If the wall moves, we can move with it; and if it does not move it cannot, save in extreme cases, hinder us.

Have we the brains to do this?

Here in the past we have easily landed into a morass of criticism, without faith in the ability of American Negroes to extricate themselves from their present plight. Our former panacea emphasized by Booker T. Washington was flight of class from mass in wealth with the idea of escaping the masses or ruling the masses through power placed by white capitalists into the hands of those with larger income. My own panacea of earlier days was flight of class from mass through the development of a Talented Tenth; but the power of this aristocracy of talent was to lie in its knowledge and character and not in its wealth. The problem which I did not then attack was that of leadership and authority within the group, which by implication left controls to wealth—a contingency of which I never dreamed. But now the whole economic trend of the world has changed. That mass and class must unite for the world's salvation is clear. We who have had least class differentiation in wealth, can follow in the new trend and indeed lead it.

Most Negroes do not believe that this can be done. They not only share American public opinion in distrusting the inherent ability of the Negro group, but they see no way in which the present classes who have proven their intelligence and efficiency can gain leadership over their own people. On the contrary, they fear desperately a vulgarization of emerging culture among them, by contact with the ignorant and antisocial mass. This fear has been accentuated by recent radical agitation; unwashed and unshaven black demagogues have scared and brow-beaten cultured Negroes; have convinced them that their leadership can only be secured through demagoguery. It is for this reason that we see in large Northern centers like Chicago and New York, intelligent, efficient Negroes conniving with crime, gambling and prostitution, in order to secure control of the Negro vote and gain place and income for black folk. Their procedure is not justified by the fact that often excellent and well-trained Negro officials are thus often raised to power. The price paid is deliberate surrender of any attempt at acculturation of the mass in exchange for increased income among the few.

Yet American Negroes must know that the advance of the Negro people since emancipation has been the extraordinary success in education, technique and character among a small number of Negroes and that the emergence of these exceptional men has been largely a matter of chance; that their triumph proves that down among the mass, ten times their number with equal ability could be discovered and developed, if sustained effort and sacrifice and intelligence were put to this task. That, on the contrary, today poverty, sickness and crime are choking the paths to Negro uplift, and that salvation of the Negro race is to come by planned and sustained efforts to open ways of development to those who now form the unrisen mass of the Negro group.

That this can be done by force, by the power of wealth and of the police is true. Along that path of progress most of the nineteenth century acculturation of the masses of men has come; but it has been an unsatisfactory, unsteady method. It has not developed the majority of men to anywhere near the top of their possibilities, and it has pitifully submerged certain groups among whites, and colored groups, like Negroes in America, the West Indies and Africa. Here comes then a special chance for a new trial of democratic development without force among some of the worst victims of force. How can it be done? It can be done through consumers' groups and the mutual interests that these members have in the success of the groups. It can bring the cultured face to face with the untrained and it can accomplish by determined effort and planned foresight the acculturation of the many through the few, rather than the opposite possibility of pulling the better classes down through ignorance, carelessness, and crime.

It is to be admitted this will be a real battle. There are chances of failure, but there are also splendid chances of success. In the African communal group, ties of family and blood, of mother and child, of group relationship, made the group leadership strong, even if not always toward the highest culture. In the case of the more artificial group among American Negroes, there are sources of strength in common memories of suffering in the past; in present threats of degradation and extinction; in common ambitions and ideals; in emulation and the determination to prove ability and desert. Here in subtle but real ways the communalism of the African clan can be transferred to the Negro American group, implemented by higher ideals of human accomplishment through the education and culture which have arisen and may further arise through contact of black folk with the modern world. The emotional wealth of the American Negro, the nascent art in song, dance, and drama can all be applied, not to amuse the white audience, but to inspire and direct the acting Negro group itself. I can conceive no more magnificent nor promising crusade in modern times. We have a chance here to teach industrial and cultural democracy to a world that bitterly needs it.

A nation can depend on force and therefore carry through plans of capitalistic industry, or state socialism, or co-operative commonwealth, despite the opposition of large and powerful minorities. They can use police and the militia to enforce their will, but this is dangerous. In the long run force defeats itself. It is only the consensus of the intelligent men of good will in a community or in a state that really can carry out a great program with absolute and ultimate authority. And by that same token, without the authority of the state, without force of police and army, a group of people who can attain such consensus is able to do anything to which the group agrees.

It is too much to expect that any such guiding consensus will entirely eliminate dissent, but it will make agreement so overwhelming that eventual clear irrational dissent can safely be ignored. When real and open democratic control is intelligent enough to select of its own accord on the whole the best, most courageous, most expert and scholarly leadership, then the problem of democracy within the Negro group is solved and by that same token the possibility of American Negroes entering into world democracy and taking their rightful place according to their knowledge and power is also sure. Here then is the economic ladder by which the American Negro, achieving new social institutions, can move pari passu with the modern world into a new heaven and a new earth.

Chapter 8

PROPAGANDA AND WORLD WAR

My discussions of the concept of race, and of the white and colored worlds, are not to be regarded as digressions from the history of my life; rather my autobiography is a digressive illustration and exemplification of what race has meant in the world in the nineteenth and twentieth centuries. It is for this reason that I have named and tried to make this book an autobiography of race rather than merely a personal reminiscence, with the idea that peculiar racial situation and problems could best be explained in the life history of one who has lived them. My living gains its importance from the problems and not the problems from me.

Nothing illustrates this more than my experiences from the time I left Atlanta until the period of reconstruction after the first World War. These days were the climacteric of my pilgrimage. I had come to the place where I was convinced that science, the careful social study of the Negro problems, was not sufficient to settle them; that they were not basically, as I had assumed, difficulties due to ignorance but rather difficulties due to the determination of certain people to suppress and mistreat the darker races. I believed that this evil group formed a minority and a small minority of the nation and of all civilized peoples, and that once the majority of well-meaning folk realized their evil machinations, we would be able to secure justice.

A still further step I was not yet prepared to realize must be taken: not simply knowledge, not simply direct repression of evil, will reform the world. In long, indirect pressure and action of various and intricate sorts, the actions of men which are not due to lack of knowledge nor to evil intent, must be changed by influencing folkways, habits, customs and subconscious deeds. Here perhaps is a realm of physical and cosmic law which science does not yet control. But of all this in 1910 I had no clear concept. It took twenty more years of living and striving to bring this revolution to my thought. Stepping, therefore, in 1910, out of my ivory tower of statistics and investigation, I sought with bare hands to lift the earth and put it in the path in which I conceived it ought to go. Little did I realize in August, 1910, that the earth was about to be shaken with earthquake, deluged with blood, whipped and starved into disaster, and that race hate and wholesale color and group subordination, not only was a prime cause of this disaster, but emphasized and sharpened its course and hindered consequent recovery.

These were the years between the Roosevelts, including the administration of Taft, the two reigns of Wilson, the interlude of Harding and Coolidge and the disaster of Hoover. The United States was living not to itself, but as part of the strain and stress of the world. I knew something of Europe in these days. I went to the Paris Exposition in 1900 with the stipend that I had received for an exhibit on Negro development prepared in my office. By grace of an English friend, Frances Hoggan, I roamed through England, Scotland and a bit of France in 1906 on a bicycle and saw the Island of Skye and Edinburgh, the Lake and Shakespeare countries and London. I saw a Europe of past beauty and present culture, fit as I fondly dreamed to realize a democracy in which I and my people could find a welcome place.

I came home rested and ready to follow the steps that led from the Niagara Movement meeting of 1906 to the Negro conference of 1909. These steps were not only the indirect ones illustrated by the difficulty of raising money for the Atlanta work, but also the series of events which led to the New York conference. Lynching continued in the United States but raised curiously enough little protest. Three hundred twenty-seven victims were publicly murdered by the mob during the years 1910 to 1914, and in 1915 the number leaped incredibly to one hundred in one year. The pulpit, the social reformers, the statesmen continued in silence before the greatest affront to civilization which the modern world has known. In 1909 William English Walling and his wife Anna Strunsky went out to investigate a lynching and anti-Negro riot in Springfield, Illinois, the birthplace of Abraham Lincoln. The upheaval took place on the one hundredth anniversary of his birth. Eventually one hundred seventeen indictments were brought in against the rioters but there was almost no actual punishment.

Walling protested in the press. He asked America if the time had not come when the work of the Great Emancipator must be finished and the Negro race not simply in law and theory, but in fact, set free. Working with Mary White Ovington, Charles Edward Russell and Oswald Garrison Villard, after meetings and correspondence, he and others called a conference in New York City. The timeliness of such a conference and such action was manifest by the formation of the Niagara Movement in 1905 and its great meeting at Harper's Ferry in 1906. Heartened and at the same time warned by the Niagara Movement, the conference of 1909 invited the members of that body to participate. They were heartened by the fact that young radical opinion among Negroes saw the necessity of immediate organized intelligent effort to complete the emancipation of the Negro; but they were also warned that this radical movement had been initiated in direct opposition to the policy and action of the greatest Negro leader since the Civil War. To a degree never before accomplished, this Negro had united liberal opinion North and South in friendliness for the Negro and it was doubtful if any organization could make headway on an anti-Washington platform. The Niagara Movement itself had made little progress, beyond its inspirational fervor, toward a united and constructive program of work.

It was therefore not without misgiving that the members of the Niagara Movement were invited into the new conference, but all save Trotter and Ida Wells Barnett came to form the backbone of the new organization. In 1910 this was incorporated as the National Association for the Advancement of Colored People. It was inevitable that I should be offered an executive position in this organization; but there again many felt that I must not be allowed to direct its policy too openly against Mr. Washington and that the work which I did should as far as possible be a continuation of what I had done in studying the American Negro and making his accomplishment known.

This was in direct accord with my own desires and plans. I did not wish to attack Booker Washington; I wished to give him credit for much good, but to oppose certain of his words and policies which could be interpreted against our best interests; I wanted to do this through propaganda of the truth and for this reason I wished to continue in New York so far as possible my studies in Atlanta, and to add to this a periodical of fact and agitation which I should edit.

I tried to accomplish this with help of the Slater Fund and actually edited the four last studies of the Atlanta series from New York with the collaboration of Augustus Dill who succeeded me in Atlanta. But President Ware was strongly advised to cut the University off from the National Association for the Advancement of Colored People entirely, and did so in 1915. The studies ceased in 1917.

I arrived in New York to find a bare office; the treasurer, Mr. Villard, said frankly: "I don't know who is going to pay your salary; I have no money." The secretary then in charge was alarmed about her own job and suspicious of my designs; and a generally critical, if not hostile, public expected the National Association to launch a bitter attack upon Booker T. Washington and Tuskegee. I placated the secretary by disclaiming any design or desire for executive work; and I heartened the treasurer, a newspaper man, by my plan to publish a periodical which should be the organ of the Association. There was, however, opposition to this. First of all, magazines of this sort were costly and the organization had no money. Secondly, organs are usually of doubtful efficiency. My good friend, Albert E. Pillsbury, then Attorney-General of Massachusetts, wrote feelingly: "If you have not decided upon a periodical, for heaven's sake don't. They are as numerous as flies." And he meant, to conclude, about as useful.

My first job was to get the *Crisis* going; and arriving on August 1, 1910, I finally got the first copy off the press in November. Later I had the collaboration and advice of a young English woman, Mary McLean, then staff writer for the Sunday edition of the New York *Times*. I owe her more than I can say. The *Crisis* came at the psychological moment and its success was phenomenal. From the one thousand which I ventured to publish first, it went up a thousand a month until by 1918 (due, of course, to special circumstances) we published and sold over a hundred thousand.

In November, 1913, and at my earnest solicitation, Augustus

G. Dill, who had succeeded me at Atlanta University, left his academic work and came to be business manager of the *Crisis* magazine. From then until early in 1928 he gave to the work his utmost devotion and to him was due much of its phenomenal business success. In five years the *Crisis* became self-supporting, January 1, 1916, with an annual income increasing from $6,500 in 1911 to $24,000 in 1915. Its total income during these years was over $84,000, and it circulated nearly a million and a half copies, net paid circulation. It reached every state in the Union, beside Europe, Africa, and the South Seas.

With this organ of propaganda and defense and with its legal bureau, lecturers and writers, the National Association for the Advancement of Colored People was able to organize one of the most effective assaults of liberalism upon prejudice and reaction that the modern world has seen. We secured extraordinary helpers: great lawyers like Moorfield Storey and Louis Marshall; earnest liberals like Milholland, John Haynes Holmes, and Jane Addams; sympathetic friends from the whole land.

Naturally the real and effective work of the organization was done by the group which centered in the office first at 20 Vesey Street, and then at 70 Fifth Avenue, where we stayed until Ginn and Company's Southern patrons forced us to move to 69. These persons were assiduous in their attendance, unfailing in their interest, and gave a large amount of their time to the work. As a result the organization was not a secretary-dominated center, with the power in the hands of one man. It was an intelligent group of considerable size which was willing and eager to learn and help.

There was one initial difficulty common to all interracial effort in the United States. Ordinarily the white members of a committee formed of Negroes and whites become dominant. Either by superior training or their influence or their wealth they take charge of the committee, guide it and use the colored membership as their helpers and executive workers in certain directions. Usually if the opposite policy is attempted, if the Negroes attempt to dominate and conduct the committee, the whites become dissatisfied and gradually withdraw. In the NAACP it was our primary effort to achieve an equality of racial influence without stressing race and without allowing undue predominance to either group. I think we accomplished this for a time to an unusual degree.

The members studied the situations. They were expert in various lines of inquiry and effort, once we had settled down to effective work. The outstanding members of this inner group were Oswald Garrison Villard, Mary Ovington, William English Walling, Paul Kennaday, Joel Spingarn, and Charles Edward Russell. Villard became chairman of the board but in 1913 was not wholly in agreement with me and was replaced by a young man to whom I have dedicated this book and who stands out vividly in my mind as a scholar and a knight.

With the combined aid of these workers and many others, we could, through the *Crisis* and our officers, our secretaries and friends, place consistently and continuously before the country a clear-cut statement of the legitimate aims of the American Negro and the facts concerning his condition. We began to organize his political power and make it influential and we started a campaign against lynching and mob law which was the most effective ever organized and eventually brought the end of the evil in sight. Especially we gained a series of court victories before the highest courts of the land which perhaps never have been equaled; beginning with the overthrow of the vicious "Grandfather Clauses" in 1916 and the breaking of the backbone of residential segregation in 1917.

One of the first difficulties that the National Association met was bound to be the matter of its attitude toward Mr. Washington. I carefully tried to avoid any exaggeration of differences of thought; but to discuss the Negro question in 1910 was to discuss Booker T. Washington and almost before we were conscious of the inevitable trends, we were challenged from Europe. Mr. Washington was in Europe in 1910 and made some speeches in England on his usual conciliatory lines. John Milholland, who had been so dominant in the organization of the National Association, immediately wrote me and said that American Negroes must combat the idea that they were satisfied with conditions. I, therefore, wrote an appeal to England and Europe, under the signature of a group of colored friends so as not to involve the NAACP officially:

"If Mr. Booker T. Washington, or any other person, is giving the impression abroad that the Negro problem in America is in process of satisfactory solution, he is giving an impression which is not true. We say this without personal bitterness toward Mr. Washington. He is a distinguished American and has a perfect right to his opinion. But we are compelled to point out that Mr. Washington's large financial responsibilities have made him dependent on the rich charitable public and that, for this reason, he has for years been compelled to tell, not the whole truth, but that part of it which certain powerful interests in America wish to appear as the truth. In flat contradiction, however, to the pleasant pictures thus pointed out, let us not forget that the consensus of opinion among eminent European scholars who know the race problem in America, from De Tocqueville to Von Halle, De Laveleys, Archer and Johnston, is that it forms the gravest of American problems. We black men who live and suffer under present conditions, and who have no reason, and refuse to accept reasons for silence, can substantiate this nearly unanimous testimony."

In further emphasis of this statement and in anticipation of the meeting of the proposed Races Congress, Mr. Milholland arranged that I should go early to London and make some addresses. The plan simmered down to an address before the Lyceum Club, the leading woman's club of London. There it encountered opposition. An American woman member wrote: "I think there is serious objection to entertaining Dr. Du Bois at the Lyceum." The result was an acrimonious controversy from which I tried to withdraw gently but was unable. Finally led by Her Highness, the then Ranee of Sarawak and Dr. Etta Sayre, a luncheon was held at the Lyceum Club with a bishop and two countesses; several knights and ladies, and men like Maurice Hewlett and Sir Harry Johnston; I was the chief speaker.

The Races Congress, held in July, 1911, in London, would have marked an epoch in the cultural history of the world, if it had not been followed so quickly by the World War. As it was, it turned out to be a great and inspiring occasion, bringing together representatives of numerous ethnic and cultural groups, and new and frank conceptions of the scientific bases of racial and social relations of people.

The congress was planned with meticulous care and thoroughness by the clear-sighted Gustav Spiller, the organizer, working under the auspices of the English Ethical Culture movement. The papers of the Congress were printed and put into the hands of the delegates before the meeting and yet kept from general publication. An extraordinary number of distinguished persons took part and, together with Felix Adler, I was named as co-secretary to represent the United States. To be sure the Congress encountered a certain air of questioning and lack of high official sanction. There were even those in England who professed to think that it had something to do with horse-racing; but even papers like the *Times* had to notice its impressive meetings and the caliber of the participants. There were dramatic incidents like the arraignment of Christianity by the delegate from Ceylon, "where every prospect pleases and only man is vile."

I had not only my regular assigned part, but due to the sudden illness of Sir Harry Johnston from his chronic tropical fever, represented him at one of the chief sessions and made a speech which gained wide reading. Thus I had a chance twice to address the Congress and I wrote one of the two poems which greeted the assembly:

> Save us, World-Spirit, from our lesser selves,
> Grant us that war and hatred cease,
> Reveal our souls in every race and hue;
> Help us, O Human God, in this Thy Truce,
> To make Humanity divine.

Even while the Races Congress was meeting came the forewarning of coming doom: in a characteristic way a German war vessel sailed into an African port, notifying the world that Germany was determined to have larger ownership and control of cheap black labor; a demand camouflaged as the need of "a place in the sun." I fancied at the time that I knew my Europe pretty well, but familiarity with the dangers of the European scene had bred contempt of disaster. I thought with other philosophers that a general European war was impossible. The economic and cultural strands among the nations had grown too strong to be snapped by war. World peace, world organization, conference and conciliation, the gradual breaking down of trade barriers, the spread of civilization to backward peoples, the emancipation of suppressed groups like the American Negro—seem to me the natural, the inevitable path of world progress. I did not assess at the right value the envy and jealousy of those imperial powers which did not share profit in colored labor, nor did I realize that the intertwining threads of culture bound colored folk in slavery to, and not in mutual co-operation with, the whites.

Indeed it was not easily possible for the student of international affairs trained in white institutions and by European ideology to follow the partially concealed and hidden action of international intrigue, which was turning colonial empire into the threat of armed competition for markets, cheap materials and cheap labor. Colonies still meant religious and social uplift in current propaganda. There were indications of strain in the determination of Germany to increase her sea power and to rival England in the technique of her manufactures. It was evident that the understanding between England and France both in Africa and in Asia was relegating Germany to a second place in colonial imperialism. It was evident too that the defeat of Russia by Japan had given rise to a fear of colored revolt against white exploitation.

The general outlines of this I had followed, but like most of the world I was thrown into consternation when later with sudden and unawaited violence, world war burst in 1914. I had come to New York and the editorship of the *Crisis* during the administration of Taft. William Taft, fat, genial and mediocre, had no grasp of world affairs nor international trends. Despite his Philippine experience, he began his reactionary administration by promising the South that he would appoint no Federal official to whom the Southern people were opposed; and thus blandly announced that eight million black Southerners were not people. Not only this but his handling of the revolt of irritated and goaded black soldiers at Brownsville, Texas, and his general cynical attitude toward the race problem led me to one of my first efforts to make political solution of the race problem.

Returning to New York after the Races Congress, I was faced by the political campaign of 1912. Disappointed at the attitude of Taft, I turned eagerly toward Roosevelt and the "Bull Moose" movement, thinking that I saw there a splendid chance for a third party movement, on a broad platform of votes for Negroes and the democratization of industry. Sitting in the office of the *Crisis*, I wrote out a proposed plank for the Progressives to adopt at their Chicago meeting in 1912: "The Progressive Party recognizes that distinctions of race or class in political life have no place in a democracy. Especially does the party realize that a group of 10,000,000 people who have in a generation changed from a slave to a free labor system, re-established family life, accumulated $1,000,000,000 of real property, including 20,000,000 acres of land, and reduced their illiteracy from 80 to 30 per cent, deserves and must have justice, opportunity and a voice in their own government. The party, therefore, demands for the Americans of Negro descent the repeal of unfair discriminatory laws and the right to vote on the same terms on which other citizens vote."

This was taken to Chicago by my friend and fellow official of the NAACP, Joel Spingarn, and supported by two other directors of the Association, Dr. Henry Moskowitz and Jane Addams. They worked in vain for its adoption. Theodore Roosevelt would have none of it. He told Mr. Spingarn frankly that he should be careful of "that man Du Bois," who was in his opinion a "dangerous" person. The "Bull Moose" convention not only refused to adopt a plank anything like this, but refused to seat most of the colored delegates. They elected a Southern "lily-white" to run on the ticket with Mr. Roosevelt, and finally succeeded in splitting the Republican Party and giving Woodrow Wilson an opportunity of becoming President of the United States.

Immediately Bishop Walters of the African Zion Church, who had joined the Democratic Party in 1909, approached me with the idea that Mr. Wilson might be influenced in the Negro's behalf. I proposed, if he could, to throw the weight of the *Crisis* against Roosevelt and Taft, and for Wilson. Bishop

Walters went to see Wilson. He secured from him in October, 1912, a categorical expression over his signature "of his earnest wish to see justice done the colored people in every matter; and not mere grudging justice, but justice executed with liberality and cordial good feeling. . . . I want to assure them that should I become President of the United States they may count upon me for absolute fair dealing, for everything by which I could assist in advancing the interests of their race in the United States."

I espoused the cause of Woodrow Wilson, fully aware of the political risk involved and yet impelled to this path by the reaction of Taft and disappointment at Roosevelt. I resigned from New York Local No. 1 of the Socialist Party which I had joined, to escape discipline for not voting the Socialist ticket. I could not let Negroes throw away votes. I wrote in the *Crisis* just before the election: "We sincerely believe that even in the face of promises disconcertingly vague, and in the face of the solid caste-ridden South, it is better to elect Woodrow Wilson President of the United States and prove once for all if the Democratic Party dares to be democratic when it comes to black men. It has proven that it can be in many Northern states and cities. Can it be in the nation? We hope so, and we are willing to risk a trial."

We estimated that in the North a hundred thousand black voters had supported Woodrow Wilson in 1912, and had been so distributed in strategic places as to do much to help his election. This was an unusually successful effort to divide the Negro vote; but as many Negroes had feared it brought disappointment and encouraged unexpected reaction. Among minor indications of this reaction was Wilson's odd demand of Bishop Walters. The Bishop had been called to the White House for consultation concerning the colored people in 1915. "By the way," said the President, " what about that letter that I wrote you during the campaign. I do not seem to remember it." "I have it right here," said the Bishop eagerly, and handed it to him. The President forgot to return it.

With the accession of Woodrow Wilson to the presidency in 1913 there opened for the American Negro a period, lasting through and long after the World War and culminating in 1919, which was an extraordinary test for their courage and a time of cruelty, discrimination and wholesale murder. For this there were several causes: the return to power for the first time since the Civil War of the Southern Democracy; secondly, the apprehension and resentment aroused in the South by the campaign of the NAACP; but above and beyond that, the rising economic rivalry between colored and white workers in the United States and back of this the whole economic stress of the modern world with its industrial imperialism.

The Southern white workers had for years been lashed into enmity against the Negro by Tillman, Vardaman, Blease, and Jeff Davis of Arkansas. Representatives of these Southern workers, now seated in Congress, proceeded to demand stricter legal and economic caste; and at the meeting of Wilson's first Congress there came the greatest flood of bills proposing discriminatory legislation against Negroes that has ever been introduced into an American Congress. There were no less than twenty bills advocating "Jim Crow" cars in the District of Columbia, race segregation of Federal employees, excluding Negroes from commissions in the army and navy, forbidding the intermarriage of Negroes and whites, and excluding all immigrants of Negro descent.

Quite suddenly the program for the NAACP, which up to this time had been more or less indefinite, was made clear and intensive. Every ounce of effort was made not only against lynching and segregation, but against this new proposed discriminatory legislation in Congress and in a dozen different states, where with evident collusion similar legislation had been proposed. Most of this legislation was eventually killed; in only one state was such a measure—an anti-intermarriage bill—passed; but in Washington one proposal was put through by executive order: Wilson proceeded to segregate nearly all of the colored Federal employees, of whom there were a considerable number, herding them so far as possible in separate rooms with separate eating and toilet facilities. This was a serious reversal of Federal usage and despite repeated assaults, much of this segregation still remains in the departments of the national capital. When the militant Monroe Trotter headed a delegation to protest to the President this segregation of colored officeholders, Wilson angrily dismissed him, declaring his language "insulting."

We found that our political efforts were abortive for a reason which, while possible, did not seem to us probable. We had calculated that increased independence in the Negro vote would bring a bid for the Negro vote from opposing parties; but it did not until many years later. Indeed, it was not until the re-election of the second Roosevelt in 1936 that the Negro vote in the North came to be eagerly contended for by the two major parties. In 1914 we tried to make congressional candidates declare themselves as to our demands, but were only partially successful. The Sixty-fourth Congress saw eleven bills introduced advocating color caste and the state legislatures continued to be bombarded by similar legislation. Thus, in 1916, we found ourselves politically helpless. We had no choice. We could vote for Wilson who had segregated us or for Hughes who, despite all our requests, remained doggedly dumb on our problems.

The spread of disaster throughout the world shown by the Chinese Revolution of 1912 and the Balkan War of 1913, and the World War of 1914, was illustrated in the United States by the meeting of the National Conference of Charities and Correction in Memphis in May, 1914. Not only were there no accommodations for colored delegates, but the conference refused even to put in the agenda anything touching the race problem. As a result, Joel Spingarn, William Pickens and myself went down to Memphis and advertised during the conference a public meeting "for all persons who love the truth and dare to hear it." A large crowd of persons black and white, including many delegates to the conference, were present.

For sometime after the opening of the World War, its possible influence upon the Negro race in America was not clear. However, this world convulsion found America spiritually ill-prepared to cope with it, so far as race difficulties were concerned. In 1912 there arose the agitation for residential race segregation. It grew out of the fact that Negroes, as they increased in intelligence and property holding, were dissatisfied with the living quarters, where by long custom they had been confined in the chief cities of the land. In Baltimore came one of their first efforts to buy their way out of the back alleys and the slums into the better-paved, better-lighted main streets. This movement was encouraged by the wish of many of the owners of this property to move to newly developed suburban districts. A fierce conflict developed and Baltimore, by city ordinance, proceeded to segregate Negroes by law. This agitation throughout the North was increased by the emigration of Southern Negroes. Cheap foreign labor had been cut off by the war and Northern manufacturers began to encourage migration from the South. The stream began as soon as the European war opened. It caused not only increasing congestion in the colored districts of the North; it also began to deplete the supply of agricultural labor and common city labor in the South, and to encourage racial friction according to current social patterns.

Beginning in Baltimore this agitation with a series of ordinances and laws spread West, North and South. For a period of ten years it called for every resource and ingenuity on the part of the National Association for the Advancement of Colored People to fight the legislation in courts, to repel mob violence on home-buyers, and to seek a supporting white public opinion.

But all this was but a prelude to deeper and more serious race oppression. The United States seized Haiti in 1915. It was not alone the intrinsic importance of the country, but Haiti stood with Liberia as a continuing symbol of Negro revolt against slavery and oppression, and capacity for self-rule; and the sudden extinction of its independence by a President whom we had helped to elect, followed by exploitation at the hands of New York City banks and plundering speculators, and the killing of at least three thousand Haitians by American soldiers, was a bitter pre-war pill.

That same year occurred another, and in the end, much more insidious and hurtful attack: the new technique of the moving picture had come to America and the world. But this method of popular entertainment suddenly became great when David Griffith made the film "The Birth of a Nation." He set the pace for a new art and method: the thundering horses, the masked riders, the suspense of plot and the defense of innocent womanhood; all this was thrilling even if melodramatic and overdrawn. This would have been a great step in the development of a motion-picture art, if it had not happened that the director deliberately used as the vehicle of his picture one of the least defensible attacks upon the Negro race, made by Thomas Dixon in his books beginning with the "Leopard's Spots," and in his play "The Clansman." There was fed to the youth of the nation and to the unthinking masses as well as to the world a story which twisted the emancipation and enfranchisement of the slave in a great effort toward universal democracy, into an orgy of theft and degradation and wide rape of white women.

In combating this film, our Association was placed in a miserable dilemma. We had to ask liberals to oppose freedom of art and expression, and it was senseless for them to reply: "Use this art in your own defense." The cost of picture making and the scarcity of appropriate artistic talent made any such immediate answer beyond question. Without doubt the increase of lynching in 1915 and later was directly encouraged by this film. We did what we could to stop its showing and thereby probably succeeded in advertising it even beyond its admittedly notable merits. The combined result of these various events caused a sudden increase of lynching. The number of mob murders so increased that nearly one hundred Negroes were lynched during 1915 and a score of whites, a larger number than had occurred for more than a decade.

The year 1916 brought one decided note of hope. The Supreme Court of the United States, after having dodged the plain issue for a decade, finally at our insistence and with the help of our corps of lawyers headed by Moorfield Storey, handed down a decision which outlawed the infamous "Grandfather Clauses" of the disfranchising constitutions of the South. These clauses had given an hereditary right to vote to white illiterates while excluding colored illiterates. To overbalance this sign of hope there came, however, continued prevalence of lynching in unusually serious form. Five Negroes in Lee County, Georgia, were lynched en masse and there came the horrible public burning of Jesse Washington in Waco, Texas, before a mob of thousands of men, women and children. "While a fire was being prepared of boxes, the naked boy was stabbed and the chain put over the tree. He tried to get away, but could not. He reached up to grab the chain and they cut off his fingers. The big man struck the boy on the back of the neck with a knife just as they were pulling him up on the tree. Mr. —— thought that was practically the death blow. He was lowered into the fire several times by means of the chain around his neck. Someone said they would estimate the boy had about twenty-five stab wounds, each one of them death-dealing."

In October, Anthony Crawford, well-to-do colored farmer of South Carolina, worth $20,000, and the owner of four hundred acres of land, was set upon and whipped for "impudence" in refusing to agree to a price for his cotton seed; he was then jailed, mobbed, mutilated and killed, and his family driven out of the county.

The death of Booker Washington in 1915 coincided with a change in Negro attitudes. The political defeat of Roosevelt and Taft had deprived Mr. Washington of his political influence. The Tuskegee Machine gradually ceased to function, and Tuskegee came to realize its natural place as a center of education rather than of propaganda. For some time Mr. Washington's general influence among American Negroes, especially in the face of the rising importance of the NAACP and the *Crisis*, had waned. Once he had said a word seeming to condone residential segregation which raised a storm; but on the whole the Washington controversy began to subside. The morning that I heard of Mr. Washington's death I knew that an era in the history of the American Negro had ended, and I wrote:

"The death of Mr. Washington marks an epoch in the history of America. He was the greatest Negro leader since Frederick Douglass, and the most distinguished man, white or black, who has come out of the South since the Civil War. His fame was international and his influence far-reaching. Of the good that he accomplished there can be no doubt: he directed the attention of the Negro race in America to the pressing necessity of economic development; he emphasized technical education, and he did much to pave the way for an understanding between the white and the darker races.

"On the other hand, there can be no doubt of Mr. Washington's mistakes and shortcomings: he never adequately grasped the growing bond of politics and industry; he did not understand the deeper foundations of human training, and his basis of better understanding between white and black was founded on caste.

"We may generously and with deep earnestness lay on the grave of Booker T. Washington, testimony of our thankfulness for his undoubted help in the accumulation of Negro land and property, his establishment of Tuskegee and spreading of industrial education, and his compelling of the white South to think at least of the Negro as a possible man. On the other hand, in stern justice, we must lay on the soul of this man a heavy responsibility for the consummation of Negro disfranchisement, the decline of the Negro college and public school, and the firmer establishment of color caste in this land."

By the middle of the year 1916, it was evident to thinking people that the American Negroes were achieving a unity in thought and action, partly caused by the removal of Mr. Washington's powerful personality and partly because of pressure of outward circumstances. This realization was not entirely voluntary on our part; it was forced upon us by the concentration of effort and unity of thought which rising race segregation, discrimination and mob murder were compelling us to follow. We had to stand together; we were already in 1916 standing together to an extent unparalleled since Reconstruction. Joel Spingarn was among the first to realize this and he proposed to call in August a conference of persons interested in the race problem at his beautiful home Troutbeck, in the peace and quiet of Amenia, where once John Burroughs dreamed and wrote. Here colored and white men of all shades of opinion might sit down, and rest and talk, and find agreement so far as possible with regard to the Negro problems.

The Amenia Conference, as Spingarn conceived it, was to be "under the auspices of the NAACP," but wholly independent of it, and the invitations definitely said this. They were issued by Mr. Spingarn personally, and the guests were assured that they would not be bound by any program of the NAACP. Thus the Conference was intended primarily to bring about as large a degree as possible of unity of purpose among Negro leaders and to do this regardless of its effect upon any organization, although, of course, most of us hoped that some central organization and preferably the NAACP would eventually represent this new united purpose.

One can hardly realize today how difficult and intricate a matter it was to arrange such a conference, to say who should come and who should not, to gloss over old hurts and enmities. About two hundred invitations to white and colored people were actually issued, and sixty or more persons expressed their willingness to attend, including not only many founders of the Niagara Movement, but close personal friends of Booker Washington. There were messages of good will from many who could not attend: from Taft, Roosevelt, Hughes, Woodrow Wilson, and others.

I doubt if ever before so small a conference of American Negroes had so many colored men of distinction who represented at the same time so complete a picture of all phases of Negro thought. Its very completeness in this respect was its salvation. If it had represented one party or clique it would have been less harmonious. As it was, we all learned what the majority of us knew. None of us in the present pressure of race hate could afford to hold uncompromising and unchangeable views. It was, after all, a matter of emphasis. We all believed in thrift, we all wanted the Negro to vote, we all wanted the laws enforced, we all wanted to abolish lynching, we all wanted assertion of our essential manhood; but how to get these things—there, of course, must be wide divergence of opinion.

The Conference marked the beginning of the new era. As we said in our resolutions: "The Amenia Conference believes that its members have arrived at a virtual unanimity of opinion in regard to certain principles and that a more or less definite result may be expected from its deliberations."

Probably on account of our meeting the Negro race was more united and more ready to meet the problems of the world than it could possibly have been without these beautiful days of understanding. How appropriate that so fateful a thing should have taken place in the midst of so much quiet and beauty, in a place of poets and fishermen, of dreamers and farmers, a place far apart and away from the bustle of the world and the centers of activity.

As if in anticipation of the whirl of circumstances and stress of soul through which the next few years were to thrust me, at the very beginning of the year 1917, I went down into the valley of the shadow of death. Save for typhoid fever at the age of seventeen, I had never been sick, but now a serious operation was indicated and a second one seemed advisable following fast upon the first. I came to know what hospitals and the magic of modern surgery were. I lay for two or three weeks shrouded by the curtains of pain and then arose apparently as strong as ever, if not stronger, for the fight ahead. I needed my strength for the fight came with a surge.

Finally and in a sense inevitably, the World War actually touched America. With our participation and in anticipation of it came an extraordinary exacerbation of race hate and turmoil. Beginning with increased lynchings in 1915, there came in 1916 lynching, burning and murder. In 1917 came the draft with its discrimination and mob rule; in 1918, the turmoil and discrimination of actual war; and finally in 1919 the worst experience of mob law and race hate that the United States had seen since Reconstruction.

The war was preceded by a spy scare—a national psychosis of fear that German intrigue would accomplish among Negroes that disloyalty and urge toward sabotage and revenge which their situation and treatment would certainly justify. It was not so much that this fear had any real support in fact; it was rather that it had every justification in reason. It was succeeded by witch-hunting—feverish endeavor to find out who dared to think differently from the increasingly major thought of the nation. Not only did Germans suffer and other foreigners, but Negroes were especially suspected. Suspicious state and Federal agents invaded even the offices of the *Crisis* and the National Association for the Advancement of Colored People and asked searching questions: "Just what, after all, were our objects and activities?" I took great satisfaction in being able to sit back in my chair and answer blandly, "We are seeking to have the Constitution of the United States thoroughly and completely enforced." It took some ingenuity, even for Southerners, to make treason out of that.

Then came the refusal to allow colored soldiers to volunteer into the army; but we consoled ourselves there by saying,

"Why should we want to fight for America or America's friends; and how sure could we be that America's enemies were our enemies too?" With the actual declaration of war in April, 1917, and the forced draft May 18, the pattern of racial segregation which our organization had been fighting from the beginning was written into law and custom. The races by law must be mustered and trained separately. Eighty-three thousand Negro draftees, raised at the first call, had to go into separate units, and so far as possible, separate encampments. Hundreds of colored unfortunates found themselves called with no place prepared where they could be legally received. Colored militia units already enrolled in the North were sent South to be insulted and kicked in Southern cantonments, while thousands of draftees were engulfed in a hell of prejudice and discrimination. Not only that, but hundreds of Negroes were drafted regardless of their home duties and physical health. The government had to dismiss the Draft Board of Atlanta in a body for flagrant and open race discrimination. When sent to camp, a concerted effort was made to train Negro draftees as laborers and not as soldiers. There have been few periods in the history of the American Negro when he has been more discouraged and exasperated.

The National Association fought with its back to the wall and with all its energies, failing in some cases, and in some cases having conspicuous and unexpected success. From the beginning of the war, however, the efforts of the Association involved, in a sense, a retreat from the high ideal toward which it aimed and yet a retreat absolutely necessary and pointing the way to future deployment of its forces in the offensive against race hate. The situation arose in our attempt to secure decent treatment in encampments for colored draftees; to see that a reasonable proportion of them went to the front as soldiers bearing arms, and not merely as laborers; and to assure, above all, that some Negroes should act as commissioned officers in the army.

The opposition to Negro officers was intense and bitter; but on the other hand, the administration was alarmed. After all, this nation, with its diverse ethnic elements, with a large number of Germans and Slavs who at best could not be enthusiastic supporters of the Allies, did not dare further to complicate the situation by driving ten million Negroes into justifiable protest and opposition.

In May a conference of Negro organizations called in Washington adopted resolutions which I wrote: "We trace the real cause of this World War to the despising of the darker races by the dominant groups of men, and the consequent fierce rivalry among European nations in their effort to use darker and backward people for purposes of selfish gain regardless of the ultimate good of the oppressed. We see permanent peace only in the extension of the principle of government by the consent of the governed, not simply among the smaller nations of Europe, but among the natives of Asia and Africa, the Western Indies and the Negroes of the United States."

Efforts at last were made to placate the Negroes. First they were given a representative in Washington in the person of Emmett Scott, formerly private secretary to Booker T. Washington; Mr. Scott was without actual power, but he had access to the Secretary of War so as to be able to lay before him directly complaints voiced by the Negroes. Negroes were promised enrollment not merely as stevedores, but as actual soldiers, and also two full divisions of Negro soldiers, the Ninety-second and Ninety-third, were planned. Immediately this brought up the question of Negro officers.

In the so-called Ninety-third Division, a number of Negro units from the organized state militia who had been drafted into the war, already had Negro officers. Two regiments of draftees with white officers were added, and these units were early hurried to France and incorporated with French troops. The complete organization of this Ninety-third Division was never actually accomplished and most of the higher Negro officers were gradually dismissed on various excuses.

On the other hand, the Ninety-second Division of Negro draftees was actually organized and immediately a demand arose for Negro officers over these troops. The official answer was a decided negative: there were no trained Negro officers—or at most, only two or three; there were no camps where new Negro officers could be trained and it was illegal under the draft law to train them in camps with white officers.

Our Association itself here hesitated. It had fought segregation and discrimination in the army valiantly, but lost. Then when, as the only alternative, we must accept a separate officers' training camp or no Negro officers, many members demurred at openly advocating segregation. Had it not been for Joel Spingarn, chairman of our Board, no Negro officers would have been trained or appointed. But Spingarn started a country-wide crusade, aided wholeheartedly by the *Crisis*. First of all, he got the Negro students interested. He spoke at Howard and corresponded with students at Fisk, Atlanta, and elsewhere. They arose en masse to demand a Negro officers' camp and the campus of Howard was even offered as a place for it.

The War Department squirmed. We had to fight even to be segregated. We fell out among ourselves. A large and important section of the Negro press led by the *Afro-American* and the *Chicago Defender* firmly opposed a Negro officers' camp on any terms. We struggled from March until May, and then suddenly a camp was opened for the training of Negro officers at Des Moines, Iowa.

The man eminently fitted and almost selected by fate for the heading of this camp was a black man, Charles Young, then lieutenant-colonel in the regular United States Army. He had an unblemished army record and a splendid character. He had recently accompanied Pershing in the Mexican foray and received distinguished commendation from the future commander-in-chief of the American Expeditionary Force. He was strong, fit, and only 49 years of age, and in the accelerated promotion of war-time would have been a general in the army by 1918. This, of course, the army did not propose to have, and although the Des Moines camp was established in May, the medical board of the army in June, when Young came up for examination for his colonelcy, hastened to retire him for "high blood pressure." It was a miserable ruse. An entire corps of white officers was appointed to train the colored cadets. Only colored captains and lieutenants were to be trained; the high officers were to be white.

Even then our difficulties were not finished; there was segregation against the cadets within and without their camp. General Ballou tried to lay down certain general rules as to what Negroes should strive for. A three-months period of training ensued. At the end of that time, after hesitation, it was decided to add another month. There was widespread suspicion that the War Department did not intend actually to commission these officers. I went down to Washington and talked with the Secretary of War, Newton Baker. He said coldly, "We are not trying by this war to settle the Negro problem." "True," I retorted, "but you are trying to settle as much of it as interferes with winning the war."

Finally, October 14, 1917, six hundred thirty-nine Negro officers were commissioned: 106 captains, 329 first lieutenants and 204 second lieutenants. It was as Champ Clark, Speaker of the House, said, a "new day" for the Negro and despite all we had been through, we felt tremendously uplifted.

In the very hour of our exaltation, the whirlwind struck us again; or perhaps I might better say, throughout this period the succession of uplift and downfall was continuous and bewildering. The very month that the Des Moines camp was authorized, a Negro was publicly burned alive in Tennessee under circumstances unusually atrocious. The mobbing and burning were publicly advertised in the press beforehand. Three thousand automobiles brought the audience, including mothers carrying children. Ten gallons of gasoline were poured over the wretch and he was burned alive, while hundreds fought for bits of his body, clothing, and the rope.

The migration of Negro workers out of the South had increased steadily. It was opposed by illegal and legal methods throughout the South, but by 1917 it had expanded to a stream and from my own travel and observation, I calculated that during the year at least a quarter of a million workers had migrated from South to North. In July came the first Northern repercussion in the East St. Louis riot, when one hundred twenty-five Negroes were killed by their white fellow laborers; their homes looted and destroyed; and hundreds of others maimed. It was a riot notable for its passion, cruelty and obvious economic motive.

In helpless exasperation we turned to symbolism and staged in New York City, and on Fifth Avenue, a silent parade to protest against mobs and lynching. Many hesitated to join us, but thousands fell in line, men, women, and children, headed by the officials of the National Association and other prominent Negroes.

In September of 1917 came another terrible occurrence arising out of the war. The Twenty-fourth colored Infantry of the regular army had been quartered at Houston, Texas. It was treated by the white population with discrimination and insult, and then kept from retaliating by being disarmed. Contrary to all army regulations, a soldier in Federal uniform could be insulted with impunity. At last some of these soldiers, goaded into desperation, broke into rioting, seized arms, and killed seventeen whites. As a result thirteen Negro soldiers were hanged, forty-one imprisoned for life, and forty others held for trial.

In my effort to reconstruct in memory my thought and the fight of the National Association for the Advancement of Colored People during the World War, I have difficulty in thinking clearly. In the midst of arms, not only laws but ideas are silent. I was, in principle, opposed to war. Everyone is. I pointed out in the *Atlantic Monthly* in 1915 how the partition of Africa was a cause of the conflict. Through my knowledge of Germany, I wished to see her militarism defeated and for that reason when America entered the war I believed we would in reality fight for democracy including colored folk and not merely for war investments.

But my main attention and interest was distracted from the facts of the war in Europe to the struggle of Color Caste in America and its repercussions on the conflict. Our partial triumph in this conflict often heartened me. I felt for a moment during the war that I could be without reservation a patriotic American. The government was making sincere efforts to meet our demands. They had commissioned over seven hundred Negro officers; we had been given representation in the Departments of War and Labor; the segregation ordinances had been mostly suppressed and even the Red Cross had reluctantly promised to use Negro nurses, although it later broke its word; Newton Baker, Secretary of War, tried to be fair and just; Wilson, overcoming long reluctance at last, spoke out against lynching. At other times I was bowed down and sickened by the public burnings, the treatment of colored troops and the widespread mob law.

At one of my periods of exaltation in July, 1918, after Negro officers had been commissioned, after news of achievement by our soldiers already in France began to come over the cables, and just as President Wilson was breaking his long silence on lynching, I wrote the editorial "Close Ranks."—"That which the German power represents today spells death to the aspirations of Negroes and all darker races for equality, freedom and democracy. Let us not hesitate. Let us, while this war lasts, forget our special grievances and close our ranks shoulder to shoulder with our own white fellow citizens and the allied nations that are fighting for democracy. We make no ordinary sacrifice, but we make it gladly and willingly with our eyes lifted to the hills."

The words were hardly out of my mouth when strong criticism was rained upon it. Who was I to talk of forgetting grievances, when my life had been given to protest against them? I replied in August, "First, This is Our Country: we have worked for it, we have suffered for it, we have fought for it; we have made its music, we have tinged its ideals, its poetry, its religion, its dreams; we have reached in this land our highest modern development and nothing, humanly speaking, can prevent us from eventually reaching here the full stature of our manhood. Our country is at war. The war is critical, dangerous and world-wide. If this is OUR country, then this is OUR war. We must fight it with every ounce of blood and treasure. . . . But what of our wrongs, cry a million voices with strained faces and bitter eyes. Our wrongs are still wrong. War does not excuse disfranchisement, 'Jim Crow' cars and social injustices, but it does make our first duty clear. It does say deep to the heart of every Negro American:—We will not bargain with our loyalty. We will not profiteer with our country's blood. We will not hesitate the fraction of a second when the God of Battles summons his dusky warriors to stand before the armposts of His Throne. Let them who call for sacrifice in this awful hour of Pain fight for the rights that should be ours; let them who make the laws writhe beneath each enactment that oppresses us,—but we? Our duty lies inexorable and splendid before us, and we shall not shirk."

I am less sure now than then of the soundness of this war

attitude. I did not realize the full horror of war and its wide impotence as a method of social reform. Perhaps, despite words, I was thinking narrowly of the interest of my group and was willing to let the world go to hell, if the black man went free. Today I do not know; and I doubt if the triumph of Germany in 1918 could have had worse results than the triumph of the Allies. Possibly passive resistance of my twelve millions to any war activity might have saved the world for black and white. Almost certainly such a proposal on my part would have fallen flat and perhaps slaughtered the American Negro body and soul. I do not know. I am puzzled.

The recent death of Joel Spingarn brings vividly to my mind the influence which he had at that time upon my thought and action. I do not think that any other white man ever touched me emotionally so closely as Joel Spingarn. He was one of those vivid, enthusiastic but clear-thinking idealists which from age to age the Jewish race has given the world. He had learned of the National Association for the Advancement of Colored People just after a crisis in his life and he joined us eagerly, ready for a new fight, a new thrill and new allegiances. I was both fascinated by his character and antagonized by some of his quick and positive judgments.

We fought each other continually in the councils of the Association, but always our admiration and basic faith in each other kept us going hand in hand. We disagreed over the editorial power which I should have in the conduct of the *Crisis* and yet the *Crisis* had no firmer friend than Spingarn. Of greatest influence on me undoubtedly was Spingarn's attitude toward the war. He was fired with consuming patriotism, he believed in America and feared Germany. He wanted me and my people not merely as a matter of policy, but in recognition of a fact, to join wholeheartedly in the war. It was due to his advice and influence that I became during the World War nearer to feeling myself a real and full American than ever before or since. Not only did Spingarn work for the better treatment of Negro soldiers, for the commissioning of Negro officers, but he himself took training at Plattsburg and entered the army as a major. He was assigned to the Intelligence Department in Washington and worked out a bold and far-sighted plan.

His basic idea was that his department would be a center for guiding the government into such an attitude and such action toward the Negroes that their loyalty, co-operation and sense of unity with the country would be assured. He urged on Secretary Baker not only the commissioning of Negro officers, but the placating of the Negro press and the appointment of Negroes to positions of authority in the government. He urged that President Wilson break his long silence and say a clear sharp word against lynching. Especially did he want me associated with him in his unit of the Intelligence Department, to be used for my firsthand knowledge of the American Negro and my ability to express their needs and plan a consistent program.

I was more than astonished when, June first, I was called to the War Department and asked if I would accept a captaincy in a bureau of the General Staff for the purpose "of far-reaching constructive effort to satisfy the pressing grievances of colored Americans." Urged by Spingarn, I replied that I would accept, provided that I could retain general oversight of the *Crisis* magazine. The military authorities saw no objection to this. But the board of directors of the NAACP, while recognizing that I ought and indeed must accept this offer, were not all of them convinced that I should retain control of the *Crisis*.

Fortunately the matter never came to an issue. Reaction and suspicion against Spingarn arose in the War Department. Late in 1917, his persistent energy and overwork had put him in the hospital and subjected him to a dangerous operation. On his recovery he had gone back to his project. Now, however, reluctance arose in Washington so far as I was concerned: many Negroes feared that once in the clutches of the war machine, my freedom of utterance would be curbed and instead of being able to influence the government toward a recognition of Negro rights, I would be reduced to the role of a cog in their organization of war spies. White Southern influence, on the other hand, was aghast when it learned from Negro sources just who it was that the War Department was about to add to its staff, and what my activities and words in the past had been. Spingarn was even urging that instead of being merely a captain I should be given from the first a commission as major, so as to be of equal rank with most of the fellow officers in his division. The final result was that the establishment of the new bureau was postponed since its broad scope might "lead beyond the proper limits of military activities." I was left to my work in the *Crisis* which was probably by far the best result; while Spingarn went to the front as major in the AEF.

In the midst of this phantasmagoria of war, race hate and mob-law, I finished fifty years of living. Life, with all its difficulties and disappointments, was still good. With all its bitter fruit I enjoyed it. Above all, my soul-child, the *Crisis*, prospered. In the years from 1916 to 1919, the *Crisis* expanded enormously, reaching one year a net paid circulation of over 100,000 copies. Its income in 1920 was over $77,000 and it had sold since 1910 four and a half million copies. This was the peak of its material prosperity.

During the year I had one of my curiously seldom intimate contacts with fellow human beings across the color line. In all this chronicle of the events of my life I have said little of interracial contact, because it was limited. At Atlanta University there were white teachers and we mingled freely and nearly forgot color differences. When I came to New York my acquaintance with white people was not large, and outside the pleasant and close contacts with co-workers in the office, I met white people chiefly as I lectured and attended conferences and committees, and at radical and Socialist dinners. Once in a while, I had tea in Miss Ovington's studio; more often Mary McLean and I sat in my office or in her rooms and planned the *Crisis*. It was only now and then that outside of the work of the Association, I was invited to or sought the company of white folk.

During the Races Congress in London, 1911, I had my broadest contact with white folk of position in the modern world. I met the kindly but rather ineffective Lord Weardale and was entertained at dinner by the Buxtons where I met Sir Roger Casement, afterward hanged. I came to know Fisher Unwin who married Cobden's daughter, and later I met H. G. Wells, whose friendship has lasted over many years. Mrs. Havelock Ellis became one of my acquaintances. I visited her cottage in the country and afterward she came to see me and dined with me in New York. I deeply enjoyed this social contact; but in America, I met little that was analogous. In part this was my own fault. I early assumed that most Americans did not wish my personal acquaintance or contact with me except in purely business relations, and that many of them would repay any approach on my part with deliberate insult, while most of them would be at least embarrassed. Probably I was often wrong in this assumption, but I was right often enough to prove to myself that my rule was wise and a great help to my own peace and quiet. Consequently on the street, in travel, in public assembly and the like, where I came in contact with white people, I spoke to them only when it was necessary, and then briefly. For the most part I did not speak at all, unless they addressed me. This whole assumption and attitude may be explained as arising from an inferiority complex; but it seems to me that in my case it was born mainly of humiliating experience, and involved on my part no attempt to conceal an inferiority of which I certainly was never consciously aware.

In 1918 I had a dinner in Boston with Glendower Evans, Margaret Deland and William James. It was small and intimate and thoroughly enjoyable. I would like to have known other and wider circles of Americans in this manner, but it was not easily possible. Only by something like accident and at long intervals did I emerge from my colored world. On my fiftieth birthday I was given a dinner which brought me in pleasant contact not only with many colored friends but with white folk, many of whom I did not think knew or appreciated my work. Up to this time I had never seen Theodore Roosevelt; but in November, 1918, I presided at a meeting in Carnegie Hall where he spoke together with Irvin Cobb and Knecht of the French High Commission. I remember my words of introduction. "I have the honor to present—Theodore Roosevelt." This was his last public speech.

Immediately after the Armistice came an unexpected change in my life program. Out of a clear sky the board of directors of the NAACP asked me to go to France for the purpose of investigating the treatment of Negro soldiers and for collecting and perfecting the historic record of their participation in the war. Already I and a number of Negroes in the United States had been talking of the advisability and necessity of having the American Negro and the Negroes of the world represented in some way before the Peace Congress. The problems of Africa were going to be discussed; the question of the color bar was coming up; but there was no provision, so far as we could see, to allow the Negro to speak for himself. We proposed sending delegates in some capacity, but at the time war restrictions made this impossible. When it was learned that I was to go, I was delegated to be their representative and I determined to call in Paris a Pan-African Congress.

Only quick and adroit work on the part of myself and friends got me the chance of joining the newspaper men on George Creel's press boat "Orizaba." There was every disposition to refuse me, even as a representative of the *Crisis* magazine. But it happened that President Wilson was sending on that same boat Robert R. Moton, principal of Tuskegee and successor to Booker T. Washington. His duty was to speak to the returning Negro soldiers, pacify them and forestall any attempt at agitation or open expression of resentment on their return to the United States. Under these circumstances my request also to go could hardly be denied.

Thus without premeditation I was thrown into direct touch with what I came later to know was the real crux of the problems of my time; and that is the widespread effort of white Europe to use the labor and material of the colored world for its own wealth and power. My plan to have Africa in some way voice its complaints to the world during the Peace Congress at Versailles, was an ambitious project conceived in time of war, without political backing and indeed without widespread backing of any kind. Had it not been for one circumstance, it would have utterly failed; and that circumstance was that black Africa had the right to send from Senegal a member to the French Parliament.

This member, Blaise Diagne, as high commissioner during the World War had caused a hundred eighty thousand black soldiers to come from Africa to Europe to stand the shock of the German onslaught in Flanders Field. He stood high in French public esteem. With infinite difficulty and with the studied opposition of America, I succeeded in getting through him the consent of Clemenceau to hold in February, 1919, at the Grand Hotel in Paris, a Pan-African Congress of fifty-seven delegates, including sixteen American Negroes, twenty West Indians, and twelve Africans. France, Belgium, and Portugal were represented by officials. The English government refused passports to English delegates, and the American Secretary of State assured Negro delegates that no congress would be held. My greatest helper in this Congress was Madame Calman-Levy, widow of the Paris publisher. This quiet, charming woman became enthusiastic over the idea of my Congress and brought together in her salon groups of interested persons including Otlet and Fontaine of Belgium and several French officials.

The results of this meeting were small. But it had some influence. I talked with Colonel House and a number of lower officials among the French, English and Portuguese. On the other hand, there came increasing disillusion. I saw the mud and dirt of the trenches; I heard from the mouths of soldiers the kind of treatment that black men got in the American army; I was convinced and said that American white officers fought more valiantly against Negroes than they did against the Germans. I still believe this was largely true. I collected some astonishing documents of systematic slander and attack upon Negroes and demands upon the French for insulting attitudes toward them. Not daring to transport these myself, I sent them to America in the hands of my friend, Frederic Howe. Later when I published these documents in America, the government started to interfere by refusing the *Crisis* mailing facilities. Then realizing that this was a partial confession of guilt, the Post Office withdrew its prohibition. We sold 100,000 copies that month.

The whole history of the American Negro and other black folk in the World War, has never been written. I collected while I was in France and since a mass of documents covering this episode in our history. They deserve publication, not simply as a part of the Negro's history, but as an unforgettable lesson in the spiritual lesions of race conflict during a critical period of American history. I hope sometime that a careful history based on these documents may see the light.

John Rolfe wrote that the last of August, 1619, there came

to Virginia "a dutch man of warre that sold us twenty Negars." These Negroes were not slaves and they were not the first Negroes who saw America; but their descendants became slaves and they formed the first permanent black settlers in the United States. As early as October, 1918, I planned a national Negro celebration of the Tercentenary of the landing of these Negroes; but alas, almost exactly three hundred years later there occurred race riots in Chicago and Washington which were among the worst in their significance that the Negro had encountered during his three hundred years of slavery and emancipation.

The year 1919 was for the American Negro one of extraordinary and unexpected reaction. This reaction had two main causes: first, the competition of emigrating Negro workers, pouring into Northern industry out of the South and leaving the Southern plantations with a shortage of their customary cheap labor. The other cause was the resentment of American soldiers, especially those from the South, at the recognition and kudos which Negroes received in the World War; and particularly their treatment in France. In the last case, the sex motive, the brutal sadism into which race hate always falls, was all too evident. The facts concerning the year 1919 are almost unbelievable as one looks back upon them today. During that year seventy-seven Negroes were lynched, of whom one was a woman and eleven were soldiers; of these, fourteen were publicly burned, eleven of them being burned alive.

That year there were race riots large and small in twenty-six American cities including thirty-eight killed in a Chicago riot of August; from twenty-five to fifty in Phillips County, Arkansas; and six killed in Washington. For a day, the city of Washington in July, 1919, was actually in the hands of a black mob fighting against the aggression of the whites with hand grenades.

The white secretary of the NAACP was mobbed in Texas in 1919, where he had gone for investigation and eventually resigned his position, because of the hopelessness of the race situation as he had viewed it. James Weldon Johnson, who had been our Field Secretary, was selected to succeed him. I hated to see the fine soul of a poet and litterateur thus dulled and frayed in the rough work of actual propaganda and agitation. Johnson made an excellent secretary, but at fatal cost to his health and strength. In Arkansas, despite the slaughter of Negroes, ninety-four other victims were arrested; twelve were condemned to death, and eighty sentenced to imprisonment. On top of that, not only did the agitation for residential segregation increase, but there was an open and wide revival of the Ku Klux Klan.

In north Georgia a reign of terror began. Governor Dorsey in April, 1921, called a conference of citizens in Atlanta and placed before them one hundred thirty-five examples of mistreatment of Negroes in Georgia within two years. He made no effort to collect all cases and said that if he had, the number could be multiplied. "In some counties the Negro is being driven out as though he were a wild animal; in others he is being held as a slave; in others no Negroes remain. In only two of the one hundred and thirty-five cases cited is the 'usual crime' against white women involved."

In 1919 the National Association staged a determined fight on lynching and concentrated all its energy in this direction. A national Conference on lynching was called in May, 1919, in New York City. The address to the nation was signed by one hundred fifty citizens including an ex-President of the United States, the attorney-general, governors of seven states, and heads of leading universities. The chief speaker at the Carnegie Hall meeting was the present Chief Justice of the United States. Mary Talbert started the anti-lynching crusade, raising a defense fund of $12,000; and James Weldon Johnson, secretary of the National Association for the Advancement of Colored People, succeeded in 1921 in forcing the Dyer Anti-lynching Bill on the attention of the Sixty-seventh Congress. Two thousand public meetings were held against lynching during that year and a thorough investigation of the causes of the Chicago riot was instigated and an investigation also headed by Mr. Johnson was made in Haiti where he charged that three thousand Haitians had been killed during the American occupation.

Meantime in the United States the battle of liberalism against race prejudice went on. I found myself trying to adjust war and post-war problems to the questions of racial justice; trying to show from the injustices of war time what the new vision must encompass; fighting mobs and lynching; encouraging Negro migration; helping woman suffrage; encouraging the new rush of young blacks to college; watching and explaining the political situation and traveling thousands of miles and lecturing in hundreds of centers.

The Dyer Anti-lynching Bill went through the House of Representatives and on to the floor of the Senate. There in 1924 it died with a filibuster and the abject surrender of its friends. It was not until years after that I knew what killed that anti-lynching bill. It was a bargain between the South and the West. By this bargain, lynching was let to go on uncurbed by Federal law, on condition that the Japanese be excluded from the United States.

Court cases kept pressing upon us: there were the Elaine riots and the Arkansas cases; there was the Sweet case in Detroit and, equally significant to my mind, although not to all my colleagues, the Sacco-Vanzetti case in Massachusetts. James Weldon Johnson, our secretary, raised from the public and the Garland Fund nearly $80,000 for a civil rights defense fund. We continued winning court victories, but somehow despite them, we did not seem to be getting far. We added to the "Grandfather" Case of 1916 and the Segregation Case of 1917 the victories in the Arkansas case, the white primary case and another segregation case in the high courts, in addition to the eventful freeing of Dr. Sweet and his family, who had been sentenced to death in Detroit for defending their home against a mob.

The most important work of the decade, as I now look back upon it, was my travel. Before 1918, I had made three trips to Europe; but now between 1918 and 1928 I made four more trips of extraordinary meaning: to France directly after the close of the war and during the Congress of Versailles; to England, Belgium, France and Geneva in the earliest days of the League of Nations; to Spain, Portugal and Africa in 1923 and 1924; and to Germany, Russia, and Constantinople in 1927. I could scarcely have encompassed a more vital part of the modern world picture than in those stirring journeys. They gave me a depth of knowledge and a breadth of view which was of incalculable value for realizing and judging modern conditions and, above all, the problem of race in America and in the world.

Chapter 9

REVOLUTION

AFTER THE WAR, with most Americans, I was seeking to return to normalcy. I tried three paths, one of which represented an old ideal and ambition, the development of literature and art among Negroes through my own writing and the encouragement of others. The second path was new and had arisen out of war; and that was the development of the idea back of the Pan-African Congress. The third idea was quite new, and proved in a way of greater importance in my thinking than even the other two; and that was the economic rehabilitation and defense of the American Negro after the change and dislocation of war. Of course, it would have been impossible for me successfully to follow more than one of these paths and indeed with my work on the *Crisis* and for the National Association, perhaps I could do nothing but experiment in all three; but I did think that I might point ways for others to follow.

It had always been my ambition to write; to seek through the written word the expression of my relation to the world and of the world to me. I had begun that writing early; while at Fisk I had an article tentatively accepted by the *Century*, although it was never actually printed. Later while in college I wrote for various colored periodicals. Then after my graduation from Harvard came my first book. This work had been my doctor's thesis which I had succeeded in some degree in transforming from a dry historical treatise into readable literature. That was published in 1896 and to my gratification was the first volume in the Harvard Historical Studies. It was followed in 1899 by the "Philadelphia Negro," a huge volume of five hundred pages but not unreadable. And from 1897 to 1914, the sixteen Atlanta University Studies which I edited and largely wrote appeared, each varying in size from pamphlet to volume. They covered more than two thousand pages. Then came, in 1903, my collection of essays called "The Souls of Black Folk," of which I have spoken.

In 1909, I published my biography of John Brown which I

regarded as one of the best things that I had done; but it met a curious fate. Unconsciously I had entrenched on the chosen field of a writer who controlled two powerful literary vehicles. He severely criticized the work, most unfairly as it seemed to me, and would give me no chance for rejoinder. In 1911, I tried my hand at fiction and published "The Quest of the Silver Fleece" which was really an economic study of some merit. Beginning in 1910, beside editing the *Crisis* continuously for twenty-three years, I published "The Negro," a sketch of racial history, in 1915; and a series of essays called "Darkwater" in 1920. In 1924, with the subvention of the publishing fund of the Knights of Columbus, I brought out "The Gift of Black Folk," basically sound as I believe, but too hurriedly done, with several unpardonable errors. The article on Georgia in "These United States" came the same year and a chapter in "The New Negro" in 1925. In 1928 came another novel, "Dark Princess," my favorite book. In addition to this I published a considerable number of magazine articles in many of the leading periodicals.

My writing up to this time and since has brought me but scant financial returns. From my twelve and more volumes I have not averaged altogether in forty years as much as five hundred dollars a year; but I have written what I wanted to say and not what men would rather hear. I have loved the writing and the chance to do it has fully repaid me and more.

More especially I tried to encourage other Negro writers through the columns of the *Crisis*. By 1920, we could point out that most of the young writers among American Negroes had made first publication in the columns of the *Crisis*. In the next few years we published work from Claude McKay, Langston Hughes, Jean Toomer, Countee Cullen, Anne Spencer, Abram Harris and Jessie Fauset. In 1924, through the generosity of Amy Spingarn, wife of Joel, we were enabled to offer a series of prizes for young Negro writers, and our contemporary, *Opportunity*, organ of the Urban League, offered similar prizes. For several years this competition went on until it grew into what has been called the renaissance of Negro literature, late in the twenties. Here again the World War and its aftermath balked us. No authentic group literature can rise save at the demand and with the support of the group which is calling for self-expression. The depression of industry, which came with a crash in 1929, was foreshadowed in the Negro group several years before, despite the apparent industrial boom. The circulation of the *Crisis* went down, the contributions to the National Association were curtailed and the New Negro literature was forced to place its dependence almost entirely upon a white audience and that audience had its own distinct patterns and preferences for Negro writing.

We were particularly proud to have had the chance to publish some bits of real literature; like that great poem of the black man's part in the war by Roscoe Jamison:

> These truly are the Brave,
> These men who cast aside
> Old memories, to walk the blood-stained pave
> Of Sacrifice, joining the solemn tide
> That moves away, to suffer and to die
> For Freedom—when their own is yet denied!
> O Pride! O Prejudice! When they pass you by,
> Hail them, the Brave, for you now crucified!

I sought to encourage the graphic arts not only by magazine covers with Negro themes and faces, but as often as I could afford, I portrayed the faces and features of colored folk. One cannot realize today how rare that was in 1910. The colored papers carried few or no illustrations; the white papers none. In many great periodicals, it was the standing rule that no Negro portrait was to appear and that rule still holds in some American periodicals. Through our "Men of the Month," our children's edition and our education edition, we published large numbers of most interesting and intriguing portraits.

In these days, 1920 and 1921, I made one effort toward which I look back with infinite satisfaction: an attempt in the *Brownie's Book* to furnish a little magazine for Negro children, in which my efforts were ably seconded by Augustus Dill and Jessie Fauset; it was really a beautiful publication, but it did not pay its way.

In another realm of art I made essay. From my childhood I have been impressed with the beauty of Negro skin-color and astonished at the blindness of whites who cannot see it. In addition I recognized, not perhaps so much a native Negro dramatic ability, as lack of those inhibitions which keep most folk from natural self-expression. Combining these two things, I believed that the pageant, with masses of costumed colored folk and a dramatic theme carried out chiefly by movement, dancing and music, could be made effective. I even hoped that such a movement might be placed on a paying basis. I tried first in 1913, when New York made an appropriation to celebrate the fiftieth anniversary of emancipation. The colored contractor who handled my printing was head of the new colored Tammany organization in Harlem. He put me on the celebration committee and through all kinds of difficulties, I wrote and staged an historic pageant of the history of the Negro race, calling it "The Star of Ethiopia." Before a total attendance of thirty thousand persons, we played it on the floor of an armory with three hundred fifty actors. Led by Charles Burroughs, they did scenes whose imagery and beauty have not often been surpassed.

Encouraged by this response I undertook in 1915 to reproduce this in Washington. We used the great ball field of the American League, a massive background of an Egyptian temple painted by young Richard Brown, and a thousand actors. A committee of the most distinguished colored citizens of Washington co-operated with me. Audiences aggregating fourteen thousand saw the pageant. We faced every discouragement from rain to lack of funds. "Then," as I wrote, "it was, as it always is in things of this sort. Suddenly a great new spirit seemed born. The thing that you have exorcised becomes a living, mighty, moving spirit. It sweeps on and you hang trembling to its skirts. Nothing can stop it. It is. It will. Wonderfully, irresistibly the dream comes true. You feel no exaltation, you feel no personal merit. It is not yours. It is its own. You have simply called it, and it comes. I shall never forget that last night. Six thousand human faces looked down from the shifting blaze of lights and on the field the shimmering streams of colors came and went, silently, miraculously save for the great cloud of music that hovered over them and enveloped them. It was no mere picture: it was reality."

A difficulty, of course, with dramatic effort of this sort, was that it could not be made to pay unless organized with considerable capital. That I did not have and could not command. Nevertheless, once more I made the experiment in Philadelphia in 1916, to celebrate the one hundredth general conference of the African M. E. Church. "It was," says the *Friend's Intelligencer*, "a signal contribution to the fine art of pageantry." A settlement worker added: "I wish I could find the words I need to thank you for the beautiful thing you have given us in the pageant; but perhaps my best tribute is the very wordlessness, the tear-salted eyes with which I watched it, and shall always remember it. It was not only the pathos and the tragedy of the story that made the tears, but something deeper than that. In spite of the hurt, you'll keep right on being a poet, won't you, please?"

But alas, neither poetry nor pageants pay dividends, and in my case they scarcely paid expenses. My pageant died with an expiring gasp in Los Angeles in 1925. But it died not solely for lack of support; rather from the tremendous and expanding vogue of the motion picture and the power of the radio and loud speaker. We had no capital for entering into this field and indeed in face of monopoly, who has? Yet, my final pageant took place significantly in Hollywood Bowl, and was still a beautiful thing: "Hard and loving, costly and adventurous has been the effort that brought the 'Star of Ethiopia' to Los Angeles. It cost five thousand dollars and weeks of work; and doubt and travail, harsh words and with it, all curiously inwrought, a love and wonder, a working hand in hand and heart in heart, which paid. And sitting again tonight I see the trees darkly, solemnly uplifted to God; I hear the wild, sad music; and then comes thrilling the light—the light of dancing feet and soft, brown skins and beautiful, beautiful eyes: the eyes of Ethiopia on the Black Rock, beneath the gleaming of her sword."

Of the Pan-African Congresses, I have explained their rather hurriedly conceived beginning. I was convinced, however, by my experience in Paris in 1919 that here was a real vision and an actual need. Contacts of Negroes of different origins and nationality, which I had then and before at other congresses and the Races Congress were most inspiring. My plans as they developed had in them nothing spectacular nor revolutionary. If in decades or a century they resulted in such world organization of black men as would oppose a united front to European aggression, that certainly would not have been beyond my dream. But on the other hand, in practical reality, I knew the power and guns of Europe and America, and what I wanted to do was in the face of this power to sit down hand in hand with colored groups and across the council table to learn of each other, our condition, our aspirations, our chances for concerted thought and action. Out of this there might come, not race war and opposition, but broader co-operation with the white rulers of the world, and a chance for peaceful and accelerated development of black folk. With this in mind I started to organize and hold a Pan-African Congress in 1921 which would be better attended and more carefully organized than that in 1919.

I found the board of directors of the NAACP not particularly interested. The older liberalism among the white people did not envisage Africa and the colored peoples of the world. They were interested in America and securing American citizens of all and any color, their rights. They had no schemes for internationalism in race problems and to many of them, it seemed quixotic to undertake anything of the sort. Then too, there were colored members who had inherited the fierce repugnance toward anything African, which was the natural result of the older colonization schemes, where efforts at assisted and even forcible expatriation of American Negroes had always included Africa. Negroes were bitterly opposed because such schemes were at bottom an effort to make slavery in the United States more secure and to get rid of the free Negroes. Beyond this they felt themselves Americans, not Africans. They resented and feared any coupling with Africa.

My scheme then for the Pan-African movement had to depend upon voluntary organization largely outside the NAACP. This to some degree I secured and planned a congress to sit successively in three capitals of Europe: London, Brussels, and Paris, from August 29 to September 6, 1921. This congress really deserved to be called Pan-African and it attracted world-wide attention. There were one hundred thirteen accredited delegates from twenty-six different groups, including thirty-five persons from the United States, thirty-nine from Africa and the rest from the West Indies and Europe.

Among the speakers were Sir Sidney, now Lord Olivier, and Norman Leys of England; Paul Otlet, often called the "father of the League of Nations"; and Senator La Fontaine of Belgium; Dr. Vitellian, former physician of Menelik of Abyssinia; General Sorelas of Spain; Blaise Diagne of France; and Florence Kelly and Bishop Hurst of America. The attention which the Congress attracted all over Europe was astonishing. It was discussed in the London *Times*, the *Observer* and *Daily Graphic*; in the Paris *Petit Parisien*, *Matin* and *Temps*; in the *Manchester Guardian* and in practically all the daily papers of Belgium. It led to heated debate in Brussels touching the rights of these delegates to discuss at all the relation of colonies, and it emphasized in the minds of all of us the importance of such discussions. Two of us visited the League of Nations and the International Labor Office with petitions and suggestions.

On the other hand the Pan-African movement ran into two fatal difficulties: first of all, it was much too early to assume, as I had assumed, that in 1921 the war was over. In fact the whole tremendous drama which followed the war, political and social revolution, economic upheaval and depression, national and racial hatred, all these things made a setting in which any such movement as I envisaged was probably at the time impossible. I sensed this in the bitter and deep opposition which our resolutions invoked in Belgium. Both the Belgian and French governments were aroused and disturbed and the English opposition hovered in the background.

There came, too, a second difficulty which had elements of comedy and curious social frustration, but nevertheless was real and in a sense tragic. Marcus Garvey walked into the scene. I had heard of Garvey when in 1915 I took a short vacation trip to Jamaica, where I was surprisingly well-received by colored people and white, because of the wide publicity given me from my participation in the Races Congress of London in 1911. Garvey and his associates, "The United Improvement and Conservation Association," joined in the welcome.

After the war he came to America, launched a widely advertised plan for commerce between Negro groups and eventually of Negro domination of Africa. It was a grandiose and bombastic scheme, utterly impracticable as a whole, but it was sincere and had some practical features; and Garvey proved not only an astonishing popular leader, but a master of propaganda. Within a few years, news of his movement, of his promises and plans, reached Europe and Asia, and penetrated every corner of Africa. He actually bought two small boats, summoned huge conventions to New York, and paraded the streets of Harlem with uniformed troops and "Black Cross" nurses. News of his astonishing plans reached Europe and the various colonial offices, even before my much more modest proposals. Often the Pan-African Congress was confounded with the Garvey movement with consequent suspicion and attack.

My first effort was to explain away the Garvey movement and ignore it; but it was a mass movement that could not be ignored. I noted this movement from time to time in the *Crisis* and said in 1920 that Garvey was "an extraordinary leader of men" and declared that he had "with singular success capitalized and made vocal the great and long-suffering grievances and spirit of protest among the West Indian peasantry." Later when he began to collect money for his steamship line, I characterized him as a hard-working idealist, but called his methods bombastic, wasteful, illogical, and almost illegal. I begged his friends not to allow him foolishly to overwhelm with bankruptcy and disaster "one of the most interesting spiritual movements of the modern world." But he went ahead, wasted his money, got in trouble with the authorities and was deported from the United States. He made a few abortive efforts later, but finally died in London in 1940, poor and neglected.

The unfortunate debacle of his over-advertised schemes naturally hurt and made difficult further effective development of the Pan-African Congress idea. Nevertheless, a third Pan-African Congress was attempted in 1923. It was less broadly representative than the second, but of some importance, and was held in London, Paris and Lisbon. Thence I went to Africa and for the first time saw the homeland of the black race.

At the London meeting of the third Pan-African Congress, Harold Laski, H. G. Wells, and Lord Olivier spoke, and Ramsay MacDonald had promised to speak to us but was hindered by the sudden opening of the campaign which made him prime minister of England. Among other things we held conferences with members of the Labor Party of England at which Mrs. Sidney Webb, Mr. Clynes and others were present. We emphasized the importance of labor solidarity between white and black labor in England, America, and elsewhere. In Portugal our meeting was attended by cabinet ministers and deputies and though small, was of exceeding interest.

In my ensuing trip to Africa, of which I have spoken elsewhere, and which in a way was a culmination of this Congress, I was further encouraged in my belief in the soundness of its underlying idea. I met in Sierra Leone members and promoters of the Congress of West Africa. Starting after the war, this organization made such cogent and persistent representations to the British colonial office in 1920 and later, that they secured for the first time in British West Africa, popular representation in the governors' councils. Their movement resembled our National Association in the United States and I was convinced that acquaintance and correspondence between colored persons promoting such movements all over the world would be a great and wise step from many points of view.

A fourth Pan-African Congress was held in New York in 1927, chiefly as a rather empty gesture to keep the idea alive. Dantès Bellegarde and Georges Sylvain of Haiti and other speakers took part. A fifth Pan-African Congress was proposed for Tunis, Africa, in 1929, but the French government vetoed the project. Then we tried to charter a boat and hold the congress in the West Indies. There was no boat available. No further efforts have been made, yet the idea is not entirely dead.

My third effort after the war was toward the economic stabilization and rehabilitation of the Negro, and was, as I see it now, more fundamental and prophetic than any of these three lines of endeavor. It started with an effort to establish consumers' co-operation among American Negroes. On

August 26, 1918, there met in the *Crisis* office, twelve colored men from seven different states, to establish the Negro Co-operative Guild. This was in response to a series of editorials and explanations in the *Crisis*, advocating consumers' co-operation for Negroes. The meeting determined to induce individuals and groups to study consumers' co-operation, to hold an annual meeting for encouraging co-operative stores and to form a central committee.

Several co-operative stores were established. The most ambitious came in Memphis where the Citizens Co-operative Stores opened five places of business in 1919 and carried on a good trade. Then the manager conceived the idea of turning this co-operative effort into a stock company. The result was that eventually he was driven out of business by competition of the chain stores. An excellent effort in the colored state school at Bluefield, West Virginia, planned to teach the students the basic theories of co-operation in a school co-operative store. From the Harvard University Graduate School of Education came a comment to the manager, W. C. Matney: "I am convinced that you are doing a splendid piece of work with this enterprise." It was successful for many years, but the state of West Virginia eventually forbade its continuance. There were four or five other attempts. My trip to Europe, the disasters of the year 1919, my concentration of interest in Pan Africa and the depression left this, perhaps the most promising of my projected movements, without further encouragement. The whole movement needed more careful preliminary spade work, with popular education both of consumers and managers; and for lack of this, it temporarily failed. It must and will be revived.

In general, the decade from 1918 to 1928 was one of infinite effort and discouraging turmoil as I suppose it had to be. The economic boom and depression in the United States were necessarily for all Americans a time of heart searching and intellectual stock-taking. I was nervous and restless; in addition to all my activities, I ranged the country from North to South and from the Atlantic to the Pacific in series of lectures, conferences, and expositions. I do not doubt but the directors of the Association and my friends would like to have seen me settle down to fewer lines of effort; but at the time this was impossible. I had to be a part of the revolution through which the world was going and to feel in my own soul the scars of its battle.

Still racial injustice prevailed. At the time of the Mississippi flood, the Red Cross allowed the Negroes to be treated like slaves and peons; and in Okolona, Mississippi, a national organization of the Episcopal Church refused to prosecute a white murderer who killed a black professor in cold blood on his own school ground. There came disquieting situations among Negro students: a strike at Hampton, disturbed conditions at Wilberforce, turmoil at Howard and an uprising at Fisk.

Into this last battle I had to throw myself; to resurrect and re-publish the *Fisk Herald* and to fight until Fisk deposed its dictatorial president. The struggle here was epoch-making. How far can a Negro college, dominated by white trustees and a white president and supported by white wealth, carry on in defiance of the wishes and best interests of its colored constituency? There was room at first for argument as to whether the Fisk of 1924 was inimical to our best interests. This matter, by tongue and pen, I helped to settle. The proof was unanswerable. The effort cost me friends and influence, even though eventually the righteousness of the fight was acknowledged by the most reactionary.

Gradually, however, even in the midst of my activities and distractions I began to pause and take stock; I began to look back critically at the twenty years of my life which had passed since I gave up my work at Atlanta University, joined the National Association for the Advancement of Colored People and founded and edited the *Crisis*. My basic theory had been that race prejudice was primarily a matter of ignorance on the part of the mass of men, giving the evil and anti-social a chance to work their way; that when the truth was properly presented, the monstrous wrong of race hate must melt and melt quickly before it. All human action to me in those days was conscious and rational. There was no twilight zone.

To some extent I saw in two decades of work a justification of this theory. Much of the statement, assertion and habit of thought characteristic of the latter part of the nineteenth century regarding the Negro had passed away. Wild Tillmans had stopped talking of the growing "degeneracy of American Negroes." Tom Watsons were ceasing to assert that the Negro race had always been and would always be barbarians. Even the basic excuse for lynching, the rape of white women, had been successfully countered and denied with statistical proof. And from a day when the legality of the Fifteenth Amendment had been openly denied and that denial in some cases supported by judicial decision, we had come to the recognition of full citizenship rights by the Supreme Court. All this was gratifying to the leaders of the National Association for the Advancement of Colored People and to me. In a sense it was an epoch-making achievement. No longer was it possible or thinkable anywhere in the United States to study and discuss the Negro without letting him speak for himself and without having that speaking done by a well-equipped person, if such person was wanted.

On the other hand, I began to be deeply and disturbingly aware that with all the success of our agitation and propaganda, with the wide circulation, reading and attention which the *Crisis* enjoyed, with the appearance of Negroes on the lecture platform everywhere, and the emergence of a distinct and creditable Negro literature, nevertheless the barriers of race prejudice were certainly as strong in 1930 as in 1910 the world over, and in certain aspects, from certain points of view, even stronger.

Or, in other words, beyond my conception of ignorance and deliberate ill-will as causes of race prejudice, there must be other and stronger and more threatening forces, forming the founding stones of race antagonisms, which we had only begun to attack or perhaps in reality had not attacked at all. Moreover, the attack upon these hidden and partially concealed causes of race hate, must be led by Negroes in a program which was not merely negative in the sense of calling on white folk to desist from certain practices and give up certain beliefs; but direct in the sense that Negroes must proceed constructively in new and comprehensive plans of their own.

I think it was the Russian Revolution which first illuminated and made clear this change in my basic thought. It was not that I at any time conceived of Bolshevik Russia as ushering in any present millennium. I was painfully sensitive to all its failures, to all the difficulties which it faced; but the clear and basic thing which appeared to me in unquestioned brightness, was that in the year 1917 and then, after a struggle with the world and famine ten years later, one of the largest nations of the world made up its mind frankly to face a set of problems which no nation was at the time willing to face, and which many nations including our own are unwilling fully to face even to this day.

Those questions involved the problem of the poverty of the mass of men in an age when an abundance of goods and technical efficiency of work seemed able to provide a sufficiency for all men, so that the mass of men could be fed and clothed and sheltered, live in health and have their intellectual faculties trained. Russia was trying to accomplish this by eventually putting into the hands of those people who do the world's work the power to guide and rule the state for the best welfare of the masses. It made the assumption, long disputed, that out of the downtrodden mass of people, ability and character, sufficient to do this task effectively, could and would be found. I believed this dictum passionately. It was, in fact, the foundation stone of my fight for black folk; it explained me.

I had been brought up with the democratic idea that this general welfare was the object of democratic action in the state, of allowing the governed a voice in government. But through the crimson illumination of war, I realized and, afterward by travel around the world, saw even more clearly that so-called democracy today was allowing the mass of people to have only limited voice in government; that democratic control of what are at present the most important functions of men: work and earning a living and distributing goods and services; that here we did not have democracy; we had oligarchy, and oligarchy based on monopoly and income; and this oligarchy was as determined to deny democracy in industry as it had once been determined to deny democracy in legislation and choice of officials.

My thoughts in this line were made more firm by a visit to Russia. Sometime in 1927, I met three Russian visitors to the United States. They were probably clandestine agents of the communist dictatorship. They sought me out, probably because they recognized that I had been for some time a leader of what was called the liberal if not the radical wing among Negroes; and Russia was conceiving the distinct idea that the revolution in the United States might be promoted certainly in some degree by stirring up discontent among the most oppressed tenth of the American nation, namely, the American Negroes.

Two of these Russians, a man and wife, were persons of education and culture and sought to learn my ideas and reactions rather than to press upon me their theories. The third was a blond German and an active revolutionist. He was unwilling to wait. He wanted something done and done now. After I had sought firmly to show him that no revolution in America could be started by Negroes and succeed, and even if that were possible, that after what I had seen of the effects of war, I could never regard violence as an effective, much less necessary, step to reform the American state, he gradually faded out of the picture and ceased to visit me. I do not know what became of him. I never saw him again.

From the other two Russians I learned much. We had pleasant social relations and I sat at their feet to hear what was taking place and what was planned in Russia. I asserted my inability to judge the situation fairly, because I did not know enough of the facts and stressed my continuing doubt as to whether the Russian pattern could be and should be applied in the United States. They said I ought to visit Russia and I expressed my eagerness to do so. Finally, they offered to finance a visit to Russia, which I accepted with a written proviso which I insisted upon, that this visit entail no promise on my part of action or agreement of any kind. I was to go on a journey of free inquiry to see the most momentous change in modern human history which had taken place since the French Revolution. I went to Russia in 1928, traveling by way of Germany, where passport difficulties held me for two or more weeks.

The sight of the German Republic struggling on the ruins of the empire and tottering under a load of poverty, oppression and disorganization made upon me an unforgettable impression. But never in my life have I been so stirred as by what I saw during two months in Russia. I visited Leningrad and Moscow, Nijni Novgorod and Kiev and came home by way of Odessa and Constantinople. I was allowed, so far as I could see, every opportunity to investigate. I saw the wild waifs of the sewers, the fifty thousand children who marched in the Red Square on Youth Day, the new art galleries and the new factories, the beginnings of the new agriculture. But this was physical. Mentally I came to know Karl Marx and Lenin, their critics and defenders. Since that trip my mental outlook and the aspect of the world will never be the same.

My day in Russia was the day of communist beginnings; the red weal of war-suffering and of famine still lay across the land. Only yesterday England, France, America and the Czechs had invaded their land without shadow of right. The people were ragged and hungry, the cities were half in ruins. The masses of men who crowded the streets and fought for places on the packed street cars, were truculent and over-assertive in manner. Moscow did not have a half dozen automobiles. Yet, there lay an unforgettable spirit upon the land, in spite of almost insurmountable obstacles; in the face of contempt and chicanery and the armed force of the civilized world, this nation was determined to go forward and establish a government of men, such as the world had never seen.

Since that they have reeled on; their path has been strewn with blood and failure; but at the same time their accomplishment today is such that they have compelled the world to face the kind of problem which they determined to face; and no matter how much the Fascism of Mussolini and the National Socialism of Hitler, the New Deal of Roosevelt and the appeasement of Chamberlain and the new World War, may assert and believe that they have found ways of abolishing poverty, increasing the efficiency of work, allowing the worker to earn a living and curtailing the power of wealth by means short of revolution, confiscation and force; nevertheless every honest observer must admit that human civilization today has by these very efforts moved toward socialism and accepted many of the tenets of Russian communism. We may, with dogged persistency, declare that deliberate murder, organized destruction and brute force cannot in the end bring and preserve human culture; but we must admit that nothing that Russia has done in war and mass murder exceeds what has been done and is being done by the rest of the civilized world.

Gradually it dawned upon me with increasing clarity just what the essential change in the world has been since the first World War and depression; and how the tactics of those who live for the widest development of men must change accordingly. It is not simply a matter of change in ideals, but even more of a decisive change in the methods by which ideals are to be approximated. As I now look back, I see in the crusade waged by the National Association for the Advancement of Colored People from 1910 to 1930, one of the finest efforts of liberalism to achieve human emancipation; and much was accomplished. But the essential difficulty with the liberalism of the twentieth century was not to realize the fundamental change brought about by the world-wide organization of work and trade and commerce.

During the nineteenth century the overwhelming influence of the economic activities of men upon their thought and action was, as Marx insisted, clear; but it was not until the twentieth century that the industrial situation called not only for understanding but for action. Modern business enterprise organized for private profit was throttling democratic government, choking art and literature and leading work and industry into a dangerous paradox by increasing the production of things for sale and yet decreasing even more rapidly the number of persons able to buy and the amount of money they could spend; thus throwing industry into periodic convulsions. The number of persons who see this economic impasse is becoming larger and larger until it includes today the leading thinkers of the world.

But the difficulty was to know how, without revolution, violence, and dislocation of human civilization, the wrong could be righted and human culture started again upon its upward path. One thing, at any rate, was clear to me in my particular problem, and that was that a continued agitation which had for its object simply free entrance into the present economy of the world, that looked at political rights as an end in itself rather than as a method of reorganizing the state; and that expected through civil rights and legal judgments to re-establish freedom on a broader and firmer basis, was not so much wrong as short-sighted; that the democracy which we had been asking for in political life must sooner or later replace the tyranny which now dominated industrial life.

In the organization whose leadership I shared at the time, I found few who envisaged the situation as I did. The bulk of my colleagues saw no essential change in the world. It was the same world with the problems to be attacked by the same methods as before the war. All we needed to do was to continue to attack lynching, to bring more cases before the courts and to insist upon our full citizenship rights. They recoiled from any consideration of the economic plight of the world or any change in the organization of industry.

My colored colleagues especially were deeply American, with the old theory of individualism, with a desire to be rich or at least well-to-do, with suspicion of organized labor and labor programs; with a horror of racial segregation. My white colleagues were still liberals and philanthropists. They wanted to help the Negroes, as they wanted to help the weak and disadvantaged of all classes in America. They realized poignantly the dislocation of industry, the present economic problems; but most of them still believed in the basic rightness of industry as at present organized and few—perhaps only one, Oswald Garrison Villard—moved from this undisturbed belief in the capitalist system toward the left, toward a conception of a new democratic control of industry.

My nearest white friend, who was executive head of the organization, Joel Spingarn, was skeptical of democracy either in industry, politics or art. He was the natural anarchist of the spirit. His interest was aroused in the Negro because of discrimination, and not in the interest of ideal methods of conducting the state. Given certain rights and opportunities, it was more than wrong, in his mind, to discriminate against certain individuals because of their race and color. He wanted for me and my people freedom to live and act; but he did not believe that voting or revolution in industry was going to bring the millennium. He was afraid that I was turning radical and dogmatic and even communistic, and he proceeded to use his power and influence in order to curb my acts and forestall any change of program of the Association on my part.

Students of sociology have not yet studied widely one method of human government used in modern times and that is the carrying out of social reform of various sorts by means of the secretary-board of directors organization. A group of intelligent men of good will come together for the purpose of studying a certain problem and improving conditions. They may elect the conventional officers, but eventually they put effective power in the hands of a secretary. There ensues a peculiarly effective unity: the members of the committee consult and discuss, arrive at conclusions which the secretary carries out. In the end, the secretary, to all essential purposes, becomes the organization and his effective consultants are his office staff whom he appoints and pays. All this goes smoothly until changes in the policy, ideals, and objects are indicated. Logically these changes should come by decision of the board of directors; but the board by this time has probably become a co-opting body, whose members are suggested by the secretary, so that they are, in fact, his creatures. Moreover, the secretary is naturally tempted to fill his board with "window-dressing"; with persons who are in general agreement with his policies, but who take no active part either in attendance or discussion; and whose names, on the other hand, lend high prestige to the organization. These persons are not apt to know that changes in object are necessary or to care much, so long as the organization remains respectable.

In part the NAACP followed this development but not entirely. In any such united effort for social betterment as ours, there is bound to be some cultural gap between white and black workers. The wider the gap, the easier the collaboration which resolves itself into the standard pattern of white leaders and black followers. If the cultural gap is narrow it calls for some degree of submission of white to Negro leadership. This in the United States is so unusual a pattern that it must be handled carefully.

Our original constituents upon the board of directors were intensely and vividly interested in finding some practical solution to the Negro problems. They were not for the most part rich men, and it was necessary to secure funds. The original idea was that rich philanthropists would gladly contribute, but this assumption was to no large extent realized. On the contrary, large numbers of colored people and many white people of small means contributed through membership and donations. The major support of the organization during its effective years came from the colored people themselves, as was natural and logical.

The secretary at first was little more than an office executive. Then we hired a trained white man at a high salary, who knew methods of modern publicity and propaganda. He came at a critical time, 1917, and did a fine job, especially in increasing membership and funds. In 1920 he resigned, and was replaced by James Weldon Johnson, whose power as executive was shared with the chairman of the board. The chairman represented the board and gave considerable time as real executive. The executive power was also shared in another and rather unusual way, and that was with the editor and publisher of the *Crisis*.

The National Association for the Advancement of Colored People never accepted financial responsibility for the *Crisis*. When they first allowed me to publish it in November, 1910, it was on condition that the Association would be willing to meet any deficit which did not exceed fifty dollars a month. It was for a long time a source of great pride to me that it was never called upon to pay any deficit. On the other hand, the Association paid my salary and a part of the office expense up until January 1, 1916. From that time until 1933, the *Crisis* was self-supporting, and received and disbursed over a half million dollars and distributed seven and a half million copies. The *Crisis* came thus to form a distinct department of the NAACP, with its own office and clerical force and its own funds kept separate from those of the organization.

There soon came the delicate matter of policy; of how far I should express my own ideas and reactions in the *Crisis*, or the studied judgment of the organization. From the first to last, I thought strongly on this point and as I still think, rightly; I determined to make the opinion expressed in the *Crisis* a personal opinion; because, as I argued, no organization can express definite and clear-cut opinions; so far as this organization as such came to conclusions, it would state them in its annual resolutions; but the *Crisis* would state openly the opinion of its editor, so long, of course, as that opinion was in general agreement with that of the organization. This was a dangerous and delicate matter, bound eventually to break down, in case there arose any considerable divergence of opinion between the organization and editor. It was perhaps rather unusual that for two decades, the two lines of thinking ran so largely in agreement.

If, on the other hand, the *Crisis* had not been in a sense a personal organ and the expression of myself, it could not possibly have attained its popularity and effectiveness. It would have been the dry kind of organ that so many societies support for purposes of reference and not for reading. The editor was thus allowed wide latitude for his expression of opinion, chiefly because that freedom cost the Association nothing, gave it free publicity which otherwise would have cost thousands of dollars, and was backed by readers and subscribers who increased more rapidly than the direct membership of the Association, and became in time a body of perhaps a quarter of a million persons. The first real although tacit decision as to my power over the policy of the *Crisis* led to a change in the chairmanship of the board, which Joel Spingarn then assumed.

The next question arose over the matter of political advice in the first Wilson election. No action was taken, but some members of the board doubted the wisdom of our support of the Democratic Party. The question of a segregated camp for Negro officers again split the board; but as the chairman and the editor were in agreement, the power of the Association was used for the establishment of the camp and later the board agreed that this had been the proper procedure. After I had gone to Europe and held the first Pan-African Congress and began to advocate Pan Africanism, the board quite decidedly refused to accept this new activity as part of its program; but it did not for a moment object to my further advocacy of Pan Africanism so long as I was responsible for any costs.

Then came the depression. The revenue of the *Crisis* began to fall off as early as 1924 and 1925. Our circulation dropped steadily until by 1933 it was scarcely more than ten thousand paid subscriptions. If the magazine was to be carried on, evidently the Association would have to share its cost, and if it did so, it would have a right to a larger voice in its conduct and policy.

If the *Crisis* had continued self-supporting during the depression, I would have felt myself free gradually to force upon the thinking Negro world and the NAACP a new economic program. But the *Crisis* was no longer self-supporting. The mass of Negroes, even the intelligent and educated, progressively being thrown out of work, did not have money for food, much less for magazines. I found myself, therefore, seeking support from an organization for a program in which they did not wholeheartedly believe; and particularly this disbelief and growing suspicion centered around the new conception which I had for mass action on the part of the Negro.

By 1930, I had become convinced that the basic policies and ideals of the Association must be modified and changed; that in a world where economic dislocation had become so great as in ours, a mere appeal based on the old liberalism, a mere appeal to justice and further effort at legal decision, was missing the essential need; that the essential need was to guard and better the chances of Negroes, educated and ignorant, to earn a living, safeguard their income, and raise the level of their employment. I did not believe that a further prolongation of looking for salvation from the whites was feasible. So far as they were ignorant of the results of race prejudice, we had taught them; but so far as their race prejudice was built and increasingly built on the basis of the income which they enjoyed and their anti-Negro bias consciously or unconsciously formulated in order to protect their wealth and power, in so far our whole program must be changed, and we must seek to increase the power and particularly the economic organization among Negroes to meet this new situation. It was this change of emphasis that I proposed to discuss and promote through the columns of the *Crisis*.

In addition to this, the meaning and implications of the new psychology had begun slowly to penetrate my thought. My own study of psychology under William James had predated the Freudian era, but it had prepared me for it. I now began to realize that in the fight against race prejudice, we were not facing simply the rational, conscious determination of white folk to oppress us; we were facing age-long complexes sunk now largely to unconscious habit and irrational urge, which demanded on our part not only the patience to wait, but the power to entrench ourselves for a long siege against the strongholds of color caste. It was this long-term program, which called first of all for economic stability on the part of the Negro; for such economic foundations as would enable the colored people of America to earn a living, provide for their own social uplift, so far as this was neglected by the state and nation, and at the same time carry out even more systematically and with greater and better-planned determination, the fight that the NAACP had inaugurated in 1910.

Meantime, the Association itself was receiving less of its income from colored supporters and more from white charity. It was illogical to expect that white philanthropy would be willing to support the economic program which I had in mind. Moreover, the colored group did not wholly agree with me. I realized that too much in later years the Association had attracted the higher income group of colored people, who regarded it as a weapon to attack the sort of social discrimination which especially irked them; rather than as an organization to improve the status and power of the whole Negro group. If now the Association was willing to allow me the same freedom of expression in the crippled *Crisis* that I had had when the *Crisis* was economically independent, I was willing to try to set forth my new point of view while giving anyone else who had an idea, full opportunity to express it. I wanted, not dogmatically but inquiringly, to find out the function of a minority group like ours, in the impending social change. I thought that this was the highest service that any real periodical of opinion could do for its constituents. If we had had at this time leisure for thought and argument, my program could have been carried out; but unfortunately it happened that here dogma entered and dogma from a source that made my new point of view easily misinterpreted and suspected and this was the dogma of the American Communist Party applied first and most unfortunately to the Scottsboro cases, in which our organization was deeply interested and involved. Had it not been for their senseless interference, these poor victims of Southern injustice would today be free. To insure their freedom, we had followed a tried and successful pattern: we had secured the services of Clarence Darrow and with him a respectable firm of local white lawyers. With quiet and careful methods, the Scottsboro victims would have been freed in a couple of years without fanfare or much publicity.

But in the case of the Communists the actual fate of these victims was a minor matter. The leaders of Russian communism thought that they saw here a chance to foment revolution in the United States. This crass instance of cruelty and injustice; where ignorant colored boys, stealing a ride on a freight train, were faced with the ridiculous charge of attacking two white prostitutes on the same train, who were amply protected, if they needed protection, by white hoodlums, seemed to Russia an unusual opportunity to expose American race prejudice and to arouse the Negroes and the working classes of America and the world. All this was based on abysmal ignorance of the pattern of race prejudice in the United States. About the last thing calculated to arouse the white workers of America would be the defense of a Negro accused of attacking a white woman, even though the Negro was probably innocent and the woman a prostitute. This fact the Communists either did not know or ignored. They seized the occasion for agitation in order to forward "the Revolution." They scared respectable lawyers out of the case; they repudiated Clarence Darrow; they made the whole issue turn on property rights and race, and spread this propaganda all over the world. Right as they undoubtedly were on the merits of the case, they were tragically wrong in their methods if they were seeking to free these victims.

This, of course, exasperated our office, the *Crisis* as well as the executive office. But while in the case of the *Crisis*, it left me still determined to work for economic reform as the immediate method of attacking the Negro problem, in the case of the executive office it had the opposite effect of making both Spingarn and others determined to avoid this discussion and any drastic change in the object of the Association.

For this reason the Second Amenia Conference was called, seventeen years after the first. The first Amenia Conference in 1916 met at a strategic time. Our essential agreement on a program of advance was gratifying and epoch-making; but as

I now realize, we had not only been hammered into unity by culminating oppression, but prepared for it by spade-work which had gone before, and which for ten years had been preparing the minds of Americans, black and white, for a new deal in race relations and renewed effort toward racial equality. In 1933, the situation was different. We met at the beginning rather than at the end of a period of preparatory discussion. We were still mentally whirling in a sea of inconclusive world discussion. We could not really reach agreement as a group, because of the fact that so many of us as individuals had not made up our own minds on the essentials of coming social change. The attendance was sifted—perhaps too much so; outside of four of the Elder Statesmen, the median age was thirty—persons just out of college; their life work begun but not settled. They were teachers, social workers, professional men, and two artisans.

The discussion and resolutions, while disappointing to both Spingarn and myself, as I now see them, threw a flood of light upon our situation. Four threads of thought entered into our conference: *first*, the fight against race segregation and color discrimination in any form. This was age-old among Negroes and also the bitterly felt contribution of those younger folk, who had experienced race prejudice during the war and the difficulties of getting a decent opportunity to work and live after the war. The *second* thread was Marxian economic determinism. Most of the younger trained college group were convinced that the economic pattern of any civilization determined its development along all cultural lines. In the *third* place everybody present, old and young, was seized with a new concern for the welfare of the great mass of Negro laboring people. They felt that too much in the past we had been thinking of the exceptional folk, the Talented Tenth, the well-to-do; that we must now turn our attention toward the welfare and social uplift of the masses. *Finally*, the old liberalism, resurgent in the leadership of the NAACP officials, wished to reiterate and strengthen everything that we had done in the past, as the only program for the future.

Out of these trends of thought, one can imagine the turmoil and contradiction of our discussion. Our argument was indeterminate and our resolutions contradictory. It was agreed that the primary problem before us was economic, but it was equally certain that this economic problem could not be approached from the point of view of race. The only approach to it must be through the white labor masses who were supposed to accept without great reluctance the new scientific argument that there was no such thing as "race"; and in the midst of this, nearly all the older men and some of the younger men were still trying to insist that the uplift of the Negro in the past and in the future could only take place through the development of superimposed economic and cultural classes; and that we needed in the future to reinforce the liberal program which we had been carrying out in the past.

I was disappointed. I had hoped for such insistence upon the compelling importance of the economic factor that this would lead to a project for a planned program for using the racial segregation, which was at present inevitable, in order that the laboring masses might be able to have built beneath them a strong foundation for self-support and social uplift; and while this fundamental economic process was going on, we could, from a haven of economic security, continue even more effectively than ever to agitate for the utter erasure of the color line.

I stood, as it seemed to me, between paths diverging to extreme communism and violence on the one hand, and extreme reaction toward plutocracy on the other. I saw disaster for American Negroes in following a set determination to ignore race hate and nearing instead a creed of eventual violence and revolution; simply because a single great nation, having perhaps no other alternative, had started this way, this path was for American Negroes, to my mind, nonsense. The nonsense did not end here; it was just as nonsensical for us to assume that the program which we had espoused in 1910 was going to work in 1950. We had got to prepare ourselves for a reorganization of society especially and fundamentally in industry. And for that reason we had got to work as a group toward the socialization of our own wealth and the establishment of such social objects in the nation and in the world.

Spingarn was disappointed and in some degree impatient. I remember one amusing incident: there was a young man in attendance (we will call him Jones), well-educated and in some ways brilliant, but on the other hand, a communist and also irresponsible and unreliable. The members of the conference had been invited up one day to the Spingarn home, a beautiful spacious country mansion with pools and gardens in the English style. Jones stood in the parlor and grinned; and said aloud to the visitors: "Comes the revolution, and Commissar Jones will live here!" Spingarn did not appreciate the joke.

The end of it all was inconclusive resolutions and no agreement; and greater conviction on the part of the executive office that discussion of economic change and organization among colored people to affect a stronger economic position, was not in the line of the policy of the NAACP; and that neither the *Crisis* nor anyone else ought to discuss these matters nor agitate them. I began to see that for a second time in my life my occupation was gone, unless I made a very complete surrender of my convictions. I was not and am not a communist. I do not believe in the dogma of inevitable revolution in order to right economic wrong. I think war is worse than hell, and that it seldom or never forwards the advance of the world.

On the other hand, I believed and still believe that Karl Marx was one of the greatest men of modern times and that he put his finger squarely upon our difficulties when he said that economic foundations, the way in which men earn their living, are the determining factors in the development of civilization, in literature, religion, and the basic pattern of culture. And this conviction I had to express or spiritually die.

My leadership was a leadership solely of ideas. I never was, nor ever will be, personally popular. This was not simply because of my idiosyncrasies but because I despise the essential demagoguery of personal leadership; of that hypnotic ascendancy over men which carries out objectives regardless of their value or validity, simply by personal loyalty and admiration. In my case I withdrew sometimes ostentatiously from the personal nexus, but I sought all the more determinedly to force home essential ideas.

I think I may say without boasting that in the period from 1910 to 1930 I was a main factor in revolutionizing the attitude of the American Negro toward caste. My stinging hammer blows made Negroes aware of themselves, confident of their possibilities and determined in self-assertion. So much so that today common slogans among the Negro people are taken bodily from the words of my mouth.

But of course, no idea is perfect and forever valid. Always to be living and apposite and timely, it must be modified and adapted to changing facts. What I began to realize was that the heights and fastnesses which we black folk were assailing, could not in America be gained by sheer force of assault, because of our relatively small numbers. They could only be gained as the majority of Americans were persuaded of the rightness of our cause and joined with us in demanding our recognition as full citizens. This process must deal not only with conscious rational action, but with irrational and unconscious habit, long buried in folkways and custom. Intelligent propaganda, legal enactment and reasoned action must attack the conditioned reflexes of race hate and change them.

Slowly but surely I came to see that for many years, perhaps many generations, we could not count on any such majority; that the whole set of the white world in America, in Europe and in the world was too determinedly against racial equality, to give power and persuasiveness to our agitation. Therefore, I began to emphasize and restate certain implicit aspects of my former ideas. I tried to say to the American Negro: during the time of this frontal attack which you are making upon American and European prejudice, and with your unwavering statement and restatement of what is right and just, not only for us, but in the long run, for all men; during this time, there are certain things you must do for your own survival and self-preservation. You must work together and in unison; you must evolve and support your own social institutions; you must transform your attack from the foray of self-assertive individuals to the massed might of an organized body. You must put behind your demands, not simply American Negroes, but West Indians and Africans, and all the colored races of the world. These things I began to say with no lessening, or thought of lessening of my emphasis upon the essential rightness of what we had been asking for a generation in the political and civic and social equality.

It was clear to me that agitation against race prejudice and a planned economy for bettering the economic condition of the American Negro were not antagonistic ideals but part of one ideal; that it did not increase segregation; the segregation was there and would remain for many years. But now I proposed that in economic lines, just as in lines of literature and religion, segregation should be planned and organized and carefully thought through. This plan did not establish a new segregation; it did not advocate segregation as the final solution of the race problem; exactly the contrary; but it did face the facts and faced them with thoughtfully mapped effort.

Of course I soon realized that in this matter of segregation I was touching an old and bleeding sore in Negro thought. From the eighteenth century down the Negro intelligentsia has regarded segregation as the visible badge of their servitude and as the object of their unceasing attack. The upper class Negro has almost never been nationalistic. He has never planned or thought of a Negro state or a Negro church or a Negro school. This solution has always been a thought upsurging from the mass, because of pressure which they could not withstand and which compelled a racial institution or chaos. Continually such institutions were founded and developed, but this took place against the advice and best thought of the intelligentsia.

American Negroes have always feared with perfect fear their eventual expulsion from America. They have been willing to submit to caste rather than face this. The reasons have varied but today they are clear: Negroes have no Zion. There is no place where they can go today and not be subject to worse caste and greater disabilities from the dominant white imperialistic world than they suffer here today. On the other hand there is no likelihood just now of their being forcibly expelled. So far as that is concerned, there was no likelihood ten years ago of the Jews being expelled from Germany. The cases are far from parallel. There is a good deal more profit in cheap Negro labor than in Jewish fellow citizens, which brings together strange bed-fellows for the protection of the Negro. On the other hand one must remember that this is a day of astonishing change, injustice and cruelty; and that many Americans of stature have favored the transportation of

Negroes and they were not all of the mental caliber of the present junior senator from Mississippi. As the Negro develops from an easily exploitable, profit-furnishing laborer to an intelligent independent self-supporting citizen, the possibility of his being pushed out of his American fatherland may easily be increased rather than diminished. We may be expelled from the United States as the Jew is being expelled from Germany.

At any rate it is the duty of American Negroes today to examine this situation not with hysteria and anger but with calm forethought. Whether self-segregation for his protection, for inner development and growth in intelligence and social efficiency, will increase his acceptability to white Americans or not, that growth must go on. And whatever the event may bring, it must be faced as men face crises and not with surprise and helpless amazement. It was astonishing and disconcerting, and yet for the philosopher perfectly natural, that this change of my emphasis was crassly and stupidly misinterpreted by the Negroes. Appropriating as their own (and indeed now it was their own) my long insistence on self-respect and self-assertion and the demand for every equality on the part of the Negro, they seemed determined to insist that my newer emphasis was a repudiation of the older; that now I wanted segregation; that now I did not want equality; that now I was asking for black people to act as black people and forcibly overthrow the dominance of the white.

I can see an assembly in Philadelphia, when I went down to say to the colored people that the demand of Leslie Hill to make the Cheyney school a college supported by the state of Pennsylvania, was wise and inevitable. "It will be a Negro college!" shouted the audience, as though such a thing had never been heard of. "It will be Segregation," said a woman, who had given much of her life to furthering the fight for Negro equality. I can see her now, brown, tense, bitter, as she lashed me with the accusation of advocating the very segregation that I had been fighting. It was in vain that I pointed out that Cheyney was already segregated; that without the help of the state, the school would die; that with the help of the state it could be a great school, regardless of the fact that its teachers and students were Negroes. And moreover, there was no reason in the world why some of the teachers and some of its students could not eventually be white.

Another incident occurred during these years, which shows the increasing paradox of race segregation in the United States. The Rosenwald Fund proposed in 1931 to start a crusade for better hospitalization for Negroes. Negro health needed to be safeguarded and improved and one of the main reasons for the Negro sickness and death rate was the fact that Negroes were not furnished hospital facilities; and that their physicians were very often not admitted to medical schools for study nor to hospitals for practice. They proposed therefore to help in the building and equipment of Negro hospitals and in the education of Negro physicians.

Just how far they proposed to go, they did not make clear because before they had thoroughly matured their plans they were bitterly attacked by Dr. Louis Wright of New York and others. Louis Wright was a special favorite of mine. The stepfather who brought him up was my own family physician for years. I had followed Wright's career as he fought his way through Harvard and made a fine record. He began practice in New York and then at the time of the World War went to France as a captain in a colored medical unit of the AEF and there had a distinguished career. He came back and fought his way into prominence in the Harlem Hospital of New York, which up to his time had admitted no Negro physicians, although nearly all the patients were Negroes. In time Louis Wright became an authority in many branches of surgery and medicine; he was with reluctance admitted to the American College of Surgeons and was appointed one of the seven members of the Board of Surgeons of the Police Department of New York. He is an outstanding man; gifted and thoroughly unselfish, and the one thing that he fought with unceasing energy was discrimination against Negroes in hospitals, whether as medical practitioners or patients. He violently attacked the Rosenwald board saying that the method of segregated hospitals and segregated training for Negro physicians was not the way to go at the matter; that what ought to be done was to insist in season and out that Negroes be admitted to medical schools and hospital practice without regard to color.

I saw and saw clearly the argument on both sides to this controversy. I was heart and soul with Louis Wright in his fight against segregation and yet I knew that for a hundred years in this America of ours it was going to be at least partially in vain. I was heart and soul with the Rosenwald Fund; what Negroes need is hospital treatment now; and what Negro physicians need is hospital practice; and to meet their present need, poor hospitals are better than none; segregated hospitals are better than those where the Negro patients are neglected or relegated to the cellar.

Yet in this case I was unable to decide or take part. I wrote a rather perfunctory editorial in general upholding Dr. Wright, but I was sorry to see the larger plan of the Rosenwald Fund curtailed and cut down to a mere ghost of its first self. Whatever the merits of this particular controversy were, I am certain that for many generations American Negroes in the United States have got to accept separate medical institutions. They may dislike it; they may and ought to protest against it; nevertheless it will remain for a long time their only path to health, to education, to economic survival.

The NAACP from the beginning faced this bogey. It was not, never had been, and never could be an organization that took an absolute stand against race segregation of any sort under all circumstances. This would be a stupid stand in the face of clear and incontrovertible facts. When the NAACP was formed, the great mass of Negro children were being trained in Negro schools; the great mass of Negro churchgoers were members of Negro churches; the great mass of Negro citizens lived in Negro neighborhoods; the great mass of Negro voters voted with the same political party; and the mass of Negroes joined with Negroes and co-operated with Negroes in order to fight the extension of this segregation and to move toward better conditions. What was true in 1910 was still true in 1940 and will be true in 1970. But with this vast difference: that the segregated Negro institutions are better organized, more intelligently planned and more efficiently conducted, and today form in themselves the best and most compelling argument for the ultimate abolition of the color line.

To have started out in this organization with a slogan "no

segregation," would have been impossible. What we did say was no increase in segregation; but even that stand we were unable to maintain. Whenever we found that an increase of segregation was in the interest of the Negro race, naturally we had to advocate it. We had to advocate better teachers for Negro schools and larger appropriation of funds. We had to advocate a segregated camp for the training of Negro officers in the World War. We had to advocate group action of Negro voters in elections. We had to advocate all sorts of organized movement among Negroes to fight oppression and in the long run end segregation.

On the other side, white friends and enemies were rather gleeful in having so apt a club fashioned to their hands. "Chauvinism!" they said, when I urged Pan African solidarity for the accomplishment of universal democracy. "Race prejudice," they intimated, was just as reprehensible when shown by black toward white as when shown by white toward black. Here again it was nearly useless to reiterate. So long as we were fighting a color line, we must strive by color organization. We have no choice. If in time, the fight for Negro equality degenerates into organized murder for the suppression of whites, then our last case is no better than our first; but this need not be, if we are level-headed and clear-sighted, and work for the emancipation of all men from caste through the organization and determination of the present victims of caste.

All this is bound to right itself logically in the minds of American Negroes and Africans, and West Indians, once it has been thoroughly digested and thought through. But the domination of ideas always has this disadvantage in the presence of active, living, personal dictatorship. It is slow, painfully slow. It works with the vast deliberation or perhaps that lack of rational thought which is characteristic of the human mind; but its ultimate triumph is inevitable and complete, so long as the ideas are kept clear and before the minds of men. I shall not live to see entirely the triumph of this, my newer emphasis; but it will triumph just as much and just as completely as did my advocacy of agitation and self-assertion. It is indeed a part of that same original program; it is its natural and inevitable fulfillment.

No sooner had I come to this conclusion than I soon saw that I was out of touch with my organization and that the question of leaving it was only a matter of time. This was not an easy decision; to give up the *Crisis* was like giving up a child; to leave the National Association was leaving the friends of a quarter of a century. But on the other hand, staying meant silence, a repudiation of what I was thinking and planning. Under such circumstances, what could I do? I had seen the modern world as few of my fellow workers had: West African villages, Jamaican homes, Russian communism, German disaster, Italian fascism, Portuguese and Spanish life, France and England repeatedly, and every state in the United States. I knew something of the seething world. I could seek through my editorship of the *Crisis* slowly but certainly to change the ideology of the NAACP and of the Negro race into a racial program for economic salvation along the paths of peace and organization.

There were two alternatives: to change the board of directors of the NAACP so as to substitute a group which agreed with this program, or to leave the Association. If the first could be done without a prolonged fight, I was willing to undertake it. I was appointed a member of the next nominating committee; five new members were proposed who would have begun the reorganization. When, however, the committee gave its report the majority had changed from the persons agreed upon and substituted two or three excellent persons who unfortunately were either absolutely reactionary in their social and economic outlook or basically ignorant.

The Association seemed to me not only unwilling to move toward the left in its program but even stepped decidedly toward the right. And what astonished me most was that this economic reaction was voiced even more by the colored members of the Board of Directors than the white. One could realize why a rich white liberal should suspect fundamental economic change, but it was most difficult for me to understand that the younger and more prosperous Negro professional men, merchants, and investors were clinging to the older ideas of property, ownership and profits even more firmly than the whites. The liberal white world saw the change that was coming despite their wish. The upper class colored world did not anticipate nor understand it.

When now I came advocating new, deliberate and purposeful segregation for economic defense in precisely the lines of business and industry whither the NAACP was not prepared to follow it was not an absolute difference of principle, but it was a grave difference as to further procedure. When I criticized the Secretary for his unsound explanation of the historic stand of the NAACP on segregation, the Board of Directors voted May 21, 1934, "that the *Crisis* is the organ of the Association and no salaried officer of the Association shall criticize the policy, work or officers of the Association in the pages of the *Crisis*." Thereupon I forthwith gave up my connection with the Association saying:

"In thirty-five years of public service my contribution to the settlement of the Negro problems has been mainly candid criticism based on a careful effort to know the facts. I have not always been right, but I have been sincere, and I am unwilling at this late day to be limited in the expression of my honest opinions in the way in which the Board proposes. . . . I am, therefore, resigning, . . . this resignation to take effect immediately." The board refused to accept this resignation and asked me to reconsider. I did so, but finally wrote, June 26, "I appreciate the good will and genuine desire to bridge an awkward break which your action indicated, and yet it is clear to me, and I think to the majority of the Board, that under the circumstances my resignation must stand."

In finally accepting my resignation the Board was kind enough to say in part: "He founded the *Crisis* without a cent of capital, and for many years made it completely self-supporting, reaching a maximum monthly circulation at the end of the World War of 100,000. This is an unprecedented achievement in American journalism, and in itself worthy of a distinguished tribute. But the ideas which he propounded in it and in his books and essays transformed the Negro world as well as a large portion of the liberal white world, so that the whole problem of the relation of black and white races has ever since had a completely new orientation. He created, what never existed before, a Negro intelligentsia, and many who have never read a word of his writings are his spiritual disciples and descendants. Without him the Association could never have been what it was and is.

"The Board has not always seen eye to eye with him in regard to various matters, and cannot subscribe to some of his criticism of the Association and its officials. But such differences in the past have in no way interfered with his usefulness, but rather on the contrary. For he had been selected because of his independence of judgment, his fearlessness in expressing his convictions, and his acute and wide-reaching intelligence. A mere yes-man could not have attracted the attention of the world, could not even have stimulated the Board itself to further study of various important problems. We shall be the poorer for his loss, in intellectual stimulus, and in searching analysis of the vital problems of the American Negro; no one in the Association can fill his place with the same intellectual grasp. We therefore offer him our sincere thanks for the services he has rendered, and we wish him all happiness in all that he may now undertake."

I had already for some years begun to canvass the possibility of a change of work. This, of course, is not easy when a person is over sixty years of age. If he has not had the grace to die before this, he ought, in accordance with prevalent public opinion, at least to be willing to stop acting and thinking. I did not agree with that. I thought of many possibilities, but at last determined to accept an offer that had been made to me quietly in 1929, and periodically repeated from time to time when John Hope of Atlanta came to town. We had been close friends since 1897. We taught together until 1910. Hope had joined the Niagara Movement and the NAACP. We met in France in 1918 while he was a YMCA secretary, and I promoting Pan Africa. Always when he came to New York, we did a theater and a dinner, and discussed the reformation of the world. When he became President of the newly organized Atlanta University, he invited me to join him.

Of course, this change of work had certain unpleasant necessities. It would not only involve giving up the *Crisis* and my connection with the Association. It also involved the cold douche of a return to life in the South. I knew the South. In part I had been educated there. I had spent thirteen years teaching in Georgia and during my connection with the NAACP nearly every year I traveled in the South to keep myself closely acquainted with its problems. The South of 1933 was not the South of 1897. In many respects it had improved and the relations between the races were better. Nevertheless the South is not a place where a man of Negro descent would voluntarily and without good reason choose to live. Its civilization is decidedly lower than that of the North. Its state and local governments are poor and full of incompetency and graft, and its whole polity is menaced by mass hysteria and mob-law. Its police system is wretched and the low grade white policeman full of crude race hate is the ruler who comes closest and in most immediate contact with black folk of all classes. There is a caste system based on color, fortified in law and even more deeply entrenched in custom, which meets and coerces the dark man at nearly every step: in trains, in street cars, in elevators, in offices, in education, in recreation, in religion and in graveyards. The economic organization is still in the nineteenth century with ruthless exploitation, low wages, child labor, debt peonage, and profit in crime. The better classes, with gracious manners and liberal outlook, exist and slowly grow; but with these I would have little contact and fear of the mob would restrain their meeting me or listening to me.

All this I faced, but I saw too the compensations. After all, the place to study a social problem is where it centers and not elsewhere. The Negro problem in the United States centers in the southern South. There in the place of its greatest concentration, forces are working for its solution and the greatest of these forces are institutions like Atlanta University. The university throws around its professors and students a certain protective coloration. It is an inner community surrounded by beauty with unusual chances for intellectual and social contact. To a degree it furnishes recreation and avenues to culture. Our library without doubt is the best in Atlanta; our music is unsurpassed and the chances here for quiet contemplation and the intellectual life are considerable.

Then too, I could not forget that even in New York, with all its opportunity for human contact, with its unrivaled facilities for a center of world thought and culture, it was nevertheless no heaven for black folk. Negroes were not welcome to its hotels and restaurants nor to most of its clubs and organizations. Contact with human beings despite color is far wider than in Georgia; but yet, it is not wide. Theaters and great music center in New York as nowhere else in America. But they are very costly; a theater once a month and opera once a year was as much as I could afford. By careful choice and delicate prevision I may in New York foot a path of broad cultural contact and wide physical freedom; it would be difficult to find a quiet, clean place to live; but if I can earn a living, I can be fairly content. I should certainly have there no such dread of the white mob and the police as Negroes must have in the southern South. Weighing and balancing all these considerations, I came back to Atlanta. In a sense I returned to my ivory tower, not so much for new scientific research, as for interpretation and reflection; and for making a record of what I had seen and experienced.

The situation to which I returned was new. Back as early as 1905, I had proposed to the seven colored colleges of Atlanta the beginning of efforts toward uniting these various institutions into one university. We actually once had a meeting at Spelman, but the dean was definitely opposed. She said crisply that if her head was going to be taken off, she would prefer to bite it off herself. I turned then in 1909 to John Hope, the president of Morehouse, and we worked out an interchange of lectures between Morehouse and Atlanta University. He wrote me in 1910: "I hope and believe this is the beginning of new and larger things in an educational way among our colored institutions. . . . I feel down-right enthusiasm over the beginning that our two schools made this year and hope that, now that we have made a start and have some slight idea of what can be accomplished, the two schools may next year do larger things." Hope was then president of Morehouse College, but in 1929, he realized our dream in the affiliation of three Negro colleges of Atlanta in the new Atlanta University, with himself as first president.

Far back in 1910 before leaving Atlanta University I had read before the American Historical Association a paper on "Reconstruction and Its Benefits," which greatly exercised Ulrich Phillips, protagonist of the slave South, but brought praise from Dunning of Columbia, Hart of Harvard and others. I was convinced then, and am more certain since, that the reason for certain adjectives applied to Reconstruction is purely racial. Reconstruction was "tragic," "terrible," a "great mistake," and a "humiliation," not because of what actually happened: people suffered after the Civil War, but people suffer after all wars; and the suffering in the South was no greater than in dozens of other centers of murder and destruction. No, the "tragedy" of Reconstruction was because here an attempt was initiated to make American democracy and the tenets of the Declaration of Independence apply not only to white men, but to black men. While still in the *Crisis* office, through a grant from the Rosenwald Fund I had begun a history of the black man's part in Reconstruction. This was my thesis. Two years' work at Atlanta University finished my "Black Reconstruction" and it was published in 1935.

Next I naturally turned my thought toward putting into permanent form that economic program of the Negro which I believed should succeed, and implement the long fight for political and civil rights and social equality which it was my privilege for a quarter of a century to champion. I tried to do this in a preliminary way, through a little study of the "Negro and the New Deal" which I was asked to undertake in 1936 by the colored "Associates in Negro Folk Education," working under the American Association for Adult Education. The editor of this series, Alain Locke, pressed me for the manuscript and by working hard I finished it and was paid for it just before my trip abroad in 1936. I think I made a fair and pretty exhaustive study of the experience of the Negro from 1933 to 1936 and by way of summing up I appended a statement and credo which I had worked out through correspondence with a number of the younger Negro scholars. It was this:

1. We American Negroes are threatened today with lack of opportunity to work according to gifts and training and lack of income sufficient to support healthy families according to standards demanded by modern culture.

2. In industry, we are a labor reservoir, fitfully employed and paid a wage below subsistence; in agriculture, we are largely disfranchised

peons; in public education, we tend to be disinherited illiterates; in higher education, we are the parasites of reluctant and hesitant philanthropy.

3. In the current reorganization of industry, there is no adequate effort to secure us a place in industry, to open opportunity for Negro ability, or to give us security in age or unemployment.

4. Not by the development of upper classes anxious to exploit the workers, nor by the escape of individual genius into the white world, can we effect the salvation of our group in America. And the salvation of this group carries with it the emancipation not only of the darker races of men who make the vast majority of mankind, but of all men of all races. We, therefore, propose this:

BASIC AMERICAN NEGRO CREED

A. As American Negroes, we believe in unity of racial effort, so far as this is necessary for self-defense and self-expression, leading ultimately to the goal of a united humanity and the abolition of all racial distinctions.

B. We repudiate all artificial and hate-engendering deification of race separation as such; but just as sternly, we repudiate an enervating philosophy of Negro escape into an artificially privileged white race which has long sought to enslave, exploit and tyrannize over all mankind.

C. We believe that the Talented Tenth among American Negroes, fitted by education and character to think and do, should find primary employment in determining by study and measurement the present field and demand for racial action and the method by which the masses may be guided along this path.

D. We believe that the problems which now call for such racial planning are Employment, Education and Health; these three: but the greatest of these is Employment.

E. We believe that the labor force and intelligence of twelve million people is more than sufficient to supply their own wants and make their advancement secure. Therefore, we believe that, if carefully and intelligently planned, a co-operative Negro industrial system in America can be established in the midst of and in conjunction with the surrounding national industrial organization and in intelligent accord with that reconstruction of the economic basis of the nation which must sooner or later be accomplished.

F. We believe that Negro workers should join the labor movement and affiliate with such trade unions as welcome them and treat them fairly. We believe that Workers' Councils organized by Negroes for interracial understanding should strive to fight race prejudice in the working class.

G. We believe in the ultimate triumph of some form of Socialism the world over; that is, common ownership and control of the means of production and equality of income.

H. We do not believe in lynching as a cure for crime; nor in war as a necessary defense of culture; nor in violence as the only path to economic revolution. Whatever may have been true in other times and places, we believe that today in America we can abolish poverty by reason and the intelligent use of the ballot, and above all by that dynamic discipline of soul and sacrifice of comfort which, revolution or no revolution, must ever be the only real path to economic justice and world peace.

I. We conceive this matter of work and equality of adequate income as not the end of our effort, but the beginning of the rise of the Negro race in this land and the world over, in power, learning and accomplishment.

J. We believe in the use of our vote for equalizing wealth through taxation, for vesting the ultimate power of the state in the hands of the workers; and as an integral part of the working class, we demand our proportionate share in administration and public expenditure.

K. This is and is designed to be a program of racial effort and this narrowed goal is forced upon us today by the unyielding determination of the mass of the white race to enslave, exploit and insult Negroes; but to this vision of work, organization and service, we welcome all men of all colors so long as their subscription to this basic creed is sincere and is proven by their deeds.

This creed proved unacceptable both to the Adult Education Association and to its colored affiliates. Consequently when I returned from abroad the manuscript, although ordered and already paid for, was returned to me as rejected for publication. Just who pronounced the veto I do not know.

I had next two other projects: first, that large mass of material relating to the Negro in the World War, which the NAACP had never made an effort to use or publish. I had been working at that off and on since 1919, and one year had a grant from the Social Science Council. But I had not yet got it in shape for publication. Another project in which I had long been interested was an Encyclopaedia of the Negro. As early as 1909, I had planned an Encyclopaedia Africana and secured on my board of advisers Sir Flinders Petrie, Sir Harry Johnston, Giuseppe Sergi, Dr. J. Deniker, William James, and Franz Boas; and on my proposed board of editors I had practically all the leading Negroes of the United States who were then inclined toward research. My change to New York and the work of starting the *Crisis*, and finally the World War, put this quite out of my mind.

In 1931, the Phelps-Stokes Fund called together a committee to consider a plan of arranging for the preparation and publication of an Encyclopaedia of the Negro. To this first meeting I was not invited as my relations to some of the executives of the Fund during the past had not been cordial. But those who met insisted upon myself and others being invited to the second meeting. Overcoming a natural hesitation I went. Eventually and to me quite unexpectedly I was designated as future chairman of the editorial board, in case the funds for the enterprise should ever be found.

Since the incorporation of the Encyclopaedia in 1932, by the help of a small appropriation from the Phelps-Stokes Fund, I have been planning and working on preliminary arrangements for such an undertaking. We found the great Funds, from bitter experience, encyclopaedia-shy. But, in addition to that, I fear that no money sufficient for the publication of such an encyclopaedia under the leadership of colored scholars and the collaboration of white men can be soon found. I doubt if men would formulate their objection to such a procedure, but after all it would seem to them natural that any such work should be under the domination of white men. At any rate, we have gotten together a definite and completely worked-out plan, even to the subjects and many of the proposed writers, which can in the future be used for an Encyclopaedia of the Negro, a publication sure to come in time.

In 1936, my application to the Oberlaender Trust for a chance to restudy Germany was granted. I spent five months in Germany, and some time in England, France, and Austria, interviewing scholars on the encyclopaedia project. I then took a two months' trip around the world. I was not allowed to stop as long in Russia as I would have liked; but I traversed it in a swift week from Moscow to Otpur. Then I spent a week in Manchoukuo, ten days in China, and two weeks in Japan. I seemed confirmed in the wisdom of my life choice by the panorama of the world which swept before me in London and Paris; Berlin and Vienna; Moscow and Mukden; Peiping and Shanghai; Kyoto and Tokyo; and heavenly Hawaii. Singularly enough in that journey I was most impressed with the poignant beauty of the world in the midst of its distress.

For several years I had been importuning my publishers to get out a new edition of the little book called "The Negro" published first in 1915 in the Home University Series. Finally in 1938 they consented by suggesting an entirely new book. This entailed a good deal of work of the highest interest and in which I took much satisfaction. The resulting volume, "Black Folk: Then and Now," was published in 1939. Since then I have been interested in the book I am now writing, a further essay into fiction, and a university review of race and culture, *Phylon*, born this year.

In February, 1938, I reached the arresting age of seventy and despite some effort on my part to escape the immediate consequences of this indiscretion, two of my younger colleagues, Ira Reid and Rayford Logan, initiated and carried through a University celebration, with a convocation, a bust by Portnoff, a dinner and a talk. In that talk I was called upon to set forth something of my philosophy of life after traversing so many years. The essence of what I said can be summed up in these words:

I have been favored among the majority of men in never being compelled to earn my bread and butter by doing work that was uninteresting or which I did not enjoy or of the sort in which I did not find my greatest life interest. This rendered me so content in my vocation that I seldom thought about salary or haggled over it. My first job paid me eight hundred dollars a year and to take it I refused one which offered ten hundred and fifty. I served over a year at the University of Pennsylvania for the munificent sum of six hundred dollars and never railed at fate. I taught and worked at Atlanta University for twelve hundred a year during thirteen effective and happy years. I never once asked for an increase. I went to New York for the salary offered and only asked for an increase there when an efficient new white secretary was hired at a wage above mine. I then asked equal salary. I did not want the shadow of racial discrimination to creep into our salary schedule. I realize now that this rather specious monetary independence may in the end cost me dearly, and land me in time upon some convenient street corner with a tin cup. For I have saved nearly nothing and lost my life insurance in the depression. Nevertheless, I insist that regardless of income, work worth while which one wants to do as compared with highly paid drudgery is exactly the difference between heaven and hell.

I am especially glad of the divine gift of laughter; it has made the world human and lovable, despite all its pain and wrong. I am glad that the partial Puritanism of my upbringing has never made me afraid of life. I have lived completely, testing every normal appetite, feasting on sunset, sea and hill, and enjoying wine, women, and song. I have seen the face of beauty from the Grand Canyon to the great Wall of China; from the Alps to Lake Baikal; from the African bush to the Venus of Milo.

Perhaps above all I am proud of a straightforward clearness of reason, in part a gift of the gods, but also to no little degree due to scientific training and inner discipline. By means of this I have met life face to face, I have loved a fight and I have realized that Love is God and Work is His prophet; that His ministers are Age and Death.

This makes it the more incomprehensible for me to see persons quite panic-stricken at the approach of their thirtieth birthday and prepared for dissolution at forty. Few of my friends have openly celebrated their fiftieth birthdays, and near none their sixtieth. Of course, one sees some reasons: the disappointment at meager accomplishment which all of us to some extent share; the haunting shadow of possible decline; the fear of death. I have been fortunate in having health and wise in keeping it. I have never shared what seems to me the essentially childish desire to live forever. Life has its pain and evil—its bitter disappointments; but I like a good novel and in healthful length of days, there is infinite joy in seeing the World, the most interesting of continued stories, unfold, even though one misses THE END.

Index

ESSAYS AND ARTICLES

Contents

Essays

Articles from THE CRISIS

ESSAYS

Jefferson Davis as a Representative of Civilization

JEFFERSON DAVIS was a typical Teutonic hero; the history of civilization during the last millenium has been the developement of the idea of the Strong Man of which he was the embodiment. The Anglo-Saxon loves a soldier—Jefferson Davis was an Anglo-Saxon, Jefferson Davis was a soldier. There was not a phase in that familiarly strange life that would not have graced a mediaeval romance: from the fiery and impetuous young lieutenant who stole as his bride the daughter of a ruler-elect of the land, to the cool and ambitious politician in the Senate hall. So boldly and surely did that cadaverous figure with the thin nervous lips and flashing eye, write the first line of the new page of American history, that the historian of the future must ever see back of the war of Secession, the strong arm of one imperious man, who defied disease, trampled on precedent, would not be defeated, and never surrendered. A soldier and a lover, a statesman and a ruler; passionate, ambitious and indomitable; bold reckless guardian of a people's All—judged by the whole standard of Teutonic civilization, there is something noble in the figure of Jefferson Davis; and judged by every canon of human justice, there is something fundamentally incomplete about that standard.

I wish to consider not the man, but the type of civilization which his life represented: its foundation is the idea of the strong man—Individualism coupled with the rule of might—and it is this idea that has made the logic of even modern history, the cool logic of the Club. It made a naturally brave and generous man, Jefferson Davis—now advancing civilization by murdering Indians, now hero of a national disgrace called by courtesy, the Mexican War, and finally, as the crowning absurdity, the peculiar champion of a people fighting to be free in order that another people should not be free. Whenever this idea has for a moment escaped from the individual realm, it has found an even more secure foothold in the policy and philosophy of the State. The Strong Man and his mighty Right Arm has become the Strong Nation with its armies. Under whatever guise, however a Jefferson Davis may appear, as man, as race, or as nation, his life can only logically mean this: the advance of a part of the world at the expence of the whole: the overweening sense of the I and the consequent forgetting of the Thou. It has thus happened, that advance in civilization has always been handicapped by shortsighted national selfishness. The vital principle of division of labor has been stifled not only in industry, but also in civilization, so as to render it well nigh impossible for a new race to introduce a new idea into the world except by means of the cudgel. To say that a nation is in the way of civilization is a contradiction in terms, and a system of human culture whose principle is the rise of one race on the ruins of another is a farce and a lie. Yet this is the type of civilization which Jefferson Davis represented: it represents a field for stalwart manhood and heroic character, and at the same time for moral obtuseness and refined brutality. These striking contradictions of character always arise when a people seemingly become convinced that the object of the world is not civilization, but Teutonic civilization. Such a type is not wholly evil or fruitless: the world has needed and will need its Jefferson Davises; but such a type is incomplete and never can serve its best purpose until checked by its complementary ideas. Whence shall these come?

To the most casual observer, it must have occurred that the Rod of Empire has in these days, turned towards the South. In every Southern country, however, destined to play a future part in the world—in Southern North America, South America, Australia, and Africa—a new nation has a more or less firm foothold. This circumstance has, however, attracted but incidental notice, hitherto; for wherever the Negro people have touched civilization their rise has been singularly unromantic and unscientific. Through the glamour of history, the rise of a nation has ever been typified by the Strong Man crushing out an effete civilization. That brutality buried aught else beside Rome when it descended golden haired and drunk from the blue north has scarcely entered human imagination. Not as the muscular warrior came the Negro, but as the cringing slave. The Teutonic met civilization and crushed it—the

Negro met civilization and was crushed by it. The one was the hero the world has ever worshipped, who gained unthought of triumphs and made unthought of mistakes; the other was the personification of dogged patience bending to the inevitable, and waiting. In the history of this people, we seek in vain the elements of Teutonic deification of Self, and Roman brute force, but we do find an idea of submission apart from cowardice, laziness or stupidity, such as the world never saw before. This is the race which by its very presence must play a part in the world of tomorrow; and this is the race whose rise, I contend, has practically illustrated an idea which is at once the check and complement of the Teutonic Strong Man. It is the doctrine of the Submissive Man—given to the world by strange coincidence, by the race of whose rights, Jefferson Davis had not heard.

What then is the change made in the conception of civilization, by adding to the idea of the Strong Man, that of the Submissive Man? It is this: the submission of the strength of the Strong to the advance of all—not in mere aimless sacrifice, but recognizing the fact that, "To no one type of mind is it given to discern the totality of Truth," that civilization cannot afford to lose the contribution of the very least of nations for its full developement: that not only the assertion of the I, but also to the submission to the Thou is the highest Individualism.

The Teuton stands today as the champion of the idea of Personal Assertion: the Negro as the peculiar embodiment of the idea of Personal Submission: either, alone, tends to an abnormal developement—towards Despotism on the one hand which the world has just cause to fear, and yet covertly admires, or towards slavery on the other which the world despises and which, yet is not wholly despicable. No matter how great and striking the Teutonic type of impetuous manhood may be, it must receive the cool purposeful "Ich Dien" of the African for its round and full developement. In the rise of Negro people and developement of this idea, you whose nation was founded on the loftiest ideals, and who many times forgot those ideals with a strange forgetfulness, have more than a sentimental interest, more than a sentimental duty. You owe a debt to humanity for this Ethiopia of the

Out-stretched Arm, who has made her beauty, patience, and her grandeur, law.

Commencement Address, Harvard University, 1890

The Conservation of Races

THE AMERICAN NEGRO has always felt an intense personal interest in discussions as to the origins and destinies of races: primarily because back of most discussions of race with which he is familiar, have lurked certain assumptions as to his natural abilities, as to his political, intellectual and moral status, which he felt were wrong. He has, consequently, been led to deprecate and minimize race distinctions, to believe intensely that out of one blood God created all nations, and to speak of human brotherhood as though it were the possibility of an already dawning to-morrow.

Nevertheless, in our calmer moments we must acknowledge that human beings are divided into races; that in this country the two most extreme types of the world's races have met, and the resulting problem as to the future relations of these types is not only of intense and living interest to us, but forms an epoch in the history of mankind.

It is necessary, therefore, in planning our movements, in guiding our future development, that at times we rise above the pressing, but smaller questions of separate schools and cars, wage-discrimination and lynch law, to survey the whole question of race in human philosophy and to lay, on a basis of broad knowledge and careful insight, those large lines of policy and higher ideals which may form our guiding lines and boundaries in the practical difficulties of every day. For it is certain that all human striving must recognize the hard limits of natural law, and that any striving, no matter how intense and earnest, which is against the constitution of the world, is vain. The question, then, which we must seriously consider is this: What is the real meaning of Race; what has, in the past, been the law of race development, and what lessons has the past history of race development to teach the rising Negro people?

When we thus come to inquire into the essential difference of races we find it hard to come at once to any definite conclusion. Many criteria of race differences have in the past been proposed, as color, hair, cranial measurements and language. And manifestly, in each of these respects, human beings differ widely. They vary in color, for instance, from the marble-like pallor of the Scandinavian to the rich, dark brown of the Zulu, passing by the creamy Slav, the yellow Chinese, the light brown Sicilian and the brown Egyptian. Men vary, too, in the texture of hair from the obstinately straight hair of the Chinese to the obstinately tufted and frizzled hair of the Bushman. In measurement of heads, again, men vary; from the broad-headed Tartar to the medium-headed European and the narrow-headed Hottentot; or, again in language, from the highly-inflected Roman tongue to the monosyllabic Chinese. All these physical characteristics are patent enough, and if they agreed with each other it would be very easy to classify mankind. Unfortunately for scientists, however, these criteria of race are most exasperatingly intermingled. Color does not agree with texture of hair, for many of the dark races have straight hair; nor does color agree with the breadth of the head, for the yellow Tartar has a broader head than the German; nor, again, has the science of language as yet succeeded in clearing up the relative authority of these various and contradictory criteria. The final word of science, so far, is that we have at least two, perhaps three, great families of human beings—the whites and Negroes, possibly the yellow race. That other races have arisen from the intermingling of the blood of these two. This broad division of the world's races which men like Huxley and Raetzel have introduced as more nearly true than the old five-race scheme of Blumenbach, is nothing more than an acknowledgment that, so far as purely physical characteristics are concerned, the differences between men do not explain all the differences of their history. It declares, as Darwin himself said, that great as is the physical unlikeness of the various races of men their likenesses are greater, and upon this rests the whole scientific doctrine of Human Brotherhood.

Although the wonderful developments of human history teach that the grosser physical differences of color, hair and bone go but a short way toward explaining the different roles which groups of men have played in Human Progress, yet there are differences—subtle, delicate and elusive, though they may be—which have silently but definitely separated men into groups. While these subtle forces have generally followed the natural cleavage of common blood, descent and physical peculiarities, they have at other times swept across and ignored these. At all times, however, they have divided human beings into races, which, while they perhaps transcend scientific definition, nevertheless, are clearly defined to the eye of the Historian and Sociologist.

If this be true, then the history of the world is the history, not of individuals, but of groups, not of nations, but of races, and he who ignores or seeks to override the race idea in human history ignores and overrides the central thought of all history. What, then, is a race? It is a vast family of human beings, generally of common blood and language, always of common history, traditions and impulses, who are both voluntarily and involuntarily striving together for the accomplishment of certain more or less vividly conceived ideals of life.

Turning to real history, there can be no doubt, first, as to the widespread, nay, universal, prevalence of the race idea, the race spirit, the race ideal, and as to its efficiency as the vastest and most ingenious invention for human progress. We, who have been reared and trained under the individualistic philosophy of the Declaration of Independence and the laisser-faire philosophy of Adam Smith, are loath to see and loath to acknowledge this patent fact of human history. We see the Pharaohs, Caesars, Toussaints and Napoleons of history and forget the vast races of which they were but epitomized expressions. We are apt to think in our American impatience, that while it may have been true in the past that closed race groups made history, that here in conglomerate America *nous avons changer tout cela*—we have changed all that, and have no need of this ancient instrument of progress. This assumption of which the Negro people are especially fond, can not be established by a careful consideration of history.

We find upon the world's stage today eight distinctly differentiated races, in the sense in which History tells us the word must be used. They are, the Slavs of eastern Europe, the Teutons of middle Europe, the English of Great Britain and America, the Romance nations of Southern and Western Europe, the Negroes of Africa and America, the Semitic people of Western Asia and Northern Africa, the Hindoos of Central

Asia and the Mongolians of Eastern Asia. There are, of course, other minor race groups, as the American Indians, the Esquimaux and the South Sea Islanders; these larger races, too, are far from homogeneous; the Slav includes the Czech, the Magyar, the Pole and the Russian; the Teuton includes the German, the Scandinavian and the Dutch; the English include the Scotch, the Irish and the conglomerate American. Under Romance nations the widely-differing Frenchman, Italian, Sicilian and Spaniard are comprehended. The term Negro is, perhaps, the most indefinite of all, combining the Mulattoes and Zamboes of America and the Egyptians, Bantus and Bushmen of Africa. Among the Hindoos are traces of widely differing nations, while the great Chinese, Tartar, Corean and Japanese families fall under the one designation—Mongolian.

The question now is: What is the real distinction between these nations? Is it the physical differences of blood, color and cranial measurements? Certainly we must all acknowledge that physical differences play a great part, and that, with wide exceptions and qualifications, these eight great races of to-day follow the cleavage of physical race distinctions; the English and Teuton represent the white variety of mankind; the Mongolian, the yellow; the Negroes, the black. Between these are many crosses and mixtures, where Mongolian and Teuton have blended into the Slav, and other mixtures have produced the Romance nations and the Semites. But while race differences have followed mainly physical race lines, yet no mere physical distinctions would really define or explain the deeper differences—the cohesiveness and continuity of these groups. The deeper differences are spiritual, psychical, differences—undoubtedly based on the physical, but infinitely transcending them. The forces that bind together the Teuton nations are, then, first, their race identity and common blood; secondly, and more important, a common history, common laws and religion, similar habits of thought and a conscious striving together for certain ideals of life. The whole process which has brought about these race differentiations has been a growth, and the great characteristic of this growth has been the differentiation of spiritual and mental differences between great races of mankind and the integration of physical differences.

The age of nomadic tribes of closely related individuals represents the maximum of physical differences. They were practically vast families, and there were as many groups as families. As the families came together to form cities the physical differences lessened, purity of blood was replaced by the requirement of domicile, and all who lived within the city bounds became gradually to be regarded as members of the group; *i. e.*, there was a slight and slow breaking down of physical barriers. This, however, was accompanied by an increase of the spiritual and social differences between cities. This city became husbandmen, this, merchants, another warriors, and so on. The *ideals of life* for which the different cities struggled were different. When at last cities began to coalesce into nations there was another breaking down of barriers which separated groups of men. The larger and broader differences of color, hair and physical proportions were not by any means ignored, but myriads of minor differences disappeared, and the sociological and historical races of men began to approximate the present division of races as indicated by physical researches. At the same time the spiritual and physical differences of race groups which constituted the nations became deep and decisive. The English nation stood for constitutional liberty and commercial freedom; the German nation for science and philosophy; the Romance nations stood for literature and art, and the other race groups are striving, each in its own way, to develope for civilization its particular message, its particular ideal, which shall help to guide the world nearer and nearer that perfection of human life for which we all long, that

"one far off Divine event."

This has been the function of race differences up to the present time. What shall be its function in the future? Manifestly some of the great races of today—particularly the Negro race—have not as yet given to civilization the full spiritual message which they are capable of giving. I will not say that the Negro race has as yet given no message to the world, for it is still a mooted question among scientists as to just how far Egyptian civilization was Negro in its origin; if it was not wholly Negro, it was certainly very closely allied. Be that as it may, however, the fact still remains that the full, complete Negro message of the whole Negro race has not as yet been given to the world: that the messages and ideal of the yellow race have not been completed, and that the striving of the mighty Slavs has but begun. The question is, then: How shall this message be delivered; how shall these various ideals be realized? The answer is plain: By the development of these race groups, not as individuals, but as races. For the development of Japanese genius, Japanese literature and art, Japanese spirit, only Japanese, bound and welded together, Japanese inspired by one vast ideal, can work out in its fullness the wonderful message which Japan has for the nations of the earth. For the development of Negro genius, of Negro literature and art, of Negro spirit, only Negroes bound and welded together, Negroes inspired by one vast ideal, can work out in its fullness the great message we have for humanity. We cannot reverse history; we are subject to the same natural laws as other races, and if the Negro is ever to be a factor in the world's history—if among the gaily-colored banners that deck the broad ramparts of civilization is to hang one uncompromising black, then it must be placed there by black hands, fashioned by black heads and hallowed by the travail of 200,000,000 black hearts beating in one glad song of jubilee.

For this reason, the advance guard of the Negro people—the 8,000,000 people of Negro blood in the United States of America—must soon come to realize that if they are to take their just place in the van of Pan-Negroism, then their destiny is *not* absorption by the white Americans. That if in America it is to be proven for the first time in the modern world that not only Negroes are capable of evolving individual men like Toussaint, the Saviour, but are a nation stored with wonderful possibilities of culture, then their destiny is not a servile imitation of Anglo-Saxon culture, but a stalwart originality which shall unswervingly follow Negro ideals.

It may, however, be objected here that the situation of our race in America renders this attitude impossible; that our sole hope of salvation lies in our being able to lose our race identity in the commingled blood of the nation; and that any other course would merely increase the friction of races which we call race prejudice, and against which we have so long and so earnestly fought.

Here, then, is the dilemma, and it is a puzzling one, I admit. No Negro who has given earnest thought to the situation of his people in America has failed, at some time in life, to find himself at these cross-roads; has failed to ask himself at some time: What, after all, am I? Am I an American or am I a Negro? Can I be both? Or is it my duty to cease to be a Negro as soon as possible and be an American? If I strive as a Negro, am I not perpetuating the very cleft that threatens and separates Black and White America? Is not my only possible practical aim the subduction of all that is Negro in me to the American? Does my black blood place upon me any more obligation to assert my nationality than German, or Irish or Italian blood would?

It is such incessant self-questioning and the hesitation that arises from it, that is making the present period a time of vacillation and contradiction for the American Negro; combined race action is stifled, race responsibility is shirked, race enterprises languish, and the best blood, the best talent, the best energy of the Negro people cannot be marshalled to do the bidding of the race. They stand back to make room for every rascal and demagogue who chooses to cloak his selfish deviltry under the veil of race pride.

Is this right? Is it rational? Is it good policy? Have we in America a distinct mission as a race—a distinct sphere of action and an opportunity for race development, or is self-obliteration the highest end to which Negro blood dare aspire?

If we carefully consider what race prejudice really is, we find it, historically, to be nothing but the friction between different groups of people; it is the difference in aim, in feeling, in ideals of two different races; if, now, this difference exists touching territory, laws, language, or even religion, it is manifest that these people cannot live in the same territory without fatal collision; but if, on the other hand, there is substantial agreement in laws, language and religion; if there is a satisfactory adjustment of economic life, then there is no reason why, in the same country and on the same street, two or three great national ideals might not thrive and develop, that men of different races might not strive together for their race ideals as well, perhaps even better, than in isolation. Here, it seems to me, is the reading of the riddle that puzzles so many of us. We are Americans, not only by birth and by citizenship, but by our political ideals, our language, our religion. Farther than that, our Americanism does not go. At that point, we are Negroes, members of a vast historic race that from the very dawn of creation has slept, but half awakening in the dark forests of its African fatherland. We are the first fruits of this new nation, the harbinger of that black to-morrow which is yet destined to soften the whiteness of the Teutonic to-day. We are that people whose subtle sense of song has given America its only American music, its only American fairy tales, its only touch of pathos and humor amid its mad money-getting plutocracy. As such, it is our duty to conserve our physical powers, our intellectual endowments, our spiritual ideals; as a race we must strive by race organization, by race solidarity, by race unity to the realization of that broader humanity which freely recognizes differences in men, but sternly deprecates inequality in their opportunities of development.

For the accomplishment of these ends we need race organizations: Negro colleges, Negro newspapers, Negro business organizations, a Negro school of literature and art, and an intellectual clearing house, for all these products of the Negro mind, which we may call a Negro Academy. Not only is all this necessary for positive advance, it is absolutely imperative for negative defense. Let us not deceive ourselves at our situation in this country. Weighted with a heritage of moral iniquity from our past history, hard pressed in the economic world by foreign immigrants and native prejudice, hated here, despised there and pitied everywhere; our one haven of refuge is ourselves, and but one means of advance, our own belief in our great destiny, our own implicit trust in our ability and worth. There is no power under God's high heaven that can stop the advance of eight thousand thousand honest, earnest, inspired and united people. But—and here is the rub—they *must* be honest, fearlessly criticising their own faults, zealously correcting them; they must be *earnest*. No people that laughs at itself, and ridicules itself, and wishes to God it was anything but itself ever wrote its name in history; it *must* be inspired with the Divine faith of our black mothers, that out of the blood and dust of battle will march a victorious host, a mighty nation, a peculiar people, to speak to the nations of earth a Divine truth that shall make them free. And such a people must be united; not merely united for the organized theft of political spoils, not united to disgrace religion with whoremongers and ward-heelers; not united merely to protest and pass resolutions, but united to stop the ravages of consumption among the Negro people, united to keep black boys from loafing, gambling and crime; united to guard the purity of black women and to reduce that vast army of black prostitutes that is today marching to hell; and united in serious organizations, to determine by careful conference and thoughtful interchange of opinion the broad lines of policy and action for the American Negro.

This, is the reason for being which the Amerian Negro Academy has. It aims at once to be the epitome and expression of the intellect of the black-blooded people of America, the exponent of the race ideals of one of the world's great races. As such, the Academy must, if successful, be

(*a*). Representative in character.
(*b*). Impartial in conduct.
(*c*). Firm in leadership.

It must be representative in character; not in that it represents all interests or all factions, but in that it seeks to comprise something of the *best* thought, the most unselfish striving and the highest ideals. There are scattered in forgotten nooks and corners throughout the land, Negroes of some considerable training, of high minds, and high motives, who are unknown to their fellows, who exert far too little influence. These the Negro Academy should strive to bring into touch with each other and to give them a common mouthpiece.

The Academy should be impartial in conduct; while it aims to exalt the people it should aim to do so by truth—not by lies, by honesty—not by flattery. It should continually impress the fact upon the Negro people that they must not expect to have things done for them—they MUST DO FOR

THEMSELVES; that they have on their hands a vast work of self-reformation to do, and that a little less complaint and whining, and a little more dogged work and manly striving would do us more credit and benefit than a thousand Force or Civil Rights bills.

Finally, the American Negro Academy must point out a practical path of advance to the Negro people; there lie before every Negro today hundreds of questions of policy and right which must be settled and which each one settles now, not in accordance with any rule, but by impulse or individual preference; for instance: What should be the attitude of Negroes toward the educational qualification for voters? What should be our attitude toward separate schools? How should we meet discriminations on railways and in hotels? Such questions need not so much specific answers for each part as a general expression of policy, and nobody should be better fitted to announce such a policy than a representative honest Negro Academy.

All this, however, must come in time after careful organization and long conference. The immediate work before us should be practical and have direct bearing upon the situation of the Negro. The historical work of collecting the laws of the United States and of the various States of the Union with regard to the Negro is a work of such magnitude and importance that no body but one like this could think of undertaking it. If we could accomplish that one task we would justify our existence.

In the field of Sociology an appalling work lies before us. First, we must unflinchingly and bravely face the truth, not with apologies, but with solemn earnestness. The Negro Academy ought to sound a note of warning that would echo in every black cabin in the land: *Unless we conquer our present vices they will conquer us;* we are diseased, we are developing criminal tendencies, and an alarmingly large percentage of our men and women are sexually impure. The Negro Academy should stand and proclaim this over the housetops, crying with Garrison: *I will not equivocate, I will not retreat a single inch, and I will be heard.* The Academy should seek to gather about it the talented, unselfish men, the pure and noble-minded women, to fight an army of devils that disgraces our manhood and our womanhood. There does not stand today upon God's earth a race more capable in muscle, in intellect, in morals, than the American Negro, if he will bend his energies in the right direction; if he will

> Burst his birth's invidious bar
> And grasp the skirts of happy chance,
> And breast the blows of circumstance,
> And grapple with his evil star.

In science and morals, I have indicated two fields of work for the Academy. Finally, in practical policy, I wish to suggest the following *Academy Creed*:

1. We believe that the Negro people, as a race, have a contribution to make to civilization and humanity, which no other race can make.

2. We believe it the duty of the Americans of Negro descent, as a body, to maintain their race identity until this mission of the Negro people is accomplished, and the ideal of human brotherhood has become a practical possibility.

3. We believe that, unless modern civilization is a failure, it is entirely feasible and practicable for two races in such essential political, economic, and religious harmony as the white and colored people of America, to develop side by side in peace and mutual happiness, the peculiar contribution which each has to make to the culture of their common country.

4. As a means to this end we advocate, not such social equality between these races as would disregard human likes and dislikes, but such a social equilibrium as would, throughout all the complicated relations of life, give due and just consideration to culture, ability, and moral worth, whether they be found under white or black skins.

5. We believe that the first and greatest step toward the settlement of the present friction between the races—commonly called the Negro Problem—lies in the correction of the immorality, crime and laziness among the Negroes themselves, which still remains as a heritage from slavery. We believe that only earnest and long continued efforts on our own part can cure these social ills.

6. We believe that the second great step toward a better adjustment of the relations between the races, should be a more impartial selection of ability in the economic and intellectual world, and a greater respect for personal liberty and worth, regardless of race. We believe that only earnest efforts on the part of the white people of this country will bring much needed reform in these matters.

7. On the basis of the foregoing declaration, and firmly believing in our high destiny, we, as American Negroes, are resolved to strive in every honorable way for the realization of the best and highest aims, for the development of strong manhood and pure womanhood, and for the rearing of a race ideal in America and Africa, to the glory of God and the uplifting of the Negro people.

American Negro Academy, *Occasional Papers*, No. 2, 1897

Careers Open to College-Bred Negroes

TO THE YOUNG ears that hearken behind college walls at the confused murmur of the world beyond, there comes at times a strangely discordant note to mar the music of their lives. Men tell them that college is a play world—the mirage of real life; the place where men climb or seek to climb heights whence they must sooner or later sink into the dust of real life. Scarcely a commencement season passes but what, amid congratulation and rejoicing, amid high resolve and lofty sentiment, stalks this pale, half-mocking ghost, crying to the new born bachelor in arts: You have played—now comes work.

And, therefore, students of the class of '98, I have thought to take this oft-repeated idea and talk with you in this last hour of your college days about the relation which, in your lives, a liberal education bears to bread-winning.

And first, young men and women, I heartily join in congratulating you to whom has been vouchsafed the vision splendid—you who stand where once I stood,

> "When meadow, grove, and stream,
> The earth, and every common sight,
> To me did seem
> Apparelled in celestial light,
> The glory and the freshness of a dream."

And yet, not a dream, but a mighty reality—a glimpse of the higher life, the broader possibilities of humanity, which is granted to the man who, amid the rush and roar of living, pauses four short years to learn what living means.

The vision of the rich meaning of life, which comes to you as students, as men of culture, comes dimly or not at all to the plodding masses of men, and even to men of high estate it comes too often blurred and distorted by selfishness and greed. But you have seen it in the freshness and sunshine of youth; here you have talked with Aristotle and Shakespeare, have learned of Euclid, have heard the solemn drama of a world, and thought the thoughts of seers and heroes of the world that was. Out of such lore, out of such light and shade, has the vision of the world appeared before you: you have not all comprehended it; you have, many of you, but glanced at its brilliant hues, and have missed the speaking splendor of the background.

I remember how once I stood near the ancient cathedral at Berne, looking at the Alps; I heard the rushing waters below and knew their music; I saw the rolling fields beyond and thought them pretty; then I saw the hills and the towering masses of dark mountains; they were beautiful, and yet I saw them with a tinge of disappointment, but even as I turned away, I glanced toward the sky, and then my heart leaped—for there above the meadows and the waters, above the hills and the mountains, blazed in the evening sunshine, the mighty, snow-clad peaks of the high Alps, glistening and glorious with the hues of the rainbow, in spotless purity and awful majesty. And so many a man to whom opportunity has unveiled some revelation of the broader, truer world, has turned away from it, half seen and half known.

But some have seen the vision, have comprehended all the meaning of a liberal education; and now, as you turn away half-regretfully, half gladly, what relation has this day of transfiguration to the hard, cold paths of the world beyond these walls? Is it to be but a memory and a longing, or if more than this, how much more?

I presume that few of you have fully realized that with tomorrow morning you begin to earn your own bread and butter; that to-day is the commencement of a new life on which you are to find self-support by daily toil. And I am glad if you have not given this matter too much thought or worry, for, surely, if you have done well your college work you have had other things to think of, problems of life and humanity far broader than your own single destiny; not that you have neglected dreams and plans of parts that you might play in life, but that you have scarce thought out its dry details. And, therefore, to most of you the nearness of real life dawned this morning with a certain suddenness; with something of that dark dismay with which the human creator faces his own creature—with some thought, too, half of rebellion and an aimless asking: Why must I turn from so pleasant a life to one hard and matter of fact? Why must I leave the pleasures of study and dear companionship and high inspiration to "bear the whips and scorns of time, the oppressor's wrong, the proud man's contumely?"

To-day the paradox of life rises over you as never before, and you wonder why you, of all men, should not have been born rich and privileged, not to see the vision of the world and all the glory that shall be, fade into some distant future, leaving long paths of dirt and rocks between. All these questions you have asked, I have asked, and all men have asked, who, whether on the college rostrum or with the pick and shovel, have, on a commencement morning, turned from study to deeds, from ideals to realization, from thought to life.

All this I cannot answer plainly, and yet the shadow of answer falls on us all; for why should the sun rise if there be neither noon nor evening, and what is a life that is all beginning? And have not these, your college days, been all the happier for the promise and prophecy of a life to come?

Three universal laws underlie the necessity of earning a living: the law of work, the law of sacrifice, the law of service. The law of work declares that to live one must toil, continuously, zealously; the apple may hang ripe upon the tree, but to eat we must pick it; grain will sprout and grow, but not till we plant it; houses will shelter us and clothes cover us only as we build and weave. Sometimes, to be sure, it may seem that enjoyment came without work and sacrifice—but it is not so. Some one toils, some one delves, and though we may shift our burden on the bowed shoulders of others—yet that is the necessity of the sick, or the shame of the lazy, or the crime of the coward.

Blind toil alone, however, will not satisfy the wants of aught but the lowest and simplest culture; the greater satisfaction comes from the sacrifice of to-day's enjoyment that tomorrow's may be greater; of this year's consumption to increase next year's production; of the indulgence of youth to the vigor of old age, of the pleasure of one life to the richer heritage of humanity; this is the law of sacrifice, and we see it everywhere: in the fruit we save to ripen, in the fields that lie fallow, in the years given to training and education, and in the self-sacrifice of a Socrates, a Darwin, or a David Livingstone.

Even this does not complete the laws of life as we find it in the twilight of the nineteenth century. We must not only work and sacrifice for ourselves and others, but also render each other mutual service. The physician must heal not himself, but all men; the tailor must mend the whole village; the farmer must plant for all. Thus in the civilized world each serves all, and all serve each, and the binding force is faith and skill, and the skill is bounded only by human possibility and genius, and the faith is faithful even to the untrue.

Such are the laws of that life, young people, which you enter to-day. And upon these laws have been built through the ages, in sweat of brow and sorrow of soul, all that fair world whose darkly glorious vision has made its study sweet to you, and its knowledge precious.

While these be the laws of universal life, their application differs in each age, and an equipment in life suitable to one century may be fatally unsuited to another. Therefore, you must not make the mistake of misunderstanding the age in which you live; and I especially warn you here, because as American Negroes, in the strange environment and unusual conditions of life which surround you, it will be peculiarly easy for you to fail to catch the spirit of the times; to distort the proportions of life, to seek to do what others have done better, and to seek quickly to undo what cannot legally be undone. I have often feared that the failure of many a promising young Negro was due largely to this natural ignorance. Young Negroes are born in a social system of caste that belongs to the middle ages; they inherit the moral looseness of a sixteenth century; they learn to lisp the religious controversies of the seventeenth century; they are stirred by discussions of the rights of man that belong to the eighteenth century, and it is not wonderful if they hardly realize that they live upon the threshold of the twentieth century. You, men of Fisk, must not misunderstand your age; you must know that the world does not feel the injustice of caste as it once did, but rather sees in it some antidote for a vulgar democracy; you must remember that there are central elementary moral precepts which the world utterly refuses to excuse or palliate;

you must realize that the controversies of Methodists and Baptists chiefly interest antiquarians and not active Christians of to-day; that we insist to-day on men's duties rather than their rights, and that the spirit of the century in which you will work is service not indulgence.

And surely no century more richly deserves understanding than the nineteenth. It has not the romantic interest of the fifteenth, when the world rose in a dream and wandered in the sunshine of its new discovered self, and poetry and art and tales from over seas; it has not the rugged might of that sixteenth century, when the dark monk faced the emperor of all the world, daring to be honest rather than orthodox, and crying, "Here I stand. God help me! I cannot waver."

But whatever the nineteenth century may lack in romantic or striking interest, it repays and more than repays in human opportunity; in the broadness of its conception of humanity, in the wonderful organization of effort to serve humanity. Never before have work and sacrifice and service meant so much, never before were there so many workers, such wide-spread sacrifice, such world-service. In the business of governing men, never before did so many take part. The issue is not altogether successful, and yet its measure of success far exceeds the wildest dreams of the world of long ago.

Never before have so many hands and heads joined to make the earth yield her increase, to make glad the waste places of the earth, to ply the loom, and whirl the spindle, and transform the useless and the worthless. On our breakfast table lies each morning the toil of Europe, Asia, and Africa, and the isles of the sea; we sow and spin for unseen millions, and countless myriads weave and plant for us; we have made the earth smaller and life broader by annihilating distance, magnifying the human voice and the stars, binding nation to nation, until to-day, for the first time in history, there is one standard of human culture as well in New York as in London, in Cape Town as in Paris, in Bombay as in Berlin.

Is not this, then, a century worth living in—a day worth serving? And though toil, hard, heavy toil, be the price of life, shall we not, young men and women, gladly work and sacrifice and serve

"That one, far off, divine event,
Toward which the whole creation moves"?

And we serve first for the sake of serving—to develop our own powers, gain the mastery of this human machine, and come to the broadest, deepest self-realization. And then we serve for real end of service, to make life no narrow, selfish thing, but to let it sweep as sweeps the morning—broad and full and free for all men and all time, that you and I and all may earn a living and earn, too, much more than that—a life worth living.

This, fellow-workers, is the veil of toil that hangs before the vision glorious. And yet, when on commencement morning, we leave behind the vivid hues of this, our inspiration, believe me, it is not easy to guard the sacred image, to keep alive the holy fire that lights and lightens life; to hold amid the toil and turmoil of living those old ideals fixed and tranquil before the soul. How often do we see young collegians enter life with high resolve and lofty purpose and then watch them shrink and shrink and shrink into sordid, selfish, shrewd plodders, full of distrust and sneers. Woe to the man, who, with the revelation of the world once before him, as it stands before you now, has let it fade and whiten into common day—life is death.

But you who, firm and inspired, turn toward the work of living, undismayed, knowing the world that was, loving the world that is, and believing in the world that is to be, just what can you do—what careers may you follow to realize the ideals and hopes of this day?

You cannot surely be knights and kings and magicians, but you can choose careers fully as wonderful and much more useful. You look about you in the world and see servants, they whose function it is to help the helpless, the weak and the busy—to cook, that Washington may command armies; to sweep, that Edison may have time to think. You see the laborer, that wizard who places his weak shoulders against the physical world and overturns mountains and pushes away forests, and guides the rivers, and garners the harvests. You see the manufacturer guiding the laborer with brains and with capital: he is the alchemist in whose alembic dirt turns to houses, grass to coats, and stones to food. The merchant you see standing beside him, the prophet who enables us to laugh at famine, and want, and waste, by bringing together buyer and seller, maker and user, reader and writer. There is the teacher, the giver of immortal life, the one who makes the child to start where his fathers left off, that the world may think on with one mind. Yonder stands the physician with the long sought elixir of life, the lawyer clothed in justice, the minister who seeks to add to justice righteousness, and to life ideals higher than life. Your restless eye may easily overlook the corner where sits the scientist seeking the truth that shall make us free, or the other, where the artist dies that there may live a poem or painting or a thought.

All these ways of earning a living you may see in the world, and many more. But it does not follow that you may idly or thoughtlessly choose one as you pick a flower on a summer's day. To choose a life calling is a serious thing: first, you must consider not so much what you want to do as what wants to be done; secondly, you cannot wander at will over all the world of work that wants workers, but duty and privilege and special advantage calls to the work that lies nearest your hands. The German works for Germany, the Englishman serves England, and it is the duty of the Negro to serve his blood and lineage, and so working, each for each, and all for each, we realize the goal of each for all.

The concrete question, then, that faces you of the class of '98, is What part can I best take in the striving of the eight million men and women who are bound to me by a common sorrow and a common hope, that through the striving of the Negro people this land of our fathers may live and thrive?

The most useful and universal work, and the type of all other work, is that of the servant and common laborer. The ordinary, unskilled part of this work I pass over—it is useful, it is honorable, but you have been trained for skilled work, and it is throwing away the money of this institution if its college graduates are to become Pullman porters. Even the higher branches of house-service, as cooking and nursing, and the great field of skilled labor, are rather for different training, and you will rightly leave them to the skilled graduates of our great industrial schools, with the sincere hope that so useful and promising avenues will soon be filled by able and honest artisans.

The first field that opens itself to you is the calling of the farmer. I do not mean the farm hand or the milkmaid, nor even the agricultural scientist. I mean the man who, by rational methods and business sense, with a knowledge of the world market, the methods of transportation, and the possibilities of the soil, will make this land of the South to bloom and blossom like Belgium and Holland, France and Germany; who will transform the slipshod, wasteful, happy-go-lucky farming of the South into the scientific business methods of New England and the West. There is little more reason for leaving farming to people without brains or culture than there would be in thus abandoning the other great fields of industry. Especially, however, do the Negro people need the country gentleman—the man of air and health and home and morals; and to-day we have an unparalleled chance to supply such an aristocracy. Throughout Tennessee and Georgia and Virginia, where the young people are hurrying to the industries of the cities, stand the fine old abandoned farms and decaying mansions of a gentry that has passed. You are the ones to buy these farms at a nominal price, start a new agriculture, and a balance for the sickly crowding of cities and to furnish the food and material which these cities increasingly demand, and thus help to solve some of the most intricate of our social problems.

The next great field open to you is that of the merchant, where again there is among Negroes no discouraging competition, and a broad field for development.

Those Negroes who urge the blight of color prejudice as a barrier to their entering mercantile pursuits, quite forget that they have before them an undeveloped market of eight million souls, and that these millions spend every year $150,000,000 to $300,000,000, and that a part of this expenditure, at least, could be made through Negro merchants, if well trained, educated, active men would only enter this field and cultivate it. Of course, the training of slavery was most unfortunate for business qualities. There linger among the freedmen's sons habits of laziness, of being perpetually five minutes behind time, of inattention to detail, which are fatal to modern business methods. All this can and must be unlearned, and the college man who, making himself familiar with the best business methods of a business age, starts in to open this field, will not only earn and deserve a living for himself, but will make it easier for thousands to follow his example.

And this brings me to a thought that I want especially to impress upon college men: The time has come when the American Negro is being expected to take care of himself, and not much longer to depend on alms and charity; he must become self-supporting—a source of strength and power instead of a menace and a burden to the nation; the hindrance that to-day prevents him from fulfilling this expectation with reasonable quickness is his anomalous economic condition—his lack of remunerative employment. And you, young men and women, are the ones to supply this lack. We have workers enough, brawny and willing; we have some skill, and the industrial schools are furnishing more; moreover, a people that have to-day more then $26,000,000 invested in church property alone, and who spend at least $10,000,000 each year in those churches, have capital enough to collect in savings banks and put into industrial enterprises. But what we do lack, and what schools like this must begin to supply in increasing numbers is the captain of industry, the man who can marshal and guide workers in industrial enterprises, who can foresee the demand and supply it—note the special aptitude of laborers and turn it to advantage—so guide with eye and brain the work of these black millions, that, instead of adding to the poverty of the nation and subtracting from its wealth, we may add to the wealth of the land and make Negro poverty no longer a by-word.

Here is a field for development such as few ages offer—a body of willing workers such as few nations furnish. And this field calls not for mere money-makers, or those who would ape the silly display and ostentation of certain classes of Americans; nor does it call for men narrowed and shrunk by the soul destroying commercialism of the hour, that philosophy which imagines men made for industry and not industry for men; but rather here is a chance to set a nation working, to make their work more effective, to build and fortify Negro homes, to educate Negro children, to establish institutions of protection, reform, and rescue, and to make the Negro people able to help others even as others have helped us.

Let us turn now to the professional class and ask about the openings there for college bred men. As to the demand in one department there can be no doubt. If ever a nation needed the gospel of health presented to them, it is the negro race, with its alarming death rate, its careless habits, its widows and orphans, and its sick and maimed. For the well trained physician, as distinguished from the quack, and the man who is too hurried to learn, there is a large and important work. The remuneration which a poor people can pay will not be large, but the chance for usefulness and far-reaching influence on the future of our race and country can scarcely be over-estimated. Especially is the calling open to young women, who ought to find here congenial, useful employment, and employment, perhaps, next in nobility to that of the noblest and best—motherhood.

When we come to the profession of law we have a narrower and less obvious field, one in which there is plenty of room for success, but against the peculiar difficulties of which, young people need warning and advice. These difficulties arise from the fact that, first, the Negro himself furnishes little important or lucrative law business, and, secondly, even among the whites, the profession is overcrowded, and only men of ability or some wealth and much influence can expect much success. Thus, many changes must come before the handicap of color prejudice will allow Negroes to start in this profession with an even chance. Yet, here as elsewhere, blood will tell.

For thirty years the chief function of the Negro college has been that of furnishing teachers for the Negro schools, and the extraordinary success and value of this work has not yet been adequately recognized. Nevertheless, it is evident that this work has already passed through many phases and is about to pass through others. Fisk University at first furnished common school teachers, then teachers of schools that teach common school teachers; finally, teachers of men who teach the teachers; with each of these steps comes, to be sure, a demand for better quality, but also for a smaller quantity.

The field for teaching, therefore, open to the class of '98, is smaller than that open to former classes and more exacting in its demands. What is true now is apt to be emphasized in the future; specially trained teachers of high attainments will ever find some demand for their services. On the other hand, most college graduates will slowly turn to other work. Hereafter, when Negro education is more firmly founded, the better trained college men will be more in demand. This, then, is a field still open—of broad usefulness and demanding the very best in character, and the better in training and knowledge, only the competition is sharp, and is destined to be sharper.

I now turn to the Christian ministry with something of diffidence. The development of the Negro church has been so extraordinary, and of such deep sociological interest that its future course is a matter of great concern. As it is now, churches organized among Negroes are, for the most part, curiously composite institutions, which combine the work of churches, theaters, newspapers, homes, schools, and lodges. As a social and business institution the church has had marvelous success and has done much for the Negro people. As a religious institution, also, it has played some part, but it is needless to say that its many other activities have not increased the efficiency of its function as a teacher of morals and inspirer to the high ideals of Christianity. An institution so popular that there is now in the United States one organization for every sixty Negro families, has, naturally, already attracted to its leadership a vast army of men. Moreover, the severest charge that can be brought against the Christian education of the Negro in the South during the last thirty years, is the reckless way in which sap-headed young fellows, without ability, and, in some cases, without character, have been urged and pushed into the ministry. It is time now to halt. It is time to say to young men like you: Qualifications that would be of no service elsewhere are not needed in the church; a general desire to be good, joined to a glib tongue, is not the sort of combination that is going to make the Negro people stop stealing and committing adultery. And, instead of aimless, wholesale invitations to enter this calling of life, we need to put our hands kindly on the shoulders of some young candidates, and tell them firmly that they are not fitted to be heads of the church of Christ. What we need is not more but fewer ministers, but in that lesser number we certainly need earnest, broad, and cultured men; men who do a good deal more than they say; men of broad plans and far-seeing thought; men who will extend the charitable and rescue work of the churches, encourage home getting, guard the children of the flock, not on Sundays, but on week days, make the people use savings banks, and, in fine, men who will really be active agents of social and moral reform in their communities. There, and there only, is the soil which will transform the mysticism of Negro religion into the righteousness of Christianity.

There is then an opening for college men in this field, but it is a field to be entered with more care than others, not with less; to be chosen by men of more stable character than others, not of less; and it is the one field where the man who doubts his fitness had best give the world the benefit of the doubt. But to those consecrated men who can and will place themselves to-day at the head of Negro religious life and guide this wavering people to a Christianity pure and holy and true—to those men in the day of reckoning shall surely come the benediction of a useful life, and the "Well done!" of the Master.

Finally, I come to the field of the scientist and the artist—of the men who seek to know and create. And here little can be said of openings or of hindrances—for the way of such men is the dim and unfenced moor that wends its path beyond the world into the unknown; the man who enters here must expect long journeys, poor and unknown and often discouraged. To do in science and literature to-day anything worth the doing, anything that is really good and lasting, is hard to any one, impossible to many. And here the young Negro so often forgets that "art is long, and time is fleeting." The first applause of his good-natured race too often turns his head; lets him rest on his oars, and instead of pursuing more doggedly the faint chance of doing some little masterpiece, he lingers upon his notoriety, and puts his picture and biography in the papers. For the man who will work, and dig, and starve, there is a chance to do here incalculable good for the Negro race; for the woman in whose soul the divine music of our fathers has touched some answering chord of genius, there is a chance to do more than follow the masters; to all of you in whom the tragedy of life, or its fitful comedy, has created a tale worth the telling, there is a chance to gain listeners who will know no color line. Everywhere there is work to be done; in physical and social science, in literature, painting and architecture, in music and sculpture, in every place where genius and toil will unite and strive.

Let me now briefly review these fields of work:

A broad field of scientific, business-like farming.

The uncultivated but promising field of the Negro merchant, with a constituency of eight millions.

The pressing demands for captains of industry to employ the labor, to direct the work, and develop the capacity of Negro workmen by industrial enterprise.

The large field for well trained physicians.

Some small demand for lawyers.

A considerable field for specially trained teachers.

The pressing necessity for fewer ministers of better type and more thorough devotion.

An ever open field for talent and application in literature, science, and art.

Such are some of the paths that open before you, class of '98, and along these you go toward the goal you have set for yourselves. Which path you will take you must choose, and the choice is difficult. Nevertheless, it cannot be long put off—for no choice is a choice. And when you have chosen, stand by it, for the man who ever is wavering and choosing again is wasting God's time. Choose, then, remembering that failure is the lot of many men, and that no success will be so marvelous but what it beckons to greater goals beyond.

And with the life work chosen, remember that it can become, as you will it, drudgery or heroism, prosaic or romantic, brutal or divine. Who of the world to-day cares whether Washington was a farmer or a merchant? Who thinks of Lincoln as a country lawyer, or reads of St. Peter, the fisherman, prays to Jesus Christ, the carpenter? If you make the object of your life calling food and drink, food and drink it will yield you grudgingly—but if above and beyond mere existence you seek to play well your part because it is worth playing—to do your duty because the world thirsts for your service, to perform clean, honest, thorough work, not for cheap applause, but because the work needs to be done, then is all your toil and drudgery transfigured into divine service and joins the mighty lives that have swept beyond time into the everlasting world. In this sense, is it, young men and women, that the vision of life you have gained here is truer and holier and more real than the narrow, sordid views of life which you meet on the streets and in the homes of smaller souls. Cling to those ideals, cherish them, and in travail and sorrow, if need be, make them more true.

It is now ten years since I stood amid these walls on my commencement morning, ten years full of toil and happiness and sorrow, and the full delight of hard work. And as I look back on that youthful gleam, and see the vision splendid, the trailing clouds of glory that lighted then the wide way of life, I am ever glad that I stepped into the world guided of strong faith in its promises, and inspired by no sordid aims. And from that world I come back to welcome you, my brothers and my sisters. I cannot promise you happiness always, but I can promise you divine discontent with the imperfect. I cannot promise you success—'tis not in mortals to command success.

But as you step into life I can give you three watchwords: First, you are Negroes, members of that dark, historic race that from the world's dawn has slept to hear the trumpet summons sound through our ears. Cherish unwavering faith in the blood of your fathers, and make sure this last triumph of humanity. Remember next, that you are gentlemen and ladies, trained in the liberal arts and subjects in that vast kingdom of culture that has lighted the world from its infancy and guided it through bigotry and falsehood and sin. As such, let us see in you an unfaltering honesty wedded to that finer courtesy and breeding which is the heritage of the well trained and the well born. And, finally, remember that you are the sons of Fisk University, that venerable mother who rose out of the blood and dust of battle to work the triumphs of the Prince of Peace. The mighty blessing of all her sons and daughters encompass you, and the sad sacrifice of every pure soul, living and dead, that has made her what she is, bend its dark wings about you and make you brave and good! And then through the weary striving and disappointment of life fear not for the end, even though you fail:

> "Truth forever on the scaffold,
>   Wrong forever on the throne,
> Yet that scaffold sways the future,
>   And behind the dim unknown
> Standeth God within the shadow,
>   Keeping watch above his own."

Commencement Address, Fisk University, June 1898

The Talented Tenth

THE NEGRO RACE, like all races, is going to be saved by its exceptional men. The problem of education, then, among Negroes must first of all deal with the Talented Tenth; it is the problem of developing the Best of this race that they may guide the Mass away from the contamination and death of the Worst, in their own and other races. Now the training of men is a difficult and intricate task. Its technique is a matter for educational experts, but its object is for the vision of seers. If we make money the object of man-training, we shall develop money-makers but not necessarily men; if we make technical skill the object of education, we may possess artisans but not, in nature, men. Men we shall have only as we make manhood the object of the work of the schools—intelligence, broad sympathy, knowledge of the world that was and is, and of the relation of men to it—this is the curriculum of that Higher Education which must underlie true life. On this foundation we may build bread winning, skill of hand and quickness of brain, with never a fear lest the child and man mistake the means of living for the object of life.

If this be true—and who can deny it—three tasks lay before me; first to show from the past that the Talented Tenth as they have risen among American Negroes have been worthy of leadership; secondly, to show how these men may be educated and developed; and thirdly, to show their relation to the Negro problem.

You misjudge us because you do not know us. From the very first it has been the educated and intelligent of the Negro people that have led and elevated the mass, and the sole obstacles that nullified and retarded their efforts were slavery and race prejudice; for what is slavery but the legalized survival of the unfit and the nullification of the work of natural internal leadership? Negro leadership, therefore, sought from the first to rid the race of this awful incubus that it might make way for natural selection and the survival of the fittest. In colonial days came Phillis Wheatley and Paul Cuffe striving against the bars of prejudice; and Benjamin Banneker, the almanac maker, voiced their longings when he said to Thomas Jefferson, "I freely and cheerfully acknowledge that I am of the African race, and in colour which is natural to them, of the deepest dye; and it is under a sense of the most profound gratitude to the Supreme Ruler of the Universe, that I now confess to you that I am not under that state of tyrannical thraldom and inhuman captivity to which too many of my brethren are doomed, but that I have abundantly tasted of the fruition of those blessings which proceed from that free and unequalled liberty with which you are favored, and which I hope you will willingly allow, you have mercifully received from the immediate hand of that Being from whom proceedeth every good and perfect gift.

"Suffer me to recall to your mind that time, in which the arms of the British crown were exerted with every powerful effort, in order to reduce you to a state of servitude; look back, I entreat you, on the variety of dangers to which you were exposed; reflect on that period in which every human aid appeared unavailable, and in which even hope and fortitude wore the aspect of inability to the conflict, and you cannot but be led to a serious and grateful sense of your miraculous and providential preservation, you cannot but acknowledge, that the present freedom and tranquility which you enjoy, you have mercifully received, and that a peculiar blessing of heaven.

"This, sir, was a time when you clearly saw into the injustice of a state of Slavery, and in which you had just apprehensions of the horrors of its condition. It was then that your abhorrence thereof was so excited, that you publicly held forth this true and invaluable doctrine, which is worthy to be recorded and remembered in all succeeding ages: 'We hold these truths to be self evident, that all men are created equal; that they are endowed with certain inalienable rights, and that among these are life, liberty and the pursuit of happiness.' "

Then came Dr. James Derham, who could tell even the learned Dr. Rush something of medicine, and Lemuel Haynes, to whom Middlebury College gave a honorary A. M.

in 1804. These and others we may call the Revolutionary group of distinguished Negroes—they were persons of marked ability, leaders of a Talented Tenth, standing conspicuously among the best of their time. They strove by word and deed to save the color line from becoming the line between the bond and free, but all they could do was nullified by Eli Whitney and the Curse of Gold. So they passed into forgetfulness.

But their spirit did not wholly die; here and there in the early part of the century came other exceptional men. Some were natural sons of unnatural fathers and were given often a liberal training and thus a race of educated mulattoes sprang up to plead for black men's rights. There was Ira Aldridge, whom all Europe loved to honor; there was that Voice crying in the Wilderness, David Walker, and saying:

"I declare it does appear to me as though some nations think God is asleep, or that he made the Africans for nothing else but to dig their mines and work their farms, or they cannot believe history, sacred or profane. I ask every man who has a heart, and is blessed with the privilege of believing—Is not God a God of justice to all his creatures? Do you say he is? Then if he gives peace and tranquility to tyrants and permits them to keep our fathers, our mothers, ourselves and our children in eternal ignorance and wretchedness to support them and their families, would he be to us a God of Justice? I ask, O, ye Christians, who hold us and our children in the most abject ignorance and degradation that ever a people were afflicted with since the world began—I say if God gives you peace and tranquility, and suffers you thus to go on afflicting us, and our children, who have never given you the least provocation—would He be to us a God of Justice? If you will allow that we are men, who feel for each other, does not the blood of our fathers and of us, their children, cry aloud to the Lord of Sabaoth against you for the cruelties and murders with which you have and do continue to afflict us?"

This was the wild voice that first aroused Southern legislators in 1829 to the terrors of abolitionism.

In 1831 there met that first Negro convention in Philadelphia, at which the world gaped curiously but which bravely attacked the problems of race and slavery, crying out against persecution and declaring that "Laws as cruel in themselves as they were unconstitutional and unjust, have in many places been enacted against our poor, unfriended and unoffending brethren (without a shadow of provocation on our part), at whose bare recital the very savage draws himself up for fear of contagion—looks noble and prides himself because he bears not the name of Christian." Side by side this free Negro movement, and the movement for abolition, strove until they merged into one strong stream. Too little notice has been taken of the work which the Talented Tenth among Negroes took in the great abolition crusade. From the very day that a Philadelphia colored man became the first subscriber to Garrison's "Liberator," to the day when Negro soldiers made the Emancipation Proclamation possible, black leaders worked shoulder to shoulder with white men in a movement, the success of which would have been impossible without them. There was Purvis and Remond, Pennington and Highland Garnett, Sojourner Truth and Alexander Crummell, and above all, Frederick Douglass—what would the abolition movement have been without them? They stood as living examples of the possibilities of the Negro race, their own hard experiences and well wrought culture said silently more than all the drawn periods of orators—they were the men who made American slavery impossible. As Maria Weston Chapman once said, from the school of anti-slavery agitation "a throng of authors, editors, lawyers, orators and accomplished gentlemen of color have taken their degree! It has equally implanted hopes and aspirations, noble thoughts, and sublime purposes, in the hearts of both races. It has prepared the white man for the freedom of the black man, and it has made the black man scorn the thought of enslavement, as does a white man, as far as its influence has extended. Strengthen that noble influence! Before its organization, the country only saw here and there in slavery some faithful Cudjoe or Dinah, whose strong natures blossomed even in bondage, like a fine plant beneath a heavy stone. Now, under the elevating and cherishing influence of the American Anti-slavery Society, the colored race, like the white, furnishes Corinthian capitals for the noblest temples."

Where were these black abolitionists trained? Some, like

Frederick Douglass, were self-trained, but yet trained liberally; others, like Alexander Crummell and McCune Smith, graduated from famous foreign universities. Most of them rose up through the colored schools of New York and Philadelphia and Boston, taught by college-bred men like Russworm, of Dartmouth, and college-bred white men like Neau and Benezet.

After emancipation came a new group of educated and gifted leaders: Langston, Bruce and Elliot, Greener, Williams and Payne. Through political organization, historical and polemic writing and moral regeneration, these men strove to uplift their people. It is the fashion of to-day to sneer at them and to say that with freedom Negro leadership should have begun at the plow and not in the Senate—a foolish and mischievous lie; two hundred and fifty years that black serf toiled at the plow and yet that toiling was in vain till the Senate passed the war amendments; and two hundred and fifty years more the half-free serf of to-day may toil at his plow, but unless he have political rights and righteously guarded civic status, he will still remain the poverty-stricken and ignorant plaything of rascals, that he now is. This all sane men know even if they dare not say it.

And so we come to the present—a day of cowardice and vacillation, of strident wide-voiced wrong and faint hearted compromise; of double-faced dallying with Truth and Right. Who are to-day guiding the work of the Negro people? The "exceptions" of course. And yet so sure as this Talented Tenth is pointed out, the blind worshippers of the Average cry out in alarm: "These are exceptions, look here at death, disease and crime—these are the happy rule." Of course they are the rule, because a silly nation made them the rule: Because for three long centuries this people lynched Negroes who dared to be brave, raped black women who dared to be virtuous, crushed dark-hued youth who dared to be ambitious, and encouraged and made to flourish servility and lewdness and apathy. But not even this was able to crush all manhood and chastity and aspiration from black folk. A saving remnant continually survives and persists, continually aspires, continually shows itself in thrift and ability and character. Exceptional it is to be sure, but this is its chiefest promise; it shows the capability of Negro blood, the promise of black men. Do Americans ever stop to reflect that there are in this land a million men of Negro blood, well-educated, owners of homes, against the honor of whose womanhood no breath was ever raised, whose men occupy positions of trust and usefulness, and who, judged by any standard, have reached the full measure of the best type of modern European culture? Is it fair, is it decent, is it Christian to ignore these facts of the Negro problem, to belittle such aspiration, to nullify such leadership and seek to crush these people back into the mass out of which by toil and travail, they and their fathers have raised themselves?

Can the masses of the Negro people be in any possible way more quickly raised than by the effort and example of this aristocracy of talent and character? Was there ever a nation on God's fair earth civilized from the bottom upward? Never; it is, ever was and ever will be from the top downward that culture filters. The Talented Tenth rises and pulls all that are worth the saving up to their vantage ground. This is the history of human progress; and the two historic mistakes which have hindered that progress were the thinking first that no more could ever rise save the few already risen; or second, that it would better the unrisen to pull the risen down.

How then shall the leaders of a struggling people be trained and the hands of the risen few strengthened? There can be but one answer: The best and most capable of their youth must be schooled in the colleges and universities of the land. We will not quarrel as to just what the university of the Negro should teach or how it should teach it—I willingly admit that each soul and each race-soul needs its own peculiar curriculum. But this is true: A university is a human invention for the transmission of knowledge and culture from generation to generation, through the training of quick minds and pure hearts, and for this work no other human invention will suffice, not even trade and industrial schools.

All men cannot go to college but some men must; every isolated group or nation must have its yeast, must have for the talented few centers of training where men are not so mystified and befuddled by the hard and necessary toil of earning a living, as to have no aims higher than their bellies, and no God greater than Gold. This is true training, and thus in the beginning were the favored sons of the freedmen trained. Out of the colleges of the North came, after the blood of war, Ware, Cravath, Chase, Andrews, Bumstead and Spence to build the foundations of knowledge and civilization in the black South. Where ought they to have begun to build? At the bottom, of course, quibbles the mole with his eyes in the earth. Aye! truly at the bottom, at the very bottom; at the bottom of knowledge, down in the very depths of knowledge there where the roots of justice strike into the lowest soil of Truth. And so they did begin; they founded colleges, and up from the colleges shot normal schools, and out from the normal schools went teachers, and around the normal teachers clustered other teachers to teach the public schools; the college trained in Greek and Latin and mathematics, 2,000 men; and these men trained full 50,000 others in morals and manners, and they in turn taught thrift and the alphabet to nine millions of men, who to-day hold $300,000,000 of property. It was a miracle—the most wonderful peace-battle of the 19th century, and yet to-day men smile at it, and in fine superiority tell us that it was all a strange mistake; that a proper way to found a system of education is first to gather the children and buy them spelling books and hoes; afterward men may look about for teachers, if haply they may find them; or again they would teach men Work, but as for Life—why, what has Work to do with Life, they ask vacantly.

Was the work of these college founders successful; did it stand the test of time? Did the college graduates, with all their fine theories of life, really live? Are they useful men helping to civilize and elevate their less fortunate fellows? Let us see. Omitting all institutions which have not actually graduated students from a college course, there are to-day in the United States thirty-four institutions giving something above high school training to Negroes and designed especially for this race.

Three of these were established in border States before the War; thirteen were planted by the Freedmen's Bureau in the years 1864–1869; nine were established between 1870 and 1880 by various church bodies; five were established after 1881 by Negro churches, and four are state institutions supported by United States' agricultural funds. In most cases the college departments are small adjuncts to high and common school work. As a matter of fact six institutions—Atlanta, Fisk, Howard, Shaw, Wilberforce and Leland, are the important Negro colleges so far as actual work and number of students are concerned. In all these institutions, seven hundred and fifty Negro college students are enrolled. In grade the best of these colleges are about a year behind the smaller New England colleges and a typical curriculum is that of Atlanta University. Here students from the grammar grades, after a three years' high school course, take a college course of 136 weeks. One-fourth of this time is given to Latin and Greek; one-fifth, to English and modern languages; one-sixth, to history and social science; one-seventh, to natural science; one-eighth to mathematics, and one-eighth to philosophy and pedagogy.

In addition to these students in the South, Negroes have attended Northern colleges for many years. As early as 1826 one was graduated from Bowdoin College, and from that time till to-day nearly every year has seen elsewhere, other such graduates. They have, of course, met much color prejudice. Fifty years ago very few colleges would admit them at all. Even to-day no Negro has ever been admitted to Princeton, and at some other leading institutions they are rather endured than encouraged. Oberlin was the great pioneer in the work of blotting out the color line in colleges, and has more Negro graduates by far than any other Northern college.

The total number of Negro college graduates up to 1899, (several of the graduates of that year not being reported), was as follows:

	Negro Colleges.	White Colleges.
Before '76	137	75
'75–80	143	22
'80–85	250	31
'85–90	413	43
'90–95	465	66
'95–99	.475	88
Class Unknown	57	64
Total	1,914	390

Of these graduates 2,079 were men and 252 were women; 50 per cent. of Northern-born college men come South to work among the masses of their people, at a sacrifice which few people realize; nearly 90 per cent. of the Southern-born graduates instead of seeking that personal freedom and broader intellectual atmosphere which their training has led them, in some degree, to conceive, stay and labor and wait in the midst of their black neighbors and relatives.

The most interesting question, and in many respects the crucial question, to be asked concerning college-bred Negroes, is: Do they earn a living? It has been intimated more than once that the higher training of Negroes has resulted in sending into the world of work, men who could find nothing to do suitable to their talents. Now and then there comes a rumor of a colored college man working at menial service, etc. Fortunately, returns as to occupations of college-bred Negroes, gathered by the Atlanta conference, are quite full—nearly sixty per cent. of the total number of graduates.

This enables us to reach fairly certain conclusions as to the occupations of all college-bred Negroes. Of 1,312 persons reported, there were:

	Per Cent.	
Teachers, ...	. . . 53.4	
Clergymen, ...	. . . 16.8	
Physicians, etc., ...	. . . 6.3	
Students, ...	. . . 5.6	
Lawyers, ...	. . . 4.7	
In Govt. Service, ...	. . . 4.0	
In Business, ...	. . . 3.6	
Farmers and Artisans, .	. . . 2.7	
Editors, Secretaries and Clerks, ...	. . . 2.4	
Miscellaneous	5	

Over half are teachers, a sixth are preachers, another sixth are students and professional men; over 6 per cent. are farmers, artisans and merchants, and 4 per cent. are in government service. In detail the occupations are as follows:

Occupations of College-Bred Men.

Teachers:		
Presidents and Deans,	19	
Teacher of Music,	7	
Professors, Principals and Teachers,	675	Total 701
Clergymen:		
Bishop,	1	
Chaplains U. S. Army,	2	
Missionaries,	9	
Presiding Elders,	12	
Preachers,	197	Total 221
Physicians:		
Doctors of Medicine,.	76	
Druggists,	4	
Dentists,.	3	Total 83
Students,		74
Lawyers,		62
Civil Service:		
U. S. Minister Plenipotentiary,	1	
U. S. Consul,	1	
U. S. Deputy Collector,	1	
U. S. Gauger,	1	
U. S. Postmasters,.	2	
U. S. Clerks,	44	
State Civil Service,	2	
City Civil Service,	1	Total 53
Business Men:		
Merchants, etc.,	30	
Managers,	13	
Real Estate Dealers,	4	Total 47
Farmers,		26
Clerks and Secretaries:		
Secretary of National Societies,	7	
Clerks, etc.,	15	Total 22
Artisans,		9
Editors,		9
Miscellaneous,		5

These figures illustrate vividly the function of the college-bred Negro. He is, as he ought to be, the group leader, the man who sets the ideals of the community where he lives, directs its thoughts and heads its social movements. It need hardly be argued that the Negro people need social leadership more than most groups; that they have no traditions to fall back upon, no long established customs, no strong family ties, no well defined social classes. All these things must be slowly and painfully evolved. The preacher was, even before the war, the group leader of the Negroes, and the church their greatest social institution. Naturally this preacher was ignorant and often immoral, and the problem of replacing the older type by better educated men has been a difficult one. Both by direct work and by direct influence on other preachers, and on congregations, the college-bred preacher has an opportunity for reformatory work and moral inspiration, the value of which cannot be overestimated.

It has, however, been in the furnishing of teachers that the Negro college has found its peculiar function. Few persons realize how vast a work, how mighty a revolution has been thus accomplished. To furnish five millions and more of ignorant people with teachers of their own race and blood, in one generation, was not only a very difficult undertaking, but a very important one, in that, it placed before the eyes of almost every Negro child an attainable ideal. It brought the masses of the blacks in contact with modern civilization, made black men the leaders of their communities and trainers of the new generation. In this work college-bred Negroes were first teachers, and then teachers of teachers. And here it is that the broad culture of college work has been of peculiar value. Knowledge of life and its wider meaning, has been the point of the Negro's deepest ignorance, and the sending out of teachers whose training has not been simply for bread winning, but also for human culture, has been of inestimable value in the training of these men.

In earlier years the two occupations of preacher and teacher were practically the only ones open to the black college graduate. Of later years a larger diversity of life among his people, has opened new avenues of employment. Nor have these college men been paupers and spendthrifts; 557 college-bred Negroes owned in 1899, $1,342,862.50 worth of real estate, (assessed value) or $2,411 per family. The real value of the total accumulations of the whole group is perhaps about $10,000,000, or $5,000 a piece. Pitiful, is it not, beside the fortunes of oil kings and steel trusts, but after all is the fortune of the millionaire the only stamp of true and successful living? Alas! it is, with many, and there's the rub.

The problem of training the Negro is to-day immensely complicated by the fact that the whole question of the efficiency and appropriateness of our present systems of education, for any kind of child, is a matter of active debate, in which final settlement seems still afar off. Consequently it often happens that persons arguing for or against certain systems of education for Negroes, have these controversies in mind and miss the real question at issue. The main question, so far as the Southern Negro is concerned, is: What under the present circumstance, must a system of education do in order to raise the Negro as quickly as possible in the scale of civilization? The answer to this question seems to me clear: It must strengthen the Negro's character, increase his knowledge and teach him to earn a living. Now it goes without saying, that it is hard to do all these things simultaneously or suddenly, and that at the same time it will not do to give all the attention to one and neglect the others; we could give black boys trades, but that alone will not civilize a race of ex-slaves; we might simply increase their knowledge of the world, but this would not necessarily make them wish to use this knowledge honestly; we might seek to strengthen character and purpose, but to what end if this people have nothing to eat or to wear? A system of education is not one thing, nor does it have a single definite object, nor is it a mere matter of schools. Education is that whole system of human training within and without the school house walls, which molds and develops men. If then we start out to train an ignorant and unskilled people with a heritage of bad habits, our system of training must set before itself two great aims—the one dealing with knowledge and character, the other part seeking to give the child the technical knowledge necessary for him to earn a living under the present circumstances. These objects are accomplished in part by the opening of the common schools on the one, and of the industrial schools on the other. But only in part, for there must also be trained those who are to teach these schools—men and women of knowledge and culture and technical skill who understand modern civilization, and have the training and aptitude to impart it to the children under them. There must be teachers, and teachers of teachers, and to attempt to establish any sort of a system of common and industrial school training, without *first* (and I say *first* advisedly) without *first* providing for the higher training of the very best teachers, is simply throwing your money to the winds. School houses do not teach themselves—piles of brick and mortar and machinery do not send out *men*. It is the trained, living human soul, cultivated and strengthened by long study and thought, that breathes the real breath of life into boys and girls and makes them human, whether they be black or white, Greek, Russian or American. Nothing, in these latter days, has so dampened the faith of thinking Negroes in recent educational movements, as the fact that such movements have been accompanied by ridicule and denouncement and decrying of those very institutions of higher training which made the Negro public school possible, and make Negro industrial schools thinkable. It was Fisk, Atlanta, Howard and Straight, those colleges born of the faith and sacrifice of the abolitionists, that placed in the black schools of the South the 30,000 teachers and more, which some, who depreciate the work of these higher schools, are using to teach their own new experiments. If Hampton, Tuskegee and the hundred other industrial schools prove in the future to be as successful as they deserve to be, then their success in training black artisans for the South, will be due primarily to the white colleges of the North and the black colleges of the South, which trained the teachers who to-day conduct these institutions. There was a time when the American people believed pretty devoutly that a log of wood with a boy at one end and Mark Hopkins at the other, represented the highest ideal of human training. But in these eager days it would seem that we have changed all that and think it necessary to add a couple of saw-mills and a hammer to this outfit, and, at a pinch, to dispense with the services of Mark Hopkins.

I would not deny, or for a moment seem to deny, the paramount necessity of teaching the Negro to work, and to work steadily and skillfully; or seem to depreciate in the slightest degree the important part industrial schools must play in the accomplishment of these ends, but I *do* say, and insist upon it, that it is industrialism drunk with its vision of success, to imagine that its own work can be accomplished without providing for the training of broadly cultured men and women to teach its own teachers, and to teach the teachers of the public schools.

But I have already said that human education is not simply a matter of schools; it is much more a matter of family and group life—the training of one's home, of one's daily companions, of one's social class. Now the black boy of the South moves in a black world—a world with its own leaders, its own thoughts, its own ideals. In this world he gets by far the larger part of his life training, and through the eyes of this dark world he peers into the veiled world beyond. Who guides and determines the education which he receives in his world? His teachers here are the group-leaders of the Negro people—the physicians and clergymen, the trained fathers and mothers, the influential and forceful men about him of all kinds; here it is, if at all, that the culture of the surrounding world trickles through and is handed on by the graduates of the higher schools. Can such culture training of group leaders be neglected? Can we afford to ignore it? Do you think that if the leaders of thought among Negroes are not trained and educated thinkers, that they will have no leaders? On the contrary a hundred half-trained demagogues will still hold the places they so largely occupy now, and hundreds of vociferous busy-bodies will multiply. You have no choice; either you must help furnish this race from within its own ranks with thoughtful men of trained leadership, or you must suffer the evil consequences of a headless misguided rabble.

I am an earnest advocate of manual training and trade teaching for black boys, and for white boys, too. I believe that next to the founding of Negro colleges the most valuable addition to Negro education since the war, has been industrial training for black boys. Nevertheless, I insist that the object of all true education is not to make men carpenters, it is to make carpenters men; there are two means of making the carpenter a man, each equally important: the first is to give the group and community in which he works, liberally trained teachers and leaders to teach him and his family what life means; the second is to give him sufficient intelligence and technical skill to make him an efficient workman; the first object demands the Negro college and college-bred men—not a quantity of such colleges, but a few of excellent quality; not too many college-bred men, but enough to leaven the lump, to inspire the masses, to raise the Talented Tenth to leadership; the second object demands a good system of common schools, well-taught, conveniently located and properly equipped.

The Sixth Atlanta Conference truly said in 1901:

"We call the attention of the Nation to the fact that less than one million of the three million Negro children of school age, are at present regularly attending school, and these attend a session which lasts only a few months.

"We are to-day deliberately rearing millions of our citizens in ignorance, and at the same time limiting the rights of citizenship by educational qualifications. This is unjust. Half the black youth of the land have no opportunities open to them for learning to read, write and cipher. In the discussion as to the proper training of Negro children after they leave the public schools, we have forgotten that they are not yet decently provided with public schools.

"Propositions are beginning to be made in the South to reduce the already meagre school facilities of Negroes. We congratulate the South on resisting, as much as it has, this pressure, and on the many millions it has spent on Negro education. But it is only fair to point out that Negro taxes and the Negroes' share of the income from indirect taxes and endowments have fully repaid this expenditure, so that the Negro public school system has not in all probability cost the white taxpayers a single cent since the war.

"This is not fair. Negro schools should be a public burden, since they are a public benefit. The Negro has a right to demand good common school training at the hands of the States and the Nation since by their fault he is not in position to pay for this himself."

What is the chief need for the building up of the Negro public school in the South? The Negro race in the South needs teachers to-day above all else. This is the concurrent testimony of all who know the situation. For the supply of this great demand two things are needed—institutions of higher education and money for school houses and salaries. It is usually assumed that a hundred or more institutions for Negro training are to-day turning out so many teachers and college-bred men that the race is threatened with an over-supply. This is sheer nonsense. There are to-day less than 3,000 living Negro college graduates in the United States, and less than 1,000 Negroes in college. Moreover, in the 164 schools for Negroes, 95 per cent. of their students are doing elementary and secondary work, work which should be done in the public schools. Over half the remaining 2,157 students are taking high school studies. The mass of so-called "normal" schools for the Negro, are simply doing elementary common school work, or, at most, high school work, with a little instruction in methods. The Negro colleges and the post-graduate courses at other institutions are the only agencies for the broader and more careful training of teachers. The work of these institutions is hampered for lack of funds. It is getting increasingly difficult to get funds for training teachers in the best modern methods, and yet all over the South, from State Superintendents, county officials, city boards and school principals comes the wail, "We need TEACHERS!" and teachers must be trained. As the fairest minded of all white Southerners, Atticus G. Haygood, once said: "The defects of colored teachers are so great as to create an urgent necessity for training better ones. Their excellencies and their successes are sufficient to justify the best hopes of success in the effort, and to vindicate the judgment of those who make large investments of money and service, to give to colored students opportunity for thoroughly preparing themselves for the work of teaching children of their people."

The truth of this has been strikingly shown in the marked improvement of white teachers in the South. Twenty years ago the rank and file of white public school teachers were not as good as the Negro teachers. But they, by scholarships and good salaries, have been encouraged to thorough normal and collegiate preparation, while the Negro teachers have been discouraged by starvation wages and the idea that any training will do for a black teacher. If carpenters are needed it is well and good to train men as carpenters. But to train men as carpenters, and then set them to teaching is wasteful and criminal; and to train men as teachers and then refuse them living wages, unless they become carpenters, is rank nonsense.

The United States Commissioner of Education says in his report for 1900: "For comparison between the white and colored enrollment in secondary and higher education, I have added together the enrollment in high schools and secondary schools, with the attendance on colleges and universities, not being sure of the actual grade of work done in the colleges and universities. The work done in the secondary schools is reported in such detail in this office, that there can be no doubt of its grade."

He then makes the following comparisons of persons in every million enrolled in secondary and higher education:

	Whole Country.	*Negroes.*
1880	4,362	1,289
1900	10,743	2,061

And he concludes: "While the number in colored high schools and colleges had increased somewhat faster than the population, it had not kept pace with the average of the whole country, for it had fallen from 30 per cent. to 24 per cent. of the average quota. Of all colored pupils, one (1) in one hundred was engaged in secondary and higher work, and that ratio has continued substantially for the past twenty years. If the ratio of colored population in secondary and higher education is to be equal to the average for the whole country, it must be increased to five times its present average." And if this be true of the secondary and higher education, it is safe to say that the Negro has not one-tenth his quota in college studies. How baseless, therefore, is the charge of too much training! We need Negro teachers for the Negro common schools, and we need first-class normal schools and colleges to train them. This is the work of higher Negro education and it must be done.

Further than this, after being provided with group leaders of civilization, and a foundation of intelligence in the public schools, the carpenter, in order to be a man, needs technical skill. This calls for trade schools. Now trade schools are not nearly such simple things as people once thought. The original idea was that the "Industrial" school was to furnish education, practically free, to those willing to work for it; it was to "do" things—i. e.: become a center of productive industry, it was to be partially, if not wholly, self-supporting, and it was to teach trades. Admirable as were some of the ideas underlying this scheme, the whole thing simply would not work in practice; it was found that if you were to use time and material to teach trades thoroughly, you could not at the same time keep the industries on a commercial basis and make them pay. Many schools started out to do this on a large scale and went into virtual bankruptcy. Moreover, it was found also that it was possible to teach a boy a trade mechanically, without giving him the full educative benefit of the process, and, vice versa, that there was a distinctive educative value in teaching a boy to use his hands and eyes in carrying out certain physical processes, even though he did not actually learn a trade. It has happened, therefore, in the last decade, that a noticeable change has come over the industrial schools. In the first place the idea of commercially remunerative industry in a school is being pushed rapidly to the background. There are still schools with shops and farms that bring an income, and schools that use student labor partially for the erection of their buildings and the furnishing of equipment. It is coming to be seen, however, in the education of the Negro, as clearly as it has been seen in the education of the youths the world over, that it is the *boy* and not the material product, that is the true object of education. Consequently the object of the industrial school came to be the thorough training of boys regardless of the cost of the training, so long as it was thoroughly well done.

Even at this point, however, the difficulties were not surmounted. In the first place modern industry has taken great strides since the war, and the teaching of trades is no longer a simple matter. Machinery and long processes of work have greatly changed the work of the carpenter, the ironworker and the shoemaker. A really efficient workman must be today an intelligent man who has had good technical training in addition to thorough common school, and perhaps even higher training. To meet this situation the industrial schools began a further development; they established distinct Trade

Schools for the thorough training of better class artisans, and at the same time they sought to preserve for the purposes of general education, such of the simpler processes of elementary trade learning as were best suited therefor. In this differentiation of the Trade School and manual training, the best of the industrial schools simply followed the plain trend of the present educational epoch. A prominent educator tells us that, in Sweden, "In the beginning the economic conception was generally adopted, and everywhere manual training was looked upon as a means of preparing the children of the common people to earn their living. But gradually it came to be recognized that manual training has a more elevated purpose, and one, indeed, more useful in the deeper meaning of the term. It came to be considered as an educative process for the complete moral, physical and intellectual development of the child."

Thus, again, in the manning of trade schools and manual training schools we are thrown back upon the higher training as its source and chief support. There was a time when any aged and wornout carpenter could teach in a trade school. But not so to-day. Indeed the demand for college-bred men by a school like Tuskegee, ought to make Mr. Booker T. Washington the firmest friend of higher training. Here he has as helpers the son of a Negro senator, trained in Greek and the humanities, and graduated at Harvard; the son of a Negro congressman and lawyer, trained in Latin and mathematics, and graduated at Oberlin; he has as his wife, a woman who read Virgil and Homer in the same class room with me; he has as college chaplain, a classical graduate of Atlanta University; as teacher of science, a graduate of Fisk; as teacher of history, a graduate of Smith,—indeed some thirty of his chief teachers are college graduates, and instead of studying French grammars in the midst of weeds, or buying pianos for dirty cabins, they are at Mr. Washington's right hand helping him in a noble work. And yet one of the effects of Mr. Washington's propaganda has been to throw doubt upon the expediency of such training for Negroes, as these persons have had.

Men of America, the problem is plain before you. Here is a race transplanted through the criminal foolishness of your fathers. Whether you like it or not the millions are here, and here they will remain. If you do not lift them up, they will pull you down. Education and work are the levers to uplift a people. Work alone will not do it unless inspired by the right ideals and guided by intelligence. Education must not simply teach work—it must teach Life. The Talented Tenth of the Negro race must be made leaders of thought and missionaries of culture among their people. No others can do this work and Negro colleges must train men for it. The Negro race, like all other races, is going to be saved by its exceptional men.

The Negro Problem, 1903

The Negro in Literature and Art

THE NEGRO is primarily an artist. The usual way of putting this is to speak disdainfully of his sensuous nature. This means that the only race which has held at bay the life destroying forces of the tropics, has gained therefrom in some slight compensation a sense of beauty, particularly for sound and color, which characterizes the race. The Negro blood which flowed in the veins of many of the mightiest of the Pharaohs accounts for much of Egyptian art, and indeed, Egyptian civilization owes much in its origins to the development of the large strain of Negro blood which manifested itself in every grade of Egyptian society.

Semitic civilization also had its Negroid influences, and these continually turn toward art as in the case of Nosseyeb, one of the five great poets of Damascus under the Ommiades. It was therefore not to be wondered at that in modern days one of the greatest of modern literatures, the Russian, should have been founded by Pushkin, the grandson of a full blooded Negro, and that among the painters of Spain was the mulatto slave, Gomez. Back of all this development by way of contact, comes the artistic sense of the indigenous Negro as shown in the stone figures of Sherbro, the bronzes of Benin, the marvelous handwork in iron and other metals which has characterized the Negro race so long that archeologists today, with less and less hesitation, are ascribing the discovery of the welding of iron to the Negro race.

To America, the Negro could bring only his music, but that was quite enough. The only real American music is that of the Negro American, except the meagre contribution of the Indian. Negro music divides itself into many parts: the older African wails and chants, the distinctively Afro-American folk song set to religious words and Calvinistic symbolism, and the newer music which the slaves adapted from surrounding themes. To this may be added the American music built on Negro themes such as "Suwanee River," "John Brown's Body," "Old Black Joe," etc. In our day Negro artists like Johnson and Will Marion Cook have taken up this music and begun a newer and most important development, using the syncopated measure popularly known as "rag time," but destined in the minds of musical students to a great career in the future.

The expression in words of the tragic experiences of the Negro race is to be found in various places. First, of course, there are those, like Harriet Beecher Stowe, who wrote from without the race. Then there are black men like Es-Sadi who wrote the Epic of the Sudan, in Arabic, that great history of the fall of the greatest of Negro empires, the Songhay. In America the literary expression of Negroes has had a regular development. As early as the eighteenth century, and even before the Revolutionary War the first voices of Negro authors were heard in the United States.

Phyllis Wheatley, the black poetess, was easily the pioneer, her first poems appearing in 1773, and other editions in 1774 and 1793. Her earliest poem was in memory of George Whitefield. She was followed by the Negro, Olaudah Equiano—known by his English name of Gustavus Vassa—whose autobiography of 350 pages, published in 1787, was the beginning of that long series of personal appeals of which Booker T. Washington's *Up from Slavery* is the latest. Benjamin Banneker's almanacs represented the first scientific work of American Negroes, and began to be issued in 1792.

Coming now to the first decades of the nineteenth century we find some essays on freedom by the African Society of Boston, and an apology for the new Negro church formed in Philadelphia. Paul Cuffe, disgusted with America, wrote an early account of Sierra Leone, while the celebrated Lemuel Haynes, ignoring the race question, dipped deeply into the New England theological controversy about 1815. In 1829 came the first full-voiced, almost hysterical, protest against slavery and the color line in David Walker's *Appeal* which aroused Southern legislatures to action. This was followed by the earliest Negro conventions which issued interesting minutes, and a strong appeal against disfranchisement in Pennsylvania.

In 1840 some strong writers began to appear. Henry Highland Garnet and J. W. C. Pennington preached powerful sermons and gave some attention to Negro history in their pamphlets; R. B. Lewis made a more elaborate attempt at

Negro history. Whitfield's poems appeared in 1846, and William Wells Brown began a career of writing which lasted from 1847 until after the war. In 1845 Douglass' autobiography made its first appearance, destined to run through endless editions up until the last in 1893. Moreover it was in 1841 that the first Negro magazine appeared in America, edited by George Hogarth and published by the A. M. E. Church.

In the fifties William Wells Brown published his *Three Years in Europe*; James Whitfield published further poems, and a new poet arose in the person of Frances E. W. Harper, a woman of no little ability who died lately; Martin R. Delaney and William Nell wrote further of Negro history, Nell especially making valuable contributions to the history of the Negro soldiers. Three interesting biographies were added to this decade to the growing number: Josiah Henson, Samuel G. Ward and Samuel Northrop; while Catto, leaving general history, came down to the better known history of the Negro church.

In the sixties slave narratives multiplied, like that of Linda Brent, while two studies of Africa based on actual visits were made by Robert Campbell and Dr. Alexander Crummell; William Douglass and Bishop Daniel Payne continued the history of the Negro church, while William Wells Brown carried forward his work in general Negro history. In this decade, too, Bishop Tanner began his work in Negro theology.

Most of the Negro talent in the seventies was taken up in politics; the older men like Bishop Wayman wrote of their experiences; William Wells Brown wrote the *Rising Son*, and Sojourner Truth added her story to the slave narratives. A new poet arose in the person of A. A. Whitman, while James M. Trotter was the first to take literary note of the musical ability of his race. Indeed this section might have been begun by some reference to the music and folklore of the Negro race; the music contained much primitive poetry and the folklore was one of the great contributions to American civilization.

In the eighties there are signs of unrest and different conflicting streams of thought. On the one hand the rapid growth of the Negro church is shown by the writers on church subjects like Moore and Wayman. The historical spirit was especially strong. Still wrote of the *Underground Railroad*; Simmons issued his interesting biographical dictionary, and the greatest historian of the race appeared when George W. Williams issued his two-volume history of the *Negro Race in America*. The political turmoil was reflected in Langston's *Freedom and Citizenship*, Fortune's *Black and White*, and Straker's *New South*, and found its bitterest arraignment in Turner's pamphlets; but with all this went other new thought; a black man published his *First Greek Lessons*, Bishop Payne issued his *Treatise on Domestic Education*, and Stewart studied Liberia.

In the nineties came histories, essays, novels and poems, together with biographies and social studies. The history was represented by Payne's *History of the A. M. E. Church*, Hood's *History of the A. M. E. Zion Church*, Anderson's sketch of *Negro Presbyterianism* and Hagood's *Colored Man in the M. E. Church*; general history of the older type by R. L. Perry's *Cushite* and the newer type in Johnson's history, while one of the secret societies found their historian in Brooks; Crogman's essays appeared and Archibald Grimke's biographies. The race question was discussed in Frank Grimke's published sermons, while social studies were made by Penn, Wright, Mossell, Crummell, Majors and others. Most notable, however, was the rise of the Negro novelist and poet with national recognition; Frances Harper was still writing and Griggs began his racial novels, but both of these spoke primarily to the Negro race; on the other hand, Chesnutt's six novels and Dunbar's inimitable works spoke to the whole nation.

Since 1900 the stream of Negro writing has continued. Dunbar has found a worthy successor in the less-known but more carefully cultured Braithwaite; Booker T. Washington has given us his biography and *Story of the Negro*; Kelly Miller's trenchant essays have appeared in book form; Sinclair's *Aftermath of Slavery* has attracted attention, as have the studies made by Atlanta University. The forward movement in Negro music is represented by J. W. and F. J. Work in one direction and Rosamond Johnson, Harry Burleigh and Will Marion Cook in another.

On the whole, the literary output of the American Negro

has been both large and creditable, although, of course, comparatively little known; few great names have appeared and only here and there work that could be called first class, but this is not a peculiarity of Negro literature.

The time has not yet come for the great development of American Negro literature. The economic stress is too great and the racial persecution too bitter to allow the leisure and the poise for which literature calls. On the other hand, never in the world has a richer mass of material been accumulated by a people than that which the Negroes possess today and are becoming conscious of. Slowly but surely they are developing artists of technic who will be able to use this material. The nation does not notice this for everything touching the Negro is banned by magazines and publishers unless it takes the form of caricature or bitter attack, or is so thoroughly innocuous as to have no literary flavor.

Outside of literature the American Negro has distinguished himself in other lines of art. One need only mention Henry O. Tanner whose pictures hang in the great galleries of the world, including the Luxembourg. There are a score of other less known colored painters of ability including Bannister, Harper, Scott and Brown. To these may be added the actors headed by Ira Aldridge, who played in Covent Garden, was decorated by the King of Prussia and the Emperor of Russia, and made a member of learned societies.

There have been many colored composers of music. Popular songs like Grandfather's Clock, Listen to the Mocking Bird, Carry Me Back to Old Virginia, etc., were composed by colored men. There were a half dozen composers of ability among New Orleans freedmen and Harry Burleigh, Cook and Johnson are well known today. There have been sculptors like Edmonia Lewis, and singers like Flora Batson, whose color alone kept her from the grand opera stage.

To appraise rightly this body of art one must remember that it represents the work of those artists only whom accident set free; if the artist had a white face his Negro blood did not militate against him in the fight for recognition; if his Negro blood was visible white relatives may have helped him; in a few cases ability was united to indomitable will. But the shrinking, modest, black artist without special encouragement had little or no chance in a world determined to make him a menial. So this sum of accomplishment is but an imperfect indication of what the Negro race is capable of in America and in the world.

Annals of the American Academy of Political and Social Science,
September 1913

Negro Education

THE CASUAL reader has greeted this study of Negro education with pleasure.* It is the first attempt to cover the field of secondary and higher education among colored Americans with anything like completeness. It is published with the sanction and prestige of the United States government and has many excellent points as, for instance, full statistics on such matters as the public expenditure for Negro school systems, the amount of philanthropy given private schools, Negro property, etc.; there is excellent and continued insistence upon the poor support which the colored public schools are receiving today. The need of continued philanthropic aid to private schools is emphasized and there are several good maps. Despite, then, some evidently careless proofreading (pages 59, 129, 157), the ordinary reader unacquainted with the tremendous ramifications of the Negro problem will hail this report with unstinted praise.

Thinking Negroes, however, and other persons who know the problem of educating the American Negro will regard the Jones' report, despite its many praiseworthy features, as a dangerous and in many respects unfortunate publication.

The Thesis of the Report

This report again and again insists by direct statements, by inference, and by continued repetition on three principles of a thesis which we may state as follows: *First*, that the present tendency toward academic and higher education among Negroes should be restricted and replaced by a larger insistence on manual training, industrial education, and agricultural training; *secondly*, the private schools in the South must "co-operate" with the Southern whites; and, *third*, that there should be more thorough-going unity of

*Negro Education, a Study of the Private and Higher Schools for Colored People in the United States; prepared in co-operation with the Phelps-Stokes Fund, under the direction of Thomas Jesse Jones, specialist in education of racial groups. Bureau of Education. Two volumes, 8 vo., 424, 724 pages. Washington, 1917.

purpose among education boards and foundations working among Negroes.

The Negro College

The whole trend of Mr. Jones' study and of his general recommendations is to make the higher training of Negroes practically difficult, if not impossible, despite the fact that his statistics show (in 1914–15) only 1643 colored students studying college subjects in all the private Negro schools out of 12,726 pupils. He shows that there are (in proportion to population) ten times as many whites in the public high schools as there are colored pupils and only sixty-four public high schools for Negroes in the whole South! He shows that even at present there are few Negro colleges and that they have no easy chance for survival. What he is criticising, then, is not the fact that Negroes are tumbling into college in enormous numbers, but their wish to go to college and their endeavor to support and maintain even poor college departments.

What, in fact, is back of this wish? Is it merely a silly desire to study "Greek," as Mr. Jones several times intimates, or is it not rather a desire on the part of American Negroes to develop a class of thoroughly educated men according to modern standards? If such a class is to be developed these Negro colleges must be planned as far as possible according to the standards of white colleges, otherwise colored students would be shut out of the best colleges of the country.

The curriculum offered at the colored southern colleges, however, brings the author's caustic criticism. Why, for instance, should "Greek and Latin" be maintained to the exclusion of economics, sociology, and "a strong course in biology"?

The reason for the maintenance of these older courses of study in the colored colleges is not at all, as the author assumes, that Negroes have a childish love for "classics." It is very easily and simply explicable. Take, for instance, Fisk University. Fisk University maintained Greek longer than most northern colleges, for the reason that it had in Adam K. Spence not simply a finished Greek scholar, pupil of the great D'Ooge, but a man of singularly strong personality and fine soul. It did not make much difference whether the students were studying Greek or Biology—the great thing was that they were studying under Spence. So, in a large number of cases the curriculum of the southern Negro college has been determined by the personnel of the available men. These men were beyond price and working for their devotion to the cause. The college was unable to call men representing the newer sciences—young sociologists and biologists. They were unable to equip laboratories, but they did with infinite pains and often heart-breaking endeavor keep within touch of the standard set by the higher northern schools and the proof that they did well came from the men they turned out and not simply from the courses they studied.

This, Mr. Jones either forgets or does not know and is thus led into exceedingly unfortunate statements as when, for instance, he says that the underlying principle of the industrial school "is the adaptation of educational activities whether industrial or literary to the needs of the pupils and the community," which is, of course, the object of any educational institution and it is grossly unfair to speak of it as being the object of only a part of the great Negro schools of the South. Any school that does not have this for its object is not a school but a fraud.

The Public Schools

Not only does this report continually decry the Negro college and its curriculum but, on the other hand, it seeks to put in its place schools and courses of study which make it absolutely impossible for Negro students to be thoroughly trained according to modern standards. To illustrate: Mr. Jones shows (page 90) that in Butte, Mont., manual training has been put into the elementary schools at the rate of *half a day a week* during the first six years and *two half days a week* in the seventh and eighth grades. When, however, it comes to the smaller elementary industrial schools of the South Mr. Jones recommends *one-half day* classroom work and *one-half* practise in the field and shops *every day*.

What, now, is the real difference between these two schemes of education? The difference is that in the Butte schools for white pupils a chance is held open for the pupil to go through high school and college and to advance at the rate which the modern curriculum demands; that in the colored schools, on the other hand, a program is being made out that will land the boy at the time he becomes self-conscious and aware of his own possibilities in an educational *impasse*. He cannot go on in the public schools even if he should move to a place where there are good public schools because he is too old. Even if he has done the elementary work in twice the time that a student is supposed to it has been work of a kind that will not admit him to a northern high school. No matter, then, how gifted the boy may be he is absolutely estopped from a higher education. This is not only unfair to the boy but it is grossly unfair to the Negro race.

The argument, then, against the kind of school that is being foisted upon Negroes in the name of industrial education is not any dislike on the part of the Negroes for having their children trained in vocations, or in having manual training used as a means of education; it is rather in having a series of schools established which deliberately shut the door of opportunity in the face of bright Negro students.

Industrial Training

With the drive that has been made to industrialize elementary schools before the children have learned to read and write and to turn the high schools to vocational teaching without giving any of the pupils a chance to train for college, it is, of course, beside the mark to criticize the colored colleges because the children that come to them are poorly trained.

Much of the criticism of colored teachers is also unfair. Even well-trained teachers are having curious pressure put upon them. Here is a teacher with eighty or one hundred pupils trying to teach them three r's in a country district. The Jeanes Fund sends a supervisor and introduces, to quote the report (page 35), "shuck mat work, simple sewing, patch quilting for girls, repair of buildings and woodworking for boys." It *might* be possible with money and teachers so to interlock this work with the teaching of the three r's as to help the net result; but when the stress, the emphasis, and the inspection has to do mainly with the *industrial work as such*, and nobody knows or cares about the chief work for which the school ought to exist; when the white community demands of these schools servants and laborers and *not* educated men and women, what is the result bound to be?

With its insistent criticising of Negro colleges this report touches with curious hesitation and diffidence upon the shortcomings of industrial schools. Their failure to distinguish between general education and technical trade training has resulted in sending out numbers of so-called teachers from educational schools who cannot read and write the English language and who are yet put in public and other schools as teachers. They may show children how to make tin pans and cobble shoes, but they are not the right persons to train youth, mentally or morally. In the second place, most of the trades taught by these trade schools are, because of hostile public opinion and poverty, decadent trades: carpentry, which is rapidly falling below the level of skilled trades; the patching of shoes; blacksmithing, in the sense of repair work, etc. The important trades of the world that are today assembled in factories and call for skilled technique and costly machinery are not taught in the vast majority of Negro industrial schools. Moreover, the higher industrial training calls for more education than the industrial schools give. I remember some ten years ago going into the wheelwrighting shop at Hampton. I said to the white instructor: "How are your students getting on?" He said: "Fairly well, only *they haven't enough mathematics*." Yet here is a report that has much to say over the foolishness of teaching mathematics!

That the course of study in the Southern schools as well as in the schools of the nation has got to be changed and adapted is absolutely true, but the object of a school system is to carry the child as far as possible in its knowledge of the accumulated wisdom of the world and then when economic or physical reasons demand that this education must stop, vocational training to prepare for life work should follow. That some of this vocational training may be made educational in object is true; that normal training may use manual training and even to some extent vocational training is true, but it is not true that the industrializing of any curriculum necessarily makes it better or that you can at one and the same time educate the race in modern civilization and train it simply to be servants and laborers. Anyone who suggests by sneering at books and "literary courses" that the great heritage of human thought ought to be displaced simply for the reason of teaching the technique of modern industry is pitifully wrong and, if the comparison must be made, more wrong than the man who would sacrifice modern technique to the heritage of ancient thought.

Cooperation

The second part of Mr. Jones' thesis lies in an insistence that the private schools of the Negro should "cooperate" with the South. He stresses the adaptation of education to the needs of the "community" (page 18), evidently meaning the *white* community. He quotes on page 25 the resolution of the white Southern Educational Association which deplores that the Negro schools are isolated from the "community," meaning again the *white* community. He instances Willcox County, Ala., where there are almost no public schools and recommends that the private schools established there be put under "community" authorities (page 149). Now what is this "community" with which the colored people are to cooperate?

In the first place, Mr. Jones admits (pages 4 and 5), that it is only the progressive few in the white South that care anything at all about Negro schools. He might go even further and acknowledge that if a plebescite were taken tomorrow in the South the popular vote of white people would shut every single Negro school by a large majority. The hostile majority is kept from such radical action by the more progressive minority and by fear of northern interference, but the condition in which they have today left the colored schools is shown by this report to be truly lamentable.

Mr. Jones quotes from Southern white men who speak of Negro school houses as "miserable beyond all description," of teachers as "absolutely untrained" and paid "the princely fortune of $80.92 for the whole term." He goes on with fact after fact to show the absolute inadequacy in the provision for colored children in the public schools of the South. On the other hand, he shows the increase in Negro property, the larger and larger amounts which Negroes are contributing to the school funds; and with all this he practically asks that the domination of the Negro private schools, which are now bearing the burden of nearly all the secondary and higher education of the Negro and much of the elementary education—that the domination of these schools be put into the hands of the same people who are doing so little for the public schools!

There is not in the whole report a single word about *taxation without representation*. There is not a single protest against a public school system in which the public which it serves has absolutely no voice, vote, or influence. There is no defense of those colored people of vision who see the public schools being used as training schools for cheap labor and menial servants instead of for education and who are protesting against this by submitting to double taxation in the support of private schools; who cannot see that these schools should be turned over to people who by their actions prove themselves to be enemies of the Negro race and its advancement.

Until the southern Negro has a vote and representation on school boards public control of his education will mean his spiritual and economic death and that despite the good intentions of the small white minority in the South who believe in justice for the Negro. It is, therefore, contradictory for this report to insist, on the one hand, on the continuation of northern philanthropy for these schools and, on the other, to commend various southern schools in proportion as they have gained the approval of the white community.

Compare, for instance, Fisk University and Atlanta University. Both Cravath of Fisk and Ware of Atlanta were men radical in their belief in Negro possibility and in their determination to establish well equipped Negro colleges. Cravath, however, lived in a more enlightened community which was earlier converted to his ideals. He did not yield his opinion any more than Ware, but Ware lived in a community that to this day will not furnish even a high school for its colored pupils. To say that Fisk should receive on this account more support than Atlanta is rank injustice; if anything Atlanta deserves the greater credit.

Cooperation with the white South means in many cases the surrender of the very foundations of self-respect. Mr. Jones inserts in his report one picture of a colored principal and his assistant waiting on table while the white trustees of his school eat. The colored people of the South do not care a rap whether white folks eat with them or not, but if white officials are coming into their schools as persons in control or advisors, then to ask that in those schools and in their homes the colored people shall voluntarily treat themselves as inferiors is to ask more than any self-respecting man is going to do.

The white community, undoubtedly, wants to keep the Negro in the country as a peasant under working conditions least removed from slavery. The colored man wishes to escape from those conditions. Mr. Jones seeks to persuade him to stay there by asserting that the advance of the Negro in the rural South has been greatest (pages 97 and 123), and he refers to the "delusion" of city life even among white people. This may be all good enough propaganda but, in fact, it is untrue. Civilization has always depended upon the cities. The advance of the cities has been greatest for all people, white and colored, and for any colored man to take his family to the country districts of South Georgia in order to grow and develop and secure education and uplift would be idiotic.

Mr. Jones touches the State schools very lightly. Here are cases where the whites have control and stories of graft and misappropriation of funds and poor organization are well known to everybody with the slightest knowledge of southern conditions. Teachers there and in the public schools are often selected not from the best available, but from the worst or most complacent. In small towns and country districts white trustees may maintain their mistresses as teachers and the protest of the colored people has fallen upon deaf ears. Until, then, colored people have a voice in the community, surrender to the domination of the white South is unthinkable.

Northern Philanthropy

This brings us to the third part of Mr. Jones' thesis, namely, that the boards working for southern education should unite as far as possible with one policy. This is an unfortunate and dangerous proposal for the simple reason that the great dominating philanthropic agency, the General Education Board, long ago surrendered to the white South by practically saying that the educational needs of the white South must be attended to before any attention should be paid to the education of Negroes; that the Negro must be trained according to the will of the white South and not as the Negro desires to be trained. It is this board that is spending more money today in helping Negroes learn how to can vegetables than in helping them to go through college. It is this board that by a system of interlocking directorates bids fair to dominate philanthropy toward the Negro in the United States. Indeed, the moving thought back of the present report is the idea of a single authority who is to say which Negro school is right or is wrong, which system is right and which is wrong, etc.

No one doubts the efficiency of concentration and unity in certain lines of work but always, even in work that can be unified, the question is *whose* influence is going to dominate; it may well be that diversity and even a certain chaos would be better than unity under a wrong idea. This is even more true in educational than in economic matters. Of course, the economic foundation of all recent educational philanthropy, particularly toward the Negro, is evident. Mr. Jones rather naively speaks of the fact that at certain times of the year "it is exceedingly difficult to prevail upon children to attend school" in the colored South which is, of course, another way of saying that bread and butter in the cotton fields is of more importance than trained intelligence.

Undoubtedly, there has already been a strong public opinion manufactured in the country which looks upon the training of Negroes in the South as cheap, contented labor to be used in emergency and for keeping white union labor from extravagant demands as a feasible and workable program. It is, in fact, one of the most dangerous programs ever thought out and is responsible for much of the lynching, unrest, and unhappiness in the South. Its genesis came easily with the idea of working *for* the Negro rather than working *with* him, a thing which Mr. Jones condemns, but hardly lives up to his condemnation.

In this very report the Negro was practically unrepresented. Instead of choosing a strong, experienced colored man to represent the Negro race (like W. T. B. Williams, or President Young of Tallahassee, or President Hope of Morehouse) an inexperienced young man was taken, of excellent character but absolutely without weight or influence. Of course, back of all this is the great difficulty or ordinary social intercourse. The reason that boards of trustees like those that control the Phelps-Stokes Fund find it so much easier to work *for* the Negro than *with* him; the reason that forgetting the investigations by Negroes at Atlanta University they turned to white institutions to encourage investigation and neglected established and worthy work is because if they are going to cooperate with the dominant white South and even with certain classes of Northerners they cannot meet Negroes as men. The propaganda that is so largely carried on and the influence that is so often formed through social intercourse must always, at present, be offered with the Negro unrepresented and unheard.

There follows easily the habit of having no patience with the man who does not agree with the decisions of such boards. The Negro who comes with his hat in his hand and flatters and cajoles the philanthropist—that Negro gets money. If these foundations raise, as they do in this report, the cry of fraud they have themselves to thank. They more than any other agency have encouraged that kind of person. On the other hand, the Negro who shows the slightest independence of thought or character is apt to be read out of all possible influence not only by the white South but by the philanthropic North.

If philanthropic agencies could unite for certain obvious great movements how splendid it would be! Take, for instance, the duplication of higher educational schools which Mr. Jones repeatedly denounces and which, undoubtedly, is a source of weakness. The General Education Board could settle the matter with the greatest ease. Let it offer in Atlanta an endowment of $500,000 for a single Negro college, provided that there be but one college there for Negroes. The boards of the different schools immediately would have something to act upon. As it is nothing that they can do individually would really better the situation. A new college formed by a federation of colored colleges in Atlanta, Marshall, Texas, and elsewhere, would be easily possible if an endowment was in sight.

Summary

Here, then, is the weakness and sinister danger of Mr. Jones' report. It calls for a union of philanthropic effort with no attempt to make sure of the proper and just lines along which this united effort should work. It calls for cooperation with the white South without insisting on the Negro being represented by voice and vote in such "cooperation," and it calls for a re-casting of the educational program for Negroes without insisting on leaving the door of opportunity open for the development of a thoroughly trained class of leaders at the bottom, in the very beginnings of education, as well as at the top.

The Crisis, February 1918

An Essay Toward a History of the Black Man in the Great War

THE MAYOR of Domfront stood in the village inn, high on the hill that hovers green in the blue sky of Normandy; and he sang as we sang: *"Allons, enfants de la patrie!"* God! How we sang! How the low, grey-clouded room rang with the strong voice of the little Frenchman in the corner, swinging his arms in deep emotion; with the vibrant voices of a score of black American officers who sat round about. Their hearts were swelling—torn in sunder. Never have I seen black folk—and I have seen many—so bitter and disillusioned at the seemingly bottomless depths of American color hatred—so uplifted at the vision of real democracy dawning on them in France.

The mayor apologized gravely: if he had known of my coming, he would have received me formally at the Hotel de Ville—me whom most of my fellow-countrymen receive at naught but back doors, save with apology. But how could I explain in Domfront, that reborn feudal town of ancient memories? I could not—I did not. But I sang the Marseillaise—*"Le jour de gloire est arrivé!"*

Arrived to the world and to ever widening circles of men—but not yet to us. Up yonder hill, transported bodily from America, sits "Jim-Crow"—in a hotel for white officers only; in a Massachusetts Colonel who frankly hates "niggers" and segregates them at every opportunity; in the General from Georgia who openly and officially stigmatizes his black officers as no gentlemen by ordering them never to speak to French women in public or receive the spontaneously offered social recognition. All this ancient and American race hatred and insult in a purling sea of French sympathy and kindliness, of human uplift and giant endeavor, amid the mightiest crusade humanity ever saw for Justice!

"Contre nous de la tyrannie,
L'etendard sanglant est levé."

This, then, is a first attempt at the story of the Hell which war in the fateful years of 1914–1919 meant to Black Folk, and particularly to American Negroes. It is only an attempt, full of the mistakes which nearness to the scene and many necessarily missing facts, such as only time can supply, combine to foil in part. And yet, written now in the heat of strong memories and in the place of skulls, it contains truth which cold delay can never alter or bring back. Later, in the light of official reports and supplementary information and with a corps of co-workers, consisting of officers and soldiers and scholars, I shall revise and expand this story into a volume for popular reading; and still later, with the passing of years, I hope to lay before historians and sociologists the documents and statistics upon which my final views are based.

Senegalese and Others

To everyone war is, and, thank God, must be, disillusion. This war has disillusioned millions of fighting white men—disillusioned them with its frank truth of dirt, disease, cold, wet and discomfort; murder, maiming and hatred. But the disillusion of Negro American troops was more than this, or rather it was this and more—the flat, frank realization that however high the ideals of America or however noble her tasks, her great duty as conceived by an astonishing number of able men, brave and good, as well as of other sorts of men, is to hate "niggers."

Not that this double disillusion has for a moment made black men doubt the wisdom of their wholehearted help of the Allies. Given the chance again, they would again do their duty—for have they not seen and known France? But these young men see today with opened eyes and strained faces the true and hateful visage of the Negro problem in America.

When the German host—grey, grim, irresistible, poured through Belgium, out of Africa France called her sons; they came; 280,000 black Senegalese, first and last—volunteers, not drafted; they hurled the Boches back across the Ourcq and the Marne on a ghastly bridge of their own dead. It was the crisis—four long, bitter years the war wore on; but Germany was beaten at the first battle of the Marne, and by Negroes. Beside the Belgians, too, stood, first and last, 30,000 black Congolese, not to mention the 20,000 black English West Indians who fought in the East and the thousands of black troops who conquered German Africa.

Stevedores

But the story of stories is that of the American Negro. Here was a man who bravely let his head go where his heart at first could not follow, who for the first time as a nation within a nation did his bitter duty because it was his duty, knowing what might be expected, but scarcely foreseeing the whole truth.

We gained the right to fight for civilization at the cost of being "Jim-Crowed" and insulted; we were segregated in the draft; we were segregated in the first officers' training camp; and we were allowed to volunteer only as servants in the Navy and as common laborers in the Army, outside of the four regular Negro regiments. The Army wanted stevedores, road builders, wood choppers, railroad hands, etc., and American Negroes were among the first to volunteer. Of the 200,000 Negroes in the American Expeditionary Force, approximately 150,000 were stevedores and laborers, doing the hardest work under, in some cases, the most trying conditions faced by any soldiers during the war. And it is the verdict of men who know that the most efficient and remarkable service has been rendered by these men. Patient, loyal, intelligent, not grouchy, knowing all that they were up against among their countrymen as well as the enemy, these American black men won the war as perhaps no other set of S. O. S. men of any other race or army won it.

Where were these men stationed? At almost every seaport in France and in some English ports; at many of the interior depots and bases; at the various assembling places where automobiles, airplanes, cars and locomotives were got ready for use; in the forests, on the mountains and in the valleys, cutting wood; building roads from ports of entry right up to the view and touch of Germans in the front-lines; burying the dead; salvaging at great risk to their own lives millions of shells and other dangerous war material, actually piling up and detonating the most deadly devices in order that French battlefields might be safe to those who walk the ways of peace.

Who commanded these thousands of black men assembled from all parts of the United States and representing in culture all the way from absolute illiterates from under-taught Southern States to well-educated men from southern private schools and colleges and even from many northern universities and colleges? By a queer twist of American reasoning on the Negro it is assumed that he is best known and best "handled" by white people from the South, who more than any other white people refuse and condemn that sort of association that would most surely acquaint the white man with the very best that is in the Negro. Therefore, when officers were to be chosen for the Negro S. O. S. men, it seems that there was a preference expressed or felt for southern white officers. Some of these were fine men, but the majority were "nigger" drivers of the most offensive type.

The big, outstanding fact about the command of these colored soldiers is that southern men of a narrow, harsh type dictated the policy and method and so forced it that it became unpopular for officers to be generous to these men. When it is considered that these soldiers were abjectly under such men, with no practical opportunity for redress, it is easy to imagine the extremes to which harsh treatment could be carried. So thoroughly understood was it that the Negro had to be "properly handled and kept in his place," even in France, large use was made even of the white non-commissioned officer so that many companies and units of Negro soldiers had no higher Negro command than corporal. This harsh method showed itself in long hours, excessive tasks, little opportunity for leaves and recreation, holding of black soldiers to barracks when in the same community white soldiers had the privilege of the town, severe punishments for slight offenses, abusive language and sometimes corporal punishment. To such extremes of "handling niggers" was this carried that Negro Y. M. C. A. secretaries were refused some units on the ground, frankly stated by officers, that it would be better to have white secretaries, and in many places separate "Y" huts were demanded for white and colored soldiers so that there would be no association or fraternizing between the races.

Worked often like slaves, twelve and fourteen hours a day, these men were well-fed, poorly clad, indifferently housed, often beaten, always "Jim-Crowed" and insulted, and yet they saw the vision—they saw a nation of splendid people threatened and torn by a ruthless enemy; they saw a democracy which simply could not understand color prejudice. They received a thousand little kindnesses and half-known words of sympathy from the puzzled French, and French law and custom stepped in repeatedly to protect them, so that their only regret was the average white American. But they worked—how they worked! Everybody joins to testify to this: the white slave-drivers, the army officers, the French, the visitors—all say that the American Negro was the best laborer in France, of all the world's peoples gathered there; and if American food and materials saved France in the end from utter exhaustion, it was the Negro stevedore who made that aid effective.

The 805th

To illustrate the kind of work which the stevedore and pioneer regiments did, we cite the history of one of the pioneer Negro regiments: Under the act of May 18, 1917, the President ordered the formation of eight colored infantry regiments. Two of these, the 805th and 806th, were organized at Camp Funston. The 805th became a Pioneer regiment and when it left camp had 3,526 men and 99 officers. It included 25 regulars from the 25th Infantry of the Regular Army, 38 mechanics from Prairie View, 20 horse-shoers from Tuskegee and 8 carpenters from Howard. The regiment was drilled and had target practice. The regiment proceeded to Camp Upton late in August, 1918, and sailed, a part from Montreal and a part from Quebec, Canada, early in September. Early in October the whole regiment arrived in the southern end of the Argonne forest. The men began their work of repairing roads as follows:

A—First 2,000 meters of Clermont-Neuvilly road from Clermont road past Apremont;

B—Second 2,000 meters of Clermont-Neuvilly road, Charpentry cut-off road;

C—Locheres crossroad on Clermont-Neuvilly road, north 2,000 meters, roads at Very;
D—Clermont-Neuvilly road from point 1,000 south of Neuvilly bridge to Neuvilly, ammunition detour road at Neuvilly, Charpentry roads;
E—Auzeville railhead, Varennes railhead; railhead work at St. Juvin and Briquenay;
F—Auzeville railhead, Varennes railhead, roads at Montblainville, roads at Landros-St. George;
G—Roads at Avocourt, roads at Sommerance;
H—Roads at Avocourt, roads at Fleville;
I—Construction of ammunition dump, Neuvilly, and railhead construction between Neuvilly and Varennes and Apremont, railroad repair work March and St. Juvin, construction of Verdun-Etain railroad from November 11;
K—Railhead details and road work Aubreville, road work Varennes and Charpentry;
M—Road and railhead work Aubreville, road work Varennes.

The outlying companies were continually in immediate sight of the sausage balloons and witnessed many an air battle. Raids were frequent.

A concentration had been ordered at Varennes, November 18, and several companies had taken up their abode there or at Camp Mahout, but to carry out the salvage program, a redistribution over the Argonne-Meuse area had to be affected immediately.

The area assigned the 805th Pioneer Infantry extended from Boult-aux-Bois, almost due south to a point one kilometre west of Les Islettes; thence to Aubreville and Avocourt and Esnes; thence to Montfaucon via Bethincourt and Cuisy; thence north through Nantillois and Cunel to Bantheville; thence southwest through Romagne, Gesnes and Exermont to the main road just south of Fleville; and then north to Boult-aux-Bois through Fleville, St. Juvin, Grand Pré and Briquenay.

The area comprised all of the Argonne forest, from Clermont north and the Varennes-Malancourt-Montfaucon-Romagne sections. More than five hundred square miles of battlefield was included.

A list of the articles to be salvaged would require a page. Chiefly they were Allied and enemy weapons and cannon, web and leather equipment, clothing and blankets, rolling stock, aviation electrical and engineer equipment. It was a gigantic task and did not near completion until the first week in March when more than 3,000 French carloads had been shipped.

For some weeks truck transportation was scarce and work was slow and consisted largely in getting material to roadsides.

As companies of the 805th neared the completion of their areas they were put to work at the railheads where they helped load the salvage they had gathered and that which many other organizations of the area had brought, and sent it on its way to designated depots.

With the slackening of the salvage work, the regiment found a few days when it was possible to devote time to drilling, athletics and study. School and agricultural books were obtained in large numbers and each company organized classes which, though not compulsory, were eagerly attended by the men.

Curtailment of this work was necessitated by instructions from Advance Section Headquarters to assist in every way possible the restoration of French farmlands to a point where they could be cultivated.

This meant principally the filling of trenches across fields and upon this work the regiment entered March 15 with all its strength, except what was required for the functioning of the railheads not yet closed.

There was up to this time no regimental band.

At Camp Funston instruments had been requisitioned, but had not arrived before the regiment left. Efforts were made to enlist a colored band at Kansas City whose members wished to enter the Army as a band and be assigned to the 805th Pioneer Infantry. General Wood approved and took the matter up with the War Department. Qualified assent was obtained, but subsequent rulings prevented taking advantage of it, in view of the early date anticipated for an overseas move.

The rush of events when the regiment reached Europe

precluded immediate attention being given the matter and, meanwhile, general orders had been issued against equipping bands not in the Regular Army.

Left to itself, without divisional connections, the regiment had to rely upon its own resources for diversion. The men needed music after the hard work they were doing and Colonel Humphrey sent his Adjutant to Paris to present the matter to the Y. M. C. A., Knights of Columbus and Red Cross.

The Red Cross was able to respond immediately and Captain Bliss returned January 1, 1919, with seven cornets, six clarinets, five saxophones, four slide trombones, four alto horns, two bass tubas, two baritones and a piccolo and, also, some "jazz band effects."

The band was organized on the spot and as more instruments and music were obtained, eventually reached almost its tabular strength while it reached proficiency almost over night.

The following commendation of the work of the regiment was received: "The Chief Engineer desires to express his highest appreciation to you and to your regiment for the services rendered to the 1st Army in the offensive between the Meuse and the Argonne, starting September 26, and the continuation of that offensive on November 1 and concluding with the Armistice of November 11.

"The success of the operations of the Army Engineer Troops toward constructing and maintaining supply lines, both roads and railway, of the Army was in no small measure made possible by the excellent work performed by your troops.

"It is desired that the terms of this letter be published to all the officers and enlisted men of your command at the earliest opportunity."

A soldier writes us:

"Our regiment is composed of colored and white officers. You will find a number of complimentary things on the regiment's record in the Argonne in the history. We were, as you know, the fighting reserves of the Army and that we were right on this front from September to November 11. We kept the lines of communication going and, of course, we were raided and shelled by German long-range guns and subject to gas raids, too.

"We are now located in the Ardennes, between the Argonne and the Meuse. This is a wild and wooly forest, I assure you. We are hoping to reach our homes in May. We have spent over seven months in this section of the battle-front and we are hoping to get started home in a few weeks after you get this letter, at least. Our regiment is the best advertised regiment in the A. E. F. and its members are from all over the United States practically.

"A month or so ago we had a pay-day here and twenty thousand dollars was collected the first day and sent to relatives and banks in the United States. Every day our mail sergeant sends from one hundred to one thousand dollars per day to the United States for the men in our regiment,—savings of the small salary they receive as soldiers. As a whole they are and have learned many things by having had this great war experience."

Negro Officers

All this was expected. America knows the value of Negro labor. Negroes knew that in this war as in every other war they would have the drudgery and the dirt, but with set teeth they determined that this should not be the end and limit of their service. They did not make the mistake of seeking to escape labor, for they knew that modern war is mostly ordinary toil; they even took without protest the lion's share of the common labor, but they insisted from the first that black men must serve as soldiers and officers.

The white Negro-hating oligarchy was willing to have some Negro soldiers—the privilege of being shot in real war being one which they were easily persuaded to share—provided these black men did not get too much notoriety out of it. But against Negro officers they set their faces like flint.

The dogged insistence of the Negroes, backed eventually by the unexpected decision of Secretary Baker, encompassed the first defeat of this oligarchy and nearly one thousand colored officers were commissioned.

Immediately a persistent campaign began:

First, was the effort to get rid of Negro officers; second, the effort to discredit Negro soldiers; third, the effort to spread race prejudice in France; and fourth, the effort to keep Negroes out of the Regular Army.

First and foremost, war is war and military organization is, and must be, tyranny. This is, perhaps, the greatest and most barbarous cost of war and the most pressing reason for its abolition from civilization. As war means tyranny, the company officer is largely at the mercy of his superior officers.

The company officers of the colored troops were mainly colored. The field officers were with very few exceptions white. The fate of the colored officers, therefore, depended almost absolutely on those placed in higher command. Moreover, American military trials and legal procedures are antiquated and may be grossly unfair. They give the accused little chance if the accuser is determined and influential.

The success, then, of the Negro troops depended first of all on their field officers; given strong, devoted men of knowledge and training there was no doubt of their being able to weed out and train company officers and organize the best body of fighters on the western front. This was precisely what the Negro-haters feared. Above all, they feared Charles Young.

Charles Young

There was one man in the United States Army who by every consideration of justice, efficiency and long, faithful service should have been given the command of a division of colored troops. Colonel Charles Young is a graduate of West Point and by universal admission is one of the best officers in the Army. He has served in Cuba, Haiti, the Philippines, Mexico, Africa and the West with distinction. Under him the Negro divison would have been the most efficient in the Army. This rightful place was denied him. For a technical physical reason ("high blood pressure") he was quickly retired from the Regular Army. He was not allowed a minor command or even a chance to act as instructor during the war.

On the contrary, the 92d and 93d Divisions of Negro

troops were given Commanding Officers who with a half-dozen exceptions either distrusted Negroes or actively and persistently opposed colored officers under any circumstances. The 92d Division particularly was made a dumping ground for poor and inexperienced field officers seeking promotion. A considerable number of these white officers from the first spent more time and ingenuity in making the lot of the Negro officer hard and the chance of the Negro soldier limited than in preparing to whip the Germans.

Prejudice

These efforts fell under various heads: giving the colored officers no instruction in certain lines and then claiming that none were fitted for the work, as in artillery and engineering; persistently picking the poorest Negro candidates instead of the best for examinations and tests so as to make any failure conspicuous; using court martials and efficiency boards for trivial offenses and wholesale removals of the Negroes; subjecting Negro officers and men to persistent insult and discrimination by refusing salutes, "Jim-Crowing" places of accommodation and amusement, refusing leaves, etc.; by failing to supply the colored troops with proper equipment and decent clothing; and finally by a systematic attempt to poison the minds of the French against the Negroes and compel them to follow the dictates of American prejudice.

These are serious charges. The full proof of them cannot be attempted here, but a few examples will serve to indicate the nature of the proof.

At the colored Officers' Training Camp no instruction was given in artillery and a dead-line was established by which no one was commissioned higher than Captain, despite several recommendations. Certain Captains' positions, like those of the Headquarters Companies, were reserved for whites, and former non-commissioned officers were given preference with the hope that they would be more tractable than college-bred men—a hope that usually proved delusive.

The colored divisions were never assembled as units this side of the water. General Ballou, a timid, changeable white man, was put in command of the 92d Division and he antagonized it from the beginning.

General Ballou's attitude toward the men of his command, as expressed in his famous, or rather infamous, Bulletin 35, which was issued during the period of training in the United States, was manifested throughout the division during the entire time that he was in command in France. Whenever any occasion arose where trouble had occurred between white and colored soldiers, the burden of proof always rested on the colored man. All discrimination was passed unnoticed and nothing was done to protect the men who were under his command. Previous to General Bullard's suggestion that some order be issued encouraging the troops for the good work that they had done on the Vosges and Marbache fronts, there had been nothing done to encourage the men and officers, and it seemed that instead of trying to increase the morale of the division, it was General Ballou's intention to discourage the men as much as possible. His action in censuring officers in the presence of enlisted men was an act that tended toward breaking down the confidence that the men had in their officers, and he pursued this method on innumerable occasions. On one occasion he referred to his division, in talking to another officer, as the "rapist division"; he constantly cast aspersion on the work of the colored officer and permitted other officers to do the same in his presence, as is evidenced by the following incident which took place in the office of the Assistant Chief of Staff, G-3, at Bourbon-les-Bains:

The staff had just been organized and several General Headquarters officers were at Headquarters advising relative to the organization of the different offices. These officers were in conversation with General Ballou, Colonel Greer, the Chief of Staff, Major Hickox, and Brigadier-General Hay. In the course of the conversation Brigadier-General Hay made the remark that "In my opinion there is no better soldier than the Negro, but God damn a 'nigger' officer"! This remark was made in the presence of General Ballou and was the occasion for much laughter.

After the 92d Division moved from the Argonne forest to the Marbache Sector the 368th Infantry was held in reserve at Pompey. It was at this place that General Ballou ordered all of the enlisted men and officers of this unit to congregate and receive an address to be delivered to them by him. No one had any idea as to the nature of this address; but on the afternoon designated, the men and officers assembled on the ground, which was used as a drill-ground, and the officers were severely censured relative to the operation that had taken place in the Argonne forest. The General advised the officers, in the presence of the enlisted men, that in his opinion they were cowards; that they had failed; and that "they did not have the guts" that made brave men. This speech was made to the officers in the presence of all of the enlisted men of the 368th Infantry and was an act contrary to all traditions of the Army.

When Mr. Ralph Tyler, the accredited correspondent of the War Department, reached the Headquarters of the 92d Division and was presented to General Ballou, he was received with the utmost indifference and nothing was done to enable him to reach the units at the front in order to gain the information which he desired. After Mr. Tyler was presented to General Ballou, the General walked out of the office of the Chief of Staff with Mr. Tyler, came into the office of the Adjutant, where all of the enlisted men worked, and stood directly in front of the desk of the colored officer, who was seated in the office of the Adjutant, and in a loud voice said to Mr. Tyler: "I regard the colored officer as a distinct failure. He is cowardly and has none of the traits which go to make a successful officer." This expression was made in the presence of all of the enlisted personnel and in a tone of voice loud enough for all of them to hear.

General Ballou's Chief of Staff was a white Georgian and from first to last his malign influence was felt and he openly sought political influence to antagonize his own troops.

General ———, Commanding Officer of the ——— (92d Division), said to Major Patterson (colored), Division Judge-Advocate, that there was a concerted action on the part of the white officers throughout France to discredit the work of the colored troops in France and that everything was being done to advertise those things that would reflect discredit upon the men and officers and to withhold anything that would bring to these men praise or commendation.

On the afternoon of November 8, the Distinguished Service Cross was awarded to Lieutenant Campbell and Private Bernard Lewis, 368th Infantry, the presentation of which was made with the prescribed ceremonies, taking place on a large field just outside of Villers-en-Haye and making a very impressive sight. The following morning a private from the 804th Pioneer Infantry was executed at Belleville, for rape. The official photographer attached to the 92d Division arose at 5 A. M. on the morning of the execution, which took place at 6 A. M., and made a moving-picture film of the hanging of this private. Although the presentation of the Distinguished Service Crosses occurred at 3 P. M. on the previous day, the official photographer did not see fit to make a picture of this and when asked if he had made a picture of the presentation, he replied that he had forgotten about it.

The campaign against Negro officers began in the cantonments. At Camp Dix every effort was made to keep competent colored artillery officers from being trained. Most of the Colonels began a campaign for wholesale removals of Negro officers from the moment of embarkation.

At first an attempt was made to have General Headquarters in France assent to the blanket proposition that white and Negro officers would not get on in the same organization; this was unsuccessful and was followed by the charge that Negroes were incompetent as officers. This charge was made wholesale and before the colored officers had had a chance to prove themselves, "Efficiency Boards" immediately began wholesale removals and as such boards could act on the mere opinion of field officers the colored company officers began to be removed wholesale and to be replaced by whites.

The court martials of Negro officers were often outrageous in their contravention of common sense and military law. The experience of one Captain will illustrate. He was a college man, with militia training, who secured a Captaincy at Des Moines—a very difficult accomplishment—and was from the first regarded as an efficient officer by his fellows; when he reached Europe, however, the Major of his battalion was from Georgia, and this Captain was too independent to suit him. The Major suddenly ordered the Captain under close arrest and after long delay preferred twenty-three charges against him. These he afterward reduced to seven, continuing meantime to heap restrictions and insults on the accused, but untried, officer. Instead of breaking arrest or resenting his treatment the Captain kept cool, hired a good colored lawyer in his division and put up so strong a fight that the court martial acquitted him and restored him to his command, and sent the Major to the stevedores.

Not every officer was able thus to preserve his calm and poise.

One colored officer turned and cursed his unfair superiors and the court martial, and revealed an astonishing story of the way in which he had been hounded.

A Lieutenant of a Machine Gun Battalion was employed at Intelligence and Personnel work. He was dismissed and reinstated three times because the white officers who succeeded him could not do the work. Finally he was under arrest for one and one-half months and was dismissed from service, but General Headquarters investigated the case and restored him to his rank.

Most of the Negro officers had no chance to fight. Some were naturally incompetent and deserved demotion or removal, but these men were not objects of attack as often as the more competent and independent men.

Here, however, as so often afterward, the French stepped in, quite unconsciously, and upset careful plans. While the American officers were convinced of the Negro officers' incompetency and were besieging General Headquarters to remove them *en masse*, the French instructors at the Gondricourt Training School, where Captains and selected Lieutenants were sent for training, reported that the Negroes were among the best Americans sent there.

Moreover, the 93d Division, which had never been assembled or even completed as a unit and stood unrecognized and unattached, was suddenly called in the desperate French need, to be brigaded with French soldiers. The Americans were thoroughly scared. Negroes and Negro officers were about to be introduced to French democracy without the watchful eye of American color hatred to guard them. Something must be done.

As the Negro troops began moving toward the Vosges sector of the battlefront, August 6, 1918, active anti-Negro propaganda became evident. From the General Headquarters of the American Army at Chaumont the French Military Mission suddenly sent out, not simply to the French Army, but to all the Prefects and Sous-Prefects of France (corresponding to our governors and mayors), data setting forth at length the American attitude toward Negroes; warning against social recognition; stating that Negroes were prone to deeds of violence and were threatening America with degeneration, etc. The white troops backed this propaganda by warnings and tales wherever they preceded the blacks.

This misguided effort was lost on the French. In some cases peasants and villagers were scared at the approach of Negro troops, but this was but temporary and the colored troops everywhere they went soon became easily the best liked of all foreign soldiers. They were received in the best homes, and where they could speak French or their hosts understood English, there poured forth their story of injustice and wrong into deeply sympathetic ears. The impudent swagger of many white troops, with their openly expressed contempt for "Frogs" and their evident failure to understand the first principles of democracy in the most democratic of lands, finished the work thus begun.

No sounding words of President Wilson can offset in the minds of thousands of Frenchmen the impression of disloyalty and coarseness which the attempt to force color prejudice made on a people who just owed their salvation to black West Africa!

Little was published or openly said, but when the circular on American Negro prejudice was brought to the attention of the French ministry, it was quietly collected and burned. And in a thousand delicate ways the French expressed their silent disapprobation. For instance, in a provincial town a colored officer entered a full dining-room; the smiling landlady hastened to seat him (how natural!) at a table with white American officers, who immediately began to show their displeasure. A French officer at a neighboring table with French officers quietly glanced at the astonished landlady. Not a word was said, no one in the dining-room took any apparent notice, but the black officer was soon seated with the courteous Frenchmen.

On the Negroes this double experience of deliberate and devilish persecution from their own countrymen, coupled with a taste of real democracy and world-old culture, was revolutionizing. They began to hate prejudice and discrimination as they had never hated it before. They began to realize its eternal meaning and complications. Far from filling them with a desire to escape from their race and country, they were filled with a bitter, dogged determination never to give up the fight for Negro equality in America. If American color prejudice counted on this war experience to break the spirit of the young Negro, it counted without its host. A new, radical Negro spirit has been born in France, which leaves us older radicals far behind. Thousands of young black men have offered their lives for the Lilies of France and they return ready to offer them again for the Sun-flowers of Afro-America.

The 93rd Division

The first American Negroes to arrive in France were the Labor Battalions, comprising all told some 150,000 men.

The Negro fighting units were the 92nd and 93rd Divisions.

The so-called 93rd Division was from the first a thorn in the flesh of the Bourbons. It consisted of Negro National Guard troops almost exclusively officered by Negroes,—the 8th Illinois, the 15th New York, and units from the District of Columbia, Maryland, Ohio, Tennessee and Massachusetts. The division was thus incomplete and never really functioned as a division. For a time it was hoped that Colonel Young might be given his chance here, but nothing came of this. Early in April when the need of the French for re-enforcements was sorest, these black troops were hurriedly transported to France and were soon brigaded with the French armies.

The 369th

This regiment was originally authorized by Governor Sulzer, but its formation was long prevented. Finally it was organized with but one Negro officer. Eventually the regiment sailed with colored and white officers, landing in France, January 1, 1918, and went into the second battle of the Marne in July, east of Verdun, near Ville-sur-Turbe. It was thus the first American Negro unit in battle and one of the first American units. Colored officers took part in this battle and some were cited for bravery. Nevertheless the white Colonel, Hayward, after the battle secured the transfer of every single colored officer, except the bandmaster and chaplain.

The regiment was in a state of irritation many times, but it was restrained by the influence of the non-commissioned officers—very strong in this case because the regiment was all from New York and mainly from Harlem—and especially because being brigaded with the French they were from the first treated on such terms of equality and brotherhood that they were eager to fight. There were charges that Colonel Hayward and his white officers needlessly sacrificed the lives of these men. This, of course, is hard to prove; but certainly the casualties in this regiment were heavy and in the great attack in the Champagne, in September and October, two hundred were killed and eight hundred were wounded and gassed. The regiment went into battle with the French on the left and the Moroccans on the right and got into its own barrage by advancing faster than the other units. It was in line seven and one-half days, when three to four days is usually the limit.

In all, the regiment was under fire 191 days—a record for any American unit. It received over 170 citations for the *Croix de Guerre* and Distinguished Service Cross and was the first unit of the Allied armies to reach the Rhine, November 18, with the Second French Army.

THE 371ST AND 372ND

The 371st Regiment was drafted from South Carolina and had southern white officers from the first, many of whom were arrogant and overbearing. The regiment mobilized at Camp Jackson, October 5–17, and embarked for France, April 9, from Newport News, Va. It was trained at Rembercourt-aux-Ports (Meuse) and left for the region near Bar-le-Duc, June 5. The troops arrived in the Argonne June 22. They were brigaded with the 157th French Division, 13th Army Corps, and remained in the battle-line, front and reserve, until the Armistice was signed.

There are few data at present available for the history of this regiment because there were no colored officers to preserve it. It is rumored, however, that after the first battle the number of casualties among the meanest of their officers led to some mutual understandings. The regiment received a number of citations for bravery.

As this regiment was brigaded usually with the 372nd, a part of its history follows:

The official records show that the 372nd Infantry was organized at Camp Stuart, January 1, 1918, Colonel Glendie B. Young, Infantry, U. S. N. G., commanding, and included the following National Guard units: First Separate Battalion, District of Columbia, Infantry; Ninth Battalion of Ohio, Infantry; Company L, Sixth Massachusetts, Infantry; and one company each from Maryland, Tennessee and Connecticut. To these were added later 250 men from Camp Custer; excepting the Staff, Machine Gun, Headquarters and Supply Companies, the regiment was officered by colored men.

The regiment was brigaded with the 371st into the 186th Infantry Brigade, a unit of the Provisional 93rd Division. It was understood that the 93rd Division, which was to be composed of all Negro troops, would be fully organized in France; but when the 372nd arrived at St. Nazaire, April 14, 1918, the organization was placed under command of the French. Four weeks later the brigade was dissolved and the 93rd Division ceased to be mentioned. Its four regiments were all subject to orders of the French G. Q. G., General Petain, commanding.

The regiment spent five weeks in training and re-organization at Conde-en-Barrois (Meuse), as a unit of the 13th French Army Corps. The men were trained in French methods by French officers and non-commissioned officers with French ordnance equipment. They developed so rapidly that a French Major exclaimed enthusiastically on the street: "These men are intelligent and alert. Their regiment will have a glorious career." Thus, from the beginning the worth of our troops was recognized by a veteran of the French Army.

To complete its training under actual war conditions, the

regiment was sent to a "quiet sector"—sub-sector, Argonne West, on June 8, where it spent twenty days learning the organization of defensive positions and how to hold these positions under shell fire from the enemy. During this time it was a part of the 63rd French Division and during the last ten days it was a part of the 35th French Division. On July 2, the 372nd Infantry became permanently identified with the 157th French Division, commanded by General Goybet. The division consisted of two colored American regiments and one French regiment of infantry. The artillery units, engineers, sanitary train, etc., were all French. On his first inspection tour, at Vanquois, General Goybet asked one of our men if he thought the Germans could pass if they started over. The little brown private replied: "Not if the boches can't do a good job in killing all of us." That pleased the new General very much and clinched his confidence in the black troops.

On July 13 the regiment retired to a reserve position near the village of Locheres (Meuse), for temporary rest and to help sustain the coming blow. The next day Colonel Young was relieved of command by Colonel Herschel Tupes, a regular army officer. In the afternoon the regiment was assembled and prepared for action, but it later was found that it would not be needed. The attack of the Germans was launched near Rheims on the night of July 14 and the next evening the world read of the decisive defeat of the Germans by General Gouraud's army.

The following Sunday found the regiment billeted in the town of Sivry-la-Perche, not very far from Verdun. After a band concert in the afternoon Colonel Tupes introduced himself to his command. In the course of his remarks, he said that he had always commanded regulars, but he had little doubt that the 372nd Infantry could become as good as any regiment in France.

On July 26 the regiment occupied sub-sector 304. The occupation of this sub-sector was marked by hard work and discontentment. The whole position had to be re-organized, and in doing this the men maintained their previous reputation for good work. The total stay in the sector was seven weeks. The regiment took part in two raids and several individuals distinguished themselves: one man received a *Croix de Guerre* because he held his trench mortar between his legs to continue firing when the base had been damaged by a shell; another carried a wounded French comrade from "No Man's Land" under heavy fire, and was also decorated. Several days after a raid, the Germans were retaliating by shelling the demolished village of Montzeville, situated in the valley below the Post-of-Command and occupied by some of the reserves; Private Rufus Pinckney rushed through the heavy fire and rescued a wounded French soldier.

On another occasion, Private Kenneth Lewis of the Medical Detachment, later killed at his post, displayed such fine qualities of coolness and disdain for danger by sticking to duty until the end that two post-mortem decorations: the *Croix de Guerre* with Palm and *Medaille Militaire* were awarded. The latter is a very distinguished recognition in the French Army.

So well had the regiment worked in the Argonne that it was sent to relieve the 123rd French Infantry Regiment in the sub-sector Vanquois, on July 28. An attack by the Germans in the valley of the Aire, of which Vanquois was a key, was expected at any moment. New defenses were to be constructed and old ones strengthened. The men applied themselves with a courageous devotion, night and day, to their tasks and after two weeks of watchful working under fire, Vanquois became a formidable defensive system.

Besides the gallantry of Private Pinckney, Montzeville must be remembered in connection with the removal of colored officers from the regiment. It was there that a board of officers (all white) requested by Colonel Young and appointed by Colonel Tupes, sat on the cases of twenty-one colored officers charged with inefficiency. Only one out of that number was acquitted: he was later killed in action. The charges of inefficiency were based on physical disability, insufficient training, unsuitability. The other colored officers who had been removed were either transferred to other units or sent to re-classification depots.

The Colonel told the Commanding General through an interpreter: "The colored officers in this regiment know as much about their duties as a child." The General was surprised and whispered to another French officer that the

Colonel himself was not so brilliant and that he believed it was prejudice that caused the Colonel to make such a change. A few moments after, the Colonel told the General that he had requested that no more colored officers be sent to the regiment. In reply to this the General explained how unwise it was because the colored officers had been trained along with their men at a great expenditure of time and money by the American and French governments; and, also, he doubted if well-qualified white officers could be spared him from other American units. The General insisted that the time was at hand for the great autumn drive and that it would be a hindrance because he feared the men would not be pleased with the change. The Colonel heeded not his General and forwarded two requests for an anti-colored-officer regiment. He went so far as to tell the Lieutenant-Colonel that he believed the regiment should have white men for non-commissioned officers. Of course, the men would not have stood for this at any price. The Colonel often would tell the Adjutant to never trust a "damned black clerk" and that he considered "one white man worth a million Negroes."

About September 8 the regiment was relieved by the 129th United States Infantry and was sent to the rear for period of rest. Twenty-four hours after arrival in the rest area, orders were received to proceed farther. The nightly marches began. The regiment marched from place to place in the Aube, the Marne and the Haute Marne until it went into the great Champagne battle on September 27.

For nine days it helped push the Hun toward the Belgian frontier. Those days were hard, but these men did their duty and came out with glory. Fortunately, all the colored officers had not left the regiment and it was they and the brave sergeants who led the men to victory and fame. The new white officers had just arrived, some of them the night before the regiment went into battle, several of whom had never been under fire in any capacity, having just come out of the training school at Langres. Nevertheless, the regiment was cited by the French and the regimental colors were decorated by Vice-Admiral Moreau at Brest, January 24, 1919.

After the relief on the battlefield, the regiment reached Somme Bionne (Marne) October 8. Congratulations came in from everywhere except American Headquarters. After a brief rest of three days the regiment was sent to a quiet sector in the Vosges, on the frontier of Alsace. The Colonel finally disposed of the remaining colored officers, except the two dentists and the two chaplains. All the officers were instructed to carry their arms at all times and virtually to shoot any soldier on the least provocation. As a consequence, a corporal of Company L was shot and killed by First Lieutenant James B. Coggins, from North Carolina, for a reason that no one has ever been able to explain. The signing of the Armistice and the cessation of hostilities, perhaps, prevented a general, armed opposition to a system of prejudice encouraged by the Commanding Officer of the Regiment.

Despite the prejudice of officers toward the men, the regiment marched from Ban-de-Laveline to Granges of Vologne, a distance of forty-five kilometers, in one day and maintained such remarkable discipline that the officers themselves were compelled to accord them praise.

While stationed at Granges, individuals in the regiment were decorated on December 17 for various deeds of gallantry in the Champagne battle. General Goybet presented four military medals and seventy-two *Croix de Guerre* to enlisted men. Colonel Tupes presented four Distinguished Service Crosses to enlisted men. At the time, the regiment had just been returned to the American command, the following order was read:

157th Division Hqrs. December 15th, 1918.
Staff.

General Order No. 246.

On the date of the 12th of December, 1918, the 371st and the 372nd R. I., U. S. have been returned to the disposal of the American Command. It is not without profound emotion that I come in the name of the 157th (French) Division and in my personal name, to say good-bye to our valiant comrades of combat.

For seven months we have lived as brothers of arms, sharing the same works, the same hardships, the same dangers;

side by side we have taken part in the great battle of the Champagne, that a wonderful victory has ended.

The 157th (French) Division will never forget the wonderful impetus irresistible, the rush heroic of the colored American regiments on the "Observatories Crest" and in the Plain of Menthois. The most formidable defense, the nests of machine guns, the best organized positions, the artillery barrages most crushing, could not stop them. These best regiments have gone through all with disdain of death and thanks to their courage devotedness, the "Red Hand" Division has during nine hard days of battle been ahead in the victorious advance of the Fourth (French) Army.

Officers and non-commissioned officers and privates of the 371st and 372nd Regiments Infantry, U. S., I respectfully salute your glorious dead and I bow down before your standards, which by the side of the 333rd R. I., led us to victory.

Dear Friends from America, when you have crossed back over the ocean, don't forget the "Red Hand" Division. Our fraternity of arms has been soaked in the blood of the brave. Those bonds will be indestructible.

Keep a faithful remembrance to your General, so proud to have commanded you, and remember that his thankful affection is gained to you forever.

(Signed) General Goybet,
Commanding the 157th (French) Division, Infantry.

Colonel Tupes, in addressing the regiment, congratulated them on the achievements and expressed his satisfaction with their conduct. He asked the men to take a just pride in their accomplishments and their spirit of loyalty.

Can this be surpassed for eccentricity?

The seven weeks at Granges were pleasant and profitable socially. Lectures were given to the men by French officers, outdoor recreation was provided and the civilian population opened their hearts and their homes to the Negro heroes. Like previous attempts, the efforts of the white officers to prevent the mingling of Negroes with the French girls of the village were futile. Every man was taken on his merits. The mayor of Granges gave the regiment an enthusiastic farewell.

On January 1, 1919, the regiment entrained for Le Mans

(Sarthe). After complying with the red-tape preparatory to embarkation and the delousing process it went to Brest, arriving there January 13, 1919.

The 370th

Up to this point the anti-Negro propaganda is clear and fairly consistent and unopposed. General Headquarters had not only witnessed instructions in Negro prejudice to the French, but had, also, consented to wholesale removals of officers among the engineers and infantry, on the main ground of color. Even the French, in at least one case, had been persuaded that Negro officers were the cause of certain inefficiencies in Negro units.

Undoubtedly the cruel losses of the 369th Regiment were due in part to the assumption of the French at first that the American Negroes were like the Senegalese; these half-civilized troops could not in the time given them be trained in modern machine warfare, and they were rushed at the enemy almost with naked hands. The resulting slaughter was horrible. Our troops tell of great black fields of stark and crimson dead after some of these superhuman onrushes.

It was this kind of fighting that the French expected of the black Americans at first and some white American officers did not greatly care so long as white men got the glory. The French easily misunderstood the situation at first and assumed that the Negro officers were to blame, especially as this was continually suggested to them by the Americans.

It was another story, however, when the 370th Regiment came. This was the famous 8th Illinois, and it had a full quota of Negro officers, from Colonel down. It had seen service on the Mexican border; it went to Houston, Tex., after the Thirteen had died for Freedom; and it was treated with wholesome respect. It was sent to Newport News, Va., for embarkation; once Colonel Dennison refused to embark his troops and marched them back to camp because he learned they were to be "Jim-Crowed" on the way over.

The regiment arrived at Brest, April 22, and was assigned to the 72nd French Division, remaining near Belfort until June 17. Then it went with the 34th French Division into the front-line, at St. Mihiel, for a month and later with the 36th French Divison into the Argonne, where they fought. They were given a short period of rest and then they went into the front-line, at Soissons, with the 59th French Division. In September and October they were fighting again.

On September 15, in the Vauxaillion area, they captured Mt. Dessinges and the adjacent woods after severe fighting. They held a sector alone afterward on the Canal L'Oise et Aisne and when attacked, repulsed the Germans and moved forward, gaining the praise of the French General. On October 24, the regiment went into the front-line again, near Grand Lup, and performed excellent service; the Armistice found part of the regiment across the Belgian frontier.

The general conduct of the regiment was excellent. No case of rape was reported and only one murder. The regiment received sixteen Distinguished Service Crosses and seventy-five *Croix de Guerre*, beside company citations.

When at first the regiment did not adopt the tactics of "shock" troops, the white Americans again took their cue and inspired a speech from the French General, which the colored men could not understand. It was not long, however, before the French General publicly apologized for his first and hasty criticism and afterward he repeatedly commended both officers and men for their bravery, intelligence and daring. This regiment received more citations than any other American regiment for bravery on the field of battle. There was, of course, the fly in the ointment,—the effort to substitute white officers was strong and continuous, notwithstanding the fact that many of the black officers of this regiment were among the most efficient in the American Army.

General Headquarters by this time had begun to change its attitude and curb the Bourbons. It announced that it was not the policy of the American Army to make wholesale removals simply on account of color and it allowed the citations for bravery of Negro troops to be approved.

Nevertheless, the pressure continued. First the colored Colonel, the ranking Negro officer in France, was sent home. The reason for this is not clear. At any rate Colonel Dennison was replaced by a white Colonel, who afterward accepted a *Croix de Guerre* for an exploit which the Negro officers to a man declare was actually performed by a Negro officer while he was sitting snugly in his tent. The men of the regiment openly jeered him, crying out: "Blue Eyes ain't our Colonel; Duncan's our Colonel!" referring to the colored Lieutenant-Colonel. But the white Colonel was diplomatic; he let the colored officers run the regiment, posed as the "Moses" of the colored race (to the open amusement of the Negroes) and quietly tried to induct white officers. "I cannot understand why they sent this white Lieutenant," he said plaintively to a colored officer. The officer at that moment had in his pocket a copy of the Colonel's telegram asking General Headquarters for white officers. But the Armistice came before the Colonel succeeded in getting but two white officers,—his brother as Major (without a battalion) and one Lieutenant.

The organization that ranked all America in distinction remained, therefore, a Negro organization, for the white Colonel was only "commanding" and Dennison was still titular head.

The 92nd Division

So much for the 93rd Division. Its troops fought magnificently in the Champagne, the Argonne and elsewhere and were given unstinted praise by the French and even commendation by the Americans. They fought well, too, despite the color of their officers—371st Regiment under white, the 369th and 372nd Regiments under white and colored, and the 370th Regiment under colored were equally brave, except that the 370th Regiment made the most conspicuous record.

One might conclude under ordinary circumstances that it was a matter of efficiency in officers and not of race, but, unfortunately, the efficient colored officer had almost no chance even to try except in the 370th Regiment and in the Champagne battle with the 372nd Regiment. With a fair chance there is no doubt that he could have led every one of these regiments just as well as the white officers. It must, too, be remembered that all the non-commissioned officers in all these regiments were Negroes.

The storm center of the Negro troops was the 92nd Division. The brigading of the 93rd Division with the French made wholesale attack and depreciation difficult, since it was continually annulled by the generous appreciation of the French. The 92nd Division, however, was planned as a complete Negro division, manned by Negro company officers. Everything depended, then, on the General and field officers as to how fair this experiment should be.

From the very first there was open and covert opposition and trouble. Instead of putting Colonel Young at the head, the white General Ballou was chosen and surrounded by southern white officers who despised "nigger" officers.

General Ballou himself was well-meaning, but weak, vacillating, without great ability and afraid of southern criticism. He was morbidly impressed by the horror of this "experiment" and proceeded from the first to kill the morale of his troops by orders and speeches. He sought to make his Negro officers feel personal responsibility for the Houston outbreak; he tried to accuse them indirectly of German propaganda; he virtually ordered them to submit to certain personal humiliations and discriminations without protest. Thus, before the 92nd Division was fully formed, General Ballou had spread hatred and distrust among his officers and men. "That old Ballou stuff!" became a by-word in the division for anti-Negro propaganda. Ballou was finally dismissed from his command for "tactical inefficiency."

The main difficulty, however, lay in a curious misapprehension in white men of the meaning and method of race contact in America. They sought desperately to reproduce in the Negro division and in France the racial restrictions of America, on the theory that any new freedom would "spoil" the blacks. But they did not understand the fact that men of the types who became Negro officers protect themselves from continuous insult and discrimination by making and moving in a world of their own; they associate socially where they are more than welcome; they live for the most part beside neighbors who like them; they attend schools where they are not insulted; and they work where their work is appreciated. Of course, every once in a while they have to unite to resent encroachments upon their world—

new discriminations in law and custom; but this is occasional and not continuous.

The world which General Ballou and his field officers tried to re-create for Negro officers was a world of continuous daily insult and discrimination to an extent that none had ever experienced, and they did this in a country where the discrimination was artificial and entirely unnecessary, arousing the liveliest astonishment and mystification.

For instance, when the Headquarters Company of the 92nd Division sailed for Brest, elaborate quarters in the best hotel were reserved for white officers, and unfinished barracks, without beds and in the cold and mud, were assigned Negro officers. The colored officers went to their quarters and then returned to the city. They found that the white Americans, unable to make themselves understood in French, had not been given their reservation, but had gone to another and poorer hotel. The black officers immediately explained and took the fine reservations.

As no Negroes had been trained in artillery, it was claimed immediately that none were competent. Nevertheless, some were finally found to qualify. Then it was claimed that technically trained privates were impossible to find. There were plenty to be had if they could be gathered from the various camps. Permission to do this was long refused, but after endless other delays and troubles, the Field Artillery finally came into being with a few colored officers. Before the artillery was ready, the division mobilized at Camp Upton, between May 28 and June 4, and was embarked by the tenth of June for France.

The entire 92nd Division arrived at Brest by June 20. A week later the whole division went to Bourbonne-les-Bains, where it stayed in training until August 6. Here a determined effort at wholesale replacement of the colored officers took place. Fifty white Lieutenants were sent to the camp to replace Negro officers. "Efficiency" boards began to weed out colored men.

Without doubt there was among colored as among white American officers much inefficiency, due to lack of adaptability, training and the hurry of preparation. But in the case of the Negro officers repeatedly the race question came to the fore and permission was asked to remove them because they were colored, while the inefficiency charge was a wholesale one against their "race and nature."

General Headquarters by this time, however, had settled down to a policy of requiring individual, rather than wholesale, accusation, and while this made a difference, yet in the army no officer can hold his position long if his superiors for any reason wish to get rid of him. While, then, many of the waiting white Lieutenants went away, the colored officers began to be systematically reduced in number.

On August 6 the division entered the front-line trenches in the Vosges sector and stayed here until September 20. It was a quiet sector, with only an occasional German raid to repel. About September 20, the division began to move to the Argonne, where the great American drive to cut off the Germans was to take place. The colored troops were not to enter the front-lines, as General Pershing himself afterward said, as they were entirely unequipped for front-line service. Nevertheless, the 368th Regiment, which arrived in the Argonne September 24, was suddenly sent into battle on the front-line on the morning of September 26. As this is a typical instance of the difficulties of Negro officers and troops, it deserves recital in detail.

It is the story of the failure of white field officers to do their duty and the partially successful and long-continued effort of company officers and men to do their duty despite this. That there was inexperience and incompetency among the colored officers is probable, but it was not confined to them; in their case the greater responsibility lay elsewhere, for it was the plain duty of the field officers: First, to see that their men were equipped for battle; second, to have the plans clearly explained, at least, step by step, to the company officers; third, to maintain liaison between battalions and between the regiment and the French and other American units.

Here follows the story as it was told to me point by point by those who were actually on the spot. They were earnest, able men, mostly Lieutenants and Captains, and one could not doubt, there in the dim, smoke-filled tents about Le Mans, their absolute conscientiousness and frankness.

THE 368TH

The 368th Regiment went into the Argonne September 24 and was put into the drive on the morning of September 26. Its duty was "combat liaison," with the French 37th Division and the 77th (white) Division of Americans. The regiment as a whole was not equipped for battle in the front-line. It had no artillery support until the sixth day of the battle; it had no grenades, no trench fires, trombones, or signal flares, no airplane panels for signaling and no shears for German wire. The wire-cutting shears given them were absolutely useless with the heavy German barbed wire and they were able to borrow only sixteen large shears, which had to serve the whole attacking battalion.* Finally, they had no maps and were at no time given definite objectives.

The Second Battalion of the 368th Regiment entered battle on the morning of September 26, with Major Elser in command; all the company officers were colored; Company F went "over the top" at 5:30 A. M.; Company H, with which the Major was, went "over" at 12:30 noon; advancing four kilometers the battalion met the enemy's fire; the Machine Gun Company silenced the fire; Major Elser, who had halted in the woods to collect souvenirs from dead German bodies,

*"On advancing from the French trenches the morning of the twenty-sixth much wire was met with by organizations and owing to the fact that none had wirecutters, considerable disorganization resulted in the companies, especially in the matter of liaison."

"As it was almost dark at this time and having no liaison with any of the other units, I decided to withdraw until I could get in touch with the Commanding Officer, 368th Infantry. The enemy searched along the trails with their artillery during our withdrawal, but none of the shells fell near us; it was pitch dark by this time and we had just reached the German's first trench. There was much confusion owing to the mass of wire we had to contend with in the dark before the companies reached the French trenches."

"Company G spent the entire day of the twenty-sixth working its way through the wire entanglements. Great difficulty was experienced in this work because of the lack of wirecutters."

—*Reports of Major M. A. Elser.*

immediately withdrew part of the battalion to the rear in single file about dark without notifying the rest of the battalion. Captain Dabney and Lieutenant Powell of the Machine Gun Company led the rest of the men out in order about 10:00 P. M. When the broadside opened on September 26, Major Elser stood wringing his hands and crying: "What shall I do! What shall I do!" At night he deplored the occurrence, said it was all his fault, and the next morning Major Elser commended the Machine Gun Company for extricating the deserted part of the battalion. Moving forward again at 11 A. M., two companies went "over the top" at 4 P. M. without liaison. With the rest of the battalion again, these companies went forward one and one-half kilometers. Major Elser stayed back with the Post-of-Command. Enemy fire and darkness again stopped the advancing companies and Captain Jones fell back 500 metres and sent a message about 6 A. M. on the morning of September 28 to the Major asking for re-enforcements. Captain Jones stayed under snipers' fire until about 3 P. M. and when no answer to his request came from the Major, he went "over the top" again and retraced the same 500 metres. Heavy machine gun and rifle fire again greeted him. He took refuge in nearby trenches, but his men began to drift away in confusion. All this time the Major was in the rear. On September 28, however, Major Elser was relieved of the command of the battalion and entered the hospital for "psychoneurosis," or "shell-shock,"—a phrase which often covers a multitude of sins. Later he was promoted to Lieutenant-Colonel and transferred to a Labor Battalion.

Meantime, on September 27, at 4:30 P. M., the Third Battalion of the 368th Infantry moved forward. It was commanded by Major B. F. Norris, a white New York lawyer, a graduate of Plattsburg, and until this battle a Headquarters Captain with no experience on the line. Three companies of the battalion advanced two and one-half kilometres and about 6:30 P. M. were fired on by enemy machine guns. The Major, who was in support with one company and a platoon of machine guns, ordered the machine guns to trenches seventy-five yards in the rear. The Major's orders were confusing and the company as well as the platoon retreated to the trenches, leaving the firing-line unsupported. Subjected to heavy artillery, grenade, machine gun and rifle fire during the whole night of September 27 and being without artillery support or grenades, the firing line broke and the men took refuge in the trench with the Major, where all spent a terrible night under rain and bombardment. Next morning, September 28, at 7:30 A. M., the firing-line was restored and an advance ordered. The men led by their colored officers responded. They swept forward two and one-half kilometres and advanced beyond both French and Americans on the left and right. Their field officers failed to keep liaison with the French and American white units and even lost track of their own Second Battalion, which was dribbling away in one of the front trenches. The advancing firing-line of the Third Battalion met a withering fire of trench mortars, seventy-sevens, machine guns, etc. It still had no artillery support and being too far in advance received the German fire front, flank and rear and this they endured five hours. The line broke at 12:30 and the men retreated to the support trench, where the Major was. He reprimanded the colored officers severely. They reported the intense artillery fire and their lack of equipment, their ignorance of objectives and their lack of maps for which they had asked. They were ordered to re-form and take up positions, which they did. Many contradictory orders passed to the Company Commanders during the day: to advance, to halt, to hold, to withdraw, to leave woods as quickly as possible. Finally, at 6:30 P. M., they were definitely ordered to advance. They advanced three kilometres and met exactly the same conditions as before,—heavy artillery fire on all sides. The Company Commanders were unable to hold all their men and the Colonel ordered the Major to withdraw his battalion from the line. Utter confusion resulted,—there were many casualties and many were gassed. Major Norris withdrew, leaving a platoon under Lieutenant Dent on the line ignorant of the command to withdraw. They escaped finally unaided during the night.

The Chief of Staff said in his letter to Senator McKellar: "One of our majors commanding a battalion said: 'The men are rank cowards, there is no other words for it.' "

A colored officer writes:

"I was the only colored person present when this was

uttered: It was on the 27th of last September in the second line trenches of Vienne Le Chateau in our attack in the Argonne and was uttered by Major B. F. Norris, commanding the 3rd Battalion. Major Norris, himself, was probably the biggest coward because he left his Battalion out in the front lines and came back to the Colonel's dugout a nervous wreck. I was there in a bunk alongside of the wall and this major came and laid down beside me and he moaned and groaned so terribly all night that I couldn't hardly close my eyes—he jumped and twisted worse than anything I have ever seen in my life. He was a rank coward himself and left his unit on some trifling pretext and remained back all night."

From September 26–29 the First Battalion of the 368th Infantry, under Major J. N. Merrill, was in the front-line French trenches. On the night of September 28 it prepared to advance, but after being kept standing under shell-fire for two hours it was ordered back to the trenches. A patrol was sent out to locate the Third Battalion, but being refused maps by the Colonel it was a long time on the quest and before it returned the First Battalion was ordered to advance, on the morning of September 29. By 1:00 P. M. they had advanced one mile when they were halted to find Major Merrill. Finally Major Merrill was located after two hours' search. A French Lieutenant guided them to positions in an old German trench. The Major ordered them forward 600 yards to other deserted German trenches. Terrific shell-fire met them here, and there were many casualties. They stayed in the trench during the night of September 29 and at noon on September 30 were ordered to advance. They advanced three kilometres through the woods, through shell and machine gun fire and artillery barrage. They dug in and stayed all night under fire. On October 1 the French Artillery came up and put over a barrage. Unfortunately, it fell short and the battalion was caught between the German and French barrages and compelled hastily to withdraw.

The regiment was soon after relieved by a French unit and taken by train to the Marbache sector. Major Elser, of the Second Battalion, made no charges against his colored officers and verbally assumed responsibility for the failure of his battalion. There was for a time strong talk of a court martial for him. Major Merrill made no charges; but Major Norris on account of the two breaks in the line of the Third Battalion on September 28 ordered five of his colored line officers court-martialed for cowardice and abandonment of positions—a Captain, two First Lieutenants, and a Second Lieutenant were accused. Only one case,—that of the Second Lieutenant, had been decided at this writing. He was found guilty by the court-martial, but on review of his case by General Headquarters he was acquitted and restored to his command.

Colonel Greer in the letter to Senator McKellar on December 6, writes as follows: "From there we went to the Argonne and in the offensive starting there on September 26, had one regiment in the line, attached to the 38th French Corps. They failed there in all their missions, laid down and sneaked to the rear, until they were withdrawn."

This is what Colonel Durand, the French General who was in command in this action, said in a French General Order: *"L'Honneur de la prise de Binarville doit revenir au 368th R. I. U. S."*

And this is what Colonel Greer himself issued in General Order No. 38, Headquarters 92nd Division, the same day he wrote his infamous letter to this senator: "The Division Commander desires to commend in order the meritorious conduct of Private Charles E. Boykin, Company C, 326th Field Signal Battalion. On the afternoon of September 26, 1918, while the 368th Infantry was in action in the Argonne forest the Regimental Commander moved forward to establish a P. C. and came upon a number of Germans who fled to the woods which were FOUND TO BE ALIVE WITH MACHINE GUNS. The Commanding Officer ordered the woods searched to the top of the hill, the officer in charge of scouting (2nd Lieutenant C. W. Carpenter) called for volunteers and Private Boykin, a telephone linesman, offered his services and set out with the rest of the detail. While trying to flank an enemy machine gun another opened fire killing him instantly."

This effort of the 368th Regiment was seized upon by Army gossip and widely heralded as a "failure" of Negro troops, and particularly of Negro officers. Yet the same sort of troops and many Negro officers in the Champagne and afterward in the Argonne under French leadership covered themselves with glory. The real failure in the initial Argonne drive was in American field strategy which was totally unequal to German methods and had to learn by bitter experience. It is worse than unfair to write off the first experience to the discredit of Negro troops and company officers who did all that was humanly possible under the circumstances.

Other Units

The 365th, 366th and 367th Regiments did not enter the battle-line at all in the Argonne. The whole division after the withdrawal of the 368th Regiment was, beginning with September 29, transferred to the Metz sector, preparatory to the great drive on that fortress which was begun, rather needlessly, as the civilian would judge, on the day before the signing of the Armistice, November 10.

According to plan, the 56th white American Division was on the left, the 92nd Division was in the center and the French Army was on the right. The 367th Regiment led the advance and forged ahead of the flanking units, the entire First Battalion being awarded the *Croix de Guerre*;—but this time wise field direction held them back, and for the first time they were supported by their own Negro Field Artillery. Beside the four Infantry Regiments the 92nd Division had the usual other units.

The 325th Field Signal Battalion, attached to Division Headquarters, was composed of four companies organized at Camp Sherman. It had ten colored and twenty white officers. It was in France at Bourbonne-les-Bains and then went to the Vosges, where it was split into detachments and attached to regiments under the Chief Signal Officer. While at school at Gondricourt, July 13–August 18, it made one of the best records of any unit. Many of its men were cited for bravery.

The 167th Field Artillery Brigade consisted of two regiments of Light Artillery (75s) trained at Camp Dix (the 349th and 350th) and one regiment of Heavy Artillery (the 351st) trained at Camp Meade, which used 155 howitzers. They experienced extraordinary difficulties in training. There can be no doubt but that deliberate effort was made to send up for examination in artillery not the best, but the poorest equipped candidates. Difficulty was encountered in getting colored men with the requisite technical training transferred to the artillery service. If the Commanding Officer in this case had been as prejudiced as in the case of the engineer and other units, there would have been no Negro Artillery. But Colonel Moore, although a Southerner, insisted on being fair to his men. The brigade landed in Brest June 26 and was trained at Montmorillon (Vienne). They were favorites in the town and were received into the social life on terms of perfect equality. There were five colored company officers and eight medical officers. The officers were sent to school at La Cortine and the Colonel in charge of this French school said that the work of the colored artillery brigade was better at the end of two weeks than that of any other American unit that had attended the school. The brigade went into battle in the Metz drive and did its work without a hitch, despite the fact that it had no transport facilities for their guns and had to handle them largely by hand.

The 317th Ammunition Train, which was attached to Division Headquarters, but was under the artillery in battle, was organized at Camp Funston in December, and had 1,333 officers and men, divided into two battalions, one motor and one horse, with seven companies. There were thirty-three colored and three white officers. The battalion landed in France June 27 and went to Montmorillon, and to the Artillery Training School at La Cortine, with the 167th Field Artillery. It arrived at Marbache October 18 and took part in the Metz drive. It had charge, also, of the Corps Ammunition dumps. During the drive all the officers were colored and Major Dean was in command. General Sherbourne, one of the few Commanding Officers fair to Negro troops, warmly commended the work of the artillery. No general court martial took place in the organization from the beginning and no efficiency boards sat. This was one of the very few units in which Negroes were promoted: four being made Captains, three First Lieutenants, eleven Second Lieutenants, and one a Major.

Near the close of the war thirty-five Lieutenants commissioned at Camp Taylor arrived in France and were sent to school near Nantes. They were subjected to many indignities by the American officers and were compelled to enter the class-room after the whites; they were refused leaves to town; reprimanded for conversing with the women of the city, who were anxious to be kind and sympathetic to the obviously oppressed strangers. Notwithstanding all this the men made good records and joined their command after the Armistice.

The 317th Engineers were assembled at Camp Sherman in December with 1,350 officers and men. There were two battalions and all the officers were colored, except four field officers. The Commanding Officers, however, were from the first determined to get rid of the Negroes. On May 10 the colored Captains were relieved, and sent to the 365th and 366th Regiments. The regiment came to France in June and was trained near Bourbonne-les-Bains until July 20. On July 22 all the remaining colored officers, except two Lieutenants, the chaplain and the medical officers, were relieved at the repeated requests of Colonel Brown, of Georgia, and others. The regiment went to the Vosges in August, and then to the Argonne, doing excellent technical work in building and construction. All but one company were attached to the Fourth French Army Corps until December 22; only Company E remained with the 92nd Division.

The 366th Field Hospital was a colored unit with only two or three whites. It handled 10,000 cases before and during the Metz drive, four weeks, and was rated best in the American Expeditionary Force. Lieutenant Wright, the colored physician in charge, was promoted to a Captaincy.

The final engagement immediately preceding the signing of the Armistice was fought in the Marbache sector, south of Metz, and was the most important event in which all the units of the 92nd Division actively participated. The division entered this sector October 7 and established headquarters in the village of Marbache, October 10, 1918. The several regiments were stationed in the front lines of the Division sector, with supporting units and reserves in the rear. Almost immediately upon entering this sector active operations were begun; patrols and reconnoitering parties were sent out from our lines; raiding parties were active and both sides found it necessary to be constantly on the alert. As the time for the advance of the whole Second Army grew nearer heavy shelling became more frequent, patrolling more active and raiding parties bolder. It was necessary to obtain all possible information regarding the enemy's movements and intentions before the advance began. There were many thrilling experiences in the sector during the four weeks preceding the final struggle.

On the tenth day of November came the order announcing the great drive and outlining the position of the 92nd Division in the line.

At 7 A. M. on the eleventh, the artillery broke loose with a terrific bombardment; this preparation lasted for a period of 42 minutes and was delivered upon the village of Bois Frehaut and the neighboring woods through which the infantry was to pass in its advance. In the meantime, the boys in the several companies composing the first assault line sprang from their trenches and with grim determination pushed themselves into "No Man's Land" and into the woods in the direction of the great German fortification, the city of Metz. The first objective of the 365th Infantry was Bois Frehaut (woods) three miles in depth and two miles in width. Barbed wire entanglements were everywhere and German machine guns were sputtering and large cannon were sending forth their messengers of death in all directions. The 365th Machine Gun Company, the 37-M M Platoon and our artillery and infantrymen repulsed this murderous attack and after two hours of desperate fighting Bois Frehaut was taken by the 365th and held by the Second Battalion of that organization until the bugle sounded the call to cease firing at 11 o'clock on the following morning.

The attack was led by Company H under the command of Captain William W. Green with a detachment of Company A commanded by Lieutenant Gus Mathews of Chicago with Company G and two other units in support. In fighting through the dense woods, made more difficult by large volumes of smoke from bursting shells, the attacking line in Company H became thinned and before many of the men arrived after the Company merged from the woods a flanking movement was attempted by the German machine gunners, but the timely arrival of Company G under the command of

Lieutenant Walter Lyons saved Company H from this added danger. During this attack the Machine Gun Company of the 365th was active in covering the advancing infantry and kept the enemy on the run, thus making it impossible for them to deliver an effective fire against the men in the assault waive. The second assault waive was under the command of Captain Walter R. Sanders who was, also, second in command of the Second Battalion of the 365th Infantry. The second waive, under heavy shell fire and gas bombs from the artillery, moved up to occupy the position first held by the Second Battalion. While making this advance Lieutenant Walter Lowe, commanding Company A, was gassed, but he remained with his company, directing its movements until a short time before the order came to cease firing on the morning of the eleventh.

While the 365th Infantry was fighting like real heroes the units in the other battalions were doing exactly the same thing. The first objective reached by the 366th was Bois-de-Boivotte. The units in the first assault waive moved over the top at exactly seven o'clock on the morning of November 10. The artillery laid down a barrage for the advancing troops and protected their advance as far as possible, but the terrific bombardment with gas, shrapnel and machine gun fire from the German trenches made progress difficult as well as extremely dangerous. The troops, accustomed as they were by this time to bursting shells and gas bombs, ignored all personal danger and fought their way to their first objective with but few casualties. The fighting was furious during the early part of the day, but the organization was able to capture and hold much ground, varying from three to five kilometers in depth.

The 367th Infantry occupied a position on the west side of the Mosselle River. Two companies of the Second Battalion were in the first assault waive with others in support and reserve. The fighting units reached and held their objective and although the fighting was brisk the 367th did not lose a single man. With the darkness came a cessation of intensive action, the troops were reorganized and plans formulated for a renewal of the attack early the next morning.

In this general engagement the 92nd Division occupied a position a little southeast of the strong fortifications of Metz.

The 165th French Division was on our right and the Seventh American Division was on our left and we kept in touch with both these divisions during the night and prepared for what subsequently proved to be the final struggle of the great world war the following morning.

At dawn the air was cool and damp; it was slightly cloudy, with a little fog in the atmosphere, just enough to give it a dull-gray color and to prevent the soldiers from seeing more than a few hundred yards in the direction of the enemy.

The keen whistling noises made by the shells from our supporting artillery as they passed over our heads on their missions of death told us that the hour was 4:30 A. M., for at that time the 351st Field Artillery Regiment began its advance upon Bois La Cote and Champey. This fire was kept up continuously until 10:45. The 350th Field Artillery Regiment, also, renewed its attack upon the woods in the neighborhood of Bois Frehaut, but ceased firing at 10 o'clock A. M., forty-five minutes earlier than the 351st. At five o'clock the First Battalion of the 350th Field Artillery laid a rolling barrage across and just north of Bouxieres-sur-Froidmont in support of the advancing infantry. Many of the same units that engaged the enemy the day before were again struggling for additional gains in the direction of Metz. Several fresh companies were brought up from the support to join those who had so gallantly repulsed the enemy on Saturday and together made a supreme effort to deliver a blow that would silence the German guns and put the Huns to flight in disorder. The only thing that saved the Kaiser's army in this sector from a crushing defeat was the order to cease firing at 11 o'clock.

At one time during the morning engagement the 56th Infantry (white) of the 7th Division, while advancing, ran into a strong barbed wire entanglement that had not been destroyed by artillery. Further advance was impossible and to retire under heavy fire from the German's big guns and merciless machine gun fire meant annihilation. Major Charles L. Appleton of the 367th Infantry, seeing the desperate situation into which the 56th Infantry had worked itself, manœuvered several platoons to a position where they could hit the Germans from the flank and cover the retirement of the 56th. This timely act on the part of Major Appleton probably saved the 56th from complete destruction.

When the bugle sounded the call to cease firing, Company H of the 365th Infantry held 800 yards of the battle-front, five kilometers of which was taken from the Germans under the heavy guns of Metz, and held against odds five to one under intense shell and machine gun fire.

Other Agencies

So much for the 92d Division. It never had a fighting chance until the last day of the war. It was a centre of intrigue from the beginning and its weak and vacillating General spent most of his time placating the Negro haters on his staff and among his field officers, who wished nothing so much as the failure of the division as a fighting unit. How different a story if Charles Young had been let to lead his own!

Of the assisting agencies the only one that paid any attention to Negro troops was the Young Men's Christian Association. The few who came to Red Cross hospitals were, with a few exceptions, not only "Jim-Crowed" but officers were put in wards with their men. The white Young Men's Christian Association secretaries usually refused to serve Negroes in any way. Very few colored secretaries were sent and an attempt was made at first to get rid of the best of these, on the ground that their beliefs on the manhood rights and human equality of Negroes were "seditious." Matters were greatly improved when a colored man was placed in general charge of the colored work. He was never, however, furnished enough men and only three women for his vast field until after the Armistice.

On one subject the white Commanding Officers of all colored units showed more solicitude than on the organization and fighting efficiency of the troops,—that was the relations of the colored officers and men with the women of France. They began by officially stigmatizing the Negroes as rapists; they solemnly warned the troops in speeches and general orders not even to speak to women on the street; ordered the white military police to spy on the blacks and arrest them if they found them talking with French women. The white troops, taking their cue from all this senseless pother, spread tales and rumors among the peasants and villagers and sought to chastise Negroes and offending women. One officer, a high-minded gentleman, graduate and Phi Beta Kappa man of a leading American institution, was court-martialed for keeping company with a perfectly respectable girl of a family of standing in one of the towns where Negroes were quartered and while General Headquarters did not uphold the court-martial, it took occasion severely to reprimand the officer and remove him to a Labor Battalion.

The result of all this a-do was simply unnecessary bitterness among Negroes and mystification among the French. The Negroes resented being publicly stigmatized by their own countrymen as unfit for association with decent people, but the French men and women much preferred the courtesy and bonhomie of the Negroes to the impudence and swagger of many of the whites. In practically every French town where the Negro troops stayed they left close and sympathetic friends among men, women and children.

While the 92nd Division was in France there were fourteen trials for attacks on women, six of which were acquitted; of the other eight, three men were convicted of simple assault, leaving five possible cases of grave crime against women; of these, three cases are still undecided at this writing, one has been acquitted by the court, but the verdict has not been reviewed, and ONE man has been found guilty and hanged. It is only fair to add that this man belonged to a Labor Battalion and was sent to the division simply for trial. No other American division in France has a better record in this respect.

The End

This is a partial and preliminary statement of the part the Negro played in the Great War. There is much in the tale that is missing and some mistakes, to be corrected by fuller information and reference to documents. But the main outlines are clear.

A nation with a great disease set out to rescue civilization; it took the disease with it in virulent form and that disease of race-hatred and prejudice hampered its actions and discredited its finest professions.

No adequate excuse for America's actions can be offered: Grant that many of the dismissed and transferred colored officers were incompetent, there is no possible excuse for the persistent and studied harrowing of admittedly competent men, to which every black officer testifies with a bitterness unexampled in Negro American history; there was no excuse for the persistent refusal to promote Negroes, despite their records testified to even by the French; there was no excuse for systematically refusing Negro officers and soldiers a chance to see something of greater and more beautiful France by curtailing their leaves and quartering them in the back districts.

On the other hand, there is not a black soldier but who is glad he went,—glad to fight for France, the only real white Democracy; glad to have a new, clear vision of the real, inner spirit of American prejudice. The day of camouflage is past.

This history will be enlarged and expanded, embellished with maps and pictures and with the aid of an editorial board, consisting of the leading Negro American scholars and the most distinguished of the black soldiers who fought in France, will be issued by the National Association for the Advancement of Colored People and THE CRISIS, in three volumes, in honor of the first great struggle of the modern Negro race for liberty.

The Crisis, June 1919

The Souls of White Folk

HIGH IN the tower, where I sit above the loud complaining of the human sea, I know many souls that toss and whirl and pass, but none there are that intrigue me more than the Souls of White Folk.

Of them I am singularly clairvoyant. I see in and through them. I view them from unusual points of vantage. Not as a foreigner do I come, for I am native, not foreign, bone of their thought and flesh of their language. Mine is not the knowledge of the traveler or the colonial composite of dear memories, words and wonder. Nor yet is my knowledge that which servants have of masters, or mass of class, or capitalist of artisan. Rather I see these souls undressed and from the back and side. I see the working of their entrails. I know their thoughts and they know that I know. This knowledge makes them now embarrassed, now furious! They deny my right to live and be and call me misbirth! My word is to them mere bitterness and my soul, pessimism. And yet as they preach and strut and shout and threaten, crouching as they clutch at rags of facts and fancies to hide their nakedness, they go twisting, flying by my tired eyes and I see them ever stripped,—ugly, human.

The discovery of personal whiteness among the world's peoples is a very modern thing,—a nineteenth and twentieth century matter, indeed. The ancient world would have laughed at such a distinction. The Middle Age regarded skin color with mild curiosity; and even up into the eighteenth century we were hammering our national manikins into one, great, Universal Man, with fine frenzy which ignored color and race even more than birth. Today we have changed all that, and the world in a sudden, emotional conversion has discovered that it is white and by that token, wonderful!

This assumption that of all the hues of God whiteness alone is inherently and obviously better than brownness or tan leads to curious acts; even the sweeter souls of the dominant world as they discourse with me on weather, weal, and woe are continually playing above their actual words an obligato of tune and tone, saying:

"My poor, un-white thing! Weep not nor rage. I know, too well, that the curse of God lies heavy on you. Why? That is not for me to say, but be brave! Do your work in your lowly sphere, praying the good Lord that into heaven above, where all is love, you may, one day, be born—white!"

I do not laugh. I am quite straight-faced as I ask soberly:

"But what on earth is whiteness that one should so desire it?" Then always, somehow, some way, silently but clearly, I am given to understand that whiteness is the ownership of the earth forever and ever, Amen!

Now what is the effect on a man or a nation when it comes passionately to believe such an extraordinary dictum as this? That nations are coming to believe it is manifest daily. Wave on wave, each with increasing virulence, is dashing this new religion of whiteness on the shores of our time. Its first effects are funny: the strut of the Southerner, the arrogance of the Englishman amuck, the whoop of the hoodlum who vicariously leads your mob. Next it appears dampening generous enthusiasm in what we once counted glorious; to free the slave is discovered to be tolerable only in so far as it freed his master! Do we sense somnolent writhings in black Africa or angry groans in India or triumphant banzais in Japan? "To your tents, O Israel!" These nations are not white!

After the more comic manifestations and the chilling of generous enthusiasm come subtler, darker deeds. Everything considered, the title to the universe claimed by White Folk is faulty. It ought, at least, to look plausible. How easy, then, by emphasis and omission to make children believe that every great soul the world ever saw was a white man's soul; that every great thought the world ever knew was a white man's thought; that every great deed the world ever did was a white man's deed; that every great dream the world ever sang was a white man's dream. In fine, that if from the world were dropped everything that could not fairly be attributed to White Folk, the world would, if anything, be even greater, truer, better than now. And if all this be a lie, is it not a lie in a great cause?

Here it is that the comedy verges to tragedy. The first minor note is struck, all unconsciously, by those worthy souls in whom consciousness of high descent brings burning desire to spread the gift abroad,—the obligation of nobility to the ignoble. Such sense of duty assumes two things: a real possession of the heritage and its frank appreciation by the humbleborn. So long, then, as humble black folk, voluble with thanks, receive barrels of old clothes from lordly and generous whites, there is much mental peace and moral satisfaction. But when the black man begins to dispute the white man's title to certain alleged bequests of the Fathers in wage and position, authority and training; and when his attitude toward charity is sullen anger rather than humble jollity; when he insists on his human right to swagger and swear and waste,—then the spell is suddenly broken and the philanthropist is ready to believe that Negroes are impudent, that the South is right, and that Japan wants to fight America.

After this the descent to Hell is easy. On the pale, white faces which the great billows whirl upward to my tower I see again and again, often and still more often, a writing of human hatred, a deep and passionate hatred, vast by the very vagueness of its expressions. Down through the green waters, on the bottom of the world, where men move to and fro, I have seen a man—an educated gentleman—grow livid with anger because a little, silent, black woman was sitting by herself in a Pullman car. He was a white man. I have seen a great, grown man curse a little child, who had wandered into the wrong waiting-room, searching for its mother: "Here, you damned black——" He was white. In Central Park I have seen the upper lip of a quiet, peaceful man curl back in a tigerish snarl of rage because black folk rode by in a motor car. He was a white man. We have seen, you and I, city after city drunk and furious with ungovernable lust of blood; mad with murder, destroying, killing, and cursing; torturing human victims because somebody accused of crime happened to be of the same color as the mob's innocent victims and because that color was not white! We have seen,—Merciful God! in these wild days and in the name of Civilization, Justice, and Motherhood,—what have we not seen, right here in America, of orgy, cruelty, barbarism, and murder done to men and women of Negro descent.

Up through the foam of green and weltering waters wells this great mass of hatred, in wilder, fiercer violence, until I look down and know that today to the millions of my people no misfortune could happen,—of death and pestilence, failure and defeat—that would not make the hearts of millions of their fellows beat with fierce, vindictive joy! Do you doubt it? Ask your own soul what it would say if the next census were to report that half of black America was dead and the other half dying.

Unfortunate? Unfortunate. But where is the misfortune? Mine? Am I, in my blackness, the sole sufferer? I suffer. And yet, somehow, above the suffering, above the shackled anger that beats the bars, above the hurt that crazes there surges in me a vast pity,—pity for a people imprisoned and enthralled, hampered and made miserable for such a cause, for such a phantasy!

Conceive this nation, of all human peoples, engaged in a crusade to make the "World Safe for Democracy"! Can you imagine the United States protesting against Turkish atrocities in Armenia, while the Turks are silent about mobs in Chicago and St. Louis; what is Louvain compared with Memphis, Waco, Washington, Dyersburg, and Estill Springs? In short, what is the black man but America's Belgium, and how could America condemn in Germany that which she commits, just as brutally, within her own borders?

A true and worthy ideal frees and uplifts a people; a false ideal imprisons and lowers. Say to men, earnestly and repeatedly: "Honesty is best, knowledge is power; do unto others as you would be done by." Say this and act it and the nation must move toward it, if not to it. But say to a people: "The one virtue is to be white," and the people rush to the inevitable conclusion, "Kill the 'nigger'!"

Is not this the record of present America? Is not this its headlong progress? Are we not coming more and more, day by day, to making the statement "I am white," the one fundamental tenet of our practical morality? Only when this basic, iron rule is involved is our defense of right nation-wide and prompt. Murder may swagger, theft may rule and prostitution may flourish and the nation gives but spasmodic, intermittent and lukewarm attention. But let the murderer be black or the thief brown or the violator of womanhood have a drop of Negro blood, and the righteousness of the indignation sweeps the world. Nor would this fact make the indignation less justifiable did not we all know that it was blackness that was condemned and not crime.

In the awful cataclysm of World War, where from beating, slandering, and murdering us the white world turned temporarily aside to kill each other, we of the Darker Peoples looked on in mild amaze.

Among some of us, I doubt not, this sudden descent of Europe into hell brought unbounded surprise; to others, over wide area, it brought the *Schaden Freude* of the bitterly hurt; but most of us, I judge, looked on silently and sorrowfully, in sober thought, seeing sadly the prophecy of our own souls.

Here is a civilization that has boasted much. Neither Roman nor Arab, Greek nor Egyptian, Persian nor Mongol ever took himself and his own perfectness with such disconcerting seriousness as the modern white man. We whose shame, humiliation, and deep insult his aggrandizement so often involved were never deceived. We looked at him clearly, with world-old eyes, and saw simply a human thing, weak and pitiable and cruel, even as we are and were.

These super-men and world-mastering demi-gods listened, however, to no low tongues of ours, even when we pointed silently to their feet of clay. Perhaps we, as folk of simpler soul and more primitive type, have been most struck in the welter of recent years by the utter failure of white religion. We have curled our lips in something like contempt as we have witnessed glib apology and weary explanation. Nothing of the sort deceived us. A nation's religion is its life, and as such white Christianity is a miserable failure.

Nor would we be unfair in this criticism: We know that we, too, have failed, as you have, and have rejected many a Buddha, even as you have denied Christ; but we acknowledge our human frailty, while you, claiming super-humanity, scoff endlessly at our shortcomings.

The number of white individuals who are practising with even reasonable approximation the democracy and unselfishness of Jesus Christ is so small and unimportant as to be fit subject for jest in Sunday supplements and in *Punch*, *Life*, *Le Rire*, and *Fliegende Blätter*. In her foreign mission work the extraordinary self-deception of white religion is epitomized:

solemnly the white world sends five million dollars worth of missionary propaganda to Africa each year and in the same twelve months adds twenty-five million dollars worth of the vilest gin manufactured. Peace to the augurs of Rome!

We may, however, grant without argument that religious ideals have always far outrun their very human devotees. Let us, then, turn to more mundane matters of honor and fairness. The world today is trade. The world has turned shopkeeper; history is economic history; living is earning a living. Is it necessary to ask how much of high emprise and honorable conduct has been found here? Something, to be sure. The establishment of world credit systems is built on splendid and realizable faith in fellow-men. But it is, after all, so low and elementary a step that sometimes it looks merely like honor among thieves, for the revelations of highway robbery and low cheating in the business world and in all its great modern centers have raised in the hearts of all true men in our day an exceeding great cry for revolution in our basic methods and conceptions of industry and commerce.

We do not, for a moment, forget the robbery of other times and races when trade was a most uncertain gamble; but was there not a certain honesty and frankness in the evil that argued a saner morality? There are more merchants today, surer deliveries, and wider well-being, but are there not, also, bigger thieves, deeper injustice, and more calloused selfishness in well-being? Be that as it may,—certainly the nicer sense of honor that has risen ever and again in groups of forward-thinking men has been curiously and broadly blunted. Consider our chiefest industry,—fighting. Laboriously the Middle Ages built its rules of fairness—equal armament, equal notice, equal conditions. What do we see today? Machine-guns against assegais; conquest sugared with religion; mutilation and rape masquerading as culture,—all this, with vast applause at the superiority of white over black soldiers!

War is horrible! This the dark world knows to its awful cost. But has it just become horrible, in these last days, when under essentially equal conditions, equal armament, and equal waste of wealth white men are fighting white men, with surgeons and nurses hovering near?

Think of the wars through which we have lived in the last

decade: in German Africa, in British Nigeria, in French and Spanish Morocco, in China, in Persia, in the Balkans, in Tripoli, in Mexico, and in a dozen lesser places—were not these horrible, too? Mind you, there were for most of these wars no Red Cross funds.

Behold little Belgium and her pitiable plight, but has the world forgotten Congo? What Belgium now suffers is not half, not even a tenth, of what she has done to black Congo since Stanley's great dream of 1880. Down the dark forests of inmost Africa sailed this modern Sir Galahad, in the name of "the noble-minded men of several nations," to introduce commerce and civilization. What came of it? "Rubber and murder, slavery in its worst form," wrote Glave in 1895.

Harris declares that King Leopold's régime meant the death of twelve million natives, "but what we who were behind the scenes felt most keenly was the fact that the real catastrophe in the Congo was desolation and murder in the larger sense. The invasion of family life, the ruthless destruction of every social barrier, the shattering of every tribal law, the introduction of criminal practices which struck the chiefs of the people dumb with horror—in a word, a veritable avalanche of filth and immorality overwhelmed the Congo tribes."

Yet the fields of Belgium laughed, the cities were gay, art and science flourished; the groans that helped to nourish this civilization fell on deaf ears because the world round about was doing the same sort of thing elsewhere on its own account.

As we saw the dead dimly through rifts of battle-smoke and heard faintly the cursings and accusations of blood brothers, we darker men said: This is not Europe gone mad; this is not aberration nor insanity; this *is* Europe; this seeming Terrible is the real soul of white culture—back of all culture,—stripped and visible today. This is where the world has arrived,—these dark and awful depths and not the shining and ineffable heights of which it boasted. Here is whither the might and energy of modern humanity has really gone.

But may not the world cry back at us and ask: "What better thing have you to show? What have you done or would do better than this if you had today the world rule? Paint with all riot of hateful colors the thin skin of European culture,—is it not better than any culture that arose in Africa or Asia?"

It is. Of this there is no doubt and never has been; but why is it better? Is it better because Europeans are better, nobler, greater, and more gifted than other folk? It is not. Europe has never produced and never will in our day bring forth a single human soul who cannot be matched and over-matched in every line of human endeavor by Asia and Africa. Run the gamut, if you will, and let us have the Europeans who in sober truth over-match Nefertari, Mohammed, Rameses and Askia, Confucius, Buddha, and Jesus Christ. If we could scan the calendar of thousands of lesser men, in like comparison, the result would be the same; but we cannot do this because of the deliberately educated ignorance of white schools by which they remember Napoleon and forget Sonni Ali.

The greatness of Europe has lain in the width of the stage on which she has played her part, the strength of the foundations on which she has builded, and a natural, human ability no whit greater (if as great) than that of other days and races. In other words, the deeper reasons for the triumph of European civilization lie quite outside and beyond Europe,—back in the universal struggles of all mankind.

Why, then, is Europe great? Because of the foundations which the mighty past have furnished her to build upon: the iron trade of ancient, black Africa, the religion and empire-building of yellow Asia, the art and science of the "dago" Mediterranean shore, east, south, and west, as well as north. And where she has builded securely upon this great past and learned from it she has gone forward to greater and more splendid human triumph; but where she has ignored this past and forgotten and sneered at it, she has shown the cloven hoof of poor, crucified humanity,—she has played, like other empires gone, the world fool!

If, then, European triumphs in culture have been greater, so, too, may her failures have been greater. How great a failure and a failure in what does the World War betoken? Was it national jealousy of the sort of the seventeenth century? But Europe has done more to break down national barriers than any preceding culture. Was it fear of the balance of power in Europe? Hardly, save in the half-Asiatic problems of the

Balkans. What, then, does Hauptmann mean when he says: "Our jealous enemies forged an iron ring about our breasts and we knew our breasts had to expand,—that we had to split asunder this ring or else we had to cease breathing. But Germany will not cease to breathe and so it came to pass that the iron ring was forced apart."

Whither is this expansion? What is that breath of life, thought to be so indispensable to a great European nation? Manifestly it is expansion overseas; it is colonial aggrandizement which explains, and alone adequately explains, the World War. How many of us today fully realize the current theory of colonial expansion, of the relation of Europe which is white, to the world which is black and brown and yellow? Bluntly put, that theory is this: It is the duty of white Europe to divide up the darker world and administer it for Europe's good.

This Europe has largely done. The European world is using black and brown men for all the uses which men know. Slowly but surely white culture is evolving the theory that "darkies" are born beasts of burden for white folk. It were silly to think otherwise, cries the cultured world, with stronger and shriller accord. The supporting arguments grow and twist themselves in the mouths of merchant, scientist, soldier, traveler, writer, and missionary: Darker peoples are dark in mind as well as in body; of dark, uncertain, and imperfect descent; of frailer, cheaper stuff; they are cowards in the face of mausers and maxims; they have no feelings, aspirations, and loves; they are fools, illogical idiots,—"half-devil and half-child."

Such as they are civilization must, naturally, raise them, but soberly and in limited ways. They are not simply dark white men. They are not "men" in the sense that Europeans are men. To the very limited extent of their shallow capacities lift them to be useful to whites, to raise cotton, gather rubber, fetch ivory, dig diamonds,—and let them be paid what men think they are worth—white men who know them to be well-nigh worthless.

Such degrading of men by men is as old as mankind and the invention of no one race or people. Ever have men striven to conceive of their victims as different from the victors, endlessly different, in soul and blood, strength and cunning, race and lineage. It has been left, however, to Europe and to modern days to discover the eternal world-wide mark of meanness,—color!

Such is the silent revolution that has gripped modern European culture in the later nineteenth and twentieth centuries. Its zenith came in Boxer times: White supremacy was all but world-wide, Africa was dead, India conquered, Japan isolated, and China prostrate, while white America whetted her sword for mongrel Mexico and mulatto South America, lynching her own Negroes the while. Temporary halt in this program was made by little Japan and the white world immediately sensed the peril of such "yellow" presumption! What sort of a world would this be if yellow men must be treated "white"? Immediately the eventual overthrow of Japan became a subject of deep thought and intrigue, from St. Petersburg to San Francisco, from the Key of Heaven to the Little Brother of the Poor.

The using of men for the benefit of masters is no new invention of modern Europe. It is quite as old as the world. But Europe proposed to apply it on a scale and with an elaborateness of detail of which no former world ever dreamed. The imperial width of the thing,—the heaven-defying audacity—makes its modern newness.

The scheme of Europe was no sudden invention, but a way out of long-pressing difficulties. It is plain to modern white civilization that the subjection of the white working classes cannot much longer be maintained. Education, political power, and increased knowledge of the technique and meaning of the industrial process are destined to make a more and more equitable distribution of wealth in the near future. The day of the very rich is drawing to a close, so far as individual white nations are concerned. But there is a loophole. There is a chance for exploitation on an immense scale for inordinate profit, not simply to the very rich, but to the middle class and to the laborers. This chance lies in the exploitation of darker peoples. It is here that the golden hand beckons. Here are no labor unions or votes or questioning onlookers or inconvenient consciences. These men may be used down to the very bone, and shot and maimed in "punitive" expeditions when they revolt. In these dark lands "industrial development" may repeat in exaggerated form every horror of the industrial history of Europe, from slavery and rape to disease and maiming, with only one test of success,—dividends!

This theory of human culture and its aims has worked itself through warp and woof of our daily thought with a thoroughness that few realize. Everything great, good, efficient, fair, and honorable is "white"; everything mean, bad, blundering, cheating, and dishonorable is "yellow"; a bad taste is "brown"; and the devil is "black." The changes of this theme are continually rung in picture and story, in newspaper heading and moving-picture, in sermon and school book, until, of course, the King can do no wrong,—a White Man is always right and a Black Man has no rights which a white man is bound to respect.

There must come the necessary despisings and hatreds of these savage half-men, this unclean *canaille* of the world—these dogs of men. All through the world this gospel is preaching. It has its literature, it has its priests, it has its secret propaganda and above all—it pays!

There's the rub,—it pays. Rubber, ivory, and palm-oil; tea, coffee, and cocoa; bananas, oranges, and other fruit; cotton, gold, and copper—they, and a hundred other things which dark and sweating bodies hand up to the white world from their pits of slime, pay and pay well, but of all that the world gets the black world gets only the pittance that the white world throws it disdainfully.

Small wonder, then, that in the practical world of things-that-be there is jealousy and strife for the possession of the labor of dark millions, for the right to bleed and exploit the colonies of the world where this golden stream may be had, not always for the asking, but surely for the whipping and shooting. It was this competition for the labor of yellow, brown, and black folks that was the cause of the World War. Other causes have been glibly given and other contributing causes there doubtless were, but they were subsidiary and subordinate to this vast quest of the dark world's wealth and toil.

Colonies, we call them, these places where "niggers" are cheap and the earth is rich; they are those outlands where like a swarm of hungry locusts white masters may settle to be served as kings, wield the lash of slave-drivers, rape girls and wives, grow as rich as Croesus and send homeward a golden stream. They belt the earth, these places, but they cluster in the tropics, with its darkened peoples: in Hong Kong and Anam, in Borneo and Rhodesia, in Sierra Leone and Nigeria, in Panama and Havana—these are the El Dorados toward which the world powers stretch itching palms.

Germany, at last one and united and secure on land, looked across the seas and seeing England with sources of wealth insuring a luxury and power which Germany could not hope to rival by the slower processes of exploiting her own peasants and workingmen, especially with these workers half in revolt, immediately built her navy and entered into a desperate competition for possession of colonies of darker peoples. To South America, to China, to Africa, to Asia Minor, she turned like a hound quivering on the leash, impatient, suspicious, irritable, with blood-shot eyes and dripping fangs, ready for the awful word. England and France crouched watchfully over their bones, growling and wary, but gnawing industriously, while the blood of the dark world whetted their greedy appetites. In the background, shut out from the highway to the seven seas, sat Russia and Austria, snarling and snapping at each other and at the last Mediterranean gate to the El Dorado, where the Sick Man enjoyed bad health, and where millions of serfs in the Balkans, Russia, and Asia offered a feast to greed well-nigh as great as Africa.

The fateful day came. It had to come. The cause of war is preparation for war; and of all that Europe has done in a century there is nothing that has equaled in energy, thought, and time her preparation for wholesale murder. The only adequate cause of this preparation was conquest and conquest, not in Europe, but primarily among the darker peoples of Asia and Africa; conquest, not for assimilation and uplift, but for commerce and degradation. For this, and this mainly, did Europe gird herself at frightful cost for war.

The red day dawned when the tinder was lighted in the Balkans and Austro-Hungary seized a bit which brought her a step nearer to the world's highway; she seized one bit and poised herself for another. Then came that curious chorus of challenges, those leaping suspicions, raking all causes for distrust and rivalry and hatred, but saying little of the real and greatest cause.

Each nation felt its deep interests involved. But how? Not, surely, in the death of Ferdinand the Warlike; not, surely, in the old, half-forgotten *revanche* for Alsace-Lorraine; not even in the neutrality of Belgium. No! But in the possession of land overseas, in the right to colonies, the chance to levy endless tribute on the darker world,—on coolies in China, on starving peasants in India, on black savages in Africa, on dying South Sea Islanders, on Indians of the Amazon—all this and nothing more.

Even the broken reed on which we had rested high hopes of eternal peace,—the guild of the laborers—the front of that very important movement for human justice on which we had builded most, even this flew like a straw before the breath of king and kaiser. Indeed, the flying had been foreshadowed when in Germany and America "international" Socialists had all but read yellow and black men out of the kingdom of industrial justice. Subtly had they been bribed, but effectively: Were they not lordly whites and should they not share in the spoils of rape? High wages in the United States and England might be the skilfully manipulated result of slavery in Africa and of peonage in Asia.

With the dog-in-the-manger theory of trade, with the determination to reap inordinate profits and to exploit the weakest to the utmost there came a new imperialism,—the rage for one's own nation to own the earth or, at least, a large enough portion of it to insure as big profits as the next nation. Where sections could not be owned by one dominant nation there came a policy of "open door," but the "door" was open to "white people only." As to the darkest and weakest of peoples there was but one unanimity in Europe,—that which Herr Dernberg of the German Colonial Office called the agreement with England to maintain white "prestige" in Africa,—the doctrine of the divine right of white people to steal.

Thus the world market most wildly and desperately sought today is the market where labor is cheapest and most helpless and profit is most abundant. This labor is kept cheap and helpless because the white world despises "darkies." If one has the temerity to suggest that these workingmen may walk the way of white workingmen and climb by votes and self-assertion and education to the rank of men, he is howled out of court. They cannot do it and if they could, they shall not, for they are the enemies of the white race and the whites shall rule forever and forever and everywhere. Thus the hatred and despising of human beings from whom Europe wishes to extort her luxuries has led to such jealousy and bickering between European nations that they have fallen afoul of each other and have fought like crazed beasts. Such is the fruit of human hatred.

But what of the darker world that watches? Most men belong to this world. With Negro and Negroid, East Indian, Chinese, and Japanese they form two-thirds of the population of the world. A belief in humanity is a belief in colored men. If the uplift of mankind must be done by men, then the destinies of this world will rest ultimately in the hands of darker nations.

What, then, is this dark world thinking? It is thinking that as wild and awful as this shameful war was, *it is nothing to compare with that fight for freedom which black and brown and yellow men must and will make unless their oppression and humiliation and insult at the hands of the White World cease. The Dark World is going to submit to its present treatment just as long as it must and not one moment longer.*

Let me say this again and emphasize it and leave no room for mistaken meaning: The World War was primarily the jealous and avaricious struggle for the largest share in exploiting darker races. As such it is and must be but the prelude to the armed and indignant protest of these despised and raped peoples. Today Japan is hammering on the door of justice, China is raising her half-manacled hands to knock next, India is writhing for the freedom to knock, Egypt is sullenly muttering, the Negroes of South and West Africa, of the West Indies, and of the United States are just awakening to their shameful slavery. Is, then, this war the end of wars? Can it be the end, so long as sits enthroned, even in the souls of those who cry peace, the despising and robbing of darker peoples?

If Europe hugs this delusion, then this is not the end of world war,—it is but the beginning!

We see Europe's greatest sin precisely where we found Africa's and Asia's,—in human hatred, the despising of men; with this difference, however: Europe has the awful lesson of the past before her, has the splendid results of widened areas of tolerance, sympathy, and love among men, and she faces a greater, an infinitely greater, world of men than any preceding civilization ever faced.

It is curious to see America, the United States, looking on herself, first, as a sort of natural peacemaker, then as a moral protagonist in this terrible time. No nation is less fitted for this rôle. For two or more centuries America has marched proudly in the van of human hatred,—making bonfires of human flesh and laughing at them hideously, and making the insulting of millions more than a matter of dislike,—rather a great religion, a world war-cry: Up white, down black; to your tents, O white folk, and world war with black and particolored mongrel beasts!

Instead of standing as a great example of the success of democracy and the possibility of human brotherhood America has taken her place as an awful example of its pitfalls and failures, so far as black and brown and yellow peoples are concerned. And this, too, in spite of the fact that there has been no actual failure; the Indian is not dying out, the Japanese and Chinese have not menaced the land, and the experiment of Negro suffrage has resulted in the uplift of twelve million people at a rate probably unparalleled in history. But what of this? America, Land of Democracy, wanted to believe in the failure of democracy so far as darker peoples were concerned. Absolutely without excuse she established a caste system, rushed into preparation for war, and conquered tropical colonies. She stands today shoulder to shoulder with Europe in Europe's worst sin against civilization. She aspires to sit among the great nations who arbitrate the fate of "lesser breeds without the law" and she is at times heartily ashamed even of the large number of "new" white people whom her democracy has admitted to place and power. Against this surging forward of Irish and German, of Russian Jew, Slav and "dago" her social bars have not availed, but against

Negroes she can and does take her unflinching and immovable stand, backed by this new public policy of Europe. She trains her immigrants to this despising of "niggers" from the day of their landing, and they carry and send the news back to the submerged classes in the fatherlands.

All this I see and hear up in my tower, above the thunder of the seven seas. From my narrowed windows I stare into the night that looms beneath the cloud-swept stars. Eastward and westward storms are breaking,—great, ugly whirlwinds of hatred and blood and cruelty. I will not believe them inevitable. I will not believe that all that was must be, that all the shameful drama of the past must be done again today before the sunlight sweeps the silver seas.

If I cry amid this roar of elemental forces, must my cry be in vain, because it is but a cry,—a small and human cry amid Promethean gloom?

Back beyond the world and swept by these wild, white faces of the awful dead, why will this Soul of White Folk,—this modern Prometheus,—hang bound by his own binding, tethered by a fable of the past? I hear his mighty cry reverberating through the world, "I am white!" Well and good, O Prometheus, divine thief! Is not the world wide enough for two colors, for many little shinings of the sun? Why, then, devour your own vitals if I answer even as proudly, "I am black!"

Darkwater, 1920

The Hands of Ethiopia

"*Semper novi quid ex Africa,*" cried the Roman proconsul, and he voiced the verdict of forty centuries. Yet there are those who would write world history and leave out of account this most marvelous of continents. Particularly today most men assume that Africa is far afield from the center of our burning social problems and especially from our problem of world war.

Always Africa is giving us something new or some metempsychosis of a world-old thing. On its black bosom arose one of the earliest, if not the earliest, of self-protecting civilizations, which grew so mightily that it still furnishes superlatives to thinking and speaking men. Out of its darker and more remote forest fastnesses came, if we may credit many recent scientists, the first welding of iron, and we know that agriculture and trade flourished there when Europe was a wilderness.

Nearly every human empire that has arisen in the world, material and spiritual, has found some of its greatest crises on this continent of Africa, from Greece to Great Britain. As Mommsen says: "It was through Africa that Christianity became the religion of the world." In Africa the last flood of Germanic invasions spent itself within hearing of the last gasp of Byzantium, and it was through Africa that Islam came to play its great rôle of conqueror and civilizer.

With the Renaissance and the widened world of modern thought Africa came no less suddenly with her new-old gift. Shakespeare's "Ancient Pistol" cries:

> A foutre for the world and worldlings base!
> I speak of Africa and golden joys!

He echoes a legend of gold from the days of Punt and Ophir to those of Ghana, the Gold Coast, and the Rand. This thought has sent the word's greed scurrying down the hot, mysterious coasts of Africa to the Good Hope of gain, until for the first time a real world-commerce was born, albeit it started as a commerce mainly in the bodies and souls of men.

The present problem of problems is nothing more than democracy beating itself helplessly against the color bar,—purling, seeping, seething, foaming to burst through, ever and again overwhelming the emerging masses of white men in its rolling backwaters and held back by those who dream of future kingdoms of greed built on black and brown and yellow slavery.

The indictment of Africa against Europe is grave. For four hundred years white Europe was the chief support of that trade in human beings which first and last robbed black Africa of a hundred million human beings, transformed the face of her social life, overthrew organized government, distorted ancient industry, and snuffed out the lights of cultural development. Today instead of removing laborers from Africa to distant slavery, industry built on a new slavery approaches Africa to deprive the natives of their land, to force them to toil, and to reap all the profit for the white world.

It is scarcely necessary to remind the reader of the essential facts underlying these broad assertions. A recent law of the Union of South Africa assigns nearly two hundred and fifty million acres of the best of natives' land to a million and a half whites and leaves thirty-six million acres of swamp and marsh for four and a half-million blacks. In Rhodesia over ninety million acres have been practically confiscated. In the Belgian Congo all the land was declared the property of the state.

Slavery in all but name has been the foundation of the cocoa industry in St. Thome and St. Principe and in the mines of the Rand. Gin has been one of the greatest of European imports, having increased fifty per cent. in ten years and reaching a total of at least twenty-five million dollars a year today. Negroes of ability have been carefully gotten rid of, deposed from authority, kept out of positions of influence, and discredited in their people's eyes, while a caste of white overseers and governing officials has appeared everywhere.

Naturally, the picture is not all lurid. David Livingstone has had his successors and Europe has given Africa something of value in the beginning of education and industry. Yet the balance of iniquity is desperately large; but worse than that, it has aroused no world protest. A great Englishman, familiar with African problems for a generation, says frankly today: "There does not exist any real international conscience to which you can appeal."

Moreover, that treatment shows no certain signs of abatement. Today in England the Empire Resources Development Committee proposes to treat African colonies as "crown estates" and by intensive scientific exploitation of both land and labor to make these colonies pay the English national debt after the war! German thinkers, knowing the tremendous demand for raw material which would follow the war, had similar plans of exploitation. "It is the clear, common sense of the African situation," says H. G. Wells, "that while these precious regions of raw material remain divided up between a number of competitive European imperialisms, each resolutely set upon the exploitation of its 'possessions' to its own advantage and the disadvantage of the others, there can be no permanent peace in the world. It is impossible."

We, then, who fought the war against war; who in a hell of blood and suffering held hardly our souls in leash by the vision of a world organized for peace; who are looking for industrial democracy and for the organization of Europe so as to avoid incentives to war,—we, least of all, should be willing to leave the backward world as the greatest temptation, not only to wars based on international jealousies, but to the most horrible of wars,—which arise from the revolt of the maddened against those who hold them in common contempt.

Consider, my reader,—if you were today a man of some education and knowledge, but born a Japanese or a Chinaman, an East Indian or a Negro, what would you do and think? What would be in the present chaos your outlook and plan for the future? Manifestly, you would want freedom for your people,—freedom from insult, from segregation, from poverty, from physical slavery. If the attitude of the European and American worlds is in the future going to be based essentially upon the same policies as in the past, then there is but one thing for the trained man of darker blood to do and that is definitely and as openly as possible to organize his world for war against Europe. He may have to do it by secret, underground propaganda, as in Egypt and India and eventually in the United States; or by open increase of armament, as in Japan; or by desperate efforts at modernization, as in China; but he must do it. He represents the vast majority of mankind. To surrender would be far worse than physical death. There is no way out unless the white world opens the door. Either the white world gives up such insult as its modern use of the adjective "yellow" indicates, or its connotation of "chink" and "nigger" implies; either it gives up the plan of color serfdom which its use of the other adjective "white" implies, as indicating everything decent and every part of the world worth living in,—or trouble is written in the stars!

It is, therefore, of singular importance after disquieting delay to see the real Pacifist appear. Both England and Germany have recently been basing their claims to parts of black Africa on the wishes and interests of the black inhabitants. Lloyd George has declared "the general principle of national self-determination applicable at least to German Africa," while Chancellor Hertling once welcomed a discussion "on the reconstruction of the world's colonial possessions."

The demand that an Africa for Africans shall replace the present barbarous scramble for exploitation by individual states comes from singularly different sources. Colored America demands that "the conquered German colonies should not be returned to Germany, neither should they be held by the Allies. Here is the opportunity for the establishment of a nation that may never recur. Thousands of colored men, sick of white arrogance and hypocrisy, see in this their race's only salvation."

Sir Harry H. Johnston recently said: "If we are to talk, as we do, sentimentally but justly about restoring the nationhood of Poland, about giving satisfaction to the separatist feeling in Ireland, and about what is to be done for European nations who are oppressed, then we can hardly exclude from this feeling the countries of Africa."

Laborers, black laborers, on the Canal Zone write: "Out of this chaos may be the great awakening of our race. There is cause for rejoicing. If we fail to embrace this opportunity now, we fail to see how we will be ever able to solve the race question. It is for the British Negro, the French Negro, and the American Negro to rise to the occasion and start a national campaign, jointly and collectively, with this aim in view."

From British West Africa comes the bitter complaint "that the West Africans should have the right or opportunity to settle their future for themselves is a thing which hardly enters the mind of the European politician. That the Balkan States should be admitted to the Council of Peace and decide the government under which they are to live is taken as a matter of course because they are Europeans, but no extra-European is credited, even by the extremest advocates of human equality, with any right except to humbly accept the fate which Europe shall decide for him."

Here, then, is the danger and the demand; and the real Pacifist will seek to organize, not simply the masses in white nations, guarding against exploitation and profiteering, but will remember that no permanent relief can come but by including in this organization the lowest and the most exploited races in the world. World philanthropy, like national philanthropy, must come as uplift and prevention and not merely as alleviation and religious conversion. Reverence for humanity, as such, must be installed in the world, and Africa should be the talisman.

Black Africa, including British, French, Belgian, Portuguese, Italian, and Spanish possessions and the independent states of Abyssinia and Liberia and leaving out of account Egypt and North Africa, on the one hand, and South Africa, on the other, has an area of 8,200,000 square miles and a population well over one hundred millions of black men, with less than one hundred thousand whites.

Commercial exploitation in Africa has already larger results to show than most people realize. Annually $200,000,000 worth of goods was coming out of black Africa before the World War, including a third of the world's supply of rubber, a quarter of all of the world's cocoa, and practically all of the world's cloves, gum-arabic, and palm-oil. In exchange there was being returned to Africa one hundred millions in cotton cloth, twenty-five millions in iron and steel, and as much in foods, and probably twenty-five millions in liquors.

Here are the beginnings of a modern industrial system: iron and steel for permanent investment, bound to yield large dividends; cloth as the cheapest exchange for invaluable raw material; liquor to tickle the appetites of the natives and render the alienation of land and the break-down of customary law easier; eventually forced and contract labor under white drivers to increase and systematize the production of raw materials. These materials are capable of indefinite expansion: cotton may yet challenge the southern United States, fruits and vegetables, hides and skins, lumber and dye-stuffs, coffee and tea, grain and tobacco, and fibers of all sorts can easily follow organized and systematic toil.

Is it a paradise of industry we thus contemplate? It is much more likely to be a hell. Under present plans there will be no voice or law or custom to protect labor, no trades unions, no eight-hour laws, no factory legislation,—nothing of that great body of legislation built up in modern days to protect mankind from sinking to the level of beasts of burden. All the industrial deviltry, which civilization has been driving to the slums and the backwaters, will have a voiceless continent to conceal it. If the slave cannot be taken from Africa, slavery can be taken to Africa.

Who are the folk who live here? They are brown and black, curly and crisp-haired, short and tall, and longheaded. Out of them in days without date flowed the beginnings of Egypt; among them rose, later, centers of culture at Ghana, Melle, and Timbuktu. Kingdoms and empires flourished in Songhay and Zymbabwe, and art and industry in Yoruba and Benin. They have fought every human calamity in its most hideous form and yet today they hold some similar vestiges of a mighty past,—their work in iron, their weaving and carving, their music and singing, their tribal government, their town-meeting and market-place, their desperate valor in war.

Missionaries and commerce have left some good with all their evil. In black Africa today there are more than a thousand government schools and some thirty thousand mission schools, with a more or less regular attendance of three-quarters of a million school children. In a few cases training of a higher order is given chiefs' sons and selected pupils. These beginnings of education are not much for so vast a land and there is no general standard or set plan of development, but, after all, the children of Africa are beginning to learn.

In black Africa today only one-seventeenth of the land and a ninth of the people in Liberia and Abyssinia are approximately independent, although menaced and policed by European capitalism. Half the land and the people are in domains under Portugal, France, and Belgium, held with the avowed idea of exploitation for the benefit of Europe under a system of caste and color serfdom. Out of this dangerous nadir of development stretch two paths: one is indicated by the condition of about three per cent of the people who in Sierra Leone, the Gold Coast, and French Senegal, are tending toward the path of modern development; the other path, followed by a fourth of the land and people, has local self-government and native customs and might evolve, if undisturbed, a native culture along their own peculiar lines. A tenth of the land, sparsely settled, is being monopolized and held for whites to make an African Australia. To these later folk must be added the four and one-half millions of the South African Union, who by every modern device are being forced into landless serfdom.

Before the World War tendencies were strongly toward the destruction of independent Africa, the industrial slavery of the mass of the blacks and the encouragement of white immigration, where possible, to hold the blacks in subjection.

Against this idea let us set the conception of a new African World State, a Black Africa, applying to these peoples the splendid pronouncements which have of late been so broadly and perhaps carelessly given the world: recognizing in Africa the declaration of the American Federation of Labor, that "no people must be forced under sovereignty under which it does not wish to live"; recognizing in President Wilson's message to the Russians, the "principle of the undictated development of all peoples"; recognizing the resolution of the recent conference of the Aborigines Protection Society of England, "that in any reconstruction of Africa, which may result from this war, the interests of the native inhabitants and also their wishes, in so far as those wishes can be clearly ascertained, should be recognized as among the principal factors upon which the decision of their destiny should be based." In other words, recognizing for the first time in the history of the modern world that black men are human.

It may not be possible to build this state at once. With the victory of the Entente Allies, the German colonies, with their million of square miles and one-half million black inhabitants, should form such a nucleus. It would give Black Africa its physical beginnings. Beginning with the German colonies two other sets of colonies could be added, for obvious reasons. Neither Portugal nor Belgium has shown any particular capacity for governing colonial peoples. Valid excuses may in both cases be advanced, but it would certainly be fair to Belgium to have her start her great task of reorganization after the World War with neither the burden nor the temptation of colonies; and in the same way Portugal has, in reality, the alternative of either giving up her colonies to an African State or to some other European State in the near future. These two sets of colonies would add 1,700,000 square miles and eighteen million inhabitants. It would not, however, be fair to despoil Germany, Belgium, and Portugal of their colonies unless, as Count Hertling once demanded, the whole question of colonies be opened.

How far shall the modern world recognize nations which are not nations, but combinations of a dominant caste and a suppressed horde of serfs? Will it not be possible to rebuild a world with compact nations, empires of self-governing elements, and colonies of backward peoples under benevolent international control?

The great test would be easy. Does England propose to erect in India and Nigeria nations brown and black which shall be eventually independent, self-governing entities, with a full voice in the British Imperial Government? If not, let these states either have independence at once or, if unfitted for that, be put under international tutelage and guardianship. It is possible that France, with her great heart, may welcome a Black France,—an enlarged Senegal in Africa; but it would seem that eventually all Africa south of twenty degrees north latitude and north of the Union of South Africa should be included in a new African State. Somaliland and Eritrea should be given to Abyssinia, and then with Liberia we would start with two small, independent African states and one large state under international control.

Does this sound like an impossible dream? No one could

be blamed for so regarding it before 1914. I, myself, would have agreed with them. But since the nightmare of 1914–1918, since we have seen the impossible happen and the unspeakable become so common as to cease to stir us; in a day when Russia has dethroned her Czar, England has granted the suffrage to women and is in the act of giving Home Rule to Ireland; when Germany has adopted parliamentary government; when Jerusalem has been delivered from the Turks; and the United States has taken control of its railroads,—is it really so far-fetched to think of an Africa for the Africans, guided by organized civilization?

No one would expect this new state to be independent and self-governing from the start. Contrary, however, to present schemes for Africa the world would expect independence and self-government as the only possible end of the experiment. At first we can conceive of no better way of governing this state than through that same international control by which we hope to govern the world for peace. A curious and instructive parallel has been drawn by Simeon Strunsky: "Just as the common ownership of the northwest territory helped to weld the colonies into the United States, so could not joint and benevolent domination of Africa and of other backward parts of the world be a cornerstone upon which the future federation of the world could be built?"

From the British Labor Party comes this declaration: "With regard to the colonies of the several belligerents in tropical Africa, from sea to sea, the British Labor Movement disclaims all sympathy with the imperialist idea that these should form the booty of any nation, should be exploited for the profit of the capitalists, or should be used for the promotion of the militarists' aims of government. In view of the fact that it is impracticable here to leave the various peoples concerned to settle their own destinies it is suggested that the interests of humanity would be best served by the full and frank abandonment by all the belligerents of any dreams of an African Empire; the transfer of the present colonies of the European Powers in tropical Africa, however, and the limits of this area may be defined to the proposed Supernational Authority, or League of Nations."

Lloyd George himself has said in regard to the German

colonies a word difficult to restrict merely to them: "I have repeatedly declared that they are held at the disposal of a conference, whose decision must have primary regard to the wishes and interests of the native inhabitants of such colonies. None of those territories is inhabited by Europeans. The governing consideration, therefore, must be that the inhabitants should be placed under the control of an administration acceptable to themselves, one of whose main purposes will be to prevent their exploitation for the benefit of European capitalists or governments."

The special commission for the government of this African State must, naturally, be chosen with great care and thought. It must represent, not simply governments, but civilization, science, commerce, social reform, religious philanthropy without sectarian propaganda. It must include, not simply white men, but educated and trained men of Negro blood. The guiding principles before such a commission should be clearly understood. In the first place, it ought by this time to be realized by the labor movement throughout the world that no industrial democracy can be built on industrial despotism, whether the two systems are in the same country or in different countries, since the world today so nearly approaches a common industrial unity. If, therefore, it is impossible in any single land to uplift permanently skilled labor without also raising common labor, so, too, there can be no permanent uplift of American or European labor as long as African laborers are slaves.

Secondly, this building of a new African State does not mean the segregation in it of all the world's black folk. It is too late in the history of the world to go back to the idea of absolute racial segregation. The new African State would not involve any idea of a vast transplantation of the twenty-seven million Negroids of the western world, of Africa, or of the gathering there of Negroid Asia. The Negroes in the United States and the other Americas have earned the right to fight out their problems where they are, but they could easily furnish from time to time technical experts, leaders of thought, and missionaries of culture for their backward brethren in the new Africa.

With these two principles, the practical policies to be followed out in the government of the new states should involve a thorough and complete system of modern education, built upon the present government, religion, and customary laws of the natives. There should be no violent tampering with the curiously efficient African institutions of local self-government through the family and the tribe; there should be no attempt at sudden "conversion" by religious propaganda. Obviously deleterious customs and unsanitary usages must gradually be abolished, but the general government, set up from without, must follow the example of the best colonial administrators and build on recognized, established foundations rather than from entirely new and theoretical plans.

The real effort to modernize Africa should be through schools rather than churches. Within ten years, twenty million black children ought to be in school. Within a generation young Africa should know the essential outlines of modern culture and groups of bright African students could be going to the world's great universities. From the beginning the actual general government should use both colored and white officials and later natives should be worked in. Taxation and industry could follow the newer ideals of industrial democracy, avoiding private land monopoly and poverty, and promoting co-operation in production and the socialization of income. Difficulties as to capital and revenue would be far less than many imagine. If a capable English administrator of British Nigeria could with $1,500 build up a cocoa industry of twenty million dollars annually, what might not be done in all Africa, without gin, thieves, and hypocrisy?

Capital could not only be accumulated in Africa, but attracted from the white world, with one great difference from present usage: no return so fabulous would be offered that civilized lands would be tempted to divert to colonial trade and invest materials and labor needed by the masses at home, but rather would receive the same modest profits as legitimate home industry offers.

There is no sense in asserting that the ideal of an African State, thus governed and directed toward independence and self-government, is impossible of realization. The first great essential is that the civilized world believe in its possibility. By reason of a crime (perhaps the greatest crime in human history) the modern world has been systematically taught to despise colored peoples. Men of education and decency ask, and ask seriously, if it is really possible to uplift Africa. Are Negroes human, or, if human, developed far enough to absorb, even under benevolent tutelage, any appreciable part of modern culture? Has not the experiment been tried in Haiti and Liberia, and failed?

One cannot ignore the extraordinary fact that a world campaign beginning with the slave-trade and ending with the refusal to capitalize the word "Negro," leading through a passionate defense of slavery by attributing every bestiality to blacks and finally culminating in the evident modern profit which lies in degrading blacks,—all this has unconsciously trained millions of honest, modern men into the belief that black folk are sub-human. This belief is not based on science, else it would be held as a postulate of the most tentative kind, ready at any time to be withdrawn in the face of facts; the belief is not based on history, for it is absolutely contradicted by Egyptian, Greek, Roman, Byzantine, and Arabian experience; nor is the belief based on any careful survey of the social development of men of Negro blood to-day in Africa and America. It is simply passionate, deep-seated heritage, and as such can be moved by neither argument nor fact. Only faith in humanity will lead the world to rise above its present color prejudice.

Those who do believe in men, who know what black men have done in human history, who have taken pains to follow even superficially the story of the rise of the Negro in Africa, the West Indies, and the Americas of our day know that our modern contempt of Negroes rests upon no scientific foundation worth a moment's attention. It is nothing more than a vicious habit of mind. It could as easily be overthrown as our belief in war, as our international hatreds, as our old conception of the status of women, as our fear of educating the masses, and as our belief in the necessity of poverty. We can, if we will, inaugurate on the Dark Continent a last great crusade for humanity. With Africa redeemed Asia would be safe and Europe indeed triumphant.

I have not mentioned North and South Africa, because my eye was centered on the main mass of the Negro race. Yet it is clear that for the development of Central Africa, Egypt should be free and independent, there along the highway to a free and independent India; while Morocco, Algeria, Tunis, and Tripoli must become a part of Europe, with modern development and home rule. South Africa, stripped of its black serfs and their lands, must admit the resident natives and colored folk to its body politic as equals.

The hands which Ethiopia shall soon stretch out unto God are not mere hands of helplessness and supplication, but rather are they hands of pain and promise; hard, gnarled, and muscled for the world's real work; they are hands of fellowship for the half-submerged masses of a distempered world; they are hands of helpfulness for an agonized God!

Twenty centuries before Christ a great cloud swept over seas and settled on Africa, darkening and well-nigh blotting out the culture of the land of Egypt. For half a thousand years it rested there, until a black woman, Queen Nefertari, "the most venerated figure in Egyptian history," rose to the throne of the Pharaohs and redeemed the world and her people. Twenty centuries after Christ, Black Africa,—prostrated, raped, and shamed, lies at the feet of the conquering Philistines of Europe. Beyond the awful sea a black woman is weeping and waiting, with her sons on her breast. What shall the end be? The world-old and fearful things,—war and wealth, murder and luxury? Or shall it be a new thing,—a new peace and a new democracy of all races,—a great humanity of equal men? *"Semper novi quid ex Africa!"*

Darkwater, 1920

The Damnation of Women

I REMEMBER four women of my boyhood: my mother, cousin Inez, Emma, and Ide Fuller. They represented the problem of the widow, the wife, the maiden, and the outcast. They were, in color, brown and light-brown, yellow with brown freckles, and white. They existed not for themselves, but for men; they were named after the men to whom they were related and not after the fashion of their own souls.

They were not beings, they were relations and these relations were enfilmed with mystery and secrecy. We did not know the truth or believe it when we heard it. Motherhood! What was it? We did not know or greatly care. My mother and I were good chums. I liked her. After she was dead I loved her with a fierce sense of personal loss.

Inez was a pretty, brown cousin who married. What was marriage? We did not know, neither did she, poor thing! It came to mean for her a litter of children, poverty, a drunken, cruel companion, sickness, and death. Why?

There was no sweeter sight than Emma,—slim, straight, and dainty, darkly flushed with the passion of youth; but her life was a wild, awful struggle to crush her natural, fierce joy of love. She crushed it and became a cold, calculating mockery.

Last there was that awful outcast of the town, the white woman, Ide Fuller. What she was, we did not know. She stood to us as embodied filth and wrong,—but whose filth, whose wrong?

Grown up I see the problem of these women transfused; I hear all about me the unanswered call of youthful love, none the less glorious because of its clean, honest, physical passion. Why unanswered? Because the youth are too poor to marry or if they marry, too poor to have children. They turn aside, then, in three directions: to marry for support, to what men call shame, or to that which is more evil than nothing. It is an unendurable paradox; it must be changed or the bases of culture will totter and fall.

The world wants healthy babies and intelligent workers. Today we refuse to allow the combination and force thousands of intelligent workers to go childless at a horrible expenditure of moral force, or we damn them if they break our idiotic conventions. Only at the sacrifice of intelligence and the chance to do their best work can the majority of modern women bear children. This is the damnation of women.

All womanhood is hampered today because the world on which it is emerging is a world that tries to worship both virgins and mothers and in the end despises motherhood and despoils virgins.

The future woman must have a life work and economic independence. She must have knowledge. She must have the right of motherhood at her own discretion. The present mincing horror at free womanhood must pass if we are ever to be rid of the bestiality of free manhood; not by guarding the weak in weakness do we gain strength, but by making weakness free and strong.

The world must choose the free woman or the white wraith of the prostitute. Today it wavers between the prostitute and the nun. Civilization must show two things: the glory and beauty of creating life and the need and duty of power and intelligence. This and this only will make the perfect marriage of love and work.

God is Love,
Love is God;
There is no God but Love
And Work is His Prophet!

All this of woman,—but what of black women?

The world that wills to worship womankind studiously forgets its darker sisters. They seem in a sense to typify that veiled Melancholy:

"Whose saintly visage is too bright
To hit the sense of human sight,
And, therefore, to our weaker view
O'er-laid with black."

Yet the world must heed these daughters of sorrow, from the primal black All-Mother of men down through the ghostly throng of mighty womanhood, who walked in the mysterious dawn of Asia and Africa; from Neith, the primal mother of all, whose feet rest on hell, and whose almighty hands uphold the heavens; all religion, from beauty to beast, lies on her eager breasts; her body bears the stars, while her shoulders are necklaced by the dragon; from black Neith down to

> "That starr'd Ethiop queen who strove
> To set her beauty's praise above
> The sea-nymphs,"

through dusky Cleopatras, dark Candaces, and darker, fiercer Zinghas, to our own day and our own land,—in gentle Phillis; Harriet, the crude Moses; the sybil, Sojourner Truth; and the martyr, Louise De Mortie.

The father and his worship is Asia; Europe is the precocious, self-centered, forward-striving child; but the land of the mother is and was Africa. In subtle and mysterious way, despite her curious history, her slavery, polygamy, and toil, the spell of the African mother pervades her land. Isis, the mother, is still titular goddess, in thought if not in name, of the dark continent. Nor does this all seem to be solely a survival of the historic matriarchate through which all nations pass,—it appears to be more than this,—as if the great black race in passing up the steps of human culture gave the world, not only the Iron Age, the cultivation of the soil, and the domestication of animals, but also, in peculiar emphasis, the mother-idea.

"No mother can love more tenderly and none is more tenderly loved than the Negro mother," writes Schneider. Robin tells of the slave who bought his mother's freedom instead of his own. Mungo Park writes: "Everywhere in Africa, I have noticed that no greater affront can be offered a Negro than insulting his mother. 'Strike me,' cries a Mandingo to his enemy, 'but revile not my mother!' " And the Krus and Fantis say the same. The peoples on the Zambezi and the great lakes cry in sudden fear or joy: "O, my mother!" And the Herero swear (endless oath) "By my mother's tears!" "As the mist in the swamps," cries the Angola Negro, "so lives the love of father and mother."

A student of the present Gold Coast life describes the work of the village headman, and adds: "It is a difficult task that he is set to, but in this matter he has all-powerful helpers in the female members of the family, who will be either the aunts or the sisters or the cousins or the nieces of the headman, and as their interests are identical with his in every particular, the good women spontaneously train up their children to implicit obedience to the headman, whose rule in the family thus becomes a simple and an easy matter. 'The hand that rocks the cradle rules the world.' What a power for good in the native state system would the mothers of the Gold Coast and Ashanti become by judicious training upon native lines!"

Schweinfurth declares of one tribe: "A bond between mother and child which lasts for life is the measure of affection shown among the Dyoor" and Ratzel adds:

"Agreeable to the natural relation the mother stands first among the chief influences affecting the children. From the Zulus to the Waganda, we find the mother the most influential counsellor at the court of ferocious sovereigns, like Chaka or Mtesa; sometimes sisters take her place. Thus even with chiefs who possess wives by hundreds the bonds of blood are the strongest and that the woman, though often heavily burdened, is in herself held in no small esteem among the Negroes is clear from the numerous Negro queens, from the medicine women, from the participation in public meetings permitted to women by many Negro peoples."

As I remember through memories of others, backward among my own family, it is the mother I ever recall,—the little, far-off mother of my grandmothers, who sobbed her life away in song, longing for her lost palm-trees and scented waters; the tall and bronzen grandmother, with beaked nose and shrewish eyes, who loved and scolded her black and laughing husband as he smoked lazily in his high oak chair; above all, my own mother, with all her soft brownness,—the brown velvet of her skin, the sorrowful black-brown of her eyes, and the tiny brown-capped waves of her midnight hair as it lay new parted on her forehead. All the way back in these dim distances it is mothers and mothers of mothers who seem to count, while fathers are shadowy memories.

Upon this African mother-idea, the westward slave trade and American slavery struck like doom. In the cruel exigencies of the traffic in men and in the sudden, unprepared emancipation the great pendulum of social equilibrium swung from a time, in 1800,—when America had but eight or less black women to every ten black men,—all too swiftly to a day, in 1870,—when there were nearly eleven women to ten men in our Negro population. This was but the outward numerical fact of social dislocation; within lay polygamy, polyandry, concubinage, and moral degradation. They fought against all this desperately, did these black slaves in the West Indies, especially among the half-free artisans; they set up their ancient household gods, and when Toussaint and Cristophe founded their kingdom in Haiti, it was based on old African tribal ties and beneath it was the mother-idea.

The crushing weight of slavery fell on black women. Under it there was no legal marriage, no legal family, no legal control over children. To be sure, custom and religion replaced here and there what the law denied, yet one has but to read advertisements like the following to see the hell beneath the system:

"One hundred dollars reward will be given for my two fellows, Abram and Frank. Abram has a wife at Colonel Stewart's, in Liberty County, and a mother at Thunderbolt, and a sister in Savannah.

"WILLIAM ROBERTS."

"Fifty dollars reward—Ran away from the subscriber a Negro girl named Maria. She is of a copper color, between thirteen and fourteen years of age—bare-headed and barefooted. She is small for her age—very sprightly and very likely. She stated she was going to see her mother at Maysville.

"SANFORD THOMSON."

"Fifty dollars reward—Ran away from the subscriber his Negro man Pauladore, commonly called Paul. I understand General R. Y. Hayne has purchased his wife and children from H. L. Pinckney, Esq., and has them now on his plantation at Goose Creek, where, no doubt, the fellow is frequently lurking.

"T. Davis."

The Presbyterian synod of Kentucky said to the churches under its care in 1835: "Brothers and sisters, parents and children, husbands and wives, are torn asunder and permitted to see each other no more. These acts are daily occurring in the midst of us. The shrieks and agony often witnessed on such occasions proclaim, with a trumpet tongue, the iniquity of our system. There is not a neighborhood where these heart-rending scenes are not displayed. There is not a village or road that does not behold the sad procession of manacled outcasts whose mournful countenances tell that they are exiled by force from all that their hearts hold dear."

A sister of a president of the United States declared: "We Southern ladies are complimented with the names of wives, but we are only the mistresses of seraglios."

Out of this, what sort of black women could be born into the world of today? There are those who hasten to answer this query in scathing terms and who say lightly and repeatedly that out of black slavery came nothing decent in womanhood; that adultery and uncleanness were their heritage and are their continued portion.

Fortunately so exaggerated a charge is humanly impossible of truth. The half-million women of Negro descent who lived at the beginning of the 19th century had become the mothers of two and one-fourth million daughters at the time of the Civil War and five million granddaughters in 1910. Can all these women be vile and the hunted race continue to grow in wealth and character? Impossible. Yet to save from the past the shreds and vestiges of self-respect has been a terrible task. I most sincerely doubt if any other race of women could have brought its fineness up through so devilish a fire.

Alexander Crummell once said of his sister in the blood: "In her girlhood all the delicate tenderness of her sex has been rudely outraged. In the field, in the rude cabin, in the press-room, in the factory she was thrown into the companionship of coarse and ignorant men. No chance was given her for delicate reserve or tender modesty. From her childhood she was the doomed victim of the grossest passion. All the virtues of her sex were utterly ignored. If the instinct of chastity asserted itself, then she had to fight like a tiger for the ownership and possession of her own person and ofttimes had to suffer pain and lacerations for her virtuous self-assertion. When she reached maturity, all the tender instincts of her womanhood were ruthlessly violated. At the age of marriage,—always prematurely anticipated under slavery—she was mated as the stock of the plantation were mated, not to be the companion of a loved and chosen husband, but to be the breeder of human cattle for the field or the auction block."

Down in such mire has the black motherhood of this race struggled,—starving its own wailing offspring to nurse to the world their swaggering masters; welding for its children chains which affronted even the moral sense of an unmoral world. Many a man and woman in the South have lived in wedlock as holy as Adam and Eve and brought forth their brown and golden children, but because the darker woman was helpless, her chivalrous and whiter mate could cast her off at his pleasure and publicly sneer at the body he had privately blasphemed.

I shall forgive the white South much in its final judgment day: I shall forgive its slavery, for slavery is a world-old habit; I shall forgive its fighting for a well-lost cause, and for remembering that struggle with tender tears; I shall forgive its so-called "pride of race," the passion of its hot blood, and even its dear, old, laughable strutting and posing; but one thing I shall never forgive, neither in this world nor the world to come: its wanton and continued and persistent insulting of the black womanhood which it sought and seeks to prostitute to its lust. I cannot forget that it is such Southern gentlemen into whose hands smug Northern hypocrites of today are seeking to place our women's eternal destiny,—men who insist upon withholding from my mother and wife and daughter those signs and appellations of courtesy and respect which elsewhere he withholds only from bawds and courtesans.

The result of this history of insult and degradation has been both fearful and glorious. It has birthed the haunting prostitute, the brawler, and the beast of burden; but it has also given the world an efficient womanhood, whose strength lies in its freedom and whose chastity was won in the teeth of temptation and not in prison and swaddling clothes.

To no modern race does its women mean so much as to the Negro nor come so near to the fulfilment of its meaning. As one of our women writes: "Only the black woman can say 'when and where I enter, in the quiet, undisputed dignity of my womanhood, without violence and without suing or special patronage, then and there the whole Negro race enters with me.' "

They came first, in earlier days, like foam flashing on dark, silent waters,—bits of stern, dark womanhood here and there tossed almost carelessly aloft to the world's notice. First and naturally they assumed the panoply of the ancient African mother of men, strong and black, whose very nature beat back the wilderness of oppression and contempt. Such a one was that cousin of my grandmother, whom western Massachusetts remembers as "Mum Bett." Scarred for life by a blow received in defense of a sister, she ran away to Great Barrington and was the first slave, or one of the first, to be declared free under the Bill of Rights of 1780. The son of the judge who freed her, writes:

> "Even in her humble station, she had, when occasion required it, an air of command which conferred a degree of dignity and gave her an ascendancy over those of her rank, which is very unusual in persons of any rank or color. Her determined and resolute character, which enabled her to limit the ravages of Shay's mob, was manifested in her conduct and deportment during her whole life. She claimed no distinction, but it was yielded to her from her superior experience, energy, skill, and sagacity. Having known this woman as familiarly as I knew either of my parents, I cannot believe in the moral or physical inferiority of the race to which she belonged. The degradation of the African must have been otherwise caused than by natural inferiority."

It was such strong women that laid the foundations of the great Negro church of today, with its five million members and ninety millions of dollars in property. One of the early mothers of the church, Mary Still, writes thus quaintly, in the forties:

> "When we were as castouts and spurned from the large churches, driven from our knees, pointed at by the proud, neglected by the careless, without a place of worship, Allen, faithful to the heavenly calling, came forward and laid the foundation of this connection. The women, like the women at the sepulcher, were early to aid in laying the foundation of the temple and in helping to carry up the noble structure and in the name of their God set up their banner; most of our aged mothers are gone from this to a better state of things. Yet some linger still on their staves, watching with intense interest the ark as it moves over the tempestuous waves of opposition and ignorance. . . .
>
> "But the labors of these women stopped not here, for they knew well that they were subject to affliction and death. For the purpose of mutual aid, they banded themselves together in society capacity, that they might be better able to administer to each others' sufferings and to soften their own pillows. So we find the females in the early history of the church abounding in good works and in acts of true benevolence."

From such spiritual ancestry came two striking figures of war-time,—Harriet Tubman and Sojourner Truth.

For eight or ten years previous to the breaking out of the Civil War, Harriet Tubman was a constant attendant at anti-slavery conventions, lectures, and other meetings; she was a black woman of medium size, smiling countenance, with her upper front teeth gone, attired in coarse but neat clothes, and carrying always an old-fashioned reticule at her side. Usually as soon as she sat down she would drop off in sound sleep.

She was born a slave in Maryland, in 1820, bore the marks of the lash on her flesh; and had been made partially deaf, and perhaps to some degree mentally unbalanced by a blow on the head in childhood. Yet she was one of the most important agents of the Underground Railroad and a leader of fugitive slaves. She ran away in 1849 and went to Boston in 1854, where she was welcomed into the homes of the leading abolitionists and where every one listened with tense interest to her strange stories. She was absolutely illiterate, with no knowledge of geography, and yet year after year she penetrated the slave states and personally led North over three hundred fugitives without losing a single one. A standing reward of $10,000 was offered for her, but as she said: "The whites cannot catch us, for I was born with the charm, and the Lord has given me the power." She was one of John Brown's closest advisers and only severe sickness prevented her presence at Harper's Ferry.

When the war cloud broke, she hastened to the front, flitting down along her own mysterious paths, haunting the armies in the field, and serving as guide and nurse and spy. She followed Sherman in his great march to the sea and was with Grant at Petersburg, and always in the camps the Union officers silently saluted her.

The other woman belonged to a different type,—a tall, gaunt, black, unsmiling sybil, weighted with the woe of the world. She ran away from slavery and giving up her own name took the name of Sojourner Truth. She says: "I can remember when I was a little, young girl, how my old mammy would sit out of doors in the evenings and look up at the stars and groan, and I would say, 'Mammy, what makes you groan so?' And she would say, 'I am groaning to think of my poor children; they do not know where I be and I don't know where they be. I look up at the stars and they look up at the stars!' "

Her determination was founded on unwavering faith in ultimate good. Wendell Phillips says that he was once in Faneuil Hall, when Frederick Douglass was one of the chief speakers. Douglass had been describing the wrongs of the Negro race and as he proceeded he grew more and more excited and finally ended by saying that they had no hope of justice from the whites, no possible hope except in their own right arms. It must come to blood! They must fight for themselves. Sojourner Truth was sitting, tall and dark, on the very front seat facing the platform, and in the hush of feeling when Douglass sat down she spoke out in her deep, peculiar voice, heard all over the hall:

"Frederick, is God dead?"

Such strong, primitive types of Negro womanhood in

America seem to some to exhaust its capabilities. They know less of a not more worthy, but a finer type of black woman wherein trembles all of that delicate sense of beauty and striving for self-realization, which is as characteristic of the Negro soul as is its quaint strength and sweet laughter. George Washington wrote in grave and gentle courtesy to a Negro woman, in 1776, that he would "be happy to see" at his headquarters at any time, a person "to whom nature has been so liberal and beneficial in her dispensations." This child, Phillis Wheatley, sang her trite and halting strain to a world that wondered and could not produce her like. Measured today her muse was slight and yet, feeling her striving spirit, we call to her still in her own words:

"Through thickest glooms look back, immortal shade."

Perhaps even higher than strength and art loom human sympathy and sacrifice as characteristic of Negro womanhood. Long years ago, before the Declaration of Independence, Kate Ferguson was born in New York. Freed, widowed, and bereaved of her children before she was twenty, she took the children of the streets of New York, white and black, to her empty arms, taught them, found them homes, and with Dr. Mason of Murray Street Church established the first modern Sunday School in Manhattan.

Sixty years later came Mary Shadd up out of Delaware. She was tall and slim, of that ravishing dream-born beauty,—that twilight of the races which we call mulatto. Well-educated, vivacious, with determination shining from her sharp eyes, she threw herself singlehanded into the great Canadian pilgrimage when thousands of hunted black men hurried northward and crept beneath the protection of the lion's paw. She became teacher, editor, and lecturer; tramping afoot through winter snows, pushing without blot or blemish through crowd and turmoil to conventions and meetings, and finally becoming recruiting agent for the United States government in gathering Negro soldiers in the West.

After the war the sacrifice of Negro women for freedom and uplift is one of the finest chapters in their history. Let one life typify all: Louise De Mortie, a free-born Virginia girl, had lived most of her life in Boston. Her high forehead, swelling lips, and dark eyes marked her for a woman of feeling and intellect. She began a successful career as a public reader. Then came the War and the Call. She went to the orphaned colored children of New Orleans,—out of freedom into insult and oppression and into the teeth of the yellow fever. She toiled and dreamed. In 1887 she had raised money and built an orphan home and that same year, in the thirty-fourth of her young life, she died, saying simply: "I belong to God."

As I look about me today in this veiled world of mine, despite the noisier and more spectacular advance of my brothers, I instinctively feel and know that it is the five million women of my race who really count. Black women (and women whose grandmothers were black) are today furnishing our teachers; they are the main pillars of those social settlements which we call churches; and they have with small doubt raised three-fourths of our church property. If we have today, as seems likely, over a billion dollars of accumulated goods, who shall say how much of it has been wrung from the hearts of servant girls and washerwomen and women toilers in the fields? As makers of two million homes these women are today seeking in marvelous ways to show forth our strength and beauty and our conception of the truth.

In the United States in 1910 there were 4,931,882 women of Negro descent; over twelve hundred thousand of these were children, another million were girls and young women under twenty, and two and a half-million were adults. As a mass these women were unlettered,—a fourth of those from fifteen to twenty-five years of age were unable to write. These women are passing through, not only a moral, but an economic revolution. Their grandmothers married at twelve and fifteen, but twenty-seven per cent of these women today who have passed fifteen are still single.

Yet these black women toil and toil hard. There were in 1910 two and a half million Negro homes in the United States. Out of these homes walked daily to work two million women and girls over ten years of age,—over half of the colored female population as against a fifth in the case of white women. These, then, are a group of workers, fighting for their daily bread like men; independent and approaching economic freedom! They furnished a million farm laborers, 80,000 farmers, 22,000 teachers, 600,000 servants and washerwomen, and 50,000 in trades and merchandizing.

The family group, however, which is the ideal of the culture with which these folk have been born, is not based on the idea of an economically independent working mother. Rather its ideal harks back to the sheltered harem with the mother emerging at first as nurse and homemaker, while the man remains the sole breadwinner. What is the inevitable result of the clash of such ideals and such facts in the colored group? Broken families.

Among native white women one in ten is separated from her husband by death, divorce, or desertion. Among Negroes the ratio is one in seven. Is the cause racial? No, it is economic, because there is the same high ratio among the white foreign-born. The breaking up of the present family is the result of modern working and sex conditions and it hits the laborers with terrible force. The Negroes are put in a peculiarly difficult position, because the wage of the male breadwinner is below the standard, while the openings for colored women in certain lines of domestic work, and now in industries, are many. Thus while toil holds the father and brother in country and town at low wages, the sisters and mothers are called to the city. As a result the Negro women outnumber the men nine or ten to eight in many cities, making what Charlotte Gilman bluntly calls "cheap women."

What shall we say to this new economic equality in a great laboring class? Some people within and without the race deplore it. "Back to the homes with the women," they cry, "and higher wage for the men." But how impossible this is has been shown by war conditions. Cessation of foreign migration has raised Negro men's wages, to be sure—but it has not only raised Negro women's wages, it has opened to them a score of new avenues of earning a living. Indeed, here, in microcosm and with differences emphasizing sex equality, is the industrial history of labor in the 19th and 20th centuries. We cannot abolish the new economic freedom of women. We cannot imprison women again in a home or require them all on pain of death to be nurses and housekeepers.

What is today the message of these black women to America and to the world? The uplift of women is, next to the problem of the color line and the peace movement, our greatest modern cause. When, now, two of these movements—woman and color—combine in one, the combination has deep meaning.

In other years women's way was clear: to be beautiful, to be petted, to bear children. Such has been their theoretic destiny and if perchance they have been ugly, hurt, and barren, that has been forgotten with studied silence. In partial compensation for this narrowed destiny the white world has lavished its politeness on its womankind,—its chivalry and bows, its uncoverings and courtesies—all the accumulated homage disused for courts and kings and craving exercise. The revolt of white women against this preordained destiny has in these latter days reached splendid proportions, but it is the revolt of an aristocracy of brains and ability,—the middle class and rank and file still plod on in the appointed path, paid by the homage, the almost mocking homage, of men.

From black women of America, however, (and from some others, too, but chiefly from black women and their daughters' daughters) this gauze has been withheld and without semblance of such apology they have been frankly trodden under the feet of men. They are and have been objected to, apparently for reasons peculiarly exasperating to reasoning human beings. When in this world a man comes forward with a thought, a deed, a vision, we ask not, how does he look,—but what is his message? It is of but passing interest whether or not the messenger is beautiful or ugly,—the *message* is the thing. This, which is axiomatic among men, has been in past ages but partially true if the messenger was a woman. The world still wants to ask that a woman primarily be pretty and if she is not, the mob pouts and asks querulously, "What else are women for?" Beauty "is its own excuse for being," but there are other excuses, as most men know, and when the white world objects to black women because it does not consider them beautiful, the black world of right asks two questions: "What is beauty?" and, "Suppose you think them ugly, what then? If ugliness and unconventionality and eccentricity of face and deed do not hinder men from doing the world's work and reaping the world's reward, why should it hinder women?"

Other things being equal, all of us, black and white, would prefer to be beautiful in face and form and suitably clothed; but most of us are not so, and one of the mightiest revolts of the century is against the devilish decree that no woman is a woman who is not by present standards a beautiful woman. This decree the black women of America have in large measure escaped from the first. Not being expected to be merely ornamental, they have girded themselves for work, instead of adorning their bodies only for play. Their sturdier minds have concluded that if a woman be clean, healthy, and educated, she is as pleasing as God wills and far more useful than most of her sisters. If in addition to this she is pink and white and straight-haired, and some of her fellow-men prefer this, well and good; but if she is black or brown and crowned in curled mists (and this to us is the most beautiful thing on earth), this is surely the flimsiest excuse for spiritual incarceration or banishment.

The very attempt to do this in the case of Negro Americans has strangely over-reached itself. By so much as the defective eyesight of the white world rejects black women as beauties, by so much the more it needs them as human beings,—an enviable alternative, as many a white woman knows. Consequently, for black women alone, as a group, "handsome is that handsome does" and they are asked to be no more beautiful than God made them, but they are asked to be efficient, to be strong, fertile, muscled, and able to work. If they marry, they must as independent workers be able to help support their children, for their men are paid on a scale which makes sole support of the family often impossible.

On the whole, colored working women are paid as well as white working women for similar work, save in some higher grades, while colored men get from one-fourth to three-fourths less than white men. The result is curious and threefold: the economic independence of black women is increased, the breaking up of Negro families must be more frequent, and the number of illegitimate children is decreased more slowly among them than other evidences of culture are increased, just as was once true in Scotland and Bavaria.

What does this mean? It forecasts a mighty dilemma which the whole world of civilization, despite its will, must one time frankly face: the unhusbanded mother or the childless wife. God send us a world with woman's freedom and married motherhood inextricably wed, but until He sends it, I see more of future promise in the betrayed girl-mothers of the black belt than in the childless wives of the white North, and I have more respect for the colored servant who yields to her frank longing for motherhood than for her white sister who offers up children for clothes. Out of a sex freedom that today makes us shudder will come in time a day when we will no longer pay men for work they do not do, for the sake of their harem; we will pay women what they earn and insist on their working and earning it; we will allow those persons to vote who know enough to vote, whether they be black or female, white or male; and we will ward race suicide, not by further burdening the over-burdened, but by honoring motherhood, even when the sneaking father shirks his duty.

"Wait till the lady passes," said a Nashville white boy.

"She's no lady; she's a nigger," answered another.

So some few women are born free, and some amid insult and scarlet letters achieve freedom; but our women in black had freedom thrust contemptuously upon them. With that freedom they are buying an untrammeled independence and dear as is the price they pay for it, it will in the end be worth every taunt and groan. Today the dreams of the mothers are coming true. We have still our poverty and degradation, our lewdness and our cruel toil; but we have, too, a vast group of women of Negro blood who for strength of character, cleanness of soul, and unselfish devotion of purpose, is today easily the peer of any group of women in the civilized world. And more than that, in the great rank and file of our five million women we have the up-working of new revolutionary ideals, which must in time have vast influence on the thought and action of this land.

For this, their promise, and for their hard past, I honor the women of my race. Their beauty,—their dark and mysterious beauty of midnight eyes, crumpled hair, and soft, full-featured faces—is perhaps more to me than to you, because I was born to its warm and subtle spell; but their worth is yours as well as mine. No other women on earth could have emerged from the hell of force and temptation which once engulfed and still surrounds black women in America with half the modesty and womanliness that they retain. I have always felt like bowing myself before them in all abasement, searching to bring some tribute to these long-suffering victims, these burdened sisters of mine, whom the world, the wise, white world, loves to affront and ridicule and wantonly to insult. I have known the women of many lands and nations,—I have known and seen and lived beside them, but none have I known more sweetly feminine, more unswervingly loyal, more desperately earnest, and more instinctively pure in body and in soul than the daughters of my black mothers. This, then,—a little thing—to their memory and inspiration.

Darkwater, 1920

Marcus Garvey

MARCUS GARVEY was born at St. Ann's Bay, Jamaica, about 1885. He was educated at the public school and then for a short time attended the Church of England Grammar School, although he was a Roman Catholic by religion. On leaving school he learned the printing trade and followed it for many years. In Costa Rica he was associated with Marclam Taylor in publishing the *Bluefield's Messenger*. Later he was on the staff of *La Nacion*. He then returned to Jamaica and worked as a printer, being foreman of the printing department of P. Benjamin's Manufacturing Company of Kingston. Later he visited Europe and spent some time in England and France and while abroad conceived his scheme of organizing the Negro Improvement Society. This society was launched August 1, 1914, in Jamaica, with these general objects among others:

"To establish a Universal Confraternity among the race"; "to promote the spirit of race pride and love"; "to administer to and assist the needy"; "to strengthen the imperialism of independent African States"; "to conduct a world-wide commercial and industrial intercourse".

His first practical object was to be the establishment of a farm school. Meetings were held and the Roman Catholic Bishop, the Mayor of Kingston, and many others addressed them. Nevertheless the project did not succeed and Mr. Garvey was soon in financial difficulties. He therefore practically abandoned the Jamaica field and came to the United States. In the United States his movement for many years languished until at last with the increased migration from the West Indies during the war he succeeded in establishing a strong nucleus in the Harlem district of New York City.

His program now enlarged and changed somewhat in emphasis. He began especially to emphasize the commercial development of the Negroes and as an islander familiar with the necessities of ship traffic he planned the "Black Star Line". The public for a long time regarded this as simply a scheme of exploitation, when they were startled by hearing that Garvey had bought a ship. This boat was a former coasting vessel, 32 years old, but it was put into commission with a black crew and a black captain and was announced as the first of a fleet of vessels which would trade between the colored peoples of America, the West Indies and Africa. With this beginning, the popularity and reputation of Mr. Garvey and his association increased quickly.

In addition to the *Yarmouth* he is said to have purchased two small boats, the *Shadyside*, a small excursion steamer which made daily excursions up the Hudson, and a yacht which was designed to cruise among the West Indies and collect cargo in some central spot for the *Yarmouth*. He had first announced the Black Star Line as a Five Million Dollar corporation, but in February, 1920, he announced that it was going to be a Ten Million Dollar corporation with shares selling at Five Dollars. To this he added in a few months the Negro Factories Corporation capitalized at One Million Dollars with two hundred thousand one dollar shares, and finally he announced the subscription of Five Million Dollars to free Liberia and Haiti from debt.

Early in 1920 he called a convention of Negroes to meet in New York City from the 1st to the 31st of August, "to outline a constructive plan and program for the uplifting of the Negroes and the redemption of Africa". He also took title to three apartment houses to be used as offices and purchased the foundation of an unfinished Baptist church which he covered over and used for meetings, calling it "Liberty Hall". In August, 1920, his convention met with representatives from various parts of the United States, several of the West India Islands and the Canal Zone and a few from Africa. The convention carried out its plan of a month's meetings and culminated with a mass meeting which filled Madison Square Garden. Finally the convention adopted a "Declaration of Independence" with 66 articles, a universal anthem and colors,—red, black and green—and elected Mr. Garvey as "His Excellency, the Provisional President of Africa", together with a number of various other leaders from the various parts of the Negro world. This in brief is the history of the Garvey movement.

The question comes (1) Is it an honest, sincere movement?

(2) Are its industrial and commercial projects business like and effective? (3) Are its general objects plausible and capable of being carried out?

The central and dynamic force of the movement is Garvey. He has with singular success capitalized and made vocal the great and long suffering grievances and spirit of protest among the West Indian peasantry. Hitherto the black peasantry of the West Indies has been almost leaderless. Its natural leaders, both mulatto and black, have crossed the color line and practically obliterated social distinction, and to some extent economic distinction, between them and the white English world on the Islands. This has left a peasantry with only the rudiments of education and with almost no economic chances, grovelling at the bottom. Their distress and needs gave Garvey his vision.

It is a little difficult to characterize the man Garvey. He has been charged with dishonesty and graft, but he seems to me essentially an honest and sincere man with a tremendous vision, great dynamic force, stubborn determination and unselfish desire to serve; but also he has very serious defects of temperament and training: he is dictatorial, domineering, inordinately vain and very suspicious. He cannot get on with his fellow-workers. His entourage has continually changed.[1] He has had endless law suits and some cases of fisticuffs with his subordinates and has even divorced the young wife whom he married with great fanfare of trumpets about a year ago. All these things militate against him and his reputation. Nevertheless I have not found the slightest proof that his objects were not sincere or that he was consciously diverting money to his own uses. The great difficulty with him is that he has absolutely no business sense, no *flair* for real organization and his general objects are so shot through with bombast and exaggeration that it is difficult to pin them down for careful examination.

On the other hand, Garvey is an extraordinary leader of

[1]Of the 15 names of his fellow officers in 1914 not a single one appears in 1918; of the 18 names of officers published in 1918 only 6 survive in 1919; among the small list of principal officers published in 1920 I do not find a single name mentioned in 1919.

men. Thousands of people believe in him. He is able to stir them with singular eloquence and the general run of his thought is of a high plane. He has become to thousands of people a sort of religion. He allows and encourages all sorts of personal adulation, even printing in his paper the addresses of some of the delegates who hailed him as "His Majesty". He dons on state occasion, a costume consisting of an academic cap and gown flounced in red and green!

Of Garvey's curious credulity and suspicions one example will suffice: In March, 1919, he held a large mass meeting at Palace Casino which was presided over by Chandler Owen and addressed by himself and Phillip Randolph. Here he collected $204 in contributions on the plea that while in France, W. E. B. DuBois had interfered with the work of his "High Commissioner" by "defeating" his articles in the French press and "repudiating" his statements as to lynching and injustice in America! The truth was that Mr. DuBois never saw or heard of his "High Commissioner", never denied his nor anyone's statements of the wretched American conditions, did everything possible to arouse rather than quiet the French press and would have been delighted to welcome and cooperate with any colored fellow-worker.

When it comes to Mr. Garvey's industrial and commercial enterprises there is more ground for doubt and misgiving than in the matter of his character. First of all, his enterprises are incorporated in Delaware, where the corporation laws are loose and where no financial statements are required.[1] So far as I can find, and I have searched with care, Mr. Garvey has never published a complete statement of the income and expenditures of the Negro Improvement Association or of the

[1]Mr. Garvey boasts Feb. 14, 1920:

"This week I present you with the Black Star Line Steamship Corporation recapitalized at ten million dollars. They told us when we incorporated this corporation that we could not make it, but we are now gone from a $5,000,000 corporation to one of $10,000,000."

This sounds impressive, but means almost nothing. The fee for incorporating a $5,000,000 concern in Delaware is $350. By *paying $250 more the corporation may incorporate with $10,000,000 authorized capital without having a cent of capital actually paid in!* Cf. "General Corporation Laws of the State of Delaware", edition of 1917.

Black Star Line or of any of his enterprises, which really revealed his financial situation. A courteous letter of inquiry sent to him July 22, 1920, asking for such financial data as he was willing for the public to know, remains to this day unacknowledged and unanswered.

Now a refusal to publish a financial statement is no proof of dishonesty, but it *is* proof that either Garvey is ill-advised and unnecessarily courting suspicion, or that his industrial enterprises are not on a sound business basis; otherwise he is too good an advertiser not to use a promising balance-sheet for all it is worth.

There has been one balance sheet, published July 26, 1920, purporting to give the financial condition of the Black Star Line after one year of operation; neither profit or loss is shown, there is no way to tell the actual cash receipts or the true condition of the business. Nevertheless it does make some interesting revelations.

The total amount of stock subscribed for is $590,860. Of this $118,153.28 is not yet paid for, leaving the actual amount of paid-in capital charged against the corporation, $472,706.72. Against this stands only $355,214.59 of assets (viz.: $21,985.21 in cash deposits and loans receivable; $12,975.01 in furniture and equipment, $288,515.37 which is the alleged value of his boats, $26,000 in real estate and $5,739 of insurance paid in advance). To offset the assets he has $152,264.14 of other liabilities (accrued salaries, $1,539.30; notes and accounts payable, $129,224.84; mortgages due $21,500). In other words, his capital stock of $472,706.72 is after a year's business impaired to such extent that he has only $202,950.45 to show for it.

Even this does not reveal the precariousness of his actual business condition. Banks before the war in lending their credit refused to recognize any business as safe unless for every dollar of current liabilities there were *two* dollars of current assets. Today, since the war, they require *three* dollars of current assets to every *one* of current liabilities. The Black Star Line had July 26, $16,485.21 in current assets and $130,764.14 in current liabilities, when recognition by any reputable bank called for $390,000 in current assets.

Moreover, another sinister admission appears in this statement: the cost of floating the Black Star Line to date has been

$289,066.27. In other words, it has cost nearly $300,000 to collect a capital of less than half a million. Garvey has, in other words, spent more for advertisement than he has for his boats!

This is a serious situation, and even this does not tell the whole story: the real estate, furniture, etc., listed above, are probably valued correctly. But how about the boats? The *Yarmouth* is a wooden steamer of 1,452 gross tons, built in 1887. It is old and unseaworthy; it came near sinking a year ago and it has cost a great deal for repairs. It is said that it is now laid up for repairs with a large bill due. Without doubt the inexperienced purchasers of this vessel paid far more than it is worth, and it will soon be utterly worthless unless rebuilt at a very high cost.[1]

The cases of the *Kanawha* (or *Antonio Maceo*) and the *Shadyside* are puzzling. Neither of these boats is registered as belonging to the Black Star Line at all. The former is recorded as belonging to C. L. Dimon, and the latter to the North and East River Steamboat Company. Does the Black Star Line really own these boats, or is it buying them by installments, or only leasing them? We do not know the facts and have been unable to find out. Under the circumstances they look like dubious "assets".

The majority of the Black Star stock is apparently owned by the Universal Negro Improvement Association. There is no reason why this association, if it will and can, should not continue to pour money into its corporation. Let us therefore consider then Mr. Garvey's other resources.

Mr. Garvey's income consists of (a) dues from members of the U. N. I. Association; (b) shares in the Black Star Line and other enterprises, and (c) gifts and "loans" for specific objects. If the U. N. I. Association has "3,000,000 members" then the income from that source alone would be certainly over a million dollars a year. If, as is more likely, it

[1]Technically the *Yarmouth* does not belong to the Black Star Line of Delaware, but to the "Black Star Line of Canada, Limited," incorporated in Canada, March 23, 1920, with one million dollars capital. This capital consists of $500 cash and $999,500 "assets." Probably the Black Star Line of Delaware controls this corporation, but this is not known.

has under 300,000 paying members, he may collect $150,000 annually from this source. Stock in the Black Star Line is still being sold. Garvey himself tells of one woman who had saved about four hundred dollars in gold: "She brought out all the gold and bought shares in the Black Star Line." Another man writes this touching letter from the Canal Zone: "I have sent twice to buy shares amounting to $125, (numbers of certificates 3752 and 9617). Now I am sending $35 for seven more shares. You might think I have money, but the truth, as I stated before, is that I have no money now. But if I'm to die of hunger it will be all right because I'm determined to do all that's in my power to better the conditions of my race."[1]

In addition to this he has asked for special contributions. In the spring of 1920 he demanded for his coming convention in August, "a fund of two million dollars ($2,000,000) to capitalize this, the greatest of all conventions." In October he acknowledged a total of something over $16,000 in small contributions. Immediately he announced "a constructive loan" of $2,000,000, which he is presumably still seeking to raise.[2]

From these sources of income Mr. Garvey has financed his enterprises and carried on a wide and determined propaganda, maintained a large staff of salaried officials, clerks and agents, and published a weekly newspaper. Notwithstanding this considerable income, there is no doubt that Garvey's expenditures are pressing hard on his income, and that his financial methods are so essentially unsound that unless he

[1]P. N. Gordon.

[2]"The Universal Negro Improvement Association is raising a constructive loan of two million dollars from its members. Three hundred thousand dollars out of this two million has been allotted to the New York Local as its quota, and already the members in New York have started to subscribe to the loan, and in the *next seven* days the three hundred thousand dollars will be oversubscribed. The great divisions of Pittsburgh, Philadelphia, Boston, Chicago, Cleveland, Wilmington, Baltimore and Washington will also oversubscribe their quota to make up the two million dollars.

"Constructive work will be started in *January*, 1921, when the first ship of the Black Star Line on the African trade will sail from New York with materials and workmen for this constructive work."

Eleven days later, November 6th, the *Negro World* is still "raising the loan" but there is no report of the amount raised.

speedily revises them the investors will certainly get no dividends and worse may happen[1]. He is apparently using the familiar method of "Kiting"—*i. e.*, the money which comes in as investment in stock is being used in current expenses, especially in heavy overhead costs, for clerk hire, interest and display. Even his boats are being used for advertisement more than for business—lying in harbors as exhibits, taking excursion parties, etc. These methods have necessitated mortgages on property and continually new and more grandiose schemes to collect larger and larger amounts of ready cash. Meantime, lacking business men of experience, his actual business ventures have brought in few returns, involved heavy expense and threatened him continually with disaster or legal complication.

On the other hand, full credit must be given Garvey for a bold effort and some success. He has at least put vessels manned and owned by black men on the seas and they have carried passengers and cargoes. The difficulty is that he does not know the shipping business, he does not understand the investment of capital, and he has few trained and staunch assistants.

The present financial plight of an inexperienced and headstrong promoter may therefore decide the fate of the whole movement. This would be a calamity. Garvey is the beloved leader of tens of thousands of poor and bewildered people who have been cheated all their lives. His failure would mean a blow to their faith, and a loss of their little savings, which it would take generations to undo.

Moreover, shorn of its bombast and exaggeration, the main

[1]It might be argued that it is not absolutely necessary that the Black Star Line, etc., should pay financially. It is quite conceivable that Garvey should launch a business philanthropy, and that without expectation of return, colored people should contribute for a series of years to support Negro enterprise. But this is not Garvey's idea. He says plainly in a circular:

"The Black Star Line corporation presents to every Black Man, Woman and Child the opportunity to climb the great ladder of industrial and commercial progress. If you have ten dollars, one hundred dollars, or one or five thousand dollars to invest for profit, then take out shares in The Black Star Line, Inc. This corporation is chartered to trade on every sea and all waters. The Black Star Line will turn over large profits and dividends to stockholders, and operate to their interest even whilst they will be asleep."

lines of the Garvey plan are perfectly feasible. What he is trying to say and do is this: American Negroes can, by accumulating and ministering their own capital, organize industry, join the black centers of the south Atlantic by commercial enterprise and in this way ultimately redeem Africa as a fit and free home for black men. This is true. It is *feasible*. It is, in a sense, practical; but it will take for its accomplishment long years of painstaking, self-sacrificing effort. It will call for every ounce of ability, knowledge, experience and devotion in the whole Negro race. It is not a task for one man or one organization, but for co-ordinate effort on the part of millions. The plan is not original with Garvey but he has popularized it, made it a living, vocal ideal and swept thousands with him with intense belief in the possible accomplishment of the ideal.

This is a great, human service; but when Garvey forges ahead and almost single-handed attempts to realize his dream in a few years, with large words and wild gestures, he grievously minimizes his task and endangers his cause.

To instance one illustrative fact: there is no doubt but what Garvey has sought to import to America and capitalize the antagonism between blacks and mulattoes in the West Indies. This has been the cause of the West Indian failures to gain headway against the whites. Yet Garvey imports it into a land where it has never had any substantial footing and where today, of all days, it is absolutely repudiated by every thinking Negro; Garvey capitalizes it, has sought to get the coöperation of men like R. R. Moton on this basis, and has aroused more bitter color enmity inside the race than has ever before existed. The whites are delighted at the prospect of a division of our solidifying phalanx, but their hopes are vain. American Negroes recognize no color line in or out of the race, and they will in the end punish the man who attempts to establish it.

Then too Garvey increases his difficulties in other directions. He is a British subject. He wants to trade in British territory. Why then does he needlessly antagonize and even insult Britain? He wants to unite all Negroes. Why then does he sneer at the work of the powerful group of his race in the United States where he finds asylum and sympathy? Particularly, why does he decry the excellent and rising business enterprises of Harlem—intimating that his schemes alone are honest and sound when the facts flatly contradict him? He proposes to settle his headquarters in Liberia—but has he asked permission of the Liberian government? Does he presume to usurp authority in a land which has successfully withstood England, France and the United States,—but is expected tamely to submit to Marcus Garvey? How long does Mr. Garvey think that President King would permit his anti-English propaganda on Liberian soil, when the government is straining every nerve to escape the Lion's Paw?

And, finally, without arms, money, effective organization or base of operations, Mr. Garvey openly and wildly talks of "Conquest" and of telling white Europeans in Africa to "get out!" and of becoming himself a black Napoleon![1]

Suppose Mr. Garvey should drop from the clouds and concentrate on his industrial schemes as a practical first step toward his dreams: the first duty of a great commercial enterprise is to carry on effective commerce. A man who sees in industry the key to a situation, must establish sufficient business-like industries. Here Mr. Garvey has failed lamentably.

The *Yarmouth*, for instance, has not been a commercial success. Stories have been published alleging its dirty condition and the inexcusable conduct of its captain and crew. To this Mr. Garvey may reply that it was no easy matter to get efficient persons to run his boats and to keep a schedule. This is certainly true, but if it is difficult to secure one black boat crew, how much more difficult is it going to be to "build and operate factories in the big industrial centers of the United States, Central America, the West Indies and Africa to manufacture every marketable commodity"? and also "to purchase and build ships of larger tonnage for the African and South American trade"? and also to raise "Five Million Dollars to free Liberia" where "new buildings are to be erected, admin-

[1]He said in his "inaugural" address:

"The signal honor of being Provisional President of Africa is mine. It is a political job; it is a political calling for me to redeem Africa. It is like asking Napoleon to take the world. He took a certain portion of the world in his time. He failed and died at St. Helena. But may I not say that the lessons of Napoleon are but stepping stones by which we shall guide ourselves to African liberation?"

istrative buildings are to be built, colleges and universities are to be constructed"? and finally to accomplish what Mr. Garvey calls the "Conquest of Africa"!

To sum up: Garvey is a sincere, hard-working idealist; he is also a stubborn, domineering leader of the mass; he has worthy industrial and commercial schemes but he is an inexperienced business man. His dreams of Negro industry, commerce and the ultimate freedom of Africa are feasible; but his methods are bombastic, wasteful, illogical and ineffective and almost illegal. If he learns by experience, attracts strong and capable friends and helpers instead of making needless enemies; if he gives up secrecy and suspicion and substitutes open and frank reports as to his income and expenses, and above all if he is willing to be a co-worker and not a czar, he may yet in time succeed in at least starting some of his schemes toward accomplishment. But unless he does these things and does them quickly he cannot escape failure.

Let the followers of Mr. Garvey insist that he get down to bed-rock business and make income and expense balance; let them gag Garvey's wilder words, and still preserve his wide power and influence. American Negro leaders are not jealous of Garvey—they are not envious of his success; they are simply afraid of his failure, for his failure would be theirs. He can have all the power and money that he can efficiently and honestly use, and if in addition he wants to prance down Broadway in a green shirt, let him—but do not let him foolishly overwhelm with bankruptcy and disaster one of the most interesting spiritual movements of the modern Negro world.

The Crisis, December 1920, January 1921

The Black Star Line

THE MAIN economic venture of Marcus Garvey was the Black Star Line.

This steamship venture was the foundation stone of Garvey's rise to popularity among Negroes. African migration is a century old and a pretty thoroughly discredited dream. Autonomous African Negro States have been forecast by scorces of Negro leaders and writers. But a definite plan to unite Negrodom by a line of steamships was a brilliant suggestion and Garvey's only original contribution to the race problem. But, asked the critic, can it be done? Has Garvey the business sense, can he raise the capital, can he gather the men?

The answer lies in the history of the Black Star fleet. The *Yarmouth* was a steamer of 1,452 gross tons, built in 1887. The Black Star Line bought this boat in 1919 and in its report for the year 1920, it was put down as worth $178,156.36. At the Orr trial, Garvey swore under oath that he paid $140,000 cash for it. We will tell the rest of this story in Garvey's own words[1]:

> We contracted to bring a carload of whiskey valued at five million dollars and the ship, in sailing out between here and Sandy Hook, was caught in a gale and was damaged badly and put back into port, and there were several raids on the whiskey; when it came back, Prohibition was in effect; the ship was raided several times, whiskey was stolen; we had a great deal of trouble with the Federal Government, costing us thousands of dollars; ultimately the ship was repaired in Cuba; we experienced a tie-up of two months with this cargo of whiskey with a crew of over fifty men and we experienced some trouble in Cuba in handling the whiskey; when she did clear from Cuba, she went to the West Indies and also had an accident there and returned, and we lost on that trip from 250 to 300 thousand dollars, and on another trip we lost about 75 thousand dollars; there were extensive repairs done on the boat, and even

[1]Orr, a stockholder, sued Garvey. The following extracts are from a certified copy of the sworn testimony at this trial.

against our instructions because the captain of the boat did things on his own account, and we were held liable for it.

Q. What did you mean by testifying you lost about a quarter of a million dollars on that cargo? A. Because we had to pay the cost of the undelivered cargo; we had to pay the cost of the repairs of the boat.

THE COURT: You had to pay for what disappeared?

A. Yes.

Q. Did all of that cargo disappear, or a few cases?

A. Part of the cargo.

Q. Do you mean for the Court to understand that you, at the head of a corporation that had a load of whiskey on their boat, that because it was destroyed or confiscated, you had to pay for it, is that what you want the Court to believe? A. We had to pay for the cargo that was not delivered for which we contracted to deliver.

Q. Did you insure the cargo? A. No, I did not.

Q. You mean for the Court to believe you had to pay for the cargo of whiskey?

THE COURT: That is what he said.

On another voyage, Luc Dorsinville, who claimed to have been Haitian agent of the line, stated that it took the *Yarmouth* three months to make a single voyage between New York, Cuba, Haiti and Jamaica; that the voyage cost between fifteen and twenty thousand dollars and that at the end of the three months the cargo did not pay half the cost. This agent claims that he had 77 passengers booked for passage and a cargo of freight, but the boat was so dirty that most of the people would not take passage. He said that he sold 27 passages beside paying many bills for the ship. Nevertheless, the ship went to Jamaica instead of New York and left the agent to settle the claims for passage money paid and other matters. There was a good deal of controversy as to just who was to blame for all this and why the *Yarmouth* did not return to ship the cargo worth over $30,000 which the agent claims was waiting for her.

Of the staggering losses on the *Yarmouth* no hint appears in Mr. Garvey's glowing speeches concerning the Black Star Line, or in the advertisements in the *Negro World*, or even in the first annual financial report issued in 1920—July 26. No losses whatsoever are recorded there. The *Yarmouth* is entered at full value and an organization expense of $289,066.27 is put down as an asset because it is an "organization expense." It was also recorded: "We have much to be thankful for in that no unfortunate accident has befallen us!"

The *Yarmouth* made three trips to the West Indies in three years. It was then docked for repairs. This bill was apparently not paid, for the *Nauticus* announced, October 15, 1921, an attachment against the Black Star Line for $20,285.57 by the National Dry Dock and Repair Company.[1] This was presumably for unpaid repairs on the *Yarmouth*, although it may have applied to other boats also. At any rate, in the *Nauticus* of December 10, 1921, appears this obituary of the first boat of the Black Star Line:

> *Yarmouth* (S.S.) 1452 tons gross 725 net, built at Dumbarton 1887 and owned by the B. S. L., N. Y., was sold by U. S. Marshall as she lay at the National Dry Dock, N. Y., December 2 [1921], to Frederic Townsend, c/o Walter Welsh, 32 Broadway, for $1,625.[2]

The *Kanawha* or *Antonio Maceo* was listed in the Black Star report as worth $75,359.01. Garvey swore that he paid $60,000 for it. It was apparently bought to do a small carrying trade between the West Indian Islands. The *Kanawha* left New York about Easter time 1921 and sailed for Cuba and the West Indies. Garvey testified that she with another ship "was repaired in drydock and sailed from here; she broke down between Cuba and the Virginia Coast and we had to tow her back to New York. We had to spend seventy or eighty thousand dollars on that boat." The *Negro World* announced that this boat "arrived in Cuba in a blaze of glory, April 16."

According to the New York *Evening World*, the boat was held up in Cuba because of boiler troubles, although several thousand dollars had been recently spent on new boilers. Finally she was tied up in Santiago de Cuba and the United

[1]A judgment of $526.70 was also obtained by the Garcia Sugar Corporation.

[2]In addition to this sum the buyer probably had to pay the attachment noted above, making the total selling price of the ship at auction $21,910.57.

States Government brought the crew back. The boat itself has never reappeared.

The *Shadyside* was listed by the Black Star Line as worth $35,000. It did a small excursion business up the Hudson during one summer.

In March, 1921, the *Shadyside* lay on the beach beside North River at the foot of 157th Street and was in a hopeless condition, quite beyond repair.

Thus the three first boats of the Garvey fleet disappeared and if the Black Star's own figures and Mr. Garvey's statements of losses are true, this involves a total disappearance of at least $630,000 of the hard-earned savings of colored folk.

But this is not all.

On Sunday night, April 10, according to the *Negro World* of April 16, 1921:

> Unexpectedly, like a bolt of lightning, came the announcement at Liberty Hall tonight that the Black Star Line Steamship Corporation expected by May 1, next, to float the *Phyllis Wheatley*, its latest addition to the corporation's line of steamships to engage in transportation between this country and Africa. The news was hailed with wild expressions of joy and delight by the immense audience that filled the great hall.

The ship was said to carry 4,500 tons of cargo and 2,000 passengers, was equipped with electric lights, fans, music and smoking rooms and refrigerating machinery.[1]

Already, as early as January, 1921, Black Star Line sailings for Liberia, West Africa, had been given display advertising in the *Negro World*. They were announced for "on or about the 27th of March, 1921, at 3 P.M." Beginning in April and continuing for seven or more months, there appeared advertisements announcing "passengers and freight" for the West Indies and West Africa by the S.S. *Phyllis Wheatley*, "sailing on or about April 25" or without definite date.

When the delegates came to the convention August 1, they naturally asked to see the *Phyllis Wheatley*, but a delegate, Noah Thompson, says in the California *New Age* of September 23, 1921:

[1]In the Orr trial.

None of the boasted ships were shown the delegates, who were daily promised that on "tomorrow" the ships would be shown. Mr. Thompson said that he was in New York thirty-five days, and with others persisted in demanding to be shown the ships, but was told daily that they could see the ships "tomorrow," and "later," but "tomorrow" never came.

September 30, 1921, Mr. Garvey defended himself, declaring:

> It was announced before the convention adjourned, that the United States Shipping Board had awarded the S.S. *Orion* to the Black Star Line, Inc., the ship for which we are to pay $250,000 and on which we have a deposit of $25,000.

Finally the truth came out. In an editorial in the *Negro World*, February 18, 1922, Mr. Garvey alleges:

> A "group" have robbed the Black Star Line and desires to cover up their robbery, in that within recent months a thorough investigation has been started to find out what has been done in the matter of over $25,000 which is said to be deposited with the United States Shipping Board for the purchase of a ship, and the continuous deception of the said parties in promising the president of the Black Star Line, the Board of Directors and stockholders, that a ship by the name of the S.S. *Orion*, which should have been named the S.S. *Phyllis Wheatley*, should have been delivered since April of 1921 and is not yet delivered up to the time of writing, and for which over a thousand and one excuses have been given.

Moreover, Mr. Garvey virtually acknowledged that the Black Star Line after collecting nearly three-quarters of a million dollars did not have in 1921 enough money to deposit $25,000 on the new ship, but said that part of the purchase money of the ship was to be raised in America and that he went to the West Indies to raise the balance. No sooner had Mr. Garvey left, however, than, as he alleges:

> Certain parties who assumed the active management of affairs of the Black Star Line in the United States planned,

in conjunction with others, that I should never return to America, and that during my absence from the country, plunderings of all kinds would have been indulged in. . . .

Changes were made in the plans that were laid out for the acquirements of the African boat; new arrangements were made, contracts were signed and for four months, whilst all these changes had been going on, not even a word of information was sent to me to acquaint me of what was being done.

The S.S. *Phyllis Wheatley* that should have been secured since April, and which I had every reason to believe was either at anchor in New York, or had sailed for Africa, was nowhere to be found!

Finally Mr. Garvey concludes:

Patience dragged on and on, until I took definite steps to locate either the money or the ship, and then to my surprise where $25,000 should have been only $12,500 was credited.

In other words, Mr. Garvey says that officials of the Black Star Line, whom he is careful not to name, stole so much of the deposit money that the *Phyllis Wheatley* could not be secured for the line!

Just when Mr. Garvey made this astonishing discovery, we are not informed; but after he returned to America in July, the sailing of the *Phyllis Wheatley* continued to be advertised until October and tickets offered for sale. As a result, Mr.

BLACK STAR LINE

PASSENGERS AND FREIGHT

FOR

HAVANA,
SANTO DOMINGO
St. KITTS, DOMINICA,
BARBADOS,
TRINIDAD,
DEMERARA,
DAKAR SECONDEE,
MONROVIA, AFRICA

By the S. S. "PHYLLIS WHEATLEY"

BOOK YOUR PASSAGE NOW

SPACE IS LIMITED

BLACK STAR LINE, Inc.

54-56 West 135th Street, New York City

TRAFFIC DEPARTMENT

ADVERTISEMENT IN THE "NEGRO WORLD"
OCT. 22, 1921.

Garvey and three of his chief officials were indicted by the Grand Jury of the District Court of the United States for the Southern District of New York, for "using the mails in furtherance of a scheme to defraud and conspiring so to do."

Several states questioned the honesty of the corporation and refused to let Mr. Garvey sell stock. In the city of Chicago, he was convicted of violating the Illinois Stock Law and fined one hundred dollars. In Virginia, John A. George was sent to jail for selling stock after the Corporation Commission had investigated the scheme through Pinkerton detectives. This was in February, 1921.

What excuses does Mr. Garvey offer for his failure? His excuses are various and extraordinary. *First* and perhaps the most astonishing is the following statement in the *Negro World* of January 21, 1922:

> *All the troubles we have had on our ships have been caused because men were paid to make this trouble by certain organizations calling themselves Negro Advancement Associations. They paid men to dismantle our machinery and otherwise damage it so as to bring about the downfall of the movement.*

Secondly, Mr. Garvey alleges gigantic "conspiracies." He said, as reported in the *Negro World*, May 13, 1922, at Liberty Hall:

> Millions of dollars were expended in the shipping industries to boycott and put out of existence the Black Star Line.

In the *Negro World* of January 28, 1922, he adds:

> The matter of my arrest last week for the alleged fraudulent use of the mails is but a concoction decided upon by the unseen forces operating against us to find some criminal excuse by which the promoter of the greatest movement among Negroes could be held up to world scorn and ridicule, thereby exposing the movement to contempt. It is a mean, low-down, contemptible method of embarrassing any movement for human uplift.

He also says that "Bolshevists" are paying for attacks on the line. (*Negro World*, December 14, 1921.)

Thirdly and chiefly, Mr. Garvey accuses his associates and employees of dishonesty. In the *Negro World* of February 18,

1922, Mr. Garvey writes of a "treacherous plot" against him and a "great state of demoralization" in the Black Star Line during his absence, and of "the tricks and dishonesty of a few employees of the Black Star Line."

In the *Negro World* of December 24, 1921, he says:

> Through the dishonesty of some of the "so-called educated," Garvey has had to suffer many reverses. Business transactions and financial arrangements which Garvey was too busy to attend to himself and left to others opened the door for several of these "so-called educated" (whom he trusted to represent him) to rob and cheat the organization, and thus make it harder for Garvey to protect and represent the interests of the people.
>
> As often as found out the "so-called educated" tramps and villains have been kicked out of the organization. Several of them have formed new organizations, started newspapers and journals. And some of the organizations, newspapers and journals, after collecting a few thousand dollars from the poor, innocent people, have gone out of existence; but the villains still hover around, connecting themselves with other papers and organizations that keep up a fight against the Universal Negro Improvement Association and Garvey.
>
> Observe carefully the composition of any anti-Garvey organization or paper and you will find there a congregation of dismissed, disgraced and so-called resigned employees of either the Universal Negro Improvement Association, the *Negro World* or the Black Star Line Corporation. All birds of a feather flock together. All villains keep together.

In the *Negro World* of July 8, 1922, he writes:

> No head of any steamship company can guarantee what will be the action of the captain of one of his ships when he clears port. If a captain wants to sell or confiscate your goods; if a captain wants to pile up debts on a steamship company for his own selfish profit, what can the president of that corporation do, especially when the individual may be in league with some powers that be, and especially the only powers that could punish him if he creates a criminal offense against the corporation? . . .

> What can Marcus Garvey do if men are employed to do their work and they prove to be dishonest and dishonorable in the performance of that work? What could Jesus do dealing with a dishonest man but to wait and punish him at His judgment? And judgment is not just now. What will happen in the meanwhile—Jesus would be robbed.

Finally, Mr. Garvey alleges his own lack of experience in the shipping business:

> Marcus Garvey is not a navigator; he is not a marine engineer; he is not even a good sailor; therefore the individual who would criticize Marcus Garvey for a ship of the Black Star Line not making a success at sea is a fool.—(*Negro World*, July 8, 1922.)

Mr. Garvey consequently writes in the *Negro World* of April 1, 1922, "We have suspended the activities of the Black Star Line."

Here then is the collapse of the only thing in the Garvey movement which was original or promising. Of course, Mr. Garvey promises repayment, reorganization and a "new" Black Star Line.

What are his statements and promises worth? Knowing, as he did, that he had lost $250,000 on a single voyage and $75,000 on another and that his capital had practically disappeared, he declared according to a report in the *Negro World*, March 5, 1921:

> Nothing engineered by Negroes within the last 500 years has been as big or as stupendous as the Black Star Line. . . .
>
> Today we control three-quarters of a million dollars (applause); not three-quarters of a million on mere paper, but in property value—money that can be realized in twenty-four hours if the stockholders desire that their money be refunded to them. By a majority vote at any meeting we can sell out the property of the Black Star Line and realize every nickel we have placed in it.

In spite of this, Mr. Garvey made the following statements under oath in the Orr trial:

> THE COURT: The people in your community have a great deal of faith in you?

A. Yes, they have.

THE COURT: Any statements you made in 1919 were relied on by the members of your community?

A. Yes.

THE COURT: *You did not paint the possibilities of the Black Star Line in hues of rose color, did you?*

A. *No, I did not; it was still a business proposition like any other business proposition.—(Italics ours.)*

Small wonder that at the end of this trial Judge Panken said:

> "It seems to me that you have been praying upon the gullibility of your own people, having kept no proper accounts of the money received for investment, being an organization of high finance in which the officers received outrageously high salaries and were permitted to have exorbitant expense accounts for pleasure jaunts throughout the country. I advise these 'dupes' who have contributed to these organizations to go into court and ask for the appointment of a receiver. You should have taken this $600,000 and built a hospital for colored people in this city instead of purchasing a few old boats. There is a form of paranoia which manifests itself in believing oneself to be a great man."

To this let us add this pitiful document from San Diego, Cal., to Noah Thompson:

> I am forced to write you, asking if it is wise for a widow-woman who makes her living by working in service and doing day's work, to continue to make the sacrifice by sending $5.00 per month on payment of shares in the Black Star Line.
>
> After reading that part of your report, stating that you and many other delegates were unable to see the ships supposed to be owned by said company, I began to think, maybe I had better keep my hard earnings at home, for I have an aged mother to support and I haven't one penny to throw away. So I am writing you for facts in regard to what I have asked you.
>
> ELLA ROSS HUTSON.

The Crisis, September 1922

A Lunatic or a Traitor

IN ITS ENDEAVOR to avoid any injustice toward Marcus Garvey and his followers, THE CRISIS has almost leaned backward. Notwithstanding his wanton squandering of hundreds of thousands of dollars we have refused to assume that he was a common thief. In spite of his monumental and persistent lying we have discussed only the larger and truer aspects of his propaganda. We have refrained from all comment on his trial and conviction for fraud. We have done this too in spite of his personal vituperation of the editor of THE CRISIS and persistent and unremitting repetition of falsehood after falsehood as to the editor's beliefs and acts and as to the program of the N. A. A. C. P.

In the face, however, of the unbelievable depths of debasement and humiliation to which this demagog has descended in order to keep himself out of jail, it is our duty to say openly and clearly:

Marcus Garvey is, without doubt, the most dangerous enemy of the Negro race in America and in the world. He is either a lunatic or a traitor. He is sending all over this country tons of letters and pamphlets appealing to Congressmen, business men, philanthropists and educators to join him on a platform whose half concealed planks may be interpreted as follows:

That no person of Negro descent can ever hope to become an American citizen.

That forcible separation of the races and the banishment of Negroes to Africa is the only solution of the Negro problem.

That race war is sure to follow any attempt to realize the program of the N. A. A. C. P.

We would have refused to believe that any man of Negro descent could have fathered such a propaganda if the evidence did not lie before us in black and white signed by this man. Here is a letter and part of a symposium sent to one of the most prominent business men of America and turned over to us; we select but a few phrases; the italics are ours:

Do you believe the Negro to be a *human being*?

Do you believe the Negro *entitled to all the rights of humanity*?

Do you believe that the Negro should be taught *not to aspire to the highest political positions in Governments of the white race*, but to such positions among his own race in a Government of his own?

Would you help morally *or otherwise* to bring about such a possibility? Do you believe that the Negro should be *encouraged to aspire* to the highest industrial and commercial positions in the countries of the white man in competition with him and to his exclusion?

Do you believe that the Negro should be encouraged to regard and *respect the rights of all other races* in the same manner as other races would respect the rights of the Negro.

The pamphlets include one of the worst articles recently written *by a Southern white man* advocating the deportation of American Negroes to Liberia and several articles by Garvey and his friends. From one of Garvey's articles we abstract one phrase:

"THE WHITE RACE CAN BEST HELP THE NEGRO BY TELLING HIM THE TRUTH, AND NOT BY FLATTERING HIM INTO BELIEVING THAT HE IS AS GOOD AS ANY WHITE MAN."

Not even Tom Dixon or Ben Tillman or the hatefulest enemies of the Negro have ever stooped to a more vicious campaign than Marcus Garvey, sane or insane, is carrying on. He is not attacking white prejudice, he is grovelling before it and applauding it; his only attack is on men of his own race who are striving for freedom; his only contempt is for Negroes; his only threats are for black blood. And this leads us to a few plain words:

1. No Negro in America ever had a fairer and more patient trial than Marcus Garvey. He convicted himself by his own admissions, his swaggering monkey-shines in the court room with monocle and long tailed coat and his insults to the judge and prosecuting attorney.

2. Marcus Garvey was long refused bail, not because of his color, but because of the repeated threats and cold blooded assaults charged against his organization. He himself openly threatened to "get" the District Attorney. His followers had repeatedly to be warned from intimidating witnesses and one was sent to jail therefor. One of his former trusted officials after being put out of the Garvey organization

brought the long concealed cash account of the organization to this office and we published it. Within two weeks the man was shot in the back in New Orleans and killed. We know nothing of Garvey's personal connection with these cases but we do know that today his former representative lies in jail in Liberia sentenced to death for murder. The District Attorney believed that Garvey's "army" had arms and ammunition and was prepared to "shoot up" colored Harlem if he was released. For these and no other reasons Garvey was held in the Tombs so long without bail and until he had made abject promises, apologizing to the judge and withdrawing his threats against the District Attorney. Since his release he has not dared to print a single word against white folk. All his vituperation has been heaped on his own race.

Everybody, including the writer, who has dared to make the slightest criticism of Garvey has been intimidated by threats and threatened with libel suits. Over fifty court cases have been brought by Garvey in ten years. After my first and favorable article on Garvey, I was not only threatened with death by men declaring themselves his followers, but received letters of such unbelievable filth that they were absolutely unprintable. When I landed in this country from my trip to Africa I learned with disgust that my friends stirred by Garvey's threats had actually felt compelled to have secret police protection for me on the dock!

Friends have even begged me not to publish this editorial lest I be assassinated. To such depths have we dropped in free black America! I have been exposing white traitors for a quarter century. If the day has come when I cannot tell the truth about black traitors it is high time that I died.

The American Negroes have endured this wretch all too long with fine restraint and every effort at cooperation and understanding. But the end has come. Every man who apologizes for or defends Marcus Garvey from this day forth writes himself down as unworthy of the countenance of decent Americans. As for Garvey himself, this open ally of the Ku Klux Klan should be locked up or sent home.

The Crisis, May 1924

Criteria of Negro Art

I DO NOT doubt but there are some in this audience who are a little disturbed at the subject of this meeting, and particularly at the subject I have chosen. Such people are thinking something like this: "How is it that an organization like this, a group of radicals trying to bring new things into the world, a fighting organization which has come up out of the blood and dust of battle, struggling for the right of black men to be ordinary human beings—how is it that an organization of this kind can turn aside to talk about Art? After all, what have we who are slaves and black to do with Art?"

Or perhaps there are others who feel a certain relief and are saying, "After all it is rather satisfactory after all this talk about rights and fighting to sit and dream of something which leaves a nice taste in the mouth".

Let me tell you that neither of these groups is right. The thing we are talking about tonight is part of the great fight we are carrying on and it represents a forward and an upward look—a pushing onward. You and I have been breasting hills; we have been climbing upward; there has been progress and we can see it day by day looking back along blood-filled paths. But as you go through the valleys and over the foothills, so long as you are climbing, the direction,—north, south, east or west,—is of less importance. But when gradually the vista widens and you begin to see the world at your feet and the far horizon, then it is time to know more precisely whither you are going and what you really want.

What do we want? What is the thing we are after? As it was phrased last night it had a certain truth: We want to be Americans, full-fledged Americans, with all the rights of other American citizens. But is that all? Do we want simply to be Americans? Once in a while through all of us there flashes some clairvoyance, some clear idea, of what America really is. We who are dark can see America in a way that white Americans can not. And seeing our country thus, are we satisfied with its present goals and ideals?

In the high school where I studied we learned most of Scott's "Lady of the Lake" by heart. In after life once it was my privilege to see the lake. It was Sunday. It was quiet. You could glimpse the deer wandering in unbroken forests; you could hear the soft ripple of romance on the waters. Around me fell the cadence of that poetry of my youth. I fell asleep full of the enchantment of the Scottish border. A new day broke and with it came a sudden rush of excursionists. They were mostly Americans and they were loud and strident. They poured upon the little pleasure boat,—men with their hats a little on one side and drooping cigars in the wet corners of their mouths; women who shared their conversation with the world. They all tried to get everywhere first. They pushed other people out of the way. They made all sorts of incoherent noises and gestures so that the quiet home folk and the visitors from other lands silently and half-wonderingly gave way before them. They struck a note not evil but wrong. They carried, perhaps, a sense of strength and accomplishment, but their hearts had no conception of the beauty which pervaded this holy place.

If you tonight suddenly should become full-fledged Americans; if your color faded, or the color line here in Chicago was miraculously forgotten; suppose, too, you became at the same time rich and powerful;—what is it that you would want? What would you immediately seek? Would you buy the most powerful of motor cars and outrace Cook County? Would you buy the most elaborate estate on the North Shore? Would you be a Rotarian or a Lion or a What-not of the very last degree? Would you wear the most striking clothes, give the richest dinners and buy the longest press notices?

Even as you visualize such ideals you know in your hearts that these are not the things you really want. You realize this sooner than the average white American because, pushed aside as we have been in America, there has come to us not only a certain distaste for the tawdry and flamboyant but a vision of what the world could be if it were really a beautiful world; if we had the true spirit; if we had the Seeing Eye, the Cunning Hand, the Feeling Heart; if we had, to be sure, not perfect happiness, but plenty of good hard work, the inevitable suffering that always comes with life; sacrifice and waiting, all that—but, nevertheless, lived in a world where men know, where men create, where they realize themselves and where they enjoy life. It is that sort of a world we want to create for ourselves and for all America.

After all, who shall describe Beauty? What is it? I remember tonight four beautiful things: The Cathedral at Cologne, a forest in stone, set in light and changing shadow, echoing with sunlight and solemn song; a village of the Veys in West Africa, a little thing of mauve and purple, quiet, lying content and shining in the sun; a black and velvet room where on a throne rests, in old and yellowing marble, the broken curves of the Venus of Milo; a single phrase of music in the Southern South—utter melody, haunting and appealing, suddenly arising out of night and eternity, beneath the moon.

Such is Beauty. Its variety is infinite, its possibility is endless. In normal life all may have it and have it yet again. The world is full of it; and yet today the mass of human beings are choked away from it, and their lives distorted and made ugly. This is not only wrong, it is silly. Who shall right this well-nigh universal failing? Who shall let this world be beautiful? Who shall restore to men the glory of sunsets and the peace of quiet sleep?

We black folk may help for we have within us as a race new stirrings; stirrings of the beginning of a new appreciation of joy, of a new desire to create, of a new will to be; as though in this morning of group life we had awakened from some sleep that at once dimly mourns the past and dreams a splendid future; and there has come the conviction that the Youth that is here today, the Negro Youth, is a different kind of Youth, because in some new way it bears this mighty prophecy on its breast, with a new realization of itself, with new determination for all mankind.

What has this Beauty to do with the world? What has Beauty to do with Truth and Goodness—with the facts of the world and the right actions of men? "Nothing", the artists rush to answer. They may be right. I am but an humble disciple of art and cannot presume to say. I am one who tells the truth and exposes evil and seeks with Beauty and for Beauty to set the world right. That somehow, somewhere eternal and perfect Beauty sits above Truth and Right I can conceive, but here and now and in the world in which I work they are for me unseparated and inseparable.

This is brought to us peculiarly when as artists we face our own past as a people. There has come to us—and it has come especially through the man we are going to honor tonight[1]—a realization of that past, of which for long years we have been ashamed, for which we have apologized. We thought nothing could come out of that past which we wanted to remember; which we wanted to hand down to our children. Suddenly, this same past is taking on form, color and reality, and in a half shamefaced way we are beginning to be proud of it. We are remembering that the romance of the world did not die and lie forgotten in the Middle Age; that if you want romance to deal with you must have it here and now and in your own hands.

I once knew a man and woman. They had two children, a daughter who was white and a daughter who was brown; the daughter who was white married a white man; and when her wedding was preparing the daughter who was brown prepared to go and celebrate. But the mother said, "No!" and the brown daughter went into her room and turned on the gas and died. Do you want Greek tragedy swifter than that?

Or again, here is a little Southern town and you are in the public square. On one side of the square is the office of a colored lawyer and on all the other sides are men who do not like colored lawyers. A white woman goes into the black man's office and points to the white-filled square and says, "I want five hundred dollars now and if I do not get it I am going to scream."

Have you heard the story of the conquest of German East Africa? Listen to the untold tale: There were 40,000 black men and 4,000 white men who talked German. There were 20,000 black men and 12,000 white men who talked English. There were 10,000 black men and 400 white men who talked French. In Africa then where the Mountains of the Moon raised their white and snow-capped heads into the mouth of the tropic sun, where Nile and Congo rise and the Great Lakes swim, these men fought; they struggled on mountain, hill and valley, in river, lake and swamp, until in masses they sickened, crawled and died; until the 4,000 white Germans

[1]Carter Godwin Woodson, 12th Spingarn Medallist.

had become mostly bleached bones; until nearly all the 12,000 white Englishmen had returned to South Africa, and the 400 Frenchmen to Belgium and Heaven; all except a mere handful of the white men died; but thousands of black men from East, West and South Africa, from Nigeria and the Valley of the Nile, and from the West Indies still struggled, fought and died. For four years they fought and won and lost German East Africa; and all you hear about it is that England and Belgium conquered German Africa for the allies!

Such is the true and stirring stuff of which Romance is born and from this stuff come the stirrings of men who are beginning to remember that this kind of material is theirs; and this vital life of their own kind is beckoning them on.

The question comes next as to the interpretation of these new stirrings, of this new spirit: Of what is the colored artist capable? We have had on the part of both colored and white people singular unanimity of judgment in the past. Colored people have said: "This work must be inferior because it comes from colored people." White people have said: "It is inferior because it is done by colored people." But today there is coming to both the realization that the work of the black man is not always inferior. Interesting stories come to us. A professor in the University of Chicago read to a class that had studied literature a passage of poetry and asked them to guess the author. They guessed a goodly company from Shelley and Robert Browning down to Tennyson and Masefield. The author was Countée Cullen. Or again the English critic John Drinkwater went down to a Southern seminary, one of the sort which "finishes" young white women of the South. The students sat with their wooden faces while he tried to get some response out of them. Finally he said, "Name me some of your Southern poets". They hesitated. He said finally, "I'll start out with your best: Paul Laurence Dunbar"!

With the growing recognition of Negro artists in spite of the severe handicaps, one comforting thing is occurring to both white and black. They are whispering, "Here is a way out. Here is the real solution of the color problem. The recognition accorded Cullen, Hughes, Fauset, White and others shows there is no real color line. Keep quiet! Don't complain! Work! All will be well!"

I will not say that already this chorus amounts to a conspiracy. Perhaps I am naturally too suspicious. But I will say that there are today a surprising number of white people who are getting great satisfaction out of these younger Negro writers because they think it is going to stop agitation of the Negro question. They say, "What is the use of your fighting and complaining; do the great thing and the reward is there". And many colored people are all too eager to follow this advice; especially those who are weary of the eternal struggle along the color line, who are afraid to fight and to whom the money of philanthropists and the alluring publicity are subtle and deadly bribes. They say, "What is the use of fighting? Why not show simply what we deserve and let the reward come to us?"

And it is right here that the National Association for the Advancement of Colored People comes upon the field, comes with its great call to a new battle, a new fight and new things to fight before the old things are wholly won; and to say that the Beauty of Truth and Freedom which shall some day be our heritage and the heritage of all civilized men is not in our hands yet and that we ourselves must not fail to realize.

There is in New York tonight a black woman molding clay by herself in a little bare room, because there is not a single school of sculpture in New York where she is welcome. Surely there are doors she might burst through, but when God makes a sculptor He does not always make the pushing sort of person who beats his way through doors thrust in his face. This girl is working her hands off to get out of this country so that she can get some sort of training.

There was Richard Brown. If he had been white he would have been alive today instead of dead of neglect. Many helped him when he asked but he was not the kind of boy that always asks. He was simply one who made colors sing.

There is a colored woman in Chicago who is a great musician. She thought she would like to study at Fontainebleau this summer where Walter Damrosch and a score of leaders of Art have an American school of music. But the application blank of this school says: "I am a white American and I apply for admission to the school."

We can go on the stage; we can be just as funny as white Americans wish us to be; we can play all the sordid parts that America likes to assign to Negroes; but for any thing else there is still small place for us.

And so I might go on. But let me sum up with this: Suppose the only Negro who survived some centuries hence was the Negro painted by white Americans in the novels and essays they have written. What would people in a hundred years say of black Americans? Now turn it around. Suppose you were to write a story and put in it the kind of people you know and like and imagine. You might get it published and you might not. And the "might not" is still far bigger than the "might". The white publishers catering to white folk would say, "It is not interesting"—to white folk, naturally not. They want Uncle Toms, Topsies, good "darkies" and clowns. I have in my office a story with all the earmarks of truth. A young man says that he started out to write and had his stories accepted. Then he began to write about the things he knew best about, that is, about his own people. He submitted a story to a magazine which said, "We are sorry, but we cannot take it". "I sat down and revised my story, changing the color of the characters and the locale and sent it under an assumed name with a change of address and it was accepted by the same magazine that had refused it, the editor promising to take anything else I might send in providing it was good enough."

We have, to be sure, a few recognized and successful Negro artists; but they are not all those fit to survive or even a good minority. They are but the remnants of that ability and genius among us whom the accidents of education and opportunity have raised on the tidal waves of chance. We black folk are not altogether peculiar in this. After all, in the world at large, it is only the accident, the remnant, that gets the chance to make the most of itself; but if this is true of the white world it is infinitely more true of the colored world. It is not simply the great clear tenor of Roland Hayes that opened the ears of America. We have had many voices of all kinds as fine as his and America was and is as deaf as she was for years to him. Then a foreign land heard Hayes and put its imprint on him and immediately America with all its imitative snobbery woke up. We approved Hayes because London, Paris and Berlin approved him and not simply because he was a great singer.

Thus it is the bounden duty of black America to begin this great work of the creation of Beauty, of the preservation of Beauty, of the realization of Beauty, and we must use in this work all the methods that men have used before. And what have been the tools of the artist in times gone by? First of all, he has used the Truth—not for the sake of truth, not as a scientist seeking truth, but as one upon whom Truth eternally thrusts itself as the highest handmaid of imagination, as the one great vehicle of universal understanding. Again artists have used Goodness—goodness in all its aspects of justice, honor and right—not for sake of an ethical sanction but as the one true method of gaining sympathy and human interest.

The apostle of Beauty thus becomes the apostle of Truth and Right not by choice but by inner and outer compulsion. Free he is but his freedom is ever bounded by Truth and Justice; and slavery only dogs him when he is denied the right to tell the Truth or recognize an ideal of Justice.

Thus all Art is propaganda and ever must be, despite the wailing of the purists. I stand in utter shamelessness and say that whatever art I have for writing has been used always for propaganda for gaining the right of black folk to love and enjoy. I do not care a damn for any art that is not used for propaganda. But I do care when propaganda is confined to one side while the other is stripped and silent.

In New York we have two plays: "White Cargo" and "Congo". In "White Cargo" there is a fallen woman. She is black. In "Congo" the fallen woman is white. In "White Cargo" the black woman goes down further and further and in "Congo" the white woman begins with degradation but in the end is one of the angels of the Lord.

You know the current magazine story: A young white man goes down to Central America and the most beautiful colored woman there falls in love with him. She crawls across the whole isthmus to get to him. The white man says nobly, "No". He goes back to his white sweetheart in New York.

In such cases, it is not the positive propaganda of people who believe white blood divine, infallible and holy to which

I object. It is the denial of a similar right of propaganda to those who believe black blood human, lovable and inspired with new ideals for the world. White artists themselves suffer from this narrowing of their field. They cry for freedom in dealing with Negroes because they have so little freedom in dealing with whites. DuBose Heywood writes "Porgy" and writes beautifully of the black Charleston underworld. But why does he do this? Because he cannot do a similar thing for the white people of Charleston, or they would drum him out of town. The only chance he had to tell the truth of pitiful human degradation was to tell it of colored people. I should not be surprised if Octavius Roy Cohen had approached the *Saturday Evening Post* and asked permission to write about a different kind of colored folk than the monstrosities he has created; but if he has, the *Post* has replied, "No. You are getting paid to write about the kind of colored people you are writing about."

In other words, the white public today demands from its artists, literary and pictorial, racial pre-judgment which deliberately distorts Truth and Justice, as far as colored races are concerned, and it will pay for no other.

On the other hand, the young and slowly growing black public still wants its prophets almost equally unfree. We are bound by all sorts of customs that have come down as second-hand soul clothes of white patrons. We are ashamed of sex and we lower our eyes when people will talk of it. Our religion holds us in superstition. Our worst side has been so shamelessly emphasized that we are denying we have or ever had a worst side. In all sorts of ways we are hemmed in and our new young artists have got to fight their way to freedom.

The ultimate judge has got to be you and you have got to build yourselves up into that wide judgment, that catholicity of temper which is going to enable the artist to have his widest chance for freedom. We can afford the Truth. White folk today cannot. As it is now we are handing everything over to a white jury. If a colored man wants to publish a book, he has got to get a white publisher and a white newspaper to say it is great; and then you and I say so. We must come to the place where the work of art when it appears is reviewed and acclaimed by our own free and unfettered judgment. And we are going to have a real and valuable and eternal judgment only as we make ourselves free of mind, proud of body and just of soul to all men.

And then do you know what will be said? It is already saying. Just as soon as true Art emerges; just as soon as the black artist appears, someone touches the race on the shoulder and says, "He did that because he was an American, not because he was a Negro; he was born here; he was trained here; he is not a Negro—what is a Negro anyhow? He is just human; it is the kind of thing you ought to expect".

I do not doubt that the ultimate art coming from black folk is going to be just as beautiful, and beautiful largely in the same ways, as the art that comes from white folk, or yellow, or red; but the point today is that until the art of the black folk compells recognition they will not be rated as human. And when through art they compell recognition then let the world discover if it will that their art is as new as it is old and as old as new.

I had a classmate once who did three beautiful things and died. One of them was a story of a folk who found fire and then went wandering in the gloom of night seeking again the stars they had once known and lost; suddenly out of blackness they looked up and there loomed the heavens; and what was it that they said? They raised a mighty cry: "It is the stars, it is the ancient stars, it is the young and everlasting stars!"

The Crisis, October 1926

So the Girl Marries

THE PROBLEM of marriage among our present American Negroes is a difficult one. On the one hand go conflicting philosophies: should we black folk breed children or commit biological suicide? On the other, should we seek larger sex freedom or closer conventional rules? Should we guide and mate our children like the French or leave the whole matter of sex intermingling to the chance of the street, like Americans? These are puzzling questions and all the more so because we do not often honestly face them.

I was a little startled when I became father of a girl. I scented far-off difficulties. But she became soon a round little bunch of Joy: plump and jolly, full of smiles and fun—a flash of twinkling legs and bubbling mischief. Always there on the broad campus of Atlanta University she was in scrapes and escapades—how many I never dreamed until years after: running away from her sleepy nurse; riding old Billy, the sage and dignified draft horse; climbing walls; bullying the Matron; cajoling the cooks and becoming the thoroughly spoiled and immeasurably loved Baby of the Campus. How far the spoiling had gone I became suddenly aware one summer, when we stopped a while to breathe the salt sea air at Atlantic City. This tot of four years marched beside me down the Boardwalk amid the unmoved and almost unnoticing crowd. She was puzzled. Never before in her memory had the world treated her quite so indifferently.

"Papa," she exclaimed at last, impatiently, "I guess they don't know I'm here!"

As the Girl grew so grew her problems: School; Multiplication Tables; Playmates; Latin; Clothes—Boys! No sooner had we faced one than the other loomed, the last lingered—the next threatened. She went to Kindergarten with her playmates of the Campus—kids and half-grown-ups. The half-grown-ups, Normal students, did me the special courtesy of letting the Girl dawdle and play and cut up. So when she came at the age of ten to the Ethical Culture School in New York there loomed the unlearned Multiplication Table; and a time we had! For despite all proposals of "letting the Child develop as it Will!", she must learn to read and count; and the school taught her—but at a price!

Then came the days of gawky growth; the impossible children of the street; someone to play with; wild tears at going to bed; excursions, games—and far, far in the offing, the shadow of the Fear of the Color Line.

I had a Grand Idea. Before the time loomed—before the Hurt pierced and lingered and festered, off to England she should go for high school and come back armed with manners and knowledge, cap-a-pie, to fight American race hate and insult. Off the Girl went to Bedale's, just as war thundered in the world. As a professor of Economics and History, I knew the war would be short—a few months. So away went Mother and Girl. Two mighty years rolled turbulently by and back came both through the Submarine Zone. The Girl had grown. She was a reticent stranger with whom soul-revealing converse was difficult. I found myself groping for continual introductions.

Then came Latin. The English teacher talked Latin and his class at Bedale's romped with Caesar through a living Gallia. The American teacher in the Brooklyn Girl's High did not even talk English and regarded Latin as a crossword puzzle with three inches of daily solution. "Decline Stella!"; "Conjugate Amo"; "What is the subject of 'Gallia est omnis divisa——' ". "Nonsense," said the Girl (which was quite true), "I've dropped Latin!"

"But the colleges haven't," I moaned. "Why college?" countered the Girl.

Why indeed? I tried Cicero "pro Archia Poeta". The Girl was cold. Then I pleaded for my own spiritual integrity: "I have told 12 millions to go to college—what will they say if you don't go?" The Girl admitted that that was reasonable but she said she was considering marriage and really thought she knew about all that schools could teach effectively. I, too, was reasonable and most considerate, despite the fact that I was internally aghast. This baby—married—My God!—but, of course, I said aloud: Honorable state and all that; and "Go ahead, if you like—but how about a year in college as a sort of, well, introduction to life in general and for furnishing topics of conversation in the long years to come? How about it?"

"Fair enough," said the Girl and she went to college.

Boys! queer animals. Hereditary enemies of Fathers-with-daughters and Mothers! Mother had chaperoned the Girl relentlessly through High School. Most Mothers didn't bother. It was a bore and one felt like the uninvited guest or the veritable Death's Head. The Girl didn't mind much, only—"Well, really Mother you don't need to go or even to sit up." But Mother stuck to her job. I've always had the feeling that the real trick was turned in those years, by a very soft-voiced and persistent Mother who was always hanging about unobtrusively. The boys liked her, the girls were good-naturedly condescending; the Girl laughed. It was so funny. Father, of course, was busy with larger matters and weightier problems, including himself.

Clothes. In the midst of high school came sudden clothes. The problem of raiment. The astonishing transformation of the hoyden and hiker and basket ball expert into an amazing butterfly. We parents had expressed lofty disdain for the new colored beauty parlors—straightening and bleaching, the very idea! But they didn't straighten, they cleaned and curled; they didn't whiten, they delicately darkened. They did for colored girls' style of beauty what two sophisticated centuries had been doing for blonde frights. When the finished product stood forth all silked and embroidered, briefly skirted and long-limbed with impudent lip-stick and jaunty toque—well, Thrift hung its diminished head and Philosophy stammered. What shall we do about our daughter's extravagant dress? The beauty of colored girls has increased 100% in a decade because they give to it time and trouble. Can we stop it? Should we? Where shall we draw the line, with good silk stockings at $1.95 per pair?

"Girl! You take so long to dress! I can dress in fifteen minutes."

"Yes—Mamma and you look it!" came the frankly unfilial answer.

College. College was absence and premonition. Empty

absence and occasional letters and abrupt pauses. One wondered uneasily what they were doing with the Girl; *who* rather than what was educating her. Four years of vague uneasiness with flashes of hectic and puzzling vacations. Once with startling abruptness there arose the Shadow of Death—acute appendicitis; the hospital—the cold, sharp knife; the horror of waiting and the namelessly sweet thrill of recovery. Of course, all the spoiling began again and it literally rained silk and gold.

Absence, too, resulted in the unexpected increase in Parent-valuation. Mother was enshrined and worshipped by the absent Girl; no longer was she merely convenient and at times in the way. She was desperately adored. Even Father took on unaccustomed importance and dignity and found new place in the scheme of things. We both felt quite set up.

Then graduation and a Woman appeared in the family. A sudden woman—sedate, self-contained, casual, grown; with a personality—with wants, expenses, plans. "There will be a caller tonight."—"Tomorrow night I'm going out."

It was a bit disconcerting, this transforming of a rubber ball of childish joy into a lady whose address was at your own house. I acquired the habit of discussing the world with this stranger—as impersonally and coolly as possible: teaching—travel—reading—art—marriage. I achieved quite a detached air, letting the domineering daddy burst through only at intervals, when it seemed impossible not to remark—"It's midnight, my dear," and "when is the gentleman going? You need sleep!"

My part in Mate-selection was admittedly small but I flatter myself not altogether negligible. We talked the young men over—their fathers and grandfathers; their education; their ability to earn particular sorts of living; their dispositions. All this incidentally mind you—not didactically or systematically. Once or twice I went on long letter hunts for facts; usually facts were all too clear and only deductions necessary. What was the result? I really don't know. Sometimes I half suspect that the Girl arranged it all and that I was the large and solemn fly on the wheel. At other times I flatter myself that I was astute, secret, wise and powerful. Truth doubtless lurks between. So the Girl marries.

I remember the Boy came to me somewhat breathlessly one Christmas eve with a ring in his pocket. I told him as I had told others. "Ask her—she'll settle the matter; not I." But he was a nice boy. A rather unusual boy with a promise of fine manhood. I wished him luck. But I did not dare plead his cause. I had learned—well, I had learned.

Thus the world grew and blossomed and changed and so the Girl marries. It is the end of an era—a sudden break and beginning. I rub my eyes and re-adjust my soul. I plan frantically. It will be a simple, quiet ceremony—

"In a church, father!"

"Oh! in a church? Of course, in a church. Well, a church wedding would be a little larger, but——"

"With Countée's father and the Reverend Frazier Miller assisting."

"To be sure—well, that is possible and, indeed, probable."

"And there will be sixteen bridesmaids."

One has to be firm somewhere—"But my dear! who ever *heard* of sixteen bridesmaids!"

"But Papa, there are eleven Moles, and five indispensables and Margaret—"

Why argue? What has to be, must be; and this evidently had to be. I struggled faintly but succumbed. Now with sixteen bridesmaids and ten ushers must go at least as many invited guests.

You who in travail of soul have struggled with the devastating puzzle of selecting a small bridge party out of your total of twenty-five intimate friends, lend me your sympathy! For we faced the world-shattering problem of selecting for two only children, the friends of a pastor with twenty-five years service in one church; and the friends of a man who knows good people in forty-five states and three continents. I may recover from it but I shall never look quite the same. I shall always have a furtive feeling in my soul. I know that at the next corner I shall meet my Best Friend and remember that I forgot to invite him. Never in all eternity can I explain. How can I say: "Bill, I just forgot you!" Or "My *dear* Mrs.

Blubenski, I didn't remember where on earth you were or indeed if you were at all or ever!" No, one can't say such things. I shall only stare at them pleadingly, in doubt and pain, and slink wordlessly away.

Thirteen hundred were bidden to the marriage and no human being has one thousand three hundred friends! Five hundred came down to greet the bride at a jolly reception which I had originally planned for twenty-five. Of course, I was glad they were there. I expanded and wished for a thousand. Three thousand saw the marriage and a thousand waited on the streets. It was a great pageant; a heart-swelling throng; birds sang and Melville Charlton let the organ roll and swell beneath his quivering hands. A sweet young voice sang of Love; and then came the holy:

"Freudig gefuert, Ziehet dahin!"

The symbolism of that procession was tremendous. It was not the mere marriage of a maiden. It was not simply the wedding of a fine young poet. It was the symbolic march of young and black America. America, because there was Harvard, Columbia, Smith, Brown, Howard, Chicago, Syracuse, Penn and Cornell. There were three Masters of Arts and fourteen Bachelors. There were poets and teachers, actors, artists and students. But it was not simply conventional America—it had a dark and shimmering beauty all its own; a calm and high restraint and sense of new power; it was a new race; a new thought; a new thing rejoicing in a ceremony as old as the world. (And after it all and before it, such a jolly, happy crowd; some of the girls even smoked cigarettes!)

Why should there have been so much of pomp and ceremony—flowers and carriages and silk hats; wedding cake and wedding music? After all marriage in its essence is and should be very simple: a clasp of friendly hands; a walking away together of Two who say: "Let us try to be One and face and fight a lonely world together!" What more? Is that not enough? Quite; and were I merely white I should have sought to make it end with this.

But it seems to me that I owe something extra to an Idea, a Tradition. We who are black and panting up hurried hills of hate and hindrance—we have got to establish new footholds on the slipping by-paths through which we come. They must at once be footholds of the free and the eternal, the new and the enthralled. With all of our just flouting of white convention and black religion, some things remain eternally so—Birth, Death, Pain, Mating, Children, Age. Ever and anon we must point to these truths and if the pointing be beautiful with music and ceremony or bare with silence and darkness—what matter? The width or narrowness of the gesture is a matter of choice. That one will have it stripped to the essence. It is still good and true. This soul wants color with bursting cords and scores of smiling eyes in happy raiment. It must be as this soul wills. The Girl wills this. So the Girl marries.

The Crisis, June 1928

The Negro College

IT HAS BEEN said many times that a Negro University is nothing more and nothing less than a university. Quite recently one of the great leaders of education in the United States, Abraham Flexner, said something of that sort concerning Howard. As President of the Board of Trustees, he said he was seeking to build not a Negro university, but a University. And by those words he brought again before our eyes the ideal of a great institution of learning which becomes a center of universal culture. With all good will toward them that say such words—it is the object of this paper to insist that there can be no college for Negroes which is not a Negro college and that while an American Negro university, just like a German or Swiss university may rightly aspire to a universal culture unhampered by limitations of race and culture, yet it must start on the earth where we sit and not in the skies whither we aspire. May I develop this thought.

In the first place, we have got to remember that here in America, in the year 1933, we have a situation which cannot be ignored. There was a time when it seemed as though we might best attack the Negro problem by ignoring its most unpleasant features. It was not and is not yet in good taste to speak generally about certain facts which characterize our situation in America. We are politically ham-strung. We have the greatest difficulty in getting suitable and remunerative work. Our education is more and more not only being confined to our own schools but to a segregated public school system far below the average of the nation with one-third of our children continuously out of school. And above all, and this we like least to mention, we suffer social ostracism which is so deadening and discouraging that we are compelled either to lie about it or to turn our faces to the red flag of revolution. It consists of studied and repeated and emphasized public insult of the sort which during all the long history of the world has led men to kill or be killed. And in the full face of any effort which any black man may make to escape this ostracism for himself, stands this flaming sword of racial doctrine which will distract his effort and energy if it does not lead him to spiritual suicide.

We boast and have right to boast of our accomplishment between the days that I studied here and this 45th Anniversary of my graduation. It is a calm appraisal of fact to say that the history of modern civilization cannot surpass if it can parallel the advance of American Negroes in every essential line of culture in these years. And yet, when we have said this we must have the common courage honestly to admit that every step we have made forward has been greeted by a step backward on the part of the American public in caste intolerance, mob law and racial hatred.

I need but remind you that when I graduated from Fisk there was no "Jim Crow" car in Tennessee and I saw Hunter of '89 once sweep a brakeman aside at the Union Station and escort a crowd of Fisk students into the first-class seats for which they had paid. There was no legal disfranchisement and a black Fiskite sat in the Legislature; and while the Chancellor of the Vanderbilt University had annually to be re-introduced to the President of Fisk, yet no white Southern group presumed to dictate the internal social life of this institution.

Manifestly with all that can be said, pro and con, and in extenuation, and by way of excuse and hope, this is the situation and we know it. There is no human way by which these facts can be ignored. We cannot do our daily work, sing a song or write a book or carry on a university and act as though these things were not.

If this is true, then no matter how much we may dislike the statement, the American Negro problem is and must be the center of the Negro American university. It has got to be. You are teaching Negroes. There is no use pretending that you are teaching Chinese or that you are teaching white Americans or that you are teaching citizens of the world. You are teaching American Negroes in 1933, and they are the subjects of a caste system in the Republic of the United States of America and their life problem is primarily this problem of caste.

Upon these foundations, therefore, your university must start and build. Nor is the thing so entirely unusual or unheard of as it sounds. A university in Spain is not simply a university. It is a Spanish university. It is a university located in Spain. It uses the Spanish language. It starts with Spanish history and makes conditions in Spain the starting point of its teaching. Its education is for Spaniards,—not for them as they may be or ought to be, but as they are with their present problems and disadvantages and opportunities.

In other words, the Spanish university is founded and grounded in Spain, just as surely as a French university is French. There are some people who have difficulty in apprehending this very clear truth. They assume, for instance, that the French university is in a singular sense universal, and is based on a comprehension and inclusion of all mankind and of their problems. But it is not so, and the assumption that it is arises simply because so much of French culture has been built into universal civilization. A French university is founded in France; it uses the French language and assumes a knowledge of French history. The present problems of the French people are its major problems and it becomes universal only so far as other peoples of the world comprehend and are at one with France in its mighty and beautiful history.

In the same way, a Negro university in the United States of America begins with Negroes. It uses that variety of the English idiom which they understand; and above all, it is founded or it should be founded on a knowledge of the history of their people in Africa and in the United States, and their present condition. Without white-washing or translating wish into fact, it begins with that; and then it asks how shall these young men and women be trained to earn a living and live a life under the circumstances in which they find themselves or with such changing of those circumstances as time and work and determination will permit.

Is this statement of the field of a Negro university a denial of aspiration or a change from older ideals? I do not think it is, although I admit in my own mind some change of thought and modification of method. The system of learning which bases its self upon the actual condition of certain classes and groups of human beings is tempted to suppress a minor premise of fatal menace. It proposes that the knowledge given and the methods pursued in such institutions of learning shall be for the definite object of perpetuating present conditions or of leaving their amelioration in the hands of and at the initiative of other forces and other folk. This was the great criticism that those of us who fought for higher education of Negroes thirty years ago, brought against the industrial school.

The industrial school founded itself and rightly upon the actual situation of American Negroes and said: "What can be done to change this situation?" And its answer was: "A training in technique and method such as would incorporate the disadvantaged group into the industrial organization of the country, and in that organization the leaders of the Negro had perfect faith. Since that day the industrial machine has cracked and groaned. Its technique has changed faster than any school could teach; the relations of capital and labor have increased in complication and it has become so clear that Negro poverty is not primarily caused by ignorance of technical knowledge that the industrial school has almost surrendered its program.

In opposition to that, the opponents of college training in those earlier years said: "What black men need is the broader and more universal training so that they can apply the general principle of knowledge to the particular circumstances of their condition."

Here again was the indubitable truth but incomplete truth. The technical problem lay in the method of teaching this broader and more universal truth and here just as in the industrial program, we must start where we are and not where we wish to be.

As I said a few years ago at Howard University, both these positions had thus something of truth and right. Because of the peculiar economic situation in our country the program of the industrial school came to grief first and has practically been given up. Starting even though we may with the actual condition of the Negro peasant and artisan, we cannot ameliorate his condition simply by learning a trade which is the technique of a passing era. More vision and knowledge is needed than that. But on the other hand, while the Negro college of a generation ago set down a defensible and true program of applying knowledge to facts, it unfortunately could not completely carry it out, and it did not carry it out, because the one thing that the industrial philosophy gave to education, the Negro college did not take and that was that the university education of black men in the United States must be grounded in the condition and work of those black men!

On the other hand, it would be of course idiotic to say, as the former industrial philosophy almost said, that so far as most black men are concerned education must stop with this. No, starting with present conditions and using the facts and the knowledge of the present situation of American Negroes, the Negro university expands toward the possession and the conquest of all knowledge. It seeks from a beginning of the history of the Negro in America and in Africa to interpret all history; from a beginning of social development among Negro slaves and freedmen in America and Negro tribes and kingdoms in Africa, to interpret and understand the social development of all mankind in all ages. It seeks to reach modern science of matter and life from the surroundings and habits and aptitudes of American Negroes and thus lead up to understanding of life and matter in the universe.

And this is a different program than a similar function would be in a white university or in a Russian university or in an English university, because it starts from a different point. It is a matter of beginnings and integrations of one group which sweep instinctive knowledge and inheritance and current reactions into a universal world of science, sociology and art. In no other way can the American Negro College function. It cannot begin with history and lead to Negro History. It cannot start with sociology and lead to Negro sociology.

Why was it that the Renaissance of literature which began among Negroes ten years ago has never taken real and lasting root? It was because it was a transplanted and exotic thing. It was a literature written for the benefit of white people and at the behest of white readers, and starting out privately from the white point of view. It never had a real Negro constituency and it did not grow out of the inmost heart and frank experience of Negroes; on such an artificial basis no real literature can grow.

On the other hand, if starting in a great Negro university

you have knowledge, beginning with the particular, and going out to universal comprehension and unhampered expression, you are going to begin to realize for the American Negro the full life which is denied him now. And then after that comes a realization of the older object of our college—to bring this universal culture down and apply it to the individual life and individual conditions of living Negroes.

The university must become not simply a center of knowledge but a center of applied knowledge and guide of action. And this is all the more necessary now since we easily see that planned action, especially in economic life, is going to be the watchword of civilization.

If the college does not thus root itself in the group life and afterward apply its knowledge and culture to actual living, other social organs must replace the college in this function. A strong, intelligent family life may adjust the student to higher culture; and, too, a social clan may receive the graduate and induct him into life. This has happened and is happening among a minority of privileged people. But it costs society a fatal price. It tends to hinder progress and hamper change; it makes Education, propaganda for things as they are. It leaves the mass of those without family training and without social standing misfits and rebels who despite their education are uneducated in its meaning and application. The only college which stands for the progress of all, mass as well as aristocracy, functions in root and blossom as well as in the overshadowing and heaven-filling tree. No system of learning—no university—can be universal before it is German, French, Negro. Grounded in inexorable fact and condition, in Poland, Italy or elsewhere, it may seek the universal and haply it may find it—and finding it, bring it down to earth and us.

We have imbibed from the surrounding white world a childish idea of Progress. Progress means bigger and better results always and forever. But there is no such rule of Life. In 6000 years of human culture, the losses and retrogressions have been enormous. We have no assurance this twentieth century civilization will survive. We do not know that American Negroes will survive. There are sinister signs about us, antecedent to and unconnected with the Great Depression.

The organized might of industry north and south is relegating the Negro to the edge of survival and using him as a labor reservoir on starvation wage. No secure professional class, no science, literature, nor art can live on such a sub-soil. It is an insistent, deep-throated cry for rescue, guidance and organized advance that greets the black leader today, and the college that trains him has got to let him know at least as much about the great black miners' strike in Alabama as about the age of Pericles.

We are on the threshold of a new era. Let us not deceive ourselves with outworn ideals of wealth and servants and luxuries, reared on a foundation of ignorance, starvation and want. Instinctively, we have absorbed these ideals from our twisted white American environment. This new economic planning is not for us unless we do it. Unless the American Negro today, led by trained university men of broad vision, sits down to work out by economics and mathematics, by physics and chemistry, by history and sociology, exactly how and where he is to earn a living and how he is to establish a reasonable Life in the United States or elsewhere—unless this is done, the university has missed its field and function and the American Negro is doomed to be a suppressed and inferior caste in the United States for incalculable time.

Here, then, is a job for the American Negro university. It cannot be successfully ignored or dodged without the growing menace of disaster. I lay the problem before you as one which you must not ignore.

To carry out this plan, two things and only two things are necessary,—teachers and students. Buildings and endowments may help, but they are not indispensable. It is necessary first to have teachers who comprehend this program and know how to make it live among their students. This is calling for a good deal, because it asks that teachers teach that which they have learned in no American school and which they never will learn until we have a Negro university of the sort that I am visioning. No teacher, black or white, who comes to a university like Fisk, filled simply with general ideas of human culture or general knowledge of disembodied science, is going to make a university of this school. Because a university is made of human beings, learning of the things they do not know from the things they do know in their own lives.

And secondly, we must have students. They must be chosen for their ability to learn. There is always the temptation to assume that the children of privileged classes, the rich, the noble, the white, are those who can best take education. One has but to express this to realize its utter futility. But perhaps the most dangerous thing among us is for us, without thought, to imitate the white world and assume that we can choose students at Fisk because of the amount of money which their parents have happened to get hold of. That basis of selection is going to give us an extraordinary aggregation. We want, by the nicest methods possible, to seek out the talented and the gifted among our constituency, quite regardless of their wealth or position, and to fill this university and similar institutions with persons who have got brains enough to take fullest advantage of what the university offers. There is no other way. With teachers who know what they are teaching and whom they are teaching, and the life that surrounds both the knowledge and the knower, and with students who have the capacity and the will to absorb this knowledge, we can build the sort of Negro university which will emancipate not simply the black folk of the United States, but those white folk who in their effort to suppress Negroes have killed their own culture.

Men in their desperate effort to replace equality with caste and to build inordinate wealth on a foundation of abject poverty have succeeded in killing democracy, art and religion.

Only a universal system of learning, rooted in the will and condition of the masses and blossoming from that manure up toward the stars is worth the name. Once builded it can only grow as it brings down sunlight and starshine and impregnates the mud.

The chief obstacle in this rich land endowed with every national resource and with the abilities of a hundred different peoples—the chief and only obstacle to the coming of that kingdom of economic equality which is the only logical end of work, is the determination of the white world to keep the black world poor and make themselves rich. The disaster which this selfish and short-sighted policy has brought, lies at the bottom of this present depression, and too, its cure lies beside it. Your clear vision of a world without wealth, of capital without profit, of income based on work alone, is the path out not only for you but for all men.

Is not this a program of segregation, emphasis of race and particularism as against national unity and universal humanity? It is and it is not by choice but by force; you do not get humanity by wishing it nor do you become American citizens simply because you want to. A Negro university, from its high ground of unfaltering facing of the Truth, from its unblinking stare at hard facts does not advocate segregation by race; it simply accepts the bald fact that we are segregated, apart, hammered into a separate unity by spiritual intolerance and legal sanction backed by mob law, and that this separation is growing in strength and fixation; that it is worse today than a half century ago and that no character, address, culture or desert is going to change it in our day or for centuries to come. Recognizing this brute fact, groups of cultured, trained and devoted men gathering in great institutions of learning proceed to ask: What are we going to do about it? It is silly to ignore the gloss of truth; it is idiotic to proceed as though we were white or yellow, English or Russian. Here we stand. We are American Negroes. It is beside the point to ask whether we form a real race. Biologically we are mingled of all conceivable elements, but race is psychology, not biology; and psychologically we are a unified race with one history, one red memory and one revolt. It is not ours to argue whether we will be segregated or whether we ought to be a caste. We are segregated; we are caste. This is our given and at present unalterable fact. Our problem is: How far and in what way can we consciously and scientifically guide our future so as to insure our physical survival, our spiritual freedom and our social growth? Either we do this or we die. There is no alternative. If America proposed the murder of this group, its moral descent into imbecility and crime and its utter loss of manhood, self-assertion and courage, the sooner we realize this the better. By that great line of McKay:

"If we must die, let it not be like hogs."

But the alternative of not dying like hogs is not that of dying or killing like snarling dogs. It is rather conquering the world by thought and brain and plan; by expression and organized cultural ideals. Therefore let us not beat futile wings in impotent frenzy, but carefully plan and guide our segregated life, organize in industry and politics to protect it and expand it and above all to give it unhampered spiritual expression in art and literature. It is the counsel of fear and cowardice to say this cannot be done. What must be can be and it is only a question of Science and Sacrifice to bring the great consummation.

What that will be, no one knows. It may be a great physical segregation of the world along the Color Line; it may be an economic rebirth which ensures spiritual and group integrity amid physical diversity. It may be utter annihilation of class and race and color barriers in one ultimate mankind, differentiated by talent, susceptibility and gift—but any of these ends are matters of long centuries and not years. We live in years, swift-flying, transient years. We hold the possible future in our hands but not by wish and will, only by thought, plan, knowledge and organization. If the college can pour into the coming age an American Negro who knows himself and his plight and how to protect himself and fight race prejudice, then the world of our dream will come and not otherwise.

The Crisis, August 1933

On Being Ashamed of Oneself

AN ESSAY ON RACE PRIDE

MY GRANDFATHER left a passage in his diary expressing his indignation at receiving an invitation to a "Negro" picnic. Alexander DuBois, born in the Bahamas, son of Dr. James DuBois of the well-known DuBois family of Poughkeepsie, N. Y., had been trained as a gentleman in the Cheshire School of Connecticut, and the implications of a Negro picnic were anathema to his fastidious soul. It meant close association with poverty, ignorance and suppressed and disadvantaged people, dirty and with bad manners.

This was in 1856. Seventy years later, Marcus Garvey discovered that a black skin was in itself a sort of patent to nobility, and that Negroes ought to be proud of themselves and their ancestors, for the same or analogous reasons that made white folk feel superior.

Thus, within the space of three-fourths of a century, the pendulum has swung between race pride and race suicide, between attempts to build up a racial ethos and attempts to escape from ourselves. In the years between emancipation and 1900, the theory of escape was dominant. We were, by birth, law and training, American citizens. We were going to escape into the mass of Americans in the same way that the Irish and Scandinavians and even the Italians were beginning to disappear. The process was going to be slower on account of the badge of color; but then, after all, it was not so much the matter of physical assimilation as of spiritual and psychic amalgamation with the American people.

For this reason, we must oppose all segregation and all racial patriotism; we must salute the American flag and sing "Our Country 'Tis of Thee" with devotion and fervor, and we must fight for our rights with long and carefully planned campaign; uniting for this purpose with all sympathetic people, colored and white.

This is still the dominant philosophy of most American Negroes and it is back of the objection to even using a special designation like "Negro" or even "Afro-American" or any such term.

But there are certain practical difficulties connected with this program which are becoming more and more clear today. First of all comes the fact that we are still ashamed of ourselves and are thus estopped from valid objection when white folks are ashamed to call us human. The reasons of course, are not as emphatic as they were in the case of my grandfather. I remember a colored man, now ex-patriate, who made this discovery in my company, some twenty-five years ago. He was a handsome burning brown, tall, straight and well-educated, and he occupied a position which he had won, across and in spite of the color line. He did not believe in Negroes, for himself or his family, and he planned elaborately to escape the trammels of race. Yet, he had responded to a call for a meeting of colored folk which touched his interests, and he came. He found men of his own calibre and training; he found men charming and companionable. He was thoroughly delighted. I know that never before, or I doubt if ever since, he had been in such congenial company. He could not help mentioning his joy continually and reiterating it.

All colored folk had gone through the same experience, for more and more largely in the last twenty-five years, colored America has discovered itself; has discovered groups of people, association with whom is a poignant joy and despite their ideal of American assimilation, in more and more cases and with more and more determined object they seek each other.

That involves, however, a drawing of class lines inside the Negro race, and it means the emergence of a certain social aristocracy, who by reasons of looks and income, education and contact, form the sort of upper social group which the world has long known and helped to manufacture and preserve. The early basis of this Negro group was simply color and a bald imitation of the white environment. Later, it tended, more and more, to be based on wealth and still more recently on education and social position.

This leaves a mass of untrained and uncultured colored folk and even of trained but ill-mannered people and groups of impoverished workers of whom this upper class of colored Americans are ashamed. They are ashamed both directly and indirectly, just as any richer or better sustained group in a nation is ashamed of those less fortunate and withdraws its skirts from touching them. But more than that, because the upper colored group is desperately afraid of being represented before American whites by this lower group, or being mistaken for them, or being treated as though they were part of it, they are pushed to the extreme of effort to avoid contact with the poorest classes of Negroes. This exaggerates, at once, the secret shame of being identified with such people and the anomaly of insisting that the physical characteristics of these folk which the upper class shares, are not the stigmata of degradation.

When, therefore, in offense or defense, the leading group of Negroes must make common cause with the masses of their own race, the embarrassment or hesitation becomes apparent. They are embarrassed and indignant because an educated man should be treated as a Negro, and that no Negroes receive credit for social standing. They are ashamed and embarrassed because of the compulsion of being classed with a mass of people over whom they have no real control and whose action they can influence only with difficulty and compromise and with every risk of defeat.

Especially is all natural control over this group difficult—I mean control of law and police, of economic power, of guiding standards and ideals, of news propaganda. On this comes even greater difficulty because of the incompatibility of any action which looks toward racial integrity and race action with previous ideals. What are we really aiming at? The building of a new nation or the integration of a new group into an old nation? The latter has long been our ideal. Must it be changed? Should it be changed? If we seek new group loyalty, new pride of race, new racial integrity—how, where, and by what method shall these things be attained? A new plan must be built up. It cannot be the mere rhodomontade and fatuous propaganda on which Garveyism was based. It has got to be far-sighted planning. It will involve increased segregation and perhaps migration. It will be pounced upon and aided and encouraged by every "nigger-hater" in the land.

Moreover, in further comment on all this, it may be pointed out that this is not the day for the experiment of new nations or the emphasis of racial lines. This is, or at least we thought it was, the day of the Inter-nation, of Humanity, and the disappearance of "race" from our vocabulary. Are we American Negroes seeking to move against, or into the face of this fine philosophy? Here then is the real problem, the real new dilemma between rights of American citizens and racial pride, which faces American Negroes today and which is not always or often clearly faced.

The situation is this: America, in denying equality of rights, of employment and social recognition to American Negroes, has said in the past that the Negro was so far below the average nation in social position, that he could not be recognized until he had developed further. In the answer to this, the Negro has eliminated five-sixths of his illiteracy according to official figures, and greatly increased the number of colored persons who have received education of the higher sort. They still are poor with a large number of delinquents and dependents. Nevertheless, their average situation in this respect has been greatly improved and, on the other hand, the emergence and accomplishment of colored men of ability has been undoubted. Notwithstanding this, the Negro is still a group apart, with almost no social recognition, subject to insult and discrimination, with income and wage far below the average of the nation and the most deliberately exploited industrial class in America. Even trained Negroes have increasing difficulty in making a living sufficient to sustain a civilized standard of life. Particularly in the recent vast economic changes, color discrimination as it now goes on, is going to make it increasingly difficult for the Negro to remain an integral part of the industrial machine or to increase his participation in accordance with his ability.

The integration of industry is making it more and more possible for executives to exercise their judgment in choosing for key positions, persons who can guide the industrial machine, and the exclusion of persons from such positions merely on the basis of race and color or even Negro descent is a widely recognized and easily defended prerogative. All that is necessary for any Christian American gentleman of high position and wide power to say in denying place and promotion to an eligible candidate is: "He is of Negro descent." The answer and excuse is final and all but universally accepted. For this reason, the Negro's opportunity in State directed industry and his opportunity in the great private organization of industry if not actually growing less, is certainly much smaller than his growth in education and ability. Either the industry of the nation in the future is to be conducted by private trusts or by government control. There seems in both to be little or no chance of advancement for the Negro worker, the educated artisan and the educated leader.

On the other hand, organized labor is giving Negroes less recognition today than ever. It has practically excluded them from all the higher lines of skilled work, on railroads, in machine-shops, in manufacture and in the basic industries. In agriculture, where the Negro has theoretically the largest opportunity, he is excluded from successful participation, not only by conditions common to all farmers, but by special conditions due to lynching, lawlessness, disfranchisement and social degradation.

Facing these indisputable facts, there is on the part of the leaders of public opinion in America, no effective response to our agitation or organized propaganda. Our advance in the last quarter century has been in segregated, racially integrated institutions and efforts and not in effective entrance into American national life. In Negro churches, Negro schools, Negro colleges, Negro business and Negro art and literature our advance has been determined and inspiring; but in industry, general professional careers and national life, we have fought battle after battle and lost more often than we have won. There seems no hope that America in our day will yield in its color or race hatred any substantial ground and we have no physical nor economic power, nor any alliance with other social or economic classes that will force compliance with decent civilized ideals in Church, State, industry or art.

The next step, then, is certainly one on the part of the Negro and it involves group action. It involves the organization of intelligent and earnest people of Negro descent for their preservation and advancement in America, in the West Indies and in Africa; and no sentimental distaste for racial or national unity can be allowed to hold them back from a step which sheer necessity demands.

A new organized group action along economic lines, guided by intelligence and with the express object of making it possible for Negroes to earn a better living and, therefore, more effectively to support agencies for social uplift, is without the slightest doubt the next step. It will involve no opposition from white America because they do not believe we can accomplish it. They expect always to be able to crush, insult, ignore and exploit 12,000,000 individual Negroes without intelligent organized opposition. This organization is going to involve deliberate propaganda for race pride. That is, it is going to start out by convincing American Negroes that there is no reason for their being ashamed of themselves; that their record is one which should make them proud; that their history in Africa and the world is a history of effort, success and trial, comparable with that of any other people.

Such measured statements can, and will be exaggerated. There will be those who will want to say that the black race is the first and greatest of races, that its accomplishments are most extraordinary, that its desert is most obvious and its mistakes negligible. This is the kind of talk we hear from people with the superiority complex among the white and the yellow race.

We cannot entirely escape it, since it is just as true, and just as false as such statements among other races; but we can use intelligence in modifying and restraining it. We can refuse deliberately to lie about our history, while at the same time taking just pride in Nefertari, Askia, Moshesh, Toussaint and Frederick Douglass, and testing and encouraging belief in our own ability by organized economic and social action.

There is no other way; let us not be deceived. American Negroes will be beaten into submission and degradation if they merely wait unorganized to find some place voluntarily given them in the new reconstruction of the economic world. They must themselves force their race into the new economic set-up and bring with them the millions of West Indians and Africans by peaceful organization for normative action or else drift into greater poverty, greater crime, greater helplessness until there is no resort but the last red alternative of revolt, revenge and war.

The Crisis, September 1933

The Propaganda of History

How the facts of American history have in the last half century been falsified because the nation was ashamed. The South was ashamed because it fought to perpetuate human slavery. The North was ashamed because it had to call in the black men to save the Union, abolish slavery and establish democracy

WHAT ARE American children taught today about Reconstruction? Helen Boardman has made a study of current textbooks and notes these three dominant theses:

1. *All Negroes were ignorant.*

"All were ignorant of public business." (Woodburn and Moran, "Elementary American History and Government," p. 397.)

"Although the Negroes were now free, they were also ignorant and unfit to govern themselves." (Everett Barnes, "American History for Grammar Grades," p. 334.)

"The Negroes got control of these states. They had been slaves all their lives, and were so ignorant they did not even know the letters of the alphabet. Yet they now sat in the state legislatures and made the laws." (D. H. Montgomery, "The Leading Facts of American History," p. 332.)

"In the South, the Negroes who had so suddenly gained their freedom did not know what to do with it." (Hubert Cornish and Thomas Hughes, "History of the United States for Schools," p. 345.)

"In the legislatures, the Negroes were so ignorant that they could only watch their white leaders—carpetbaggers, and vote aye or no as they were told." (S. E. Forman, "Advanced American History," Revised Edition, p. 452.)

"Some legislatures were made up of a few dishonest white men and several Negroes, many too ignorant to know anything about law-making." (Hubert Cornish and Thomas Hughes, "History of the United States for Schools," p. 349.)

2. *All Negroes were lazy, dishonest and extravagant.*

"These men knew not only nothing about the government, but also cared for nothing except what they could gain for themselves." (Helen F. Giles, "How the United States Became a World Power," p. 7.)

"Legislatures were often at the mercy of Negroes, childishly ignorant, who sold their votes openly, and whose 'loyalty' was gained by allowing them to eat, drink and clothe themselves at the state's expense." (William J. Long, "America—A History of Our Country," p. 392.)

"Some Negroes spent their money foolishly, and were worse off than they had been before." (Carl Russell Fish, "History of America," p. 385.)

"This assistance led many freed men to believe that they need no longer work. They also ignorantly believed that the lands of their former masters were to be turned over by Congress to them, and that every Negro was to have as his allotment 'forty acres and a mule.'" (W. F. Gordy, "History of the United States," Part II, p. 336.)

"Thinking that slavery meant toil and that freedom meant only idleness, the slave after he was set free was disposed to try out his freedom by refusing to work." (S. E. Forman, "Advanced American History," Revised Edition.)

"They began to wander about, stealing and plundering. In one week, in a Georgia town, 150 Negroes were arrested for thieving." (Helen F. Giles,"How the United States Became a World Power," p. 6.)

3. *Negroes were responsible for bad government during Reconstruction*:

"Foolish laws were passed by the black law-makers, the public money was wasted terribly and thousands of dollars were stolen straight. Self-respecting Southerners chafed under the horrible régime." (Emerson David Fite, "These United States," p. 37.)

"In the exhausted states already amply 'punished' by the desolation of war, the rule of the Negro and his unscrupulous carpetbagger and scalawag patrons, was an orgy of extravagance, fraud and disgusting incompetency." (David Saville Muzzey, "History of the American People," p. 408.)

"The picture of Reconstruction which the average pupil in these sixteen States receives is limited to the South. The South found it necessary to pass Black-Codes for the control of the shiftless and sometimes vicious freedmen. The Freedmen's Bureau caused the Negroes to look to the North rather than to the South for support and by giving them a false sense of equality did more harm than good. With the scalawags, the ignorant and non-propertyholding Negroes under the leadership of the carpetbaggers, engaged in a wild orgy of spending in the legislatures. The humiliation and distress of the Southern whites was in part relieved by the Ku Klux Klan, a secret organization which frightened the superstitious blacks."[1]

Grounded in such elementary and high school teaching, an American youth attending college today would learn from current textbooks of history that the Constitution recognized slavery; that the chance of getting rid of slavery by peaceful methods was ruined by the Abolitionists; that after the period of Andrew Jackson, the two sections of the United States "had become fully conscious of their conflicting interests. Two irreconcilable forms of civilization . . . in the North, the democratic . . . in the South, a more stationary and aristocratic civilization." He would read that Harriet Beecher Stowe brought on the Civil War; that the assault on Charles Sumner was due to his "coarse invective" against a South Carolina Senator; and that Negroes were the only people to achieve emancipation with no effort on their part. That Reconstruction was a disgraceful attempt to subject white people to ignorant Negro rule; and that, according to a Harvard professor of history (the italics are ours), "Legislative expenses were grotesquely extravagant; the *colored members in some states engaging in a saturnalia of corrupt expenditure*" (Encyclopaedia Britannica, 14th Edition, Volume 22, p. 815, by Frederick Jackson Turner).

In other words, he would in all probability complete his education without any idea of the part which the black race has played in America; of the tremendous moral problem of abolition; of the cause and meaning of the Civil War and the relation which Reconstruction had to democratic government and the labor movement today.

Herein lies more than mere omission and difference of emphasis. The treatment of the period of Reconstruction reflects small credit upon American historians as scientists. We have too often a deliberate attempt so to change the facts of history

[1]"Racial Attitudes in American History Textbooks," *Journal of Negro History*, XIX, p. 257.

that the story will make pleasant reading for Americans. The editors of the fourteenth edition of the Encyclopaedia Britannica asked me for an article on the history of the American Negro. From my manuscript they cut out all my references to Reconstruction. I insisted on including the following statement:

"White historians have ascribed the faults and failures of Reconstruction to Negro ignorance and corruption. But the Negro insists that it was Negro loyalty and the Negro vote alone that restored the South to the Union; established the new democracy, both for white and black, and instituted the public schools."

This the editor refused to print, although he said that the article otherwise was "in my judgment, and in the judgment of others in the office, an excellent one, and one with which it seems to me we may all be well satisfied." I was not satisfied and refused to allow the article to appear.

War and especially civil strife leave terrible wounds. It is the duty of humanity to heal them. It was therefore soon conceived as neither wise not patriotic to speak of all the causes of strife and the terrible results to which sectional differences in the United States had led. And so, first of all, we minimized the slavery controversy which convulsed the nation from the Missouri Compromise down to the Civil War. On top of that, we passed by Reconstruction with a phrase of regret or disgust.

But are these reasons of courtesy and philanthropy sufficient for denying Truth? If history is going to be scientific, if the record of human action is going to be set down with that accuracy and faithfulness of detail which will allow its use as a measuring rod and guidepost for the future of nations, there must be set some standards of ethics in research and interpretation.

If, on the other hand, we are going to use history for our pleasure and amusement, for inflating our national ego, and giving us a false but pleasurable sense of accomplishment, then we must give up the idea of history either as a science or as an art using the results of science, and admit frankly that we are using a version of historic fact in order to influence and educate the new generation along the way we wish.

It is propaganda like this that has led men in the past to insist that history is "lies agreed upon"; and to point out the danger in such misinformation. It is indeed extremely doubtful if any permanent benefit comes to the world through such action. Nations reel and stagger on their way; they make hideous mistakes; they commit frightful wrongs; they do great and beautiful things. And shall we not best guide humanity by telling the truth about all this, so far as the truth is ascertainable?

Here in the United States we have a clear example. It was morally wrong and economically retrogressive to build human slavery in the United States in the eighteenth century. We know that now, perfectly well; and there were many Americans North and South who knew this and said it in the eighteenth century. Today, in the face of new slavery established elsewhere in the world under other names and guises, we ought to emphasize this lesson of the past. Moreover, it is not well to be reticent in describing that past. Our histories tend to discuss American slavery so impartially, that in the end nobody seems to have done wrong and everybody was right. Slavery appears to have been thrust upon unwilling helpless America, while the South was blameless in becoming its center. The difference of development, North and South, is explained as a sort of working out of cosmic social and economic law.

One reads, for instance, Charles and Mary Beard's "Rise of American Civilization," with a confortable feeling that nothing right or wrong is involved. Manufacturing and industry develop in the North; agrarian feudalism develops in the South. They clash, as winds and waters strive, and the stronger forces develop the tremendous industrial machine that governs us so magnificently and selfishly today.

Yet in this sweeping mechanistic interpretation, there is no room for the real plot of the story, for the clear mistake and guilt of rebuilding a new slavery of the working class in the midst of a fateful experiment in democracy; for the triumph of sheer moral courage and sacrifice in the abolition crusade; and for the hurt and struggle of degraded black millions in their fight for freedom and their attempt to enter democracy. Can all this be omitted or half suppressed in a treatise that calls itself scientific?

Or, to come nearer the center and climax of this fascinating history: What was slavery in the United States? Just what did it mean to the owner and the owned? Shall we accept the conventional story of the old slave plantation and its owner's fine, aristocratic life of cultured leisure? Or shall we note slave biographies, like those of Charles Ball, Sojourner Truth, Harriet Tubman and Frederick Douglass; the careful observations of Olmsted and the indictment of Hinton Helper?

No one can read that first thin autobiography of Frederick Douglass and have left many illusions about slavery. And if truth is our object, no amount of flowery romance and the personal reminiscences of its protected beneficiaries can keep the world from knowing that slavery was a cruel, dirty, costly and inexcusable anachronism, which nearly ruined the world's greatest experiment in democracy. No serious and unbiased student can be deceived by the fairy tale of a beautiful Southern slave civilization. If those who really had opportunity to know the South before the war wrote the truth, it was a center of widespread ignorance, undeveloped resources, suppressed humanity and unrestrained passions, with whatever veneer of manners and culture that could lie above these depths.

Coming now to the Civil War, how for a moment can anyone who reads the *Congressional Globe* from 1850 to 1860, the lives of contemporary statesmen and public characters, North and South, the discourses in the newspapers and accounts of meetings and speeches, doubt that Negro slavery was the cause of the Civil War? What do we gain by evading this clear fact, and talking in vague ways about "Union" and "State Rights" and differences in civilization as the cause of that catastrophe?

Of all historic facts there can be none clearer than that for four long and fearful years the South fought to perpetuate human slavery; and that the nation which "rose so bright and fair and died so pure of stain" was one that had a perfect right to be ashamed of its birth and glad of its death. Yet one monument in North Carolina achieves the impossible by recording of Confederate soldiers: "They died fighting for liberty!"

On the other hand, consider the North and the Civil War. Why should we be deliberately false, like Woodward, in

"Meet General Grant," and represent the North as magnanimously freeing the slave without any effort on his part?

"The American Negroes are the only people in the history of the world, so far as I know, that ever became free without any effort of their own. . . .

"They had not started the war nor ended it. They twanged banjos around the railroad stations, sang melodious spirituals, and believed that some Yankee would soon come along and give each of them forty acres of land and a mule."[1]

The North went to war without the slightest idea of freeing the slave. The great majority of Northerners from Lincoln down pledged themselves to protect slavery, and they hated and harried Abolitionists. But on the other hand, the thesis which Beale tends to support that the whole North during and after the war was chiefly interested in making money, is only half true; it was abolition and belief in democracy that gained for a time the upper hand after the war and led the North in Reconstruction; business followed abolition in order to maintain the tariff, pay the bonds and defend the banks. To call this business program "the program of the North" and ignore abolition is unhistorical. In growing ascendancy for a calculable time was a great moral movement which turned the North from its economic defense of slavery and led it to Emancipation. Abolitionists attacked slavery because it was wrong and their moral battle cannot be truthfully minimized or forgotten. Nor does this fact deny that the majority of Northerners before the war were not abolitionists, that they attacked slavery only in order to win the war and enfranchised the Negro to secure this result.

One has but to read the debates in Congress and state papers from Abraham Lincoln down to know that the decisive action which ended the Civil War was the emancipation and arming of the black slave; that, as Lincoln said: "Without the military help of black freedmen, the war against the South could not have been won." The freedmen, far from being the inert recipients of freedom at the hands of philanthropists, furnished 200,000 soldiers in the Civil War who took part in

[1]W. E. Woodward, *Meet General Grant*, p. 372.

nearly 200 battles and skirmishes, and in addition perhaps 300,000 others as effective laborers and helpers. In proportion to population, more Negroes than whites fought in the Civil War. These people, withdrawn from the support of the Confederacy, with threat of the withdrawal of millions more, made the opposition of the slaveholder useless, unless they themselves freed and armed their own slaves. This was exactly what they started to do; they were only restrained by realizing that such action removed the very cause for which they began fighting. Yet one would search current American histories almost in vain to find a clear statement or even faint recognition of these perfectly well-authenticated facts.

All this is but preliminary to the kernel of the historic problem with which this book deals, and that is Reconstruction. The chorus of agreement concerning the attempt to reconstruct and organize the South after the Civil War and emancipation is overwhelming. There is scarce a child in the street that cannot tell you that the whole effort was a hideous mistake and an unfortunate incident, based on ignorance, revenge and the perverse determination to attempt the impossible; that the history of the United States from 1866 to 1876 is something of which the nation ought to be ashamed and which did more to retard and set back the American Negro than anything that has happened to him; while at the same time it grievously and wantonly wounded again a part of the nation already hurt to death.

True it is that the Northern historians writing just after the war had scant sympathy for the South, and wrote ruthlessly of "rebels" and "slave-drivers." They had at least the excuse of a war psychosis.

As a young labor leader, Will Herberg, writes: "The great traditions of this period and especially of Reconstruction are shamelessly repudiated by the official heirs of Stevens and Sumner. In the last quarter of a century hardly a single book has appeared consistently championing or sympathetically interpreting the great ideals of the crusade against slavery, whereas scores and hundreds have dropped from the presses in ignoble 'extenuation' of the North, in open apology for the Confederacy, in measureless abuse of the Radical figures of Reconstruction. The Reconstruction period as the logical culmination of decades of previous development, has borne the brunt of the reaction."[1]

First of all, we have James Ford Rhodes' history of the United States. Rhodes was trained not as an historian but as an Ohio business man. He had no broad formal education. When he had accumulated a fortune, he surrounded himself with a retinue of clerks and proceeded to manufacture a history of the United States by mass production. His method was simple. He gathered a vast number of authorities; he selected from these authorities those whose testimony supported his thesis, and he discarded the others. The majority report of the great Ku Klux investigation, for instance, he laid aside in favor of the minority report, simply because the latter supported his sincere belief. In the report and testimony of the Reconstruction Committee of Fifteen, he did practically the same thing.

Above all, he begins his inquiry convinced, without admitting any necessity of investigation, that Negroes are an inferior race:

"No large policy in our country has ever been so conspicuous a failure as that of forcing universal Negro suffrage upon the South. The Negroes who simply acted out their nature, were not to blame. How indeed could they acquire political honesty? What idea could barbarism thrust into slavery obtain of the rights of property? . . .

"From the Republican policy came no real good to the Negroes. Most of them developed no political capacity, and the few who raised themselves above the mass, did not reach a high order of intelligence."[2]

Rhodes was primarily the historian of property; of economic history and the labor movement, he knew nothing; of democratic government, he was contemptuous. He was trained to make profits. He used his profits to write history. He speaks again and again of the rulership of "intelligence and property" and he makes a plea that intelligent use of the ballot for the benefit of property is the only real foundation of democracy.

The real frontal attack on Reconstruction, as interpreted by

[1]Will Herberg, *The Heritage of the Civil War*, p. 3.

[2]Rhodes, *History of the United States*, VII, pp. 232–233.

the leaders of national thought in 1870 and for some time thereafter, came from the universities and particularly from Columbia and Johns Hopkins.

The movement began with Columbia University and with the advent of John W. Burgess of Tennessee and William A. Dunning of New Jersey as professors of political science and history.

Burgess was an ex-Confederate soldier who started to a little Southern college with a box of books, a box of tallow candles and a Negro boy; and his attitude toward the Negro race in after years was subtly colored by this early conception of Negroes as essentially property like books and candles. Dunning was a kindly and impressive professor who was deeply influenced by a growing group of young Southern students and began with them to re-write the history of the nation from 1860 to 1880, in more or less conscious opposition to the classic interpretations of New England.

Burgess was frank and determined in his anti-Negro thought. He expounded his theory of Nordic supremacy which colored all his political theories:

"The claim that there is nothing in the color of the skin from the point of view of political ethics is a great sophism. A black skin means membership in a race of men which has never of itself succeeded in subjecting passion to reason, has never, therefore, created any civilization of any kind. To put such a race of men in possession of a 'state' government in a system of federal government is to trust them with the development of political and legal civilization upon the most important subjects of human life, and to do this in communities with a large white population is simply to establish barbarism in power over civilization."

Burgess is a Tory and open apostle of reaction. He tells us that the nation now believes "that it is the white man's mission, his duty and his right, to hold the reins of political power in his own hands for the civilization of the world and the welfare of mankind."[1]

For this reason America is following "the European idea of the duty of civilized races to impose their political sovereignty

[1]Burgess, *Reconstruction and the Constitution*, pp. viii, ix.

upon civilized, or half civilized, or not fully civilized, races anywhere and everywhere in the world."[1]

He complacently believes that "There is something natural in the subordination of an inferior race to a superior race, even to the point of the enslavement of the inferior race, but there is nothing natural in the opposite."[2] He therefore denominates Reconstruction as the rule "of the uncivilized Negroes over the whites of the South."[3] This has been the teaching of one of our greatest universities for nearly fifty years.

Dunning was less dogmatic as a writer, and his own statements are often judicious. But even Dunning can declare that "all the forces [in the South] that made for civilization were dominated by a mass of barbarous freedmen"; and that "the antithesis and antipathy of race and color were crucial and ineradicable."[4] The work of most of the students whom he taught and encouraged has been one-sided and partisan to the last degree. Johns Hopkins University has issued a series of studies similar to Columbia's; Southern teachers have been welcomed to many Northern universities, where often Negro students have been systematically discouraged, and thus a nation-wide university attitude has arisen by which propaganda against the Negro has been carried on unquestioned.

The Columbia school of historians and social investigators have issued between 1895 and the present time sixteen studies of Reconstruction in the Southern States, all based on the same thesis and all done according to the same method: first, endless sympathy with the white South; second, ridicule, contempt or silence for the Negro; third, a judicial attitude towards the North, which concludes that the North under great misapprehension did a grievous wrong, but eventually saw its mistake and retreated.

These studies vary, of course, in their methods. Dunning's own work is usually silent so far as the Negro is concerned. Burgess is more than fair in law but reactionary in matters of race and property, regarding the treatment of a Negro as a

[1]Burgess, *Reconstruction and the Constitution*, p. 218.

[2]Ibid., pp. 244–245.

[3]Ibid., p. 218.

[4]Dunning, *Reconstruction, Political and Economic*, pp. 212, 213.

man as nothing less than a crime, and admitting that "the mainstay of property is the courts."

In the books on Reconstruction written by graduates of these universities and others, the studies of Texas, North Carolina, Florida, Virginia and Louisiana are thoroughly bad, giving no complete picture of what happened during Reconstruction, written for the most part by men and women without broad historical or social background, and all designed not to seek the truth but to prove a thesis. Hamilton reaches the climax of this school when he characterizes the black codes, which even Burgess condemned, as "not only . . . on the whole reasonable, temperate and kindly, but, in the main, necessary."[1]

Thompson's "Georgia" is another case in point. It seeks to be fair, but silly stories about Negroes indicating utter lack of even common sense are included, and every noble sentiment from white people. When two Negro workers, William and Jim, put a straightforward advertisement in a local paper, the author says that it was "evidently written by a white friend." There is not the slightest historical evidence to prove this, and there were plenty of educated Negroes in Augusta at the time who might have written this. Lonn's "Louisiana" puts Sheridan's words in Sherman's mouth to prove a petty point.

There are certain of these studies which, though influenced by the same general attitude, nevertheless have more of scientific poise and cultural background. Garner's "Reconstruction in Mississippi" conceives the Negro as an integral part of the scene and treats him as a human being. With this should be bracketed the recent study of "Reconstruction in South Carolina" by Simkins and Woody. This is not as fair as Garner's, but in the midst of conventional judgment and conclusion, and reproductions of all available caricatures of Negroes, it does not hesitate to give a fair account of the Negroes and of some of their work. It gives the impression of combining in one book two antagonistic points of view, but in the clash much truth emerges.

Ficklen's "Louisiana" and the works of Fleming are anti-Negro in spirit, but, nevertheless, they have a certain fairness

[1]Hamilton, "Southern Legislation in Respect to Freedmen," in *Studies in Southern History and Politics*, p. 156.

and sense of historic honesty. Fleming's "Documentary History of Reconstruction" is done by a man who has a thesis to support, and his selection of documents supports the thesis. His study of Alabama is pure propaganda.

Next come a number of books which are openly and blatantly propaganda, like Herbert's "Solid South," and the books by Pike and Reynolds on South Carolina, the works by Pollard and Carpenter, and especially those by Ulrich Phillips. One of the latest and most popular of this series is "The Tragic Era" by Claude Bowers, which is an excellent and readable piece of current newspaper reporting, absolutely devoid of historical judgment or sociological knowledge. It is a classic example of historical propaganda of the cheaper sort.

We have books like Milton's "Age of Hate" and Winston's "Andrew Johnson" which attempt to re-write the character of Andrew Johnson. They certainly add to our knowledge of the man and our sympathy for his weakness. But they cannot, for students, change the calm testimony of unshaken historical facts. Fuess' "Carl Schurz" paints the picture of this fine liberal, and yet goes out of its way to show that he was quite wrong in what he said he saw in the South.

The chief witness in Reconstruction, the emancipated slave himself, has been almost barred from court. His written Reconstruction record has been largely destroyed and nearly always neglected. Only three or four states have preserved the debates in the Reconstruction conventions; there are few biographies of black leaders. The Negro is refused a hearing because he was poor and ignorant. It is therefore assumed that all Negroes in Reconstruction were ignorant and silly and that therefore a history of Reconstruction in any state can quite ignore him. The result is that most unfair caricatures of Negroes have been carefully preserved; but serious speeches, successful administration and upright character are almost universally ignored and forgotten. Wherever a black head rises to historic view, it is promptly slain by an adjective—"shrewd," "notorious," "cunning"—or pilloried by a sneer; or put out of view by some quite unproven charge of bad moral character. In other words, every effort has been made to treat the Negro's part in Reconstruction with silence and contempt.

When recently a student tried to write on education in

Florida, he found that the official records of the excellent administration of the colored Superintendent of Education, Gibbs, who virtually established the Florida public school, had been destroyed. Alabama has tried to obliterate all printed records of Reconstruction.

Especially noticeable is the fact that little attempt has been made to trace carefully the rise and economic development of the poor whites and their relation to the planters and to Negro labor after the war. There were five million or more non-slaveholding whites in the South in 1860 and less than two million in the families of all slaveholders. Yet one might almost gather from contemporary history that the five million left no history and had no descendants. The extraordinary history of the rise and triumph of the poor whites has been largely neglected, even by Southern white students.[1]

The whole development of Reconstruction was primarily an economic development, but no economic history or proper material for it has been written. It has been regarded as a purely political matter, and of politics most naturally divorced from industry.[2]

All this is reflected in the textbooks of the day and in the encyclopedias, until we have got to the place where we cannot use our experiences during and after the Civil War for the uplift and enlightenment of mankind. We have spoiled and misconceived the position of the historian. If we are going, in the future, not simply with regard to this one question, but with regard to all social problems, to be able to use human experience for the guidance of mankind, we have got clearly to distinguish between fact and desire.

In the first place, somebody in each era must make clear the facts with utter disregard to his own wish and desire and belief. What we have got to know, so far as possible, are the things that actually happened in the world. Then with that much clear and open to every reader, the philosopher and prophet has a chance to interpret these facts; but the historian has no right, posing as scientist, to conceal or distort facts; and until we distinguish between these two functions of the

[1]Interesting exceptions are Moore's and Ambler's monographs.

[2]*The Economic History of the South* by E. Q. Hawk is merely a compilation of census reports and conventionalities.

chronicler of human action, we are going to render it easy for a muddled world out of sheer ignorance to make the same mistake ten times over.

One is astonished in the study of history at the recurrence of the idea that evil must be forgotten, distorted, skimmed over. We must not remember that Daniel Webster got drunk but only remember that he was a splendid constitutional lawyer. We must forget that George Washington was a slave owner, or that Thomas Jefferson had mulatto children, or that Alexander Hamilton had Negro blood, and simply remember the things we regard as creditable and inspiring. The difficulty, of course, with this philosophy is that history loses its value as an incentive and example; it paints perfect men and noble nations, but it does not tell the truth.

No one reading the history of the United States during 1850–1860 can have the slightest doubt left in his mind that Negro slavery was the cause of the Civil War, and yet during and since we learn that a great nation murdered thousands and destroyed millions on account of abstract doctrines concerning the nature of the Federal Union. Since the attitude of the nation concerning state rights has been revolutionized by the development of the central government since the war, the whole argument becomes an astonishing *reductio ad absurdum*, leaving us apparently with no cause for the Civil War except the recent reiteration of statements which make the great public men on one side narrow, hypocritical fanatics and liars, while the leaders on the other side were extraordinary and unexampled for their beauty, unselfishness and fairness.

Not a single great leader of the nation during the Civil War and Reconstruction has escaped attack and libel. The magnificent figures of Charles Sumner and Thaddeus Stevens have been besmirched almost beyond recognition. We have been cajoling and flattering the South and slurring the North, because the South is determined to re-write the history of slavery and the North is not interested in history but in wealth.

This, then, is the book basis upon which today we judge Reconstruction. In order to paint the South as a martyr to inescapable fate, to make the North the magnanimous emancipator, and to ridicule the Negro as the impossible joke in the whole development, we have in fifty years, by libel, innuendo and silence, so completely misstated and obliterated the history of the Negro in America and his relation to its work and government that today it is almost unknown. This may be fine romance, but it is not science. It may be inspiring, but it is certainly not the truth. And beyond this it is dangerous. It is not only part foundation of our present lawlessness and loss of democratic ideals; it has, more than that, led the world to embrace and worship the color bar as social salvation and it is helping to range mankind in ranks of mutual hatred and contempt, at the summons of a cheap and false myth.

Nearly all recent books on Reconstruction agree with each other in discarding the government reports and substituting selected diaries, letters, and gossip. Yet it happens that the government records are an historic source of wide and unrivaled authenticity. There is the report of the select Committee of Fifteen, which delved painstakingly into the situation all over the South and called all kinds and conditions of men to testify; there are the report of Carl Schurz and the twelve volumes of reports made on the Ku Klux conspiracy; and above all, the *Congressional Globe*. None who has not read page by page the *Congressional Globe*, especially the sessions of the 39th Congress, can possibly have any idea of what the problems of Reconstruction facing the United States were in 1865–1866. Then there were the reports of the Freedmen's Bureau and the executive and other documentary reports of government officials, expecially in the war and treasury departments, which give the historian the only groundwork upon which he can build a real and truthful picture. There are certain historians who have not tried deliberately to falsify the picture: Southern whites like Frances Butler Leigh and Susan Smedes; Northern historians, like McPherson, Oberholtzer, and Nicolay and Hay. There are foreign travelers like Sir George Campbell, Georges Clemenceau and Robert Somers. There are the personal reminiscences of Augustus Beard, George Julian, George F. Hoar, Carl Schurz and John Sherman. There are the invaluable work of Edward McPherson and the more recent studies by Paul Haworth, A. A. Taylor, and Charles Wesley. Beale simply does not take Negroes into account in the critical year of 1866.

Certain monographs deserve all praise, like those of

Kendrick and Pierce. The work of Flack is prejudiced but built on study. The defense of the carpetbag régime by Tourgée and Allen, Powell Clayton, Holden and Warmoth are worthy antidotes to the certain writers.

The lives of Stevens and Sumner are revealing even when slightly apologetic because of the Negro; while Andrew Johnson is beginning to suffer from writers who are trying to prove how seldom he got drunk, and think that important.

It will be noted that for my authority in this work I have depended very largely upon secondary material; upon state histories of Reconstruction, written in the main by those who were convinced before they began to write that the Negro was incapable of government, or of becoming a constituent part of a civilized state. The fairest of these histories have not tried to conceal facts; in other cases, the black man has been largely ignored; while in still others, he has been traduced and ridiculed. If I had had time and money and opportunity to go back to the original sources in all cases, there can be no doubt that the weight of this work would have been vastly strengthened, and as I firmly believe, the case of the Negro more convincingly set forth.

Various volumes of papers in the great libraries like the Johnson papers in the Library of Congress, the Sumner manuscripts at Harvard, the Schurz correspondence, the Wells papers, the Chase papers, the Fessenden and Greeley collections, the McCulloch, McPherson, Sherman, Stevens and Trumbull papers, all must have much of great interest to the historians of the American Negro. I have not had time nor opportunity to examine these, and most of those who have examined them had little interest in black folk.

Negroes have done some excellent work on their own history and defense. It suffers of course from natural partisanship and a desire to prove a case in the face of a chorus of unfair attacks. Its best work also suffers from the fact that Negroes with difficulty reach an audience. But this is also true of such white writers as Skaggs and Bancroft who could not get first-class publishers because they were saying something that the nation did not like.

The Negro historians began with autobiographies and reminiscences. The older historians were George W. Williams and

Joseph T. Wilson; the new school of historians is led by Carter G. Woodson; and I have been greatly helped by the unpublished theses of four of the youngest Negro students. It is most unfortunate that while many young white Southerners can get funds to attack and ridicule the Negro and his friends, it is almost impossible for first-class Negro students to get a chance for research or to get finished work in print.

I write then in a field devastated by passion and belief. Naturally, as a Negro, I cannot do this writing without believing in the essential humanity of Negroes, in their ability to be educated, to do the work of the modern world, to take their place as equal citizens with others. I cannot for a moment subscribe to that bizarre doctrine of race that makes most men inferior to the few. But, too, as a student of science, I want to be fair, objective and judicial; to let no searing of the memory by intolerable insult and cruelty make me fail to sympathize with human frailties and contradiction, in the eternal paradox of good and evil. But armed and warned by all this, and fortified by long study of the facts, I stand at the end of this writing, literally aghast at what American historians have done to this field.

What is the object of writing the history of Reconstruction? Is it to wipe out the disgrace of a people which fought to make slaves of Negroes? Is it to show that the North had higher motives than freeing black men? Is it to prove that Negroes were black angels? No, it is simply to establish the Truth, on which Right in the future may be built. We shall never have a science of history until we have in our colleges men who regard the truth as more important than the defense of the white race, and who will not deliberately encourage students to gather thesis material in order to support a prejudice or buttress a lie.

Three-fourths of the testimony against the Negro in Reconstruction is on the unsupported evidence of men who hated and despised Negroes and regarded it as loyalty to blood, partriotism to country, and filial tribute to the fathers to lie, steal or kill in order to discredit these black folk. This may be a natural result when a people have been humbled and impoverished and degraded in their own life; but what is inconceivable is that another generation and another group should regard this testimony as scientific truth, when it is contradicted by logic and by fact. This chapter, therefore, which in logic should be a survey of books and sources, becomes of sheer necessity an arraignment of American historians and an indictment of their ideals. With a determination unparalleled in science, the mass of American writers have started out so to distort the facts of the greatest critical period of American history as to prove right wrong and wrong right. I am not familiar enough with the vast field of human history to pronounce on the relative guilt of these and historians of other times and fields; but I do say that if the history of the past has been written in the same fashion, it is useless as science and misleading as ethics. It simply shows that with sufficient general agreement and determination among the dominant classes, the truth of history may be utterly distorted and contradicted and changed to any convenient fairy tale that the masters of men wish.

I cannot believe that any unbiased mind, with an ideal of truth and of scientific judgment, can read the plain, authentic facts of our history, during 1860–1880, and come to conclusions essentially different from mine; and yet I stand virtually alone in this interpretation. So much so that the very cogency of my facts would make me hesitate, did I not seem to see plain reasons. Subtract from Burgess his belief that only white people can rule, and he is in essential agreement with me. Remember that Rhodes was an uneducated money-maker who hired clerks to find the facts which he needed to support his thesis, and one is convinced that the same labor and expense could easily produce quite opposite results.

One fact and one alone explains the attitude of most recent writers toward Reconstruction; they cannot conceive Negroes as men; in their minds the word "Negro" connotes "inferiority" and "stupidity" lightened only by unreasoning gayety and humor. Suppose the slaves of 1860 had been white folk. Stevens would have been a great statesman, Sumner a great democrat, and Schurz a keen prophet, in a mighty revolution of rising humanity. Ignorance and poverty would easily have been explained by history, and the demand for land and the franchise would have been justified as the birthright of natural freemen.

But Burgess was a slaveholder, Dunning a Copperhead and Rhodes an exploiter of wage labor. Not one of them apparently ever met an educated Negro of force and ability. Around such impressive thinkers gathered the young post-war students from the South. They had been born and reared in the bitterest period of Southern race hatred, fear and contempt. Their instinctive reactions were confirmed and encouraged in the best of American universities. Their scholarship, when it regarded black men, became deaf, dumb and blind. The clearest evidence of Negro ability, work, honesty, patience, learning and efficiency became distorted into cunning, brute toil, shrewd evasion, cowardice and imitation—a stupid effort to transcend nature's law.

For those seven mystic years between Johnson's "swing 'round the circle" and the panic of 1873, a majority of thinking Americans in the North believed in the equal manhood of black folk. They acted accordingly with a clear-cut decisiveness and thorough logic, utterly incomprehensible to a day like ours which does not share this human faith; and to Southern whites this period can only be explained by deliberate vengeance and hate.

The panic of 1873 brought sudden disillusion in business enterprise, economic organization, religious belief and political standards. A flood of appeal from the white South reënforced this reaction—appeal with no longer the arrogant bluster of slave oligarchy, but the simple moving annals of the plight of a conquered people. The resulting emotional and intellectual rebound of the nation made it nearly inconceivable in 1876 that ten years earlier most men had believed in human equality.

Assuming, therefore, as axiomatic the endless inferiority of the Negro race, these newer historians, mostly Southerners, some Northerners who deeply sympathized with the South, misinterpreted, distorted, even deliberately ignored any fact that challenged or contradicted this assumption. If the Negro was admittedly sub-human, what need to waste time delving into his Reconstruction history? Consequently historians of Reconstruction with a few exceptions ignore the Negro as completely as possible, leaving the reader wondering why an element apparently so insignificant filled the whole Southern picture at the time. The only real excuse for this attitude is loyalty to a lost cause, reverence for brave fathers and suffering mothers and sisters, and fidelity to the ideals of a clan and class. But in propaganda against the Negro since emancipation in this land, we face one of the most stupendous efforts the world ever saw to discredit human beings, an effort involving universities, history, science, social life and religion.

The most magnificent drama in the last thousand years of human history is the transportation of ten million human beings out of the dark beauty of their mother continent into the new-found Eldorado of the West. They descended into Hell; and in the third century they arose from the dead, in the finest effort to achieve democracy for the working millions which this world had ever seen. It was a tragedy that beggared the Greek; it was an upheaval of humanity like the Reformation and the French Revolution. Yet we are blind and led by the blind. We discern in it no part of our labor movement; no part of our industrial triumph; no part of our religious experience. Before the dumb eyes of ten generations of ten million children, it is made mockery of and spit upon; a degradation of the eternal mother; a sneer at human effort; with aspiration and art deliberately and elaborately distorted. And why? Because in a day when the human mind aspired to a science of human action, a history and psychology of the mighty effort of the mightiest century, we fell under the leadership of those who would compromise with truth in the past in order to make peace in the present and guide policy in the future.

One reads the truer deeper facts of Reconstruction with a great despair. It is at once so simple and human, and yet so futile. There is no villain, no idiot, no saint. There are just men; men who crave ease and power, men who know want and hunger, men who have crawled. They all dream and strive with ecstasy of fear and strain of effort, balked of hope and hate. Yet the rich world is wide enough for all, wants all, needs all. So slight a gesture, a word, might set the strife in order, not with full content, but with growing dawn of fulfillment. Instead roars the crash of hell; and after its whirlwind a teacher sits in academic halls, learned in the tradition of its elms and its elders. He looks into the upturned face of youth and in him youth sees the gowned shape of wisdom and hears the voice of God. Cynically he sneers at "chinks" and "niggers." He says that the nation "has changed its views in regard to the political relation of races and has at last virtually accepted the ideas of the South upon that subject. The white men of the South need now have no further fear that the Republican party, or Republican Administrations, will ever again give themselves over to the vain imagination of the political equality of man."[1]

Immediately in Africa, a black back runs red with the blood of the lash; in India, a brown girl is raped; in China, a coolie starves; in Alabama, seven darkies are more than lynched; while in London, the white limbs of a prostitute are hung with jewels and silk. Flames of jealous murder sweep the earth, while brains of little children smear the hills.

This is education in the Nineteen Hundred and Thirty-fifth year of the Christ; this is modern and exact social science; this is the university course in "History 12" set down by the Senatus academicus; ad quos hae literae pervenerint: Salutem in Domino, sempeternam!

In Babylon, dark Babylon
  Who take the wage of Shame?
The scribe and singer, one by one,
  That toil for gold and fame.
They grovel to their masters' mood;
  The blood upon the pen
Assigns their souls to servitude—
  Yea! and the souls of men.

GEORGE STERLING

[1]Burgess, *Reconstruction and the Constitution*, p. 298.

Black Reconstruction, 1935

The Revelation of Saint Orgne the Damned

SAINT ORGNE stood facing the morning and asked: What is this life I see? Is the dark damnation of color, real? or simply mine own imagining? Can it be true that souls wrapped in black velvet have a destiny different from those swathed in white satin or yellow silk, when all these covering are fruit of the same worm, and threaded by the same hands? Or must I, ignoring all seeming difference, rise to some upper realm where there is no color nor race, sex, wealth nor age, but all men stand equal in the Sun?

Thus Orgne questioned Life on his Commencement morning, in the full springtide of his day. And this is the Revelation and the answer that came to Saint Orgne the Damned as he came to be called, as he stood on his Mount of Transfiguration, looking full at life as it is and not as it might be or haply as he would have it.

"In very truth, thou art damned, and may not escape by vain imagining nor fruitless repining. When a man faces evil, he does not call it good, nor evade it; he meets it breast-forward, with no whimper of regret nor fear of foe."

"Blessed is he that reads and they that hear the words of this prophecy for the time is at hand. Grace be unto you and peace, from him which was and which is and is to come and from the seven spirits which are before his throne."

I, who also am your brother and companion in tribulation and in the kingdom and the patience, was in the isle that is called America. I was in the spirit and heard behind me a great Voice saying, "I am Alpha and Omega, the first and the last; and what thou seest write." I turned to the voice. I saw seven golden candlesticks with one in the midst of the candlesticks; and in his hands seven stars and out of his mouth went a sharp two edged sword. And when I saw him I fell at his feet as dead and he laid his right hand upon me saying unto me "Fear not. Write thou the things which thou has seen; the mystery of the seven stars and the seven golden candlesticks."

So Orgne turned and climbed the Seven Heights of Hell to view the Seven Stars of Heaven. The seven heights are Birth and Family; School and Learning; the University and Wisdom;

the great snow-capped peak of Work; the naked crag of Right and Wrong; the rolling hills of the Freedom of Art and Beauty; and at last, the plateau that is the Democracy of Race; beyond this there are no vales of Gloom—for the star above is the sun itself and all shadows fall straight before it.

Orgne descended into the valleys of the Shadow, lit only by the waving light of single candles set in seven golden candlesticks, struggling through noisome refuse of body and mind. Long years he strove, uphill and down, around and through seven groups of seven years until in the end he came back to the beginning, world-weary, but staunch; and this is the revelation of his life and thought which I, his disciple, bring you from his own hands.

A golden candlestick stood beneath a silver star, atop a high mountain and in the cold gray dawn of a northern spring. There was the first hint of apple blossoms and faint melody in the air; within the melody was the whisper of a Voice, which sighed and said: "Why should we breed black folk in this world and to what end? Wherefor should we found families and how? Is not the world for such as are born white and rich?"

Then Orgne, half grown, lying prone, reared himself suddenly to his feet and shivering looked upward to light. The sun rose slowly above the mountain and with its light spake. Hear ye the Wisdom of the families of black folk:

Gentlemen are bred and not born. They are trained in childhood and receive manners from those who surround them and not from their blood. Manners maketh Man, and are the essence of good breeding. They have to do with forms of salutation between civilized persons; with the care and cleanliness and grooming of the body. They avoid the stink of bodily excretions; they eat their food without offense to others; they know that dirt is matter misplaced and they seek to replace it. The elementary rules of health become to them second nature and their inbred courtesy one to another makes life liveable and gracious even among crowds.

Now this breeding and infinite detail of training is not learned in college and may not be taught in school. It is the duty and task of the family group and once the infinite value of that training is missed it can seldom be replaced through any later agency. It is in vain that the university seeks to cope with ill-bred youngsters, foul-mouthed loafers and unwashed persons who have happened to pass the entrance examinations. Once in the earlier mission schools among American Negroes men tried to do this, knowing of the irreparable harm slavery had done the family group. They had some success right here in this institution; but the day when such effort is possible is gone. Unless a new type of Negro family takes the burden of this duty, we are destined to be, as we are too largely today, a bad-mannered, unclean crowd of ill-bred young men and women who are under the impression that they are educated.

For this task we have got to create a new family group; and a cultural group rather than a group merely biological. The biology and blood relationship of families is entirely subordinate and unimportant as compared with its cultural entity; with the presence of two persons who take upon themselves voluntarily the sacrificial priesthood of parents to children, limited in number and interval by intelligent and scientific birth-control, who can and will train in the elements of being civilized human beings: how to eat, how to sleep, how to wash, how to stand, how to walk, how to laugh, how to be reverent and how to obey.

It is not entirely our fault that we have missed, forgotten or are even entirely unaware of the cultural place of the family. In European and American civilization we have tried to carry out the most idiotic paradox that ever civilized folk attempted. We have tried to make babies both sins and angels. We have regarded sex as a disgrace and as eternal life. We talk in one breath of the Virgin Mary and of the Mother of God. And at the critical age of life for both men and women, we compel them to strain the last sinew of moral strength to repress a natural and beautiful appetite, or to smear it with deception and crime. We base female eligibility for marriage on exotic personal beauty and childlike innocence, and yet pretend to desire brains, common sense and strength of body. If an age thus immolates its ugly virgins, it will crucify its beautiful fools, with the result of making marriage a martyrdom that few enter with open eyes. The change from this has got to recognize the sin of virginity in a world that needs proper children; the right of the so-called unfathered child to be; the legal adoption into the cultural family of gifted and promising children and the placing of black sheep, no matter who their parents are, under necessary restraint and correction. Amen.

———

The Voice ceased. As Orgne walked slowly down the mountain, he brooded long over the word he had heard, wondering vaguely how far the revelation was within or without his own soul; and then turning the message over in his mind, he thought of his own home, of the three small rooms, of the careful, busy mother and grandmother, of the dead father; and he mused: if one's start in life depends on breeding and not on color or unchangeable and unfathomable compulsions before birth, surely I may live, even though I am black and poor.

There came a long space of Seven years. Orgne stood by the bank of the Golden River, with the second candlestick in his hand. He could not see the stars above, for it was nine o'clock of a sun-washed morning; but he knew they were there. He was celebrating all alone his entry into High School. None of his people save only his dead grandfather had ever gotten so far; but with the wave of disappointment which comes with all accomplishment, he muttered, "And why should they, why should I, dawdle here with elements of things and mere tools of Knowledge while both I and the world wait." The river flowed softly as he slept in the summer mildness. Daisies and buttercups waved above him. The grey fleecy clouds gathered and swiftly low thunder rolled; a bolt of heat lightning flashed across the sky. He slept on, yet heard the second star as it spoke:

Hear ye! This is the wisdom of the elementary school.

———

The difficulty and essential difficulty with Negro education lies in the elementary school; lies in the fact that the number of Negroes in the United States today who have learned thoroughly to read, write, and count is small; and that the proportion of those who cannot read, cannot express their thoughts and cannot understand the fundamentals of arithmetic, algebra and geometry is discouragingly large. The reason that we cannot do thorough college work and cannot keep high university standards is that the students in institutions like this are fundamentally weak in mastery of those essential tools to human learning. Not even the dumbest college professor can spoil the education of the man who as a child has learned to read, write, and cipher; so too Aristotle, Emmanuel Kant and Mark Hopkins together are powerless before the illiterate who cannot reason.

The trouble lies primarily, of course, in the elementary schools of the South; in schools with short terms; with teachers inadequate both as to numbers and training; with quarters ill-suited physically and morally to the work in hand; with colored principals chosen not for executive ability but for their agility in avoiding race problems; and with white superintendents who try to see how large a statistical showing can be made without expenditure of funds, thought nor effort.

This is the fault of a nation which does not thoroughly believe in the education of Negroes, and of the South which still to a large extent does not believe in any training for black folk which is not of direct commercial profit to those who dominate the state.

But the fault does not end there. The fault lies with the Negroes themselves for not realizing this major problem in their education and for not being willing and eager and untiring in their effort to establish the elementary school on a fundamental basis. Necessary as are laws against lynching and race segregation, we should put more money, effort, and breath in perfecting the Negro elementary school than in anything else, and not pause nor think of pausing until every Negro child between five and fifteen is getting at least nine months a year, five hours a day, five days in the week, in a modern school room, with the best trained teachers, under principals selected for training and executive ability, and serving with their teachers during efficiency and good behavior; and with the school under the control of those whose children are educated there.

Until this is done and so far as it is not done the bulk of

university endowment is being wasted and high schools strive partially in vain. Amen.

Again flew seven years. Orgne was far from home and school and land. He was speaking an unknown tongue and looking upon the walls and towers, colors and sounds of another world. It was high noon and autumn. He sat in a lofty cathedral, glorious in the fretted stone lace-work of its proudly vaulted roof. Its flying buttresses looked down upon a grey and rippled lake; beyond lay fields of flowers, golden chrysanthemums and flaming dahlias and further the ancient university, where for a thousand years men had sought Truth. Around rose a symphony of sound, a miraculous blending of strings and brass, trumpet and drum which was the Seventh Symphony with its lovely interlacing of melody and soft solemn marches, breaking to little hymns and dances. He listened to its revelation gazing rapt at candlesticks and gilded star and whispered: "Why should I know and What, and what is the end of knowing? Is it not enough to feel?" The angels in the choir sang No—Hear ye! For Wisdom is the principal thing.

There can be no iota of doubt that the chief trouble with the world and the overwhelming difficulty with American Negroes is widespread ignorance; the fact that we are not thoroughly acquainted with human history; of what men and peoples have thought and done in the seven thousand years of our cultural life. We are especially unacquainted with modern science; with the facts of matter and its constitution; with the meaning of time and space; with chemical reaction and electrical phenomena; with the history of the machine and the tool; with the unfolding of life in the vegetable and animal kingdoms; with the history of human labor; the development of our knowledge of the mind; the practical use of the languages of the world; and the methods of logical reasoning, beginning and ending with mathematics.

This great body of knowledge has been growing and developing for thousands of years, and yet today its mastery is in the hands of so few men, that a comparative small death roll would mean the end of human culture. Without this knowledge there can be no planning in economy; no substantial guidance in character building; no intelligent development of art. It is for acquaintanceship with this knowledge and the broadening of its field that the college and university exist. This is the reason and the only reason for its building among American Negroes and the work that it is accomplishing today is so infinitely less than that which with any real effort it might accomplish that one has a right to shudder at the misuse of the word university. Amen.

Orgne stood at twilight in the swamp. In seven more years, all the romance and glamour of Europe had sunk to the winter of America. It was twilight, and the swamp glowed with the mystery of sunset—long shafts of level burning light,—greens and yellows, purples and red; the whisper of leaves, the ghosts of dead and dying life. The sun died dismally, and the clouds gathered and a drizzling rain began to fall with slow determination. Orgne shrank within himself. He saw the toil of labor and revolted. He felt the pinch of poverty and wept. "What is this stuff I hear," he cried: "how can we marry and support a family without money? How can we control our schools without economic resource? How can we turn our churches from centers of superstition into intelligent building of character; and beyond this how shall we have time for real knowledge; and freedom of art; and effort toward world-wide democracy, until we have the opportunity to work decently and the resources to spend, which shall enable us to be civilized human beings?"

Suddenly across the swamp and across the world and up from the cotton fields of Georgia rolled a Negro folk song. Orgne saw in music Jehovah and his angels, the Wheel in a Wheel. He saw the Golden Candlestick and heard the revelation of the Star: Hear ye! This is the teaching of the World of Work.

The most distressing fact in the present world is poverty; not absolute poverty, because some folk are rich and many are well-to-do; not poverty as great as some lands and other historical ages have known; but poverty more poignant and discouraging because it comes after a dream of wealth; of riotous, wasteful and even vulgar accumulation of individual riches, which suddenly leaves the majority of mankind today without enough to eat; without proper shelter; without sufficient clothing.

Nowhere was the dream of wealth, for all who would work and save, more vivid than here in the United States. We Negroes sought to share that vision and heritage. Moreover, the poverty which the world now experiences, comes after a startling realization of our national endowment of rich natural resources and our power to produce. We have the material goods and forces at command, the machines and technique sufficient to feed, clothe the world, educate children and free the human soul for creative beauty and for the truth that will widen the bounds of all freedom.

That does not mean that we could have enough goods and services for present extravagance, display and waste; but if there were neither idle rich nor idle poor; if sharing of wealth were based not on owning but only on effort, and if all who are able did their share of the world's work or starved, and limited their consumption to reasonable wants, we could abolish poverty.

Why have we not done this? It is because of greed in the production and distribution of goods and human labor. We discovered widely in the 18th century and the 19th the use of capital and it was a great and beneficent discovery; it was the rule of sacrificing present wealth for greater wealth to come. But instead of distributing this increase of wealth primarily among those who make it we left most workers as poor as possible in order further to increase the wealth of a few. We produced more wealth than the wealthy could consume and yet used this increased wealth to monopolize materials and machines; to buy and sell labor in return for monopoly ownership in the products of labor and for further wealth.

We thus not only today produce primarily for the profit of owners and not for use of the mass of people, but we have grown to think that this is the only way in which we can produce. We organize industry for private wealth and not for public weal, and we argue often honestly and conscientiously, that no human planning can change the essentials of this process. Yet the process itself has failed so many times and so abysmally, that we are bound to change or starve in the midst of plenty. We are encouraging war through fear of poverty that need not exist; we face the breakdown of production by persistent overproduction of the kinds of goods which we cannot afford to consume.

What can we do? There is only one thing for civilized human beings to do when facing such a problem, and that is to learn the facts, to reason out their connection and to plan the future; to know the truth; to arrange it logically and to contrive a better way. In some way, as all intelligent men acknowledge, we must in the end, produce for the satisfaction of human needs and distribute in accordance with human want. To contend that this cannot be done is to face the Impossible Must. The blind cry of reaction on the one hand, which says that we cannot have a planned economy and, therefore, must not try; and the cry of blood which says that only by force can selfishness be curbed, are equally wrong. Is it not a question of deliberate guilt but of selfish stupidity. The economic world can only be reformed by Spartan restraint in the consumption of goods and the use of services; by the will to work not simply for individual profit but for group weal; not simply for one group but for all groups; and the freedom to dream and plan.

This reformation of the world is beginning with agony of soul and strain of muscle. It can and must go on, and we black folk of America are faced with the most difficult problem of realizing and knowing the part which we have got to play in this economic revolution for our own salvation and for the salvation of the world. This is not easy, for we are cut off from the main effort by the lesions of race; by the segregation of color; by the domination of caste. And yet nothing could be more fatal to our own ideals and the better ideals of the world than for us with unconscious ignorance or conscious perversity or momentary applause to join the forces of reaction; to talk as though the 20th century presented the same oversimplified path of economic progress which seemed the rule in the 19th: work, thrift and wealth by individual effort no matter what the social cost.

The economic illiteracy prevalent among American Negroes is discouraging. In a day when every thinker sees the disorganization of our economic life and the need of radical change, we find the teachers of economics in colored colleges, the Negro business men, Negro preachers and writers to a very large extent talking the language of the early 19th century; seeking to make themselves believe that work for any kind of wages, saving at any sacrifice and wealth on any terms not excluding cheating, murder, and theft, are ways of the world still open and beckoning to us. Selah!

Orgne listened and sat staring at the sodden cotton field beyond the somber swamp. Always the swinging thunder of song surged above—Jordan rolled; the rocks and the mountains fled away, the Way was crowded; and Moses went down, away down among the cabins in the cotton patch to the crazy church and hysterical crowd of penitents all praying madly to escape debt. Orgne talked to the planter and said "let my people go," and worked with the tenants seven long years.

Seven years he toiled and in the end had a little nest of land holders owning one large unmortgaged farm in twenty shares; working their crops and buying their provisions in common and dividing them with equal justice. Poor, Orgne came to them and poor he finally went away leaving them poor too but fed and sheltered. They called him Saint. He smiled and looked upward to the star; but the preacher looked down to the dirt and mortgaged it behind the backs of the trusting flock and ran away with the money.

Saint Orgne cursed and cried how shall we plan a new earth without honest men and what is this thing we call a church. So, angry, disillusioned and weary he came to a land where it was always afternoon, and he laid him prone on the earth and slept.

Seven years he slept and in seven years came a thousand miles and more to Ohio, to teach in college. At high noon he stood before the chapel and heard the singing of a hymn in the haze of early spring time. Around him stretched the wide, undulating valleys of the Miami, the Ohio, and the realm of the Mississippi. He looked up and suddenly hated the walls that shut out the stars; he hated the maudlin words of the hymn quite as much as he loved the lilt of the voices that raised it. He loved the flowers—the violets and morning glory, the blossoming fruit that filled the yards about. Then came the earthquake; then the earth trembled and swayed; far off in San Francisco a city fell and around the nation quivered. In the midst of the rushing, swaying crowd, again Orgne, after seven years, awoke and found the Golden Candlestick in his hands, and heard the low clear revelation of the Star:

Saint Orgne the Damned, behold the Vision of the Seven Black Churches of America,—the Baptist, the four wings of Methodism, the Roman and Episcopal Catholics.

Their five millions of members in 40,000 groups, holding $200,000,000 in their hands, are the most strongly organized body among us; the first source of our group culture, the beginning of our education—what is this church doing today toward its primary task of teaching men right and wrong, and the duty of doing right?

The flat answer is nothing if not less than nothing. Like other churches and other religions of other peoples and ages, our church has veered off on every conceivable side path, which interferes with and nullifies its chief duty of character building.

It has built up a body of dogma and fairy tale, fantastic fables of sin and salvation, impossible creeds and impossible demands for ignorant unquestioning belief and obedience. Ask any thorough churchman today and he will tell you, not that the object of the church is to get men to do right and make the majority of mankind happy, but rather that the whole duty of man is to "believe in the Lord Jesus Christ and be saved;" or to believe "that God is God and Mohammed is his prophet;" or to believe in the "one Holy and Catholic church," infallible and omniscient; or to keep the tomb of one's grandfather intact and his ideas undisputed.

Considering how desperately, great and good men have inveighed against these continuing foibles of priesthood for many thousand years, and how little in essence has been accomplished, it may seem hopeless to return to the attack today, but that is precisely what this generation has to do. The function of the Negro church, instead of being that of building edifices, paying old debts, holding revivals and staging entertainments, has got to be brought back, or shall we say forward, to the simple duty of teaching ethics. For this purpose the Hebrew scriptures and the New Testament canon will not suffice. We must stop telling children that the lying and deceitful Jacob was better than the lazy Esau, or that the plan of salvation is anything but the picture of the indecent anger and revenge of a bully.

We can do this, not so much by the attacking of outworn superstition and conventional belief as by hearty research into real ethical questions. When is it right to lie? Do low wages mean stealing? Does the prosperity of a country depend upon the number of its millionaires? Should the state kill a murderer? How much money should you give to the poor? Should there be any poor? And as long as there are, what is crime and who are the criminals?

So Saint Orgne preached the word of life from Jeremiah, Shakespeare and Jesus, Confucius, Buddha and John Brown; and organized a church with a cooperative store in the Sunday school room; with physician, dentist, nurse and lawyer to help, serve and defend the congregation; with library, nursery school, and a regular succession of paid and trained lecturers and discussion; they had radio and moving pictures and out beyond the city a farm with house and lake. They had a credit union, group insurance and building and loan association. The members paid for this not by contributions but by ten dollars a month each of regular dues and those who would join this church must do more than profess to love God.

Seven years he served and married a woman not for her hair and color but for her education, good manners, common sense and health. Together they made a home and begot two strong intelligent children. Looking one day into their eyes

Orgne became suddenly frightened for their future. He prayed "Oh life let them be free!"

———

So soon, so soon, Orgne sighed, the world rolls around its sevens of years. It was midsummer and he was sailing upon the sea. He was bound for Africa on a mission of world brotherhood. Behind and waiting were wife and children, home and work. Ahead was the darker world of men yellow, brown, and black. Dinner was done and the deck empty save for himself; all were within the magnificent saloon massed with tall vases of roses and lilies, priceless with tapestry and gilding, listening to the great organ which the master played. The largo whispered, smiled and swelled upward to tears. Then the storm swept down. Then the ocean, lashed to fury by the wind, bellowed and burned; the vast ship tossed like a tortured soul, groaned and twisted in its agony. But Orgne smiled. He knew that behind the storm and above the cloud the evening stars were singing, and he listened to the rhythm of their words: Hear Ye! This is the Freedom of Art which is the Beauty of Life.

———

Life is more than meat, even though life without food dies. Living is not for earning, earning is for living. The man that spends his life earning a living, has never lived. The education that trains men simply for earning a living is not education.

What then is Life—What is it for—What is its great End? Manifestly in the light of all knowledge, and according to the testimony of all men who have lived, Life is the fullest, most complete enjoyment of the possibilities of human existence. It is the development and broadening of the feelings and emotions, through sound and color, line and form. It is technical mastery of the media that these paths and emotions need for expression of their full meaning. It is the free enjoyment of every normal appetite. It is giving rein to the creative impulse, in thought and imagination. Here roots the rise of the Joy of Living, of music, painting, drawing, sculpture and building; hence come literature with romance, poetry, and essay; hence rise Love, Friendship, emulation, and ambition, and the ever widening realms of thought, in increasing circles of apprehended and interpreted Truth.

It is the contradiction and paradox of this day that those who seek to choke and conventionalize art, restrict and censor thought and repress imagination are demanding for their shriveled selves, freedom in precisely those lines of human activity where control and regimentation are necessary; and necessary because upon this foundation is to be built the widest conceivable freedom in a realm infinitely larger and more meaningful than the realm of economic production and distribution of wealth. The less freedom we leave for business exploitation the greater freedom we shall have for expression in art.

We have got to think of the time when poverty approaches abolition; when men no longer fear starvation and unemployment; when health is so guarded that we may normally expect to live our seventy years and more, without excess of pain and suffering. In such a world living begins; in such a world we will have freedom of thought and expression, and just as much freedom of action as maintenance of the necessary economic basis of life permits; that is, given three or six hours of work under rule and duress, we ought to be sure of at least eighteen hours of recreation, joy, and creation with a minimum of compulsion for anybody.

Freedom is the path of art, and living in the fuller and broader sense of the term is the expression of art. Yet those who speak of freedom talk usually as fools talk. So far as the laws of gravitation are concerned there can be no freedom; so far as the physical constitution of the universe is concerned, we must produce and consume goods in accordance with that which is inexorable, unmoved by sentiment or dream. But this realm of the physical need be only the smaller part of life and above it, is planning, emotion and dream; in the exercising of creative power; in building, painting and literature there is a chance for the free exercise of the human spirit, broad enough and lofty enough to satisfy every ambition of the free human soul. Limited though it be by birth and death, by time and space, by health and mysterious native gift, nevertheless its realm is so magnificent that those who fear that freedom may end with the abolition of poverty or that disease is needed to insure room on the earth or that war and murder are the only handmaids of courage are all talking utter nonsense.

The freedom to create within the limits of natural law; the freedom to love without limit; the freedom to dream of the utter marriage of beauty and art; all this men may have if they are sufficiently well-bred to make human contact bearable; if they have learned to read and write and reason; if they have character enough to distinguish between right and wrong and strength enough to do right; if they can earn a decent living and know the world in which they live.

The vastest and finest truth of all, is that while wealth diminishes by sharing and consuming and calls for control; Art, which is experience of life, increases and grows, the more widely it is shared. Here lie the rock foundations of Democracy. Selah.

———

So now again pass seven years. It is midnight of an autumn day; and Saint Orgne, risen beatified on the dark frustration of his soul, to the quiet peace of pain, stands in an old forest amid falling leaves, with the starry heavens above him. He knows where, months before, the heavy fragrance of purple wisteria had hallowed this air and dipped great festoons of blooms down into a scented world. But tonight these are gone. All is death. There is no sound; and yet somehow somewhere beneath lies some Tone too deep for sound—a silent chord of infinite harmony. Saint Orgne lifts his hands and waves back to the skies the seven golden candlesticks and the seven silver stars, and speaks, saying, "It is enough!" But the Voice replies:

"I see a new Heaven and a new Earth." "How can that be," wails Saint Orgne. "What is new about War and Murder? What is new in deified and organized race hate? What is new in breadlines and starvation, crime and disease? Is not our dream of Democracy done?"

The stars shine silently on, but in his own heart Saint Orgne's answer comes—Hear ye! This is the Truth of Democracy and Race.

———

The world compels us today as never before to examine and re-examine the problem of democracy. In theory we know it by heart: all men are equal and should have equal voice in their own government. This dictum has been vigorously attacked. All men are not equal. Ignorance cannot speak logically or clearly even when given voice. If sloth, dullness and mediocrity hold power, civilization is diluted and lowered, and government approaches anarchy. The mob cannot rule itself and will not choose the wise and able and give them the power to rule.

This attack began in 1787 during the French Revolution and it rose to crescendo sixty years later in 1867 when our fathers were enfranchised. The original dictum of human equality and the right of the governed to a voice in their government has never been universally accepted and only seldom has it been attempted. In the world today, universal suffrage is coerced by force as was true here in the South during reconstruction; or by intimidation as was true in the South after 1876; or by economic pressure, either through threat of poverty or bribery of increased income, as has been true in the United States for years. Today finally we have entered the period of propaganda, when people to be sure may vote but cannot think freely nor clearly because of falsehood forced on their eyes and ears; or equally by the deliberate suppression of the whole truth. It is thus that there has arisen in our day, on an astonishing scale, the fascism of despair; the acquiescence of great masses of men in irresponsible tyranny, not because they want it, but because they see no other escape from greater disaster.

Let us then examine anew the basic thesis of democracy. It does not really mean to say that all men are equal; but it does assert that every individual who is a part of the state must have his experience and his necessities regarded by that state if the state survive; that the best and only ultimate authority on an individual's hurt and desire is that individual himself no matter how inarticulate his inner soul may be; that life, as any man has lived it, is part of that great national reservoir of knowledge without use of which no government can do justice.

But this is not the main end of democracy. It is not only

that the complaints of all should be heard, or the hurts of the humblest healed; it is for the vastly larger object of loosing the possibilities of mankind for the development of a higher and broader and more varied human culture. Democracy then forms not merely a reservoir of complaint but of ability, hidden otherwise in poverty and ignorance. It is the astonishing result of an age of enlightenment, when the ruling classes of the world are the children of peasants, slaves and gutter snipes, that the still dominant thought is that education and ability are not today matters of chance, but mainly of individual desert and effort. As a matter of fact the chances of real ability today getting opportunity for development are not one-tenth as great as the chance of their owners dying in child-birth, being stunted by poverty or ending in prison or on the gallows. Democracy means the opening of opportunity to the disinherited to contribute to civilization and the happiness of men.

Given a chance for the majority of mankind, to be educated, healthy and free to act, it may well turn out that human equality is not so wild a dream as many seem to hope.

The intelligent democratic control of a state by its citizens does not of itself and by any mechanical formula mean good government. It must be supplemented by the thrift and unselfishness of its citizens. The citizen of a democracy who thinks of democratic government chiefly as a means of his own advancement, meets and ought to meet disappointment. Only in so far as he conceives of democracy as the only way to advance the interests of the mass of people, even when those interests conflict with his, is he playing the heroic role of a patriot. And whenever he excludes from that mass the interests of the poor and the foolish; the Jew and Negro; the Asiatic and the South Sea Islander; he kills the effort at democracy.

Democracy does not and cannot mean freedom. On the contrary it means coercion. It means submission of the individual will to the general will and it is justified in this compulsion only if the will is general and not the will of special privilege.

Far from this broad conception of democracy, we have increasingly allowed the idea to be confined to the opportunity of electing certain persons to power without regard as to whether they can or will exercise power or for what. Even this choice of the voter, in current democracies, is confined mostly to comparatively minor matters of administration; but in the great realm of making a living, the fundamental interest of all; in the matter of determining what goods shall be produced, what services shall be rendered, and how goods and services shall be shared by all, there has been deep and bitter determination, that here democracy shall never enter; that here the Tyrant or the King by the grace of God shall always and forever rule.

It is widely in vain that the basic argument for democratic control has here been brought to bear; that these goods and services are the product of the labor of the mass of men and not solely of the rich and talented; and that therefore all men must have some decisive voice in the conduct of industry and the division of wealth. To be sure this calls for more intelligence, technical knowledge of intricate facts and forces, and greater will to work and sacrifice than most men today have; which is only saying that the mass of men must more and more largely acquire this knowledge, skill and character; and that meantime its wide absence, is no valid excuse for surrendering the control of industry to the anarchy of greed and the tyranny of chance.

This faces us directly with our problem in America. Our best brains are taught and want to be taught in large northern universities where dominant economic patterns and European culture, not only prevail, but prevail almost to the exclusion of anything else.

Naturally these men are then grabbed up with rolling eyes and eager mien by the best Southern Negro schools. Now if these Negro universities have any real meaning it is that in them other points of view, should be evolved. They may or may not be radically different. They may bring something entirely new or be an adaptation of surrounding civilization; but certainly they should logically bring a newness of view and a re-examination of the old, of the European, and of the white, which would be stimulating and which would be real education.

But right here we have not simply little or no advance, but

we have attitudes which make advance impossible. On the matter of race, for instance, we are ultra-modern. There are certainly no biological races in the sense of people with large groups of unvarying inherited gifts and instincts thus set apart by nature as eternally separate. We have seen the whole world reluctantly but surely approaching this truth. We have therefore hastened to conclude there is no sense in studying racial subjects or inculcating racial ideals or writing racial textbooks or projecting vocational guidance from the point of view of race. And yet standing in stark contradiction of all this are the surrounding facts of race: the Jim Crow seats on the street cars every day, the Jim Crow coaches on the railroads, the separate sections of the city where the races dwell; the discrimination in occupations and opportunities and in law; and beyond that the widespread division of the world by custom into white, yellow and black, ruler and eternally ruled.

We American Negroes form and long will form a perfectly definite group, not entirely segregated and isolated from our surroundings, but differentiated to such a degree that we have very largely a life and thought of our own. And it is this fact that we as scientists, and teachers and persons engaged in living, earning a living, have got to take into account and make our major problem. In the face of that, we have these young intellectual exquisites who smile if they do not laugh outright at our writhings. Their practical program is so far as our race or group is concerned: Do nothing, think nothing, become absorbed in the nation.

To which the flat answer is: this is impossible. We have got to do something about race. We have got to think and think clearly about our present situation. Absorption into the nation, save as a long, slow intellectual process, is unthinkable and while it may eventually come, its trend and result depends very largely upon what kind of a group is being absorbed; whether such racial integration has to do with poverty-stricken and half starved criminals; or whether with intelligent self-guided, independently acting men, who know what they want and propose at any civilized cost to get it. No, separated and isolated as we are so largely, we form in America an integral group, call it by any name you will, and this fact in itself has its meaning, its worth and its values.

In no line is this clearer than in the democratization of industry. We are still a poor people, a mass of laborers, with few rich folk and little exploitation of labor. We can be among the first to help restore the idea of high culture and limited income and dispel the fable that riotous wealth alone is civilization. Acting together, voluntarily or by outer compulsion, we can be the units through which universal democracy may be accomplished.

We black folk have striven to be Americans. And like all other Americans, we have longed to become rich Americans. Wealth comes easiest today through the exploitation of labor by paying low wages; and if we have not widely exploited our own and other labor the praise belongs not to us, but to those whites whose monopoly of wealth and ruthless methods have out-run our tardy and feeble efforts. This is the place to pause and look about, as well, backward as forward. The leaders of the labor movement in America as in Europe, deceived us just as they deceived themselves. They left us out. They paid no attention to us, whether we were drudging in colonies or slaving in cotton fields or pleading in vain at the door of union labor factories. The object of white labor was not the uplift of all labor; it was to join capital in sharing the loot from exploited colored labor. So we too, only half emancipated, hurled ourselves forward, too willing if it had but been possible, to climb up to a bourgeois heaven on the prone bodies of our fellows. But white folk occupied and crowded these stairs. And white labor loved the white exploiter of black folk far more than it loved its fellow black proletarian.

Such is the plight of democracy today. Where in this picture does the American Negro come? With few exceptions, we are all today "white folks' niggers." No, do not wince. I mean nothing insulting or derogatory, but this is a concrete designation which indicates that very very many colored folk: Japanese, Chinese, Indians, Negroes; and, of course, the vast majority of white folk; have been so enthused, oppressed, and suppressed by current white civilization that they think and judge everything by its terms. They have no norms that are not set in the 19th and 20th centuries. They can conceive of no future world which is not dominated by present white nations and thoroughly shot through with their ideals, their method of government, their economic organization, their literature and their art; or in other words their throttling of democracy, their exploitation of labor, their industrial imperalism and their color hate. To broach before such persons any suggestion of radical change; any idea of intrusion, physical or spiritual, on the part of alien races is to bring down upon one's devoted head the most tremendous astonishment and contempt.

What to do? We went to school. But our industrial schools taught no industrial history, no labor movement, no social reform,—only technique just when the technique of skilled trades was changing to mass industry. Our colleges taught the reactionary economics of Northern Schools. We landed in bitter and justifiable complaint and sought a way out by complaining. Our mistake lay not in the injustice of our cause, but in our naive assumption that a system of industrial monopoly that was making money out of our exploitation, was going voluntarily to help us escape its talons.

On the other hand when we turn to join the forces of progress and reform we find again no easy or obvious path. As the disinherited both of labor and capital; as those discriminated against by employer and employee, we are forced to a most careful and thorough-going program of minority planning. We may call this self-segregation if we will but the compulsion is from without and inevitable. We may call it racial chauvinism but we may make it the path to democracy through group culture. This path includes sympathy and cooperation with the labor movement; with the efforts of those who produce wealth, to assert their right to control it. It has been no easy path. What with organized, intelligent and powerful opposition and ignorant and venal and dogmatic leadership, the white labor movement has staggered drunkenly for two hundred years or more and yet it has given the world a vision of real democracy, of universal education and of a living wage. It is the most promising movement of modern days and we who are primarily laborers must eventually join it.

In addition to this, no matter how great our political disfranchisement and social exclusion, we have in our hands a voting power which is enormous, and that is the control we can exercise over the production and distribution of goods through our expenditure as consumers. The might and efficiency of this method of economic reform is continually minimized by the obvious fact that it does not involve radical change and that without other and more thorough-going changes it can bring no immediate millenium. But notwithstanding for a minority group it is the most powerful weapon at hand and to refuse to use an instrument of power because it is not all powerful is silly.

A people who buy each year at least a half billion dollars worth of goods and services are not helpless. If they starve it is their own fault. If they do not achieve a respected place in the surrounding industrial organization, it is because they are stupid.

Here then is the plight and the steps toward remedy. Yet we are not awake. We have let obvious opportunities slip by during these awful days of depression when we have lost much of the land we used to own; when our savings have been dissipated; when our business enterprises have failed and when if not a majority a strikingly large minority of us are existing on public charity. We have not asked for the advantage of public housing as we should. We have not taken advantage of the possibilities of the TVA. We have not pushed energetically into plans of resettlement and the establishment of model villages. We have almost refused the subsistence homestead. We have not begun to think of socialized medicine and consumers' cooperation. We have no comprehensive plans concerning our unemployment, our economic dependence, the profit economy and the changing technique of industry. The day of our reckoning is at hand. Awake, Awake, put on thy strength Oh Zion.

The martyrdom of man may be increased and prolonged through primitive, biological racial propaganda, but on the other hand through cooperation, education and understanding the cultural race unit may be the pipe line through which human civilization may extend to wider and wider areas to the fertilization of mankind.

It is to this use of our racial unity and loyalty that the United States impels us. We cannot escape it. Only through racial effort today can we achieve economic stability, cultural growth and human understanding. The way to democracy lies through race loyalty if only that is its real and consciously comprehended end. Selah and Amen.

This then is the revelation of Saint Orgne the Damned, as given me by his hand; and the philosophy of life out of which he strove to climb, despite the curse, to broader and more abundant life. Bearing this revelation, Men and Women of the Class of 1938, there return to you today, three pilgrims, and the ghosts of three others, whose memories await us. Fifty years ago we stood where you stand and received the Light of the Seven Stars. We return, not all-wise, but wise; for we have seen ten presidents rule in America and five kings reign in England; we have seen the fall of three great empires; a whole world at war to commit 26 million murders; the rise of dark Japan and fall of darker Ethiopia. We have seen our own race in America nearly double in number from less than seven to more than twelve million souls.

We return home today worn and travel stained, yet with the Light which Alma Mater laid upon our hands; it does not burn so high nor flash so fiercely—yet it has lighted thousands of other candles, and it is still aflame. We hand it on to you, that fifty years hence you give it again to others—and so on forever.

Commencement Address, Fisk University, 1938

The Trial

I HAVE FACED during my life many unpleasant experiences: the growl of a mob; the personal threat of murder; the scowling distaste of an audience. But nothing has so cowed me as that day, November 8, 1951, when I took my seat in a Washington courtroom as an indicted criminal. I was not a criminal. I had broken no law, consciously or unwittingly. Yet I sat with four other American citizens of unblemished character, never before accused even of misdemeanor, in the seats often occupied by murderers, forgers and thieves; accused of a felony and liable to be sentenced before leaving this court to five years of imprisonment, a fine of $10,000 and loss of my civil and political rights as a citizen, representing five generations of Americans.

It was a well-furnished room, not large, and poorly ventilated. Within the rail were tables for the lawyers, and back of these, seats for the defendants, with their backs to the audience behind. In front, on a low platform, sat the clerks and court stenographer; and behind, to a dais, came the black-gowned judge, announced by the marshal—"God save the United States of America!"

On either side were seats for the jurors, from whom twelve would soon be chosen to declare our guilt, or innocence, or a mistrial. All these seats were now filled with the jury panel, and an unusually large panel overflowed into the seats usually occupied by the public. There must have been 200 persons present; white and colored, from which juries for several cases would be drawn. Our first worry was this matter of the jury.

The jury system in the United States has fallen on evil days. The old English concept of a man's guilt being decided by presentation of the facts before twelve of his fellow citizens too often fails. Juries are selected in devious ways and by secret manipulation. Most Negroes are sent to jail by persons who hate or despise them. Many ordinary workers are found guilty by well-to-do "blue-ribbon" people who have no conception of the problems that face the poor. Juries are too often filled with professional jurors selected and chosen by the prosecution and expected to convict.

Our first hurdle was a long examination of the panel anent their affiliations, opinions and prejudices. The prosecution asked, among other things, if they had any prejudice against convicting a person of advanced years. The defendants asked a long series of more searching questions as to the prospective juror's attitude toward color, discrimination, and membership in certain organizations. One woman admitted that she was formerly a member of the K.K.K. and was excused.

No one on the panel admitted that he had at any time advocated segregation of the races, or racial discrimination in housing, transportation, employment, recreation, education; or in the use of places of public accommodation in the District of Columbia. Looking at the persons, this seemed to me hardly believable. Probably most of the whites had belonged to some such organizations but would not now admit it. They were asked about their attitude toward the House Committee on Un-American Activities, but none admitted prejudice. A number said that they had relatives in the armed forces, but declared that if they were convinced of the defendants' innocence they would be willing to say so even if a majority of the jury disagreed with them.

In our case there came another angle—the colored juror. In many parts of the nation, Negroes seldom or never serve on juries. But in the District of Columbia, lately, continually there are many Negro jurors drawn, so much so that there has been a distinct movement to curb their choice. Something of this was heard by the lawyers in our case, and they were prepared to fight it. But on the other hand, we sensed another and more hurtful method of opposition. There is a considerable proportion of Negroes in government employ: in the post office, as teachers in the public schools, as civil servants in dozens of branches. All such employees in Washington, white as well as black, are in fear of attack by witch hunts and loyalty tests, where often the accused have no chance to know or answer their accusers. Also, they are faced with severe competition and political influence. Negroes suffer especially, because their chance for employment outside government is narrow, and because their political influence is curtailed; and finally because of race discrimination which makes even civil service rules bow to prejudice. Suppose, now, a Negro government employee is given jury service in a case where he knows that the government is out for conviction and where the case appeals to current popular hysteria. In our case the government had allowed the distinct impression to prevail that it had unanswerable evidence in hand to prove our direct connection with Communist movements abroad against the United States. Suppose, then, a Negro with a government job and a home and family is drawn for this jury: no matter what the facts show, how will he vote? How will he dare to vote?

These facts faced us and one solution was to try to exclude government employees from the panel. This the judge offered to do, and he had the panel polled. The poll showed that if government employees were excluded, practically no Negroes would be left, since employment for educated Negroes in the District of Columbia is practically confined to government service. We faced a perfect dilemma: if we excluded government employees, we indirectly helped draw the color line; if we accepted government employees, more Negroes would face a greater risk of dismissal on trumped up charges than the whites. The white non-government worker would usually be in a job which did not employ Negroes, which would mean that he had had no contact with them and would be prejudiced. The lawyers consulted, and then Marcantonio came over and put this dilemma squarely before me. "Accept government employees!" I answered.

We did, and to my amazement got a jury of eight Negroes and four whites! I did not know whether to be glad or scared. The prosecution usually knows the jury panel fairly well, and it is thought that the panel may often be sprinkled with stooges. Was it possible that these eight Negroes might be owned? As I looked at their intelligent faces, veiled and noncommittal as some were, I did not think so. My impulse was to follow the conclusion of Earl Dickerson, who said: "No eight American Negroes will ever agree to convict you!" Then he added reflectively, "If they do, I'll never defend another!" I was afraid his practice might be curtailed. Yet I could not believe that many American Negroes believed that I was a paid spy.

Next in importance came the problem of the judge who

would preside. Judge Holtzoff, who had charge over our preliminary hearing in May, made a bad impression: pompous and opinionated; fond of talking about himself. He plainly disliked New York lawyers, and had a low opinion of women. On one occasion he summoned me to the bar, threatened to cancel my bond and send me to jail because of printed publicity found in the courtroom. Abbott Simon immediately stepped forward and took the blame for what was at worst an unintentional mistake, and more probably an attempt to frame us by some smart newspaper men. The judge finally dismissed us with a sharp warning against such "tirades" in his courtroom.

When, therefore, I heard that Judge McGuire had finally been assigned to our case, I was elated, until I heard that he was rumored to be the most reactionary judge on the District bench, and worse than Holtzoff! His appearance, however, was reassuring. He was from first to last, courteous and intelligent. He did not put on judicial airs; he never lost his temper; he was firm but kindly. Had it not been for the nature of our indictment and the impossibility of reconciling the attitude of Judge McGuire with that of the Department of Justice, through whose employment he had risen to the bench, I would call Judge James McGuire a great jurist, who in this case held the scales of justice absolutely level.

But my considered opinion is that what happened was that this judge at the last moment freed himself from the political pressures of the day to which so many had succumbed and that both he and the Department of State realized that the eyes of the world were fixed on this case.

In strictly legal aspect, remember what this trial was: it was not a question of our opinions and beliefs; it involved no question as to whether we were Communists, Socialists, Jehovah's Witnesses or Nudists; it involved no imputation of moral turpitude except in so far as it is a statutory crime to say what foreigners are saying at the command of those foreigners. The judge said:

> "The point in this case is whether or not this organization acted as an agent or in a capacity similar to that for a foreign organization or foreign political power, whether

> advocating peace, advocating this, or advocating that. They can advocate the distribution of wealth; they can advocate that all red-headed men be shot. It doesn't make any difference what they advocate."

It was not even fully admitted until the third week of the trial that the government did not allege that the Soviet Union was connected with the "foreign principal" accused in the indictment. It was never alleged that we had no right to advocate peace. It was only the question: were we "agents" of a foreign principal? Yet and despite all this, the public was deliberately given to understand by spokesmen of government and by the press that we were accused of lying, spying, and treason in the pay of the Soviet Union. As one of the attendants said in the ante-room of the court, scowling at us: "If the damned Communists don't like this country, why don't they go back to Russia?"

Jurisdictional questions were first raised, based on the fact that the organization was defunct, and on the question of the jurisdiction of the court over individual defendants. These motions were denied, although the court admitted that there was still some question as to the liability of the officers of the Peace Information Center, if it were proven that the Peace Information Center no longer existed. Marcantonio said:

> "The plea of not guilty did not in any manner, shape or form revive the dead. In other words, if John Jones were indicted and he died, and died before the indictment, certainly, he could not be found guilty and considered in being simply because counsel pleaded not guilty. And pleading not guilty they pleaded not guilty for all purposes, including the establishment of the non-existence of the individual."
>
> "The Court: You have just said what I have said, much better. So, we will leave it that way."

One of the basic reasons for the repeated miscarriages of justice in this country, is the lack of attention on the part of the respectable public to the procedures of court trials. Most persons assume that trials have to do with criminals, tricky lawyers, peremptory judges, and hard court officials. Such folk keep as far from courts as possible and let flagrant and cruel injustice escape without remark or attention. We knew this, and from the first appealed to our friends and the friends of justice everywhere to attend this trial and see what went on. As a result the sessions were crowded by a quiet, intelligent audience, who came from New York, New England, Chicago, the South and West, with usually a waiting line to be admitted. It was in every sense a public trial, and the Department of Justice knew it.

The jury having been selected, the trial began Thursday, November 8, and lasted five days, during three weeks, because of adjournments for weekends and holidays. A fussy little fat man, Maddrix, chief of the prosecution, and former Attorney-General of Maryland, stated the case for the prosecution:

> "The first count states that the Peace Information Center was an unincorporated organization, having its headquarters in New York City. It further alleges that the Peace Information Center was an agent of a foreign principal, in that it acted as and held itself out as a publicity agent for the Committee of the World Congress of the Defenders of Peace, and the World Peace Council . . . and because of it being an agent of a foreign principal, it was under a liability to file a registration statement with the Attorney General of the United States. . . .
>
> "The material disseminated within the United States by Peace Information Center as publicity agent for its said foreign principal consisted of information about peace, war, instruments of war, and the consequences of peace and of war. . . .
>
> "The agency relationship of the Peace Information Center with the Committee of the World Congress of the Defenders of Peace and the World Peace Council is not claimed to have existed pursuant to contractual relationship."

Maddrix added that the government intended to call twenty-seven witnesses.

Our lawyers postponed rejoinder, since the jury seemed more bewildered than impressed by the bill of particulars. We elected to await the development of the government case before stating ours. We were puzzled by the fairness of the judge, and were awaiting the nature of the evidence which the prosecution could produce. The prosecution reminded us that we had not named our prospective witnesses, as was the practice in the District of Columbia. We had determined to confine ourselves to as few witnesses as possible and to rely on the strength of our case rather than corroborative repetition. I had been chosen as the main witness, with two other witnesses to substantiate certain occurrences which took place during my absence in Europe. These were named; and then Marcantonio added that we might subpoena the Secretary of State and the Attorney-General. Later, when it seemed that I might need character witnesses, Albert Einstein offered to do "Whatever he could."

We may never know just what reactions took place in government circles concerning this indictment. At first, certainly, the government meant to scare us by the "Communist" bogey. Then by threatening indictment they aimed to cut off contributions to the Peace Information Center, or make us try to escape persecution. When we began to fight back and the volume of protest from white and black arose, and from Europe and Asia as well as Africa, the government began frantically to collect evidence which they had never possessed. They sent out agents. They interviewed and tried to intimidate every person connected in any way with the founding of the Peace Information Center. They subpoenaed a host of witnesses, including some of the defendants, which was illegal. They kept giving out intimations of the unanswerable evidence which they possessed. They scared off lawyers: one widely known attorney listened to our offer, and then told us he was dining with the Attorney-General. He finally refused his services. When the head of the Criminal Division of the Department of Justice went to Paris and interviewed the Secretary of the Defenders of Peace, he returned quite willing to postpone the case, and as we hoped, never to press it. When, by insistence of his superiors, long postponement was refused, he did not enter the case, and the three lawyers who took charge of the prosecution were distinctly not experienced or first class men.

Whatever design there was to confront us with manufactured testimony from professional spies, liars and agents-provocateurs, it was abandoned. But the very fairness of the trial raised the query as to why the government ever was induced to bring this case on so flimsy a basis? They had no case and they knew it. Their only hope of success was to raise national hysteria against us to the flaming point. This our campaign rendered impossible. No ex-spy could get away with testimony about seeing me emerge from the Kremlin with a bag of gold; no stooge could make black America believe that I was an undercover conspirator, when for fifty years I had always blurted out the truth on all occasions.

The judge continued to be fair and courteous. The prosecution was inept if not stupid. The defense was prepared to the last comma; it knew law and procedure; it was on its toes every minute with its eyes on the possible appeal to higher courts. The government spent precious time and money on proving the obvious: that the Peace Information Center existed; that it had a bank account; that it rented offices; that it distributed literature. Cautious F.B.I. men and newspaper reporters introduced literature which anyone could have gotten at any time, and which we freely admitted we had written and distributed.

The chief dependence of the prosecution was on John Rogge. Rogge the witness was a caricature of Rogge the crusader for Peace and Reform. In place of the erect, self-confident if not arrogant leader, came a worn man, whose clothes hung loosely on him, and who in a courtroom where he had conducted many cases, had difficulty locating me in the defendants' chairs. I voluntarily stood up to help him out.

He admitted his membership in the Peace Information Center. He admitted his attendance at the World Peace Congress; and declared that its actual objective was not peace, but that it was an agency for the foreign policy of the Soviet Union.

Mr. Maddrix in his opening said that the government did not intend to show and would not show that there was any contract of agency between the World Congress of the Defenders of Peace and the Peace Information Center. The Court said:

> "The responsibility of the government is to prove beyond a reasonable doubt, first of all, the nexus; and in doing that, you will have to establish, of course, that there was a foreign group, whether that group takes the aspect of a foreign political party, a foreign government or a foreign association within the purview of the statute."

The government introduced twenty copies of the magazine *In Defense of Peace*, issued by the Defenders of Peace, which led to argument as to whether their contents should be admitted. The judge said that he did not think that the prosecution ought to go into the nature and character of the activities of the principal, but to establish first the fact of agency. The prosecution insisted that it should have the right to show that the propaganda of the Defenders of Peace was political, but the judge insisted that first the prosecution should prove or indicate to the jury that the foreign group was a government, or party, or some organization within the purview of the statute, and that then it should establish a nexus between the Defenders of Peace and the Peace Information Center.

The prosecution then tried to say that the Defenders of Peace had said there was a terrible plot against humanity, and that the United States was the center of this plot, and for that reason the Defenders of Peace were attacking the United States. The defendants' lawyers objected to this. The judge reminded the prosecution that they had established the existence of a foreign group with headquarters in Paris. They should now indicate to the jury the evidence seeking to show the connection between that foreign group and the Peace Information Center.

This led to a long argument in which Marcantonio stressed the fact that it was absurd to argue that parallelism in thought or expression established the relationship of agency. "Two people may have parallel views, one at the north pole and one at the south pole. That does not establish agency." The Court agreed that two parallel lines never meet, but said that he assumed that the connection between the two lines of thought was going to be indicated. The Court said that unless this nexus was shown, "I think that at the proper time you would be entitled to a directed verdict." This was the first intimation that our case might never reach the jury; but this seemed at the time too good ever to become true. Mr. Jaffe, our Constitutional lawyer, insisted that if the government was first going into a characterization of the Defenders of Peace, that that would be damaging in the minds of the jury, and prejudice them. The judge responded:

> "I indicated that to Mr. Maddrix; but he says that he cannot (omit this), by virtue of the way his case is set up. Then Mr. Marcantonio very well says that if he expects to show the so-called connection by virtue of the similarity of activity in the nature of propaganda, then that would be, as he very aptly described it, parallelism; and the two could never meet, either in time or eternity. So there has to be a nexus shown; and I am assuming that will be shown. If it isn't shown, the Government doesn't make out a case and that is all."

Mr. Maddrix stressed the fact that the propaganda of the Defenders of Peace was that Anglo-American imperialism was the foremost champion of a new war, and the Soviet Union a great peace-loving power, the champion of peace; and that the evidence of this propaganda was admissible. Marcantonio replied:

> "After he makes that statement, all we need is a band to play 'Stars and Stripes Forever'—the United States is warlike; the Soviet Union is peaceful—you have a speech in Congress."

The defendants' lawyers had not read the twenty copies of the magazine *In Defense of Peace* which the prosecution had introduced, and had little time now to do so. I therefore undertook to read them over the weekend, and said in a memorandum to our lawyers:

> "My opinion is that we have nothing to fear from this magazine. Its references to the United States are on the whole temperate, even when critical; it does not mention this country often: during 1950, out of 156 articles only 6 were on the United States. In general, the United States is

treated generously and hopefully. After the outbreak of the war in Korea, criticism is more frequent and specific but seldom or never nasty.

"There is clear evidence of the character of the Defenders of Peace, and no assumption of any nexus of agent and principal. I have noted instances where this might be inferred by the reader but they are not important. On the other hand, the statements on peace are strong and well put. I do not believe that the prosecution can get any support for its contentions from these magazines."

On the other hand, the prosecution might easily quote single sentences or references inimical to the United States; and we had to insist that whatever this magazine said was not material until it had been proven that we were agents of the Defenders of Peace, and shared responsibility for its propaganda. The judge took the matter under advisement while he examined the magazines. He must have found much that he would be unwilling to place before the jury, for reasons which the prosecution might have shared, had they read the copies themselves carefully. The judge finally excluded all except four copies, and admitted them only to identify the Stockholm Appeal and the fact that it was sponsored by the publishers of this magazine, and that the magazine was published in a foreign country. When the prosecution wished to have all the contents of the magazine admitted, the judge said that he was not going to put mere propaganda before the jury.

It was at this juncture that Judge McGuire called the lawyers to his chambers and went straight to the kernel of Rogge's testimony. Rogge had said that the object of the Defenders of Peace was ostensibly peace, but really to carry out the policies of the Soviet Union. This was, as we suspected from the beginning, the whole intention of the Rogge testimony, and the method by which the government hoped to put us in jail. If, by this testimony, Russian and Communist controversy could be smeared across the case, current popular hysteria could be aroused against us. Witnesses like J. B. Matthews, long the propagandist of the Dies Committee, could be brought on the stand with his lurid stories about

Communists, corroborated by the F.B.I. and its Budenzes and Bentleys.

The judge, therefore, came straight to the point: referring to Rogge he said:

> "This witness was permitted to state that while the stated purpose was peace, the real purpose was to promote the foreign policy of the Soviet Union.
>
> "Do you expect to show that the World Council for Peace was in fact an agent of another principal, namely the Soviet Union?"

Mr. Maddrix did not answer this directly, but the judge continued, saying that he let in reference to the Soviet Union because he thought the prosecution was going to show that the Soviet Union actually was the foreign principal, and that the World Council for Peace was merely the conduit to use the activity of the Peace Information Center. If this was not their case, he was going to tell the jury to disregard any reference to the Soviet Union. Mr. Maddrix objected to being restricted, but the Court insisted:

> "You cannot blow hot and cold. I have got to be advised now as to what you expect to show. . . . You are not, I take it, predicating your case or the theory of your case on the ground that the World Council for Peace was, in effect, the agent of the Soviet Union?"
>
> Mr. Maddrix: "We are not making that statement, no."
>
> The Court: "What you do not intend to prove, and I am so advised now, is that you are not going to attempt to prove formally that the activities of the World Council for Peace were the activities of the Soviet Union?"
>
> Mr. Maddrix: "I could not state it any better. . . . We do not intend to show that the Committee of the Congress of the World Defenders of Peace was an agent of the Soviet Union."

As a result of this admission the Court said:

> "I thought I ought to be advised at this juncture just exactly what the Government expected to show with reference to the Soviet Union being the principal or the so-

called principal of the Peace Information Center. I understand the Government expects not to show, under any circumstances, the existence of another principal behind the principal we are concerned with, namely, the Soviet Union. If that is not my understanding here of what transpired at the bench, I would like to be so advised."

The prosecution then again admitted:

"We do not charge in our indictment that the foreign principal in any way involves an element of agency as I understand this case, between the foreign principal, the Committee of the World Congress, and the Soviet Union."

The Court: "You have answered my question. You are contending that the only foreign principal involved in this case is the World Congress for Peace?"

Mr. Cunningham: "Absolutely."

The Court: "I am not going to try the Soviet Union or make any comparison between the Soviet Union with respect to peace and America. I am going to stick to the issue."

With the jury out of the room, there was a conference of the judge and lawyers concerning other points in Rogge's testimony. Rogge had said that the purpose of the Stockholm Appeal was to concentrate the eyes of the world on the atom bomb in the possession of the United States, and to take the eyes of the world off any aggression that might and which did come from the East. The Court asked Mr. Maddrix if he considered Mr. Rogge an expert. He said no, but that no one was in a better position than Mr. Rogge to know what was going on and to answer this particular question. He was a member of the policy-making group, and had attended its meetings. The Court then said:

"I am not trying any propaganda lines. I am not trying any foreign policy questions involving any country, including our own. You have a very simple case here. You charged this Peace Information Center and these individuals, as officers and directors, as being agent of a foreign principal, and disseminating propaganda in the United States. You have got to show a tie-up between the principal so-called and the so-called agent. If you don't do that, you are out of court."

The prosecution insisted that the agency of the Peace Information Center was going to be proved by circumstantial evidence. The judge said:

"You have to show the connection. . . . I may be in Timbuctoo and you may be in some place in South America. I may be shaving and using Gillette brushless shaving cream and you may be doing the same thing, but there is no connection except we are both using Gillette."

Thereupon, when the jury had returned, the judge addressed them, saying that when Rogge was on the stand he was asked what the purpose of the World Council for Peace was, and he answered. The judge went on:

"You are now instructed by the Court, as emphatically as I can make words that lend emphasis to what I say, that you are to disregard Mr. Rogge's opinion of what he thought the purpose of the Stockholm Peace Appeal was. It is a very simple rule of evidence that excludes that type of opinion, because opinion is excluded, and the only opinion that is permitted to be introduced in a court of law, in certain circumstances, is the opinion of an expert. So, therefore, you will disregard entirely the characterization of the witness Rogge with reference to what he thought the World Council for Peace had in view."

Although we did not at the time realize it, and still watched narrowly for trumped up testimony, it was right here that we won our case. The prosecution had rested its whole case on Rogge's testimony that we were representing the Soviet Union through the Defenders of Peace organization in Paris. They had naturally not an iota of real proof of this, but they planned to depend on public opinion. But Rogge's own testimony convicted him. He was a member of the Peace Information Center; he was a member of the policy-making bureau of the Defenders of Peace. He had visited the Soviet Union and spoken as a representative of the Defenders of Peace and the Peace Information Center. He had sworn on oath when he himself became an agent of Yugoslavia that he was not a member of any other foreign agency.

Mr. Rogge continued his testimony, mentioning the meeting of the Bureau of the Defenders of Peace in Prague. When asked as to the substance of my speech he said: "The substance of Dr. Du Bois' speech was that all the difficulties of the world stem from what he described as the capitalistic warmongers in the United States."

Mr. Marcantonio asked that that be stricken out, and the Court said that he was not going to get off on any ideological discussion with reference to capitalism or any other form of enterprise; that the essential question was whether or not Dr. Du Bois was present. "What was said and who else was there is immaterial." The judge told the jury to disregard what Mr. Rogge had said. Later he excluded testimony about mention at Stockholm of setting up a peace movement in the United States.

Rogge was asked if he had a meeting in his home in February, 1949, with regard to the establishment of a peace organization in the United States. He answered that he had permitted such a meeting to be held. He admitted allowing telegrams to be sent out over his name inviting people to the meeting; and that it did result in appointing a committee on organization.

Then Mr. Marcantonio turned to the Congress of the Defenders of Peace in Paris, and brought out the fact that Mr. Rogge had sent a letter to Dr. Du Bois asking him to attend that Congress, showing him the letter.

Rogge admitted that when he attended the meeting in Prague in August, 1951, he was agent of a foreign country, and Marcantonio tried to get the letter which he had written in Prague, agreeing with the purposes of the World Defenders of Peace, admitted as evidence, but it was excluded.

Later in chambers Mr. Marcantonio interjected, angrily: "You have no case and why don't you admit it? I think this is one of the most deliberate diabolical plots ever pulled which is being pulled on these defendants."

He apologized for losing his temper, but added that the "prosecution wants to convict these defendants on their political views."

"You are trying to frighten us," said Mr. Maddrix.

Marcantonio replied, "I am not trying to frighten you at all. I am exposing you."

The Court finally said: "Mr. Marcantonio, you have indicated your surprise and your righteous indignation. They say of nuns they never get angry; it is always righteous indignation."

Mr. Cunningham of the prosecution intervened and tried to say that the Peace Information Center acted and held itself out to be a publicity agent, "that the proof of that does not require the showing of any nexus or any direct connection between the Peace Information Center and the foreign principal."

The Court: "Let's stop right there. Why doesn't the statute require that?"

Mr. Cunningham tried to refer to the legislative history of the bill, but this the Court refused to allow, and said: "You have got to show nexus and you have got to show nexus either by direct or circumstantial evidence. If you do not do that, the case fails."

The next witness, Victor Lasky, a screen writer formerly on the New York *World-Telegram and Sun*, testified that he had visited the offices of the Peace Information Center and received copies of the Stockholm Petition, and that "I made it quite clear that I abhorred the Petition." The Court excluded that because, as he said, the jury is not concerned with the witness' views on the petition.

Mr. Maddrix tried to get in the record the fact that Lasky had written a book against Communism, but that was excluded.

An F.B.I. agent, John J. Kearney, came next, and told about attending a meeting of the Peace Information Center at the Hotel Capitol. He tried to refer to Peace Information Center propaganda among Catholics, but the judge excluded all matters about race and religion:

> "Now, as I said before, no matter what form of political

propaganda it takes, if it is propaganda upon the part of the foreign principal, then, the American people, under the statute, are entitled to know who is paying the bill or who is behind the gun. That is all there is to it. For that reason I excluded everything else, foreign policy of Russia, foreign policy of the United States, the appeals to Catholics, appeals to Jews, appeals to all sorts of groups, minority or otherwise; that is out of the picture."

He also excluded hearsay evidence and pictures of certain persons produced in the magazine, *In Defense of Peace*, which Mr. Maddrix introduced. Mr. Marcantonio asked, "Is Dick Tracy coming in next?" When the judge was asked to admit the picture of Dr. Du Bois, the Court rejoined that he was in the courtroom, and that the picture was not material.

The prosecution asked if reference to the withdrawal of soldiers from Korea by the Committee of the World Congress and the Peace Information Center should be offered. The Court rejoined that it had not been offered. All that had been offered was the Stockholm Appeal and the statement made in the "Peacegrams" that the Peace Information Center was not affiliated with the World Congress of Peace.

Then came a nervous medical student, William B. Reed, who testified that he had visited the offices of the Peace Information Center four times, and once had listened in on a telephone conversation. He finally admitted that he had been in the employ of the F.B.I. He identified certain material which he had been given in the office of the Peace Information Center, and said that he had entrusted it to "somebody," which somebody finally proved to be J. B. Matthews, formerly Chief Investigator of the House Committee on Un-American Activities, who expected to testify but was never called by the government.

A letter to the public on the Peace Information Center letterhead was admitted in evidence to show our criminal activities:

"Dear Friend,

"You will be interested to learn that a Peace Information Center has been set up in New York City. It will, we believe, be of help to the millions of people in our country who ardently seek peace and an end to the cold war.

"The purpose of the office is to bring news of peace activities here and throughout the world. We plan to do this by issuing Fact Sheets and Bulletins from time to time; by co-operating in arranging for delegations from the United States to attend Peace Conferences; and co-operating in the tours of persons who come to this country to speak for peace.

"The interests of peace transcend all boundaries and all present and past differences. All people must unite who agree with the proposition that war must and can be averted, that the horrors of a Third World War are unthinkable, and with its corollaries that universal disarmament should start immediately and atomic weapons be outlawed. . . .

"Peace sentiment is growing throughout the United States, petitions are being circulated and meetings held. We would appreciate any information about peace activities in your area. Copies of material being used or news items would be most helpful to us.

"We hope you will indicate your interest and desire to continue to receive our material by sending us the enclosed card.

Sincerely yours,

(signed) W. E. B. Du Bois
Chairman"

The prosecution, out of hearing of the jury, called attention to the fact that the Department of Justice had made repeated demands on the defendants to register as foreign agents; intimating that our failure was wilful. The judge reminded them that the statute did not require the government to make any demands on anybody to register. The statute merely said that if the person representing a foreign principal did not register and did not maintain that it came within the exemptions, then that person was liable to the penalty imposed. The Court also pointed out that wilful failure to register must be proven, and said that he assumed that the defense was going to allege that the failure to register was not wilful.

The question of Miss Soloff's connection with the case was then discussed, and she was, the following day, acquitted by the Court on the ground that she was evidently a salaried employee and not a policy-making official. This ruling, which was based on a perfectly clear fact, we had tried to get at our first arraignment in May. Judge Holtzoff refused, and for eight months Miss Soloff was an indicted criminal, with absolutely no grounds for the charge.

The government then, to our surprise, rested its case, having called but seven of its twenty-seven witnesses. We immediately began to prepare for our presentation of our case. I was to be the main witness, and the only one of the defendants to take the stand. There was, however, a period when I was absent in Prague, and corroborative witnesses would be needed for certain actions.

We would call two members of our advisory board, the business manager of the *National Guardian*, and a professor of anthropology at Columbia, for this purpose.

Then, too, we had the sworn testimony of the executive secretary of the World Defenders of Peace, accused of being our "foreign principal." At considerable cost we had sent three of our lawyers to Paris in July. The government also sent three of their representatives, including the head of the Criminal Division of the Department of Justice, to take depositions from Jean Laffitte, the Secretary of the World Defenders of Peace. At this interesting inquiry, held at the offices of the United States Embassy, sworn testimony was taken, which we were ready to introduce but never got the opportunity. Mr. Laffitte, a man of training and manners, member of the Legion of Honor, declared that the Committee of which he was Secretary General was

> ". . . instituted by the First World Congress of the Defenders of Peace. Its definite task was to circulate and make known the information given and the decisions taken by the Congress. It was also in charge of circulating the various information concerning activities on behalf of Peace throughout the world. Its task was also to denounce all propaganda which predisposed public opinion in favor of war and to support all initiatives tending towards peace. It

had the duty of encouraging all cultural activities in favor of peace. And it was in charge of preparing a further World Congress of Peace."

He was asked if he had ever heard of the Peace Information Center and if the Center had authority to act as publicity agent. He answered that he had heard of the Peace Information Center, but that it had never had such authority; that the Committee had not appointed the Peace Information Center as its agent for the circulation of the Stockholm Appeal, nor had the Peace Information Center asked to act as publicity agent; that it expended no funds belonging to the Committee, and had no authority to make contracts; that it made no reports orally or in writing to this Committee.

He was then asked about national committees which were in co-operation with the World Committee. He said there were such committees in about eighty countries, but that there was none in the United States. He said that his committee had co-operated with the Peace Information Center in a very simple way:

> "We had heard of the formation of an Information Center in the United States which had assumed the task of circulating information relating to the furtherance of peace. This naturally resulted in our sending the Center information concerning peace movements, and allowed us to hope that in this way such information would become more widely known than other matter which we sent to the United States."

Then came an interesting colloquy. Mr. Laffitte was asked, "Do you regard Soviet Russia as the strongest advocate for peace among governments?" Mr. Laffitte's attorney immediately objected to his client's answering. Mr. McInerney, head of the Criminal Division of the Department of Justice of the United States, demurred and said that he was unable to understand Laffitte's "reluctance to express a viewpoint which he has proclaimed to the world." Mr. Laffitte's attorney replied that his client had made a point of answering all questions which were closely or remotely related to this matter, but that there was no obligation on his part to answer as to his personal opinions and beliefs:

"If he were called to testify before a French court, and if inconceivably he were asked to what political party he belonged or what was his belief concerning a given problem (a thing which could never happen), I would urge him not to answer such a question, since he is a French citizen entirely free as to his opinions; a freedom guaranteed by the Constitution of his country."

Mr. McInerney, taken aback, and probably remembering the Constitution of his own country, replied, "I wish to apologize if I have intruded upon his constitutional rights under French law."

When Mr. Laffitte was further asked if he had been in direct communication at any time with the Peace Information Center, he said that he had not. He was asked if the Peace Information Center was organized at the time that Dr. Du Bois was present in Paris at the Peace Congress. He replied that it was not, and that the Paris Committee did not hear of its organization until a year later. He was then asked if he had had personal correspondence with Dr. Du Bois, and he replied:

"I told you that I had not had any personal correspondence, properly so-called, with Dr. Du Bois. We confined ourselves to sending Professor Dr. Du Bois, who is a member of the World Committee, the information which we transmit without distinction to all members of the World Committee; that is to say, the Secretariat regularly sends all members of the World Committee information concerning the different meetings of the Bureau or the decisions taken at such meetings, and also any publications which may arise therefrom,—always with a covering letter which we send as a matter of courtesy and a mark of respect for these personalities."

He denied that he had ever requested the Peace Information Center to disseminate the Stockholm Appeal as an agent of the Committee. This interesting testimony we were given no chance to introduce.

The prosecution had rested before the morning session was finished. We prepared during the remainder of the morning to present certain motions, and then if they were denied, to go into our defense, introducing the Paris depositions, then character witnesses for me, after which I would take the stand. I was ready.

In Battle for Peace, 1952

The Acquittal

ARMISTICE DAY, November 11, had interrupted the trial and given a three day recess. I took the occasion to fill a conditional promise to speak at the Community Church in Boston, where for some years I have made annual addresses. Mr. Lathrop, the minister, in introducing me, reminded the congregation that a spiritual founder of this church, Theodore Parker, had also once been an indicted criminal. I said in part:

"The real causes of World War will persist and threaten so long as peoples of Europe and America are determined to control the wealth of most of the world by means of cheap labor and monopolies. Against this a resurgence of the revolt of the poor will raise a new Russia from the dead if we kill this one, and birth a new theory of communism so long as Africa, Asia and South America see the impossibility of otherwise escaping poverty, ignorance and disease. . . .

"We who have known a better America find the present scene almost unbelievable. A great silence has fallen on the real soul of the nation. We are smearing loyal citizens on the paid testimony of self-confessed liars, traitors and spies. We are making the voice of America the babble of cowards paid to travel. . . .

"My words are not a counsel of despair. Rather they are a call to new courage and determination to know the Truth. Four times this nation has faced disaster and recovered: Once at the end of the 18th century when we hesitated between separate independent colonies and a disciplined federal state; again when in the age of Jackson the uncouth, democratic west overbore the oligarchical well-mannered east; once more in the 19th century when human slavery cut the heart of the nation in two and we had to cement it with blood; finally, when in 1929 our boasted industries fell in vast ruin and begged on their knees for government aid, until Roosevelt rescued them with socialist planning, and gave his life to rebuilding our economy.

> "What we have done, we can do again. But not by silence—not by refusing to face the ugly facts."

On Tuesday afternoon, November 20, the defense began its argument for a judgment of acquittal. It first based a plea for dismissal on the ground of "lack of jurisdiction." The Peace Information Center in order to be under the jurisdiction of the court must be in existence, and the government must prove its existence. The judge remarked: "You say that the Peace Information Center is dead. I say to you, there is a general presumption that a condition of affairs once existing is presumed to continue to exist until the contrary is shown."

Marcantonio replied: "There is only one presumption in criminal law, the presumption of innocence."

Here Marcantonio gave the prosecution an opportunity to give up the case on a technicality which would have saved their faces. He tried to get Maddrix to admit that the Peace Information Center had ceased to exist before its indictment. Had Maddrix admitted this, the case would undoubtedly have been thrown out of court then and there. But Maddrix stubbornly and indignantly refused to make the admission. On the other hand, while this fact was true, it would have been difficult for us to prove. When does an organization close? We voted in October to close and did no new work after that; but all vestiges of the old work could not suddenly stop. Letters concerning peace and peace movements continued to pour into the office and we answered them; we could not easily cancel our lease. So that while we transacted no new business we were closing out odds and ends in January and February.

Marcantonio then turned to the argument for a directed acquittal:

> "The organization did not register because it is not an 'agent.' If it is not an agent as defined in the statute, therefore, the defendants could not have failed to cause it to register; and, hence, the judgment of acquittal should, by right, be directed to the individuals as well as the organization."

Attacking the Government's brief, he continued:

"The Government is seeking to spell out here a theory of the law which is something out of this world. And I read that language:

'While it is believed that evidence of a connection between Peace Information Center and the Committee has material probative value, the statute does not include "connection" as a necessary element in the proof of this phase of the charge.'

"Now, I submit, and I think that your Honor has indicated quite clearly, that connection must be established. Here, again, the Government reveals itself in its very last sentence.

"Now what is the Government saying here? It is saying that a statute states that the relationship does not have to be one pursuant to a contractual relationship; therefore no connection has to be established; no connection has to be established because no contractual relationship is required to be shown.

"I contend, and I believe Your Honor has indicated time and time again, that unless connection has been shown, there is no relationship of agency and principal. . . ."

Marcantonio insisted that the basic definition of "agency" in the law of 1938 was not changed by the law of 1942, and that 1) the Government must establish that the Peace Information Center was acting in behalf of the Partisans of Peace; 2) that the Peace Information Center was subject to control of the Partisans of Peace; 3) that the Partisans of Peace had consented to the fact that the Peace Information Center should act on its behalf; 4) that the Peace Information Center consented to the control of the Partisans of Peace; 5) that the Peace Information Center consented to act for the Partisans of Peace, and 6) that there was a consent on the part of the Peace Information Center to be subject to the control of the Partisans of Peace. "All these are musts; if any one of these fails, the case fails."

The Court brought up the case of interlocking directorate, where, for instance, Dr. Du Bois was a member of the Partisans of Peace, and also a member of the Peace Information Center. The judge admitted that this in itself did not necessarily prove that one was subject to the control of either, but he asked if that wasn't a circumstance which, along with other evidence, might prove it. Marcantonio answered:

> "No, sir. I will tell you why it is not. Because you have no evidence of control. Let me put it this way. All you have here, so far as Dr. Du Bois is concerned, is that he was a member of the Congress of the Defenders of Peace, and that he is president of this organization; period."

He said there was no testimony that the organization of which Dr. Du Bois was a member decided to have an organization over here; nor that there were directions given which Dr. Du Bois had to carry out over here.

The argument went over into the afternoon. The judge intervened with the following analogy, directed to Mr. Maddrix of the Prosecution. He said suppose you were living in Vienna and published a pamphlet on taxation which I liked. I ask your permission to republish your pamphlet in New York at my expense. The Government asks me to register as your agent. I refuse. I maintain that while I agree with your thought I am not your agent and therefore will not register. Is not that right?

Mr. Maddrix replied that the Government insisted that the agency was implied by the similarity of ideas.

Here Mr. Cunningham of the Government prosecution, a lank Texan with a perpetually anxious scowl, came up with the extraordinary plea that no connection need be proven. He maintained that a publicity agent as defined by the law of 1942 was not an agency in the sense of the law of 1938:

> "You have to go further and show, as your Honor points out, that one was doing it for the other, not necessarily by contract, and not necessarily by any agreement at all. The foreign principal may never have heard of the person here, as I have said before. We have to show it was the subjective intent of these people here to disseminate information in the United States, propaganda for and on behalf of, and further the propaganda objectives of the European organization."

The judge leaned forward and asked how a person disseminating propaganda of the type that the statute prohibits could be found guilty of acting for a foreign principal, "if the principal never heard of the disseminator and the disseminator never heard of the principal?" The judge continued, "Your contention is this: that if there is an argument about salt and pepper, Congress, by virtue of its power, said, 'pepper could be salt and salt could be pepper'."

Mr. Cunningham answered, "Yes, sir. That is exactly what is confusing the issue here."

Mr. Marcantonio retorted: "Except that the English language is still the same. Salt is salt and pepper is pepper. Principal is principal and agent is agent."

The court recessed until the afternoon. Mr. Marcantonio then insisted that the Government had not proved its contention of agency.

> "Again, I repeat, repeat, repeat and repeat again there was no evidence of control and direction. Furthermore, even if they went so far (and let's assume for the sake of argument only) that the Stockholm Appeal which we circulated was the propaganda of a foreign organization, we still would not be guilty and there still would be no evidence of our being guilty under this act, unless they showed control, unless they showed relationship. Merely circulating the Stockholm Peace Petition in and of itself is not evidence. It is not any evidence of control. It is not any evidence of consensual relationship. . . . What is more—in the Government's case, we grasp something that is positive. We find in all of the documentary evidence adduced time and time again there appears the affirmative statement that the Peace Information Center is not affiliated with anybody."

Mr. Maddrix of the prosecution followed and stressed the testimony of Rogge; he showed the various things done by the Peace Information Center which corresponded to the actions of the World Defenders of Peace. He referred to Mrs. Moos and Dr. Du Bois and to the fact that while Dr. Du Bois was Chairman of the Peace Information Center, he had been to Paris; he was a member of the World Congress; and had made other trips. He spoke of Abbott Simon's activities. He said:

> ". . . people who represent in the United States foreign interests in the form of disseminating propaganda, do not do so as openly as business contracts are made. There is not available the type of specific agreements which we would ordinarily desire; and the framers of this Act, Congressman McCormick and the rest, knew what they were up against; and so in 1942, they did amend it considerably. I am not going into that. I am saying that to show that under the 1942 Act, less evidence was needed than is needed under the 1938 Act."

Here the arguments ended. The jury had not yet been summoned. Without giving us any chance to offer our testimony or the sworn depositions of the Defenders of Peace; without waiting for the character witnesses, Judge McGuire, sitting at his high rostrum, rendered his verdict. We still were waiting for that overwhelming proof of guilt which for nine months the Department of Justice had promised. It never came. The judge said:

> "Now, we are faced with a situation as it comes in every criminal case, where the responsibility is upon the Court to interpose its ruling in the matter of a determination as to whether the case shall continue and as to whether or not, under those circumstances, the defendants shall be obliged to place defense on the stand as to the charge made against them before the jury.
>
> "I don't know whether or not these individual defendants who sit here at the bar of this court are sincere or misguided, or whether or not they have deliberately and designedly set out to subvert the very liberties under which they live and we live.
>
> "It is an old aphorism, however, that has been more or less channeled by the Supreme Court in the Bennis case, and that is this: I may hate the very things you say, but I respect your right to say them, and as Americans, we have confidence both in our material strength, which is important, and our spiritual strength; that is, in the validity of the institutions in which we live. . . .

"First of all, with reference to the motion for dismissal predicated upon jurisdictional ground, that is denied and the record will so indicate."

We sighed. Here came, we were sure, what we were expecting—denial of our plea and introduction of a misleading interpretation of the evidence. We sat back and listened. The judge continued:

"The Government has alleged that 'Peace Information Center' was the agent of a foreign principal. They proved the existence, in my judgment, of the Peace Information Center. They certainly proved the existence of the World Council for Peace. Mrs. Moos may very well have gone to Prague, may very well have gone to Moscow. There may have been, and I take it as proven, there were individuals who were officers of both; but, applying the test, as laid down here, in a case which, presumably, is the law of the land (because on appeal to the Supreme Court of the United States certiorari was denied in the case)—in this case the Government has failed to support, on the evidence adduced, the allegations laid down in the indictment. So, therefore, the motion, under the circumstances, for a judgment of acquittal will be granted."

For a moment a wave of surprised excitement passed over the audience, which had been listening breathlessly. Applause seemed on the edge of bursting out. Behind me, as I afterwards learned, my wife fainted. I, myself, felt slightly numb. Someone on my left kissed my cheek.

But the judge, changing his position slightly, but with no change of tone, quickly warned against any demonstration, and continued to speak. I thought that perhaps I had misunderstood, and that some modification of his words was coming. The judge proceeded:

"The judge's function is exhausted when he determines that the evidence does or does not permit the conclusion of guilt beyond reasonable doubt within a fair operation of a reasonable mind. So, therefore, if the case should go to the jury, I would be permitting the jury to conjecture in a field of conjecture, and, in addition to that, I would have to inform the jury and to instruct them that, if they could resolve the evidence in the case with any reasonable hypothesis looking toward the defendants, then, under the circumstances, they are obliged to do so, and then, as a consequence, they would have to be so instructed.

"So the case goes off, in my view, on a conception of the law.

"The government maintains one point of view and the defense maintains another. I think that the position of the defense is maintained and supported by the opinion mentioned and that opinion is conclusive in my mind; and that is my ruling."

The jury was then brought in, the ruling of the Court explained to them, and they were discharged. We were free for the first time in nine months.

We left Washington as quickly as possible. I was, frankly, bewildered. Of all the results of this fantastic and utterly unfair indictment, this was quite the last which I had awaited. At first I had confidently expected that after conference and explanation, the indictment would be quashed. Then, when it was relentlessly pushed, and the case set for trial, I had expected that after a series of delays and postponements, the actual trial would never take place. This would have been unsatisfactory, and left us long in unease, but it would have been better than a criminal procedure. Then, when the indictment was pushed and the trial opened, our best hope was for a failure to agree on the part of the jury where Negroes outnumbered whites two to one. This would have left a bad taste and brought the charge that narrow race loyalty had defeated Justice—an argument for excluding Negro jurors hereafter. With the acceptance of the jury there could be but one conclusion, and that was that the government thought it had absolute proof to convict us.

Indeed, there is evidence that this is what the highest authorities said, and allowed the public to believe. But we knew that even if the government thought it had such proof, it was either mistaken or the alleged proof was based on a deliberate lie. We had never asked or been offered opportunity to act as agent of any foreign person, organization or government;

our organization had never received a cent of money from abroad or from representatives of foreigners for its work, so far as we knew or believed. Indeed, the total amount of our funds was far too modest, and its expenditure too easily proven to indicate any foreign aid. It would have been possible to prove the source of every penny, if we had been pushed to divulge each contributor. But this would have been a betrayal of trust, and grossly unfair to donors, who were often so afraid of the F.B.I. as to refuse to give anything to any cause. But the facts were clear enough without this resort. We had received no large sums; never more than single gifts of a hundred dollars, and very seldom as much as that. We had books and testimony to show receipts and every dollar of expenses.

Of course, there were many who continually intimated that while I or even most of my colleagues knew nothing of treachery and bribery, nevertheless someone in the organization might have been a spy or foreign agent. Anybody can sometimes be deceived, but to those of us who knew this group, such accusation or suspicion was simply silly.

Why, then, had the Department of Justice been so arrogant, determined, and certain? Why did it so impudently brush off my offer to explain our whole work? If, after explanation, the Department had indicated any way in which we had transgressed the law, I was quite ready to change our methods or give up the whole project. But one thing we could not do, and that was to say under oath that we had been and were "agents of a foreign principal." This was a lie that no government could compel us to tell no matter what the penalty.

When, therefore, the Department of Justice refused conference, and insisted on trial, we had to fight, and fight not only with facts and law, but to be ready to meet any deliberate attempt at deception, which we had no means of anticipating. This was our expectation during every minute of that three weeks trial. I was looking for it down to the very last word of the decision of the judge. It did not come, and that was the basis of my bewilderment as I left the courtroom. I even forgot to call attention to one minor victory of this major case.

One of our chief headaches of this trial was that it must take place in this "Jim Crow" capital of our fatherland, where a Negro could not be sure of hotel accommodations or an opportunity to eat a meal, and sometimes even had difficulty with cabs. Moreover, there was even the more serious problem as to where this racially mixed group of lawyers and defendants, men and women, could meet privately for consultation. These are real problems which most white Americans, and no foreigners, can for a moment envisage. Yet for a white woman to go to a colored hotel; or a colored person to go to a white hotel; for white persons and colored, men and women, to be closeted together, morning, noon or night—such goings on are not only not customary but in at least a third of the states of this union illegal, and would in Alabama, Georgia, or Mississippi lead to arrest if not riot or murder.

Washington is geographically at the edge of the slave South, but has always been Southern in culture. Today its citizens are disfranchised and ruled by an irresponsible Congressional committee, because if Washington had democratic government, Negroes would vote and hold office, go to hotels, and sit in restaurants.

We sought to settle this problem at first by asking change of venue to some more civilized part of the nation. This was promptly denied. Then someone proposed that we hire an apartment and all live together. This I vetoed. It could put us all in jail if the press got wind of it.

At our first arraignment, we tried all stopping at a colored hotel. The accommodations were poor, however, and Mrs. Du Bois and I then procured lodging with a young colored man and his wife, who were not so afraid as their frightened friends. Our white colleagues went to white hotels and the colored attorneys stopped at home. A local trade union furnished us a meeting place for consultation. Thus matters went on for a week. Then one of the white defendants put the case up to the management of the Statler, the newest and best hotel in Washington. They had no space then, but made reservations for the week of the trial, which proved the last. We all stopped there, and were courteously entertained. Indeed, we held our Victory celebration there, in the center of one of their best dining rooms, with white and black persons, lawyers, defendants, and colored newspaper reporters present. Thus we won at least a temporary battle "along the Color Line" just as we won our liberty from a jail sentence.

There remained, however, my quandary. The government not only went to trouble and large expense, risked its own reputation, but also forced us to extraordinary and world-wide effort, to escape punishment. Personally, I had no funds for such a case. I am retired from work, with a pension too small for normal expenses of living. My wife's work and income were seriously curtailed by her complete immersion in this case. We have no rich friends. None of the defendants were able personally to finance this case. Had it not been for the almost miraculous rise of American friends, we would have gone to jail by default. Not a cent of money for the trial came from abroad. Even had this been possible, it would have been used to convict us. But in this nation by popular appeal to poor and middle-class folk, Negroes and white, trade unions and other groups, we raised funds for these purposes:

Legal fees	$18,400
Publicity	5,600
Office	5,250
Salaries	3,600
Travel	2,365

To this should be added additional legal fees of at least $13,000; $3,000 paid to an attorney hired by one of the defendants and not paid for by the Committee, and at least $10,000 which Marcantonio earned but would not accept. This amounts to a total of $40,215. To this should be added at least $2,000 in travel expenses paid by localities. How much the case cost the government we cannot know, but it could not have been less than $100,000, and it might have been much more.

The net result of this extraordinary trial, of wasted time and strength, and at least $150,000 of the earnings of the poor, was neither to prove nor allege that any one of the five defendants had committed any act involving moral turpitude; it did not prove or even allege that the World Peace Council, representing over seventy nations including our own, was guilty of anything but trying to stop war. When the government of the United States alleged that the defendants were agents of the World Peace Council, it was unable with all its power and money to convince one of its own judges that it had sufficient evidence to lay before a jury; and that therefore the demand of the Department of Justice that the defendants register as foreign agents was not sustained.

But of course this unjustified effort to make five persons register as the source of foreign propaganda for peace and particularly to scare fifteen million Negroes from complaint, was not the real object of this long and relentless persecution. The real object was to prevent American citizens of any sort from daring to think or talk against the determination of Big Business to reduce Asia to colonial subserviency to American industry; to reweld the chains on Africa; to consolidate United States control of the Caribbean and South America; and above all to crush Socialism in the Soviet Union and China. That was the object of this case.

This object every intelligent American knew. Our leading thinkers and educators were perfectly aware of this assault on the basis of the democratic process in America. Even if some thought peace at present dangerous and did not believe in socialism, they knew that if democracy was to survive in modern culture and in this vaunted "Land of the Free" and leader of "free nations," the right to think and to speak; the right to know what others were thinking; particularly to know opinion in that Europe which, despite our provincial and vulgar boasting and the golgotha of world wars, is still our main source of science and culture—that this democratic right of freedom of thought and speech must be preserved from Truman and McGrath; McCarran and Smith; from McCarthy and little Georgia Wood leading the reactionary slave South, or America was dead.

Despite this, most Americans of education and stature did not say a word or move a hand. This is the most astonishing and frightening result of this trial. We five are free but America is not. The absence of moral courage and intellectual integrity which our persecution revealed still stands to frighten our own nation and the better world. It is clear still today, that freedom of speech and of thinking can be attacked in the

United States without the intellectual and moral leaders of this land raising a hand or saying a word in protest or defense, except in the case of the Saving Few. Their ranks did not include the heads of the great universities, the leaders of religion, or most of the great names in science. Than this fateful silence there is on earth no greater menace to present civilization.

It was the State Department which started this prosecution to quell Communists, and retard the peace movement which was beginning to annoy the Pentagon. The inclusion of myself, a Negro, in the dragnet, was probably at first fortuitous, but quickly backed by the Military as a needed warning to complaining Negroes. When rising public opinion fastened on me as the key figure, the determination of the government to convict me increased, especially when I refused to plead "Nolle Contendere" and my contumacious speeches continued. The continued appeals to Truman and McGrath must have had effect, but were ignored at the insistence of the State Department, until the volume of protest abroad compelled attention, centered emphasis on the Negro question in America, and made even the Catholic Church aware that the growing extent of its proselytizing among Negroes might suffer from the fact that the Attorney-General was a Catholic.

When Marcantonio became our chief counsel, the Catholic hierarchy must also have remembered that around him was a large group of voters with Catholic background. The State Department sent down emissaries to mingle with the audience at the trial, and to make inquiries about me, since apparently they had never heard of me previously.

The Department of Justice evidently put its main faith in Rogge's testimony to secure a conviction, but when the judge excluded testimony about the foreign policy of the Soviet Union, and testimony about the aims and acts of the World Defenders of Peace, demanding first that evidence of our agency of the Defenders of Peace be introduced, the value of Rogge's testimony was very small, and more damning against him than us. Hearing this, the Department of Justice had made a frantic last minute search of all possible sources of information for possible discovery of spies and stoolpigeons. Practically every person who had attended any meetings of the Peace Information Center or been connected in any way was visited by F.B.I. agents, often two or three times, and many of them subpoenaed. So little was discovered, however, that at the last moment most of these witnesses were never summoned.

As public opinion against this prosecution belted the earth and threatened to erupt into the Assembly of the United Nations, and when despite free trips abroad for prominent Negroes, and threats against Negro professionals, civil servants and business men, the volume of Negro protest increased rather than stopped, Truman and the National Democratic Committee began to listen to the warning of the highest placed Negro Democrats, and the pressure for conviction lessened.

There was some indication that an attack on colored jurors might be tried, but that seemed too risky. All Jews on the panel were barred, but Negroes, most of them office-holders and subject to intimidation, were accepted. But any verdict of conviction with a jury of eight Negroes and four whites was hardly probable. A devout Catholic judge, who once faced trouble for refusing to grant any divorces, was assigned to the case.

What turns me cold in all this experience is the certainty that thousands of innocent victims are in jail today because they had neither money, experience nor friends to help them. The eyes of the world were on our trial despite the desperate effort of press and radio to suppress the facts and cloud the real issues; the courage and money of friends and of strangers who dared stand for a principle freed me; but God only knows how many who were as innocent as I and my colleagues are today in hell. They daily stagger out of prison doors embittered, vengeful, hopeless, ruined. And of this army of the wronged, the proportion of Negroes is frightful. We protect and defend sensational cases where Negroes are involved. But the great mass of arrested or accused black folk have no defense. There is desperate need of nation-wide organizations to oppose this national racket of railroading to jails and chain-gangs the poor, friendless and black.

Only a minority of the business and professional Negroes of Harlem attended my birthday dinner after the indictment was known. Of the fifty presidents of Negro colleges, every one of which I had known and visited—and often many times as speaker and adviser—of these only one, Charles Johnson of Fisk University, publicly professed belief in my integrity before the trial; and only one congratulated me after the acquittal.

The Negro churches varied: the Baptists of Philadelphia strongly supported me, but the National Baptist Convention took no action; several bishops of the A.M.E. and Zion Church connections expressed sympathy, and my undergraduate Negro fraternity, the Alpha Phi Alpha, was divided in opinion. The colored Elks supported me through their chief official, but none of the other colored secret orders did.

Colored public school teachers sat in almost complete silence. All this shows not necessarily lack of sympathy for me in my persecution, but the wide fear and intimidation of the Negro people of America, afraid for jobs, appointments, business opportunities, and even of personal safety.

In contrast to all this lethargy and fright, the mass support which I gained from the Negroes of the nation began slowly as soon as they could understand the facts, and then swelled in astonishing volume as the trial neared. From the beginning of the trial the courtroom was continuously crowded, and largely by out-of-town colored people and white, some of whom came from long distances. The coverage by Negro newspapers attested the nation-wide demand for news and sympathy for the accused. The F.B.I. and the Departments of State and Justice had observers seeking information from Negroes present. Republican and Democratic National Committees kept in touch. There is no doubt that increasing apprehension of repercussions of the possible results of this trial on the Negro vote played a great part in its result.

We must admit that the majority of the American Negro intelligentsia, together with much of the West Indian and West African leadership, shows symptoms of following in the footsteps of western acquisitive society, with its exploitation of labor, monopoly of land and its resources, and with private profit for the smart and unscrupulous in a world of poverty, disease and ignorance, as the natural end of human culture. I have long noted and fought this all too evident tendency, and built my faith in its ultimate change on an inner Negro cultural ideal. I thought this ideal would be built on ancient African communism, supported and developed by memory of slavery and experience of caste, which would drive the Negro group into a spiritual unity precluding the development of economic classes and inner class struggle. This was once possible, but it is now improbable. I strove hard to accomplish this while I was yet editor of the *Crisis*, and afterward in my teaching at Atlanta University.

Just before I lost my position there by compulsory age retirement, I had finished plans for uniting all the powerful colored Land Grant colleges into an organization under the leadership of my department in Atlanta University, to pursue co-operative social studies covering the black South. If once this had become established, my guidance of the young Negro intelligentsia might have been increased and implemented, and the science of sociology might have immeasurably benefited by a laboratory test of extraordinary breadth and opportunity. This, as I fondly hoped, might have revived my Atlanta University studies of the late 19th century, which white "philanthropy" starved to untimely death. All this, petty envy killed, just as it was reborn.

The very loosening of outer racial discriminatory pressures has not, as I had once believed, left Negroes free to become a group cemented into a new cultural unity, capable of absorbing socialism, tolerance and democracy, and helping to lead America into a new heaven and new earth. But rather, partial emancipation is freeing some of them to ape the worst of American and Anglo-Saxon chauvinism, luxury, showing-off and "social climbing."

I find, curiously enough then, that my experience in this fantastic accusation and criminal process is tending to free me from that racial provincialism which I always recognized but which I was sure would eventually land me in an upper realm of cultural unity, led by "My People." I have discovered that a large and powerful portion of the educated and well-to-do Negroes are refusing to forge forward in social leadership of anyone, even their own people, but are eager to fight social medicine for sick whites or sicker Negroes; are opposing trade unionism not only for white labor but for the far more helpless black worker; are willing to get "rich quick" not simply by shady business enterprise, but even by organized gambling and the "dope" racket.

On the other hand, I am free from jail today, not only by the efforts of that smaller part of the Negro intelligentsia which has shared my vision, but also by the steadily increasing help of Negro masses and of whites who have risen above race prejudice not by philanthropy but by brotherly and sympathetic sharing of the Negro's burden and identification with it as part of their own. Without the help of the trade unionists, white and black, without the Progressives and radicals, without Socialists and Communists and lovers of peace all over the world, my voice would now be stilled forever.

In Battle for Peace, 1952

A Vista of Ninety Fruitful Years

THIS IS the month of my 90th birthday. I have lived to an age which is increasingly distasteful to this nation. Unless by 60 a man has gained possession of enough to support himself without paid employment, he faces the distinct possibility of starvation. He is liable to lose his job and to refusal if he seeks another. At 70 he is frowned upon by the Church and if he is foolish enough to survive until 90, he is often regarded as a freak.

This is because in the face of human experience the United States has discovered that Youth knows more than Age. When a man of 35 becomes president of a great institution of learning or United State Senator or head of a multi-million dollar corporation, a cry of triumph rings in the land. Why? To pretend that 15 years bring of themselves more wisdom and understanding than 50 is a contradiction in terms.

Given a fool, a hundred years will not make him wise; but given an idiot, he will not be wise at 20. Youth is more courageous than age because it knows less. Age is wiser than youth because it knows more. This all mankind has affirmed from Egypt and China 5,000 years ago to Britain and Germany today.

The United States knows better. I would have been hailed with approval if I had died at 50. At 75 my death was practically requested. If living does not give value, wisdom and meaning to life, then there is no sense in living at all. If immature and inexperienced men rule the earth, then the earth deserves what it gets: the repetition of age-old mistakes, and wild welcome for what men knew a thousand years ago was disaster.

I do not apologize for living long. High on the ramparts of this blistering hell of life, I sit and see the Truth. I look it full in the face, and I will not lie about it, neither to myself nor to the world. I see my country as what Cedric Belfrage aptly characterizes as a "Frightened Giant," afraid of the Truth, afraid of Peace. I see a land which is degenerating and faces decadence, unless it has sense enough to turn about and start back.

It is no sin to fail. It is the habit of man. It is disaster to go on when you know you are going wrong. I judge this land not merely by statistics or reading lies agreed upon by historians. I judge by what I have seen, heard, and lived through for near a century.

There was a day when the world rightly called Americans honest even if crude; earning their living by hard work; telling the truth no matter whom it hurt; and going to war only in what they believed a just cause after nothing else seemed possible.

Today we are lying, stealing, and killing. We call all this by finer names: Advertising, Free Enterprise, and National Defense. But names in the end deceive no one; today we use science to help us deceive our fellows; we take wealth that we never earned and we are devoting all our energies to kill, maim, and drive insane, men, women and children who dare refuse to do what we want done.

No nation threatens us. We threaten the world. Our President says that Foster Dulles is the wisest man he knows. If Dulles is wise, God help our fools—the fools who rule us.

They know why we fail—these military masters of men—we haven't taught our children mathematics and physics. No, it is because we have not taught our children to read and write or to behave like human beings and not like hoodlums. Every child on my street is whooping it up with toy guns and big boys with real pistols. When Elvis Presley goes through the motions of copulation on the public stage it takes the city police force to hold back teen-age children from hysteria.

What are we doing about it? Half the Christian churches of New York are trying to ruin the free public schools in order to replace them by religious dogma; and the other half are too interested in Venezuelan oil to assist the best center in Brooklyn in fighting youthful delinquency, or to prevent a bishop from kicking William Howard Melish into the street and closing his church. Which of the hundreds of churches sitting half empty protests about this? None. They hire Billy Graham to replace the circus in Madison Square Garden.

All this must not be mentioned even if you know it and see it. America must never be criticized even by honest and sincere men. America must always be praised, or you lose your job or are ostracized or land in jail.

Criticism is treason, and treason or the hint of treason testified to by hired liars may be punished by shameful death. I saw Ethel Rosenberg lying beautiful in her coffin beside her mate. I tried to stammer futile words above her grave. But not over graves should we shout this failure of justice, but from the housetops of the world.

Honest men may and must criticize America: describe how she has ruined her democracy, sold out her jury system, and led her seats of justice astray. The only question that may arise is whether this criticism is based on truth, not whether it may be openly expressed.

What is truth? What can it be when the President of the United States, guiding the nation, stands up in public and says: *"The world also thinks of us as a land which has never enslaved anyone."* Everyone who heard this knew it was not true. Yet here stands the successor of George Washington who bought, owned, and sold slaves; the successor of Abraham Lincoln who freed four million slaves after they had helped him win victory over the slave-holding South. And so far as I have seen, not a single periodical, not even a Negro weekly, has dared challenge or even criticize that extraordinary falsehood.

This is what I call decadence. It could not have happened 50 years ago. In the day of our fiercest controversy we have not dared thus publicly to silence opinion. I have lived through disagreement, vilification, and war and war again. But in all that time, I have never seen the right of human beings to think so challenged and denied as today.

The day after I was born, Andrew Johnson was impeached. He deserved punishment as a traitor to the poor Southern whites and poorer freedmen. Yet during his life, no one denied him the right to defend himself.

A half century ago, in 1910, I tried to state and carry into realization unpopular ideas against a powerful opposition—in the white South, in the reactionary North, and even among my own people. I found my thought being misconstrued and I planned an organ of propaganda—*The Crisis*—where I would be free to say what I believed.

This was no easy sailing. My magazine reached but a fraction of the nation. It was bitterly attacked and once the government suppressed it. But in the end I maintained a platform of radical thinking on the Negro question which influenced many minds. War and depression ended my independence of thought and forced me to return to teaching, but with the certainty that I had at least started a new line of belief and action.

As a result of my work and that of others, the Supreme Court began to restore democracy in the South and finally outlawed discrimination in public services based on color. This caused rebellion in the South which the nation is afraid to meet.

The Negro stands bewildered and attempt is made by appointments to unimportant offices and trips abroad to bribe him into silence. His art and literature cease to function. He is scared. Only the children like those at Little Rock stand and fight.

The Yale sophomore who replaced a periodical of brains by a book of pictures concealed in advertisements, proposed that America rule the world. This failed because we could not rule ourselves. But Texas to the rescue, as Lyndon Johnson proposes that America take over outer space. Somewhere beyond the moon there must be sentient creatures rolling in inextinguishable laughter at the antics of our earth.

We tax ourselves into poverty and crime so as to make the rich richer and bring more crime and poverty. We know the cause of this: it is to permit our rich business interests to stop socialism and to prevent the ideals of communism from ever triumphing on earth. The aim is impossible.

Socialism progresses and will progress. All we can do is to silence and jail its promoters. I believe in socialism. I seek a world where the ideals of communism will triumph—to each according to his need; from each according to his ability. For this I will work as long as I live. And I still live.

National Guardian, February 17, 1958

To an American Born Last Christmas Day

THE MOST distinguished guest of this festive occasion is none other than my great-grandson, Arthur Edward McFarlane II, who was born this last Christmas day. He has kindly consented to permit me to read to you a bit of advice which, as he remarked with a sigh of resignation, great-grandparents are supposed usually to inflict on the helpless young. This then is my word of advice.

As men go, I have had a reasonably happy and successful life. I have had enough to eat and drink, have been suitably clothed and, as you see, have had many friends. But the thing which has been the secret of whatever I have done is the fact that I have been able to earn a living by doing the work which I wanted to do and that work was what the world needed done.

I want to stress this. You will soon learn, my dear young man, that most human beings spend their lives doing work which they hate and work which the world does not need. It is therefore of prime importance that you early learn what you want to do; how you are fit to do it and whether or not the world needs this service.

Here, in the next 20 years, your parents can be of use to you. You will soon begin to wonder just what parents are for besides interfering with your natural wishes. Let me therefore tell you: parents and their parents are inflicted upon you in order to show what kind of person you are, what sort of world you live in and what the persons who dwell here need for their happiness and well-being.

It was my unusual good fortune in the first 25 years of my life to learn by effort and hard competition just what I could do; then to get a fairly good idea of what the world was in which I must work. In these years I had seen the United States, North and South; I had lived in England, France, Germany and Italy; I had listened to the advice of some of the world's greatest minds and I had heard from the lips of human beings just what their problems were. Beside this, I had seen the Atlantic Ocean, the high Alps at Berne, the Venus of Milo and the Sistine Madonna.

Then I came home prepared to work. It was then, in the summer of 1892, 66 years ago, that I made a quite unconscious choice: I chose to begin my life work for the pleasure of doing it and the need of its being done and not for the money I was going to be paid for doing it. This was no great and advertised occasion; I asked no advice and none was proffered. I chose without hesitancy or question.

It was in this wise: after borrowing money to pay for postage stamps, I wrote the nation and offered my services. The response was slow and unenthusiastic. But at last three offers came. Wilberforce, a Negro college in Ohio, offered me $750 a year as a teacher. A state school in Missouri offered me $1,050.

I went to Wilberforce not because of any martyr complex but because I knew something about Wilberforce. I knew that in 1787, when this nation was declaring all men equal, two black men were on their knees praying to God in the fashionable church of St. George's in Philadelphia. While St. George's was glad to see Negroes practice the true religion, they did not like them to clutter up the aisles of this church and to assail God with such vehemence. Two deacons therefore approached these black men and whispered gently that it would be more seemly if they would finish their prayers in the balcony. The balcony was much nearer heaven than the main floor.

But these Negroes were stubborn. They said, "No, we are going to finish our prayers right here and now. Then we are going to get up and leave this church and we are never coming back." So one of these men, Richard Allen, left the white Methodist church and founded the African Methodist Episcopal church which today is one of the largest Negro organizations in the world.

And one of Allen's successors, Bishop Daniel Payne, bought a site in Southern Ohio and founded a college called Wilberforce. And Wilberforce in 1892 offered me a job teaching which I hastened to accept because at Wilberforce I planned to develop a university like the University of Berlin for the uplift of the Negro race in America.

Quite incidentally, Wilberforce offered me enough to live on during this work. The fact that the Missouri state school offered me $300 more seemed to me of no importance.

Right here, my esteemed great-grandson, may I ask you to stick a pin. You will find it the fashion in the America where eventually you will live and work to judge that life's work by the amount of money it brings you. This is a grave mistake.

The return from your work must be the satisfaction which that work brings you and the world's need of that work. With this, life is heaven or as near heaven as you can get. Without this—with work which you despise, which bores you and which the world does not need—this life is hell. And believe me, many a $25,000-a-year executive is living in just such a hell today.

Income is not greenbacks, it is satisfaction; it is creation; it is beauty. It is the supreme sense of a world of men going forward, lurch and stagger though it may, but slowly, inevitably going forward, and you, you yourself with your hand on the wheels. Make this choice then, my son. Never hesitate, never falter.

And now comes the word of warning: the satisfaction with your work even at best will never be complete, since nothing on earth can be perfect. The forward pace of the world which you are pushing will be painfully slow. But what of that: the difference between a hundred and thousand years is less than you now think. But doing what must be done, that is eternal even when it walks with poverty.

And I care not to garner while others
Know only to harvest and reap.
For mine is the reaping of sowing
Till the spirit of rest gives me sleep.

National Guardian, March 10, 1958

My Character

WHEN I WAS a young man, we talked much of character. At Fisk University character was discussed and emphasized more than scholarship. I knew what was meant and agreed that the sort of person a man was would in the long run prove more important for the world than what he knew or how logically he could think. It is typical of our time that insistence on character today in the country has almost ceased. Freud and others have stressed the unconscious factors of our personality so that today we do not advise youth about their development of character; we watch and count their actions with almost helpless disassociation from thought of advice.

Nevertheless, from that older generation which formed my youth I still retain an interest in what men are rather than what they do; and at the age of 50, I began to take stock of myself and ask what I really was as a person. Of course I knew that self-examination is not a true unbiased picture; but on the other hand without it no picture is quite complete.

From childhood I tried to be honest; I did not mean to take anything which did not belong to me. I told the truth even when there was no call for the telling and when silence would have been golden. I did not usually speak in malice but often blurted out the truth when the story was incomplete and was therefore as seemed to me wrong. I had strict ideas about money and its earning. I worked and worked hard for the first 25 cents a week which I earned. I could never induce myself to gamble or take silly chances because I figured the loss vividly in fatigue and pain. Once on a French train I played the pea in a shell game and lost two dollars. Forty years later in Mexico I won two dollars on a horse race. These were my first and last games of chance.

I was careful about debt. My folk were poor but seldom in debt. I have before me a statement of my indebtedness, September 1, 1894, when I started on my first life job. My salary was $800 a year and my living expense I calculated at: Board $100; Room $35; Clothes $65; Books $100; Debts $350; Sundries $25—Total $675; Savings $125. This proved too optimistic but still I kept out of debt. When I taught at Atlanta at a salary of $1,200 a year for 12 years, I owed nobody. I had a wife and child and each year I took them somewhere north so as to give them fresh air and civilization. It took every cent of my salary, together with small fees from lectures and writing, to pay our way and yet only once was I compelled to overdraw my salary for a month ahead.

Saving I neglected. I had had no experience in saving. My mother's family with whom I lived as a child never had a bank account nor insurance; and seldom a spare dollar. I took out a small life insurance of $1,000 when I was 27. I was cheated unmercifully by the white Pennsylvania company in the fee charged because I was colored. Later after marriage I took out $10,000 of insurance in a Negro company, the Standard Life. Eventually the company went bankrupt and I lost every cent. I was then too old to obtain more insurance on terms which I could afford.

My income has always been low. During my 23 years with the NAACP, I received for the first five years $2,500 a year. For the next 18 years, $5,000. With savings from this I bought a home and then sold it later for an apartment building in Harlem. There were five apartments, one of which my family was to occupy and the others I calculated would pay me a permanent income. But the house was overpriced; neglected orders for expensive sewer repairs were overdue. The down payment which I could afford was low and the property was overloaded with three mortgages on which I had to pay bonuses for renewal. Downtown banks began to squeeze black Harlem property holders and taxes increased. With the depression, tenants could not pay or moved.

There was one recourse: to turn the property into a rooming house for prostitution and gambling. I gave it to the owners of the mortgages and shouldered the loss of all my savings at 60 years of age. In all this I had followed the advice of a friend skilled in the handling of real estate but who assumed that I was trying to make money and not dreaming of model housing conditions. As many of my friends have since informed me, I was a fool; but I was not a thief which I count to my credit.

I returned to Atlanta University in 1934 at a salary of $4,500 a year but still out of debt. When ten years later I was retired without notice, I had no insurance and but small savings. A white classmate, grandson of a railway magnate, berated me for not wishing to give up work. He could not conceive of a man working for 50 years without saving enough to live on the rest of his days. In money matters I was surely negligent and ignorant; but that was not because I was gambling, drinking or carousing; it was because I spent my income in making myself and my family comfortable instead of "saving for a rainy day." I may have been wrong, but I am not sure of that.

On one aspect of my life, I look back upon with mixed feelings; and that is on matters of friendship and sex. I couple them designedly because I think they belong together. I have always had more friends among women than among men. This began with the close companionship I had with my mother. Friends used to praise me for my attention to my mother; we always went out together arm in arm and had our few indoor amusements together. This seemed quite normal to me; my mother was lame, why should I not guide her steps? And who knew better about my thoughts and ambitions? Later in my life among my own colored people the women began to have more education, while the men imitated an American culture which I did not share: I drank no alcoholic beverages until I went to Germany and there I drank light beer and Rhine wine. Most of the American men I knew drank whiskey and frequented saloons which from my boyhood were out of bounds.

Indeed the chief blame which I lay on my New England schooling was the inexcusable ignorance of sex which I had when I went south to Fisk at 17. I was precipitated into a region, with loose sex morals among black and white, while I actually did not know the physical difference between men and women. At first my fellows jeered in disbelief and then became sorry and made many offers to guide my abysmal ignorance. This built for me inexcusable and startling temptations. It began to turn one of the most beautiful of earth's experiences into a thing of temptation and horror. I fought and feared amid what should have been a climax of true living. I avoided women about whom anybody gossiped and as

I tried to solve the contradiction of virginity and motherhood, I was inevitably faced with the other contradiction of prostitution and adultery. In my hometown sex was deliberately excluded from talk and if possible from thought. In public school there were no sexual indulgences of which I ever heard. We talked of girls, looked at their legs, and there was rare kissing of a most unsatisfactory sort. We teased about sweethearts, but quite innocently. When I went South, my fellow students being much older and reared in a region of loose sexual customs regarded me as liar or freak when I asserted my innocence. I liked girls and sought their company, but my wildest exploits were kissing them.

Then, as teacher in the rural districts of East Tennessee, I was literally raped by the unhappy wife who was my landlady. From that time through my college course at Harvard and my study in Europe, I went through a desperately recurring fight to keep the sex instinct in control. A brief trial with prostitution in Paris affronted my sense of decency. I lived more or less regularly with a shop girl in Berlin, but was ashamed. Then when I returned home to teach, I was faced with the connivance of certain fellow teachers at adultery with their wives. I was literally frightened into marriage before I was able to support a family. I married a girl whose rare beauty and excellent household training from her dead mother attracted and held me.

I married at 29 and we lived together for 53 years. It was not an absolutely ideal union, but it was happier than most, so far as I could perceive. It suffered from the fundamental drawback of modern American marriage: a difference in aim and function between its partners; my wife and children were incidents of my main life work. I was not neglectful of my family; I furnished a good home. I educated the child and planned vacations and recreation. But my main work was out in the world and not at home. That work out there my wife appreciated but was too busy to share because of cooking, marketing, sweeping and cleaning and the endless demands of children. This she did naturally without complaint until our firstborn died—died not out of neglect but because of a city's careless sewage. His death tore our lives in two. I threw myself more completely into my work, while most reason for living left the soul of my wife. Another child, a girl, came later, but my wife never forgave God for the unhealable wound.

As I wandered across the world to wider and higher goals, I sensed two complaints against the pairing of the sexes in modern life: one, that ties between human beings are usually assumed to be sexual if a man and woman are concerned; and two, that normal friendships between men and women could not exist without sex being assumed to be the main ingredient. Also, if a man and woman are friends, they must be married and their friendship may become a cloying intimacy, often lasting 24 hours a day, with few outside friends of the opposite sex on pain of gossip, scandal and even crime engulfing the family. My travel and work away from home saved us from this. One difficulty of married life we faced as many others must have. My wife's life-long training as a virgin, made it almost impossible for her ever to regard sexual intercourse as not fundamentally indecent. It took careful restraint on my part not to make her unhappy at this most beautiful of human experiences. This was no easy task for a normal and lusty young man.

Most of my friends and helpers have been women; from my mother, aunts and cousins, to my fellow teachers, students, secretaries, and dreamers toward a better world. Sex indulgence was never the cause or aim of these friendships. I do not think my women friends ever gave my wife harm or unease. I was thoughtful of her comfort and support and of her treatment in public and private. My absence from home so much helped in the household drudgery. I still make my own bed of mornings; for many years I prepared my own breakfast, especially my coffee; I always leave a bathroom cleaner than when I enter; but sewing and sweeping I neglect. I have often wondered if her limitation to a few women friends and they chiefly housekeepers; and if her lack of contact with men, because of her conventional upbringing and her surroundings—if this did not make her life unnecessarily narrow and confined. My life on the other hand threw me widely with women of brains and great effort to work on the widest scale. I am endlessly grateful for these contacts.

My first married life lasted over half a century, and its

ending was normal and sad, with the loneliness which is always the price of death. To fill this great gap, and let my work go on, I married again near the end of my days. She was a woman 40 years my junior but her work and aim in life had been close to mine because her father had long believed in what I was trying to do. The faith of Shirley Graham in me was therefore inherited and received as a joy and not merely as a duty. She has made these days rich and rewarding.

In the midst of my career there burst on me a new and undreamed of aspect of sex. A young man, long my disciple and student, then my co-helper and successor to part of my work, was suddenly arrested for molesting men in public places. I had before that time no conception of homosexuality. I had never understood the tragedy of an Oscar Wilde. I dismissed my co-worker forthwith, and spent heavy days regretting my act.

I knew far too few of my contemporaries. I was on occasion incomprehensibly shy, and almost invariably loath to interrupt others in seeking to explain myself. This in the case of my fellow Negroes was balanced by our common experiences and shared knowledge of what each other had lived through; but in the case of white companions, and especially those newly met, we could not talk together, we lived in different worlds. We belonged to no social clubs, and did not visit the same people or even stand at the same liquor bars. We did not lunch together. I did not play cards, and could never get wildly enthusiastic even over baseball. Naturally we could not share stories of sex.

Thus I did not seek white acquaintances, I let them make the advances, and they therefore thought me arrogant. In a sense I was, but after all I was in fact rather desperately hanging on to my self-respect. I was not fighting to dominate others; I was fighting against my own degradation. I wanted to meet my fellows as an equal; they offered or seemed to offer only a status of inferiority and submission.

I did not for the most part meet my great contemporaries. Doubtless this was largely my own fault. I did not seek them. I deliberately refused invitations to spend weekends with Henry James and H. G. Wells. I did not follow up an offer of the wife of Havelock Ellis to meet him and Bernard Shaw.

Later, when I tried to call on Shaw he was coy. Several times I could have met Presidents of the United States and did not. Great statesmen, writers and artists of America, I might have met, and in some cases, might have known intimately. I did not try to accomplish this. This was partly because of my fear that color caste would interfere with our meeting and understanding; if not with the persons themselves, certainly with their friends. But even beyond this, I was not what Americans called a "good fellow."

This too illustrates a certain lack of sympathy and understanding which I had for my students. I was for instance a good teacher. I stimulated inquiry and accuracy. I met every question honestly and never dodged an earnest doubt. I read my examination papers carefully and marked them with sedulous care. But I did not know my students as human beings; they were to me apt to be intellects and not souls. To the world in general I was nearly always the isolated outsider looking in and seldom part of that inner life. Partly that role was thrust upon me because of the color of my skin. But I was not a prig. I was a lusty man with all normal appetites. I loved "Wine, Women and Song." I worked hard and slept soundly; and if, as many said, I was hard to know, it was that with all my belligerency I was in reality unreasonably shy.

One thing I avoided, and that was envy. I tried to give the other fellow his due even when I disliked him personally and disagreed with him logically. It became to me a point of honor never to refuse appreciation to one who had earned it, no matter who he was. I loved living, physically as well as spiritually. I could not waste my time on baseball but I could appreciate a home run. My own exercise was walking, but there again I walked alone. I knew life and death. The passing of my first-born boy was an experience from which I never quite recovered. I wrote:

"The world loved him; the women kissed his curls, the men looked gravely into his wonderful eyes, and the children hovered and fluttered about him. I can see him now, changing like the sky from sparkling laughter to darkening frowns, and then to wondering thoughtfulness as he watched the world. He knew no color-line, poor dear—and the veil, though it shadowed him, had not yet darkened half his sun. He loved the white matron, he loved his black nurse; and in his little world walked souls alone, uncolored and unclothed. I—yea, all men—are larger and purer by the infinite breadth of that one little life. She who in simple clearness of vision sees beyond the stars said when he had flown—'He will be happy There; he ever loved beautiful things.' And I, far more ignorant, and blind by the web of my own weaving, sit alone winding words and muttering, 'If still he be, and he be There, and there be a There, let him be happy, O Fate!'

"Blithe was the morning of his burial, with bird and song and sweet-smelling flowers. The trees whispered to the grass, but the children sat with hushed faces. And yet it seemed a ghostly unreal day—the wraith of Life. We seemed to rumble down an unknown street behind a little white bundle of posies, with the shadow of a song in our ears. The busy city dinned about us; they did not say much, those pale-faced hurrying men and women; they did not say much—they only glanced and said 'Niggers.' "

My religious development has been slow and uncertain. I grew up in a liberal Congregational Sunday School and listened once a week to a sermon on doing good as a reasonable duty. Theology played a minor part and our teachers had to face some searching questions. At 17 I was in a missionary college where religious orthodoxy was stressed; but I was more developed to meet it with argument, which I did. My "morals" were sound, even a bit puritanic, but when a hidebound old deacon inveighed against dancing I rebelled. By the time of graduation I was still a "believer" in orthodox religion, but had strong questions which were encouraged at Harvard. In Germany I became a freethinker and when I came to teach at an orthodox Methodist Negro school I was soon regarded with suspicion, especially when I refused to lead the students in public prayer. When I became head of a department at Atlanta, the engagement was held up because again I balked at leading in prayer, but the liberal president let me substitute the Episcopal prayer book on most occasions. Later I improvised prayers on my own. Finally I faced a crisis: I was using Crapsey's *Religion and Politics* as a Sunday School text. When Crapsey was hauled up for heresy, I refused further to teach Sunday School. When Archdeacon

Henry Phillips, my last rector, died, I flatly refused again to join any church or sign any church creed. From my 30th year on I have increasingly regarded the church as an institution which defended such evils as slavery, color caste, exploitation of labor and war. I think the greatest gift of the Soviet Union to modern civilization was the dethronement of the clergy and the refusal to let religion be taught in the public schools.

Religion helped and hindered my artistic sense. I know the old English and German hymns by heart. I loved their music but ignored their silly words with studied inattention. Great music came at last in the religious oratorios which we learned at Fisk University but it burst on me in Berlin with the Ninth Symphony and its Hymn of Joy. I worshipped Cathedral and ceremony which I saw in Europe but I knew what I was looking at when in New York a Cardinal became a strike-breaker and the Church of Christ fought the Communism of Christianity.

I revered life. I have never killed a bird nor shot a rabbit. I never liked fishing and always let others kill even the chickens which I ate. Nearly all my schoolmates in the South carried pistols. I never owned one. I could never conceive myself killing a human being. But in 1906 I rushed back from Alabama to Atlanta where my wife and six-year old child were living. A mob had raged for days killing Negroes. I bought a Winchester double-barreled shotgun and two dozen rounds of shells filled with buckshot. If a white mob had stepped on the campus where I lived I would without hesitation have sprayed their guts over the grass. They did not come. They went to south Atlanta where the police let them steal and kill. My gun was fired but once and then by error into a row of *Congressional Records*, which lined the lower shelf of my library.

My attitude toward current problems arose from my long habit of keeping in touch with world affairs by repeated trips to Europe and other parts of the world. I became internationally-minded during my four years at Harvard, two in college and two in the graduate school. Since that first trip in 1892, I have made 15 trips to Europe, one of which circled the globe. I have been in most European countries and traveled in Asia, Africa and the West Indies. Travel became a habit and knowledge of current thought in modern countries was always a part of my study, since before the First World War when the best of American newspapers took but small account of what Europe was thinking.

I can remember meeting in London in 1911 a colored man who explained to me his plan of leading a black army out of Africa and across the Pyrenees. I was thrilled at his earnestness! But gradually all that disappeared, and I began building a new picture of human progress.

This picture was made more real in 1926 when it became possible for me to take a trip to Russia. I saw on this trip not only Russia, but prostrate Germany, which I had not seen for 30 years. It was a terrible contrast.

By 1945 all these contacts with foreign peoples and foreign problems and the combination of these problems with the race problem here was forced into one line of thought by the Second World War. This strengthened my growing conviction that the first step toward settling the world's problems was Peace on Earth.

Many men have judged me, favorably and harshly. But the verdict of two I cherish. One knew me in mid-life for 50 years and was without doubt my closest friend. John Hope wrote me in 1918:

"Until the last minute I have been hoping that I would have an opportunity to be with you next Monday when you celebrate the rounding out of 50 years in this turbulent but attractive world. But now I am absolutely certain that I cannot come, so I am writing Mr. Shillady expressing my regret and shall have to content myself with telling you in this letter how glad I am that your 50th birthday is going to be such a happy one because you can look back on so much good work done. But not the good work alone. What you may look upon with greatest comfort is good intention. The fact that every step of the way you have purposed to be a man and to serve other people rather than yourself must be a tremendous comfort to you. Sometime soon if I chance to be back in New York I am going to have you take your deferred birthday dinner with *me*. You do not realize how much that hour or two which we usually spend together when I am in New York means to me."

Joel Spingarn said:

"I should like to have given public expression by my presence and by my words, not merely to the sense of personal friendship which has bound us together for 15 years, but to the gratitude which in common with all other Americans I feel we owe you for your public service. It so happens that by an accident of fate, you have been in the forefront of the great American battle, not merely for justice to a single race, but against the universal prejudice which is in danger of clouding the whole American tradition of toleration and human equality.

"I congratulate you on your public service, and I congratulate you also on the power of language by which you have made it effective. I know that some people think that an artist is a man who has nothing to say and who writes in order to prove it. The great writers of the world have not so conceived their task, and neither have you. Though your service has been for the most part the noble one of teacher and prophet (not merely to one race or nation but to the world), I challenge the artists of America to show more beautiful passages than some of those in *Darkwater* and *The Souls of Black Folk*."

Let one incident illustrate the paradox of my life.

Robert Morse Lovett was perhaps the closest white student friend I made at Harvard; when not long before his last visit to New York about 1950 he wanted to see and talk with me, he proposed the Harvard Club of which he was a member. I was not. No Negro graduate of Harvard was ever elected to membership in a Harvard club. For a while Jews were excluded, but no longer. I swallowed my pride and met Lovett at the Club. A few months later he died.

The Autobiography, 1968

Articles from
THE CRISIS
1910–1934

The Crisis

November 1910

The object of this publication is to set forth those facts and arguments which show the danger of race prejudice, particularly as manifested to-day toward colored people. It takes its name from the fact that the editors believe that this is a critical time in the history of the advancement of men. Catholicity and tolerance, reason and forbearance can to-day make the world-old dream of human brotherhood approach realization; while bigotry and prejudice, emphasized race consciousness and force can repeat the awful history of the contact of nations and groups in the past. We strive for this higher and broader vision of Peace and Good Will.

The policy of THE CRISIS will be simple and well defined:

It will first and foremost be a newspaper: it will record important happenings and movements in the world which bear on the great problem of inter-racial relations, and especially those which affect the Negro-American.

Secondly, it will be a review of opinion and literature, recording briefly books, articles, and important expressions of opinion in the white and colored press on the race problem.

Thirdly, it will publish a few short articles.

Finally, its editorial page will stand for the rights of men, irrespective of color or race, for the highest ideals of American democracy, and for reasonable but earnest and persistent attempt to gain these rights and realize these ideals. The magazine will be the organ of no clique or party and will avoid personal rancor of all sorts. In the absence of proof to the contrary it will assume honesty of purpose on the part of all men, North and South, white and black.

Agitation

November 1910

Some good friends of the cause we represent fear agitation. They say: "Do not agitate—do not make a noise; *work*." They add, "Agitation is destructive or at best negative—what is wanted is positive constructive work."

Such honest critics mistake the function of agitation. A toothache is agitation. Is a toothache a good thing? No. Is it therefore useless? No. It is supremely useful, for it tells the body of decay, dyspepsia and death. Without it the body would suffer unknowingly. It would think: All is well, when lo! danger lurks.

The same is true of the Social Body. Agitation is a necessary evil to tell of the ills of the Suffering. Without it many a nation has been lulled to false security and preened itself with virtues it did not possess.

The function of this Association is to tell this nation the crying evil of race prejudice. It is a hard duty but a necessary one—a divine one. It is Pain; Pain is not good but Pain is necessary. Pain does not aggravate disease—Disease causes Pain. Agitation does not mean Aggravation—Aggravation calls for Agitation in order that Remedy may be found.

Pink Franklin

February 1911

The commutation of the death sentence of Pink Franklin, of South Carolina, to imprisonment for life is the latest step in an astounding American tragedy, but not, please God! the last.

Here is a colored boy, the son of a Southern white man, a boy with a fair common school education, good-tempered, pleasant to look upon and a regular worker. He is arrested under a law the essential principle of which has since been declared unconstitutional by the Supreme Courts of both South Carolina and the United States.

His plea of self-defense in killing an armed and unannounced midnight intruder into the very bedroom of himself and his wife, after he himself had been shot, would have absolutely freed any white man on earth from the slightest guilt or punishment. Yet it could not free a colored man in South Carolina. It brought a sentence of murder in the first degree.

Governor Ansell in commuting his sentence to imprisonment for life did a brave thing. Why was it brave? Because it was just? No, it was unjust. To punish this innocent man with a terrible sentence—one almost worse than death, were it not for the hope ahead—is a terribly unjust deed. Yet Governor Ansell's act was brave because of public opinion in South Carolina; because the dominant public opinion of that State demanded this boy's blood; because Governor Ansell took his political future in his hands when he defied this opinion. Honor, then, to Governor Ansell and to strong papers like the Columbia State; but what shall we say of the civilization of a community which makes moral heroism of the scantiest justice?

Rampant Democracy

February 1911

There is an artist in New York who rose from the humblest circumstances and now lives in a suburb of the city. In his rise he has evidently learned the essentials of democracy, for his wife in an interview says that they want separate Negro schools in that suburb. They need to have them, but a very foolish law interfered, she laments: "We got along here very well with our separate Negro school. At the same time the Catholic Church maintained a parochial school, to which most of the Italian children went, so that public schools had practically no problem to solve at all as to the commingling of children of different races."

Exquisite! Add to this the demand for separate Asiatic schools in California and we have a splendid start; we have but to demand, then, separate public schools for the rich and cultured. Why should Reginald De Courcey sit in school with Skinny Flynn and Isaac Baumgarten? Perish the thought! Then, too, we must in time distinguish between the Rich and the New Rich, the Real Thing and the Bounder. For instance, why should a Kentucky drummer presume to school his children with the lineal descendant of a patroon—but, noticing a deep red flush on the cheek of the artist's wife, we forbear to push this point. We merely pause to ask: What is democracy anyhow?

A Golden Wedding

June 1911

A golden nuptial mass for a colored man and wife was celebrated for the first time in this country on May 1, in honor of the 50th anniversary of the marriage of Mr. and Mrs. George E. Wibecan, Sr. They were married in Liverpool, England, in 1861, came to this country shortly afterward, and settled in Ridgewood, Long Island. For half a century they have been prominently identified with every forward movement in their section of the country, and are among the most respected citizens of Long Island. The parish, white and colored, turned out to honor the pair on their golden anniversary, and the parish priest paid a high tribute to their influence in the community.

George E. Wibecan, Jr., is one of Brooklyn's well-known colored men, and is high in the councils of the Republican party.

Business and Philanthropy

June 1911

The talented, systematic, hard-headed youth of our nation are put into business. We tell them that the object of business is to make money. Our dull, soft-headed, unsystematic youth we let stray into philanthropy to work for the good of men. Then we wonder at our inability to stop stealing. This is the great American paradox.

Small wonder that we see in our world two armies: one large and successful, well dressed and prosperous. They say bluntly: "We are not in business for our health—business pays!" The other army is seedy and diffident and usually apologetic. It says: "There are things that ought to be done, and we are trying to do them—philanthropy begs." Between the business men, pure and simple, and the professional philanthropists waver the world's hosts—physicians, lawyers, teachers, and servants, some regarding their work as philanthropy, most of them looking at it as business and testing its success by its pay.

Business pays.

Philanthropy begs.

Business is reality, philanthropy is dream: business first, philanthropy afterward—is this true? No, it is not. It is the foundation falsehood of our perverted social order.

In reality it is business enterprise that continually tends to defeat its own ability to pay and it is philanthropy that works to preserve a social order that will make the larger and broader and better business enterprises pay.

What is meant when we say a business pays? Simply this: that for the service rendered or the thing given, the public will to-day pay a valued equivalent in services or goods. Men do this because of their present wants. Given a people wanting certain things and corresponding business enterprises follow. Will this demand continue? That depends: if the satisfaction of these wants minister to the real health and happiness of the community, the demand will continue and grow; if not, eventually either the business or the nation will die. The fact then that a business pays to-day is no criterion for the future. The liquor traffic pays and so does the publishing of school books; houses of prostitution pay and so do homes for renting purposes: and yet alcoholism and prostitution mean death while education and homes mean life to this land.

The amount then that a business pays is no test of its social value. It may pay and yet gradually destroy the larger part of all business enterprise. Here enters philanthropy. Its object is to do for men not what they want done, but that which, for their own health, they ought to want done. Will such service pay? Possibly it will: possibly the people will want the service as soon as they learn of it and lo! "Philanthropy and five per cent." appears. More often, however, the people do not recognize the value of the new thing—do not want it; will not use baths or have anything to do with coffee rooms. Will they pay, then? If they perform a service necessary to human welfare and if the people are gradually learning what is really for their good, then sometimes such philanthropy pays. If it does not pay then the service offered was really unnecessary or the people to whom it was offered have ceased to advance toward betterment and are in danger of death.

The test, then, of business is philanthropy; that is, the question as to how far business enterprise is doing for men the things they ought to have done for them, when we consider not simply their present desires, but their future welfare. Just here it is that past civilizations have failed. Their economic organization catered to fatal wants and persisted in doing so, and refused to let philanthropy guide them. Just so to-day. Whenever a community seats itself helplessly before a dangerous public desire, or an ingrained prejudice, recognizing clearly its evil, but saying, "We must cater to it simply because it exists," it is final; change is impossible. Beware; the epitaph of that people is being written.

It is just as contemptible for a man to go into the grocery business for personal gain as it is for a man to go into the ministry for the sake of the salary.

There is not a particle of ethical difference in the two callings. The legitimate object of both men is social service. The service of one is advice, inspiration and personal sympathy; the service of the other is fresh eggs and prompt delivery. Thus "from the blackening of boots to the whitening of souls" there stretches a chain of services to be done for the comfort and salvation of men.

Those who are doing these things are doing holy work, and the *work done*, not the *pay received*, is the test of the working. Pay is simply the indication of present human appreciation of the work, but most of the world's best work has been, and is being done, unappreciated.

"Ah, yes," says the cynic, "but do you expect men will work for the sake of working?" Yes, I do. That's the reason most men work. Men want work. They love work. Only give them the work they love and they will ask no pay but their own soul's "Well done!" True it is that it is difficult to assign to each of the world's workers the work he loves; true it is that much of the world's drudgery will ever be disagreeable; but pay will never destroy inherent distaste, nor (above the starvation line) will it form a greater incentive than social service, if we were but trained to think so.

These things are true, fellow-Americans; therefore, let us, with one accord, attack the bottom lie that supports graft and greed and selfishness and race prejudice: namely, that any decent man has at any time any right to adopt any calling or profession for the sole end of personal gain.

"Surely," gasp the thrifty, "the first duty of man is to earn a living!" This means that a man must at least do the world a service such as men, constituted as they are to-day, will requite with the necessities of life. This is true for some men always; perhaps for most men to-day. We pray for some sweet morning when it will be true for all men. But is was not true for Socrates, nor for Jesus Christ.

I Am Resolved

January 1912

I am resolved *in this New Year to play the man—to stand straight, look the world squarely in the eye, and walk to my work with no shuffle or slouch.*

I am resolved *to be satisfied with no treatment which ignores my manhood and my right to be counted as one among men.*

I am resolved *to be quiet and law abiding, but to refuse to cringe in body or in soul, to resent deliberate insult, and to assert my just rights in the face of wanton aggression.*

I am resolved *to defend and assert the absolute equality of the Negro race with any and all other human races and its divine right to equal and just treatment.*

I am resolved *to be ready at all times and in all places to bear witness with pen, voice, money and deed against the horrible crime of lynching, the shame of "Jim Crow" legislation, the injustice of all color discrimination, the wrong of disfranchisement for race or sex, the iniquity of war under any circumstances and the deep damnation of present methods of distributing the world's work and wealth.*

I am resolved *to defend the poor and the weak of every race and hue, and especially to guard my mother, my wife, my daughter and all my darker sisters from the insults and aggressions of white men and black, with the last strength of my body and the last suffering of my soul.*

For all these things, I am resolved *unflinchingly to stand, and if this resolve cost me pain, poverty, slander and even life itself, I will remember the Word of the Prophet, how he sang:*

"Though Love repine and Reason chafe,
There came a Voice, without reply,
'Tis man's Perdition to be safe
When for the Truth he ought to die!"

A Mild Suggestion

January 1912

They were sitting on the leeward deck of the vessel and the colored man was there with his usual look of unconcern. Before the seasickness his presence aboard had caused some upheaval. The Woman, for instance, glancing at the Southerner, had refused point blank to sit beside him at meals, so she had changed places with the Little Old Lady. The Westerner, who sat opposite, said he did not care a ——, then he looked at the Little Old Lady, and added in a lower voice to the New Yorker that there was no accounting for tastes. The Southerner from the other table broadened his back and tried to express with his shoulders both ancestors and hauteur. All this, however, was half forgotten during the seasickness, and the Woman sat beside the colored man for a full half hour before she noticed it, and then was glad to realize that the Southerner was too sick to see. Now again with sunshine and smiling weather, they all quite naturally reverted (did the Southerner suggest it?) to the Negro problem. The usual solutions had been suggested: education, work, emigration, etc.

They had not noticed the back of the colored man, until the thoughtless Westerner turned toward him and said breezily: "Well, now, what do you say? I guess you are rather interested." The colored man was leaning over the rail and about to light his cigarette—he had several such bad habits, as the Little Old Lady noticed. The Southerner simply stared. Over the face of the colored man went the shadow of several expressions; some the New Yorker could interpret, others he could not.

"I have," said the colored man, with deliberation, "a perfect solution." The Southerner selected a look of disdain from his repertoire, and assumed it. The Woman moved nearer, but partly turned her back. The Westerner and the Little Old Lady sat down. "Yes," repeated the colored man, "I have a perfect solution. The trouble with most of the solutions which are generally suggested is that they aggravate the disease." The Southerner could not help looking interested. "For instance," proceeded the colored man, airily waving his hand, "take education; education means ambition, dissatisfaction and revolt. You cannot both educate people and hold them down."

"Then stop educating them," growled the Southerner aside.

"Or," continued the colored man, "if the black man works, he must come into competition with whites——"

"He sure will, and it ought to be stopped," returned the Westerner. "It brings down wages."

"Precisely," said the speaker, "and if by underselling the labor market he develops a few millionaires, how now would you protect your residential districts or your select social circles or—your daughters?"

The Southerner started angrily, but the colored man was continuing placidly with a far-off look in his eyes. "Now, migration is both costly and inhuman; the transportation would be the smallest matter. You must buy up perhaps a thousand millions' worth of Negro property; you must furnish some capital for the masses of poor; you must get some place for them to go; you must protect them there, and here you must pay not only higher wages to white men, but still higher on account of the labor scarcity. Meantime, the Negroes suddenly removed from one climate and social system to another climate and utterly new conditions would die in droves—it would be simply prolonged murder at enormous cost.

"Very well," continued the colored man, seating himself and throwing away his cigarette, "listen to my plan," looking almost quizzically at the Little Old Lady; "you must not be alarmed at its severity—it may seem radical, but really it is—it is—well, it is quite the only practical thing and it has surely one advantage: it settles the problem once, suddenly, and forever. My plan is this: You now outnumber us nearly ten to one. I propose that on a certain date, shall we say next Christmas, or possibly Easter, 1912? No, come to think of it, the first of January, 1913, would, for historical reasons, probably be best. Well, then, on the first of January, 1913, let each person who has a colored friend invite him to dinner. This would take care of a few; among such friends might be included the black mammies and faithful old servants of the South; in this way we could get together quite a number. Then those who have not the pleasure of black friends might arrange for meetings, especially in 'white' churches and Young Men's and Young Women's Christian Associations, where Negroes are not expected. At such meetings, contrary to custom, the black people should not be seated by themselves, but distributed very carefully among the whites. The remaining Negroes who could not be flattered or attracted by these invitations should be induced to assemble among themselves at their own churches or at little parties and house warmings.

"The few stragglers, vagrants and wanderers could be put under careful watch and ward. Now, then, we have the thing in shape. First, the hosts of those invited to dine should provide themselves with a sufficient quantity of cyanide of potassium, placing it carefully in the proper cups, and being careful not to mix the cups. Those at church and prayer meeting could choose between long sharp stilettoes and pistols—I should recommend the former as less noisy. Those who guard the colored assemblies and the stragglers without should carefully surround the groups and use Winchesters. Then, at a given signal, let the colored folk of the United States be quietly dispatched; the signal might be a church bell or the singing of the national hymn; probably the bell would be best, for the diners would be eating."

By this time the auditors of the colored man were staring; the Southerner had forgotten to pose; the Woman had forgotten to watch the Southerner; the Westerner was staring with admiration; there were tears in the eyes of the Little Old Lady, while the New Yorker was smiling; but the colored man held up a deprecating hand: "Now don't prejudge my plan," he urged. "The next morning there would be ten million funerals, and therefore no Negro problem. Think how quietly the thing would be settled; no more bother, no more argument; the whole country united and happy. Even the

Negroes would be a great deal happier than they are at present. Instead of being made heirs to hope by education, or ambitious by wealth, or exiled invalids on the fever coast, they would all be happily ensconced in Heaven. Of course, I admit that at first the plan may seem a little abrupt and cruel, and yet is it more cruel than present conditions, and would it not be well to be a little more abrupt in our social solutions? At any rate think it over," and the colored man dropped lazily into his steamer chair and felt for another cigarette.

The crowd slowly dispersed; the Southerner chose the Woman, but was heard to say something about fools. The Westerner turned to the New Yorker and said: "Now, what in hell do you suppose that darky meant?" But the Little Old Lady went silently to her cabin.

An Open Letter to Woodrow Wilson

March 1913

Sir: Your inauguration to the Presidency of the United States is to the colored people, to the white South and to the nation a momentous occasion. For the first time since the emancipation of slaves the government of this nation—the Presidency, the Senate, the House of Representatives and, practically, the Supreme Court—passes on the 4th of March into the hands of the party which a half century ago fought desperately to keep black men as real estate in the eyes of the law.

Your elevation to the chief magistracy of the nation at this time shows not simply a splendid national faith in the perpetuity of free government in this land, but even more, a personal faith in you.

We black men by our votes helped to put you in your high position. It is true that in your overwhelming triumph at the polls you might have succeeded without our aid, but the fact remains that our votes helped elect you this time, and that the time may easily come in the near future when without our 500,000 ballots neither you nor your party can control the government.

True as this is, we would not be misunderstood. We do not

ask or expect special consideration or treatment in return for our franchises. We did not vote for you and your party because you represented our best judgment. It was not because we loved Democrats more, but Republicans less and Roosevelt least, that led to our action.

Calmly reviewing our action we are glad of it. It was a step toward political independence, and it was helping to put into power a man who has to-day the power to become the greatest benefactor of his country since Abraham Lincoln.

We say this to you, sir, advisedly. We believe that the Negro problem is in many respects the greatest problem facing the nation, and we believe that you have the opportunity of beginning a just and righteous solution of this burning human wrong. This opportunity is yours because, while a Southerner in birth and tradition, you have escaped the provincial training of the South and you have not had burned into your soul desperate hatred and despising of your darker fellow men.

You start then where no Northerner could start, and perhaps your only real handicap is peculiar lack of personal acquaintance with individual black men, a lack which is the pitiable cause of much social misery and hurt. A president of Harvard or Columbia would have known a few black men as men. It is sad that this privilege is denied a president of Princeton, sad for him and for his students.

But waiving this, you face no insoluble problem. The only time when the Negro problem is insoluble is when men insist on settling it wrong by asking absolutely contradictory things. You cannot make 10,000,000 people at one and the same time servile and dignified, docile and self-reliant, servants and independent leaders, segregated and yet part of the industrial organism, disfranchised and citizens of a democracy, ignorant and intelligent. This is impossible and the impossibility is not factitious; it is in the very nature of things.

On the other hand, a determination on the part of intelligent and decent Americans to see that no man is denied a reasonable chance for life, liberty and happiness simply because of the color of his skin is a simple, sane and practical solution of the race problem in this land. The education of colored children, the opening of the gates of industrial opportunity to colored workers, absolute equality of all citizens before the law, the civil rights of all decently behaving citizens in places of public accommodation and entertainment, absolute impartiality in the granting of the right of suffrage—these things are the bedrock of a just solution of the rights of man in the American Republic.

Nor does this solution of color, race and class discrimination abate one jot or tittle the just fight of humanity against crime, ignorance, inefficiency and the right to choose one's own wife and dinner companions.

Against this plain straight truth the forces of hell in this country are fighting a terrific and momentarily successful battle. You may not realize this, Mr. Wilson. To the quiet walls of Princeton where no Negro student is admitted the noise of the fight and the reek of its blood may have penetrated but vaguely and dimly.

But the fight is on, and you, sir, are this month stepping into its arena. Its virulence will doubtless surprise you and it may scare you as it scared one William Howard Taft. But we trust not; we think not.

First you will be urged to surrender your conscience and intelligence in these matters to the keeping of your Southern friends. They "know the Negro," as they will continually tell you. And this is true. They do know "the Negro," but the question for you to settle is whether or not the Negro whom they know is the real Negro or the Negro of their vivid imaginations and violent prejudices.

Whatever Negro it is that your Southern friends know, it is your duty to know the real Negro and know him personally. This will be no easy task. The embattled Bourbons, from the distinguished Blease to the gifted Hoke Smith, will evince grim determination to keep you from contact with any colored person. It will take more than general good will on your part to foil the wide conspiracy to make Negroes known to their fellow Americans not as flesh and blood but as beasts of fiction.

You must remember that the ability, sincerity and worth of one-tenth of the population of your country will be absolutely veiled from you unless you make effort to lift the veil. When you make that effort, then more trouble will follow. If you tell your Southern friends that you have discovered that the internal revenue of New York is well collected and administered, they are going to regard you in pained surprise. Can a Negro administer! they will exclaim, ignoring the fact that he does.

But it is not the offices at your disposal, President Woodrow Wilson, that is the burden of our great cry to you. We want to be treated as men. We want to vote. We want our children educated. We want lynching stopped. We want no longer to be herded as cattle on street cars and railroads. We want the right to earn a living, to own our own property and to spend our income unhindered and uncursed. Your power is limited? We know that, but the power of the American people is unlimited. To-day you embody that power, you typify its ideals. In the name then of that common country for which your fathers and ours have bled and toiled, be not untrue, President Wilson, to the highest ideals of American Democracy.

Respectfully yours,
THE CRISIS.

Another Open Letter to Woodrow Wilson

September 1913

Sir: On the occasion of your inauguration as President of the United States, THE CRISIS took the liberty of addressing to you an open letter. THE CRISIS spoke for no inconsiderable part of ten millions of human beings, American born, American citizens. THE CRISIS said in that letter, among other things:

"The only time when the Negro problem is insoluble is when men insist on settling wrong by asking absolutely contradictory things. You cannot make 10,000,000 people at one and the same time servile and dignified, docile and self-reliant, servants and independent leaders, segregated and yet part of the industrial organism, disfranchised and citizens of a democracy, ignorant and intelligent. This is impossible and the impossibility is not factitious; it is in the very nature of things.

"On the other hand, a determination on the part of intelligent and decent Americans to see that no man is denied a reasonable chance for life, liberty and happiness simply because of the color of his skin is a simple, sane and practical solution of the race problem in this land."

Sir, you have now been President of the United States for six months and what is the result? It is no exaggeration to say that every enemy of the Negro race is greatly encouraged; that every man who dreams of making the Negro race a group of menials and pariahs is alert and hopeful. Vardaman, Tillman, Hoke Smith, Cole Blease and Burleson are evidently assuming that their theory of the place and destiny of the Negro race is the theory of your administration. They and others are assuming this because not a single act and not a single word of yours since election has given anyone reason to infer that you have the slightest interest in the colored people or desire to alleviate their intolerable position. A dozen worthy Negro officials have been removed from office, and you have nominated but one black man for office, and he, such a contemptible cur, that his very nomination was an insult to every Negro in the land.

To this negative appearance of indifference has been added positive action on the part of your advisers, with or without your knowledge, which constitutes the gravest attack on the liberties of our people since emancipation. Public segregation of civil servants in government employ, necessarily involving personal insult and humiliation, has for the first time in history been made the policy of the United States government.

In the Treasury and Postoffice Departments colored clerks have been herded to themselves as though they were not human beings. We are told that one colored clerk who could not actually be segregated on account of the nature of his work has consequently had a cage built around him to separate him from his white companions of many years. Mr. Wilson, do you know these things? Are you responsible for them? Did you advise them? Do you not know that no other group of American citizens has ever been treated in this way and that no President of the United States ever dared to propose such treatment? Here is a plain, flat, disgraceful spitting in the face of people whose darkened countenances are already dark with the slime of insult. Do you consent to this,

President Wilson? Do you believe in it? Have you been able to persuade yourself that national insult is best for a people struggling into self-respect?

President Wilson, we do not, we cannot believe this. THE CRISIS still clings to the conviction that a vote for Woodrow Wilson was NOT a vote for Cole Blease or Hoke Smith. But whether it was or not segregation is going to be resented as it ought to be resented by the colored people. We would not be men if we did not resent it. The policy adopted, whether with your consent or knowledge or not, is an indefensible attack on a people who have in the past been shamefully humiliated. There are foolish people who think that such policy has no limit and that lynching, "Jim Crowism," segregation and insult are to be permanent institutions in America.

We have appealed in the past, Mr. Wilson, to you as a man and statesman; to your sense of fairness and broad cosmopolitan outlook on the world. We renew this appeal and to it we venture to add some plain considerations of political expediency.

We black men still vote. In spite of the fact that the triumph of your party last fall was possible only because Southern white men have, through our disfranchisement, from twice to seven times the political power of Northern white men—notwithstanding this, we black men of the North have a growing nest egg of 500,000 ballots, and ballots that are counted, which no sane party can ignore. Does your Mr. Burleson expect the Democratic party to carry New York, New Jersey, Pennsylvania, Ohio, Indiana, Illinois, by 200,000 votes? If he does will it not be well for him to remember that there are 237,942 black voters in these States. We have been trying to tell these voters that the Democratic party wants their votes. Have we been wrong, Mr. Wilson? Have we assumed too great and quick a growth of intelligence in the party that once made slavery its cornerstone?

In view of all this, we beg to ask the President of the United States and the leader of the Democractic party a few plain questions:

1. Do you want Negro votes?
2. Do you think that a "Jim Crow" civil service will get these votes?

3. Is your Negro policy to be dictated by Tillman and Vardaman?
4. Are you going to appoint black men to office on the same terms that you choose white men?

This is information, Mr. Wilson, which we are very anxious to have.

THE CRISIS advocated sincerely and strongly your election to the Presidency. THE CRISIS has no desire to be compelled to apologize to its constituency for this course. But at the present rate it looks as though some apology or explanation was going to be in order very soon.

We are still hoping that present indications are deceptive. We are still trying to believe that the President of the United States is the President of 10,000,000 as well as of 90,000,000, and that though the 10,000,000 are black and poor, he is too honest and cultured a gentleman to yield to the clamors of ignorance and prejudice and hatred. We are still hoping all this, Mr. Wilson, but hope deferred maketh the heart sick.

Very respectfully yours,
THE CRISIS.

Howells and Black Folk

November 1913

In the composite picture which William Dean Howells, as his life work, has painted of America he has not hesitated to be truthful and to include the most significant thing in the land—the black man. With lie and twistings most Americans seek to ignore the mighty and portentous shadow of ten growing millions, or, if it insists on darkening the landscape, to label it as joke or crime. But Howells, in his "Imperative Duty," faced our national foolishness and shuffling and evasion. Here was a white girl engaged to a white man who discovers herself to be "black." The problem looms before her as tremendous, awful. The world wavers. She peers beyond the Veil and shudders and then—tells her story frankly, marries her man, and goes her way as thousands of others have done and are doing.

It was Howells, too, that discovered Dunbar. We have had

a score of artists and poets in black America, but few critics dared call them so. Most of them, therefore, starved; or, like Timrod, "passed" as white. Howells dared take Dunbar by the hand and say to the world, not simply here is a black artist, but here is an artist who happens to be black. Not only that, but as an artist Dunbar had studied black folk and realized the soul of this most artistic of all races. "I said," wrote Howells, "that a race which had come to this effect in any member of it had attained civilization in him, and I permitted myself the imaginative prophecy that the hostilities and the prejudices which had so long constrained his race were destined to vanish in the arts; that these were to be the final proof that God had made one blood of all nations of men."

Finally when, on the centenary of Lincoln's birth, a band of earnest men said, we must finish the work of Negro emancipation and break the spiritual bonds that still enslave this people, William Dean Howells was among the first to sign the call. From this call came the National Association for the Advancement of Colored People and THE CRISIS magazine.

The Three Wise Men

December 1913

The comet was blazing down from the sky on the midnight before Christmas. Three songs were dying away in the East: one from the rich and ornate chapel of the great cathedral on the hills beyond 110th Street—a song of beauty and exquisite finish but coldly and formally sung. Another, a chant from the dim synagogue on the lower East Side—heavy with droning and passionate; the last from West 53d Street—a minor wail of utter melody. The songs had died away and the three priests, looking at the midnight sky, saw the comet at the same moment. The priest in the ornate chapel, gowned in his silken vestments, paused and stared wonderingly at the star; it seemed drawing near to him and guiding him. Almost before he knew it he had thrown a rich fur cloak about himself and was whirling downtown in a taxicab, watching the star with fascinated gaze. The rabbi on the lower East Side no sooner saw that blaze in the heavens than a low cry of joy left his lips and he followed swiftly, boarding a passing Grand Street car and changing up Broadway; he hung on the footboard to watch unmindful of the gibes at his white beard and Jewish gabardine. The old black preacher of 53d Street, with sad and wrinkled face, looked at the moving star thoughtfully and walked slowly with it. So the three men threaded the maze of the Christmas-mad streets, neither looking on the surging crowds nor listening to the shouts of the people, but seeing only the star. The "honk, honk" of the priest's taxicab warned the black priest scarcely too soon, and he staggered with difficulty aside as it whizzed by and made the motorman of the car, which bore the Jew, swear at the carelessness of the chauffeur. One flew, the other whirred swiftly and the third walked slowly; yet because of their differing ways they all came to the steps of the great apartment house at the same moment, and they bowed gravely to each other, yet not without curiosity, as each ascended the steps. The porter was strangely deferential and they rose swiftly to the seventh floor, where a wide hall door flew silently open.

Within and before the wide log fire of the drawing room sat a woman. She was tall and shapely and well gowned. She sat alone. The guests had gone an hour since and the last footsteps of the servants were echoing above; yet she sat there weary, still gazing into the mystery of the fire. She had seen many Christmas Eves and they were growing all to be alike—wretchedly alike. All equally lonely, aimless—almost artificial. She arose once and walked to the window, sweeping aside the heavy curtains, and the brilliancy of the star blazed in upon her. She looked upon it with a start. She remembered how once long, long years ago she had looked upon stars and such things as very real and shining fingers of fate. She remembered especially on a night like this how some such star had told her future. How out of her soul wonderful things were to be born, and she had said unto the star: "How shall this be?" And something had answered: "That holy thing that shall be born of you shall be called the

Son of God." And then she had cried in all her maiden faith and mystery: "Behold the hand-maiden of the Lord, be it according to thy word." And the angel departed from her, and it never came back again. Here she was reaching the portals of middle age with no prospects and few ambitions; to live and wait and sleep; to work a soulless work, to eat in some great manger like this—that was the life that seemed stretching before her endless and without change, until the End and the Change of Changing. And yet she had dreamed such dreams and fancied such fair destiny! As she thought of these dreams to-night a tear gathered and wandered down her face. It was then that she became suddenly aware of two men standing on either side of her, and she felt, but did not see, a third man, who stood behind. But for the soft voice of the first speaker she would have sprung up in alarm, but he was an old man and deferential with soft ascetic Jewish face, with white-forked beard and gabardine, and he bowed in deep humility as he spoke, saying:

"Where is He that is born King of the Jews, for we have seen His star in the East, and have come to worship Him?"

The other surpliced figure, who stood upon her right hand, said the same thing, only less:

"Where is He who is born King, for we have seen His star in the East, and have come to worship Him?" And scarcely had his voice ceased than the strong low rolling of another voice came from behind, saying:

"Where is He, for we have seen His star in the East, and have come to worship Him?"

She sank back in her chair and smiled. There was evidently some mistake, and she said to the Jew courteously:

"There is no King here."

"But," said the Jew, eagerly, tremulously, "it is a child we seek, and the star has guided us hither; we have brought gifts of gold and frankincense and myrrh." Still the woman shook her head.

"Children are not allowed in these apartments," she said, "and besides, I am unwed."

The face of the Jew grew radiant.

"The Scriptures say He shall be born of a Virgin," he chanted. But the woman smiled bitterly.

"The children of Virgins are not welcome in the twentieth century, even though they be Sons of God!"

"And in a manger," continued the Jew.

"This is, indeed, a manger," laughed the woman, "but He is not here—He is not here—only—cattle feed here."

Then the silk-robed priest on the left interrupted:

"You do not understand," he said, "it is not a child of the body we seek, but of the Word. The Word which was with God and the Word which was God. We seek the illuminating truth which shall settle all our wild gropings and bring light to this blind world." But the woman laughed even more bitterly.

"I was foolish enough once to think," she said, "that out of my brain would leap some wondrous illuminating word which should give light and warmth to the world, but nothing has been born, save here and there an epigram and the smartness of a phrase. No, He is not here."

The surpliced priest drew back with disappointed mien, and then suddenly, in the face of priest and Jew, as they turned toward the unseen figure at her back, she saw the birth of new and wonderful comprehension—Jew and Gentile sank to their knees—and she heard a soft and mighty voice that came up out of the shadows behind her as she bent forward, almost crouching, and it said:

"Him whom we seek is child neither of thy body nor of thy brain, but of thy heart. Strong Son of God, immortal love. We seek not the king of the world nor the light of the world, but the love of the world, and of all men, for all men; and lo! this thou bearest beneath thy heart, O woman of mankind. This night it shall be born!"

Slowly her heart rose and surged within as she struggled to her feet; a wonderful revelation lighted in her whirling brain. She, of all women; she, the chosen one—the bride of Almighty God; her lips babbled noiselessly searching for that old and saintly hymn: "My soul doth magnify the Lord, and my spirit hath rejoiced in God, my saviour. For he hath regarded the low estate of his hand-maiden, for behold! from henceforth all generations shall call me blessed." A great new strength gripped her limbs. Slowly she arose, and as she rose, the roof rose silently with her—the walls of the vast room widened—the cold wet pavement touched her satined feet, and the pale-blue brilliance of the star rained on her coiled hair and naked shoulders. The shouting, careless, noisy midnight crowds surged by and brushed her gown. Slowly she turned herself, with strange new gladness in her heart, and the last words of the hymn on her lips: "He hath put down the Mighty from their seats and hath exalted them of low degree; he hath filled the hungry with good things and the rich he hath sent empty away." She turned, and lo! before her stood that third figure, an old, bent black man, sad faced and pitiful, and yet with brilliant caverned eyes and mighty wings that curved to Heaven. And suddenly there was with the angel a multitude of the heavenly host praising God and saying:

"Glory to God in the highest; and on earth peace, good will toward men."

SELAH!

A Question of Policy

May 1914

The Editor of THE CRISIS:

I wish the best success of your cause. May I therefore call your attention and that of your readers to certain rather characteristic points in your interesting Easter number of the magazine, in which I suspect that you tend to defeat your main purpose? First, I doubt whether your judgment of the late Mr. Robert C. Ogden was fair. If he did not admire "a self-conscious" Negro, he did not like self-consciousness in anyone. The ideal type of man, black or white, is not thinking about himself. Granting, however, that you put your finger on a certain limitation in Mr. Ogden's democracy, my point is that we ought to give "the benefit of the doubt" to the men of Mr. Ogden's type. If they are not the *best* friends of the *most* progressive movement, still let us claim them heartily as friends. Otherwise we tend to halt the procession. To claim them as friends tends to move such men our way. For what end do we talk if not to persuade? To persuade those who agree with us? That is cheap work. We want to persuade those who are on the fence, hesitating whether to come further.

Secondly, what you say of capitalizing the word Negro strikes me again as characteristic of the same attitude (shall I say it?) of carrying a chip on the shoulder. For I must confess that, though brought up in the sturdiest old anti-slavery traditions, I was never taught to spell either Negro or white with a capital. I still object to spell " white" after this new convention, and yet I wish to treat my colored friends as well as I treat white people. I suspect that most people do not know this new style of capitalization, and are quite innocent of the intent to give offense.

Thirdly, I think you go off the line of useful persuasion and create needless antagonism in what you say on page 286 of Mr. Roosevelt's remark that "the best men in the United States believe in treating each man, of whatever color, absolutely on his worth," etc. You and I wish this to become true. Do you imagine that it is the slightest help to our purpose to denounce Mr. Roosevelt's statement as a "falsehood"? Why not better keep the fine sentence in print in every issue of THE CRISIS, till the colonel comes back from South America? The more people who are made to see this sentence the sooner the world will come to believe it, and act up to it. The oftener you call such a word false the slower you inevitably make human progress toward our ideal.

We wonder sometimes at educated people who seem never to have grappled with the philosophy of evolution! Is it possible that the management of THE CRISIS, a progressive paper, is still living in the period of dualism, and thinks that we civilize the world in proportion to the number of people whom we can stir up to feel ugly?

Finally, why do you hurt and spoil the touching effect of the story of lynching at Leland, Miss., by what seems a clear slur at President Wilson and President Eliot? Has either of them ever given encouragement to lynching? Here are ninety millions of people emerging from the barbarism of only a few generations ago. The wonder is that there is so little killing; the fact is that society is steadily setting its face against it. Please say every positive word you like to establish the manliness, the patience and the courage of your leaders. Please do the least possible to arouse resentment of bitterness, which is sure to react upon those who stir it. Please do more of what you are doing every month, to show the growth of a kindly good will among all kinds of people. For good will is the only irresistible power in the universe.

Respectfully your friend,
CHARLES F. DOLE.

THE PHILOSOPHY OF MR. DOLE

We publish very gladly Mr. Dole's criticism of THE CRISIS, because of our deep respect for the writer and because he voices a real and vital disagreement with our policy which is continually, in one way or another, coming to expression. It is briefly this thesis: "Don't antagonize, don't be bitter; say the conciliatory thing; make friends and do not repel them; insist on and emphasize the cheerful and good and dwell as little as possible on wrong and evil."

THE CRISIS does not believe in this policy so far as the present status of the American Negro problem is concerned. We could imagine many social problems, and many phases in a particular problem, when the watchful waiting, the tactfully conciliatory attitude would be commendable and worth while. At other times it would be suicidal and this, in our opinion, is one of the times.

It was ever so. When the Hebrew prophets cried aloud there were respectable persons by the score who said:

"Unfortunate exaggeration!"

"Unnecessary feeling!"

"Ungodly bitterness!"

Yet the jeremiads were needed to redeem a people. When the abolitionists began, not simply to say, but to act as if slavery were a "covenant with hell," there were plenty of timid souls "on the fence, hesitating," who scrambled down hastily on the popular side and were willing to lynch Garrison and ostracize Phillips.

All this might be beside the mark if we had not already tried Mr. Dole's prescriptions. For now nearly twenty years we have made of ourselves mudsills for the feet of this Western world. We have echoed and applauded every shameful accusation made against 10,000,000 victims of slavery. Did they call us inferior half-beasts? We nodded our simple heads and whispered: "We is." Did they call our women prostitutes and our children bastards? We smiled and cast a stone at the bruised breasts of our wives and daughters. Did they accuse of laziness 4,000,000 sweating, struggling laborers, half paid and cheated out of much of that? We shrieked: "Ain't it so?" We laughed with them at our color, we joked at our sad past, and we told chicken stories to get alms.

And what was the result? We got "friends." I do not believe any people ever had so many "friends" as the American Negro to-day! He has nothing but "friends" and may the good God deliver him from most of them, for they are like to lynch his soul.

What is it to be a friend of the Negro? It is to believe in anything for him except, perhaps, total and immediate annihilation. Short of that, good and kind friends of colored folk believe that he is, in Mr. Dooley's charming phrase, "aisily lynched," and ought to be occasionally. Even if 2,662 accused black people have been publicly lynched, burned and mutilated in twenty-eight years (not to mention the murder of perhaps 10,000 other black folk), our friends think we ought not to disturb the good President of these United States because *"the wonder is that there is so little killing!"*

It is the old battle of the better and the best. The worst foes of Negro manhood to-day are those compromising friends who are willingly satisfied with even less than half a loaf. They want the Negro educated; but the South objects to Negro colleges. Oh, very well, then, high schools; but the South objects to "literary" training for "niggers!" Dear, dear! Then "industrial" training; but the South objects to training any considerable number of Negroes for industry; it wants them for menial service. Very well, train them as servants and field hands—anything as long as it is "education!" Then we and THE CRISIS rise and say: *"But——"* Our friends raise deprecating hands; they adjust the sofa pillows, shade the light, and say: "Now, now! *Give them the benefit of the doubt!"*

Or we clamor for the right to vote. "Of course you should

vote," say our friends. "But," says the South, "they are too ignorant and inexperienced; we will vote for them." "Excellent," cry our friends, "vote for them and guard them in their civil rights." "What's this?" asks the South. "We mean their economic rights," say our friends glibly, "their right to work and get property." "Yes," answers the South calmly, "the right to work, and we'll work them." "But——" cries THE CRISIS and the black man who has been worked long enough. "Sh!" answer our friends. *"You'll halt the procession!"*

That's precisely what we intend to do. For twenty-five years we have let the procession go by until the systematic denial of manhood rights to black men in America is the crying disgrace of the century. We have wrongs, deep and bitter wrongs. There are local and individual exceptions; there are some mitigating circumstances; there is much to be excused; there is much to be said; and yet for the great mass of 10,000,000 Americans of Negro descent these things are true:

We are denied education.

We are driven out of the Church of Christ.

We are forced out of hotels, theatres and public places.

We are publicly labeled like dogs when we travel.

We can seldom get decent employment.

We are forced down to the lowest wage scale.

We pay the highest rent for the poorest homes.

We cannot buy property in decent neighborhoods.

We are held up to ridicule in the press and on the platform and stage.

We are disfranchised.

We are taxed without representation.

We are denied the right to choose our friends or to be chosen by them, but must publicly announce ourselves as social pariahs or be suggestively kicked by the *Survey*.

In law and custom our women have no rights which a white man is bound to respect.

We cannot get justice in the courts.

We are lynched with impunity.

We are publicly, continuously and shamefully insulted from the day of our birth to the day of our death.

And yet we are told not to be "self-conscious;" to lie about the truth in order to make it "come true;" to grapple with the "philosophy of evolution;" and not to make people "feel ugly" by telling them "ugly facts."

Few admire Mr. Dole, personally, more than the editor of THE CRISIS. Mr. Dole is the type of what the American of the future may be: fine in feeling, delicate in touch, sensitive to the subtle beauties of the world. But Mr. Dole's feet never walked the way we tread. He does not know—he cannot conceive this darker world of insult, repression, hunger and murder. He and Charles William Eliot and Woodrow Wilson and millions of others have given no encouragement to lynching, except by silence!

Except by silence!

EXCEPT BY SILENCE!

Who ever tried harder than the Negro and his "friends" to use the lie for social betterment? We have lied about the South so strenuously that this may account for the persistent blackness of our faces. Oh, yes: the South is the true, tried friend of Negroes; the South wants them educated; the South detests lynching; the South loves black mammies and buries them handsomely; the little playful antics of mobs are but ebullitions of Anglo-Saxon energy or at worst the faults of "poor white trash," who do not count. Moreover, those who dispute these statements are either meddling white Northerners or impudent Negroes who want to marry white women.

All of this we black folk and our "friends" have been saying glibly and frequently. We were lying, and we knew we were lying, *to make the "falsehood come true;"* but did the world know this? Did we not lull this nation to false security and fatuous insensibility? And is the uneasiness of our friends at the plain talk of THE CRISIS the cause of ugly feeling or the necessary result of ridiculous lies? How far may we indeed meddle with the truth? Where is the boundary line between getting people "to come and believe" what is untrue and telling them on your honor that black is white? We have a sincere desire to see a little brochure by Mr. Dole—with hand-made paper, deckle edged and privately printed—on "The Uses of the Lie as a Means of Social Salvation." We would like to distribute a few copies in Heaven among Mr. Dole's Puritan ancestors and listen to the ensuing profanity.

It is the palpable evasions of our friends, and our earnest

friends like Mr. Dole, that are most discouraging. When we protest at the plain insult of "negro," Mr. Dole answers that we do not capitalize "white." But white is not the correlative of Negro, as Mr. Dole knows right well. "Black" and "colored" are the correlatives to "white," while Negro is used exactly as the words Malay or German or Jew or Indian are used. To refuse a word so used capitalization is a petty and usually a deliberate insult.

Humanity is progressing toward an ideal; but not, please God, solely by help of men who sit in cloistered ease, hesitate from action and seek sweetness and light; rather we progress to-day, as in the past, by the soul-torn strength of those who can never sit still and silent while the disinherited and the damned clog our gutters and gasp their lives out on our front porches. These are the men who go down in the blood and dust of battle. They say ugly things to an ugly world. They spew the lukewarm fence straddlers out of their mouths, like God of old; they cry aloud and spare not; they shout from the housetops, and they make this world so damned uncomfortable with its nasty burden of evil that it tries to get good and does get better.

Evolution is evolving the millennium, but one of the unescapable factors in evolution are the men who hate wickedness and oppression with perfect hatred, who will not equivocate, will not excuse, and will be heard. With the sainted spirits of such as these THE CRISIS would weakly but earnestly stand and cry in the world's four corners of the way; and it claims no man as friend who dare not stand and cry with it.

Votes for Women

August 1914

This fall the voters of six states certainly, and possibly eight, will vote on woman's suffrage. In North and South Dakota, Montana, Nevada, Missouri and Nebraska elections are scheduled and attempts are being made to include this question in the fall elections of Oklahoma and Ohio. The Negro population of these eight states is 552,054. Assuming that the black voters of Oklahoma will be largely disfranchised it is, nevertheless, probable that 80,000 Negro voters will be asked to vote for or against the extension of the right of suffrage to women. How should they vote? A colored woman writes us from New Haven:

> May I ask if through your columns you will answer some questions regarding Woman Suffrage and the colored woman? Our white friends come and tell us that we can do so much for ourselves when we get the ballot. Please tell me how we are going to do so much for ourselves? Will not the proportionate vote be the same as now? Should not the white women consider the betterment of the colored people as well as the foreigner who comes to our shores, because conditions are better here than in his own country? I attended a meeting a short time ago and the speaker invited questions. She had spoken of almost everything possible except the problems that vitally concern the people addressed. I asked her why the women were silent on the lynching of colored people in the South and on the unjust marriage laws and other laws discriminating against the Negro. She replied: "We have to take up the most important subjects, we cannot bother with everything under the sun and there are so many other things more important than lynching. As for marriage laws, we have to have some laws regulating marriage between races. For my part, I do not believe in marriage between Americans and Europeans." Now, Mr. Editor, this woman is a highly educated woman, but does not that sound like shallow reasoning? Are not Americans made up of all nations of Europe? Now what are we trying to do for ourselves if that is the way that the women who are working for votes for women feel towards the problem of the colored woman? Have we any right to believe that they will work for our cause after they get the ballot, if they do not feel willing to take up such questions now? Has the past history of our race anything to give us such encouragement?

Let us answer frankly, there is not the slightest reason for supposing that white American women under ordinary circumstances are going to be any more intelligent, liberal or humane toward the black, the poor and unfortunate than white men are. On the contrary, considering what the subjection of a race, a class or a sex must mean, there will undoubtedly manifest itself among women voters at first more prejudice and petty meanness toward Negroes than we have now. It is the awful penalty of injustice and oppression to breed in the oppressed the desire to oppress others. The southern white women who form one of the most repressed and enslaved groups of modern civilized women will undoubtedly, at first, help willingly and zealously to disfranchise Negroes, cripple their schools and publicly insult them.

Nevertheless, votes for women must and ought to come and the Negroes should help bring this to pass for these reasons:

1. Any extension of democracy involves a discussion of the fundamentals of democracy.

2. If it is acknowledged to be unjust to disfranchise a sex it cannot be denied that it is absurd to disfranchise a color.

3. If the North enfranchises women, the proportion of unselfish intelligent voters among Negroes will be increased, and the proportion of Negro voters whom white politicians have trained to venality will be decreased.

4. If when the North enfranchises women the South refuses, or enfranchises only the whites, then the discrepancy between North and South in the votes cast will be even greater than now; at present the southern white voter has from five to seven times the power of the northern voter. How long would the nation endure an increase or even a doubling of this power? It would not take long before southern representatives in Congress would be cut down or colored women enfranchised.

5. Granting that first tendencies would make the woman voter as unfair in race rights as the man, there would be in the long run a better chance to appeal to a group that knows the disadvantage and injustice of disfranchisement by experience, than to one arrogant and careless with power. And in all cases the broader the basis of democracy the surer is the universal appeal for justice to win ultimate hearing and sympathy.

Therefore: Votes for Women.

The Prize Fighter

August 1914

Boxing is an ancient sport. It is mentioned in Homer's Iliad and Virgil's Aeneid and was a recognized branch of the celebrated Olympic games. During the middle age boxing went out of style among most nations, the preference being given to various sorts of encounters with weapons. In England it was revived in the Seventeenth Century, and fighting with bare fists became a national sport in the Eighteenth Century. Boxing gloves were invented late in that century, and in the beginning of the Nineteenth Century, John Jackson (note the prophecy!) became champion and teacher of Lord Byron and other great and titled personages.

Gradually the more brutal features of the sport were eliminated and the eighth Marquess of Queensberry drew up a set of rules in the sixties which have since prevailed.

There is still today some brutality connected with boxing, but as compared with football and boat racing it may be seriously questioned whether boxing deserves to be put in a separate class by reason of its cruelty. Certainly it is a highly civilized pastime as compared with the international game of war which produces so many "heroes" and national monuments.

Despite all this, boxing has fallen into disfavor—into very great disfavor. To see publications like the New York *Times* roll their eyes in shivery horror at the news from Paris (to which it is compelled to give a front page) makes one realize the depths to which we have fallen.

The cause is clear: Jack Johnson, successor of the Eighteenth Century John Jackson, has out-sparred an Irishman. He did it with little brutality, the utmost fairness and great good nature. He did not "knock" his opponent senseless. Apparently he did not even try. Neither he nor his race invented prize fighting or particularly like it. Why then this thrill of national disgust? Because Johnson is black. Of course, some pretend to object to Mr. Johnson's character. But we have yet to hear, in the case of white America, that marital troubles have disqualified prize fighters or ball players or even statesmen. It comes down, then, after all to this unforgivable blackness. Wherefore we conclude that at present prize fighting is very, very immoral, and that we must rely on football and war for pastime until Mr. Johnson retires or permits himself to be "knocked out."

Does Race Antagonism Serve Any Good Purpose

September 1914

There are four classes of reasons usually given in defense of Race Antagonism.

1. It is an instinctive repulsion from something harmful and is, therefore, a subtle condition of ultimate survival.

The difficulty with this theory is that it does not square with the facts: race antipathy is not instinctive but a matter of careful education. Black and white children play together gladly and know no prejudice until it is implanted precept upon precept and by strong social pressure; and when it is so implanted it is just as strong in cases where there is no physical difference as it is where physical differences are striking. The racial repulsion in the Balkans among peoples of practically the same blood is to-day greater than it was between whites and blacks on the Virginia plantations.

2. Racial antagonism, whether instinctive or not, is a reasonable measure of self-defense against undesirable racial traits.

This second proposition is the one which usually follows careful examination of the first. After all, it is admitted "instinct" is an unimportant fact. Instincts are simply accumulated reasons in the individual or in the race. The reasons for antagonizing inferior races are clear and may be summed up as follows:

Poor health and stamina.
Low ability.
Harmful ideals of life.

We are now on surer ground because we can now appeal to facts. But no sooner do we make this appeal than we are astonished to find that there are surprising little data. Is it true that the Negro as a physical animal is inferior to the white man or is he superior? Is the high death rate of the

Indian a proof of his poor physique or is it proof of wretched conditions of life which would long ago have killed off a weaker people? And, again, is spiritual superiority always in direct proportion to physical strength in races any more than in individuals? Connected with this matter of health comes the question of physical beauty, but surely, if beauty were to become a standard of survival how small our world population would be!

It is argued, however, that it may be granted that the physical stamina of all races is probably approximately the same and that physical comeliness is rather a matter of taste and selection than of absolute racial difference. However, when it comes to intellectual ability the races differ so enormously that superior races must in self-defense repel the inferior sternly, even brutally. Two things, however, must be said in answer to this: First, the prejudice against the Jews, age long and world wide is surely not based on inferior ability. We have only to name Jeremiah, D'Israeli and Jesus Christ to set our minds at rest on that point. Moreover, if we compare the intellectual ability of Teuton and Chinese which is inferior? Or, if we take Englishman and Bantu, is the difference a difference of native ability or of training and environment? The answer to this is simple: We do not know. But arguing from all known facts and analogies we must certainly admit in the words of the secretary of the First International Races Congress, that "an impartial investigator would be inclined to look upon the various important peoples of the world as, to all intents and purposes, essentially equals in intellect, enterprise, morality and physique."

3. Racial antipathy is a method of Race Development.

We may admit so far as physique and native ability go, that as Ratzel says: "There is only one species of man; the variations are numerous, but do not go deep." At the same time it is plain that Europe has out-stripped China in civilization, and China has out-stripped Africa. Here at least are plain facts. Is not racial antipathy a method of maintaining the European level of culture? But is it necessary for the runner to hate and despise the man he is out-distancing? Can we only maintain culture in one race by increasing barbarism in others? Does it enhance the "superiority" of white men to allow them to steal from yellow men and enslave black men and reduce colored women to concubinage and prostitution? Surely not. Admitting that in the world's history again and again this or that race has out-stripped another in culture, it is impossible to prove that inherent racial superiority was the cause or that the level of culture has been permanently raised in one race by keeping other races down.

4. Race Antipathy is a method of group specialization.

This argument admits the essential equality of races but insists on the difference in gifts and argues that antipathy between races allows each to develop its own peculiar gifts and aptitudes. Does it? That depends on the "antipathy." If antipathy means the enslaving of the African, the exploitation of the Chinese, the peonage of Mexicans and the denial of schools to American Negroes then it is hard to see where the "encouragement" comes in. If it means the generous encouragement of all men according to their gifts and ability then why speak of race "antipathy" or encourage it? Let us call it Human Uplift and Universal Brotherhood and be done with it.

Such are the arguments. Most persons use all four at once and skillfully skip from one to the other. Each argument has in other days been applied to individuals and social classes, but we have outgrown that. We apply it to-day to "races" because race is a vague, unknown term which may be made to cover a multitude of sins. After all, what is a "Race?" and how many races are there? Von Luschan, one of the greatest of modern anthropologists, says: "The question of the number of human races has quite lost its *raison d' etre*, and has become a subject rather of philosophic speculation than of scientific research." What we have on earth is men. Shall we help them or hinder them? Shall we hate and kill them or love and preserve and uplift them? Which method will do us most good? This is the real question of "Race" antipathy.

From the Boston "Globe"

January 1915

The following editorial on "The Alleged Failure of Democracy" was written by the editor of THE CRISIS and printed in the Boston Sunday *Globe*:

We are becoming more democratic, but not easily, not without struggle and misgivings. Our progress seems even slower than it is because we have really experienced so little real democracy in the past. We founded a republic in 1787 which was in reality an aristocracy of the most pronounced tendencies. The democracy ushered in by Andrew Jackson was the beginning of that system of government by deception where "the people" are congratulated on the possession of all powers of government, while the real rulers hide in the background so effectually that their very existence often is not sensed. Since the Civil War we have driven these rulers into the open, and frankly acknowledged, weighed and studied their power.

From this knowledge we have started well on the way toward dethroning the ward heeler and the petty boss, and are hammering at the strongholds of the greater bosses. Our real difficulty comes in settling in our own minds a proper, permanent repository for the power thus regained. In other words, we are facing to-day still the elementary problem of democracy: How far do we dare trust the mass of the people, not with sham power and sounding phrases, but with real power?

Those on the one hand who call for commission government, and those on the other hand who ask for the initiative and the recall represent the two different answers to this problem. True it is, that there are those far-sighted ones who combine both demands. For the most part, however, we may distinguish those who would deposit the power won from the bosses with one or more strong men for safekeeping; and those who would try and place that power just as far as possible in the hands of the masses.

There can be no doubt that the former type of thinkers gains great strength and support from the supposed failure of certain democratic experiments in the past, particularly in the case of the foreign vote in our cities and of the Negro vote during reconstruction times. The alleged failure of democracy in reconstruction times especially has been used in the past and is still used as a tremendous argument against democracy in the nation and in the world. The argument runs something like this: "Ignorant freedmen failed as voters. This proves that democratic government cannot rest on ignorance." But how much learning is necessary to a share in the government? Immediately our ideas enlarge: "Government is for the educated and the expert. It is a reward, not a right. Democracy is an evolution that may come to fruition in a thousand years. To-day we need the strength and efficiency found only in a few." In the face of such argument it is high time that the people of this country asked themselves seriously two questions: What is democracy? Did democracy fail in reconstruction?

Democracy is not a gift of power, but a reservoir of knowledge. Only the soul that suffers knows its suffering. Only the one who needs knows what need means. Ignorance may vitiate the expression of needs and vice may deceive, but it remains true that despotism and aristocracy have displayed far more ignorance of the real needs of the people than the most ignorant of democracies. The people alone are the sources of that real knowledge which enables a State to be ruled for the best good of its inhabitants. And only by putting power in the hands of each inhabitant can we hope to approximate in the ultimate use of that power the greatest good to the greatest number.

Seldom in the history of the world has this great truth been so well proved as in the experience of the American Negro. Without civil or political rights, and admitting every claim of benevolence on the part of his master, he became a slave, whose very existence threatened the industrial and spiritual life of the nation. Emancipated and given a vote, despite his ignorance and inexperience, he gave the South three gifts, so valuable that no one to-day would dream of giving them up:

1. The public-school system.
2. The enfranchisement of the poor whites.
3. The beginning of modern social legislation in land reform, eleemosynary institutions and social uplift.

The Negro was not disfranchised because he had failed in democratic government, but because there was every reason to believe that he would succeed, and it was his success which the beaten masters feared more than his failure.

Having disfranchised him with this fiction of failure, that same fiction is being used to-day to discredit democracy throughout the nation, to stop the just enfranchisement of women, to curtail the power of the foreign born and their descendants, and to support the argument in the twentieth century that the democratic ideals of the nineteenth century were in vain.

To the help of this program comes the wholesale exploitation and despising of colored races and the suicidal career of universal conquest to which Europe stands committed.

But the march of real democracy goes on. Slowly but surely the masses of men will become the great depositors of the bulk of both political and economical power, for their own good. Only democratic government can be both enlightened and selfish, both bond and free.

An Amazing Island

June 1915

Jamaica is a most amazing island. I have seen something of the earth, more especially Europe and America which leave, to be sure, much unseen; but of the lands that I have looked upon hitherto Jamaica is the most startling. The ride from Spanishtown to the northwestern sea is one of the great rides of the world to be likened to the Horse Shoe Bend or St. Gotthard. The Wag Water is a beautiful stream and Montego Bay is the bay of Naples. The whole island is a mass of gray, green mountains thrown on the face of the sea with gash and shadow and veil. The rain of Jamaica is the maddest, wildest and wettest of rains and the sunshine is God's. There in Jamaica the world is met. Africa and Asia and Europe all meet which may mean little and yet may be the most fateful meeting the world ever saw. In Jamaica for the first time in my life I lived beyond the color line—not on one side of it but beyond its end. There in strange places I could sense its curious paths stopping and wavering and fading into uncertain threads. Of course, I was ever looking for it. That is my inborn nature. I saw that the moving picture films, for instance, were "approved" by "His Worship, the Mayor," and when I sat beside His Worship, the Mayor at dinner, behold, His Worship was colored. I almost hesitated at the barber shops but the barbers did not hesitate. It was a strange sort of luxury to ride on railways where engineers, firemen, conductor and brakemen were black. The smart, dark Constables in their gleaming white hats and coats gave me a double sense of security. In the stores there was usually a curl or a tint in the clerk that proclaimed the most ancient of blood and it was the same in the post office, the telephone exchange and the government buildings. In fact, though somewhat of an expert in knowing mine own, I confess that in Jamaica it was quite impossible for me to pick out the alleged 15,000 white people out of the 900,000 of population.

The peasants—a great mass of hard working black laborers—were to me perhaps more alluring. I can see now those black, straight and strong and full-bosomed forms, supple of hip and thigh and lithe of limb, sinewy yet fine and calm, treading their silent miles like fate. Soft of word and slow but sweet of smile and uncomplaining, of the blood and tears of such as these was built Jamaica. Threaded through all this curious beauty, with palm and mahogany, the scent of orange blossoms and the gleam of bananas, threaded through all this is the tragedy of a poverty almost incomprehensible. Think of a woman carrying sand all day, twelve endless hours in a Jamaica sun, for eighteen cents! Think of able-bodied men working for twenty-five cents and less a day. Think of walking fifty miles and carrying a hundred pound burden for forty cents. Think of raising and selling oranges at two cents a hundred!

Here is an island rich beyond dream; out of it for three centuries and more the white world has reaped its millions. Yet today the island lies poverty-stricken but facing the world proudly with one great gift, the gift of racial peace, the utter overturning of the barbaric war of color, with a chance for men to lift themselves regardless of the complexion of their grandfathers. It is the most marvelous paradox of this paradoxical western world.

Woman Suffrage

November 1915

This month 200,000 Negro voters will be called upon to vote on the question of giving the right of suffrage to women. THE CRISIS sincerely trusts that everyone of them will vote *Yes*. But THE CRISIS would not have them go to the polls without having considered every side of the question. Intelligence in voting is the only real support of democracy. For this reason we publish with pleasure Dean Kelly Miller's article against woman suffrage. We trust that our readers will give it careful attention and that they will compare it with that marvelous symposium which we had the pleasure to publish in our August number. Meantime, Dean Miller will pardon us for a word in answer to his argument.

Briefly put, Mr. Miller believes that the bearing and rearing of the young is a function which makes it practically impossible for women to take any large part in general, industrial and public affairs; that women are weaker than men; that women are adequately protected under man's suffrage; that no adequate results have appeared from woman suffrage and that office-holding by women is "risky."

All these arguments sound today ancient. If we turn to easily available statistics we find that instead of the women of this country or of any other country being confined chiefly to child-bearing they are as a matter of fact engaged and engaged successfully in practically every pursuit in which men are engaged. The actual work of the world today depends more largely upon women than upon men. Consequently this man-ruled world faces an astonishing dilemma: either Woman the Worker is doing the world's work successfully or not. If she is not doing it well why do we not take from her the necessity of working? If she is doing it well why not treat her as a worker with a voice in the direction of work?

The statement that woman is weaker than man is sheer rot: It is the same sort of thing that we hear about "darker races" and "lower classes." Difference, either physical or spiritual, does not argue weakness or inferiority. That the average woman is spiritually different from the average man is undoubtedly just as true as the fact that the average white man differs from the average Negro; but this is no reason for disfranchising the Negro or lynching him. It is inconceivable that any person looking upon the accomplishments of women today in every field of endeavor, realizing their humiliating handicap and the astonishing prejudices which they face and yet seeing despite this that in government, in the professions, in sciences, art and literature and the industries they are leading and dominating forces and growing in power as their emancipation grows,—it is inconceivable that any fair-minded person could for a moment talk about a "weaker" sex. The sex of Judith, Candace, Queen Elizabeth, Sojourner Truth and Jane Addams was the merest incident of human function and not a mark of weakness and inferiority.

To say that men protect women with their votes is to overlook the flat testimony of the facts. In the first place there are millions of women who have no natural men protectors: the unmarried, the widowed, the deserted and those who have married failures. To put this whole army incontinently out of court and leave them unprotected and without voice in political life is more than unjust, it is a crime.

There was a day in the world when it was considered that by marriage a woman lost all her individuality as a human soul and simply became a machine for making men. We have outgrown that idea. A woman is just as much a thinking, feeling, acting person after marriage as before. She has opinions and she has a right to have them and she has a right to express them. It is conceivable, of course, for a country to decide that its unit of representation should be the family and that one person in that family should express its will. But by what possible process of rational thought can it be decided that the person to express that will should always be the male, whether he be genius or drunkard, imbecile or captain of industry? The meaning of the twentieth century is the freeing of the individual soul; the soul longest in slavery and still in the most disgusting and indefensible slavery is the soul of womanhood. God give her increased freedom this November!

Mr. Miller is right in saying that the results from woman suffrage have as yet been small but the answer is obvious: the experiment has been small. As for the risks of allowing women to hold office: Are they nearly as great as the risks of allowing working men to hold office loomed once in the eyes of the Intelligent Fearful?

A Singer

October 1916

Miss Marion E. Anderson was one of the leading singers with the People's Choral Society of one hundred and twenty-five voices in the rendition of Handel's "Messiah" at Musical Fund Hall, Philadelphia, Pa., last April.

Miss Anderson is in her second year at the William Penn High School in Philadelphia. She has been singing before the public for the past two years and the People's Choral Society has contributed $144 toward a scholarship for her. She is now studying under a German teacher and anticipates going abroad after her schooling if she can secure sufficient engagements; but her father is dead and Miss Anderson is one of a family of four.

"We Should Worry"

June 1917

The American Negro more unanimously than any other American group has offered his services in this war as officer and soldier. He has done this earnestly and unselfishly, overlooking his just resentment and grievous wrongs.

Up to the present his offer has been received with sullen and ungracious silence, or at best in awkward complaisance.

Nevertheless, the offer stands as it stood in 1776, 1812, 1861, and 1898.

But——

Certain Americans,—Southern Bourbons, and Northern Copperheads—fear Negro soldiers. They do not fear that they will not fight—they fear that they WILL fight and fight bravely and well. Just as in Reconstruction days, it was not bad Negro voters they feared but good, intelligent ones.

Selah!

These Bourbons and Copperheads know that if Negroes fight well in this war they will get credit for it. They cannot "Carrizal" the news and boost the white putty-head who blundered, forgetting the very name of the brave black subalterns. No! those fool French will tell the truth and the Associated Press will not be able to edit "Niggers"; so the Copperheads and Bourbons do not want Negro soldiers. They think they can trust Southern state officers to juggle that little "agricultural laborer joker" and keep us out of the ranks.

Very good.

"We should worry."

If they do not want us to fight, we will work. We will walk into the industrial shoes of a few million whites who go to the front. We will get higher wages and we cannot be stopped from migrating by all the deviltry of the slave South; particularly with the white lynchers and mob leaders away at war.

Will we be ousted when the white soldiers come back?

THEY WON'T COME BACK!

So there you are, gentlemen, and take your choice,——

We'll fight or work.

We'll fight and work.

If we fight we'll learn the fighting game and cease to be so "aisily lynched."

If we don't fight we'll learn the more lucrative trades and cease to be so easily robbed and exploited.

Take your choice, gentlemen.

"We should worry."

Houston

October 1917

It is difficult for one of Negro blood to write of Houston. Is not the ink within the very wells crimsoned with the blood of black martyrs? Do they not cry unavenged, saying:—Always WE pay; always WE die; always, whether right or wrong, it is SO MANY NEGROES killed, so many

NEGROES wounded. But here, at last, at Houston is a change. Here, at last, white folk died. Innocent, adventitious strangers, perhaps, as innocent as the thousands of Negroes done to death in the last two centuries. Our hands tremble to rise and exult, our lips strive to cry.

And yet our hands are not raised in exultation; and yet our lips are silent, as we face another great human wrong.

We did not have to have Houston in order to know that black men will not always be mere victims. But we did have Houston in order to ask, Why? Why must this all be? At Waco, at Memphis, at East St. Louis, at Chester, at Houston, at Lexington, and all along that crimsoned list of death and slaughter and orgy and torture.

This, at least, remember, you who jump to judgment—Houston was not an ordinary outburst. Just before the riot the acting chaplain of the regiment writes us: "The battalion has made good and all doubts as to the conduct of the Negro soldier have been dissipated. We are striving to add another page to the glorious record of our regiment."

What it was they had to stand, we learn only in tortuous driblets from sources bitterly prejudiced. These facts, at least, are clear: Contrary to all military precedent the Negro provost guard had been disarmed and was at the mercy of citizen police who insulted them until blood ran. At last, they stole their own arms and turned and fought. They were not young recruits; they were not wild and drunken wastrels; they were disciplined men who said—"This is enough; we'll stand no more!" That they faced and faced fearlessly the vision of a shameful death, we do not doubt. We ask no mitigation of their punishment. They broke the law. They must suffer. But before Almighty God, if those guiltless of their black brothers' blood shot the punishing shot, there would be no dead men in that regiment.

The Black Man and the Unions

March 1918

I am among the few colored men who have tried conscientiously to bring about understanding and co-operation between American Negroes and the Labor Unions. I have sought to look upon the Sons of Freedom as simply a part of the great mass of the earth's Disinherited, and to realize that world movements which have lifted the lowly in the past and are opening the gates of opportunity to them today are of equal value for all men, white and black, then and now.

I carry on the title page, for instance, of this magazine the Union label, and yet I know, and everyone of my Negro readers knows, that the very fact that this label is there is an advertisement that no Negro's hand is engaged in the printing of this magazine, since the International Typographical Union systematically and deliberately excludes every Negro that it dares from membership, no matter what his qualifications.

Even here, however, and beyond the hurt of mine own, I have always striven to recognize the real cogency of the Union argument. Collective bargaining has, undoubtedly, raised modern labor from something like chattel slavery to the threshold of industrial freedom, and in this advance of labor white and black have shared.

I have tried, therefore, to see a vision of vast union between the laboring forces, particularly in the South, and hoped for no distant day when the black laborer and the white laborer, instead of being used against each other as helpless pawns, should unite to bring real democracy in the South.

On the other hand, the whole scheme of settling the Negro problem, inaugurated by philanthropists and carried out during the last twenty years, has been based upon the idea of playing off black workers against white. That it is essentially a mischievous and dangerous program no sane thinker can deny, but it is peculiarly disheartening to realize that it is the Labor Unions themselves that have given this movement its greatest impulse and that today, at last, in East St. Louis have brought the most unwilling of us to acknowledge that in the present Union movement, as represented by the American Federation of Labor, there is absolutely no hope of justice for an American of Negro descent.

Personally, I have come to this decision reluctantly and in the past have written and spoken little of the closed door of opportunity, shut impudently in the faces of black men by organized white workingmen. I realize that by heredity and century-long lack of opportunity one cannot expect in the laborer that larger sense of justice and duty which we ought to demand of the privileged classes. I have, therefore, inveighed against color discrimination by employers and by the rich and well-to-do, knowing at the same time in silence that it is practically impossible for any colored man or woman to become a boiler maker or book binder, an electrical worker or glass maker, a worker in jewelry or leather, a machinist or metal polisher, a paper maker or piano builder, a plumber or a potter, a printer or a pressman, a telegrapher or a railway trackman, an electrotyper or stove mounter, a textile worker or tile layer, a trunk maker, upholsterer, carpenter, locomotive engineer, switchman, stone cutter, baker, blacksmith, boot and shoemaker, tailor, or any of a dozen other important well-paid employments, without encountering the open determination and unscrupulous opposition of the whole united labor movement of America. That further than this, if he should want to become a painter, mason, carpenter, plasterer, brickmaker or fireman he would be subject to humiliating discriminations by his fellow Union workers and be deprived of work at every possible opportunity, even in defiance of their own Union laws. If, braving this outrageous attitude of the Unions, he succeeds in some small establishment or at some exceptional time at gaining employment, he must be labeled as a "scab" throughout the length and breadth of the land and written down as one who, for his selfish advantage, seeks to overthrow the labor uplift of a century.

Paul Le Roy Robeson

March 1918

This athlete is only nineteen years old, but he is six feet, two inches high, and weighs 210 pounds.

He is the son of the Rev. W. D. Robeson, a Methodist clergyman in Somerville, N. J. He was graduated from the Somerville, N. J., High School in 1915, at the head of his class.

In high school he was full-back on the football team. He entered Rutgers College on a four years' scholarship, won in competitive examination, in which he made the highest average in the state. He became a member of the varsity football team in his first year at Rutgers. He came into prominence, however, only recently, when he played with his colleagues and gained the victory over the Newport Naval Reserves, a team composed of former All-American players and led by Cupid Black, captain of Yale's team last year. Mr. Robeson has since been placed on the All-American and All-Eastern teams of practically every critic. His coach, Mr. George Foster Sanford, says: "Robeson is the best football player in the country today."

Mr. Robeson, also, has maintained a high scholastic record. He has won the class oratorical prize for two years, a feat never before accomplished in the school. He is varsity debater, plays guard in basketball, throws weights in track, catches in baseball, and is a baritone soloist.

Tillman

August 1918

It can hardly be expected that any Negro would regret the death of Benjamin L. Tillman, Senator from South Carolina. His attacks on our race have been too unbridled and outrageous for that. And yet it is our duty to understand this man in relation to his time. He represented the rebound of the unlettered white proletariat of the South from the oppression of slavery to new industrial and political freedom. The visible sign of their former degradation was the Negro. They kicked him because he was kickable and stood for what they hated; but they must as they grow in knowledge and power come to realize that the Negro far from being the cause of their former suffering was but a co-sufferer with them. Some day a greater than Tillman, Blease and Vardaman will rise in the South to lead the white laborers and small farmer, and he will greet the Negro as a friend and helper and build with him and not on him. This leader is not yet come, but the death of Tillman foretells his coming and the real enfranchisement of the Negro will herald his birth.

"Jim Crow"

January 1919

We colored folk stand at the parting of ways, and we must take counsel. The objection to segregation and "Jim-Crowism" was in other days the fact that compelling Negroes to associate only with Negroes meant to exclude them from contact with the best culture of the day. How could we learn manners or get knowledge if the heritage of the past was locked away from us?

Gradually, however, conditions have changed. Culture is no longer the monopoly of the white nor is poverty and ignorance the sole heritage of the black. Many a colored man in our day called to conference with his own and rather dreading the contact with uncultivated people even though they were of his own blood has been astonished and deeply gratified at the kind of people he has met—at the evidence of good manners and thoughtfulness among his own.

This together with the natural human love of herding like with like has in the last decade set up a tremendous current within the colored race against any contact with whites that can be avoided. They have welcomed separate racial institutions. They have voluntarily segregated themselves and asked for more segregation. The North is full of instances of practically colored schools which colored people have demanded and, of course, the colored church and social organization of every sort are ubiquitous.

Today both these wings of opinion are getting suspicious of each other and there are plenty of whites to help the feeling along. Whites and Blacks ask the Negro who fights separation: "Are you ashamed of your race?" Blacks and Whites ask the Negro who welcomes and encourages separation: "Do you want to give up your rights? Do you acknowledge your inferiority?"

Neither attitude is correct. Segregation is impolitic, because it is impossible. You can not build up a logical scheme of a self-sufficing, separate Negro America inside America or a Negro world with no close relations to the white world. If there are relations between races they must be based on the knowledge and sympathy that come alone from the long and intimate human contact of individuals.

On the other hand, if the Negro is to develop his own power and gifts; if he is not only to fight prejudices and oppression successfully, but also to unite for ideals higher than the world has realized in art and industry and social life, then he must unite and work with Negroes and build a new and great Negro ethos.

Here, then, we face the curious paradox and we remember contradictory facts. Unless we had fought segregation with determination, our whole race would have been pushed into an ill-lighted, unpaved, un-sewered ghetto. Unless we had built great church organizations and manned our own southern schools, we should be shepherdless sheep. Unless we had welcomed the segregation of Fort Des Moines, we would have had no officers in the National Army. Unless we had beaten open the doors of northern universities, we would have had no men fit to be officers.

Here is a dilemma calling for thought and forbearance. Not every builder of racial co-operation and solidarity is a "Jim-Crow" advocate, a hater of white folk. Not every Negro who fights prejudice and segregation is ashamed of his race.

Reconstruction and Africa

February 1919

The suggestion has been made that these colonies which Germany has lost should not be handed over to any other nation of Europe but should, under the guidance of *organized civilization*, be brought to a point of development which shall finally result in an autonomous state. This plan has met with much criticism and ridicule. Let the natives develop along their own lines and they will "go back," has been the cry. Back to what, in Heaven's name?

Is a civilization naturally backward because it is different? Outside of cannibalism, which can be matched in this country, at least, by lynching, there is no vice and no degradation in native African customs which can begin to touch the horrors thrust upon them by white masters. Drunkenness, terrible diseases, immorality, all these things have been the gifts of European civilization. There is no need to dwell on German and Belgian atrocities, the world knows them too well. Nor have France and England been blameless. But even supposing that these masters had been models of kindness and rectitude, who shall say that any civilization is in itself so superior that it must be superimposed upon another nation without the expressed and intelligent consent of the people most concerned. The culture indigenous to a country, its folk-customs, its art, all this must have free scope or there is no such thing as freedom for the world.

The truth is, white men are merely juggling with words—or worse—when they declare that the withdrawal of Europeans from Africa will plunge that continent into chaos. What Europe, and indeed only a small group in Europe, wants in Africa is not a field for the spread of European civilization, but a field for exploitation. They covet the raw materials,—ivory, diamonds, copper and rubber in which the land abounds, and even more do they covet cheap native labor to mine and produce these things. Greed,—naked, pitiless lust for wealth and power, lie back of all of Europe's interest in Africa and the white world knows it and is not ashamed.

Any readjustment of Africa is not fair and cannot be lasting which does not consider the interests of native Africans and peoples of African descent. Prejudice, in European colonies in Africa, against the ambitious Negro is greater than in America, and that is saying much. But with the establishment of a form of government which shall be based on the concept that Africa is for Africans, there would be a chance for the colored American to emigrate and to go as a pioneer to a country which must, sentimentally at least, possess for him the same fascination as England does for Indian-born Englishmen.

Returning Soldiers

May 1919

We are returning from war! THE CRISIS and tens of thousands of black men were drafted into a great struggle. For bleeding France and what she means and has meant and will mean to us and humanity and against the threat of German race arrogance, we fought gladly and to the last drop of blood; for America and her highest ideals, we fought in far-off hope; for the dominant southern oligarchy entrenched in Washington, we fought in bitter resignation. For the America that represents and gloats in lynching, disfranchisement, caste, brutality and devilish insult—for this, in the hateful upturning and mixing of things, we were forced by vindictive fate to fight, also.

But today we return! We return from the slavery of uniform which the world's madness demanded us to don to the freedom of civil garb. We stand again to look America squarely in the face and call a spade a spade. We sing: This country of ours, despite all its better souls have done and dreamed, is yet a shameful land.

It *lynches*.

And lynching is barbarism of a degree of contemptible nastiness unparalleled in human history. Yet for fifty years we have lynched two Negroes a week, and we have kept this up right through the war.

It *disfranchises* its own citizens.

Disfranchisement is the deliberate theft and robbery of the only protection of poor against rich and black against white. The land that disfranchises its citizens and calls itself a democracy lies and knows it lies.

It encourages *ignorance*.

It has never really tried to educate the Negro. A dominant minority does not want Negroes educated. It wants servants, dogs, whores and monkeys. And when this land allows a reactionary group by its stolen political power to force as many black folk into these categories as it possibly can, it cries in contemptible hypocrisy: "They threaten us with degeneracy; they cannot be educated."

It *steals* from us.

It organizes industry to cheat us. It cheats us out of our land; it cheats us out of our labor. It confiscates our savings. It reduces our wages. It raises our rent. It steals our profit. It taxes us without representation. It keeps us consistently and universally poor, and then feeds us on charity and derides our poverty.

It *insults* us.

It has organized a nation-wide and latterly a world-wide propaganda of deliberate and continuous insult and defamation of black blood wherever found. It decrees that it shall not be possible in travel nor residence, work nor play, education nor instruction for a black man to exist without tacit or open acknowledgment of his inferiority to the dirtiest white dog. And it looks upon any attempt to question or even discuss this dogma as arrogance, unwarranted assumption and treason.

This is the country to which we Soldiers of Democracy return. This is the fatherland for which we fought! But it is *our* fatherland. It was right for us to fight. The faults of *our* country are *our* faults. Under similar circumstances, we would fight again. But by the God of Heaven, we are cowards and jackasses if now that that war is over, we do not marshal every ounce of our brain and brawn to fight a sterner, longer, more unbending battle against the forces of hell in our own land.

We *return.*

We *return from fighting.*

We *return fighting.*

Make way for Democracy! We saved it in France, and by the Great Jehovah, we will save it in the United States of America, or know the reason why.

Race Intelligence

July 1920

For a century or more it has been the dream of those who do not believe Negroes are human that their wish should find some scientific basis. For years they depended on the weight of the human brain, trusting that the alleged underweight of less than a thousand Negro brains, measured without reference to age, stature, nutrition or cause of death, would convince the world that black men simply could not be educated. Today scientists acknowledge that there is no warrant for such a conclusion and that in any case the absolute weight of the brain is no criterion of racial ability.

Measurements of the bony skeleton followed and great hopes of the scientific demonstration of race inferiority were held for a while. But they had to be surrendered when Zulus and Englishmen were found in the same dolichocephalic class.

Then came psychology: the children of the public schools were studied and it was discovered that some colored children ranked lower than white children. This gave wide satisfaction even though it was pointed out that the average included most of both races and that considering the educational opportunities and social environment of the races the differences were measurements simply of the ignorance and poverty of the black child's surroundings.

Today, however, all is settled. "A workably accurate scientific classification of brain power" has been discovered and by none other than our astute army officers. The tests were in two sets for literates and illiterates and were simplicity itself. For instance, among other things the literates were asked in three minutes "to look at each row of numbers below and on the two dotted lines write the two numbers that should come next."

3	4	5	6	7	8	. . .	. . .
8	7	6	5	4	3	. . .	. . .
10	15	20	25	30	35	. . .	. . .
81	27	9	3	1	1/3	. . .	. . .
1	4	9	16	25	36	. . .	. . .
16	17	15	18	14	19	. . .	. . .
3	6	8	16	18	36	. . .	. . .

Illiterates were asked, for example, to complete pictures where the net was missing in a tennis court or a ball in a bowling alley!

For these tests were chosen 4730 Negroes *from Louisiana and Mississippi* and 28,052 white recruits *from Illinois*. The result? Do you need to ask? M. R. Trabue, Director, Bureau of Educational Service, Columbia University, assures us that the intelligence of the average southern Negro is equal to that of a 9-year-old white boy and that we should arrange our educational program to make "waiters, porters, scavengers and the like" of most Negroes!

Is it conceivable that a great university should employ a man whose "science" consists of such utter rot?

An Open Letter to Warren Gamaliel Harding

March 1921

Sir:

By an unprecedented vote you have been called to the most powerful position in the gift of mankind. Of the more than hundred million human beings whose destiny rests so largely with you in the next four years, one in every ten is of Negro descent.

Your enemies in the campaign sought to count you among this number and if it were true it would give us deep satisfaction to welcome you to the old and mystic chrism of Negroland, whence many mighty souls have stepped since time began.

But blood and physical descent are little and idle things as compared with spiritual heritage. And here we would see you son of the highest: a child of Abraham Lincoln and Lloyd Garrison and Frederick Douglass; a grandson of Thomas Jefferson and John Quincy Adams; and a lineal descendant of the martyred Fathers of the Free of all times and lands.

We appeal to you: we the outcast and lynched, the mobbed and murdered, the despoiled and insulted; and yet withal, the indomitable, unconquered, unbending and unafraid black children of kings and slaves and of the best blood of the workers of the earth—

WE WANT THE RIGHT TO VOTE.

WE WANT TO TRAVEL WITHOUT INSULT.

WE WANT LYNCHING AND MOB-LAW QUELLED FOREVER.

WE WANT FREEDOM FOR OUR BROTHERS IN HAITI.

We know that the power to do these things is not entirely in your hands, but its beginnings lie there. After the fourth of March, on you more than on any other human being rests the redemption of the blood of Africa and through it the peace of the world. All the cruelty, rape and atrocities of slavery; all the groans and humiliations of half-freedom; all the theft and degradation of that spirit of the Ku Klux mob that seeks to build a free America on racial, religious and class hatred—the weight of all this woe is yours.

You, Sir, whether you will or no, stand responsible. You are responsible for the truth back of the pictures of the burning of Americans circulated in European drawing-rooms; for the spectacle of 82% of the voters of the South disfranchised under a government called a democracy; for the hypocrisy of a nation seeking to lend idealism to the world for peace when within its own borders there is more murder, theft, riot and crucifixion than was ever even charged against Bolshevik Russia.

In the name of our fathers, President Harding, our fathers black and white who toiled and bled and died to make this a free and decent nation, will you not tear aside the cobwebs of politics, and lies of society, and the grip of industrial thieves, and give us an administration which will say and mean: *the first and fundamental and inescapable problem of American democracy is Justice to the American Negro.* If races cannot live together in peace and happiness in America, they cannot live together in the world. Race isolation died a century ago. Human unity within and without Nations, must and will succeed—and you, Sir, must start bringing this to pass.

The Negro and Radical Thought

July 1921

Mr. Claude McKay, one of the editors of *The Liberator* and a Negro poet of distinction, writes us as follows:

> "I am surprised and sorry that in your editorial, 'The Drive', published in THE CRISIS for May, you should leap out of your sphere to sneer at the Russian Revolu-

tion, the greatest event in the history of humanity; much greater than the French Revolution, which is held up as a wonderful achievement to Negro children and students in white and black schools. For American Negroes the indisputable and outstanding fact of the Russian revolution is that a mere handful of Jews, much less in ratio to the number of Negroes in the American population, have attained, through the Revolution, all the political and social rights that were denied to them under the regime of the Czar.

"Although no thinking Negro can deny the great work that the N. A. A. C. P. is doing, it must yet be admitted that from its platform and personnel the Association cannot function as a revolutionary working class organization. And the overwhelming majority of American Negroes belong by birth, condition and repression to the working class. Your aim is to get for the American Negro the political and social rights that are his by virtue of the Constitution, the rights which are denied him by the Southern oligarchy with the active co-operation of the state governments and the tacit support of northern business interests. And your aim is a noble one, which deserves the support of all progressive Negroes.

"But the Negro in politics and social life is ostracized only technically by the distinction of color; in reality the Negro is discriminated against because he is of the lowest type of worker. . . .

"Obviously, this economic difference between the white and black workers manifests itself in various forms, in color prejudice, race hatred, political and social boycotting and lynching of Negroes. And all the entrenched institutions of white America,—law courts, churches, schools, the fighting forces and the Press,—condone these iniquities perpetrated upon black men; iniquities that are dismissed indifferently as the inevitable result of the social system. Still, whenever it suits the business interests controlling these institutions to mitigate the persecutions against Negroes, they do so with impunity. When organized white workers quit their jobs, Negroes, who are discouraged by the whites to organize, are sought to take their places. And these strike-

> breaking Negroes work under the protection of the military and the police. But as ordinary citizens and workers, Negroes are not protected by the military and the police from the mob. The ruling classes will not grant Negroes those rights which, on a lesser scale and more plausibly, are withheld from the white proletariat. The concession of these rights would immediately cause a Revolution in the economic life of this country."

We are aware that some of our friends have been disappointed with THE CRISIS during and since the war. Some have assumed that we aimed chiefly at mounting the band wagon with our cause during the madness of war; others thought that we were playing safe so as to avoid the Department of Justice; and still a third class found us curiously stupid in our attitude toward the broader matters of human reform. Such critics, and Mr. McKay is among them, must give us credit for standing to our guns in the past at no little cost in many influential quarters, and they must also remember that we have one chief cause,—the emancipation of the Negro, and to this all else must be subordinated—not because other questions are not important but because to our mind the most important social question today is recognition of the darker races.

Turning now to that marvelous set of phenomena known as the Russian Revolution, Mr. McKay is wrong in thinking that we have ever intentionally sneered at it. On the contrary, time may prove, as he believes, that the Russian Revolution is the greatest event of the nineteenth and twentieth centuries, and its leaders the most unselfish prophets. At the same time THE CRISIS does not know this to be true. Russia is incredibly vast, and the happenings there in the last five years have been intricate to a degree that must make any student pause. We sit, therefore, with waiting hands and listening ears, seeing some splendid results from Russia, like the cartoons for public education recently exhibited in America, and hearing of other things which frighten us.

We are moved neither by the superficial omniscience of Wells nor the reports in the New York *Times*; but this alone we do know: that the immediate work for the American

Negro lies in America and not in Russia, and this, too, in spite of the fact that the Third Internationale has made a pronouncement which cannot but have our entire sympathy:

> "The Communist Internationale once forever breaks with the traditions of the Second Internationale which in reality only recognized the white race. The Communist Internationale makes it its task to emancipate the workers of the entire world. The ranks of the Communist Internationale fraternally unite men of all colors: white, yellow and black—the toilers of the entire world."

Despite this there come to us black men two insistent questions: What is today the right program of socialism? The editor of THE CRISIS considers himself a Socialist but he does not believe that German State Socialism or the dictatorship of the proletariat are perfect panaceas. He believes with most thinking men that the present method of creating, controlling and distributing wealth is desperately wrong; that there must come and is coming a social control of wealth; but he does not know just what form that control is going to take, and he is not prepared to dogmatize with Marx or Lenin. Further than that, and more fundamental to the duty and outlook of THE CRISIS, is this question: How far can the colored people of the world, and particularly the Negroes of the United States, trust the working classes?

Many honest thinking Negroes assume, and Mr. McKay seems to be one of these, that we have only to embrace the working class program to have the working class embrace ours; that we have only to join trade Unionism and Socialism or even Communism, as they are today expounded, to have Union Labor and Socialists and Communists believe and act on the equality of mankind and the abolition of the color line. THE CRISIS wishes that this were true, but it is forced to the conclusion that it is not.

The American Federation of Labor, as representing the trade unions in America, has been grossly unfair and discriminatory toward Negroes and still is. American Socialism has discriminated against black folk and before the war was prepared to go further with this discrimination. European Socialism has openly discriminated against Asiatics. Nor is this surprising. Why should we assume on the part of unlettered and suppressed masses of white workers, a clearness of thought, a sense of human brotherhood, that is sadly lacking in the most educated classes?

Our task, therefore, as it seems to THE CRISIS, is clear: We have to convince the working classes of the world that black men, brown men, and yellow men are human beings and suffer the same discrimination that white workers suffer. We have in addition to this to espouse the cause of the white workers, only being careful that we do not in this way allow them to jeopardize our cause. We must, for instance, have bread. If our white fellow workers drive us out of decent jobs, we are compelled to accept indecent wages even at the price of "scabbing". It is a hard choice, but whose is the blame? Finally despite public prejudice and clamour, we should examine with open mind in literature, debate and in real life the great programs of social reform that are day by day being put forward.

This was the true thought and meaning back of our May editorial. We have an immediate program for Negro emancipation laid down and thought out by the N. A. A. C. P. It is foolish for us to give up this practical program for mirage in Africa or by seeking to join a revolution which we do not at present understand. On the other hand, as Mr. McKay says, it would be just as foolish for us to sneer or even seem to sneer at the blood-entwined writhing of hundreds of millions of our whiter human brothers.

President Harding and Social Equality

December 1921

For fifty years we who, *pro* and *con*, have discussed the Negro Problem, have been skulking behind a phrase—"Social Equality." Today President Harding's speech, like sudden thunder in blue skies, ends the hiding and drives us all into the clear light of truth.

We had our excuses perhaps in the past: about every problem of human relations lurks a penumbra of shadowing possibilities, which we would not discuss. It seems unnecessary, inappropriate, beside the point. And so defenders of the higher training of women have hestitated to explore sex freedom for females; and lovers of democracy have declined to consider the possibility of the masses voting their own wages. It is not that we have denied the ensuing problems that shadow our main object, but we have said with a certain truth: sufficient unto the present tangle is the obvious evil thereof. Let us follow the clear light and afterward turn to other darknesses.

But sometimes this becomes suddenly impossible. Sometimes the so-considered minor problem is so tremendous and insistent that it leaps to the fore and demands examination and honest facing. This is particularly so when we have not simply ignored the problem but have deliberately and cynically lied about it, denied it, and said not that "Social Equality" was not a pertinent and pressing problem; but rather that it was no problem at all.

THE BIRMINGHAM SPEECH

And now comes President Harding's Birmingham speech when unwittingly or deliberately the President brings the crisis. We may no longer dodge nor hesitate. We must all, black or white, Northerner or Southerner, stand in the light and speak plain words.

The President must not for a moment be blamed because, when invited to the semi-centennial of a great southern city of industry, he talked of the Negro instead of the results of profitable mining. There is but one subject in the South. The Southerners themselves can speak no other, think no other, act no other. The eternal and inevitable southern topic is and has been and will be the Black Man.

Moreover, the President laid down three theses with which no American can disagree without a degree of self-stultification almost inconceivable, namely:

1. The Negro must vote on the same terms that white folk vote.
2. The Negro must be educated.
3. The Negro must have economic Justice.

The sensitive may note that the President qualified these demands somewhat, even dangerously, and yet they stand out so clearly in his speech that he must be credited with meaning to give them their real significance. And in this the President made a braver, clearer utterance than Theodore Roosevelt ever dared to make or than William Taft or William McKinley ever dreamed of. For this let us give him every ounce of credit he deserves.

SOCIAL EQUALITY

But President Harding did not stop here. Indeed he did not begin here. Either because he had no adequate view of the end of the fatal path he was treading or because, in his desire to placate the white South, he was careless of consequences, he put *first* on his program of racial settlement a statement which could have been understood and was understood and we fear was intended to be understood to pledge the nation, the Negro race and the world to a doctrine so utterly inadmissible in the twentieth century, in a Republic of free citizens and in an age of Humanity that one stands aghast at the motives and the reasons for the pronouncement.

It may to some seem that this statement is overdrawn. Some puzzled persons may say: but Negroes themselves have told me that they repudiate "Social Equality" and amalgamation of race; in fact, right there at Birmingham, Negro applause of the President was audible.

All this does not minimize—rather it emphasizes the grave crisis precipitated by the President's speech. It emphasizes the fact of our mental skulking or transparent and deliberate dishonesty in dealing with the Negro.

Social equality may mean two things. The obvious and clear meaning is the right of a human being to accept companionship with his fellow on terms of equal and reciprocal courtesy. In this sense the term is understood and defended by modern men. It has not been denied by any civilized man since the French Revolution. It is the foundation of democracy and to bring it into being, the world went through revolution, war, murder and hell.

But there is another narrow, stilted and unreal meaning,

that is sometimes dragged from these words, namely: Social Equality is the right to demand private social companionship with another.

Or to put it more simply: the real meaning of "social equality" is eligibility to association with men, and the forced and illogical meaning is the right to demand private association with any particular person. Such a demand as the latter is idiotic and was never made by any sane person; while on the contrary, for any person to admit that his character is such that he is physically and morally unfit to talk or travel or eat with his fellow-men, or that he has no desire to associate with decent people, would be an admission which none but a leper, a criminal or a liar could possibly make. It is the very essence of self respect and human equality and it carries with it no jot of arrogance or assumption—it is simply *Homo Sum*.

SELF-DECEPTION

Despite this, for fifty years the Southern white man has said to the Negro: Do you mean to say that you consider yourself fit to associate with white people? And the Negro has answered; but the question which he answered was not the one asked, but rather the other totally different question: Do you mean to say that you want to force your friendship and company on persons who do not want them? The answer to this is obviously an emphatic and indignant *No*. But when the Negro said *No*, he knew that he was not answering the question the white man intended to ask and the white man knew that the Negro knew this, and that he himself had purposely asked a question of double and irreconcilable meaning, when he said, "Do you want Social Equality?"

And so this undeceiving deception has gone on for fifty years until the President of the United States, throwing caution to the winds, has either boldly or unwittingly announced as a national policy that "men of both races may well stand uncompromisingly against every suggestion of Social Equality."

Or in other words, that no man, no matter how civilized,

decent or gifted he may be, shall be permitted to associate with his fellow men on terms of equality or want to associate with them, if he be a Negro or of Negro descent.

Let us sweep away all quibbling: Let us assume that the President was sane and serious and could not and did not mean by "social equality" anything so inconceivable as the right of a man to invite himself to another man's dinner table. No. Mr. Harding meant that the American Negro must acknowledge that it was a wrong and a disgrace for Booker T. Washington to dine with President Roosevelt!

The answer to this inconceivably dangerous and undemocratic demand must come with the unanimous ring of 12 million voices, enforced by the voice of every American who believes in Humanity.

Let us henceforward frankly admit that which we hitherto have always known; that *no system of social uplift which begins by denying the manhood of a man can end by giving him a free ballot, a real education and a just wage.*

RACE EQUALITY

Let us confess that the pseudo-science to which the President unhappily referred as authority, and the guilty philanthropy which has greedily levelled racial barriers and now seeks with the bloodstained hands of a Lugard to rearrange them so that profit may emerge and manhood be dammed—let us confess that all this is vain, wrong and hypocritical and that every honest soul today who seeks peace, disarmament and the uplift of all men must say with the Pan-African Congress:

"The absolute equality of races,—physical, political and social—is the founding stone of world peace and human advancement. No one denies great differences of gift, capacity and attainment among individuals of all races, but the voice of science, religion and practical politics is one in denying the God-appointed existence of superior races, or of races naturally and inevitably and eternally inferior."

To deny this fact is to throw open the door of the world to a future of hatred, war and murder such as never yet has staggered a bowed and crucified humanity. How can a man bring himself to conceive that the majority of mankind—Chinese, Japanese, Indians and Negroes are going to stand up and acknowledge to the world that they are unfit to be men or to associate with men, when they know they *are* men?

AMALGAMATION

But President Harding does not stop even here. He declares "Racial amalgamation there cannot be."

What does the President mean?

Does he mean that the White and Negro races in this land never have mixed? There are by census reports over two million acknowledged mulattoes in the United States today; and without doubt there are, in fact, no less than four million persons with white and Negro blood.

Does he mean that there is no amalgamation today? Between 1850 and 1921 the mulattoes have increased over 400 per cent. Does he mean there will be no future amalgamation? How does he know?

Or does he mean that it would be better for Whites and Blacks not to amalgamate? If he meant that, why did he not say so plainly? And if he had said so, 99 per cent of the Negroes would agree with him. We have not asked amalgamation; we have resisted it. It has been forced on us by brute strength, ignorance, poverty, degradation and fraud. It is the white race, roaming the world, that has left its trail of bastards and outraged women and then raised holy hands to heaven and deplored "race mixture." No, we are not demanding and do not want amalgamation, but the reasons are ours and not yours. It is not because we are unworthy of intermarriage—either physically or mentally or morally. It is not because the mingling of races has not and will not bring mighty offspring in its Dumas and Pushkin and Coleridge-Taylor and Booker Washington. It is because no real men accept any alliance except on terms of absolute equal regard and because we are abundantly satisfied with our own race and blood. And at the same time we say and as free men must say that whenever two human beings of any nation or race desire each other in marriage, the denial of their legal right to marry is not simply wrong—it is lewd.

SEGREGATION AND RACE PRIDE

And this brings us to the last word of President Harding: He says in one breath:

> Especially would I appeal to the self respect of the colored race. I would inculcate in it the wish to improve itself as a distinct race with a heredity, a set of traditions, an array of aspirations all its own. Out of such racial ambitions and pride will come natural segregations.

> The one thing we must sedulously avoid is the development of group and class organizations in this country. There has been a time when we heard too much about the labor vote, the business vote, the Irish vote, the Scandinavian vote, the Italian vote, and so on. But the demagogues who would array class against class and group against group have fortunately found little to reward their efforts.

Is the President calling himself a demagogue? Does he not realize the logical contradictions of his thought? Can he not see his failure to recognize the Universal in the Particular, the menace of all group exclusiveness and segregation in the forced segregation of American Negroes? Can he not in this day of days with foreigners of every race flocking to Washington and the eyes of a blood-weary world strained after them—can he not realize the vast, the awful implications of this appeal to the Frankenstein of race exclusiveness—that hateful thing which has murdered peace and culture and nations? Does he not hear the answer that leaps to our lips? For when Warren Harding or any white man comes to teach Negroes pride of race, we answer that our pride is our business and not theirs, and a thing they would better fear rather than evoke: For the day that Black men love Black men simply because they are Black, is the day they will hate White men simply because they are White.

And then, God help us all!

Charles Young

February 1922

The life of Charles Young was a triumph of tragedy. No one ever knew the truth about the Hell he went through at West Point. He seldom even mentioned it. The pain was too great. Few knew what faced him always in his army life. It was not enough for him to do well—he must always do better; and so much and so conspicuously better, as to disarm the scoundrels that ever trailed him. He lived in the army surrounded by insult and intrigue and yet he set his teeth and kept his soul serene and triumphed.

He was one of the few men I know who literally turned the other cheek with Jesus Christ. He was laughed at for it and his own people chided him bitterly, yet he persisted. When a white Southern pigmy at West Point protested at taking food from a dish passed first to Young, Young passed it to him first and afterward to himself. When officers of inferior rank refused to salute a "nigger", he saluted them. Seldom did he lose his temper, seldom complain.

With his own people he was always the genial, hearty, half-boyish friend. He kissed the girls, slapped the boys on the back, threw his arms about his friends, scattered his money in charity; only now and then behind the Veil did his nearest comrades see the Hurt and Pain graven on his heart; and when it appeared he promptly drowned it in his music—his beloved music, which always poured from his quick, nervous fingers, to caress and bathe his soul.

Steadily, unswervingly he did his duty. And Duty to him, as to few modern men, was spelled in capitals. It was his lodestar, his soul; and neither force nor reason swerved him from it. His second going to Africa, after a terrible attack of black water fever, was suicide. He knew it. His wife knew it. His friends knew it. He had been sent to *Africa* because the Army considered his blood pressure too high to let him go to *Europe*! They sent him there to die. They sent him there because he was one of the very best officers in the service and if he had gone to Europe he could not have been denied the stars of a General. They could not stand a black American General. Therefore they sent him to the fever coast of Africa. They ordered him to make roads back in the haunted jungle. He knew what they wanted and intended. He could have escaped it by accepting his retirement from active service, refusing his call to active duty and then he could have lounged and lived at leisure on his retirement pay. But Africa needed him. He did not yell and collect money and advertise great schemes and parade in crimson—he just went quietly, ignoring appeal and protest.

He is dead. But the heart of the Great Black Race, the Ancient of Days—the Undying and Eternal—rises and salutes his shining memory: Well done! Charles Young, Soldier and Man and unswerving Friend.

Abraham Lincoln

May 1922

Abraham Lincoln was a Southern poor white, of illegitimate birth, poorly educated and unusually ugly, awkward, ill-dressed. He liked smutty stories and was a politician down to his toes. Aristocrats—Jeff Davis, Seward and their ilk—despised him, and indeed he had little outwardly that compelled respect. But in that curious human way he was big inside. He had reserves and depths and when habit and convention were torn away there was something left to Lincoln—nothing to most of his contemners. There was something left, so that at the crisis he was big enough to be inconsistent—cruel, merciful; peace-loving, a fighter; despising Negroes and letting them fight and vote; protecting slavery and freeing slaves. He was a man—a big, inconsistent, brave man.

Ten Phrases

July 1922

The following ten phrases are recommended to white students in Southern colleges as quite sufficient for all possible discussions of the race problem:

1. The Southerner is the Negro's Best Friend.
2. Slavery was Beneficial to the Negro.
3. The Races will Never Mix.
4. All Negro Leaders are Mulattoes.
5. The Place for the Negro is in the South.
6. I love My Black Mammy.
7. Do you want your sister to marry a Nigger?
8. Do not disturb the present friendly relations between the races.
9. The Negro must be kept in his place.
10. Lynching is the defense of Southern womanhood.

Again, Lincoln

September 1922

We love to think of the Great as flawless. We yearn in our imperfection toward Perfection—sinful, we envisage Righteousness.

As a result of this, no sooner does a great man die than we begin to whitewash him. We seek to forget all that was small and mean and unpleasant and remember the fine and brave and good. We slur over and explain away his inconsistencies and at last there begins to appear, not the real man, but the tradition of the man—remote, immense, perfect, cold and dead!

This sort of falsehood appeals to some folk. They want to dream their heroes true; they want their heroes all heroic with no feet of clay; and they are astonished, angered, hurt if some one speaks the grim, forgotten truth. They can see but one motive for such digging up of filth, for such evil speaking of the dead—and that is prurient love of evil.

Thus many of my readers were hurt by what I said of Lincoln in the July CRISIS.

I am sorry to hurt them, for some of them were tried friends of me and my cause—particularly one like the veteran, wounded at Chickamauga and a staunch defender of our rights, who thinks my words "unkind and uncalled for."

First and foremost, there comes a question of fact. Was what I said true or false? This I shall not argue. Any good library will supply the books, and let each interested reader judge. Only they should remember that, as one of my naive critics writes, "I know that there are among his early biographers those who say something to the same effect"; but against these he marshalls the later words of those who want to forget. I leave the matter there. If my facts were false, my words were wrong—but were my facts false?

Beyond this, there is another and deeper question on which most of my critics dwell. They say, What is the use of recalling evil? What good will it do? or as one phrases, "Is this proper food for your people"? I think it is.

Abraham Lincoln was perhaps the greatest figure of the nineteenth century. Certainly of the five masters,—Napoleon, Bismarck, Victoria, Browning and Lincoln, Lincoln is to me the most human and lovable. And I love him not because he was perfect but because he was not and yet triumphed. The world is full of illegitimate children. The world is full of folk whose taste was educated in the gutter. The world is full of people born hating and despising their fellows. To these I love to say: See this man. He was one of you and yet he became Abraham Lincoln.

Some may prefer to believe (as one correspondent intimates) that he was of Mayflower ancestry through the "Lincolns of Hingham!" Others may refuse to believe his taste in jokes and political maneuvers and list him as an original abolitionist and defender of Negroes. But personally I revere him the more because up out of his contradictions and inconsistencies he fought his way to the pinnacles of earth and his fight was within as well as without. I care more for Lincoln's great toe than for the whole body of the perfect George Washington, of spotless ancestry, who "never told a lie" and never did anything else interesting.

No! I do not love evil as evil; I do not retail foul gossip about either the living or the dead; but I glory in that crucified humanity that can push itself up out of the mud of a miserable, dirty ancestry; who despite the clinging smirch of low tastes and shifty political methods, rose to be a great and good man and the noblest friend of the slave.

Do my colored friends really believe the picture would be fairer and finer if we forgot Lincoln's unfortunate speech at Charleston, Illinois, in 1858? I commend that speech to the editors who have been having hysterics. Abraham Lincoln said:

> I will say, then, that I am not, nor ever have been, in favor of bringing about in any way the social and political equality of the white and black races—that I am not, nor ever have been, in favor of making voters or jurors of Negroes, nor of qualifying them to hold office, nor to intermarry with white people; and I will say in addition to this, that there is a physical difference between the white and black races which I believe will forever forbid the two races living together on terms of social and political equality. And inasmuch as they cannot so live, while they do remain together there must be the position of superior and inferior, and I, as much as any other man, am in favor of having the superior position assigned to the white race.

This was Lincoln's word in 1858. Five years later he declared that black slaves "are and henceforward shall be free." And in 1864 he was writing to Hahn of Louisiana in favor of Negro suffrage.

The difficulty is that ignorant folk and inexperienced try continually to paint humanity as all good or all evil. Was Lincoln great and good? He was! Well, then, all evil alleged against him are malicious lies, even if they are true.

"Why should you wish to hold up to public gaze those defects of character you claim he possessed, knowing that he wrought so well?"

That is the very reason for telling the Truth. That is the reason for painting Cromwell's mole as it was and not as some artists conceive it ought to have been.

The scars and foibles and contradictions of the Great do not diminish but enhance the worth and meaning of their upward struggle: it was the bloody sweat that proved the human Christ divine; it was his true history and antecedents that proved Abraham Lincoln a Prince of Men.

On Being Crazy

June 1923

It was one o'clock and I was hungry. I walked into a restaurant, seated myself and reached for the bill-of-fare. My table companion rose.

"Sir," said he, "do you wish to force your company on those who do not want you?"

No, said I, I wish to eat.

"Are you aware, Sir, that this is social equality?"

Nothing of the sort, Sir, it is hunger,—and I ate.

The day's work done, I sought the theatre. As I sank into my seat, the lady shrank and squirmed.

I beg pardon, I said.

"Do you enjoy being where you are not wanted?" she asked coldly.

Oh no, I said.

"Well you are not wanted here."

I was surprised. I fear you are mistaken, I said. I certainly want the music and I like to think the music wants me to listen to it.

"Usher," said the lady, "this is social equality."

No, madame, said the usher, it is the second movement of Beethoven's Fifth Symphony.

After the theatre, I sought the hotel where I had sent my baggage. The clerk scowled.

"What do you want?" he asked.

Rest, I said.

"This is a white hotel," he said.

I looked around. Such a color scheme requires a great deal of cleaning, I said, but I don't know that I object.

"We object," said he.

Then why—, I began, but he interrupted.

"We don't keep 'niggers'," he said, " we don't want social equality."

Neither do I. I replied gently, I want a bed.

I walked thoughtfully to the train. I'll take a sleeper through Texas. I'm a bit dissatisfied with this town.

"Can't sell you one."

I only want to hire it, said I, for a couple of nights.

"Can't sell you a sleeper in Texas," he maintained. "They consider that social equality."

I consider it barbarism, I said, and I think I'll walk.

Walking, I met a wayfarer who immediately walked to the other side of the road where it was muddy. I asked his reasons.

" 'Niggers' is dirty," he said.

So is mud, said I. Moreover I added, I am not as dirty as you—at least, not yet.

"But you're a 'nigger', ain't you?" he asked.

My grandfather was so-called.

"Well then!" he answered triumphantly.

Do you live in the South? I persisted, pleasantly.

"Sure," he growled, "and starve there."

I should think you and the Negroes might get together and vote out starvation.

"We don't let them vote."

We? Why not? I said in surprise.

" 'Niggers' is too ignorant to vote."

But, I said, I am not so ignorant as you.

"But you're a 'nigger'."

Yes, I'm certainly what you mean by that.

"Well then!" he returned, with that curiously inconsequential note of triumph. "Moreover," he said, "I don't want my sister to marry a nigger."

I had not seen his sister, so I merely murmured, let her say, no.

"By God you shan't marry her, even if she said yes."

But,—but I don't want to marry her, I answered a little perturbed at the personal turn.

"Why not!" he yelled, angrier than ever.

Because I'm already married and I rather like my wife.

"Is she a 'nigger'?" he asked suspiciously.

Well, I said again, her grandmother—was called that.

"Well then!" he shouted in that oddly illogical way.

I gave up. Go on, I said, either you are crazy or I am.

"We both are," he said as he trotted along in the mud.

The Tuskegee Hospital

July 1923

We have strong reasons for believing that the following are the actual facts concerning the Tuskegee Hospital:

1. The Harding administration, without consultation with

Negro leaders, made Dr. R. R. Moton a sort of referee for 12 million Negroes as to the personnel of the hospital and the Veterans' Bureau promised him categorically that he would be consulted before anybody was appointed superintendent of the hospital.

2. Colonel Robert H. Stanley, a white man, was made superintendent of the hospital and arrived at Tuskegee two days before Dr. Moton was notified.

3. Plans were made to open the hospital April first with a full white staff of white doctors and *white nurses* with *colored nurse-maids* for each white nurse, in order to save them from contact with colored patients!

4. On February 14th Dr. Moton wrote President Harding and told him that if Negro physicians and nurses were debarred from service in the hospital without at least being given a chance to qualify under the Civil Service rules it would bring justifiable criticism upon him and upon the Harding administration.

5. Dr. Moton wrote to the Superintendent of the hospital asking that the opening of the hospital be delayed. The Superintendent replied that there could be no mixture of races in the staff.

6. Strong pressure was put upon Dr. Moton to make him change his position and the Governor of Alabama, together with General R. E. Steiner, telegraphed the President protesting against a mixed staff and demanding a full white staff. Steiner is the head of the American Legion in Alabama and he is the one who in New Orleans fought to keep Negro ex-service men from membership in the Legion; consequently no Negro ex-service men in Alabama can have any affiliation whatsoever with the American Legion. Meantime Dr. Moton was threatened by the Ku Klux Klan and others and Tuskegee school had to place armed guards at his home.

7. On February 23 President Harding called Dr. Moton into conference after which the President issued an executive order calling for a special examination for Negro applicants for places on the hospital staff.

8. The only interest of white people in Alabama in this hospital is economic and racial. They want to draw the gov-

ernment salaries and they do not want any Negro officials in Alabama whom the state cannot dominate. To illustrate this: the contract for burying soldiers was given to a white undertaker from Greenville, South Carolina, before the bids of local colored undertakers had a chance even to be submitted.

9. The Civil Service Commission is delaying unnecessarily and unreasonably in arranging for examinations and qualifying colored physicians and without doubt are going to cheat in every possible way.

In commenting on all this we can simply gasp. Is it not inconceivable? Human hatred, meanness and cupidity gone stark mad! Separating races in hospitals and graveyards and fighting to put white men over a Negro hospital! Giving nurses black *maids* to do the work while the white "ladies" eat with the internes, dance at the balls and flirt with the doctors and black men die! Lying, postponing, deceiving, threatening to keep out black doctors and nurses. What will be the result? What *can* be the result? What decent Negro physician or devoted black nurse will dare go to this nest of barbarism?

We honor Moton for his present stand and sympathize with him in his undoubted danger and humiliation. But this leads us to condemn him all the more sharply and unsparingly for the last part which he has played in inter-racial politics.

Here was a great government duty to take care of black soldiers wounded in soul and body by their awful experience in the Great War. They ought to have been cared for without discrimination in the same hospitals and under the same circumstances as white soldiers. But even if this were impossible because of race hatred, certainly the last place on God's green earth to put a segregated Negro hospital was in the lynching belt of mob-ridden Alabama, Georgia, Mississippi and their ilk.

It occurred to some of our bright Northern white philanthropists and politicians that the shunting of this institution to Tuskegee was exactly the thing; and the tool they found ready to their hand to carry this out was Dr. R. R. Moton.

"Chickens come home to roost." Tuskegee is no place for

such a hospital. It is not and cannot be an integral part of the school, which the public opinion of the world of the memory of Booker T. Washington partially protects from Alabama mobs. Outside of such schools as Tuskegee and the larger cities, there is no protection in central Alabama for a decent Negro pig-pen, much less for an institution to restore the life and health of those very black servants of the nation, whom Alabama, led by the cowardly Steiner, has kicked out of the American Legion.

Any Negro in such a hospital, under Southern white men and women of the type who are now fighting like beasts to control it, would be a subject of torture and murder rather than of restoration of health. The only decent method would have been to have placed the institution in the law-abiding North where it belongs; and even now, despite the fact that these millions of dollars of brick and equipment have been sunk into the morass of the black belt, the best way out of the mess would be to tear the hospital down and rebuild it within the confines of civilization.

The Technique of Race Prejudice

August 1923

We have developed in the United States a technique of race discrimination which gains its despicable ends by methods so subtle and evasive that the man on the street not only cannot place the blame but after a few bewildered gestures is tempted to look upon the whole thing as an "Act of God".

Consider, for instance, the now well-known case of Miss Augusta Savage. Miss Savage struggled up through the wretched public schools of Florida; came to New York and eventually began studying art at Cooper Union. "Miss Savage's record," writes the Art Director, "has been excellent and her conduct irreproachable." The friends of Miss Savage sought to get her a chance to do some study abroad in the "Fontainebleau School of the Fine Arts", financed by Americans and established as "a summer school for American architects, painters and sculptors".

The Executive Committee of this school is impressive: The Chairman of the Department of Architecture, is Whitney Warren, a leading architect, member of the National Institute of Arts and Sciences, with an honorary degree from Harvard. The Chairman of the Department of Painting and Sculpture is Ernest C. Peixotto, a pupil of Benjamin Constant and Chevalier of the French Legion of Honor; well known as a painter and illustrator. Other members of the Committee are Edwin Blashfield, who decorated the great central dome of the Library of Congress; Howard Greenley, President of the Architectural League; Thomas Hastings, who designed the New York Public Library and is a member of the American Academy of Arts and Letters; J. Monroe Hewlett, President of the Mural Painters; Hermon MacNeil, President of the National Sculpture Society; and James Gamble Rogers, who designed the great Harkness Memorial Quadrangle at Yale.

Here then, are representatives of the best America; leaders in Art and Literature; members of the world's most exclusive clubs and organizations. This Committee told Miss Savage that she could not study at the Fontainebleau School of Fine Arts and that the reason was because she was black. But do not think that this action was straightforward, clear and definite. The only clear and definite thing about it was that Miss Savage's deposit was returned to her and that she did not go to Fontainebleau. But the responsibility for this action and the reasons for it are most difficult to trace and yet the hunt has its points of interest.

THE CRISIS has addressed a politely-worded note to each one of the eight gentlemen mentioned above. Mr. Peixotto, Mr. Warren and Mr. Greenley have not answered. However, Mr. Peixotto had already written a letter to another person which we feel at liberty to quote: He hopes she will "understand our position" and starts off with a technical excuse based on Miss Savage's alleged failure to furnish "two letters of recommendation". He hastens, however, to admit that this is a small matter and proceeds to say: "To be perfectly frank with you, we did learn that Miss Savage was of the colored race and the question was put before our Advisory Committee who strongly felt that in a school such as the Fontainebleau School it would not be wise to have a colored student."

Then come five varying points of view; first there are two alibis: Thomas Hastings says: "I believe it is needless for me to say that I personally would have no sympathy with keeping Miss Augusta Savage away from the Fontainebleau School of Arts because of Negro Descent."

Edwin Blashfield says: "I was not present at any meeting where the question of Miss Savage's application came up or was discussed and I am entirely without knowledge of what happened."

James Gamble Rogers also has an alibi handy: "I did not know anything about the case of the colored girl you mention until I read it in the newspapers." But he adds this interesting point of view: "When we try to take advantage of this Fontainebleau School for the benefit of people here, we have to have sponsors for certain financial conditions, such as guaranteeing the payment to the boats that so many staterooms will be paid for, etc., and it is not easy to get the sponsors. Therefore, I hope that you will do nothing that will prevent us getting the sponsors."

Hermon A. MacNeil says nothing of responsibility but is, "Extremely sorry that a story of this kind should have gotten about as I know the gentlemen of the committee are men of the broadest vision and are trying to do the very best possible. It may be that her work was not very high in quality."

So far, poor Mr. Peixotto stands apparently alone; but finally, J. Monroe Hewlett adds this bit: "The accepted applicants come from all parts of the United States. It seemed clear to the committee that any race prejudice that manifested itself among the students might easily affect the entire morale of the School during its first year. . . . I am satisfied in my own mind that the decision reached in regard to Miss Savage was due quite as much to consideration for her as to any other thought or feeling."

To us who have experience, there is nothing mystifying in all this. These men, either by shirking their plain responsibility or by disingenuous excuses have connived at a miserable piece of race discrimination; and yet every last one of them has "ducked" responsibility: they have no knowledge; they spared her feelings; they need money. Many of them prayed that the reason should be that Miss Savage had no ability, but that is disproved by the records at Cooper Union and by the fact that no very high standards of ability were required of the sensitive white Southerners. Other Directors emphasized the terrible and explosive possibilities of social contact. But the Art Director at Cooper Union writes of his own accord: "It may be added that Miss Savage's treatment at the hands of her fellow-students, whether in the classes, in the lunch room or in their social relations generally, has been as irreproachable as has been her own conduct: indeed it appears that she has been rather a favorite."

In fact, here you have in its naked shame, the technique of American race prejudice. It is idle to charge up lynching solely to the "poor white trash"; it is silly to talk of race prejudice as simply a child of ignorance and poverty. The ignorant and poor may lynch and discriminate but the real deep and the basic race hatred in the United States is a matter of the educated and distinguished leaders of white civilization. They are the ones who are determined to keep black folk from developing talent and sharing in civilization. The only thing to their credit is that they are ashamed of what they do and say and cover their tracks desperately even if ineffectually with excuses and surprises and alibis. But the discrimination goes on and they not only do not raise a hand to stop it—they even gently and politely but in strict secrecy put their shoulders to the wheel and push it forward.

One can only sum it up in the words of Daisy King, a white sculptor:

> "Have you seen this latest example of 'White Supremacy'. Sounds like good old Texas, doesn't it? That Thomas Hastings, the architect of the 42nd Street Library, and our foremost architect since the death of Stanford White, with his own training safely completed should stoop to place a stone in the path of a little colored girl who has won a distinctive honor, against odds, is unbelievable. That Ernest Peixotto, himself a Spanish Jew, should feel

it necessary to deprive a young colored woman of a well-earned scholarship in order to protect from 'contamination' these young Southern girls who have apparently, no honors to their credit, is, to say the least, 'instructive'."

The Younger Literary Movement

February 1924

There have been times when we writers of the older set have been afraid that the procession of those who seek to express the life of the American Negro was thinning and that none were coming forward to fill the footsteps of the fathers. Dunbar is dead; Chesnutt is silent; and Kelly Miller is mooning after false gods while Brawley and Woodson are writing history rather than literature. But even as we ask "Where are the young Negro artists to mold and weld this mighty material about us?"—even as we ask, they come.

There are two books before me, which, if I mistake not, will mark an epoch: a novel by Jessie Fauset and a book of stories and poems by Jean Toomer. There are besides these, five poets writing: Langston Hughes, Countée Cullen, Georgia Johnson, Gwendolyn Bennett and Claude McKay. Finally, Negro men are appearing as essayists and reviewers, like Walter White and Eric Walrond. (And even as I write comes the news that a novel by Mr. White has just found a publisher.) Here then is promise sufficient to attract us.

We recognize the exquisite abandon of a new day in Langston Hughes' "Song For a Banjo". He sings:

Shake your brown feet, Liza,
Shake 'em Liza, chile,
Shake your brown feet, Liza,
(The music's soft and wile).
Shake your brown feet, Liza,
(The Banjo's sobbin' low),
The sun's goin' down this very night—
Might never rise no mo'.

Countée Cullen in his "Ballad of the Brown Girl" achieves eight lyric lines that are as true as life itself. There is in Claude

McKay's "If We Must Die" a strain martial and mutinous. There are other echoes—two from dead poets Jamison and Cotter who achieved in their young years long life if not immortality. But this essay is of two books.

The world of black folk will some day arise and point to Jean Toomer as a writer who first dared to emancipate the colored world from the conventions of sex. It is quite impossible for most Americans to realize how straightlaced and conventional thought is within the Negro World, despite the very unconventional acts of the group. Yet this contradiction is true. And Jean Toomer is the first of our writers to hurl his pen across the very face of our sex conventionality. In "Cane",[1] one has only to take his women characters *seriatim* to realize this: Here is Karintha, an innocent prostitute; Becky, a fallen white woman; Carma, a tender Amazon of unbridled desire; Fern, an unconscious wanton; Esther, a woman who looks age and bastardy in the face and flees in despair; Louise, with a white and a black lover; Avey, unfeeling and unmoral; and Doris, the cheap chorus girl. These are his women, painted with a frankness that is going to make his black readers shrink and criticize; and yet they are done with a certain splendid, careless truth.

Toomer does not impress me as one who knows his Georgia but he does know human beings; and, from the background which he has seen slightly and heard of all his life through the lips of others, he paints things that are true, not with Dutch exactness, but rather with an impressionist's sweep of color. He is an artist with words but a conscious artist who offends often by his apparently undue striving for effect. On the other hand his powerful book is filled with felicitous phrases—Karintha, "carrying beauty perfect as the dusk when the sun goes down",—

"Hair—
Silver-grey
Like streams of stars"

Or again, "face flowed into her eyes—flowed in soft creamy foam and plaintive ripples". His emotion is for the most part entirely objective. One does not feel that he feels

[1]Boni & Liveright, New York.

much and yet the fervor of his descriptions shows that he has felt or knows what feeling is. His art carries much that is difficult or even impossible to understand. The artist, of course, has a right deliberately to make his art a puzzle to the interpreter (the whole world is a puzzle) but on the other hand I am myself unduly irritated by this sort of thing. I cannot, for the life of me, for instance see why Toomer could not have made the tragedy of Carma something that I could understand instead of vaguely guess at; "Box Seat" muddles me to the last degree and I am not sure that I know what "Kabnis" is about. All of these essays and stories, even when I do not understand them, have their strange flashes of power, their numerous messages and numberless reasons for being. But still for me they are partially spoiled. Toomer strikes me as a man who has written a powerful book but who is still watching for the fullness of his strength and for that calm certainty of his art which will undoubtedly come with years.

The Challenge of Detroit

November 1925

In Detroit, Michigan, a black man has shot into a mob which was threatening him, his family, his friends and his home in order to make him move out of the neighborhood. He killed one man and wounded another.

Immediately a red and awful challenge confronts the nation. Must black folk shoot and shoot to kill in order to maintain their rights or is this unnecessary and wanton bloodshed for fancied ill? The answer depends on the facts. The Mayor of Detroit has publicly warned both mob and Negroes. He has repudiated mob law but he adds, turning to his darker audience, that they ought not to invite aggression by going where they are not wanted. There are thus two interpretations:

1. A prosperous Negro physician of Detroit, seeking to get away from his people, moves into a white residential section where his presence for social reasons is distasteful to his neighbors.

2. A prosperous Negro physician of Detroit, seeking a better home with more light, air, space and quiet, finds it naturally in the parts of the city where white folk with similar wants have gone rather than in the slums where most of the colored are crowded.

Which version is true? See the figures:

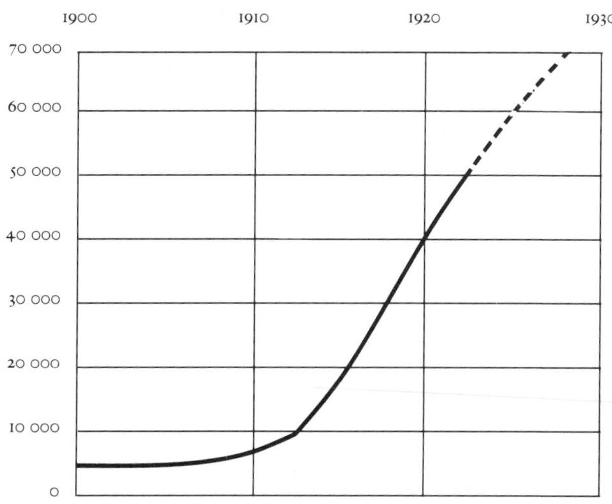

Negro Population of Detroit

1900 . .	4,111
1910 . .	5,741
1920 . .	40,838
1925 . .	60,000 (estimated)

Two thirds of this population in 1920 were crowded into three wards—the Third, Fifth and Seventh. Meantime the total population of Detroit has more than doubled in ten years and the people have reached out on all sides to new dwelling places. Have the Negroes no right to rush too? Is it not their duty to seek better homes and, if they do, are they not bound to "move into white neighborhoods" which is simply another way of saying "move out of congested slums"?

Why do they not make their own new settlements then? Because no individual can make a modern real estate development; no group of ordinary individuals can compete with organized real estate interests and get a decent deal. When Negroes have tried it they have usually had miserable results; in Birmingham, Alabama, twenty years since, they bought a nice street and lined it with pretty homes; the city took all its prostitutes and stuck them into a segregated vice district right behind the pretty homes! In Macon, Savannah, New Orleans and Atlanta crime and prostitution have been kept and protected in Negro residence districts. In New York City, for years, no Negro could rent or buy a home in Manhattan outside the "Tenderloin"; and white Religion and Respectability far from stretching a helping hand turned and cursed the blacks when by bribery, politics and brute force they broke into the light and air of Harlem. Some great leaders in Negro philanthropy like Clarence Kelsey formed a financial bloc to push the Negroes out of Harlem, to refuse mortgages to landlords renting to them; but only one practical project of furnishing them decent quarters came to fruition.

Dear God! Must we not live? And if we live may we not live somewhere? And when a whole city full of white folk led and helped by banks, Chambers of Commerce, mortgage companies and "realtors" are combing the earth for every decent bit of residential property for whites, where in the name of God can we live and live decently if not by these same whites? If some of the horror-struck and law-worshipping white leaders of Detroit instead of winking at the Ku Klux Klan and admonishing the Negroes to allow themselves to be kicked and killed with impunity—if these would finance and administer a decent scheme of housing relief for Negroes it would not be necessary for us to kill white mob leaders in order to live in peace and decency. These whited sepulchres pulled that trigger and not the man that held the gun.

But, wail the idiots, Negroes depress real estate values! This is a lie—an ancient and bearded lie. Race prejudice decreases values both real estate and human; crime, ignorance and filth decrease values. But a decent, quiet, educated family buying property in a decent neighborhood will not affect values a bit unless the people in that neighborhood hate a colored skin more than they regard the value of their own property. This has been proven in a thousand instances. Sudden fall in values comes through propaganda and hysteria manipulated by real estate agents or by Southern slave drivers who want their labor to return South; or by ignorant gossip mongers. Usually Negroes do not move into new developments but into districts which well-to-do whites are deserting. The fall in values is not due to race but to a series of economic readjustments and often, as in Baltimore, real estate values were actually saved and raised, not lowered, when black folk bought Druid Hill Avenue and adjacent streets. Certainly a flood of noisy dirty black folk will ruin any neighborhood but they ruin black property as well as white, and the reason is not their color but their condition. And whom, High Heaven, shall we blame for that?

But these facts make no difference to organized American Negro haters. They are using every effort to maintain and increase race friction. In the South time and time again communities have almost forgotten race lines until the bitter, hate-preaching liar stirred it up again. The whole present "Anglo-Saxon" and "race purity" agitation in Virginia has arisen because one white family openly acknowledged its colored grandmother! The whole crusade in Detroit has come to a head because, in 1920, 663,000 Southern whites had migrated and were living in Wisconsin, Michigan, Illinois, Indiana and Ohio. Their numbers are swelling. They are largely clerks, artisans and laborers, not illiterate but ignorant of the modern world and forming by habit the lawless material of mobs. They are ruining the finer democracy of the Middle West and using the Negro as an excuse.

What shall we do? I know a black man. He is a professional man and a graduate of a great eastern school. He has studied abroad. His wife was educated in a good western school and is a quiet housewife. His son is a college graduate and a high school teacher. They have never been arrested. They conduct themselves as cultured folk. This man is living in an apartment in Harlem. He would like more air and sunlight and less noise. He would like a new, small, modern house in the further Bronx or in the hills of Westchester or New Jersey or in the higher part of Queens. He sees daily in the papers new homes advertised suitable to his means—$500, $1,000 even $2000 down, the rest as rent. Can he buy one of these? Not without plotting, deception, insult or murder.

For instance: A man bought a modest home in Staten Island. He was a mail carrier with a fine record; his wife was a school teacher, educated and well-bred. They had four sturdy children in school. As a result he has been mobbed and insulted, his property injured, his glass and shrubbery broken, his insurance cancelled, his life threatened, his existence made miserable. His neighbors do everything to insult him and his, even to crossing the street to avoid passing him. He sticks to his home even though offered a profit to sell, "on principle". He is "colored".

Another man in Detroit bought a fine home in a former exclusive district which is now changing. He was a physician with a large practice, the founder of a hospital, public-spirited and well-liked. He had married the daughter of perhaps the greatest of the interpreters of Negro folk songs with worldwide reputation. He moved in. A mob of thousands appeared, yelling and cursing. They broke his windows, threw out his furniture and he and his family escaped under police protection. He gave up his home, made no resistance, moved back whence he came, filed no protest, made no public complaint. He was "colored".

A little later another physician in Detroit bought another beautiful home and moved in. A mob—almost the same mob—came, cursed, threw stones and ordered him to move. He gathered his family and friends within and locked the door. Five or six thousand people lined the streets. The police set traffic officers to divert the traffic that could not get through. The mob invaded his yard and approached his doors. He shot and shot to kill. His wife and his friends are now in jail charged with *Murder in the first degree!* He was "colored".

Gentle Reader, which of these three examples shall my friend of Harlem follow? Which would you follow if you were "free", black and 21?

"Porgy," by DuBose Heyward

March 1926

Porgy. By DuBose Heyward. George H. Doran Company. New York. 1925. 196 pages.

DuBose Heyward's little novel of colored Charleston life, "Porgy", is a beautiful piece of work. It is the Iliad of a small black beggar in the underworld of labor and crime surrounded by whiskey and lust and sanctified with music, a queer and quaint religion and a great yearning flood of love.

Seldom before has a white Southern writer done black folk with so much of sympathy and subtle understanding. Heyward knows Porgy and his fellows; but his very knowledge brings forward the old and ever young criticism: Charleston has 35,000 persons of Negro descent. They include not only pitiful and terrible figures—beggars, drunkards and prostitutes—but self-supporting and self-respecting laborers and servants, artisans and merchants, professional men and housewives. There is a group of educated and well-to-do folk, beautiful in character and face, who look back on generations of freedom and comfort and accomplishment. Out of Charleston for a hundred years has flowed leadership of the colored folk of America and in Charleston still rest men and women who would be a credit to any modern nation.

And yet if Charleston were swept by a cataclysm tomorrow, and the archaeologists of the 40th century searched white men's writings to learn of its inhabitants in the 20th century, "Porgy" would remain as the best, almost the only picture. It would be a fine picture of the best type of Negro which DuBose Heyward could really know. Into the black underworld he can go almost unhindered save by that subtle veil he so delicately paints. But between him and the main mass of Charleston Negroes there is an unpassable gulf. Whose ever the fault is, the loss to art is irreparable.

Books

(VAN VECHTEN'S "NIGGER HEAVEN")

December 1926

Carl Van Vechten's "Nigger Heaven" is a blow in the face. It is an affront to the hospitality of black folk and to the intelligence of white. First, as to its title: my objection is based on no provincial dislike of the nickname. "Nigger" is an English word of wide use and definite connotation. As employed by Conrad, Sheldon, Allen and even Firbanks, its use was justifiable. But the phrase, "Nigger Heaven", as applied to Harlem is a misnomer. "Nigger Heaven" does not mean, as Van Vechten once or twice intimates, (pages 15, 199) a haven for Negroes—a city of refuge for dark and tired souls; it means in common parlance, a nasty, sordid corner into which black folk are herded, and yet a place which they in crass ignorance are fools enough to enjoy. Harlem is no such place as that, and no one knows this better than Carl Van Vechten.

But after all, a title is only a title, and a book must be judged eventually by its fidelity to truth and its artistic merit. I find this novel neither truthful nor artistic. It is not a true picture of Harlem life, even allowing for some justifiable impressionistic exaggeration. It is a caricature. It is worse than untruth because it is a mass of half-truths. Probably some time and somewhere in Harlem every incident of the book has happened; and yet the resultant picture built out of these parts is ludicrously out of focus and undeniably misleading.

The author counts among his friends numbers of Negroes of all classes. He is an authority on dives and cabarets. But he masses this knowledge without rule or reason and seeks to express all of Harlem life in its cabarets. To him the black cabaret is Harlem; around it all his characters gravitate. Here is their stage of action. Such a theory of Harlem is nonsense. The overwhelming majority of black folk there never go to cabarets. The average colored man in Harlem is an everyday laborer, attending church, lodge and movie and as conservative and as conventional as ordinary working folk everywhere.

Something they have which is racial, something distinctively Negroid can be found; but it is expressed by subtle, almost delicate nuance, and not by the wildly, barbaric drunken orgy in whose details Van Vechten revels. There is laughter, color and spontaneity at Harlem's core, but in the current cabaret, financed and supported largely by white New York, this core is so overlaid and enwrapped with cheaper stuff that no one but a fool could mistake it for the genuine exhibition of the spirit of the people.

To all this the author has a right to reply that even if the title is an unhappy catch-phrase for penny purposes and his picture of truth untruthful, that his book has a right to be judged primarily as a work of art. Does it please? Does it entertain? Is it a good and human story? In my opinion it is not; and I am one who likes stories and I do not insist that they be written solely for my point of view. "Nigger Heaven" is to me an astonishing and wearisome hodgepodge of laboriously stated facts, quotations and expressions, illuminated here and there with something that comes near to being nothing but cheap melodrama. Real human feelings are laughed at. Love is degraded. The love of Byron and Mary is stark cruelty and that of Lasca and Byron is simply nasty. Compare this slum picture with Porgy. In his degradation, Porgy is human and interesting. But in "Nigger Heaven" there is not a single loveable character. There is scarcely a generous impulse or a beautiful ideal. The characters are singularly wooden and inhuman. Van Vechten is not the great artist who with remorseless scalpel probes the awful depths of life. To him there are no depths. It is the surface mud he slops about in. His women's bodies have no souls; no children palpitate upon his hands; he has never looked upon his dead with bitter tears. Life to him is just one damned orgy after another, with hate, hurt, gin and sadism.

Both Langston Hughes and Carl Van Vechten know Harlem cabarets; but it is Hughes who whispers

"One said he heard the jazz band sob
When the little dawn was grey".

Van Vechten never heard a sob in a cabaret. All he hears is noise and brawling. Again and again with singular lack of invention he reverts to the same climax of two creatures tearing and scratching over "mah man"; lost souls who once had women's bodies; and to Van Vechten this spells comedy, not tragedy.

I seem to see that Mr. Van Vechten began a good tale with the promising figure of Anatol, but that he keeps turning aside to write in from his notebook every fact he has heard about Negroes and their problems; singularly irrelevant quotations, Haitian history, Chesnutt's novels, race-poetry, "blues" written by white folk. Into this mass he drops characters which are in most cases thin disguises; and those who know the originals have only to compare their life and this death, to realize the failure in truth and human interest. The final climax is an utterly senseless murder which appears without preparation or reason from the clouds.

I cannot for the life of me see in this work either sincerity or art, deep thought, or truthful industry. It seems to me that Mr. Van Vechten tried to do something bizarre and he certainly succeeded. I read "Nigger Heaven" and read it through because I had to. But I advise others who are impelled by a sense of duty or curiosity to drop the book gently in the grate and to try the *Police Gazette*.

Flood

July 1927

We hope that every Negro that can escape from the slave camps guarded by the National Red Cross for the benefit of the big planters of Mississippi and Louisiana and the lynchers of Arkansas will leave this land of deviltry at the first opportunity. Let them ride, run and crawl out of this hell. There is no hope for the black man there today. Relief funds are being used to pamper white folk and in some cases are actually being sold to black folk as the basis of contracts for their compulsory services in the future. Fully 75 per cent of the refugees have been Negroes and we doubt if they have received 25 per cent of the relief funds.

We do not know where the refugees from the Mississippi bottoms can go, but we are frank to say it would be better for them to starve in Memphis and Chicago than to be slaves in Arkansas and Mississippi. Even if eventually they have to return, they can make better terms than by staying.

And they can expect no help from Coolidge or Hoover. Mr. Hoover is too busy having his picture taken and Mr. Coolidge, when the Arkansas mob burns the body of an imbecile, feeding the bonfire with lumber torn from a Negro church, while the Mayor of the city keeps the Negro leaders imprisoned in their own business block—Mr. Coolidge tells the world of the privileges of American civilization.

Lynchings

August 1927

The recent horrible lynchings in the United States, even the almost incredible burning of human beings alive, have raised not a ripple of interest, not a single protest from the United States Government, scarcely a word from the pulpit and not a syllable of horror or suggestion from the Defenders of the Republic, the 100% Americans, or the propagandists of the army and navy. And this in spite of the fact that the cause of the Louisville, Mississippi, bestiality was, according to the Memphis *Commercial-Appeal*, "widespread indignation at the refusal of the Negroes traveling in slow, second-handed Fords to give road to faster cars". And yet hiding and concealing this barbarism by every resource of American silence we are sitting in council at Geneva and Peking and trying to make the world believe that we are a civilized nation.

The Name "Negro"

March 1928

South Bend, Ind.

Dear Sir:

I am only a high school student in my Sophomore year, and have not the understanding of you college educated men.

It seems to me that since THE CRISIS is the Official Organ of the National Association for the Advancement of Colored People which stand for equality for all Americans, why would it designate, and segregate us as "Negroes", and not as "Americans".

The most piercing thing that hurts me in this February CRISIS, which forced me to write, was the notice that called the natives of Africa, "Negroes", instead of calling them "Africans", or "natives".

The word, "Negro", or "nigger", is a white man's word to make us feel inferior. I hope to be a worker for my race, that is why I wrote this letter. I hope that by the time I become a man, that this word, "Negro", will be abolished.

ROLAND A. BARTON.

My dear Roland:

Do not at the outset of your career make the all too common error of mistaking names for things. Names are only conventional signs for identifying things. Things are the reality that counts. If a thing is despised, either because of ignorance or because it is despicable, you will not alter matters by changing its name. If men despise Negroes, they will not despise them less if Negroes are called "colored" or "Afro-Americans".

Moreover, you cannot change the name of a thing at will. Names are not merely matters of thought and reason; they are growths and habits. As long as the majority of men mean black or brown folk when they say "Negro", so long will Negro be the name of folks brown and black. And neither anger nor wailing nor tears can or will change the name until the name-habit changes.

But why seek to change the name? "Negro" is a fine word. Etymologically and phonetically it is much better and more logical than "African" or "colored" or any of the various hyphenated circumlocutions. Of course, it is not "historically" accurate. No name ever was historically accurate: neither "English," "French," "German," "White," "Jew," "Nordic" nor "Anglo-Saxon." They were all at first nicknames, misnomers, accidents, grown eventually to conventional habits and achieving accuracy because, and simply because, wide and continued usage rendered them accurate. In this sense "Negro" is quite as accurate, quite as old and quite as definite as any name of any great group of people.

Suppose now we could change the name. Suppose we arose tomorrow morning and lo! instead of being "Negroes", all the world called us "Cheiropolidi",—do you really think this would make a vast and momentous difference to you and to me? Would the Negro problem be suddenly and eternally settled? Would you be any less ashamed of being descended from a black man, or would your schoolmates feel any less superior to you? The feeling of inferiority is in you, not in any name. The name merely evokes what is already there. Exorcise the hateful complex and no name can ever make you hang your head.

Or, on the other hand, suppose that we slip out of the whole thing by calling ourselves "Americans". But in that case, what word shall we use when we want to talk about those descendants of dark slaves who are largely excluded still from full American citizenship and from complete social privilege with white folk? Here is Something that we want to talk about; that we do talk about; that we Negroes could not live without talking about. In that case, we need a name for it, do we not? In order to talk logically and easily and be understood. If you do not believe in the necessity of such a name, watch the antics of a colored newspaper which has determined in a fit of New Year's Resolutions not to use the word "Negro!"

And then too, without the word that means Us, where are all those spiritual ideals, those inner bonds, those group ideals and forward strivings of this mighty army of 12 millions? Shall we abolish these with the abolition of a name? Do we want to abolish them? Of course we do not. They are our most precious heritage.

Historically, of course, your dislike of the word Negro is easily explained: "Negroes" among your grandfathers meant black folk; "Colored" people were mulattoes. The mulattoes hated and despised the blacks and were insulted if called "Negroes". But we are not insulted—not you and I. We are quite as proud of our black ancestors as of our white. And perhaps a little prouder. What hurts us is the mere memory that any man of Negro descent was ever so cowardly as to despise any part of his own blood.

Your real work, my dear young man, does not lie with names. It is not a matter of changing them, losing them, or forgetting them. Names are nothing but little guideposts along the Way. The Way would be there and just as hard and just as long if there were no guideposts,—but not quite as easily followed! Your real work as a Negro lies in two directions: *First*, to let the world know what there is fine and genuine about the Negro race. And *secondly*, to see that there is nothing about that race which is worth contempt; your contempt, my contempt; or the contempt of the wide, wide world.

Get this then, Roland, and get it straight even if it pierces your soul: a Negro by any other name would be just as black and just as white; just as ashamed of himself and just as shamed by others, as today. It is not the name—it's the Thing that counts. Come on, Kid, let's go get the Thing!

Robert E. Lee

March 1928

Each year on the 19th of January there is renewed effort to canonize Robert E. Lee, the great confederate general. His personal comeliness, his aristocratic birth and his military prowess all call for the verdict of greatness and genius. But one thing—one terrible fact—militates against this and that is the inescapable truth that Robert E. Lee led a bloody war to perpetuate human slavery. Copperheads like the New York *Times* may magisterially declare: "of course, he never fought for slavery". Well, for what did he fight? State rights? Nonsense. The South cared only for State Rights as a weapon to defend slavery. If nationalism had been a stronger defense of the slave system than particularism, the South would have been as nationalist in 1861 as it had been in 1812.

No. People do not go to war for abstract theories of government. They fight for property and privilege and that was what Virginia fought for in the Civil War. And Lee followed

Virginia. He followed Virginia not because he particularly loved slavery (although he certainly did not hate it), but because he did not have the moral courage to stand against his family and his clan. Lee hesitated and hung his head in shame because he was asked to lead armies against human progress and Christian decency and did not dare refuse. He surrendered not to Grant, but to Negro Emancipation.

Today we can best perpetuate his memory and his nobler traits, not by falsifying his moral débacle, but by explaining it to the young white South. What Lee did in 1861, other Lees are doing in 1928. They lack the moral courage to stand up for justice to the Negro because of the overwhelming public opinion of their social environment. Their fathers in the past have condoned lynching and mob violence, just as today they acquiesce in the disfranchisement of educated and worthy black citizens, provide wretchedly inadequate public schools for Negro children and endorse a public treatment of sickness, poverty and crime which disgraces civilization.

It is the punishment of the South that its Robert Lees and Jefferson Davises will always be tall, handsome and well-born. That their courage will be physical and not moral. That their leadership will be weak compliance with public opinion and never costly and unswerving revolt for justice and right. It is ridiculous to seek to excuse Robert Lee as the most formidable agency this nation ever raised to make 4 million human beings goods instead of men. Either he knew what slavery meant when he helped maim and murder thousands in its defense, or he did not. If he did not he was a fool. If he did, Robert Lee was a traitor and a rebel—not indeed to his country, but to humanity and humanity's God.

DePriest

February 1929

We have received the following letter from Margaret Deland, the well-known writer:

"I remember with great pleasure meeting you very many

years ago at the house of my friend, Mrs. Evans, in Boston. I recall that William James was there also, and that we four had a delightful time. As I have always been profoundly interested in the political, industrial and spiritual welfare of the people who were so deeply wronged some three hundred years ago, I am keenly alive to the advancement of Negro Americans to-day.

"So, remembering your good nature in answering the questions I asked that day at Mrs. Evans', I am venturing to send you the enclosed clipping in regard to the election to Congress of Oscar DePriest. I have a feeling that few things would be so impressive to persons who desire not only justice, but spiritual advancement, for the colored people, as to have a colored man of your eminence protest against the political advancement of any person of his race who does not display intellectual and moral integrity. Of course, the same protest should be made to the political advancement of any unethical white man—and, as we both know well, there have been many opportunities for such protest! But political indignation expressed against white scoundrels, in papers conducted by white men—desirable as such expression of opinion is—can not draw forth the same approval, as that same indignation expressed against an unethical colored man, in a magazine such as THE CRISIS.

"I am sure that you will see my point in this, and I most earnestly hope that THE CRISIS will repudiate this man in no uncertain terms."

THE CRISIS regrets that it cannot do this. On the contrary, it congratulates Oscar DePriest upon his election. We do not approve of all that Mr. DePriest has done in the past and probably shall not approve of much that he will do in the future, but we do know that Oscar DePriest stands solidly and unwaveringly for the following things:

1. The enforcement of the 13th, 14th and 15th Amendments of the Constitution of the United States.

2. The passage of the Dyer Anti-Lynching Bill.

3. The abolition of the "Jim-Crow" car in interstate commerce.

4. The abolition of color segregation and discrimination in the Civil Service of the United States.

We wish that in addition to this, Mr. DePriest believed in clean politics; in the smashing of Big Business, bootlegging and crime in their present alliance for political power; and in the organization of political life in Chicago so that the intelligent will of the majority could be openly and efficiently expressed.

We wish that Mr. DePriest stood for these things, but we acknowledge with bowed head that if he had stood for such a program as this he never would have been Congressman from Illinois. In other words, the only organized interests in the United States who could be induced to send a colored man to Congress or any man who stands for the five things outlined above, are the same interests which are allied with the rule of wealth and crime.

We find ourselves compelled in political life, therefore, to choose the least of evils. If we remember that Senator Borah stands for clean politics, we also are compelled to remember that he stands for the disfranchisement of Negroes; that he did not vote for the Dyer Anti Lynching Bill, and that he has grown dumb in the fight for Haiti. We would like to admire Al Smith because of the high level of his appointments to office, and his fight against the power trust. But we are compelled to vote against him because never in all his career has he given the slightest attention to the American Negro or expressed the slightest interests in his problems. We support Oscar DePriest, therefore, for the same reasons that we oppose Borah and Smith, namely: the things that DePriest stands for are more vital to the future of democracy in America than prohibition, crime and privilege. Given democracy in this land and we can fight drunkedness, prostitution and monopoly; without democracy and with a "Solid South" we can only wobble between Hoover and Raskob.

Gambling

January 1930

As compared with crap-shooting, always supposed to be the peculiar diversion of Negroes, nine-tenths of the operations of the Wall Street Stock Exchange favors craps, by every consideration of morals and social welfare. Unless the dice are loaded, crap-shooting is a game of pure chance, and the utmost that can happen is the transfer of actual wealth from one gambler to another. But in Wall Street, we have something much more complicated and much less defensible.

We have a great gambling pool, forming nine-tenths of a set of operations, of which the remaining tenth is legitimate and under present conditions necessary effort to sell capital to the highest bidder.

If the government owned all capital and distributed it by science, reason and welfare, as both Russia and President Hoover are now attempting to do, stock gambling would cease.

Around this, at present necessary operation, has arisen the habit of open betting on the future profit of the various industries seeking capital. Some of this betting takes the form of buying stock with the object of selling it for a higher price. There is an element of gambling here but it is the necessary gambling of privately owned capital and is as legitimate as crap-shooting.

Beyond this, however, there is a custom so wide-spread that it involved, during 1928, as high as seven billion dollars of borrowed funds in addition to 30 or more billions of owned wealth. This consists of betting on the price of stock without buying it and with only the deposit of enough actual funds to insure the head gambler from sudden loss. It is this dealing in "futures", that has set the United States crazy for the last few years, taking funds from legitimate industry, depleting thrift accounts and stealing the wages of millions of people; it has made an astonishing number of level-headed Americans dream that they were going to gamble themselves into a financial heaven, where they would subsist on honey and illegal wine, and would sing, dance and do no work forever and forever.

Moreover, the dice in this gambling are nearly always loaded. Everybody who knew anything knew that they were loaded. The head gamblers know the present value of stocks and the reasonable future values. They deliberately deceive their clients by subtle propaganda to pay unreasonable prices.

The President of the United States, the Secretary of the Treasury, the heads of great industries, the leaders of social welfare, all knew that stock prices were unreasonably high, yet, for the most part, they were dumb until the crash came. They knew that prices were being paid for part-ownership in industrial enterprises, which were far beyond anything which the enterprise could ever legitimately earn, and yet, they were silent. They listened in silence to a shameless propaganda that explained how a Miracle was happening and that miracle was involved in American financial leadership of the world; that in some magic way values were going to be re-cast so as to make Steel Common worth two or three times what it was really worth by any sane measurement.

Every professional gambler in Wall Street, backed by the money distributing power of the Federal Banking System, assured the world that this was so, with the idea of making profit by the gullability of ignorant investors. Every person of ordinary wisdom knew that the crash must come because the market had gone out beyond the steadying influence of real values and was depending solely on gamblers' lies and the gullability of morons.

Just as there were gamblers who were gambling for a rise, and lied to make it, so there were other gamblers who, as the crest approached, gambled for a fall, and did not spare the truth to bring it about. The result was a crash so stupendous that it shook the world.

What was that crash in its essence? If it had been merely the transfer of money from gambler to gambler, it would have resembled a huge crap game and have been negligible save in its moral results. There would have been the same amount of wealth and work as before and the same number of idle blood-suckers. This is what the *New York Times* assured us was true after the crash, while President Hoover and Secretary Mellon joined in similar statements.

But these were half-truths. For the stock crash was far more than a transfer of hard-earned wealth and thrifty savings from poor people to the gambling rich. It involved destruction of wealth, work and faith—these three and the greatest of these is the Faith, called Credit. We count as wealth today in organized industry not only what we have but what we expect to have; not only what we do but what we plan to do. Destroy plans and overthrow legitimate expectation and industry is sick or dies. Of the great structure of modern time production and space distribution, the actual present goods, the pittance of cash money and the current days work are bagatelles compared with the expected value of goods to be finished, the value which goods now Here will have when they are There. Destroy the faith built on present Work—the Credit reared on present Cash and Goods and you have destroyed wealth and more than wealth.

That is the reason the President and Cabinet and millionaires are rushing about and crying all is well when no one knows better than they that all is not well because gamblers have been squandering the nation's wealth which industry needed and expected.

The collapse of the Stock Market was not only loss of capital taken from legitimate industry and sunk and destroyed in wild-cat schemes; it was above all, a shaking of the faith of Americans in American industrial organization and in all private capitalistic enterprise. It was the most tremendous blow to the integrity and efficiency of the capitalistic and privately-owned industry of America which that organization ever received. American capitalism was stabbed in the house of its friends. Nothing that Socialists have said or thought for one hundred years has so openly and crassly pointed out the weakness and injustice of industrial life in America.

The end is not yet. The President may repudiate all his individualism and deny the *laissez-faire* of private enterprise by hurriedly summoning the captains of industry and pleading with them for that co-operation, scientific foresight and submergence of the profit motive which only an efficient State can supply in fullest measure. The fundamental weakness of our system still remains. We are gambling with loaded dice. If gamble we must, we would far better confine ourselves to craps.

Patient Asses

March 1930

I met my friend one morning on Seventh Avenue as we were hurrying opposite ways to our work. She asked:

"Did you attend the Smuts lecture?"

I did not.

She said: "He does not strike me as sincere."

I quite agreed with her.

And then she said: "You were wise in advocating Pan-Africanism."

I thanked her. I was glad that she saw the point. I wished again, as I have often wished, that other people would see it. Here was a statesman from the Union of South Africa. Effort was made before his visit to the United States to commit the colored people to support of him and his policy in order that their action might influence their colored brethren in South Africa. As he was about to arrive, a movement was put on foot to get colored leaders to sign a laudatory address and thank Jans Smuts for his South African Negro program! This was fortunately blocked. Then a quiet conference was arranged in Washington by the Phelps Stokes Fund in which the program was confined to carefully restricted discussion of the American race problem and arranged so as to include no single Negro who had been in South Africa or had expert knowledge of the South African situation.

In the meantime, however, Mr. Smuts, himself, supplied a good deal of missing information. He had no sooner opened his mouth at Town Hall, New York City, than he put his own foot deeply and completely in it. He compared Negroes to patient asses and wanted them to dance and sing! Negroes have been more patient than most asses and asses do not usually dance and sing. Indeed, the animals that dance and sing best are the least patient with demagogues like Smuts.

Dr. Moton of Tuskegee, who among a half-dozen Negro leaders sat upon the platform, was the only one who had the courage to challenge Smuts then and there. We congratulate him upon the deed.

Smuts explained. He meant nothing derogative. He was complimenting Negroes. That is Smuts all over! Shrewd, wary, insincere, distrusted throughout South Africa by black and white, Boer and Briton, desperately trying to pose in Europe and America as a great Liberal and forever damned by his determination to keep black folk in eternal subjection to white, while salving the fools with fair words. Herzog, his opponent and the present Premier, is at least sincere. He is as narrow in his "Nigger" hatred as Smuts, but his narrowness is lack of knowledge and not deliberate and suave hypocrisy. Herzog wants to learn. Smuts will never learn. He knows it all now.

And he ought to know it. He and his party established the color caste of South Africa in its present form. From the founding of the Union of South Africa until 1924, Smuts has been a member of the Cabinet and often Prime Minister. During this time he helped establish and vigorously defended the following caste system for black men:

1. Disfranchisement of all persons of Negro descent, except in Cape Colony, and even there Negro voters can not vote for Negro candidates.

2. Disarming the natives by excluding them from the militia.

3. Depriving natives of their land and prohibiting them from buying land except in restricted areas. This legislation gave a million and a half whites 87 per cent of the land and five million natives 13 per cent.

4. Excluding Negroes from the Civil Service.

5. "Jim Crow" regulations for railroads and public buildings. There are separate Post Offices for blacks, either at the back of the white Post Office or underground. Even here, no native clerk is employed and natives must take off their hats when entering any public building. In some cases they cannot walk on the sidewalk.

6. Direct taxation on natives, at the rate of $5 to $10 a year and using most of this money for the benefit of the whites, who pay no poll tax.

7. Educational facilities are so meagre that 95 per cent of the natives are illiterate. In the Transvaal for a long time the government grant to native schools was about the same sum

as they expended for the upkeep of animals in the Pretoria Zoo.

8. The pass system which compells every native to be registered and carry a pass without which he is subject to arrest and imprisonment.

Some of these regulations do not apply to persons of mixed blood and educated natives not living in tribes, but even for them the caste discrimination and restrictions are humiliating and disgraceful and make South Africa the worst place on earth for colored folk to live.

Conceive what would happen to an Englishman who had treated Irishmen in this way and who came to the United States to lecture? How many Irishmen would be sitting on his platform grinning at him? We certainly are patient asses. We shall never secure emancipation from the tyranny of the white oppressor until we have achieved it in our own souls.

Protest

October 1930

American Negroes are gradually learning the power and necessity of determined agitation and protest. But they are still a little under the influence of the idea that unless the protest is successful or seems to have a reasonable chance for success, it is worse than useless. They would say, for instance, fight Senator Allen of Kansas if you know you can defeat him, but if there is any doubt, don't fight. Fight against McCulloch of Ohio if he can be beaten in a normally Republican state. If you have any doubt, vote for him.

This is of course idiotic advice. Protest is for two purposes: first, for its effect upon your political enemies, and secondly, for its effect upon yourself. The effect upon your political enemies can be registered through successful protest which ends in their defeat but also through unsuccessful effort which gives them clear notice of what your attitude of mind is.

Senator Allen knows today that three-fourths of the Negro voters of Kansas voted against him. He is going to think twice before he opposes these voters in the future, even though they have not yet succeeded in defeating him. So, too, McCulloch of Ohio deserves defeat and it will be good for his soul to know that black voters did all they could to help defeat him, even though they may not be successful.

But above all this, the black man that takes his medicine of insult, discourtesy and prejudice sitting down and saying nothing, loses his own self-respect. Even if the offending politician does not hear of your opposition; does not feel your lone vote, you know and you feel, and it is an awful thing to have to be ashamed of one's self.

Books

March 1931

A Philadelphia correspondent writes to the Secretary of the N. A. A. C. P.:

> I am a Negro father, twenty-six years of age, and I am anxious to include in my library such books as my limited budget of $1 to $2 a week will allow. Although preference will be given to current literature, I want also to consider meritorious works of any date about the Negro or written by Negroes. In this way I am hoping within the next eight or ten years to possess a good collection of Negro literature. I assure you that any information you may give will be most gratefully appreciated.

The answer to this letter deserves to be broadcast. Here is a man of small income, who has got the vision to see that a sum between $12 and $25 a year will be well spent for books. He should not, of course, in his spending neglect the daily paper, the weekly paper and the monthly magazine. He must subscribe to one of the large colored weeklies and at least one colored magazine. Beside that, a weekly, like the *Nation* or *Literary Digest* and a monthly like the *American Mercury*, *Harpers'* or *The Forum* will give the necessary broad outlook of an American citizen.

In buying books, he must not neglect general literature; the Haldeman-Julius little Blue Books at five cents each, the

Modern Library at 75 cents, and other volumes at $1 to $3 must be bought now and then.

But the specific quest is spending $12 to $25 a year for Negro literature. Some of these books are recently published, some can only be found in second-hand stores; but all are indispensable to a good Negro library. They can be bought gradually from year to year:

"The American Negro" published by the Annals of the American Academy
Balch's "Occupied Haiti"
Brawley's "The Negro in Literature and Art"
Buell's "Native Problem in Africa"
Bullock's "In Spite of Handicaps"
Chesnutt's Novels
Cullen's Poems
Du Bois' "Souls of Black Folk," "The Negro," "Darkwater"
Fauset's "For Freedom"
Jessie Fauset's Novels
Finot's "Race Prejudice"
Frobenius' "The Voice of Africa"
Henson's "The Negro Explorer at the North Pole"
Hill's "Toussaint L'Overture"
Hughes' Poems and "Not Without Laughter"
Ingram's "History of Slavery and Serfdom"
Johnson's Poems and "Black Manhattan"
Johnsons' Negro Spirituals
Nella Larsen's Novels
Leys' "Kenya"
Life of John Brown
Locke and Montgomery's "Negro Plays"
Locke and others, "The New Negro"
Lugard's "Tropical Dependency"
Lynch's "Facts of Reconstruction"
Mckay's Poems
Kelley Miller's "Race Adjustment"
Moton's "What the Negro Thinks"
Ovington's "Portraits in Color"
Olivier's "The Anatomy of African Misery" and "White Capital and Colored Labor"

Pickens' "Bursting Bonds"
Reuter's "American Race Problem"
Robeson's "The Life of Paul Robeson"
Simmons' "Men of Mark"
Spero and Harris' "The Negro Worker"
Starr's "Liberia"
Stowe's "Uncle Tom's Cabin"
Toomer's "Cane"
Vandercook's "Black Majesty"
Washington's "Up from Slavery"
Wesley's "Negro Labor in the United States"
White's Novels and "Rope and Faggot"
Williams' "History of the Negro Race"
Wilson's "The Black Phalanx"
Woodson's "Negro Orators" and "The Negro in Our History"
Woolf's "Empire and Commerce in Africa"

Here are something over 60 volumes which should cost in all less than $150; or at $25 a year they could be bought in 6 years. After that, we shall have further valuable suggestions.

P. S. Have we made serious omissions already? If so, write us.

P. S. No. 2. THE CRISIS sells most of these books.

Chesnutt

January 1933

Charles Waddell Chesnutt, genial American gentleman and dean of Negro literature in this land, is dead. We have lost a fine intellect, a keen sense of humor and a broad tolerant philosophy. Chesnutt was of that group of white folk who because of a more or less remote Negro ancestor identified himself voluntarily with the darker group, studied them, expressed them, defended them, and yet never forgot the absurdity of this artificial position and always refused to admit its logic or its ethical sanction. He was not a Negro; he was a man. But this fact never drove him to the opposite extreme. He did not repudiate persons of Negro blood as social equals and close friends. If his white friends (and he had legion) could not tolerate colored friends, they need not come to Mr. Chesnutt's home. If colored friends demanded racial segregation and hatred, he had no patience with them. Merit and friendship in his broad and tolerant mind knew no lines of color or race, and all men, good, bad and indifferent, were simply men. God rest his beautiful memory.

The Right to Work

April 1933

We have been taught to regard the industrial system today as fixed and permanent. Our problem has been looked upon as the static one of adjusting ourselves to American industry and entering it on its own terms. Our first awakening came when we found that the technique of industry changes so fast and the machine displaces and modifies human labor in so many ways, that it is practically impossible for our Negro industrial schools to equip themselves so as to train youth for current work, while the actual shops and apprentice systems are largely closed to us.

Our second lesson is to realize that the whole industrial system in the United States and in the world is changing and will change radically, either by swift evolution or here and there by revolution; and instead of our sitting like dumb and patient fools awaiting the salvation of the white industrial Lord, it is our duty now to prepare for a new organization and a new status, new modes of making a living, and a new organization of industry.

It is immaterial to us whether this change in the surrounding white world comes in ten, twenty-five or one hundred years. The fact is that the change is inevitable. No system of human culture can stand world war and industrial cataclysm repeatedly, without radical reorganization, either by reasoned reform or irrational collapse.

What, then, shall we do? What can we do? Parties of reform, of socialism and communism beckon us. None of these offers us anything concrete or dependable. From Brook Farm down to the L.I.P.A., the face of reform has been set to lift the white producer and consumer, leaving the black man and his peculiar problems severely alone, with the fond hope that better white men will hate Negroes less and better white conditions make race contact more human and respectable. This has sometimes happened, but more often it has not.

Socialists and Communists assume that state control of industry by a majority of citizens or by a dictatorship of laborers, is going in some magic way to abolish race prejudice of its own accord without special effort or special study or special plan; and they want us Negroes to assume on faith that this will be the result.

Yet nothing in the history of American socialism gives us the slightest assurance on this point, and with American communism led by a group of pitiable mental equipment, who give no thought to the intricacies of the American situation, the vertical and horizontal divisions of the American working classes; and who plan simply to raise hell on any and all occasions, with Negroes as shock troops,—these offer in reality nothing to us except social equality in jail.

On the other hand, we would be idiots not to recognize the imminence of industrial change along socialistic and even communistic lines, which the American revolution sooner or later is bound to take. If we simply mill contentedly after the streaming herd, with no clear idea of our own solutions of our problem, what can we expect but the contempt of reformers and slavery to a white proletariat? If we expect to enter present or future industry upon our own terms, we must have terms; we must have power; we must learn the secret of economic organization; we must submit to leadership, not of words but of ideas; we must weld the civilized part of these 12 millions of our race into an industrial phalanx that cannot be ignored, and which America and the world will come to regard as a strong asset under any system and not merely as a weak and despicable liability.

What, then, shall we do? We cannot use the power of a State because we do not form a State. We cannot dictate as a proletariat, because we are a minority, and not as Marxism and Socialism usually assume an overwhelming majority with power in the reach of its outstretched arms.

On the contrary, we are a despised minority, whose social chains are not loosed, and who have the contempt of the white workers, even more than of capitalists and investors. Despite this, we are strong. Our unrealized strength is so enormous that the world wonders at our stupid apathy. We are physically able to survive slavery, lynching, debauchery, mob-rule, cheating and poverty, and yet remain the most prolific, original element in America, with good health and strength. We have brains, energy, and even taste and genius. From our depths of poverty, we have amassed some wealth. Out of charity, our schools, colleges and universities are growing to be real centers of learning, and Negro literature and art has been distilled from our blood and sweat. There is no way of keeping us in continued industrial slavery, unless we continue to enslave ourselves, and remain content to work as servants for white folk and dumb driven laborers for nothing.

What can we do? We can work for ourselves. We can consume mainly what we ourselves produce, and produce as large a proportion as possible of that which we consume.

Going back to the preaching of Robert Owen and Charles Fourier, we can by consumers and producers co-operation, by phalanstéres and garden cities, establish a progressively self-supporting economy that will weld the majority of our people into an impregnable, economic phalanx.

I am aware of the gale of laughter which such a proposal produces, not only from fools, but from serious students of economics. Of course, we are told, that 1848 scotched socialism; that "labor exchanges" failed; that New Harmony died; that Proudhon's Bank of Exchange became a joke; and much else in this line. But the basic idea beneath all this did not fail, as thousands of successful co-operatives throughout the world testify; as Denmark and Russia are living witnesses; as the working men's homes of Vienna prove. Remember production is already gone co-operative with technocratic control, oligarchic ownership and built on Democratic stupidity under a plutocracy. Consumption in all America is disorganized, blind and bamboozled by lying advertising and "high-powered" selling. Why may not Negroes begin consumers' co-operation under intelligent democratic control and expand at least to the productive and consuming energy of this one group? There would be white monopoly and privilege to fight, but only stupidity and disloyalty could actually stop progress. Expell both unflinchingly.

Moreover, our strength in Negro America lies in many respects precisely where the weaknesses of former co-operation and association lurked. We have a motive such as they never had. We are fleeing, not simply from poverty, but from insult and murder and social death. We have an instinct of race and a bond of color, in place of a protective tariff for our infant industry. We have, as police power, social ostracism within to coerce a race thrown back upon itself by ostracism without; and behind us, if we will survive, is Must, not May.

Negro American consumer's co-operation will cost us something. It will mean inner subordination and obedience. It will call for inflexible discipline. It will mean years of poverty and sacrifice, but not aimless, rather to one great End. It will invite ridicule, retaliation and discrimination. All this and more. But if we succeed, we have conquered a world. No future revolution can ignore us. No nation, here or elsewhere, can oppress us. No capital can enslave us. We open the gates, not only to our own twelve millions, but to five million West Indians, and eight million black South Americans, and one hundred and fifty million and more Africans. We stretch hands and hands of strength and sinew and understanding to India and China, and all Asia. We become in truth, free.

Our Music

July 1933

If a trained Negro singer gives a concert in New York, or a trained colored chorus sings there or elsewhere in the North, there is a type of comment, always made concerning their singing which is stereotyped and inevitable and repeated from year to year ad nauseum. For instance, Olin Downes, of *The New York Times*, voiced it after hearing the Fisk University Choir at Carnegie Hall; and asks the listener to "compare last night's singing of spirituals with the manner of the singing in the drama of 'Porgy,' or the performances of the Hall Johnson Choir in 'Green Pastures,' which contributed so memorably to the effect of that production. Or let him attend a real religious revival in Harlem, as the writer has done. He will hear hymns and spirituals, but they will have an emotion that was not to be felt last night. That was one thing. Quite another thing is the wildness, the melancholy, the intense religious feeling communicated when Negroes sing in the sacred spirit and the uncorrupted manner of their race."

All this is to our humble opinion pure and unadulterated nonsense. What it really means is that Negroes must not be allowed to attempt anything more than the frenzy of the primitive, religious revival. "Listen to the Lambs" according to Dett, or "Deep River," as translated by Burleigh, or any attempt to sing Italian music or German music, in some inexplicable manner, leads them off their preserves and is not "natural." To which the answer is, Art is not natural and is not supposed to be natural. And just because it is not natural, it may be great Art. The Negro chorus has a right to sing music of any sort it likes and to be judged by its accomplishment rather than by what foolish critics think that it ought to be doing. It is to be trusted that our leaders in music, holding on to the beautiful heritage of the past, will not on that account, either be coerced or frightened from taking all music for their province and showing the world how to sing.

Segregation in the North

April 1934

I have read with interest the various criticisms on my recent discussions of segregation. Those like that of Mr. Pierce of Cleveland, do not impress me. I am not worried about being inconsistent. What worries me is the Truth. I am talking about conditions in 1934 and not in 1910. I do not care what I said in 1910 or 1810 or in B.C. 700.

The arguments of Walter White, George Schuyler and Kelly Miller have logic, but they seem to me quite beside the point. In the first place, Walter White is white. He has more white companions and friends than colored. He goes where he will in New York City and naturally meets no Color Line, for the simple and sufficient reason that he isn't "colored"; he feels his new freedom in bitter contrast to what he was born to in Georgia. This is perfectly natural and he does what anyone else of his complexion would do.

But it is fantastic to assume that this has anything to do with the color problem in the United States. It naturally makes Mr. White an extreme opponent of any segregation based on a myth of race. But this argument does not apply to Schuyler or Miller or me. Moreover, Mr. White knows this. He moved once into a white apartment house and it went black on him. He now lives in a colored apartment house with attendant limitations. He once took a friend to dine with him at the celebrated café of the Lafayette Hotel, where he had often been welcomed. The management humiliated him by refusing to serve Roland Hayes.

The attitudes of Schuyler and Kelly Miller are historically based on the amiable assumption that there is little or no segregation in the North, and that agitation and a firm stand is making this disappear; that obvious desert and accomplishment by Negroes can break down prejudice. This is a fable. I once believed it passionately. It may become true in 250 or 1,000 years. Now it is not true. No black man whatever his culture or ability is today in America regarded as a man by any considerable number of white Americans. The difference between North and South in the matter of segregation is largely a difference of degree; of wide degree certainly, but still of degree.

In the North, neither Schuyler nor Kelly Miller nor anyone with a visible admixture of Negro blood can frequent hotels or restaurants. They have difficulty in finding dwelling places in better class neighborhoods. They occupy "Lower 1" on Pullmans, and if they are wise, they do not go into dining cars when any large number of white people is there. Their children either go to colored schools or to schools nominally for both races, but actually attended almost exclusively by colored children. In other words, they are confined by unyielding public opinion to a Negro world. They earn a living on colored newspapers or in colored colleges, or other racial institutions. They treat colored patients and preach to colored pews. Not one of the 12 colored Ph.D.'s of last year, trained by highest American and European standards, is going to get a job in any white university. Even when Negroes in the North work side by side with whites, they are segregated like the postal clerks, or refused by white unions or denied merited promotion.

No matter how much we may fulminate about "No segregation," there stand the flat facts. Moreover, this situation has in the last quarter century been steadily growing worse. Mr. Spingarn may ask judicially as to whether or not the N.A.A.C.P. should change its attitude toward segregation. The point that he does not realize is that segregation has changed its attitude toward the N.A.A.C.P. The higher the Negro climbs or tries to climb, the more pitiless and unyielding the color ban. Segregation may be just as evil today as it was in 1910, but it is more insistent, more prevalent and more unassailable by appeal or argument. The pressing problem is: What are we going to do about it?

In 1910, colored men could be entertained in the best hotels in Cleveland, Detroit and Chicago. Today, there is not a single Northern city, except New York, where a Negro can be a guest at a first-class hotel. Not even in Boston is he welcome; and in New York, the number of hotels where he can go is very small. Roland Hayes was unable to get regular hotel accommodations, and Dr. Moton only succeeds by powerful white influence and by refraining from use of the public dining room or the public lobbies.

If as Spingarn asserts, the N.A.A.C.P. has conducted a quarter-century campaign against segregation, the net result has been a little less than nothing. We have by legal action steadied the foundation so that in the future, segregation must be by wish and will and not law, but beyond that we have not made the slightest impress on the determination of the overwhelming mass of white Americans not to treat Negroes as men.

These are unpleasant facts. We do not like to voice them. The theory is that by maintaining certain fictions of law and administration, by whistling and keeping our courage up, we can stand on the "principle" of no segregation and wait until public opinion meets our position. But can we do this? When we were living in times of prosperity; when we were making post-war incomes; when our labor was in demand, we perhaps could afford to wait. But today, faced by starvation and economic upheaval, and by the question of being able to survive at all in this land in the reconstruction that is upon us, it is ridiculous not to see, and criminal not to tell, the colored people that they can not base their salvation upon the empty reiteration of a slogan.

What then can we do? The only thing that we not only can, but must do, is voluntarily and insistently to organize our economic and social power, no matter how much segregation it involves. Learn to associate with ourselves and to train ourselves for effective association. Organize our strength as consumers; learn to co-operate and use machines and power as producers; train ourselves in methods of democratic control within our own group. Run and support our own institutions.

We are doing this partially now, only we are doing it under a peculiar attitude of protest, and with only transient and distracted interest. A number of excellent young gentlemen in Washington, having formed a Negro Alliance, proceed to read me out of the congregation of the righteous because I dare even discuss segregation. But who are these young men? The products of a segregated school system; the talent selected by Negro teachers; the persons who can today, in nine cases out of ten, earn only a living through segregated Negro social institutions. These are the men who are yelling against segregation. If most of them had been educated in the mixed schools in New York instead of the segregated schools of Washington, they never would have seen college, because Washington picks out and sends ten times as many Negroes to college as New York does.

It would, of course, be full easy to deny that this voluntary association for great social and economic ends is segregation; and if I had done this in the beginning of this debate, many people would have been easily deceived, and would have yelled "No segregation" with one side of their mouths and "Race pride and Race initiative" with the other side. No such distinction can possibly be drawn. Segregation may be compulsory by law or it may be compulsory by economic or social condition, or it may be a matter of free choice. At any rate, it is the separation of human beings and separation despite the will to humanity. Such separation is evil; it leads to jealousy, greed, nationalism and war; and yet it is today and in this world inevitable; inevitable to Jews because of Hitler; inevitable to Japanese because of white Europe; inevitable to Russia because of organized greed over all the white world; inevitable to Ethiopia because of white armies and navies; inevitable, because without it, the American Negro will suffer evils greater than any possible evil of separation: we would suffer the loss of self-respect, the lack of faith in ourselves, the lack of knowledge about ourselves, the lack of ability to make a decent living by our own efforts and not by philanthropy.

This situation has been plunged into crisis and precipitated to an open demand for thought and action by the Depression and the New Deal. The government, national and state, is helping and guiding the individual. It has entered and entered for good into the social and economic organization of life. We could wish, we could pray, that this entrance could absolutely ignore lines of race and color, but we know perfectly well it does not and will not, and with the present American opinion, it cannot. The question is then, are we going to stand out and refuse the inevitable and inescapable government aid because we first wish to abolish the Color Line? This is not simply tilting at windmills; it is, if we are not careful, committing race suicide.

"NO SEGREGATION"

Back of all slogans lies the difficulty that the meanings may change without changing the words. For instance, "no segregation" may mean two very different things:

1. A chance for the Negro to advance without the hindrances which arise when he is segregated from the main group, and the main social institutions upon which society depends. He becomes, thus, an outsider, a hanger on, with no chance to function properly as a man.

2. It may mean utter lack of faith of Negroes in Negroes, and the desire to escape into another group, shirking, on the other hand, all responsibility for ignorance, degradation and lack of experience among Negroes, while asking admission into the other group on terms of full equality and with full chance for individual development.

It is in the first sense that I have always believed and used the slogan: "No Segregation." On the other hand, in the second sense, I have no desire or right to hinder or estop those persons who do not want to be Negroes. But I am compelled to ask the very plain and pertinent question: Assuming for the moment that the group into which you demand admission does not want you, what are you going to do about it? Can you demand that they want you? Can you make them by law or public opinion admit you when they are supreme over this same public opinion and make these laws? Manifestly, you cannot. Manifestly your admission to the other group on the basis of your individual desert and wish, can only be accomplished if they, too, join in the wish to have you. If they do so join, all problems based mostly on race and color disappear, and there remains only the human problems of social uplift and intelligence and group action. But there is in the United States today no sign that this objection to the social and even civic recognition of persons of Negro blood is going to occur during the life of persons now living. In which case there can be only one meaning to the slogan "No Segregation;" and that is, no hindrance to my effort to be a man. If you do not wish to associate with me, I am more than willing to associate with myself. Indeed, I deem it a privilege to work with and for Negroes, only asking that my hands be not tied nor my feet hobbled.

OBJECTS OF SEGREGATION

What is the object of those persons who insist by law, custom and propaganda to keep the American Negro separate in rights and privileges from other citizens of the United States? The real object, confessed or semiconscious, is to so isolate the Negro that he will be spiritually bankrupt, physically degenerate, and economically dependent.

Against this it is the bounden duty of every Negro and every enlightened American to protest; to oppose the policy so far as it is manifest by laws; to agitate against customs by revealing facts; and to appeal to the sense of decency and justice in all American citizens.

I have never known an American Negro who did not agree that this was a proper program. Some have disagreed as to the emphasis to be put on this and that method of protest; on the efficacy of any appeal against American prejudice; but all Negroes have agreed that segregation is bad and should be opposed.

Suppose, however, that this appeal is ineffective or nearly so? What is the Negro going to do? There is one thing that he can or must do, and that is to see to it that segregation does *not* undermine his health; does *not* leave him spiritually bankrupt; and does *not* make him an economic slave; and he must do this at any cost.

If he cannot live in sanitary and decent sections of a city, he must build his own residential quarters, and raise and keep them on a plane fit for living. If he cannot educate his children in decent schools with other children, he must, nevertheless, educate his children in decent Negro schools and arrange and conduct and oversee such schools. If he cannot enter American industry at a living wage, or find work suited to his education and talent, or receive promotion and advancement according to his desserts, he must organize his own economic life so that just as far as possible these discriminations will not reduce him to abject exploitation.

Everyone of these movements on the part of colored people are not only necessary, but inevitable. And at the same time, they involve more or less active segregation and acquiescence in segregation.

Here again, if there be any number of American Negroes who have not in practical life made this fight of self-segregation and self-association against the compulsory segregation forced upon them, I am unacquainted with such persons. They may, of course, explain their compulsory retreat from a great ideal, by calling segregation by some other name. They may affirm with fierce insistency that they will never, no never, under any circumstances acquiesce in segregation. But if they live in the United States in the year of our Lord 1934, or in any previous year since the foundation of the government, they are segregated; they accept segregation, and they segregate themselves, because they must. From this dilemma I see no issue.

BOYCOTT

Whither does all this sudden talk of segregation lead? May I illustrate by an appositive example. Several times The Crisis has commended what seemed to us the epoch-making work of The *Chicago Whip* when it instituted boycotts against stores in the black belt which refused to employ Negro clerks. Recently, in Washington, a group of young intellectuals sought to do the same thing but fell afoul of the ordinances against picketing. These efforts illustrate the use of mass action by Negroes who take advantage of segregation in order to strengthen their economic foundation. The Chicago success was applauded by every Negro in the land and the Washington failure deserved success. Today the same sort of move is being made in Richmond.

Yet, mind you, both these efforts were efforts toward segregation. The movement meant, in essence, Negro clerks for Negro customers. Of course, this was not directly said but this is what it amounted to. The proponents knew that Negro clerks would only be hired if Negro customers demanded it, and if the Negro customers, as happened in some cases, did not want to be waited on by Negro clerks, or even felt insulted if the Negro clerk came to them, then the proprietors had a perfect right to refuse to employ Negro clerks. Indeed, this happened in several cases in Harlem, New York.

And yet given the practically compulsory segregation of residence, and the Negro race is not only justified but compelled to invoke the additional gesture which involves segregation by asking Negro clerks for Negro customers. Of course, the logical demand of those who refuse to contemplate any measure of segregation, would be to demand the employment of Negro clerks everywhere in the city, and in all stores, at least in the same proportion that the Negro population bears to the total population. This was not demanded because such a demand would be futile and have no implement for its enforcement. But you can enforce the employment of Negroes by commercial houses in a Negro community and this ought to be done and must be done, and this use of the boycott by American Negroes must be widened and systematized, with care, of course, to avoid the ridiculous laws which make boycotts in so many cases illegal.

The funny postscript to all this, is that the same group of young Negroes who sought in Washington to fight segregation with segregation, or better to build a decent living on compulsory segregation, immediately set up a yell of "No Segregation," when they read THE CRISIS.

INTEGRATION

Extreme opponents of segregation act as though there was but one solution of the race problem, and that, complete integration of the black race with the white race in America, with no distinction of color in political, civil or social life. There is no doubt but what this is the great end toward which humanity is tending, and that so long as there are artificially emphasized differences of nationality, race and color, not to mention the fundamental discriminations of economic class, there will be no real Humanity.

On the other hand, it is just as clear, that not for a century and more probably not for ten centuries, will any such consummation be reached. No person born will ever live to see national and racial distinctions altogether abolished, and economic distinctions will last many a day.

Since this is true, the practical problem that faces us is not a choice between segregation and no segregation, between compulsory interferences with human intercourse and complete liberty of contact; the thing that faces us is given varying degrees of segregation. How shall we conduct ourselves so that in the end human differences will not be emphasized at the expense of human advance.

It is perfectly certain that, not only shall we be compelled to submit to much segregation, but that sometimes it will be necessary to our survival and a step toward the ultimate breaking down of barriers, to increase by voluntary action our separation from our fellowmen.

When my room-mate gets too noisy and dirty, I leave him; when my neighbors get too annoying and insulting I seek another home; when white Americans refuse to treat me as a man, I will cut my intercourse with white Americans to the minimum demanded by decent living.

It may be and often has been true that oppression and insult have become so intense and so unremitting that there is no alternative left to self-respecting men but to herd by themselves in self-defense, until the attitude of the world changes. It happens that today is peculiarly a day when such voluntary union for self-expression and self-defense is forced upon large numbers of people. We may rail against this. We may say that it is not our fault, and it certainly is not. Nevertheless, to do nothing in the face of it: to accept opposition without united counter opposition is the program of fools.

Moreover if association and contact with Negroes is distasteful to you, what is it to white people? Remember that the white people of America will certainly never want us until we want ourselves. We excuse ourselves in this case and say we do not hate Negroes but we do hate their condition, and immediately the answer is thrown back on us in the very words. Whose job is it to change that condition? The job of the white people or the job of the black people themselves, and especially of their uplifted classes?

William Monroe Trotter

May 1934

Monroe Trotter was a man of heroic proportions, and probably one of the most selfless of Negro leaders during all our American history. His father was Recorder of Deeds for the District of Columbia, at the time when Recorders were paid by fees; and as a result, he retired from office with a small fortune, which he husbanded carefully. Thus, his son was born in comfortable circumstances, and with his talent for business, and his wide acquaintanceship with the best class of young Massachusetts men in his day, might easily have accumulated wealth.

But he turned aside. He had in his soul all that went to make a fanatic, a knight errant. Ready to sacrifice himself, fearing nobody and nothing, strong in body, sturdy in conviction, full of unbending belief.

I remember when I first saw him as a student at Harvard. He was several classes below me. I should liked to have known him and spoken to him, but he was curiously aloof. He was even then forming his philosophy of life. Colored students must not herd together, just because they were colored. He had his white friends and companions, and they liked him. He was no hanger-on, but a leader among them. But he did not seek other colored students as companions. I was a bit lonesome in those days, but I saw his point, and I did not seek him.

Out of this rose his life-long philosophy: Intense hatred of all racial discrimination and segregation. He was particularly incensed at the compromising philosophy of Booker T. Washington; at his industrialism, and his condoning of the deeds of the South.

In the first years of the 20th Century, with George Forbes, Monroe Trotter began the publication of *The Guardian*. Several times young men have started radical sheets among us, like *The Messenger*, and others. But nothing, I think, that for sheer biting invective and unswerving courage, ever quite equaled the *Boston Guardian* in its earlier days. Mr. Washington and his followers literally shrivelled before it, and it was, of course, often as unfair as it was inspired.

I had come to know Trotter, then, especially because I knew Deenie Pindell as a girl before they were married. We were to stop with them one summer. Mrs. Du Bois was already there when I arrived in Boston, and on the elevated platform, I learned of the Zion Church riot. It was called a riot in the newspapers, and they were full of it. As a matter of fact, Trotter and Forbes had tried to ask Booker T. Washington certain pointed questions, after a speech which he made in the colored church; and immediately he was arrested, according to the careful plans which William L. Lewis, Washington's attorney, had laid. I was incensed at Trotter. I thought that he had been needlessly violent, and had compromised me as his guest; but when I learned the exact facts, and how little cause for riot there was, and when they clapped Trotter in the Charles Street Jail, all of us more conservative, younger men rose in revolt.

Out of this incident, within a year or two, arose the Niagara movement, and Trotter was present.

But Trotter was not an organization man. He was a free lance; too intense and sturdy to loan himself to that compromise which is the basis of all real organization. Trouble arose in the Niagara movement, and afterward when the Niagara movement joined the new N.A.A.C.P., Trotter stood out in revolt, and curiously enough, did not join the new organization because of his suspicion of the white elements who were co-operating with us.

He devoted himself to *The Guardian*, and it became one of the first of the nation-wide colored weeklies. His wife worked with him in utter devotion; giving up all thought of children; giving up her pretty home in Roxbury; living and lunching with him in the *Guardian Office*, and knowing hunger and cold. It was a magnificent partnership, and she died to pay for it.

The Trotter philosophy was carried out remorselessly in his paper, and his philosophy. He stood unflinchingly for fighting separation and discrimination in church and school, and in professional and business life. He would not allow a colored Y. M. C. A. in Boston, and he hated to recognize colored churches, or colored colleges. On this battle line he fought a long, exhausting fight for over a quarter of a century. What has been the result? There are fewer Negroes in Boston churches today than when Trotter began a crusade, and colored people sat in the pews under Phillips Brooks' preaching. There may be more colored teachers in the schools, but certainly they are playing no such part as Maria

Baldwin did, as principal of the best Cambridge Grammar School.

When Trotter began, not a single hotel in Boston dared to refuse colored guests. Today, there are few Boston hotels where colored people are received. There is still no colored Y. M. C. A., but on the other hand, there are practically no colored members of the white "Y," and young colored men are deprived of club house and recreational facilities which they sorely need. In the professions, in general employment, and in business, there is certainly not less, and probably more discrimination than there used to be.

Does this mean that Monroe Trotter's life was a failure? Never. He lived up to his belief to the best of his ability. He fought like a man. The ultimate object of his fighting was absolutely right, but he miscalculated the opposition. He thought that Boston and America would yield to clear reason and determined agitation. They did not. On the contrary, to some extent, the very agitation carried on in these years has solidified opposition. This does not mean that agitation does not pay; but it means that you cannot necessarily cash in quickly upon it. It means that sacrifice, even to blood and tears, must be given to this great fight; and not one but a thousand lives, like that of Monroe Trotter, is necessary to victory.

More than that, inner organization is demanded. The free lance like Trotter is not strong enough. The mailed fist has got to be clenched. The united effort of twelve millions has got to be made to mean more than the individual effort of those who think aright. Yet this very inner organization involves segregation. It involves voluntary racial organization, and this racial grouping invites further effort at enforced segregation by law and custom from without. Nevertheless, there is no alternative. We have got to unite to save ourselves, and while the unbending devotion to principle, such as Monroe Trotter shows, has and must ever have, its value, with sorrow, and yet with conviction, we know that this is not enough.

I can understand his death. I can see a man of sixty, tired and disappointed, facing poverty and defeat. Standing amid indifferent friends and triumphant enemies. So he went to the window of his Dark Tower, and beckoned to Death; up from where She lay among the lilies. And Death, like a whirlwind, swept up to him. I shall think of him as lying silent, cold and still; at last at peace, dreamless and serene. Let no trump of doom disturb him from his perfect and eternal rest.

The Board of Directors on Segregation

May 1934

This is the vote which was proposed to the Board of Directors by W. E. B. Du Bois:

> "The segregation of human beings purely on a basis of race and color, is not only stupid and unjust, but positively dangerous, since it is a path that leads straight to national jealousies, racial antagonisms, and war.
>
> "The N.A.A.C.P., therefore, has always opposed the underlying principle of racial segregation, and will oppose it.
>
> "On the other hand, it has, with equal clearness, recognized that when a group like the American Negroes suffers continuous and systematic segregation, against which argument and appeal are either useless or very slow in effecting changes, such a group must make up its mind to associate and co-operate for its own uplift and in defense of its self-respect.
>
> "The N.A.A.C.P., therefore, has always recognized and encouraged the Negro church, the Negro college, the Negro public school, Negro business and industrial enterprises, and believes they should be made the very best and most efficient institutions of their kind judged by any standard; not with the idea of perpetuating artificial separations of mankind, but rather with the distinct object of proving Negro efficiency, showing Negro ability and discipline, and demonstrating how useless and wasteful race segregation is."

This is the modification of the Du Bois proposal, as rewritten by the Committee of Administration, and placed before the Board at its April meeting:

"The National Association for the Advancement of Colored People has always opposed the segregation of human beings on the basis of race and color. We have always as a basic principle of our organization opposed such segregation and we will always continue to oppose it.

"It is true that we have always recognized and encouraged the Negro church, the Negro college, the Negro school, and Negro business and industrial enterprises, and we shall continue to encourage them, so that they may serve as proofs of Negro efficiency, ability and discipline. Not merely external necessity but our faith in the genius of the Negro race has made us do this. But this does not alter our conviction that the necessity which has brought them into being is an evil, and that this evil should be combated to the greatest extent possible.

"We reserve to ourselves complete liberty of action in any specific case that may arise, since such liberty is essential to the statesmanship necessary to carry out any ideal; but we give assurance to the white and colored peoples of the world that this organization stands where it has always stood, as the chief champion of equal rights for black and white, and as unalterably opposed to the basic principle of racial segregation."

This is the resolution passed by the Board:

"The National Association for the advancement of Colored People is opposed both to the principle and the practice of enforced segregation of human beings on the basis of race and color.

"Enforced segregation by its very existence carries with it the implication of a superior and inferior group and invariably results in the imposition of a lower status on the group deemed inferior. Thus both principle and practice necessitate unyielding opposition to any and every form of enforced segregation."

These proposals and this vote will be discussed in the June issue of THE CRISIS.

It would be interesting to know what the Board means by the resolution.

Does it mean that it does not approve of the Negro Church or believe in its segregated activities in its 26,000 edifices where most branches of the N.A.A.C.P. meet and raise money to support it?

Does it mean that it lends no aid or countenance to Fisk, Atlanta, Talladega, Hampton, Howard, Wiley and a dozen other Negro Colleges?

Does it disapprove of the segregated public school system where two million Negro children are taught by 50,000 Negro teachers?

Does it believe in 200 Negro newspapers which spread N.A.A.C.P. news and propaganda?

Does it disapprove of slum clearance like the Dunbar Apartments in New York, the Rosenwald Apartments in Chicago and the $2,000,000 projects in Atlanta?

Does it believe in Negro business enterprise of any sort?

Does it believe in Negro history, Negro literature and Negro art?

Does it believe in the Negro spirituals?

And if it does believe in these things is the Board of Directors of the N.A.A.C.P., afraid to say so?

Counsels of Despair

June 1934

Many persons have interpreted my reassertion of our current attitude toward segregation as a counsel of despair. We can't win, therefore, give up and accept the inevitable. Never, and nonsense. Our business in this world is to fight and fight again, and never to yield. But after all, one must fight with his brains, if he has any. He gathers strength to fight. He gathers knowledge, and he raises children who are proud to fight and who know what they are fighting about. And above all, they learn that what they are fighting for is the opportunity and the chance to know and associate with black folk. They are not fighting to escape themselves. They are fighting to say to the world: the opportunity of knowing Negroes is worth so much to us and is so appreciated, that we want you to know them too.

Negroes are not extraordinary human beings. They are just like other human beings, with all their foibles and ignorance and mistakes. But they are human beings, and human nature is always worth knowing, and withal, splendid in its manifestations. Therefore, we are fighting to keep open the avenues of human contact; but in the meantime, we are taking every advantage of what opportunities of contact are already open to us, and among those opportunities which are open, and which are splendid and inspiring, is the opportunity of Negroes to work together in the twentieth century for the uplift and development of the Negro race. It is no counsel of despair to emphasize and hail the opportunity for such work.

Surely then, in this period of frustration and disappointment, we must turn from negation to affirmation, from the ever-lasting "No" to the ever-lasting "Yes". Instead of sitting, sapped of all initiative and independence; instead of drowning our originality in imitation of mediocre white folks; instead of being afraid of ourselves and cultivating the art of skulking to escape the Color Line; we have got to renounce a program that always involves humiliating self-stultifying scrambling to crawl somewhere where we are not wanted; where we crouch panting like a whipped dog. We have got to stop this and learn that on such a program they cannot build manhood. No, by God, stand erect in a mud-puddle and tell the white world to go to hell, rather than lick boots in a parlor.

Affirm, as you have a right to affirm, that the Negro race is one of the great human races, inferior to none in its accomplishment and in its ability. Different, it is true, and for most of the difference, let us reverently thank God. And this race, with its vantage grounds in modern days, can go forward of its own will, of its own power, and its own initiative. It is led by twelve million American Negroes of average modern intelligence; three or four million educated African Negroes are their full equals, and several million Negroes in the West Indies and South America. This body of at least twenty-five million modern men are not called upon to commit suicide because somebody doesn't like their complexion or their hair. It is their opportunity and their day to stand up and make themselves heard and felt in the modern world.

Indeed, there is nothing else we can do. If you have passed your resolution, "No segregation, Never and Nowhere," what are you going to do about it? Let me tell you what you are going to do. You are going back to continue to make your living in a Jim-Crow school; you are going to dwell in a segregated section of the city; you are going to pastor a Jim-Crow Church; you are going to occupy political office because of Jim-Crow political organizations that stand back of you and force you into office. All these things and a thousand others you are going to do because you have got to.

If you are going to do this, why not say so? What are you afraid of? Do you believe in the Negro race or do you not? If you do not, naturally, you are justified in keeping still. But if you do believe in the extraordinary accomplishment of the Negro church and the Negro college, the Negro school and the Negro newspaper, then say so and say so plainly, not only for the sake of those who have given their lives to make these things worthwhile, but for those young people whom you are teaching, by that negative attitude, that there is nothing that they can do, nobody that they can emulate, and no field worthwhile working in. Think of what Negro art and literature has yet to accomplish if it can only be free and untrammeled by the necessity of pleasing white folks! Think of the splendid moral appeal that you can make to a million children tomorrow, if once you can get them to see the possibilities of the American Negro today and now, whether he is segregated or not, or in spite of all possible segregation.

THE ANTI-SEGREGATION CAMPAIGN

The assumptions of the anti-segregation campaign have been all wrong. This is not our fault, but it is our is misfortune. When I went to Atlanta University to teach in 1897, and to study the Negro problem, I said, confidently, that the basic problem is our racial ignorance and lack of culture. That once Negroes know civilization, and whites know Negroes, then the problem is solved. This proposition is still true, but the solution is much further away than my youth dreamed. Negroes are still ignorant, but the disconcerting thing is that white people on the whole are just as much opposed to

Negroes of education and culture, as to any other kind, and perhaps more so. Not all whites, to be sure, but the overwhelming majority.

Our main method, then, falls flat. We stop training ability. We lose our manners. We swallow our pride, and beg for things. We agitate and get angry. And with all that, we face the blank fact: Negroes are not wanted; neither as scholars nor as business men; neither as clerks nor as artisans; neither as artists nor as writers. What can we do about it? We cannot use force. We cannot enforce law, even if we get it on the statute books. So long as overwhelming public opinion sanctions and justifies and defends color segregation, we are helpless, and without remedy. We are segregated. We are cast back upon ourselves, to an Island Within; "To your tents, Oh Israel!"

PROTEST

Some people seem to think that the fight against segregation consists merely of one damned protest after another. That the technique is to protest and wail and protest again, and to keep this thing up until the gates of public opinion and the walls of segregation fall down.

The difficulty with this program is that it is physically and psychologically impossible. It would be stopped by cold and hunger and strained voices, and it is an undignified and impossible attitude and method to maintain indefinitely. Let us, therefore, remember that this program must be modified by adding to it a positive side. Make the protest, and keep on making it, systematically and thoughtfully. Perhaps now and then even hysterically and theatrically; but at the same time, go to work to prepare methods and institutions which will supply those things and those opportunities which we lack because of segregation. Stage boycotts which will put Negro clerks in the stores which exploit Negro neighborhoods. Build a 15th Street Presbyterian Church, when the First Presbyterian would rather love Jesus without your presence. Establish and elaborate a Washington system of public schools, comparable to any set of public schools in the nation; and then when you have done this, and as you are doing it, and while in the process you are saving your voice and your temper, say softly to the world: see what a precious fool you are. Here are stores as efficiently clerked as any where you trade. Here is a church better than most of yours. Here are a set of schools where you should be proud to send your children.

METHODS OF ATTACK

When an army moves to attack, there are two methods which it may pursue. The older method, included brilliant forays with bugles and loud fanfare of trumpets, with waving swords, and shining uniforms. In Coryn's "The Black Eagle", which tells the story of Bertrand du Guesclin, one sees that kind of fighting power in the fourteenth century. It was thrilling, but messy, and on the whole rather ineffective.

The modern method of fighting, is not nearly as spectacular. It is preceded by careful, very careful planning. Soldiers are clad in drab and rather dirty khaki. Officers are not riding out in front and using their swords; they sit in the rear and use their brains. The whole army digs in and stays hidden. The advance is a slow, calculated forward mass movement. Now going forward, now advancing in the center, now running around by the flank. Often retreating to positions that can be better defended. And the whole thing depending upon G.H.Q.; that is, the thought and knowledge and calculations of the great general staff. This is not nearly as spectacular as the older method of fighting, but it is much more effective, and against the enemy of present days, it is the only effective way. It is common sense based on modern technique.

And this is the kind of method which we must use to solve the Negro problem and to win our fight against segregation. There are times when a brilliant display of eloquence and picketing and other theatrical and spectacular things are not only excusable but actually gain ground. But in practically all cases, this is true simply because of the careful thought and planning that has gone before. And it is a waste of time and effort to think that the spectacular demonstration is the real battle.

The real battle is a matter of study and thought; of the building up of loyalties; of the long training of men; of the growth of institutions; of the inculcation of racial and national ideals. It is not a publicity stunt. It is a life.

Dr. DuBois Resigns

August 1934

The Board of Directors of the National Association for the advancement of Colored people at the June meeting took no action upon the resignation of Dr. DuBois, tendered as of June 11, but named a committee to confer with Dr. DuBois and see if some satisfactory settlement of differences could not be arranged.

Under date of June 26, however, Dr. DuBois addressed the following letter to the Board and released it to the press as of July 1, eight days before it came officially to the notice of the Board at its regular meeting July 9:

> "In deference to your desire to postpone action on my resignation of June 11, I have allowed my nominal connection with THE CRISIS to extend to July 1, and have meantime entered into communication with the Chairman of the Board, and with your Committee on Reconciliation.
>
> "I appreciate the good will and genuine desire to bridge an awkward break which your action indicated, and yet it is clear to me, and I think to the majority of the Board that under the circumstances my resignation must stand. I owe it, however, to the Board and to the public to make clear at this time the deeper reasons for my action, lest the apparent causes of my resignation seem inadequate.
>
> "Many friends have truthfully asserted that the segregation argument was not the main reason for my wishing to leave this organization. It was an occasion and an important occasion, but it could have been adjusted. In fact, no matter what the Board of the National Association for the Advancement of Colored People says, its action towards segregation has got to approximate, in the future as in the past, the pattern which it followed in the case of the separate camp for Negro officers during the World War and in the case of the Tuskegee Veterans' Hospital. In both

instances, we protested vigorously and to the limit of our ability the segregation policy. Then, when we had failed and knew we had failed, we bent every effort toward making the colored camp at Des Moines the best officers' camp possible, and the Tuskegee Hospital, with its Negro personnel, one of the most efficient in the land. This is shown by the 8th and 14th Annual Reports of the National Association for the Advancement of Colored People.

"The only thing, therefore, that remains for us is to decide whether we are openly to recognize this procedure as inevitable, or be silent about it and still pursue it. Under these circumstances, the argument must be more or less academic, but there is no essential reason that those who see different sides of this same shield should not be able to agree to live together in the same house.

"The whole matter assumed, however, a serious aspect when the Board peremptorily forbade all criticism of the officers and policies in THE CRISIS. I had planned to continue constructive criticism of the National Association for the Advancement of Colored People in THE CRISIS because I firmly believe that the National Association for the Advancement of Colored People faces the most gruelling of tests which come to an old organization: founded in a day when a negative program of protest was imperative and effective, it succeeded so well that the program seemed perfect and unlimited. Suddenly, by World War and chaos, we are called to formulate a positive program of construction and inspiration. We have been thus far unable to comply.

"Today this organization, which has been great and effective for nearly a quarter of a century, finds itself in a time of crisis and change, without a program, without effective organization, without executive officers, who have either the ability or disposition to guide the National Association for the Advancement of Colored People in the right direction.

"These are harsh and arresting charges. I make them deliberately, and after long thought, earnest effort, and with infinite writhing of spirit. To the very best of my ability, and every ounce of my strength, I have since the beginning of the Great Depression, tried to work inside the organization for its realignment and readjustment to new duties.

I have been almost absolutely unsuccessful. My program for economic readjustment has been totally ignored. My demand for a change in personnel has been considered as mere petty jealousy, and my protest against our mistakes and blunders has been looked upon as disloyalty to the organization.

"So long as I sit by quietly consenting, I share responsibility. If I criticize within, my words fall on deaf ears. If I criticize openly, I seem to be washing dirty linen in public. There is but one recourse, complete and final withdrawal, not because all is hopeless nor because there are no signs of realization of the possibilities of reform and of the imperative demand for men and vision, but because evidently I personally can do nothing more.

"I leave behind me in the organization many who have long thought with me, and yet hesitated at action; many persons of large ideals who see no agents at hand to realize them, and who fear that the dearth of ability and will to sacrifice within this organization, indicates a similar lack within the whole race. I know that both sets of friends are wrong, and while I desert them with deep reluctance, it is distinctly in the hope that the fact of my going may arouse to action and bring a great and gifted race to the rescue, with a re-birth of that fine idealism and devotion that founded the National Association for the Advancement of Colored People.

"Under these circumstances, there is but one thing for me to do, and that is to make the supreme sacrifice of taking myself absolutely and unequivocably out of the picture, so that hereafter the leaders of the National Association for the Advancement of Colored People, without the distraction of personalities and accumulated animosities, can give their whole thought and attention to the rescuing of the greatest organization for the emancipation of Negroes that America has ever had.

"I am, therefore, insisting upon my resignation, and on July 1st, whether the Board of Directors acts or does not act, I automatically cease to have any connection whatsoever in any shape or form with the National Association for the Advancement of Colored People. I do not, however, cease to wish it well, to follow it with personal and palpitating interest, and to applaud it when it is able to rescue itself from its present impossible position and reorganize itself according to the demands of the present crisis.

"Very respectfully yours,

("Signed) W. E. B. Du Bois."

At its meeting July 9, the Board adopted the following resolution:

RESOLVED, That it is with the deepest regret that we hereby accept the resignation of Dr. W. E. B. DuBois as editor of the Crisis, as a member of the Board of Directors, as Director of Publications and Research, as a member of the Board of the Crisis Publishing Company, and as a member of the Spingarn Medal Award Committee; and we desire at the same time to record our sense of the loss which his resignation will bring not only to the members of this Board but to every loyal member of the Association.

Dr. Du Bois joined the Association in 1910 as Director of Publications and Research. The Association was then a few months old. He was already a distinguished teacher, scholar and man of letters, Professor of Sociology in Atlanta University, and author of "Souls of Black Folk" and other works which had deeply moved the white world as well as the black. The ideas which he had propounded for a decade were the same ideas that had brought the Association into being.

He founded the Crisis without a cent of capital, and for many years made it completely self-supporting, reaching a maximum monthly circulation at the end of the World War of 106,000. This is an unprecedented achievement in American journalism, and in itself worthy of a distinguished tribute. But the ideas which he propounded in it and in his books and essays transformed the Negro world as well as a large portion of the liberal white world, so that the whole problem of the relation of black and white races has ever since had a completely new orientation. He created, what never existed before, a Negro intelligentsia, and many who have never read a word of his writings are his spiritual disciples and descendants. Without him the Association could never have been what it was and is.

The Board has not always seen eye to eye with him in regard to various matters, and cannot subscribe to some of his criticism of the Association and its officials. But such differences in the past have in no way interfered with his usefulness, but rather the contrary. For he had been selected because of his independence of judgment, his fearlessness in expressing his convictions, and his acute and wide-reaching intelligence. A mere yes-man could not have attracted the attention of the world, could not even have stimulated the Board itself to further study of various important problems. We shall be the poorer for his loss, in intellectual stimulus, and in searching analysis of the vital problems of the American Negro; no one in the Association can fill his place with the same intellectual grasp. We therefore offer him our sincere thanks for the services he has rendered, and we wish him all happiness in all that he may now undertake.

Index

Chronology

1868–71 Born William Edward Burghardt Du Bois, February 23, 1868, on Church Street, Great Barrington, Massachusetts, only child of Alfred Du Bois and Mary Silvina Burghardt. (Great-grandfather, James Du Bois, a physician descended from seventeenth-century French Huguenot immigrants, emigrated to the Bahamas from Poughkeepsie, New York, after the American Revolution, became a slave-owning plantation farmer, and had two sons by a mulatto woman. Grandfather Alexander Du Bois, born 1803, came to the United States, briefly attended school in Connecticut, lived in Haiti, then returned to New England and worked as a storekeeper and boat steward. Father Alfred Du Bois, born in Haiti in 1825, worked as a barber throughout eastern New England before coming to Great Barrington in 1867. Maternal great-great-grandfather Tom Burghardt, born around 1730, was enslaved in West Africa and brought to western Massachusetts. Freed during the Revolutionary War, he settled on a small farm on the South Egremont Plain outside of Great Barrington; his descendants farmed and worked as laborers and servants throughout the region. Mother Mary Burghardt, born in 1831 of African and Dutch ancestry, worked as a domestic servant, had a son, Idelbert, by her first cousin John Burghardt in 1861, and married Alfred Du Bois against her family's wishes in February 1867.) Moves with mother to home of grandparents when father goes to New Milford, Connecticut, in 1868. Father writes asking mother to join him; she refuses. Father never returns and Du Bois never sees him again (father may have died in New Milford about 1870).

1872–73 Grandfather Othello Burghardt dies, September 19, 1872. Family moves from Burghardt farm on South Egremont Plain into Great Barrington, where they live above former stables. Mother works as a domestic servant.

1874–78 Enters public school; excels in most subjects, advancing through grades more quickly than his peers. Plays marbles, duck-on-a-rock, I Spy, and Indians with friends.

1879 Grandmother Sally Burghardt dies, January 19. Moves with mother to rooms above store near railroad station. Mother suffers paralytic stroke that leaves her left arm withered and left leg lame.

1880–82 Enters high school. Works at various jobs: shoveling coal, splitting kindling, mowing lawns, selling the *New York Globe*, a black weekly, distributing tea for A&P company. Throughout high school years, lives with mother in four rooms in the rear of a widow's house on Church Street. Mother takes in brother as boarder and works sporadically as a domestic servant; receives financial assistance from Burghardt family and occasional gifts from white neighbors. Co-edits short-lived high school newspaper, *The Howler*. Encouraged by high school principal Frank Hosmer, takes college preparatory courses, including algebra, geometry, Greek, and Latin. Mrs. Russell, wife of local mill-owner, whose handicapped son Du Bois plays with, buys schoolbooks for him. Frequents town bookstore, reading newspapers and studying pictures of political figures; buys five-volume edition of Macaulay's *History of England* on time installments. Climbs hills, explores caves, swims, and plays baseball in spare time.

1883 Becomes occasional Great Barrington correspondent for the *Springfield Republican* and begins to report on the local black community for the *New York Globe*. Goes to New Bedford, Massachusetts, in summer to meet grandfather Alexander Du Bois and is impressed by his elegance. Attends annual picnic at Rocky Point, Rhode Island, celebrating West Indian emancipation, August 1. Festivities there and at nearby Oakland Beach draw over 3,000 people from northeastern black communities; event makes enduring impression on Du Bois (there are fewer than fifty blacks living in Great Barrington). Returns to Great Barrington via Springfield and Albany, New York, where he sees electric streetlights for the first time and stays with his half-brother, Idelbert.

1884 Graduates from high school, the only black student in class of thirteen. Delivers oration on abolitionist Wendell Phillips. Aspires to attend Harvard, but his youth, lack of funds, concern about mother's poverty and poor health, and doubts about academic preparation prevent application. Frank Hosmer, Edward Van Lennep, superintendent of Du Bois's Congregational Sunday school, and Congregational minister C. C. Painter consider ways to secure Du Bois a scholarship. Summer, hired as timekeeper by contractors building blue granite mansion in Great Barrington for the widow of railroad tycoon Mark Hopkins; works on site for a year at wage of one dollar a day.

1885 Mother dies March 23, age 54. Great Barrington Sunday school and three Connecticut Congregational churches contribute $25 each to fund organized by Painter, who arranges for Du Bois to attend Fisk University in Nashville, Tennessee. Enters Fisk with sophomore standing in autumn, still hoping to attend Harvard. Nearly dies of typhoid fever in October. Joins college Congregational church, where he becomes involved in a dispute over his allegedly sinful social dancing. Begins long friendship with fellow student Thomas Calloway. Edits the *Fisk Herald*, school newspaper, with Calloway serving as business manager; raises funds with him for college's first gymnasium. Studies German, Greek, Latin, classical literature, philosophy, ethics, chemistry, and physics.

1886–87 Teaches school for two summers in poor black hamlet near Alexandria, Tennessee; hears black folk songs and spirituals "sung with primitive beauty and grandeur." Sings with Mozart Society at Fisk. Urges convention of black college students to vote independently of the Republican Party in the pursuit of black interests.

1888–89 Graduates from Fisk with A.B. degree in June 1888 in class of five; gives oration on Bismarck. Admitted to Harvard College as a junior; awarded Price-Greenleaf grant of $250. During summer works as a busboy at Lake Minnetonka, Minnesota, resort hotel while serving as business manager for Fisk glee club quartet performing there; arranges concerts for them in the Midwest. Autumn, rents room in home of black woman at 20 Flagg Street in Cambridge; lives there during his four years at Harvard, taking meals at Memorial Hall and eventually becoming a member of the Foxcraft dining club. Studies philosophy with William James and George Santayana, economics with Frank Taussig, history with Albert Bushnell Hart, as well as chemistry and geology. Rejected by Harvard glee club for what he is convinced are racial reasons. Does not submit work to Harvard publications and has little involvement in student life. Awarded Matthews scholarship in 1889. During summer earns money by giving lectures and readings to church groups. Develops social life among Boston black community and participates in amateur theatricals. Befriended by Josephine Ruffin, a founder of the National Association of Negro Women and publisher of the *Courant*, a weekly black paper, to which Du Bois contributes many of his Harvard essays. Becomes engaged to Maud Cuney, a student at the New England Conservatory of Music, but marriage never takes place.

1890 Wins second prize in Boylston oratorical competition. Awarded B.A. cum laude in philosophy. Gives one of five student commencement orations, speaking on Jefferson Davis. Address receives wide press attention, *The Nation* commenting that he handled the theme with "almost contemptuous fairness." Receives $400 bequest from estate of Alexander Du Bois. Applies to Harvard graduate school in political science and is accepted and appointed Henry Bromfield Rogers Fellow for 1890–91 (renewed 1891–92). Begins looking for ways to finance study in Europe. Writes to Rutherford B. Hayes, chairman of the Slater Fund for the Education of Negroes, asking for fellowship after reading newspaper account of speech in which Hayes offered the Fund's help to southern blacks wishing to study abroad while describing "their chief and almost only gift" as "that of oratory."

1891 Receives letter from Hayes stating that the newspaper report was in error and that no program for European study exists. Writes to Hayes: " . . . the injury you have—unwittingly I trust—done the race I represent, and am not ashamed of, is almost irreparable. . . . I find men willing to help me thro' cheap theological schools, I find men willing to help me use my hands before I have got my brains in working order, I have an abundance of good wishes on hand, but I never found a man willing to help me get a Harvard Ph.D." Hayes responds apologetically. Du Bois criticizes Boston black community in speech "Does Education Pay?" for its lack of cultural development. Receives M.A. degree in history from Harvard. Works on thesis on suppression of African slave trade, a topic suggested by Hart; delivers paper drawn from it at December meeting of the American Historical Association in Washington.

1892 Visits 12-year-old Helen Keller at her school in Boston with William James. Reapplies to Slater Fund. Awarded $375 grant and $375 loan to study in Germany for one year. Arrives in Rotterdam in August. After short stay in Holland, travels up the Rhine into Germany. Boards with German family in Thuringian town of Eisenach for seven weeks, then enters Friedrich Wilhelm University in Berlin in October. Studies history, economics, politics, and political economy; teachers include Gustav Schmoller, Adolf Wagner, and Heinrich von Treitschke. December, travels through southern Germany, studying village life and visiting art centers.

1893 Celebrates 25th birthday, February 23, by dedicating his personal library to the memory of his mother and by writing a meditation on life and his destiny. Attends lectures of Max Weber. Aid renewed for one year by Slater Fund. Goes to opera, symphony concerts, and meetings of the Social Democratic Party. Travels during summer throughout Germany and in Switzerland, Austria, Italy, Hungary, and Poland. Writes thesis for Schmoller on agricultural economics in the American South.

1894 Denied doctoral degree by Friedrich Wilhelm authorities due to short period of study in Germany. Unable to get further assistance from Slater Fund, spends month in Paris and returns to the United States in June, traveling in steerage. Goes to Great Barrington to see family, writes to black colleges seeking teaching job. Rejected by Fisk, Howard University, Hampton Institute, and Tuskegee Institute. Accepts chair in classics at Wilberforce University, administered by the African Methodist Church, in Xenia, Ohio. Turns down higher-paying position at Lincoln Institute in Missouri after committing himself to Wilberforce, as well as new offer from Booker T. Washington to teach mathematics at Tuskegee. Teaches Latin, Greek, English, and German for annual salary of $800; unsuccessfully tries to add sociology to the curriculum. Becomes increasingly frustrated by college's lack of funds, administration's religious and educational conservatism, and campus political tensions. Forms friendship with Charles Young, recent West Point graduate (Young becomes one of the outstanding black officers in the army; Du Bois writes often on his behalf).

1895 Writes Booker T. Washington after his speech at Atlanta Cotton Exposition in September envisioning rapprochement between southern whites and blacks: "Let me heartily congratulate you upon your phenomenal success at Atlanta—it was a word fitly spoken." Receives Ph.D. from Harvard, the first black to do so.

1896 May 12, marries Nina Gomer (b. 1872), a student at Wilberforce, in Cedar Rapids, Iowa, where her father is a hotel chef. *The Suppression of the African Slave-Trade to the United States of America, 1638–1870*, doctoral thesis, published as first volume of the Harvard Historical Monograph Series by Longmans, Green, and Co. Autumn, hired by the University of Pennsylvania as an "investigator" at salary of $900 to prepare sociological study of Philadelphia black population. Moves with wife into room over settlement cafeteria in impoverished Seventh Ward and interviews five thousand people for study.

1897 Helps found the American Negro Academy, an early black scholarly society. Delivers address to Academy, "The Conservation of Races," manifesto calling on American blacks to act as the "advance guard" of black racial development worldwide and to maintain a separate identity within American society (speech is later published as a pamphlet). Accepts professorship in economics and history at Atlanta University. Begins correspondence with Carroll D. Wright, commissioner of the United States Bureau of Labor Statistics, resulting in publication of several of Du Bois's studies in the *Bulletin of the Department of Labor* before Wright resigns in 1905. Spends summer in rural Virginia, studying areas many Philadelphia blacks had moved from. Moves to house on Atlanta University campus, refuses to attend segregated concerts, theaters, parks, museums, or ride on segregated streetcars; uses horse and carriage in the countryside when possible to avoid segregated transportation. Takes over existing Atlanta conferences devoted to problems of urban blacks; plans and supervises series of sociological studies of black American life, eventually intending each subject to be reexamined after ten years; entire project is to run for ten decade-long cycles. Research is conducted mainly by unpaid part-time volunteer interviewers, mostly graduates of black colleges, and through questionnaires. Results, edited and annotated by Du Bois, are published in sixteen reports between 1898 and 1914; subjects include black businesses, artisans, and economic cooperation and social self-improvement organizations; college-educated blacks; public school education for blacks; causes and conditions of health, crime, and morality in black communities; black family life and the role of churches; and a special bibliographic volume. Annual budget of $5,000 covers cost of facilities, research, publication, and yearly meetings, as well as Du Bois's $1,200 university salary. Son, Burghardt Gomer Du Bois, born October 2 in Great Barrington, where Nina Du Bois had gone to give birth. November, addresses American Academy of Political and Social Sciences in Philadelphia. Proposes extensive scientific study of American blacks and urges the establishment of a modern research center at a southern black college to be linked to Harvard, Columbia, Johns Hopkins, and the University of Pennsylvania. Plan is ignored.

1898 Forms close and lasting friendship with John Hope, professor of classics at Morehouse College. Delivers address, "Careers Open to College-Bred Negroes," at Fisk commencement. Urges graduates to become scientific farmers, merchants, industrial leaders, and professionals and to serve their "blood and lineage" by economically and culturally developing the black community.

1899 Results of Philadelphia study published as *The Philadelphia Negro* by the University of Pennsylvania. Son Burghardt dies of dysentery in Atlanta, May 24; buried in Great Barrington. Marriage is permanently strained; Du Bois concentrates increasingly on his work. After Sam Hose, a poor Georgia black, is accused of murder, Du Bois prepares a statement urging a fair trial, then learns on his way to discuss the case with Joel Chandler Harris at the *Atlanta Constitution* that Hose has been lynched. (Later writes: ". . . one could not be a calm, cool, and detached scientist while Negroes were lynched, murdered, and starved . . .") Writes and lobbies against legislation that would disenfranchise Georgia blacks. Has articles published in *Atlantic Monthly* and *The Independent*, first of many to appear in national magazines over the next five decades.

1900 Begins unsuccessful proceedings against the Southern Railway System for denying him a sleeping berth on racial grounds (in 1905 the Interstate Commerce Commission indefinitely postpones hearing the case). Petitions Georgia state legislature, protesting cuts in funds for black public schools. Designs exhibit on black economic development for Paris Exposition. Travels by steerage to Europe to install exhibit, which wins grand prize; Du Bois receives Gold Medal. Attends Pan-African conference in London, July; states in speech that "the problem of the twentieth century is the problem of the color line." Daughter, Nina Yolande (known throughout life as Yolande), born October 21 in Great Barrington.

1901 "The Freedman's Bureau," article defending Reconstruction organization and its efforts to establish black rights, published in March *Atlantic Monthly*.

1902 Becomes increasingly sympathetic with William Monroe Trotter (an 1895 Harvard graduate Du Bois had known slightly), co-founder of the *Boston Guardian*, and other "radicals" who reject Booker T. Washington's accommodation with white supremacy in favor of a determined campaign for political and civil rights. Urged by wealthy northern supporters of Washington to leave Atlanta and teach at Tuskegee Institute, with significant increase in salary. Meets Washington for the first time to discuss offer; declines, uncertain of possible role at Tuskegee and determined to preserve his independence.

1903 Becomes involved in complex negotiations with Washington over plans for private conference of black leaders intended to unite various factions. *The Souls of Black Folk*, reworking of magazine articles with new material, published by A. C. McClurg in April. Book's success (six printings appear by 1905) brings Du Bois to national prominence. Chapter critically evaluating career of Booker T. Washington elicits attacks from Washington supporters in the black press. Writes to *Boston Guardian* defending

Trotter after he is arrested for disrupting Washington's attempted address to a July 30 Boston rally. Essay "The Talented Tenth," published in anthology *The Negro Problem*, argues that liberal arts education is essential for creating the "aristocracy of talent and character" that will raise "the masses of the Negro people." Helps Jessie Fauset, future novelist and one of few black students at Cornell, to secure a teaching job, beginning long association.

1904 Made Fellow of American Association for the Advancement of Science. January, attends long-delayed black leadership conference, held at Carnegie Hall in New York. Conference ends with speeches by Du Bois and Washington who, along with Washington supporter Hugh Browne, are chosen to select a Committee of Twelve for the Advancement of the Negro Race. Resigns in summer, frustrated by Washington's control of the committee. "Credo" published in the *Independent*, October 6. Corresponds with social worker and reformer Mary White Ovington, beginning long professional and personal association.

1905 January, writes article for magazine *Voice of the Negro* accusing unnamed black newspapers of receiving "hush money" from the Washington forces. Charge provokes fierce controversy, threatening Du Bois's position at Atlanta University. Unsuccessfully seeks funding from northern philanthropist Jacob Schiff for monthly political journal. Invites 59 blacks to meeting in Fort Erie, Ontario, beginning July 11; 29 attend and organize as the Niagara Movement, dedicated to uncompromising pursuit of political and economic rights. Du Bois elected general secretary; membership, intended to be drawn from educated elite, reaches 150 by end of year. Conflict with Washington forces intensifies. Begins correspondence with lawyer, writer, and musical performer James Weldon Johnson, a Niagara Movement supporter. December, founds and edits *The Moon Illustrated Weekly*, magazine published in Memphis (it ceases publication in the summer of 1906).

1906 In homage to John Brown, Niagara Movement meets at Storer College in Harpers Ferry, West Virginia. Conducts social and economic study of Lowndes County, Alabama, using official records and house-to-house canvassing; it appears as "The Negro Farmer," in U.S. Census Bureau publication *Special Reports*. September, in Alabama when white mobs begin attacking and killing blacks in Atlanta; immediately returns home, buys shotgun and buckshot, and stands guard on his porch until rioting ends. Writes poem, "A Litany at Atlanta," on train returning to Alabama. In aftermath of riot, Nina and Yolande move to Great Barrington, where Yolande attends elementary school.

1907 Founds and edits (jointly until 1909, then solely until last issue in 1910) *Horizon*, small monthly "Journal of the Color Line" published in Washington, D.C. Niagara Movement meets in Boston. Despite modest successes in challenging discrimination, organization is in debt and split internally by personal tension between Du Bois and Monroe Trotter. Travels, sometimes by bicycle, during summer vacation in France, England, and Scotland.

1908 Endorses William Jennings Bryan, Democratic candidate for president, and arouses controversy by urging black voters to abandon their traditional allegiance to the Republicans. Niagara Movement holds sparsely attended conference in Oberlin, Ohio. Atlanta studies nearly end for lack of money; saved by $1,000 grant from Slater Fund. Du Bois attributes financial difficulties to Washington's opposition and influence.

1909 Joins with 52 prominent professionals in calling for national civil rights conference. Call, written by New York publisher Oswald Garrison Villard, is inspired by William English Walling's report in the *Independent* on 1908 lynchings in Springfield, Illinois. Appeal issued on centennial of Lincoln's birth, February 12; conference meets in New York, May 31. Meeting, dominated by white liberals, results in formation of National Negro Committee; Du Bois a member. Biography *John Brown* published by George W. Jacobs and Company. Book criticized as historically inaccurate by Villard (whose own biography of Brown appears in 1910). Begins preparations for an *Encyclopedia Africana*, historical and sociological study of black life worldwide, to be written by international staff of black scholars under Du Bois's editorship. Niagara Movement holds fifth and final meeting at Sea Isle City, New Jersey.

1910 National Negro Committee reorganized as the National Association for the Advancement of Colored People. Du Bois hired as Director of Publications and Research with $2,500 salary (increased to $5,000 in 1923). Elected to board of directors, becoming its only black member. Moves to New York in August to found, edit, and write (several pieces every issue) for *The Crisis*, monthly magazine of the NAACP. First issue appears in November, with circulation of 1,000. Family moves to 3059 Villa Avenue in the Bronx. Has first of many clashes with board over his outspokenness, editorial independence, and radicalism. Continues to edit Atlanta Conference monographs. Writes pamphlet "Race Relations in the United States: An Appeal to England," attacking Washington for recent optimistic and conciliatory speeches in Britain; elicits signed endorsements of appeal from several prominent black public figures.

1911 Attends Universal Races Congress in London, organized by the English Ethical Culture movement. Meeting devoted primarily to scientific refutations of racist theories; avoids explicit political actions or appeals. First novel, *The Quest of the Silver Fleece*, romantic melodrama set against detailed exploration of the cotton industry, published by A. C. McClurg. Joins Socialist Party. Circulation of *The Crisis* reaches 16,000.

1912 Writes anti-discrimination plank for Progressive Party platform. Advocated at Chicago convention by NAACP official Joel Spingarn, it is rejected by Theodore Roosevelt, who calls Du Bois "dangerous." Angered by the Taft administration's racial policies, endorses Woodrow Wilson in *The Crisis* and resigns from the Socialist Party.

1913 Writes and stages *The Star of Ethiopia*, pageant celebrating black history, presented in New York to commemorate the fiftieth anniversary of emancipation (over a period of several years it is performed in Washington, D.C., Philadelphia, and Los Angeles). Becomes disillusioned by the Wilson administration's discriminatory policies. *Crisis* circulation rises to 30,000. Villard resigns as chairman of the NAACP board of directors after failing repeatedly to curb Du Bois's editorial independence and is succeeded by Joel Spingarn, a close friend of Du Bois.

1914 Arouses intense controversy by criticizing the quality of the black press in *The Crisis*. Attends Memphis meeting of the National Conference of Charities and Correction; helps organize integrated public meeting to address issues relating to blacks ignored by conference. Supports women's suffrage in *Crisis* editorial. Views imperialist rivalries of European powers as major cause of World War I; judges French and British colonialism preferable to that of Germany and hopes for Allied victory. Wife accompanies daughter to England, where Yolande enters the progressive Bedales preparatory school (outbreak of war and subsequent fear of submarine attack causes prolonged separation from Du Bois). Du Bois moves to 248 West 64th St. in New York City.

1915 *The Negro*, overview of African and Afro-American history, published by Henry Holt. Takes active role in NAACP campaign against D. W. Griffith's film *The Birth of a Nation* and its glorification of the Ku Klux Klan. Strongly protests the American occupation of Haiti. Vacations in Jamaica. Writes balanced assessment of Booker T. Washington after his death on November 14.

1916 Wife and daughter return from England; family moves to 650 Greene Avenue in Brooklyn. Attends conference organized by Joel Spingarn and held at Spingarn's Amenia, New York, estate, August 24–26. Meeting, attended by over fifty people, is intended to reconcile pro- and anti-Washington factions; it achieves spirit of unity but fundamental divisions remain. Writes to President Wilson reminding him of past promises, stating that "you have grievously disappointed us." Does not receive direct reply; endorses Republican Charles Evans Hughes in election. Urges James Weldon Johnson to assume leadership role at NAACP (Johnson serves as executive secretary 1917–18 and 1920–31).

1917 Seriously ill at start of year, undergoes two kidney operations. Campaigns for establishment of separate training camp for black army officers, convinced that there is no alternative to accepting their segregation and that black participation in America's war effort, especially in combat, is crucial to future political and economic gains. Writes editorial "We Should Worry" in June *Crisis*, urging blacks to seek work in war industries if they are barred from military service and arguing that the acquisition of military and industrial skills would seriously weaken white racial domination. Collects testimony for NAACP from survivors of East St. Louis massacre of blacks. Marches in front ranks of NAACP-organized silent parade down Fifth Avenue in New York City, protesting increase in racial violence.

1918 Warned by Department of Justice that he risks prosecution for his criticism of racism in the military. At urging of Joel Spingarn, War Department offers Du Bois commission as army captain and position in special military intelligence bureau designed to address racial problems. After securing continuing control over *The Crisis*, Du Bois accepts. Writes "Close Ranks" in July *Crisis*: "Let us while this war lasts, forget our special grievances and close our ranks shoulder to shoulder with our white fellow citizens and the allied nations that are fighting for democracy." Editorial and acceptance of commission strongly criticized, especially in the District of Columbia NAACP chapter. War Department withdraws offer of commission. Helps organize Negro Cooperative Guild to study and coordinate black-run cooperatives. Sails for France in December to investigate the treatment of black troops for the NAACP.

1919 Gathers material on achievements of black units in battle, the strong appreciation shown them by the French, and their unfair treatment by white officers. Organizes First Pan-African Congress and, with the help of Blaise Diagne, Senegalese member of the French Chamber of Deputies, persuades Premier Georges Clemenceau to permit the Congress to meet in Paris, February 19–21. Despite British and American interference, 57 delegates from the United States, the West Indies, Europe, and Africa attend. Du Bois elected executive secretary and observes conference for the NAACP. Congress passes resolutions calling on Paris Peace Conference to acknowledge and protect the rights of Africans living under colonial rule. Reports on the conference for *The Crisis*, then returns to the United States in early spring. May, publishes documents collected in France detailing official American attempts to prevent fraternization between black soldiers and French civilians. Post Office delays mailing of issue for one day while contemplating its suppression; it sells 106,000 copies, highest circulation ever. Writes long essay in June *Crisis* on the role of African and American blacks in the war (a book on the subject is begun but never finished). Attacked in House of Representatives for allegedly inciting race riots; investigated along with other black journalists by Department of Justice. September, Jessie Fauset joins staff of *The Crisis* as literary editor (over the next decade she and Du Bois publish, promote, and encourage many emerging black writers, including Countee Cullen, Langston Hughes, Claude McKay, and Jean Toomer).

1920 Founds and edits *The Brownies' Book*, a monthly magazine for black children, with Augustus Dill and Jessie Fauset, January (publication ends in December 1921 due to lack of funds). *Darkwater: Voices from within the Veil*, collection of essays published by Harcourt, Brace and Howe, arouses controversy by warning of possibility of worldwide race war. December, writes first article for *The Crisis* on black nationalist Marcus Garvey, praising Garvey's inspirational vision while criticizing his dictatorial style of leadership and responding mildly to Garvey's bitter and personal attacks. Monthly circulation of *The Crisis* falls to 65,000.

1921 Moves to 108 Edgecombe Avenue in upper Harlem. January, writes article in *The Crisis* questioning the finances of Garvey's Black Star Line and criticizing his attacks on American mulattoes. Signs protest with 118 other "American Christians" against Henry Ford's propagation of the anti-Semitic forgery *Protocols of the Elders of Zion*. Organizes and attends Second Pan-African Congress, held successively in London, Brussels, and Paris, August 28–September 6, attended by 113 official delegates including 35 Americans, 41 Africans, and representatives from the West Indies and Europe. London meeting produces resolutions critical of European colonialism, calling for international defense of African rights. Brussels and Paris sessions marked by sharp divisions between British and American delegates supporting confrontational policies and French and Belgian delegates, led by Blaise Diagne, seeking accommodation with their governments. Du Bois presents resolutions to League of Nations in Geneva and urges the International Labor Bureau to investigate working conditions in colonies (a small office is eventually established). Retires as secretary of the Pan-African movement.

1922 Campaigns for passage of the Dyer Anti-Lynching Bill, urging northern blacks to vote against its opponents; bill adopted by House of Representatives but blocked by Senate. Writes detailed examination of the Black Star Line's troubled finances in *The Crisis*.

1923 Moves within Harlem to 606 St. Nicholas Avenue. "Back to Africa," article strongly condemning Garvey for promoting racial division, appears in February *Century*. Awarded Spingarn Medal by NAACP. Plans trip to Liberia, his first visit to Africa. On recommendation of Boston attorney William Lewis, is appointed envoy extraordinary and minister plenipotentiary to the inauguration of Liberian president Charles King by President Coolidge. Organizes Third Pan-African Congress, held in London, Paris, and Lisbon, November. Does not attend Paris session due to split with assimilationist French delegates; movement suffers from declining membership and lack of funds. Arrives in Monrovia, Liberia, December 22.

1924 Delivers speech during inaugural ceremonies, January 1. Travels in Liberia for a month, returns to the United States in March after stops in Sierra Leone, Guinea, and Senegal. *The Gift of Black Folk: The Negroes in the Making of America*, written for the Knights of Columbus as part of a series devoted to interracial understanding, published by The Stratford Co. Writes "A Lunatic or a Traitor," vehement denunciation of Garvey, for May *Crisis*. Joins opposition to Fisk president Fayette McKenzie, accusing him of racism and suppressing student life. Revives *Fisk Herald*, publishing it from New York, and delivers sharply critical speech to Fisk alumni at daughter's graduation (McKenzie eventually resigns after a student strike). Endorses Robert LaFollette, Progressive Party candidate for president.

1925 Contributes essay "The Negro Mind Reaches Out," overview of contemporary Africa, to *The New Negro: An Interpretation*, a key work of the Harlem Renaissance, edited by Alain Locke.

1926 Founds Krigwa Players, a Harlem theater group dedicated to writing and performing plays depicting black life. Accepts invitation to visit Soviet Union on expense-paid, fact-finding trip on condition that his right of independent judgment be respected. Travels in autumn to Germany, then sails across Baltic to Kronstadt. Visits Leningrad, Moscow, Nizhni Novgorod (now Gorki), Kiev, and Odessa during two-month stay; meets former Comintern leader Karl Radek. Stops in Turkey, Greece, and Italy on return. Profoundly impressed, writes article for *The Crisis* praising the achievements of the Bolshevik Revolution.

1927 Buys apartment at 226 West 150th St. in the Dunbar Apartments, first cooperative housing development for blacks in New York City. Krigwa Players win second prize in international Little Theater competition. August, Fourth Pan-African Congress meets in New York; condemns American intervention in Haiti and the economic exploitation of Liberia. (A Fifth Congress, planned for the end of the decade, is never held.)

1928 Daughter Yolande marries poet Countee Cullen in Harlem; 3,000 people attend wedding (marriage dissolves within a year). Receives South Egremont Plain home of grandfather Othello Burghardt as birthday gift from group of friends. (Plans to make it into a country home but is forced to sell it in 1955, unable to afford cost of restoration.) Novel *Dark Princess: A Romance*, depicting an international alliance of Africans, Asians, and American blacks, published by Harcourt, Brace.

1929 Withdraws article "The Negro in the United States," written for the fourteenth edition of the *Encyclopedia Britannica*, after refusing to eliminate his assertions that blacks played a crucial and positive role during Reconstruction. Forced by increasing yearly losses (over $4,000 in 1928) to seek subsidy for *The Crisis* from the NAACP board. Opposed by acting secretary Walter White, who favors using limited Association funds for anti-lynching, legal, and lobbying work. Receives nearly $5,000 over next two years, but financial difficulties persist.

1930 Receives honorary Doctor of Laws degree from Howard

University and delivers commencement address "Education and Work," denouncing materialism, hedonism, and failure to provide leadership among recent black college graduates; calls on black colleges to train industrial planners and build black economic power.

1931 Contributes articles to *Louisiana Weekly*, the Philadelphia *Tribune*, and the New York *Amsterdam News*. Criticizes the Communist Party for its handling of the Scottsboro case. Secures position on committee established by the Phelps-Stokes Fund to publish a Negro encyclopedia after having been initially passed over. Attempts unsuccessfully to limit power of NAACP board and to expand role of general membership in order to preserve independence of the increasingly debt-ridden *Crisis*.

1932 February, defends Liberia in *The Crisis* against charges of labor exploitation made by George Schuyler in 1931 exposé, *Slaves Today*. Granddaughter, Du Bois Williams, born to Yolande and her second husband, Arnett Williams. Writes columns for the short-lived New York *National News*.

1933 Begins to reevaluate his position on segregation in *The Crisis*. Deeply pessimistic about prospects for integration and increasingly concerned about effects of the Depression, advocates reliance on separate black institutions and economic and social self-help measures. Conflict with NAACP board and Walter White intensifies. Accepts offer of one-year visiting professorship from John Hope, now president of Atlanta University. Journalists George Streator and Roy Wilkins (later executive secretary of the NAACP) assume editing responsibilities for *The Crisis*, with Du Bois retaining overall control. Helps organize and attends Second Amenia Conference, held August 18–21 at Joel Spingarn's country home. Meeting attempts to devise new strategy for black progress, but fails to achieve any lasting consensus. Teaches seminar at Atlanta on "Marx and the Negro."

1934 Continues editorials on segregation and black strategy, praising positive aspects of voluntary segregation and criticizing resolutely integrationist NAACP policy as unrealistic, inconsistent, and lacking in pride. May, NAACP board votes that paid officers of the Association may no longer criticize its policies in *The Crisis* without prior board approval. Du Bois resigns as editor of *The Crisis* and from the NAACP, May 21. Board votes not to accept resignation and asks him to reconsider. Resigns again, June 26, effective July 1. Already past normal retirement age, appointed chairman of the department of sociology at Atlanta University at salary of $4,500 (no agreement is made regarding eventual retirement). Nina refuses to return to Atlanta and remains in New York; Du Bois stays in a faculty dormitory suite and visits her when possible. Seeks to revive Atlanta studies series and establish a university-affiliated scholarly journal devoted to racial and cultural issues, but is frustrated by lack of funds. Begins frequent travel throughout South by automobile, conducting research and discussing racial issues; packs lunch to avoid segregated restaurants, carries tools and coveralls so that in event of breakdown he does not have to approach white-run garages. Chosen as editor-in-chief of Phelps-Stokes Fund-supported *Encyclopedia of the Negro* and begins preparatory work on the project, which soon encounters financial difficulties.

1935 *Black Reconstruction*, lengthy historical study arguing that blacks played the vital role in the restoration of southern democracy, published by Harcourt, Brace. Receives $1,600 grant from Oberlaender Trust, Philadelphia-based foundation, to study industrial education in Germany and Austria.

1936–37 February, begins writing weekly column in the *Pittsburgh Courier* (it runs until January 1938). John Hope dies, February 20. Moves New York residence to 210 West 150th St., another building in Dunbar complex. Leaves United States in June; visits England, France, Belgium, and Austria, spends five months in Germany in autumn and winter of 1936. Reports on Germany for the *Pittsburgh Courier*, attributing Hitler's success to his use of socialist methods in reducing unemployment and his skill at propaganda; denounces anti-Semitic persecutions as cruel and barbaric. Travels through Poland to Moscow and, after short stay, takes Trans-Siberian Railroad to the Far East, visiting Manchuria, China, and Japan. Returns to the United States by way of Hawaii in early 1937. Begins never-finished novel

"A Search for Democracy," about black American professor exploring fascism, communism, and democracy.

1938 Receives honorary Doctor of Laws degree from Atlanta University and honorary Doctor of Letters degree from Fisk, where he gives commencement address, "The Revelation of Saint Orgne the Damned." Delivers autobiographical address, "A Pageant in Seven Decades, 1868–1938," at convocation of Atlanta University, Morehouse College, and Spelman College held in celebration of his birthday.

1939 *Black Folk, Then and Now*, revised and expanded version of *The Negro*, published by Henry Holt. October, begins column for New York *Amsterdam News* (it runs until October 1944).

1940 Autobiography, *Dusk of Dawn*, published by Harcourt, Brace. Founds *Phylon*, long-planned quarterly magazine for the study of black issues worldwide, editing and writing for it until 1944. Receives honorary Doctorate of Humane Letters from Wilberforce. Meets writer Richard Wright during Midwest lecture tour. Short story collection, "The Sorcery of Color," rejected by Henry Holt (the manuscript has not been found). Nina moves to house at 2302 Montebello Terrace (built on lot purchased by Du Bois several years before) in Baltimore, where Yolande teaches English and history at Dunbar High School.

1941 Proposes social science study of southern blacks in address to presidents of black land-grant colleges meeting in Chicago.

1942 Proposed study plan is adopted; Du Bois is appointed coordinator of project.

1943 First study conference of black land-grant colleges held at Atlanta University; Du Bois greatly satisfied. Edits conference report. November, informed by the board of trustees that he will be retired on June 30, 1944. Suspects opposition to his activism by John Hope's successor Rufus Clement and Spelman College president Florence Read to be instrumental in decision. Has less than $5,000 in savings and is dismayed by threat to new study program; begins unsuccessful campaign to have decision reversed.

1944 Second Atlanta conference held in spring (program ends for lack of funds several years later). Becomes first black member of the National Institute of Arts and Letters. Atlanta University trustees vote to provide Du Bois with year's full salary and pension of $1,800 a year for five years and $1,200 a year thereafter. Offered positions by Fisk and Howard University; persuaded by Arthur Spingarn and Louis Wright to accept offer from Walter White of position as NAACP director of special research. Despite reluctance to work with White, accepts with unwritten understanding of $5,000 annual salary, office space for library and staff, and freedom to write and speak independently. Spends summer speaking to teachers in Haiti. Begins work at the NAACP in New York, September. Essay "My Evolving Program for Negro Freedom" published in *What the Negro Wants*, edited by Rayford Logan. Moves into apartment at 409 Edgecombe Avenue, found for him by Shirley Graham. (A 39-year-old writer, teacher, and civil rights activist, Graham met Du Bois as a child in 1920 and had corresponded with him over the previous decade; she becomes a close friend and supporter.)

1945 January, begins writing weekly column in the Chicago *Defender* (it runs until May 1948). Spring, attends San Francisco conference that drafts United Nations Charter. Serves under Walter White as associate NAACP consultant to the American delegation; strongly criticizes charter for failing to oppose colonialism. Resigns from American Association of University Professors in protest against their scheduling of meetings in segregated hotels. Helps organize Fifth Pan-African Congress, held in Manchester, England, October 15–19. Meets Kwame Nkrumah, Jomo Kenyatta, and other Africans who now dominate Pan-African movement and explicitly demand independence from European rule. Autumn, Nina suffers stroke and is partially paralyzed on her left side; spends eight months in hospital. *Encyclopedia of the Negro: Preparatory Volume with Reference Lists and Reports*, written with Guy B. Johnson, published by the Phelps-Stokes Fund; volume represents ten years of intermittent work on the unfinished project. *Color and Democracy: Colonies and Peace*, anti-imperialist analysis of the post-war world, published by Harcourt, Brace.

1946 Delivers address "Behold the Land" to Southern Negro Youth Congress in Columbia, South Carolina, urging young blacks to stay and fight in the South for black freedom worldwide. Calls representatives of twenty organizations to New York conference to draft petition to the United Nations on behalf of American blacks; appeal becomes NAACP project directed by Du Bois.

1947 March, begins writing weekly column for New York paper, *People's Voice* (appears until March 1948). Edits and writes introduction to *An Appeal to the World*, NAACP-sponsored collection of six essays by five authors intended to enlist world opinion in the fight against racial discrimination in the United States. Presented to the United Nations Commission on Human Rights, its hearing is supported by the Soviet Union but blocked by the United States. Visits Jamaica, Grenada, Trinidad, and Cuba. *The World and Africa* published by the Viking Press.

1948 Continued criticism of American foreign policy and expressions of sympathy for the Soviet Union intensify long-standing conflict with Walter White. Actively supports Henry Wallace, Progressive Party candidate for president. September, writes memorandum to NAACP board of directors criticizing White's appointment to the American delegation to the United Nations and predicting that White's acceptance of the position would "align the Association with the reactionary, war-mongering colonial imperialism of the present Administration." Memorandum appears in *The New York Times* and White quickly has the board dismiss Du Bois from NAACP staff. Becomes vice-chairman of the Council of African Affairs (serving until 1956), an organization listed as "subversive" by the attorney general. Position is unpaid, but provides Du Bois with office space. November, begins writing for *National Guardian* (contributes regularly until May 1961).

1949 Helps sponsor Cultural and Scientific Conference for World Peace, held in New York in March. Serves as chairman of writers' panel, with Soviet novelist Aleksandr Fadeev, poet Louis Untermeyer, critic F. O. Matthiessen, and Norman Mailer as members. Addresses closing rally at Madison Square Garden. Attends First World Congress of the Defenders of Peace, held in Paris in April, and is the only one of 25 invited Americans to attend the All-Union Conference of Peace Proponents held in Moscow in August.

1950 April, helps found and is elected chairman of the Peace Information Center. Organization disseminates information about international peace movement and collects signatures for petition in support of the Stockholm Appeal calling for the unconditional prohibition of the use of atomic weapons. Nina Gomer Du Bois dies in Baltimore, July 1, and is buried in Great Barrington next to her son. August, attends meeting of the World Peace Committee in Prague and visits Poland after encountering difficulties in obtaining passport. Peace Information Center informed by the Department of Justice that it must register as an "agent of a foreign principal." Center refuses to register and is formally disbanded in October to avoid further legal pressure. Nominated by American Labor Party as candidate for United States Senate seat from New York held by Democrat Herbert Lehman. Sees campaign as possibly his last chance to present views to a wide audience and as opportunity to help fellow Labor Party candidate Congressman Vito Marcantonio. Makes ten public speeches and gives seven radio addresses. Receives four percent of the vote statewide, fifteen percent in Harlem.

1951 February 9, indicted under the Foreign Agents Registration Act of 1938 along with four other officers of the Peace Information Center. Indictment alleges that the Center acted as an unregistered agent of the Committee of the World Congress of the Defenders of Peace and its successor, the World Peace Council; offense carries maximum penalty of five years imprisonment and a $10,000 fine. February 14, secretly marries Shirley Graham, ensuring her visiting rights if he is jailed. Fingerprinted, searched, briefly handcuffed, and then released on bail at arraignment in Washington, D.C., February 16. Essex House, New York City hotel, cancels reservation for long-planned testimonial birthday dinner; sponsored by Council on African Affairs, it is held instead at Small's Paradise, a Harlem cabaret, and is attended by several hundred people, including Paul Robeson and sociologist E. Franklin Frazier. February 27, formal public marriage to Shirley Graham, attended by daughter Yolande and Shirley

Graham's son David (whom Du Bois later adopts), followed by three-week trip to the Bahamas. Buys house at 31 Grace Court in Brooklyn from playwright Arthur Miller. Makes two national lecture tours with Shirley Graham Du Bois in spring and fall to publicize court case and raise money to meet legal expenses; tours, along with efforts of defense committee, yield over $35,000. Embittered by efforts of the NAACP and many black leaders, newspapers, and intellectuals to distance themselves from him. Trial begins in Washington, November 8, and ends November 13 when Judge Matthew McGuire grants motion of acquittal for all defendants made by defense counsel Vito Marcantonio, ruling that the government had failed to show any organizational link between the Peace Information Center and any foreign organization.

1952 Continued advocacy of controversial left-wing positions causes further estrangement from black American mainstream. Department of State refuses to issue Du Bois a passport on grounds that his foreign travel is not in the national interest (later demands that he sign statement declaring that he is not a Communist Party member; Du Bois refuses to sign). Despite passport denial, is able to make trip to the Virgin Islands. *In Battle for Peace*, account of his indictment and trial, published by Masses and Mainstream.

1953 Eulogizes Stalin in the *National Guardian*. Takes part in unsuccessful campaign to save Julius and Ethel Rosenberg from execution; reads 23rd Psalm at their funeral. Awarded International Peace Prize by the World Peace Council.

1954 Delivers eulogy at funeral of Vito Marcantonio. Surprised by the Supreme Court *Brown* decision overturning school segregation, writes, "I have seen the impossible happen."

1955 Visits Grenada and Barbados. Denied passport to attend World Youth Festival in Warsaw.

1956 Sends message of support to the Reverend Dr. Martin Luther King, Jr., during Montgomery bus boycott. Invited to lecture in the People's Republic of China; prevented from accepting by passport restrictions. Prevented by local officials from speaking at American Labor Party rally in Levittown, Long Island. Challenges William Faulkner to debate on segregation in Mississippi; Faulkner declines.

1957 *The Ordeal of Mansart*, first volume of *The Black Flame*, trilogy of historical novels depicting black American life from Reconstruction onward, published by Mainstream. Bust of Du Bois unveiled in Schomburg Collection for Negro Literature and History (later the Schomburg Center for the Research in Black Culture) of the New York Public Library; Du Bois attends ceremony. Invited by Kwame Nkrumah, now prime minister of Ghana, to its independence ceremonies; prevented from attending by passport restrictions. Great-grandson Arthur Edward McFarlane II born in December.

1958 Two thousand people attend ninetieth birthday celebration at Roosevelt Hotel, New York. Elected alumni member of Fisk chapter of Phi Beta Kappa. Begins work on new autobiography, drawn almost entirely from previously published works (published in 1968 as *The Autobiography of W.E.B. Du Bois* by International Publishers). Obtains passport after Supreme Court overturns political affidavit requirement. Leaves in August on world tour. Visits England, France, Belgium, and Holland during summer and then travels to Czechoslovakia, East Germany, and the Soviet Union in autumn, attending conference of African and Asian writers in Tashkent and receiving honorary Doctorate of Economics from Humboldt (formerly Friedrich Wilhelm) University in East Berlin. Invited to address All-African conference in Accra, Ghana, but is forced by exhaustion to rest in Soviet sanitarium; his speech, urging Africans to reject Western capital and accept aid from the Soviet Union and China, is delivered by Shirley Graham Du Bois.

1959 Meets with Nikita Khruschev. Travels to Beijing in February and spends two months in China. Makes broadcast to Africa over Radio Beijing; meets with Mao Zedong and Zhou Enlai. Returns to the Soviet Union and then travels to Sweden and England before returning to the United States on July 1. Awarded the International Lenin

Prize in September. *Mansart Builds a School*, second volume of *The Black Flame*, published by Mainstream.

1960 Visits Ghana to participate in celebrations of its establishment as a republic and Nigeria to attend the inauguration of its first African governor-general.

1961 *Worlds of Color*, final novel in *The Black Flame* trilogy, published by Mainstream. Daughter Yolande dies of heart attack in Baltimore, March 21. Du Bois attends burial in Great Barrington. Accepts invitation of Nkrumah to move to Ghana and become director of revived *Encyclopedia Africana* project. Applies for membership in the Communist Party of the United States shortly before leaving for Accra in October, where he and his wife are assigned a seven-room house.

1962 Undergoes operations in Accra and Bucharest for enlarged and infected prostate gland before having it removed in London. Meets Charles Chaplin in Switzerland. Travels to China in autumn.

1963 Receives honorary Doctor of Letters degree from the University of Ghana on 95th birthday, February 23. Becomes citizen of Ghana. Follows preparations for the civil rights march on Washington. Dies in Accra on its eve, at 11:40 P.M., August 27. Buried outside of Christianborg Castle in Accra after a state funeral, August 29.

Note on the Texts

The Suppression of the African Slave-Trade to the United States of America, 1638–1870, W.E.B. Du Bois's first book, was a revised version of his doctoral dissertation (Harvard University, 1895). It was published in 1896 by Longmans, Green, and Co. of New York as Volume I of the Harvard Historical Studies series. Only two other printings of the work appeared during Du Bois's life: a reprinting by Longmans, Green, and Co. in 1904 (no corrections or revisions were made in the plates) and a photo-offset version of the 1896 text published by The Social Science Press in New York City in 1954. Du Bois added a three-page "Apologia," which was inserted between Appendix D and the index, for the 1954 volume, but no changes were made in the text. The present volume reprints the Longmans, Green, and Co. 1896 text. The later "Apologia" is included in the notes.

Many of the chapters in *The Souls of Black Folk* are revised versions of essays that had appeared earlier in *The Atlantic Monthly*, *The World's Work*, *The Dial*, *The New World*, and *Annals of the American Academy*. One essay, "Of the Black Belt," had been commissioned but not printed by *McClure's Magazine*. Other essays, such as "Of the Passing of the First-Born" and "Of the Coming of John," though written earlier, had not previously been printed. Two essays, "Of Mr. Booker T. Washington and Others" and "The Sorrow Songs," were written expressly for *The Souls of Black Folk*. The book, published by A. C. McClurg and Co. of Chicago in 1903, went through at least 22 additional printings before 1938. Some time before 1951, Du Bois purchased the plates, and the Blue Heron Press of New York used these plates in a 1953 reprinting. That reprint contained a preface, "Fifty Years Later," in which Du Bois writes:

> Several times I planned to revise the book and bring it abreast of my own thought and to answer criticism. But I hesitated and finally decided to leave the book as first printed, as a monument to what I thought and felt in 1903.

I hoped in other books to set down changes of fact and reaction.

In the present Jubilee Edition I have clung to this decision, and my thoughts of fifty years ago appear again as then written. Only in a few cases have I made less than a half-dozen alterations in word or phrase and then not to change my thought as previously set down but to avoid any possible misunderstanding today of what I meant to say yesterday.

In the correspondence between Du Bois and the Blue Heron Press there is a list of specific revisions requested (page and line numbers are changed here to correspond to this volume):

March 16, 1953

CHANGES IN SOULS OF BLACK FOLK

p. 448, line 9, capitalize "Negroes".
p. 450, ?
p. 454, line 11, change to read "native and foreign, seized it. The returns of the"
p. 480, 26 lines from bottom, change to read, "enterprising capitalist who sold it to him pocketed"

TO BE ADDED TO CHAPTER VII, p. 455:

In the foregoing chapter, "Jews" have been mentioned five times, and the late Jacob Schiff once complained that this gave an impression of anti-Semitism. This at the time I stoutly denied; but as I read the passages again in the light of subsequent history, I see how I laid myself open to this possible misapprehension. What, of course, I meant to condemn was exploitation of black labor and that it was in this county and at that time in part a matter of immigrant Jews, was incidental and not essential. My inner sympathy with the Jewish people was expressed better in the last paragraph of page 520. But this illustrates how easily one slips into unconscious condemnation of a whole group.

Despite all this, however, none of the changes were ever made. The 1953 printing, apart from Du Bois's new preface and "Comments" by his wife, Shirley Graham Du Bois, is an exact reprint from the plates of the 1903 McClurg edition. Therefore, as is the case with *The Suppression of the African Slave-Trade*, there has been only one authorial edition of *The Souls of Black Folk*, and the text of its original McClurg printing of 1903 is used here.

The choice of text for *Dusk of Dawn: An Essay Toward an Autobiography of a Race Concept*, published by Harcourt, Brace and Company of New York in 1940, is even simpler. No other printing of the work was made during Du Bois's lifetime; the 1940 text is printed here.

For the essays and articles, this volume prints the texts of their original periodical or book publication, with the exception of the three essays from *Darkwater* (1920). "Souls of White Folk" was made up of an essay in the *Independent*, August 18, 1910, and part of another essay, "Of the Culture of White Folk," in *Journal of Race Development*, April 1917; "The Hands of Ethiopia" was first published as "The African Roots of the War" in *The Atlantic Monthly* May 15, 1915; and part of "The Damnation of Women" appeared under the title "On Being Black" in *The New Republic* February 18, 1920. Since all of these essays were heavily revised for publication in the book *Darkwater*, the revised versions have been selected for inclusion here. Articles from *The Crisis*, with a few exceptions, are grouped together in a final section of this volume. The exceptions are the pieces that Du Bois printed as essays or addresses and for this reason they are included in the earlier section.

Although later versions of some of the essays included here form parts of *The Autobiography of W.E.B. Du Bois: A Soliloquy on Viewing My Life from the Last Decade of Its First Century* (New York: International Publishers, 1968), the book versions of those essays have not been chosen as the texts to be printed because *The Autobiography* appeared five years after Du Bois died, and he did not have the opportunity to exercise authorial control. Collation has shown that the work is mainly made up of previously published material. For example, some two hundred pages are drawn from *Dusk of Dawn*; the account of the trial and acquittal comes from *In Battle for Peace: The Story of My 83rd Birthday* (New York: Masses & Mainstream, 1952); and the Postlude chapter is taken from "A

Vista of Ninety Fruitful Years" in the *National Guardian* February 17, 1958. Therefore, only the chapter "My Character," which does not appear elsewhere, is selected from *The Autobiography* for inclusion in this volume.

The source and date for each essay and article are given below.

ESSAYS:

"Jefferson Davis as a Representative of Civilization," Commencement Address, Harvard University, 1890. Typescript, Harvard Archives.

"The Conservation of Races" (American Negro Academy, *Occasional Papers*, No. 2), Washington, D.C.: American Negro Academy, 1897.

"Careers Open to College-Bred Negroes," *Two Addresses Delivered by Alumni of Fisk University, in connection with the Anniversary Exercises of their Alma Mater, June, 1898*. Nashville, Fisk University, 1898.

"The Talented Tenth," *The Negro Problem: A Series of Articles by Representative American Negroes of To-day*. Contributions by Booker T. Washington, W. E. Burghardt Du Bois, Paul Laurence Dunbar, Charles W. Chesnutt, and others. New York: James Pott & Co., 1903, pp. 33–75.

"The Negro in Literature and Art," *The Annals of the American Academy*, 49 (September 1913), 233–37.

"Negro Education," *The Crisis*, 15 (February 1918), 173–78.

"An Essay Toward a History of the Black Man in the Great War," *The Crisis*, 18 (June 1919), 63–87.

"The Souls of White Folk," "The Hands of Ethiopia," and "The Damnation of Women," *Darkwater: Voices from within the Veil*. New York: Harcourt, Brace and Howe, Inc., 1920, pp. 19–52, 56–74, and 163–86.

"Marcus Garvey," *The Crisis*, 21 (December 1920 and January 1921), 58, 60, 112–15.

"The Black Star Line," *The Crisis*, 24 (September 1922), 210–14.

"A Lunatic or a Traitor," *The Crisis*, 28 (May 1924), 8–9.

"Criteria of Negro Art," *The Crisis*, 32 (October 1926), 290, 292, 294, 296–97.

"So the Girl Marries," *The Crisis*, 35 (June 1928), 192–93, 207–09.
"The Negro College," *The Crisis*, 40 (August 1933), 175–77.
"On Being Ashamed of Oneself: An Essay on Race Pride," *The Crisis*, 40 (September 1933), 199–200.
"The Propaganda of History," *Black Reconstruction*. New York: Harcourt Brace and Company, 1935, pp. 711–29.
"The Revelation of Saint Orgne the Damned," Commencement Address, 1938, Fisk University. Nashville: Hemphill Co., 1939.
"The Trial" and "The Acquittal," *In Battle for Peace: The Story of My 83rd Birthday*. New York: Masses & Mainstream, 1952, pp. 119–39, 140–59.
"A Vista of Ninety Fruitful Years," *National Guardian*, 10 (February 17, 1958), 7.
"To an American Born Last Christmas Day," *National Guardian*, 10 (March 10, 1958), 4.
"My Character," *The Autobiography of W.E.B. Du Bois: A Soliloquy on Viewing My Life from the Last Decade of Its First Century*. New York: International Publishers, 1968, pp. 277–88.

Articles from The Crisis:

"The Crisis," 1 (November 1910), 10.
"Agitation," 1 (November 1910), 11.
"Pink Franklin," 1 (February 1911), 17.
"Rampant Democracy," 1 (February 1911), 21.
"A Golden Wedding," 2 (June 1911), 55.
"Business and Philanthropy," 2 (June 1911), 64–65.
"I Am Resolved," 3 (January 1912), 113.
"A Mild Suggestion," 3 (January 1912), 115–16.
"An Open Letter to Woodrow Wilson," 5 (March 1913), 236–37.
"Another Open Letter to Woodrow Wilson," 6 (September 1913), 232–33, 236.
"Howells and Black Folk," 7 (November 1913), 338.
"The Three Wise Men," 7 (December 1913), 80–82.
"A Question of Policy—The Philosophy of Mr. Dole," 8 (May 1914), 23–26.

"Votes for Women," 8 (August 1914), 179–80.
"The Prize Fighter," 8 (August 1914), 181.
"Does Race Antagonism Serve Any Good Purpose," 8 (September 1914), 232–33.
"From the Boston 'Globe,' " 9 (January 1915), 129, 132.
"An Amazing Island," 10 (June 1915), 80–81.
"Woman Suffrage," 11 (November 1915), 29–30.
"A Singer," 12 (October 1916), 281.
" 'We Should Worry,' " 14 (June 1917), 61–62.
"Houston," 14 (October 1917), 284–85.
"The Black Man and the Unions," 15 (March 1918), 216–17.
"Paul Le Roy Robeson," 15 (March 1918), 229–31.
"Tillman," 16 (August 1918), 165.
" 'Jim Crow,' " 17 (January 1919), 112–13.
"Reconstruction and Africa," 17 (February 1919), 165–66.
"Returning Soldiers," 18 (May 1919), 13–14.
"Race Intelligence," 20 (July 1920), 118–19.
"An Open Letter to Warren Gamaliel Harding," 21 (March 1921), 197–98.
"The Negro and Radical Thought," 22 (July 1921), 102–04.
"President Harding and Social Equality," 23 (December 1921), 53–56.
"Charles Young," 23 (February 1922), 155.
"Abraham Lincoln," 24 (May 1922), 103.
"Ten Phrases," 24 (July 1922), 107.
"Again, Lincoln," 24 (September 1922), 199–201.
"On Being Crazy," 26 (June 1923), 56–57.
"The Tuskegee Hospital," 26 (July 1923), 106–07.
"The Technique of Race Prejudice," 26 (August 1923), 152–54.
"The Younger Literary Movement," 27 (February 1924), 161–62.
"The Challenge of Detroit," 31 (November 1925), 7–10.
" 'Porgy,' by DuBose Heyward," 31 (March 1926), 240.
"Books (Van Vechten's 'Nigger Heaven')," 33 (December 1926), 81–82.
"Flood," 34 (July 1927), 168.
"Lynchings," 34 (August 1927), 203.
"The Name 'Negro,' " 35 (March 1928), 96–97.
"Robert E. Lee," 35 (March 1928), 97.
"DePriest," 36 (February 1929), 57.

"Gambling," 37 (January 1930), 29–30.
"Patient Asses," 37 (March 1930), 100–01.
"Protest," 37 (October 1930), 352–53.
"Books," 38 (March 1931), 102.
"Chesnutt," 40 (January 1933), 20.
"The Right to Work," 40 (April 1933), 93–94.
"Our Music," 40 (July 1933), 165.
"Segregation in the North—'No Segregation'—Objects of Segregation—Boycott—Integration," 41 (April 1934), 115–17.
"William Monroe Trotter," 41 (May 1934), 134.
"The Board of Directors on Segregation," 41 (May 1934), 149.
"Councils of Despair—The Anti-Segregation Campaign—Protest—Methods of Attack," 41 (June 1934), 182–83.
"Dr. DuBois Resigns," 41 (August 1934), 245–46.

The original indexes to *The Suppression of the African Slave-Trade* and *Dusk of Dawn* are reproduced here with a few necessary corrections. The numbers have been changed to refer to this volume. A new index was made for the Essays and Articles section.

This volume presents the texts of the original editions chosen for inclusion here. It does not attempt to reproduce features of the typographic design, such as the display capitalization of chapter openings. The texts are reproduced without change, except for the correction of typographical errors. Spelling, punctuation, and capitalization often are expressive features and they are not altered, even when inconsistent or irregular. The following is a list of the typographical errors corrected, cited by page and line number: 43.19, Middleton; 168.5, Convention; 190.34, Godon; 193.3, arose; 224.26, Provided; 228.1, 1779,; 228.35, o[]; 239.35, *Be*; 278.20, 2.; 311.37, p.; 448.9, negroes; 535.29, "Freulig; 577.11, Greenlead; 619.20, title; 743.28, McClean; 788.19–20, ennervating; 818.40, menta[]; 820.3, however; 845.18, Crummel; 862.21, indigeneous; 864.28, *Sun*; 868.31, through-going; 896.22, Morrocans; 898.26, Gourand; 906.10, Ballou,; 916.15, Bourbonne-les Bains; 956.12, degradation,; 1004.27, true); 1005.20, distain; 1012.32, negro; 1015.11, action; 1015.28, university; 1042.1, Hendricks; 1048.29, write.; 1051.15, births; 1052.34, months'; 1053.18, feel?; 1054.29, beings?; 1057.20, go."; 1062.34, done?; 1068.18, it; 1069.2–3, mimimized; 1069.26, consumers; 1080.22, admissable; 1124.38, 39, Grapsey; 1149.10, maize; 1160.10, disfranchize; 1163.24, anologies; 1176.26, proletarist; 1195.16, Young.; 1204.23, dispicable; 1208.4, 'instructive'.; 1224.15, persons; 1224.37, Dyer-Anti Lynching; 1226.24, addition 30; 1227.20, and depending; 1245.4–5, degenrate; 1256.36, that.

Notes

In the notes below, the numbers refer to page and line of this volume (the line count includes chapter headings). No note is made for material included in a standard desk-reference book. Notes at the foot of the page are Du Bois's own. Many complete names of people and titles are supplied in the index to the Essays and Articles section. For more detailed notes, references to other studies, and further biographical background, see *The Correspondence of W.E.B. Du Bois*, 3 volumes (Amherst: University of Massachusetts Press, 1973–78), edited by Herbert Aptheker; *The Seventh Son* (New York: Random House, 1971), edited by Julius Lester; *W.E.B. Du Bois on Sociology and the Black Community* (Chicago: University of Chicago Press, 1978), edited by Dan S. Green and Edwin D. Driver; Paul G. Partington, *W.E.B. Du Bois: A Bibliography of His Published Writings* (Whittier, California: privately printed, 1979); Francis L. Broderick, *W.E.B. Du Bois: Negro Leader in a Time of Crisis* (Stanford: Stanford University Press, 1959); *Black Titan: W.E.B. Du Bois* (Boston: Beacon Press, 1970), edited by John Henrik Clarke, Esther Jackson, Ernest Kaiser, and J. H. O'Dell; Jack B. Moore, *W.E.B. Du Bois* (Boston: Twayne Publishers, 1981); Elliott Rudwick, *W.E.B. Du Bois* (Champaign: University of Illinois Press, new edition, 1982); *Dictionary of American Negro Biography* (New York: W. W. Norton, 1982), edited by Rayford W. Logan and Michael R. Winston; *Encyclopedia of Black America* (New York: McGraw-Hill, 1981; paperback, Da Capo Press, 1984), edited by W. Augustus Low and Virgil A. Clift.

THE SUPPRESSION OF THE AFRICAN SLAVE-TRADE

11.23 The war interrupted] The War of Austrian Succession, 1740–49.

345.32 1872–7] For the 1954 reprint of *The Suppression of the African Slave-Trade* by The Social Science Press of New York, Du Bois added the following "Apologia" after Appendix D:

As I read again this work of mine written over sixty years ago, I am on the one hand gratified to realize how hard and honestly I worked on my subject as a young man of twenty-four. As a piece of documented historical research, it was well done and has in the last half century received very little criticism as to accuracy and completeness.

There are, however, certain criticisms which are evident. One relates to the monographic method which sets a man to segregating from the total flow of history a small part for intensive study; when he knows nothing or little of the mass of facts of which his minute study is a part. This fault would tend to limit special research to men of wide knowledge, such as I certainly did not have in 1896, if even now; and might thus confine monographs to a very few writers. I was fortunate that the bit of history which I selected was unusually susceptible to segregation without too much danger of misinterpretation from lack of broader understanding.

There is, however, another area of criticism which I have not seen voiced but which disturbs me. That is my ignorance in the waning nineteenth century of the significance of the work of Freud and Marx. I had received at Harvard excellent preparation for understanding Freud under the tutelage of William James, Josiah Royce, and George Santayana. At this time psychological measurements were beginning at Harvard with Munsterberg; but the work of Freud and his companions and their epoch-making contribution to science was not generally known when I was writing this book, and consequently I did not realize the psychological reasons behind the trends of human action which the African slave trade involved.

Trained in the New England ethic of life as a series of conscious moral judgments, I was continually thrown back on what men "ought" to have done to avoid evil consequence. My book's last admonition was "to do things at the very moment when they ought to be done." Some knowledge of Freud would have made my conclusion less pat and simple.

While Harvard's department of Philosophy was perhaps the best in its day, certainly in America, the teaching in the social sciences was poor and as a scientific field unrecognized. Our best known professor of economics was absorbed in a re-interpretation of the Ricardean "Wages Fund" and never mentioned Marx. Some of the young, new instructors like Edward Cummings in fields now included in Sociology, mentioned Marx but only in passing and did not stress his significance. In Germany I heard much more of Marxism but in rebuttal of his theories rather than in explanation. I got the idea that his teaching already had been superceded and consequently gave little time to first hand study of his work.

This was important in my interpretation of the history of slavery and the slave trade. For if the influence of economic motives on the action of mankind ever had clearer illustration it was in the modern history of the African race, and particularly in America. No real conception of this appears in my book. There are some approaches, some illusions, but no complete realization of the application of the philosophy of Karl Marx to my subject. That concept came much later when I began intensive study of the facts of society, culminating in my Black Reconstruction in 1935.

Naturally in my study of the slave trade I noted economic facts and influences. In my preface I said: "facts and statistics bearing on the economic side of the study have been difficult to find, and my conclusions, are consequently liable to modification from this source." I mentioned the economic motives behind the signing of the Asiento, and the declaration of the British in the 18th century that the slave trade was the "very life of the colonies," but how could I or my advisers have neglected that classic word of Marx on the colonies as the source of primary capitalistic accumulation? I saw that the farming colonies restricted slavery because it "did not pay." I noted the profits of the trading colonies from the slave trade. I saw "that vast economic revolution in which American slavery was to play so prominent and fatal a role." Nevertheless, in examining the motives behind the attempt to stop the slave trade during the Revolution, I seemed to have missed the strength of the economic reasons for its failure, although I mention them.

I still saw slavery and the trade as chiefly the result of moral lassitude—"the policy of laissez-faire, laissez-passez." I wanted the young nation to call "the whole moral energy of the people into action" instead of accepting a "bargain" on "one of the most threatening of the social and political ills" which faced the nation. But apparently I did not clearly see that the real difficulty rested in the willingness of a privileged class of Americans to get power and comfort at the expense of degrading a class of black slaves, by not paying them what their labor produced.

When the slave trade and slavery were debated in the early sessions of Congress I recorded the way in which "property" was stressed by the South in a new way, and how the reopened slave trade meant "fortunes to the planters and Charleston slave merchants." Nevertheless when the Cotton Kingdom was rising to power after 1820, and I studied the Economic Revolution, the new inventions and the rise in cotton sales and prices, I still seemed to miss the clear conclusion that slavery was a matter of income more than of morals. I do say "that this problem arose principally from the cupidity and carelessness of our ancestors. It was the plain duty of the colonies to crush the trade and the system in its infancy; they preferred to enrich themselves on its profits." Yet I conclude: "No persons would have seen the Civil War with more surprise and horror than the Revolutionists of 1776; yet from the small and apparently dying institution of their day arose the walled and castled Slave-Power. From this we may conclude that it behooves nations as well as men to do things at the very moment when they ought to be done."

What I needed was to add to my terribly conscientious search into the facts of the slave trade the clear concept of Marx on the class struggle for income and power, beneath which all considerations of right or morals were twisted or utterly crushed. Yet naturally it is too much to ask that I should have been as wise in 1896 as I think I am in 1954. I am proud to see that at the beginning of my career I made no more mistakes than apparently I did.

THE SOULS OF BLACK FOLK

372.2 *Of . . . Freedom*] Revision of the article "The Freedman's Bureau" in the *Atlantic Monthly*, March 1901.

372.14–15 THE PROBLEM . . . color-line] Statement was first made by Du Bois in his address "To the Nations of the World" at the Pan-African Congress in London, July 1900.

374.7 Pierce of Boston] Edward Lillie Pierce (1829–97) was also the official biographer of Charles Sumner.

386.22–387.21 In a . . . commendation.] In an editorial in *The Crisis*, April 1912, entitled "Modest Me," Du Bois wrote:

The editor of THE CRISIS assumes to be a fairly modest man as modesty goes in these trumpeting times; but with some diffidence he admits to a swelling of pardonable pride at a certain occurrence in South Carolina which the papers of that realm, with somewhat singular unanimity, have omitted to notice.

Some time since—to be exact, in 1901—the editor and certain other persons (among them the Hon. Woodrow Wilson, then unknown to a newer kind of fame) were asked to write on "Reconstruction" for the Atlantic. The editor concocted an article which he liked quite well and in turn the Atlantic was persuaded to publish it. It was called "The Freedman's Bureau." It caused no stir in the world, but the editor kept it carefully in his archives to gloat over now and then in the fastnesses of his study when the family had retired. Very well.

Some time in 1911 the Wade Hampton Chapter of the United Daughters of the Confederacy offered a medal to the student of the University of South Carolina writing the best article on "The Freedman's Bureau." Mr. Colin W. Covington, of Bennettsville, S.C., won the coveted prize, and his essay was published in the Columbia State, January 28, 1912.

Imagine, now, the editor's gratification on reading this work of genius to discover that nearly one-half of the essay, and that the important and concluding half, was the editor's own work from his Atlantic essay of 1901. A single quotation will indicate more clearly this new instance of racial concord:

> In a distracted land, where slavery had hardly fallen, to keep the strong from wanton abuse of the weak, and the weak from staring with hate over the half-shorn strength of the strong, was a thankless, hopeless task. The former masters of the land were absolutely ordered about, seized and imprisoned, and punished over and again, with almost no courtesy from army officers. The former slaves were intimidated, beaten, raped and butchered by angry and revengeful men. Bureau courts tended to become centers simply for punishing whites, while the regular civil courts tended to become solely institutions for perpetuating the slavery of blacks. Almost every law and method ingenuity could devise was employed by the legislatures to reduce the Negroes to serfdom—to make them the slaves of the State, if not of individual owners; while the bureau officials too often were found striving to put the "bottom rail on top," and give the freedmen a power and independence which they could not yet use. It is all well enough for us of another generation to wax wise with advice to those who bore the burden in the heat of the day. It is full easy now to see that the man who lost home, fortune and family at a stroke, and saw his land ruled by "mules and niggers," was really benefited by the passing of slavery. It is not difficult now to say to the young freedman, cheated and beaten about, who has seen his father's head beaten to a jelly and his own mother namelessly assaulted that "the meek shall inherit the earth." Above all, nothing

is more convenient than to heap on the freedmen's bureau all the evils of that evil day and damn it utterly for every mistake and blunder that was made.

All this is easy, but it is neither sensible nor right. Someone had blundered before Oliver Howard was born; there was criminal aggression and heedless neglect, but without some system of control there would have been far more than there was. Had that control been from within the Negro would have been re-enslaved to all intents and purposes. Coming, as the control did, from without, perfect men and methods would have bettered all things and even with imperfect agents and questionable methods, the work accomplished was not without much praise.

There is nothing to mar the fulness of the tribute here involved—not even quotation marks!

More might be quoted to the extent of two or three of these pages, but let us forbear. Were the editor a grasping man he might (either for himself or for his race) ask to have a large share of that medal clipped from the proud young Southern breast that bears it and pinned on his own. But no. Sufficient be the secret sense of desert and warmest flattery, and the editor yields to vanity only to the extent of bringing all this to the attention of his assiduous friend, the Charleston News and Courier, whose frequent sallies have in the past caused him much innocent amusement.

In the *Crisis* article, Du Bois quotes from his own essay in a parallel column.

396.9–10 the terrible . . . Stono] Historical incidents of violent resistance by black slaves. Throughout the 18th century, colonies of fugitive slaves called Maroons formed communities in the swamps and forests of the South. They lived from their own labor and by raids on nearby settlements and plantations; their presence (or the suspicion of their proximity) was a source of fear. In 1733, slaves gained control of St. John in the Virgin Islands (then known as the Danish West Indies) and held it for six months. An international force broke the insurrection and many of the slaves committed suicide rather than return to slavery. Cato of Stono was a slave who led what was estimated to be over one hundred slaves in insurrection and flight from Stono, South Carolina, in 1739. Their purpose was to escape to the Spanish colony of Florida. While many were captured and executed, it is believed that some did escape. The Stono Rebellion is said to be the cause of the South Carolina colonial legislature's restricting for the first time the importation of African slaves, as blacks had become a majority in that colony.

396.15–18 songs . . . Cuffes] Phillis Wheatley (c. 1753–84), born in West Africa and brought as a slave to Boston in 1761 at the age of seven or eight, was purchased by John and Susannah Wheatley, who treated her as a member of the family and taught her to read and write at an early age. She developed an interest in Latin and read Horace, Virgil, and Ovid. Her first published poem was "On the Death of the Reverend George Whitefield"

(1770). She was manumitted in 1773, but remained a servant and friend of the Wheatley family. She traveled to London in 1773, where her book *Poems on Various Subjects, Religious and Moral* was published (the second American woman after Anne Bradstreet to have a book published). Crispus Attucks (1723?–70), the first man to fall in the Boston Massacre, was believed to have been a slave from Framingham, Massachusetts, who had escaped at the age of seventeen. Peter Salem (1750–1816), born in Framingham, Massachusetts, the slave of Jeremiah Belnap, was one of the Minutemen in the Battle of Concord, April 19, 1775, and fought at Bunker (Breed's) Hill, Saratoga, and Stony Point, serving in the Continental Army until the end of the war. He died in poverty. Salem Poor (1758–?), a free-born black of Massachusetts, served in the Continental Army in the American Revolution. He saw action at Bunker (Breed's) Hill, Valley Forge, and White Plains. Benjamin Banneker (1731–1806), born in Philadelphia of free black parents, was a self-taught mathematician and astronomer. He assisted in the survey of the Federal Territory in 1791 and calculated ephemerides for almanacs for the years 1792–97. Dr. James Derham, black physician, was described by Benjamin Rush in 1788 as "very learned." Paul Cuffe (1759–1817), born in Cuttyhunk, Massachusetts, of a freed-slave father and American Indian mother, became a wealthy merchant in New Bedford. In 1780, Cuffe and his brother John petitioned the Massachusetts General Court in protest of a clause in the Massachusetts Constitution of 1778 that withheld the vote from Negroes and Indians. The petition requested relief from taxes for Negroes and Indians, using the argument of no taxation without representation. The right to vote was granted by court decision in 1783. Cuffe is also known for his effort to establish a colony of Afro-Americans in Sierra Leone, transporting at his own expense some 38 settlers in 1815.

396.34 Walker's wild appeal] David Walker (1785–1830), born of a free mother and slave father in Wilmington, N.C., took the status of his mother, traveled widely, then settled in Boston and taught himself to read and write. His pamphlet *David Walker's Appeal in four articles together with a Preamble to the Colored Citizens of the World, but in particular and very expressly to those of The United States of America* (1829) advocated total, worldwide revolt of African peoples from the yoke of European oppression. The *Appeal* caused great anxiety in the slave states, and Walker's mysterious death in Cambridge, Massachusetts, was sometimes attributed to foul play by a pro-slavery group.

397.3–4 Forten . . . Boston] James Forten, Sr. (1766–1842), was trained in the trade of sail-making and became the owner of his own firm in Philadelphia in 1798. By 1832 he had amassed a fortune of $100,000. He attacked various schemes to settle American blacks in Africa and was one of the organizers and supporters of a series of Negro conventions which began in 1830 and continued sporadically until the Civil War. Robert Purvis, Sr. (1810–98), born of mixed parentage, inherited $120,000 upon his father's death. He became an abolitionist leader in Philadelphia, and with William Lloyd Garrison was one of the founders of the American Anti-Slavery Society in Philadelphia in 1833. Mary Ann Shad (or Shadd, 1823–93), born in Wilmington, Delaware, spent twelve years as an expatriate in Canada, where she edited the fugitive slave newspaper *Provincial Freemen*; she may have been involved in the conspiracy that led to John Brown's raid on Harpers Ferry in 1859. Alexander Du Bois, W.E.B. Du Bois's grandfather. James G. Barbadoes (c. 1796–1841) was one of the founders of the American Anti-Slavery Society, 1833. He and two of his children died of fever in Jamaica, where they had gone with a group of blacks to test the possibilities of emigration.

397.15 Remond . . . Douglass] Charles Lenox Remond (1810–74), born in Salem, Massachusetts, was a journalist, lecturer, and an active member of the Massachusetts Anti-Slavery Society. William C. Nell (1816–74), born in Boston, Massachusetts, was a lecturer, journalist, and historian and was active in the Underground Railroad. William Wells Brown (c. 1814–84), fugitive slave and author of a famous slave narrative describing his life in slavery and his escape on January 1, 1834. Frederick Douglass (c. 1817–95), born a slave on the eastern shore of Maryland, taught himself to read and write and took up the caulking trade. He escaped from slavery to become one of the principal orators on the abolitionist circuit and published and edited *The North Star*, which became a major organ of the abolition and women's rights movements. Following the Civil War, Douglass became a minor figure in the Republican Party, holding several offices. He remained until his death an agitator for reform and civil rights for blacks.

397.24–27 Elliot . . . Payne] Robert Brown Elliott (1842–84), who claimed to have been born in Boston and educated in Jamaica and England (Eton College), is now believed to have been born and educated in Liverpool, England, where he learned the printing trade. He arrived in Boston in 1867 after service in the British Navy and worked as a typesetter. After a few months he moved to South Carolina to become an editor of the *South Carolina Leader*, one of the early southern papers published by blacks. He was elected to the South Carolina House of Representatives and in 1870 to the United States House of Representatives. In 1873, after losing a bid for the Senate, he returned to the House of Representatives. He resigned suddenly from the House to return to South Carolina in an effort to reform corrupt political practices there. He was elected attorney general but was removed from office with other Republicans in 1877 with the return of Democratic rule in the state. Blanche K. Bruce (1841–98), runaway slave, teacher, and planter, became the first, and last, black to serve a full term as senator from Mississippi, 1875–81; he later held appointed offices in government under Republican administrations. John Mercer Langston (1829–97), lawyer, founder and dean of the Law Department at Howard University (1869–73), vice-president (1870–73) and acting president of the university (1873–75); he later was president of Virginia Normal and Collegiate Institute, Petersburg, Virginia (1885–87). He served as chargé d'affaires to the Dominican Republic from 1877–85 and was the first black elected to the House of Representatives from Virginia, serving one term, 1890–92. For Alexander Crummell (1819–98), see

Chapter XII, "Of Alexander Crummell," pp. 512–20. Daniel A. Payne (1811–93), educator, church historian, civic leader, and bishop of the African Methodist Episcopal Church, was instrumental in founding Wilberforce University and served as its president for sixteen years.

397.33 Price . . . leader] Joseph C. Price (1854–93), son of a slave father and free mother, was ordained by the African Methodist Episcopal Zion Church. He was a powerful orator and worked to raise funds for black education, in particular the establishment of Livingstone College in Salisbury, North Carolina.

400.14 the Grimkes . . . Bowen] Archibald H. Grimké (1849–1930), lawyer, editor, and author, and his brother Francis J. Grimké (1850–1937), clergyman and author, were both active civil rights leaders. Kelly Miller (1863–1939) taught at Howard University from 1890 to 1934 and was dean of the College of Arts and Sciences (1907–19). A mathematician by training, he added sociology to the curriculum at Howard; as a journalist and pamphleteer, he attempted to resolve conflicts among black leaders. John Wesley Edward Bowen (1855–1933), Methodist clergyman, earned a Ph.D. in philosophy from Boston University, the second black in America to do so. He was a professor at various institutions and became the first black to attain a regular professorship at Gammon Theological Seminary. He was an unsuccessful candidate for the office of bishop, and he continually worked for the full and equal assimilation of black clergymen into the Methodist establishment. He was a chautauqua lecturer of great power and eloquence.

403.1–3 praising . . . Tillman] Charles Brantley Aycock (1859–1912), governor of North Carolina from 1901–05, was a champion of educational reform in his state, attempting to overcome the illiteracy of both whites and blacks through funding of public education. John Tyler Morgan (1824–1907), senator from Alabama 1876–1907, was a strong advocate of white supremacy. Thomas Nelson Page's (1853–1922) novels promoted a romantic view of the Old South and plantation life. Benjamin Ryan ("Pitchfork Ben") Tillman (1847–1918), demagogue, orator, and advocate of "white democracy," was governor of South Carolina from 1890 to 1894 and senator from South Carolina from 1894 until 1918. Noted for his speeches provoking whites to the violent suppression of blacks, he presented the views of southern extremists in addresses to the Senate and on the chautauqua platform. He justified lynching in cases of rape, advocated the use of force to disenfranchise blacks, and favored the repeal of the Fifteenth Amendment. See Du Bois's remarks on Tillman in *The Crisis* (pp. 1176–77 in this volume).

405.3–11 Willst . . . SCHILLER.] "Wouldst Thou make Thy power known / Choose the sinless within Thy Eternal House! / The immortal ones, the pure ones, / The tough hearted and tearless. / Do not choose the tender virgin, / Nor the soft soul of the shepherdess." From *Die Jungfrau von Orleans*, IV, i, (1801).

408.33 Cicero . . . Poeta"] The oration is a forceful argument on behalf of literature, detailing the benefits provided by the artist and his claim to honor and commendation from society.

420.28 "Entbehren . . . entbehren."] "Deny yourself, you must deny yourself." Johann Wolfgang von Goethe, *Faust*, I, *Studierzimmer*.

432.9 FORMER TEACHER AND FRIEND] Edmund Asa Ware (1837–85), founder (1867) and first president of Atlanta University.

439.24 Sam Hose] A black farm laborer of Palmetto, Georgia, accused of murdering his employer in a quarrel over wages early in April 1899. He escaped, and while still at large was accused of raping his employer's wife. After his capture he confessed to the murder but refused even under duress to admit to the rape charge. He was lynched, burned alive, and mutilated, with a mob of nearly 2,000 men, women, and children looking on; the tree on which he was hanged was chopped up by souvenir salesmen.

440.15 prayers of Whitefield] George Whitefield (1714–70), English evangelist and revivalist preacher, after spending a few months in Georgia in 1738, had given support to the freeholders who were petitioning the trustees of the colony to remove the restrictions on importing slave labor. Though believing slaves should be treated kindly, he defended the idea of slavery on biblical grounds.

440.18 Darien . . . place] In McIntosh County, Georgia, August 23, 1899, hundreds of blacks, who for days had been hearing rumors of a threatened lynching, assembled at the ringing of a church bell, and their presence prevented the removal of a prisoner. They were later tried for insurrection and 21 were sent to convict farms for a year.

440.20–21 the Moravians of Ebenezea] Moravians founded two early settlements near Savannah, Georgia: Ebenezer, in 1734, and New Ebenezer, in 1736. Most settlers had moved to Pennsylvania by 1740, partly to avoid military service against the Spanish.

440.23 statute of 1808] Congress passed March 2, 1807, "An Act to prohibit the importation of Slaves into any port or place within the jurisdiction of the United States, from and after the first day of January, in the year of our Lord one thousand eight hundred and eight."

475.3–6 Life . . . BROWNING.] From "A Vision of Poets," conclusion.

492.23–25 "That . . . vaster."] Alfred Lord Tennyson, *In Memoriam*, prologue.

493.13 FIONA MACLEOD.] Pseudonym of William Sharp (1855–1905).

505.4 *Dum . . . vivamus.*] "While we live, let us live."

506.3–9 O sister . . . SWINBURNE.] From "Itylus."

518.4–8 " . . . bear . . . takes,"] William Shakespeare, *Hamlet*, III, i, 69–73.

535.29 "Freudig . . . dahin."] From "The Wedding March," Richard Wagner, *Lohengrin*, III, i. The first two lines are: *Treulich geführt, ziehet dahin / Wo euch der Segen der Liebe bewahr!* (Faithfully led, be drawn to that place / Where the blessings of love watch over you!) Du Bois changes *Treulich* (faithfully) to *Freudig* (joyfully).

537.12–13 Port Royal experiment] In 1861 the extensive cotton plantations of Port Royal, South Carolina, came under federal control. The Port Royal Relief Committee, organized in Philadelphia by James M. McKim, managed the cultivation of these lands as an experiment in free labor and supervision by former slaves. The enterprise was successful enough to cause the free blacks to assume they would eventually own the land, but at the end of the Civil War the land was returned to the former slave-owning planters.

537.21–22 Thomas . . . McKim] Higginson's (1823–1911) account of his experience leading the 1st South Carolina Volunteers from 1862–64, in *Army Life in a Black Regiment* (1870), includes the first serious attention to slave songs and black folk music. Lucy McKim Garrison (1842–77), daughter of James McKim, was the only trained musician among northerners who collected slave songs in the Sea Islands of South Carolina during the Civil War. When she published "Poor Rosy, Poor Gal" (*Dwight's Journal of Music*, 1862) and "Roll, Jordan, Roll" (1862), music was included along with the words for the first time.

DUSK OF DAWN

559.3 As . . . elsewhere,] In *Darkwater* (1920), Chapter I, "The Shadow of Years."

559.34–35 Abyssinian expedition] A large military force under Sir Robert Napier, sent by England to free its consul, Charles Duncan Cameron, and other European prisoners held by Emperor Theodore II (1818–68) of Abyssinia. Napier's army seized the capital, Magdala, and rescued the prisoners in April 1868. Theodore committed suicide during the attack.

566.34–35 revolution . . . South] In return for their acceptance of the special electoral commission's decision in the disputed 1876 Tilden-Hayes presidential election, southern Democrats in the House of Representatives received assurances from Republican leaders that Rutherford B. Hayes would withdraw federal troops from the South and end Reconstruction, promises Hayes fulfilled after his inauguration in 1877.

578.7–8 heresy . . . Briggs] Charles Augustus Briggs (1841–1913), biblical scholar and professor at Union Theological Seminary in New York.

589.23 Force bills] Congress passed four acts between 1870 and 1875 to enforce civil and political rights as guaranteed by the Fourteenth and Fifteenth Amendments. They were repealed in 1894.

593.40–594.2 foray . . . Atlanta] On the night of August 13, 1906, shots were fired around Fort Brown (Brownsville), Texas, where three companies of the black 25th Infantry Regiment were stationed, resulting in the death of one white man and the wounding of two others. The soldiers, who had previously complained of racial harassment by local civilians, signed affidavits disclaiming any knowledge of the incident. There was no public hearing, and the three companies were dishonorably discharged by order of President Theodore Roosevelt, a decision executed by his successor, William Howard Taft. The next month a bloodier riot occurred in Atlanta, Georgia. Du Bois believed that Georgia politicians Tom Watson (a former Populist who had turned away from supporting black enfranchisement) and Hoke Smith (who had been elected governor in August 1906; see note 1143.31) had deliberately provoked whites to attack blacks.

595.12 Charles Young] See Du Bois's remarks in *The Crisis*, pp. 1195–96.

595.13 Charles Burroughs] Burroughs later helped Du Bois direct the pageant "The Star of Ethiopia" and was a director of the Krigwa Players.

606.35–36 Monroe . . . Forbes] William Monroe Trotter (1872–1934), businessman and editor, was, along with Du Bois, one of the early critics of Booker T. Washington. He is believed to have been a suicide. See Du Bois's article on him, pp. 1248–52 in this volume. George Forbes (1864–1927), lawyer, editor, and librarian. Though Forbes later quarreled with Trotter and left the *Guardian*, he supported Du Bois's Niagara Movement in 1907.

627.10 Odum . . . Brigham] Howard W. Odum (1884–1954) was Kenan Professor of Sociology at the University of North Carolina at Chapel Hill. His first book, *Social and Mental Traits of the Negro* (1910), explained black social status by assuming that racial traits determined character and capability. William McDougall (1871–1938), an English-born and -educated Harvard professor of psychology, wrote *Is America Safe for Democracy?* (1921), which proclaimed the innate mental superiority of the Nordic race due to hereditary factors. Carl C. Brigham (1890–1943) taught at Princeton from 1920 until his death. His principal works included *Two Studies in Mental Tests* (1917) and *Study of American Intelligence* (1923). Both McDougall's and Brigham's work drew heavily upon the now widely discredited intelligence testing conducted by the U.S. Army during World War I.

646.35 the Veys] Sometimes spelled Vai or Vei; a West African people who inhabit the region of present-day Liberia.

659.38 the Jukes] The fictitious name of a family in New York State believed to have had an unusual and chronic record of crime and pauperism. Richard L. Dugdale reported that this family history, extending back into the 18th century, proved the existence of innate hereditary traits. Geneticists and sociologists now reject the conclusions and charge that evidence and photographs were deliberately manipulated to obtain the results Dugdale promoted.

661.35 "When Malinda Sings"] A poem by Paul Laurence Dunbar.

695.13–14 Walker's Appeal] See note 396.34.

697.21 Bishop Turner's] Henry McNeal Turner (1834–1915), bishop of the African Methodist Episcopal Church, was appointed chaplain to black army troops in 1863 by President Lincoln. He helped organize the Republican Party in Georgia during Reconstruction, and held various positions, the last being postmaster of Macon, Georgia. Disillusioned with the prospects for blacks in the United States, he became the foremost black advocate of colonizing Afro-Americans in West Africa, particularly in Liberia. Between 1891 and 1898, he took four trips to Africa.

702.32–33 Woodson's] Carter G. Woodson (1875–1950), historian and scholar, founded the Association for the Study of Negro Life and History and the *Journal of Negro History* in 1916.

727.10–11 Tillman . . . Arkansas.] Benjamin Tillman, see note 403.1–3. James Kimble Vardaman (1861–1930), governor of Mississippi (1904–08) and U.S. senator (1913–19), was noted for his impassioned oratory and his exploitation of racial and class prejudices, asserting that the political dominance of whites was endangered by the education of blacks. Coleman L. Blease (1868–1942), flamboyant and controversial governor of South Carolina from 1911 to 1915, openly defended the lynching of blacks accused of the rape or murder of whites. Jefferson Davis (1862–1913) was governor of Arkansas from 1900 to 1907 and U.S. senator from 1907 to 1913.

728.24 William Pickens] Pickens (1881–1954), a member of the Niagara Movement, became one of the original members of the NAACP. He was field secretary from 1920 until his dismissal in 1942 over a policy disagreement with the national board. He was director of the Interracial Division of the Treasury Department's Savings (War) Bonds Division from 1941 to 1945.

740.5 "Close Ranks."] The beginning of the original *Crisis* editorial (July 1918):

This is the crisis of the world. For all the long years to come men will point to the year 1918 as the great Day of Decision, the day when the world decided whether it would submit to military despotism and an endless armed peace—if peace it could be called—or whether they would put down the menace of German militarism and inaugurate the United States of the World.

We of the colored race have no ordinary interest in the outcome. . . .

748.26 Mary Talbert] Mary Burnett Talbert (1862?–1923) served as a Red Cross nurse with the American Expeditionary Force in France during

World War I. She was president of the National Association of Colored Women from 1916 to 1920.

749.14–15 the Elaine . . . cases] In the fall of 1919 disputes arose between black sharecroppers and tenant farmers of Elaine, Phillips County, Arkansas, and white landowners and merchants. Blacks protesting the lack of itemized accounts for cotton brought to mill formed the Progressive Farmers and Household Union of America. The union's use of passwords, secret handshakes, and insignia fostered the suspicions of whites, and about October 1, 1919, a rumor that blacks were plotting an insurrection and were planning to massacre whites touched off days of violence that took an estimated five white and 25 black lives. Governor Charles H. Brough called for federal troops and 500 were mobilized "to repel the attack of a black army." One thousand blacks were arrested and 122 indicted. Twelve men were sentenced to death and 75 were sentenced to convict farms. The trials lasted only five to ten minutes each. No witnesses for the defense were called. The NAACP appealed these convictions and gained a favorable verdict from the Supreme Court (Moore *v.* Dempsey, 1923). The Court held that if a trial is so dominated by a mob that justice is interfered with, the principle of due process has been violated.

749.15 the Sweet . . . Detroit] See Du Bois's article in *The Crisis*, page 1210 in this volume.

757.19 said . . . Garvey] See pp. 969–79 in this volume.

778.2 junior . . . Mississippi] Theodore G. Bilbo (1877–1947), elected to the Senate in 1934, was noted for oratorical flights and racist demagoguery. He supported much of the New Deal but opposed anti-lynching legislation, and on June 6, 1938, he proposed legislation to deport 12,000,000 black citizens to Liberia.

783.15–784.19 "In thirty . . . undertake."] For the full text, see pp. 1259–63.

ESSAYS AND ARTICLES

818.11 Zamboes of America] Of mixed American Indian and black ancestry.

819.32 "one . . . event."] Tennyson, *In Memoriam*, Conclusion, stanza xxxvi.

824.37–38 *I will . . . heard.*] William Lloyd Garrison, "Salutatory Address," *The Liberator*, January 1, 1831.

825.5–8 Burst . . . star.] Tennyson, *In Memoriam*, lxiv. The first line is altered from "Who breaks his birth's invidious bar," and the verb tenses have been changed from the original's "grasps," "breasts," and "grapples."

827.20–24 "When . . . dream."] William Wordsworth, "Intimations of Immortality from Recollections of Early Childhood," i, with slight variation in line indentation.

829.3–4 "bear . . . contumely?"] See note 518.4–8.

831.11–14 monk . . . waver."] Martin Luther's speech at the Diet of Worms, April 18, 1521. The lines are engraved on his monument at Worms. The emperor was Charles V.

832.1–2 "That . . . moves"?] See note 819.32.

838.22–23 "Well . . . Master.] Cf. Matthew 25:21, 23 and Luke 19:17.

841.4–9 "Truth . . . own."] James Russell Lowell, "The Present Crisis."

843.2–3 Phillis . . . Banneker,] See note 396.15–18.

844.15 David Walker,] See note 396.34.

845.17 Purvis and Remond] See notes 397.3–4 and 397.15.

845.17 Pennington] Pennington (1807–70) wrote an important autobiography, *The Fugitive Blacksmith, or, Events in the History of James W. C. Pennington . . . formerly a Slave in the State of Maryland, United States*, published in London in 1849.

845.18 Alexander Crummell] See the essay "Of Alexander Crummell," Chapter XII in *The Souls of Black Folk*, pp. 512–20 in this volume.

845.24 Maria Weston Chapman] Chapman (1806–85) was an active Boston editor and abolitionist who worked closely with William Lloyd Garrison.

846.2 McCune Smith] James McCune Smith (1813–65), son of a slave, was educated at the African Free School in New York City and at Glasgow University. He practiced law, wrote scholarly historical articles, and was active in anti-slavery causes.

846.5–7 Russworm . . . Benezet.] "Russworm" is probably John Brown Russwurm (1799–1851), born in Jamaica and educated in Canada and Maine and later at Bowdoin College. Although he had no direct connection with Dartmouth College, he taught at the Smith School for blacks in Boston, which was founded and supported by Dartmouth alumni, before entering Bowdoin in 1822. Russwurm subsequently published a newspaper, *Freedom's Journal*, in New York City and in 1829 emigrated to Liberia, where he was superintendent of schools, editor and publisher of the *Liberia Herald*, and governor of the Maryland Colony at Cape Palmas. Elias Neau (d. 1722) was a French-born member of the Society for the Propagation of the Gospel in Foreign Parts who taught a catechizing school at Trinity Church in New York City from 1704 until his death. Anthony Benezet (1713–84) was born in France of a Huguenot family, joined a society of Quakers in London, and came with them to America. He established and endowed a school for blacks in Philadelphia.

846.9–10 Langston . . . Payne.] For Langston, Bruce, Elliot, and Payne, see note 397.24–27. Dr. Daniel Hale Williams (1856–1931), surgeon, opened the first hospital, the Chicago Provident, where blacks and whites served on the same staff and was the first to operate successfully on the heart. Richard Theodore Greener (1844–1922), the first black to receive a degree from Harvard, became an educator, lawyer, and consular officer.

849.18–19 As early . . . College,] John Brown Russwurm; see note 846.5–7.

857.23 Atticus G. Haygood] Haygood (1839–96), born in Georgia and a chaplain in the Confederate Army, wrote *Our Brother in Black, His Freedom and His Future* (1881), which offended many white southerners. He believed in federal aid for black education and opposed the leasing of convict laborers.

903.30–31 Houston . . . Freedom] See note 1172.31.

926.19–20 Chicago . . . Estill Springs] In Chicago, Illinois, in July 1919, 38 people were killed and more than 500 injured in race riots and bombings. During rioting in East St. Louis, Illinois, in July 1917, at least forty blacks and nine whites were murdered by mobs, often abetted by police and state militia. In Memphis, Tennessee, on May 22, 1917, Ell Person, a black accused of the murder of a white girl, was taken from deputies by a mob and burned at the stake before a crowd estimated at 15,000. In Waco, Texas, in May 1916, a mentally retarded black teenager, convicted of murdering a white woman, was taken from the courtroom by a mob and tortured and burned in the public square before 15,000 people. Six people were killed in rioting in Washington, D.C., during the summer of 1919. There were lynchings in Dyersburg, Tennessee, in March 1916 and December 1917. In Estill Springs, Tennessee, on February 8, 1918, Jim McIlherron killed two white men in a quarrel. A black clergyman who helped him escape was shot and killed by a mob. McIlherron was later captured, tortured, and burned alive.

927.10 *Schaden Freude*] Malicious joy or glee.

929.13 Glave in 1895.] E. J. Glave served with Sir Henry Morton Stanley in Africa and wrote *In Savage Africa, Or, Six Years of Adventure in Congo-Land* (1892).

929.14–23 Harris . . . tribes."] John Hobbis Harris wrote several well-known books on Africa, including *Down in Darkest Africa* (1912) and *Africa: Slave or Free* (1919).

930.10–11 Nefertari . . . Askia,] Variant spelling for Nefertiti of Egypt. Askia Muhammad I (c. 1493–1528) was ruler of Songhay, largest of the ancient native empires of West Africa.

930.15 Sonni Ali] (1464–92) Immediate predecessor of Askia Muhammad I; see preceeding note.

939.2 *Semper* . . . proconsul,] Pliny, *Historia Naturalis*, II, viii, 42: "It is commonly said among the Greeks that 'Africa always offers something new.' " Pliny's nephew, known as "the Younger," was consul in A.D. 100.

939.28–30 Shakespeare's . . . joys!] *2 Henry IV*, V, iii.

939.31–32 days . . . Ophir] Punt, exact location unknown, was an area south of Egypt and accessible through the Red Sea that supplied Egypt with slaves and gold between 1486–68 B.C. Ophir was a port in the Old Testament from which Solomon's ships brought cargoes of gold and ivory; its location also is unknown.

972.22 fellow-worker.] The first installment in *The Crisis* ended here. The second installment began with the succeeding paragraph.

993.1 *Criteria . . . Art*] The text of the address delivered at the Chicago Conference of the NAACP in 1926.

1000.28 "White Cargo"] A melodrama by Leon Gordon about a beautiful mulatto woman despoiled by the degenerate white men engaged in uplifting Africa. Du Bois wrote it was "about as delicious a piece of hypocrisy as we have witnessed."

1008.15 "Freudig . . . dahin!"] See note 535.29.

1010.1 *The Negro College*] Part of an address on "The Field and Function of a Negro College," delivered at the annual alumni reunion during commencement week at Fisk University, June 1933.

1016.8 miners' strike] Over 9,000 members of the United Mine Workers (probably about half of them black) went on strike in 1904 when the district's furnace companies, which operated about 60 percent of Alabama's coal mines, refused to renew their contract. Led by the Tennessee Coal and Iron Co., the companies imported black strikebreakers, sent large forces of deputies to intimidate the miners, and tried to split the white and black miners by offering blacks the choice jobs in the mines if they agreed to return. Though the president of the company had predicted that over 80 percent of the black miners would be back at work in less than a month, only fifty of the 2,000 black strikers at the Pratt City Mines, for example, were at work after four months. When the strike was called off after sixteen months, only 300 of the 9,000 strikers were back at work.

1025.25 Nefertari . . . Moshesh] For Nefertari and Askia, see note 930.10–11. Moshesh (c. 1790–1870), Sotho tribal leader, founded the Basuto nation in South Africa, defeated several British armed expeditions, and successfully resisted Boer expansion into Basutoland (now Lesotho).

1031.6–7 Charles . . . Tubman] For Harriet Tubman and Sojourner Truth, see "The Damnation of Women," pp. 960–61 of this volume. Charles Ball wrote *Slavery in the United States: A Narrative of the Life & Adventures of Charles Ball, a Black Man* (1836), and *Fifty Years in Chains: Or, the Life of an American Slave* (1859).

1042.24–25 Wells papers] Probably the papers of Gideon Welles, Secretary of the Navy in Lincoln's cabinet, in the Library of Congress.

1047.23–31 In Babylon . . . STERLING] From "In the Market Place," *Selected Poems* (1923).

1107.3–4 Charles . . . University,] Charles S. Johnson (1893–1956) was editor of the Urban League's magazine, *Opportunity*, and a strong supporter of writers and artists of the Harlem Renaissance. He was the first black president of Fisk University, serving from 1946 until his death.

1113.35 live.] Most of this article was reprinted in the "Postlude" chapter of *The Autobiography of W.E.B. Du Bois*, where the following two paragraphs were added at the end:

I just live. I plan my work, but plan less for shorter periods. I live from year to year and day to day. I expect snatches of pain and discomfort to come and go. And then reaching back to my archives, I whisper to the great Majority: To the Almighty Dead, into whose pale approaching faces, I stand and stare; you whose thoughts, deeds and dreams have made men wise with all wisdom and stupid with utter evil. In every name of God, bend out and down, you who are the infinite majority of all mankind and with your thoughts, deeds, dreams and memories, overwhelm, outvote, and coerce this remnant of human life which lingers on, imagining themselves wisest of all who have lived just because they still survive. Whither with wide revelation will they go with their stinking pride and empty boasting, whose ever recurring lies only you the Dead have known all too well? Teach living man to jeer at this last civilization which seeks to build heaven on Want and Ill of most men and vainly builds on color and hair rather than on decency of hand and heart. Let your memories teach these wilful fools all which you have forgotten and ruined and done to death.

You are not and yet you are: your thoughts, your deeds, above all your dreams still live. So too, your deeds and what you forgot—these lived as your bodies died. With these we also live and die, realize and kill. Our dreams seek Heaven, our deeds plumb Hell. Hell lies about us in our Age; blithely we push into its stench and flame. Suffer us not, Eternal Dead to stew in this Evil—the Evil of South Africa, the Evil of Mississippi; the Evil of Evils which is what we hope to hold in Asia and Africa, in the southern Americas and islands of the Seven Seas. Reveal, Ancient of Days, the Present in the Past and prophesy the End in the Beginning. For this is a beautiful world; this is a wonderful America, which the founding fathers dreamed until their sons drowned it in the blood of slavery and devoured it in greed. Our children must rebuild it. Let then the Dreams of the Dead rebuke the Blind who think that what is will be forever and teach them that what was worth living for must live again and that which merited death must stay dead. Teach us, Forever Dead, there is no Dream but Deed, there is no Deed but Memory.

1131.1 *The Crisis.*] This editorial appeared in the first issue of *The Crisis.*

1132.35 Governor Ansell] Martin F. Ansell (1850–1945), governor of South Carolina from 1907–11.

1143.31 Blease] See note 727.10–11.

1143.31 Hoke Smith] Democratic politician from Georgia (1855–1931), advocate of white supremacy and states rights. Owner and editor of *Atlanta Journal* (1887–1900); secretary of interior in Grover Cleveland's cabinet (1893–96); twice governor of Georgia (1907–09 and 1911); U.S. senator from Georgia (1911–20), unseated in 1920 by Tom Watson. His campaigns and his newspaper openly provoked violence against blacks, and he supported election controls that disenfranchised black voters in Georgia.

1144.2–5 internal . . . does.] Charles W. Anderson (1866–1938), black New York Republican and friend of Booker T. Washington, was appointed collector of internal revenue for Second District in New York City by President Theodore Roosevelt in 1905 and served until 1915.

1145.9 Vardaman] See note 727.10–11.

1145.10 Tillman] See note 403.1–3.

1145.10 Burleson] Albert S. Burleson (1863–1937), congressman from Ninth (later Tenth) District of Texas, 1898–1913, became postmaster general in Wilson's cabinet (1913–21), where he had large responsibility for patronage and political appointments.

1145.18–19 but one . . . cur,] President Wilson nominated A. E. Patterson, a black lawyer from Oklahoma, to be register of the treasury, one of the few seats traditionally held by a black appointee. Senators Vardaman of Mississippi, Tillman of South Carolina, and Smith of Georgia vigorously opposed the appointment, and Patterson, under pressure, withdrew his name. He was sharply criticized for failing to stand up to the opposition by black spokesmen who thought him cowardly and considered the loss of the position a setback for the race. President Wilson, however, did delay the resignation of Charles W. Anderson (see note 1144.2–5), and he successfully supported the reappointment of Robert H. Terrell as municipal judge in Washington, D.C.

1152.25 Robert C. Ogden] Ogden (1836–1913), a merchant who was influenced by Samuel C. Armstrong, the founder of Hampton Institute, served as president of Hampton's board of trustees and as trustee of Tuskegee Institute. His principal interest was the education of southern whites, and he inspired the so-called "Ogden movement" of educational reform that swept the South in the early 20th century. He headed the Southern Education Board and was a member of the General Education Board, which dispensed funds with the policy that racially separate and unequal education was an acceptable price for educational reform.

1153.34 lynching . . . Miss.,] On February 24, 1914, Sam Petty, accused of killing a deputy sheriff who had attempted to arrest him on minor charges, was captured by a posse and burned alive.

1154.8 CHARLES F. DOLE.] Dole (1845–1927) was a Congregational clergyman, author of numerous religious and inspirational publications, trustee of Tuskegee Institute (1893–1916), supporter of Hampton Institute, and father of James Drummond Dole, magnate of the Hawaiian pineapple industry.

1156.32 suggestively . . . *Survey*.] In responding to an article Du Bois had submitted, Paul U. Kellog, editor of *The Survey*, had written him, December 17, 1913: "Members of the staff who read your 'Black Man's Program for 1914' felt as a matter of tactics the clause 'to marry any sane grown person who wants to marry him' would be regarded as the semi-official utterance of the Association for the Advancement of Colored People, and would be misconstrued and prove a boomerang; and as friends of you and the Association we raised the question of its advisability with you from the organization standpoint." Du Bois suggested dropping the last lines, where he had referred to the NAACP, but *The Survey* printed an article by May Childs Neerney, a secretary of the NAACP, instead.

1172.4 "Carrizal" the news] On June 21, 1916, during the American punitive expedition against Pancho Villa, white officers led black troops of the Tenth Cavalry into the town of Carrizal, Mexico, where they were routed by superior Mexican forces. In the fighting sixteen Americans, including the officers, were killed and 24 were captured. Blame for the defeat fell on the black soldiers. Du Bois wrote in the August 1916 issue of *The Crisis*:

> Carrizal was a glory and a blunder, a joke and a crucifixion; a blunder on the part of a President who sent an army on a fool's errand and on the part of a gay, young officer who needlessly risked human life on the theory that Mexicans always run.
>
> Carrizal was a glory for the Mexicans who dared to defend their country from invasion and for Negro troopers who went singing to their death. And the greater glory was the glory of the black men, for Mexicans died for a land they love, while Negroes sang for a country that despises, cheats and lynches them. Even across the sunlit desert as they died came the last wild shriek of a human bon-fire in Texas where Southern "gentlemen" and "ladies" capered in glee—brave, filthy Texas. Laugh? Why shouldn't they laugh at simple death and grim duty? Have they not faced harsher and more horrible things? "Jim Crow" cars, helpless disenfranchisement and organized insult? Why should they not laugh at death for a country which honors them dying and kicks and buffets them living? God laughed. It was a Joke.

1172.31 *Houston*] Soldiers of the black 24th Infantry Regiment stationed in Houston, Texas, had been disarmed by army officials following weeks of hostile tensions with white civilians and the Houston police. On August 26, 1917, an unarmed black military policeman confronted two white civilian policemen arresting a black woman on charges of abusive language and was beaten and fired upon by the white officers. When reports that the man had died reached the black troops, they seized arms and marched on the town, where two blacks and seventeen whites (including five policemen) were killed. In the aftermath 63 black soldiers were court-martialed; thirteen were executed on December 11, 1917, and five on September 13, 1918; 51 received life sentences, and five were sentenced to shorter terms.

1173.11–12 Waco . . . Lexington,] See note 926.18–20 for Waco, Memphis, and East St. Louis. In Chester, Pennsylvania, three blacks and three whites died during rioting in August 1917. In Lexington, Tennessee, Berry Noyes, a black man, was lynched on April 22, 1918, for killing a sheriff.

1183.36 HAITI.] In 1915, United States Marines intervened to restore order after Haitian president Guillaume Sam was murdered by a mob. The American occupation continued until 1934. This particular reference may be to a revolt in the interior that began in 1918 and was suppressed by U.S. Marines after more than a year of fighting and the deaths of an estimated 3,000 Haitians. Instances were also reported of torture, forced labor, and censorship of the press.

1192.27–28 Pan-African Congress] Congress of African and Afro-American representatives sponsored by the NAACP and held in Paris in February 1919 to coincide with the Paris Peace Conference that led to the Treaty of Versailles.

1199.17 Hahn of Louisiana] Georg Michael Decker Hahn (1830–86), born in Bavaria, came as a child to New Orleans. A bitter opponent of slavery and secession, he was elected the first Republican governor of Louisiana, February 22, 1864. He resigned March 4, 1865, to become U.S. senator, but never took his seat because of his opposition to President Johnson's policies.

1204.29 Augusta Savage] Savage (1892–1962) later received a Rosenwald scholarship and studied in Europe 1929–31. On her return, she opened a studio and helped many younger artists, becoming a legendary figure in Harlem.

1208.12 Kelly Miller] See note 400.14.

1208.13 Brawley and Woodson] Benjamin G. Brawley (1882–1939), professor of English at Howard University and other institutions, wrote on literary and historical subjects, and is probably best known for *The Negro in Literature and Art* (1918), reissued as *The Negro Genius* in 1937. For Carter G. Woodson, see note 702.32–33.

1212.16 Clarence Kelsey] Kelsey (1856–1930), financier and real estate developer, was a trustee and later chairman of the board of Hampton Institute, succeeding William Howard Taft. He was chairman of the Hampton-Tuskegee endowment campaign in 1923 that raised five million dollars.

1214.33–1215.2 physician . . . "colored".] Dr. Ossian Hayes Sweet

(b. 1895) was educated at Wilberforce University, Howard University Medical College, the University of Vienna, and the Sorbonne. His defense was organized by the NAACP. He was represented by Clarence Darrow and Arthur Garfield Hayes and won a complete acquittal.

1223.34 Margaret Deland] Deland (1857–1945) was the author of genteel novels of traditional values and stories of small-town Protestant America. Although an advocate of women's rights, she refused to support women's suffrage, and is reported to have said, "We have suffered many things at the hands of Patrick, and now the New Woman would add Bridget!"

1224.37 Dyer Anti-Lynching Bill.] Introduced in 1922 by Leonidas Carstarphen Dyer (1871–1957), Republican congressman from Missouri (1911–13 and 1915–33), and supported by the NAACP, the bill sought to make lynching a federal offense. Although it passed the House of Representatives, it was defeated by a filibuster in the Senate.

1225.18 Borah] William E. Borah (1865–1940), United States senator from Idaho from 1907 until his death, was known as a progressive and independent legislator.

1226.22 Haiti.] See note 1183.36.

1226.34 Raskob.] John J. Raskob (1879–1950), financier, national chairman of Democratic Party, and supporter of Al Smith in the 1928 election. He later helped found the American Liberty League, in opposition to Roosevelt's New Deal.

1232.24 Senator Allen] Henry J. Allen (1868–1950), former governor of Kansas (1919–23), was appointed in 1929 to fill the Senate seat left vacant when Charles Curtis resigned to become vice-president under Hoover. Allen was defeated in his bid for re-election in 1930 by George McGill.

1232.25–26 McCulloch of Ohio] Roscoe Conkling McCulloch (1880–1958), former member of the House from Ohio (1915–19), was appointed in 1929 to the U.S. Senate seat left vacant by the death of Theodore E. Burton. He was defeated for re-election in 1930.

1248.34 *William Monroe Trotter*] See note 606.35–36.

CATALOGING INFORMATION

Du Bois, William Edward Burghardt, 1868–1963.
Writings: The suppression of the African slave-trade; The souls of black folk; Dusk of dawn; Essays and articles from The Crisis.
Ed. by Nathan Huggins

(The Library of America ; 34)
1. Afro-Americans—Collected works. I. Title. II. The suppression of the African slave-trade. III. The souls of black folk. IV. Dusk of dawn. V. The Crisis. VI. Series.
E185.97.D73A2 1986 973′.0496073 86–10565
ISBN 0–940450–33–X

This book is set in 10 point Linotron Galliard, a face designed for photocomposition by Matthew Carter and based on the sixteenth-century face Granjon. The paper is acid-free Ecusta Nyalite and meets the requirements for permanence of the American National Standards Institute. The binding material is Brillianta, a 100% woven rayon cloth made by Van Heek-Scholco Textielfabrieken, Holland. The composition is by Haddon Craftsmen, Inc., and The Clarinda Company. Printing and binding by R. R. Donnelley & Sons Company. Designed by Bruce Campbell.

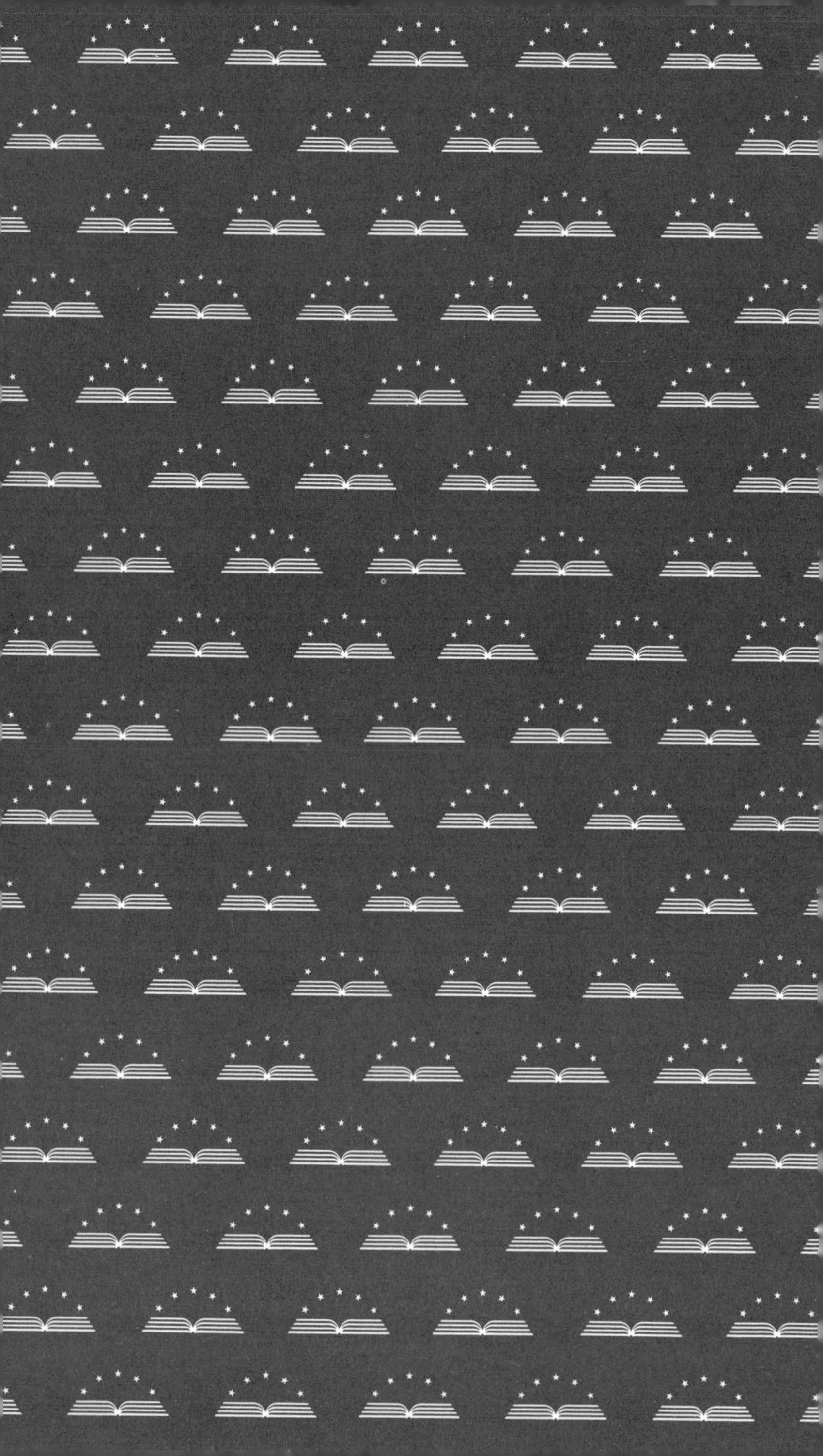